ECONOMICS

The McGraw-Hill Economics Series

SURVEY OF ECONOMICS

Brue, McConnell, and Flynn
Essentials of Economics
Third Edition

Mandel
M: Economics—The Basics
Third Edition

Schiller and Gebhardt
Essentials of Economics
Tenth Edition

PRINCIPLES OF ECONOMICS

Asarta and Butters
Connect Master: Economics
First Edition

Colander
Economics, Microeconomics, and Macroeconomics
Tenth Edition

Frank, Bernanke, Antonovics, and Heffetz
Principles of Economics, Principles of Microeconomics, Principles of Macroeconomics
Sixth Edition

Frank, Bernanke, Antonovics, and Heffetz
Streamlined Editions: Principles of Economics, Principles of Microeconomics, Principles of Macroeconomics
Third Edition

Karlan and Morduch
Economics, Microeconomics, Macroeconomics
Second Edition

McConnell, Brue, and Flynn
Economics, Microeconomics, Macroeconomics
Twenty-First Edition

Samuelson and Nordhaus
Economics, Microeconomics, and Macroeconomics
Nineteenth Edition

Schiller and Gebhardt
The Economy Today, The Micro Economy Today, and The Macro Economy Today
Fourteenth Edition

Slavin
Economics, Microeconomics, and Macroeconomics
Eleventh Edition

ECONOMICS OF SOCIAL ISSUES

Guell
Issues in Economics Today
Eighth Edition

Register and Grimes
Economics of Social Issues
Twenty-First Edition

ECONOMETRICS

Gujarati and Porter
Basic Econometrics
Fifth Edition

Hilmer and Hilmer
Practical Econometrics
First Edition

MANAGERIAL ECONOMICS

Baye and Prince
Managerial Economics and Business Strategy
Ninth Edition

Brickley, Smith, and Zimmerman
Managerial Economics and Organizational Architecture
Sixth Edition

Thomas and Maurice
Managerial Economics
Twelfth Edition

INTERMEDIATE ECONOMICS

Bernheim and Whinston
Microeconomics
Second Edition

Dornbusch, Fischer, and Startz
Macroeconomics
Twelfth Edition

Frank
Microeconomics and Behavior
Ninth Edition

ADVANCED ECONOMICS

Romer
Advanced Macroeconomics
Fourth Edition

MONEY AND BANKING

Cecchetti and Schoenholtz
Money, Banking, and Financial Markets
Fifth Edition

URBAN ECONOMICS

O'Sullivan
Urban Economics
Eighth Edition

LABOR ECONOMICS

Borjas
Labor Economics
Seventh Edition

McConnell, Brue, and Macpherson
Contemporary Labor Economics
Eleventh Edition

PUBLIC FINANCE

Rosen and Gayer
Public Finance
Tenth Edition

ENVIRONMENTAL ECONOMICS

Field and Field
Environmental Economics: An Introduction
Seventh Edition

INTERNATIONAL ECONOMICS

Appleyard and Field
International Economics
Ninth Edition

Pugel
International Economics
Sixteenth Edition

ECONOMICS

SECOND EDITION

Dean Karlan
Yale University and Innovations for Poverty Action

Jonathan Morduch
New York University

ECONOMICS, SECOND EDITION

Published by McGraw-Hill Education, 2 Penn Plaza, New York, NY 10121. Copyright © 2018 by McGraw-Hill Education. All rights reserved. Printed in the United States of America. Previous editions © 2014. No part of this publication may be reproduced or distributed in any form or by any means, or stored in a database or retrieval system, without the prior written consent of McGraw-Hill Education, including, but not limited to, in any network or other electronic storage or transmission, or broadcast for distance learning.

Some ancillaries, including electronic and print components, may not be available to customers outside the United States.

This book is printed on acid-free paper.

1 2 3 4 5 6 7 8 9 LWI 21 20 19 18 17

ISBN 978-1-259-19314-9
MHID 1-259-19314-4

Chief Product Officer, SVP Products & Markets: *G. Scott Virkler*
Vice President, General Manager, Products & Markets: *Marty Lange*
Vice President, Content Design & Delivery: *Betsy Whalen*
Managing Director: *James Heine*
Brand Manager: *Katie Hoenicke*
Director, Product Development: *Rose Koos*
Product Developer: *Alyssa Lincoln*
Lead Product Developer: *Michele Janicek*
Lead Product Developer: *Ann Torbert*
Marketing Manager: *Virgil Lloyd*
Marketing Coordinator: *Dave O'Donnell*
Market Development Manager: *Trina Maurer*
Director of Digital Content Development: *Douglas Ruby*
Director, Content Design & Delivery: *Linda Avenarius*
Program Manager: *Mark Christianson*
Content Project Managers: *Kathryn D. Wright, Kristin Bradley, and Karen Jozefowicz*
Buyer: *Laura M. Fuller*
Design: *Matt Diamond*
Content Licensing Specialists: *Beth Thole and Melissa Homer*
Cover Image: © *Godruma/Getty Images*
Compositor: *SPi Global*
Printer: *LSC Communications*

All credits appearing on page or at the end of the book are considered to be an extension of the copyright page.

Library of Congress Cataloging-in-Publication Data
Names: Karlan, Dean S., author. | Morduch, Jonathan, author.
Title: Economics / Dean Karlan, Yale University and Innovations for Poverty
    Action, Jonathan Morduch, New York University.
Description: Second Edition. | Dubuque : McGraw-Hill Education, 2017. |
    Revised edition of the authors's Economics, 2014.
Identifiers: LCCN 2016030925 | ISBN 9781259193149 (alk. paper)
Subjects: LCSH: Economics.
Classification: LCC HB171.5 .K297 2017 | DDC 330—dc23 LC record available at
https://lccn.loc.gov/2016030925

The Internet addresses listed in the text were accurate at the time of publication. The inclusion of a website does not indicate an endorsement by the authors or McGraw-Hill Education, and McGraw-Hill Education does not guarantee the accuracy of the information presented at these sites.

www.mhhe.com

dedication

We dedicate this book to our families.

—Dean and Jonathan

about the authors

Dean Karlan

Dean Karlan is Professor of Economics at Yale University and President and Founder of Innovations for Poverty Action (IPA). Dean started IPA in 2002 with two aims: to help learn what works and what does not in the fight against poverty and other social problems around the world, and then to implement successful ideas at scale. IPA has worked in over 50 countries, with 1,000 employees around the world. Dean's personal research focuses on using field experiments to learn more about the effectiveness of financial services for low-income households, with a focus on using behavioral economics approaches to improve financial products and services. His research includes related areas, such as building income for those in extreme poverty, charitable fundraising, voting, health, and education. Dean is also cofounder of stickK.com, a start-up that helps people use commitment contracts to achieve personal goals, such as losing weight or completing a problem set on time, and in 2015 he founded ImpactMatters, an organization that helps assess whether charitable organizations are using and producing appropriate evidence of impact. Dean is a Sloan Foundation Research Fellow, a Guggenheim Fellow, and an Executive Committee member of the Board of the M.I.T. Jameel Poverty Action Lab. In 2007 he was awarded a Presidential Early Career Award for Scientists and Engineers. He is coeditor of the *Journal of Development Economics* and on the editorial board of *American Economic Journal: Applied Economics*. He holds a BA from University of Virginia, an MPP and MBA from University of Chicago, and a PhD in Economics from MIT. In 2016 he coauthored *Failing in the Field,* and in 2011 he coauthored *More Than Good Intentions: Improving the Ways the World's Poor Borrow, Save, Farm, Learn, and Stay Healthy.*

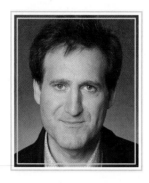

Jonathan Morduch

Jonathan Morduch is Professor of Public Policy and Economics at New York University's Wagner Graduate School of Public Service. Jonathan focuses on innovations that expand the frontiers of finance and how financial markets shape economic growth and inequality. Jonathan has lived and worked in Asia, but his newest book, *The Financial Diaries: How American Families Cope in a World of Uncertainty* (written with Rachel Schneider and published by Princeton University Press, 2017), follows families in California, Mississippi, Ohio, Kentucky, and New York as they cope with economic ups and downs over a year. The new work jumps off from ideas in *Portfolios of the Poor: How the World's Poor Live on $2 a Day* (Princeton University Press, 2009), which Jonathan coauthored and which describes how families in Bangladesh, India, and South Africa devise ways to make it through a year living on $2 a day or less. Jonathan's research on financial markets is collected in *The Economics of Microfinance* and *Banking the World,* both published by MIT Press. At NYU, Jonathan is executive director of the Financial Access Initiative, a center that supports research on extending access to finance in low-income communities. Jonathan's ideas have also shaped policy through work with the United Nations, World Bank, and other international organizations. In 2009, the Free University of Brussels awarded Jonathan an honorary doctorate to recognize his work on microfinance. He holds a BA from Brown and a PhD from Harvard, both in Economics.

Karlan and **Morduch** first met in 2001 and have been friends and colleagues ever since. Before writing this text, they collaborated on research on financial institutions. Together, they've written about new directions in financial access for the middle class and poor, and in Peru they set up a laboratory to study incentives in financial contracts for loans to women to start small enterprises. In 2006, together with Sendhil Mullainathan, they started the Financial Access Initiative, a center dedicated to expanding knowledge about financial solutions for the 40 percent of the world's adults who lack access to banks. This text reflects their shared passion for using economics as a tool to improve one's own life and to promote better business and public policies in the broader world.

brief contents

preface

We offer the second edition of this text as a resource for professors who, like us, want to show students that *economics can make a positive impact*—in their own lives and in society as a whole. We designed the text with our own version of a "dual mandate":

- to *deliver core economic concepts* along with *exciting new ideas* in economic thought and
- to *keep student learners engaged by confronting issues that are important in the world.*

Our intention is that this approach will help students see economics as a tool to better one's own life, promote better public policies, and run better businesses around the world.

Why Study Economics?

Whenever we've been asked why we teach economics, or why students should study the topic, our answer is simple: *"Economics helps make the world a better place."* It's unfortunate that economics often has a reputation for being the "dismal science." We believe fundamentally that *economics is a good thing.* Economic principles can help students understand and respond to everyday situations. Economic ideas also help us tackle big challenges, such as fixing our health care system and keeping the government fiscally solvent. We show students how economic ideas are shaping their world in important, positive ways, and we provide them with a wide-ranging set of practical insights to help develop their economic intuition.

We have built engagement with real-world problems into the fabric of our chapters, and we present data-driven economic thinking as a way to help solve these problems. Faculty and students will find that our impact-based focus *breaks down barriers* between what goes on in the classroom and what is going on in communities, both at home and around the world.

By keeping the discussion down-to-earth and lively, we aim to make the learning materials easier to use and compelling. The chapters are organized around a familiar curriculum of introductory concepts while adding empirical context for ideas that students often find overly abstract or too simplified. The innovative, empirical orientation of the book enables us to incorporate intriguing findings from recent studies and to address material from such areas as game theory, finance, behavioral economics, and political economy. This approach connects concepts in introductory economics to important *new developments* in economic research, while placing a premium on *easy-to-understand explanations.* In every chapter we fulfill four fundamental commitments:

- **Show how economics connects to important ideas and issues in the world.** This text engages students by approaching economics as a way of explaining real people and their decisions and by providing a set of tools that serve to solve many different types of problems. *We show students that economics can make the world a better place,* while challenging them to reach their own conclusions about what "better" really means.
- **Teach principles as evidence-based tools for dealing with real situations.** The text is centered on examples and issues that resonate with students' experience. Applications come *first,* reinforcing the relevance of the tools that students acquire. Engaging empirical cases are interspersed throughout the content. The applications open up puzzles, anomalies, and possibilities that basic economic principles help explain. The aim is, first and foremost, to ensure that students gain an intuitive grasp of basic ideas.
- **Appeal to today's globally engaged students.** Students today live in a digital, globalized world. We recognize that they are knowledgeable and care about both local and international issues. *Economics* takes a global perspective, with the United States as a leading example. We draw on a world of examples to bring to life topics like how to encourage fair

competition, create jobs, strengthen markets, protect the environment, engage in international trade, and reduce poverty.

- **Provide a balanced, data-driven view.** Economics provides a way to organize insights, integrate data, and enrich worldviews—no matter one's personal politics. Many topics are uncontroversial; others are hotly debated. Our aim is to provide balanced approaches that help students sharpen and enrich their own understandings of the argument. We do this by focusing on the data and evidence behind the effects we see.

In the second edition of this text, we continue to offer stand-alone chapters that dig into some of the new topics in economics. We've watched as topics like behavioral economics, game theory, political economy, and inequality figure more and more prominently in undergraduate curricula with each passing year. We believe it is important to provide teachers with ways to share new ideas and evidence with their students—important concepts that most nonmajors would usually miss.

At the same time, we realize how selective teachers must be in choosing which material to cover in the limited time available. In light of this, we've been especially glad for the guidance from many teachers in finding ways to present, in a time- and space-efficient way, some of the newer, and most exciting, parts of economics today. We promise you will find the topics, discussions, and writing style of *Economics* clear, concise, accessible, easy to teach from, and fun to read.

Motivation

Who are we? Why did we write this text?

Economics draws on our own experiences as academic economists, teachers, and policy advisors. We are based at large research universities and often work with and advise nonprofit organizations, governments, international agencies, donors, and private firms. Much of our research involves figuring out how to improve the way real markets function. Working with partners in the United States and on six continents, we are involved in testing new economic ideas. *Economics* draws on the spirit of that work, as well as similar research, taking students through the process of engaging with real problems, using analytical tools to devise solutions, and ultimately showing what works and why.

One of the best parts of writing this text, promoting its first edition, and revising for the second edition has been the opportunity to spend time with instructors across the country. We've been inspired by their creativity and passion and have learned from their pedagogical ideas. One of the questions we often ask fellow instructors is why they originally became interested in economics. A common response—one we share—is an attraction to the logic and power of economics as a social science. We also often hear instructors describe something slightly different: the way that economics appealed to them as a tool for making sense of life's complexities, whether in business, politics, or daily life. We wrote this book to give instructors a way to share with their students both of those ways that economics matters.

We also are grateful to the many adopters and near-adopters of the first edition who provided many helpful suggestions for ways to make the second edition an even better resource for instructors and students. As you'll see in the list of chapter-by-chapter changes that starts on page xviii, we've worked hard to fulfill your expectations and meet that goal.

We hope this product will provide students a solid foundation for considering important issues they will confront in their lives. We hope to inspire students to continue their studies in economics, and we promise this text will give them something useful to take away even if they choose other areas of study. Finally, we hope that, in ways small and large, the tools they learn in these pages and this course will help them to think critically about their environment, to live better lives, and to make an impact on their world.

Dean Karlan
Yale University

Jonathan Morduch
New York University

guided tour of features that benefit student learning

What makes this product different? Here's a quick guided tour of some key features that will engage students as they use the Karlan/Morduch content.

Four questions about how economists think

The text's evidence-based approach is framed by *four questions* that economists ask to break down a new challenge and analyze it methodically. We explore these four questions in Chapter 1 and then carry them throughout. They shape a consistent data-driven and impact-based approach to a wide variety of examples and case studies, demonstrating how the questions can be used to address real issues. By teaching the *right questions to ask,* the text provides students with a method for working through decisions they'll face as consumers, employees, entrepreneurs, and voters. Here are the four questions:

- **Question 1:** *What are the wants and constraints of those involved?* This question introduces the concept of *scarcity.* It asks students to think critically about the preferences and resources driving decision making in a given situation. It links into discussions of utility functions, budget constraints, strategic behavior, and new ideas that expand our thinking about rationality and behavioral economics.
- **Question 2:** *What are the trade-offs?* This question focuses on *opportunity cost.* It asks students to understand trade-offs in any decision, including factors that might go beyond the immediate financial costs and benefits. Consideration of trade-offs takes us to discussions of marginal decision making, sunk costs, nonmonetary costs, and discounting.
- **Question 3:** *How will others respond?* This question asks students to focus on *incentives,* both their incentives and the incentives of others. Students consider how individual choices aggregate in both expected and unexpected ways, and what happens when incentives change. The question links into understanding supply and demand, elasticity, competition, taxation, game theory, and monetary and fiscal policy.
- **Question 4:** *Why isn't someone already doing it?* This question relates to *efficiency.* It asks students to start from an assumption that markets work to provide desired goods and services, and then to think carefully about why something that seems like a good idea isn't already being done. We encourage students to revisit their answers to the previous three questions, to see whether they missed something about the trade-offs, incentives, or other forces at work, or are looking at a genuine market failure. This fourth question links topics such as public goods, externalities, information gaps, monopoly, arbitrage, and how the economy operates in the long run versus the short run.

Unique coverage

Economics presents the *core principles* of economics but also seeks to present some of the new ideas that are *expanding* the basics of economic theory. The sequence of chapters follows a fairly traditional route through the core principles. In a departure from the norm, we present the chapters on individual decision making (Part 3) before firm decisions (Part 4). We believe that by thinking first about the choices faced by individuals, students become better prepared to understand the choices of firms, groups, and governments. The text proceeds step-by-step from the personal to the public, allowing students to build toward an understanding of aggregate decisions on a solid foundation of individual decision making.

Two changes, based on market feedback, took place in the second edition chapter organization:

- We switched the sequence of two macroeconomic chapters, putting the "Unemployment and the Labor Market" chapter before the "Economic Growth" chapter.
- We added a new "Aggregate Expenditure" chapter.

Economics offers several stand-alone chapters focused on new ideas that are expanding economic theory, which can add nuance and depth to the core principles curriculum: behavioral economics, game theory, information, time and uncertainty, political choices, choice architecture, and development economics.

In addition, because students sometimes need reinforcement with the math requirements of the course, *Economics* contains seven unique math appendixes that explain math topics important to understanding economics. **McGraw-Hill Create**™ enables you to select and arrange the combination of traditional and unique chapters and appendixes that will be perfect for *your* course, at an affordable price for *your* students.

Engaging pedagogical features

Interesting examples open each chapter. These chapter-opening stories, presented in an engaging, journalistic style, feature issues that consumers, voters, businesspeople, and family members face. The examples then take students through relevant principles that can help frame and solve the economic problem at hand.

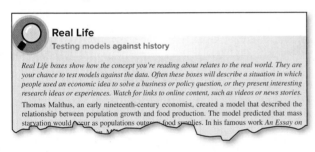

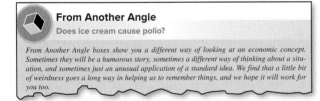

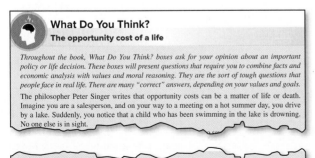

Boxed features build interest. Four different types of boxed stories add interesting real-world details:

- **Real Life** boxes describe a short case or policy question, findings from history or academic studies, and anecdotes from the field.
- **From Another Angle** boxes show a different way of looking at an economic concept—a different way of thinking about a situation, a humorous story, or sometimes just an unusual application of a standard idea.
- **What Do You Think?** boxes offer a longer case study, with implications for public policy and student-related issues. They present relevant data or historical evidence and ask students to employ both economic analysis and normative arguments to defend a position. We leave the student with open-ended questions, which professors can assign as homework or use for classroom discussion.
- **Where Can It Take You?** boxes direct students to further classes, resources, or jobs related to the topic at hand, to show students how they might apply economics in their careers and as consumers.

In addition, two other types of boxes—**Potentially Confusing** and **Hints**—offer in-depth explanations of a concept or use of terminology. These boxes call attention to common misunderstandings or provide further explanation of tricky concepts. Students appreciate that rather than smoothing over confusing ideas and language, we offer the support they need to understand economic language and reasoning on a deeper level.

Throughout this book, every chapter contains built-in review tools and study devices for student use. **Concept Check questions tied to learning objectives** appear at the end of each major section and prompt students to make sure they understand the topics covered before moving on. **Conclusions** at the end of each chapter sum up the overall lessons learned. **Summaries** give a deeper synopsis of what each learning objective covered. **Key Terms** provide a convenient list of the economic terminology introduced and defined in the chapter.

Also located at the ends of chapters and smoothly integrated with the chapter text are questions and problems for each learning objective:

- **Review Questions** guide students through review and application of the concepts covered in the chapter. These range from straightforward questions about theories or formulas to more open-ended narrative questions.
- High-quality **Problems and Applications** problem sets provide quantitative homework opportunities.

Both sets of content, plus additional Extra Practice Questions, are **fully integrated with Connect®**, enabling online assignments and grading.

The Karlan and Morduch product was built "from the ground up" with the expectation of *complete digital integration* of the text and related hands-on learning materials. All content in the chapter and online is tagged to the chapter learning objectives. Further, this text comes with a robust line-up of learning and teaching products, built for simple and reliable usability. See below for the highlights of our digital offer within Connect.

McGraw-Hill Connect

Adaptive reading experience. SmartBook contains the same content as the print book, but actively tailors that content to the needs of the individual through adaptive probing. Instructors can assign SmartBook reading assignments for points to create incentives for students to come to class prepared.

Extensive algorithmic and graphing assessment. Robust, auto-gradable question banks for each chapter now include even more questions that make use of the Connect graphing tool. More questions featuring algorithimic variations have also been added.

Interactive graphs. This new assignable resource within Connect helps students see the relevance of subject matter by providing visual displays of real data for students to manipulate. All graphs are accompanied by assignable assessment questions and feedback to guide students through the experience of learning to read and interpret graphs and data.

Videos. New to this edition are videos that provide support for key economics topics. These short, engaging explanations are presented at the moment a student is struggling to help the student connect the dots and grasp challenging concepts.

Math preparedness tutorials. Our math preparedness assignments have been reworked to help students refresh on important prerequisite topics necessary to be successful in economics.

Chapter 0 Orientation Assignments. New video assignments have been added to Connect on topics such as SmartBook, graphing exercises, and the interactive graphs. These videos provide students with information about the different assignment types they will encounter in Connect, to help them be successful on their assignments and ensure a smooth start to the term.

New Student Interface. Connect's new, intuitive interface gives students a view of assignments and deadlines across all courses in Connect, to help them be more organized. Students also have access to a personalized analytics dashboard designed to help them allocate study time appropriately for maximum success in the course.

Supplementary Materials

All supplements accompany this text in a completely seamless integration. The following ancillaries are available for quick download and convenient access via the Online Learning Center at www.mhhe.com/karlanmorduch2e and within Connect. Instructor resources are password protected for security.

Test bank

The test bank has been extensively revised for this edition by Aaron Finkle at University of Maryland and Michael Machiorlatti at Oklahoma City Community College. All test bank items were also thoroughly accuracy-checked by Cindy Clement at University of Maryland and Ida Mirzaie at Ohio State University. The test bank contains thousands of quality multiple-choice questions. Each question is tagged with the corresponding learning objective, level of difficulty, economic concept, AACSB learning category, and Bloom's Taxonomy objective. All of the test bank content is available to assign within Connect.

The test bank is also available in TestGen, a complete, state-of-the-art test generator and editing application software that allows instructors to quickly and easily select test items from McGraw-Hill's test bank content. The instructors can then organize, edit, and customize questions and answers to rapidly generate tests for paper or online administration. Questions can include stylized text, symbols, graphics, and equations that are inserted directly into questions using built-in mathematical templates. TestGen's random generator provides the option to display different text or calculated number values each time questions are used. With both quick-and-simple test creation and flexible and robust editing tools, TestGen is a complete test generator system for today's educators.

PowerPoint presentations

Revised for this edition by Gregory Gilpin at Montana State University, the PowerPoint presentations have been carefully crafted to ensure maximum usefulness in the classroom. Each presentation covers crucial information and supplies animated figures that are identical to those in the book. The presentations also contain sample exercises, instructor notes, and more.

In addition to the instructor PowerPoint presentations, a student version is also provided. The student PowerPoints provide a review of each chapter's main points and graphs in a static, PDF form. Some information is intentionally missing from these PDFs so that students are prompted to follow along with the instructor and fill information in as it is discussed in class.

Instructor's manual

The instructor's manual provides a wealth of resources to help organize and enrich the course. Elements include:

- **Learning Objectives:** Lists the learning objectives for each chapter.
- **Chapter Outline:** Shows an outline of the chapter organization for a quick review.
- **Beyond the Lecture:** Presents ideas and activities you can use to start discussion and engage students in class, along with team exercises and assignments you can use outside of class, revised by Dave Brown, Penn State University.
- **Clicker Questions:** Offer additional opportunities for classroom engagement, created by Dave Brown, Penn State University.
- **End-of-Chapter Solutions:** Provides answers to all end-of-chapter questions and problems, revised for this edition by Nora Underwood at University of Central Florida and Erin Moody at University of Maryland. All end-of-chapter answers and solutions have been accuracy checked by Susan Bell at Seminole State College and Greg Gilpin, Montana State University.

Assurance of Learning Ready

Many educational institutions today are focused on the notion of *assurance of learning,* an important element of some accreditation standards. Karlan and Morduch's *Economics* is designed specifically to support your assurance of learning initiatives with a simple, yet powerful solution. Each test bank question for *Economics* maps to a specific chapter learning outcome/objective listed in the text. You can use our test bank software, TestGen, or Connect to easily query for learning outcomes/objectives that directly relate to the learning objectives for your course. You can then use the reporting features to aggregate student results in similar fashion, making the collection and presentation of assurance of learning data simple and easy.

AACSB Statement

McGraw-Hill Education is a proud corporate member of AACSB International. Understanding the importance and value of AACSB accreditation, Karlan and Morduch's *Economics* recognizes the curricula guidelines detailed in the AACSB standards for business accreditation by connecting selected questions in the text and the test bank to the eight general knowledge and skill guidelines in the AACSB standards.

The statements contained in *Economics* are provided only as a guide for the users of this textbook. The AACSB leaves content coverage and assessment within the purview of individual schools, the mission of the school, and the faculty. While *Economics* and the teaching package make no claim of any specific AACSB qualification or evaluation, we have within *Economics* labeled selected questions according to the eight general knowledge and skills areas.

McGraw-Hill Customer Care Contact Information

At McGraw-Hill, we understand that getting the most from new technology can be challenging. That's why our services don't stop after you purchase our products. You can email our Product Specialists 24 hours a day to get product training online. Or you can search our knowledge bank of Frequently Asked Questions on our support website. For Customer Support, call **800-331-5094**, email hmsupport@mcgraw-hill.com, or visit www.mhhe.com/support. One of our Technical Support Analysts will be able to assist you in a timely fashion.

McGraw-Hill Connect®
Learn Without Limits

Connect is a teaching and learning platform that is proven to deliver better results for students and instructors.

Connect empowers students by continually adapting to deliver precisely what they need, when they need it, and how they need it, so your class time is more engaging and effective.

73% of instructors who use **Connect** require it; instructor satisfaction **increases** by 28% when **Connect** is required.

Connect's Impact on Retention Rates, Pass Rates, and Average Exam Scores

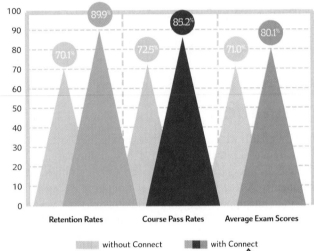

Using **Connect** improves retention rates by **19.8%**, passing rates by **12.7%**, and exam scores by **9.1%**.

Analytics

Connect Insight®

Connect Insight is Connect's new one-of-a-kind visual analytics dashboard that provides at-a-glance information regarding student performance, which is immediately actionable. By presenting assignment, assessment, and topical performance results together with a time metric that is easily visible for aggregate or individual results, Connect Insight gives the user the ability to take a just-in-time approach to teaching and learning, which was never before available. Connect Insight presents data that helps instructors improve class performance in a way that is efficient and effective.

Impact on Final Course Grade Distribution

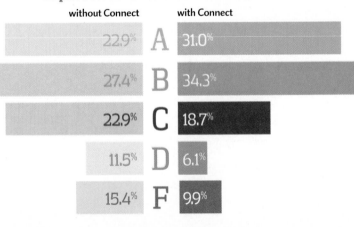

Adaptive

THE **ADAPTIVE** READING EXPERIENCE DESIGNED TO TRANSFORM THE WAY STUDENTS READ

More students earn **A's** and **B's** when they use McGraw-Hill Education **Adaptive** products.

SmartBook®

Proven to help students improve grades and study more efficiently, SmartBook contains the same content within the print book, but actively tailors that content to the needs of the individual. SmartBook's adaptive technology provides precise, personalized instruction on what the student should do next, guiding the student to master and remember key concepts, targeting gaps in knowledge and offering customized feedback, and driving the student toward comprehension and retention of the subject matter. Available on tablets, SmartBook puts learning at the student's fingertips—anywhere, anytime.

Over **8 billion questions** have been answered, making McGraw-Hill Education products more intelligent, reliable, and precise.

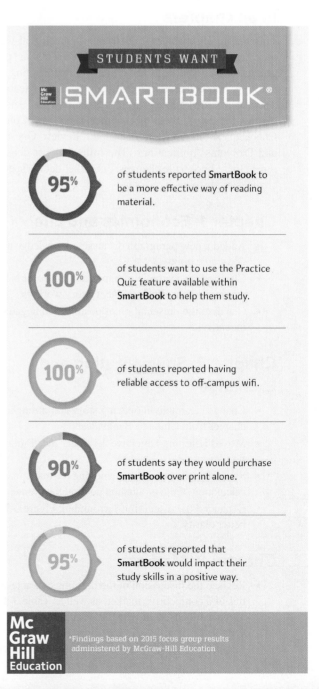

STUDENTS WANT

SMARTBOOK®

95% of students reported **SmartBook** to be a more effective way of reading material.

100% of students want to use the Practice Quiz feature available within **SmartBook** to help them study.

100% of students reported having reliable access to off-campus wifi.

90% of students say they would purchase **SmartBook** over print alone.

95% of students reported that **SmartBook** would impact their study skills in a positive way.

McGraw Hill Education

*Findings based on 2015 focus group results administered by McGraw-Hill Education

www.mheducation.com

detailed content changes

Numerous changes were made to the second edition of this text; this section provides a detailed, chapter-by-chapter list of changes. The hope is that this list will help users of the text quickly see what has changed in each chapter so they can adjust lesson plans as needed.

In all chapters

Throughout all chapters, the authors updated real-world data, reformatted long paragraphs into smaller paragraphs or bulleted lists for easier student reading and learning, and added additional eBook-only box features. They also added more learning objectives (as detailed below) for text subsections, with related new Concept Check questions and end-of-chapter Review Questions and Problems/Applications. The following list does not repeat these bookwide changes, but rather details specific changes made to each chapter.

Chapter 1: Economics and Life

- Added a new paragraph discussing knowledge as a nonscarce good.
- Clarified the example of opportunity cost for self-employed consultants versus factory workers.
- Clarified the presentation of positive and negative incentives.

Chapter 2: Specialization and Exchange

- Changed example in opening story and throughout chapter from China to Bangladesh.
- Moved Learning Objective 2.1 under the "Production Possibilities" header.
- Simplified the chapter by removing the mathematical calculation of the production possibilities frontier.
- Expanded the discussion surrounding Figure 2-7 for better clarity.

Chapter 3: Markets

- Revised the discussion of the defining characteristics of a competitive market, as well as Table 3-1, to make it consistent with the discussion in Chapter 13.
- Slightly expanded the explanation of *ceteris paribus*.

Chapter 4: Elasticity

- Changed the presentation of price elasticity of demand to show only the mid-point method and made more explicit the equations for percentage change in quantity demanded and percentage change in price.
- Added a new table (Table 4-1) to show estimated price elasticities of demand for some common goods.
- Added a new paragraph to further explain nonprice determinants in cross-price elasticity of demand.

Chapter 5: Efficiency

- Clarified and simplified the examples of willingness to pay and willingness to sell.
- Expanded the discussion of total surplus, as shown in Figure 5-5.
- Expanded the discussion of deadweight loss, as shown in Figure 5-8.
- Revised text to clarify the concept of missing markets.
- Added a Concept Check question for Learning Objective 5.6 about how price changes affect the distribution of surplus between consumers and producers.

Chapter 6: Government Intervention

- Changed the sequence of the three reasons to intervene in markets, moving market failures last.
- Introduced the term *welfare effects* in the discussion of deadweight loss.
- Added a new paragraph further explaining the effects of payday lending rates to the "Put a cap on payday lending?" box.
- Added a new Concept Check question for Learning Objective 6.2 about what can cause a price floor to become nonbinding.
- Added a new equation (Equation 6.3) on calculation of government subsidy expenditure.
- Added two new figures: Figure 6-12 shows the deadweight loss from a subsidy and Figure 6-13 shows the effect of a subsidy on surplus.
- Added a new Concept Check question for Learning Objective 6.3 about what determines the incidence of a tax.

Chapter 7: Consumer Behavior

- Divided what used to be one learning objective in the first edition (LO 7.5) into two learning objectives (LOs 7.5 and 7.6).
- Added a short parenthetical explanation that utility numbers have no concrete meaning other than relative to each other.
- Added a new table (Table 7.1) to show marginal utility, with clarified explanation of diminishing marginal utility.
- Added a new Potentially Confusing box on the difference between inferior and normal goods to the "Changes in prices" header, under the income effect discussion.
- Added a new paragraph summarizing the income and substitution effects.
- Added a new Concept Check question for Learning Objective 7.5 about the influence of opinions on utility.

Appendix E: Using Indifference Curves

- Added two new learning objectives: LO E.3 (shapes of indifference curves for perfect substitutes and perfect complements) and LO E.6 (how to build an individual's demand curve using indifference curves).
- Revised the appendix to better differentiate the example used in the body of Chapter 7 ("Cody") and the example used in the appendix ("Malik").

Chapter 8: Behavioral Economics

- Revised the box about stickK, a company that helps people reach their goals by committing to a course of action and facing a penalty if they fail to follow through.

Chapter 9: Game Theory and Strategic Thinking

- Added new learning objectives: LOs 9.3 (dominant strategy in a one-time game), 9.4 (whether a Nash equilibrium will be reached in a one-time game), and 9.5 (how a commitment strategy can be used to achieve cooperation in a one-time game).
- Added a new figure (Figure 9.5) showing the payoffs in the driving game of "chicken."
- Added a new Concept Check about how to identify whether a strategy is dominant.

- Under the "Sequential Games" header, added a new "What Do You Think?" box about strategy on the TV show *Survivor*.
- Added a new Concept Check question about backward induction.

Chapter 10: Information

- Expanded and clarified the discussion of adverse selection.

Chapter 11: Time and Uncertainty

- Added new Learning Objectove 11.5 (risk-averse versus risk-seeking behaviors).
- Revised the formula for the future value of a sum (Equation 11.3).
- Expanded the explanation of present value computation.

Chapter 12: The Costs of Production

- Revised the numbers in Table 12-2 that shows production and marginal product of labor.
- Revised the discussion of total, average, and marginal costs, including the columns and numbers in the costs of production table (Table 12-3).
- Revised and expanded the discussion of marginal cost.
- Changed the terminology *returns to scale* to *economies and diseconomies of scale.*

Chapter 13: Perfect Competition

- Revised the discussion of characteristics of competitive markets to match the discussion in Chapter 3.
- Added a "Potentially Confusing" box in the discussion of the optimal quantity of output, discussing the terminology "profit increased" when referring to a negative amount.
- Added a section-concluding paragraph about why firms continue to produce when they are making negative profits.
- Added equations showing the calculation of profit using average revenue and average total cost.
- In the discussion of deciding when to operate, separated out discussions of firms' short-run versus long-run decisions, to clarify difference between shutting down and exiting the market.
- Added new Table 13-4 showing revenue, cost, and profit data when price falls.

- Added a "Potentially Confusing" box elaborating on economists' use of the terminology *exiting* versus *shutting down*.
- Added new subheadings to differentiate the discussions of the effects of market entry on the long-run and short-run supply curves.
- Added a "Potentially Confusing" box reviewing the difference between accounting profit and economic profit.

Chapter 14: Monopoly

- Adjusted the curves in Figures 14-2, 14-3, 14-4, 14-5, and 14-6.
- Revised the labels in Figure 14-1, part A.
- Added new Table 14-2 to compare the characteristics of perfect competition and monopoly markets.
- Made changes in panel A of Figure 14-6 to highlight and differentiate private monopoly price and government monopoly price.
- Added a Concept Check question asking how aggressive tactics create barriers to entry.

Chapter 15: Monopolistic Competition and Oligopoly

- Added a paragraph further explaining market categories of record companies (oligopolists) and individual musicians (monopolistic competitors).
- Adjusted the curves in Figures 15-2, 15-3, and 15-4.
- Added new Table 15-1 comparing the characteristics of market models (perfect competition, monopoly, monopolistic competition).
- Revised Figure 15-6 to show marginal revenue curve and expanded the text discussion of the profit-maximizing quantity for monopolies and perfectly competitive firms.
- Clarified the discussion of quantity effect and price effect in oligopolies.
- Added new Figure 15-7 that compares the market equilibrium in different types of markets for music albums—monopoly, duopoly, three-firm, and perfectly competitive.
- Revised and slightly expanded Learning Objective 15.7 to clarify the application of game theory to oligopolies' decision to compete or collude.
- Expanded the section on Nash equilibriums.
- Added a new Concept Check question for Learning Objective 15.7 about collusion in repeated games.

Chapter 16: The Factors of Production

- Clarified the text discussion of the value of marginal product (VMP) and added a new formula for calculating VMP.
- Added new Table 16-2 about nonprice determinants of labor demand and Table 16-3 about nonprice determinants of labor supply, to clarify discussion of labor supply and labor demand.
- Combined previously separate text discussions of determinants of labor demand and labor, for greater clarity.

Chapter 17: International Trade

- Changed China to Bangladesh in chapter-opening example.
- Added new Learning Objective 17.4 addressing when and how an economy's trade policies affect world supply of and world demand for a good.
- Added a new summary paragraph under "Incomplete Specialization" header.
- Clarified the text explanations, relating to Figures 17-4 and 17-5, about becoming a net importer and a net exporter.
- Added new Concept Check questions for Learning Objective 17.3 (what happens to domestic consumer surplus when a country becomes a net-importer of a good) and Learning Objective 17.4 (what happens to world supply and world demand when a large economy moves from restricted to unrestricted trade).

Chapter 18: Externalities

- Major revision and reorganization of the "What Are Externalities?" section. The revised content now features separate subsections on negative externalities and positive externalities.
- The negative externalities section covers the problem of "too much"—negative production externality and negative consumption externality.
- The positive externalities section covers the problem of "too little"—positive consumption externality and positive production externality.
- The new section on private solutions to externalities discusses why private solutions don't always occur.

- The new section on public solutions to externalities addresses taxes and subsidies, and quotas and tradable allowances.
- New "What Do You Think?" box, "Reclining Transactions," applying the Coase theorem to the problem of people reclining their seats on airplanes.
- New figures throughout the chapter.

Chapter 19: Public Goods and Common Resources

- Slightly expanded the discussion of nonrival goods.
- Expanded and reorganized the content dealing with the tragedy of the commons and use of government regulation to solve common resources problems.
- Revised the Concept Check question related to Learning Objective 19.3 about the effect of social norms on potential free riders.
- Added a new Concept Check question for Learning Objective 19.4 about how the tragedy of the commons affects demand for common resources and equilibrium quantity.

Chapter 20: Taxation and the Public Budget

- Numbered the tax-revenue computation formula (Equation 20-1).
- Revised Figure 20-4 that graphs the price and quantity effects of a tax increase.
- Added subheaders to highlight and better differentiate proportional, progressive, and regressive taxation.
- Added a text discussion and table comparing tax rates of various countries.
- Moved and reformatted the discussion of personal income tax collection.

Chapter 21: Poverty, Inequality, and Discrimination

- Added new Learning Objective 21.2 about why poverty persists.
- Expanded the "Real Life" box on "Getting out of the neighborhood?" to include recent evidence on a policy experiment that tests the effects of moving poor families out of areas with concentrated poverty.
- Added a new "What Do You Think?" box about the super-wealthy that invites students to consider the implications of widening inequality.
- Added new Learning Objective 21.7 about why economists differentiate between correlation and causation when measuring discrimination and why markets do not always eliminate discrimination.

Chapter 22: Political Choices

- Added new Learning Objective 22.6 about major features of political structures and how they can affect policy choices.

Chapter 23: Public Policy and Choice Architecture

- Expanded the explanation of SMartT™ retirement-savings program and the effectiveness of commitment devices, which illustrates an idea from behavioral economics that helps workers save more.
- Added a list summarizing important rules for creating effective commitment devices.
- Added new Learning Objective 23.4 about how well-presented information can help people make decisions that are good for them and a related Concept Check question asking for definition of a heuristic.

Chapter 24: Measuring GDP

- Changed chapter title to "Measuring GDP."
- Tightened introductory section about valuing an economy.
- Moved, to earlier under the "Approaches to Measuring GDP" header, the paragraph discussing why there are three approaches to measuring GDP.
- Slightly expanded the discussion of real versus nominal GDP.
- Added a new Concept Check question for Learning Objective 24.1 about why only final goods and services are counted under GDP and why sales of used goods are not counted.
- Added a new Concept Check question for Learning Objective 24.2 about why total income in a country is equal to total expenditures on goods produced in that country.

- Added a Concept Check question related to Learning Objective 24.3 about how the expenditure approach and the income approach capture two sides of the same transactions.
- Added a new, separate Learning Objective 24.5 about calculating the GDP deflator.

Chapter 25: The Cost of Living

- Slightly expanded the introductory discussion of measuring price changes over time.
- Simplified Learning Objective 25.4 so that it asks students to calculate inflation by just the CPI method and to recognize alternative inflation measures (PPI and GDP deflator).
- Added new Learning Objective 25.5 about using a price index to adjust nominal values into real values.
- Added new Learning Objective 25.6 about how indexing keeps the real value of a payment constant over time.

Chapter 26: Unemployment and the Labor Market

- Changed sequence of two chapters so that "Unemployment and the Labor Market" (now Chapter 26) comes before "Economic Growth" (now Chapter 27).
- Added the formula for computation of the size of the labor force (Equation 26-1).
- Added subheaders to better highlight and differentiate discussions of frictional, structural, and real-wage (classical) unemployment.

Chapter 27: Economic Growth

- Changed sequence of two chapters so that "Economic Growth" (now Chapter 27) follows "Unemployment and the Labor Market" (now Chapter 26).
- Added new text discussion (new Learning Objective 27.4) about the growth accounting framework, including the growth accounting equation (Equation 27-4) and discussion of how technology, labor, and capital contribute to economic growth.
- Added subheaders to better differentiate discussions of domestic savings and foreign direct investment.
- Expanded text discussion of government involvement in R&D and innovation.

Chapter 28: Aggregate Expenditure

- **NEW chapter!** The new chapter "Aggregate Expenditure" introduces the Keynesian approach to addressing business cycles, showing how economies can get stuck due to low aggregate demand. It introduces tools that policy-makers use to try to get economies out of recessions.

Appendix G: Algebra and Aggregate Expenditure

- **NEW appendix!** The new appendix "Algebra and Aggregate Expenditure" shows how to solve for equilibrium AE algebraically.

Chapter 29: Aggregate Demand and Aggregate Supply

- Added new Figure 29.1, which shows how price-driven shifts in planned aggregate expenditure trace out the aggregate demand curve.
- Added new "Hint" box explaining the labeling of the horizontal axis in this chapter as "output," equivalent to aggregate expenditure.
- Added new discussion, including new Figure 29-1, of graphing price-level changes.
- Added new text discussion (new Learning Objective 29.3) section about the differences in the multiplier effects for aggregate demand due to changes in government spending versus changes in taxes.
- Added new Concept Check questions related to Learning Objective 29.6 about shifts in the SRAS and LRAS curves.
- Expanded the discussion of the effect of a decrease in aggregate demand, as shown in Figure 29-11.
- Deleted the "Real Life" box on recessions and remittances.
- Added subheaders to differentiate discussions of temporary supply shocks from permanent supply shocks.
- Added new Learning Objective 29.9 that asks students to use the AD/AS framework to determine whether an observed change in output and prices was due to a demand shock or a supply shock.
- Added new Figure 29-14 showing the different short-run impacts of decreases in aggregate demand versus aggregate supply.

Chapter 30: Fiscal Policy

- Corrected caption for Figure 30-1.
- Added new Learning Objective 30.3 about the effect of time lags on fiscal policy.
- Added subheaders to highlight difference among information lags, formulation lags, and implementation lags.
- Added new Learning Objective 30.4 about how stabilizers can automatically adjust fiscal policy as the economy changes and revised text discussion about automatic stabilizers.
- Added new Learning Objective 30.5, with related text discussion, about the theory and evidence of Ricardian equivalence. The section explains why government policy to lift economies from recessions may be ineffective, highlighting key empirical assumptions and the available evidence.
- Moved section on the multiplier model out of this chapter.
- Slightly expanded discussion of on revenue and spending under "The Government Budget" header.
- Added new Learning Objective 30.8, with related text discussion, about how the government goes into debt and how Treasury securities work.
- Added new Figure 30-7 that shows top foreign holders of U.S. debt.

Chapter 31: The Basics of Finance

- Added new Learning Objective 31.1, with related text discussion, about asymmetry problems that can occur in financial markets.
- Added panel B to Figure 31-2.
- Added new Learning Objective 31.2 about functions of financial markets and banks.
- Added new Learning Objective 31.3 about the market for loanable funds and the difference between savings and investment.
- Highlighted the conceptual difference in economics between savings and investment by formatting discussion as a list and adding a new "Hint" box.
- Added new Figure 31-4 showing how a change in the underlying determinants of investment opportunities shifts the demand curve for loanable funds.
- Added new Learning Objective 31.4 about factors that affect the supply and demand for loanable funds and revised the discussions of the determinants of savings and investment.

- Added new Learning Objective 31.5 about how interest rates on loans vary with the length of the loan and the riskiness of the transaction.
- Added new Learning Objective 31.6 about the key functions of the financial system (intermediating between buyers and sellers, providing liquidity, and diversifying risk).
- Added new discussion of asset bubbles.
- Expanded Learning Objective 31.11 about why savings equals investment in a closed economy and how government spending and foreign capital flows affect the saving-investment relationship.

Chapter 32: Money and the Monetary System

- Replaced old Figure 31-1 of a simple money-creation process with new Table 32-1.
- Revised discussion of money creation in today's economy through bank loans, including new Figure 32-1.
- Revised discussion of measuring money, including change to use of the terminology *monetary base*.
- Clarified discussions of expansionary and contractionary monetary policies.
- Added new paragraph introducing the concept of zero lower bound. The section highlights why policy that depends on reducing interest rates may not work (since the interest rates can't be reduced far enough), leading to a discussion of new tools used by policy-makers like "quantitative easing."
- Added new Figure 32-6, "The Economic Effects of Monetary Policy," showing the effect of the slope of the money demand curve on interest rates.
- Deleted short section from first edition "Coming full circle: Back to the market for loanable funds."

Chapter 33: Inflation

- Added new Learning Objective 33.1 about various definitions of inflation: inflation, deflation, headline inflation, and core inflation.
- Clarified text example of bracket creep, to show how inflation can reduce the resources available to families, even when their income rises with inflation.
- Added subheaders to further highlight sections on disinflation and hyperinflation.
- Added new Learning Objective 33.8 about why policy-makers favor a small amount of inflation

Chapter 34: Financial Crisis

- Revised the chapter-opening story to emphasize how the government's role entails crisis management, not just steering the economy through business cycles.
- Added text discussion of the leverage ratio (part of Learning Objective 34.1).
- Added new Learning Objective 34.2 about the causes of two famous historical financial crises (the South Seas Bubble and the Great Crash of 1929).
- Reformatted discussion of the timeline of the 2007–2008 financial crisis for greater clarity.

Chapter 35: Open-Market Macroeconomics

- Clarified text discussion of the effects of foreign investment.
- Added new Learning Objective 35.7 about the determinants of demand and supply in the forex market and added subheadings under "A model of the exchange-rate market" to clarify discussion.
- Added a "Hint" box to discuss economists' use of the terminology *devalued* and *revalued.*

- Added new Learning Objective 35.9 about why monetary policy is ineffective when maintaining a fixed exchange rate.
- Changed labels on the y-axis in Figures 35-11 and 35-13.
- Fixed label on the x-axis in Figure 35-12, part B.
- Corrected the droplines in Figure 35-16.
- Added new Learning Objective 35.11 about the role of the IMF and how financial crises are created by excessive debt and unsustainable exchange rates.

Chapter 36: Development Economics

- Added new Learning Objective 36.7 about the aims of foreign aid, the role of poverty traps, the main institutions delivering aid, and criticisms of foreign aid.
- Added new Learning Objective 36.8 about how impact investing provides a new tool for creating social impact—the idea that some investors make decisions to earn a financial return while also having social impacts by channeling money to companies with social missions like improving health and reducing poverty.

acknowledgments

Many people helped us create this text. It's said that "it takes a village," but it often felt like we had the benefit of an entire town.

We thank Meredith Startz, Ted Barnett, and Andrew Wright for the foundational work they contributed to the first edition, which still shines through in this edition. Thanks, too, to Victor Matheson (College of the Holy Cross), Diana Beck (New York University), Amanda Freeman (Kansas State University), and John Kane (SUNY--Oswego) for their contributions to and thoughts about early drafts of chapters.

An energetic group of collaborators helped us shape second-edition content in ways that are relevant and engaging for a student audience: David "Dukes" Love (Williams College) steered us through the writing of the macro chapters, helping us revamp our treatment of the aggregate expenditure model and how it leads into the aggregate demand and aggregate supply model. These changes in turn provide simple ways to introduce students to recently added tools of macro policy. Erin Moody (University of Maryland) applied her extensive classroom experience as an essential contributor throughout the micro chapters, ensuring that we addressed the many suggestions we received from users and reviewers of our text since the first edition published. Camille Soltau Nelson (Oregon State University) analyzed Chapter 18, "Externalities," and ensured that this time around the chapter fits the needs of our users. Our IPA team of researchers, Radhika Lokur and Noor Sethi, brought a recent-student perspective to the text and helped us update many of our examples and figures with the most current data.

We couldn't have produced the second edition without all of these talented individuals. We thank them for their expertise and also for their willingness to provide feedback at a moment's notice.

Many other talented individuals contributed on and off throughout this project. We thank Bob Schwab, Kevin Stanley, Ross vanWassenhove, and James Peyton for closely reviewing a draft of our revised Chapter 18 and helping guide us toward a final version. We thank John Neri and Murat Doral for providing detailed feedback on all the macro chapters of the text. We appreciate Jodi Begg's help in providing a base to work from for Chapter 28, "Aggregate Expenditure." We thank Chiuping Chen, Ashley Hodgson, Michael Machiorlatti, and Germain Pichop for reviewing said chapter in its draft stages to ensure we were on the right track.

We thank Nora Underwood (University of Central Florida) and Erin Moody (University of Maryland) for their many and varied contributions to end-of-chapter content, both in the text and in Connect. We are very appreciative of the extensive work done by Susan Bell (Seminole State College) and Greg Gilpin (Montana State University) in accuracy-checking this content. In addition, we thank Russell Kellogg (University of Colorado Denver) for authoring the LearnSmart content.

We also want to share our appreciation to the following people at McGraw-Hill for the hard work they put into creating the product you see before you: Katie Hoenicke, Senior Brand Manager, helped us communicate the overarching vision and promoted our revision. Virgil Lloyd, Marketing Manager, guided us in visiting schools and working with the sales team. Ann Torbert, Lead Product Developer, has been an exemplary editor, improving the exposition on each page and keeping attention on both the big picture and key details. Alyssa Lincoln, Senior Product Developer, and Michele Janicek, Lead Product Developer, managed innumerable and indispensable details—reviews, manuscript, and the many aspects of the digital products and overall package. Kathryn Wright, Core Content Project Manager, helped turn our manuscript into the finished, polished product you see before you. Kristin Bradley, Assessment Content Project Manager, skillfully guided the digital plan. Thanks, too, to Douglas Ruby, Senior Director of Digital Content, and Kevin Shanahan, Senior Product Manager, CPO, for their careful shepherding of the digital materials that accompany the text.

Thank You!

Creating the second edition of a book is a daunting task. We wanted to do everything we could to improve upon the first edition, and we couldn't have done this without professors who told us honestly what they thought we could do better. To everyone who helped shape this edition, we thank you for sharing your insights and recommendations.

Symposia

Luca Bossi
University of Pennsylvania

Regina Cassady
Valencia College

June Charles
North Lake College

Monica Cherry
St. John Fisher College and State University of New York at Buffalo

George Chikhladze
University of Missouri–Columbia

Patrick Crowley
Texas A&M University–Corpus Christi

Attila Cseh
Valdosta State University

Susan Doty
University of Texas at Tyler

Irene Foster
George Washington University

Don Holley
Boise State University

Ricot Jean
Valencia College

Sarah Jenyk
Youngstown State University

Stephanie Jozefowicz
Indiana University of Pennsylvania

Nkongolo Kalala
Bluegrass Community and Technical College

Carrie Kerekes
Florida Gulf Coast University

Brandon Koford
Weber State University

Soloman Kone
City University of New York

W. J. Lane
University of New Orleans

Jose Lopez-Calleja
Miami Dade College

Erika Martinez
University of South Florida–Tampa

Geri Mason
Seattle Pacific University

ABM Nasir
North Carolina Central University

Eric Nielsen
Saint Louis Community College

Rich Numrich
College of Southern Nevada

Michael Polcen
Northern Virginia Community College

Martin Sabo
Community College of Denver

Latisha Settlage
University of Arkansas–Fort Smith

Mark Showalter
Brigham Young University

Warren Smith
Palm Beach State College

Kay Strong
Baldwin Wallace University

Ryan Umbeck
Ivy Tech Community College

Ross VanWassenhove
University of Houston

Terry Von Ende
Texas Tech University

Jennifer Wissink
Cornell University

Focus Groups

Siddiq Abdullah
University of Massachusetts–Boston

Seemi Ahmad
Dutchess Community College

Nurul Aman
University of Massachusetts–Boston

Aimee Chin
University of Houston

Can Erbil
Boston College

Varun Gupta
Wharton County Junior College

Moon Han
North Shore Community College

Hilaire Jean-Gilles
Bunker Hill Community College

Jennifer Lehman
Wharton County Junior College

Mikko Manner,
Dutchess Community College

Nara Mijid
Central Connecticut State University

Shahruz Mohtadi
Suffolk University

Victor Moussoki
Lone Star College

Kevin Nguyen
Lone Star College

Jan Palmer
Ohio University

Julia Paxton
Ohio University

Tracy Regan
Boston College

Christina Robinson
Central Connecticut State University

Rosemary Rossiter
Ohio University

Sara Saderion
Houston Community College

Reviews

Steve Abid
Grand Rapids Community College

Eric Abrams
McKendree University

Richard Ugunzi Agesa
Marshall University

Seemi Ahmad
Dutchess Community College

Jason A. Aimone
Baylor University

Donald L. Alexander
Western Michigan University

Ricky Ascher
Broward College and Palm Beach State College

Shannon Aucoin
University of Louisiana at Lafayette

Gyanendra Baral
Oklahoma City Community College

Klaus Becker
Texas Tech University

Pedro Bento
West Virginia University

Jennifer Bossard
Doane College

Kristen Broady
Fort Valley State University

Gregory Brock
Georgia Southern University

Giuliana Andreopoulos Campanelli
William Paterson University

Joni Charles
Texas State University

Chiuping Chen
American River College

Tom Creahan
Morehead State University

Can Dogan
North American University

Brandon Dupont
Western Washington University

Matthew J. Easton
Pueblo Community College

Linda K. English
Baylor University

Irene R. Foster
George Washington University

Alka Gandhi
Northern Virginia Community College

Soma Ghosh
Albright College

Gregory Gilpin
Montana State University

Lisa Workman Gloege
Grand Rapids Community College

Cynthia Harter
Eastern Kentucky University

Darcy Hartman
Ohio State University

Ashley Hodgson
St. Olaf College

Don Holley
Boise State University

Harvey James
University of Missouri

Sarah Jenyk
Youngstown State University

Russell Kellogg
University of Colorado Denver

Greg Lindeblom
Broward College

Michael Machiorlatti
Oklahoma City Community College

Rita Madarassy
Santa Clara University

Edouard Mafoua
State University of New York at Canton

C. Lucy Malakar
Lorain County Community College

Geri Mason
Seattle Pacific University

Katherine McClain
University of Georgia

Bruce McClung
Texas State University

Robin McCutcheon
Marshall University

Tia M. McDonald
Ohio University

John Min
Northern Virginia Community College

Sam Mirmirani
Bryant University

Ida A. Mirzaie
Ohio State University

Franklin G. Mixon Jr.
Columbus State University

Erin Moody
University of Maryland

Barbara Moore
University of Central Florida

Christopher Mushrush
Illinois State University

Charles Myrick
Oklahoma City Community College

Camille Nelson
Oregon State University

Per Norander
University of North Carolina–Charlotte

Ronald Oertel
Western Washington University

Constantin Ogloblin
Georgia Southern University

Alex Olbrecht
Ramapo College of New Jersey

Tomi Ovaska
Youngstown State University

Jan Palmer
Ohio University

Julia Paxton
Ohio University

James Peyton
Highline College

Germain Pichop
Oklahoma City Community College

Brennan Platt
Brigham Young University

Elizabeth Porter
University of North Carolina–Asheville

Mathew Price
Oklahoma City Community College

Christina Robinson
Central Connecticut State University

Matthew Roelofs
Western Washington University

Randall R. Rojas
University of California–Los Angeles

John Rykowski
Kalamazoo Valley Community College

Robert M. Schwab
University of Maryland

Gasper Sekelj
Clarkson University

James K. Self
Indiana University

Mark Showalter
Brigham Young University

Kevin Stanley
Highline College

Steve Trost
Virginia Polytechnic Institute and State University

Ross S. vanWassenhove
University of Houston

In addition, we continue to be grateful to the first-edition contributors, who over the course of several years of development attended focus groups or symposia or provided content reviews. Thanks to the following, whose insights, recommendations, and feedback helped immeasurably as the project took shape.

Mark Abajian
San Diego Mesa College

Tom Adamson
Midland University

Richard Agesa
Marshall University

Rashid Al-Hmoud
Texas Tech University

Frank Albritton
Seminole State College-Sanford

Terence Alexander
Iowa State University

Clifford Althoff
Joliet Junior College

Diane Anstine
North Central College

Michael Applegate
Oklahoma State University–Stillwater Campus

Ali Ataiifar
Delaware County Community College

Roberto Ayala
California State Polytechnic University–Pomona

Jim Barbour
Elon University

Gary Benson
Southwest Community College

Laura Jean Bhadra
Northern Virginia Community College–Manassas

Prasun Bhattacharjee
East Tennessee State University–Johnson City

Radha Bhattacharya
California State University–Fullerton

Michael Bonnal
University of Tennessee–Chattanooga

Camelia Bouzerdan
Middlesex Community College

Dale Bremmer
Rose-Hulman Institute of Technology

Anne Bresnock
University of California–Los Angeles

Bruce Brown
California State Polytechnic University–Pomona

Ken Brown
University of Northern Iowa

Laura Bucila
Texas Christian University

Andrew Cassey
Washington State University

Kalyan Chakraborty
Emporia State University

Catherine Chambers
University of Central Missouri

Britton Chapman
State College of Florida–Manatee

Sanjukta Chaudhuri
University of Wisconsin–Eau Claire

Chiuping Chen
American River College

Ron Cheung
Oberlin College

Young Back Choi
Saint John's University

Dmitriy Chulkov
Indiana University–Kokomo

Cindy Clement
University of Maryland–College Park

Howard Cochran
Belmont University

Jim Cox
Georgia Perimeter College

Matt Critcher
University of Arkansas Community College–Batesville

Chifeng Dai
Southern Illinois University–Carbondale

Thomas Davidson
Principia College

Rafael Donoso
Lone State College–North Harris

Floyd Duncan
Virginia Military Institute

David Eaton
Murray State University

Eric Eide
Brigham Young University–Provo

Marwan El Nasser
State University of New York–Fredonia

Harry Ellis
University of North Texas

Maxwell Eseonu
Virginia State University

Brent Evans
Mississippi State University

Russell Evans
Oklahoma State University

Fidelis Ezeala-Harrison
Jackson State University

Chris Fant
Spartanburg Community College

Michael Fenick
Broward College

Abdollah Ferdowsi
Ferris State University

Tawni Ferrarini
Northern Michigan University

Herbert Flaig
Milwaukee Area Technical College

Irene Foster
George Washington University

Joseph Franklin
Newberry College

Shelby Frost
Georgia State University

Fran Lara Garib
San Jacinto College

Deborah Gaspard
Southeast Community College

Karen Gebhardt
Colorado State University

Juan Alejandro Gelves
Midwestern State University

Kirk Gifford
Brigham Young University–Idaho

Otis Gilley
Louisiana Technical University

Gregory Gilpin
Montana State University–Bozeman

Bill (Wayne) Goffe
State University of New York–Oswego

Michael Gootzeit
University of Memphis

George Greenlee
St. Petersburg College

Galina Hale
Federal Reserve Bank of San Francisco

Oskar Harmon
University of Connecticut–Stamford

David Hedrick
Central Washington University–Ellensburg

Dennis Heiner
College of Southern Idaho

Andrew Helms
Washington College

David Hickman
Frederick Community College

Ashley Hodgson
Saint Olaf College

Vanessa Holmes
Pennsylvania State University–Scranton

Scott Houser
Colorado School of Mines

Gregrey Hunter
California Polytechnic University–Pomona

Kyle Hurst
University of Colorado–Denver

Jonathan Ikoba
Scott Community College

Onur Ince
Appalachian State University

Dennis Jansen
Texas A&M University

Shuyi Jiang
Emmanuel College

Barbara Heroy John
University of Dayton

James Johnson
University of Arkansas Community College–Batesville

Mahbubul Kabir
Lyon College

Ahmad Kader
University of Nevada–Las Vegas

John Kane
State University of New York–Oswego

Tsvetanka Karagyozova
Lawrence University

Joel Kazy
State Fair Community College

Daniel Kuester
Kansas State University

Gary Langer
Roosevelt University

Daniel Lawson
Oakland Community College

Richard Le
Cosumnes River College

Jim Lee
Texas A&M University–Corpus Christi

Willis Lewis
Winthrop University

Qing Li
College of the Mainland

Tin-Chun Lin
Indiana University Northwest–Gary

Delwin Long
San Jacinto College

Katie Lotz
Lake Land College

Karla Lynch
North Central Texas College

Arindam Mandal
Siena College

Daniel Marburger
Arkansas State University–Jonesboro

Geri Mason
Seattle Pacific University

Victor Matheson
College of the Holy Cross

Bryan McCannon
Saint Bonaventure University

Michael McIlhon
Century Community and Technical College

Hannah McKinney
Kalamazoo College

Al Mickens
State University of New York–Old Westbury

Nara Mijid
Central Connecticut State University

Martin Milkman
Murray State University

Douglas Miller
University of Missouri–Columbia

Gregory Miller
Wallace Community College–Selma

Edward Millner
Virginia Commonwealth University

Mitch Mitchell
Bladen Community College

Daniel Morvey
Piedmont Technical College

Rebecca Moryl
Emmanuel College

Tina Mosleh
Ohlone College

Thaddaeus Mounkurai
Daytona State College–Daytona Beach

Chris Mushrush
Illinois State University

Muhammad Mustafa
South Carolina State University

Tony Mutsune
Iowa Wesleyan College

Max Grunbaum Nagiel
Daytona State College–Daytona Beach

John Nordstrom
College of Western Idaho

Emlyn Norman
Texas Southern University

Christian Nsiah
Black Hills State University

Jan Ojdana
University of Cincinnati

Ronald O'Neal
Camden County College

Serkan Ozbeklik
Claremont McKenna College

Debashis Pal
University of Cincinnati–Cincinnati

Robert Pennington
University of Central Florida–Orlando

Andrew Perumal
University of Massachusetts–Boston

Steven Peterson
University of Idaho

Brennan Platt
Brigham Young University

Sanela Porca
University of South Carolina–Aiken

Gregory Pratt
Mesa Community College

William Prosser
Cayuga Community College

Gregory Randolph
Southern New Hampshire University

Mitchell Redlo
Monroe Community College

Timothy Reynolds
Alvin Community College

Michael Rolleigh
Williams College

Amanda Ross
West Virginia University–Morgantown

Jason Rudbeck
University of Georgia

Michael Ryan
Gainesville State College

Robert Rycroft
University of Mary Washington

Michael Salemi
University of North Carolina–Chapel Hill

Gregory Saltzman
Albion College

Ravi Samitamana
Daytona State College

Saied Sarkarat
West Virginia University–Parkersburg

Naveen Sarna
Northern Virginia Community College–Alexandria

Jesse Schwartz
Kennesaw State University

Abdelkhalik Shabayek
Lane College

Mark Showalter
Brigham Young University

Cheri Sides
Lane College

Megan Silbert
Salem College

Sovathana Sokhom
Loyola Marymount University

Souren Soumbatiants
Franklin University

Marilyn Spencer
Texas A&M University–Corpus Christi

Brad Stamm
Cornerstone University

Karl Strauss
Saint Bonaventure University

Chuck Stull
Kalamazoo College

Abdulhamid Sukar
Cameron University

Albert Sumell
Youngstown State University

Philip Isak Szmedra
Georgia Southwestern State University

Christine Tarasevich
Del Mar College

Noreen Templin
Butler Community College

Darryl Thorne
Valencia College East

Kiril Tochkov
Texas Christian University

Demetri Tsanacas
Ferrum College

George Tvelia
Suffolk County Community College

Nora Underwood
University of Central Florida

Jose Vazquez
University of Illinois–Champaign

Marieta Velikova
Belmont University

Jeffery Vicek
Parkland College

Jennifer Vincent
Champlain College

Terry von Ende
Texas Tech University

Craig Walker
Oklahoma Baptist University

Jennifer Ward-Batts
Wayne State University

Tarteashia Williams
Valencia College–West Campus

Melissa Wiseman
Houston Baptist University

Jim Wollscheid
University of Arkansas–Fort Smith

Jeff Woods
University of Indianapolis

Ranita Wyatt
Pasco-Hernando Community College–West Campus

Suthathip Yaisawarng
Union College

Jim Yates
Darton College

Daehyun Yoo
Elon University

Ceren Ertan Yoruk
Sage College of Albany

Chuck Zalonka
Oklahoma State University–Oklahoma City

Finally, thanks to the following instructors, and their students, who class-tested chapters of the first edition before publication. Their engagement with the content and their feedback from the "test drive" made this a better product.

Richard Agesa
Marshall University

Anne Bresnock
University of California–Los Angeles

Chiuping Chen
American River College

John Kane
State University of New York–Oswego

Jim Lee
Texas A&M University–Corpus Christi

Martin Milkman
Murray State University

Kolleen Rask
College of the Holy Cross

Jesse Schwartz
Kennesaw State University

Jennifer Vincent
Champlain College

detailed contents

feature boxes

Part One

The Power of Economics

The two chapters in Part 1 will introduce you to . . .

the tools and intuition essential to the study of economics. Chapter 1, "Economics and Life," presents four questions that introduce the fundamental concepts of economic problem solving. We also describe how economists think about data and analyze policies: You'll see that we typically separate how one *wants* the world to look ("normative" analysis) from how the world *actually* works ("positive" analysis).

Chapter 2, "Specialization and Exchange," presents the ideas of absolute and comparative advantage, to explain how people (and countries) can most effectively use their resources and talents. Should you hire a plumber or fix the pipes yourself? Should you become a pop star or an economist? We develop these ideas to show how trade can make everyone better off, on both a personal and a national level.

This is just a start. Throughout the book, we'll use these tools to gain a deeper understanding of how people interact and manage their resources, which in turn gives insight into tough problems of all sorts. Economic ideas weave a common thread through many subjects, from the purely economic to political, environmental, and cultural issues, as well as personal decisions encountered in everyday life. Economics is much more than just the study of money, and we hope you'll find that what you learn here will shed light far beyond your economics classes.

Economics and Life

MAKING AN IMPACT WITH SMALL LOANS

On the morning of October 13, 2006, Bangladeshi economist Muhammad Yunus received an unexpected telephone call from Oslo, Norway. Later that day, the Nobel committee announced that Yunus and the Grameen Bank, which he founded in 1976, would share the 2006 Nobel Peace Prize. Past recipients of the Nobel Peace Prize include Mother Teresa, who spent over 50 years ministering to beggars and lepers; Martin Luther King Jr., who used peaceful protest to oppose racial segregation; and the Dalai Lama, an exiled Tibetan Buddhist leader who symbolizes the struggle for religious and cultural tolerance. What were an economist and his bank doing in such company?

Grameen is not a typical bank. Yes, it makes loans and offers savings accounts, charging customers for its services, just like other banks. But it serves some of the poorest people in the poorest villages in one of the poorest countries in the world. It makes loans so small that it's hard for people in wealthy countries to imagine what good they can do: The first group of loans Yunus made totaled only $27. Before Grameen came along, other banks had been unwilling to work in these poor communities. They believed it wasn't worth bothering to lend such small amounts; many believed the poor could not be counted on to repay their loans.

© *Karen Kasmauski/Corbis*

Yunus disagreed. He was convinced that even small loans would allow poor villagers to expand their small businesses—maybe buying a sewing machine or a cow to produce milk for the local market—and earn more money. Or perhaps a villager wouldn't expand a small business but would instead use the money to pay for a health emergency or to buy food when faced with hunger. Regardless of the way the loans were used, villagers' lives would be more comfortable and secure, and their children would have a better future. Yunus claimed that they would be able to repay the loan and that his new bank would earn a profit.

Yunus proved the skeptics wrong. Today, Grameen Bank serves more than 8 million customers, and it reports that 98 percent of its loans are repaid—a better rate than some banks in rich countries.[1] Grameen also reports steady profits. Such results have inspired other banks to start serving poor communities on nearly every continent, including recent start-ups in the United States in New York City and Omaha, Nebraska.

Muhammad Yunus was trained as an economist. He earned a PhD at Vanderbilt University in Nashville and then taught in Tennessee before becoming a professor in Bangladesh. When a devastating famine struck Bangladesh, Yunus became disillusioned with teaching. What did abstract equations and stylized graphs have to do with the suffering he saw around him?

Ultimately, Yunus realized that economic thinking holds the key to solving hard problems that truly matter. The genius of Grameen Bank is that it is neither a traditional charity nor a traditional bank. Instead, it is a business that harnesses basic economic insights to make the world a better place.

In this book, we'll introduce you to the tools economists are using to tackle some of the world's biggest challenges, from health care reform, to climate change, to lifting people out of poverty. Of course, these tools are not just for taking on causes worthy of Nobel Prizes. Economics can also help you become a savvier consumer, successfully launch a new cell phone app, or simply make smarter decisions about how to spend your time and money. Throughout this book, we promise we'll ask you not just to memorize theories, but also to apply the ideas you read about to the everyday decisions you face in your own life.

The Basic Insights of Economics

When people think of economics, they often think of the stock market, the unemployment rate, or media reports saying things like "the Federal Reserve has raised its target for the federal funds rate." Although economics does include these topics, its reach is much broader.

Economics is the study of how people manage resources. Decisions about how to allocate resources can be made by individuals, but also by groups of people in families, firms, governments, and other organizations. In economics, *resources* are not just physical things like cash and gold mines. They are also intangible things, such as time, ideas, technology, job experience, and even personal relationships.

Traditionally, economics has been divided into two broad fields: microeconomics and macroeconomics. **Microeconomics** is the study of how individuals and firms manage resources. **Macroeconomics** is the study of the economy as a whole, and how policymakers manage the growth and behavior of the overall economy. Microeconomics and macroeconomics are highly related and interdependent; we need both to fully understand how economies work.

Economics starts with the idea that people compare the choices available to them and purposefully behave in the way that will best achieve their goals. As human beings, we have ambitions and we make plans to realize them. We strategize. We marshal our resources. When people make choices to achieve their goals in the most effective way possible given the resources they have, economists say they are exhibiting **rational behavior**. The assumption that people behave rationally isn't perfect. As we'll see later in the book, people can sometimes be short-sighted or swayed merely by the way choices are presented. Nevertheless, the assumption of rational behavior helps to explain a lot about the world.

People use economics every day, from Wall Street to Walmart, from state capitol buildings to Bangladeshi villages. They apply economic ideas to everything from shoe shopping to baseball, from running a hospital to running for political office. What ties these topics together is a common approach to problem solving.

Economists tend to break down problems by asking a set of four questions:

1. What are the wants and constraints of those involved?
2. What are the trade-offs?
3. How will others respond?
4. Why isn't someone already doing it?

Underneath these questions are some important economics concepts, which we will begin to explore in this chapter. The questions and the underlying concepts are based on just a few common-sense assumptions about how people behave, yet they offer a surprising amount of insight into tough problems of all sorts. They are so important to economic problem solving that they will come up again and again in this book. In this chapter we'll take a bird's-eye view of economics, focusing on the fundamental concepts and skimming over the details. Later in the book, we'll return to each question in more depth.

economics the study of how people, individually and collectively, manage resources

microeconomics the study of how individuals and firms manage resources

macroeconomics the study of the economy as a whole, and how policymakers manage the growth and behavior of the overall economy

rational behavior making choices to achieve goals in the most effective way possible

Scarcity

Question 1: What are the wants and constraints of those involved?

LO 1.1 Explain the economic concept of scarcity.

scarcity
the condition of wanting more than we can get with available resources

For the most part, people make decisions that are aimed at getting the things they want. Of course, you can't always get what you want. People want a lot of things, but they are *constrained* by limited resources. Economists define **scarcity** as the condition of wanting more than we can get with available resources. Scarcity is a fact of life. You have only so much time and only so much money. You can arrange your resources in a lot of different ways—studying or watching TV, buying a car, or traveling to Las Vegas—but at any given time, you have a fixed range of possibilities. Scarcity also describes the world on a collective level: As a society, we can produce only so many things, and we have to decide how those things are divided among many people.

On the other hand, some things are not restricted by resources. Consider, for example, knowledge. The total quantity of available knowledge does not diminish as more and more people acquire it. Similarly, sunlight and air can also be considered nonscarce goods. In economic terms, however, it is safe to say that most goods are considered to be scarce.

The first question to ask in untangling a complex economic problem is, "What are the wants and constraints of those involved?" Given both rational behavior and scarcity, we can expect people to try to get what they want but to be constrained by the limited resources available to them. Suppose you *want* to spend as much time as possible this summer taking road trips around the country. You are *constrained* by the available time (three months of summer vacation) and by the amount of money you have available to pay for gas, food, and places to stay. Behaving rationally, you might choose to work double shifts for two months to earn enough to spend one month on the road. Since you are now *constrained* by having only one month to travel, you'll have to prioritize your time, activities, and expenses.

Now put yourself in Muhammad Yunus's shoes, back in 1976. He sees extremely poor but entrepreneurial Bangladeshi villagers and thinks they could improve their lives with access to loans. Why aren't banks providing financial services for these people? We can apply the first of the economists' questions to start to untangle this puzzle: *What are the wants and constraints of those involved?* In this case, those involved are traditional Bangladeshi banks and poor Bangladeshi villagers.

Let's look at both:

- The banks *want* to make profits by lending money to people who will pay them back with interest. The banks are *constrained* by having limited funds available to lend and needing to pay employees and branch expenses. We can therefore expect banks to prioritize making large loans to customers they believe are likely to pay them back. Before 1976, that meant wealthier, urban Bangladeshis, not the very poor in remote rural villages.
- The villagers *want* the chance to increase their incomes. They have energy and business ideas but are *constrained* in their ability to borrow money because banks believe they are too poor to repay loans.

Analyzing the wants and constraints of those involved gives us some valuable information about why poor Bangladeshis didn't have access to loans. Banks *wanted* to earn profits and managed their *constrained* funds to prioritize those they thought would be profitable customers. Bangladeshi villagers *wanted* to increase their incomes but couldn't follow up on business opportunities due to *constrained* start-up money.

That's good information, but we haven't yet come up with the solution that Dr. Yunus was looking for. To take the next step in solving the puzzle, we turn to another question economists often ask.

Opportunity cost and marginal decision making

Question 2: What are the trade-offs?

LO 1.2 Explain the economic concepts of opportunity cost and marginal decision making.

Every decision in life involves weighing the *trade-off* between costs and benefits. We look at our options and decide whether it is worth giving up one in order to get the other. We choose to do things only when we think the benefits will be greater than the costs. The potential *benefit* of taking an action is often easy to see: You would have fun road-tripping for a month. Bank customers who take out a loan would have the opportunity to expand their businesses or pay for emergency expenses. The *costs* of a decision, on the other hand, are not always clear.

You might think it *is* clear—that the cost of your road trip is simply the amount of money you spend on gas, hotels, and food. But something is missing from that way of thinking. The true cost of something is not just the amount you have to pay for it. Rather, the cost also includes the *opportunity you must now give up for something that you might have enjoyed otherwise.* Suppose if you hadn't gone on your road trip, your second choice would have been to spend that money to buy a big-screen TV and spend that month at home watching movies with friends. The true cost of your road trip is passing up the enjoyment you would have gained from owning the TV and hanging out with friends for a month. Behaving rationally, you should go on the road trip only if it will be more valuable to you than the best alternative use for your time and money. This is a matter of personal preference. Because people have different alternatives and place different values on things like a road trip or a TV, they will make different decisions.

Economists call this true cost of your choice the **opportunity cost**, which is equal to the value to you of what you have to give up in order to get something. Put another way, opportunity cost is the value you could have gained by choosing your next-best alternative—the "opportunity" you have to pass up in order to take your first choice.

Let's return to the road trip. Say you're going with a friend and her plan B would have been buying a new computer, taking a summer class, and visiting her cousins. The opportunity cost of her vacation is different from yours. For her, the opportunity cost is the pleasure she would have gained from owning a new computer, the benefits she would have taken from the course, and the fun she would have had with her cousins. If she's behaving rationally, she will go with you on the road trip only if she believes it will be more valuable to her than what she's giving up.

Opportunity cost helps us think more clearly about trade-offs. If someone asked you how much your road trip cost and you responded by adding up the cost of gas, hotels, and food, you would be failing to capture some of the most important and interesting aspects of the trade-offs you made. Opportunity cost helps us to see why, for example, a self-employed consultant and an equally paid factory worker may face truly different trade-offs when they contemplate taking the same vacation for the same price. The self-employed consultant likely forgoes earning income in order to take a vacation; the factory worker likely gets paid vacation days. The opportunity cost for the consultant includes the value of what he or she would buy with the money earned by working instead of taking the vacation. Thus the opportunity cost of a vacation for the consultant is much higher than it is for the factory worker. That difference makes it much more expensive for the consultant to take a vacation than the factory worker.

Economists often express opportunity cost as a dollar value. Suppose you've been given a gift certificate worth $15 at a restaurant. The restaurant has a short menu: pizza or spaghetti, each of which costs $15. The gift certificate can be used only at this particular restaurant, so the only thing you give up to get pizza is spaghetti, and vice versa. If you didn't have the certificate, you would be willing to pay as much as $15 for the pizza but no more than $10 for the spaghetti. What are your trade-offs?

opportunity cost
the value to you of what you have to give up in order to get something; the value you could have gained by choosing the next-best alternative

- What is the opportunity cost of choosing the pizza? Even though the price on the menu is $15, the opportunity cost is only $10—because $10 is the value you place on your best (and only) alternative, the spaghetti.
- What is the opportunity cost of choosing the spaghetti? It's $15, the value you place on the pizza.

Which meal do you choose? One choice has an opportunity cost of $10, the other $15. Behaving rationally, you should choose the pizza because it has the lower opportunity cost. (You give up less by choosing the lower opportunity cost.)

A simpler way of describing this trade-off would be simply to say that you prefer pizza over spaghetti. The opportunity cost of spaghetti is higher because to get it, you have to give up something you like more. But putting it in terms of opportunity cost can be helpful when there are more choices, or more nuances to the choices.

For example, suppose the gift certificate could be used only to buy spaghetti. Now what is the opportunity cost of choosing the spaghetti? It is $0 because you can't do anything else with the gift certificate—your choice is spaghetti or nothing. The opportunity cost of pizza is now $15 because you'd have to pay for it with money you could have spent on $15 worth of other purchases outside the restaurant. So even though you like pizza better, you might now choose the spaghetti because it has a lower opportunity cost in this particular situation.

Once you start to think about opportunity costs, you see them everywhere. For an application of opportunity cost to a serious moral question, read the What Do You Think? box "The opportunity cost of a life."

What Do You Think?
The opportunity cost of a life

Throughout the book, What Do You Think? boxes ask for your opinion about an important policy or life decision. These boxes will present questions that require you to combine facts and economic analysis with values and moral reasoning. They are the sort of tough questions that people face in real life. There are many "correct" answers, depending on your values and goals.

The philosopher Peter Singer writes that opportunity costs can be a matter of life or death. Imagine you are a salesperson, and on your way to a meeting on a hot summer day, you drive by a lake. Suddenly, you notice that a child who has been swimming in the lake is drowning. No one else is in sight.

You have a choice. If you stop the car and dive into the lake to save the child, you will be late for your meeting, miss out on making a sale, and lose $250. The *opportunity cost* of saving the child's life is $250.

Alternatively, if you continue on to your meeting, you earn the $250, but you lose the opportunity to dive into the lake and save the child's life. The *opportunity cost* of going to the meeting is one child's life.

What would you do? Most people don't hesitate. They immediately say they would stop the car, dive into the lake, and save the drowning child. After all, a child's life is worth more than $250.

Now suppose you're thinking about spending $250 on a new iPod. That $250 could instead have been used for some charitable purpose, such as immunizing children in another country against yellow fever. Suppose that for every $250 donated, an average of one child's life ends up being saved. (In fact, $250 to save one child's life is not far from reality in many cases.) What is the opportunity cost of buying an iPod? According to Peter Singer, it is the same as the opportunity cost of going straight to the meeting: a child's life.

These two situations are not exactly the same, of course, but why does the first choice (jump in the lake) seem so obvious to most people, while the second seems much less obvious?

WHAT DO YOU THINK?

1. In what ways do the two situations presented by Singer—the sales meeting and the drowning child versus the iPod and the unvaccinated child—differ?
2. Singer argues that even something like buying an iPod is a surprisingly serious moral decision. Do you agree? What sort of opportunity costs do you typically consider when making such a decision?
3. What might be missing from Singer's analysis of the trade-offs people face when making a decision about how to spend money?

Another important principle for understanding trade-offs is the idea that rational people make decisions *at the margin.* **Marginal decision making** describes the idea that rational people compare the *additional* benefits of a choice against the *additional* costs, without considering related benefits and costs of past choices.

For example, suppose an amusement park has a $20 admission price and charges $2 per ride. If you are standing outside the park, the cost of the first ride is $22: You will have to pay the admission price and buy a ticket for the ride. Once you are inside the park, the *marginal* cost of each additional ride is $2. When deciding whether to go on the roller coaster a second or third time, you should compare only the benefit or enjoyment you will get from one more ride to the opportunity cost of that additional ride.

This may sound obvious, but in practice, many people don't make decisions on the margin. Suppose you get into the amusement park and start to feel sick shortly thereafter. If doing something else with your $2 and your time would bring you more enjoyment than another roller-coaster ride while feeling sick, the rational thing to do would be to leave. The relevant trade-off is between the *additional* benefits that going on another ride would bring versus the additional costs. You cannot get back the $20 admission fee or any of the other money you've already spent on rides. Economists call a cost that has already been incurred and cannot be recovered a **sunk cost**. Sunk costs should not have any bearing on your *marginal* decision about what to do next. But many people feel the need to go on a few more rides to psychologically justify the $20 admission.

Trade-offs play a crucial role in businesses' decisions about what goods and services to produce. Let's return to the example that started this chapter and apply the idea to a bank in Bangladesh: *What are the trade-offs involved in making a small loan?*

- For traditional banks, the opportunity cost of making small loans to the poor was the money that the bank could have earned by making loans to wealthier clients instead.
- For poor borrowers, the opportunity cost of borrowing was whatever else they would have done with the time they spent traveling to the bank and with the money they would pay in fees and interest on the loan. The benefit, of course, was whatever the loan would enable them to do that they could not have done otherwise, such as starting a small business or buying food or livestock.

Based on this analysis of trade-offs, we can see why traditional banks made few loans to poor Bangladeshis. Banks perceived the poor to be risky clients. The opportunity cost of making small loans to the poor seemed to outweigh the benefits—unless the banks charged very high fees. From the perspective of poor rural villagers, high fees meant that the opportunity cost of borrowing was higher than the benefits; they chose not to borrow under the terms offered by banks.

Notice that the answer to this question built off the answer to the first: We had to know the wants and constraints of each party before we could assess the trade-offs they faced. Now that we understand the motivations and the trade-offs that led to the situation Dr. Yunus observed, we can turn to a third question he might have asked himself when considering what would happen when he founded the Grameen Bank.

marginal decision making
comparison of additional benefits of a choice against the additional costs it would bring, without considering related benefits and costs of past choices

sunk cost
a cost that has already been incurred and cannot be recovered or refunded

Incentives

Question 3: How will others respond?

LO 1.3 Explain the economic concept of incentives.

You're in the mood for pizza, so you decide to go back to the restaurant with the short menu. When you get there, you discover that the prices have changed. Pizza now costs $50 instead of $15.

What will you do? Remember that your gift certificate is good for only $15. Unless you can easily afford to shell out $50 for a pizza or you just really hate spaghetti, you probably won't be ordering the pizza. We're sure that you can think of ways to spend $35 that are worth more to you than your preference for pizza over spaghetti. But what if the prices had changed less drastically—say, $18 for pizza? That might be a tougher call.

As the trade-offs change, so will the choices people make. When the restaurant owner considers how much to charge for each dish, she must consider *how others will respond* to changing prices. If she knows the pizza is popular, she might be tempted to try charging more to boost her profits. But as she increases the price, fewer diners will decide to order it.

If a trade-off faced by a lot of people changes, even by a small amount, the combined change in behavior by everyone involved can add up to a big shift. Asking "How will others respond?" to a trade-off that affects a lot of people gives us a complete picture of how a particular decision affects the world. The collective reaction to a changing trade-off is a central idea in economics; it will come up in almost every chapter of this book. You'll see it in questions such as

- What happens when prices change?
- What happens when the government implements a new policy?
- What happens when a company introduces a new product?

Answering any of these questions requires us to consider a large-scale reaction, rather than the behavior of just one person, company, or policy-maker.

In answering this question about trade-offs, economists commonly make two assumptions. The first is that people respond to incentives. An **incentive** is something that causes people to behave in a certain way by changing the trade-offs they face. Incentives can be positive or negative:

incentive
something that causes people to behave in a certain way by changing the trade-offs they face

- A *positive* incentive (sometimes just called an *incentive*) makes people *more likely* to do something. For example, lowering the price of spaghetti creates a positive incentive for people to order it because it lowers the opportunity cost: When you pay less for spaghetti, you give up fewer other things you could have spent the money on.
- A *negative* incentive (sometimes called a *disincentive*) makes them *less likely* to do it. Charging people more for pizza is a negative incentive to buy pizza because they now have to give up more alternative purchases.

The second assumption economists make about trade-offs is that nothing happens in a vacuum. That is, you can't change just one thing in the world without eliciting a response from others. If you change your behavior—even if only in a small way—that action will change the incentives of the people around you, causing them to change their behavior in response. If you invent a new product, competitors will copy it. If you raise prices, consumers will buy less. If you tax a good or service, people will produce less of it.

Asking *how others will respond* can help prevent bad decisions by predicting the undesirable side-effects of a change in prices or policies. The question can also be used to design changes that elicit positive responses. When Muhammad Yunus was setting up Grameen Bank, he had to think carefully about the incentives that both rural villagers and traditional banks faced; he considered how those incentives could be changed without incurring negative side-effects.

One reason banks saw rural villagers as risky customers is that they were too poor to have collateral to offer the bank. *Collateral* is a possession, like a house or a car, pledged by a borrower to a lender. If the borrower cannot repay the loan, the lender keeps the collateral. The threat of losing the collateral increases the cost of choosing to not repay the loan; collateral gives the borrower a positive incentive to repay. When traditional banks thought about lending to poor Bangladeshis, they believed that without the threat of losing collateral, the villagers would be unlikely to repay their loans.

Yunus needed to think up a different way of creating a positive incentive for poor customers to repay their loans. His best-known solution was to require borrowers to apply for loans in five-person groups. Every person in the group would have a stake in the success of the other members. If one person didn't repay a loan, no one else in the group could borrow from the bank again.

Yunus's idea, called *group responsibility,* was simple but hugely significant. Yunus concluded that borrowers would have a strong incentive to repay their loans: They wouldn't want to ruin relationships with other members of the group—their fellow villagers, with whom they live every day and rely on for mutual support in hard times. This incentive, in turn, changed the trade-off faced by banks; they responded by being more willing to lend to the poor at lower rates. By asking himself how villagers would respond to the new kind of loan and how banks in turn would respond to the villagers' response, Yunus was able to predict that his idea could be the key to spreading banking services to the poor.

Dr. Yunus's predictions proved to be correct. Seeing that poor villagers nearly always repaid their loans under Grameen's system gave other banks confidence that small borrowers could be reliable customers. Banks offering microloans, savings accounts, and other services to the very poor have spread around the world. As a result of Yunus's creativity and thoughtfulness about incentives, the poor have better access to financial services, and banks earn money from providing them. Today, other ideas have proved even more effective in providing the right incentives for small borrowers, continuing in the tradition of experimentation and innovation pioneered by Yunus and Grameen Bank.

Throughout this book, you will see many examples of how the power of incentives can be harnessed to accomplish everything from increasing a company's profits to protecting the environment. But before we get carried away with brilliant economic innovations, we have to ask ourselves one more question, the final test for any ideas that come out of our problem-solving process.

Efficiency

Question 4: Why isn't someone already doing it?

LO 1.4 Explain the economic concept of efficiency.

People tend to behave rationally. We clip coupons, compare car models before buying, and think hard about which major to choose in college. Although people are not calculating machines, we usually weigh trade-offs, respond to incentives, and are on the lookout for opportunities to get what we want in the most effective way possible.

The same goes for businesses. There are millions of businesses in the world, each trying to make a profit. When consumers want a good or service, some business will take the opportunity to earn money by providing it. That fact leads to our final assumption: *Under normal circumstances, individuals and firms will act to provide the things people want.* If a genuine profit-making opportunity exists, someone will take advantage of it, and usually sooner rather than later.

This final assumption comes from the idea of **efficiency**. Efficiency describes a situation in which resources are used in the most productive way possible to produce the goods and services that have the greatest total economic value to society. Increasing efficiency means finding a way to better use resources to produce the things that people want.

The definition of efficiency might raise some questions. How do we determine *value,* for example? What exactly do we mean by *resources*? Over the course of the book, we'll dive deeper

efficiency
use of resources in the most productive way possible to produce the goods and services that have the greatest total economic value to society

into these issues. For now, we'll take a broad view: Something is *valuable* if someone wants it. A *resource* is anything that can be used to make something of value, from natural resources (such as water and trees) to human resources (such as talents and knowledge). This broad view leads to an important idea: When the economy is working efficiently, resources are *already* being allocated to valuable ends.

So when you think you see a big, unexploited opportunity—a new product, policy, technology, or business model that could change the world or earn you millions of dollars—ask yourself: If it's such a great idea, *why isn't someone* already *doing it?*

One possible answer is simply that nobody has thought of it before. That's possible. Perhaps you *have* seen an efficient way to allocate resources in a way that produces economic value for society. But if *you* have seen the opportunity, doesn't it seem likely that at least one of the billions of other smart, rational people in the world will have seen it too?

Don't get us wrong: We're not saying there is never an opportunity to do something new in the world. Great new ideas happen all the time—they drive progress. But there's a strong possibility that other people have already thought about the idea, and if they chose not to take advantage of it, that's a hint that you might be missing something. The first thing to do is backtrack to the first three economists' questions:

- Have you misjudged people's wants and constraints?
- Have you miscalculated the trade-offs they face?
- Have you misunderstood how people will respond to incentives?

If you think back through those questions and still think you're on to something, here are some more possibilities to consider. We said that *under normal circumstances,* the economy is operating efficiently and individuals or firms provide the things people want. What are some ways in which circumstances might not be normal?

- ***Innovation:*** Innovation is the explanation you're hoping is correct. Maybe your idea has not been used yet because it is too new. If you have come up with a truly new idea, whether it is new technology or a new business model, people cannot have taken advantage of it yet because it didn't exist before.

- ***Market failure:*** Market failures are an important cause of inefficiency. Sometimes people and firms fail to take advantage of opportunities because something prevents them from capturing the benefits of the opportunity, or imposes additional costs on them. For instance, maybe your great new idea won't work because it would be impossible to prevent others from quickly copying it. Or perhaps your great new idea won't work because a few big companies already have the market for it sewn up. Economists call such situations *market failures.* We will discuss market failures in much greater depth later in the book.

- ***Intervention:*** If a powerful force—often the government—intervenes in the economy, transactions cannot take place the way they normally would. We'll see later in the book that many government economic policies intentionally or unintentionally interfere with people's ability to take advantage of profit-making opportunities.

- ***Unprofitable idea:*** Maybe your idea won't produce a profit. Individuals and governments have goals other than profit, of course—for example, creating great art or promoting social justice. But if your idea doesn't also generate a profit, then it is less surprising that no one has taken advantage of it.

When Muhammad Yunus asked himself the question "Why isn't someone already lending to the poor?" he first identified a market failure involving lack of collateral. Understanding the market-failure problem enabled him to come up with the idea of group responsibility to fix it.

But then he had to ask himself, "Why aren't other banks already using the group responsibility idea?"

Disney Movie Club
IRON-ON TRANSFER
It's fun and easy to apply your transfer on a T-shirt or Sweatshirt!
Have an adult iron on this design for you.

Apply to cotton or cotton poly blends only. Pre-washed garments are recommended.

1. Pre-heat hand iron to setting between wool and cotton. Remove all water from a steam iron.

2. Place thin towel on a hard, clean surface. **Do not** use an ironing board. Lay out garment, smooth out wrinkles and position transfer on garment, image side down.

3. Iron transfer pressing down firmly and steadily, constantly moving the iron back and forth for 30 seconds. If the transfer is larger than the surface of iron, repeat this step several times until entire area has been covered.

4. Let garment cool completely before removing paper.

*If transfer will not release from paper or is not adhered to fabric then repeat step 3 and 4. **Do not** re-iron directly over the surface of an applied transfer. If garment must be repressed then cover with this paper.

Before washing, turn garment inside-out. Wash cool water, tumble dry low or line dry.

FAC-033679-19182 | Made in the U.S.A. | #DisneyMovieClub | © 2019 Disney

...tted. Maybe some government pol-
...nd decided it still wouldn't generate
...fit, of course—he was interested in
...rofit for the banks even with group
...dy doing it.
...s a case in which the answer to *why*
...inely new. Grameen Bank was able
...oney, while making enough profit to
...people in Bangladesh can get small
...d the world, over 200 million low-
...s, something that seems like a great

...ese questions test your understanding of the ...nswering any of the questions, go back and ...ideas.

...ade-offs that people face when making

...t isn't already in the market. **[LO 1.4]**

An Economist's Problem-Solving Toolbox

The four questions we've just discussed are some of the fundamental insights of economics. Using them to understand how the world *might* work is only half the battle. Understanding when and how to apply them is the other half. In the second part of this chapter, we will describe some tools economists use to apply these insights to real situations.

Accurately spotting the fundamental economic concepts at work in the world is sometimes less obvious than you might think. Throughout history, people have observed the world around them and drawn conclusions that have proved hilariously—or sometimes tragically—wrong. We now know that the sun doesn't revolve around the earth. Droughts are not caused by witches giving people the evil eye. Yet, intelligent people once believed these things. It's human nature to draw meaning from the patterns we observe around us, but our conclusions are not always correct.

Economic analysis requires us to combine theory with observations and to subject both to tough scrutiny before drawing conclusions. In this section we will see how to put together theories and facts to determine what causes what. We will also distinguish between the way things *are* and the way we think they *should be*. You can apply these tools to all sorts of situations, from personal life choices to business decisions and policy analysis.

Correlation and causation

LO 1.5 Distinguish between correlation and causation.

A die-hard sports fan may wear a particular jersey while watching his or her team win the NBA finals or Super Bowl, and then forever insist that jersey is lucky. This is an exaggerated example of a common human tendency: When we see that two events occur together, we tend

to assume that one causes the other. Economists, however, try to be particularly careful about what causes what.

To differentiate between two variables that move together and two variables that have a cause-and-effect relationship, we use two different terms. For the instance in which two variables have a consistent relationship, we say there is a **correlation** between them. Correlation can be positive or negative:

correlation
a consistently observed relationship between two variables

- If both variables tend to move in the same direction, we say they are *positively correlated.* For example, wearing raincoats is positively correlated with rain.
- When two variables move in opposite directions, we say they are *negatively correlated.* High temperatures are negatively correlated with people wearing down jackets.

If there is no consistent relationship between two variables, we say they are *uncorrelated.*

Correlation differs from causation. **Causation** means that one variable causes the other. As the preceding examples show, causation and correlation often go together. Weather and clothing are often correlated because weather *causes* people to make certain choices about the clothing they wear.

causation
a relationship between two events in which one brings about the other

Correlation and causation do not *always* go together in a straightforward way. Correlation and causation can be confused in three major ways: coincidence, omitted variables, and reverse causation.

Coincidence

Does the result of the Super Bowl predict the performance of the stock market? A few years ago, some people thought it might. The Super Bowl pits the top team from the American Football Conference against the top team from the National Football Conference. For a long time, when a team from the AFC won, the stock market had a bad year; when a team from the NFC won, the stock market had a great year. In fact, this pattern held true 85 percent of the time between 1967 and 1997.

Would it have been a good idea to base your investment strategy on the results of the Super Bowl? We think not. There is no plausible cause-and-effect relationship here. Stock market outcomes happened to be *correlated with* Super Bowl outcomes for a number of years, but there is no logical way they could be *caused by* them. If you search long enough for odd coincidences, you will eventually find some.

Omitted variables

Consider the following statement: There is a positive correlation between the presence of firefighters and people with serious burn injuries. Does this statement mean that firefighters cause burn injuries? Of course not. We know that firefighters are not burning people; they're trying to save them. Instead, there must be some common underlying variable behind both observed outcomes—fires, in this case.

Sometimes, two events that are correlated occur together because both are caused by the same underlying factor. Each has a causal relationship with a third factor, but not with each other. The underlying factor is called an *omitted variable*—despite the fact that it is an important part of the cause-and-effect story, it has been left out of the analysis. The From Another Angle box "Does ice cream cause polio?" tells the story of an omitted variable that convinced some doctors to mistakenly campaign against a staple of summer fun: ice cream.

From Another Angle
Does ice cream cause polio?

From Another Angle boxes show you a different way of looking at an economic concept. Sometimes they will be a humorous story, sometimes a different way of thinking about a situation, and sometimes just an unusual application of a standard idea. We find that a little bit of weirdness goes a long way in helping us to remember things, and we hope it will work for you too.

A disease called polio once crippled or killed thousands of children in the United States every year. Before it was known what caused polio, doctors observed that polio infections seemed to be more common in children who had been eating lots of ice cream. Observing this *correlation* led some people to assume that there was a *causal* relationship between the two. Some doctors recommended an anti-polio diet that avoided eating ice cream. Many fearful parents understandably took their advice.

We now know that polio is caused by a virus that is transmitted from one person to another. The virus was spread through contaminated food and water—for example, dirty swimming pools or water fountains. It had nothing at all to do with how much ice cream a child ate.

The ice cream confusion was caused by an *omitted variable*: warm weather. In warm weather, children are more likely to use swimming pools and water fountains. And in warm weather, children are also more likely to eat ice cream. Polio was therefore *correlated* with eating ice cream, but it certainly wasn't *caused* by it.

Dr. Jonas Salk developed a polio vaccine in 1952 that stopped the fear of the disease and its spread.

Source: Steve Lohr, "For Today's Graduate, Just One Word: Statistics," *New York Times*, August 5, 2009.

Reverse causation

A third common source of confusion between correlation and causation is *reverse causation*: Did A cause B, or did B cause A? When two events always happen together, it can be hard to say which caused the other.

Let's return to the correlation between rain and raincoats. If we knew nothing about rain, we might observe that it often appears together with raincoats; we might conclude that wearing a raincoat (A) causes rain (B). In this case, we all know that the causation goes the other way, but observation alone does not tell us that.

Looking at the timing of two correlated events can sometimes provide clues. Often, if A happens before B, it hints that A causes B rather than vice versa. But grabbing a raincoat as you leave home in the morning frequently happens *before* it rains in the afternoon. The timing notwithstanding, taking your raincoat with you in the morning clearly does not *cause* rain later in the day. In this case, your *anticipation* of B causes A to happen.

An important lesson for economists and noneconomists alike is never to take observations at face value. Always make sure you can explain *why* two events are related. To do so, you need another tool in the economist's toolbox: a model.

Models

LO 1.6 List the characteristics of a good economic model.

model
a simplified
representation of the
important parts of a
complicated situation

A **model** is a simplified representation of a complicated situation. In economics, models show how people, firms, and governments make decisions about managing resources and how their decisions interact. An economic model can represent a situation as basic as how people decide what car to buy or as complex as what causes a global recession.

Because models simplify complex problems, they allow us to focus our attention on the most important parts. Models rarely include every detail of a given situation, but that is a good thing. If we had to describe the entire world with perfect accuracy before solving a problem, we'd be so overwhelmed with details that we'd never get the answer. By carefully simplifying the situation to its essentials, we can get useful answers that are *approximately* right.

circular flow model
a simplified
representation of how the
economy's transactions
work together

One of the most basic models of the economy is the **circular flow model**. The economy involves billions of transactions every day, and the circular flow model helps show how all of those transactions work together. The model slashes through complexity to show important patterns. Figure 1-1 shows the circular flow of economic transactions in a graphic format called the *circular flow diagram.*

The first simplification of the circular flow model is to narrow our focus to the two most important types of actors in the economy, households and firms:

- *Households* are vital in two ways. First, they supply land and labor to firms and invest capital in firms. (Land, labor, and capital are called the *factors of production.*) Second, they buy the goods and services that firms produce.
- *Firms* too are vital but do the opposite of households: They buy or rent the land, labor, and capital supplied by households, and they produce and sell goods and services.

The circular flow model shows that firms and households are tightly connected through both production and consumption.

In another helpful simplification, the circular flow model narrows the focus to two markets that connect households and firms:

- The *market for goods and services* is exactly what it sounds: It reflects all of the activity involved in the buying and selling of goods and services. In this market, households spend their wages from labor and their income from land and capital, and firms earn revenue from selling their goods and services.
- The second market is the *market for the factors of production.* Here, households supply land, labor, and capital, and firms hire and purchase or rent these inputs.

FIGURE 1-1
Circular flow diagram

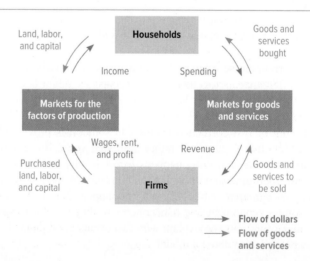

The model puts all of this together. The transactions we have described are part of two loops:

- One is a loop of inputs and outputs as they travel throughout the economy. The *inputs* are the land, labor, and capital firms use to produce goods. The *outputs* are the goods and services that firms produce using the factors of production.
- Another loop represents the flow of dollars. Households buy goods and services using the money they get from firms for using their factors of production. Firms get revenues from selling these goods and services—and, in turn, firms can then use the money to buy or rent factors of production.

You might be a little dizzy at this point, with everything spinning in loops. To help straighten things out, let's follow $5 from your wallet as it flows through the economy. You could spend this $5 in any number of ways. As you're walking down the street, you see a box of donuts sitting in the window of your local bakery. You head in and give the baker your $5, a transaction in the market for goods. The money represents revenue for the baker and spending by you. The donuts are an output of the bakery.

The story of your $5 is not over, though. In order to make more donuts, the baker puts that $5 toward buying inputs in the market for the factors of production. This might include paying rent for the bakery or paying wages for an assistant. The baker's spending represents income for the households that provide the labor in the bakery or rent out the space. Once the baker pays wages or rent with that $5, it has made it through a cycle in the circular flow.

As the circular flow model shows, an economic model approximates what happens in the real economy. Later in the book, we'll discuss other models that focus on specific questions—like how much gasoline prices will go up when the government raises taxes or how fast the economy is likely to grow in the next decade.

The best models lead us to clearer answers about complicated questions. What makes a good economic model? We have already said that good models can leave out details that are not crucial, and they focus on the important aspects of a situation. To be useful, a model *should* also do three things:

1. *A good model predicts cause and effect.* The circular flow model gives a useful description of the basics of the economy. Often, though, we want to go further. Many times we want a model not only to describe economic connections but also to predict how things will happen in the future. To do that, we have to get cause and effect right. If your model says that A causes B, you should be able to explain why. In the "Markets" chapter we'll learn about a central model in economics that shows that for most goods and services, the quantity people want to buy goes down as the price goes up. Why? As the cost of an item rises, but the benefit of owning it remains the same, more people will decide that the trade-off is not worth it.

2. *A good model states its assumptions clearly.* Although models are usually too simple to fit the real world perfectly, it's important that they be clear about their simplifying assumptions. Doing so helps us to know when the model will predict real events accurately and when it will not. For example, we said earlier that economists often assume that people behave rationally. We know that isn't always true, but we accept it as an assumption because it is *approximately* accurate in many situations. As long as we are clear that we are making this assumption, we will know that the model may not be accurate when people fail to behave rationally.

3. *A good model describes the real world accurately.* If a model does not describe what actually happens in the real world, something about the model is wrong. We've admitted that models are not perfectly accurate because they are intentionally simpler than the real world. But if a model predicts things that are not usually or approximately true, it is not useful. How do we tell if a model is realistic? Economists test their models by observing what happens in the real world and collecting data, which they use to verify or reject the

model. In the Real Life box "Testing models against history," take a look at a model that has been tested over and over again in the last few hundred years.

Real Life
Testing models against history

Real Life boxes show how the concept you're reading about relates to the real world. They are your chance to test models against the data. Often these boxes will describe a situation in which people used an economic idea to solve a business or policy question, or they present interesting research ideas or experiences. Watch for links to online content, such as videos or news stories.

Thomas Malthus, an early nineteenth-century economist, created a model that described the relationship between population growth and food production. The model predicted that mass starvation would occur as populations outgrew food supplies. In his famous work *An Essay on the Principle of Population,* Malthus wrote:

> The power of population is so superior to the power of the earth to produce subsistence for man, that premature death must in some shape or other visit the human race. . . . [G]igantic inevitable famine stalks . . .

Since Malthus wrote these words, famines have in fact killed millions of people. However, they have not been related to population growth in the way that Malthus predicted. Instead, the population of the world has increased from under a billion in 1800 to about 7.4 billion today. At the same time, nutrition standards have risen in almost every country.

Malthus's model left out a crucial part of the story: human ingenuity and technological progress. As the world's population has grown, people have found new ways to grow better food more efficiently and to make more land usable for growing food. They have also found better ways to limit population growth.

Malthus's idea has not died out, though. Today, neo-Malthusian theory predicts that population will still outstrip the world's productive capacity. This theory updates Malthus's model to address more modern concerns, such as increasing environmental degradation that makes land unfit for farming. Others argue that nonrenewable resources, such as oil, will be depleted. Still others warn that even if the world's farmers can produce enough food, unequal access to resources like fresh water will cause local famines and wars.

Critics of these arguments point out that human ingenuity has somehow averted catastrophe at every point in recent history when a Malthusian disaster seemed imminent. The population boom that followed World War II was supposed to lead to starvation, but it was counteracted by the Green Revolution, which increased food production manyfold.

Is the neo-Malthusian model accurate, then, or is it too missing some critical factor? Time will provide the data to answer this question.

Source: T. R. Malthus, *An Essay on the Principle of Population,* 1798.

Positive and normative analysis

LO 1.7 Distinguish between positive and normative analysis.

Economics is a field of study in which people frequently confuse facts with judgments that are based on beliefs. Think about the following example:

- *Statement #1:* Income taxes reduce the number of hours that people want to work.

- *Statement #2:* Income taxes should be reduced or abolished.

Many people have trouble separating these two statements. Some feel that the second statement flows logically from the first. Others disagree with the second statement, so they assume the first can't possibly be true.

If you read carefully, however, you'll see that the first sentence is a statement about cause and effect. Thus, it can be proved true or false by data and evidence. A statement that makes a factual claim about how the world *actually* works is called a **positive statement**.

The second sentence, on the other hand, cannot be proved true or false. Instead, it indicates what *should be* done—but only if we share certain goals, understandings, and moral beliefs. A statement that makes a claim about how the world *should be* is called a **normative statement**.

To see how important the distinction between positive and normative statements can be, consider two claims that a physicist might make:

- *Positive statement:* A nuclear weapon with the explosive power of 10 kilotons of TNT will have a fallout radius of up to six miles.
- *Normative statement:* The United States was right to use nuclear weapons in World War II.

Although people could disagree about both of these statements, the first is a question of scientific fact; the second depends heavily on a person's ethical and political beliefs. The first statement may inform your opinion of the second, but you can still agree with one and not the other.

Earlier in this chapter, we introduced a feature called "What Do You Think?" that asks for your opinion about an important policy or life decision. From this point forward, you can use your understanding of the differences between normative and positive analysis to untangle the questions asked in these boxes and combine the two kinds of analysis to arrive at a conclusion. Begin trying your hand at this with the What Do You Think? box "The cost of college cash."

positive statement
a factual claim about how the world actually works

normative statement
a claim about how the world should be

A famous quote makes this point nicely: "Everyone has a right to their own opinion, but not to their own facts." If you search the internet for this quote, you'll see that it has been attributed to many people.
http://www.glasbergen. com/?count=14&s=teaching

"You're certainly entitled to your opinion."

What Do You Think?
The cost of college cash

In 2012–2013, the average yearly cost of a college education ranged from $15,022 at public universities to $34,483 at private universities. Students have a number of options for paying the bill. They can take out federal loans, private loans, or a combination of the two to defer payments until later, or they can use savings or earnings to foot the bill.

Students who qualify for federal loans enjoy benefits such as limits on the interest rate they can be charged or the total payments they can be expected to make. They also have the possibility of loan forgiveness if they enter certain fields after graduation.

Lending to students is a controversial topic. Some people argue for more controls on private lending institutions, such as interest-rate caps and greater protection for students who default. They reason that lending programs should support students who would not otherwise be able to afford college. Furthermore, they argue, graduating with a lot of debt discourages students from going into lower-paid public service jobs.

Other people maintain that the existing lending system is fine. Getting a college degree, they argue, increases a person's future earning power so much that graduates should be able to handle the debt, even at high interest rates. They worry that overregulation will discourage private lenders from offering student loans, defeating the purpose of giving students better access to financial assistance.

(continued)

WHAT DO YOU THINK?

Use the four basic questions economists ask to break down the problem. Remember that your answer can draw on both positive analysis (what *will* happen if a certain policy is followed) and normative analysis (what *should* be done, given your values and goals). You should be able to say which parts of your answers fall into each category.

1. What motivations and constraints apply to students who are considering different schools and loan options? What motivations and constraints apply to private lenders?
2. What opportunity costs do students face when deciding how to pay for college? Should they avoid loans by skipping college altogether or by working their way through college?
3. How would prospective students respond to government limits on the interest rate on student loans? How would private banks that offer student loans respond?
4. Why do you think the federal government has not yet implemented interest-rate caps on private student loans? Do you anticipate any unintended side-effects of that policy?
5. Consider your arguments in response to questions 1 through 4. Which parts were based on normative statements and which on positive statements?

Sources: National Center for Education Statistics, "Trends in college pricing," http://nces.ed.gov/fastfacts/display.asp?id=76; "How much student debt is too much?" http://roomfordebate.blogs.nytimes.com/2009/06/14/how-much-student-debt-is-too-much/?scp=1&sq=student%20loans&st=cse.

Throughout this book, remember that *you don't have to buy into a particular moral or political outlook in order for economics to be useful to you.* Our goal is to provide you with a toolbox of economic concepts that you can use to engage in positive analysis. We will also highlight important decisions you may face that will require you to engage in normative thinking, informed by economic analysis. You will find that economics can help you to make better decisions and identify the most effective policies, regardless of your goals and beliefs.

✓ CONCEPT CHECK

☐ What does it mean when two variables are positively correlated? **[LO 1.5]**
☐ What are the characteristics of a good economic model? **[LO 1.6]**
☐ What is the difference between a positive statement and a normative statement? **[LO 1.7]**

Conclusion

Economists approach problems differently from many other people. A basic principle of human behavior underlies economics—the idea that people typically make choices to achieve their goals in the most effective way possible, subject to the constraints they face.

In this chapter we have introduced the basic concepts economists use, as well as four questions they ask to break down problems. Throughout this book, you will see these concepts and questions over and over again:

1. Scarcity: *What are the wants and constraints of those involved?*
2. Opportunity cost: *What are the trade-offs?*
3. Incentives: *How will others respond?*
4. Efficiency: *Why isn't someone already doing it?*

In later chapters, as we progress to more complicated problems, try using these four questions to break down problems into manageable pieces. Then you can tackle those smaller pieces using the four fundamental concepts presented in this chapter.

Key Terms

economics, p. 5

microeconomics, p. 5

macroeconomics, p. 5

rational behavior, p. 5

scarcity, p. 6

opportunity cost, p. 7

marginal decision making, p. 9

sunk costs, p. 9

incentive, p. 10

efficiency, p. 11

correlation, p. 14

causation, p. 14

model, p. 16

circular flow model, p. 16

positive statement, p. 19

normative statement, p. 19

Summary

LO 1.1 Explain the economic concept of scarcity.

Economists usually assume that people behave rationally and live within a condition of scarcity. Answering the question *What are the wants and constraints of those involved?* tells you what to expect from each player in the situation you are analyzing. Given rational behavior and scarcity, you can expect people to work to get what they want (their motivations) using the limited resources at their disposal (their constraints).

LO 1.2 Explain the economic concepts of opportunity cost and marginal decision making.

Trade-offs arise when you must give up something to get something else. Answering *What are the trade-offs?* will tell you about the costs and benefits associated with a decision. The full cost of doing something is its *opportunity cost*—the value to you of what you have to give up in order to get something, or the value you could have gained by choosing the next-best alternative.

Economists assume that rational people make decisions "at the margin," by comparing any additional benefits of a choice to the extra costs it brings. If people are behaving rationally when they face trade-offs, they will always choose to do something if the marginal benefit is greater than the opportunity cost. They will never do it if the opportunity cost is greater than the marginal benefit.

LO 1.3 Explain the economic concept of incentives.

The collective reaction to changing trade-offs is a central idea in economics. Asking *How will others respond?* will give you a complete picture of how a particular decision affects the world. You can assume that any action will bring a response because people react to changes in their incentives.

LO 1.4 Explain the economic concept of efficiency.

Efficiency occurs when resources are used in the most productive way possible to produce the goods and services that have the greatest total economic value to society. In other words, *efficiency* means using resources to produce the things that people want. Under normal circumstances, markets are efficient.

So when you see what seems to be unexploited opportunity, you should ask: If it's such a great idea, *why isn't someone already doing it?* Markets usually allocate resources efficiently. When they don't, other explanations might be in play: a market failure may have occurred; government may have intervened in the economy; there may be goals other than profit involved; or there may be a genuine opportunity for innovation.

LO 1.5 Distinguish between correlation and causation.

When there is a consistently observed relationship between two variables, we say they are *correlated*. This is different from a *causal* relationship, in which one variable brings about the other. Three common ways in which correlation and causation are confused are coincidence, omitted variables, and reverse causation.

LO 1.6 List the characteristics of a good economic model.

A model is a simplified representation of the important parts of a complicated situation. In economics, models usually show how people, firms, and governments make decisions about managing resources and how their decisions interact. The *circular flow model* is a representation of how the transactions of households and firms flow through the economy.

A good economic model should predict cause and effect, describe the world accurately, and state its assumptions clearly. Economists test their models by observing what happens in the world and collecting data that can be used to support or reject their models.

> **LO 1.7** Distinguish between positive and normative analysis.

A statement that makes a factual claim about how the world actually works is called a *positive* statement. A statement that makes a claim about how the world should be is called a *normative* statement. Economics is a field in which people frequently confuse positive statements with normative statements. You do not have to adopt a particular moral or political point of view to use economic concepts and models.

Review Questions

1. Suppose you are shopping for new clothes to wear to job interviews, but you're on a tight budget. In this situation, what are your wants and constraints? What does it mean to behave rationally in the face of scarcity? **[LO 1.1]**

2. You are a student with a demanding schedule of classes. You also work part time and your supervisor allows you to determine your schedule. In this situation, what is your scarce resource? How do you decide how many hours to work? **[LO 1.1]**

3. Think about the definition of scarcity that you learned in this chapter. Name three ways that you confront scarcity in your own life. **[LO 1.1]**

4. When shopping for your interview clothes, what are some trade-offs you face? What is the opportunity cost of buying new clothes? What are the benefits? How do you balance the two? **[LO 1.2]**

5. You have an 8:30 class this morning, but you are feeling extremely tired. How do you decide whether to get some extra sleep or go to class? **[LO 1.2]**

6. It's Friday night. You already have a ticket to a concert, which cost you $30. A friend invites you to go out for a game of paintball instead. Admission would cost you $25, and you think you'd get $25 worth of enjoyment out of it. Your concert ticket is nonrefundable. What is your opportunity cost (in dollars) of playing paintball? **[LO 1.2]**

7. Suppose you have two job offers and are considering the trade-offs between them. Job A pays $45,000 per year; it includes health insurance and two weeks of paid vacation. Job B pays $30,000 per year; it includes four weeks of paid vacation but no health insurance. **[LO 1.2]**

   a. List the benefits of Job A and the benefits of Job B.

   b. List the opportunity cost of Job A and the opportunity cost of Job B.

8. Your former neighbor gave you his lawnmower when he moved. You are thinking of using this gift to mow lawns in your neighborhood this summer for extra cash. As you think about what to charge your neighbors and whether this idea is worth your effort, what opportunity costs do you need to consider? **[LO 1.2]**

9. Think of a few examples of incentives in your daily life. How do you respond to those incentives? **[LO 1.3]**

10. You supervise a team of salespeople. Your employees already receive a company discount. Suggest a positive incentive and a negative incentive you could use to improve their productivity. **[LO 1.3]**

11. Your boss decides to pair workers in teams and offer bonuses to the most productive team. Why might your boss offer team bonuses instead of individual bonuses? **[LO 1.3]**

12. Think of a public policy—a local or national law, tax, or public service—that offers an incentive for a particular behavior. Explain what the incentive is, who is offering it, and what they are trying encourage or discourage. Does the incentive work? **[LO 1.3]**

13. Why do individuals or firms usually provide the goods and services people want? **[LO 1.4]**

14. You may have seen TV advertisements for products or programs that claim to teach a sure-fire way to make millions on the stock market. Apply the *Why isn't someone already doing it?* test to this situation. Do you believe the ads? Why or why not? **[LO 1.4]**

15. Describe an innovation in technology, business, or culture that had a major economic impact in your lifetime. **[LO 1.4]**

16. Why do people confuse correlation with causation? **[LO 1.5]**

17. Name two things that are positively correlated and two things that are negatively correlated. **[LO 1.5]**

18. Why is it important for a good economic model to predict cause and effect? **[LO 1.6]**

19. Why is it important for a good economic model to make clear assumptions? **[LO 1.6]**

20. Describe an economic model you know. What does the model predict about cause and effect? **[LO 1.6]**

21. Describe an economic model you know. What assumptions does the model make? Are the assumptions reasonable? **[LO 1.6]**

22. What is the difference between disagreeing about a positive statement and disagreeing about a normative statement? [**LO 1.7**]

23. Would a good economic model be more likely to address a positive statement or a normative statement? Why? [**LO 1.7**]

24. Write a positive statement and a normative statement about your favorite hobby. [**LO 1.7**]

Problems and Applications

1. Think about how and why goods and resources are scarce. Goods and resources can be scarce for reasons that are inherent to their nature at all times, that are temporary or seasonal, or that are artificially created. Separate the goods listed below into two groups; indicate which (if any) are artificially scarce (AS) and which (if any) are inherently scarce (IS). [**LO 1.1**]

    a. air of any quality _____

    b. land _____

    c. patented goods _____

    d. original Picasso paintings _____

2. You are looking for a new apartment in Manhattan. Your income is $4,000 per month, and you know that you should not spend more than 25 percent of your income on rent. You have come across the listings for one-bedroom apartments shown in Table 1P-1. You are indifferent about location, and transportation costs are the same to each neighborhood. [**LO 1.1**]

    a. Which apartments fall within your budget? (Check all that apply.)

    b. Suppose that you adhere to the 25 percent guideline but also receive a $1,000 cost-of-living supplement because you are living and working in Manhattan. Which apartments fall within your budget now?

3. Suppose the price of a sweater is $15. Julia's benefit from purchasing each additional sweater is given in

TABLE 1P-1

Location	Monthly Rent
Chelsea	$1,200
Battery Park	2,200
Delancey	950
Midtown	1,500

TABLE 1P-2

	Marginal benefit ($)
1st sweater	50
2nd sweater	35
3rd sweater	30
4th sweater	23
5th sweater	12
6th sweater	8

Table 1P-2. Julia gets the most benefit from the first sweater and less benefit from each additional sweater. If Julia is behaving rationally, how many sweaters will she purchase? [**LO 1.2**]

4. Sweaters sell for $15 at the crafts fair. Allie knits sweaters; her marginal costs are given in Table 1P-3. Allie's costs increase with each additional sweater. If Allie is behaving rationally, how many sweaters will she sell? [**LO 1.2**]

5. Last year, you estimated you would earn $5 million in sales revenues from developing a new product. So far, you have spent $3 million developing the product, but it is not yet complete. Meanwhile, this year you have new sales projections that show expected revenues from the new product will actually be only $4 million. How much should you be willing to spend to complete the product development? [**LO 1.2**]

    a. $0.

    b. Up to $1 million.

    c. Up to $4 million.

    d. Whatever it takes.

TABLE 1P-3

	Marginal cost ($)
1st sweater	5
2nd sweater	8
3rd sweater	12
4th sweater	18
5th sweater	25
6th sweater	32

TABLE 1P-4

		Affected good
a.	A local movie theater offers a student discount.	Movie tickets
b.	A tax on soft drinks passes in your state.	Soft drinks
c.	Subsidies on corn are cut in half.	Corn subsidies
d.	Your student health center begins offering flu shots for free.	Flu shots

6. Consider the following examples. For each one, say whether the incentive is positive or negative. **[LO 1.3]**

    a. Bosses who offer time-and-a-half for working on national holidays.

    b. Mandatory minimum sentencing for drug offenses.

    c. Fines for littering.

    d. Parents who offer their children extra allowance money for good grades.

7. Consider the events that change prices as described in Table 1P-4. For each one, say whether the opportunity cost of consuming the affected good increases or decreases. **[LO 1.3]**

8. Your best friend has an idea for a drive-through bar. Indicate the best explanation for why others have not taken advantage of her idea: true innovation, market failure, government intervention, or unprofitability. **[LO 1.4]**

9. Your best friend has an idea for a long-distance car service to drive people across the country. Indicate the best explanation for why others have not taken advantage of her idea: true innovation, market failure, intervention, or unprofitability. **[LO 1.4]**

10. Determine whether each of the following questionable statements is best explained by coincidence, an omitted variable, or reverse causation. **[LO 1.5]**

    a. In cities that have more police, crime rates are higher.

    b. Many retired people live in states where everyone uses air conditioning during the summer.

    c. More people come down with the flu during the Winter Olympics than during the Summer Olympics.

    d. For the last five years, Punxsutawney Phil has seen his shadow on Groundhog Day, and spring has come late.

11. For each of the pairs below, determine whether they are positively correlated, negatively correlated, or uncorrelated. **[LO 1.5]**

    a. Time spent studying and test scores.

    b. Vaccination and illness.

    c. Soft drink preference and music preference.

    d. Income and education.

12. Each statement below is part of an economic model. Indicate whether the statement is a prediction of cause and effect or an assumption. **[LO 1.6]**

    a. People behave rationally.

    b. If the price of a good falls, people will consume more of that good.

    c. Mass starvation will occur as population outgrows the food supply.

    d. Firms want to maximize profits.

13. From the list below, select the characteristics that describe a good economic model. **[LO 1.6]**

    a. Includes every detail of a given situation.

    b. Predicts that A causes B.

    c. Makes approximately accurate assumptions.

    d. Fits the real world perfectly.

    e. Predicts things that are usually true.

14. Determine whether each of the following statements is positive or normative. (Remember that a positive statement isn't necessarily *correct;* it just makes a factual claim rather than a moral judgment.) **[LO 1.7]**

    a. People who pay their bills on time are less likely than others to get into debt.

    b. Hard work is a virtue.

    c. Everyone should pay his or her bills on time.

    d. China has a bigger population than any other country in the world.

    e. China's One-Child Policy (which limits families to one child each) helped to spur the country's rapid economic growth.

    f. Lower taxes are good for the country.

15. You just received your midterm exam results and your professor wrote the following note: "You received a 70 on this exam, the average score. If you want to improve your grade, you should study more." Evaluate your professor's note. **[LO 1.7]**

    a. Is the first sentence positive or normative?

    b. Is the second sentence positive or normative?

Endnotes

1. Grameen Bank, "Monthly Report 2-2016," http://www. grameen-info.org/monthly-reports-2-2016/.

Specialization and Exchange

Learning Objectives

LO 2.1 Construct a production possibilities graph and describe what causes shifts in production possibilities curves.

LO 2.2 Define absolute and comparative advantage.

LO 2.3 Explain why people specialize.

LO 2.4 Explain how the gains from trade follow from comparative advantage.

THE ORIGINS OF A T-SHIRT

How can we get the most out of available resources? It's one of the most basic economic questions. Factory managers ask it when looking for ways to increase production. National leaders ask it as they design economic policy. Activists ask it when they look for ways to reduce poverty or conserve the environment. And, in a different way, it's a question we all ask ourselves when thinking about what to do in life and how to make sure that we're taking full advantage of our talents.

To get a handle on this question, we start by thinking about resources at the highest level: the logic of international trade and the specialization of production between countries. By the end of the chapter, we hope that you'll see how the same ideas apply to decisions at any scale, right down to whether it makes more sense to fix your own computer or pay a specialist to do it for you.

We'll start with what seems to be a simple question: Where did your T-shirt come from? Look at the tag. We're betting it was made in a place you've never been to, and maybe never thought of visiting. Bangladesh? Honduras? Malaysia? Sri Lanka?

That "made in" label tells only part of the story. Chances are that your shirt's history spans other parts of the globe. Consider a standard T-shirt: The cotton might have been grown in Mali and then shipped to Pakistan, where it was spun into yarn. The yarn might have been sent to Bangladesh, where it was woven into cloth, cut into pieces, and assembled into a shirt. That shirt might then have traveled all the way to the United States, where it was shipped to a store near you. A couple of years from now, when you are cleaning out your closet, you may donate the shirt to a charity, which may ship it to a second-hand clothing vendor in Mali—right back where your shirt's travels began.

Of course, this is not only the story of shirts. It is remarkably similar to the story of shoes, computers, phones, and cars, among many other manufactured goods. Today, the products and services most of us take for granted come to us through an incredibly complex global network of farms, mines, factories, traders, and stores. Why is the production of even a simple T-shirt spread across the world? Why is the cotton grown in Mali and the sewing done in Bangladesh, rather than vice versa? Why isn't the whole shirt made in the United States, so that it doesn't have to travel so far to reach you?

© igor kisselev/Alamy

This chapter addresses fundamental economic questions about who produces which goods and why. The fact that millions of people and firms around the globe coordinate their activities to provide consumers with the right combination of goods and services seems like magic.

This feat of coordination doesn't happen by chance, nor does a super-planner tell everyone where to go and what to do. Instead, the global production line is a natural outcome of people everywhere acting in their own self-interest to improve their own lives. Economists call this coordination mechanism the *invisible hand,* an idea that was first suggested by the eighteenth-century economic thinker Adam Smith.

To get some insight into the *who* and *why* of production, consider how the story of shirts has changed over the last few centuries. For most of the 1800s, Americans wore shirts made in the United States. Today, however, most shirts are made in Bangladesh, China, and other countries where factory wages are low. Have American workers become worse at making shirts over the last two centuries? Definitely not. In fact, as we'll see in this chapter, it doesn't even mean that Bangladeshi workers are better than American workers at making shirts. Instead, each good tends to be produced by the country, company, or person with the lowest opportunity cost for producing that good.

Countries and firms *specialize* in making goods for which they have the lowest opportunity cost. They then trade with one another to get the combination of goods they want to consume. The resulting *gains from trade* can be shared such that everyone ends up better off. It's no surprise that trade has taken off as transportation and communication between countries have become cheaper and better.

The concepts in this chapter apply not just to the wealth of nations and international trade. They also illuminate the daily choices most people face: Who should cook which dishes at Thanksgiving dinner? Should you hire a plumber or fix the pipes yourself? Should you become a rock star or an economist? The concepts these questions raise can be subtle and are sometimes misunderstood. We hope this chapter will provide insights that will help you become a better resource manager in all areas of your life.

Production Possibilities

LO 2.1 Construct a production possibilities graph and describe what causes shifts in production possibilities curves.

In Chapter 1, "Economics and Life," we talked about economic models. Good models help us understand complex situations through simplifying assumptions that allow us to zero in on the important aspects. The story of why Bangladesh now produces shirts for Americans that Americans themselves were producing 200 years ago is a complex one, as you'd expect. But by simplifying it into a model, we can reach useful insights.

Let's assume the United States and Bangladesh produce only two things—shirts and, say, bushels of wheat. (In reality, of course, they produce many things, but we're trying not to get bogged down in details right now.) The model uses "wheat" to stand in for "stuff other than shirts," allowing us to focus on what we're really interested in—shirts.

Using this model we'll perform a thought experiment about production using a tool called the *production possibilities frontier.* This tool is used in other contexts as well, many of which have no connection to international trade. Here we use it to show what has changed over the last couple of centuries to explain why Americans now buy shirts from Bangladesh.

Drawing the production possibilities frontier

Let's step back in time to the United States in 1800. In our simple model, there are 2 million American workers, and they have two choices of where to work: shirt factories or wheat farms. In shirt factories, each worker produces 1 shirt per day. On wheat farms, each worker produces 2 bushels of wheat per day.

What would happen if everyone worked on a wheat farm? The United States would produce 4 million bushels of wheat per day (2 bushels of wheat per worker × 2 million workers). This is one "production possibility." Alternatively, what would happen if everyone went to work in a shirt factory? The United States would produce 2 million shirts per day (1 shirt per worker × 2 million workers). Those production possibilities are represented as entries A and E (the top and bottom rows) in panel A of Figure 2-1.

Of course, the United States wouldn't want just shirts or just wheat—and there is no reason that all workers have to produce the same thing. There are many different combinations of shirts and wheat that American workers could produce. Some of these are shown as rows B, C, and D in panel A of Figure 2-1. For example, if one-quarter of the workers go to the shirt factory, they can make 500,000 (0.5 million) shirts (1 shirt per worker × 500,000 workers); the remaining workers can produce 3 million bushels of wheat (2 bushels per worker × 1.5 million workers). This production possibility is represented by row B. Or maybe 1 million workers would make shirts (1 million shirts) and 1 million would produce wheat (2 million bushels). That's row C.

For a graphic look at the production possibilities, we can plot them as points on a graph, as shown in panel B of Figure 2-1. If we fill in enough points, we create the solid green line shown in Figure 2-2. This is the **production possibilities frontier (PPF)**. It is a line or curve that shows all the possible combinations of outputs that can be produced using all available resources. In this case, the frontier plots all combinations of shirts and wheat that can be produced using all available workers in the United States. Points inside the frontier (such as point T) are achievable but don't make full use of all available resources.

The production possibilities frontier helps us answer the first of the economists' questions discussed in Chapter 1, "Economics and Life": *What are the wants and constraints of those involved?* People in the United States *want* to consume shirts and wheat (and other things, of course; remember, we're simplifying). The production possibilities frontier gives us a way to represent the *constraints* on production. The United States cannot produce combinations of shirts

production possibilities frontier (PPF)

a line or curve that shows all the possible combinations of two outputs that can be produced using all available resources

FIGURE 2-1

Possible production combinations

(A)

Production possibilities	Bushels of wheat (millions)	Shirts (millions)
A	4	0
B	3	0.5
C	2	1.0
D	1	1.5
E	0	2.0

(B)

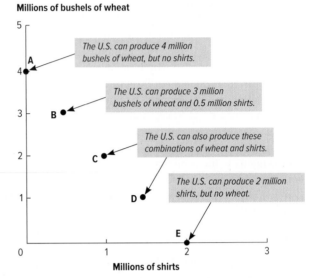

The United States can produce the maximum number of shirts or the maximum amount of wheat by devoting all its resources to one good or the other. But by allocating some resources to the production of each good, the United States can also produce many different combinations of wheat and shirts.

FIGURE 2-2

Production possibilities frontier

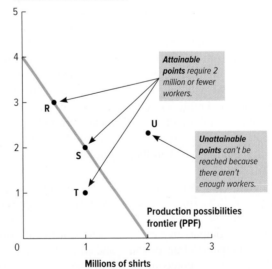

Points on or below the production possibilities frontier, such as R, S, and T, represent combinations of goods that the United States can produce with available resources. Points outside the frontier, such as U, are unattainable because there aren't enough resources.

and wheat that lie outside the frontier—such as point U in Figure 2-2. There just aren't enough workers or hours in the day to produce at point U, no matter how workers are allocated between shirts and wheat.

The production possibilities frontier also addresses the second economists' question: *What are the trade-offs?* Each worker can make *either* 1 shirt *or* 2 bushels of wheat per day. In other words, there is a trade-off between the quantity of wheat produced and the quantity of shirts produced. If we want an extra shirt, one worker has to stop producing bushels of wheat for a day. Therefore, the opportunity cost of 1 shirt is 2 bushels of wheat. Each bushel of wheat takes one worker half a day, so the opportunity cost of a bushel of wheat is half a shirt.

This opportunity cost is represented graphically by the *slope* of the production possibilities frontier. Moving up the frontier means getting more wheat at the cost of fewer shirts. Moving down the frontier means less wheat and more shirts. Looking at Figure 2-2, you'll notice that the slope of the line is −2. This is the same as saying that the opportunity cost of 1 shirt is always 2 bushels of wheat.

> For a refresher on calculating and interpreting slopes, see Appendix A, "Math Essentials: Understanding Graphs and Slope," which follows this chapter.

Production possibilities frontiers when opportunity costs differ

So far, we've made the assumption that all workers are able to make the same amount of each good. In reality, some workers will probably be nimble-fingered and great at making shirts; others will be more naturally gifted at farming. What happens if we adjust our simple model to reflect this reality?

Let's start off with all workers producing wheat and nobody making shirts. If we reallocate the workers who are best at making shirts, we can get a lot of shirts without giving up too much wheat. In other words, the opportunity cost of making the first few shirts is quite low.

Now imagine almost all workers are making shirts, so that only the best farmers are left producing wheat. If we reallocate most of the remaining workers to shirt making, we give up a lot of wheat to get only a few extra shirts. The opportunity cost of getting those last few shirts is very high.

We can add a little more nuance to the model, to include land and machinery as resources also needed for production. We would find that the same pattern holds: As more of each resource is allocated to production, the opportunity cost of producing an additional unit of a good typically increases. This happens because we expect producers to always produce as efficiently as they can, which means, all else equal, using the resources with the lowest opportunity cost.

Let's start with everyone producing wheat. With wheat production pushed to the maximum, some farmers probably have to work on land that isn't well-suited to producing wheat. It could be that the land is swampy, or the soil has been overfarmed and depleted of nutrients. When farmers who had been working on this poor land switch over to making shirts, the economy will lose only a little wheat and gain many shirts in return. In contrast, if only a small amount of wheat is being grown using only the best, most fertile land, reallocating the last few farmers will cause a relatively large decrease in wheat production for each additional shirt.

Returning to the simplest model where workers are the only input to production, we can translate this increasing opportunity cost into the production possibilities frontier. Doing so, we get a curve that bows out (a concave curve) instead of a straight line, as shown in Figure 2-3. Panel A shows what happens if we have just three types of workers:

- For every bushel of wheat, some can make 1 shirt; they're the workers between points C_1 and C_2.
- For every bushel of wheat, some can make only $\frac{1}{2}$ of a shirt (between points C_2 and C_3).
- For every bushel of wheat, some can make only $\frac{1}{4}$ of a shirt (between points C_3 and C_4).

In other words, as we go down the curve, we move from those who are better at making shirts to those who are better at producing wheat. As we do so, the opportunity cost of making

FIGURE 2-3

Bowed-out (concave) production possibilities frontier

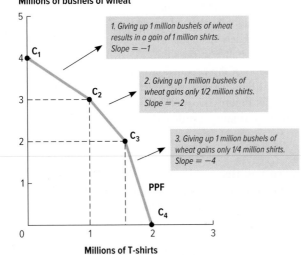

(A) Constructing the PPF

At point C_1, all workers produce wheat, and switching the best sewers to making shirts will result in a big gain in the quantity of shirts. As more and better farmers switch to making shirts, however, the gain in shirts produced decreases relative to the loss in the quantity of wheat. As a result the slope of the PPF is steeper from C_2 to C_3, and again from C_3 to C_4.

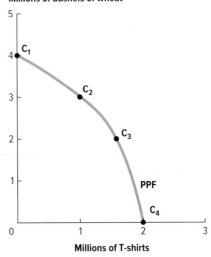

(B) The PPF

In reality, each worker has slightly different skills and therefore a slightly different opportunity cost of making shirts in terms of wheat. As a result, we get a smoothly curved production possibilities frontier.

shirts in terms of producing wheat increases. As that happens, the slope of the curve gets steeper (-1 between C_1 and C_2, -2 between C_2 and C_3, and -4 between C_3 and C_4).

In reality there aren't just three types of workers—each of the 2 million workers will have slightly different skills. The many possibilities will result in a curve that looks smooth, as in panel B of Figure 2-3. At each point of the curved production possibilities frontier, the slope represents the opportunity cost of getting more wheat or more shirts, based on the skills of the next worker who could switch.

Choosing among production possibilities

What can the production possibilities frontier tell us about what combination of goods an economy will choose to produce? Earlier, we noted that economies can produce at points inside the frontier, as well as points on it. However, choosing a production point *inside* the frontier means a country could get more wheat, more shirts, or both, just by using all available workers. For instance, in Figure 2-4, the United States can get more wheat without giving up any shirts, by moving from point B_1 to point B_2. It can do the same by moving from point B_2 to B_3.

efficient points
combinations of production possibilities that squeeze the most output possible from all available resources

But once at the frontier, the United States will have to give up some of one good to get more of the other. Points like B_3 that lie *on* the frontier are called **efficient** because they squeeze the most output possible from all available resources. Points *within* (inside) the frontier are *inefficient* because they do not use all available resources.

In the real world, economies aren't always efficient. A variety of problems can cause some workers to be unemployed or other resources to be left idle. We'll return to these issues in detail in future chapters. For now, we'll assume that production is always efficient. People and firms usually try to squeeze as much value as they can out of the resources available to them, so efficiency is a reasonable starting assumption.

FIGURE 2-4

Choosing an efficient production combination

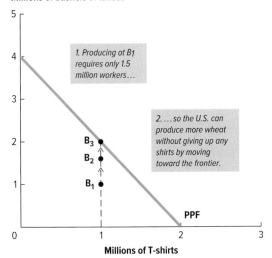

The United States needs only 1.5 million workers to reach point B_1. If the country employs more workers, it can reach point B_2 and get more wheat without giving up any shirts. The country can keep employing more workers until it reaches point B_3 (or any other point on the frontier) and there are no more workers left. Once the frontier is reached, getting more of one good requires giving up some of the other.

FIGURE 2-5

Choosing between efficient combinations

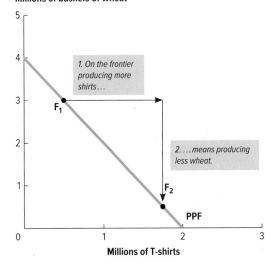

At all points on the production possibilities frontier, the United States employs the entire workforce. Because the country uses all its resources fully at each point, choosing between points on the frontier is a matter of preference when there is no trade with other countries. The United States may choose to produce more wheat and fewer shirts (point F_1) or more shirts and less wheat (point F_2), depending on what its consumers want.

Based on the assumption of efficiency, we can predict that an economy will choose to produce at a point *on* the frontier rather than inside it. What the production possibilities frontier cannot tell us is *which* point on the frontier that will be. Will it be F_1 in Figure 2-5, for example? Or will the United States choose to move down the curve to F_2, producing more shirts at the expense of less wheat? We can't say whether point F_1 or F_2 is better without knowing more about the situation. If the U.S. economy is completely self-sufficient, the decision depends on what combination of shirts and wheat people in the United States want to consume. If trade with other countries is possible, it also depends on consumers and production possibilities in those countries, as we'll see later in the chapter.

Shifting the production possibilities frontier

Thus far, we've built a simple model that tells us what combinations of T-shirts and wheat the United States could produce in 1800. However, a lot of things have changed since 1800, including incredible improvements in technology that improve production possibilities. The production possibilities frontier is a useful tool for illustrating this change and understanding how it affects the constraints and trade-offs the country faces. Two main factors drive the change in U.S. production possibilities: the number of workers and changes in technology.

First, there are more workers. The U.S. population now is about 60 times larger than it was in 1800. Having more workers means more people available to produce shirts and wheat. Graphically, we can represent this change by shifting the entire frontier outward. Panel A of Figure 2-6 shows what happens to the frontier when the U.S. population doubles, with each worker still able to produce 1 shirt or 2 bushels of wheat per day.

FIGURE 2-6

Shifting the production possibilities frontier

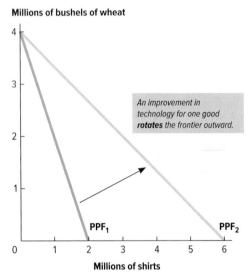

(A) Change in resources: Population growth

Millions of bushels of wheat

*An increase in available resources **shifts** the entire frontier outward.*

PPF₁ — PPF₂

Millions of shirts

Production possibilities expand when resources increase. If the working population grows, the country can make more of everything by producing at the same rate as before. *This causes the frontier to shift outward.* If the population doubled, so would the maximum possible quantities of shirts and wheat.

(B) Change in technology: Invention of the power loom

Millions of bushels of wheat

*An improvement in technology for one good **rotates** the frontier outward.*

PPF₁ — PPF₂

Millions of shirts

Production possibilities expand when technology improves. If the textile industry adopts the power loom, workers can make more shirts in the same amount of time. *This causes the frontier to rotate outward.* The rate of wheat production remains constant while the rate of shirt production increases, so the slope of the frontier changes.

The real magic of expanded productive capacity lies in the incredible technological advances that have taken place. In 1810, a businessman from Boston named Francis Cabot Lowell traveled to England to learn about British textile factories and to copy their superior technology. He brought back the power loom, which enabled workers to weave much more cotton fabric every day than they could before.[1]

We can model this change in technology through the production possibilities frontier by changing the rate of shirt production from 1 to 3 shirts per day, as shown in panel B of Figure 2-6. As the rate of shirt production increases, while the rate of wheat production remains the same, the shape of the curve changes. In this case, it pivots outward along the *x*-axis: This pivot indicates that for any given number of workers assigned to shirt-making, more shirts are produced than before. At every point except one (where all workers are producing wheat), the country can produce more with the same number of workers, thanks to improved technology.

> For a refresher about shifts and pivots in graphs, see Appendix B, "Math Essentials: Working with Linear Equations," which follows Chapter 3, "Markets."

✓CONCEPT CHECK

☐ Could a person or country ever produce a combination of goods that lies outside the production possibilities frontier? Why or why not? **[LO 2.1]**

☐ Would an increase in productivity as a result of a new technology shift a production possibilities frontier inward or outward? **[LO 2.1]**

Absolute and Comparative Advantage

In 1810, armed with power looms and a growing population, the United States was a highly effective producer of cotton shirts. For more than a century, it was the world's biggest clothing manufacturer. Since then, the U.S. population has grown larger, and manufacturing technology has improved even more. So, why do less than 5 percent of global clothing exports come from the United States?[2]

Up to now, we have worked with a very simple model of production to highlight the key trade-offs faced by individual producers. If there is no trade between countries, then the United States can consume only those goods that it produces on its own. In the real world, however, goods are made all over the world. If Americans want to buy more shirts than the United States produces, they can get them from somewhere else. Under these conditions, how can we predict which countries will produce which goods?

Understanding how resources are allocated among multiple producers is a step toward understanding why big firms work with specialized suppliers. It also helps explain why a wealthy, productive country like the United States trades with much poorer, less-productive countries. In this section we will see that trade actually increases total production, which can benefit everyone involved. To see why, let's turn to the question of why many T-shirts sold in the United States today are made in Bangladesh.

Absolute advantage

LO 2.2 Define absolute and comparative advantage.

Suppose that taking into account all the improvements in shirt-making and wheat-growing technology since 1800, an American worker can now make 50 shirts or grow 200 bushels of wheat per day.[3] A Bangladeshi worker, in comparison, can produce 25 shirts or 50 bushels of wheat. (Why the differences? Perhaps U.S. workers use faster cloth-cutting technology, or maybe because U.S. farmers use fertilizers, pesticides, and irrigation systems that farmers in Bangladesh don't.) In other words, given the same number of workers, the United States can produce twice as many shirts or four times as much wheat as Bangladesh.

If a producer can generate more output than others with a given amount of resources, that producer has an **absolute advantage**. In our simplified model, the United States has an absolute advantage over Bangladesh at producing both shirts and wheat because it can make more of both products than Bangladesh can per worker.

absolute advantage
the ability to produce more of a good or service than others can with a given amount of resources

Comparative advantage

Absolute advantage is not the end of the story, though. If it were, the United States would still be producing the world's shirts. The problem is that for every T-shirt the United States produces, it uses resources that could otherwise be spent growing wheat. Of course, the same could be said of Bangladesh. But in our model of T-shirt and wheat production, the opportunity cost of making 1 shirt in the United States is 4 bushels of wheat (200 bushels ÷ 50 shirts = 4 bushels per shirt). The opportunity cost of making 1 shirt in Bangladesh is only 2 bushels of wheat (50 bushels ÷ 25 shirts = 2 bushels per shirt). The United States has to give up more to make a shirt than Bangladesh does.

When a producer can make a good at a lower opportunity cost than other producers, we say it has a **comparative advantage** at producing that good. In our model, Bangladesh has a comparative advantage over the United States at shirt-making: Its opportunity cost of producing a shirt is only 2 bushels of wheat, compared to 4 bushels of wheat for the United States.

The United States, on the other hand, has a comparative advantage over Bangladesh at producing wheat: Each time the United States produces a bushel of wheat, it gives up the opportunity to

comparative advantage
the ability to produce a good or service at a lower opportunity cost than others

produce one-quarter of a shirt (50 shirts ÷ 200 bushels $= \frac{1}{4}$ shirt per bushel). For Bangladesh, however, the opportunity cost of producing a bushel of wheat is larger: it's one-half of a shirt (25 shirts ÷ 50 bushels $= \frac{1}{2}$ shirt per bushel). The United States has a lower opportunity cost for producing wheat than Bangladesh ($\frac{1}{4}$ shirt is less than $\frac{1}{2}$ shirt). Therefore, we say the United States has a comparative advantage over Bangladesh at wheat production.

A country can have a comparative advantage without having an absolute advantage. In our scenario, the United States has an absolute advantage over Bangladesh at producing both shirts and wheat, but it has a bigger advantage at producing wheat than at making shirts. It can make four times as much wheat per worker as Bangladesh (200 versus 50 bushels) but only twice as many shirts per worker (50 versus 25). It's better at both—but it's "more better," so to speak, at producing wheat. (We know that "more better" is not good grammar, but it nicely expresses the idea.) Likewise, Bangladesh has a comparative advantage at the good it is "less worse" at (producing shirts), even though it does not have an absolute advantage at either compared to the United States.

You may have noticed that for each country, the opportunity cost of growing wheat is the *inverse* of the opportunity cost of producing shirts. (For the United States, $\frac{1}{4}$ is the inverse of 4; for Bangladesh, $\frac{1}{2}$ is the inverse of 2.) Mathematically, this means that it is impossible for one country to have a comparative advantage at producing both goods. Each producer's opportunity cost depends on its *relative* ability at producing different goods. Logic tells us that you can't be better at A than at B and also better at B than at A. (And mathematically, if X is bigger than Y, then $\frac{1}{X}$ will be smaller than $\frac{1}{Y}$.) The United States can't be better at producing wheat than shirts relative to Bangladesh and at the same time be better at producing shirts than wheat relative to Bangladesh. As a result, no producer has a comparative advantage at everything, and each producer has a comparative advantage at something.

We can check this international trade scenario against an example closer to home. When your family makes Thanksgiving dinner, does the best cook make everything? If you have a small family, maybe one person *can* make the whole dinner. But if your family is anything like our families, you will need several cooks. Grandma is by far the most experienced cook, yet the potato peeling always gets outsourced to the kids. Is that because the grandchildren are better potato peelers than Grandma? We think that's probably not the case. Grandma has an absolute advantage at everything having to do with Thanksgiving dinner. Still, the kids may have a *comparative* advantage at potato peeling, which frees up Grandma to make those tricky pie crusts.

We can find applications of comparative advantage everywhere in life. Sports is no exception. Look at the From Another Angle box "Babe Ruth, star pitcher" for another example.

From Another Angle
Babe Ruth, star pitcher

How should baseball managers decide who should play at different positions? One approach is to assign the best player to each position. But the skills required for many positions are similar. What does a manager do when one player has an absolute advantage at multiple positions? One answer is to turn to comparative advantage.

Consider the choice that New York Yankees manager Miller Huggins faced when he acquired a player named Babe Ruth in 1920. Ruth was an excellent pitcher. In 1918 he had set a record for the most consecutive scoreless innings pitched in the World Series—a record that was not broken until 1961. He could easily have become one of the best pitchers of his generation. But Ruth didn't end up as a pitcher. Babe Ruth was both the best pitcher *and* the best hitter on the team. From a practical point of view, he couldn't do both (pitching takes too much energy), so Miller Huggins had to make a choice.

Although Ruth had an *absolute* advantage at both positions, he had a *comparative* advantage as a hitter. The opportunity cost of having Ruth pitch was the number of games the Yankees would win by having him bat. Huggins decided the opportunity cost of Ruth's pitching was higher than the opportunity cost of his batting. Ruth went on to become one of the greatest hitters of all time. In 1920 he hit 54 home runs. That year, only one other *team* collectively hit as many home runs as Ruth *alone* did.

A good manager should, as Miller Huggins did, assign players to positions according to their comparative advantage. The question is not which player is best at a particular position, but which player the team can most afford to lose at any other position. For a player seeking to play a particular position, the right argument may be not that he or she is the best at that position, but that he or she is worth less at any other!

Source: 2016 Family of Babe Ruth and Babe Ruth League c/o Luminary Group LLC.

✓ CONCEPT CHECK

☐ What does it mean to have an absolute advantage at producing a good? **[LO 2.2]**

☐ What does it mean to have a comparative advantage at producing a good? **[LO 2.2]**

☐ Can more than one producer have an absolute advantage at producing the same good? Why or why not? **[LO 2.2]**

Why Trade?

The United States is perfectly capable of producing its own shirts and its own wheat. In fact, in our simple model, it has an absolute advantage at producing both goods. So, why buy shirts from Bangladesh? We are about to see that both countries are actually able to consume more when they specialize in producing the good for which they have a comparative advantage and then trade with one another.

Specialization

LO 2.3 Explain why people specialize.

If you lived 200 years ago, your everyday life would have been full of tasks that probably never even cross your mind today. You might have milked a cow, hauled water from a well, split wood, cured meat, mended a hole in a sock, and repaired a roof.

Contrast that with life today. Almost everything we use comes from someone who specializes in providing a particular good or service. We bet you don't churn the butter you put on your toast. You probably wouldn't begin to know how to construct the parts in your smartphone. We are guessing you don't usually sew your own clothes or grow your own wheat. In today's world, all of us are dependent on one another for the things we need on a daily basis.

In our model, when the United States and Bangladesh work in isolation, each produces some shirts and some wheat—each in the combinations that its consumers prefer. Suppose the United States has 150 million workers and Bangladesh has 80 million. As before,

- each U.S. worker can make 50 shirts or 200 bushels of wheat and
- each Bangladeshi worker can make 25 shirts or 50 bushels of wheat.

TABLE 2-1

Production with and without specialization

When Bangladesh and the United States each specializes in the production of one good, the two countries can produce an extra 0.5 billion T-shirts and 1 billion bushels of wheat using the same number of workers and the same technology.

	Country	Wheat (billions of bushels)	T-shirts (billions)
Without specialization	United States	26	1
	Bangladesh	3	0.5
	Total	**29**	**1.5**
With specialization	United States	30	0
	Bangladesh	0	2
	Total	**30**	**2**

Now, suppose these production combinations occur:

- Based on U.S. consumers' preferences, U.S. workers are split so that they produce 1 billion shirts and 26 billion bushels of wheat.
- In Bangladesh, workers are allocated to produce 0.5 billion shirts and 3 billion bushels of wheat.

Even though Bangladesh's productivity per worker is lower, it has a large number of workers and so is able to produce a large total quantity of goods. (The quantities of shirts and wheat are unrealistically large because we are assuming they are the only goods being produced. In reality, of course, countries produce many different goods, but this simplifying assumption helps us to zero in on a real-world truth.)

We have seen that if the United States and Bangladesh are self-sufficient (each producing what its people want to consume), then together the two countries can make 1.5 billion T-shirts and 29 billion bushels of wheat, as shown at the top of Table 2-1 ("without specialization"). What would happen if, instead, Bangladesh put all its resources into making shirts and the United States put all its resources into producing wheat?

If each country focuses on producing the good for which it has a comparative advantage, total production increases. Focusing in this way is called **specialization**. It's the practice of spending all of your resources producing a particular good. When each country specializes in making a particular good according to its comparative advantage, total production possibilities are greater than if each produced the exact combination of goods its own consumers want.

The bottom section of Table 2-1 ("with specialization") shows us:

specialization
spending all of your time producing a particular good

United States

$$200 \text{ bushels per worker} \times 150 \text{ million workers} = 30 \text{ billion bushels}$$

Bangladesh

$$25 \text{ shirts per worker} \times 80 \text{ million workers} = 2 \text{ billion shirts}$$

By specializing, the two countries together can produce 1 billion bushels of wheat more than before, *plus* 0.5 billion more shirts. Specialization increases total production, using the same number of workers and the same technology.

This rule applies to all sorts of goods and services. It explains why dentists hire roofers to fix a roof leak and why roofers hire dentists to fill a cavity. See the Real Life box "Specialization sauce" for an example of the power of specialization in a setting you are probably somewhat familiar with—McDonald's.

Real Life

Specialization sauce

Henry Ford pioneered the assembly-line method of automobile manufacturing: Each worker does just one small task on each car before it moves down the line to the next worker, who does a different small task. Ford proved that he could build more cars in less time when each employee specialized in this way. Restaurants use the same principle: They can serve more customers faster if they split the work among managers, waitstaff, and chefs. Fast-food restaurants take specialization even further.

Fast food as we know it was born in 1948, when McDonald's founders Dick and Mac McDonald decided to implement a radically new method of preparing food. Inspired by factory assembly lines, they applied Ford's concept of specialization to the restaurant business. Instead of assigning several employees to general food preparation, they split each order into parts, parceling out the steps required to prepare a meal. One employee became the grilling specialist; another added mustard and ketchup. A different employee operated the potato fryer, and yet another mixed the milkshakes.

Any single employee would almost certainly have been able to learn how to grill a hamburger, add condiments, make fries, *and* mix a milkshake. In each restaurant, one particularly skilled employee was probably faster than everyone else at all the steps in making a meal.

Even so, specialization was more efficient. By assigning only one specific task to each employee, the founders of McDonald's revolutionized the speed and quantity of food preparation. Harnessing the power of specialization allowed them to grill more burgers, fry more potatoes, and feed more hungry customers.

Source: Eric Schlosser, *Fast Food Nation* (Boston: Houghton Mifflin, 2002), pp. 19–20.

Gains from trade

LO 2.4 Explain how the gains from trade follow from comparative advantage.

When countries specialize in producing the goods for which they have a comparative advantage, total production increases. The problem with specialization is that each producer ends up with only one good—in our model, wheat in the United States, T-shirts in Bangladesh. If Americans want to wear T-shirts and Bangladeshis want to enjoy wheat, they must trade.

Suppose that Bangladesh and the United States agree to trade 3.5 billion bushels of wheat for 1.5 billion T-shirts. As a result, each country ends up with an additional 0.5 billion bushels of wheat, and the United States also has 0.5 billion more shirts than before. The improvement in outcomes that occurs when specialized producers exchange goods and services is called the **gains from trade**.

Figure 2-7 shows how the gains from trade affect a country's consumption. Before the trade, it was impossible for the United States and Bangladesh to consume any combination of goods outside their production possibilities frontiers. After the trade between the two specialized producers, each country's consumption increases to a point that was previously unachievable. If Bangladesh consumes the same amount of shirts as before and trades the remaining, both countries are able to consume 0.5 billion bushels more wheat after opening up to trade.

In Figure 2-7, the gains from the U.S.–Bangladesh trade are distributed equally: 0.5 billion bushels more wheat for the United States and 0.5 billion bushels more wheat for Bangladesh. In reality, the distribution can vary. The gains do not have to be equal for the trading arrangement to benefit everyone. If Bangladesh takes an extra 0.25 billion bushels of wheat and the United States an extra 0.75 billion (or vice versa), both countries will still be better off than if they worked alone.

gains from trade
the improvement in outcomes that occurs when producers specialize and exchange goods and services

FIGURE 2-7
Specialization and gains from trade

(A) United States' gains from trade

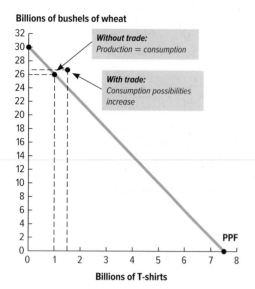

(B) Bangladesh's gains from trade

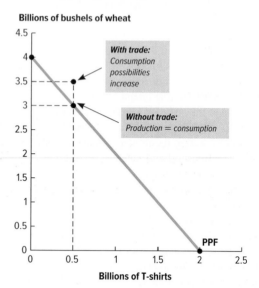

If a country does not specialize and trade, its production and consumption are both limited to points along its production possibilities frontier. By specializing and achieving gains from trading, the United States gains 0.5 million T-shirts and 0.5 billion bushels of wheat.

By opening up to trade, Bangladesh also gains 0.5 billion bushels of wheat compared to what it could produce on its production possibilities frontier.

Overall, there is room for trade as long as two things occur: (1) the two countries differ in their opportunity costs to produce a good and (2) they set a favorable trading price. A favorable trading price needs to benefit both parties. If T-shirts from Bangladesh are too expensive, the United States will refuse to buy them. Similarly, if U.S. wheat is too expensive, Bangladesh will not buy it. If the United States agrees to trade 3.5 billion bushels of wheat for 1.5 billion T-shirts, it must be because the United States values 3.5 billion bushels of wheat less than 1.5 billion T-shirts.

To see how much each country values a good, we must look at its opportunity costs. Recall that the opportunity cost of 1 T-shirt for Bangladesh is 2 bushels of wheat. In other words, the value of 1 T-shirt for Bangladesh is at least 2 bushels of wheat. If the United States offered to trade 1 bushel of wheat in exchange for 1 T-shirt, Bangladesh would refuse such a trade; Bangladesh could simply produce the wheat itself. Bangladesh needs to receive at least 2 bushels of wheat in exchange for 1 T-shirt.

To see how many bushels of wheat the United States is willing to give up in exchange for 1 T-shirt, we can look at the United States' opportunity cost. The opportunity cost of 1 T-shirt for the United States is 4 bushels of wheat. Thus, the United States will only trade up to 4 bushels of wheat in exchange for 1 T-shirt. More than 4 bushels of wheat would be worth more than 1 T-shirt. If Bangladesh tries to charge a price greater than the United States' opportunity cost, the United States will choose to make the T-shirts itself. In order for trade to benefit both countries, the trade price of 1 T-shirt must be at least 2 bushels of wheat but less than 4 bushels of wheat.

In general, two countries will benefit from a trade price that falls between their opportunity costs. In our example, the price at which Bangladesh and the United States are willing to trade T-shirts must fall between Bangladesh's opportunity cost for producing T-shirts and the

United States' opportunity cost for producing T-shirts. If Bangladesh is the country that has specialized in T-shirts, it cannot charge a price greater than the United States' opportunity cost. If it does, the United States will simply make the T-shirts itself. Conversely, Bangladesh must receive a price that covers its opportunity costs for making T-shirts or it will not be willing to trade.

Consider the *wants* that drive people to trade. When people specialize and trade, everyone gets more of the things they want than they would if they were self-sufficient. Thus, trade can be driven entirely by self-interest. Just as the United States benefits from trading with Bangladesh (even though the United States may have an absolute advantage at producing both wheat and shirts), an experienced worker or large firm benefits from trading with a less-experienced employee or a small, specialized company.

For example, when Bill Gates was the CEO of Microsoft, he hired recent college graduates to fix bugs in the computer code, even though he might have done it faster himself. Let's say Bill can fix the bug in an hour, but for every hour he's distracted from running Microsoft, the company's profits go down by $1,000. The less-experienced coder earns only $50 an hour, so even if she takes two to three times as long to do the work, it's still worth it for Bill to hire her and spend his own time keeping Microsoft's productivity up. Bill has an absolute advantage at fixing computer bugs, but the opportunity cost in lost profits means the younger coder has a comparative advantage. (Bill's comparative advantage is at running Microsoft.) Everyone ends up better off if they specialize.

In spite of the gains from specializing and trading, not everyone considers this an obvious choice in every circumstance—which brings us to our fourth question from Chapter 1, "Economics and Life": *Why isn't someone already doing it?* In the case of trade, we know that many *are* already doing it. However, some people argue that it's worth giving up the gains from trade for various reasons. For some examples, see the What Do You Think? box "Is self-sufficiency a virtue?"

What Do You Think?
Is self-sufficiency a virtue?

Why should the United States trade with other countries? If every other country in the world were to disappear tomorrow, the United States would probably manage to fend for itself. It has plenty of fertile land, natural resources, workers, and manufacturing capacity. In fact, many observers consider the value Americans place on self-sufficiency to be a cultural trait.

Based on what you now know about specialization and the gains from trade, what do you think about the value of exchange versus the value of self-sufficiency? Economists tend to line up in favor of free international trade; they argue that trade makes both countries economically better off. Serious and worthwhile arguments have also been made on the other side. The following are some reasons that have been proposed for developing national self-sufficiency. When thinking through these questions, remember the answer is rarely simple.

- **National heritage.** Many people feel that a line has been crossed when a country loses its family farms or outsources a historically important industry—for example, auto-making in the United States. Does a country lose its culture when it loses these industries and shifts into other industries instead?
- **Security.** Some people worry that trade weakens a country if it then has to rely on trade for critical goods. If foreign relations sour, wars can result. Is it safe to rely on other countries for your food supply, or does that kind of dependency pose a security risk? For example, what can happen to national security if we rely on other countries entirely for steel or uranium or oil?
- **Quality control and ethics.** When goods are imported from other countries, production standards are harder to control than if the goods are made at home. Some people argue that

(continued)

international trade undermines consumer safety and environmental regulations. Others also say that international trade fosters labor conditions that would be considered unethical or illegal in the United States.

WHAT DO YOU THINK?

1. Do you agree with any of these objections to free trade? Why? When is self-sufficiency more valuable than the gains from trade?
2. Is the choice between trade and self-sufficiency an *either/or* question? Is there a middle-of-the-road approach that would address concerns on both sides of this issue?

Comparative advantage over time

Our simplified model of production possibilities and trade helps us to understand why Americans now buy shirts from other countries. But we noted at the beginning of the chapter that this wasn't always the case: 200 years ago, the United States was selling shirts to the rest of the world. To understand this change, we can apply our model to shifts in comparative advantage over time. These shifts have caused significant changes in different countries' economies and trade patterns.

When the Industrial Revolution began, Great Britain led the world in clothing manufacturing. In the nineteenth century, the United States snatched the comparative advantage through a combination of new technology (which led to higher productivity) and cheap labor (which led to lower production costs). Gradually, the comparative advantage in clothing shifted away from the United States to other countries. Clothing manufacturing moved from country to country, searching for ever-lower costs:

- By the 1930s, 40 percent of the world's cotton goods were made in Japan, where workers from the countryside were willing to work long hours for low wages.
- In the mid-1970s, clothing manufacturing moved to Hong Kong, Taiwan, and Korea, where wages were even lower than those in Japan.
- The textile industry then moved to China in the early 1990s, when millions of young women left their farms to work for wages as much as 90 percent lower than those in Hong Kong. Similar changes happened in Bangladesh.

There's an upside to the progressive relocation of this industry and its jobs: Eventually high-wage jobs replaced low-wage jobs, and these countries experienced considerable economic growth.

Losing a comparative advantage in clothing production sounds like a bad thing at first. But as we know from our model, you can't lose comparative advantage in one thing without gaining it in another. Changes in clothing manufacturing were driven by workers in each country getting more skilled at industries that paid better than making clothes—such as making cars, or programming computers, or providing financial services. This meant the opportunity cost of making clothes increased. The comparative advantage in clothing production shifted to countries where the workers lacked skills in better-paying industries and so were willing to work in textile factories for lower wages.

Most historians would agree that it wasn't a sign of failure when countries lost their comparative advantage in clothing production—it was a sign of success. Former textile producers like Great Britain, the United States, Japan, Korea, and Hong Kong are all much wealthier now than they were when they were centers of clothing manufacturing.

However, these changes probably didn't look or feel like success at the time, especially for workers in textile factories who saw their jobs disappearing overseas. This same tension is arising today in other industries as companies "outsource" tasks that can be done more cheaply in other countries.

✓ CONCEPT CHECK

☐ Why do people or countries specialize? **[LO 2.3]**

☐ How do two countries benefit from trading with each other? **[LO 2.4]**

☐ Is it possible to not have a comparative advantage at anything? Why or why not? **[LO 2.4]**

Conclusion

Specialization and trade can make everyone better off. It is not surprising, then, that in an economy driven by individuals seeking to make a profit or improve their communities, people specialize so as to exploit their comparative advantages. That principle is as true for countries, like the United States and Bangladesh, as it is for individuals picking their careers.

No government intervention is required to coordinate production. The great economic thinker Adam Smith suggested the term *invisible hand* to describe this coordinating mechanism:

> It is not from the benevolence of the butcher, the brewer, or the baker that we expect our dinner, but from their regard to their [self-interest]. . . . he intends only his own gain, and he is in this, as in many other cases, led by an invisible hand to promote an end which was no part of his intention.[4]

The functioning of the invisible hand depends on a lot of other assumptions, such as free competition and full information. Later in the book we will discuss these assumptions, and when they work and when they do not.

Most people take for granted the prevalence of specialization and trade in their everyday lives. Few stop to think about the benefits and where they come from. In this chapter we tried to dig down to the bottom of the assumptions people make and expose the logic behind the gains from trade. As we proceed—especially when we return to topics like international trade and government intervention in the markets—try to remember the underlying incentive that drives people to interact with one another in economic exchanges.

Key Terms

production possibilities
frontier (PPF), p. 27

efficient points, p. 30

absolute advantage, p. 33

comparative advantage, p. 33

specialization, p. 36

gains from trade, p. 37

Summary

LO 2.1 Construct a production possibilities graph and describe what causes shifts in production possibilities curves.

A production possibilities graph shows all the combinations of two goods that a person or an economy can produce with a given amount of time, resources, and technology. The production possibilities frontier is a line on that graph that shows all the maximum attainable combinations of goods. Producers of goods and services are not likely to choose a combination of goods inside the production possibilities frontier because they could achieve a higher production level with the same amount of resources. They cannot choose points outside the frontier, which would require more than the available resources. The choice between combinations on the production possibilities frontier is a matter of preference.

Shifts in the production possibilities frontier can be caused by changes in technology, as well as changes in population and other resources. Increases in technological capabilities and population will shift the PPF outward; decreases in these factors will shift the PPF inward.

LO 2.2 Define absolute and comparative advantage.

Producers have an absolute advantage at making a good when they can produce more output than others with a given amount of resources. If you put two people or countries to work making the same good, the person or country that is more productive has an absolute advantage.

People or countries have a comparative advantage when they are better at producing one good than they are at producing other goods, relative to other producers. Everyone has a comparative advantage at something, whether or not they have an absolute advantage at anything.

LO 2.3 Explain why people specialize.

Specialization means spending all or much of your time producing a particular good. Production is highest when people or countries specialize in producing the good for which they have a comparative advantage. Specialization increases total production, using the same number of workers and the same technology.

LO 2.4 Explain how the gains from trade follow from comparative advantage.

The increase in total production that occurs from specialization and exchange is called the gains from trade. With specialization and trade, two parties can increase production and consumption, and each ends up better off.

Shifts in comparative advantage over time have caused significant changes in different countries' economies and trade patterns. These changes signal general economic success, although they can be painful for the individual workers and industries involved.

Review Questions

1. You've been put in charge of a bake sale for a local charity, at which you are planning to sell cookies and cupcakes. What would a production possibilities graph of this situation show? **[LO 2.1]**

2. You manage two employees at a pet salon. Your employees perform two tasks, giving flea baths and grooming animals. If you constructed a single production possibilities frontier for flea baths and grooming that combined both of your employees' work efforts, would you expect the production possibilities frontier to be linear (a straight line)? Explain why or why not. **[LO 2.1]**

3. You and another volunteer are in charge of a bake sale for a local charity, at which you are planning to sell cookies and cupcakes. What would it mean for one of you to have an absolute advantage at baking cookies or cupcakes? Could one of you have an absolute advantage at baking both items? **[LO 2.2]**

4. You and another volunteer are in charge of a bake sale for a local charity, at which you are planning to sell cookies and cupcakes. What would it mean for you or the other volunteer to have a comparative advantage at baking cookies or cupcakes? Could one of you have a comparative advantage at baking both items? **[LO 2.2]**

5. You and another volunteer are in charge of a bake sale for a local charity, at which you are planning to sell cookies and cupcakes. Suppose you have a comparative advantage at baking cookies, and the other volunteer has a comparative advantage at baking cupcakes. Make a proposal to the volunteer about how to split up the baking. Explain how you can both gain from specializing, and why. **[LO 2.3]**

6. At the flower shop, where you manage two employees, your employees perform two tasks: caring for the displays of cut flowers and making flower arrangements to fill customer orders. Explain how you would approach organizing your employees and assigning them tasks. **[LO 2.3]**

7. Suppose two countries produce the same two goods and have identical production possibilities frontiers. Do you expect these countries to trade? Explain why or why not. **[LO 2.4]**

8. Brazil is the largest coffee producer in the world, and coffee is one of Brazil's major export goods. Suppose that in 20 years, Brazil no longer produces much coffee and imports most of its coffee instead. Explain why Brazil might change its trade pattern over time. **[LO 2.4]**

Problems and Applications

1. Your friend Sam has been asked to prepare appetizers for a university reception during homecoming weekend. She has an unlimited amount of ingredients but only six hours to prepare them. Sam can make 300 mini-sandwiches or 150 servings of melon slices topped with smoked salmon and a dab of sauce per hour. **[LO 2.1]**

   a. Draw Sam's production possibilities frontier.

   b. Now suppose that the university decides to postpone the reception until after the big game, so

Sam has an extra four hours to prepare. Redraw her production possibilities frontier to show the impact of this increase in resources.

c. Now, in addition to the extra time to prepare, suppose Sam's friend Chris helps by preparing the melon slices. Sam can now make 300 mini-sandwiches or 300 melon appetizers per hour. Redraw Sam's production possibilities frontier to show the impact of increased productivity in making melon appetizers.

2. Your friend Sam has been asked to prepare appetizers for the university reception. She has an unlimited amount of ingredients and six hours in which to prepare them. Sam can make 300 mini-sandwiches or 150 servings of melon slices topped with smoked salmon and a dab of sauce per hour. **[LO 2.1]**

   a. What is Sam's opportunity cost of making one mini-sandwich?

   b. What is Sam's opportunity cost of making one melon appetizer?

   c. Suppose the reception has been postponed, so Sam has an extra four hours to prepare. What is the opportunity cost of making one mini-sandwich now?

   d. Suppose the reception has been postponed, so Sam has an extra four hours to prepare. What is the opportunity cost of making one melon appetizer now?

   e. Suppose Sam's friend Chris helps by preparing the melon slices, increasing Sam's productivity to 300 mini-sandwiches or 300 melon appetizers per hour. What is the opportunity cost of making one mini-sandwich now?

   f. Suppose Sam's friend Chris helps by preparing the melon slices, increasing Sam's productivity to 300 mini-sandwiches or 300 melon appetizers per hour. What is the opportunity cost of making one melon appetizer now?

3. Suppose that Canada produces two goods: lumber and fish. It has 18 million workers, each of whom can cut 10 feet of lumber or catch 20 fish each day. **[LO 2.1]**

   a. What is the maximum amount of lumber Canada could produce in a day?

   b. What is the maximum amount of fish it could produce in a day?

   c. Draw Canada's production possibilities frontier.

   d. Use your graph to determine how many fish can be caught if 60 million feet of lumber are cut.

FIGURE 2P-1

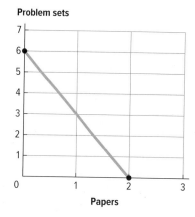

Problem sets

4. The graph in Figure 2P-1 shows Tanya's weekly production possibilities frontier for doing homework (writing papers and doing problem sets). **[LO 2.1]**

   a. What is the slope of the production possibilities frontier?

   b. What is the opportunity cost of doing one problem set?

   c. What is the opportunity cost of writing one paper?

5. Use the production possibilities frontier in Figure 2P-2 to answer the following questions. **[LO 2.1]**

   a. What is the slope of the PPF between point A and point B?

   b. What is the slope of the PPF between point B and point C?

   c. Is the opportunity cost of producing hammers higher between points A and B or between points B and C?

FIGURE 2P-2

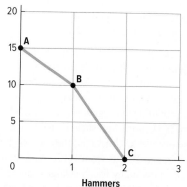

Screwdrivers

FIGURE 2P-3

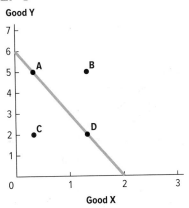

Good Y

FIGURE 2P-4

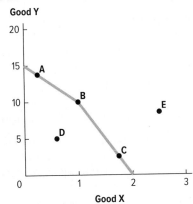

Good Y

d. Is the opportunity cost of producing screwdrivers higher between points A and B or between points B and C?

6. For each point on the PPF in Figure 2P-3, note whether the point is attainable and efficient, attainable and inefficient, or unattainable. [LO 2.1]

7. For each point on the PPF in Figure 2P-4, note whether the point is attainable and efficient, attainable and inefficient, or unattainable. [LO 2.1]

8. The Red Cross and WIC (Women, Infants, and Children) program both provide emergency food packages and first-aid kits to New York City homeless shelters. Table 2P-1 shows their weekly production possibilities in providing emergency goods to NYC homeless shelters. NYC homeless shelters need a total of 20 first-aid kits per week. Currently, they get 10 kits from the Red Cross and 10 kits from WIC. With their remaining resources, how many food packages can each organization provide to NYC homeless shelters? [LO 2.1]

TABLE 2P-1

	Red Cross	WIC
Food packages	300	200
First-aid kits	50	20

9. Suppose that three volunteers are preparing cookies and cupcakes for a bake sale. Diana can make 27 cookies or 18 cupcakes per hour; Andy can make 25 cookies or 17 cupcakes; and Sam can make 10 cookies or 12 cupcakes. [LO 2.2]

   a. Who has the absolute advantage at making cookies?

   b. At making cupcakes?

10. Paula and Carlo are coworkers. Their production possibilities frontiers for counseling clients and writing memos are given in Figure 2P-5. [LO 2.2]

FIGURE 2P-5

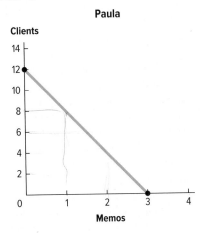

Paula

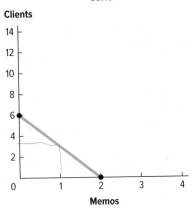

Carlo

a. Which worker has an absolute advantage in counseling clients?

b. Which worker has an absolute advantage in writing memos?

c. Which worker has a comparative advantage in counseling clients?

d. Which worker has a comparative advantage in writing memos?

11. Two students are assigned to work together on a project that requires both writing and an oral presentation. Steve can write 1 page or prepare 3 minutes of a presentation each day. Anna can write 2 pages or prepare 1 minute of a presentation each day. **[LO 2.2]**

   a. Who has a comparative advantage at writing?

   b. Suppose that Steve goes to a writing tutor and learns some tricks that enable him to write 3 pages each day. Now who has a comparative advantage at writing?

12. Suppose that the manager of a restaurant has two new employees, Rahul and Henriette, and is trying to decide which one to assign to which task. Rahul can chop 20 pounds of vegetables or wash 100 dishes per hour. Henriette can chop 30 pounds of vegetables or wash 120 dishes. **[LO 2.3]**

   a. Who should be assigned to chop vegetables?

   b. Who should be assigned to wash dishes?

13. The Dominican Republic and Nicaragua both produce coffee and rum. The Dominican Republic can produce 20 thousand tons of coffee per year or 10 thousand barrels of rum. Nicaragua can produce 30 thousand tons of coffee per year or 5 thousand barrels of rum. **[LO 2.3]**

   a. Suppose the Dominican Republic and Nicaragua sign a trade agreement in which each country would specialize in the production of either coffee or rum. Which country should specialize in producing coffee? Which country should specialize in producing rum?

   b. What are the minimum and maximum prices at which these countries will trade coffee?

14. Eleanor and her little sister Joanna are responsible for two chores on their family's farm, gathering eggs and collecting milk. Eleanor can gather 9 dozen eggs or collect 3 gallons of milk per week. Joanna can gather 2 dozen eggs or collect 2 gallons of milk per week. **[LO 2.3]**

   a. The family wants 2 gallons of milk per week and as many eggs as the sisters can gather. Currently, Eleanor and Joanna collect one gallon of milk each and as many eggs as they can. How many dozens of eggs does the family have per week?

   b. If the sisters specialized, which sister should collect the milk?

   c. If the sisters specialized, how many dozens of eggs would the family have per week?

15. Suppose Russia and Sweden each produces only paper and cars. Russia can produce 8 tons of paper or 4 million cars each year. Sweden can produce 25 tons of paper or 5 million cars each year. **[LO 2.4]**

   a. Draw the production possibilities frontier for each country.

   b. Both countries want 2 million cars each year and as much paper as they can produce along with 2 million cars. Find this point on each production possibilities frontier and label it "A."

   c. Suppose the countries specialize. Which country will produce cars?

   d. Once they specialize, suppose they work out a trade of 2 million cars for 6 tons of paper. Find the new *consumption* point for each country and label it "B."

16. Maya and Max are neighbors. They both grow lettuce and tomatoes in their gardens. Maya can grow 45 heads of lettuce or 9 pounds of tomatoes this summer. Max can grow 42 heads of lettuce or 6 pounds of tomatoes this summer. If Maya and Max specialize and trade, the price of tomatoes (in terms of lettuce) would be as follows: 1 pound of tomatoes would cost between _____ and _____ pounds of lettuce. **[LO 2.4]**

Endnotes

1. http://www.encyclopedia.com/topic/Francis_Cabot_Lowell.aspx

2. http://www.economist.com/news/leaders/21646204-asias-dominance-manufacturing-will-endure-will-make-development-harder-others-made

3. http://www.agclassroom.org/gan/timeline/farm_tech.htm

4. Adam Smith, *An Inquiry into the Nature and Causes of the Wealth of Nations*, 1776.

Math Essentials: Understanding Graphs and Slope

Learning Objectives

LO A.1 Create four quadrants using x- and y-axes and plot points on a graph.

LO A.2 Use data to calculate slope.

LO A.3 Interpret what the direction and steepness of slope indicate about a line.

Graphing is an essential component of economics. We touched on graphs in Chapter 2, "Specialization and Exchange," and we'll only see more graphs from here on out in the course. In order to truly understand the concepts of economics, you'll need to understand the basics of graphing. In this appendix, we'll discuss how to create and interpret different types of graphs.

Creating a Graph

LO A.1 Create four quadrants using x- and y-axes and plot points on a graph.

A graph is one way to visually represent data. In this book, we use graphs to describe and interpret economic relationships. For example, we use a graph called a production possibilities frontier to explore opportunity costs and trade-offs in production. We use graphs of average, variable, and marginal costs to explore production decisions facing a firm. And—the favorite of economists everywhere—we use graphs to show supply and demand and the resulting relationship between price and quantity.

Graphs of one variable

Graphs of a single variable come in three main forms: the bar chart, the pie chart, and the line graph. In school, you've probably made all three and plastered them on science-fair posters and presentations or used them in reports. These graphs are versatile; they can be used to present all sorts of information. Throughout economics, and in this book, you'll come across these graphs frequently.

   Probably the most common single-variable graph is the *bar graph*, an example of which is shown in Figure A-1. The bar graph shows the size or frequency of a variable using bars—hence the name. The size of the bar on the y-axis shows the value of the variable, while the x-axis contains the categories of the variables. In Figure A-1, for example, the bar graph shows the number

FIGURE A-1

Top five news websites

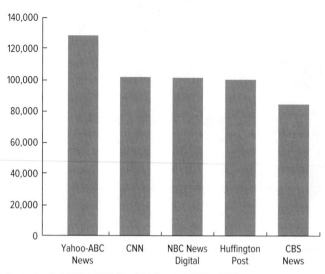

Unique visits for January 2015 (in thousands)

Source: http://www.journalism.org/media-indicators/digital-top-50-online-news-entities-2015/.

of visits received by five major news sites in the month of January 2015. Since the bars stack up next to each other, a bar graph makes it clear exactly where each news site stands in comparison to the others. As you can see, the larger bars for Yahoo-ABC News and CNN mean that these sites get more visits than CBS News.

In general, bar graphs are versatile. You can show the distribution of letter grades in a class or the average monthly high and low temperatures in your city. Any time the size of a variable is important, you are generally going to want to use a bar graph.

Pie charts are generally used to show how much of certain components make up a whole. Pie charts are usually a circle, cut into wedges that represent how much each makes up of the whole. Figure A-2 shows the sales of the 10 largest car manufacturers as a percentage of overall new-car sales (as of April 2016). The large wedges of General Motors and Ford show that these are large automakers compared to the small wedge representing Mercedes-Benz.

The most common use of pie charts is for budgeting. You'll often see government and business income and expenses broken down in a pie chart. Also, come election time, you'll see pie charts all over the news media, representing the percentage of votes in an election each candidate receives.

A final type of graph is called a *line* (or *time-series*) *graph.* This type of graph is helpful when you are trying to emphasize the trend of a single variable. In economics, the most common usage of line graphs is to show the value of a variable over time. Inflation rates, GDP, and government debt over decades are all prime candidates to be presented on a line graph.

Figure A-3 shows the GDP growth rate in Mexico since 1960 on a time-series graph. Presenting the data this way makes it clear that Mexico's GDP growth was strong during the 1960s and 70s (anything above 4 percent growth is very good), dipped below zero in 2009, and rose into positive territory in 2010 and beyond.

Ultimately, single-variable graphs can take us only so far. In order to get at some of the most fundamental issues of economics, we need to be able to plot the values of two variables (such as price and quantity) simultaneously.

FIGURE A-2

Automaker market share

This pie chart shows the relative market share of each automaker. The size of the wedge gives the share of each automaker. General Motors has a large wedge, while Mercedes-Benz has a much smaller share of the market.

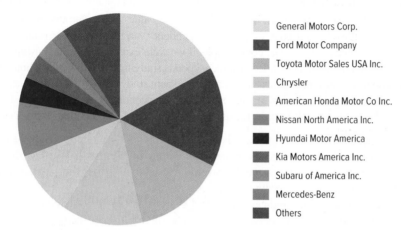

- General Motors Corp.
- Ford Motor Company
- Toyota Motor Sales USA Inc.
- Chrysler
- American Honda Motor Co Inc.
- Nissan North America Inc.
- Hyundai Motor America
- Kia Motors America Inc.
- Subaru of America Inc.
- Mercedes-Benz
- Others

Source: WSJ Markets Data Center, http://online.wsj.com/mdc/public/page/2_3022-autosales.html#autosalesE.

FIGURE A-3

GDP growth in Mexico

A line graph commonly shows a variable over a range of time. This allows the trend in the variable to be clear. In this case, you can see that GDP growth in Mexico has been highly variable, but overall, GDP growth was higher on average before 1980.

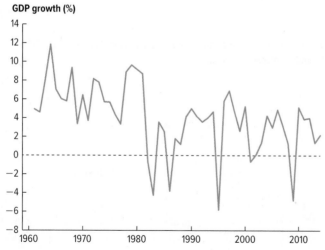

Source: World Bank World Development Indicators.

Graphs of two variables

In order to present two or more variables on a graph, we need something called the *Cartesian coordinate system.* With only two dimensions, this graphing system consists of two axes: the *x* (horizontal) axis and the *y* (vertical) axis. We can give these axes other names, depending on what economic variables we want to represent, such as price and quantity, or inputs and outputs.

In some cases, it doesn't matter which variable we put on each axis. At other times, logic or convention will determine the axes. There are two common conventions in economics that it will be useful for you to remember:

1. **Price on the *y*-axis, quantity on the *x*-axis:** When we graph the relationship between price and quantity in economics, price is always on the *y*-axis and quantity is always on the *x*-axis.

2. **The *x*-axis "causes" the *y*-axis:** In general, when the values of one variable are dependent on the values of the other variable, we put the "dependent" variable on the *y*-axis and the "independent" variable on the *x*-axis. For example, if we were exploring the relationship between test scores and the number of hours a student spends studying, we would place hours on the *x*-axis and test scores on the *y*-axis because hours spent studying affect scores, generally not vice versa. Sometimes, though, the opposite is true. In economics, we often say that price (always the *y*-axis variable) causes the quantity demanded of a good (the *x*-axis variable).

The point where the two axes intersect is called the *origin*. Points to the right of the origin have *x*-coordinates with positive values; points to the left of the origin have *x*-coordinates with negative values. Similarly, points above the origin have *y*-coordinates with positive values and points below the origin have *y*-coordinates with negative values.

To specify a particular point, indicate the *x*- and *y*-coordinates in an ordered pair. Indicate the *x*-coordinate first, and then the *y*-coordinate: (*x,y*). The intersection of the two axes creates four quadrants, as shown in Figure A-4.

Quadrant I: (*x,y*) The *x*- and *y*-coordinates are both positive.

Quadrant II: (−*x,y*) The *x*-coordinate is negative and the *y*-coordinate is positive.

Quadrant III: (−*x,−y*) The *x*- and *y*-coordinates are both negative.

Quadrant IV: (*x,−y*) The *x*-coordinate is positive and the *y*-coordinate is negative.

Origin: (0,0) The *x*- and *y*-coordinates are both zero at the origin.

FIGURE A-4

The four quadrants

The Cartesian coordinate system is a way to plot values of two variables simultaneously. Different quadrants reflect whether the values of *x* and *y* are positive or negative.

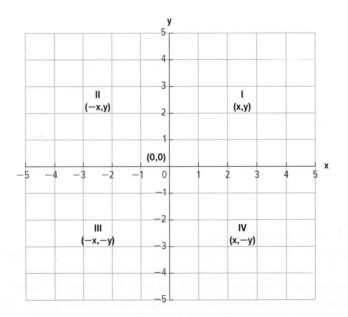

FIGURE A-5

Plotting points on a graph

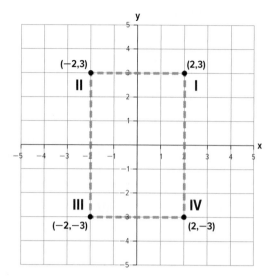

Each set of ordered pairs corresponds to a place
on the Cartesian coordinate system.

Figure A-5 shows the following points plotted on a graph.

Quadrant I: (2,3)

Quadrant II: (−2,3)

Quadrant III: (−2,−3)

Quadrant IV: (2,−3)

In economics, we often isolate quadrant I when graphing. This is because there are many economic variables for which negative values do not make sense. For example, one important graph we use in economics is the relationship between the price of a good and the quantity of that good demanded or supplied. Since it doesn't make sense to consider negative prices and quantities, we show only quadrant I when graphing supply and demand.

Figure A-6 shows a line in quadrant I that represents the relationship between the price of hot dogs at the ballpark and the quantity of hot dogs that a family wants to buy. Price is on the y-axis and the quantity of hot dogs the family demands is on the x-axis. For instance, one coordinate pair on this line is (3,2), meaning that if the price of hot dogs is $2, the family will want to buy 3 of them.

We could extend this demand curve in ways that make sense graphically but that don't represent logical price-quantity combinations in the real world. For instance, if we extend the demand curve into quadrant II, we have points such as (−2,7). If we extend the demand curve into quadrant IV, we have points such as (6,−1). However, it doesn't make sense to talk about someone demanding negative 2 hot dogs, nor does it make sense to think about a price of negative $1.

Remember that we are not just graphing arbitrary points. Rather, we are illustrating a real relationship between variables that has meaning in the real world. Both (−2,7) and (6,−1) are points that are consistent with the equation for this demand curve, but neither point makes sense to include in our analysis. For graphing this price-quantity relationship, we would limit our graph to quadrant I.

However, some variables you will study (such as revenue) may have negative values that make sense. When this is the case, graphs will show multiple quadrants.

FIGURE A-6

Thinking about the logic behind graphs

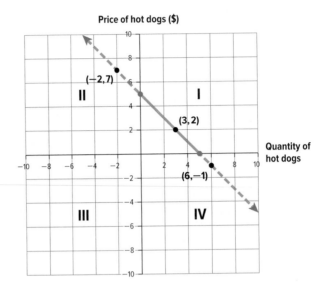

Plotting points in the four quadrants on a graph gives a line.

Slope

Both the table and the graph in Figure A-7 represent a particular relationship between two variables, *x* and *y*. For every *x*, there is a corresponding *y*. When we plot the points in the table, we see that there is a consistent relationship between the value of *x* and the value of *y*. In this case, we can see at a glance that whenever the *x* value increases by 1, the *y* value increases by 0.5. We can describe this relationship as the *slope* of the line.

FIGURE A-7

The slope of a line

X	Y
−4	2
−2	3
0	4
2	5
4	6

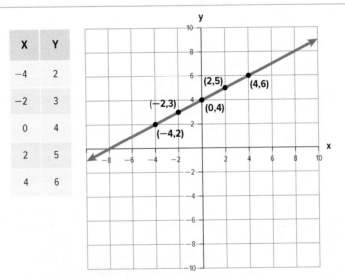

Slope refers to the shape of the line and is determined by the change in *y* and *x*.

Slope is a ratio of vertical distance (change in y) to horizontal distance (change in x). We begin to calculate slope by labeling one point along the line Point 1, which we denote (x_1, y_1), and another point along the line Point 2, which we denote (x_2, y_2). We can then calculate the horizontal distance by subtracting x_1 from x_2. We calculate vertical distance by subtracting y_1 from y_2.

slope
the ratio of vertical distance (change in y) to horizontal distance (change in x)

EQUATION A-1 $$\text{Horizontal distance} = \Delta x = (x_2 - x_1)$$

$$\text{Vertical distance} = \Delta y = (y_2 - y_1)$$

The vertical distance is sometimes referred to as the **rise**, while the horizontal distance is known as the **run**. "Rise over run" is an easy way to remember how to calculate slope.

rise
vertical distance; calculated as the change in y

EQUATION A-2 $$\text{Slope} = \frac{\text{Rise}}{\text{Run}} = \frac{\Delta y}{\Delta x} = \frac{(y_2 - y_1)}{(x_2 - x_1)}$$

When the relationship between x and y is linear (which means that it forms a straight line), the slope is constant. That is, for each one-unit change in the x-variable, the corresponding y-variable always changes by the same amount. Therefore, we can use any two points to calculate the slope of the line—it doesn't matter which ones we pick because the slope is the same everywhere on the line.

run
horizontal distance; calculated as the change in x

Slope gives us important information about the relationship between our two variables. As you'll see, slope tells us something about both the direction of the relationship between two variables (whether they move in the same direction) and the magnitude of the relationship (how much y changes in response to a change in x).

Calculating slope

LO A.2 Use data to calculate slope.

In Figure A-8, the rise, or vertical distance between point (2,3) and point (4,5), is 5 minus 3, which equals 2. The run, or horizontal distance, is 4 minus 2, which equals 2. Therefore, the slope of the line in Figure A-8 is calculated as:

$$\text{Slope} = \frac{(y_2 - y_1)}{(x_2 - x_1)} = \frac{(5 - 3)}{(4 - 2)} = \frac{2}{2} = 1$$

Let's return to Figure A-7 and apply this same calculation. Because the relationship between x and y is linear, we can use any two points to calculate the slope. Let's pick the point (2,5) to be point 1, which we call (x_1, y_1). Then, pick the point (4,6) to be point 2, which we call (x_2, y_2).

$$\frac{(y_2 - y_1)}{(x_2 - x_1)} = \frac{(6 - 5)}{(4 - 2)} = \frac{1}{2} = 0.5$$

Note that it doesn't matter which point we pick as point 1 and which as point 2. We could have chosen 5 as y_2 and 6 as y_1 rather than vice versa. All that matters is that y_1 is from the same ordered pair as x_1 and y_2 from the same pair as x_2. To prove that this is true, let's calculate slope again using (2,5) as point 2. The slope still comes out to 0.5:

$$\frac{(y_2 - y_1)}{(x_2 - x_1)} = \frac{(5 - 6)}{(2 - 4)} = \frac{(-1)}{(-2)} = \frac{1}{2} = 0.5$$

Use two different points from the table in Figure A-7 to calculate slope again. Try using the points $(-4, 2)$ and $(0,4)$. Do you get 0.5 as your answer?

FIGURE A-8

Calculating slope

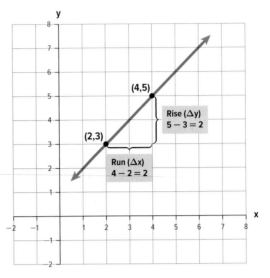

You can calculate the slope by dividing the change in the y value over the change in x—the rise over the run.

The direction of a slope

LO A.3 Interpret what the direction and steepness of slope indicate about a line.

The direction of a slope tells us something meaningful about the relationship between the two variables we are representing. For instance, when children get older, they grow taller. If we represented this relationship in a graph, we would see an upward-sloping line, telling us that height increases as age increases, rather than decreasing. Of course, it is common knowledge that children get taller, not shorter, as they get older. But if we were looking at a graph of a relationship we did not already understand, the slope of the line would show us at a glance how the two variables relate to one another.

To see how we can learn from the direction of a slope and how to calculate it, look at the graphs in panels A and B of Figure A-9.

In panel A, we can see that when x increases from 1 to 2, y also increases, from 2 to 4. If we move the other direction down the line, we see that when x decreases from 2 to 1, y also decreases, from 4 to 2. In other words, x and y move in the same direction. Therefore, x and y are said to have a *positive relationship*. Not surprisingly, this means that the slope of the line is a positive number:

$$\text{Slope} = \frac{\Delta y}{\Delta x} = \frac{2}{1} = 2$$

When the slope of a line is positive, we know that y increases as x increases, and y decreases as x decreases. If a line leans upward, then its slope is positive.

Now, turn to the graph in panel B. In this case, when x increases from 1 to 2, y decreases from 4 to 2. Reading from the other direction, when x decreases from 2 to 1, y increases from 2 to 4.

FIGURE A-9

The direction of a slope

(A) Positive relationship

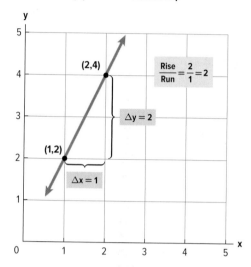

If a line slopes upward, its slope is positive; *y* increases as *x* increases, or *y* decreases as *x* decreases.

(B) Negative relationship

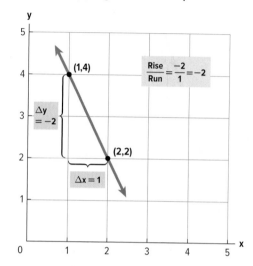

If a line slopes downward, its slope is negative: *y* decreases as *x* increases, or *y* increases as *x* decreases.

Therefore, *x* and *y* move in opposite directions and are said to have a *negative relationship.* The slope of the line is a negative number:

$$\text{Slope} = \frac{\Delta y}{\Delta x} = \frac{-2}{1} = -2$$

When the slope of a line is negative, we know that *y* decreases as *x* increases, and *y* increases as *x* decreases. If a line leans downward, then its slope is negative.

In Chapter 3, "Markets," you will see applications of these positive and negative relationships between the variables price and quantity. Here's a preview:

- You will see a positive relationship between price and quantity when you encounter a *supply curve.* You will learn the meaning of that positive relationship: As the price of a good increases, suppliers are willing to supply a larger quantity to markets. Supply curves, therefore, are upward-sloping.

- You will see a negative relationship between price and quantity when you encounter a *demand curve.* You will learn the meaning of that negative relationship: As the price of a good increases, consumers are willing to purchase a smaller quantity. Demand curves are downward-sloping.

From these examples, you can see that two variables (such as price and quantity) may have more than one relationship with each other, depending on whose choices they represent and under what circumstances.

The steepness of a slope

In addition to the *direction* of the relationship between variables, the *steepness* of the slope also gives us important information. It tells us how much *y* changes for a given change in *x*.

FIGURE A-10

The steepness of a slope

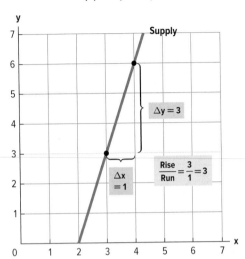

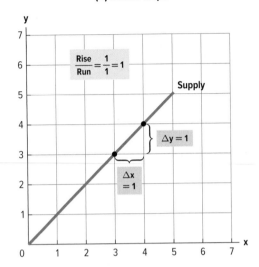

The larger the number representing slope is, the steeper the curve will be. The slope in panel A is steeper than the slope in panel B.

The closer the slope is to zero, the flatter the curve will be. The slope in panel B is flatter than the slope in panel A.

In both panels of Figure A-10, the relationship between *x* and *y* is positive (upward-sloping), and the distance between the *x* values, Δ*x*, is the same. However, the change in *y* that results from a one-unit change in *x* is greater in panel A than it is in panel B. In other words, the slope is *steeper* in panel A and *flatter* in panel B.

Numerically, the closer the number representing the slope is to zero, the flatter the curve will be. Remember that both positive and negative numbers can be close to zero. So, a slope of −1 is equally steep as a slope of 1, although one slopes downward and the other upward. Correspondingly, a line with a slope of −5 is steeper than a line with a slope of −1 or one with a slope of 1.

In general, slope is used to describe how much *y* changes in response to a one-unit change in *x*. In economics, we are sometimes interested in how much *x* changes in response to a one-unit change in *y*. For example, in Chapter 4, "Elasticity," you will see how quantity (on the *x*-axis) responds to a change in price (on the *y*-axis).

Key Terms

slope, p. 46G

rise, p. 46G

run, p. 46G

Problems and Applications

1. Create four quadrants using *x*- and *y*-axes. Use your graph to plot the following points. **[LO A.1]**

   a. (1,4)   c. (−3,−3)

   b. (−2,1)   d. (3,−2)

2. Create four quadrants using *x*- and *y*-axes. Use your graph to plot the following points. **[LO A.1]**

   a. (0,4)   c. (1,0)

   b. (0,−2)   d. (−3,0)

FIGURE AP-1

3. Use the curve labeled "Demand" in Figure AP-1 to create a table (schedule) that shows Price in one column and Quantity in another. What is the slope of the curve labeled "Demand"? **[LO A.2]**

4. Use the curve labeled "Demand" in Figure AP-2 to create a table (schedule) that shows Price in one column and Quantity in another. What is the slope of the curve labeled "Demand"? **[LO A.2]**

FIGURE AP-2

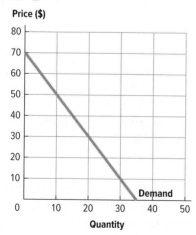

5. Use the information about price and quantity in Table AP-1 to create a graph, with Price on the y-axis and Quantity on the x-axis. Label the resulting curve "Demand." What is the slope of that curve? **[LO A.2]**

6. Use the information about price and quantity in Table AP-2 to create a graph, with Price on the y-axis and Quantity on the x-axis. Label the resulting curve "Demand." What is the slope of that curve? **[LO A.2]**

TABLE AP-1

Price ($)	Quantity
0	120
2	100
4	80
6	60
8	40
10	20
12	0

TABLE AP-2

Price ($)	Quantity
0	5
5	4
10	3
15	2
20	1
25	0

7. Use the curve labeled "Supply" in Figure AP-3 to create a table (schedule) that shows Price in one column and Quantity in another. What is the slope of the curve labeled "Supply"? **[LO A.2]**

8. Use the curve labeled "Supply" in Figure AP-4 to create a table (schedule) that shows Price in one column and Quantity in another. What is the slope of the curve labeled "Supply"? **[LO A.2]**

9. Use the information about price and quantity in Table AP-3 to create a graph, with Price on the *y*-axis and Quantity on the *x*-axis. Label the resulting curve "Supply." What is the slope of that curve? **[LO A.2]**

TABLE AP-3

Price ($)	Quantity
0	0
25	5
50	10
75	15
100	20
125	25

TABLE AP-4

Price ($)	Quantity
0	0
2	8
4	16
6	24
8	32
10	40
12	48

FIGURE AP-3

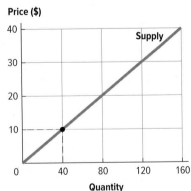

FIGURE AP-4

10. Use the information about price and quantity in Table AP-4 to create a graph, with Price on the *y*-axis and Quantity on the *x*-axis. Label the resulting curve "Supply." What is the slope of that curve? **[LO A.2]**

11. What is the direction of slope indicated by the following examples? **[LO A.3]**

   a. As the price of rice increases, consumers want less of it.

   b. As the temperature increases, the amount of people who use the town pool also increases.

   c. As farmers use more fertilizer, their output of tomatoes increases.

12. Rank the following equations by the steepness of their slope from lowest to highest. **[LO A.3]**

   a. $y = -3x + 9$

   b. $y = 4x + 2$

   c. $y = -0.5x + 4$

Part Two

Supply and Demand

The four chapters in Part 2 will introduce you to . . .

the basics of markets, which form the baseline for most economic analysis. Chapter 3, "Markets," introduces supply and demand. Any time we go into the store and decide to buy something, we act on our demand for that good. On the other side, the store figured out that it made sense for them to supply that good to us. The interaction between the forces of demand and supply determines the price we pay and how much gets bought and sold.

Chapters 4, 5 and 6 ("Elasticity," "Efficiency," and "Government Intervention") will use demand and supply to answer a variety of questions: Why do people rush to the store when Apple slashes the price of an iPhone? Why would the government ever want to set limits on prices in the market?

Together with Part 1, the chapters in this part introduce the basic concepts of economic problem solving. To start, we've stripped these ideas down to their simplest form. These same concepts will return throughout the text, and we will build on them as we turn to different problems.

Markets

Learning Objectives

LO 3.1 Identify the defining characteristics of a competitive market.

LO 3.2 Draw a demand curve and describe the external factors that determine demand.

LO 3.3 Distinguish between a shift in and a movement along the demand curve.

LO 3.4 Draw a supply curve and describe the external factors that determine supply.

LO 3.5 Distinguish between a shift in and a movement along the supply curve.

LO 3.6 Explain how supply and demand interact to drive markets to equilibrium.

LO 3.7 Evaluate the effect of changes in supply and demand on the equilibrium price and quantity.

MOBILES GO GLOBAL

For many people, a cell phone is on the list of things never to leave the house without, right up there with a wallet and keys. For better or worse, cell phones have become a fixture of everyday life.

It's hard to believe that as recently as the late 1990s, cell phones were a luxury that only a third of Americans enjoyed. Before that, in the 1980s, they were big, heavy devices, seldom bought for personal use at all. In less than a quarter of a century, this expensive sci-fi technology became a relatively cheap, universal convenience. Today there are approximately 90 cell phones for every 100 people in the United States. In fact, around half of the world's 7.4 billion people have a cell phone subscription.[1] For instance, two-thirds of Africa's 1.13 billion citizens now have cell phones.[2] This phenomenal growth makes it easier to keep up with friends and family. It also connects small-town merchants to businesses in distant cities, opening up new economic possibilities.

How does a product move from expensive to cheap, from rare to commonplace, so quickly? The answer partly lies in the relationship between supply and demand. This chapter shows how the forces of supply and demand interact to determine the quantities and prices of goods that are bought and sold in competitive markets.

The basic story of how a new product takes hold is a familiar one. In the beginning, cell phones were expensive and rare. Over time, the technology improved, the price dropped, the product caught on, and sales took off. Throughout this process of change, markets allow for ongoing communication between buyers and producers, using prices as a signal. The up-and-down movement of prices ensures that the quantity of a product that is available stays in balance with the quantity consumers want to buy.

To explain the leap in usage that cell phones have made over time, however, we need to go further than just price signals. Outside forces that influence supply and demand, such as changes in technology, fashion trends, and economic ups and downs, have driven that transformation. Markets have the remarkable ability to adjust to these changes without falling out of balance.

© Tim Robberts/Getty Images

In this chapter, we'll step into the shoes of consumers and producers to examine the trade-offs they face. We'll see that the issues that drive supply and demand in the cell phone industry are not unique. In fact, the functioning of markets, as summarized in the theory of supply and demand, is the bedrock of almost everything in this book. Mastering this theory will help you to solve all kinds of problems, from what price to sell your product for as a businessperson, to how to find the cheapest gasoline, to the causes of a shortage of hybrid cars.

Markets

In Chapter 2, "Specialization and Exchange," we discussed the power of the "invisible hand" to coordinate complex economic interactions. The key feature of an economy organized by the invisible hand is that private individuals, rather than a centralized planning authority, make the decisions. Such an economy is often referred to as a **market economy**.

market economy
an economy in which private individuals, rather than a centralized planning authority, make the decisions

What is a market?

What do we mean by a *market*? The word might make you think of a physical location where buyers and sellers come together face-to-face—like a farmers' market or a mall. But people do not have to be physically near each other to make an exchange. For example, think of online retailers like Amazon.com or of fruit that is grown in South America but sold all over the world. The term **market** actually refers to the buyers and sellers who trade a particular good or service, not to a physical location.

Which buyers and sellers are included in the market depends on the context. The manager of a clothing store at your local mall might think about the market for T-shirts in terms of people who live locally and the other places they could buy T-shirts, like competing stores, garage

market
buyers and sellers who trade a particular good or service

sales, or online retailers. The CEO of a major clothing brand, on the other hand, might include garment factories in Bangladesh and the fashion preferences of customers living all over the world in her idea of a market. Which boundaries are relevant depends on the scope of trades that are being made.

What is a competitive market?

LO 3.1 Identify the defining characteristics of a competitive market.

Making simplifying assumptions can help us zero in on important ideas. In this chapter, we will make a big simplifying assumption—that markets are *competitive*. A **competitive market** is one in which fully informed, price-taking buyers and sellers easily trade a standardized good or service. Let's unpack this multipart definition: Imagine you're driving up to an intersection where there is a gas station on each corner. This scenario demonstrates the four defining characteristics of a perfectly competitive market.

First, we bet you'd find that a gallon of gas costs the same in each station at the intersection. Why? Recall the third economists' question from Chapter 1, "Economics and Life": If one station tries to raise its price, *how will others respond?* Assuming the stations are offering standardized gallons of gas, customers should be indifferent between buying from one station or another at a given price. If one raises its price, all the drivers will simply go to a cheaper station instead. The gas station that raised prices will end up losing customers. For this reason, no individual seller has the power to change the market price. In economic terminology, a buyer or seller who cannot affect the market price is called a **price taker**.

The drivers going by are also price takers. If you try to negotiate a discount at one of the gas stations before filling your tank, you won't get far—the owner would rather wait and sell to other customers who will pay more. The price is the price; your choice is to take it or leave it. In competitive markets, both buyers and sellers are price takers.

Second, the gas sold by each station is the same—your car will run equally well regardless of *which* brand you buy. This means that the gas being sold is a **standardized good**—a good or service for which any two units of it have the same features and are interchangeable. In a competitive market, the good being bought and sold is standardized.

Third, the price at each gas station is prominently displayed on a big sign. As you drive by, you can immediately see how much a gallon of each type of gas costs at each station. In a competitive market, you have *full information* about the price and features of the good being bought and sold.

Finally, it's easy for you to choose any of the four gas stations at the intersection. The stations are very near each other, and you don't have to have special equipment to fill up your tank or pay an entrance fee to get into the station. In competitive markets, there are no **transaction costs**—the costs incurred by buyer and seller in agreeing to and executing a sale of goods or services. Thus, in competitive markets, you don't have to pay anything for the privilege of buying or selling in the market. You can easily do business in this four-station market for gasoline.

By thinking about the gas stations at a single intersection, you have learned the four characteristics of perfectly competitive markets. Table 3-1 summarizes the four characteristics of a perfectly competitive market: price-taking participants, a standardized good, full information, and no transaction costs.

In reality, few markets are truly *perfectly* competitive. Even gas stations at the same intersection might not be: Maybe one can charge a few cents more per gallon because it uses gas with less ethanol or offers regular customers an attractive loyalty scheme or has a Dunkin' Donuts to entice hungry drivers. In future chapters, we'll spend a lot of time thinking about the different ways that markets in the real world are structured and why it matters when they fall short of perfect competition.

competitive market
a market in which fully informed, price-taking buyers and sellers easily trade a standardized good or service

price taker
a buyer or seller who cannot affect the market price. In a perfectly competitive market, firms are price takers as a consequence of many sellers selling standardized goods.

standardized good
a good for which any two units have the same features and are interchangeable

transaction costs
the costs incurred by buyer and seller in agreeing to and executing a sale of goods or services

TABLE 3-1

Four characteristics of perfectly competitive markets

Characteristic	Description
Participants are price takers	Neither buyers nor sellers have the power to affect the market price.
Standardized good	Any two units of the good have the same features and are interchangeable.
Full information	Market participants know everything about the price and features of the good.
No transaction costs	There is no cost to participate in exchanges in the market.

The market for cell phones is not perfectly competitive either. Cell phones are not standardized goods—some models look cooler, or have better cameras, or have access to different apps or calling plans. You're unlikely to be completely indifferent between two different cell phones at the same price, as you are between two gallons of gas. Furthermore, the fact that there are a limited number of service providers means that sellers aren't always price takers. If only one network has good coverage in your area or has an exclusive deal with a popular type of phone, it can get away with charging a premium.

So, why *assume* perfect competition if markets in the real world are rarely perfectly competitive? The answer is that the simple model of competitive markets we will develop in this chapter leads us to useful insights, even in markets that aren't perfectly competitive. Taking the time now to make sure you understand perfect competition inside and out will better prepare you to understand why it matters when markets aren't perfectly competitive. As we go through this chapter, we'll note some ways in which the real cell phone market departs from perfect competition. By the end of the chapter, we hope you'll agree that the simple model of perfect competition tells us a lot, if not everything, about how the real cell phone market works.

✓ CONCEPT CHECK

☐ What is a market? What are the characteristics of a competitive market? **[LO 3.1]**

☐ Why are participants in competitive markets called *price takers*? **[LO 3.1]**

Demand

Demand describes how much of something people are willing and able to buy under certain circumstances. Suppose someone approached you and asked if you would like a new cell phone. What would you answer? You might think, "Sure," but as a savvy person, you would probably first ask, "For how much?" Whether you want something (or how much of it you want) depends on how much you have to pay for it.

These days most people in the United States have cell phones, but that hasn't been the case for very long. Let's assume for the sake of our model that cell phones are standardized—one model, with given features and calling plans. Now, put yourself in the position of a consumer in the mid-1990s: Maybe you've seen cell phones advertised at $499 and think it's not worth it to you. As the price goes down over time to $399, and $299, you're still not tempted to buy it. At $199, you start to consider it. Then, the first time you see a cell phone advertised for less than $125, you decide to buy.

Different people bought their first cell phone at different prices: At any given time, with any given price, some people in the population are willing and able to buy a phone and others aren't. If we add up all of these individual choices, we get overall *market demand*. The amount of a particular good that buyers in a market will purchase at a given price during a specified period is called the **quantity demanded**. For almost all goods, the lower the price goes, the higher the quantity demanded.

This inverse relationship between price and quantity demanded is so important that economists refer to it as the **law of demand**. The first requirement for the law of demand is the idea sometimes known as *ceteris paribus*, the Latin term for "all other things being the same." In other words, the law of demand says that, when all else is held equal (when all other factors remain the same), quantity demanded rises as price falls.

Economists frequently rely on the idea of *ceteris paribus* to isolate the expected effect of a single change in the economy. For example, suppose you want to predict what would happen next year to cell phone sales if cell phone prices go down. The law of demand tells us that if cell phone prices go down, *holding all else equal*, quantity demanded will go up.

But what if the economy is not doing well next year and consumers hold back on buying new cell phones? In this instance, we *cannot* say in general that "if cell phone prices go down, quantity demanded will go up" because not everything else has been held the same. Instead, the negative impact of the weak economy may offset the positive impact of the reduction in price. We need to be more specific. So, it is critical to "hold all else equal" in order to make clear statements about what we can predict.

The law of demand isn't a made-up law that economists have imposed on markets. Rather, it holds true because it describes the underlying reality of individual people's decisions. The key is to think about the *trade-offs* that people face when making the decision to buy.

What happens when the price of something falls? First, the benefit that you get from purchasing it remains the same because the item itself is unchanged. But the opportunity cost has fallen: When the price goes down, you don't have to give up as many other purchases in order to get the item. When benefits stay the same and opportunity cost goes down, this trade-off suddenly starts to look a lot better. When the trade-off between costs and benefits tips toward benefits, more people will want to buy the good.

Of course, falling prices will not have been the only consideration in people's decisions to buy their first cell phone. Some might have decided to buy one when they got a pay raise at work. Others might have bought one at the point when most of their friends owned one. Incomes, expectations, and tastes all play a role; economists call these factors *nonprice determinants* of demand. We'll discuss their potential effects later in this chapter. First, let's focus on the relationship between price and quantity demanded.

The demand curve

LO 3.2 Draw a demand curve and describe the external factors that determine demand.

The law of demand says that the quantity of cell phones demanded will be different at every price level. For this reason, it is often useful to represent demand as a table, called a **demand schedule**. A demand schedule shows the quantities of a particular good or service that consumers are willing and able to purchase (demand) at various prices. Panel A of Figure 3-1 shows a hypothetical annual demand schedule for cell phones in the United States. (Remember, we're assuming that cell phones are a standardized good. This isn't quite right, but the basic principle holds true: When cell phone prices are lower, you're more likely to buy a new one.) The demand schedule assumes that factors other than price remain the same.

Panel B of Figure 3-1 shows another way to represent demand, by drawing each price-quantity combination from the demand schedule as a point on a graph. That graph, called a **demand curve**, visually displays the demand schedule. That is, it is a graph that shows the quantities of a particular good or service that consumers will demand at various prices. The demand curve also represents consumers' *willingness to buy*: It shows the highest amount consumers will pay for any given quantity.

quantity demanded
the amount of a particular good that buyers will purchase at a given price during a specified period

law of demand
a fundamental characteristic of demand that states that, all else equal, quantity demanded rises as price falls

demand schedule
a table that shows the quantities of a particular good or service that consumers are willing and able to purchase (demand) at various prices

demand curve
a graph that shows the quantities of a particular good or service that consumers will demand at various prices

FIGURE 3-1

Demand schedule and the demand curve

(A) Demand schedule

(B) Demand curve

Cell phones (millions)	Price ($)
30	180
60	160
90	140
120	120
150	100
180	80
210	60
240	40
270	20

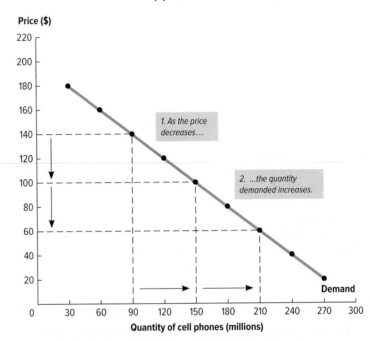

This demand schedule shows the quantity of cell phones demanded each year at various prices. As prices decrease, consumers want to purchase more cell phones.

This demand curve is a graphic representation of the demand schedule for cell phones in the United States. Each entry in the demand schedule is plotted on this curve.

Since demand curves and other material in this chapter make extensive use of lines and linear equations, you may want to review those concepts in Appendix B, "Math Essentials: Working with Linear Equations," which follows this chapter.

On the demand curve, quantity goes on the *x*-axis (the horizontal axis) and price on the *y*-axis (the vertical axis). The result is a downward-sloping line that reflects the inverse relationship between price and quantity. The demand curve in Figure 3-1 represents exactly the same information as the demand schedule.

Determinants of demand

The demand curve represents the relationship between price and quantity demanded *with everything else held constant*. If everything else is *not* held constant—that is, if one of the nonprice factors that determines demand changes—the curve will shift.

The downward-sloping demand curve reflects the trade-offs that people face between (1) the benefit they expect to receive from a good and (2) the opportunity cost they face for buying it. Therefore, any factor that changes this balance at a given price will change people's willingness to buy, and thus their purchasing decisions.

The nonprice determinants of demand can be divided into five major categories:

- Consumer preferences.
- The prices of related goods.
- Income of the consumers.
- Expectations of future prices.
- The number of buyers in the market.

Table 3-2 summarizes the impact of each factor on demand. Each of these nonprice determinants affects either the benefits or the opportunity cost of buying a good, even if the price of the good itself remains the same.

TABLE 3-2

Determinants of demand

Determinant	Examples of an increase in demand	Examples of a decrease in demand
Consumer preferences	A "Buy American" ad campaign appeals to national pride, increasing the demand for U.S.-made sneakers.	An outbreak of *E. coli* decreases the demand for spinach.
Prices of related goods	A decrease in the price of hot dogs increases the demand for relish, a complementary good.	A decrease in taxi fares decreases the demand for subway rides, a substitute good.
Incomes	An economic downturn lowers incomes, increasing the demand for ground beef, an inferior good.	An economic downturn lowers incomes, decreasing the demand for steak, a normal good.
Expectations	A hurricane destroys part of the world papaya crop, causing expectations that prices will rise and increasing the current demand for papayas.	An announcement that a new smartphone soon will be released decreases the demand for the current model.
Number of buyers	An increase in life expectancy increases the demand for nursing homes and medical care.	A falling birthrate decreases the demand for diapers.

 POTENTIALLY CONFUSING

You may notice that these five factors include price-related issues such as the price of related goods and expectations about future prices. So why do we refer to them as *nonprice determinants*? We do so in order to differentiate them from the effect of the *current price* of the good on demand for that good.

Consumer preferences

Consumer preferences are the personal likes and dislikes that make buyers more or less inclined to purchase a good. We don't need to know *why* people like what they like or to agree with their preferences; we just need to know that these likes and dislikes influence their purchases. At any given price, some consumers will get more enjoyment (i.e., benefits) out of a cell phone than do others. That enjoyment may be based simply on how much they like talking to friends, or whether they use their phones for work, or any number of other personal preferences.

Some consumer preferences are fairly constant across time, such as those that arise from personality traits or cultural attitudes and beliefs. For example, a recluse may have little desire for a cell phone; an on-the-go executive may find a cell phone (or two) to be essential. Other preferences will change over time, in response to external events or fads. For instance, it's more useful to own a cell phone when all your friends already have one. And more people may demand cell phones after a national disaster, knowing they want to be able to reach their families in emergencies.

Prices of related goods

Another factor that affects the demand for a particular good is the prices of related goods. There are two kinds of related goods: substitutes and complements.

We say that goods are **substitutes** when they serve similar-enough purposes that a consumer might purchase one in place of the other—for example, rice and pasta. If the price of rice doubles while the price of pasta stays the same, demand for pasta will increase. That's because the *opportunity cost* of pasta has decreased: You can buy less rice for the same amount of

substitutes
goods that serve a similar-enough purpose that a consumer might purchase one in place of the other

money, so you give up less potential rice when you buy pasta. If the two goods are quite similar, we call them *close substitutes*. Similar fishes, such as salmon and trout, might be considered close substitutes.

For many Americans deciding whether to buy their first cell phone, the nearest substitute would have been a landline phone. Cell phones and landlines are not very close substitutes: You can use them for the same purposes at home or the office, but only one of them can go for a walk with you. Still, if the price of U.S. landline phone service had suddenly skyrocketed, we can be sure that change would have increased the demand for cell phones.

In fact, the very high cost of landline phone services in many developing countries is one reason why cell phones spread very quickly. In the United States, almost every household had a landline phone before it had a cell phone. In many poor countries, landlines are so expensive that very few people can afford one. That's why cell phones are often called a *leapfrog technology*: People go straight from no phone to cell phone, hopping over an entire stage of older technology.

complements
goods that are consumed together, so that purchasing one will make consumers more likely to purchase the other

Related goods that are consumed together, so that purchasing one will make a consumer more likely to purchase the other, are called **complements**. Peanut butter and jelly, cereal and milk, cars and gasoline are all complements. If the price of one of the two goods increases, demand for the other will likely decrease. Why? As consumers purchase less of the first good, they will want less of the other to go with it. Conversely, if the price of one of the two goods declines, demand for the other will likely increase. For example, when the prices of new cell phones fall, consumers will be more likely to buy new accessories to go with them.

Incomes

Not surprisingly, the amount of income people earn affects their demand for goods and services: The bigger your paycheck, the more money you can afford to spend on the things you want. The smaller your paycheck, the more you have to cut back.

normal goods
goods for which demand increases as income increases

Most goods are **normal goods**, meaning that an increase in income causes an increase in demand. Likewise, for normal goods, a decrease in income causes a decrease in demand. For most people, cell phones are a normal good. If someone cannot currently afford a cell phone, she's more likely to buy one when her income rises. If someone already has a cell phone, she's more likely to upgrade to a newer, fancier cell phone when her income rises.

inferior goods
goods for which demand decreases as income increases

For some goods, called **inferior goods**, the opposite relationship holds: As income increases, demand decreases. Typically, people replace inferior goods with more expensive and appealing substitutes when their incomes rise. For many people, inexpensive grocery items like instant noodles, some canned foods, and generic store brands might be inferior goods. When their incomes rise, people replace these goods with fresher, more expensive ingredients. Decreases in income occur for many people during economic downturns; thus, the demand for inferior goods reflects the overall health of the economy. For an example, see the Real Life box "Can instant-noodle sales predict a recession?"

Real Life

Can instant-noodle sales predict a recession?

If you were to open a typical college student's kitchen cupboard, what would you find? Many students rely on a decidedly unglamorous food item: ramen instant noodles. Packed with cheap calories, this tasty snack is famously inexpensive.

Ramen noodles are an example of an inferior good. When people's budgets are tight (as are those of most students), these noodles sell well. When incomes rise, ramen sales drop and more expensive foods replace them.

In Thailand, ramen noodles have even been used as an indicator of overall economic health. The Mama Noodles Index tracks sales of a popular brand of instant ramen noodles. Because the demand for inferior goods increases when incomes go down, an increase in ramen sales could signal a downturn in incomes and an oncoming recession. In fact, observers of the Thai economy say that the Mama Noodles Index does a pretty good job of reflecting changing economic conditions.

Even the demand for inferior goods may decrease during severe economic downturns, however. Although the Mama Noodles Index has risen as expected when the Thai economy falters, the index unexpectedly dropped 15 percent during the deep recession of early 2009.

So are instant noodles an inferior good or a normal good? In Thailand, the answer may depend on who you are or how severely your income has dropped. For the middle class, who choose between ramen and more expensive foods, ramen may indeed be an inferior good. For the poor, whose choice more likely is whether or not they will get enough to eat, ramen may be a normal good. When their incomes rise, they may buy more ramen; when their incomes fall, even noodles may be a luxury.

Sources: "Using their noodles," Associated Press, September 5, 2005, http://www.theage.com.au/news/world/using-their-noodles/2005/09/04/1125772407287.html; Kwanchai Rungfapaisarn, "Downturn bites into instant-noodle market as customers tighten belts," *The Nation,* March 20, 2009, http://www.nationmultimedia.com/business/Downturn-bites-into-instant-noodle-market-as-custo-30098402.html.

Expectations

Changes in consumers' expectations about the future—especially future prices—can also affect demand. If consumers expect prices to fall in the future, they may postpone a purchase until a later date, causing current demand to decrease. If you think cell phones will go on sale in a few months, you might put off your purchase until then. Or you might delay upgrading your smartphone in the hope that when the next model releases, the current model will drop in price. When prices are expected to drop in the future, demand decreases.

Conversely, if consumers expect prices to rise in the future, they may wish to purchase a good immediately to avoid a higher price. This reasoning often occurs in speculative markets, like the stock market or sometimes the housing market. Buyers purchase stock or a house expecting prices to rise, so they can sell at a profit. In these markets, then, demand increases when prices are low and are expected to rise.

Number of buyers

The demand curve represents the demand of a particular number of potential buyers. In general, an increase in the number of potential buyers in a market will increase demand. A decrease in the number of buyers will decrease it. Major population shifts, like an increase in immigration or a drop in the birthrate, can create nationwide changes in demand. As the number of teenagers and college students increases, the demand for cell phones increases too.

Shifts in the demand curve

LO 3.3 Distinguish between a shift in and a movement along the demand curve.

What happens to the demand curve when one of the five nonprice determinants of demand changes? The entire demand curve shifts, either to the right or to the left. The shift is horizontal rather than vertical because nonprice determinants affect the quantity demanded at *each* price. When the quantity demanded at a given price is now higher, the point on the curve corresponding to that price is now further right. When the quantity demanded at a given price is lower, the point on the curve corresponding to that price is now further left.

Consider what happens, for example, when the economy is growing and people's incomes are rising. Let's assume the price of cell phones does not change ("all else held equal"). But with rising incomes, more people will choose to buy a new cell phone at any given price, causing quantity demanded to be higher at every possible price. Panel A of Figure 3-2 shows the resulting shift of the demand curve to the right, from D_A to D_B. In contrast, if the economy falls into a recession and people begin pinching pennies, quantity demanded will decrease at every price, and the curve will shift to the left, from D_A to D_C.

It is important to distinguish between these *shifts* in demand, which move the entire curve, and *movements along* a given demand curve. Remember this key point: *Shifts in the demand curve are caused by changes in the nonprice determinants of demand.* A recession, for example, would lower incomes and move the whole demand curve left. When we say "demand decreases," this is what we are talking about.

In contrast, suppose that the price of phones increases but everything else stays the same—that is, there is no change in the nonprice determinants of demand. Because the demand curve describes the quantity consumers will demand at any possible price, not just the current market price, we don't have to shift the curve to figure out what happens when the price goes up. Instead, we simply look at a different point on the curve to describe what is actually happening in the market right now.

To find the quantity that consumers will want to purchase at this new price, we move along the existing demand curve from the old price to the new one. If, for instance, the price of cell phones increases, we find the new quantity demanded by moving up along the demand curve to the new price point, as shown in panel B of Figure 3-2. The price change does not shift the curve itself because the curve already describes what consumers will do at any price.

FIGURE 3-2

Shifts in the demand curve versus movement along the demand curve

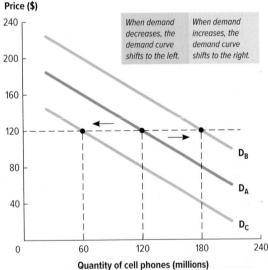

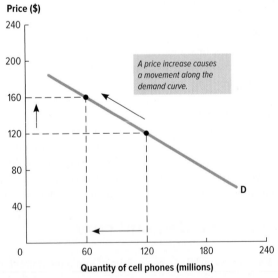

Changes in external factors cause the entire demand curve to shift. The shift from D_A to D_B represents an increase in demand, meaning that consumers want to buy more cell phones at each price. The shift from D_A to D_C represents a decrease in demand, meaning that consumers want to buy fewer cell phones at each price.

A price change causes a movement along the demand curve, but the curve itself remains constant.

To summarize, panel A of Figure 3-2 shows a *shift in demand* as the result of a change in the nonprice determinants; panel B shows a *movement along the demand curve* as the result of a change in price.

Economists use very specific terminology to distinguish between a shift in the demand curve and movement along the demand curve:

- We say that a change in one of the nonprice determinants of demand causes an "increase in demand" or "decrease in demand"—that is, a *shift* of the entire demand curve.

- To distinguish this from *movement along* the demand curve, we say that a change in price causes an "increase in the quantity demanded" or "decrease in the quantity demanded."

Just keep in mind that a "change in demand" is different from a "change in the quantity demanded." Observing this seemingly small difference in terminology prevents a great deal of confusion.

Understanding the effects of changes in both price and the nonprice determinants of demand is a key tool for businesspeople and policy-makers. Suppose you are in charge of an industry group whose members want to spur demand for cell phones. One idea might be to start an advertising campaign to increase the real or perceived benefits of owning a cell phone. If you understand the determinants of demand, you know that the advertising campaign would change consumer preferences. In other words, a successful advertising campaign would shift the demand curve for cell phones to the right. Similarly, if you are a congressional representative who is considering a tax cut to stimulate the economy, you know that a tax cut increases consumers' disposable incomes, increasing the demand for all normal goods. In other words, you are hoping that the resulting increase in incomes will shift the demand curve for cell phones to the right.

✓ CONCEPT CHECK

☐ What are the five nonprice determinants of demand? **[LO 3.2]**

☐ What is the difference between a change in demand and a change in quantity demanded? **[LO 3.3]**

Supply

We've discussed the factors that determine how many phones consumers want to buy at a given price. But are cell phone producers necessarily willing to sell that many? The concept of *supply* describes how much of a good or service producers will offer for sale under given circumstances. The **quantity supplied** is the amount of a particular good or service that producers will offer for sale at a given price during a specified period.

As with demand, we can find overall *market supply* by adding up the individual decisions of each producer. Imagine you own a factory that can produce cell phones or other consumer electronics. If the price of cell phones is $110, you might decide there's good money to be made and use your entire factory space to produce cell phones. If the price is only $80, you might produce some cell phones but decide it will be more profitable to devote part of your factory to producing laptop computers. If the cell phone price drops to $55, you might decide you'd make more money by producing only laptops. Each producer will have a different price point at which it decides it's worthwhile to supply cell phones. This rule—all else held equal, quantity supplied increases as price increases—is called the **law of supply**.

(In reality, it's costly to switch a factory from making cell phones to laptops or other goods. However, the simple version illustrates a basic truth: The higher the price of a good, the more of that good producers will want to supply. Similarly, the lower the price of a good, the less of that good producers will want to supply.)

quantity supplied
the amount of a particular good or service that producers will offer for sale at a given price during a specified period

law of supply
a fundamental characteristic of supply that states that, all else equal, quantity supplied rises as price rises

As with demand, supply varies with price because the decision to produce a good is about the *trade-off* between the benefit the producer will receive from selling the good and the opportunity cost of the time and resources that go into producing it. When the market price goes up and all other factors remain constant, the benefit of production increases relative to the opportunity cost, and the trade-off involved in production makes it more favorable to produce more.

For instance, if the price of phones goes up and the prices of raw materials stay the same, existing phone producers may open new factories, and new companies may start looking to enter the cell phone market. The same holds true across other industries. If air travelers seem willing to pay higher prices, airlines will increase the frequency of flights, add new routes, and buy new planes so they can carry more passengers. When prices drop, they cut back their flight schedules and cancel their orders for new planes.

The supply curve

supply schedule
a table that shows the quantities of a particular good or service that producers will supply at various prices

supply curve
a graph that shows the quantities of a particular good or service that producers will supply at various prices

LO 3.4 Draw a supply curve and describe the external factors that determine supply.

Like demand, supply can be represented as a table or a graph. A **supply schedule** is a table that shows the quantities of a particular good or service that producers will supply at various prices. Panel A of Figure 3-3 shows a hypothetical supply schedule for U.S. cell phone providers.

A **supply curve** is a graph of the information in the supply schedule. Just as the demand curve showed consumers' willingness to buy, so the supply curve shows producers' *willingness to sell*: It shows the minimum price producers must receive to supply any given quantity. Panel B of Figure 3-3 shows the supply curve of U.S. cell phone providers—visually representing the supply schedule.

FIGURE 3-3

Supply schedule and the supply curve

(A) Supply schedule

Cell phones (millions)	Price ($)
270	180
240	160
210	140
180	120
150	100
120	80
90	60
60	40
30	20

This supply schedule shows the quantity of cell phones supplied each year at various prices. As prices decrease, suppliers want to produce fewer cell phones.

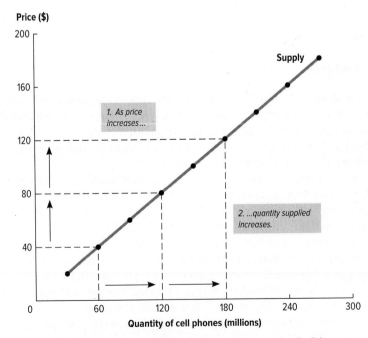

(B) Supply curve

This supply curve is a graphic representation of the supply schedule for cell phones in the United States. It shows the quantity of cell phones that suppliers will produce at various prices.

Determinants of supply

The law of supply describes how the quantity that producers are willing to supply changes as price changes. But what determines the quantity supplied at any given price? As with demand, a number of *nonprice factors* determine the opportunity cost of production and therefore producers' willingness to supply a good or service. *When a nonprice determinant of supply changes, the entire supply curve will shift.* Such shifts reflect a change in the quantity of goods supplied at *every* price.

The nonprice determinants of supply can be divided into five major categories:

- Prices of related goods.
- Technology.
- Prices of inputs.
- Expectations.
- The number of sellers.

Each of these factors determines the opportunity cost of production relative to a given benefit (i.e., the price) and therefore the trade-off that producers face. Table 3-3 shows how the supply of various products responds to changes in each determinant.

Prices of related goods

Return to your factory, where you can produce either cell phones or laptops. Just as you chose to produce more laptops and fewer cell phones when the price of cell phones dropped, you would do the same if the price of laptops increased while the price of cell phones stayed constant.

The price of related goods determines supply because it affects the opportunity cost of production. When you choose to produce cell phones, you forgo the profits you would have earned from producing something else. If the price of that something else increases, the amount you forgo in profits also increases. For instance, imagine a farmer who can grow wheat or corn (or other crops, for that matter) on his land. If the price of corn increases, the quantity of wheat (the substitute crop) he is willing to grow falls. Why? Because each acre he devotes to wheat is one fewer acre he can use to grow corn.

TABLE 3-3

Determinants of supply

Determinant	Examples of an increase in supply	Examples of a decrease in supply
Price of related goods	The price of gas rises, so an automaker increases its production of smaller, more fuel-efficient cars.	The price of clean energy production falls, so the power company reduces the amount of power it supplies using coal power plants.
Technology	The installation of robots increases productivity and lowers costs; the supply of goods increases.	New technology allows corn to be made into ethanol, so farmers plant more corn and fewer soybeans; the supply of soybeans decreases.
Prices of inputs	A drop in the price of tomatoes decreases the production cost of salsa; the supply of salsa increases.	An increase in the minimum wage increases labor costs at food factories; the supply of processed food decreases.
Expectations	New research points to the health benefits of eating papayas, leading to expectations that the demand for papayas will rise. More farmers plant papayas, increasing the supply.	Housing prices are expected to rise, so builders hold back on new construction projects today (in order to build later when housing prices are higher), decreasing the supply of homes in the near future.
Number of sellers	Subsidies make the production of corn more profitable, so more farmers plant corn; the supply of corn increases.	New licensing fees make operating a restaurant more expensive; some small restaurants close, decreasing the supply of restaurants.

In 1980, this cutting-edge technology cost $4,000. © C. Borland/Photolink/ Getty Images

Technology

Improved technology enables firms to produce more efficiently, using fewer resources to make a given product. Doing so lowers production costs, increasing the quantity producers are willing to supply at each price.

Improved technology has played a huge role in the changing popularity of cell phones. As technological innovation in the construction of screens, batteries, and mobile networks and in the processing of electronic data has leapt forward, the cost of producing a useful, consumer-friendly cell phone has plummeted. As a result, producers are now willing to supply more cell phones at lower prices.

Prices of inputs

The prices of the inputs used to produce a good are an important part of its cost. When the prices of inputs increase, production costs rise, and the quantity of the product that producers are willing to supply at any given price decreases.

Small amounts of silver and gold are used inside cell phones, for example. When the prices of these precious metals rise, the cost of manufacturing each cell phone increases, and the total number of units that producers collectively are willing to make at any given price goes down. Conversely, when input prices fall, supply increases.

Expectations

Suppliers' expectations about prices in the future also affect quantity supplied. For example, when the price of real estate is expected to rise in the future, more real estate developers will wait to embark on construction projects, decreasing the supply of houses in the near future. When expectations change and real estate prices are projected to fall in the future, many of those projects will be rushed to completion, causing the supply of houses to rise.

Number of sellers

The market supply curve represents the quantities of a product that a particular number of producers will supply at various prices in a given market. This means that the number of sellers in the market is considered to be one of the fixed parts of the supply curve. We've already seen that the sellers in the market will decide to supply more if the price of a good is higher. This does not mean that the number of sellers will change based on price in the short run.

There are, however, nonprice factors that cause the number of sellers to change in a market and move the supply curve. For example, suppose cell phone producers must meet strict licensing requirements. If those licensing requirements are dropped, more companies may enter the market, willing to supply a certain number of cell phones at each price. These additional phones must be added to the number of cell phones existing producers are already willing to supply at each price point.

Shifts in the supply curve

LO 3.5 Distinguish between a shift in and a movement along the supply curve.

Just as with demand, changes in price cause suppliers to move to a different point on the same supply curve, while changes in the nonprice determinants of supply shift the supply curve itself. A change in a nonprice determinant increases or decreases *supply*. A change in price increases or decreases the *quantity supplied*.

FIGURE 3-4

Shifts in the supply curve versus movement along the supply curve

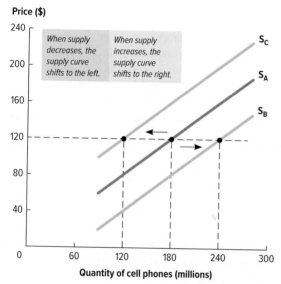

(A) Shifts in the supply curve

When supply decreases, the supply curve shifts to the left.

When supply increases, the supply curve shifts to the right.

Changes in external factors cause the entire supply curve to shift. The shift from S_A to S_B represents an increase in supply, meaning that producers are willing to supply more cell phones at each price. The shift from S_A to S_C represents a decrease in supply, meaning that producers are willing to supply fewer cell phones at each price.

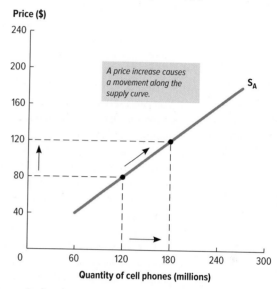

B) Movement along the supply curve

A price increase causes a movement along the supply curve.

A price change causes a movement along the supply curve, but the curve itself remains constant.

A change in one of the nonprice determinants increases or decreases the supply at any given price. These shifts are shown in panel A of Figure 3-4. An increase in supply shifts the curve to the right. A decrease in supply shifts the curve to the left. For instance, an improvement in battery technology that decreases the cost of producing cell phones will shift the entire supply curve to the right, from S_A to S_B; the quantity of phones supplied at every price is higher than before. Conversely, an increase in the price of the gold needed for cell phones raises production costs, shifting the supply curve to the left, from S_A to S_C.

As with demand, we differentiate these shifts in the supply curve from a movement along the supply curve, which is shown in panel B of Figure 3-4. If the price of cell phones changes, but the nonprice determinants of supply stay the same, we find the new quantity supplied by moving along the supply curve to the new price point.

Also, as with demand, economists use very specific terminology to distinguish between a shift in the supply curve and movement along the supply curve:

- We say that a change in one of the nonprice determinants of supply causes an "increase in supply" or "decrease in supply"—that is, a *shift* of the entire supply curve.
- To distinguish this from *movement along* the supply curve, we say that a change in price causes an "increase in the quantity supplied" or "decrease in the quantity supplied."

✓CONCEPT CHECK

☐ What does the law of supply say about the relationship between price and quantity supplied? **[LO 3.4]**

☐ In which direction does the supply curve shift when the price of inputs increases? **[LO 3.5]**

equilibrium
the situation in a market when the quantity supplied equals the quantity demanded; graphically, this convergence happens where the demand curve intersects the supply curve

equilibrium price
the price at which the quantity supplied equals the quantity demanded

equilibrium quantity
the quantity that is supplied and demanded at the equilibrium price

Market Equilibrium

We've discussed the factors that influence the quantities supplied and demanded by producers and consumers. To find out what actually happens in the market, however, we need to combine these concepts. The prices and quantities of the goods that are exchanged in the real world depend on the *interaction* of supply with demand.

Graphically, this convergence of supply with demand happens at the point where the demand curve intersects the supply curve, a point called the market **equilibrium**. The price at this point is called the **equilibrium price** and the quantity at this point is called the **equilibrium quantity**.

Bear with us for a moment as we point out the obvious: There is no sale without a purchase. You can't sell something unless someone buys it. Although this point may be obvious, the implication for markets is profound. When markets work well, the quantity supplied exactly equals the quantity demanded.

We can think of this intersection, where quantity supplied equals quantity demanded, as the point at which buyers and sellers "agree" on the quantity of a good they are willing to exchange at a given price. At higher prices, sellers want to sell more than buyers want to buy. At lower prices, buyers want to buy more than sellers are willing to sell. Because every seller finds a buyer at the equilibrium price and quantity, and no one is left standing around with extra goods or an empty shopping cart, the equilibrium price is sometimes called the *market-clearing price*.

In reality, things don't always work so smoothly: Short-run "friction" sometimes slows the process of reaching equilibrium, even in well-functioning markets. As a result, smart businesspeople may hold some inventory for future sale, and consumers may need to shop around for specific items. On the whole, though, the concept of equilibrium is incredibly accurate (and important) in describing how markets function.

Figure 3-5 shows the market equilibrium for cell phones in the United States. It was constructed by combining the market supply and demand curves shown in Figures 3-1 and 3-3. In this market, the equilibrium price is $100, and the equilibrium quantity supplied and demanded is 150 million phones.

FIGURE 3-5

Market equilibrium in the U.S. market for cell phones

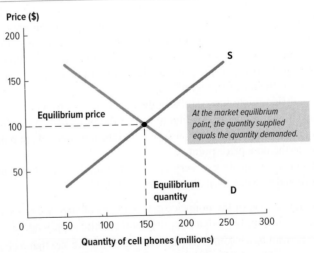

The point where the supply curve intersects the demand curve is called the equilibrium point. In this example, the equilibrium price is $100, and the equilibrium quantity is 150 million cell phones. At this point, consumers are willing to buy exactly as many cell phones as producers are willing to sell.

Reaching equilibrium

> **LO 3.6** Explain how supply and demand interact to drive markets to equilibrium.

How does a market reach equilibrium? Do sellers know intuitively what price to charge? No. Instead, they tend to set prices by trial and error, by past experience with customers, or by thinking through their costs and adding in a bit of profit. Irrespective of the firm's pricing process, typically the incentives buyers and sellers face naturally drive the market toward an equilibrium price and quantity.

Figure 3-6 shows two graphs, one in which the starting price is above the equilibrium price and the other in which it is below the equilibrium price. In panel A, we imagine that cell phone suppliers think they'll be able to charge $160 for a cell phone, so they produce 240 million phones. They find, though, that consumers will buy only 60 million. (We can read those quantities demanded and supplied at a price of $160 from the demand and supply curves.) When the quantity supplied is higher than the quantity demanded, we say that there is a **surplus** of phones, or an **excess supply**. Manufacturers are stuck holding extra phones in their warehouses; they want to sell that stock and must reduce the price to attract more customers. They have an incentive to keep lowering the price until quantity demanded increases to reach quantity supplied.

In panel B of Figure 3-6, we imagine that cell phone producers make the opposite mistake—they think they'll be able to charge only $40 per phone. They make only 60 million cell phones, but consumers actually are willing to buy 240 million cell phones at that price. When the quantity demanded is higher than the quantity supplied, we say there is a **shortage**, or **excess demand**. Producers will see long lines of people waiting to buy the few available cell phones; they will quickly realize that they could make more money by charging a higher price. They have an incentive to increase the price until quantity demanded decreases to equal quantity supplied, and no one is left standing in line.

surplus (excess supply)
a situation in which the quantity of a good that is supplied is higher than the quantity demanded

shortage (excess demand)
a situation in which the quantity of a good that is demanded is higher than the quantity supplied

FIGURE 3-6

Reaching equilibrium in the market for cell phones

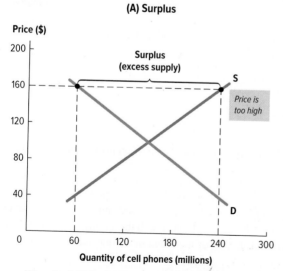

(A) Surplus

When the initial price for cell phones is above the equilibrium point, producers want to supply more cell phones than consumers want to buy. The gap between the quantity supplied and the quantity demanded is called a surplus, or excess supply.

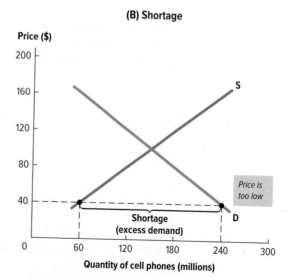

(B) Shortage

When the initial price for cell phones is below the equilibrium point, consumers want to buy more cell phones than sellers want to produce. The distance between the quantity demanded and the quantity supplied is called a shortage, or excess demand.

Thus, at any price above or below the equilibrium price, sellers face an incentive to raise or lower prices. No one needs to engineer the market equilibrium or share secret information about what price to charge. Instead, money-making incentives drive the market toward the equilibrium price, at which there is neither a surplus nor a shortage. The Real Life box "The Prius shortage of 2003" describes a case in which a producer started out charging the wrong price, but the market solved the problem.

Real Life
The Prius shortage of 2003

In 2003, Toyota introduced the first mainstream "hybrid" car, the Prius, to the U.S. auto market. A hybrid car runs on a combination of gasoline and electric power, using the engine to charge an electric battery in stop-and-go traffic. The Prius got much better gas mileage than its competitors—usually between 40 and 50 miles to the gallon. But for most families the gas savings were more than offset by the car's higher price. The car's main appeal was its environmentally friendly design.

When the Prius hit the U.S. market in October 2003, dealerships sold out immediately. Toyota had significantly underestimated the demand. Prospective buyers had to put their names on a waiting list, often for more than six months. A few years later, when gasoline prices spiked, demand was driven even higher as consumers grew more interested in good gas mileage. In the short run, Toyota could not do much to address the shortage; increasing plant capacity would take time.

Instead, the market found a way to solve the problem. As we know, price acts as a signal between buyers and sellers trying to match demand with supply. When quantity demanded exceeds quantity supplied, the price of the good will rise. As we might expect, Prius buyers began to bid up the price of the car. Dealerships were soon charging thousands of dollars more than the manufacturer's suggested price. For a while, even the price of a *used* Prius was higher than the suggested price for a new car.

Eventually, Toyota responded to the shortage by increasing production capacity of the Prius. The company moved production of the car to progressively larger plants; in 2008, total production topped 1 million. Shortages persisted, however, as increases in demand outstripped the increases in supply. As Toyota scrambled to catch up with demand, sellers happily charged a premium to clear the market.

Source: "Wait time for Prius buyers diminishing," *CNNMoney,* November 6, 2006, http://money.cnn.com/2006/11/06/autos/prius/index.htm.

Changes in equilibrium

LO 3.7 Evaluate the effect of changes in supply and demand on the equilibrium price and quantity.

We've seen what happens to the supply and demand curves when a nonprice factor changes. Because the equilibrium price and quantity are determined by the interaction of supply and demand, a shift in either curve will also change the market equilibrium. Some changes will cause only the demand curve to shift; some, only the supply curve. Some changes will affect both the supply and demand curves.

To determine the effect on market equilibrium of a change in a nonprice factor, ask yourself a few questions:

1. Does the change affect demand? If so, does demand increase or decrease?
2. Does the change affect supply? If so, does supply increase or decrease?
3. How does the combination of changes in supply and demand affect the equilibrium price and quantity?

Shifts in demand

We suggested earlier that landline service is a *substitute* for cell phones and that if the price of landline service suddenly skyrockets, then demand for cell phones increases. In other words, the demand curve shifts to the right. The price of landline service probably doesn't affect the supply of cell phones because it doesn't change the costs or expectations that cell phone manufacturers face. So the supply curve stays put.

Figure 3-7 shows the effect of the increase in landline price on the market equilibrium for cell phones. Because the new demand curve intersects the supply curve at a different point, the equilibrium price and quantity change. The new equilibrium price is $120, and the new equilibrium quantity is 180 million.

We can summarize this effect in terms of the three questions to ask following a change in a nonprice factor:

1. *Does demand increase or decrease?* Yes, the change in the price of landline phone service increases demand for cell phones at every price.

2. *Does supply increase or decrease?* No, the change in the price of landline phone service does not affect any of the nonprice determinants of supply. The supply curve stays where it is.

3. *How does the combination of changes in supply and demand affect equilibrium price and quantity?* The increase in demand shifts the demand curve to the right, pushing the equilibrium to a higher point on the stationary supply curve. The new point at which supply and demand "agree"? represents a price of $120 and a quantity of 180 million phones.

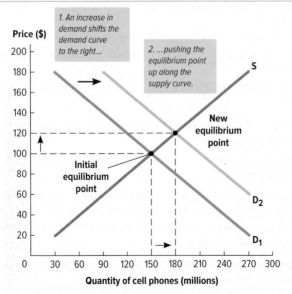

FIGURE 3-7

Shift in the demand for cell phones

When an external factor increases the demand for cell phones at all prices, the demand curve shifts to the right. This increase in demand results in a new equilibrium point. Consumers purchase more cell phones at a higher price.

FIGURE 3-8

Shift in the supply of cell phones

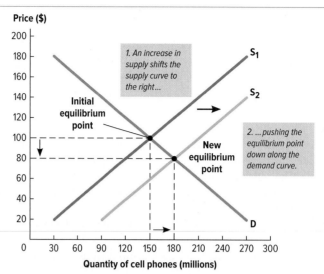

When an external factor affects the supply of cell phones at all prices, the supply curve shifts. In this example, supply increases and the market reaches a new equilibrium point. Consumers purchase more phones at a lower price.

Shifts in supply

What would happen if a breakthrough in battery technology enabled cell phone manufacturers to construct phones with the same battery life for less money? Once again, asking *How will others respond?* helps us predict the market response. We can see that the new technology does not have much impact on demand: Customers probably have no idea how much the batteries in their phones cost to make, nor will they care as long as battery life stays the same. However, cheaper batteries definitely decrease production costs, increasing the number of phones manufacturers are willing to supply at any given price. So the demand curve stays where it is, and the supply curve shifts to the right.

Figure 3-8 shows the shift in supply and the new equilibrium point. The new supply curve intersects the demand curve at a new equilibrium point, representing a price of $80 and a quantity of 180 million phones.

Once again, we can analyze the effect of the change in battery technology on the market for cell phones in three steps:

1. *Does demand increase or decrease?* No, the nonprice determinants of demand are not affected by battery technology.
2. *Does supply increase or decrease?* Yes, supply increases because the new battery technology lowers production costs.
3. *How does the combination of changes in supply and demand affect equilibrium price and quantity?* The increase in supply shifts the supply curve to the right, pushing the equilibrium to a lower point on the stationary demand curve. The new equilibrium price and quantity are $80 and 180 million phones.

Table 3-4 summarizes the effect of some other changes in demand or supply on the equilibrium price and quantity.

Shifts in both demand and supply

In our discussion so far, we've covered examples in which only demand or supply shifted. However, it's possible that factors that shift demand and supply in the market for cell phones could coincidentally happen at the same time. For example, an increase in landline cost (a demand

TABLE 3-4

Effect of changes in demand or supply on the equilibrium price and quantity

Example of change in demand or supply	Effect on equilibrium price and quantity	Shift in curve
A successful "Buy American" advertising campaign increases the demand for Fords.	The demand curve shifts to the right. The equilibrium price and quantity increase.	
An outbreak of *E. coli* reduces the demand for spinach.	The demand curve shifts to the left. The equilibrium price and quantity decrease.	
The use of robots decreases production costs.	The supply curve shifts to the right. The equilibrium price decreases and the equilibrium quantity increases.	
An increase in the minimum wage increases labor costs.	The supply curve shifts to the left. The equilibrium price increases and the equilibrium quantity decreases.	

factor) could occur simultaneously with an improvement in battery technology (a supply factor). It's also possible that a single change could affect both supply and demand.

For instance, suppose that in addition to reducing the cost of production, the new battery technology makes cell phone batteries last longer. We already know that cheaper batteries will increase supply. As we saw before with increases in supply, price decreases while the quantity increases. Asking *how consumers will respond* allows us to see that the improvement in battery life will also increase demand: Longer-lasting batteries will make a cell phone more valuable to consumers at any given price. As a result, both the demand curve and the supply curve shift to the right. Panels A and B of Figure 3-9 both show that the effect of a double change is a new equilibrium point at a higher price and a higher quantity.

Even without looking at a graph, we could have predicted that in this case the equilibrium *quantity* would rise. Increases in demand and increases in supply both independently lead to a higher equilibrium quantity—and the combination will certainly do so as well.

Without more information, however, we cannot predict the change in equilibrium *price.* Holding all else equal, an increase in demand leads to an increase in price, but an increase in supply leads to a decrease in price. To find the net effect on equilibrium price, we would have to know whether the shift in demand outweighs the shift in supply shown in panel A of Figure 3-9, or vice versa, which is shown in panel B.

FIGURE 3-9

Shifts in both demand and supply

An increase in supply and demand shifts both curves to the right, resulting in a higher quantity traded. However, the direction of the price shift depends on whether supply or demand increases more.

(A) Demand increases more

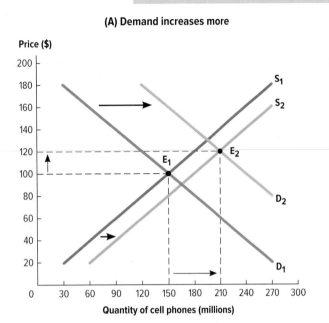

Sometimes, supply and demand shift together. In this example, both curves shift to the right, but demand increases more. At the new equilibrium point, E_2, consumers purchase more cell phones at a higher price.

(B) Supply increases more

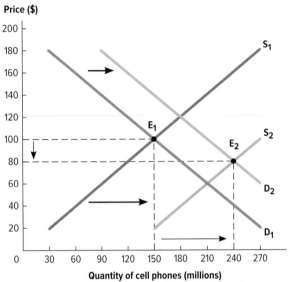

Sometimes, supply and demand shift together. In this example, both curves shift to the right, but supply increases more. At the new equilibrium point, E_2, consumers purchase more cell phones at a lower price.

We can state this idea more generally: When supply and demand shift together, it is possible to predict *either* the direction of the change in quantity *or* the direction of the change in price without knowing how much the curves shift. Table 3-5 shows some rules you can use to predict the outcome of these shifts in supply and demand. These rules are:

- When supply and demand move in the *same* direction, we can predict the direction of the change in quantity but not the direction of the change in price.
- When supply and demand move in *opposite* directions, the change in price is predictable, but not the change in quantity.

Thinking about the intuition behind these rules may help you to remember them. Any time you are considering a situation in which supply and demand shift at the same time, ask yourself,

TABLE 3-5

Predicting changes in price and quantity when supply and demand change simultaneously

Supply change	Demand change	Price change	Quantity change
Decrease	Decrease	?	↓
Decrease	Increase	↑	?
Increase	Increase	?	↑
Increase	Decrease	↓	?

"What do buyers and sellers agree on?" For instance, when both supply and demand increase, buyers and sellers "agree" that at any given price, the quantity they are willing to exchange is higher. The reverse is true when both supply and demand decrease: Buyers and sellers agree that at a given price, the quantity they are willing to exchange is lower.

Applying this reasoning to opposite shifts in supply and demand—when one increases but the other decreases—is trickier. To find out what buyers and sellers "agree" on, try rephrasing what it means for demand to increase. One way to say it is that consumers are willing to buy a *higher* quantity at the *same* price. Another way to say it is that consumers are willing to pay a *higher* price to buy the *same* quantity. So, when demand increases and supply decreases, buyers are willing to pay more for the same quantity; also, sellers are willing to supply the same quantity only if they receive a higher price. In other words, they can "agree" on a higher price at any given quantity. We can therefore predict that the equilibrium price will increase.

The opposite is true when demand decreases and supply increases. Buyers are willing to buy the same quantity as before only if the price is lower, and sellers are willing to supply the same quantity at a lower price. Because the two groups can "agree" on a lower price at any given quantity, we can predict that the price will decrease.

Of course, you can always work out the effect of simultaneous shifts in demand and supply by working through the three questions described in the previous section. Draw the shifts in each curve on a graph, as is done in two cases in panels A and B of Figure 3-9, and find the new equilibrium.

Before you finish this chapter, read the Real Life box "Give a man a fish" for some information about how cell phones affected supply and demand in one developing country.

Real Life

Give a man a fish

Are cell phones a technological luxury or a practical necessity? Maybe you can't imagine life without the ability to call or text your friends anywhere, any time. But are cell phones as important as shelter, food, or water? A study in India showed that being able to communicate may help people to meet their basic needs.

In a competitive market, the price of a particular good is found at the point where the quantity supplied equals the quantity demanded. This model assumes that everywhere in the market, buyers and sellers are fully informed about prices and can adjust their behavior accordingly. If buyers and sellers do not have good information about prices, shortages can develop in some locations and surpluses in others.

When the economist Robert Jensen studied the market for fish in Kerala, a state in southwestern India, he found that it did not reach one equilibrium price. Instead, each local fish market has its own equilibrium. In this area, many people rely on fishing for their daily income. Fishermen tend to sell their fish at a single local market; they take the price that prevails at that market on a particular day. If that market has only a few buyers that day, the fishermen end up with too much fish. At the same time, if the fishermen in a neighboring village have a poor catch that day, some buyers at that market will go home empty-handed—even if they are willing to pay a high price. Without a way to know if there is a shortage or surplus in a nearby market, the fishermen can't adjust their prices to reach equilibrium with customers.

Jensen found that the fishermen could solve this problem using cell phones. By communicating with one another and with people on land while out fishing, they were able to find out where their catches would be most profitable that day. They used that information to travel to the right village to sell their fish. Supply began to better match the demand in each village, and

(continued)

prices became more uniform across villages. Access to the right information allowed the market for fish to reach an efficient equilibrium. Sellers earned an average of 8 percent more in profits, and buyers paid an average of 4 percent less for their fish. Fishermen increased their incomes, and consumers stretched their incomes further.

As the saying goes, "Give a man a fish and he will eat for a day. Teach a man to fish and he will eat for a lifetime." To this wisdom, we might add, "Give a man a cell phone. . . ."

Source: R. Jensen, "Give a Man a Fish, " *The Quarterly Journal of Economics,* 122, 3, 2007.

✓CONCEPT CHECK

☐ What is the market equilibrium? **[LO 3.6]**

☐ What happens to the equilibrium price and quantity if the supply curve shifts right but the demand curve stays put? **[LO 3.7]**

Conclusion

By the time you reach the end of this course, you'll be quite familiar with the words *supply* and *demand.* We take our time on this subject for good reason: An understanding of supply and demand is the foundation of economic problem solving. You'll be hard-pressed to make wise economic choices without it.

Although markets are not always perfectly competitive, you may be surprised at how accurately many real-world phenomena can be described using the simple rules of supply and demand. In the next chapters we'll use these rules to explain how consumers and producers respond to price changes and government policies.

Key Terms

market economy, p. 50

market, p. 50

competitive market, p. 51

price taker, p. 51

standardized good, p. 51

transaction costs, p. 51

quantity demanded, p. 53

law of demand, p. 53

demand schedule, p. 53

demand curve, p. 53

substitutes, p. 55

complements, p. 56

normal goods, p. 56

inferior goods, p. 56

quantity supplied, p. 59

law of supply, p. 59

supply schedule, p. 60

supply curve, p. 60

equilibrium, p. 64

equilibrium price, p. 64

equilibrium quantity, p. 64

surplus (excess supply), p. 65

shortage (excess demand), p. 65

Summary

LO 3.1 Identify the defining characteristics of a competitive market.

A market is the group of buyers and sellers who trade a particular good or service. In competitive markets, a large number of buyers and sellers trade standardized goods and services. They have full information about the goods, and there is no cost to participate in exchanges in the market. Participants in competitive markets are called price takers because they can't affect the prevailing price for a good.

LO 3.2 Draw a demand curve and describe the external factors that determine demand.

A demand curve is a graph that shows the quantities of a particular good or service that consumers will demand at various prices. It also shows consumers' highest willingness to pay for a given quantity. The law of demand states that for almost all goods, the quantity demanded increases as the price decreases. This relationship results in a downward-sloping demand curve.

Several nonprice factors contribute to consumers' demand for a good at a given price: Consumer preferences, the prices of related goods, incomes, and expectations about the future all affect demand. On a marketwide level, the number of buyers also can increase or decrease total demand. When one of these underlying factors changes, the demand curve will shift to the left or the right.

LO 3.3 Distinguish between a shift in and a movement along the demand curve.

When one of the nonprice factors that drives demand changes, the entire curve *shifts* to the left or the right. With this shift, the quantity demanded at any given price changes. When demand increases, the curve shifts to the right; when demand decreases, it shifts to the left.

When the nonprice determinants of demand stay the same, a change in the price of a good leads to a *movement along* the curve, rather than a shift in the curve.

LO 3.4 Draw a supply curve and describe the external factors that determine supply.

A supply curve is a graph that shows the quantities of a particular good or service that producers will supply at various prices. It shows the minimum price producers must receive to supply any given quantity. The law of supply states that the quantity supplied increases as the price increases, resulting in an upward-sloping supply curve.

Several nonprice factors determine the supply of a good at any given price: They include the prices of related goods, technology, prices of inputs, expectations about the future, and the number of sellers in the market. If one of these underlying factors changes, the supply curve will shift to the left or the right.

LO 3.5 Distinguish between a shift in and a movement along the supply curve.

Just as with demand, a change in the nonprice determinants of supply will cause the entire supply curve to shift to the left or the right. As a result, the quantity supplied is higher or lower at any given price than it was before. When supply increases, the curve shifts to the right; when supply decreases, it shifts to the left.

A shift in the supply curve differs from movement along the supply curve. A movement along the curve happens when the price of a good increases but the nonprice determinants of supply stay the same.

LO 3.6 Explain how supply and demand interact to drive markets to equilibrium.

When a market is in equilibrium, the quantity supplied equals the quantity demanded. The incentives that individual buyers and sellers face drive a competitive market toward equilibrium. If the prevailing price is too high, a surplus will result, and sellers will lower their prices to get rid of the excess supply. If the prevailing price is too low, a shortage will result, and buyers will bid up the price until the excess demand disappears.

LO 3.7 Evaluate the effect of changes in supply and demand on the equilibrium price and quantity.

When one or more of the underlying factors that determine supply or demand change, one or both curves will shift, leading to a new market equilibrium price and quantity.

To calculate the change in the equilibrium price and quantity, you must first determine whether a change affects demand, and, if so, in which direction the curve will shift. Then you must determine whether the change also affects supply, and, if so, in which direction that curve will shift. Finally, you must determine the new equilibrium point where the two curves intersect.

Review Questions

1. Think about a competitive market in which you participate regularly. For each of the characteristics of a competitive market, explain how your market meets these requirements. **[LO 3.1]**

2. Think about a noncompetitive market in which you participate regularly. Explain which characteristic(s) of competitive markets your market does not meet. **[LO 3.1]**

3. Explain why a demand curve slopes downward. **[LO 3.2]**

4. In each of the following examples, name the factor that affects demand and describe its impact on your demand for a new cell phone. **[LO 3.2]**
   a. You hear a rumor that a new and improved model of the phone you want is coming out next year.
   b. Your grandparents give you $500.
   c. A cellular network announces a holiday sale on a data package that includes the purchase of a new smartphone.
   d. A friend tells you how great his new phone is and suggests that you get one, too.

5. Consider the following events:
   a. The price of cell phones goes down by 25 percent during a sale.
   b. You get a 25 percent raise at your job.

Which event represents a shift in the demand curve? Which represents a movement along the curve? What is the difference? **[LO 3.3]**

6. What is the difference between a change in demand and a change in quantity demanded? **[LO 3.3]**

7. Explain why a supply curve slopes upward. **[LO 3.4]**

8. In each of the following examples, name the factor that affects supply and describe its impact on the supply of cell phones. **[LO 3.4]**

    a. Economic forecasts suggest that the demand for cell phones will increase in the future.

    b. The price of plastic goes up.

    c. A new screen technology reduces the cost of making cell phones.

9. Consider the following events:

    a. A fruitworm infestation ruins a large number of apple orchards in Washington state.

    b. Demand for apples goes down, causing the price to fall.

    Which event represents a shift in the supply curve? Which represents a movement along the curve? What is the difference? **[LO 3.5]**

10. What is the difference between a change in supply and a change in quantity supplied? **[LO 3.5]**

11. What is the relationship between supply and demand when a market is in equilibrium? Explain how the incentives facing cell phone companies and consumers cause the market for cell phones to reach equilibrium. **[LO 3.6]**

12. Explain why the equilibrium price is often called the market-clearing price. **[LO 3.6]**

13. Suppose an economic boom causes incomes to increase. Explain what will happen to the demand and supply of phones, and predict the direction of the change in the equilibrium price and quantity. **[LO 3.7]**

14. Suppose an economic boom drives up wages for the sales representatives who work for cell phone companies. Explain what will happen to the demand and supply of phones, and predict the direction of the change in the equilibrium price and quantity. **[LO 3.7]**

15. Suppose an economic boom causes incomes to increase and at the same time drives up wages for the sales representatives who work for cell phone companies. Explain what will happen to the demand for and supply of phones and predict the direction of the change in the equilibrium price and quantity. **[LO 3.7]**

Problems and Applications

1. Consider shopping for cucumbers in a farmers' market. For each statement below, note which characteristic of competitive markets the statement describes. *Choose from:* standardized good, full information, no transaction costs, and participants are price takers. **[LO 3.1]**

    a. All of the farmers have their prices posted prominently in front of their stalls.

    b. Cucumbers are the same price at each stall.

    c. There is no difficulty moving around between stalls as you shop and choosing between farmers.

    d. You and the other customers all seem indifferent about which cucumbers to buy.

2. Suppose two artists are selling paintings for the same price in adjacent booths at an art fair. By the end of the day, one artist has nearly sold out of her paintings while the other artist has sold nothing. Which characteristic of competitive markets has not been met and best explains this outcome? **[LO 3.1]**

    a. Standardized good.

    b. Full information.

    c. No transaction costs.

    d. Participants are price takers.

3. Using the demand schedule in Table 3P-1, draw the daily demand curve for slices of pizza in a college town. **[LO 3.2]**

TABLE 3P-1

Price ($)	Quantity demanded (slices)
0.00	350
0.50	300
1.00	250
1.50	200
2.00	150
2.50	100
3.00	50
3.50	0

4. Consider the market for cars. Which determinant of demand is affected by each of the following events? *Choose from:* consumer preferences, prices of related goods, incomes, expectations, and the number of buyers. **[LO 3.2]**

   a. Environmentalists launch a successful One Family, One Car campaign.

   b. A baby boom occurred 16 years ago.

   c. Layoffs increase as the economy sheds millions of jobs.

   d. An oil shortage causes the price of gasoline to soar.

   e. The government offers tax rebates in return for the purchase of commuter rail tickets.

   f. The government announces a massive plan to bail out the auto industry and subsidize production costs.

5. If a decrease in the price of laptops causes the demand for tablets to increase, are laptops and tablets substitutes or complements? **[LO 3.2]**

6. If rising incomes cause the demand for beer to decrease, is beer a normal or inferior good? **[LO 3.2]**

7. Consider the market for corn. Say whether each of the following events will cause a shift in the demand curve or a movement along the curve. If it will cause a shift, specify the direction. **[LO 3.3]**

   a. A drought hits corn-growing regions, cutting the supply of corn.

   b. The government announces a new subsidy for biofuels made from corn.

   c. A global recession reduces the incomes of consumers in poor countries, who rely on corn as a staple food.

   d. A new hybrid variety of corn seed causes a 15 percent increase in the yield of corn per acre.

   e. An advertising campaign by the beef producers' association highlights the health benefits of corn-fed beef.

8. The demand curve in Figure 3P-1 shows the monthly market for sweaters at a local clothing store. For each of the following events, draw the new outcome. **[LO 3.3]**

   a. Sweaters fall out of fashion.

   b. There is a shortage of wool.

   c. The winter is particularly long and cold this year.

   d. Sweater vendors offer a sale.

FIGURE 3P-1

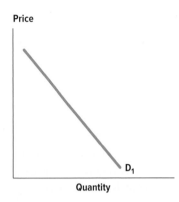

9. Using the supply schedule found in Table 3P-2, draw the daily supply curve for slices of pizza in a college town. **[LO 3.4]**

10. Consider the market for cars. Which determinant of supply is affected by each of the following events? *Choose from:* prices of related goods, technology, prices of inputs, expectations, and the number of sellers in the market. **[LO 3.4]**

    a. A steel tariff increases the price of steel.

    b. Improvements in robotics increase efficiency and reduce costs.

    c. Factories close because of an economic downturn.

    d. The government announces a plan to offer tax rebates for the purchase of commuter rail tickets.

TABLE 3P-2

Price ($)	Quantity supplied (slices)
0.00	0
0.50	50
1.00	100
1.50	150
2.00	200
2.50	250
3.00	300
3.50	350

e. The price of trucks falls, so factories produce more cars.

f. The government announces that it will dramatically rewrite efficiency standards, making it much harder for automakers to produce their cars.

11. Consider the market for corn. Say whether each of the following events will cause a shift in the supply curve or a movement along the curve. If it will cause a shift, specify the direction. **[LO 3.5]**

a. A drought hits corn-growing regions.

b. The government announces a new subsidy for biofuels made from corn.

c. A global recession reduces the incomes of consumers in poor countries, who rely on corn as a staple food.

d. A new hybrid variety of corn seed causes a 15 percent increase in the yield of corn per acre.

e. An advertising campaign by the beef producers' association highlights the health benefits of corn-fed beef.

12. The supply curve in Figure 3P-2 shows the monthly market for sweaters at a local craft market. For each of the following events, draw the new outcome. **[LO 3.5]**

a. The price of wool increases.

b. Demand for sweaters decreases.

c. A particularly cold winter is expected to begin next month.

d. Demand for sweaters increases.

FIGURE 3P-2

TABLE 3P-3

Price ($)	Quantity demanded (slices)	Quantity supplied (slices)
0.00	350	0
0.50	300	50
1.00	250	100
1.50	200	150
2.00	150	200
2.50	100	250
3.00	50	300
3.50	0	350

13. Refer to the demand and supply schedule shown in Table 3P-3. **[LO 3.6]**

a. If pizza parlors charge $3.50 per slice, will there be excess supply or excess demand? What is the amount of excess supply or excess demand at that price?

b. If pizza parlors charge $1.00 per slice, will there be excess supply or excess demand? What is the amount of excess supply or excess demand at that price?

c. What are the equilibrium price and quantity in this market?

FIGURE 3P-3

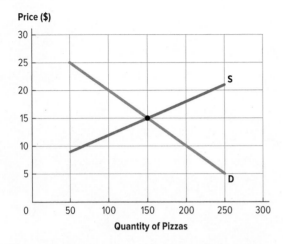

Price ($)

Quantity of Pizzas

FIGURE 3P-4

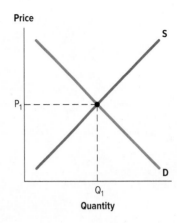

Price

Quantity

The graph in Figure 3P-3 shows the weekly market for pizzas in a small town. Use this graph to answer Problems 14–16.

14. Which of the following events will occur at a price of $20? **[LO 3.6]**

    a. Equilibrium.

    b. Excess demand.

    c. Excess supply.

    d. No pizzas supplied.

    e. No pizzas demanded.

15. Which of the following events will occur at a price of $10? **[LO 3.6]**

    a. Equilibrium.

    b. Excess demand.

    c. Excess supply.

    d. No pizzas supplied.

    e. No pizzas demanded.

16. What are the equilibrium price and quantity of pizzas? **[LO 3.6]**

17. The graph in Figure 3P-4 shows supply and demand in the market for automobiles. For each of the following events, draw the new market outcome and say whether the equilibrium price and quantity will increase or decrease. **[LO 3.7]**

    a. Environmentalists launch a successful One Family, One Car campaign.

    b. A steel tariff increases the price of steel.

    c. A baby boom occurred 16 years ago.

    d. An oil shortage causes the price of gasoline to soar.

    e. Improvements in robotics increase efficiency and reduce costs.

    f. The government offers a tax rebate for the purchase of commuter rail tickets.

18. Say whether each of the following changes will increase or decrease the equilibrium price and quantity, or whether the effect cannot be predicted. **[LO 3.7]**

    a. Demand increases; supply remains constant.

    b. Supply increases; demand remains constant.

    c. Demand decreases; supply remains constant.

    d. Supply decreases; demand remains constant.

    e. Demand increases; supply increases.

    f. Demand decreases; supply decreases.

    g. Demand increases; supply decreases.

    h. Demand decreases; supply increases.

Endnotes

1. http://www.gsmamobileeconomy.com/GSMA_Global_Mobile_Economy_Report_2015.pdf

2. http://www.ngrguardiannews.com/2015/06/africas-mobile-phone-penetration-now-67/

Math Essentials: Working with Linear Equations

Learning Objectives	
LO B.1	Use linear equations to interpret the equation of a line.
LO B.2	Use linear equations to explain shifts and pivots.
LO B.3	Use linear equations to solve for equilibrium.

Relationships between variables can be represented with algebraic equations, as well as graphs and tables. You should be comfortable moving among all three representations. We addressed graphs in Appendix A, "Math Essentials: Understanding Graphs and Slope"; if you didn't read it then, you might want to do so now.

Interpreting the Equation of a Line

LO B.1 Use linear equations to interpret the equation of a line.

If the relationship between two variables is linear, it can be represented by the equation for a line, which is commonly written as:

EQUATION B-1
$$y = mx + b$$

In this form, called the *slope intercept form, m* is the slope of the line and *b* is the *y*-intercept.

All linear equations provide information about the slope and *y*-intercept of the line. From our discussion in Appendix A, "Math Essentials: Understanding Graphs and Slope," we already know that slope is the ratio of vertical distance (change in *y*) to horizontal distance (change in *x*). So what does the *y*-intercept tell us? It is the point at which the line crosses the *y*-axis. Put another way, it is the value of *y* when *x* is 0. Knowing these values is useful in turning an equation into a graph. Also, as we'll see, they can allow us to get information about the real economic relationship being represented without even having to graph it.

Although you might see the equation for a line rearranged in several different forms, just remember that if *y* is on the left-hand side of the equation, whatever number is multiplying *x* (known as the *coefficient of x*) is your slope. If you don't see a number in front of *x,* the slope is 1. The number being added to or subtracted from a multiple of *x* is a constant that represents the *y*-intercept. If you don't see this number, you know that the *y*-intercept is zero. Take a look at a few examples in Table B-1.

TABLE B-1

Examples of linear equations

The steepness and position of a line in the Cartesian coordinate system is determined by two things: its slope and its intercept. Slope refers to steepness; the intercept determines where the line is positioned.

Equation	Slope	y-intercept
$y = 6x + 4$	6	4
$y = -x - 2$	−1	−2
$y = 10 - 2x$	−2	10
$y = -4x$	−4	0

Turning a graph into an equation

To see how to translate a graph into an algebraic equation, look at Figure B-1. What is the equation that represents this relationship? To derive this equation, we need to find the values of the slope and the y-intercept. We can calculate the slope at any point along the line:

$$\text{Slope} = \frac{\Delta y}{\Delta x} = \frac{(y_2 - y_1)}{(x_2 - x_1)}$$

$$= \frac{(6 - 5)}{(4 - 2)} = \frac{1}{2} = 0.5$$

By looking at the graph to see where the line intersects the y-axis, we can tell that the y-intercept is 4. Therefore, if we write the equation in the form $y = mx + b$, we get $y = 0.5x + 4$. Our table, graph, and equation all give us the same information about the relationship between x and y.

Turning an equation into a graph

Let's work in the opposite direction now, starting with an equation and seeing what information it gives us. The following equation takes the form $y = mx + b$, with P and Q substituted for y and x, respectively.

$$P = -5Q + 25$$

We know from looking at this equation that it represents a line with a slope of −5 and a y-intercept of 25. Suppose that we know this equation represents supply or demand, but we're not sure which. How can we tell whether this is a demand equation or a supply equation? Easy. The slope is negative. We don't need a graph to tell us that the relationship between P and Q is negative and the line will be downward-sloping. Therefore, the equation must represent demand rather than supply.

Because the y-intercept in our equation is 25, we know that the demand curve will cross the y-axis at 25. This tells us that when price is 25, quantity demanded is 0. In order for consumers to demand a positive quantity, price must be lower than 25.

If we need to know more about the relationship represented by the equation, we can graph the demand curve. Since we know that 25 is the y-intercept, we can use the point (0,25) to begin plotting our graph as shown in Figure B-2.

It takes only two points to define a line, and we already have one from the y-intercept. To find a second point, we can plug in any value of Q and solve for the corresponding P (or vice versa). For example, if we let Q = 2 and solve for P, we get:

$$P = -5(2) + 25$$

$$P = -10 + 25$$

$$P = 15$$

We can now plot the point (2,15) and connect it to the y-intercept at (0,25).

FIGURE B-1

Translating a graph into an algebraic equation

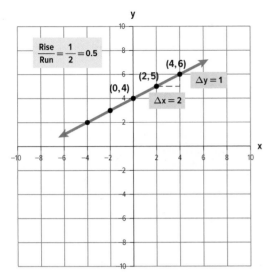

By using information provided on a graph, you can easily construct an equation of the line in the form $y = mx + b$. The slope, m, is calculated by taking the rise of a line over its run. The value of the y-intercept provides the b part of the equation.

FIGURE B-2

Translating an algebraic equation into a graph

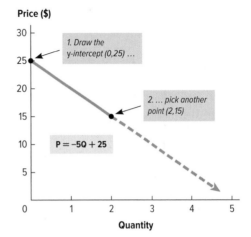

The first step in graphing the equation of a line in the form $y = mx + b$ is to plot the y intercept, given by b. Then pick another point by choosing any value of x or y, and solving the equation for the other variable to get an ordered pair that represents another point on the line. Connecting these two points gives the line.

Rather than plugging in random points, though, it is often useful to know the x-intercept as well as the y-intercept. On a demand curve, this will tell us what quantity is demanded when price is 0. To find this intercept, we can let $P = 0$ and solve for Q:

$$0 = -5Q + 25$$

$$-25 = -5Q$$

$$5 = Q$$

We can now plot the point (5,0) and connect it to (0,25) to graph the demand curve.

Finding intercepts is useful for interpreting other types of graphs as well. In a production possibilities frontier, the intercepts tell you how much of one good will be produced if all resources are used to produce that good and none are used to produce the other good. In the production possibilities frontier shown in Figure B-3, for example, we can find the y-intercept to see that by devoting all workers to making shirts and none to producing wheat, 2 million T-shirts can be produced. Alternatively, we can find the x-intercept to see that if all workers grow wheat and none make shirts, 4 million bushels of wheat can be produced.

We saw in Chapter 2, "Specialization and Exchange," that the slope of the frontier represents the trade-off between producing two goods. We can use our intercepts as the two points we need to calculate the slope.

$$\text{Slope} = \frac{\Delta y}{\Delta x} = \frac{(4 \text{ million} - 0)}{(0 - 2 \text{ million})} = \frac{4}{-2} = -2$$

You know that the slope of the frontier will be negative because it represents a trade-off: You can't make more wheat without giving up some shirts. Because an increase in wheat means a decrease in shirts, the two variables move in opposite directions and have a negative relationship.

FIGURE B-3

Using intercepts to interpret a production possibilities frontier

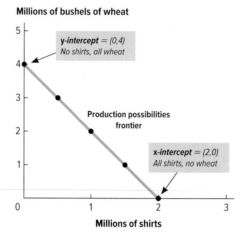

The intercepts of a production possibilities frontier give the maximum amount of a good a country can produce by dedicating all resources in the economy to the production of that good. In this case, with all workers dedicated to the production of one good or the other, the economy can make either 4 million bushels of wheat or 2 million shirts.

This frontier has a constant slope, which means that the trade-off between the two goods—which we can also think of as the opportunity cost of producing shirts in terms of wheat—is also constant.

Equations with *x* and *y* reversed

Thus far, we have represented demand and supply equations with P (or *y*) isolated on the left side of the equation. For example, our demand equation was given as P = −5Q + 25. You may find, however, that in some places, demand and supply equations are given with Q (or *x*) isolated on the left side of the equation instead.

When you see this, you cannot read the equation as giving you the slope and the *y*-intercept. Instead, when an equation is in this form, you have the inverse of slope and the *x*-intercept.

Look at our demand equation again. If we rearrange the equation to solve for Q, we have an equation of the form *x = ny + a:*

$$P = -5Q + 25$$
$$P - 25 = -5Q$$
$$-\frac{1}{5}P + 5 = Q \quad \text{or} \quad Q = -\frac{1}{5}P + 5$$

We know that the starting equation represents the same underlying relationship as the final equation. For instance, we know that our slope is −5, but in the rearranged form where we have solved for Q, the coefficient multiplying P is the inverse of slope, or $-\frac{1}{5}$. We can generalize this observation to say that when we have an equation of the form $x = ny + a$, $n = \frac{1}{m}$, where *m* is the slope of the line from the same equation expressed in the form $y = mx + b$. We also know that 25 is the *y*-intercept. But in our rearranged form, *a* represents the *x*-intercept,

FIGURE B-4

Same line, different equation forms

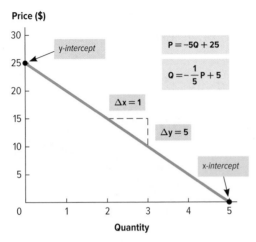

Regardless of whether you solve an equation
for P or Q, the resulting line is the same.

which is 5. The graph in Figure B-4 shows that these two equations represent different aspects of the same line.

Keep in mind that $P = -5Q + 25$ is the same equation as $Q = -\frac{1}{5}P + 5$; we have simply rearranged it to solve for Q instead of P.

Shifts and Pivots

LO B.2 Use linear equations to explain shifts and pivots.

Imagine that your campus cafeteria has a deli with a salad bar and that the price of a salad depends on the number of ingredients you add to it. This relationship is represented by the following equation:

$$y = 0.5x + 4$$

where

y = total price of the salad

x = number of added ingredients

Because our variables are the price of a salad and the number of ingredients, negative quantities do not make sense: You can't have negative carrots in your salad, and we doubt that the cafeteria is paying you to buy salads. Therefore, we can isolate the graph of this equation to the first quadrant, as shown in panel A of Figure B-5.

Our y-intercept of 4 represents the price of a salad if you add zero ingredients. In other words, a plain bowl of lettuce costs $4. The slope of 0.5 represents the cost of adding ingredients to the salad. Each additional ingredient costs 50 cents. The fact that (2,5) is a point along the line shows that the price of a salad with two added ingredients is $5.

FIGURE B-5

Shifting a line to change the intercept

(A) Restrict the graph to Quadrant I

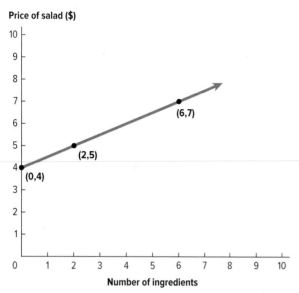

In order to easily change the intercept, first restrict the line to values in the first quadrant. This will clearly show the *y*-intercept of the line.

(B) Shift the line upward by moving the intercept

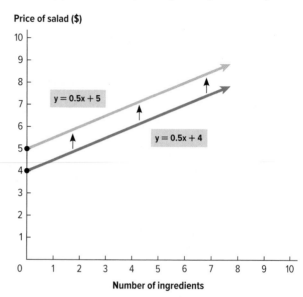

Once the *y*-intercept is clear, you can shift the line to the new intercept indicated by the equation of the line.

How much is a salad with six added ingredients?

$$y = 0.5(6) + 4$$

$$y = 3 + 4$$

$$y = 7$$

A salad with six added ingredients is $7, and (6,7) is another point on the graph.

Now, let's see what happens to our graph when the baseline price of a bowl of lettuce without additional ingredients increases to $5. This baseline price is represented by the *y*-intercept, which changes from 4 to 5. The slope of the graph does not change because each additional ingredient still costs 50 cents.

Thus, our equation changes to $y = 0.5x + 5$. Rather than regraphing this new question from scratch, we can simply *shift* the original line to account for the change in the *y*-intercept, as shown in panel B of Figure B-5.

Suppose, instead, that the price of lettuce remains at $4, but the price of additional ingredients increases to $1 each. How will this change the graph and equation?

If the price of lettuce with zero additional ingredients remains at $4, the *y*-intercept will also stay the same. However, the slope will change, increasing from 50 cents to $1. Figure B-6 shows that this change of slope will *pivot* the line in our graph.

Our equation changes as well. This time, we substitute 1 in place of 0.5 for the slope. Thus, $y = x + 4$. (Remember that no coefficient on *x* indicates that the slope is 1.)

What happens if the baseline price of lettuce goes up to $5 *and* the price of toppings goes up to $1? We have to both *shift and pivot* the line to represent the change in the intercept and the slope. (Sounds like a fitness routine, doesn't it?) Figure B-7 shows both changes.

FIGURE B-6

Pivoting a line to change the slope

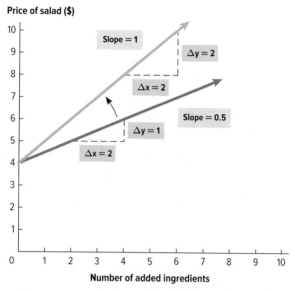

Changes in slope will pivot the equation of a line. Increases in slope will rotate the line upward; decreases in slope will rotate the line downward.

FIGURE B-7

Shift and pivot

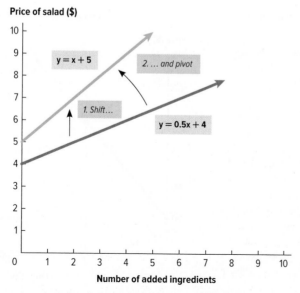

In order to handle a change in slope and intercept, you first shift the line to the new intercept and then pivot the line to reflect the new slope.

You will need to shift and pivot lines in many places throughout this book to represent changes in the relationship between two variables. For instance, we saw in Chapter 3, "Markets," that when a nonprice determinant of demand changes, you need to *shift* the demand curve to show that people demand a higher or lower quantity of a good at any given price. When consumers become more or less sensitive to changes in price, you need to *pivot* the demand curve to represent a change in slope.

Solving for Equilibrium

LO B.3 Use linear equations to solve for equilibrium.

One graph can show multiple relationships between the same two variables. The most frequent case we encounter in this book is graphs showing both the demand relationship and the supply relationship between price and quantity.

Panel A of Figure B-8 shows data from supply and demand schedules. Remember from Chapter 3, "Markets," that as P increases, the quantity *demanded* decreases. Since P and Q are moving in opposite directions, the relationship is negative. When these values are plotted in panel B, we have a downward-sloping line for the demand curve. Conversely, as P increases, the quantity *supplied* increases. Plotting these points yields an upward-sloping supply curve.

When we use one graph to show multiple equations of the same variables, we do so in order to show something meaningful about the relationship between them. For instance, when we show supply and demand on the same graph, we usually want to find the equilibrium point—the point at which the quantity supplied and the quantity demanded are equal to one another at the same price.

FIGURE B-8

Supply and demand

(A) Supply and demand schedules

Price ($)	Q_{demand}	Q_{supply}
20	180	0
30	160	10
40	140	20
50	120	30
80	60	60
90	40	70
100	20	80
110	0	90

(B) Graphing the schedules

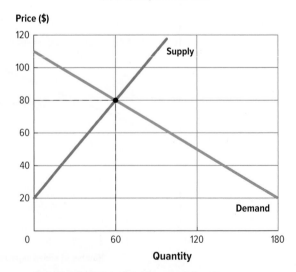

The supply and demand schedules show the quantities demanded and supplied for a given price.

Graphing the values from the schedules gives a downward-sloping demand curve and an upward-sloping supply curve.

We can find the equilibrium point in several ways. If we have schedules showing both demand and supply data, the easiest way to find equilibrium is to locate the price that corresponds to *equal supply and demand quantities*. What is that price in panel A of Figure B-8? At a price of 80, Q is 60 in the demand schedule as well as in the supply schedule.

We can also find the equilibrium point easily by looking at a graph showing both supply and demand. The one-and-only point where the two lines intersect is the equilibrium.

Sometimes, however, it is useful to find equilibrium from equations alone, without having to graph them or to calculate a whole schedule of points by plugging in different prices. Usually you'll want to use this method when you are given equations but no graph or schedule. However, just for practice, let's first derive the supply and demand equations from Figure B-8 and then figure out the equilibrium point.

We want to start by representing supply and demand as equations of the form $y = mx + b$. Let y = price and x = quantity. We need to determine the slope (m) and the y-intercept (b) for each equation.

First, the demand equation: What is the y-intercept? It is the value of y when x is 0. Looking at panel A in Figure B-8, we can see that when Q is zero, P is 110. The y-intercept of the demand equation is 110. Now we need the slope. Because this is a linear relationship and the slope is constant, we can determine the slope using any two points. Let's use the points (180,20) and (160,30).

$$\frac{\Delta y}{\Delta x} = \frac{(P_2 - P_1)}{(Q_2 - Q_1)} = \frac{(20 - 30)}{(180 - 160)} = \frac{-10}{20} = -0.5$$

Thus, our demand equation is: $P = -0.5Q + 110$.

We'll use the same procedure to derive the supply equation. Looking at the supply schedule, we can see that when Q is zero, P is 20. The y-intercept is 20. To determine slope, let's use the points (0,20) and (10,30).

$$\frac{\Delta y}{\Delta x} = \frac{(P_2 - P_1)}{(Q_2 - Q_1)} = \frac{(20 - 30)}{(0 - 10)} = \frac{-10}{-10} = 1$$

Thus, our supply equation is: $P = Q + 20$.

Now that we have our equations, we can use them to solve for equilibrium. Equilibrium represents a point that is on both the demand and supply curves; graphically, it is where the two curves intersect. This means that P on the demand curve must equal P on the supply curve, and the same for Q. Therefore, it makes sense that we find this point by setting the two equations equal to each other.

$$P_D = -0.5Q + 110$$

$$P_S = Q + 20$$

$$P_D = P_S$$

therefore,

$$-0.5Q + 110 = Q + 20$$

This allows us to solve for a numeric value for Q.

$$1.5Q + 20 = 110$$

$$1.5Q = 90$$

$$Q = 60$$

Now that we have a value for Q, we can plug it in either the supply or demand equation to get the value for P. Let's use our supply equation.

$$P = 20 + Q$$

$$P = 20 + 60$$

$$P = 80$$

Solving for equilibrium using the equations gives us the same point we found using the demand and supply schedules: Q = 60 and P = 80 (60,80).

Problems and Applications

1. Use the demand curve in Figure BP-1 to derive a demand equation. **[LO B.1]**

2. Use the demand schedule in Table BP-1 to derive a demand equation. **[LO B.1]**

3. Use the supply curve in Figure BP-2 to derive a supply equation. **[LO B.1]**

4. Use the supply schedule in Table BP-2 to derive a supply equation. **[LO B.1]**

5. Graph the equation P = 2Q + 3. Is this a supply curve or a demand curve? **[LO B.1]**

6. Graph the equation P = −8Q + 10. Is this a supply curve or a demand curve? **[LO B.1]**

7. Rearrange the equation Q = 5 − 0.25P and sketch the graph. Is this a supply curve or a demand curve? **[LO B.1]**

8. Rearrange the equation Q = 0.2P and sketch the graph. Is this a supply curve or a demand curve? **[LO B.1]**

TABLE BP-1

Price ($)	Quantity
0	320
10	280
20	240
30	200
40	160
50	120
60	80
70	40
80	0

FIGURE BP-1

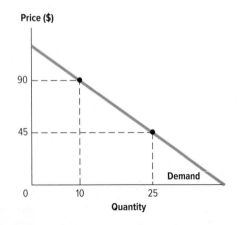

FIGURE BP-2

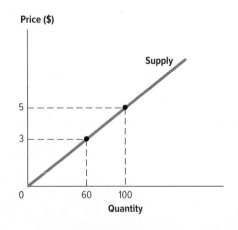

TABLE BP-2

Price ($)	Quantity
100	0
200	25
300	50
400	75
500	100
600	125

9. The entrance fee at your local amusement park is $20 for the day. The entrance fee includes all rides except roller coasters. Roller coasters cost an extra $2 per ride. **[LO B.2]**

a. Write an equation that represents how much money you will spend on rides as a function of the number of rides you go on: S = total spending on rides; Q = the quantity of roller coaster rides.

b. What is your total spending on rides if you ride 4 roller coasters?

c. Draw a graph of the relationship between total spending on rides and the number of roller coaster rides.

d. Redraw the graph from part (c) to show what changes if the entrance fee increases to $25.

e. Rewrite the equation from part (a) to incorporate the increased entrance fee of $25.

f. After the entrance fee increases to $25, what is your total spending on rides if you ride 4 roller coasters?

10. Use the following two equations: **[LO B.3]**

(1) P = 12 − 2Q

(2) P = 3 + Q

a. Find the equilibrium price and quantity.

b. Graph the demand and supply equations. Illustrate the equilibrium point.

11. With reference to Table BP-3: **[LO B.3]**

a. Use the information from the table to create the demand and supply equations.

b. Use your demand and supply equations to solve for equilibrium.

c. Graph supply and demand curves. Illustrate the equilibrium point.

TABLE BP-3

Price ($)	Quantity demanded	Quantity supplied
0	12	0
20	10	4
40	8	8
60	6	12
80	4	16
100	2	20
120	0	24

Elasticity

Learning Objectives

LO 4.1 Calculate price elasticity of demand using the mid-point method.

LO 4.2 Explain how the determinants of price elasticity of demand affect the degree of elasticity.

LO 4.3 Calculate price elasticity of supply using the mid-point method.

LO 4.4 Explain how the determinants of price elasticity of supply affect the degree of elasticity.

LO 4.5 Calculate cross-price elasticity of demand, and interpret the sign of the elasticity.

LO 4.6 Calculate income elasticity of demand, and interpret the sign of the elasticity.

COFFEE BECOMES CHIC

In the 1990s, a coffeehouse craze rippled through middle-class communities in the United States, as a strong economy bolstered sales of high-priced espresso drinks. Soon, Americans were making daily pilgrimages to a place called Starbucks, where a cup of coffee had been transformed into the "Starbucks experience," complete with soundtrack, mints, and charity-themed water bottles. For 15 years the Starbucks business model was highly successful. From 1992 through 2007, the company expanded by over 15,000 stores.

When the U.S. economy stumbled in 2008, however, Starbucks's growth rate dropped to an all-time low. Competitors and customers began to ask, "How much is too much for a cup of coffee?" Presumably, Starbucks executives had asked themselves that very question over the course of more than a decade. Given the company's phenomenal rate of expansion, they must have had the right answer—at least until the economy started having problems.

How do businesses like Starbucks make pricing decisions? How do they anticipate and react to changing circumstances? We learned in the prior chapter that when price changes, quantity demanded changes. If Starbucks raised the price of its lattes—perhaps due to a coffee supply shortage caused by poor weather in Ethiopia—that change would reduce the quantity demanded

© Somsak Sudthangtum/123RF

by consumers. This chapter introduces the idea of elasticity, which describes *how much* this change in prices will affect consumers.

Like the market for cell phones, the market for gourmet coffee is not perfectly competitive. Managers of a big company like Starbucks have some ability to set prices, and they try to choose prices that will earn the largest profits. They also try to respond to changing market conditions: How much will sales fall if the price of coffee beans drives up the cost of a latte? How much will people decrease their coffee consumption during a recession? How many customers will be lost if competitors like Dunkin' Donuts and McDonald's offer less-expensive coffee? Even in perfectly competitive markets, producers want to predict how their profits will change in response to economic conditions and changes in the market price.

Nonprofit service providers also often need to think about price elasticity. For instance, a nonprofit hospital wants to set the price of care so as to cover costs without driving away too many patients. Similarly, colleges and universities want to cover costs and keep education affordable for students.

The ability to address issues like these is critical for any public or private organization. Understanding how to price a Starbucks latte requires the same kind of thinking as figuring out whether to raise entrance fees to national parks to cover the costs of maintaining the wilderness. Solving these challenges relies on a tool called *elasticity,* a measure of how much supply and demand will respond to changes in price and income.

In this chapter, you will learn how to calculate the effect of a price change on the quantity supplied or demanded. You will become familiar with some rules that businesses and policy-makers follow when they cannot measure elasticity exactly. Using what you know about supply and demand, you will be able to categorize different types of goods by noting whether their elasticities are positive or negative. You will also learn how to use a rough approximation of price elasticity to tell whether raising prices will raise or lower an organization's total revenue.

What Is Elasticity?

If Starbucks raises the price of a latte, we can expect the quantity of lattes demanded to fall. But by how much? Although we saw in Chapter 3, "Markets," that price increases cause the quantity demanded to fall in a competitive market, we have not yet been able to say *how big* that movement will be. That question is the subject of this chapter.

elasticity
a measure of how much consumers and producers will respond to a change in market conditions

Elasticity is a measure of how much consumers and producers will respond to a change in market conditions. The concept can be applied to supply or demand. Also, it can be used to measure responses to a change in the price of a good, a change in the price of a related good, or a change in income.

The concept of elasticity allows economic decision makers to anticipate *how others will respond* to changes in market conditions. Whether you are a business owner trying to sell cars or a public official trying to set sales taxes, you need to know how much a change in prices will affect consumers' willingness to buy.

The most commonly used measures of elasticity are *price elasticity of demand* and *price elasticity of supply.* These two concepts describe how much the quantity demanded and the quantity supplied change when the price of a good changes. The *cross-price elasticity of demand* describes how much the demand curve shifts when the price of another good changes. It tells us how much the quantity of coffee demanded changes, for example, when the price of tea increases. Another helpful measure, *income elasticity of demand,* measures how much the demand curve shifts when consumers' incomes change. We'll examine these four elasticity concepts in this chapter. Let's begin with price elasticity of demand.

Price Elasticity of Demand

Price elasticity of demand describes the size of the change in the quantity demanded of a good or service when its price changes. We showed in Chapter 3, "Markets" that quantity demanded generally decreases when the price increases, but so far we have not been able to say *how much* it decreases. Price elasticity of demand fills this gap in our understanding of supply and demand.

Another way to think about price elasticity of demand is as a measure of consumers' sensitivity to price changes. Sensitivity to price changes is measured as more or less elastic:

- When consumers' buying decisions are highly influenced by price, we say that their demand is *more elastic.* By that, we mean that a small change in price causes a large change in the quantity demanded.

- When consumers are not very sensitive to price changes—that is, when they will buy approximately the same quantity, regardless of the price—we say that their demand is *more inelastic.*

Calculating price elasticity of demand

LO 4.1 Calculate price elasticity of demand using the mid-point method.

Consider the challenge Starbucks faced in shoring up falling sales during the recession. In this situation, a business might lower its prices by offering a sale. But would a sale work? How much could Starbucks's managers expect purchases to increase as a result of the sale? In other words, *How will customers respond* to a sale? The ability to answer this question is a critical tool for businesses. To do so, we need to know the price elasticity of demand for Starbucks coffee.

Let's say that Starbucks usually charges $2 for a cup of coffee. What might happen if it offers a special sale price of $1.50? Suppose that before the sale, Starbucks sold 10 million cups of coffee each day. Now, say that consumers react to the sale by increasing the quantity demanded to 15 million cups per day. Figure 4-1 shows the quantity demanded before and after the sale as two points on the demand curve for coffee. Based on the results of this sale, what can we say about consumers' sensitivity to the price of coffee at Starbucks?

Mathematically, price elasticity is the percentage change in the quantity of a good that is demanded in response to a given percentage change in price. The basic formula looks like Equation 4-1.

EQUATION 4-1 $$\text{Price elasticity of demand} = \frac{\%\text{ change in Q demanded}}{\%\text{ change in P}}$$

To calculate percentage change, we will be using the **mid-point method**. The mid-point method measures the percentage change relative to a point *midway between the two points.* The mid-point method can be used to calculate the percentage change in quantity demanded, for example

price elasticity of demand
the size of the change in the quantity demanded of a good or service when its price changes

mid-point method
method that measures percentage change in quantity demanded (or quantity supplied) relative to a point midway between two points on a curve; used to estimate elasticity

FIGURE 4-1

Elasticity of the demand for coffee

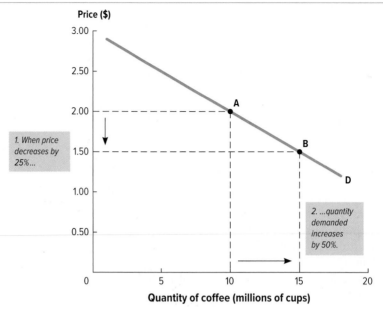

When the price of coffee is $2 a cup, consumers demand 10 million cups. If the price falls to $1.50 per cup, the quantity demanded increases to 15 million cups.

(the numerator in Equation 4-1). We do that by dividing the change in quantity demanded by the mid-point (average) quantity, as shown in Equation 4-2.

EQUATION 4-2

$$\% \text{ change in Q demanded} = \frac{Q_2 - Q_1}{\text{Average of Q}} = \frac{Q_2 - Q_1}{\left(\dfrac{Q_2 + Q_1}{2}\right)}$$

In the denominator of this expression, the mid-point (average) quantity is equal to the sum of the two quantities divided by 2.

We can find the percentage change in price (the denominator of Equation 4-1) in the same way, as shown in Equation 4-3.

EQUATION 4-3

$$\% \text{ change in P} = \frac{P_2 - P_1}{\text{Average of P}} = \frac{P_2 - P_1}{\left(\dfrac{P_2 + P_1}{2}\right)}$$

? POTENTIALLY CONFUSING

Another way of calculating *percentage change* is to divide the difference between the starting and ending levels by the starting level. Using this method, the percentage change in quantity demanded would be expressed as:

$$\% \text{ change in quantity demanded} = \left[\frac{(Q_2 - Q_1)}{Q_1}\right]$$

Notice that the denominator of this expression is simply the starting value of quantity demanded. While you may have used this method before, this method causes a measurement problem when we use it to calculate elasticity: The elasticity changes depending on which direction we move along the demand curve. To avoid this problem, we will be using the mid-point method for calculating percentage change in this chapter.

Putting Equation 4-2 and Equation 4-3 together, we get Equation 4-4, which is the mid-point method for calculating the price elasticity of demand. This is a fully fleshed-out version of Equation 4-1.

EQUATION 4-4 $$\text{Price elasticity of demand} = \frac{(Q_2 - Q_1)/[(Q_2 + Q_1)/2]}{(P_2 - P_1)/[(P_2 + P_1)/2]}$$

Looking at our example, we find that the demand for coffee went from 10 million cups at $2 to 15 million cups at $1.50. So the average (mid-point) quantity demanded was 12.5 million cups. The average (mid-point) price was $1.75. If we plug the original and sale quantities and prices into Equation 4-4, what do we find? The price was cut by 29 percent and the quantity demanded rose by 40 percent. That tells us that the price elasticity of demand is −1.38.

$$\text{Price elasticity of demand} = \frac{\left(\dfrac{15 \text{ million} - 10 \text{ million}}{12.5 \text{ million}}\right)}{\left(\dfrac{1.50 - 2.00}{1.75}\right)} = \frac{0.40}{-0.29} = -1.38$$

What does it mean for the price elasticity of demand to be −1.38? Remember that the elasticity describes the size of the change in the quantity demanded of a good when its price changes. A measure of −1.38 price elasticity of demand for cups of coffee means that a 1 percent decrease in the price of coffee will lead to a 1.38 percent increase in the quantity of coffee cups demanded. (Alternatively, we could also say that a 1 percent *increase* in the price of coffee will lead to a 1.38 percent *decrease* in the quantity of coffee cups demanded.)

The *price elasticity of demand will always be a negative number.* Why? Because price and quantity demanded *move in opposite directions:*

- A positive change in price will cause a negative change in the quantity demanded.
- A negative change in price will cause a positive change in the quantity demanded.

In our example, the price of coffee decreased and the quantity demanded increased.

However, be aware that economists often drop the negative sign and express the price elasticity of demand as a positive number, just for the sake of convenience. Don't be fooled! Under normal circumstances, price elasticity of demand is always negative, whether or not the negative sign is printed.

? POTENTIALLY CONFUSING

Some books include the negative sign, and others drop the negative sign. Another way to think of an elasticity measure is as an absolute value. The *absolute value* of a number is its distance from zero, or its numerical value without regard to its sign. For example, the absolute values of 4 and −4 are both 4. The absolute value of elasticity measures the "size" of the response, while the sign measures its direction. Sometimes only the absolute value will be printed, when it is assumed that you know the direction of the change.

You might be wondering why we work with percentages in calculating elasticity. Why not just compare the change in the quantity demanded to the change in price? The answer is that percentages allow us to avoid some practical problems. Think about what would happen if one person measured coffee in 12-ounce cups, while another measured it by the pot or the gallon. Without percentages, we would have several different measures of price elasticity, depending on which unit of measurement we used. To avoid this problem, economists use the *percentage change* in quantity rather than the *absolute change* in quantity. That way, the elasticity of demand for coffee is the same whether we measure the quantity in cups, pots, or gallons.

Determinants of price elasticity of demand

> **LO 4.2** Explain how the determinants of price elasticity of demand affect the degree of elasticity.

How would the quantity demanded of lattes (or your drink of choice) change if the price fell from $3 to $1.50? Now, how much would the quantity demanded of cotton socks change if the price fell from $10 per pack to $5? Although both represent a 50 percent price reduction, we suspect that the former might change your buying habits more than the latter. Socks are socks, and $5 savings probably won't make you rush out and buy twice as many. To state this more formally, we would say that the demand for lattes is more elastic than the demand for socks.

The underlying idea here is that consumers are more sensitive to price changes for some goods and services than for others. As said earlier, we can classify the degree of sensitivity to price changes by labeling the demand for a particular good as elastic or inelastic. More rigorous definitions of these terms will be given later, but for now remember this: When consumers are very responsive to price changes for a particular good, we say that the demand for that good is *more elastic.* When consumers are not very responsive to price changes for a particular good, we say the demand for that good is *more inelastic.*

Why isn't price elasticity of demand the same for all goods and services? Many factors determine consumers' responsiveness to price changes. The availability of substitutes, relative need and relative cost, and the time needed to adjust to price changes all affect price elasticity of demand.

Would you expect this price change to reduce the quantity demanded of lobsters? www.CartoonStock.com

"Great idea, Pete!"

Availability of substitutes

Recall from Chapter 3, "Markets," that substitutes are goods that are distinguishable from one another but have similar uses. When the price of a good with a close substitute increases, consumers will buy the substitute instead. If close substitutes are available for a particular good, then the demand for that good will be *more elastic* than if only distant substitutes are available. For example, the price elasticity of demand for cranberry juice is likely to be relatively elastic; if the price gets too high, many consumers may switch to grape juice.

Degree of necessity

When a good is a basic necessity, people will buy it even if its price rises. The demand for socks probably is not very elastic, nor is the demand for home heating during the winter. Although people may not like it when the prices of these goods rise, they will buy them to maintain a basic level of comfort. And when prices fall, they probably won't buy vastly more socks or make their homes a lot hotter.

In comparison, the demand for luxuries like vacations, expensive cars, and jewelry is likely to be much more elastic. Most people can easily do without these goods when their prices rise. Note, however, that the definition of a necessity depends on your standards and circumstances. In Florida, air conditioning may be a necessity and heating a luxury; the opposite is likely to be true in Alaska.

Cost relative to income

All else held equal, if consumers spend a very small share of their incomes on a good, their demand for the good will be less elastic than otherwise. For instance, most people can get a year's supply of ballpoint pens for just a few dollars. Even if the price doubled, a year's supply would still cost less than $10, so consumers probably would not bother to adjust their consumption of ballpoint pens.

The opposite is also true: If a good costs a very large proportion of a person's income, like going on a luxury three-week vacation to the beach, the demand for the good will be more elastic. If the price of rooms at high-end beachfront hotels doubles, then a lot of people will decide to do something else with their vacations.

Adjustment time

Goods often have much more elastic demand over the long run than over the short run. Often, adjusting to price changes takes some time. Consider how you might react to an increase in the price of gasoline. In the short run, you might cancel a weekend road trip, but you would still have to do the same amount of driving as usual to school, work, or the grocery store. Over a year, however, you could consider other choices that would further reduce your consumption of gas, such as buying a bus pass or a bicycle, getting a more fuel-efficient car, or moving closer to work or school.

Scope of the market

A major caveat to the determinants just described is that each depends on how you define the market for a good or service. The price elasticity of demand for bananas might be high, but the price elasticity of demand for *fruit* could still be low because there are more substitutes for bananas than for the broader category of fruit. Similarly, although water might have a very low price elasticity of demand as a basic necessity, the demand for *bottled* water could be extremely elastic.

Using price elasticity of demand

When we make decisions in the real world, we often don't know the exact price elasticity of demand. But we don't always need to estimate elasticity precisely to know that consumers will react differently to price changes for lattes than for socks. Instead, businesses and other decision makers often know something general about the shape of the demand curve they are facing. Being able to place goods into several broad categories of elasticity can facilitate real pricing decisions in situations without full information.

At the extremes, demand can be perfectly elastic or perfectly inelastic. When demand is **perfectly elastic**, the quantity demanded drops to zero when the price increases even a minuscule amount. Thus, a perfectly elastic demand curve is horizontal, as shown in panel A of Figure 4-2. This graph indicates that consumers are very sensitive to price. When demand is **perfectly inelastic**, the quantity demanded is the same no matter what the price. Thus, the demand curve is vertical, as shown in panel B of Figure 4-2. These two extremes rarely occur in real life.

perfectly elastic demand
demand for which any increase in price will cause quantity demanded to drop to zero; represented by a perfectly horizontal line

perfectly inelastic demand
demand for which quantity demanded remains the same regardless of price; represented by a perfectly vertical line

---

FIGURE 4-2

Perfectly elastic and perfectly inelastic demand

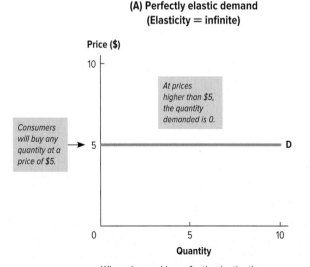

(A) Perfectly elastic demand
(Elasticity = infinite)

At prices higher than $5, the quantity demanded is 0.

Consumers will buy any quantity at a price of $5.

When demand is perfectly elastic, the demand curve is horizontal. At prices above $5, consumers will not buy any quantity of the good.

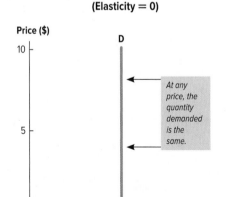

(B) Perfectly inelastic demand
(Elasticity = 0)

At any price, the quantity demanded is the same.

When demand is perfectly inelastic, the demand curve is vertical. Consumers will always demand the same quantity of a good, regardless of the price.

elastic
demand that has an absolute value of elasticity greater than 1

inelastic
demand that has an absolute value of elasticity less than 1

unit-elastic
demand that has an absolute value of elasticity exactly equal to 1

Between these two extremes, elasticity is commonly divided into three quantifiable categories: elastic, inelastic, and unit-elastic. When the absolute value of the price elasticity of demand is greater than 1, we call the associated quantity demanded **elastic**. With elastic demand, a given percentage change in the price of a good will cause an even larger percentage change in the quantity demanded. For example, Panel A of Figure 4-3 shows that for elastic demand, an 80 percent change in price could lead to a 150 percent change in the quantity demanded. Remember, we are using the mid-point method to calculate the percentage change here.

When the absolute value of the price elasticity of demand is less than 1, we say that demand is **inelastic**. With inelastic demand, a given percentage change in price will cause a smaller percentage change in the quantity demanded. Panel B of Figure 4-3 illustrates that for inelastic demand, an 80 percent change in price might lead to a 50 percent change in the quantity demanded.

If the absolute value of elasticity is exactly 1—that is, if a percentage change in price causes the same percentage change in the quantity demanded—then we say that demand is **unit-elastic**. Panel C of Figure 4-3 illustrates that for unit-elastic demand, an 80 percent change in price leads to an 80 percent change in the quantity demanded.

The concept of elasticity is not merely a theoretical tool. Businesses and policy decisions often depend on the value of particular elasticities. Table 4-1 displays actual estimates of price elasticities for a selection of goods. You can ask yourself why some price elasticities are larger than others. Why is the quantity demanded of air travel more elastic for leisure travel than business travel? Why is the quantity demanded of gasoline more elastic in the long run than the short run?

As we'll see later in this chapter, the terms *elastic, inelastic,* and *unit-elastic* can be used to describe any sort of elasticity, not just the price elasticity of demand. Although these categories may sound academic, they can have serious implications for real-world business and policy decisions. The Real Life box "Does charging for bednets decrease malaria?" describes a case in which knowing whether the price elasticity of demand is elastic or inelastic is a matter of life and death.

FIGURE 4-3

Elastic, inelastic, and unit-elastic demand

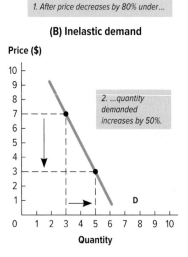
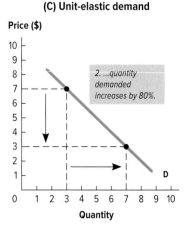

(A) Elastic demand

With an elastic demand curve, a small change in price leads to a big change in the quantity demanded. As a result, the price elasticity of demand is greater than 1.

(B) Inelastic demand

With an inelastic demand curve, even a large price change has a small effect on the quantity demanded. As a result, the price elasticity of demand is less than 1.

(C) Unit-elastic demand

When demand is unit-elastic, the percentage change in price equals the percentage change in quantity, so that the price elasticity of demand is exactly 1.

TABLE 4-1

Estimated price elasticities of demand

Good	Estimated elasticities
Oil in the short run	−0.02
Eggs	−0.27
Gasoline in the short run	−0.05 to −0.6
Water (residential)	−0.41
Alcoholic drinks	−0.44
Gasoline in the long run	−0.25 to −0.7
Electricity	−0.38 to −0.61
Soft drinks	−0.7 to −0.8
Heroin	−0.8
Business air travel	−0.8
Leisure air travel	−1.6
NFL ticket resales	−2.94

Sources: T. Andreyeva, M. W. Long, and K. D. Brownell, "The impact of food prices on consumption: A systematic review of research on the price elasticity of demand for food," *American Journal of Public Health* 100, no. 2 (2010), p. 216; T. Helbling et al., "Oil scarcity, growth, and global imbalances," in International Monetary Fund, *World Economic Outlook*, April 2011, ch. 3, https://www.imf.org/external/pubs/ft/weo/2011/01/pdf/c3.pdf; S. M. Olmstead and R. N. Stavins, "Comparing price and nonprice approaches to urban water conservation," *Water Resources Research* 45, no. 4 (2009); T. A. Olmstead, S. M. Alessi, B. Kline, R. L. Pacula, and N. M. Petry, "The price elasticity of demand for heroin: Matched longitudinal and experimental evidence," *Journal of Health Economics* 41 (2015), pp. 59–71; P. Belobaba, A. Odoni, and C. Barnhart, eds., *The Global Airline Industry* (New York: Wiley & Sons, 2015), p. 61; M. A. Diehl, J. G. Maxcy, and J. Drayer, "Price elasticity of demand in the secondary market: Evidence from the National Football League," *Journal of Sports Economics* 16, no. 6 (August 2015), pp. 557–75; A. J. Ros, "An econometric assessment of electricity demand in the United States using panel data and the impact of retail competition on prices," *Insight in Economics*, June 9, 2015, http://www.nera.com/content/dam/nera/publications/2015/PUB_Econometric_Assessment_Elec_Demand_US_0615.pdf; P. Krugman, "Prices and gasoline demand," *The New York Times*, May 9, 2008, http://krugman.blogs.nytimes.com/2008/05/09/prices-and-gasoline-demand/?_r=0; L. Levin, M. S. Lewis, and F. A. Wolak, "High frequency evidence on the demand for gasoline," April 12, 2013, http://web.stanford.edu/group/fwolak/cgi-bin/sites/default/files/files/Levin_Lewis_Wolak_demand.pdf.

Real Life

Does charging for bednets decrease malaria?

Around the world, malaria kills millions of young people every year. There is no vaccine to protect children from malaria. There is a way to escape the disease, though: sleep under a bednet that has been treated with insecticide. Bednets prevent malaria by shielding people from disease-carrying mosquitoes.

Organizations that want to promote the use of bednets to fight malaria face a practical question: Would charging a fee for bednets be more effective in reducing the illness than handing out the nets for free?

Those who advocate charging a fee argue that people who pay for the nets will value them more, and will probably use them more, than those who receive the nets for free. These advocates expect that fewer nets will be wasted on people who don't really want them and that people who do buy them will be more likely to use them. Moreover, if people pay for their bednets, organizations will be able to afford to distribute more of them. On the other hand, the law

(continued)

of demand states that the higher the price, the lower the quantity demanded. Even if charging a fee would make some people more likely to use the nets, it might dissuade others from getting them, thus undermining the aim of the anti-malaria campaign. In particular, it may lead the very poorest to not be able to have a bednet.

To settle this question, health organizations needed to know the price elasticity of the demand for bednets. Working in Kenya, economists Jessica Cohen of the Harvard School of Public Health and Pascaline Dupas of Stanford set up an experiment to try both methods and to measure the price elasticity of demand for bednets. As it turned out, charging a fee greatly reduced the quantity of the nets demanded. In the experiment, the number of people who took bednets dropped by 75 percent when the price increased from zero to $0.75. Furthermore, the people who bought bednets at that price did not use them more effectively than those who received them for free.

If profit were the goal in this campaign, a few bednets sold at $0.75 would generate more revenue than a lot of bednets given away for free. But the goal was to protect people from malaria, not to make a profit. For organizations with a social mission, free distribution of bednets seems more effective than charging a fee.

Source: J. Cohen and P. Dupas, "Free distribution or cost sharing? Evidence from a randomized malaria prevention experiment," *Quarterly Journal of Economics* 125, no. 1 (February 2010), pp. 1–45.

Knowing whether the demand for a good is elastic or inelastic is extremely useful in business. That information allows a manager to determine whether a price increase will cause total revenue to rise or fall. **Total revenue** is the amount that a firm receives from the sale of goods and services, calculated as the quantity sold multiplied by the price paid for each unit. This number is important for an obvious reason: It tells us how much money sellers receive when they sell something.

An increase in price affects total revenue in two ways:

total revenue
the amount that a firm receives from the sale of goods and services; calculated as the quantity sold multiplied by the price paid for each unit

- It causes a *quantity effect,* or a decrease in total revenue that results from selling fewer units of the good.

- It causes a *price effect,* or an increase in total revenue that results from receiving a higher price for each unit sold.

Figure 4-4 shows both the quantity effect and the price effect. When the quantity effect outweighs the price effect, a price increase will cause a drop in total revenue, as it does in Figure 4-4. When the price effect outweighs the quantity effect, a price increase will raise total revenue.

When demand is elastic, a price increase causes total revenue to fall. We already know that when demand is elastic, a change in price will cause a larger percentage change in quantity demanded. Another way of saying this is that the quantity effect outweighs the price effect. So when demand is elastic, a price increase causes a proportionally larger decrease in the quantity demanded, and total revenue falls.

Conversely, when demand is inelastic, the percentage change in price is larger than the percentage change in quantity demanded. The price effect outweighs the quantity effect, and total revenue increases. With inelastic demand, then, consumers will purchase less of a good when its price rises, but the change in the quantity demanded will be proportionally less than the change in price.

Figure 4-5 shows this trade-off between the price and quantity effects. As you can see, panel A shows an elastic demand in which a $1 change in price causes the quantity demanded to increase by 4,000. With the inelastic demand curve in panel B, a $2 decrease in price increases quantity demanded by only 1,000.

FIGURE 4-4

Effect of a price increase on total revenue

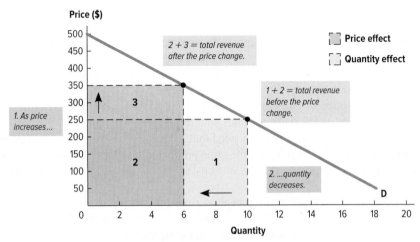

The colored rectangles represent total revenue at two different prices. As the price increases from $250 to $350, total revenue is affected in two ways. The blue rectangle represents the increase in revenue received for each unit sold (the price effect). The yellow rectangle represents the decrease in total revenue as the number of units sold drops (the quantity effect). The elasticity of demand determines which effect is larger. In this case, the yellow area is larger than the blue area, meaning that the quantity effect outweighs the price effect, and total revenue decreases.

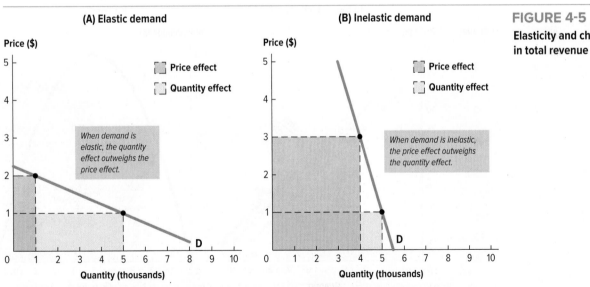

FIGURE 4-5

Elasticity and changes in total revenue

(A) Elastic demand

In this market, demand is elastic. At a price of $1, 5,000 units are sold for a total revenue of $5,000. If the price increases to $2, only 1,000 units are sold for a total revenue of only $2,000. The quantity effect outweighs the price effect.

(B) Inelastic demand

In this market, demand is inelastic. At a price of $1, 5,000 units are sold for a total revenue of $5,000. If the price increases to $3, the number of units sold drops by only 1,000, to 4,000 units. Because the price effect outweighs the quantity effect, total revenue climbs to $12,000, an increase of $7,000.

There is one final point to make. So far, everything we've said has described elasticity *at a particular spot on the demand curve.* For most goods, however, elasticity varies along the curve. So when we said that the price elasticity of demand for coffee was −1.38, we meant that it was −1.38 for a price change from $1.50 to $2 a cup. If the price changes from $2 to $2.50, the elasticity will be different.

The reasoning behind this fact is common sense. Imagine that the price of lattes plummets to 10 cents, and you get into the habit of buying one every morning. What would you do if you showed up one morning and found that the price had doubled overnight, to 20 cents? We bet you'd shrug and buy one anyway.

Now, imagine the price of lattes is $10, and you buy them only as occasional treats. If you arrive at the coffee shop and find the price has doubled to $20, what will you do? You'd probably consider very carefully whether you really need that latte. In both cases, you would be responding to a 100 percent increase in price for the same product, but you would react very differently. This makes perfect sense: In one case, the latte costs you only 10 more cents, but in the other, it costs an additional $10.

Your reactions to the latte illustrate a general rule: *Demand tends to be more elastic when price is high and more inelastic when price is low.* This brings us to an important caveat about the three graphs shown in Figure 4-3. Although the example of an elastic demand curve in panel A has a steeper *slope* than the inelastic demand curve in panel B, we now know that slope is not the same as elasticity.

In fact, the elasticity of demand is different at different points along a linear demand curve. The reasoning is nonintuitive, but straightforward when you think about it graphically. Look at Figure 4-6. The line in panel B has a constant slope, but the percentage changes in price and

FIGURE 4-6

Changes in elasticity along the demand curve

(A) Demand and revenue schedule

Price ($)	Quantity	Total revenue ($)
50	0	0
45	1	45
40	2	80
35	3	105
30	4	120
25	5	125
20	6	120
15	7	105
10	8	80
5	9	45
0	10	0

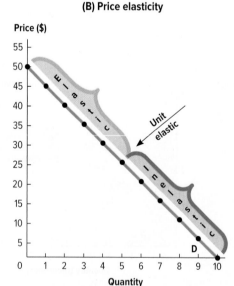

(B) Price elasticity

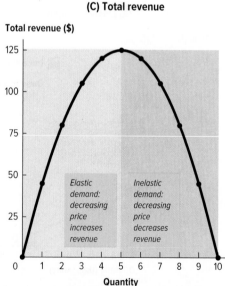

(C) Total revenue

This table lists the data shown in the graphs in panels A and B. Quantity demanded always increases as price falls. Total revenue rises until the price falls to $25, then falls at lower prices.

Price elasticity of demand varies along the demand curve. Above a certain price, demand is elastic; below it, demand is inelastic.

This graph shows total revenue along the demand curve shown above. Total revenue first rises, but then begins to fall as demand moves from elastic to inelastic.

quantity are very different at either end of the curve. For instance, going from $45 to $40 is a much smaller difference (in percentage terms) than from $10 to $5, but the slope of the curve is the same between both sets of points.

The result is that as we move along a linear demand curve starting from a price equal to zero, revenue first increases as the price increases, and then decreases with higher prices. (You can see this result in the "Total revenue" column in panel A.) The maximum revenue occurs where demand is unit-elastic.

Panel C of Figure 4-6 graphs out the total revenue curve associated with the demand curve in panel B, using calculations from the schedule in Panel A. Note that when the price is high, lowering the price will increase revenue. For example, when the price decreases from $45 to $40 (see the schedule), total revenue almost doubles, from $45 to $80. When the price is low, however, lowering it further decreases total revenue. Moving from $10 to $5, for example, decreases total revenue from $80 to $45.

Price elasticity of demand has all sorts of real-world applications. See, for example, the issue discussed in the What Do You Think? box "Should entrance fees at national parks be raised?"

> For a refresher on slope versus elasticity, see Appendix C, "Math Essentials: Calculating Percentage Change, Slope, and Elasticity," which follows this chapter.

What Do You Think?

Should entrance fees at national parks be raised?

The National Park Service is the steward of 84 million acres of America's most famous natural spaces, including Yellowstone, the Grand Canyon, and the Everglades. In 2008, the Park Service proposed higher fees at some parks. Writer John Krist argued in favor of the price increases:

> A day at Disneyland costs a family of four at least $232, not counting Mickey Mouse ears. At Six Flags Magic Mountain, the admission price would be at least $180. A seven-day pass to enter Yellowstone National Park costs $25 per car, which means that the same family spending a week among bison, elk, geysers and grizzlies would pay the equivalent of 89 cents per person, per day.
>
> Which is why it's perplexing to see such an outcry over news that the Park Service wants to raise entrance fees at 135 sites over the next two years. . . . Their principal arguments are economic: Tourism-dependent communities fret that higher fees will reduce visitation and cut into profits, while others argue that the increases will keep out those of limited financial means. It's true, in theory at least, that raising the price of something should decrease demand for it.* . . .
>
> On the other hand, it's absurd to expect a finite amount of parkland to accommodate a continually increasing number of people. Anyone who has driven into Yosemite Valley on a holiday weekend is unlikely to regard a drop in park visitation as entirely a bad thing.
>
> Slightly higher user fees are unlikely to have much effect on park use, but they could have a significant effect on the quality of the park experience. Most of that money will stay at individual parks, where it can be spent on upkeep and repairs—the sort of unglamorous expenditures that typically get shortchanged in the politically driven federal budget process. Smaller crowds and plumbing that works—what's not to like?

*You can tell that the author of this piece hadn't read this book. If he had, he would have been careful to say that raising the price decreases the *quantity demanded,* rather than saying it decreases *demand.*

WHAT DO YOU THINK?

1. Do you agree with Krist's argument that the demand for national park visits is inelastic at current price levels, so that higher fees are "unlikely to have much effect on park use"? Think about the factors that affect price elasticity, such as the availability and price of substitutes.

(continued)

2. How would you weigh the following trade-offs?

a. Should the Park Service intentionally try to shrink the demand for visits in order to reduce crowding? In order to protect parks from environmental damage?

b. Does the Park Service have a responsibility to keep national parks accessible to families who cannot afford to pay higher fees?

c. Should the Park Service be concerned about the economic impact of a reduced demand for visits on surrounding communities?

Source: John Krist, "So what if park fees go up?," *High Country News*, July 16, 2008.

✓ CONCEPT CHECK

☐ What is the formula for calculating the price elasticity of demand? **[LO 4.1]**

☐ Why should you use the mid-point method to calculate the price elasticity of demand? **[LO 4.1]**

☐ If demand is inelastic, will an increase in price lead to more, less, or the same amount of revenue **[LO 4.2]**

☐ If demand is elastic, will an increase in price lead to more, less, or the same amount of revenue? **[LO 4.2]**

☐ If demand is unit-elastic, will an increase in price lead to more, less, or the same amount of revenue? **[LO 4.2]**

Price Elasticity of Supply

What happens when an increase in coffee consumption drives up the price of coffee beans? *How will the coffee market respond* to the price change? We can predict, based on the law of supply, that coffee growers will respond to an increase in price by increasing their production. But by how much will they increase production? The concept of price elasticity of supply can help us answer that question.

price elasticity of supply
the size of the change in the quantity supplied of a good or service when its price changes

Price elasticity of supply is the size of the change in the quantity supplied of a good or service when its price changes. Price elasticity of supply measures producers' responsiveness to a change in price, just as price elasticity of demand measures consumers' responsiveness to a change in price.

Chapter 3, "Markets," showed that when prices rise, producers supply larger quantities of a good; when prices fall, they supply smaller quantities. Just as the price elasticity of demand for a good tells us how much the quantity demanded changes as we move along the demand curve, the price elasticity of supply tells us how much the quantity supplied changes as we move along the supply curve.

Calculating price elasticity of supply

LO 4.3 Calculate price elasticity of supply using the mid-point method.

Price elasticity of supply, shown in Equation 4-5, is measured in the same way as price elasticity of demand: as the percentage change in quantity divided by the percentage change in price.

EQUATION 4-5
$$\text{Price elasticity of supply} = \frac{\%\ \text{change in quantity supplied}}{\%\ \text{change in price}}$$

To ensure that elasticity will be the same whether you move up or down the supply curve, you should use the mid-point method, as in Equation 4-6.

EQUATION 4-6 $\text{Price elasticity of supply} = \dfrac{(Q_2 - Q_1)/[(Q_1 + Q_2)/2]}{(P_2 - P_1)/[(P_1 + P_2)/2]}$

Suppose that when the price of coffee beans goes from $1 to $1.20 per pound, production increases from 90 million pounds of coffee beans per year to 100 million pounds. Using the mid-point method, the percentage change in quantity supplied would be:

$$\% \text{ change in quantity supplied} = \frac{(100 \text{ million} - 90 \text{ million})}{95 \text{ million}} = 11\%$$

The percentage change in price would be:

$$\% \text{ change in price} = \frac{1.2 - 1}{1.1} = 18\%$$

So the price elasticity of supply at this point on the supply curve is:

$$\text{Price elasticity of supply} = \frac{11\%}{18\%} = 0.6$$

As with the price elasticity of demand, we can describe the price elasticity of supply using three categories:

- *Elastic,* if it has an absolute value greater than 1.
- *Inelastic,* if it has an absolute value less than 1.
- *Unit-elastic,* if it has an absolute value of exactly 1.

We can also describe the extreme cases: Supply is *perfectly elastic* if the quantity supplied could be anything at a given price, and is zero at any other price. At the other extreme, supply is *perfectly inelastic* if the quantity supplied is the same, regardless of the price.

Going back to our example, an elasticity of 0.6 tells us that the supply of coffee beans is relatively inelastic, at least in the short run. Does this result make sense? As it turns out, coffee takes a long time to grow. Coffee plants don't produce a full yield for four to six years after they are planted. Because coffee growers can't increase production quickly, it makes sense that the supply of coffee would be inelastic. (What if prices had fallen from $1.20 to $1, instead of rising from $1 to $1.20? Using the mid-point method, the elasticity would be the same.)

HINT

- Remember that the elasticity of *demand* is calculated by dividing a positive number by a negative number, or by dividing a negative number by a positive number, so the answer is always negative.
- The elasticity of *supply,* on the other hand, is calculated by dividing either a positive number by another positive number or a negative number by another negative number. In either case, the answer is always positive.

Remembering this rule can help you to check your arithmetic.

There is one important difference between the elasticities of supply and demand: The price elasticity of demand is always negative and the price elasticity of supply is always positive. The reason is simple: The quantity demanded always moves in the *opposite direction* from the price, but the quantity supplied moves in the *same direction* as the price.

Determinants of price elasticity of supply

LO 4.4 Explain how the determinants of price elasticity of supply affect the degree of elasticity.

Whether supply is elastic or inelastic depends on the supplier's ability to change the quantity produced in response to price changes. Three factors affect a supplier's ability to expand production: the availability of inputs, the flexibility of the production process, and the time needed to adjust to changes in price. Recall that this last factor—time—is also a determinant of the elasticity of demand. Just as consumers take time to change their habits, suppliers need time to ramp up production.

Availability of inputs

The production of some goods can be expanded easily, just by adding extra inputs. For example, a bakery can easily buy extra flour and yeast to produce more bread, probably at the same cost per loaf. Increasing the supply of other goods is more difficult, however, and sometimes is impossible. If the price of Picasso paintings goes up, there isn't much anyone can do to produce more of them.

In other words, the elasticity of supply depends on the elasticity of the supply of inputs. If producing more of a good will cost a lot more than the initial quantity did because the extra inputs will be harder to find or more costly, then the producer will be reluctant to increase the quantity supplied. Higher and higher prices will be needed to convince the producer to go to the extra expense.

Flexibility of the production process

The easiest way for producers to adjust the quantity supplied of a particular good is to draw production capacity away from other goods when its price rises, or to reassign capacity to other goods when its price falls. Farmers may find this sort of substitution relatively simple: When corn prices are high, they will plant more acres with corn; when corn prices are low, they will reassign acres to more profitable crops. Other producers have much less flexibility. If you own a company that manufactures specialized parts for Toyota, you might need to buy new machinery to begin making parts for Ford, let alone switch to another type of product entirely.

Adjustment time

As with demand, supply is more elastic over long periods than over short periods. That is, producers can make more adjustments in the long run than in the short run. In the short run, the number of hotel rooms at Disneyland is fixed; in the medium and long run, old rooms can be renovated and new hotels can be built. Production capacity can also increase or decrease over time as new firms start up or old ones shut down.

✓ CONCEPT CHECK

☐ How would you calculate the price elasticity of supply? **[LO 4.3]**

☐ What are the three determinants of the price elasticity of supply? **[LO 4.4]**

Other Elasticities

The demand for a good is sensitive to more than just the price of the good. Because people are clever, flexible, and always on the lookout for ways to make the most of opportunities, demand also responds to changing circumstances, such as the prices of other goods and the incomes consumers earn. Let's consider two other demand elasticities, the *cross-price elasticity of demand* and the *income elasticity of demand*.

Cross-price elasticity of demand

LO 4.5 Calculate cross-price elasticity of demand, and interpret the sign of the elasticity.

Earlier we noted that price elasticities are affected by the availability of alternative options. For example, we might expect a Starbucks latte to have relatively price-elastic demand because some people will shift to buying coffee from Dunkin' Donuts when the price of a Starbucks latte rises. Once again, recalling the four economists' questions we presented in Chapter 1, "Economics and Life," asking *How will others respond?* is the key to understanding the situation.

What happens if the price of Dunkin' Donuts regular coffee falls but the price of a Starbucks latte stays the same? **Cross-price elasticity of demand** describes how much demand changes when the price of a *different* good changes. For example, because lattes and regular coffee are substitutes, we expect the demand for lattes to decrease when the price of regular coffee falls (as some people switch from lattes to coffee). The reverse also holds: If the price of a cup of Dunkin' Donuts coffee rises, while the price of a Starbucks latte remains the same, we expect the demand for lattes to increase (as some people switch from coffee to the relatively cheaper latte). Equation 4-7 gives the formula for the cross-price elasticity of demand.

cross-price elasticity of demand a measure of how the demand for one good changes when the price of a different good changes

EQUATION 4-7

$$\text{Cross-price elasticity of demand between A and B} = \frac{\%\ \text{change in quantity of A demanded}}{\%\ \text{change in price of B}}$$

Remember that nonprice determinants (like income or tastes) will shift a demand curve. In the case of cross-price elasticity, the price of a substitute or a complement is a nonprice determinant. Thus, the entire demand curve shifts. However, we still measure this change in demand by observing the change in the quantity demanded. But in this case, the initial quantity demanded is on one demand curve and the final quantity demanded is on another demand curve.

When two goods are substitutes, we expect their cross-price elasticity of demand to be positive. That is, an increase in the price of one will cause an increase in the quantity demanded of the other. On the other hand, a decrease in the price of one good will cause a decrease in the quantity demanded of the other. Just how elastic the demand is depends on how close the two substitutes are: If they are very close substitutes, a change in the price of one will cause a large change in the quantity demanded of the other, so that cross-price elasticity will be high. If they are not close substitutes, cross-price elasticity will be low.

Cross-price elasticity can also be negative. We saw that the price elasticity of demand is always negative and can be expressed as an absolute value. In contrast, cross-price elasticity can be positive or negative. Its sign tells us about the relationship between two goods:

- When two goods are substitutes, their cross-price elasticity will be positive.
- When two goods are complements (that is, when they are consumed together), cross-price elasticity will be negative.

For example, when people drink more coffee, they want more cream to go with it. Coffee and cream are complements, not substitutes. So when the demand for coffee increases, the demand for cream will increase, all else held equal. When two goods are linked in this way, their cross-price elasticity will be negative: an increase in the price of one good will decrease the quantity demanded of both goods. Again, the relative size of the elasticity tells us how strongly the two goods are linked. If the two goods are strong complements, their cross-price elasticity will be a large negative number. If the two goods are loosely linked, their cross-price elasticity will be negative but not far below zero.

Income elasticity of demand

LO 4.6 Calculate income elasticity of demand, and interpret the sign of the elasticity.

People buy some goods in roughly the same amounts, no matter how wealthy they are. Salt, toothpaste, and toilet paper are three examples. These are not the sort of products people rush out to buy when they get a raise at work. Other goods, though, are very sensitive to changes in income. If you got a raise, you might splurge on new clothes or a meal at a fancy restaurant.

income elasticity of demand

a measure of how much the demand for a good changes in response to a change in consumers' incomes

The **income elasticity of demand** for a good describes how much demand changes in response to a change in consumers' incomes. Similar to cross-price elasticity, a change in income causes the demand curve to shift. We measure this change in demand by observing the change in the quantity demanded. As Equation 4-8 shows, the income elasticity of demand is expressed as the ratio of the percentage change in the quantity demanded to the percentage change in income:

EQUATION 4-8 $$\text{Income elasticity of demand} = \frac{\%\ \text{change in quantity demanded}}{\%\ \text{change in income}}$$

Recall from Chapter 3, "Markets," that increases in income raise the demand for normal goods and lower the demand for inferior goods. Income elasticity tells us how much the demand for these goods changes.

For example, a Starbucks Frappuccino® is a normal good that might be fairly responsive to changes in income. When people become wealthier, they will buy more of a small luxury item like this. Therefore, we would guess that the income elasticity of demand for fancy iced coffee drinks is positive (because the drink is a normal good) and relatively large (because the drink is a nonnecessity that has many cheaper substitutes).

Regular coffee is also generally a normal good, so its income elasticity should be positive. However, we might guess that it will be less elastic than a Frappuccino's. Many people consider their standard cup of coffee every day before work to be more of a necessity than a luxury and will buy it regardless of their incomes. Another way to put it is that the demand for Frappuccinos is income-elastic, while the demand for plain coffee is relatively income-inelastic.

For normal goods like these, income elasticity is positive because as incomes rise, demand increases. This then leads to an increase in quantity demanded. Both necessities and luxuries are normal goods, and although their income elasticities are positive, their sizes vary:

- If the good is a necessity, income elasticity of demand will be positive and less than 1.
- If the good is a luxury, income elasticity will be positive and greater than 1.

As with the cross-price elasticity of demand, the income elasticity of demand can be negative as well as positive. The income elasticity of demand is negative for inferior goods because quantity demanded decreases as incomes increase.

In 2009 Starbucks introduced a new retail product, VIA® Ready instant coffee. Although some coffee enthusiasts sneered, others thought it was a shrewd move at a time of economic hardship. Instant coffee mix may be an inferior good in some places: As incomes increase, people will drink more expensive beverages and *decrease* their consumption of instant coffee. During a recession, however, budgets tighten and people may increase their consumption of instant coffee as they cut back on more expensive drinks. At least, that is what Starbucks was hoping. In this scenario, the income elasticity of instant coffee would be small and negative. A less-appealing inferior good that people quickly abandon as they grow richer would have a large, negative income elasticity.

Once again, the sign and size of a good's elasticity tell us a lot about the good. Table 4-2 summarizes what we have learned about the four types of elasticity.

If you find this discussion particularly interesting, you might want to consider work as a pricing analyst. You can read more about this in the Where Can It Take You? box "Pricing analyst."

TABLE 4-2

Four measures of elasticity

Measure	Equation	Negative	Positive	More elastic	Less elastic
Price elasticity of demand	$\dfrac{\text{\% change in quantity demanded}}{\text{\% change in price}}$	Always	Never	Over time, for substitutable goods and luxury items	In the short run, for unique and necessary items
Price elasticity of supply	$\dfrac{\text{\% change in quantity supplied}}{\text{\% change in price}}$	Never	Always	Over time, with flexible production	In the short run, with production constraints
Cross-price elasticity	$\dfrac{\text{\% change in quantity demanded of A}}{\text{\% change in price of B}}$	For complements	For substitutes	For near-perfect substitutes and strong complements	For loosely related goods
Income elasticity	$\dfrac{\text{\% change in quantity demanded}}{\text{\% change in income}}$	For inferior goods	For normal goods	For luxury items with close substitutes	For unique and necessary items

Where Can it Take You?
Pricing analyst

A major task in most industries is to keep an eye on competitors' prices and respond accordingly. Large businesses hire *pricing analysts* to perform this critical function. Pricing analysts use their knowledge of elasticity and markets to help businesses determine the right price to charge for their products.

Some businesses have especially complicated pricing problems. Think about airlines, which charge different prices for every flight on every route, every day. Moreover, airlines frequently charge different prices for economy, business-class, and first-class tickets. How will air travelers respond to a change in ticket prices? What will happen if the price of a ticket to New York goes up, while tickets to Las Vegas go on sale? How will customers respond to a change in competitors' ticket prices? How will they respond to a booming economy or a recession?

The answers to these questions may differ for every type of ticket. To respond to changing market conditions in the airline industry, pricing analysts need to understand all types of elasticity.

✓CONCEPT CHECK

- ☐ Why is the cross-price elasticity of demand positive for substitutes? **[LO 4.5]**
- ☐ Why does the income-elasticity of demand depend on whether a good is normal or inferior? **[LO 4.6]**

Conclusion

Supply and *demand* may be the most common words in economics, but applying these concepts to the real world requires a bit of elaboration. Elasticity is the first of several concepts we will study that will help you to apply the concepts of supply and demand to business and policy questions. In this chapter we saw how elasticity can be used to predict how price changes will influence revenue. In the coming chapters we will use elasticity to predict the effects of government intervention in the market, and we will dig deeper into the consumer and producer choices that drive elasticity.

Key Terms

Summary

LO 4.1 Calculate price elasticity of demand using the mid-point method.

Elasticity is a measure of consumers' and producers' responsiveness to a change in market conditions. Understanding the elasticity for a good or service allows economic decision makers to anticipate the outcome of changes in market conditions and to calibrate prices so as to maximize revenues.

Price elasticity of demand is the size of the change in the quantity demanded of a good or service when its price changes. Elasticity should be calculated as a percentage using the mid-point method to avoid problems with conflicting units of measurement and with the direction of a change.

Price elasticity of demand is almost always negative because the quantity demanded falls as the price rises. It is usually represented as an absolute value, without the negative sign.

LO 4.2 Explain how the determinants of price elasticity of demand affect the degree of elasticity.

In general, demand is inelastic for goods that have no close substitutes, are basic necessities, or cost a relatively small proportion of consumers' income. Demand is also inelastic over short periods and for broadly defined markets.

When demand is elastic, a percentage change in the price of a good will cause a larger percentage change in the quantity demanded; the absolute value of the elasticity will be greater than 1. When demand is inelastic, a percentage change in price will cause a smaller percentage change in the quantity demanded; the absolute value of the elasticity will be less than 1. When demand is unit-elastic, the percentage changes in price and quantity will be equal, and the elasticity will be exactly 1.

LO 4.3 Calculate price elasticity of supply using the mid-point method.

Price elasticity of supply is the size of the change in the quantity supplied of a good or service when its price changes. Price elasticity of supply is almost always positive because the quantity supplied increases as the price increases.

LO 4.4 Explain how the determinants of price elasticity of supply affect the degree of elasticity.

Supply is generally inelastic when additional inputs to the production process are difficult to get and the production process is inflexible. Supply is also inelastic over short periods.

Supply is considered elastic when the absolute value of its price elasticity is greater than 1, inelastic when the absolute value is less than 1, and unit-elastic when it is exactly 1.

LO 4.5 Calculate cross-price elasticity of demand, and interpret the sign of the elasticity.

Cross-price elasticity of demand is the percentage change in the quantity demanded in response to a given percentage change in the price of a *different* good. The cross-price elasticity of demand between two goods will be positive if they are substitutes and negative if they are complements.

LO 4.6 Calculate income elasticity of demand, and interpret the sign of the elasticity.

Income elasticity of demand is the percentage change in the quantity of a good demanded in response to a given percentage change in income. Income elasticity of demand will be positive for normal goods and negative for inferior goods.

Review Questions

1. You are advising a coffee shop manager who wants to estimate how much sales will change if the price of a latte rises. You tell him that he should measure the change in sales using the percentage change in quantity of coffee sold rather than the number of cups of coffee or the total ounces of coffee sold. Similarly, you tell him that he should measure the price increase in percentage terms rather than in terms of absolute dollars. Explain why he should measure elasticity in percentage terms rather than in terms of dollars and cups. **[LO 4.1]**

2. Explain why the coffee shop manager should calculate elasticity using the mid-point method. **[LO 4.1]**

3. You are working as a private math tutor to raise money for a trip during spring break. First explain why the price elasticity of demand for math tutoring might be elastic. Then explain why the price elasticity of demand for math tutoring might be inelastic. **[LO 4.2]**

4. You are working as a private math tutor to raise money for a trip during spring break. You want to earn as much money as possible, and you think the demand for math tutors is currently inelastic. Should you increase or decrease the price you charge? Explain. **[LO 4.2]**

5. You have been hired by the government of Kenya, which produces a lot of coffee, to examine the supply of gourmet coffee beans. Suppose you discover that the price elasticity of supply is 0.85. Explain this number to the Kenyan government. **[LO 4.3]**

6. You have noticed that the price of tickets to your university's basketball games keeps increasing, but the supply of tickets remains the same. Why might supply be unresponsive to changes in price? **[LO 4.3]**

7. Which will have a more price-elastic supply over six months: real estate in downtown Manhattan or real estate in rural Oklahoma? Explain your reasoning. **[LO 4.4]**

8. Certain skilled labor, such as hair cutting, requires licensing or certification, which is costly and takes a long time to acquire. Explain what would happen to the price elasticity of supply for haircuts if this licensing requirement were removed. **[LO 4.4]**

9. Although we could describe both the cross-price elasticity of demand between paper coffee cups and plastic coffee lids and the cross-price elasticity of demand between sugar and artificial sweeteners as highly elastic, the first cross-price elasticity is negative and the second is positive. What is the reason for this? **[LO 4.5]**

10. Name two related goods you consume that would have a positive cross-price elasticity. What happens to your consumption of the second good if the price of the first good increases? **[LO 4.5]**

11. Name two related goods you consume that would have a negative cross-price elasticity. What happens to your consumption of the second good if the price of the first good increases? **[LO 4.5]**

12. In France, where cheese is an important and traditional part of people's meals, people eat about six times as much cheese per person as in the United States. In which country do you think the demand for cheese will be more income-elastic? Why? **[LO 4.6]**

13. Name a good you consume for which your income elasticity of demand is positive. What happens when your income increases? **[LO 4.6]**

14. Name a good you consume for which your income elasticity of demand is negative. What happens when your income increases? **[LO 4.6]**

Problems and Applications

1. When the price of a bar of chocolate is $1, the quantity demanded is 100,000 bars. When the price rises to $1.50, the quantity demanded falls to 60,000 bars. Calculate the price elasticity of demand using the mid-point method. **[LO 4.1]**

   a. Suppose the price increases from $1 to $1.50. Calculate the price elasticity of demand.

   b. Suppose the price decreases from $1.50 to $1. Calculate the price elasticity of demand.

2. If the price elasticity of demand for used cars priced between $3,000 and $5,000 is −1.2 (using the mid-point method), what will be the percent change in quantity demanded when the price of a used car falls from $5,000 to $3,000? **[LO 4.1]**

3. Three points are identified on the graph in Figure 4P-1. **[LO 4.2]**

   a. At point A, is demand inelastic, elastic, or unit-elastic?

FIGURE 4P-1

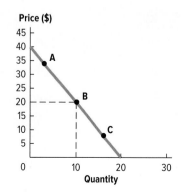

b. At point B, is demand inelastic, elastic, or unit-elastic?

c. At point C, is demand inelastic, elastic, or unit-elastic?

4. Which of the following has a more elastic demand in the short run? **[LO 4.2]**

   a. Pomegranate juice or drinking water?

   b. Cereal or Rice Krispies®?

   c. Speedboats or gourmet chocolate?

5. In each of the following instances, determine whether demand is elastic, inelastic, or unit-elastic. **[LO 4.2]**

   a. If price increases by 10 percent and quantity demanded decreases by 15 percent, demand is _____.

   b. If price decreases by 10 percent and quantity demanded increases by 5 percent, demand is _____.

6. In each of the following instances, determine whether quantity demanded will increase or decrease, and by how much. **[LO 4.2]**

   a. If price elasticity of demand is −1.3 and price increases by 2 percent, quantity demanded will _____ by _____ percent.

   b. If price elasticity of demand is −0.3 percent and price decreases by 2 percent, quantity demanded will _____ by _____ percent.

Problems 7 and 8 refer to the demand schedule shown in Table 4P-1. For each price change, say whether demand

is elastic, unit-elastic, or inelastic, and say whether total revenue increases, decreases, or stays the same.

7. Consider each of the following price increase scenarios. **[LO 4.2]**

   a. Price increases from $10 to $20. Demand is _____ and total revenue _____.

   b. Price increases from $30 to $40. Demand is _____ and total revenue _____.

   c. Price increases from $50 to $60. Demand is _____ and total revenue _____.

8. Price decreases from $70 to $60. Demand is _____ and total revenue _____. **[LO 4.2]**

Problems 9–12 refer to Figure 4P-2.

9. Draw the price effect and the quantity effect for a price change from $60 to $50. Which effect is larger? Does total revenue increase or decrease? No calculation is necessary. **[LO 4.2]**

10. Draw the price effect and the quantity effect for a price change from $30 to $20. Which effect is larger? Does total revenue increase or decrease? No calculation is necessary. **[LO 4.2]**

11. Draw the price effect and the quantity effect for a price change from $60 to $70. Which effect is larger? Does total revenue increase or decrease? No calculation is necessary. **[LO 4.2]**

12. Draw the price effect and the quantity effect for a price change from $10 to $20. Which effect is larger? Does total revenue increase or decrease? No calculation is necessary. **[LO 4.2]**

TABLE 4P-1

Price ($)	Quantity demanded
80	0
70	50
60	100
50	150
40	200
30	250
20	300
10	350
0	400

FIGURE 4P-2

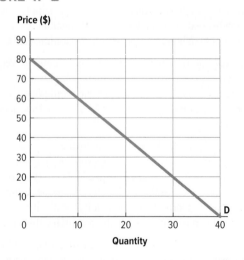

FIGURE 4P-3

13. Use the graph in Figure 4P-3 to calculate the price elasticity of supply between points A and B using the midpoint method. **[LO 4.3]**

14. If the price of a haircut is $15, the number of haircuts provided is 100. If the price rises to $30 per haircut, barbers will work much longer hours, and the supply of haircuts will increase to 300. What is the price elasticity of supply for haircuts between $15 and $30? **[LO 4.3]**

15. Which of the following has a more elastic supply in the short run? **[LO 4.4]**

    a. Hospitals or mobile clinics?

    b. Purebred dogs or mixed-breed dogs?

    c. On-campus courses or online courses?

16. In each of the following instances, determine whether supply is elastic, inelastic, or unit-elastic. **[LO 4.4]**

    a. If price increases by 10 percent and quantity supplied increases by 15 percent, supply is _____.

    b. If price decreases by 10 percent and quantity supplied decreases by 5 percent, supply is _____.

17. In each of the following instances, determine whether quantity supplied will increase or decrease, and by how much. **[LO 4.4]**

    a. If price elasticity of supply is 1.3 and price increases by 2 percent, quantity supplied will _____ by _____ percent.

    b. If price elasticity of supply is 0.3 and price decreases by 2 percent, quantity supplied will _____ by _____ percent.

18. Suppose that the price of peanut butter rises from $2 to $3 per jar. **[LO 4.5]**

    a. The quantity of jelly purchased falls from 20 million jars to 15 million jars. What is the cross-price elasticity of demand between peanut butter and jelly? Are they complements or substitutes?

    b. The quantity of jelly purchased increases from 15 million jars to 20 million jars. What is the cross-price elasticity of demand between peanut butter and jelly? Are they complements or substitutes?

19. For each of the following pairs, predict whether the cross-price elasticity of demand will be positive or negative: **[LO 4.5]**

    a. Soap and hand sanitizer.

    b. CDs and MP3s.

    c. Sheets and pillowcases.

20. Suppose that when the average family income rises from $30,000 per year to $40,000 per year, the average family's purchases of toilet paper rise from 100 rolls to 105 rolls per year. **[LO 4.6]**

    a. Calculate the income-elasticity of demand for toilet paper.

    b. Is toilet paper a normal or an inferior good?

    c. Is the demand for toilet paper income-elastic or income-inelastic?

21. In each of the following instances, determine whether the good is normal or inferior, and whether it is income-elastic or income-inelastic. **[LO 4.6]**

    a. If income increases by 10 percent and the quantity demanded of a good then increases by 5 percent, the good is _____ and _____.

    b. If income increases by 10 percent and the quantity demanded of a good decreases by 20 percent, the good is _____ and _____.

Math Essentials: Calculating Percentage Change, Slope, and Elasticity

Learning Objectives

LO C.1   Understand how to calculate percentage changes.

LO C.2   Use slope to calculate elasticity.

The math associated with the concept of elasticity covers a wide variety of topics. In order to be able to calculate elasticity, you need to be able to calculate percentage changes. In order to talk about shape of a line, and its elasticity, you need to be able to understand slope and the relationship between variables, particularly price and quantity.

Percentage Change

LO C.1 Understand how to calculate percentage changes.

In Chapter 4, "Elasticity," we calculated elasticity in all its forms. If you're not entirely comfortable calculating percentage change, though, elasticity can be a daunting idea. Percentage changes represent the relative change in a variable from an old value to a new one. In the chapter, and in this appendix, we use the mid-point method to calculate percentage change. The mid-point method measures the percentage change relative to a point *midway between the two points*.

Equation C-1 shows how to calculate percentage change using the mid-point method. There, X_1 represents the original value of any variable X, and X_2 is the new value of this variable.

EQUATION C-1
$$\text{Percentage change} = \left[\frac{(X_2 - X_1)}{\left(\frac{X_2 + X_1}{2} \right)} \right] \times 100$$

Notice that the denominator is the *mid-point* between X_1 and X_2. In other words, it is the average of X_1 and X_2. Overall, you can use this method to calculate the percentage change in variables of various kinds. A percentage change in quantity, for example, would be expressed as:

EQUATION C-1A $$\text{Percentage change in quantity} = \left[\frac{(Q_2 - Q_1)}{\left(\dfrac{Q_2 + Q_1}{2}\right)} \right] \times 100$$

where Q_2 represents the new value of quantity demanded and Q_1 the original quantity demanded. Similarly, a percentage change in price would be expressed as:

EQUATION C-1B $$\text{Percentage change in price} = \left[\frac{(P_2 - P_1)}{\left(\dfrac{P_2 + P_1}{2}\right)} \right] \times 100$$

Let's try an example for practice: For weeks, you have been watching the price of a new pair of shoes. They normally cost \$90, but you see that the store has a sale and now offers them for \$70. You find the percentage change in the price of the shoes by first subtracting the old price (\$90) from the new one (\$70) to find the change in price, which is −\$20. To find how much of a change this is, you take this −\$20 price change and divide it by the price midway between \$70 and \$90 (\$80).

$$\frac{\$70 - \$90}{\left(\dfrac{\$70 + \$90}{2}\right)} = \frac{-\$20}{\$80} = -0.25$$

You then multiply by 100 to get the percentage change: –0.25 × 100 = –25%. In this case, the \$20 price reduction was a 25 percent decrease in price. Not a bad sale!

Notice that in this case, the percentage change is negative, which indicates that the new value is less than the original. If the prices of shoes had increased instead, the associated percentage change would be a positive value.

The best way to do get comfortable with calculating percentage changes is through lots of practice. You can find a few extra problems to try on your own at the end of this appendix, and you also could challenge yourself to calculate price changes you see in your everyday life.

Slope and Elasticity

LO C.2 Use slope to calculate elasticity.

In Appendix A, "Math Essentials: Understanding Graphs and Slope," we showed that the direction of a slope tells us something meaningful about the relationship between the two variables we are representing:

- When *x* and *y* move in the *same direction,* they are said to have a *positive* relationship. Not surprisingly, this means that the slope of the line is a positive number. When the slope of a line is positive, we know that *y* increases as *x* increases, and *y* decreases as *x* decreases.
- Similarly, when *x* and *y* move in *opposite directions,* they are said to have a *negative* relationship. The slope of the line is a negative number. When the slope of a line is negative, we know that *y* decreases as *x* increases, and *y* increases as *x* decreases.

In Chapter 3, "Markets," we saw a positive relationship between price and quantity in the supply curve. We saw a negative relationship between price and quantity in the demand curve. Two variables (such as price and quantity) may have more than one relationship to each other, depending on whose choices they represent and under what circumstances.

The steepness of a slope is also important. Numerically, the closer the number representing the slope is to zero, the flatter the curve will be. Remember that both positive and negative numbers can be close to zero. So, a slope of −1 is equally steep as a slope of 1, although one slopes downward and the other upward. Correspondingly, a line with a slope of −5 is steeper than a line with a slope of −1 or one with a slope of 1.

You can tell just from looking at an equation how steep the line will be. If this idea is still a little hazy, you might want to page back to Appendix A, in the "Steepness of a slope" section, to refresh your memory. The steepness of slope is important to understanding the concept of elasticity.

Although the ideas of slope and elasticity are related, there are two basic mathematical distinctions between them:

1. Slope describes the change in y per the change in x, whereas elasticity measures are based on the change in x per the change in y.
2. We usually measure elasticity in terms of *percentage changes,* rather than absolute (unit-based) changes.

Why would we be interested in how much x changes in response to a one-unit change in y? To get at this difference, let's look at Figure C-1. It is similar to Figure A-10 (in Appendix A) but replaces the variables x and y with the quantity of a good (Q) and its price (P).

In Chapter 4, "Elasticity," you learned that *price elasticity* is a measure of the responsiveness of supply (or demand) to changes in price. In other words, it is a measure of how quantity (on the x-axis) responds to a change in price (on the y-axis). So this time, let's make the change in price (vertical distance) the same and look at how much quantity changes (horizontal distance).

Looking at Figure C-1, we can see that when price moves from P_1 to P_2, quantity supplied changes by less in panel A than it does in panel B. When price increases from P_1 to P_2 in panel A, quantity increases by 1 unit, from Q_1 to Q_2. In contrast, panel B shows an increase of 2 units from Q_1 to Q_2 for the same change in P. This means supply is less responsive to a price change in panel A compared to panel B.

FIGURE C-1

Measuring a change in Q in response to a change in P

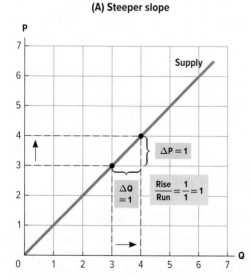

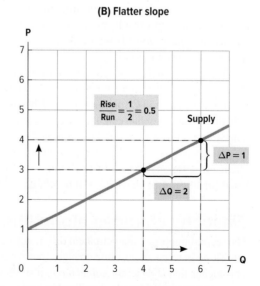

The steeper slope in panel A indicates that price changes less in panel A than in panel B in response to a change in quantity demanded.

The flatter slope in panel B indicates that price changes more in panel B than in panel A in response to a change in quantity demanded.

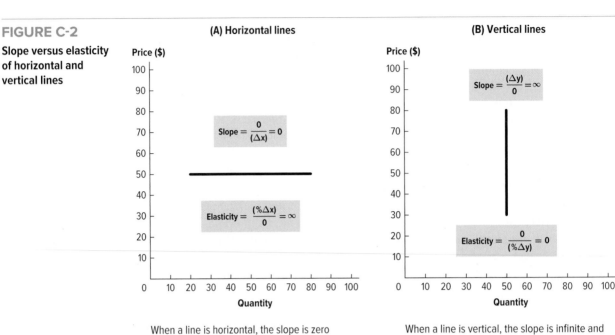

FIGURE C-2

Slope versus elasticity of horizontal and vertical lines

(A) Horizontal lines

$$\text{Slope} = \frac{0}{(\Delta x)} = 0$$

$$\text{Elasticity} = \frac{(\%\Delta x)}{0} = \infty$$

When a line is horizontal, the slope is zero and the associated elasticity is infinite. In other words, demand or supply only occurs at a single price.

(B) Vertical lines

$$\text{Slope} = \frac{(\Delta y)}{0} = \infty$$

$$\text{Elasticity} = \frac{0}{(\%\Delta y)} = 0$$

When a line is vertical, the slope is infinite and the elasticity is zero. Regardless of the price, quantity supplied or demanded is going to be the same.

X over Y, or Y over X?

We have noted that slope is indicated by $\frac{\Delta y}{\Delta x}$. In contrast, elasticity is commonly indicated by $\frac{\%\Delta Q}{\%\Delta P}$, which corresponds to $\frac{\Delta x}{\Delta y}$. In some sense, then, *elasticity is computed as the mirror image of slope.* The easiest way to picture this is to see the difference between slope and elasticity for vertical and horizontal lines.

In Figure C-2, the horizontal line pictured in panel A has a slope of zero. This is because a one-unit change in *x* results in zero change in *y*. Therefore, slope is calculated as $\frac{0}{\Delta x}$. Zero divided by any number is zero. If we think of the horizontal line as a demand curve mapping price to quantity demanded, however, the price elasticity is infinity.

How can slope be zero and elasticity infinity? Remember that slope measures how much *y* changes in response to a change in *x*. Elasticity, however, measures the sensitivity of P (on the *y*-axis) to a change in Q (on the *x*-axis). Whereas *x* is in the denominator when calculating slope, it is in the numerator when calculating elasticity. For a horizontal line, then, elasticity will be %ΔQ/0 since there is no change in P. Division by 0 is mathematically undefined, or known as infinity.

The reverse is true when we look at a vertical line. When a graph is vertical, there is zero change in *x* for any change in *y*. Therefore, slope is calculated as $\frac{\Delta y}{0}$. In this case, slope is undefined (infinity). But elasticity will be 0/%ΔP. Again, zero divided by any number is zero.

Elasticity changes along lines with constant slope

The second important mathematical difference between slope and elasticity is that we usually measure slope in terms of absolute changes, but we measure elasticity in terms of percentage changes. This means that at different points along a straight line, slope is constant, but elasticity varies.

As an example, take a look at the demand schedule in Table C-1. First, let's calculate the slope between two different sets of points. Using the first two prices and quantities at the top of the demand schedule, we see that the slope between these points is −1.

Price ($)	Quantity
80	0
70	10
60	20
50	30
40	40
30	50
20	60
10	70
0	80

TABLE C-1

Demand schedule

$$\text{Slope } \#1 = \frac{\Delta P_1}{\Delta Q_1} = \frac{(0-10)}{(80-70)} = \frac{-10}{10} = -1$$

Then, pick another two points. Using the quantities 30 and 20 and their respective prices, we can calculate that the slope is still −1.

$$\text{Slope } \#2 = \frac{\Delta P_2}{\Delta Q_2} = \frac{(30-20)}{(50-60)} = \frac{10}{-10} = -1$$

No matter what two points along the demand curve we choose, the slope is the same. *Slope is constant because the demand curve is linear.*

Now let's calculate elasticity between these same two sets of points. We will use the mid-point method described in Chapter 4, "Elasticity," to calculate elasticity:

$$\text{Elasticity} = \frac{\%\Delta Q}{\%\Delta P} = \frac{\Delta Q/Q_{\text{midpoint}}}{\Delta P/P_{\text{midpoint}}}$$

Let's start with the top of the demand curve and calculate the price elasticity of demand for a price change from 80 to 70. Using the mid-point method, we have:

$$\frac{\Delta Q/Q_{\text{midpoint}}}{\Delta P/P_{\text{midpoint}}} = \frac{(0-10)/5}{(80-70)/60} = \frac{-10/5}{10/60} = \frac{-2}{0.17} = -11.8$$

Now let's calculate the price elasticity of demand at the bottom of the demand curve for a price change of 30 to 20.

$$\frac{\Delta Q/Q_{\text{midpoint}}}{\Delta P/P_{\text{midpoint}}} = \frac{(50-60)/55}{(30-20)/25} = \frac{-10/55}{10/25} = \frac{-0.18}{0.4} = -0.45$$

Even though both of these calculations represented a 10-unit change in quantity in response to a $10 change in price, along a linear demand curve, elasticity changes. Moving down along the demand curve means less elasticity. This is because the same change in Q or P is a different *percentage* of the midpoint at different points on the line.

Problems and Applications

1. Calculate the percentage change in each of the following examples using the mid-point method. **[LO C.1]**
   a. 8 to 12.
   b. 18 to 14.
   c. 130 to 120.
   d. 95 to 105.

2. Find the percentage change in price in each of the following examples using the mid-point method. **[LO C.1]**
   a. The price of a $4.50 sandwich increases to $5.50.
   b. A sale discounts the price of a sofa from $750 to $500.

3. Use the demand curve in Figure CP-1 to answer the following questions. Use the mid-point method in your calculations. **[LO C.2]**
   a. What is the price elasticity of demand for a price change from $0 to $20?
   b. What is the price elasticity of demand for a price change from $20 to $40?
   c. What is the price elasticity of demand for a price change from $40 to $60?

4. Use the demand schedule in Table CP-1 to answer the following questions. Use the mid-point method in your calculations. **[LO C.2]**
   a. What is the price elasticity of demand for a price change from $4 to $8?
   b. What is the price elasticity of demand for a price change from $8 to $16?
   c. What is the price elasticity of demand for a price change from $20 to $24?

TABLE CP-1

Price ($)	Quantity
0	60
4	50
8	40
12	30
16	20
20	10
24	0

TABLE CP-2

Price ($)	Quantity
0	56
1	48
2	42
3	35
4	28
5	21
6	14
7	7
8	0

FIGURE CP-1

5. Use the demand schedule in Table CP-2 to answer the following questions. Use the mid-point method when calculating elasticity. **[LO C.2]**
   a. What is the price elasticity of demand for a price change from $2 to $3? What is the slope of the demand curve for a price change from $2 to $3?
   b. What is the price elasticity of demand for a price change from $3 to $5? What is the slope of the demand curve for a price change from $3 to $5?
   c. What is the price elasticity of demand for a price change from $6 to $7? What is the slope of the demand curve for a price change from $6 to $7?

Efficiency

Learning Objectives

LO 5.1 Use willingness to pay and willingness to sell to determine supply and demand at a given price.

LO 5.2 Calculate consumer surplus based on a graph or table.

LO 5.3 Calculate producer surplus based on a graph or table.

LO 5.4 Calculate total surplus based on a graph or table.

LO 5.5 Define efficiency in terms of surplus, and identify efficient and inefficient situations.

LO 5.6 Describe the distribution of surplus, or benefits to society, that results from a policy decision.

LO 5.7 Calculate deadweight loss.

LO 5.8 Explain why correcting a missing market can make everyone better off.

A BROKEN LASER POINTER STARTS AN INTERNET REVOLUTION

In 1995, a young software developer named Pierre Omidyar spent his Labor Day weekend building a website he called AuctionWeb. His idea was to create a site where people could post their old stuff for sale online and auction it off to the highest bidder. Soon after, he sold the first item on AuctionWeb for $14.83. It was a broken laser pointer, which he had posted on the site as a test, never expecting anyone to bid on it. When Pierre pointed out that the pointer was broken, the bidder explained that he was "a collector of broken laser pointers."

As you might have guessed, AuctionWeb became the wildly successful company we now know as eBay. In 2015, 20 years after the site was first conceived, the total value of items sold on eBay was $82 billion and 162 million people around the world were active buyers.[1]

Like many creation stories, the tale of eBay's first sale gives us insight into what makes it tick. People are interested in some pretty odd things (like broken laser pointers), but given a big enough crowd, matches usually can be made between buyers and sellers. When buyers and

© David Paul Morris/Bloomberg/Getty Images

sellers are matched up and they trade, each is made better off. The buyer gets an item he wants, and the seller gets money. Because both parties are willing participants, they benefit from engaging in such transactions. In fact, they even are willing to pay eBay to provide the marketplace where they can find one another. How else is someone with a broken laser pointer going to find an eager buyer?

eBay's success is based on one of the most fundamental ideas in economics: *Voluntary exchanges create value and can make everyone involved better off.* The importance of that idea stretches far beyond eBay. This principle drives a range of businesses—from grocery stores, to investment banks, to online retailers—that do not manufacture or grow anything themselves. Instead, they facilitate transactions between producers and consumers.

But this principle raises a question: How do we know that people are better off when they buy and sell things? Can we say anything about *how much* better off they are?

To answer these questions, we need a tool to describe the *size of the benefits* that result from transactions and who receives said benefits. In this chapter we will introduce the concept of *surplus.* It can measure the benefit that people receive when they buy something for less than they would have been willing to pay. It also can measure the benefit that people receive when they sell something for more than they would have been willing to accept. *Surplus* is the best way to look at the benefits people receive from successful transactions.

Surplus also shows us why the equilibrium price and quantity in a competitive market are so special: They maximize the total well-being of those involved. Even when we care about outcomes other than total well-being (like inequality in the distribution of benefits), surplus gives us a yardstick for comparing different ideas and policies. For instance, calculations of surplus can clearly show who benefits and who loses from policies such as taxes and minimum wages. As we'll see, maximizing total surplus—an idea called *efficiency*—is one of the most powerful features of a market system. Even more remarkable is that it is achieved without centralized coordination.

Surplus also shows us how simply enabling people to trade with one another can make them better off. Often, creating a new market for goods and services (as the Grameen Bank did in Bangladesh, in the example in Chapter 1, "Economics and Life") or improving an existing market (as eBay did on the Internet) can be a good way to help people. Knowing how and when to harness the power of economic exchanges to improve well-being is an important tool for businesspeople and public-minded problem solvers alike.

Willingness to Pay and Sell

LO 5.1 Use willingness to pay and willingness to sell to determine supply and demand at a given price.

eBay is an online auction platform that allows people to post items for sale that anyone else online can buy. People who want to buy the item make bids offering to pay a particular price. This decentralized marketplace supports all sorts of transactions: from real estate, to used cars, to rare books, to (in one extraordinary case) a half-eaten cheese sandwich said to look like the Virgin Mary (which sold for $28,000).[2]

Who uses eBay? What do they want? At the most basic level, they are people who want to buy or sell a particular good. We're not sure how many people want broken laser pointers or decade-old cheese sandwiches, so let's stick with something a little more typical. How about digital cameras? Just as we did in Chapter 3, "Markets," we'll make the simplifying assumption that there is just one kind of digital camera rather than thousands of slightly different models.

Imagine you see a digital camera posted for sale on eBay. Who might bid on it? What are their *wants and constraints*? Most obviously, people who bid will be those who *want* a camera. But they will also care about the price they pay: Why spend $200 for a camera if you can get it for $100 and spend the other $100 on something else? Potential buyers *want* to pay as little as possible, but on top of this general preference, each buyer has a maximum price she is willing to pay.

Economists call this maximum price the buyer's **willingness to pay** or the *reservation price.* Economists use these two terms interchangeably; in this book, we'll stick with "willingness to pay." This price is the point above which the buyer throws up her hands and says, "Never mind. I'd rather spend my money on something else." Each potential buyer wants to purchase a camera for a price that is as low as possible and no higher than her maximum *willingness to pay.*

On eBay, we can see willingness to pay in action. When the price of a product remains below a bidder's willingness to pay, he'll continue to bid on it. When the going price passes his willingness to pay, he'll drop out.

Of course, buyers are only half the story. Who posted the camera for sale on eBay in the first place? To create a functioning market for digital cameras, someone has to want to sell. Whereas buyers want to buy a camera for as low a price as possible, sellers want to sell for as high a price as possible. Why take less money if you could get more? Just as each potential buyer has a willingness to pay, each potential seller has a *willingness to sell.* **Willingness to sell** is the minimum price that a seller is willing to accept in exchange for a good or service. A seller always wants to sell for a price that is as high as possible, but never lower than his minimum.

We can see willingness to sell in action on eBay through the "reserve price" that sellers can set when they post an item. This reserve price sets a bar below which the seller will not accept any bids. If she doesn't get any higher bids, she simply keeps the item.

So far, so good: Buyers want to buy low; sellers want to sell high. What does this have to do with markets? We're about to see that willingness to pay and willingness to sell are actually the forces that drive the shape of demand and supply curves.

willingness to pay (reservation price) the maximum price that a buyer would be willing to pay for a good or service

willingness to sell the minimum price that a seller is willing to accept in exchange for a good or service

Willingness to pay and the demand curve

Let's return to potential camera buyers and take a closer look at how they choose to bid on the camera posted on eBay. To keep things simple, let's imagine that there are five potential buyers who are considering bidding on this particular camera.

- Bidder #1 is a bird watcher who cares passionately about having a good camera to document the rare birds she finds. She is willing to pay up to $500 for the camera.
- Bidder #2 is an amateur photographer. He has an outdated camera and is willing to pay $250 for this newer model.

- Bidder #3 is a real estate agent who will be willing to pay $200 or less to be able to take better pictures of her properties.
- Bidder #4 is a journalist. She wouldn't mind having a newer camera than the one her newspaper provided but would pay no more than $150 for it.
- Bidder #5 is a teacher who will spend no more than $100—the amount of the eBay gift certificate given to him by appreciative parents for his birthday.

We can plot on a graph each potential buyer's willingness to pay. In panel A of Figure 5-1, we've graphed possible prices for the camera against the number of buyers who would be willing to bid that price for it. Remember that each person's willingness to pay is a *maximum*—he or she would also be willing to buy the camera at any lower price. Therefore, at a price of $100, all five buyers are willing to bid; at $350, only one will bid.

If you squint a bit, you might notice that the graph in panel A looks a lot like a demand curve: Price is on the *y*-axis, quantity is on the *x*-axis, and there's a line showing that quantity demanded increases as price decreases. In fact this *is* a demand curve, although it represents only five potential buyers. We could conduct the same exercise in a bigger market and plot out the willingness to pay of millions of people rather than just five. In that case, we'd get a smooth demand curve, as shown in panel B of Figure 5-1. The individual steps that we see in panel A get smaller and smaller over the millions of cameras demanded, resulting in the smoothed-out curve.

Notice that although each buyer's willingness to pay is driven by different factors, we can explain the motivations behind all of their decisions by asking, *What are the trade-offs?* Money that is spent to buy a camera on eBay cannot be spent on other things. Willingness to pay is the point at which the benefit that a person will get from the camera is equal to the benefit of

FIGURE 5-1

Willingness to pay and the demand curve

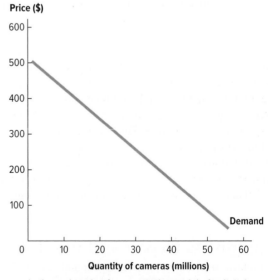

(A) Willingness to pay with few buyers

Price ($)

Bird watcher

Amateur photographer

Real estate agent

Journalist

Each step represents a camera bought by the additional buyer who becomes interested at that price.

Teacher

Potential buyers

At any given price, buyers with a higher willingness to pay will buy and those with a lower willingness to pay will not. If the price were $350, only one buyer would buy. If it were $50, all five people would buy. This demand curve has a step-like shape rather than a smooth line because there are a limited number of buyers whose prices are expressed in round dollar amounts.

(B) Willingness to pay with many buyers

Price ($)

Demand

Quantity of cameras (millions)

In the real market for a particular model of a digital camera, there are millions of cameras demanded at a particular price. The steps that we see in panel A get smaller and smaller until they disappear into a smooth curve.

spending the money on another alternative—in other words, the opportunity cost. For instance, $250 is the point at which the enjoyment that the amateur photographer gets from a camera is the same as the enjoyment he would get from, say, buying $250 worth of stamps for his stamp collection instead.

Since everyone has things they want other than cameras, the same opportunity cost logic applies to each of the potential buyers represented in the demand curve. At prices above the maximum willingness to pay, the opportunity cost is greater than the benefits. At lower prices, the benefits outweigh the opportunity cost.

To figure out which of our five individual buyers will actually purchase a camera, we have to know the market price. To find the market price, we have to know something about the supply of digital cameras. Therefore, we turn next to investigating the supply curve.

Willingness to sell and the supply curve

As you may have guessed, just as the shape of the demand curve was driven by potential buyers' willingness to pay, the shape of the supply curve for digital cameras is driven by potential sellers' *willingness to sell.* To simplify things, let's imagine five prospective sellers who have posted their cameras for sale on eBay.

- Seller #1 is a comic book collector. He was given a camera as a birthday present, but all he really cares about is having money to spend on comic books. He's willing to part with his camera for as little as $50.
- Seller #2 is a sales representative for a big company that makes digital cameras. She's authorized to sell a camera for $100 or higher.
- Seller #3 is a professional nature photographer who owns several cameras but won't sell for anything less than $200. At a lower price he'd rather give the camera as a gift to his nephew.
- Seller #4 is a sales representative for a small company that is just starting up in the camera industry and has much higher costs of production than the larger company; it can make money only by selling its cameras for $300 or more.
- Seller #5 is an art teacher who is sentimentally attached to her camera, given to her by a friend. She won't give it up unless she can get at least $400.

We can represent these five individuals by plotting on a graph their willingness to sell. Panel A of Figure 5-2 shows a graph of potential prices and the number of cameras that will be up for bid at each price. This graph is a supply curve representing only five potential sellers. As with the demand curve, if we added all of the millions of digital cameras that are actually for sale in the real world, we see the smooth supply curve we're accustomed to, as in panel B.

Sellers' willingness to sell is determined by the *trade-offs* they face, and, in particular, the opportunity cost of the sale. The opportunity cost of selling a camera for sellers #1, #3, and #5 is the use or enjoyment that the seller could get from keeping the camera. In the case of the two camera manufacturers, sellers #2 and #4, the opportunity cost is whatever else the firm would do with the money that would be required to manufacture the camera—say, marketing the camera or researching new technology. The opportunity cost of each of the five sellers will be determined by different factors—not all of them strictly monetary, as in the case of the teacher, who is sentimentally attached to her camera.

For an item that a seller just wants to get rid of (like the broken laser pointer mentioned at the start of the chapter), the starting price might be one cent. If opportunity cost is zero, anything is better than nothing!

On the other hand, in a market where manufacturers are producing and selling new products, the minimum price will have to be high enough to make it worth their while to continue making new products. This would be the case for the two camera manufacturers. If the selling price didn't cover the costs of production, the manufacturers would simply stop making the item—otherwise,

FIGURE 5-2

Willingness to sell and the supply curve

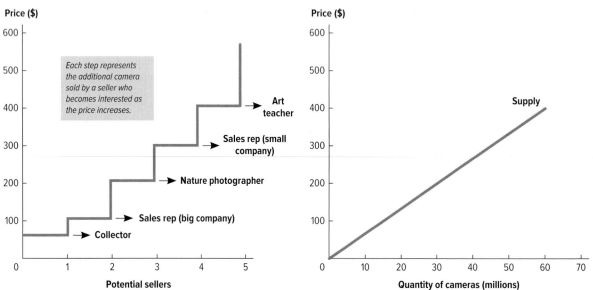

(A) Willingness to sell with few sellers

Each step represents the additional camera sold by a seller who becomes interested as the price increases.

Price ($)

Art teacher

Sales rep (small company)

Nature photographer

Sales rep (big company)

Collector

Potential sellers

(B) Willingness to sell with many sellers

Price ($)

Supply

Quantity of cameras (millions)

At any given price, sellers with a lower willingness to sell will sell, while those with a higher willingness to sell will not. At a price of $400, all five people will sell their cameras, while at a price of $200, only three sell. This rough supply curve would look smooth if there were many sellers, each with a different willingness to sell.

In the real market for a particular model of a digital camera, there are millions of cameras supplied at a particular price. The steps that we see in panel A get smaller and smaller until they disappear into a smooth curve.

they would actually lose money every time they made a sale. (Occasionally, we do see manufacturers selling below the cost of production, but only when they've made a mistake and have to get rid of already-produced goods.)

Having met five potential buyers and five potential sellers, we're now in a position to understand what happens when the two groups come together in the market to make trades. But first, take a look at the Real Life box "Haggling and bluffing" to consider how buyers' willingness to pay interacts with sellers' willingness to sell in the real world.

Real Life

Haggling and bluffing

If you've ever visited a flea market or bought a used car, you have probably haggled over price. In much of the world, haggling for goods is an integral part of daily life. Even in wealthy countries, bargaining over salaries and promotions is commonplace—employees offer to sell their time and skills, and employers offer to buy them. In any bargaining situation, the seller wants to sell for as high a price as possible, and the buyer wants to buy for as low a price as possible. How do they reach an agreement?

The idea of willingness to pay explains a lot of bargaining strategies. Usually, the seller will start with a price much higher than the minimum she is actually willing to accept. Likewise, the buyer starts with an offer much lower than what he is actually willing to pay. Neither will reveal the price he or she thinks is reasonable. Isn't this a waste of time? They both know that they'll end up somewhere in the middle. Why not just start there?

Put yourself in the shoes of a flea-market vendor. If you knew for certain how much a potential customer was willing to pay, would you accept anything short of that amount? Probably not. As the would-be buyer, then, you have a strong incentive to make sure that the vendor doesn't know your true willingness to pay. The same is true for the vendor, who wants to hide from the potential buyer the minimum price he'll accept. Both parties start bidding far from their actual reservation price, hoping to end up with the most favorable price possible.

The same principle also explains a trick that is sometimes used by hagglers: bluffing about your willingness to pay. What would you do if the cost of an item were above your maximum willingness to pay? On eBay, you'd stop bidding; in the flea market, you'd walk away. Walking away from the bargaining table signals that the current price is higher than your willingness to pay—whether or not that is truly the case. If the seller realizes he won't get a higher price, he will sometimes settle rather than lose the sale entirely. On the other hand, if you're a bad bluffer or if your offered price is below the seller's willingness to sell, you lose the deal.

The next time you hear that "labor has walked out on talks" in a union wage negotiation or that a party to a civil lawsuit has "withdrawn from mediation," you will know that they're signaling their minimum or maximum price. The question is, are they bluffing?

✓ **CONCEPT CHECK**

☐ How is willingness to pay determined by opportunity cost? **[LO 5.1]**
☐ What is the relationship between willingness to pay and the demand curve? **[LO 5.1]**

Measuring Surplus

Surplus is a way of measuring who benefits from transactions and by how much. Economists use this word to describe a fairly simple concept: If you get something for less than you would have been willing to pay, or sell it for more than the minimum you would have accepted, that's a good thing. Think about how nice it feels to buy something on sale that you would have been willing to pay full price for. That "bonus" value that you would have paid if necessary, but didn't have to, is *surplus*. We can talk about surplus for both buyers and sellers, individually and collectively.

surplus
a way of measuring who benefits from transactions and by how much

Surplus is the difference between the price at which a buyer or seller would be *willing* to trade and the actual price. Think about willingness to pay as the price at which someone is completely indifferent between buying an item and keeping his money. At a higher price, he would prefer to keep the money; at a lower price, he would prefer to buy. By looking at the distance between this "indifference point" and the actual price, we can describe the extra value the buyer (or the seller) gets from the transaction.

Surplus is a simple idea, but a surprisingly powerful one. It turns out that surplus is a better measure of the value that buyers and sellers get from participating in a market than price itself. To see why this is true, read the From Another Angle box "How much would you pay to keep the Internet from disappearing?"

From Another Angle

How much would you pay to keep the Internet from disappearing?

Why is surplus a better measure of value than how much we pay for something? Consider the difference between what we pay for the Internet versus a particular model of computer.

Most people can access the Internet for very little, or even for free. You might pay a monthly fee for high-speed access at home, but almost anyone can use the Internet for free at schools, libraries, or coffee shops. Once you're online there are millions of websites that will provide information, entertainment, and services at no charge. Computer owners, on the other hand, pay a lot for particular types of computers. For instance, consumers might pay $999 for a MacBook laptop. Does this mean that we value access to the Internet less than a MacBook? Probably not.

Simply measuring price falls short of capturing true value. To see why, think about how much you would pay to prevent the particular type of computer you own from disappearing from the market. You might pay something: After all, there's a reason you chose it in the first place, and you might be willing to cough up a bit extra to get your preferred combination of technical specifications, appearance, and so on. But if the price got very steep, you'd probably rather switch to another, similar type of computer instead of paying more money. That difference—the maximum extra amount you would pay over the current price to maintain the ability to buy something—is your *consumer surplus*. It is the difference between your willingness to pay and the actual price.

Now consider the same question for the Internet. Imagine that the Internet is going to disappear tomorrow, or, at least, that you will be unable to access it in any way. How much would you pay to keep that from happening? Remember, that means no e-mail, no Google search or maps, no Facebook, no Twitter, no YouTube, no video streaming, and no online shopping. We suspect that you might be willing to pay a lot. The amount that you're willing to pay represents the true value that you place on the Internet, even though the amount that you currently spend on it might be very little. That's the magic of surplus.

Consumer surplus

LO 5.2 Calculate consumer surplus based on a graph or table.

consumer surplus
the net benefit that a consumer receives from purchasing a good or service, measured by the difference between willingness to pay and the actual price

Let's go back to our five eBay buyers and calculate the surplus they would receive from buying a camera at a given price. This part of the transaction illustrates **consumer surplus**—the net benefit that a consumer receives from purchasing a good or service, measured by the difference between willingness to pay and the actual price.

Suppose it turns out that the going rate for cameras on eBay is $160. The bird watcher was willing to bid up to $500. Therefore, her consumer surplus from buying the camera is $340—the difference between her willingness to pay and the $160 she actually pays. Two other potential buyers will also buy a camera if the price is $160: the amateur photographer (willing to pay $250) and the real estate agent (willing to pay up to $200). The consumer surplus they receive is $90 and $40, respectively. The other two potential buyers will have dropped out of bidding when the price rose above $100 and then above $150, so they buy nothing and pay nothing. Their consumer surplus is zero.

We can add up each individual's consumer surplus to describe the overall benefits that buyers received in a market. (Somewhat confusingly, economists use the same term for individual and collective surplus, but you should be able to tell from the context whether we mean one person's consumer surplus or total consumer surplus for all buyers in the market.) If the market for digital cameras consisted only of our five individuals, then the total consumer surplus would be:

$$\$340 + \$90 + \$40 + \$0 + \$0 = \$470$$

FIGURE 5-3

Consumer surplus

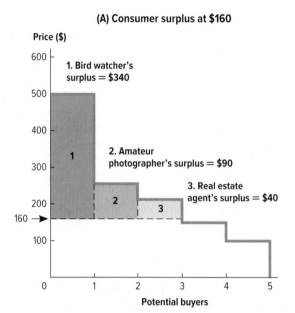

(A) Consumer surplus at $160

1. Bird watcher's surplus = $340
2. Amateur photographer's surplus = $90
3. Real estate agent's surplus = $40

This graph shows consumer surplus in the camera market when price is $160. The shaded area is the difference between willingness to pay and the market price for each buyer. The more that a buyer would have been willing to pay, the greater the surplus at a lower price. At this price, total consumer surplus is $470, the sum of the individual surpluses shown.

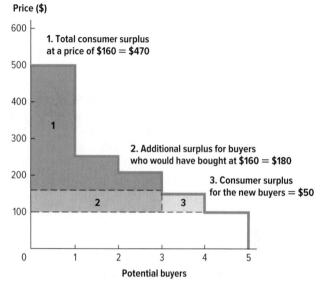

(B) Consumer surplus at $100

1. Total consumer surplus at a price of $160 = $470
2. Additional surplus for buyers who would have bought at $160 = $180
3. Consumer surplus for the new buyers = $50

When the price of cameras falls to $100, consumer surplus increases. Area 1 is consumer surplus under the old price. Area 2 is the additional surplus received by people who were willing to buy at either price. Area 3 is the surplus received by the two new buyers who enter the market when price falls. The combination of the three areas is total consumer surplus when price is $100. When the price falls, total consumer surplus increases from $470 to $700.

On a graph, we represent consumer surplus as the area underneath the demand curve and above the horizontal line of the equilibrium price. Panel A of Figure 5-3 shows consumer surplus for these five individuals when the price is $160. (Because there are only five buyers in this market, the demand curve in panel A has the step-like shape we saw earlier.)

How does a change in the market price affect buyers? Since buyers would always prefer prices to be lower, a decrease in price makes them better off, and an increase in price makes them worse off. Some people will choose not to buy at all when prices rise—which means that their surplus becomes zero. Those who do buy will have a smaller individual surplus than they had at the lower price. The opposite is true when prices fall. Measuring consumer surplus tells us *how much* better or worse off buyers are when the price changes.

Panel B of Figure 5-3 shows what happens to total consumer surplus if the going price of cameras on eBay falls to $100. You can see by comparing panel A with panel B that when the price level falls, the area representing consumer surplus gets bigger. The consumer surplus of each of the three buyers who were already willing to buy increases by $60 each. Also, two more buyers join the market: The journalist's willingness to pay is $150, so she gains consumer surplus of $50. The teacher's willingness to pay is $100; he buys a camera but gains no consumer surplus because the price is exactly equal to his willingness to pay. When the camera's price drops to $100, total consumer surplus among our five individuals totals $700 (an increase of $230):

$$\$470 + \$60 + \$60 + \$60 + \$50 + \$0 = \$700$$

> For a refresher on the area under a linear curve, see Appendix D, "Math Essentials: The Area under a Linear Curve," which follows this chapter.

Producer surplus

LO 5.3 Calculate producer surplus based on a graph or table.

producer surplus
the net benefit that a producer receives from the sale of a good or service, measured by the difference between the producer's willingness to sell and the actual price

Like buyers, sellers want to increase the distance between the price at which they are willing to trade and the actual price. Sellers are better off when the market price is higher than their minimum willingness to sell. **Producer surplus** is the net benefit that a producer receives from the sale of a good or service, measured by the difference between willingness to sell and the actual price. It's called *producer* surplus regardless of whether the sellers actually produced the good themselves or—as often happens on eBay—are selling it secondhand.

If our five potential sellers find that the going price of cameras on eBay is $160, two of them will sell; they will be happy because they will get more for their cameras than the minimum they were willing to accept. Seller #1 (the comic book collector), whose willingness to sell is $50, has a producer surplus of $110. Seller #2 (the sales rep for the bigger camera company), whose willingness to sell is $100, has a surplus of $60. Potential sellers #3, #4, and #5 won't trade at a price of $160, so each has a surplus of zero.

Just as we did for consumer surplus, we can add up each seller's producer surplus to describe the overall benefits that sellers received in a market. If our five sellers are the only ones in the market, then total producer surplus at a price of $160 is:

$$\$110 + \$60 + \$0 + \$0 + \$0 = \$170$$

Panel A of Figure 5-4 shows producer surplus for the five sellers when the price is $160. (Again, because of the small size of this market, the supply curve in panel A has a step-like shape.)

FIGURE 5-4

Producer surplus

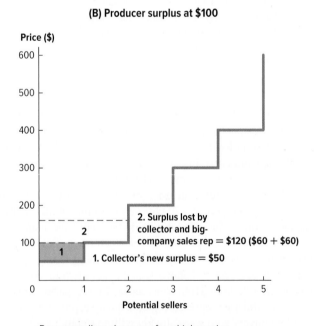

This shows the willingness to sell of all the potential sellers in our market. The shaded area (1 + 2) between the supply curve and the market prices shows total producer surplus of $170, the sum of the individual surpluses shown.

Because sellers always prefer a higher price, producer surplus goes down when the price falls to $100. At $100, two sellers are still willing to sell, but are worse off because they receive less money for their cameras. Area 1 shows the new producer surplus: $50. Area 2 shows the reduction in surplus for the two sellers.

A change in the market price affects sellers in the opposite way it affects buyers. Sellers would always prefer prices to be higher, so a decrease in price makes them worse off. Some will choose not to sell at all when prices fall; their surplus becomes zero. Those who do sell will have a smaller individual surplus than at the higher price. The opposite is true when the market price rises, which makes sellers better off. Measuring producer surplus tells us *how much* better or worse off sellers are when the price changes.

On a graph, we represent producer surplus as the area below the horizontal line of equilibrium price and above the supply curve. Panel B of Figure 5-4 shows what happens to producer surplus if the price drops from $160 to $100. Sellers #1 and #2 still sell, but their surplus is reduced. Total producer surplus falls to $50.

You can see by comparing panel A with panel B that when the price level falls, the area representing producer surplus gets smaller. On the other hand, the higher the price, the bigger the area, and the greater the producer surplus.

Total surplus

> **LO 5.4** Calculate total surplus based on a graph or table.

We now understand how to calculate consumer surplus and producer surplus at any given price. But what will the actual market price be? To find out, we have to put the demand and supply curves together and locate the point where they intersect.

Panel A of Figure 5-5 shows the demand curve for our five buyers and the supply curve for our five sellers. The two curves intersect at a price of $200. At this price, three buyers are willing to buy a camera and three sellers are willing to sell a camera. The consumer surplus of each buyer is shown as the area underneath the demand curve and above the horizontal line of the equilibrium price. Consumer surplus is $350 ($300 + $50 + $0 + $0 + $0). (Buyer #3 buys at her willingness to pay price, so she has no consumer surplus.) The producer surplus is shown as the area above the supply curve and beneath the equilibrium price. Producer surplus is $250 ($150 + $100 + $0 + $0 + $0). (Seller #3 sells at his willingness to sell price, so he has no producer surplus.)

Just as we've found total consumer surplus and total producer surplus, we can find total surplus for an entire market. **Total surplus** is a measure of the combined benefits that everyone receives from participating in an exchange of goods or services. The total surplus is the benefit received by all market participants, the sum of both consumer and producer surplus. For our camera market of five buyers and five sellers, total surplus is $600 ($350 + $250).

To better understand total surplus, let's broaden our focus beyond just five buyers and five sellers to the entire market for digital cameras on eBay. To represent this big market, we can bring back the smooth demand and supply curves from Figures 5-1 and 5-2. When we put the two together in panel B of Figure 5-5, we find that the equilibrium price is $200, and the equilibrium quantity of cameras traded is 30 million. (We're assuming a standardized model of digital camera and all the other features of a competitive market outlined in Chapter 3, "Markets.")

Total consumer surplus is represented graphically by the area underneath the demand curve and above the equilibrium price. That's the area shaded gold in panel B of Figure 5-5. Total producer surplus is represented by the area of the graph above the supply curve and below the equilibrium price—the area shaded blue. Added together, those two areas—consumer surplus and producer surplus—make up the total surplus created by those 30 million sales of digital cameras on eBay. Graphically, total surplus is equal to the total area between the supply and demand curves, to the left of the equilibrium quantity.

We can also think of total surplus as value created by the existence of the market. Total surplus is calculated by adding up the benefits that every individual participant receives ($300 consumer surplus for the bird watcher, plus $150 producer surplus for the comic book collector,

total surplus
a measure of the combined benefits that everyone receives from participating in an exchange of goods or services

FIGURE 5-5

Surplus at market equilibrium

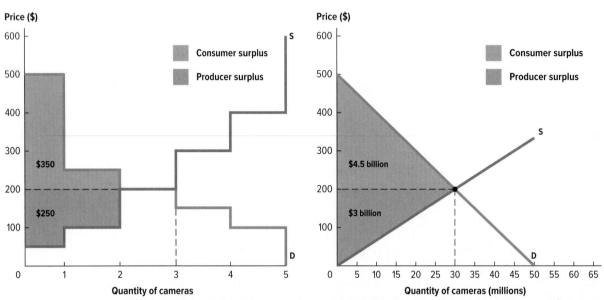

(A) Surplus at market equilibrium for the five-buyer and five-seller camera market

At the market equilibrium in our smaller market, the price of a camera is $200, and three are bought and sold. Consumer surplus is represented by the area between the demand curve and the market price, and is equal to $350. Producer surplus is represented by the area between the supply curve and the market price, and is equal to $250. Total surplus adds up to $600.

(B) Surplus at market equilibrium for the entire camera market

At the market equilibrium in our large market, the price of cameras is $200, and 30 million are bought and sold. Consumer surplus is represented by the area between the demand curve and the market price, and is equal to $4.5 billion. Producer surplus is represented by the area between the supply curve and the market price, and is equal to $3 billion. Total surplus adds up to $7.5 billion.

and so on, for every one of those 30 million sales). But these benefits exist only as a result of participation in exchanges in the market.

This is an important point because sometimes people mistakenly think of the economy as a fixed quantity of money, goods, and well-being, in which the only question is how to divide it up among people. That idea is referred to as a **zero-sum game**. A zero-sum game is a situation in which whenever one person gains, another loses an equal amount, such that the net value of a transaction is zero. Playing poker is an example of a zero-sum game: Whatever one player wins, another player, logically, has to lose.

The concept of surplus shows us that the economy generally does not work like a poker game. Voluntary transactions, like selling cameras on eBay, do not have a winner or loser. Rather, *both the buyer and seller are winners* since each gains surplus. Everyone ends up better off than he or she was before. Total surplus cannot be *less* than zero—if it were, people would simply stop buying and selling.

As a rule, markets generate value, but the distribution of that value is a more complicated issue. In the following sections, we will look at what surplus can tell us about the well-being generated by market transactions and by deviations from the market equilibrium. Then, in the next chapter, we'll use these tools to evaluate the effects of some common government policies when they are implemented in a competitive market. Later in the book, we will revisit some of the assumptions about how competitive markets operate, and we will discuss what happens to surplus when those assumptions don't hold true in the real world.

zero-sum game
a situation in which whenever one person gains, another loses an equal amount, such that the net value of any transaction is zero

✓ CONCEPT CHECK

☐ What consumer surplus is received by someone whose willingness to pay is $20 below the market price of a good? **[LO 5.2]**

☐ What is the producer surplus earned by a seller whose willingness to sell is $40 below the market price of a good? **[LO 5.3]**

☐ Why can total surplus never fall below zero in a market for goods and services? **[LO 5.4]**

Using Surplus to Compare Alternatives

In a competitive market, buyers and sellers will naturally find their way to the equilibrium price. In our eBay example, we expect that buyers and sellers of digital cameras will bargain freely, offering different prices until the number of people who want to buy is matched with the number of people who want to sell. This is the invisible hand of market forces at work. It doesn't require any eBay manager to coordinate or set prices. But as we're about to see, the magic of the invisible hand doesn't stop there.

Market equilibrium and efficiency

LO 5.5 Define efficiency in terms of surplus, and identify efficient and inefficient situations.

The concept of surplus lets us appreciate something very important about market equilibrium: Not only is it the point at which transactions occur between the buyers willing to pay the most and sellers able to produce at the lowest cost. It also is the point at which total surplus is maximized. In other words, equilibrium maximizes the total well-being of the participants in the market.

To see why this is so, let's look at what would happen to surplus if, for some reason, the market moved away from equilibrium. Suppose an eBay manager decides to set the price of cameras so that people don't have to go to the trouble of bidding. He decides that $300 seems like a reasonable price. How will potential buyers and sellers *respond* to this situation? Figure 5-6 shows us:

- There are now 10 million fewer cameras sold (the quantity sold falls from 30 million to 20 million). Buyers who wanted 10 million cameras at the equilibrium price of $200 are no longer willing to buy at $300, reducing their consumer surplus to zero.
- That means that sellers who would have sold those 10 million cameras to buyers also miss out and get producer surplus of zero.
- For the 20 million cameras that still are sold, buyers pay a higher price and lose surplus.
- The sellers of those 20 million cameras benefit from the higher price and gain the surplus lost by consumers.

Overall, total surplus in the market is lower than it was at the equilibrium price because 10 million fewer cameras are sold.

What happens if the interfering eBay manager instead decides to sell digital cameras for $100? As Figure 5-7 shows:

- Buyers are willing to purchase 40 million cameras at a price of $100. Sellers are willing to sell only 15 million at $100.
- Since 15 million fewer cameras sell (that is, 15 million instead of 30 million at equilibrium), buyers and sellers lose the surplus that would have been gained through their sale.
- For the 15 million transactions that still take place, consumers gain surplus of $1.5 billion ($100 × 15 million) from buying at a lower price (area 2). That consumer surplus is exactly equal to the surplus the remaining sellers lose from selling at a lower price.

FIGURE 5-6

Changing the distribution of surplus

When the price rises above the market equilibrium, fewer transactions take place. The surplus shown in area 2 is transferred from consumers to producers as a result of the higher price paid for transactions that do still take place. The surplus in areas 4 and 5 is lost to both consumers and producers as a result of the reduced number of transactions.

FIGURE 5-7

Surplus when price is below equilibrium

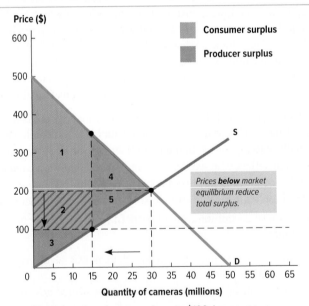

When the price of cameras drops to $100, buyers are willing to purchase 40 million, but sellers want to sell only 15 million. For those who do trade, successful buyers gain surplus of $1.5 billion (area 2) from buying at the lower price, while the sellers lose surplus of that same amount. The buyers and sellers who would have traded at equilibrium but no longer do so lose $1.875 billion of combined surplus. The surplus in areas 4 and 5 is lost to both consumers and producers as a result of the reduced number of transactions. Total surplus falls from $7.5 billion to $5.625 billion.

- The buyers and sellers who would have traded at equilibrium but no longer do so lose $1.875 billion of combined surplus. Breaking this down, we find that the 15 million buyers no longer in the market lose $1.125 billion (area 4), and sellers lose $0.75 billion (area 5) in surplus.
- This $1.875 billion total (areas 4 + 5) in lost surplus is subtracted from the amount of total surplus before the price ceiling. Overall, total surplus falls from $7.5 billion to $5.625 billion.

In both cases—when the price is $300 (above the equilibrium price) or when it is $100 (below the equilibrium price)—total surplus decreases relative to the market equilibrium. In fact, we find this same result at *any price* other than the equilibrium price. The key is that a higher or lower price causes fewer trades to take place because some people are no longer willing to buy or sell. The value that would have been gained from these voluntary trades no longer exists. As a result, *the equilibrium in a perfectly competitive, well-functioning market maximizes total surplus.*

Another way to say this is that the market is **efficient** when it is at equilibrium: There is no exchange that can make anyone better off without someone becoming worse off. Efficiency is one of the most powerful features of a market system. Even more remarkable is that it is achieved without centralized coordination.

efficient market
an arrangement such that no exchange can make anyone better off without someone becoming worse off

Changing the distribution of total surplus

LO 5.6 Describe the distribution of surplus, or benefits to society, that results from a policy decision.

A reduction in total surplus was not the only interesting thing that happened when the meddling eBay manager moved the price of digital cameras away from equilibrium. Another outcome was *reassignment of surplus* from customers to producers, or vice versa, for the transactions that did take place:

- When the price was raised, sellers gained some well-being at the expense of buyers.
- When the price was lowered, buyers gained some well-being at the expense of sellers.

In both cases, achieving this transfer of well-being from one group to the other came at the expense of *reduced total surplus.*

When an artificially high price is imposed on a market, it's bad news for consumer surplus. Consumers lose surplus due to the reduced number of transactions and the higher price buyers have to pay on the remaining transactions.

The situation for producers, though, is more complex. At the artificially high price, producers lose some surplus from the transactions that would have taken place under equilibrium and no longer do. On the other hand, they gain more surplus from the higher price on the transactions that do still take place. These two effects will compete with one another. Whichever effect "wins" will determine whether the producer surplus increases or decreases overall.

To see why, let's go back to Figure 5-6. Area 2 is surplus that is transferred from consumers to producers. Areas 4 and 5 represent surplus lost to consumers and producers, respectively, from transactions that no longer take place. Whether area 2 is bigger or smaller than area 5 will indicate whether producer surplus increases or decreases. That result depends on the shape of the demand curve and the supply curve. In this case, we can see that area 2 is bigger than area 5. The effect of the artificially high price was to make sellers better off (at the expense of making buyers even more worse off).

The opposite situation occurs when prices are lower than the market equilibrium, which you can see by looking again at Figure 5-7. Fewer transactions take place (because fewer producers are willing to sell), and so both producers and consumers lose some surplus from missed transactions. For the transactions that do still take place, consumers pay less and gain surplus at the expense of producers. Producers get paid less and lose surplus. Thus, a price below the market equilibrium will always reduce producer surplus. That price might increase or decrease consumer surplus: The outcome depends on how much surplus is gained by those who buy at a lower price compared to what is lost to those who can no longer buy at all.

We don't expect eBay managers to start imposing their own prices any time soon—that would be contrary to the whole idea of eBay as a decentralized virtual marketplace. But there are times when governments or other organizations do decide to impose minimum or maximum prices on markets. That happens because efficiency is not the only thing we care about. Many fundamental public policy questions revolve around possible trade-offs between economic efficiency and other concerns such as fairness and equity. We'll look in much more detail at this idea in the next chapter.

Deadweight loss

LO 5.7 Calculate deadweight loss.

deadweight loss
a loss of total surplus that occurs because the quantity of a good that is bought and sold is below the market equilibrium quantity

An intervention that moves a market away from equilibrium might benefit either producers or consumers, but it always comes with a decrease in total surplus. Where does that surplus go? It disappears and becomes what is known as a **deadweight loss**. Deadweight loss is the loss of total surplus that occurs when the quantity of a good that is bought and sold is below the market equilibrium quantity. Any intervention that moves a market away from the equilibrium price and quantity creates deadweight loss. Fewer exchanges take place, so there are fewer opportunities for the generation of surplus.

We can calculate deadweight loss in two ways: One way is to subtract total surplus *after* a market intervention from total surplus at the market equilibrium *before* the intervention. Or we can calculate deadweight loss directly by determining the area of the triangle on a graph. This second method is usually the easiest.

Figure 5-8 shows what happens in the eBay camera market when the price is too low at $100. Only 15 cameras are exchanged at this price, but the efficient quantity is 30. For the units between 15 and 30, consumers have a willingness to pay that is higher than producers' costs. Thus, exchanging the units would create surplus, but because the units are not exchanged, this potential surplus is lost. To calculate the exact size of this deadweight loss, we calculate the area between supply and demand for those units that aren't exchanged. The "base" of this triangle is measured

FIGURE 5-8

Deadweight loss

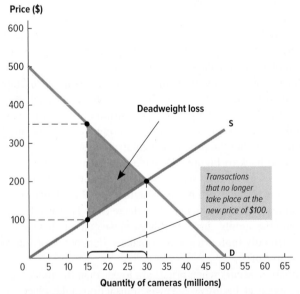

Deadweight loss represents the surplus that is lost to both producers and consumers as a result of fewer transactions taking place when the price moves away from equilibrium. Here, deadweight loss is equal to the gray shaded area.

along the *y*-axis from \$100 to \$350. The "height" is measured along the *x*-axis from 15 to 30. Then, using the formula for the area of a triangle, the deadweight loss is $\frac{b \times h}{2} = \frac{250 \times 15}{2} = 1{,}875$.

We'll see in the next chapter that deadweight loss is an incredibly important concept for understanding the costs of government intervention in markets, through mechanisms such as taxes and controls on the prices of goods.

Missing markets

LO 5.8 Explain why correcting a missing market can make everyone better off.

When there are people who would like to make exchanges but cannot, for one reason or another, we miss opportunities for mutual benefit. In this situation, we say that a market is "missing": Buyers and sellers would like to make a trade but for some reason cannot. The term "missing" can be misleading. Sometimes a market exists, so it is not literally missing, but, rather, not all trades are happening as potential buyers and sellers would together like to have happen. Asking why a market is missing is important; the answer can provide guidance to policies and businesses that can make the world a better place by allowing more people to engage in trade for mutual benefit.

Markets can be missing for a variety of reasons. Sometimes public policy prevents the market from existing—for instance, when the production or sale of a particular good or service is banned. Or sometimes a particular good or service is taxed; the tax doesn't eliminate the market but does add a cost, which leads to fewer transactions. Markets can also be missing or shrunk due to other types of holdups: a lack of accurate information or communication between potential buyers and sellers, or a lack of technology that would make the exchanges possible.

eBay and newer companies such as Airbnb, Uber, and Lyft are examples of how technology can generate new value by creating or expanding a market. Prior to the existence of such companies, people who wanted to offer a service or product, and people who wanted to buy it, often never found each other. For example, before eBay you could hold a garage sale to get rid of your extra stuff; you could go to your local stores or post an ad in a newspaper if you were looking to buy an unusual item. But it was quite difficult to find out if someone on the other side of the country was offering a rare product or a better price. eBay allows more buyers to find sellers and vice versa, encouraging more mutually beneficial trades.

The idea that we can increase total surplus by creating new markets and improving existing ones has important implications for public policy. Policies and technologies that help people share information and do business more effectively can increase well-being. For instance, ideas like creating a market for small loans by the Grameen Bank (see Chapter 1, "Economics and Life") or expanding access to cell phones in Indian fishing villages (see Chapter 3, "Markets") don't just redistribute pieces of the pie to help the poor. Instead, they make the whole pie bigger.

Think about the many situations in the world in which new technology, new strategies, and outreach to new clients have created a market that brings value to people. Also think about some controversial situations in which markets don't exist but could be created, as described in the What Do You Think? box "Kidneys for sale."

What Do You Think?
Kidneys for sale

When buyers and sellers come together to participate in voluntary transactions, the resulting markets create value that would not otherwise exist. The idea that well-functioning markets maximize surplus is an important descriptive fact.

(continued)

But people may have moral and political priorities that go beyond maximizing surplus. In fact, many important public policy questions revolve around trade-offs between economic efficiency and other goals.

For instance, the law in the United States (and many other countries) prohibits certain types of market transactions. Consider the following cases:

- It's illegal to buy or sell organs for medical transplants.
- It's illegal to buy or sell certain drugs, such as cocaine and heroin.
- It's illegal to buy or sell children for adoption.
- It's illegal to buy or sell certain types of weapons, such as nuclear devices.

Looking at it from one angle, these are all examples of missing markets. You now know that when markets are missing, we miss opportunities to create surplus by enabling voluntary transactions to take place. For instance, a market for organs could make a lot of people better off. Some healthy people would gain surplus by selling their kidneys: They would rather have money and one remaining kidney than two kidneys and no money. Meanwhile, some people with kidney disease would happily pay for the donation of a healthy kidney. Because the law prevents this transaction from happening, both miss out on surplus.

If maximizing surplus is our highest goal, it's plausible that we should allow organs and other such goods to be traded on the market. But allowing markets for organs goes against many people's moral instincts—perhaps because they hold other goals higher than maximizing surplus.

WHAT DO YOU THINK?

1. Do you agree that the law should prevent trade in organs?
2. How about drugs, children, and nuclear weapons?
3. Are there any reasons that markets for these goods might not end up maximizing surplus?
4. What values and assumptions are driving your answers?

✓ **CONCEPT CHECK**

☐ What can we say about the size and distribution of total surplus in an efficient market? **[LO 5.5]**

☐ How do price changes affect the distribution of surplus between consumers and producers? **[LO 5.6]**

☐ Why does an intervention that moves a market away from the equilibrium price and quantity create a deadweight loss? **[LO 5.7]**

☐ What does it mean to say that a market is "missing"? **[LO 5.8]**

Conclusion

In this chapter we've introduced the concepts of willingness to pay and willingness to sell, which help explain when individual buyers and sellers will choose to make a trade. We've also discussed what it means to measure consumer and producer surplus and shown that the market equilibrium is efficient because it maximizes total surplus.

As we'll see in the next chapter, surplus and deadweight loss are powerful tools for understanding the implications of business ideas and public policies. Who will benefit from the policy? Who will be harmed by it? What effect will it have on the economy overall? The language of surplus, efficiency, and distribution of benefits is particularly helpful for getting to the bottom of controversial decisions.

Later in the book, we will describe important cases in which the efficiency rule about market equilibrium does not always hold true, and we'll see how surplus can also help us understand these cases.

Key Terms

willingness to pay (reservation price), p. 105

willingness to sell, p. 105

surplus, p. 109

consumer surplus, p. 109

producer surplus, p. 112

total surplus, p. 113

zero-sum game, p. 114

efficient market, p. 117

deadweight loss, p. 118

Summary

LO 5.1 Use willingness to pay and willingness to sell to determine supply and demand at a given price.

Willingness to pay and willingness to sell describe the value that an individual places on a particular good or service. Willingness to pay (also sometimes known as the reservation price) is the maximum price that a buyer would be willing to pay for a particular good or service. Willingness to sell is the lowest price a seller is willing to accept in exchange for a particular good or service.

Consumers will buy only if the price is lower than their willingness to pay. Producers will sell only if the price is higher than their willingness to sell.

LO 5.2 Calculate consumer surplus based on a graph or table.

Surplus is a way of measuring who benefits from transactions and how much. Consumer surplus is the net benefit that consumers receive from purchasing a good or service, measured by the difference between each consumer's willingness to pay and the actual price. Graphically, it is equal to the area below the demand curve and above the market price.

LO 5.3 Calculate producer surplus based on a graph or table.

Producer surplus is a measure of the net benefits that a producer receives from the sale of a good or service, measured by the difference between the producer's willingness to sell and the actual price. Graphically, it is equal to the area above the supply curve and below the market price.

LO 5.4 Calculate total surplus based on a graph or table.

Total surplus is a measure of the combined benefits that everyone receives from participating in an exchange of goods or services. It is calculated by adding consumer surplus and producer surplus. Graphically, it is equal to the total area between the supply and demand curves, to the left of the equilibrium quantity.

LO 5.5 Define efficiency in terms of surplus, and identify efficient and inefficient situations.

A market is *efficient* if there is no exchange that can make anyone better off without someone becoming worse off. An efficient market maximizes total surplus but doesn't tell us how the surplus is distributed between consumers and producers. In a competitive market, efficiency is achieved only at the market equilibrium price and quantity; higher prices and lower prices will both decrease the quantity bought and sold and reduce total surplus.

LO 5.6 Describe the distribution of surplus, or benefits to society, that results from a policy decision.

Prices above or below the market equilibrium reduce total surplus but also redistribute surplus between producers and consumers differently. A price above the equilibrium always decreases consumer surplus. Also, at a price above equilibrium, some producers win and others lose; the overall effect on producer surplus depends on the shape of the supply and demand curves. A price below the equilibrium always decreases producer surplus; some consumers win and others lose.

LO 5.7 Calculate deadweight loss.

Deadweight loss is the loss of total surplus that occurs when the quantity of a good that is bought and sold is below the market equilibrium quantity. Any intervention that moves a market away from the equilibrium price and quantity causes deadweight loss. Fewer exchanges take place, so there are fewer opportunities for the generation of surplus.

LO 5.8 Explain why correcting a missing market can make everyone better off.

A market is "missing" when there is a situation in which people would like to engage in mutually beneficial trades of goods and services but can't because no market for them exists. A missing market is a special case of a market in which quantity is held below the equilibrium—in this case, at or close to zero. Missing markets can occur for many reasons, including government intervention or a lack of information or technology. When missing markets are filled, people are able to trade, which generates surplus.

Review Questions

1. Bill is a professional photographer. His camera is broken and he needs a new one within the next hour, or he will miss an important deadline. Lisa is a high-school student who doesn't have a camera but wants to get one to take pictures at her prom next month. Who do you think would have a higher willingness to pay for a particular camera today? Why? **[LO 5.1]**

2. You are in the market for a new couch and have found two advertisements for the kind of couch you want to buy. One seller notes in her ad that she is selling because she is moving to a smaller apartment, and the couch won't fit in the new space. The other seller says he is selling because the couch doesn't match his other furniture. Which seller do you expect to buy from? Why? (*Hint:* Think who would be the more motivated seller.) **[LO 5.1]**

3. Suppose you are at a flea market and are considering buying a box of vintage records. You are trying to bargain down the price, but the seller overhears you telling a friend that you are willing to pay up to $50. Why is your consumer surplus now likely to be lower than it would have been if the seller hadn't overheard you? **[LO 5.2]**

4. Consider a market in equilibrium. Suppose supply in this market increases. How will this affect consumer surplus? Explain. **[LO 5.2]**

5. You currently have a television that you want to sell. You can either pick a price and try to sell it at a yard sale or auction it off on eBay. Which method do you think will yield a higher producer surplus? Why? **[LO 5.3]**

6. Consider a market in equilibrium. Suppose demand in this market decreases. How will this affect producer surplus? Explain. **[LO 5.3]**

7. Consider the market for plane tickets to Hawaii. A bad winter in the mainland United States increases demand for tropical vacations, shifting the demand curve to the right. The supply curve stays constant. Does total surplus increase or decrease? (*Hint:* Sketch out a generic supply and demand curve and look at what happens to the size of the triangle that represents total surplus when the demand curve shifts right.) **[LO 5.4]**

8. You need to paint your fence, but you really hate this task. You decide to hire the kid next door to do it for you. You would be willing to pay him up to $100, but you start by offering $50, expecting to negotiate. To your great surprise, he accepts your $50 offer. When you tell your friend about the great deal you got, she is shocked that you would take advantage of someone. What can you tell your friend to assure her that you did not cheat the kid next door? **[LO 5.4]**

9. New York City has a long-standing policy of controlling rents in certain parts of the city—in essence, a price ceiling on rent. Is the market for apartments likely to be efficient or inefficient? What does this imply for the size of total surplus? **[LO 5.5]**

10. Total surplus is maximized at the equilibrium price and quantity. When demand increases, price increases. Explain how total surplus is still maximized if price increases due to an increase in demand. **[LO 5.5]**

11. When the price of gasoline was very high in the summer of 2008, several U.S. presidential candidates proposed implementing a national price ceiling to keep fuel affordable. How would this policy have affected producer and consumer surplus? How would it have affected total surplus? **[LO 5.6]**

12. Consider a policy to help struggling farmers by setting a minimum trade price for wheat. Will this be an effective way to increase their surplus? Explain. **[LO 5.6]**

13. If rent control creates deadweight loss for both consumers and suppliers of housing, why are consumers often in favor of this policy? **[LO 5.7]**

14. Suppose price is 5 percent above equilibrium in two markets: a market for a necessity and a market for a luxury good. All else equal (including supply conditions), in which market do you expect deadweight loss to be greater? Explain. **[LO 5.7]**

15. Your grandmother likes old-fashioned yard sales and doesn't understand why everyone is so excited about eBay. Explain to her why the creation of a market that enables people who don't live in the same town to buy and sell used goods increases total surplus over the yard-sale market. **[LO 5.8]**

16. At Zooey's elementary school, children are not allowed to trade lunches or components of their lunches with other students. Lunchroom monitors watch closely and strictly enforce this policy. Help Zooey make an argument about the inefficiency of this policy to her principal. **[LO 5.8]**

Problems and Applications

1. Use the information in Table 5P-1 to construct a step graph of the six consumers' willingness to pay. **[LO 5.1]**

TABLE 5P-1

Buyer	Willingness to pay for one unit ($)
Fred	8
Ann	2
Morgan	16
Andre	12
Carla	2
Hanson	4

TABLE 5P-2

Seller	Willingness to sell one unit ($)
Joseph	25
Juan	20
Kristin	60
Peter	10
Candice	25
Solomon	50

2. Use the information in Table 5P-2 to construct a step graph of the six sellers' willingness to sell. **[LO 5.1]**

3. Answer the following questions based on Tables 5P-3 and 5P-4. **[LO 5.1]**

   a. What is the quantity demanded at $10? What is the quantity supplied at $10?

   b. What is the quantity demanded at $25? What is the quantity supplied at $25?

4. Based on Table 5P-5, calculate consumer surplus for each consumer when the price is $17. What is the total consumer surplus at this price? **[LO 5.2]**

TABLE 5P-3

Buyer	A	B	C	D	E	F	G	H	I
Willingness to pay for one unit	$35	$33	$27	$22	$21	$13	$13	$12	$6

TABLE 5P-4

Seller	A	B	C	D	E	F	G	H	I
Willingness to sell for one unit	$4	$9	$12	$14	$15	$21	$23	$30	$51

TABLE 5P-5

Buyer	A	B	C	D	E	F	G	H	I
Willingness to pay for one unit	$6	$27	$13	$21	$33	$35	$12	$13	$22

FIGURE 5P-1

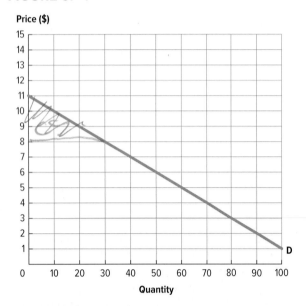

FIGURE 5P-2

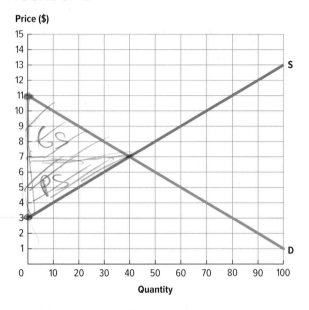

FIGURE 5P-3

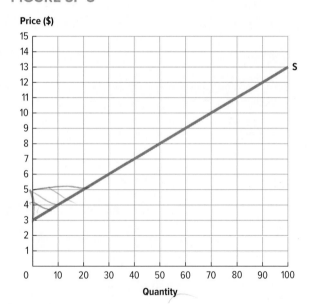

5. Use the demand curve represented in Figure 5P-1 to draw the consumer surplus when the market price is $8. What is the value of consumer surplus at this price? **[LO 5.2]**

6. Based on Figure 5P-2, consumer surplus is $0 when price is greater than or equal to what price? **[LO 5.2]**

7. Use the market represented in Figure 5P-2 to plot the equilibrium price and quantity and to draw the consumer surplus when the market is in equilibrium. What is the value of consumer surplus at the equilibrium price? **[LO 5.2]**

8. Use the market represented in Figure 5P-2 to draw the consumer surplus when the price is $5. What is the value of consumer surplus at this price? **[LO 5.2]**

9. Based on Table 5P-6, calculate producer surplus for each producer when the price is $20. What is total producer surplus at this price? **[LO 5.3]**

10. Use the supply curve represented in Figure 5P-3 to draw the producer surplus when the market price is $5. What is the value of producer surplus at this price? **[LO 5.3]**

11. Based on Figure 5P-2, producer surplus is $0 when price is less than or equal to what price? **[LO 5.3]**

12. Use the market represented in Figure 5P-2 to plot the equilibrium price and quantity and to draw the producer surplus when the market is in equilibrium. What is the value of producer surplus at the equilibrium price? **[LO 5.3]**

TABLE 5P-6

Buyer	A	B	C	D	E	F	G	H	I
Willingness to pay for one unit	$21	$4	$30	$14	$12	$15	$51	$9	$23

FIGURE 5P-4

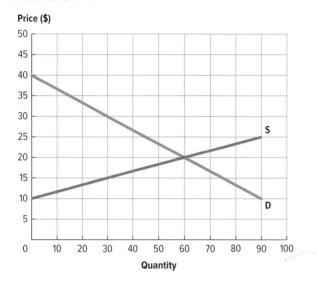

FIGURE 5P-6

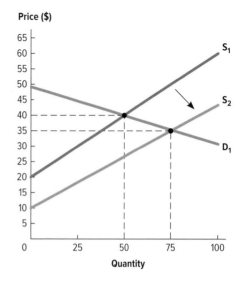

13. Use the market represented in Figure 5P-2 to draw the producer surplus if the price is $9. What is the value of producer surplus at this price? **[LO 5.3]**

14. Use the market represented in Figure 5P-4 to draw the consumer and producer surplus when the market is in equilibrium. What is the value of total surplus at equilibrium? **[LO 5.4]**

15. Consider the market represented in Figure 5P-5. **[LO 5.4]**
   a. Calculate total surplus when demand is D₁.
   b. Calculate total surplus when demand decreases to D₂.

16. Consider the market represented in Figure 5P-6. **[LO 5.4]**
   a. Calculate total surplus when supply is S₁.
   b. Calculate total surplus when supply increases to S₂.

17. Consider the market represented in Figure 5P-7. **[LO 5.5]**
   a. Draw the consumer surplus and the producer surplus at the equilibrium price and quantity. What is the value of total surplus at equilibrium?
   b. Draw the consumer surplus and the producer surplus if the price is $30. What are the values of consumer surplus, producer surplus, and total surplus at this price?
   c. Draw the consumer surplus and the producer surplus if the price is $10. What are the values of consumer surplus, producer surplus, and total surplus at this price?

FIGURE 5P-5

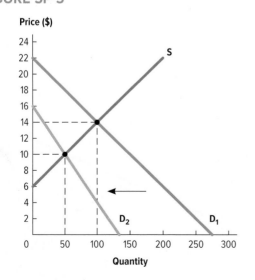

FIGURE 5P-7

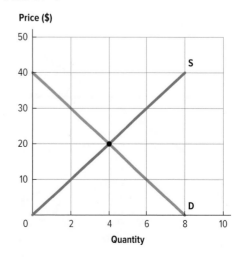

18. Assume the market for wine is functioning at its equilibrium. For each of the following situations, say whether the new market outcome will be *efficient* or *inefficient*. **[LO 5.5]**

    a. A new report shows that wine is good for heart health.

    b. The government sets a minimum price for wine, which increases the current price.

    c. An unexpected late frost ruins large crops of grapes.

    d. Grape pickers demand higher wages, increasing the price of wine.

19. Based on Figure 5P-8, choose all of the following options that are true. **[LO 5.5, 5.6]**

    a. The market is efficient.

    b. Total surplus is higher than it would be at market equilibrium.

    c. Total surplus is lower than it would be at market equilibrium.

    d. Producer surplus is lower than it would be at market equilibrium.

    e. Consumer surplus is lower than it would be at market equilibrium.

20. In which of the following situations can you say, without further information, that consumer surplus decreases relative to the market equilibrium level? **[LO 5.6]**

    a. Your state passes a law that pushes the interest rate (i.e., the price) for payday loans below the equilibrium rate.

    b. The federal government enforces a law that raises the price of dairy goods above the equilibrium.

    c. Your city passes a local property tax, under which buyers of new houses have to pay an additional 5 percent on top of the purchase price.

    d. The government lowers the effective price of food purchases through a food-stamp program.

21. Use the areas labeled in the market represented in Figure 5P-9 to answer the following questions. **[LO 5.6]**

    a. What area(s) are consumer surplus at the market equilibrium price?

    b. What area(s) are producer surplus at the market equilibrium price?

    c. Compared to the equilibrium, what area(s) do consumers lose if price is P_2?

    d. Compared to the equilibrium, what area(s) do producers lose if the price is P_2?

    e. Compared to the equilibrium, what area(s) do producers gain if the price is P_2?

    f. Compared to the equilibrium, total surplus decreases by what area(s) if the price is P_2?

22. Figure 5P-10 shows a market for cotton, with the price held at $0.80 per pound. Draw and calculate the deadweight loss caused by this policy. **[LO 5.7]**

23. Consider the market represented in Figure 5P-11. **[LO 5.7]**

    a. Suppose the government sets a minimum price of $25 in the market. Calculate the deadweight loss.

    b. Suppose the government sets a maximum price of $25 in the market. Calculate the deadweight loss.

24. What is the value of the existence of the market represented in Figure 5P-12? **[LO 5.8]**

FIGURE 5P-8

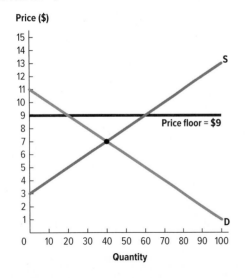

FIGURE 5P-9

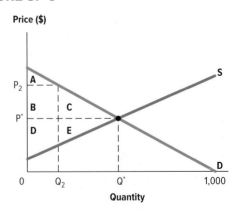

FIGURE 5P-10

Quantity (millions of lb.)

FIGURE 5P-11

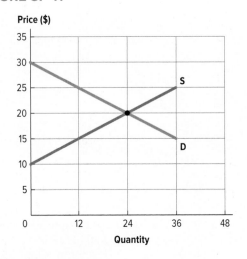

Quantity

FIGURE 5P-12

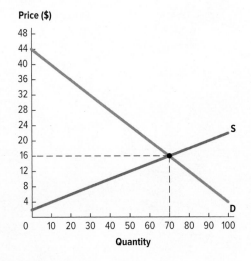

Quantity

FIGURE 5P-13

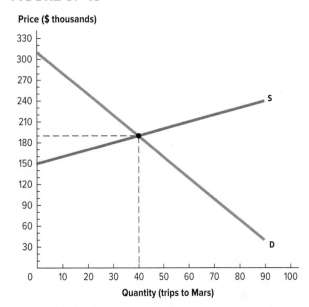

Quantity (trips to Mars)

25. We can consider the market for traveling to Mars to be missing because no technology exists that allows this service to be bought and sold. Suppose that someone has invented space-travel technology that will enable this service to be provided. Figure 5P-13 shows the estimated market for trips to Mars. Calculate the surplus that could be generated by filling in this missing market. **[LO 5.8]**

Endnotes

1 https://investors.ebayinc.com/releasedetail. cfm?ReleaseID=952024

2 http://news.bbc.co.uk/2/hi/4034787.stm

Math Essentials: The Area under a Linear Curve

Learning Objective

LO D.1 Calculate surplus by finding the area under a linear curve.

Chapter 5 introduced you to the concept of surplus. Surplus measures the gains or losses in well-being resulting from transactions in a market. You will often need to calculate a numerical value for surplus. To do that, you need to know how to find the area under a linear curve, and, therefore, we will review a little geometry.

The Area under a Linear Curve

LO D.1 Calculate surplus by finding the area under a linear curve.

Graphically, surplus is represented as the area between a supply or demand curve and the market price. The area between these curves and the market price will take the form of a triangle. In order to find surplus, you are going to need to be able to calculate the area of a triangle:

EQUATION D-1 $\text{Area of triangle} = \frac{1}{2} \times \text{Base of triangle} \times \text{Height of triangle} = \frac{1}{2}bh$

The key, then, is to figure which length to use as the base and which as the height.

In panel A of Figure D-1, consumer surplus is the shaded triangle below the demand curve and above the market price. The base of this triangle is the *horizontal distance* from the equilibrium point to the y-axis, $(12 - 0) = 12$. The height is the *vertical distance* from the equilibrium price to the y-intercept of the demand curve, $(50 - 20) = 30$. Therefore, the area of the triangle—and the consumer surplus—is:

$$\frac{1}{2} \times (12 \times 30) = \$180$$

Producer surplus is the shaded area below the market price and above the supply curve in panel B of Figure D-1. The base of the triangle is again the *horizontal distance* from the equilibrium point to the y-axis, $(12 - 0) = 12$. The height is the vertical distance from the equilibrium

FIGURE D-1

Measuring the area under a curve

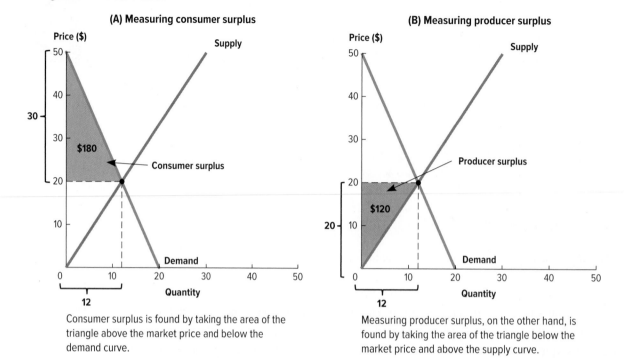

(A) Measuring consumer surplus

Consumer surplus is found by taking the area of the triangle above the market price and below the demand curve.

(B) Measuring producer surplus

Measuring producer surplus, on the other hand, is found by taking the area of the triangle below the market price and above the supply curve.

price to the y-intercept of the supply curve, $(20 - 0) = 20$. Therefore the area of the triangle—and the producer surplus—is:

$$\frac{1}{2} \times (12 \times 20) = \$120$$

You learned in Chapter 5 that total surplus is consumer surplus plus producer surplus:

$$\text{Total surplus} = \$180 + \$120 = \$300$$

We can also calculate total surplus directly by calculating the area of the larger triangle that encompasses both. This time, the calculation of this triangle is slightly different. The base is the amount of space in between the y-intercept of the supply and demand curves. This gives a base of 50. The height of the triangle, on the other hand, is the distance from the y-axis to the equilibrium point. The area is thus $\frac{1}{2} \times 50 \times 12 = \$300$, the same result as before.

Occasionally, you will see oddly shaped surplus areas. You can always calculate these by breaking them down into familiar rectangles and triangles. Then calculate the area of each using length times width (for a rectangle) and $\frac{1}{2}bh$ (for a triangle), and add the results to find the total area.

Problems and Applications

1. Use the graph in Figure DP-1 to answer the following questions. **[LO D.1]**

    a. What is the amount of consumer surplus?

    b. What is the amount of producer surplus?

    c. What is the amount of total surplus?

FIGURE DP-1

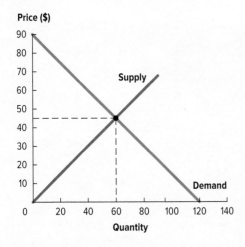

2. Use these two supply and demand equations to answer the following questions. **[LO D.1]**

    $$P = 50 - 4Q$$

    $$P = 2 + 2Q$$

    a. What is the equilibrium price? What is the equilibrium quantity?

    b. Draw a graph of supply and demand and illustrate the equilibrium.

    c. What is the amount of consumer surplus?

    d. What is the amount of producer surplus?

    e. What is the amount of total surplus?

Government Intervention

Learning Objectives

LO 6.1 Calculate the effect of a price ceiling on the equilibrium price and quantity.

LO 6.2 Calculate the effect of a price floor on the equilibrium price and quantity.

LO 6.3 Calculate the effect of a tax on the equilibrium price and quantity.

LO 6.4 Calculate the effect of a subsidy on the equilibrium price and quantity.

LO 6.5 Explain how elasticity and time period influence the impact of a market intervention.

FEEDING THE WORLD, ONE PRICE CONTROL AT A TIME

In the spring of 2008, a worldwide food shortage caused food prices to skyrocket. In just a few months, the prices of wheat, rice, and corn shot up as much as 140 percent. In the United States, the number of people living on food stamps rose to the highest level since the 1960s. By June, low-income Americans were facing tough choices, as the prices of basics like eggs and dairy products rose. Many reported giving up meat and fresh fruit; others said they began to buy cheap food past the expiration date.[1]

Rising food prices caused trouble all over the world. The *Economist* magazine reported on the political fallout:

> [In Côte d'Ivoire,] two days of violence persuaded the government to postpone planned elections. . . . In Haiti, protesters chanting "We're hungry" forced the prime minister to resign; 24 people were killed in riots in Cameroon; Egypt's president ordered the army to start baking bread; [and] the Philippines made hoarding rice punishable by life imprisonment.[2]

Faced with hunger, hardship, and angry outbursts, many governments felt obliged to respond to the crisis. But what to do? Responses varied widely. Many countries made it illegal to charge high prices for food. Other countries subsidized the price of basic necessities. In the United

© Abdurashid Abdulle/AFP/Getty Images

States and Europe, policy-makers tried to alleviate the shortage by paying farmers to grow more food. Were these responses appropriate? What, if anything, *should* governments do in such a situation?

Food is a tricky issue for policy-makers because it's a basic necessity. If prices rise too high, people go hungry. If prices fall too low, farmers go out of business, which raises the risk of food shortages in the future. So, while policy-makers aren't too concerned if the prices of many goods—like digital cameras or lattes—jump up and down, they often do care about food prices. But attempts to lower, raise, or simply stabilize prices can backfire or create unintended side effects. Sometimes the cure ends up being worse than the problem itself.

In this chapter, we'll look at the logic behind policies that governments commonly use to intervene in markets. There are often both intended and unintended consequences— and economic models and data can help think through both. We will start with *price controls,* which make it illegal to sell a good for more or less than a certain price. Then we will look at *taxes* and *subsidies,* which discourage or encourage the production of particular goods. These tools are regularly applied to a broad range of issues, from unemployment to home ownership, air pollution to education. For better or worse, they have a huge effect on our lives as workers, consumers, businesspeople, and voters.

Why Intervene?

In Chapter 3, "Markets," we saw that markets gravitate toward equilibrium. When markets work well, prices adjust until the quantity of a good that consumers demand equals the quantity that suppliers want to produce. At equilibrium, everyone gets what he or she is willing to pay for. In Chapter 5, "Efficiency," we saw that equilibrium price and quantity also maximize total surplus. At equilibrium, there is no way to make some people better off without harming others.

So, why intervene? Why not let the invisible hand of the market determine prices and allocate resources? Some would argue that's exactly what should be done. Others believe the government has to intervene sometimes—and the fact is that every single government in the world intervenes in markets in some fashion.

Three reasons to intervene

The arguments for intervention fall into three categories: changing the distribution of surplus, encouraging or discouraging consumption of certain goods, and correcting market failures. As we discuss different policy tools throughout the chapter, ask yourself which of these motivations is driving the intervention.

Changing the distribution of surplus

Efficient markets maximize total surplus, but an efficient outcome may still be seen as unfair. For example, even if the job market is efficient, wages can still drop so low that some workers fall below the poverty line while their employers make healthy profits. In such cases, some may argue for intervention in markets in order to change the distribution of surplus. The government might respond by intervening in the labor market to impose a minimum wage. This policy will change the distribution of surplus, reducing employers' profits (which may lead to higher prices) and lifting workers' incomes.

Of course, the definition of fairness is up for debate. Reasonable people can—and often do—argue about whether a policy that benefits a certain group (such as minimum-wage workers) is justified or not. Our focus will be on accurately describing the benefits and costs of such policies. Economics can help us predict whose well-being will increase, whose well-being will decrease, and who may be affected in unpredictable ways.

Encouraging or discouraging consumption

Around the world, many people judge certain products to be "good" or "bad" based on culture, health, religion, or other values. At the extreme, certain "bad" products are banned, such as many addictive drugs.

More often, governments use taxes to discourage people from consuming "bad" products, rather than simply banning them. Common examples are cigarettes and alcohol. Furthermore, in some cases consumption of a good imposes costs on others, such as second-hand smoke from cigarettes. In such cases the government may add a tax so that consumers or producers of the good have to pay more of the cost to society of consuming or producing that good. (Figuring out exactly what that cost is can be quite difficult, by the way.)

On the other hand, governments use *subsidies* to encourage people to consume "good" products or services. For instance, many governments provide public funding for schools to encourage education and for vaccinations to encourage parents to protect their children against disease.

Correcting market failures

Our model of demand and supply has so far assumed that markets work efficiently. In the real world, though, that's not always true. For example, sometimes there is only one producer of a good, who faces no competition and can charge an inefficiently high price. In other cases, one person's use of a product or service imposes costs on other people that are not captured in prices paid by the first person; an example is the pollution that others experience when smoke is ejected by your car (that is, the price you pay for the gas that is burned in your car imposes a cost on others when they must experience the pollution).

Situations in which the assumption of efficient, competitive markets fails to hold are called **market failures**. When there is a market failure, intervention can actually increase total surplus. We'll have much more to say about market failures in future chapters. In this chapter, we will stick to analyzing the effect of government interventions in efficient, competitive markets.

market failures

situations in which the assumption of efficient, competitive markets fails to hold

Four real-world interventions

In this chapter we'll look at four real-world examples of how governments have intervened or could intervene in the market for food. For each, we'll consider the motives for the intervention and what its direct and indirect consequences were or could be. These four interventions are:

1. For many Mexican families, tortillas are an important food. What happened when the Mexican government set a *maximum price* for tortillas, in an effort to keep them affordable?

2. To ensure supplies of fresh milk, the U.S. government wanted to protect dairy farmers. What happened when the government set a *minimum price* for milk?

3. Many Americans struggle with health problems caused by overeating and poor nutrition. Several states have responded by banning the use of certain fats in food products; others require that restaurants post nutritional information about the foods they serve. What would happen if governments *taxed* high-fat or high-calorie foods?

4. What would happen if, instead of setting a maximum price for tortillas, the Mexican government *subsidized* tortillas?

As we walk through these examples of real policies, we want you to apply both positive and normative analysis. Remember the difference:

- *Positive analysis* is about facts: Does the policy actually accomplish the original goal?
- *Normative analysis* is a matter of values and opinions: Do you think the policy is a good idea?

Few policies are all good or all bad. The key question is, *What are the trade-offs* involved in the intervention? Do the benefits outweigh the costs?

✓CONCEPT CHECK

☐ What are three reasons that a government might want to intervene in markets?

Price Controls

Suppose you are an economic policy advisor, and food prices are rising. What should you do? If you live in a region with many low-income consumers, you might want to take action to ensure that everyone gets enough to eat. One policy tool you might consider using is a **price control**—a regulation that sets a maximum or minimum legal price for a particular good. The direct effect of a price control is to hold the price of a good up or down when the market shifts, thus preventing the market from reaching a new equilibrium.

price control

a regulation that sets a maximum or minimum legal price for a particular good

Price controls can be divided into two opposing categories: *price ceilings* and *price floors.* We met this idea already in Chapter 5, "Efficiency," when we imagined an interfering eBay manager setting prices for digital cameras. In reality, eBay would never do such a thing, but governments often do, particularly when it comes to markets for food items. What are the effects of using price controls to intervene in a well-functioning, competitive market?

Price ceilings

LO 6.1 Calculate the effect of a price ceiling on the equilibrium price and quantity.

A **price ceiling** is a maximum legal price at which a good can be sold. Many countries have price ceilings on staple foods, gasoline, and electricity because policy-makers try to ensure everyone can afford the basic necessities.

price ceiling
a maximum legal price at which a good can be sold

Here, we come to the first of the real-world interventions in the chapter: Historically, the government of Mexico has set a price ceiling for tortillas. The intent is to guarantee that this staple food will remain affordable. Panel A of Figure 6-1 illustrates a hypothetical market for tortillas without a price ceiling. The equilibrium price is $0.50 per pound and the equilibrium quantity is 50 million pounds.

Let's say that the government of Mexico responded to rising tortilla prices by setting a price ceiling of approximately $0.25 per pound, as shown in panel B of Figure 6-1. How would we expect consumers to respond to this intervention? When the price falls, consumers will want to buy more tortillas. In this example, the price fell from $0.50 to $0.25, and as a result, quantity demanded increased from 50 million to 75 million pounds. How would we expect producers to respond to this intervention? Predictably, a lower price means fewer producers will be willing to supply tortillas. In this example, when the price fell to $0.25, the quantity supplied dropped from 50 million to 25 million pounds.

The lower price imposed by the price ceiling means higher quantity demanded but lower quantity supplied. Supply and demand were no longer in equilibrium. The price ceiling created

FIGURE 6-1

A market with and without a price ceiling

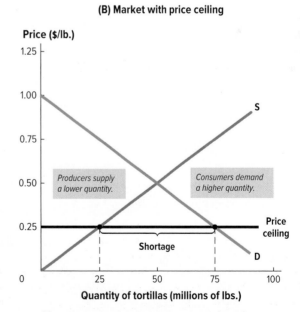

Without government intervention, the market for tortillas in Mexico would reach equilibrium at a price of $0.50 per pound and a quantity of 50 million pounds.

After government intervention, a price ceiling of $0.25 keeps the price of tortillas below the equilibrium point. At this new price, consumers want to buy more tortillas (75 million pounds) than producers want to supply (25 million pounds), resulting in a shortage of tortillas.

a *shortage* of tortillas, equal to the 50-million-pound difference between the quantity demanded (75 million) and the quantity supplied (25 million).

Did the price ceiling meet the goal of providing low-priced tortillas to consumers? Yes and no. Consumers were able to buy *some* tortillas at the low price of $0.25 a pound—but they *wanted* to buy three times as many tortillas as producers were willing to supply. We can assess the full effect of the price ceiling by looking at what happened to consumer and producer surplus. Even without looking at the graph, we already know that a price ceiling will cause producer surplus to fall: Sellers are selling fewer tortillas at a lower price.

We also know that total surplus—that is, producer and consumer surplus combined—will fall because the market has moved away from equilibrium. Some trades that would have happened at the equilibrium price do not happen. Also, the surplus that would have been generated by those mutually beneficial trades is lost entirely. This area is known as *deadweight loss* and is represented by area 1 in Figure 6-2. As discussed in Chapter 5, "Efficiency," **deadweight loss** represents the loss of total surplus that occurs because the quantity of a good that is bought and sold is below the market equilibrium quantity. Economists refer to changes in the economic well-being of market participants, as measured by changes in consumer surplus or producer surplus like deadweight loss, as *welfare effects*.

What we can't tell without looking at the graph is whether consumer surplus will increase or decrease; that response depends on the shape of the supply and demand curves. In this instance, consumers lose surplus from trades that no longer take place (from the 25 million pounds of tortillas no longer supplied). But for the trades that still do take place, consumers gain surplus from paying $0.25 instead of $0.50. In those trades, producers lose the same amount of surplus from receiving the lower price. This direct transfer of surplus from producers to consumers is represented by area 2 (the cross-hatched area) in Figure 6-2.

Did consumer surplus increase or decrease? Because area 2 in Figure 6-2 is larger than half of area 1 (the portion of deadweight loss that would have gone to consumers at equilibrium), we

deadweight loss
a loss of total surplus that occurs because the quantity of a good that is bought and sold is below the market equilibrium quantity

---

FIGURE 6-2

Welfare effects of a price ceiling

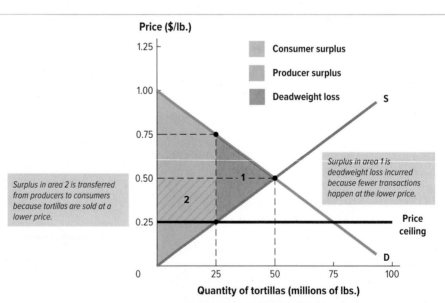

The price ceiling causes the total quantity of tortillas traded to fall by 25 million (from equilibrium at 50 million to 25 million). This results in deadweight loss. The price ceiling also causes surplus to be transferred from producers to consumers: Consumers win because they pay a lower price, and producers lose because they sell at a lower price ($0.25 instead of $0.50).

know that the intended goal of the price ceiling was achieved: a net increase in the well-being of consumers.

Was the policy worthwhile? On the one hand, consumers gained surplus. On the other hand, the surplus lost by producers was greater than that gained by consumers, meaning that total surplus decreased. Is it a price worth paying? That is a normative question about which reasonable people can disagree.

Another factor we may want to consider in our overall analysis of the price ceiling is how the scarce tortillas are allocated. Because a price ceiling causes a shortage, goods must be rationed. Rationing could be done in a number of ways. One possibility is for goods to be rationed equally, with each family entitled to buy the same amount of tortillas per week. This is what happened when food was rationed in the United States during World War II. Another possibility is to allocate goods on a first-come, first-served basis. This mode of rationing forces people to waste time standing in lines.

In still other cases, rationed goods might go to those who are given preference by the government, or to the friends and family of sellers. Finally, shortages open the door for people to bribe whoever is in charge of allocating scarce supplies. Rationing via bribery results in even more deadweight loss than in the example shown in Figure 6-2. Economists call this *rent-seeking behavior,* and it is often cited as an argument against imposing price ceilings.

The What Do You Think? box "Put a cap on payday lending?" asks you to weigh the costs and benefits of a controversial price ceiling on the interest rates of payday loans.

What Do You Think?
Put a cap on payday lending?

After the global financial crisis that began in 2008, policy-makers considered many proposals to reform financial practices. Small loans to consumers got a lot of attention because some people felt that irresponsible borrowing—through credit cards, mortgages, and consumer loans—was in part to blame for the crisis.

One of the most controversial types of borrowing is the *payday loan,* a short-term cash loan—usually for less than $1,000—that is intended to be repaid with the borrower's next paycheck. Many borrowers like these loans because they can walk out of the loan center with cash in their pockets in 30 minutes or faster. Payday loan centers tend to be located in low-income neighborhoods, where people have few other options for borrowing.

Because people with poor credit often use payday loans, lenders often charge high fees or interest rates (reflecting the higher risk of loan default). The fees also tend to be modest relative to the labor cost for the lender, but quite high relative to the amount borrowed. For example, you might not see a problem with a retailer earning a $20 profit on the sale of a $100 jacket. But if an individual must pay a $20 fee for a $100 one-week loan, that person will be paying a very high interest rate on an annualized basis.

In 2008, the U.S. Congress considered putting a price ceiling of 36 percent per year on the interest rates lenders could charge for payday loans. Since the interest rate is effectively the "price" of taking out a loan, this measure amounted to a price ceiling on a certain sort of loan service. Supporters of the proposed price ceiling argued that limiting interest rates would protect vulnerable consumers from "predatory" lenders who offer loans people can't afford. Those loans often trap borrowers in a cycle of taking out loans simply to repay prior loans.

Critics of the price ceiling countered that capping interest rates would force many payday lenders out of business. Consumers who make informed decisions to take out payday loans would be hurt by the resulting loss of credit. Those borrowers who have no other options could be driven to stop paying their bills or overdraw their checking accounts. This could lead to utilities

(continued)

being cut off or even eviction—consequences likely far worse than the fee on the payday loan. Ultimately, as expensive as payday loans are, they may be better than the next-best alternative.

Currently, 18 states (as well as the District of Columbia) have banned payday loans or set a ceiling on the interest rates that are charged for them. In 2008, for example, Ohio capped payday loan rates at 28 percent per year. Other states still allow less-restricted payday loans. In Missouri, lenders can charge up to 75 percent over a short loan period. You can learn about short-term loan regulations in your state by visiting http://www.paydayloaninfo.org/state-information.

WHAT DO YOU THINK?

1. An Internet search for *payday loan* turns up dozens of websites that promise "instant," "easy," or "no-hassle" loans. What's the cheapest rate you can find in your state? Would you consider borrowing at this price?
2. Price ceilings hold down prices, but also cause shortages and transfer surplus from payday-loan store owners to borrowers. Knowing that, would you support a cap on payday loan interest rates?
3. What would you expect the outcome of such a policy to be for buyers (borrowers) and sellers (lenders)?
4. Can you think of a way to protect potential victims of high interest rates without hurting borrowers who make informed borrowing decisions?

Source: "Payday loan consumer information," Consumer Federation of America's PayDay Loan website, http://www.paydayloaninfo.org.

Nonbinding price ceilings

A price ceiling does not always affect the market outcome. If the ceiling is set above the equilibrium price in a market, it is said to be *nonbinding*. That is, the ceiling doesn't "bind" or restrict buyers' and sellers' behavior because the current equilibrium is within the range allowed by the ceiling. In such cases, the equilibrium price and quantity will prevail.

Price ceilings are usually binding when they are first implemented. (Otherwise, why bother to create one?) Over time, though, shifts in the market can render the ceilings nonbinding. Suppose the price of corn decreases, reducing the cost of making tortillas. Figure 6-3 shows how the supply curve for tortillas would shift to the right (from S_1 to S_2) in response to this change in the market (a change in the price of inputs). This shift causes the equilibrium price to fall below the price ceiling. The new equilibrium is 80 million pounds of tortillas at $0.20 a pound, and the price ceiling becomes nonbinding.

Price floors

LO 6.2 Calculate the effect of a price floor on the equilibrium price and quantity.

---

price floor
a minimum legal price at which a good can be sold

A **price floor** is a minimum legal price at which a good can be sold. The United States has a long history of establishing price floors for certain agricultural goods. The rationale is that farming is a risky business—subject to bad weather, crop failure, and unreliable prices—but also an essential one, if people are to have enough to eat. A price floor is seen as a way to guarantee farmers a minimum income in the face of these difficulties, keeping them in business and ensuring a reliable supply of food.

We now come to the second of our four real-world interventions: The United States has maintained price floors for dairy products for over 65 years; the Milk Price Support Program began with the Agricultural Act of 1949. What effect has this program had on the market for

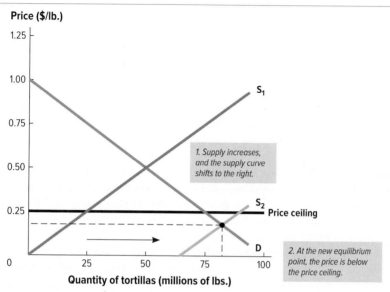

FIGURE 6-3

Nonbinding price ceiling

A price ceiling is intended to keep prices below the equilibrium level. However, changes in the market can reduce the equilibrium price to a level below the price ceiling. When that happens, the price ceiling no longer creates a shortage because the quantity supplied equals the quantity demanded.

milk? In panel A of Figure 6-4, we show a hypothetical unregulated market for milk in the United States, with an annual equilibrium quantity of 15 billion gallons and an equilibrium price of $2.50 per gallon.

Now suppose the U.S. government implements a price floor, so that the price of milk cannot fall below $3 per gallon, as shown in panel B of Figure 6-4. How will producers and

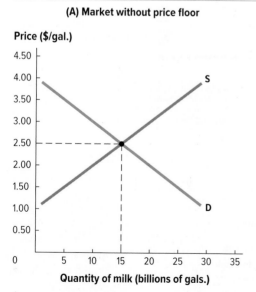

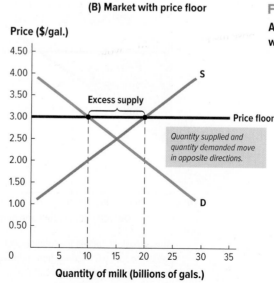

FIGURE 6-4

A market with and without a price floor

Without government intervention, the equilibrium point in the market for milk would be 15 billion gallons at a price of $2.50 per gallon.

A price floor raises the price of milk above the equilibrium point. At the new price of $3 per gallon, consumers want to buy less than suppliers want to produce, resulting in a 10-billion-gallon surplus.

consumers respond? At $3 per gallon, dairy farmers will want to increase milk production from 15 to 20 billion gallons, moving up along the supply curve. At that price, however, consumers will want to decrease their milk consumption from 15 to 10 billion gallons, moving up along the demand curve. As a result, the price floor creates an excess supply of milk that is equal to the difference between the quantity supplied and the quantity demanded—in this case, 10 billion gallons.

Has the government accomplished its aim of supporting dairy farmers and providing them with a reliable income? As with price ceilings, the answer is yes and no. Producers who can sell all their milk will be happy: They are selling more milk at a higher price. However, producers who cannot sell all their milk, because demand no longer meets supply, will be unhappy. Consumers will be unhappy because they are getting less milk at a higher price.

Again, we can apply the concept of surplus to formally analyze how this change in total surplus is distributed between consumers and producers. Before the price floor, 15 billion gallons of milk were supplied and bought; after the price floor, this number is only 10 billion. Five billion gallons of milk that could have been traded were not, reducing total surplus. This deadweight loss is represented by area 1 in Figure 6-5.

Like price ceilings, price floors change the distribution of surplus; in this case, producers win at the expense of consumers. When the price floor is in effect, the only consumers who buy are those whose willingness to pay is above $3. Their consumer surplus falls because they are buying the same milk at a higher price. Consumers' lost surplus is transferred directly to the producers who sell milk to them. This transfer of consumer surplus is represented by area 2 (the cross-hatched area) in Figure 6-5.

Did producers gain or lose overall? The answer depends on whether the area of transferred consumer surplus is bigger or smaller than the producers' share of the deadweight loss. Area 2 (the transfer of consumer surplus) is larger than the section of area 1 lost to producers; in this case, the price floor policy increased well-being for producers.

FIGURE 6-5

Welfare effects of a price floor

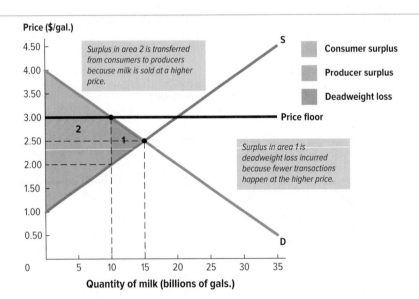

The price floor causes the total quantity of milk traded to fall by 5 billion gallons relative to equilibrium. This results in deadweight loss. The price floor also causes surplus to be transferred from consumers to producers: In this example, producers win because they sell at a higher price, and consumers lose because they pay a higher price.

Is the price of reduced total and consumer surplus worth paying to achieve increased producer surplus? One factor to consider is how the extra surplus is distributed among producers. Producers who are able to sell all their milk at the higher price will be happy. But producers who do not manage to sell all of their goods will be left holding an excess supply. They may be worse off than before the imposition of the price floor. With excess supply, customers may choose to buy from firms they like based on familiarity, political preference, or any other decision-making process they choose.

To prevent some producers from being left with excess supply, the government may decide to buy up all the excess supply of milk, ensuring that *all* producers benefit. In fact, that is how the milk price support program works in the United States. The Department of Agriculture guarantees producers that it will buy milk at a certain price, regardless of the market price. Of course, paying for the milk imposes a cost on taxpayers and is often cited as an argument against price floors. How much milk will the government have to buy? The answer is the entire amount of the excess supply created by the price floor. In the case of the hypothetical milk price floor, the government will have to buy 10 billion gallons at a price of $3. The cost to taxpayers of maintaining the price floor in this example would be $30 billion each year.

Nonbinding price floors

Price floors are not always binding. In fact, in recent years, the market prices for dairy products in the United States have usually been above the price floor. The price floor may become binding, however, in response to changes in the market. Figure 6-6 shows how such a decrease in supply could render a price floor nonbinding. Consider the effect of the increased demand for ethanol in 2007 on the market for milk. Ethanol is a fuel additive made from corn. The sudden rise in demand for ethanol pushed up the price of corn, which in turn pushed up the cost of livestock feed for dairy farmers. As a result of this change in the price of inputs, the supply curve for milk shifted to the left (from S_1 to S_2 in Figure 6-6). This shift pushed the equilibrium price for milk above the $3 price floor to $3.50.

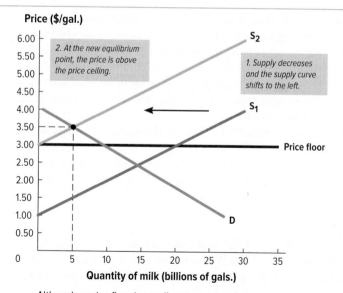

FIGURE 6-6

Nonbinding price floor

Although a price floor is usually set so as to raise prices above the equilibrium level, changes in the supply can raise the equilibrium price above the price floor. When that happens, the surplus that was created by the price floor disappears and the quantity supplied equals the quantity demanded.

✓ CONCEPT CHECK

☐ Why does a price ceiling cause a shortage? **[LO 6.1]**

☐ What can cause a price ceiling to become nonbinding? **[LO 6.1]**

☐ Explain how a government can support a price floor through purchases. **[LO 6.2]**

☐ What can cause a price floor to become nonbinding? **[LO 6.2]**

Taxes and Subsidies

Taxes are the main way that governments raise revenue to pay for public programs. Taxes and subsidies can also be used to correct market failures and encourage or discourage production and consumption of particular goods. However, like price floors and price ceilings, they can have unintended consequences.

Taxes

LO 6.3 Calculate the effect of a tax on the equilibrium price and quantity.

We began this chapter by discussing hunger, which is usually a minor problem in wealthy countries. Indeed, the United States has the opposite problem: diseases associated with overeating and poor nutrition such as obesity, heart disease, and diabetes. How can policy-makers respond to this new type of food crisis? This issue is the third of the real-world interventions in this chapter.

In 2008, the state of California banned the use of trans fats in restaurants in an effort to reduce heart disease and related problems. Trans fats are artificially produced ("partially hydrogenated") unsaturated fats. Used in many fried and packaged foods because they extend products' shelf lives, they are believed to be unhealthy if consumed in excess. For decades, trans fats have been the key to making commercially produced french fries crispy and pastries flaky.

Rather than banning trans fats, what would happen if California taxed them? When a good is taxed, either the buyer or seller must pay some extra amount to the government on top of the sale price. How should we expect people to *respond* to a tax on trans fats? Taxes have two primary effects: First, they discourage production and consumption of the good that is taxed. Second, they raise government revenue through the fees paid by those who continue buying and selling the good. Therefore, we would expect a tax both to reduce consumption of trans fats and to provide a new source of public revenue.

Figure 6-7 illustrates this scenario by showing the impact of a trans-fat tax on the market for Chocolate Whizbangs. A delicious imaginary candy, Chocolate Whizbangs are unfortunately rather high in trans fats. Suppose that, currently, 30 million Whizbangs are sold every year, at $0.50 each. To discourage consumption, a tax on Whizbangs has been proposed; the new tax could be imposed either on sellers or on buyers.

A tax on sellers

Let's say that the government of California enacts a trans-fat tax of $0.20, which the seller must pay for every Whizbang sold. *How will buyers and sellers respond?* The impact of a tax is more complicated than the impact of a price control, so let's take it one step at a time.

1. **Does a tax on sellers affect supply?** *Yes, supply decreases.*

    When a tax is imposed on sellers (producers), they must pay the government $0.20 for each Whizbang sold. At any market price, sellers will behave as if the price they are receiving is actually $0.20 lower. Put another way, for sellers to be willing to supply any given quantity, the market price must be $0.20 higher than it was before the tax.

FIGURE 6-7

Effect of a tax paid by the seller

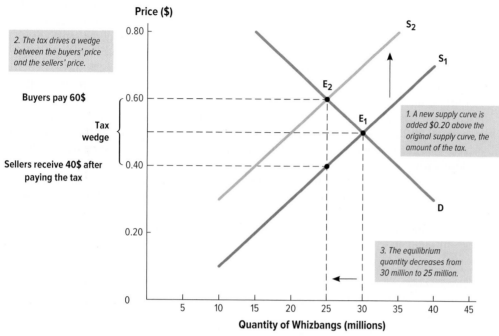

A tax levied on the seller adds a new supply curve that is $0.20 higher than the original, which is the amount of the tax. As a result, the equilibrium quantity decreases and the equilibrium price increases. At the equilibrium quantity, the price paid by buyers is now different from the amount received by sellers after the tax is paid. This "tax wedge" is equal to the amount of the tax, or $0.20.

Figure 6-7 shows this change in supply graphically, by adding a new supply curve (S_2). (Technically, this "shift" isn't really a shift of the curve but a way of showing the new equilibrium price; see the nearby Potentially Confusing box.) The new supply curve is $0.20 higher, the exact amount of the tax. At any given market price, sellers will now produce the same quantity as they would have at a price $0.20 lower before the tax: At $0.60 on curve S_2, the quantity supplied will be the same as at a price of $0.40 on curve S_1. At a price of $0.50 on curve S_2, the quantity supplied will be the same as at a price of $0.30 on curve S_1, and so on.

2. **Does a tax on sellers affect demand?** *No, demand stays the same.*

   Demand remains the same because the tax does not change any of the nonprice determinants of demand. At any given price, buyers' desire to purchase Whizbangs is unchanged. Remember, however, that the *quantity demanded* does change, although the curve itself doesn't change.

3. **How does a tax on sellers affect the market equilibrium?** *The equilibrium price rises and quantity demanded falls.*

   The new supply curve causes the equilibrium point to move up along the demand curve. At the new equilibrium point, the price paid by the buyer is $0.60. Because buyers now face a higher price, they demand fewer Whizbangs, so the quantity demanded falls from 30 million to 25 million. Notice that at the new equilibrium point, the quantity demanded is lower and the price is higher. Taxes usually reduce the quantity of a good or service that is sold, shrinking the market.

? POTENTIALLY CONFUSING

In Chapter 3, "Markets," we distinguished between a curve *shifting* to the left or right and *movement along* the same curve. A shift represents a fundamental change in the quantity demanded or supplied at any given price; a movement along the same curve simply shows a switch to a different quantity and price point. The question here is, does a tax cause a *shift* of the demand or supply curve or a *movement along* the curve?

The answer is neither, really. Here's why: When we add a tax, we're not really shifting the curve; rather, we are adding a second curve. We still need the original curve to understand what is happening. This is because the price that sellers receive is actually $0.20 lower than the price at which they sell Whizbangs, due to the tax. So we need one curve to represent what sellers receive and another curve to represent what buyers pay.

Notice in Figure 6-7 that the price suppliers receive is on the original supply curve, S_1, but the price buyers pay is on the new supply curve, S_2. The original curve *does not actually move,* but we add the second curve to indicate that because of the tax, buyers face a different price than what the sellers will get. In order for the market to be in equilibrium, the quantity that buyers demand at $0.60 must now equal the quantity that sellers supply at $0.40.

Now let's look at the new equilibrium price in Figure 6-7. The price paid by buyers to sellers is the new market price, $0.60. However, sellers do not get to keep all the money they receive. Instead, they must pay the tax to the government. Since the tax is $0.20, the price that sellers receive once they have paid the tax is only $0.40. Ultimately, sellers do not receive the full price that consumers pay; the tax creates what is known as a *tax wedge* between buyers and sellers. A **tax wedge** is the difference between the price paid by buyers and the price received by sellers, which equals the amount of the tax. In Figure 6-7, the tax wedge is calculated as shown in Equation 6-1.

tax wedge
the difference between the price paid by buyers and the price received by sellers in the presence of a tax

EQUATION 6-1 $$\text{Tax wedge} = P_{\text{buyers}} - P_{\text{sellers}} = \text{Tax}$$

For each Whizbang sold at the new equilibrium point, the government collects tax revenue, as calculated in Equation 6-2.

EQUATION 6-2 $$\text{Government tax revenue} = \text{Tax} \times Q_{\text{post-tax}}$$

Specifically, the government receives $0.20 for each of the 25 million Whizbangs sold, or $5 million total. Graphically, the government revenue equals the green-shaded area in Figure 6-8.

Just like a price control, a tax causes deadweight loss and redistributes surplus. We can see the deadweight loss caused by the reduced number of trades in Figure 6-8. It is surplus lost to buyers and sellers who would have been willing to make trades at the pre-tax equilibrium price.

The redistribution of surplus, however, is a little trickier to follow. Under a tax, *both* producers and consumers lose surplus. Consumers who still buy pay more for the same candy than they would have under equilibrium, and producers who still sell receive less for the same candy. The difference between this lost surplus and deadweight loss, however, is that it doesn't "disappear." Instead, it becomes government revenue. In fact, the area representing government revenue in Figure 6-8 is exactly the same as the surplus lost to buyers and sellers still trading in the market after the tax has been imposed. This revenue can pay for services that might transfer surplus back to producers or consumers, or both, or to people outside of the market.

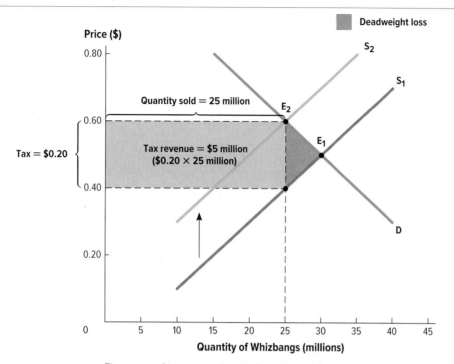

FIGURE 6-8

Government revenue and deadweight loss from a tax

The revenue from a per-unit tax is the amount of the tax multiplied by the number of units sold at the post-tax equilibrium point. The amount of tax revenue directly corresponds to the surplus lost to consumers and producers. The trades that no longer happen under the tax represent deadweight loss.

A tax on buyers

What happens if the tax is imposed on buyers instead of sellers? Surprisingly, the outcome is exactly the same. Suppose California enacts a sales tax of $0.20, which the buyer must pay for every Whizbang bought. In this case, as Figure 6-9 shows, the demand curve (rather than the supply curve) moves by the amount of the tax, but the resulting equilibrium price and quantity are the same.

To double-check this result, let's walk step by step through the effect of a tax levied on buyers.

1. **Does a tax on buyers affect the supply curve?** *No, supply stays the same.*

   The supply curve stays the same because the tax does not change the incentives producers face. None of the nonprice determinants of supply are affected.

2. **Does a tax on buyers affect the demand curve?** *Yes, demand decreases.*

   Demand decreases because the price buyers must pay per unit, including the tax, is now $0.20 higher than the original price. As Figure 6-9 shows, we take the original demand curve D_1 and factor in the amount of the tax; the result is a second demand curve D_2, which represents the price buyers pay under the tax. At any given price, buyers will now behave as if the price were actually $0.20 higher. For example, at $0.40 on curve D_2, the quantity demanded is as if the price were $0.60 on curve D_1. At $0.30 on curve D_2, the quantity demanded is as if the price were $0.50.

3. **How does a tax on buyers affect the market equilibrium?** *The equilibrium price and quantity both fall.*

   As a result, the equilibrium point with the new demand curve is further down the supply curve. The equilibrium price falls from $0.50 to $0.40 and the quantity demanded and

FIGURE 6-9

Effect of a tax paid by the buyer

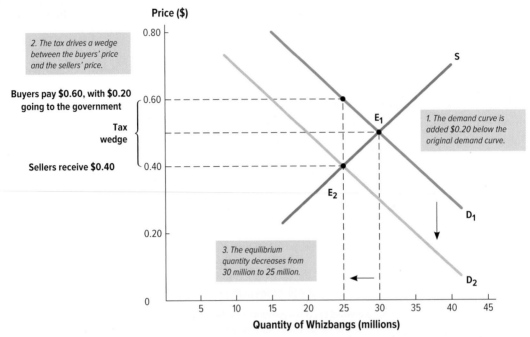

A tax levied on the buyer adds a new demand curve $0.20 below the original curve. As a result, the equilibrium quantity decreases and the equilibrium price paid by the buyer increases. These results are the same as those of a tax levied on the seller.

supplied falls from 30 million to 25 million. Although the market equilibrium price goes down instead of up, as it does with a tax on sellers, the actual amount that buyers and sellers pay is the same no matter who pays the tax. When buyers pay the tax, they pay $0.40 to the seller and $0.20 to the government, or a total of $0.60. When sellers pay the tax, buyers pay $0.60 to the seller, who then pays $0.20 to the government. Either way, buyers pay $0.60 and sellers receive $0.40.

As Figure 6-9 shows, a tax on buyers creates a tax wedge just as a tax on sellers does. At the new equilibrium point, the price sellers receive is $0.40. The buyer pays $0.40 to the seller and then the $0.20 tax to the government, so that the total effective price is $0.60. Using Equation 6-1, once again the tax wedge is $0.20, exactly equal to the amount of the tax.

$$\text{Tax wedge} = \$0.60 - \$0.40 = \$0.20$$

Furthermore, the government still collects $0.20 for every Whizbang sold, just as under a tax on sellers. Again, using Equation 6-2, the post-tax equilibrium quantity is 25 million, and the government collects $5 million in tax revenue.

$$\text{Government tax revenue} = \$0.20 \times 25 \text{ million} = \$5 \text{ million}$$

What is the overall impact of the tax on Whizbangs? Regardless of whether a tax is imposed on buyers or sellers, there are four effects that result from all taxes:

1. Equilibrium quantity falls. The goal of the tax has thus been achieved—consumption of Whizbangs has been discouraged.

2. Buyers pay more for each Whizbang and sellers receive less. This creates a tax wedge, equal to the difference between the price paid by buyers and the price received by sellers.

3. The government receives revenue equal to the amount of the tax multiplied by the new equilibrium quantity. In this case, the California state government receives an additional $5 million in revenue from the tax on Whizbangs—which could be used to offset the public health expenses caused by obesity-related diseases.

4. The tax causes deadweight loss. The value of the revenue the government collects is always less than the reduction in total surplus caused by the tax.

In evaluating a tax, then, we must weigh its goal—in this case, reducing the consumption of trans fats—against the loss of surplus in the market.

Who bears the burden of a tax?

We've seen that the outcome of a tax does not depend on who pays it. Whether a tax is levied on buyers or on sellers, the cost is shared. But which group bears more of the burden?

In our example, the burden was shared equally:

- Buyers paid $0.50 for a Whizbang before the tax; after the tax, they pay $0.60. Therefore, buyers bear $0.10 of the $0.20 tax burden.

- Sellers received $0.50 for each Whizbang before the tax; after the tax, they receive $0.40. Therefore, sellers also bear $0.10 of the $0.20 tax burden.

The shaded rectangles in panel A of Figure 6-10 represent graphically this 50-50 split. The relative tax burden borne by buyers and sellers is called the **tax incidence**.

Often, however, the tax incidence is not split equally. Sometimes one group carries much more of it than the other. Compare the example just given to another possible market for Whizbangs,

tax incidence
the relative tax burden borne by buyers and sellers

FIGURE 6-10

Tax incidence and relative elasticity

Sellers' tax burden

Buyers' tax burden

In all panels, the supply curve S_2 lies $0.20 above the original curve.

(A) Equal incidence

Price ($)

0.60

0.40

S_2 S_1 D

Buyers pay $0.60; sellers receive $0.40.

25 30

Quantity of Whizbangs (millions)

When supply and demand have the same relative elasticity, buyers and sellers share the tax burden equally.

(B) Sellers pay more

Price ($)

0.54

0.34

S_2 S_1 D

Buyers pay $0.54; sellers receive $0.34.

22 30

Quantity of Whizbangs (millions)

When demand is more elastic than supply, sellers shoulder more of the tax burden than buyers.

(C) Buyers pay more

Price ($)

0.66

0.46

S_2 S_1 D

Buyers pay $0.66; sellers receive $0.46.

22 30

Quantity of Whizbangs (millions)

When supply is more elastic than demand, buyers shoulder more of the tax burden than sellers.

represented in panel B of Figure 6-10. In this case, buyers paid $0.50 before the tax. After the tax, they pay $0.54, so their tax burden is $0.04 per Whizbang. Sellers, on the other hand, receive only $0.34 after the tax, so their tax burden, at $0.16 per Whizbang, is four times as large as that of buyers.

Panel C of Figure 6-10 shows the opposite case, in which buyers bear more of the burden than sellers. Thus, buyers pay $0.66 and sellers receive $0.48.

What determines the incidence of a tax? The answer has to do with the relative elasticity of the supply and demand curves. Recall from Chapter 4, "Elasticity," that price elasticity describes how much the quantity supplied or demanded changes in response to a change in price. Since a tax effectively changes the price of a good to both buyers and sellers, the relative responsiveness of supply and demand will determine the tax burden. Essentially, *the side of the market that is more price elastic will be more able to adjust to price changes and will shoulder less of the tax burden.*

Panel B of Figure 6-10 imagines a market in which demand is more elastic: Many consumers easily give up their Whizbang habit and buy healthier snacks instead. In that case, Whizbang producers pay a higher share of the tax. Panel C imagines a market in which demand is less elastic: Consumers are so obsessed with Whizbangs that they will buy even at the higher price. In that case, buyers pay a higher share of the tax.

Recall that the market outcome of a tax—the new equilibrium quantity and price—is the same regardless of whether a tax is imposed on buyers or on sellers. Thus, the tax burden will be the same no matter which side of the market is taxed. Note in panel C of Figure 6-10 that buyers bear the greater part of that burden, even though the tax is imposed on sellers. The situation in panels B and C shows there can be a difference between *economic incidence* (the economic effect of a tax on either buyers or sellers) and *statutory incidence* (the person who is legally responsible for paying the tax). The actual economic incidence of a tax is unrelated to the statutory incidence.

This is an important point to remember during public debates about taxes. A politician may say that companies that pollute should be held accountable for the environmental damage they cause, through a tax on pollution. Regardless of how you may feel about the idea of taxing pollution, remember that levying the tax on companies that pollute does not mean that they will end up bearing the whole tax burden. Consumers who buy from those producers will also bear part of the burden of the tax, through higher prices. Policy-makers have little control over how the tax burden is shared between buyers and sellers.

Subsidies

LO 6.4 Calculate the effect of a subsidy on the equilibrium price and quantity.

---

subsidy
a requirement that the government pay an extra amount to producers or consumers of a good

A **subsidy** is the reverse of a tax: It is a requirement that the government pay an extra amount to producers or consumers of a good. Governments use subsidies to encourage the production and consumption of a particular good or service. They can also use subsidies as an alternative to price controls to benefit certain groups without generating a shortage or an excess supply.

Let's return to the Mexican dilemma—what to do when hungry people cannot afford to buy enough tortillas. This is the last of the four real-world interventions in the chapter, and here we ask a different question: What would happen if the government *subsidized* tortillas rather than imposed a price ceiling on them?

Figure 6-11 shows the tortilla market we discussed earlier in the chapter. The figure shows that before the subsidy, the market is in equilibrium at a price of $0.70 per pound and a quantity of 50 million pounds. Now suppose the government offers tortilla makers a subsidy of $0.35 per pound. *How will buyers and sellers respond to the subsidy?* They will respond in the opposite way that they respond to a tax:

- With a tax, the quantity supplied and demanded decrease, and the government collects revenue.

- With a subsidy, the quantity supplied and demanded increase, and the government spends money.

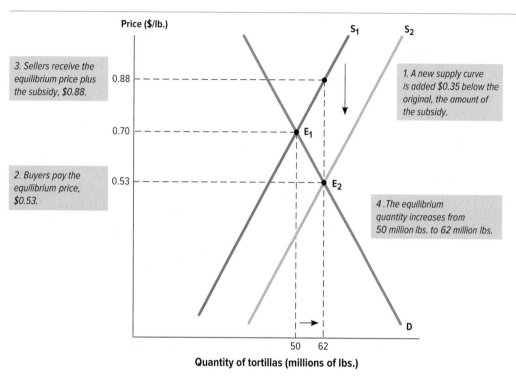

FIGURE 6-11

Effect of a subsidy to the seller

A subsidy has the opposite effect of a tax. A new supply curve is added $0.35 below the original supply curve. This decreases the equilibrium price and increases the equilibrium quantity supplied and demanded.

We can calculate the effect of a $0.35 tortilla subsidy by walking through the same three steps we used to examine the effect of a tax.

1. **Does a subsidy to sellers affect the supply curve?** *Yes, supply increases.*

   When producers receive a subsidy, the real price they receive for each unit sold is higher than the market price. At any market price, therefore, they will behave as if the price were $0.35 higher. Put another way, for sellers to supply a given quantity, the market price can be $0.35 lower than it would have to be without the subsidy. As a result, the new supply curve is drawn $0.35 below the original. In Figure 6-11, S_2 shows the new supply curve that is the result of the subsidy.

2. **Does a subsidy to sellers affect the demand curve?** *No, demand stays the same.*

   The demand curve stays where it is because consumers are not directly affected by the subsidy.

3. **How does a subsidy to sellers affect the market equilibrium?** *The equilibrium price decreases and the equilibrium quantity increases.*

   The equilibrium quantity with the new supply curve increases as consumers move down along the demand curve to the new equilibrium point. At the new, post-subsidy equilibrium, the quantity supplied increases from 50 million pounds of tortillas to 62 million pounds. As with a tax, the price buyers pay for tortillas differs from the price sellers receive after the subsidy because the subsidy creates a wedge between the two prices. This time, however, sellers receive a *higher* price than the pre-subsidy equilibrium of $0.70, and buyers pay a *lower* one. Buyers pay $0.53 per pound and sellers receive $0.88 per pound. The government pays the $0.35 difference.

The government subsidizes each pound of tortillas sold at the new equilibrium point. To calculate the total amount of government expenditure on a subsidy, we can use Equation 6-3. The government spends $0.35 for each of the 62 million pounds of tortillas sold, or $21.7 million total.

EQUATION 6-3   Government subsidy expenditure $= \text{Subsidy} \times Q_{\text{post-subsidy}}$

Like taxes, subsidies also cause deadweight loss and redistribute surplus. Panel A of Figure 6-12 shows the deadweight loss caused by the overproduction and overconsumption of tortillas. If there is no subsidy, 50 million pounds is the equilibrium quantity. Any more, and the cost to produce them would be higher than the benefit to consumers. Thus, it would be inefficient to exchange more than 50 million pounds of tortillas. The subsidy lowers the cost to the producer, thus causing producers and consumers to exchange 12 million more pounds of tortillas than is efficient. This leads to a deadweight loss.

Panel B of Figure 6-12 shows the total government expenditure on the subsidy. You may wonder why only part of the government expenditure is counted as deadweight loss. If the government is funding 12 million more pounds of tortillas than is efficient, shouldn't the entire expenditure be deadweight loss? The answer is no, because the government is increasing both consumer and producer surplus with its expenditures. However, the deadweight loss arises because not all of the expenditure becomes surplus.

Figure 6-13 shows the consumer surplus and producer surplus from a subsidy. Notice that both consumer surplus and producer surplus increase with a subsidy. However, recall that the increase in surplus is funded by the government, as shown in panel B of Figure 6-12. Notice that the amount of government expenditure is less than the total increase in producer and consumer surplus. Ultimately, that expenditure is passed on to taxpayers (both producers and individuals) in the form of more taxes.

FIGURE 6-12

Deadweight loss from a subsidy

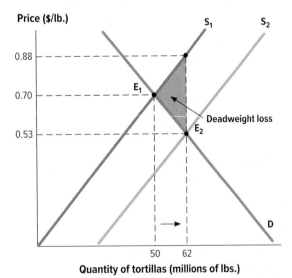

(A) Deadweight loss from tortilla subsidy

For the 12 million pounds of tortillas produced due to the subsidy, supply exceeds demand. Thus, the exchange of these tortillas causes deadweight loss.

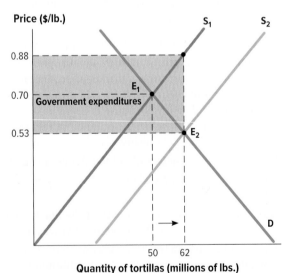

(B) Government spending on tortilla subsidy

The government subsidy expenditure is the amount of the subsidy multiplied by the post-subsidy equilibrium quantity. The subsidy increases both consumer surplus and producer surplus but imposes a cost on the government, which ultimately is paid for by taxes on consumers and producers.

FIGURE 6-13

Effect of a subsidy on surplus

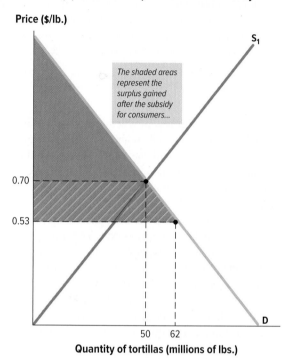

(A) Consumer surplus from tortilla subsidy

Price ($/lb.)

The shaded areas represent the surplus gained after the subsidy for consumers...

S_1

0.70

0.53

D

50　62

Quantity of tortillas (millions of lbs.)

The post-subsidy price paid by consumers ($0.53) is lower than the initial equilibrium price ($0.70), and the post-subsidy quantity (62 million pounds) is higher than the initial equilibrium quantity (50 million pounds). This results in an increase in consumer surplus.

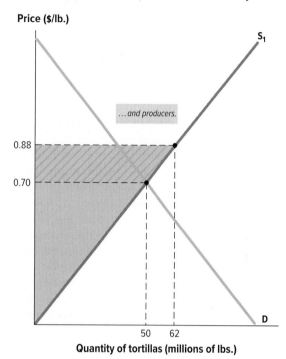

(B) Producer surplus from tortilla subsidy

Price ($/lb.)

S_1

...and producers.

0.88

0.70

D

50　62

Quantity of tortillas (millions of lbs.)

The post-subsidy price received by sellers ($0.88) is higher than the initial equilibrium price ($0.70), and the post-subsidy quantity (62 million pounds) is higher than the initial equilibrium quantity (50 million pounds). This results in an increase in producer surplus.

Are the benefits to consumers and producers worth the cost? That depends on how much we value the increased production of tortillas and their reduced cost to consumers versus the opportunity cost of the subsidy—that is, whatever other use the government or taxpayers might have made of that $21.7 million.

In addition, as the Real Life box "The unintended consequences of biofuel subsidies" shows, the obvious benefits of a subsidy can sometimes be swamped by unexpected costs.

Real Life

The unintended consequences of biofuel subsidies

The United States subsidizes the production of "biofuels" such as ethanol, a cleaner fuel than gasoline. Ethanol is fermented from many sources of starch, though it is most typically created from corn in the United States. The professed goal of the push towards biofuels such as ethanol—and thus the subsidy—is to reduce pollution. As hoped, the subsidy has caused a huge increase in the production of ethanol. Unfortunately, it has also had some unintended effects. Michael Grunwald, a journalist for *Time* magazine, argues that, indirectly, biofuels can actually increase pollution.

(continued)

> Grunwald claims that the problem is simple, and yet something policy-makers didn't antici-
> pate. In order to grow the products that ethanol is created from, farmers need land—which can
> lead to the destruction of forests, wetlands, and grasslands. This can lead to the opposite effect
> of the hoped-for reduction in air pollution. Unfortunately, unintended consequences aren't
> always just a postscript to market interventions. Sometimes, they can change the whole story.
>
> Source: M. Grunwald, "The clean energy scam," *Time*, March 27, 2008, http://www.time.com/time/magazine/
> article/0,9171,1725975,00.html. The *New York Times* had a follow-up in its environmental blog: http://green.
> blogs.nytimes.com/2008/11/03/the-biofuel-debate-good-bad-or-too-soon-to-tell/.

As with a tax, the effect of a subsidy is the same regardless of whether it is paid to producers
or consumers. If consumers received a $0.35 subsidy for every pound of tortillas they bought,
their demand curve would be $0.35 above the original, and the supply curve would remain
unchanged. In that case, the equilibrium outcome would be the same as if producers received the
subsidy: Quantity increases from 50 million pounds to 62 million pounds, buyers pay $0.53 per
pound, and sellers receive $0.88 per pound.

Also as with a tax, the way in which the benefits of a subsidy are split between buyers and
sellers depends on the relative elasticity of the demand and supply curves. *The side of the market
that is more price elastic receives more of the benefit.* In our example, both have almost the same
benefit: Buyers are better off by $0.17 per pound of tortillas, and producers by $0.18.

As with taxes, it is important to note that who gets what share of benefit from the subsidy does
not depend on who receives the subsidy. Sometimes in debates about subsidies you will hear
someone argue that a subsidy should be given either to buyers or sellers because they "deserve it
more." This argument doesn't make much sense in a competitive market (although it might in a
noncompetitive market).

In sum, a subsidy has the following effects, regardless of whether it is paid to buyers or sellers:

1. Equilibrium quantity increases, accomplishing the goal of encouraging production and
   consumption of the subsidized good.
2. Buyers pay less and sellers receive more for each unit sold. The amount of the subsidy
   forms a wedge between buyers' and sellers' prices.
3. The government has to pay for the subsidy, the cost of which equals the amount of the
   subsidy multiplied by the new equilibrium quantity.

✓ CONCEPT CHECK

☐ What is a tax wedge? **[LO 6.3]**

☐ What determines the incidence of a tax? **[LO 6.3]**

☐ How does a subsidy affect the equilibrium quantity? How does it affect the price that sellers receive and the price that buyers pay? **[LO 6.4]**

☐ Does it matter whether a subsidy is paid to buyers or sellers? Why or why not? **[LO 6.4]**

Evaluating Government Interventions

LO 6.5 Explain how elasticity and time period influence the impact of a market intervention.

We began this chapter with a discussion of three reasons why policy-makers might decide to
intervene in a market: to change the distribution of surplus, to encourage or discourage consumption, and to correct market failures. To decide whether policy-makers have achieved their goals

TABLE 6-1

Government interventions: a summary

Intervention	Reason for using	Effect on price	Effect on quantity	Who gains and who loses?
Price floor	To protect producers' income	Price cannot go below the set minimum.	Quantity demanded decreases and quantity supplied increases, creating excess supply.	Producers who can sell all their goods earn more revenue per item; other producers are stuck with an unwanted excess supply.
Price ceiling	To keep consumer costs low	Price cannot go above the set maximum.	Quantity demanded increases and quantity supplied decreases, creating a shortage.	Consumers who can buy all the goods they want benefit; other consumers suffer from shortages.
Tax	To discourage an activity or collect money to pay for its consequences; to increase government revenue	Price increases.	Equilibrium quantity decreases.	Government receives increased revenue; society may gain if the tax decreases socially harmful behavior. Buyers and sellers of the good that is taxed share the cost. Which group bears more of the burden depends on the price elasticity of supply and demand.
Subsidy	To encourage an activity; to provide benefits to a certain group	Price decreases.	Equilibrium quantity increases.	Buyers purchase more goods at a lower price. Society may benefit if the subsidy encourages socially beneficial behavior. The government and ultimately the taxpayers bear the cost.

by implementing a price control, tax, or subsidy, we need to assess the effects of each intervention, including its unintended consequences.

We've established a few rules about the expected outcomes of market interventions. Table 6-1 summarizes the key effects of price controls, taxes, and subsidies. In general, we can say the following:

- Price controls have opposing impacts on the quantities supplied and demanded, causing a shortage or excess supply. In contrast, taxes and subsidies move the quantities supplied and demanded in the same direction, allowing the market to reach equilibrium at the point where the quantity supplied equals the quantity demanded.
- Taxes discourage people from buying and selling a particular good, raise government revenue, and impose a cost on both buyers and sellers.
- Subsidies encourage people to buy and sell a particular good, cost the government money, and provide a benefit to both buyers and sellers.

In the following sections we will consider some of the more complicated details of market interventions. These details matter. Often the details of an intervention make the difference between a successful policy and a failed one.

How big is the effect of a tax or subsidy?

Regardless of the reason for a market intervention, it's important to know exactly *how much* it will change the equilibrium quantity and price. Can the effect of a tax or subsidy on the equilibrium quantity be predicted ahead of time? The answer is yes, *if* we know the price elasticity of supply and demand. A general rule applies: *The more elastic supply or demand is, the greater the change in quantity.* This rule follows directly from the definition of price elasticity, which measures buyers' and sellers' responsiveness to a change in price—and a tax or subsidy is effectively a change in price.

Figure 6-14 shows the effect of a $0.20 tax on the quantity demanded under four different combinations of price elasticity of supply and demand—again, for Whizbangs. It's worthwhile to walk through each combination, one by one:

- In panel A, both supply and demand are *relatively inelastic:* In this case the tax causes the equilibrium quantity to decrease, but not by much. Both buyers and sellers are willing to continue trading, even though they now must pay the tax.
- In panel B, *demand is more elastic than supply:* When the supply curve is $0.20 higher, the change in quantity is much larger than in panel A.
- In panel C, *supply is elastic but demand is relatively inelastic:* Again, because suppliers are highly responsive to the cost of the tax, the quantity changes more than in panel A.
- In panel D, *supply and demand are both elastic:* In this case, the quantity goes down even more than in the second and third examples.

To predict the size of the effect of a tax or subsidy, then, policy-makers need to know the price elasticity of both supply and demand. As we have seen, they can also use that information to determine who will bear more of the burden or receive more of the benefit.

If you are interested in the role of government in the economy, read the Where Can It Take You? box "Public economics" to learn more about the field.

FIGURE 6-14

Price elasticity and the effect of a $0.20 tax

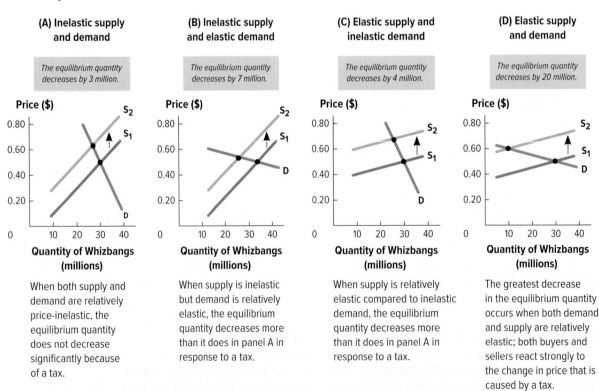

(A) Inelastic supply and demand	(B) Inelastic supply and elastic demand	(C) Elastic supply and inelastic demand	(D) Elastic supply and demand
The equilibrium quantity decreases by 3 million.	*The equilibrium quantity decreases by 7 million.*	*The equilibrium quantity decreases by 4 million.*	*The equilibrium quantity decreases by 20 million.*

When both supply and demand are relatively price-inelastic, the equilibrium quantity does not decrease significantly because of a tax.

When supply is inelastic but demand is relatively elastic, the equilibrium quantity decreases more than it does in panel A in response to a tax.

When supply is relatively elastic compared to inelastic demand, the equilibrium quantity decreases more than it does in panel A in response to a tax.

The greatest decrease in the equilibrium quantity occurs when both demand and supply are relatively elastic; both buyers and sellers react strongly to the change in price that is caused by a tax.

Where Can it Take You?

Public economics

Are you more interested in elections and legislation than in how to run a business? If so, we hope you are beginning to realize that understanding the economics behind public policy is incredibly important. Although well-designed policies can accomplish great things, well-intentioned but poorly designed policies can backfire badly.

To learn more about the economics of public policy, consider taking a *public economics* course. We will discuss policy issues throughout this book, but there is a lot more to learn, whether you want to be a politician, an analyst at a think tank, or just an informed voter.

Long-run versus short-run impact

We have seen that in addition to changing the price of a good or service, price controls cause shortages or excess supply. Because buyers and sellers take time to respond to a change in price, sometimes the full effect of price controls becomes clear only in the long run.

Suppose the U.S. government imposes a price floor on gasoline in an attempt to reduce air pollution by discouraging people from driving. Panel A of Figure 6-15 shows the short-run impact of a price floor in the market for gasoline. In the short run, the quantity of gas demanded might not change very much. Although people would cut down on unnecessary driving, the greater part of demand would still be based on driving habits that are difficult to change, such as commuting to school or work or going to the grocery store. And unless gasoline producers have a lot of unused oil wells sitting around, sellers might have trouble ramping up production quickly. In the short run, demand and supply are not very elastic, so the price floor results in only a small excess supply.

FIGURE 6-15

Government intervention in the long and short run

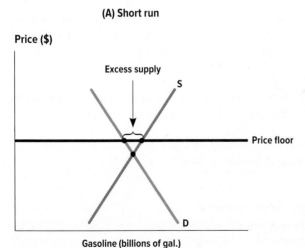

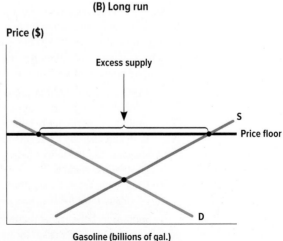

In the short run, neither the supply nor the demand for gasoline is very elastic, so the effect of a price floor on the quantity supplied is relatively small.

In the long run, both the supply and the demand for gasoline will change in response to price controls. As a result, the long-run effect on the quantity supplied is much greater than the short-run effect.

Recall that for both supply and demand, one of the determinants of price elasticity is the period over which it is measured. On both sides of the market, elasticity is often greater over a long period than over a short one:

- On the demand side, consumers might make small lifestyle changes over the medium term, such as buying a bus pass or shopping closer to home. Over the long run, they might make even bigger changes. When they need to buy a new car, for example, they will be inclined to buy a model that offers high gas mileage. If they move to a new job or home, they may place more weight than in the past on commuting distance.

- Supply will also be more elastic over the long run. Because a higher price gives suppliers an incentive to produce more, they may invest in oil exploration, dig new wells, or take steps to increase the pumping capacity of existing wells. Panel B of Figure 6-15 shows the long-run impact of a price floor in the market for gasoline. Because both supply and demand are more elastic in the long run than in the short run, the excess supply of gasoline is much larger in the long run than in the short run.

If the goal of the price floor was to reduce air pollution by giving consumers an incentive to cut down on driving, the impact might look disappointing in the short run: The quantity of gas burned will decrease very little. Over the long run, however, the quantity of gas burned will decrease further, and the policy will look more successful.

If, on the other hand, the reason for the price floor was to support gasoline suppliers, the short-run response would look deceptively rosy because suppliers will sell almost the same quantity of gas at a higher price. As the quantity falls over the long run, however, more producers will be stuck with an excess supply and the policy will start to look less successful.

In the European Union and the United States, farmers are given very generous subsidies. Without these subsidies, many farmers would be forced to quit farming. Critics argue that subsidies distort the market by keeping prices of certain foods much higher than they would be without subsidies. Read the full debate in the What Do You Think? box "Farm subsidies."

What Do You Think?

Farm subsidies

Many wealthy countries spend a lot of money on price floors and subsidies that encourage domestic agricultural production. For instance, the costs associated with Europe's Common Agricultural Policy (CAP) currently account for almost half the European Union's budget, or approximately $50 billion per year.

CAP was established in 1957 with the following objectives:

1. To increase agricultural productivity by developing technical progress and by ensuring the rational development of agricultural production and the optimum utilization of the factors of production, particularly labor.
2. To ensure thereby a fair standard of living for the agricultural population, particularly by the increasing of the individual earnings of persons engaged in agriculture.
3. To stabilize markets.
4. To guarantee regular supplies.
5. To ensure reasonable prices in supplies to consumers.

Supporters believe that these are important and worthwhile policy goals. However, CAP has come under heavy criticism for many reasons. Critics say that CAP imposes a huge cost on taxpayers; creates excess supplies of crops by distorting farmers' incentives; hurts farmers in poor countries, whose produce must compete with Europe's subsidized crops; and channels public funds to big agribusinesses.

The European Union is not alone in its policies. Every year the U.S. farm bill allocates many billions of dollars to crop price supports. Japan also intervenes heavily in agricultural markets.

WHAT DO YOU THINK?

1. Do you approve of the stated objectives of Europe's Common Agricultural Policy? Which, if any, do you think merit the market distortions they may create?
2. Do wealthy nations have a responsibility to consider the impact of their agricultural policies on poorer countries, or are domestic farming interests more important?

Source: European Commission, "The Common Agricultural Policy: A Partnership between Europe and Farmers" (2012), http://ec.europa.eu/agriculture/cap-overview/2012_en.pdf.

✓ **CONCEPT CHECK**

- ☐ If the demand for a good is inelastic, will a tax have a large or small effect on the quantity sold? Will buyers or sellers bear more of the burden of the tax? **[LO 6.5]**
- ☐ Would you expect a tax on cigarettes to be more effective over the long run or the short run? Explain your reasoning. **[LO 6.5]**

Conclusion

If you listen to the news, it might seem as if economics is all about business and the stock market. Business matters, but many of the most important, challenging, and useful applications of economic principles involve public policy.

This chapter gives you the basic tools you need to understand government interventions and some of the ways they can affect your everyday life. Of course, the real world is complicated, so this isn't our last word on the topic. Later, we discuss how to evaluate the benefits of both markets and government policies. We'll also discuss market failures and whether and when governments can fix them.

Key Terms

market failures, p. 132

price control, p. 132

price ceiling, p. 133

deadweight loss, p. 134

price floor, p. 136

tax wedge, p. 142

tax incidence, p. 145

subsidy, p. 146

Summary

LO 6.1 Calculate the effect of a price ceiling on the equilibrium price and quantity.

The government usually intervenes in a market for one or more of the following reasons: to change the distribution of a market's benefits, to encourage or discourage the consumption of particular goods and services, or to correct a market failure. Governments may also tax goods and services in order to raise public revenues.

A price ceiling is a maximum legal price at which a good can be sold. A binding price ceiling causes a shortage because at the legally mandated price, consumers will demand more than producers supply. This policy benefits some consumers because they are able to buy what they want at a lower price, but other consumers are unable to find the goods they want. Producers lose out because they sell less at a lower price than they would without the price ceiling.

LO 6.2 Calculate the effect of a price floor on the equilibrium price and quantity.

A price floor is a minimum legal price at which a good can be sold. A price floor causes an excess supply because at the minimum price, sellers will supply more than consumers demand. This policy benefits some producers, who are able to sell their goods at a higher price, but leaves other producers with goods they can't sell. Consumers lose because they buy less at a higher price. Maintaining a price floor often requires the government to buy up the excess supply, costing taxpayers money.

LO 6.3 Calculate the effect of a tax on the equilibrium price and quantity.

A tax requires either buyers or sellers to pay some extra price to the government when a good is bought and sold. A tax shrinks the size of a market, discouraging the consumption and production of the good being taxed. The effect is the same regardless of whether the tax is levied on buyers or sellers. The tax burden is split between consumers and producers, and the government collects revenues equal to the amount of the tax times the quantity sold.

LO 6.4 Calculate the effect of a subsidy on the equilibrium price and quantity.

A subsidy is a payment that the government makes to buyers or sellers of a good for each unit that is sold. Subsidies increase the size of a market, encouraging the consumption and production of the good being subsidized. The effect is the same regardless of whether the subsidy is paid to buyers or sellers. Both consumers and producers benefit from a subsidy, but taxpayers must cover the cost.

LO 6.5 Explain how elasticity and time period influence the impact of a market intervention.

In evaluating the effects of a government intervention in the market, it is important to consider both the intended and unintended consequences of the policy. The size of the impact of a tax or subsidy and the distribution of the burden or benefit will depend on the price elasticities of supply and demand. Furthermore, the impact of a government intervention is likely to change over time, as consumers and producers adjust their behavior in response to the new incentives.

Review Questions

1. You are an advisor to the Egyptian government, which has placed a price ceiling on bread. Unfortunately, many families still cannot buy the bread they need. Explain to government officials why the price ceiling has not increased consumption of bread. **[LO 6.1]**

2. Suppose there has been a long-standing price ceiling on housing in your city. Recently, population has declined and demand for housing has decreased. What will the decrease in demand do to the efficiency of the price ceiling? **[LO 6.1]**

3. Suppose the United States maintains a price floor for spinach. Why might this policy decrease revenues for spinach farmers? **[LO 6.2]**

4. Suppose Colombia maintains a price floor for coffee beans. What will happen to the size of the deadweight loss if the price floor encourages new growers to enter the market and produce coffee? **[LO 6.2]**

5. Many states tax cigarette purchases. Suppose that smokers are unhappy about paying the extra charge for their cigarettes. Will it help smokers if the state imposes the tax on the stores that sell the cigarettes rather than on smokers? Why or why not? **[LO 6.3]**

6. Consider a tax on cigarettes. Do you expect the tax incidence to fall more heavily on buyers or sellers of cigarettes? Why? **[LO 6.3]**

7. In the United States, many agricultural products (such as corn, wheat, and rice) are subsidized. What are the potential benefits of subsidizing these products? What are the costs? **[LO 6.4]**

8. A subsidy will increase consumer and producer surplus in a market and will increase the quantity of trades. Why, then, might a subsidy (such as a subsidy for producing corn in the United States) be considered inefficient? **[LO 6.4]**

9. Suppose the government imposes a price ceiling on gasoline. One month after the price ceiling, there is a shortage of gasoline, but it is much smaller than critics of the policy had warned. Explain why the critics' estimates might still be correct. **[LO 6.5]**

10. A state facing a budget shortfall decides to tax soft drinks. You are a budget analyst for the state. Do you expect to collect more revenue in the first year of the tax or in the second year? Why? **[LO 6.5]**

Problems and Applications

1. Many people are concerned about the rising price of gasoline. Suppose that government officials are thinking of capping the price of gasoline below its current

FIGURE 6P-1

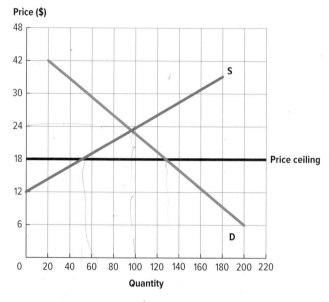

Price ($)

FIGURE 6P-3

Market for farmed halibut

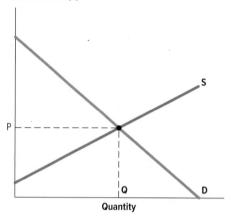

Price of halibut ($)

price. Which of the following outcomes do you predict will result from this policy? Check all that apply. **[LO 6.1]**

  a. Drivers will purchase more gasoline.

  b. Quantity demanded for gasoline will increase.

  c. Long lines will develop at gas stations.

  d. Oil companies will work to increase their pumping capacity.

2. Consider the market shown in Figure 6P-1. The government has imposed a price ceiling at $18. **[LO 6.1]**

  a. At a price ceiling of $18, what is quantity demanded? Quantity supplied?

  b. At this price ceiling, is there a shortage or a surplus? By how many units?

3. Figure 6P-2 shows a market in equilibrium. **[LO 6.1]**

FIGURE 6P-2

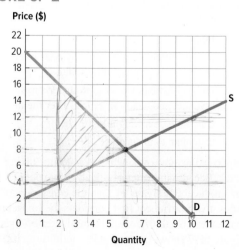

Price ($)

  a. Draw a price ceiling at $12. What is the amount of shortage at this price? Draw and calculate the deadweight loss.

  b. Draw a price ceiling at $4. What is the amount of shortage at this price? Draw and calculate the deadweight loss.

4. Decades of overfishing have dramatically reduced the world supply of cod (a type of whitefish). Farm-raised halibut is considered a close substitute for ocean-fished cod. Figure 6P-3 shows the market for farm-raised halibut. **[LO 6.1]**

  a. What effect will overfishing cod have on the price of cod? On the graph, show the effect of overfishing cod on the market for farmed halibut.

  b. A fast-food chain purchases both cod and halibut for use in its Fish 'n' Chips meals. Already hurt by the reduced supply of cod, the fast-food chain has lobbied aggressively for price controls on farmed halibut. As a result, Congress has considered imposing a price ceiling on halibut at the former equilibrium price—the price that prevailed before overfishing reduced the supply of cod. What will happen in the market for farmed halibut if Congress adopts the price control policy? Draw and label the price ceiling, quantity demanded, quantity supplied, and deadweight loss.

5. Consider the market shown in Figure 6P-4. The government has imposed a price floor at $36. **[LO 6.2]**

  a. At a price floor of $36, what is quantity demanded? Quantity supplied?

  b. At this price floor, is there a shortage or a surplus? By how many units?

FIGURE 6P-4

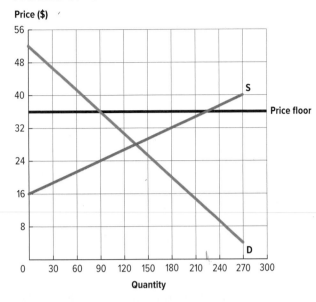

FIGURE 6P-5

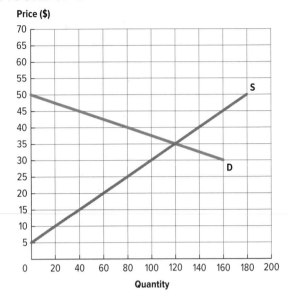

6. The Organization for the Promotion of Brussels Sprouts has convinced the government of Ironia to institute a price floor on the sale of brussels sprouts, at $8 per bushel. Demand is given by $P = 9 - Q$ and supply by $P = 2Q$, where Q is measured in thousands of bushels. **[LO 6.2]**

    a. What will be the price and quantity of brussels sprouts sold at market equilibrium?

    b. What will be the price and quantity sold with the price floor?

    c. How big will be the excess supply of brussels sprouts produced with the price floor?

7. The traditional diet of the citizens of the nation of Ironia includes a lot of red meat, and ranchers make up a vital part of Ironia's economy. The government of Ironia decides to support its ranchers through a price floor, which it will maintain by buying up excess meat supplies. Table 6P-1 shows the supply and demand

TABLE 6P-1

Price ($)	Quantity demanded (thousands of lbs.)	Quantity supplied (thousands of lbs.)
6	5	80
5	20	70
4	35	60
3	50	50
2	65	40
1	80	30

schedule for red meat; quantities are given in thousands of pounds. **[LO 6.2]**

    a. How many thousands of pounds of meat would you recommend that the government purchase to keep the price at $4/pound?

    b. How much money should the government budget for this program?

8. The market shown in Figure 6P-5 is in equilibrium. Suppose there is a $15 per unit tax levied on sellers.

    a. Draw the after-tax supply curve.

    b. Plot the after-tax price paid by consumers and the after-tax price paid by sellers.

9. The market shown in Figure 6P-6 is in equilibrium. Suppose there is a $1.50 per unit tax levied on sellers. **[LO 6.3]**

    a. Draw the after-tax supply curve.

    b. Plot the after-tax price paid by consumers and the after-tax price paid by sellers.

    c. Draw consumer surplus, producer surplus, tax revenue, and deadweight loss after the tax.

    d. Calculate deadweight loss.

    e. Calculate total surplus.

10. Suppose the government is considering taxing cigarettes. Because it is often politically more popular to tax the producers of cigarettes than the consumers of cigarettes, the government first considers the impact on the market as a result of taxing the producers of cigarettes. Figure 6P-7 shows the market in equilibrium. **[LO 6.3]**

FIGURE 6P-6

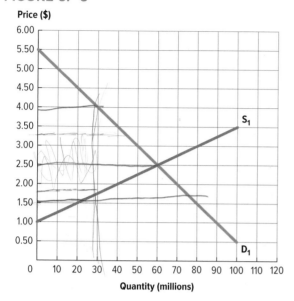

FIGURE 6P-7

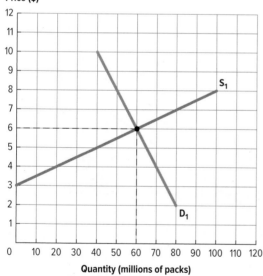

a. Draw the after-tax supply curve if the government chooses to tax cigarette producers $2.50 per pack of cigarettes.

b. Plot the after-tax price paid by consumers and the after-tax price received by sellers.

c. Do consumers or producers bear the greater burden of this tax?

d. Now suppose the government considers taxing the consumers of cigarettes instead of the producers of cigarettes. Draw the after-tax supply curve if the government chooses to tax cigarette consumers $2.50 per pack of cigarettes.

e. Plot the after-tax price paid by consumers and the after-tax price received by sellers.

f. Do consumers or producers bear the greater burden of this tax?

g. Is the price sellers receive when the government taxes consumers of cigarettes more than, less than, or the same as the price sellers receive when the government taxes producers of cigarettes?

h. Is the price buyers pay when the government taxes consumers of cigarettes more than, less than, or the same as the price buyers pay when the government taxes producers of cigarettes?

11. Suppose you have the information shown in Table 6P-2 about the quantity of a good that is supplied and demanded at various prices. **[LO 6.3]**

   a. Plot the demand and supply curves on a graph, with price on the y-axis and quantity on the x-axis.

   b. What are the equilibrium price and quantity?

   c. Suppose the government imposes a $15 per unit tax on sellers of this good. Draw the new supply curve on your graph.

   d. What is the new equilibrium quantity? How much will consumers pay? How much will sellers receive after the tax?

   e. Calculate the price elasticity of demand over this price change.

   f. If demand were less elastic (holding supply constant), would the deadweight loss be smaller or larger? **[LO 6.5]**

TABLE 6P-2

Price ($)	Quantity demanded	Quantity supplied
45	10	160
40	20	140
35	30	120
30	40	100
25	50	80
20	60	60
15	70	40
10	80	20
5	90	0

FIGURE 6P-8

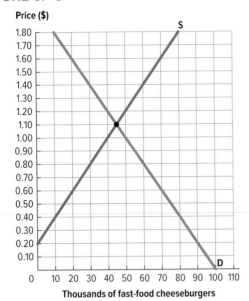

FIGURE 6P-9

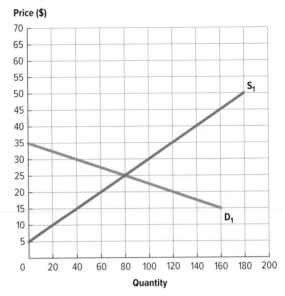

12. The weekly supply and demand for fast-food cheese-burgers in your city is shown in Figure 6P-8. In an effort to curb a looming budget deficit, the mayor recently proposed a tax that would be levied on sales at fast-food restaurants. **[LO 6.3]**

   a. The mayor's proposal includes a sales tax of 60 cents on cheeseburgers, to be paid by consumers. What is the new outcome in this market (how many cheeseburgers are sold and at what price)? Illustrate this outcome on your graph.

   b. How much of the tax burden is borne by consumers? How much by suppliers?

   c. What is the deadweight loss associated with the proposed tax?

   d. How much revenue will the government collect?

   e. What is the loss of consumer surplus from this tax?

13. The market shown in Figure 6P-9 is in equilibrium. Suppose there is a $15 per unit subsidy given to buyers. **[LO 6.4]**

   a. Draw the after-subsidy demand curve.

   b. Plot the after-subsidy price paid by consumers and the after-subsidy price paid by sellers.

14. The market shown in Figure 6P-10 is in equilibrium. Suppose there is a $15 per unit subsidy given to sellers. **[LO 6.4]**

   a. Draw the after-subsidy supply curve.

   b. Plot the after-subsidy price paid by consumers and the after-subsidy price paid by sellers.

FIGURE 6P-10

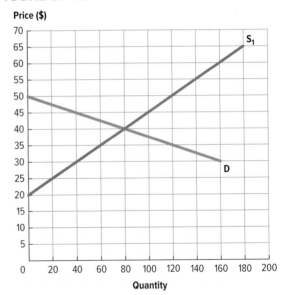

15. Demand and supply of laptop computers are given in Figure 6P-11. The quantity of laptops is given in thousands. Suppose the government provides a $300 subsidy for every laptop computer that consumers purchase. **[LO 6.4]**

   a. What will be the quantity of laptops bought and sold at the new equilibrium?

   b. What will be the price consumers pay for laptops under the subsidy?

FIGURE 6P-11

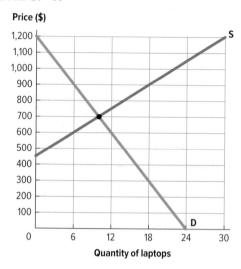

Quantity of laptops

c. What will be the price that sellers receive for laptops under the subsidy?

d. How much money should the government budget for the subsidy?

16. The market shown in Figure 6P-12 is in equilibrium. Suppose there is a $1.50 per unit subsidy given to buyers. **[LO 6.4]**

    a. Draw the after-subsidy demand curve.

    b. Plot the after-subsidy price paid by consumers and the after-subsidy price paid by sellers.

    c. Draw government expenditures for the subsidy.

    d. Calculate government expenditures.

FIGURE 6P-12

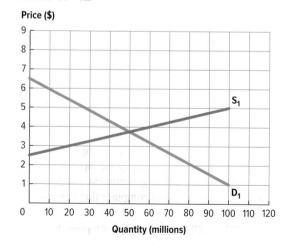

Quantity (millions)

FIGURE 6P-13

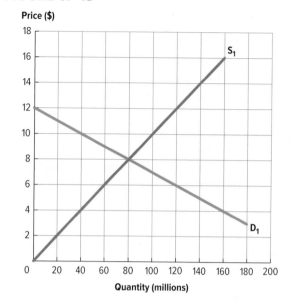

Quantity (millions)

17. The market shown in Figure 6P-13 is in equilibrium. Suppose there is a $3 per unit subsidy given to buyers. **[LO 6.4]**

    a. Draw the after-subsidy demand curve.

    b. Plot the after-subsidy price paid by consumers and the after-subsidy price paid by sellers.

    c. Draw the deadweight loss after the subsidy.

    d. Calculate deadweight loss.

18. Suppose government offers a subsidy to laptop sellers. Say whether each group of people gains or loses from this policy. **[LO 6.4]**

    a. Laptop buyers.

    b. Laptop sellers.

    c. Desktop computer sellers (assuming that they are different from laptop manufacturers).

    d. Desktop computer buyers.

19. Suppose that for health reasons, the government of the nation of Ironia wants to increase the amount of broccoli citizens consume. Which of the following policies could be used to achieve the goal? **[LO 6.1, 6.4]**

    a. A price floor to support broccoli growers.

    b. A price ceiling to ensure that broccoli remains affordable to consumers.

    c. A subsidy paid to shoppers who buy broccoli.

    d. A subsidy paid to farmers who grow broccoli.

20. The following scenarios describe the price elasticity of supply and demand for a particular good. In which scenario will a subsidy increase consumption the most? Choose only one. **[LO 6.5]**

    a. Elastic demand, inelastic supply.

    b. Inelastic demand, inelastic supply.

    c. Elastic demand, elastic supply.

    d. Inelastic demand, elastic supply.

21. The market shown in Figure 6P-14 is in equilibrium. **[LO 6.5]**

    a. If a tax was imposed on this market, would buyers or sellers bear more of the burden of the tax? Why?

22. The following scenarios describe the price elasticity of supply and demand for a particular good. All else equal (equilibrium price, equilibrium quantity, and size of the tax), in which scenario will government revenues be the highest? Choose only one. **[LO 6.5]**

    a. Elastic demand, inelastic supply.

    b. Inelastic demand, inelastic supply.

    c. Elastic demand, elastic supply.

    d. Inelastic demand, elastic supply.

Endnotes

1. http://www.time.com/time/magazine/article/ 0,9171,1727720,00.html and http://www.nytimes. com/2008/06/22/nyregion/22food.html.

2. "The new face of hunger," *The Economist,* April 17, 2008.

FIGURE 6P-14

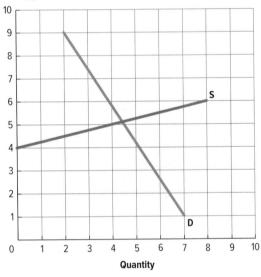

Price ($)

Individual Decisions

The five chapters in Part 3 will introduce you to . . .

how consumers make decisions. Every day we make lots of choices. Some are relatively small, like deciding whether to grab a bite to eat at a fast-food restaurant for lunch or to donate a dollar into a cash-register charity box. Some choices are large and important: One day you may meet with your academic advisor to discuss possible careers, you may consider buying a house, and—although it might not seem like an economic choice— you may choose someone with whom you want to spend the rest of your life.

How can we be sure of the right choices? What about the decisions of others? The five chapters in this part show how economics can help in getting a handle on these questions.

Chapter 7, "Consumer Behavior," introduces a fundamental concept that economists use to understand how people make decisions. Regardless of size or cost, decisions are made based on what is called *utility*. For the most part, the desire to maximize utility is what guides people when they make decisions.

Still, it is not always easy to translate good intentions into effective outcomes. Almost all of us make some decisions that we don't follow through on. Sometimes we make choices that may not seem completely rational. Chapter 8, "Behavioral Economics: A Closer Look at Decision Making," will explain why we sit through to the end of movies that we are not enjoying, or order a plate of fajitas instead of the healthy salad we had planned to eat. This is part of the field of behavioral economics. Behavioral economics enriches the understanding of decision making by bringing in social and psychological factors that influence decision making. It can help us turn good ideas into good outcomes—and it's as relevant to public policy and business as it is to choices you make every day.

When making decisions, in daily life or in politics and business, it is important to consider what others are doing. This is called thinking strategically. Chapter 9, "Game Theory and Strategic Thinking," introduces the tools of game theory and the advantages of thinking strategically. A winning strategy is key when running a tight political campaign, or picking a location for a new store, or handling a tricky negotiation with a boss. Making the right decisions wins elections, earns profit, and gets you the raise you deserve.

Overall, one of the most important parts of making a decision is having the relevant information—the topic of Chapter 10, "Information." If you are new in a city, how can you decide where to eat? If you are a manager, how can you make sure everyone's working hard—even when you're not around? What should you think about when you buy a used car or select an insurance plan? We'll see how information affects decisions and contracts, and how markets require good information. When information isn't available, markets can fail to deliver an efficient outcome, opening up possible ways that public policy might help.

Chapter 11, "Time and Uncertainty," considers two other elements of decision making: time and risk. Some decisions have benefits and costs that will come in the future (like saving or going to college). And some decisions also involve risk: The car you drive off the lot could strand you on the side of the road tomorrow, or it could be a champ and run perfectly for years. The successes of businesses and governments often hinge on how well they are prepared for unknowns that emerge over time. This chapter gives you conceptual tools to organize your thinking about life's uncertainties.

The problems we deal with in Part 3 are at the heart of economics. They show the power of economics to help you make better choices in everyday life, and, as a society, to help us better reach shared goals.

Consumer Behavior

Learning Objectives

LO 7.1 Explain how revealed preferences indicate which goods or activities give a person the most utility.

LO 7.2 Show how the budget constraint affects utility maximization.

LO 7.3 Show how a change in income affects consumption choices.

LO 7.4 Show how a change in price affects consumption choices, and distinguish between the income and substitution effects.

LO 7.5 Outline the ways in which utility is influenced by other people.

LO 7.6 Describe how people get utility from altruism and reciprocity.

THE SEASON FOR GIVING

Every holiday season, millions of Americans engage in a frenzy of gift-giving. Shopping malls fill with excited consumers searching for gifts that friends and family will treasure.

There is another way of telling this happy holiday story though: Every holiday season millions of Americans engage in a frenzy of inefficient spending. Gift-giving, according to this second story, is wasteful.[1] The giver spends money to buy something that the receiver may or may not want. In the best-case scenario, the gift is something the receiver would have purchased for himself had he been given money instead. In most cases, though, the gift-giver is an imperfect judge of what the receiver really wants. And if the giver is especially clueless, the gift ends up stuffed in the back of a closet, never to be seen again (or is regifted to somebody else).

Although people don't usually like to admit it, the second story might be closer to reality than the first. Economist Joel Waldfogel surveyed students in his class and found that, on average, the personal value they placed on the gifts they received was between 65 and 90 percent of the original price.[2] In other words, someone who bought a $20 gift would often have done better to hand that person $18 in cash (and keep the difference). Waldfogel wrote about the inefficiency of gift-giving in *Scroogenomics*—a book that was, no doubt, wrapped and ironically gifted to thousands of people during the holidays.

© Scott Kleinman/Getty Images

Which holiday story is more accurate? The answer requires us to talk more carefully about a concept—utility—that is at the heart of all microeconomic thinking. *Utility* is a way of describing the value that a person places on something, like receiving a gift, eating a meal, or experiencing something fun. The tough thing about gift-giving is that it's hard to know exactly how much value another person will place on something. Some people would like an iPod; others, a pair of running shoes. (There are probably even a few people who actually want those sweaters from Aunt Mildred.) If you're going to spend $20 on a gift (or $10, or $50, or whatever amount), the recipient probably knows better than you do what will bring her the most enjoyment for that money.

It turns out that the same idea applies to weightier choices. Should billions of dollars in foreign aid and government social programs be used to subsidize things that we think are "good" like food and health care? Or should the programs instead simply distribute cash and trust families to make their own choices?

So then, why not just give people cash and let recipients decide what to do with it? If we take a broader view, cash might *not* turn out to be better than a gift. In the case of government social programs, there's a worry that when handing out cash, the money might get diverted to the wrong people or be spent on purchases that taxpayers think are not essential.

What of your own gift-giving? The receiver might derive sentimental value from your gift, precisely because you cared enough to choose it. Or a gift might be important as a signal about your relationship with the recipient and how well you know his or her likes and dislikes. In the best case of all, you might buy a gift that is better than cash, giving something the receiver didn't know about or wouldn't have thought to buy for himself. When you surprise a friend with a movie she's never heard of but that quickly becomes her favorite, it's clear that gift-giving can be utility-enhancing.

In this chapter, we will explore the full meaning of *utility* and how it drives decision making—from simple pleasures like eating and sleeping to complex social values like behaving morally or meeting others' expectations. We'll see how economists define *utility* and how they use an abstract idea about the subjective value individuals place on things to do practical economic analysis. Utility is part of what defines economics as unique from other areas of study. Although we didn't call it by name, it's at the root of most of the questions we explored in Chapters 1 through 6. If you look back after reading this chapter, you'll see that underpinning the choices about satisfying *wants* and making *trade-offs* is the most important idea in economics: the quest to maximize utility.

The Basic Idea of Utility

The challenges of gift-giving bring up a point that is crucial to economic analysis: $20 isn't valuable in and of itself. Instead, it represents the things you could choose to buy for $20—food, music, a haircut, part of a rent payment, or savings that will let you get these things somewhere down the road. If someone gave you $20, you could probably, without too much trouble, figure out how to spend it in a way that benefits you. Most of us are pretty good at knowing our own likes and dislikes, at least when it comes to everyday things.

But it is much harder to figure out what *someone else* would want with that $20. If you could simply buy them whatever you would have wanted for yourself, that would be easy. But what makes you happiest is probably not the same as what will make them the happiest. Everyone has different likes and dislikes, situations in life, incomes, and so on. Those differences make us appreciate and prioritize different purchases and activities.

Utility and decision making

For now, let's stick with the easier scenario: Forget about what other people might like, and just think about what makes *you* happy. Imagine that it's the weekend. You have a completely free day, with no obligations. What will you do with it? Remember the first question economists ask: What are your *wants and constraints*? Here, your *constraints* are pretty clear. You have the hours available in one day and access to however much money is available in your bank account. But what can we say about your *wants*? In this chapter, we'll look more closely at the question of what it means to "want" something.

Your possibilities for what to do on a free day are almost endless. You could spend all day watching TV. You could read a thick Russian novel. You could go to the mall and buy some new running shoes. You could study. You could work the phones for your favored candidate in the upcoming election. You could buy 300 cans of tomato soup and take a bath in them. Out of these and a million other possibilities, how do you decide what you *want* to do the most with the time and money available?

This is a surprisingly complex question. Each possible way of spending your day probably involves very different mixtures of good and bad feelings. If you spend all day watching TV, you might feel very relaxed. On the other hand, if you spend the day reading a Russian novel, you might feel proud of yourself for improving your mind and experience a little thrill every time you anticipate casually discussing *The Brothers Karamazov* with that attractive literature major.

Somehow, you need to decide what combination of activities—and what blend of emotions and sensations you get from those activities—is preferable to you, on the whole. Russian novels, TV, and tomato-soup baths are pretty different things. But since we all compare options about what to do with our time and what to buy with our money every day, we must have some sort of internal yardstick that allows us to compare the value we derive from different choices. Sometimes this evaluation is subconscious: You probably don't agonize daily over whether to bathe in soup, even though you *could* do it. Sometimes it's quite conscious and requires deep thinking or extensive research, like choosing whether to buy a car and, if so, what model.

What we need is a universal measure that allows us to compare choices like reading to TV-watching, and TV-watching to working a second job to earn a little extra money. Clearly, something like this must exist inside your mind. Otherwise you wouldn't be able to make these types of decisions, consciously or subconsciously. Economists call this measure **utility**. Utility is a measure of the amount of satisfaction a person derives from something.

utility
a measure of the amount of satisfaction a person derives from something

People get utility from the goods and services they consume and experiences they have. You can get utility from consuming a tasty snack. You can also get utility from figuratively "consuming" a pleasant sensation or experience, such as scoring a goal in a soccer game or chatting with a friend. You can get utility from things you can purchase—food, clothes, cell phones, massages—and also from things that don't usually have a dollar value, like listening to music, learning new things, or doing a good deed. In short, things you like increase your utility. If something is unpleasant and you would choose not to consume it even if it were free, we say that thing reduces your utility.

The idea of utility is fundamental to economics. Think about some of the examples discussed in earlier chapters, such as buying cell phones or Starbucks lattes. People make decisions like this by choosing to do the things they think will give them the most utility, given all of the available options. That is, if you buy a Starbucks latte, it's because you think it will give you more utility than a double espresso or a soda or anything else you could have bought with that amount of money.

Economists call this method of decision making *utility maximization.* The idea that people are *rational utility maximizers* is the baseline assumption in the way economists think about the world. Later in the book, we'll see that economists sometimes relax this assumption to account for the fact that people can be short on information or self-control when making choices. But utility maximization is always the starting point in economics for thinking about how individuals behave.

Over the course of this chapter, we hope you'll see that utility is a deep idea. It encompasses even the toughest choices we make in life and can include the ways that other people influence those choices. For instance, people do unpleasant things all the time. Is that because they are failing to maximize their utility? Not at all. If we take a broad enough view, we usually see that people are doing what they *believe* will bring them the most well-being. Often, that takes into account trade-offs between things that seem nice or feel good in the short term and things that are productive or moral or pleasant in the long term. People weigh the trade-offs between ice cream and health, personal safety and joining the army to defend their country, spending now or saving for later, and so on. The idea of utility allows us to think about this internal and often instinctual calculation in all its richness and complexity.

Revealed preference

LO 7.1 Explain how revealed preferences indicate which goods or activities give a person the most utility.

Unfortunately, utility is hard to measure. If you want to know how much money you've got, you can look at your bank account and put a precise figure on it. But utility is subjective and mysterious. We can't always explain to *ourselves* why we get more utility from one thing than another. We definitely can't put a scale inside *other people's* heads to see how much utility they get from something—although scientists are hard at work to develop something that will do this. For more about methods that scientists use to paint a picture of happiness around the world and at the neural level, read the Real Life box "The science of happiness."

Real Life
The science of happiness

How to measure utility is a question that interests more than just economists. Psychologists and neuroscientists also want to find meaningful ways to compare people's mental states when they're doing different activities or living in different kinds of cultures. Increasingly, economists are teaming up with researchers in these fields to study what has become known as the "science of happiness."

For example, researchers have compiled survey data in a "World Database of Happiness." You can view their Average Happiness map at http://www1.eur.nl/fsw/happiness/hap_nat/maps/Map_AverageHappiness.php. Costa Rica ranks highest in average happiness; Tanzania has the lowest average happiness. Potentially, such studies can help us understand what features of life in different countries make people more happy or unhappy. That knowledge could help us design public policies that make citizens happier.

Survey questions such as the ones used to compile the world map of average happiness often ask people to report how happy they are or how satisfied they feel with their lives. Researchers also ask how happy people are during different activities: Study participants carry a diary with them and receive reminder messages at random points during each day. They write down what they are doing and how happy they feel on a numerical scale. This allows researchers to compare whether, on average, people are happier while commuting to work or looking after their children or playing sports or cooking dinner.

Neuroscientists gather information on happiness using brain-imaging technology. That technology allows researchers to directly observe which regions of the brain are activated in different contexts, including economic decision-making contexts. These data help increase our understanding of how a subjective feeling of well-being emerges from observable neural activities.

Economists who study happiness hope that by borrowing techniques from neuroscience, they can change the study of utility. In the future it will use more objective data about the actual brain processes involved in decision making. Although it's a tall order, some researchers even hope to create measures of utility that are comparable across people. If this sounds interesting to you, investigate interdisciplinary work in fields like behavioral economics, neuroeconomics, or economic psychology.

Sources: The World Database of Happiness, http://worlddatabaseofhappiness.eur.nl; D. Kahneman et al., "The Day Reconstruction Method (DRM): Instrument documentation," July 2004, https://dornsife.usc.edu/assets/sites/780/docs/drm_documentation_july_2004.pdf.

How can we say anything meaningful about the utility other people experience? The answer is surprisingly simple: We *observe* what people actually do, and we assume that, as rational individuals, they're doing what gives them the most utility. Their actions reveal their preferences: If you observe someone ordering a scoop of chocolate ice cream at the ice-cream counter, you can conclude she thought she would get more utility from the chocolate than the strawberry or chocolate-chip cookie dough flavors. If you observe someone buying tickets for an action movie, you can conclude that this gives him more utility than the romantic comedy he could have seen instead. This choice may not be due to the movie itself, but to his companions. For instance, maybe his companions preferred the action move, and he preferred to make his companions happy rather than see his first choice of movie. In that situation, he is maximizing his utility by agreeing to the action movie.

Economists call this idea **revealed preference**. We can tell what maximizes other people's utility by observing their behavior. The fact that someone chose to do something "reveals" that she preferred it to the other available options. Of course, this inference is specific to a particular person and situation. Different people prefer different ice-cream flavors. The same person might be in the mood for an action movie today and a romantic comedy tomorrow.

Revealed preference might sound obvious. It's actually an idea that is unique to economics, and somewhat controversial. If you're interested in understanding how economics overlaps with other disciplines such as psychology, anthropology, or political science, it's important that you understand the idea and its limitations.

Continuing our earlier example, let's say that you spent your free day watching TV instead of reading that Russian novel. Later, you tell a friend, "I really wanted to finish *The Brothers Karamazov,* but somehow I ended up spending all day watching TV." As economists, we suspect you're not being entirely honest with yourself. Observing that you spent all day in front of the TV, with *The Brothers Karamazov* lying unopened on the table next to you, revealed preference suggests that what you *really* wanted to do was watch TV. If not, why did you do it?

This is a trivial example, but it's easy to think of a more serious one. Suppose someone tells you, "I really want to stop smoking, but somehow I keep buying cigarettes." Revealed preference suggests he is getting more utility from continuing to smoke than he would get from actually quitting. If you were a policy-maker deciding how heavily to tax cigarettes, or whether to ban cigarette advertising, you'd have to think seriously about whether to give more weight to what

revealed preference
the idea that people's preferences can be determined by observing their choices and behavior

people *say* they want or to what they actually *do*. In the case of cigarettes, there's a reasonable argument that physical addiction makes it hard for people to actually do in the moment what they know they want in the long term. There might be a role for friends or policy-makers to help by taking some options out of reach. We'll come back to this issue in a later chapter.

Despite interesting debates on tough cases like cigarettes, the idea of revealed preference can take us a long way toward understanding what people want. Notice that we're not making comparisons between people; we're looking only at what one individual prefers. In other words, we can say that two people both preferred chocolate ice cream over strawberry, but not whether one of them liked chocolate more than the other did.

Utility functions

The idea of revealed preference gives us a nice framework for evaluating people's utility. But we can't just follow people around and observe all of their behavior. (That would be impractical, as well as creepy.) Instead, we need a more formal method to make revealed preferences useful in economic analysis.

In order to think systematically about how people make choices, economists construct a **utility function**. A utility function is a formula for calculating the total utility that a particular person derives from consuming a combination of goods and services. Each unique combination of goods and services that a person could choose to consume is called a **bundle**. The utility function is a map that connects each possible bundle to the corresponding level of utility that a person gets from consuming it.

Earlier, we said that utility is a subjective measure that can't be readily quantified. Yet, we also said that a utility function is a way of quantitatively describing preferences. The key to understanding this apparent contradiction is that the utility measurements that go into a utility function are *relative,* not absolute. The numbers we use in utility functions do not measure something concrete like inches or pounds or dollars. Rather, if we say that a certain activity gives a person utility of 3, what that means is that the person values the activity more highly than an activity associated with a utility measure of 2, and less than one with utility of 4. The numbers don't mean anything except an ordering for activities the person likes more or less. (Because these numbers have no meaning other than *relative to each other,* we could have said that the chosen activity has a utility of 6,000, and that the person values that activity more highly than one with utility of 5,000, and less than one with utility of 7,000. But the smaller the numbers—3 rather than 6,000, for example—the easier they are to work with.)

Let's apply the idea of a utility function to a simple utility-generating experience: eating dinner. Say that Sarah is eating a dinner of macaroni and cheese, broccoli, and ice cream. We ask her to rate the utility she gets from each part of her dinner. She responds that she gets utility of 3 from each serving of macaroni and cheese, utility of 2 from each serving of broccoli, and utility of 8 from each scoop of ice cream. (Remember that the specific numbers we use are arbitrary. What matters are the *relative numbers* attached to each good in the function, which help us understand how much more utility Sarah gets from choosing one thing over another.) For dinner, she eats one serving of mac and cheese, two servings of broccoli, and two scoops of ice cream. Her dinner utility function is therefore:

EQUATION 7-1   Total utility = $(3 \times 1$ mac and cheese$) + (2 \times 2$ broccoli$) + (8 \times 2$ ice cream$)$
$$= 3 + 4 + 16 = 23$$

This analysis raises some questions: Does it suggest that Sarah should keep eating and eating, with the idea that the more food, the more utility? Why stop, when every serving of broccoli, mac and cheese, and ice cream would add positive utility? Also, since ice cream gives her far and away the most utility, shouldn't she ditch the broccoli and mac and cheese to have an ice-cream dinner chock full of utility? In reality, we're sure you'll agree that infinite eating of ice cream is not a good idea and is unlikely to maximize anyone's utility. What is missing from this analysis? To find out, keep reading.

utility function

a formula for calculating the total utility that a particular person derives from consuming a combination of goods and services

bundle

a unique combination of goods and services that a person could choose to consume

☐ What can observing people's actual choices tell us about their preferences? What is this approach called? **[LO 7.1]**

☐ What is the word for a particular combination of goods and services that a person could choose to consume? **[LO 7.1]**

Marginal Utility

To understand when and why Sarah should stop eating ice cream, we need the concept of marginal utility. In Chapter 1, "Economics and Life," we introduced the idea of making decisions *at the margin*. The change in total utility that comes from consuming one additional unit of a good or service is called **marginal utility**.

Let's go back to ice cream. Imagine how much pleasure you'd get from a scoop of your favorite flavor. Now imagine eating a second scoop. Is it just as enjoyable? Maybe it's a bit less yummy than the very first taste. In other words, the marginal utility you get from a second scoop is a little lower than the marginal utility of the first scoop. Now eat a third scoop. We bet you'll enjoy this one less than the first two. A fourth scoop? You're not getting much additional enjoyment at all. A fifth, sixth, seventh, or eighth scoop? Less and less enjoyable; in fact, after eight scoops of ice cream, you likely are not feeling well.

We can assign some numbers to describe these changes in marginal utility. Let's say that, as Table 7-1 shows, the first scoop of ice cream yields 6 units of utility. But each scoop afterward yields less and less additional utility. From one scoop to two, you gain 5 units of marginal utility. Total utility increases, but the second scoop brings less marginal utility than the first scoop brought.

Sometimes, marginal utility diminishes so much that it actually becomes negative. When we offer you a seventh scoop of ice cream, you might feel indifferent between eating it or not. It adds nothing to your total utility, so it has zero marginal utility. And you'd rather not eat that eighth scoop, as it may make you sick. The eighth scoop would *reduce* your total utility. In other words, it would have *negative marginal utility*.

The principle demonstrated here is called **diminishing marginal utility** which states that the additional utility gained from consuming successive units of a good or service tends to be smaller than the utility gained from the previous unit. The diminishing marginal utility of food items is particularly noticeable because our bodies have a physical reaction to additional consumption. Our stomachs start to tell us that we're full, and our sense of taste fades as the novelty of a new flavor passes.

marginal utility
the change in total utility that comes from consuming one additional unit of a good or service

diminishing marginal utility
the principle that the additional utility gained from consuming successive units of a good or service tends to be smaller than the utility gained from the previous unit

TABLE 7-1
Utility from ice cream

Scoops of ice cream	Marginal utility	Total utility
1	6	6
2	5	11
3	4	15
4	3	18
5	2	20
6	1	21
7	0	21
8	−1	20

Economists observe that the principle of diminishing marginal utility applies to most goods and services. Imagine you have recently moved to a cold climate and have no sweaters. Buying one sweater makes a huge difference in your comfort. Buying a tenth sweater isn't such a big deal.

Figure 7-1 illustrates the idea of diminishing marginal utility. Panel A of Figure 7-1 shows the total utility you get from eating more and more scoops of ice cream. The curve slopes upward to begin with, flattening out as additional scoops add less and less to your total utility. At the point marked Y, the seventh scoop, your total utility peaks—and the slope of the curve is completely flat. Beyond that point, each scoop has negative marginal utility; the curve of total utility slopes downward after that point.

Panel B of Figure 7-1 shows the same idea, plotting the *marginal* utility of each scoop rather than total utility. The line in this graph slopes downward, showing that your marginal utility is diminishing with each additional scoop. Remember that even though marginal utility slopes downward, each additional scoop of ice cream still increases *total* utility as long as marginal utility is greater than zero. At point X, the marginal utility of one more scoop of ice cream is 2. Thus, consuming the fifth scoop of ice cream increases total utility, though only by a small amount. At point Y, the marginal utility is zero: You get no extra enjoyment from the seventh scoop. At scoop 8, marginal utility is negative. Point Y is a significant link between panel A and panel B: When the marginal utility of an additional unit of a good is zero, you've maxed out the total utility you can get from consuming that good.

Although many things you can do or buy have diminishing marginal utility, not all of them will end up in *negative* marginal utility. For example, most people will never get negative utility from having more savings. If you have no savings, the marginal utility of your first $1,000 is pretty high. If you already have a million dollars, the marginal utility of having another $1,000 might be pretty small. There's probably not that much difference between your life with $1,000,000 and your life with $1,001,000. But it's hard to imagine you'd ever get *reduced* total utility from having more money appear in your savings account. If you really can't think of

---

FIGURE 7-1

Diminishing marginal utility

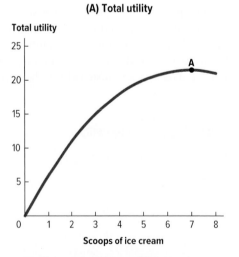

(A) Total utility

The first couple of scoops of ice cream cause big increases in utility. But as you eat more ice cream, the effect of each additional scoop on your total utility decreases until more ice cream will actually make you *un*happier, starting at point A.

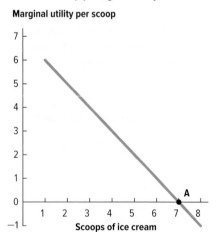

(B) Marginal utility

The marginal utility, or the additional utility from each additional scoop, is always decreasing, until it actually becomes negative at point A.

anything else to buy, after all, you can always give it away to someone else and enjoy being a philanthropist.

For most purchasing decisions, you wouldn't get anywhere near the point of negative marginal utility. Long before you buy a seventh scoop of ice cream, or a tenth sweater, or a fiftieth video game, you are likely to have decided you'd get higher marginal utility from spending that money on something else. After all, people don't usually offer you free, unlimited ice cream or sweaters or games. Rather, you usually have to pay or work for them. You are likely to conclude, before you reach the point of negative marginal utility, that having one more of any of those things just isn't worth it.

This brings us to the most important point in this chapter: What happens when we combine the concept of *diminishing marginal utility* with the concept of *wants and constraints*?

Maximizing utility within constraints

LO 7.2 Show how the budget constraint affects utility maximization.

Let's go back to the example of your free day. In reality, you're very unlikely to spend the entire day doing just one thing. Instead, you might do a number of different things: drive to the mall, shop for running shoes, and eat some lunch; go for a run in your new shoes; relax for a while by watching TV; make a little progress through *The Brothers Karamazov;* and go out with friends in the evening. Or there are millions of other possible combinations you could choose. How do you pick which bundle of activities to do within the time and money available?

Marginal utility helps make sense of this sort of decision by calling attention to the *trade-offs* involved. Why didn't you spend another hour at the mall? Because once you'd been there for four hours, the marginal utility of another hour was less than the marginal utility of going for an energizing run instead. Why didn't you run for a second hour? Because you were getting tired. The marginal utility of another hour of running was less than the marginal utility of watching some TV. And so on, with the rest of the day.

Of course, you don't have to make these choices consecutively, waiting until you get tired of one activity before deciding to move on. People can think ahead about the bundle of goods or activities that will give them the most combined utility; they can anticipate that too much of one thing isn't as good as some other option. Your choice about how to spend the day is really about selecting a *combination* of goods and activities that will maximize your utility, within the limits of time and money available to you. If you have spent your day wisely, there is no other combination of activities that could have added up to greater total utility.

There are many things that might give you positive utility that you choose not to do. They may be good and enjoyable, but the opportunity cost (passing up something even more enjoyable) is higher than the benefit you'd get. People have many wants, but they are constrained by the time and money available to them. If they are rational utility maximizers, they try to optimize within those constraints by spending their resources on the bundle of goods and activities that will give them the highest possible total utility.

We can use a quantitative model to illustrate the idea of maximizing utility within constraints. Like all models, we'll have to simplify a bit. Imagine that Cody has $120 to spend each month after paying all his bills. Assume there are only two things he considers spending the money on: movie theater tickets and concert tickets. A movie ticket costs $15 and a concert ticket costs $30. Cody could buy several possible combinations of movie and concert tickets within his budget. He could not see any concerts at all and spend $120 going to the movies. He could see four movies ($60) and two concerts ($60), and so on.

We can represent these bundle possibilities on a line called a *budget constraint,* as shown in Figure 7-2. A **budget constraint** is a line composed of all of the possible combinations of goods and services a consumer can buy with his or her income. (If this graph looks familiar to

budget constraint
a line that is composed of all of the possible combinations of goods and services that a consumer can buy with her or his income

FIGURE 7-2

The budget constraint

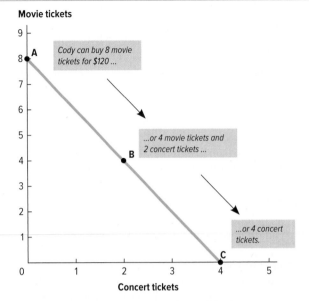

The budget constraint represents the combinations of goods that are available to Cody given his budget. Each bundle on the line costs exactly the amount of money Cody has in his budget.

the production possibilities frontier graph of Chapter 2, "Specialization and Exchange," that's no coincidence. They express very similar ideas—the concept of choosing between different combinations of things within the constraint of limited resources.)

   If Cody is a rational consumer, making choices to achieve goals in the most effective way possible, he will spend his budget on the combination of movie and concert tickets that maximizes his utility. How does he feel about going to see a movie?

- Cody feels that going to the movie theater three times in a month is very important. He'll give each of his first three movie tickets a utility score of 95.
- After that, seeing a fourth movie gives him additional utility of 80, and a fifth movie scores an additional 65 points of utility. (Remember that utility is an imaginary measure. These numbers don't refer to anything that's measurable outside of Cody's mind; they're just a way of getting an insight into his relative preferences.)
- Eventually, he'll become so sick of seeing movies that he'd rather not go an eighth time: The marginal utility of movie number eight would be negative, at −10.

How about concerts?

- Cody would not be happy if he went the entire month without going to a concert, so his first concert gives him utility of 100.
- Seeing a second concert wouldn't be as crucial, but still very enjoyable; that second concert ticket will give him utility of 85.
- After a while, Cody starts to tire of going to concerts, so the marginal utility Cody gets from each ticket decreases. By the time he's bought three tickets, he feels like that's enough, and additional tickets won't increase his total utility.

   The amount of marginal and total utility Cody gets from each movie ticket is shown in panel A of Table 7-2, while the amount of marginal and total utility Cody gets from each concert ticket is shown in panel B.

TABLE 7-2

Maximizing total utility

(A) Utility from movie tickets		
Tickets	**Marginal utility**	**Total utility**
1	95	95
2	95	190
3	95	285
4	80	365
5	65	430
6	35	465
7	10	475
8	−10	465
(B) Utility from concert tickets		
Tickets	**Marginal utility**	**Total utility**
1	100	100
2	85	185
3	25	210
4	0	210

In panel A, we see that utility greatly increases as Cody buys the first few movie tickets, and peaks when he buys 7 movie tickets. After that, utility decreases. In panel B, we see that Cody gets lots of utility from the first few concert tickets. After the third ticket, he gets no further utility.

By adding up the utility of each potential bundle of movie tickets and concert tickets, as shown in panel A of Figure 7-3, you can see that the optimal combination for Cody is to buy one concert ticket and six movie tickets, or Bundle B. If Cody is a rational, utility-maximizing consumer, then we can expect him to do just that. Out of all the available options, that's the combination that gives him the most total utility (565).

Usually, economists don't ask people to give a utility rating to the things they could buy. Instead, they try out different utility functions and make predictions about how they expect people to behave. They might look at data about how groups of people in the real world actually did behave and compare the two. They then can assess how well they understood the wants and constraints that motivated people's choices.

As always, real life is a lot more complicated than any model. In reality, people choose between thousands of different spending possibilities rather than just two, yielding millions of possible combinations. The principle, however, is the same: Rational consumers choose to spend their budgets on the combination of goods and services that will give them the highest possible total utility.

There's another real-life complication we haven't considered in this chapter: Budgets don't fall out of the sky; they're usually determined by earlier choices about what job to apply for and how much to work. In the real world, our decisions about how to maximize utility also involve this trade-off between work and available budget: Would you get more utility from working hard and having more money to spend, or having more leisure time but less money to enjoy it with? This is an idea we'll come back to later in the book.

Appendix E, "Using Indifference Curves," which follows this chapter, presents indifference curves. Economists use indifference curves as a tool to represent utility graphically and to explain how consumers maximize utility.

FIGURE 7-3
Maximizing utility

(A) Maximizing total utility

Bundle	Concert tickets	Utility from concert tickets	Movie tickets	Utility from movie tickets	Total utility
A	0	0	8	465	465
B	1	100	6	465	565
C	2	185	4	365	550
D	3	210	2	190	400
E	4	210	0	0	210

This table shows all the bundles that Cody can potentially consume. The total utility he gets from each bundle depends on the number of concert tickets and the number of movie tickets in it.

(B) Utility along the budget constraint

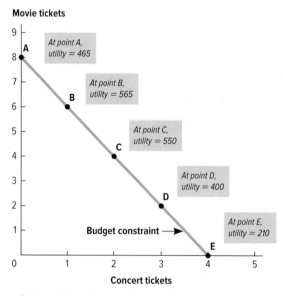

Each bundle on the budget constraint corresponds to one of the rows in the table in panel A. While each costs the same, the utility each provides varies according to Cody's preferences.

✓ CONCEPT CHECK

☐ If something has negative marginal utility, what happens to your total utility when you consume it? **[LO 7.2]**

☐ What is the budget constraint? **[LO 7.2]**

Responding to Changes in Income and Prices

Income changes all the time. You might get a raise for diligent work. Or, pressed by a lack of business, your boss may be forced to cut your hours, and you earn less money. Both of these changes in income are likely to change how much you decide to spend on the things you buy.

The same is true for changes in prices. If lattes drop in price by $0.50 one day, you'll probably decide to buy more of them. As these examples show, rational utility maximizers will change their behavior as circumstances like income and prices change.

Changes in income

LO 7.3 Show how a change in income affects consumption choices.

When a person's income increases, more bundles of goods and services become affordable. When income decreases, fewer bundles are affordable, and consumers will probably have to cut consumption of some things. We represent these changes by shifting the entire budget line to show each new range of options available to the consumer.

Why does this happen? Let's look at what happens when Cody gets $60 for his birthday from his grandparents. Suppose he decides to use all of his money this month—the $120 he normally would spend, plus the birthday cash. That means Cody now has a grand total of $180 to spend. Again, Cody will decide how many movie tickets to buy and how many concert tickets to buy:

- If he decides to buy only concert tickets, with the extra cash he can now buy six tickets instead of only four.
- If instead he decides to buy only movie tickets, he can now afford 12 tickets instead of eight.

With more money, Cody can buy more of both goods at every point. The entire budget line shifts out by the equivalent of $60, maintaining the same slope as it did before. As a result, Cody can buy more movie tickets or more concert tickets (or more of both) than he did before he received the birthday money. (*Note:* Don't confuse the budget constraint with the demand curve; it looks similar, but the y-axis here isn't price.)

Why does the slope stay the same? Even though Cody has more money, the ratio of the prices of the two goods has not changed. Movie tickets are still $15 and concert tickets, $30. The only thing that has changed is that Cody is now able to buy more tickets in whatever combination he chooses. Figure 7-4 shows the effect of this increase in income.

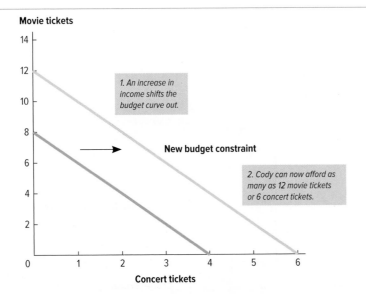

FIGURE 7-4

The effect of an increase in income

When Cody's income increases as a result of a gift, he is able to afford more goods. This shifts the budget constraint outward, and he can now buy 12 movie tickets or 6 concert tickets.

Changes in prices

LO 7.4 Show how a change in price affects consumption choices, and distinguish between the income and substitution effects.

What happens to an individual's behavior when income stays the same but the prices of goods change? Let's think about Cody again. If the price of movie tickets decreases, he can clearly afford to purchase more movie tickets. In addition, while it's not as obvious, he could also purchase more concert tickets: Now that each movie ticket is cheaper, there might be some money left over for more concert tickets. In general, changes in the price of a good have two important effects, called the *income effect* and the *substitution effect*.

Before thinking about the difference between the two, observe that any price decrease causes the budget line to rotate outward, as shown in Figure 7-5. Why does the curve rotate outward instead of shifting right in a parallel fashion? Let's return to Cody's pre-birthday budget constraint of $120. If the price of movie tickets has decreased from $15 to $10, Cody's budget constraint changes:

- If he puts all of his money into movie tickets, he is able to afford 12 tickets at the new lower price: four more than he was originally able to buy.
- But if he puts all of his money into concert tickets, he is still able to afford only six of them since the price of concert tickets has stayed the same.

Income effect

income effect
the change in consumption that results from a change in effective wealth due to higher or lower prices

The **income effect** describes the change in consumption that results from a change in effective wealth due to higher or lower prices. If the price of movie tickets falls from $15 to $10 per ticket and Cody continues to buy his usual four movie tickets a month, he is now $5 "richer" for each ticket he buys. He now has an extra $20 in comparison to last month.

In general, consumers can buy more things when the price of a good they usually purchase decreases. When goods get cheaper, consumers' money goes farther: Cody could buy more movie tickets. He also has more money left over after buying movie tickets and could put this toward buying more concert tickets. The change in consumption as a result of Cody "feeling richer" is the income effect.

FIGURE 7-5

The effect of a price change

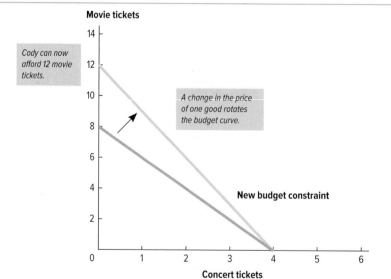

When the price of one good changes, the budget constraint rotates out to demonstrate the new consumption bundles that are available. The change in slope reflects the change in the relative prices of the two goods.

?

POTENTIALLY CONFUSING

Notice that even though this effect is called the *income* effect, it is not describing the impact that a *change in income* would have on consumption. Instead, we are saying that a change in the *price* of a good effectively makes you richer or poorer. It is *as though* your income changed. However, there has been no direct change in income.

A refresher on normal goods and inferior goods is important here. After a price change causes a change in effective wealth, we need to know whether the consumer will buy more or less of each good. Remember that *normal goods* are those for which demand increases as income increases. If Cody chooses to increase his consumption of both movie and concert tickets when his income increases, this would imply they are both normal goods. In contrast, *inferior goods* are those for which demand decreases as income increases. (Instant ramen noodles, that staple of college diets everywhere, are a classic inferior good.) The income effect impacts the demand for normal and inferior goods because the change in price mimics the effect of a change in income.

Substitution effect

Now let's look at the second important effect brought about by changes in the price of a good. The **substitution effect** describes the change in consumption that results from a change in the relative price of goods. In our example, when the price of a movie ticket decreased from $15 to $10, movie tickets became cheaper *relative to* concert tickets. (We saw that relative change represented by the change in the slope of the budget line.) Said another way, concert tickets became more expensive *relative to* movie tickets, even though the price of concert tickets did not change. This relative change causes Cody to choose more movies and fewer concerts. He substitutes the good that has become cheaper in relative terms for the one that has become more expensive, which is why it's called the "substitution" effect.

substitution effect
the change in consumption that results from a change in the relative price of goods

Another way to say this is that the *opportunity cost* of concerts and movies has changed. When movie tickets cost $15 and concert tickets cost $30, the opportunity cost of a concert was two movies. When the price of a movie ticket decreases to $10, the opportunity cost of a concert increases to three movies. The flip-side is that the opportunity cost of movies in terms of forgone concerts has decreased (from $\frac{1}{2}$ to $\frac{1}{3}$).

Why? Think about the situation as a change in the marginal utility *per dollar* that Cody gets for each good. When the price of movie tickets decreases, the marginal utility per dollar for movie tickets goes up; the marginal utility per dollar for concert tickets stays the same. Cody now gets more utility bang for his buck from movies, so he wants to spend more of his budget on them.

Occasionally, though, people may actually choose to consume *more* of a good when its price increases. This occurs for goods known as *Veblen goods*. Veblen goods are items for which the quantity demanded is higher when prices are higher. They are something that people buy *because* they are flashy and expensive. Buyers choose them to show others that they can afford flashy and expensive goods.

The idea of Veblen goods conflicts with the idea of utility we presented earlier in this chapter; there we assumed that you would make the same choices whether you were alone or not. Would you buy a luxury watch when a basic one tells time just fine, if you were the only person who could see it? Why buy a $200 handbag when a $50 one will hold all of your stuff, if no one else will see you with it? Although you may also enjoy the high quality, durability, or design of luxury items, these goods sell at least in part because people get utility from the reaction others have to items known to be expensive or exclusive. The Veblen good suggests that utility may be far from the individual measure we have talked about so far.

This example illustrates one of the many instances in which your utility is affected by other people. The perceptions of others help explain why people buy luxury items. They also influence how we donate to charity and what gifts we give to others, and even how we interact with others in everyday situations. Such examples show the remarkable breadth of the concept of utility, and we explore this idea further in the next section.

Ultimately, both the income effect and the substitution effect influence an individual's reaction to a price change. Cody may choose to buy more movie tickets but the same number of concert tickets. Or he may choose to buy more of both goods. In unusual circumstances, he might even choose to buy fewer movie tickets and more concert tickets. After observing how his choices change after the change in price, we would then know whether he was influenced more by the income effect or the substitution effect.

✓ CONCEPT CHECK

☐ What happens to the budget constraint when income increases? **[LO 7.3]**

☐ What happens to consumption of a normal good when its price increases? **[LO 7.4]**

☐ What is the difference between the income effect and the substitution effect of a price increase for a normal good? **[LO 7.4]**

Utility and Society

A common misconception about economics is that utility maximization assumes people are inward-looking consumption machines. In fact, the idea of utility is much broader and more flexible than that. Utility can help us think about envy, status, kindness, and a range of other very human emotions.

Here's an example: To avoid Scroogenomics-style waste during the holidays, why not give your aunt and uncle what anyone would want—a goat? We don't mean giving the actual goat to your relatives as an affordable and earth-friendly lawn care solution. Instead, charities like Heifer International will send a goat to a poor family in Africa or South America in your aunt's and uncle's names. A single goat can be a great help. Goats can provide milk for the family and fertilizer for crops. They can even act as a source of savings that can be sold when times are tough.

Many organizations offer the opportunity to give these "charity-gifts"—sending a goat or other useful items to a stranger in need, while giving the credit for the donation as a gift to someone else. What can the idea of utility tell us about this three-party exchange? Your aunt and uncle get a warm glow knowing that they were recognized in your donation. You get the same good feeling that accompanies a good deed. It's also possible that you get a little kick from knowing that your aunt and uncle find you both socially conscious and generous. And, of course, the family that receives the goat receives something that they value.

As the Heifer example shows, people can get utility from a variety of sources, in a way that weaves together both psychology and economics. Some people do good deeds only when others are looking because they're interested only in their reputation. Of course, many others do good deeds because they're good—every year, people give to perfect strangers who may live in the same town or thousands of miles away. In the next few sections, we'll look at all of these motivations.

Utility and status

LO 7.5 Outline the ways in which utility is influenced by other people.

The utility we get from consuming something is not always about our *direct* benefit alone. If it were, those designer handbags would be a far tougher sell. Chocolate ice cream, in contrast, is an example of something we'd probably enjoy just as much whether or not anybody else knew we were consuming it. More often, utility comes from two sources: One is the *direct effect* the product has on us and the other is the effect that *other people's reaction*s to it have on us. In the end, overall utility is a mix of outside perceptions and inner preferences, both of which contribute to decision making. Your choice of which cell phone you use, which brands of clothes you wear, or which car you drive is likely to be partly influenced by your efforts to signal personality traits, aesthetics, or social status.

Take the decision to buy a new car. There are many obvious differences between an off-road sport utility vehicle (SUV) and a Prius. The SUV grinds over rough terrain with ease; the Prius would struggle as off-road conditions get hairy. But the Prius sips gas—generally getting 50 miles per gallon—compared to the sub-20 miles per gallon for the rugged SUV. If your internal preference was the only thing that mattered, you would likely make your final decision based on characteristics such as these, and how they fit your transportation needs and lifestyle.

However, utility calculations include much more than that. Sure, gas mileage is an important consideration, but people buy cars for other reasons as well. As you silently whir through town in a Prius, for instance, the people who see you probably associate other traits with you (traits you may or may not have): They may assume that the average Prius driver lives a healthy and earth-friendly life (although any particular individual may not). We'd guess that every person who owns a Prius has at least once gotten a little kick out of knowing that he or she is perceived to have these traits.

Even more important than the opinion of random strangers, though, will be the perceptions of those who are close to you. If you're a long-time member of an environmental group, you may get more utility from showing up to a meeting in a Prius than you would if you rumbled up in a large SUV. The SUV, though, may score more points from fellow members at the local outdoors club. The idea that utility is influenced by others' opinions is not new. Utility can be related to status, and some people get lots of utility from buying goods that show off how wealthy they are.

Utility is sometimes influenced not just by what others think, but by how much others have. Assuming two jobs that are exactly the same, which would you prefer:

- A job with a salary of $36,000 at a firm where the average salary is $40,000?
- A job with a salary of $34,000 at a firm where the average salary is $30,000?

It seems like an easy question. You might assume it's your own salary that affects your utility, not anyone else's, so you'd get more utility from the extra money. Yet when researchers presented people with this scenario, 80 percent said that someone in the second position would be happier with her job situation.

What can account for this? If the only utility we get comes from pleasures like eating ice cream, then a higher salary would give us more utility: We can buy more ice cream with $36,000 than with $34,000.

But if we also get utility from *how others see us,* that starts to explain why we might prefer to earn $4,000 more than the people we spend most of our time with. Perhaps we'd get utility from driving to the office every day in a slightly newer car than our coworkers', taking calls on a slightly fancier cell phone, and being able to talk about slightly more impressive vacations.

Utility may also depend on your *frame of reference.* You'll get more utility from earning $34,000 if you are comparing yourself with coworkers earning $30,000 than if you are comparing yourself with former schoolmates earning $40,000 elsewhere. If you compare yourself with CEOs of Fortune 500 companies, then earning $34,000 will make you positively miserable. This line of thought has an unsettling implication: Simply by changing our frame of reference, we might gain or lose utility. See the What Do You Think? box "Choosing a league" to read more about this debate.

What Do You Think?
Choosing a league

Would you rather be the worst player in the major leagues or the best player in the minor leagues? Would you rather be the star soloist in your local choir or a below-average voice in a prestigious, big-city choir?

Before the age of modern communications, these questions didn't matter so much. Everyone's frame of reference was fairly local and limited. Technology has changed all that: Thanks to downloadable MP3s and streaming radio through Pandora and Spotify, our frame of reference for good music is much broader. The local diva in the church choir was probably much more exciting in a time when you couldn't compare her to Adele—and the local diva might have been much happier when she didn't have Adele to compare herself to.

The same is true of good local athletes, actors, chefs, comedians, politicians, and many other professions. To the extent that utility in these pursuits comes from *relative* status, there are fewer and fewer winners as our frame of reference becomes wider and wider. The same goes for material wealth in general: Some people argue that introducing television to remote communities can make them less happy by allowing comparisons with much more wealthy societies.

Then again, we all have some power to choose our own frames of reference. It's up to the local diva whether she chooses to enjoy performing to a small but appreciative audience at church, or stay at home feeling sad that she was turned down when she auditioned for *American Idol.*

WHAT DO YOU THINK?

1. Would you rather be the best player on a bad team or the worst player on a good team? Why?
2. Are there benefits to comparing ourselves with superstars? How do those benefits weigh against the negatives?

Of course, utility maximization is only as selfish or unselfish as we ourselves are. As you plink a few coins in the tin in front of the grocery store during the holidays and see the warm smile from the bell-ringer, it is likely that you are getting utility from that exchange. It's a mutually beneficial exchange: You get a fuzzy glow while shopping and charities receive needed donations. Utility can come from following through on our best inclinations as well as our pettiest ones, and can help explain some very noble actions.

Utility and altruism

LO 7.6 Describe how people get utility from altruism and reciprocity.

In 2010, a 7.0 magnitude earthquake shook Haiti, killing over 300,000 people; it left millions more homeless, without access to food or clean water. In the following two weeks, people in North America donated over $500 million to relief efforts. Of course, charity is not limited to sympathetic reactions to calamitous disaster. Even in the midst of the deep economic recession in 2008, Americans gave more than $300 billion to charities of every kind. They gave to religious groups and schools, arts organizations, and disaster relief. That's not counting the donations of time and expertise that people made as volunteers. Nor does it include the countless acts of everyday kindness and selflessness that people perform for family and friends and strangers.

altruism
a motive for action in which a person's utility increases simply because someone else's utility increases

How does economics account for this evidence of mass caring for others? How does it account for doctors who travel overseas to treat sick people in refugee camps? For people who care for their elderly relatives? For volunteers in after-school programs who help kids do their homework? When people behave "selflessly" by doing something for others, with no obvious benefit for themselves, we say they are behaving *altruistically.* Economists use the term **altruism** to

The concept of utility applies to more than just consumption. A person's utility can increase from altruistic behaviors such as volunteer activities.

© Amble Designs/Shutterstock

describe a motive for action in which a person's utility increases simply because someone else's utility increases.

When we do good things, we often get utility from multiple sources. A doctor who travels overseas to treat sick people in refugee camps will get utility from helping others. If she is like most people, she also will probably get utility when she tells people at parties about her charitable work. Such feelings are an undeniable part of giving behavior. Altruistic and selfish or image-conscious motivations can coexist perfectly well; a single action might produce utility for many different reasons. For instance, imagine buying an extra concert ticket for a friend: It's entirely reasonable for you to get utility both from your altruistic enjoyment of your friend's happiness and from your own increased enjoyment of the experience due to sharing it with good company.

The Product(RED) campaign, started in 2006, gives a couple dollars to fight global AIDS for every Product(RED)-branded good you buy. If people cared only about altruism, this campaign wouldn't exist. Instead of spending $20 on a T-shirt, with $5 given to charity, a truly altruistic person could forgo the more-expensive T-shirt, spend $10 on cheaper threads, and give $10 to charity. Even further, a person could instead write a check for $20 directly to the RED Global Fund. In buying that T-shirt, you are showing that you get some sort of utility beyond the simple altruism in fighting AIDS: Maybe you get a warm glow from wearing that shirt. Or maybe you just liked the design.

Economists have done experiments to get at the underlying reasons for giving. The results of these efforts are presented in the Real Life box "Why we give."

Real Life
Why we give

Economists have recently used experiments to gain insight into the psychology of charity. In one experiment, researchers sent various people door to door soliciting donations for charity. Young, attractive people visited some houses; dowdier solicitors visited others. The result? The

(continued)

attractive solicitors got significantly more donations. The impact of attractiveness was more pronounced than any other single factor that the experimenters examined. The appearance of the person collecting donations might seem like something that shouldn't matter in our conscious decisions about charity, but it's possible that people respond to beauty on a subconscious level, something that psychologists call the "halo effect."

In another experiment, researchers randomly assigned each potential donor to a certain level of matching donations. Some were told that every $1 they donated would be matched by a $3 donation from a third party. Others were offered a match of $2. Still others got a simple $1-to-$1 match. Another group was not offered any matching donation at all. Those who were offered matching donations gave more than those who weren't, but the level of matching was irrelevant. Those offered 2:1 or 3:1 matches did not give significantly more than those offered the 1:1 match. This result suggests people saw the match as a reason to give to the charity, even if the size of the match didn't matter.

The question of the *impact* of charitable giving is one that economists are also researching, and with startling results. Experiments with different ways of using international aid money show that some projects do much more good per dollar given than others. Yet this raises a troubling possibility: The charities that raise the most money aren't necessarily the ones that have the greatest impact on those in need but sometimes may be those with the flashiest fund-raising techniques.

As economic research increases our understanding of why people give and which charities do the most good, we may also find ways to bring the two together—to encourage people to give more money to the most effective charities. For example, the website GuideStar (www .guidestar.org) rates the efficiency of charities. Similarly, GiveWell (www.givewell.org) names charities that do the most good per dollar donated. Lastly, ImpactMatters (www.impactm.org), a new organization founded by one of the authors of this book, helps donors find charities that use and produce appropriate evidence of impact.

Sources: Dean Karlan and John List, "Does price matter in charitable giving? Evidence from a large-scale natural field experiment," *American Economic Review* 97, no. 5 (December 2007), pp. 1774–1793; Craig Landry et al., "Toward an understanding of the economics of charity: Evidence from a field experiment," *The Quarterly Journal of Economics* 121, no. 2 (May 2006), pp. 747–782.

In the end, when economists say things like, "We assume people are rational and act in their self-interest," they aren't saying they assume people are *selfish*. They mean only that people maximize their utility. Revealed preferences show us that many people get utility from doing things that really aren't selfish at all.

Utility and reciprocity

Revealed preference also suggests that many people get utility from punishing bad behavior and rewarding good. Imagine that a researcher asks you to take part in an experiment. You will do the experiment with a partner; you know nothing about him or her, and you will never meet. The researcher then gives you $10 and tells you that you can give any amount of the money to your partner, or decide to keep it all for yourself. The researcher lets you know that he will triple the amount that you decide to transfer—so, for example, a $3 transfer becomes a $9 transfer. Your partner will get the opportunity to transfer money back to you. If you could talk to the other person, you might agree that you'll transfer the full $10; she'll receive $30 and share the bonanza by transferring $15 back to you. But you can't talk to each other. What would you do?

When researchers ask people to play this game in real experiments, they find that, on average, the more the first person shares with a partner, the more the partner will send back in response. This suggests that people get utility from rewarding kindness with kindness in return, even when there's nothing in it for them.

We call this tendency **reciprocity**. Reciprocity means responding to another's action with a similar action. Reciprocity involves doing good things for people who did good things for us. (Note the difference from *altruism,* which involves simply wanting others to be better off.)

reciprocity
responding to another's action with a similar action

Reciprocity also occurs when we respond in kind to bad treatment. When people make an effort to decrease someone else's utility in response to being harmed themselves, they are engaging in *negative reciprocity*. When you steal toothpaste from that guy down the hall whose music has kept you up at night for a week, you're engaging in negative reciprocity.

People frequently engage in reciprocal actions even when they stand to lose out on some benefit. To see how this works, let's return to the game from the research experiment. Like before, you choose how much money to transfer to your partner, but now the researcher allows the partner to accept or reject the offer. If she rejects, then neither of you gets to keep *any* of the money. In theory, you might expect the partner to accept any offer: Even if you transfer only one cent, the partner is better off accepting it than rejecting it.

But that's not what happens when this experiment is played in practice. The partner regularly rejects the money if she deems the amount offered to be "too low." The partner willingly forfeits free money as a way to punish the other who has acted "unfairly." This outcome occurs despite the fact that the punishment has no future implications—the two participants don't know who the other person is and there will be no further rounds of the experiment. As the experiment shows, fairness is an ideal that people often are willing to sacrifice for, even when it's not rational to do so.

Reciprocity guides everyday interactions. When you bring over a pizza in exchange for help studying for an exam, or you buy the food that you were offered as a free sample in the store, you are engaging in reciprocity. Along with ideas such as altruism and status, reciprocity adds depth to our concept of utility, showing it as sometimes quirky and altogether human.

✓ CONCEPT CHECK

☐ How can other people's opinions and impressions influence our utility? **[LO 7.5]**

☐ Name two ways that an action may provide utility, other than the direct effect of consuming a good or service. **[LO 7.6]**

Conclusion

The ideas in this chapter are at the heart of economic analysis. Everything in the following chapters (and, for that matter, the preceding chapters) is in some way based on the assumption that people attempt to maximize their utility within the limitations of their resources.

We'll enrich this picture in the coming chapters, seeing that individuals have to answer many tough questions when making even commonplace decisions: What is the timing of the benefits, now or later? What is the timing of the costs? What are the risks? Am I fully informed about the situation? Are others competing with me for the same goal?

The idea of utility maximization is remarkably flexible. We'll see that people often have preferences that extend far beyond a narrow definition of their own benefit. Sometimes they pursue their goals in unexpected or not entirely rational ways. Nonetheless, the essential idea of individuals pursuing the things they want in the face of scarcity drives economic analysis from A to Z.

Key Terms

utility, p. 167

revealed preference, p. 169

utility function, p. 170

bundle, p. 170

marginal utility, p. 171

diminishing marginal utility, p. 171

budget constraint, p. 173

income effect, p. 178

substitution effect, p. 179

altruism, p. 182

reciprocity, p. 185

Summary

LO 7.1 Explain how revealed preferences indicate which goods or activities give a person the most utility.

Utility is an imaginary measure of the amount of satisfaction a person derives from something. People get utility from things they can purchase but also from things that don't usually have a dollar value. People make decisions by choosing to do the things they think will give them the most utility, given all of the available options. Economists use the term *utility maximization* to describe this method of decision making.

Economists generally assume that individuals' preferences are demonstrated through the choices that they make, a concept known as *revealed preference*. We observe what people actually do, and assume that as rational individuals, they're doing what gives them the most utility.

LO 7.2 Show how the budget constraint affects utility maximization.

The *budget constraint* is a line that shows all the possible consumption bundles available to an individual given a fixed budget. The slope of the budget line is equivalent to the ratio of prices of the two goods. A rational individual will maximize utility given the amount of goods he or she can afford.

LO 7.3 Show how a change in income affects consumption choices.

An increase in an individual's income will cause the budget line to shift outward, allowing a consumer to buy more goods on average. A decrease in income, on the other hand, will cause a person to consume fewer goods on average.

LO 7.4 Show how a change in price affects consumption choices, and distinguish between the income and substitution effects.

A change in the price of goods can have two effects on optimal consumption. The change in consumption that results from increased effective wealth due to lower prices is called the *income effect.* When prices decrease, a consumer is able to afford larger quantities, just as if her income had increased.

The *substitution effect* describes the change in consumption that results from a change in the relative price of goods. When one good becomes relatively less expensive compared with the other good than it was before the price change, consumers will be inclined to buy more of it.

LO 7.5 Outline the ways in which utility is influenced by other people.

How much utility consumers get from a good can be influenced by how others perceive their choice. Some people choose to consume expensive goods to signal to others that they can afford these goods. Utility can also be influenced by your *frame of reference*—you're far more likely to be happy with a salary if it's in line with what everyone around you earns.

LO 7.6 Describe how people get utility from altruism and reciprocity.

Altruism is a motive for action in which a person's utility increases simply because someone else's utility increases. *Reciprocity* is the idea that some people get utility from punishing bad behavior and rewarding good, even when it comes at some cost to them.

Review Questions

1. Which of the following activities give you positive utility? **[LO 7.1]**
   a. Playing sports
   b. Receiving a prestigious scholarship
   c. Buying a new TV
   d. Eating brussels sprouts
   e. All of the above

2. Your gym offers two classes at the same time: weightlifting and yoga. Both classes are included in your membership and have space available. Your friend tells you he wants to work on his strength and take the weightlifting class, but you always see him in yoga class. Which class gives him more utility? How do you know this? **[LO 7.1]**

3. Evie has a gift pass for unlimited roller-coaster rides on her birthday. Given the information about Evie's utility in Table 7Q-1, explain why she chooses to ride only three times. **[LO 7.1]**

TABLE 7Q-1

Roller-coaster rides	Total utility
1	20
2	35
3	45
4	40

TABLE 7Q-2

Roller-coaster rides	Total utility
1	20
2	35
3	45
4	40

4. Dan likes to spend his allowance on two things: candy and toys. What are the three constraints that determine the possible consumption bundles of toys and candy available to Dan? **[LO 7.2]**

5. Evan has $40 to spend at an amusement park. The roller coaster costs $10 per ride. Given the information about Evan's utility in Table 7Q-2, explain why he chooses to ride only three times. **[LO 7.2]**

6. Suppose a wedge of cheese is $10 and a loaf of bread is $5. What is the opportunity cost of purchasing a wedge of cheese (in terms of bread)? Explain what happens to the opportunity cost of purchasing a wedge of cheese (in terms of bread) if your income decreases by 20 percent. **[LO 7.3]**

7. Simone spends $200 a month on voice lessons and dance lessons. She just learned that starting next month her favorite dance instructor is moving out of town and the monthly rent for her apartment is increasing. How will each of these events affect Simone's budget constraint for voice and dance lessons? **[LO 7.3]**

8. Julian buys plants and flowers every month. Both are normal goods. When the price of flowers fell, Julian purchased fewer plants. Which effect was stronger for Julian, the income effect or the substitution effect? **[LO 7.4]**

9. Sarah spends her monthly entertainment budget on books and movies. Sarah's initial utility-maximizing combination of books and movies is five movies and two books a month. Assume the price of books falls. Sarah's new utility-maximizing combination of books and movies is five movies and four books. Given this information, can we say whether movies are a normal good? **[LO 7.4]**

10. Your friend says, "I'd rather be a big fish in a small pond than a small fish in a big pond." What concept does this comment illustrate? **[LO 7.5]**

11. Suppose that in addition to being a college student, you run your own business and earn $35,000 per year. Your friends are all in college, and their average annual income is $10,000 per year. When you graduate from college, you decide to continue running your business. Your friends accept jobs that pay $50,000 per year. Do you expect your utility to increase, decrease, or stay the same after graduation? Why? **[LO 7.5]**

12. You come home to discover that your roommate has left their dirty dishes in the sink (again!). Why might you be likely to leave your own dirty dishes in the sink (which you know annoys your roommate), even though you usually prefer a clean kitchen to a messy kitchen? **[LO 7.6]**

13. An organization that raises money to provide meals for seniors gives tote bags to its donors. Sami thinks it is wasteful to spend donated money on tote bags for donors because the money could be used to provide more meals. Explain to Sami why giving tote bags could make financial sense for the organization. **[LO 7.6]**

Problems and Applications

1. Total utility is maximized when marginal utility becomes (positive, zero, negative) _____. **[LO 7.1]**

2. Table 7P-1 shows the total utility that John gets from ice cream, for each quantity he consumes. Fill in the third column showing the marginal utility he gets from each additional scoop. **[LO 7.1]**

3. You love going to the movies. For your birthday, your friend offers to take you to a triple feature without popcorn or a double feature with two bags of popcorn. Table 7P-2 shows your utility for movies and popcorn. Which option should you choose? **[LO 7.1]**

4. Refer to the budget constraint for jeans and T-shirts in Figure 7P-1. Which of the following consumption bundles is attainable? **[LO 7.2]**
    a. 3 pairs of jeans, 1 T-shirt.
    b. 2 pairs of jeans, 4 T-shirts.
    c. 2 pairs of jeans, 3 T-shirts.
    d. 1 pair of jeans, 4 T-shirts.

TABLE 7P-1

Scoops of ice cream	Total utility	Marginal utility of the last scoop eaten
1	10	
2	17	
3	21	
4	23	
5	23	

TABLE 7P-2

Movies	Total utility	Bags of popcorn	Total utility
1	10	1	5
2	15	2	5
3	18	3	4

FIGURE 7P-1

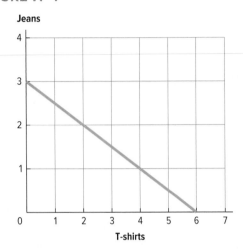

Jeans

T-shirts

5. Petra has $480 to spend on DVDs and books. A book costs $24 and a DVD costs $15. **[LO 7.2]**

    a. Write an equation for the budget constraint. Let x = books. Let y = DVDs.

    b. Use your equation to determine how many books Petra can buy if she buys 8 DVDs.

6. Jordan visits her sister several times a year. Jordan's travel budget is $600, which she uses to buy bus tickets and train tickets. The train costs $120 per trip and the bus costs $40. **[LO 7.2, 7.3]**

    a. Graph Jordan's budget constraint.

    b. How many total trips can Jordan take if she takes the train three times?

    c. Suppose Jordan's travel budget is cut to $360. Draw her new budget constraint.

    d. How many train trips can she take if she doesn't want to reduce the total number of trips she takes each year?

7. Maria has a $300 gift certificate at a spa that she can use on massages or manicures. A massage costs $100 and a manicure costs $30. **[LO 7.3, 7.4]**

    a. Write the equation for Maria's budget constraint. Let x = massages. Let y = manicures.

    b. Suppose Maria decides to split her gift certificate with a friend and transfers half of the value of her gift certificate to her friend. Write the equation for her new budget constraint.

    c. After giving away half of her gift certificate, suppose the price of massages increases by 50 percent before Maria can use her gift certificate. Write the equation for her new budget constraint.

8. Every year, Heather hosts a holiday party for her friends. Her party budget is $200. Heather spends her budget on food platters that cost $25 each and on entertainment, which costs $50 per hour. **[LO 7.4]**

    a. Graph Heather's budget constraint for food and entertainment.

    b. To reward her loyal business, the entertainment company Heather hires has offered her a 50 percent discount on entertainment purchases for this year's party. On your graph, illustrate Heather's new budget constraint for food and entertainment.

    c. Assuming that food platters and entertainment are normal goods, what can you say about the quantity of each good that Heather will purchase after the discount? Will the quantity of entertainment increase or decrease, or is the change uncertain? Will the quantity of food increase or decrease, or is the change uncertain?

9. Hideki attends baseball games and goes to movie theaters. Baseball tickets cost $15 and movie tickets cost $10. His entertainment budget is $180. **[LO 7.4]**

    a. Graph Hideki's budget constraint for baseball and movie tickets.

    b. Suppose the home team is having a good season and the price of baseball tickets goes up to $20 per game. Graph the new budget constraint.

    c. Assuming that baseball and movie tickets are normal goods, what can you say about the quantity of each good that Hideki will consume after the price of baseball tickets goes up? Will the quantity of baseball games he attends increase or decrease, or is the change uncertain? Will the quantity of movies he watches increase or decrease, or is the change uncertain?

10. For which of the following goods is the utility you get from consuming them likely to be affected by the opinions of others? **[LO 7.5]**

    a. MP3s.

    b. A new car.

    c. Running shoes.

    d. A new laptop for class.

11. Dan spends his money on baseball games and concert tickets. Baseball tickets cost $15, and concert tickets cost $25. His entertainment budget is $150.

    a. Draw Dan's budget constraint, putting baseball tickets on the x-axis.

    b. Dan decides to attend three concerts and five baseball games. Plot this point on the budget constraint.

    c. Dan's best friend Jay tells Dan that his favorite thing to do is go to concerts. In fact, going to concerts is popular with a lot of Dan's friends. Will Dan's budget constraint increase, decrease, or stay the same? Will the quantity of concerts he attends increase, decrease, or stay the same? **[LO 7.5]**

12. Samuel's utility is influenced by reciprocity. He is likely to respond to a surprisingly generous birthday gift from his best friend in what way? **[LO 7.6]**

    a. Not giving his friend a birthday gift at all.

    b. Giving his friend the birthday gift he had originally planned to give.

    c. Giving his friend a more thoughtful or more generous gift that he had originally planned to give.

    d. Returning the birthday gift he received.

13. Say whether each of the following situations is an example of altruism or reciprocity. **[LO 7.6]**

    a. Giving a few canned goods to the local food bank for its annual food drive.

    b. Helping someone move her couch after she helped you study for an upcoming exam.

    c. The biological relationship between cleaner fish and large predators in the ocean, in which cleaner fish keep the predator free from parasites and the predator keeps the cleaner fish safe.

Endnotes

1. http://www.slate.com/articles/business/moneybox/2011/12/scarves_no_surfing_lessons_yes_the_economist_s_guide_to_efficient_gift_giving_.html

2. https://www.amherst.edu/media/view/104699/original/christmas.pdf

Using Indifference Curves

Learning Objectives

LO E.1 Explain how the marginal rate of substitution relates to the shape of the indifference curve.

LO E.2 Outline the four properties that apply to all indifference curves.

LO E.3 Explain the shapes of indifference curves for perfect substitutes and perfect complements.

LO E.4 Describe the point at which a consumer maximizes utility.

LO E.5 Show how changes in income and prices affect utility maximization.

LO E.6 Show how to build an individual's demand curve using indifference curves.

Chapter 7, "Consumer Behavior," presented utility in all of its complexity. We learned how people maximize their utility given how much they are able to spend, how the consumption of goods is affected by the opinion of others, and how people decide how much to give to charity. In this appendix, we describe an important tool that economists use when looking at how people make such decisions—indifference curves.

Representing Preferences Graphically

Indifference curves are a way to represent utility graphically. We'll describe how they work and show that indifference curves come in many shapes and sizes. As you'll see, indifference curves can be applied to many different problems of consumer choice. These include how people maximize their utility, how they respond to changes in both income and prices, and how they relate to some fundamental concepts in economics.

Consumption bundles and indifference curves

LO E.1 Explain how the marginal rate of substitution relates to the shape of the indifference curve.

Think back to our example from Chapter 7, "Consumer Behavior," about Cody and his decision-making process. Here, we'll look at a situation similar to Cody's, but this time we'll think about how Cody's friend, Malik, makes decisions about how to best spend his money for the month. Malik has $120 to spend on movie and concert tickets. In Malik's hometown, movie tickets cost $10 each and concert tickets cost $40 each. Given his budget and the costs of tickets, Malik has a lot of choices:

- He could spend most of his money on movie tickets, leaving comparatively little for concert tickets.
- He could splurge on three concert tickets and not see any movies.
- He could choose combinations of tickets in between.

Each of the possible combinations Malik could choose is called a *consumption bundle*. In Chapter 7, we put these consumption bundles into a utility function. That utility function produced a number that represented the amount of utility a person receives from a certain combination of goods. This process involved some labor, going through each consumption bundle and doing the arithmetic needed to find the utility that would be gained from each possible choice.

Fortunately, there's another way, using graphs. By representing on curves the utility from various bundles, we can easily compare the bundles visually. A curve called an **indifference curve** fulfills this need, linking all the different bundles that provide a consumer with equal levels of utility. It gets its name because it shows all the options among which a consumer is truly indifferent. By "indifferent," economists don't mean that the consumer doesn't care about the options. Instead, "indifferent" means that the consumer experiences no real difference between one bundle of goods or services over another. In other words, any of the bundles would be equally acceptable.

Figure E-1 shows a set of indifference curves for our model consumer Malik. Each point on one of the curves represents a consumption bundle that gives Malik the same amount of satisfaction as the other bundles on that curve. If his consumption moves from point A on curve I_b to point B, he loses some movie tickets, but he gets enough extra concert tickets to compensate him so that he feels indifferent between the two options.

indifference curve
a curve showing all the different consumption bundles that provide a consumer with equal levels of utility

---

FIGURE E-1

Indifference curves

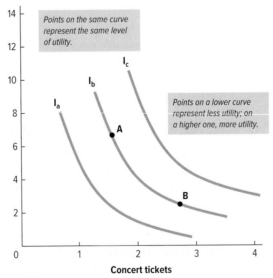

Indifference curves represent the utility provided by different combinations of goods and services. Points on the same indifference curve give the same utility. Higher indifference curves represent greater utility.

If Malik moved to a point on a *different* curve, though, he would not be indifferent. Specifically, moving to a point on a higher indifference curve, such as I_c, gives him higher utility. Moving to a point on a lower indifference curve, such as I_a, gives him lower utility.

Indifference curves gain their shape from the principle of diminishing marginal utility. At each end of the curve, Malik is indifferent between bundles that trade lots of one good for very little of the other. This is due to diminishing marginal utilities. When Malik has a lot of concert tickets, he doesn't get much utility from the last few concert tickets he buys. Buying one more movie ticket, on the other hand, gives him a lot of utility because he didn't have very many movie tickets. As a result, the slope of the curve is very steep. At the other end of the curve, the opposite is true: If Malik has a lot of movie tickets but very few concert tickets, then gaining an additional concert ticket brings him a lot of utility. In order to remain on the same indifference curve and maintain the same amount of utility, he would be willing to give up many movie tickets in exchange for the utility he gets from an extra concert ticket.

At any point, the slope of the indifference curve tells you how much more of one good Malik requires to compensate him for the loss of the other. In other words, it tells you the rate at which he would be willing to trade or substitute between the two goods. This rate is called the **marginal rate of substitution (MRS)**. Because the marginal rate of substitution is the relative satisfaction the consumer gets from two goods—in general, we'll call them X and Y—at any point, it can also be represented as the ratio of the marginal utilities of the two goods.

marginal rate of substitution (MRS) the rate at which a consumer is willing to trade or substitute between two goods

The marginal rate of substitution is also equal to the absolute value of the slope of the indifference curve at any given point:

EQUATION E-1
$$\text{Absolute value of slope} = \text{MRS} = \frac{MU_X}{MU_Y}$$

After all, the slope is just the ratio of how much the *y* variable changes for one unit of movement along the *x*-axis.

Properties of indifference curves

LO E.2 Outline the four properties that apply to all indifference curves.

There are four properties of indifference curves that are essential to the way they work. Later economics classes (if you take them, which we hope you will do) will prove these rules using math; for now, we will show why they make sense intuitively.

- *A consumer prefers a higher indifference curve to a lower one.* Since higher indifference curves contain more goods, and the average consumer gets more utility from consuming more, a higher indifference curve represents bundles of goods that provide the consumer with more utility than the bundles on lower indifference curves. Without constraints, it simply doesn't make any sense to pick a bundle on a lower indifference curve when you could pick a bundle with more goods, and more utility.

- *Indifference curves do not cross one another.* Each indifference curve represents all the bundles that provide the consumer with a certain level of utility. Suppose that one curve represents bundles with utility of 10, and a second curve represents bundles with utility of 20. If these curves crossed, the bundle at the point of intersection would simultaneously have utility of 10 and 20. That's not possible! Therefore, indifference curves do not cross each other.

- *Indifference curves usually slope downward.* Assuming that both goods are desirable, then the consumer would always prefer more of each good to less of it. A downward-sloping indifference curve—one with a negative slope—shows that when a consumer gets less of one good, her utility decreases and she requires more of the other good in order to compensate.

- *Indifference curves usually curve inward.* This inward curve, like the side of a bowl, follows from the property of diminishing marginal utility. At the top of the curve, the slope is steep because the consumer has a lot of the good on the *y*-axis and is willing to trade more of it for even a little of the good on the *x*-axis. As the curve goes downward, the consumer has less of the good represented on the *y*-axis and requires more and more of the good on the *x*-axis to compensate for the loss of that good, and the slope flattens out.

Just as utility functions are unique to a consumer and represent personal preferences, so too there is no such thing as a universal set of indifference curves for particular goods. There are only indifference curves *for a particular person.* Let's say that Cody and Malik are both trying to decide how many movie tickets to buy with the same amount of money. If Malik gets more utility from movies, he will be willing to trade many more concert tickets for movie tickets at every point along the curve.

Perfect substitutes and perfect complements

> **LO E.3** Explain the shapes of indifference curves for perfect substitutes and perfect complements.

In two special cases, indifference curves become straight lines. In Chapter 3, "Markets," we mentioned that many goods have substitutes and complements. Remember:

- *Substitutes* are two goods that have similar qualities and fulfill similar desires. These include tangerines and oranges, tea and coffee, or coal and natural gas, for example.
- *Complements* are goods that are consumed together, such as peanut butter and jelly, or cereal and milk.

Perfect substitutes

While many goods are general substitutes for each other, some are so similar that they can be called *perfect substitutes.* Different brands of milk are a good example. We'd wager that you can't tell the difference between any two brands in the store that are roughly the same price. Different brands of tomatoes, potatoes, and many other types of produce are also often perfect substitutes.

Since both goods are essentially the same, the rules of diminishing marginal utility simply don't apply to perfect substitutes. For example, let's say you have five cartons of Farmer John milk; a friend offers to trade you two cartons of his Happy Cow milk for two cartons of your Farmer John milk. If you can't tell the difference between the two brands, you'd have very little reason to make the trade. There'd be no benefit to giving up some of your Farmer John milk for the same amount of Happy Cow milk.

If the price is the same, you'd always be indifferent to having one brand versus the other, no matter how many cartons you already have of each brand. You are perfectly indifferent between the two. You could spend all of your milk money on each, or split it 50–50 between the two, or trade one Farmer John for one Happy Cow at any point along the curve and still get the same utility. This represents a marginal rate of substitution of 1 at every point.

As a result, the indifference curve for perfect substitutes, shown in panel A of Figure E-2, is always linear. In the case of the two milks, since you are willing to trade one carton for the other, the slope of the indifference curve is 1.

The marginal rate of substitution is not always going to be 1, though. In general, the slope of the indifference curve is going to depend on the relative value of the two goods. Take the example of money: In the vast majority of cases, you'd be indifferent toward having a $5 bill or five $1 bills; in the end you buy $5 worth of stuff with either combination. If you don't mind making the trade between the two, the marginal rate of substitution between $1 bills and $5 bills is 5 (or $\frac{1}{5}$ depending on which is on the *y*-axis), making for a much steeper indifference curve than what was the case for similarly priced milk.

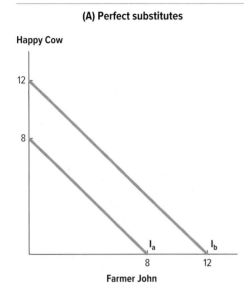

(A) Perfect substitutes

Since the two goods are perfect substitutes, a consumer is willing trade one for the other in order to maintain the same amount of utility.

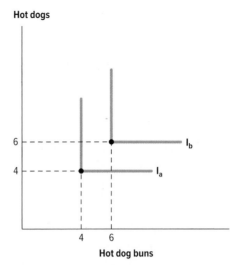

(B) Perfect complements

Once a consumer has one of each good, adding extras on either side doesn't actually add any further utility. This is because perfect complements are useless without the other good.

FIGURE E-2

Perfect substitutes and perfect complements

Perfect complements

Perfect complements, unlike substitutes, are goods that *have to be consumed together.* Pairs of shoes, socks, and gloves are all perfect complements. In each of these cases, having just one of a good without its complement isn't useful at all (unless, like Michael Jackson, you favor the single-glove look). If you are having a cookout, you're generally going to want to have enough buns for your hot dogs. Having more buns than hot dogs doesn't increase your utility, as they aren't really good for much besides holding hot dogs, and they just sit around until you get more hot dogs.

The relationship between complements creates an L-shaped indifference curve, part horizontal and part vertical. Let's say that you buy six hot dogs and six buns. Now imagine that you get another bun. Since you can't do anything with the extra bun, you still have the same amount of utility as when you had six hot dogs and six buns. The same is true whether you have eight buns or 12. You still get only the same amount of utility as when you had six of each. The same is also true for when you get more hot dogs. In most cases, it doesn't do you any good to have more hot dogs without buns. This relationship between perfect complements gives the L-shaped indifference curve shown in panel B of Figure E-2.

Understanding Consumer Choice

Even though indifference curves come in many different shapes, their relation to utility maximization is always the same. In Chapter 7, "Consumer Behavior," we worked through an example—movie and concert tickets—to find what bundle maximizes utility. We looked at each bundle on the budget line and added up the utility that a consumer (in that case, Cody) got from each good in the bundle. Whichever bundle resulted in the higher amount of utility was the correct choice.

This is a long and tedious process, though. The concepts of marginal rates of substitution and indifference curves presented in this appendix allow for a much clearer picture of how to find where a consumer maximizes utility. You'll find that either method leads to the optimal consumption bundle.

Equalizing the marginal utility of the last purchase

LO E.4 Describe the point at which a consumer maximizes utility.

Another way to think about optimal consumption is to imagine that you are "buying utility" and trying to get the best value for your money. That is, *you want to maximize your marginal utility per dollar spent.* How would you choose a consumption bundle that fits this criterion?

Let's approach this challenge from a marginal decision-making viewpoint, once again using Malik as an example. As a rational consumer, before Malik buys anything, he has to ask himself, "Could I do better by spending my dollar on something else?" Suppose he starts his purchases from scratch and chooses which good to buy next based on which will bring him the greatest marginal utility per dollar. *Marginal utility per dollar spent* is calculated by taking the extra utility gained from consuming one more unit of a good and dividing it by the cost of that unit. Panel A of Table E-1 shows the marginal utility of attending concerts, and panel B shows the marginal utility of going to the movies.

Panel C in Table E-1 puts together the the information from panels A and B to show Malik's purchase decision-making. In panel C, you'll see that starting with nothing, Malik's best move is to buy a concert ticket. (See the tan-highlighted box in the row for choice 1.) After that, for choices 2, 3, and 4, the good that brings him the highest marginal utility per dollar for his next purchase is a movie ticket. Malik continues to choose each purchase based on what gets him the most bang for his buck—the highest marginal utility for the next dollar he spends. When does this stop? When Malik reaches his budget limit. It's not a coincidence that, at this point, the marginal utility of the next dollar spent on each good is the same.

Suppose that instead of starting his purchases from scratch, Malik picks a random consumption bundle and then analyzes whether he could switch one of his purchases to achieve more utility. If he started with 12 movie tickets and no concert tickets, he could get more utility by switching some of his money over to buy a concert ticket. We can see that the marginal utility per dollar he would get from buying his first concert ticket is greater than the marginal utility per dollar he receives from his last $40 worth of movie tickets. He can continue to make these trades until he reaches a point where he can no longer get more marginal utility by switching his last dollar spent. At this point, the marginal utilities are the same for each of his choices.

The principle to remember is this: *Optimal consumption occurs at the point where the marginal utility gained from the dollar spent on good X equals the marginal utility gained from the last dollar spent on good Y.*

The marginal utility per dollar spent on good X can be written as the marginal utility divided by the price: $\frac{MU_X}{P_X}$. So, optimal consumption occurs where:

EQUATION E-2 $$\text{Optimal consumption} = \frac{MU_X}{P_X} = \frac{MU_Y}{P_Y}$$

In our example, Malik reaches the point where the marginal utilities per dollar for concerts and for movies are equal when he watches four movies and goes to two concerts.

Finding the highest indifference curve

You know that consumers prefer bundles on higher indifference curves to lower ones because those bundles give them greater utility. A final way to think about optimal consumption, therefore, is to find the highest possible indifference curve that still contains bundles within the budget constraint.

Figure E-3 shows Malik's budget constraint and several indifference curves. There are many bundles on curve I_1 that lie within his budget constraint, and even a few that fall on the budget line. But you can see that the highest possible indifference curve he can reach with the given budget constraint is I_2, which just grazes up against the budget line, intersecting it at only one point.

(A) Calculating marginal utility of concert tickets			
Tickets	**Utility**	**$ spent**	**Marginal utility/$**
0	0	0	—
1	70	40	1.75
2	130	80	1.5
3	185	120	1.375

(B) Calculating marginal utility of movie tickets			
Tickets	**Utility**	**$ spent**	**Marginal utility/$**
0	0	0	—
1	17	10	1.7
2	34	20	1.7
3	50	30	1.6
4	65	40	1.5
5	79	50	1.4

Panels A and B show the calculation of the marginal utility Malik would get from the purchase of each ticket. These numbers are used in panel C to determine the optimal amount of tickets to purchase.

(C) Purchase decisions				
Choice	**Potential marginal utility/$ from next movie ticket**	**Potential marginal utility/$ from next concert ticket**	**Buy?**	**Total $ spent**
1	1.7	1.75	Concert	40
2	1.7	1.5	Movie	50
3	1.7	1.5	Movie	60
4	1.6	1.5	Movie	70
5	1.5	1.5	Buy both!	120

Each purchase gives Malik a certain marginal utility per dollar spent. As he makes each consumption choice, he chooses the good that will bring him the highest marginal utility per dollar. At the point where the marginal utility of the next purchase of each good is equal, Malik buys one of each, and has maximized total utility.

He has no reason to choose a bundle on a lower curve. Bundles on higher curves like I_3 are unreachable given his budget.

At the optimal consumption bundle at point C, the slope of the budget line is the same as the slope of the indifference curve—they are tangent to one another. In order to find where the two meet, we need some math.

FIGURE E-3

The optimal consumption bundle

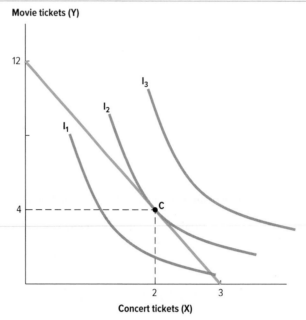

This graph shows several of Malik's indifference curves. Curves I_1 and I_2 are both within his budget. I_3 provides the most utility but will cost more than his budget allows. I_2, which just grazes the budget constraint, provides the most utility that Malik can afford.

In general, the formula for the slope of the budget line for goods X and Y is:

EQUATION E-3 $$\text{Slope of the budget line} = \frac{P_X}{P_Y}$$

The formula for the slope of the indifference curve between those same goods is:

EQUATION E-4 $$\text{Slope of the indifference curve} = \text{MRS} = \frac{MU_X}{MU_Y}$$

Since the slope of the budget line is equal to the slope of the indifference curve at the optimal consumption point and they are equal at the point where they are tangent, we can put these two formulas together:

EQUATION E-5 $$\text{Optimal consumption} = \frac{P_X}{P_Y} = \frac{MU_X}{MU_Y}$$

We can reduce this equation by rearranging terms to put X on one side of the equation and Y on the other. Doing so, we can confirm that this is exactly the same formula that we earlier found in Equation E-2:

$$\text{Optimal consumption} = \frac{MU_X}{P_X} = \frac{MU_Y}{P_Y}$$

Finding the highest-possible indifference curve turns out to be the same thing as equalizing the marginal utility per dollar for each good.

In the next few sections, maximizing utility by using indifference curves will be instrumental to figuring out how consumers respond to change. In Chapter 7, "Consumer Behavior," we were able to make only very general statements about how changes in prices and income affect overall consumption. Now we'll be able to form a more complete picture of how consumers make decisions in response to change.

How Consumers Respond to Change

LO E.5 Show how changes in income and prices affect utility maximization.

Budgets change. Prices also go up and down. Consumers respond to changes in income and prices by adjusting their consumption decisions. In this section, we'll describe how to apply the optimal-choice approaches to changes in income and prices. Although in the end we will find the same results as we did in the chapter, we now do so with a more complete conception of consumer decisions using indifference curves.

Responding to a change in income

From Chapter 7, "Consumer Behavior," you'll remember that an increase in income shifts the budget constraint out, and a decrease in income has the opposite effect. We found that an increase in income leads to more consumption—as long as both goods are normal, meaning that the consumer demands more of them as income increases. This result was taken on faith that since more is better, it is only logical that a consumer would buy more when she receives more income.

Adding indifference curves to this analysis allows us to see why this is true. Although this will be similar to what happened in the body of the chapter, we'll run through another example of a change in income—this time using indifference curves. As before, we're back to Malik's decision to buy movie and concert tickets.

Suppose Malik gets $80 for his birthday. Now Malik has $200 to spend. The increase in his income means that Malik has access to higher indifference curves that contain more tickets than before. As is the case with any optimization, the goal is to find the indifference curve that is tangent to the new budget constraint. This process is shown in Figure E-4. When his income increases by $80, he ends up buying eight movie tickets and three concert tickets.

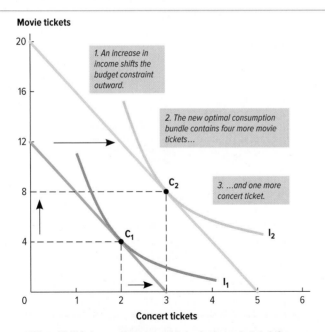

FIGURE E-4

Increases in income with normal goods

When Malik's income increases, his budget constraint shifts outward, keeping the same slope. Malik will choose to consume at the highest indifference curve possible that intersects the budget line, at point C_2. The new consumption bundle contains both more concert tickets and more movie tickets, meaning that they are both normal goods.

Responding to a change in prices

As you'll remember from the chapter, a change in price rotates the budget constraint. In a sense, the change in price is similar to a change in income: When the price of a good increases, for example, you can't afford the same amount of goods as before; the effect is the same as if you'd lost some income.

Although we'll go through and break the effect of a price change into its two parts, we'll first show the overall effect of a change in prices. Starting from our movie/concert ticket base, let's say that the local movie theater has a special discount that decreases the price of tickets to $5, and the budget constraint rotates outward. Now Malik has higher indifference curves available to him. Figure E-5 shows this effect: Malik moves from indifference curve I_1 to I_2. Thankfully, the process of optimization is still the same, even as the budget constraint changes. All you need to do is find the indifference curve that is tangent to the new budget constraint.

The income and substitution effects

If you'll remember from the body of the chapter, the change in consumption that occurs with a change in prices can be broken into two parts, the *income effect* and the *substitution effect*. Depending on the type of good, the income and substitution effects will have different impacts on the optimal consumption bundle of the consumer when prices change. For normal goods, a price increase will lead to a larger change in the income effect versus the substitution effect, and so a consumer will consume less.

Let's see what happens when we add indifference curves: Figure E-6 shows the overall response to the price change with indifference curves, in two steps. One corresponds to the substitution effect, and the other to the income effect.

Panel A shows the first step, in which consumption responds to the changes in relative prices (substitution effect). Consumption moves along the original indifference curve to the point where the marginal rate of substitution is equal to the new slope of the budget line, which is shown by the dashed green line (parallel to the original budget line).

FIGURE E-5

Overall effect of a price decrease

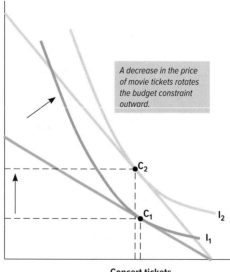

Movie tickets

A decrease in the price of movie tickets rotates the budget constraint outward.

C_2

C_1 I_2

I_1

Concert tickets

When the price of one good decreases, the budget constraint rotates outward to demonstrate the new consumption bundles that are available. The change in slope reflects the change in the relative prices of the two goods.

FIGURE E-6

The income and substitution effects of a price decrease

(A) Substitution effect

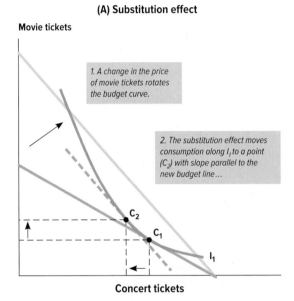

1. A change in the price of movie tickets rotates the budget curve.

2. The substitution effect moves consumption along I_1 to a point (C_2) with slope parallel to the new budget line…

The substitution effect moves the optimal consumption point along the *same* indifference curve, increasing consumption of the good whose price has been reduced (movie tickets), and decreasing consumption of the other good (concert tickets). If the substitution effect alone were at work, consumption would move to C_2. The dashed green line reflects the new slope of the budget line.

(B) Income effect

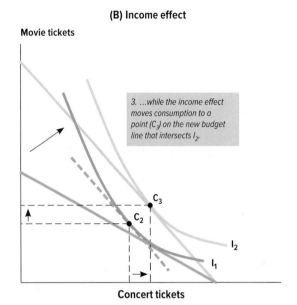

3. …while the income effect moves consumption to a point (C_3) on the new budget line that intersects I_2

The income effect will also increase consumption of the good with the newly reduced price (movie tickets), but it has the opposite effect on the item whose price has not changed (concert tickets). In this particular example, the income and substitution effects happen to have opposite effects on the number of concert tickets purchased. The combined impact of the income and substitution effect in this example is to increase the number of movie tickets purchased.

Panel B shows the second step, when consumption shifts up to the highest indifference curve that is now accessible due to the increase in purchasing power (income effect). This new consumption bundle is at point C_3, which includes more of both goods.

Indifference curves help make sense of the income and substitution effects. Before, we could make general statements only about the impact of a change in prices. Now, indifference curves allow us to see exactly how much the consumption changes under the income and substitution effects.

Deriving the demand curve using indifference curves

LO E.6 Show how to build an individual's demand curve using indifference curves.

Indifference curves can also fill in our understanding of one of the more fundamental concepts in economics: the individual demand curve. When the demand curve was originally presented in Chapter 3, "Markets," we simply said the consumer would demand a certain quantity based on price. Did you wonder, "Where did those numbers come from?" They are actually derived from indifference curves.

Since the indifference curves show where a consumer gets the most utility, it makes sense that any consumer would demand the quantity of a good that gives the most utility. Remember that indifference curves are intrinsic to a person, and that the demand curves we are making are

FIGURE E-7

Deriving the demand curve using indifference curves

(A) Optimal consumption

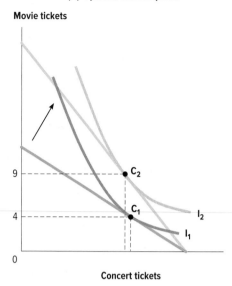

(B) The demand curve for movie tickets

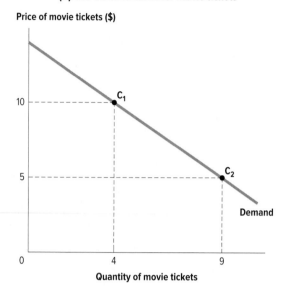

When the price of movie tickets falls from $10 to $5, rotating the budget constraint, the optimal number of movie tickets Malik wants to consume increases from 4 to 9 tickets.

These two optimal consumption bundles provide enough information to build a demand curve for movie tickets.

demand curves *for the individual*. They do not represent full-market demand. With that caveat, we'll bring back, one more time, Malik and his decision to buy concert and movie tickets.

Starting from the original $120 and $10 price for movie tickets, we know that Malik's optimal consumption bundle includes four movie tickets. That is the same as saying that at a price of $10, he demands four movie tickets. What happens if we decrease the price to $5? After the budget constraint rotates inward, his optimal consumption bundle includes five more movie tickets. At the lower price, he now demands (is willing to buy) nine tickets.

This information is all that we need to build the demand curve. Demanding four tickets when the price is $10 represents one point on the demand schedule, and demanding nine when the price is $5 represents another. Finding the slope between these two points fleshes out the rest of Malik's demand curve. Figure E-7 shows how his demand curve for movie tickets is built in this way.

Conclusion

The idea that individuals maximize utility is one of the most powerful concepts in economics. Indifference curves, though they may seem complex at first, can make understanding this concept far easier. From demand curves to price changes, indifference curves can help explain how consumers decide how much to buy and how satisfied they are with their choices.

Key Terms

indifference curve, p. 190B

marginal rate of substitution
(MRS), p. 190C

Summary

LO E.1 Explain how the marginal rate of substitution relates to the shape of the indifference curve.

An *indifference curve* links all the different bundles that provide a consumer with equal levels of utility. It is called an indifference curve because it shows all of the options among which a consumer is truly indifferent.

At any point, the slope of the indifference curve tells you how much more of one good a consumer requires to compensate for the loss of the other. In other words, it tells you the rate at which a consumer would be willing to trade or substitute between the two goods. This is the *marginal rate of substitution (MRS)*. Because the marginal rate of substitution is the relative satisfaction the consumer gets from the two goods at any point, it can also be represented as the ratio of the marginal utilities of the two goods.

The marginal rate of substitution is also equal to the absolute value of the slope of the indifference curve at any given point. The slope is just the ratio of how much the *y* variable changes for one unit of movement along the *x*-axis.

LO E.2 Outline the four rules that apply to all indifference curves.

Indifference curves generally follow four rules: Consumers prefer higher indifference curves to lower ones; indifference curves do not cross; indifference curves usually slope downward; and they curve inward.

LO E.3 Explain the shapes of indifference curves for perfect substitutes and perfect complements.

Because perfect substitutes are essentially the same, the rules of diminishing marginal utility simply don't apply to them. Therefore, the indifference curve for perfect substitutes is always linear (and downward-sloping). In general, the slope of that linear indifference curve is going to depend on the relative value of the two goods.

Perfect complements are goods that have to be consumed together. You are indifferent about having an extra unit of X if you don't have an extra unit of Y. Adding an extra unit of one of them does not increase utility. This relationship between complements creates an L-shaped indifference curve, part horizontal and part vertical.

LO E.4 Describe the point at which a consumer maximizes utility.

A consumer maximizes utility at the point where the highest indifference curve is tangent to the budget constraint. That is, the utility-maximization point is where the slope of the indifference curve equals the slope of the budget constraint.

This point can also be found through two other methods: (1) Count the utility gained from each bundle on the budget constraint to see which is the greatest. (2) Find the point where the marginal utilities for the goods in the bundle are equal.

LO E.5 Show how changes in income and prices affect utility maximization.

Changes in income shift the budget constraint. Increases in income will, on average, increase the optimal consumption of goods in a bundle. The opposite is true for decreases in income.

Changes in prices rotate the budget constraint. On average, when prices decrease, the optimal consumption bundle includes more goods than before. When prices increase, the optimal consumption bundle includes fewer goods than before.

LO E.6 Show how to build an individual's demand curve using indifference curves.

An individual's demand curve can be created using that individual's indifference curves. A consumer will demand the quantity of a good that gives the most utility, and indifference curves show precisely where that point is. Finding the optimal consumption bundle on two curves, and finding the slope between these two points, will provide the demand curve.

Review Questions

1. If an indifference curve is a vertical line, does the amount of the good on the *y*-axis influence the consumer's utility? **[LO E.1]**

2. Two friends are discussing their plans for the month. One works at a movie theater and gets 10 free movie tickets; the other works at a concert venue and gets 10 free concert tickets. What can we predict about the first person's marginal rate of substitution between movies and concerts? What can we predict about the second person's marginal rate of substitution between the two? How does this relate to the slope of each of their indifference curves? **[LO E.1]**

3. Your friend tells you that although she has a large amount of M&Ms and just a few Skittles, she would still be willing to give up the rest of her Skittles, just to get one last M&M. What characteristic of indifference curves is your friend going against? **[LO E.2]**

4. For each pair of goods listed below, state whether the indifference curves would be linear or L-shaped. **[LO E.3]**
    • Ten dollar bills and pairs of five dollar bills.
    • Coffee and tea.
    • Bagels and muffins.
    • Left shoes and right shoes.

5. Suppose that a budget constraint intersects an indifference curve at two separate points. Can either of these consumption bundles be optimal? Explain why or why not. **[LO E.4]**

6. Dan consumes two goods: peanut butter and jelly sandwiches, which are an inferior good, and chicken salad sandwiches, which are a normal good. He gets a raise at work. Will the ratio of peanut butter and jelly sandwiches to chicken salad sandwiches that he consumes increase or decrease? **[LO E.5]**

7. Haley divides her entertainment budget between movie tickets and concert tickets. Two of her indifference curves are shown in Figure EQ-1. When movie tickets are $12 and concert tickets are $20, she purchases 25 movie tickets and 45 concert tickets. This is shown on Indifference Curve 1 (IC_1). Haley finds out that she can sign up for a loyalty program with the movie theater and buy tickets at a 50% discount. When the price of movie tickets decreases, she buys 50 movie tickets and 50 concert tickets. This is shown on Indifference Curve 2 (IC_2). For which of these two goods can we draw Haley's demand curve? Explain. **[LO E.6]**

Problems and Applications

1. Your baby cousin Hubert loves lollipops and bouncy balls. Look at the indifference curves in Figure EP-1 that represent his preferences among various bundles of the two goods. Assuming the indifference curves follow the four properties outlined in this appendix, rank bundles A through D from the highest utility to the lowest, including ties. **[LO E.1]**

2. Table EP-1 shows some possible consumption bundles for a person who consumes MP3s and lattes. **[LO E.2]**

FIGURE EP-1

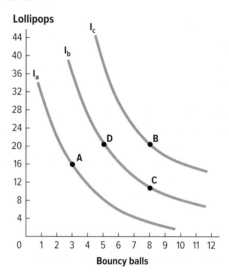

TABLE EP-1

Bundle	MP3s	Lattes	Total utility
A	13	8	20
B	3	2	12
C	13	10	23
D	6	3	15
E	9	4	17
F	6	1	12
G	17	9	23
H	4	0	11

FIGURE EQ-1

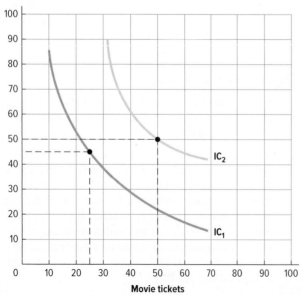

a. Which bundles fall on the lowest indifference curve?

b. Which bundles fall on the highest indifference curve?

3. Determine whether the preferences described below would be represented by an indifference curve that is L-shaped, bows inward, or is a straight line. **[LO E.2, LO E.3]**

   a. Edgar will eat carrots only if he has hummus to go with them.

   b. Andrew likes to start his day right with oatmeal, but he's just as happy starting it with steel-cut oats as he is with rolled oats.

   c. Ezekiel really enjoys coffee and donuts together, but he's also happy eating just one or the other.

4. Jonah is completely indifferent between eating the brand name version of his favorite cereal and eating the generic version. His preferences would best be represented by which indifference curve in Figure EP-2: IC_a or IC_b? Are brand-name cereal and generic cereal perfect substitutes or perfect complements? **[LO E.3]**

5. A consumer is stocking up on sodas and sports drinks at the dollar store. As you might expect at a dollar store, each bottle of each drink costs $1. He has a $10 bill to spend. Based on Table EP-2 of marginal utilities, find the optimal consumption bundle. **[LO E.4]**

6. A consumer is buying steaks for $4 each and potatoes for $1 per pound. She has $40. Plot her budget constraint on Figure EP-3 and find her optimal consumption bundle. **[LO E.4]**

7. Under utility maximization, is it possible that after an increase in income, a consumer would remain on the same indifference curve? What about after a decrease in the price of one of the goods? **[LO E.5]**

8. *True or false?* The income effect is represented by the shift in consumption of a good as the bundle moves along the old indifference curve before moving to another indifference curve tangent to the new budget line. **[LO E.5]**

9. Tyler likes to divide his entertainment between attending basketball games and attending football games. Two of his indifference curves are shown in Figure EP-4. When football games are $25 and basketball games are $20, he chooses to attend 6 football games and 7 basketball games. This is shown on Indifference Curve 1 (IC_1). The football team has been selling out every game, so they decide to raise the price to $45 per game. At this new price, Tyler chooses to attend 2 football games and 8 basketball games. This is shown on Indifference Curve 2 (IC_2). **[LO E.6]**

a. Draw Tyler's demand curve for football games.

b. What is the slope of the Tyler's demand curve for football games?

FIGURE EP-2

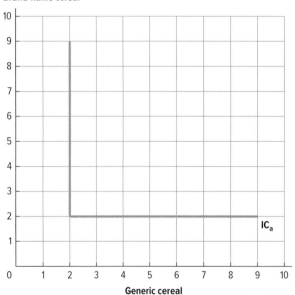

Brand-name cereal / Generic cereal

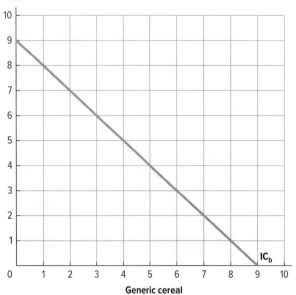

Brand-name cereal / Generic cereal

TABLE EP-2

Quantity of a good	Marginal utility of a soda	Marginal utility of a sports drink
1	10	8
2	8	7
3	6	6
4	5	5
5	4	4
6	3	3
7	2	2

FIGURE EP-4

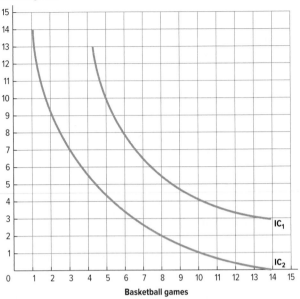

FIGURE EP-3

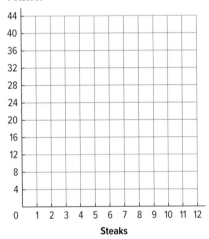

FIGURE EP-5

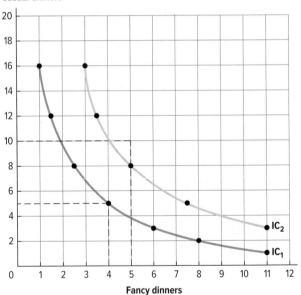

10. Gabriella divides her food budget between fancy dinners and casual dinners. Two of her indifference curves are shown in Figure EP-5. When casual dinners are $12 and fancy dinners are $25, she chooses 5 casual dinners and 4 fancy dinners. This is shown on Indifference Curve 1 (IC$_1$). A new restaurant opens near her apartment, and she can get a casual dinner for $6. At this new price, she chooses 8 casual dinners and 5 fancy dinners. This is shown on Indifference Curve 2 (IC$_2$). **[LO E.6]**

    a. Draw Gabriella's demand curve for casual dinners.

    b. What do we know about Gabriella's demand for fancy dinners?

Behavioral Economics: A Closer Look at Decision Making

Learning Objectives

LO 8.1 Explain how time inconsistency accounts for procrastination and other problems with self-control.

LO 8.2 Explain why sunk costs should not be taken into account in deciding what to do next.

LO 8.3 Identify the types of opportunity cost that people often undervalue, and recognize why undervaluing them distorts decision making.

LO 8.4 Explain why fungibility matters in financial decision making.

WHEN IS $20 NOT QUITE $20?

Imagine yourself in the following situation: Earlier today, you bought a ticket for a concert this evening. The ticket cost $20. You arrive at the concert venue, reach into your pocket for the ticket, and . . . it's not there. You must have dropped it somewhere on the way. How annoying! Tickets are still available at the door for $20. Which of the following is your reaction?

#1: "Oh well, never mind. These things happen. I'll just buy another ticket."

#2: "No way I'm going to spend $40 on this concert! I'd rather go do something else instead."

If you said #2, many are like you: When researchers presented a similar situation to them, 46 percent of people said they'd do something else with their evening. The other 54 percent said they'd swallow their annoyance enough to buy a replacement ticket.

Now imagine an alternative scenario: This time you arrive at the concert venue intending to buy your ticket at the door. You reach into your pocket for the money to pay, and . . . hold on, what's this? You definitely had five $20 bills in your pocket this morning, but now you have only four. You must have lost one of them somewhere today. How annoying! Which of the following do you then say?

#1: "Oh well, never mind. These things happen. I'll get my ticket for the concert."

#2: "You know what? Forget the concert."

This time only 12 percent chose #2 and said they'd abandon their evening plans. Fully 88 percent of people said they'd buy the ticket anyway.

You may have noticed that the economics of these two situations are *exactly the same.* In both scenarios, you arrive at the venue intending to see a concert you had previously decided was worth $20 to you, only to make the unwelcome discovery that you are $20 less well off than you'd thought you were.

© Media Union/Shutterstock

If you are short of money for things you need in the near future, it may make sense to skip the concert in *either* case. If you're not short of money, it makes sense to go to the concert in *either* case. What difference does it make if you lost the $20 *before* or *after* you'd converted a bill into a concert ticket? Objectively, it doesn't matter at all. Emotionally, however, it does matter. (Even if you would have bought a ticket in both scenarios, wouldn't you have felt just a little bit more annoyed about losing the ticket?) To a significant proportion of people, that emotional difference is so great it would make them abandon their plans if they had lost the ticket, but *not* if they had lost the $20 bill.

This is not rational behavior. Other examples that often indicate irrational behavior are:

- Saying you want to lose weight but ordering a high-calorie, fattening dessert.
- Being willing to pay more for something if you use a credit card than if you use cash.
- Stubbornly watching to the end of a movie you've decided you're not enjoying at all.

People who are rational (as defined in economics) wouldn't behave in these ways, but many people do. Yet, haven't we said throughout this book that economists assume people behave rationally to maximize their utility? Yes, we have. So what's going on?

The assumption that people are rational utility maximizers gets us a long way. It's true often enough to be useful. But it's not true all the time, and how much the exceptions matter is a hotly debated question in economics right now. In the past few decades, economists have been learning a lot from psychologists and biologists about how real people make everyday decisions that translate economic ideas into action. The resulting theories have developed into a branch of economics that expands our models of decision making. This field is called *behavioral economics,* the topic of this chapter.

Irrational behavior does *not* mean "people act randomly." The interesting insights from behavioral economics come from understanding people's decision-making patterns, whether rational or not. We then can build models that make the best prediction possible for what people will actually do in a given situation.

Behavioral economists are not just advancing our academic knowledge of how people make decisions. They also have developed some practical, easy-to-use tools that can help people enact the choices they *say* they would like to make: save more money, get healthier, give more to charity. You may even be using some of these tools without realizing it.

Formally, **behavioral economics** is a field of economics that draws on insights from psychology to expand models of individual decision making. Behavioral economics is wide-ranging, and in this chapter we'll cover just three of its more interesting applications: time inconsistency, thinking irrationally about costs, and forgetting the fungibility of money.

behavioral economics
a field of economics that draws on insights from psychology to expand models of individual decision making

Dealing with Temptation and Procrastination

When we discussed utility (in Chapter 7, "Consumer Behavior"), we already provided an example of the kind of question that interests behavioral economists: You wake up one Saturday morning with great intentions to have a useful and productive day—work out, clean the apartment, study. Later, you realize that, somehow, suddenly it's Saturday evening and you're still in your pajamas watching reruns of *Game of Thrones*. Huh. How did that happen?

As we have seen, one way to look at this common experience is to use the idea of *revealed preference*—that is, no matter what you *had thought* you wanted to do, your actions reveal that what you *actually* wanted to do was to spend the day watching TV. Another way to look at it is to consider that you simply weren't acting rationally.

Neither explanation seems very satisfying. Many of us have experienced feelings of conflict when we know we *want* to do one thing but find ourselves constantly doing another. We want to study, but instead play games; we want to diet, but instead eat dessert; we want to save, but instead spend too much. Saying that our actions must reveal our true desires goes against our understanding of ourselves. On the other hand, explaining the conflict by just saying we are irrational feels like giving up; that explanation also suggests that we have no ability to predict what decisions people will make.

There *is* a third way: We can improve our models a bit, to be more accurate in predicting how we deal with the struggles against procrastination and temptation. This can be done by using the ideas of time inconsistency, competing selves, and commitment.

Time inconsistency, competing selves, and commitment

LO 8.1 Explain how time inconsistency accounts for procrastination and other problems with self-control.

One theory of why we sometimes give in to temptation is based on the idea that people can hold two inconsistent sets of preferences:

- One set holds what we would *like to want* in the future—to study enough for exams, to lose weight, to build up a healthy savings account.
- One set holds what we *will actually want* in the future, when the future comes—to play games, to eat dessert, to go shopping.

Behavioral economists use the term **time inconsistency** to describe what is happening when we change our minds about what we want simply because of the timing of the decision.

Consider this classic example of time inconsistency: A researcher says to you, "We want to offer you a snack to thank you for taking part in a survey one week from today. Please tell

time inconsistency
a situation in which we change our minds about what we want simply because of the timing of the decision

Behavioral economics provides insights to explain time inconsistency and strategies for dealing with our future selves.

us now: Which would you like after the survey—an apple or a chocolate brownie?" Most people choose the apple. However, when the following week arrives, the researcher asks the participants whether they still want the apple; most participants instead switch to the chocolate brownie. A person with time-consistent preferences would choose the same snack, regardless of whether the choice is being made ahead of time or in the moment. We are *time inconsistent* when we say that we'll prefer the apple next week and then switch to a chocolate brownie when we get to consume it immediately.

Time inconsistency helps to explain behaviors like procrastination and lack of self-control. It is as if there are two selves inhabiting our thoughts: One is a "future-oriented self," with clear-sighted preferences to get things done, eat healthily, and so on. The other is a "present-oriented self," who backslides when faced with temptation in the here-and-now. Of course, as Hobbes, the cartoon tiger, tells his friend Calvin, "the problem with the future is that it keeps turning into the present." However wise the decisions your future-oriented self makes about the future, when that future becomes the present, your present-oriented self will be in charge again. If, after next week's survey, the researcher says, "We brought you an apple—but you can still have a chocolate brownie if you would prefer," our present-oriented self takes command and switches to the brownie.

It makes sense to think of time inconsistency as a battle between these two selves. In other words, a time-inconsistent individual is being neither irrational nor rational. Rather, future-oriented and present-oriented selves within the individual are each rationally pursuing their own objectives.

People who are aware of their time-inconsistent preferences often seek out ways to remove temptation. If you eat too many potato chips at night, you can decide not to buy chips when at the store. If you waste too much time online, you can install a browser add-on such as Leechblock (for Firefox) or StayFocusd (for Chrome) and use it to define limits to the time you can spend on certain websites. Of course, these strategies are not foolproof. You could always make a nighttime dash to the store, or uninstall Leechblock or StayFocusd. But these actions at least put obstacles in the way of your weak-willed, present-oriented self. These are simple ways of making one's vices more expensive. By doing so, we're using the law of demand (as prices go up, quantity demanded goes down!) to coax ourselves into consuming less of our vices.

For an example of how an organization can benefit by exploiting the dynamic between future- and present-oriented selves, see the Real Life box "Give more tomorrow."

Real Life

Give more tomorrow

Do you ever intend to do something good, such as volunteering or donating money, but you keep putting it off? You're not alone. Charities know that even the best-intentioned supporters can be forgetful about sending a check. That's why so many charities encourage people to sign up for monthly contributions, which will be deducted automatically from their credit cards or bank accounts.

We can view this as another example of time inconsistency. Your future-oriented self wants to give regularly to charity, but your present-oriented self never gets around to doing so. Signing up to make monthly contributions is a winning strategy for your future-oriented self; it turns that force of inertia into an advantage. It's not surprising that, on average, monthly donors give more to charity than irregular donors.

A recent collaboration between Swedish economist Anna Breman and the charity Diakonia has taken this idea one step further. Charities, of course, would like their existing monthly contributors to give more. Would it make a difference if they were asked to increase their contribution *in the future*? Breman and Diakonia conducted an experiment to find out. They split about a thousand monthly contributors into two groups. Those in the first group were asked to consider increasing their monthly donation, starting right away. Those in the second group were asked the same thing, except that the increase would take effect in two months.

The result? The second group increased their donations by one-third more than the first group. That's a big difference for a charity that relies on funding from individual donors. It seems that Diakonia's donors, like people who ask for a brownie today but an apple next week, are more willing to give more in two months' time than to give more now.

Of course, at any time, a donor's present-oriented self could cancel the increased monthly donation, but is usually too lazy to bother. The force of inertia is a powerful one: Monthly donors tend to keep giving at their promised level for an average of seven years. Rather than simply asking donors to give more, then, it seems that charities wanting to improve their fundraising should consider asking them to give more tomorrow.

Based on Anna Breman, "Give more tomorrow," *Journal of Public Economics*, 2011, vol. 95, issue 11, 1349–1357. http://econpapers.repec.org/article/eeepubeco/v_3a95_3ay_3a2011_3ai_3a11_3ap_3a1349-1357.htm.

The problem of competing selves can be alleviated using what is called a **commitment device**. A commitment device is a mechanism that allows people to voluntarily restrict their choices in order to make it easier to stick to plans. A classic example of a commitment device occurs in the ancient Greek epic poem *The Odyssey*. Odysseus and his crew know that their ship is about to pass through waters populated by sirens, sea nymphs whose beautiful magic song bewitches men, causing them to jump into the sea and descend to a watery grave. Odysseus wants to hear the sirens' song, but his future-oriented self is wise enough to know that he can't trust his present-oriented self to resist the sirens' call. So Odysseus commands his men to tie him to the mast before they enter the sirens' waters. He creates a commitment device that literally binds his present-oriented self to his decision to listen but not jump.

A more everyday example of a commitment device is an arbitrary deadline. In one experiment, a professor told his business-school class they would have three assignments due for the semester and that they could set their own due dates. Failure to meet the due dates would result

commitment device
a mechanism that allows people to voluntarily restrict their choices in order to make it easier to stick to plans

in a lower grade. Although students would not have been penalized for choosing the last day of the semester as a deadline for all three assignments, most did not take this option. They recognized that their present-oriented selves would be likely to procrastinate, leave all the work to the last minute, and be unable to complete everything. Most chose to space the deadlines evenly throughout the semester. By committing themselves to meet these arbitrary deadlines, they gave themselves a powerful incentive not to spend the whole semester procrastinating.[1]

For another example of a commitment device, see the Real Life box "Take out a contract on yourself."

Real Life
Take out a contract on yourself

In competitions between your present- and future-oriented selves, commitment strategies aren't easy to pull off. You may "commit" to punish yourself by, say, doing 100 push-ups if you give in to the temptation to order dessert. But that doesn't work, does it? By the time you get home from the restaurant, your present-oriented self is back in charge and decides that those push-ups aren't necessary after all. You, like Odysseus, need some way of binding yourself.

The website stickK.com (co-founded by one of the authors of this book) is one such way. Here's how it works: You define some measurable objective—say, that on December 1 you will weigh no more than a certain weight. Then, you sign a contract that includes incentives designed to help you keep your commitment. You can nominate a trusted friend to act as your referee—someone you can rely on to dole out tough love if you fall short, instead of letting you off the hook. You can name a friend who will be told if you succeed or fail (as a way to increase the social shame or reward). You can also define an amount of money you forfeit if you fail to reach your goal—and you enter your credit-card number, so there's no backing out.

Here's the extra twist, for those who choose to put money at stake: You nominate an organization you *hate* to get your money. If you miss your target, stickK.com takes your forfeited money from your credit card and gives it to your "anti-charity."

Giving up cigarettes and losing weight are two common personal goals, but stickK.com has also inspired some creative commitments:

- "Speak more slowly to foreigners in New York City."
- "No more dating losers." (The person's best friend was assigned to judge the definition of "loser.")
- "Conserve energy by turning off the lights and air conditioner when leaving home."
- "Study more."
- "Study less."
- "No cutting my hair for two months."

Two important principles you should follow in order to make the most out of the website (or commitment devices in general): Be specific and be realistic. Goals that are vague do not work as well as goals that provide some detail on what one is going to do. And goals that are unrealistic are easily forgotten, overlooked, or given up.

At the time of writing, over 301,000 contracts have been written, for a total of over $24 million. Contracts with financial stakes report success 74 percent of the time.

Source: www.stickK.com.

✓CONCEPT CHECK

☐ How can procrastination be explained by time inconsistency? **[LO 8.1]**

☐ What is a commitment strategy, and how can it help someone overcome time inconsistency? **[LO 8.1]**

Thinking Irrationally about Costs

In Chapter 1, "Economics and Life," we talked about how people weigh the trade-off between costs and benefits to arrive at a decision:

- If the benefits of doing something are greater than the opportunity cost, we assume that rational people will choose to do it.
- If the benefits are smaller than the opportunity cost, they won't choose to do it.

In reality, it turns out that people don't always weigh costs and benefits rationally. In this section we'll look at two common mistakes people make in thinking about costs: failing to ignore sunk costs and undervaluing opportunity costs.

These mistakes result from examples of what psychologists call *cognitive biases.* These biases are systematic patterns in how we behave that lead to consistently erroneous decisions. Cognitive biases come up a lot in behavioral economics. If you find yourself falling into the traps described below, don't be too hard on yourself—it seems that human brains simply aren't built to find it easy to think rationally in certain situations.

The sunk-cost fallacy

LO 8.2 Explain why sunk costs should not be taken into account in deciding what to do next.

Have you ever sat through to the end of a terrible movie just because you didn't want to "waste" the cost of the ticket? The logic is tempting, but it's flawed. This is an example of what economists call the *sunk-cost fallacy.* A **sunk cost** is a cost that has already been incurred and can't be refunded or recovered—such as the cost of a ticket once you've begun watching the film. It makes no sense to consider sunk costs when weighing the trade-off between opportunity costs and benefits, but people do it all the time. Why? Because we find it hard to accept our losses.

Once you've begun watching the film, the money you spent on the ticket is a sunk cost, whether you like the movie or not.
image100/Alamy

To see why it's a fallacy to consider sunk costs in your decisions, consider the following choice: Would you like to spend the next 90 minutes watching a terrible movie that's free of charge or doing something else? You'd probably want to do something else, right? Grab a coffee, hang out with a friend, maybe even pay to see a good movie. The option of watching a terrible movie, even if it's free, is not an attractive one. Yet when you have paid to see a movie that you quickly realize is terrible, this is the situation you face. The cost of the ticket is gone—you can't get it back.

sunk cost
a cost that has already been incurred and cannot be refunded or recovered

Why, then, do many people in this situation stubbornly sit through the rest of the movie? Maybe they are factoring sunk costs into their calculations: "Well, I already spent money to see this movie, so I have to watch the whole thing." They have a sense that somehow the money they spent on the ticket will have been wasted *only if* they walk out. The alternative would be to make peace with the idea that the money is *already* wasted because they're not getting pleasure from watching the movie. So to avoid feeling regret about wasting money, they stick it out. (Why not feel regret for wasting time, though? We'll come back to that question a bit later.)

A similar cognitive bias explains our chapter-opening example. Many people apparently consider that the cost of the lost ticket will be wasted *only if* they buy a replacement ticket. The rational approach is to accept that the cost of the lost ticket is wasted already and ignore it in the considerations. Doing that, the only question then is whether the *future* costs ($20 for a ticket) will outweigh the *future* benefits (the enjoyment of the concert). This trade-off is exactly the same whether you lost the ticket or a $20 bill.

Another common example of the sunk-cost fallacy is making multiple expensive repairs to a failing old car. You spend $1,000 repairing your car. The very next month it breaks down again, and the mechanic says it needs another $2,000 worth of repairs. It seems likely to keep on needing more and more repairs, totaling much more than its resale value. If you considered only *future* costs against *future* benefits, you would decide to scrap the car and buy another one. But many people feel that scrapping the car would be "wasting" the $1,000 they spent on it last month.

The sunk-cost fallacy doesn't apply only to money. Have you ever stayed in a bad relationship because you felt it would be a shame to "waste" the time and effort you'd put into it already?

Undervaluing opportunity costs

LO 8.3 Identify the types of opportunity cost that people often undervalue, and recognize why undervaluing them distorts decision making.

Remember that choosing one opportunity means choosing *not* to take advantage of another opportunity. Everything has an opportunity cost. Sometimes the trade-off is clear. If you are choosing between two similarly priced dishes on a restaurant menu, the opportunity cost of ordering one dish is obvious: It's the enjoyment you would have gotten from eating the other dish instead.

In many other cases, however, the trade-off is less clear. Often the benefit part of a trade-off is obvious because it is right in front of you—say, if you are trying on a $100 jacket in a store. But the opportunity cost is much harder to visualize: What else might you spend $100 on? It may be that if you thought very hard about how else you might spend that $100, you would come up with an alternative you prefer. But such alternatives can seem abstract and distant, while the jacket is concrete and immediate. As a result, you may overvalue the benefit you would get from the jacket and undervalue its opportunity cost.

People are especially prone to undervaluing opportunity costs when they are nonmonetary, such as time. In sitting through a terrible movie all the way to the end, people fall prey to the sunk-cost fallacy and also fail to recognize the opportunity cost of their time. They mistakenly put value on a nonretrievable monetary cost (the price of the ticket); they also fail to consider the value of their *nonmonetary opportunity cost* (time). Staying to the end of a bad movie means you will lose any utility you could have gained by doing something else instead.

The *implicit cost of ownership* is another nonmonetary opportunity cost that is often overlooked. The term refers to a cognitive bias, documented by behavioral economists, that leads people to value things more once they possess them. Everything you own has an opportunity cost because you could always choose to sell it. We don't tend to think in this way about the things we own. But by continuing to own an item, you incur an opportunity cost equal to what someone would be willing to pay you for it. Say you have a bicycle that you no longer use and you could get $200 for it on eBay. If you didn't own the bicycle, you certainly wouldn't pay $200 to buy it. So why continue to own it? You are effectively "paying" $200 to keep the bike. If you thought clearly about the opportunity cost, you would sell it.

As another example, suppose you win in a raffle courtside tickets to a basketball game, and you could sell them for $400. You may well choose to use the tickets yourself, even though you would never have considered paying anything like $400 for them if you hadn't won the raffle. It's easy to remember that you are paying when money leaves your wallet. It's harder to remember that not adding money to your wallet is essentially the same thing.

Even seasoned investors often overlook the implicit cost of ownership, as they stubbornly hold onto badly performing stocks that they would never consider buying if they didn't already own them.

✓ CONCEPT CHECK

☐ What is a sunk cost? Why is it not part of the opportunity cost of a decision? **[LO 8.2]**

☐ What is the implicit cost of ownership? **[LO 8.3]**

Forgetting about Fungibility

LO 8.4 Explain why fungibility matters in financial decision making.

If something is **fungible**, it is easily exchangeable or substitutable. Many commonly traded commodities are fungible. Any given ton of copper can be exchanged for a different ton of copper, or a barrel of oil for another barrel of oil.

fungible
easily exchangeable or substitutable

The cleanest example of a fungible object is money. A dollar is a dollar is a dollar, whether you received it as a gift, found it on the floor, or earned it by working. A dollar is also a dollar whether it's a dollar bill in your wallet, 20 nickels in a pot of loose change, or a number on the screen when you check your bank balance online. It all has the same value. Money is fungible.

This sounds like stating the obvious, but it isn't. Behavioral economists have found that people often do not behave as if money is fungible, and this leads to some odd and irrational decisions.

Creating mental categories for money

People often divide up their savings into categories, giving names to the different categories. Some people even physically label money by putting it into envelopes or jars that say "rent" or "groceries." Other people keep separate funds for special purposes, such as a vacation fund, a birthday present fund, or a rainy-day fund. Keeping separate funds helps people remember their savings goals, remain disciplined in saving toward those goals, and measure their progress toward the goals.

Consider the vacation example: You label a jar (or preferably a bank account, which is safer) "vacation money." The money you put in this fund could just as easily be spent on a whim. But if you do that regularly, you will likely never have the savings you need for that vacation. Putting the money in the vacation fund may help you "forget" all about it when you are looking for last-minute fun money. And even if you do remember you have money in the vacation fund, you might feel bad taking some out to go out and party, and you don't want to let yourself down. In this way, separating money into mental categories may help you organize your expenditures and stick to your plan.

However, in other cases, mentally labeling money as belonging to one category or another can be costly. Consider a college student who has amassed $1,000 in savings by working a weekend job. The student's friends are all planning a spring break trip, with a budget of $1,000. Perfect— the student "labels" the $1,000 savings as "spring break fund" and swears not to touch it. But a few months before spring break, the student, who also has a credit card, needs a bit of cash for books and school supplies. This student has a choice:

- Dip into the savings account and lose the little bit of interest the savings would earn.
- Borrow by paying for the books and supplies with the credit card. If the amount owed on the credit card isn't paid off at the end of the month, the student will pay interest on the outstanding balance.

Given this choice, many people would refuse to spend their savings and would instead borrow by using the credit card. But the credit-card debt almost certainly bears a higher interest rate than the savings account earns. The decision to hold on to savings rather than pay down debt is one that makes people poorer in the long run. The lesson is this: Sometimes having a mental label on savings helps us reach our goals, but sometimes it can be costly. Remember to think carefully about trade-offs and fungibility when making such decisions.

At least one credit-card company makes a point of enabling customers to mentally categorize debt, which may or may not be a good thing; see the What Do You Think? box "Credit-card categories: More realistic or more confusing?"

What Do You Think?

Credit-card categories: More realistic or more confusing?

In 2009, Chase Bank introduced a new credit-card product called Blueprint, designed with the help of an economist who specializes in behavioral finance. Blueprint helps customers categorize their credit-card bills so they can choose which categories to pay off right away and which to carry over. They can then create payment plans for the expenses they choose not to pay off immediately.

A series of television commercials supporting Blueprint's launch showed people choosing to pay off regular expenses such as groceries, gas, and rent, while creating special payment plans for one-time expenses such as an engagement ring. The ads appeal to a common intuition: Many people don't mind paying interest on big-ticket items but feel uncomfortable about getting into debt to cover their everyday living expenses.

The insight behind Chase's Blueprint product is to work with the way many people really think about money. The product aims to help customers put order into their finances—in the same way that it can be helpful to set aside cash for "rent" in its own envelope.

Looked at a different way, however, the product works by downplaying the fact that money is fungible. The fungibility of money means that the categories people create are meaningless in financial terms. Economic logic tells us that if you have a $500 credit-card bill and choose to pay only $300, the interest due on the remaining $200 will be identical, no matter whether you tell yourself you're paying off your monthly grocery bill or part of an engagement ring. The risk is that the product nurtures unclear thinking about finance by promoting a false distinction between categories of debt. Customers may be tempted to think that paying later is more acceptable for big-ticket purchases. With that mind-set, they may run up more credit-card debt on items that they could be better off saving up for instead.

WHAT DO YOU THINK?

1. Should banks design products around the way that people actually view their finances, even if the outcomes might seem irrational to outsiders?
2. Should banks design products that push customers to make choices consistent with rational economic decision making?
3. Overall, would you expect customers who use a product like Blueprint to end up with more or less debt?

Source: http://www.chaseblueprint.com/.

People place money into categories in many different ways. Above we discussed categorizing by different spending purposes, but people also sometimes put money into mental categories depending on how they received the money. This can be helpful for organizing finances, if linked to spending. But this can also lead people to take risks they wouldn't otherwise take. For example, behavioral economists have observed that people who have recently won some money are more likely to spend it recklessly. In a casino, for example, you may hear a gambler who has just won a bet say that he is "playing with the house's money"; he may take bigger risks with that money than he would have done with the money he came in with. This is an irrational distinction: Once he had won, the money was no longer "the house's," but his own.

Irrational behavior has also been documented in investment-fund managers who are entrusted with investing people's savings. They, too, seem prone to making a false mental distinction between amounts they started out with and amounts they have just gained in the market. As a result, they make more reckless investment decisions when they have recently made a profitable trade.

✓ CONCEPT CHECK

☐ Why is money considered fungible? **[LO 8.4]**

☐ How can forgetting about money's fungibility lead to poor financial decisions? **[LO 8.4]**

Conclusion

We can go a long way in economics by assuming that people act rationally to maximize their utility. Real people, though, make economic decisions in complicated, unexpected, and sometimes nonoptimal ways. Behavioral economics shows us that, in practice, we need a broader understanding of "maximizing utility" in order to build models that predict many of the quirky things people do. Understanding these human tendencies can help us to avoid common decision-making pitfalls. It can also help us to design products and policies that allow people to make better choices.

Although the behaviors explored in this chapter can be viewed as biases or mistakes, they are the sort of mistakes that can be corrected. We've also discussed some strategies designed to help people reach their intended goals and make better choices. In a later chapter (Chapter 23, "Public Policy and Choice Architecture") we'll return to some of these issues as we think about business ideas and public policies that help people make good choices and stick to their goals.

Key Terms

behavioral economics, p. 193

time inconsistency, p. 193

commitment device, p. 195

sunk cost, p. 197

fungible, p. 199

Summary

LO 8.1 Explain how time inconsistency accounts for procrastination and other problems with self-control.

Time inconsistency occurs when we change our minds about what we want simply because of the timing of the decision. That often means wanting something now that is inconsistent with what you want for yourself in the future. Time inconsistency helps to explain behaviors like procrastination and giving in to temptation. People who are time inconsistent experience an internal battle between two selves: a "future-oriented self," who might have worthy goals such as being productive and eating healthily, and a "present-oriented self," who may be prone to slacking off and backsliding. Ideas such as *commitment devices* can help us understand and manage this battle.

LO 8.2 Explain why sunk costs should not be taken into account in deciding what to do next.

Economists usually assume that people will do something if and only if the benefits of doing it are greater than the opportunity cost. But people have an irrational tendency to place value on *sunk costs*—costs that have already been incurred, and cannot be refunded or recovered. People would make better decisions if they did not consider sunk costs, instead weighing only those costs that are still to come.

LO 8.3 Identify the types of opportunity cost that people often undervalue, and recognize why undervaluing them distorts decision making.

People frequently undervalue abstract or *nonmonetary* opportunity costs, such as the value of the time they spend on an activity or the implicit cost of owning an item. Economically, turning down an opportunity to sell an item that you already own is equivalent to buying that item at the offered price.

LO 8.4 Explain why fungibility matters in financial decision making.

A good is considered *fungible* if it is easily exchangeable or substitutable. The foremost example of a fungible good is money. Even though money is fungible, this is often not reflected in people's behavior. Instead, they may put it into various mental categories. Although this approach can help people to save money or stick to a budget, it can also lead to poor financial decisions, as when people don't use their low-interest savings to pay down high-interest debts.

Review Questions

1. Describe a situation from your own experience in which you are time inconsistent. What have you done (or might you do) to accomplish the goals of your future-oriented self? **[LO 8.1]**

2. You have a friend who is always resolving to improve her grades but who never seems to find time to study. Explain to her how time inconsistency might be affecting her choices and suggest some steps she might take to meet her goal. **[LO 8.1]**

3. You've already paid to get into an all-you-can-eat buffet and have enjoyed several plates of food. You're not really hungry anymore but feel you ought to eat more to get the full value from the buffet. Does this inclination make sense? Explain why or why not. **[LO 8.2]**

4. Alda is willing to pay $2,000 to visit her favorite cousin over spring break. A month ago, she booked a trip costing $1,200. Spring break has arrived, but Alda needs one day to finish an important paper before she goes. Alda could cancel her trip and get a refund of $800. Or she could pay an additional $1,000 (on top of the $1,200 she already paid) to rebook the trip for two days later. Explain what Alda should do. **[LO 8.2]**

5. Suppose your art history professor has a small personal art collection, including some works by a famous artist. She bought this artist's paintings at a modest price, before he became well known. One of the paintings is now worth $2 million. When you ask the professor whether she would buy it now for $2 million, she says she wouldn't. Is the professor's decision making consistent? Why or why not? **[LO 8.3]**

6. Chandra received a gift certificate that covers three salsa dance lessons. After the first lesson, Chandra decided that she doesn't like salsa, yet she still plans to go to the next lesson because it doesn't cost her anything. Evaluate Chandra's logic. **[LO 8.3]**

7. You have a friend who runs up a balance on his credit card by buying new furniture to replace the furniture he has. The interest rate on the balance is 15 percent per month. The furniture store offers a layaway plan with monthly payments equivalent to an interest rate of 10 percent per month. Explain to your friend how he could manage his finances more sensibly. **[LO 8.4]**

8. Dora and Vicki are bartenders. Dora prefers her tips in cash because she can have the money right away. Credit-card tips don't get paid to bar staff until the payments are processed, which can take a few days. Vicki still prefers for her customers to put her tip on their credit card. Why might Vicki have this preference? **[LO 8.4]**

Problems and Applications

1. In which of the following cases is time inconsistency likely to be at work? **[LO 8.1]**

   a. A child plans to become a doctor when he grows up, but a month later reads a book about firefighters and decides to become a firefighter instead.

   b. A student keeps intending to finish reading *War and Peace*—next week.

   c. A parent plans to enroll his child in art class but enrolls her in dance class instead.

   d. A beginning piano player plans to practice three times a week but frequently practices only once a week.

2. You would like to save more money. Which of the following strategies will help you overcome time inconsistency? **[LO 8.1]**

   a. Deciding how much you need to save.

   b. Setting up a savings account.

   c. Putting reminders in your calendar to make deposits.

   d. Enrolling in an automatic-transfer program that will move a specified amount of money from your checking account to your savings account each month.

3. You're seated at a banquet that is beginning to become boring. Which of the following pieces of information are relevant to your decision to stay or go somewhere else? **[LO 8.2]**

   a. Another party is happening at the same time, and you've heard that it's fun.

   b. The dinner you were served was only so-so.

   c. You haven't eaten dessert yet, and it looks delicious.

    d. You paid $30 to attend the banquet.

    e. The other party you could attend has a cover charge of $10.

4. You just spent $40 on a new movie for your collection. You would have preferred the director's cut but discovered when you got home that you bought the theatrical version. The store you bought the movie from has an "all sales final" policy, but you could resell the movie online for $30. The director's cut sells for $50. By how much would you need to value the director's cut over the theatrical version for it to make sense for you to sell the version you bought and buy the director's cut? **[LO 8.2]**

5. Suppose you're bowling with friends. You've already played one game and are trying to decide whether to play another. Each game costs $6 per person, plus a one-time rental fee of $5 for the bowling shoes. It would take another hour to play the next game, which would make you late to work. Missing an hour of work would mean that you would lose pay at a rate of $12 per hour. Based on this information, how much would you have to enjoy the next bowling game, expressed in terms of dollars, to play another game? **[LO 8.3]**

6. During a holiday party at work, you pay $2 to buy a raffle ticket for a 160-gigabyte iPod. You win the drawing. Based on a little research online, you discover that the going rate for a hardly used 160-gigabyte iPod is $200. **[LO 8.3]**

    a. What was the opportunity cost of acquiring the iPod?

    b. What is the opportunity cost of choosing to keep the iPod?

7. Jamie is saving for a trip to Europe. She has an existing savings account that earns 2 percent interest and has a current balance of $4,500. Jamie doesn't want to use her current savings for the vacation, so she decides to borrow the $1,500 she needs for travel expenses. She will repay the loan in exactly one year. The annual interest rate is 5 percent. **[LO 8.4]**

    a. If Jamie were to withdraw the $1,500 from her savings account to finance the trip, how much interest would she forgo?

    b. If Jamie borrows the $1,500, how much will she pay in interest?

    c. How much does the trip cost her if she borrows rather than dips into her savings?

8. Suppose you have accumulated a credit card balance of $500, at an annual interest rate of 10 percent. You are also planning to open a new savings account that accumulates interest at an annual rate of 3 percent. You just got your paycheck and have $200 that you can use either to pay down your debt or open your savings account. **[LO 8.4]**

    a. If you use the full $200 to pay down your debt, what will your credit card balance be in one year? Assume no additional credit card payments during this time.

    b. If, instead, you put the full $200 into your savings account, what will be the balance in your savings account in one year, assuming you make no additional deposits during this time? What will your credit card balance be, assuming you make no additional payments during this time because your payment requirements have been deferred for one year?

    c. In one year, how much money will you have lost if you deposit the $200 in your savings account compared to paying down your credit card?

Endnotes

1. http://duke.edu/~dandan/Papers/PI/deadlines.pdf.

Game Theory and Strategic Thinking

Learning Objectives

LO 9.1 Understand strategic behavior and describe the components of a strategic game.

LO 9.2 Explain why noncooperation is always the outcome in the prisoners' dilemma.

LO 9.3 Identify whether or not a player has a dominant strategy in a one-time game.

LO 9.4 Identify whether or not a Nash equilibrium will be reached in a one-time game.

LO 9.5 Explain how a commitment strategy can be used to achieve cooperation in a one-time game.

LO 9.6 Explain how repeated play can enable cooperation.

LO 9.7 Explain how backward induction can be used to make decisions.

LO 9.8 Use a decision tree to solve a sequential game.

LO 9.9 Define first-mover advantage and identify it in practice.

LO 9.10 Explain why patient players have more bargaining power in repeated games.

LO 9.11 Explain how a commitment strategy can allow players to achieve their goals by limiting their options.

LITTERBUGS BEWARE

Litter is an eyesore, whether it's a candy bar wrapper on the sidewalk or a plastic bag caught on a fence along the highway. Most people would prefer clean streets, parks, and oceans over messy ones. So why is there litter?

Imagine it's a sunny day and you've had lunch at a table outside. You're just finishing up when the wind blows your sandwich wrapper to the ground. You could chase it, but the wind is blowing the paper even farther away. You're in a hurry, and it's unlikely that you will get caught and punished for not putting the wrapper in a trash can. Besides, there's other trash around; your wrapper is not going to make much difference to the overall environment. So, with a bit of guilt, you walk away.

The trouble is that once others see your trash blowing about, they're more likely to decide to litter as well. That can then lead to even more litter. The result is an increasingly dirty, trash-strewn community.

That's the paradox. Everyone would like to have a clean environment, but incentives sometimes push us to make things just a little bit worse. Over time, with *everyone* making things just a little bit worse, the outcome adds up to being a lot worse. Once everyone is littering, you'll litter more too. It's not the best outcome, but somehow that's how things unwind. The problem escalates because it's impossible to get everyone to agree, voluntarily, to not litter.

© Andrew Yahin/Shutterstock

How can the problem be fixed? One idea is to create strong norms against littering. One way to do that is to encourage families, schools, churches, and other civic organizations to reinforce the shared sense that it's good to keep communities clean. The now-iconic "Don't Mess With Texas" slogan was originally created at the request of the Texas Department of Transportation to try to create social norms against roadside litter.

The government of Singapore in Southeast Asia took a different route; it used a strong dose of economic incentives. It chose to stop the problem before it started. If you're caught in Singapore tossing trash anywhere but in the trash can, it will cost you $1,400. In addition to the fine, the Singaporean authorities usually impose what is called a "corrective work order." This order forces you to collect trash outside in bright green vests under the full scrutiny of public humiliation. If you try to dump something a little bigger—say, by tossing a full garbage bag from your car—you face up to $35,000 in fines or a year in jail, plus the loss of your vehicle.

With these harsh punishments, it's not surprising that Singapore is generally cleaner than large cities in the United States. In New York City, for example, the fine for littering ranges from $50 to $250, which doesn't have quite the same sting as the fine in Singapore! New York City also often makes it costly (in time and effort) to be clean—you sometimes have to walk for blocks to find a trash can.

By making littering expensive, Singapore left its citizens with little choice but to put their trash in the can, solving the littering problem. Singapore's policy is tough, but authorities argue that the high fines help citizens obtain the clean outcome that they want. That outcome had been impossible to achieve because of a collective failure to voluntarily quit littering. What's more, in the end, the authorities rarely have to enforce the fines. With effective incentives in place, few people end up littering.

While Singapore has found a way to reduce litter, many other places have problems with trash that simply cannot be solved through heavy fines and rules. When trash moves across borders or floats open in the sea, it is hard to create workable international solutions. Deep within state or national parks and wilderness areas, it's hard to catch litterers. But as the Singapore example shows, taking people's motivations and incentives seriously is a helpful way to start piecing together responses.

In this chapter, we'll see that the littering problem is an example of the *prisoners' dilemma*—a game of strategy in which people make rational choices that lead to a less-than-ideal result for all. It might seem to trivialize choices to think of them as a "game," but economists use the term *game* in a broader sense than its everyday use: To economists, *games* are not just recreational pursuits like chess, Monopoly, or poker; instead, games are situations in which players pursue strategies designed to achieve their goals. As we'll see in this chapter, these kind of games pop up in all kinds of real-world situations, ranging from environmental protection to business to war.

Games and Strategic Behavior

> **LO 9.1** Understand strategic behavior and describe the components of a strategic game.

Economists use the word **game** to refer to any situation involving at least two people that requires those involved to think strategically. The study of how people behave strategically under different circumstances is called **game theory**.

We have seen that people behave rationally when they look at the trade-offs they face and pursue their goals in the most effective way possible. When the trade-offs you face are determined by the choices someone else will make, behaving rationally involves **behaving strategically**. Behaving strategically means acting to achieve a goal by anticipating the interplay between your own and others' decisions. When your outcomes depend on another's choices, asking *How will others respond?* is the key to good decision making. (Remember, this is one of the four key questions economists consider, introduced in Chapter 1, "Economics and Life.")

Rules, strategies, and payoffs

All games share three features: rules, strategies, and payoffs. *Rules* define the actions that are allowed in a game. In chess, for example, each type of piece is allowed to move only in certain directions. In real life, people's behavior is constrained by laws both legislated and natural. For example, when two businesses are competing, the structure of costs each firm faces can be seen as a rule. In presidential elections, rules include the workings of the electoral college and the system of majority voting. In environmental games, the laws of nature could be seen as the rules that constrain and guide the decisions we humans make.

Strategies are the plans of action that players follow to achieve their goals. In the game Monopoly, you might decide to buy as many cheap properties as possible, to build hotels on Boardwalk and Park Place, or to become a railroads and utilities magnate. All these strategies are different approaches to the same goal: earning lots of fake money while bankrupting other players. When two businesses are competing, strategies might include producing a certain quantity of a good. One strategy in an election campaign is to use hopeful language and images to try to inspire people to vote for a certain candidate.

Payoffs are the rewards that come from particular actions. They can be monetary or nonmonetary in nature. The salary for a certain job or the profits that come from making good business decisions are monetary payoffs. In chess, the nonmonetary payoff is winning. In an election campaign, the most important payoff is usually being elected.

game
a situation involving at least two people that requires those involved to think strategically

game theory
the study of how people behave strategically under different circumstances

behaving strategically
acting to achieve a goal by anticipating the interplay between your own and others' decisions

✓**CONCEPT CHECK**

☐ What is a strategy? **[LO 9.1]**

One-Time Games and the Prisoners' Dilemma

The name *prisoners' dilemma* comes from a situation you could imagine in an episode of *Law and Order* or other police shows: You and an accomplice have been arrested on suspicion of committing both a serious crime and a more minor one. The police hold you in separate cells. A policeman candidly explains to you that he lacks the evidence to convict either of you of the serious crime, but he does have evidence to convict you both of the minor crime. He wants to get at least one conviction for the major crime, so he offers you a deal: If you confess that you both did it, and your accomplice *doesn't* confess, you'll get let off with 1 year in prison, while your accomplice gets the maximum 20-year term for committing the major crime.

Prisoners' dilemma

LO 9.2 Explain why noncooperation is always the outcome in the prisoners' dilemma.

prisoners' dilemma
a game of strategy in which two people make rational choices that lead to a less-than-ideal result for both

The classic **prisoners' dilemma** is a game of strategy in which two people make rational choices that lead to a less-than-ideal result for both. The same ideas can be applied to situations with more than two people and also to organizations rather than individuals.

What if you confess and your accomplice *also* confesses? The policeman no longer needs your evidence to get a conviction, so the 1-year deal is off. Still, he tells you you'll get some time off the maximum sentence as a reward for cooperating—you'll both get 10 years. And what if neither of you confesses? The policeman sighs: Then you'll both be convicted of the minor crime only, and you'll both serve 2 years. A thought occurs to you—is the policeman offering the same deal to your accomplice? "Of course," he confirms with a smirk.

You think to yourself, "If my accomplice confesses, then I'll get 10 years if I confess and 20 years if I don't. But if my accomplice *doesn't* confess, I'll get 1 year if I confess and 2 years if I don't. Therefore, whatever my accomplice does, I'll be better off if I confess." Although you were partners in crime, you soon realize that your accomplice will be using the same logic. This means you will both confess, and you will both get 10 years. If only you and your accomplice could somehow agree to cooperate by both staying quiet, then you could avoid this outcome and each get away with serving only 2 years.

Figure 9-1 summarizes this predicament in the form of a *decision matrix*. Reading horizontally across the top row, we see that if your accomplice confesses, your choice (shown in green)

FIGURE 9-1

The prisoners' dilemma

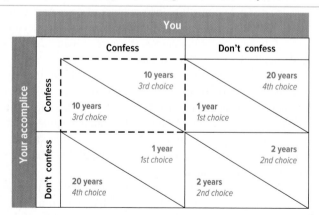

You will always choose to confess in a prisoners' dilemma because you prefer a 10-year sentence to 20 years (if your accomplice confesses) and a 1-year sentence to 2 years (if your accomplice doesn't confess). Your accomplice makes the same calculation. Both of you have a dominant strategy to confess, so you will both end up in jail for 10 years—whereas you could have both received only 2 years if you could somehow have agreed to cooperate.

is between your third-preference outcome (10 years in prison) and your fourth choice (20 years). Reading the bottom row shows that if your opponent doesn't confess, your choice is between your first-choice outcome (1 year in prison) and your second choice (2 years).

What about your accomplice? Reading vertically down the columns reveals the same set of choices for your opponent. The incentives each of you faces mean that you will both confess and end up in the top-left box, both getting your third-choice outcome. If you could have cooperated with each other, you could have ended up in the bottom-right box, both getting your second-choice outcome.

Let's see how this think-ing is mirrored in an election campaign—say, the presidential election campaign between George W. Bush and John Kerry in 2004 (considered by some to be one of the most negative in recent times). If you were running the Bush campaign, your thought process might have gone some-thing like this: "If Senator Ker-ry's campaign goes negative, we would have to attack him back or we'd look weak. But what if Sen-ator Kerry doesn't go negative? If we attack him and he doesn't attack us back, we'd destroy his chances of winning the election. So, whatever Senator Kerry does,

The Obama/Romney cam-paigns played nicer than the Bush/Kerry campaigns, but all candidates face prison-ers' dilemma–type choices. © *Spencer Platt/Getty Images*

we're better off going negative." Whoever is running Senator Kerry's campaign will be thinking the same thing. The result: Both campaigns go negative, both candidates' reputations suffer, and voters feel more and more disillusioned with the political process.

We can analyze this situation in a decision matrix (see Figure 9-2). First we have to define the payoffs. Above all, each candidate would rather win easily than face a tight race—winning easily is their top preference. And each would rather face a tight race than lose heavily—losing heav-ily is their last choice. In each case, dirty campaigning is a price worth paying. But if given the choice between a tight race in which both go negative and damage their reputations (the top-left quadrant) and a tight race in which both stay positive and enhance their reputations (the bottom-right quadrant), both candidates would prefer the positive tight race.

Just as in the original prisoners' dilemma, both candidates will look at their options and real-ize that whatever the other one does, they're better off going negative. As a result, they both end up with their third-choice outcome when they might both have had their second-choice outcome instead—if only they'd been able to cooperate.

The littering "game" described at the beginning of this chapter can also be shown in a deci-sion matrix. To do so, we've assigned points to the various outcomes in order to show their pros and cons—but the exact numbers are not what's important. Instead, what matters is their relative size and whether the points are positive, negative, or zero. The people making decisions in this example—you and your neighbor—want to earn the most points they can (or lose as few points as possible). (You can think of "your neighbor" as representing all other people in the commu-nity who might litter.)

Figure 9-3 shows the payoffs in the decision you and your neighbor face when deciding if you should let your trash blow away. As you can see, littering results in the larger payoff, regard-less of whether your neighbor litters or not. Again, the result is the third-choice outcome, even though potential litterers might have obtained their second-choice outcome instead—if you and your neighbor had been able to cooperate.

FIGURE 9-2

The prisoners' dilemma in a presidential campaign

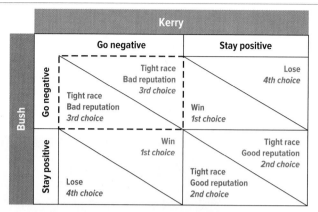

Kerry will choose to go negative because if Bush goes negative, Kerry would rather keep the race tight (even if it means damaging his reputation) than lose in a landslide; if Bush stays positive, Kerry would rather win in a landslide (even if it means damaging his reputation) than face a tight race. Bush makes the same calculation. As a result, both candidates will end up in a negative tight race, when they'd both have preferred a positive tight race instead.

FIGURE 9-3

Payoffs for littering

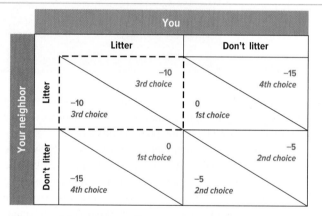

To represent the decision to litter or not, we assign points to the various outcomes (or "payoffs") of the choices that you and your neighbor make about littering. If we look at your choice to litter or not to litter, we can see that in any given situation, you'd prefer to litter—you would rather save yourself the walk to the trash can, no matter if there's litter already on the ground or not. Your neighbor faces the same trade-off; consequently, you both litter. Note that if you both had decided not to litter, you would've been better off because you would enjoy cleaner streets.

Finding the dominant strategy

> **LO 9.3** Identify whether or not a player has a dominant strategy in a one-time game.

dominant strategy
a strategy that is the best one for a player to follow no matter what strategy other players choose

In the original prisoners' dilemma, whatever your accomplice does, you're better off confessing. When a strategy is the best one to follow *no matter what strategy other players choose*, it is called a **dominant strategy**. Going negative is a dominant strategy for both candidates in an election campaign (and, as result, neither candidate looks good).

FIGURE 9-4
A game with no dominant strategy

		Player B		
		Rock	Paper	Scissors
Player A	Rock	Tie	B wins	A wins
	Paper	A wins	Tie	B wins
	Scissors	B wins	A wins	Tie

Player B's best choice depends on what Player A plans to do. Since it's a simultaneous move, however, neither can know what the other will choose. There is no one strategy that is best every time, so there is no dominant strategy.

Of course, not all games feature a dominant strategy for each player. Take the familiar children's game rock-paper-scissors (Figure 9-4). As you probably know, rock beats scissors, scissors beat paper, and paper beats rock. Because both players move at the same time, predicting your opponent's choice is tough. Reading across the rows or down the columns of the decision matrix shows that there is no single strategy that will work best for you, regardless of what your opponent plays.

Reaching equilibrium

LO 9.4 Identify whether or not a Nash equilibrium will be reached in a one-time game.

Remember the concept of equilibrium from the chapters on supply and demand: The equilibrium price and quantity are reached in a market when no individual buyer has an incentive to pay more and no individual seller has an incentive to accept less, given what all the other buyers and sellers are doing. The concept of equilibrium is often used in game theory: In particular, a special type of equilibrium called a **Nash equilibrium** is reached when all players choose the best strategy they can, *given the choices of all other players.* In other words, this is a point in a game when no player has an incentive to change his or her strategy, given what the other players are doing. This equilibrium can also be described as the *situation of no-regrets*—that is, on discovering the decisions made by other players, you have no reason to regret your own decision. The concept is named after the famous game theorist John Nash.

Nash equilibrium
an equilibrium reached when all players choose the best strategy they can, given the choices of all other players. It is a situation wherein, given the consequences, the player has no regrets about his or her decision.

In a game such as rock-paper-scissors, there is no Nash equilibrium. Let's say you play with a friend. If the friend plays scissors and you play rock, then you have no incentive to change (rock beats scissors), but the friend would have an incentive to change to paper (paper beats rock). If the friend changes to paper, though, that would give you an incentive to change to scissors (scissors beat paper). And so on. There is no stable outcome where neither of you would wish to change your strategy once you find out what the other player is doing.

In the prisoners' dilemma, there *is* a stable outcome: You both confess. If your accomplice confesses, you have no incentive to switch from confessing to not confessing. And if you are confessing, your accomplice has no incentive to switch from confessing to not confessing. Thus, there is an equilibrium where both you and your accomplice confess.

As we can see from the prisoners' dilemma, an equilibrium outcome to a game is not necessarily a good one for the participants. This negative–negative outcome is called a *noncooperative equilibrium* because the participants act independently, pursuing only their individual interests.

FIGURE 9-5

Payoffs in a driving game

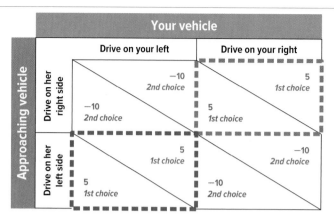

If you drive on the right side of the road and the approaching driver drives on the side to her left, you will crash. Similarly, if you choose the left side and she chooses the right, you will crash. But if you both choose to drive on the side to your right, or if you both choose to drive on the left, you avoid a crash. Neither right or left is a dominant strategy for either driver, but the game can still result in an equilibrium. In fact, there are two equilibria: one in which both drivers choose right and one in which both drivers choose left.

Some games have a stable positive–positive outcome even though everyone's acting in his or her own self-interest. Consider the "game" of driving: Suppose you are one of only two motorists on an island and you both are driving toward each other. If you decide to drive on the right and the other person drives on her left, you have a head-on collision (the least-preferred payoff for you both). This is not an equilibrium; your decision gives the other driver an incentive to drive on the right instead. When you both drive on the right, you avoid accidents (your most-preferred payoff), and neither of you has an incentive to change. Driving on the right is thus a positive–positive outcome.

Figure 9-5 shows the payoffs from this driving game. As you may have noticed from this example, games can have more than one equilibrium outcome. If both drivers drive on the right, then each receives a payoff of 5. Neither player has an incentive to change his or her strategy because doing so would result in a lower payoff. However, both of you driving on the left would also be an equilibrium. (Indeed, this is the equilibrium outcome to the driving game that has been reached by motorists in some countries outside the United States, such as the UK, Japan, and Australia.) This example also tells us a game doesn't need to have a dominant strategy to reach an equilibrium outcome: Neither driving on the right nor driving on the left is a dominant strategy—the best decision depends on what other players do.

Avoiding competition through commitment

LO 9.5 Explain how a commitment strategy can be used to achieve cooperation in a one-time game.

In our discussion of the prisoners' dilemma, we have repeatedly stressed that the players of the game would be better off if they could cooperate. So why don't they? It's not simply because they are being held in separate cells and can't talk to each other. (Bush and Kerry could have picked up the phone and agreed that each would run a positive campaign.) Nor is the problem simply one of trust: You could make a deal beforehand with your accomplice that neither of you will confess.

The problem runs much deeper: Even if you are completely sure that your accomplice can be trusted not to confess, *you* should still confess. Remember that whatever your accomplice does, you are better off confessing—that's why it's a dominant strategy. In prisoners' dilemma–type games, prearranged agreements to cooperate are tough to make work because *both* players have a strong incentive to defect.

One solution to this problem is to reduce the players' payoffs by creating a punishment for defecting. For this strategy to work, the punishment must be so bad that it outweighs the incentive not to cooperate. Is that possible? That depends on the circumstances of a particular game. In the classic prisoners' dilemma, imagine that you and your accomplice are members of an organized criminal gang in which all agree that any member who testifies against another member will be killed in retribution. This dramatically changes the payoff for confessing: a shorter prison sentence, but with the expectation of being killed at the end of it. With those options, "Don't confess" starts to look like a much more attractive option.

Agreements like this are an example of a **commitment strategy**, in which players agree to submit to a penalty in the future if they defect from a given strategy. Changing the payoffs by agreeing to future penalties can allow players to reach a mutually beneficial equilibrium that would otherwise be difficult to maintain.

commitment strategy an agreement to submit to a penalty in the future for defecting from a given strategy

What about our example of negative election campaigns? Sadly, commitment strategies are hard to make work. Rival politicians do often make high-profile public agreements to run a clean campaign. The idea is that if one of them then goes negative, voters will be angry about the broken promise to stay positive. For this strategy to work, however, voters would have to be so angry that it would outweigh the electoral advantage of going negative. Given how many of these agreements are made and then broken, this doesn't usually appear to be the case.

Promoting competition in the public interest

Reaching a positive–positive outcome through a commitment strategy can benefit everyone. In the election game, for example, the public would benefit if politicians could somehow stay positive. Voters would avoid the unpleasantness that comes with a negative campaign, and both voter turnout and public interest in politics might climb.

In some variations of the prisoners' dilemma game, however, *preventing* players from cooperating serves the public interest. The commitment strategy we imagined for the classic prisoners' dilemma is not so far from real-world reality: The famous code of *omertà,* which prohibits anyone in the community from ever talking with authorities, makes it difficult for prosecutors to persuade *mafiosi* to confess and testify against their mafia bosses. That's why the witness protection program was created: It attempts to increase the payoff for confessing by providing police protection before, during, and after a trial (and sometimes an entirely new identity). It nudges the players back toward an outcome in which they can pursue their self-interest.

Consider a more everyday example, from the world of business: Suppose that a town has only two gas stations, Conoco and Exxon. Each could choose to charge high prices or low prices. This gives us four possible outcomes and payoffs, visualized in the decision matrix in Figure 9-6:

- If both stations charge low prices, they both make low profits.
- If both stations charge high prices, they both make high profits.
- If Exxon charges high prices and Conoco charges low prices, everyone in town buys gas from Conoco. The Conoco station makes very high profits, and the Exxon station loses money.
- If Exxon charges low prices and Conoco charges high prices, the opposite occurs: Everyone buys gas from Exxon, which makes very high profits, while Conoco gets no customers and loses money.

By now the analysis should be familiar: This game is another application of the prisoners' dilemma, with a dominant strategy of charging low prices. Both gas stations will do so, though they would be better off if they could agree to keep prices high. This noncooperative equilibrium—both charging low prices—is bad news for the game's players, the two gas stations. But it is good news for the town's consumers, who pay lower prices for their gas.

FIGURE 9-6

The prisoners' dilemma in competition between two firms

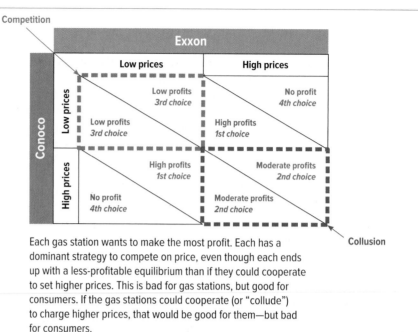

Each gas station wants to make the most profit. Each has a dominant strategy to compete on price, even though each ends up with a less-profitable equilibrium than if they could cooperate to set higher prices. This is bad for gas stations, but good for consumers. If the gas stations could cooperate (or "collude") to charge higher prices, that would be good for them—but bad for consumers.

We can expect the two gas station owners to try to think of a way they could cooperate, reaching an equilibrium in which they both make high profits. (In the next section, we'll see one way this could happen.) But the town's consumers will want to prevent this outcome from happening because it will leave them with no choice but to pay high prices for their gas. We even have a more negative word for cooperation in this business context: *collusion*. We use a more positive word to describe the noncooperative equilibrium: *competition*.

In later chapters we will see that collusion is, in fact, a common problem: Firms often try to find ways to collude so that they all charge higher prices. Governments—working on behalf of consumers—try to find ways to stop businesses from colluding. In the language of game theory, outlawing collusion changes the rules of the price-competition game.

✓CONCEPT CHECK

☐ Consider the prisoners' dilemma game. If one prisoner knows for sure that the other won't confess, what should he do? Why? **[LO 9.2]**

☐ How do you identify whether a strategy is dominant or not? **[LO 9.3]**

☐ What is the distinctive characteristic of the Nash equilibrium? **[LO 9.4]**

☐ How can a commitment strategy help two parties in a game cooperate instead of choosing their dominant strategies? **[LO 9.5]**

Repeated Play in the Prisoners' Dilemma

> **LO 9.6** Explain how repeated play can enable cooperation.

So far, we have been modeling the prisoners' dilemma game as involving a one-time simultaneous decision. In the classic version of the game, with two criminal accomplices facing the prospect of a 20-year prison sentence, this is accurate—it really is a one-time decision. But in our example of a presidential campaign, that's not the case: Decisions to run positive or negative ads are not simply made once, at the start of the campaign; they are reviewed on a daily basis.

Gas station owners decide on their prices on a day-to-day, or even hour-to-hour, basis. Economists call a game that is played more than once a **repeated game**.

repeated game
a game that is played more than once

Strategies and incentives often work quite differently when games are repeated. In particular, players no longer need commitment strategies to reach a mutually beneficial equilibrium. To see why, let's go back to our town with two gas stations. Imagine you manage the Exxon station. One morning you might think, "Today I'm going to increase my prices. Sure, I'll lose a little money at first, but it's a risk worth taking because the Conoco station manager might see the opportunity for us both to benefit in the longer run." In round one of the game, then, Exxon plays a "high prices" strategy.

Now imagine you manage the Conoco station. On seeing that the Exxon station has increased its prices, you might think, "Great, I'll start making more money because people will come here to buy gas. But hold on—that can't last for long. When the Exxon station starts losing money, it will have no choice but to cut prices again. But if I also increase my prices, perhaps the Exxon manager will keep his prices high, and we can *both* make more profits." In round two of the game, then, both Exxon and Conoco play a "high prices" strategy.

What happens in round three? Both gas station managers will think, "I could make more money by cutting my prices—if the other station keeps its prices high. But it wouldn't, would it? If I reduce my prices, the other station will be forced to reduce its prices. So I'll keep my prices high, and see if the other gas station does the same." In round three of the game, once again both gas stations play "high prices." The same reasoning holds for rounds four, five, six, and so on. Prices remain high, with the two players maintaining cooperation.

The tit-for-tat strategy

The thought processes of the Exxon and Conoco managers are an example of a type of strategy called **tit-for-tat**. Tit-for-tat is a straightforward idea: Whatever the other player does, you do the same thing in response.

tit-for-tat
a strategy in which a player in a repeated game takes the same action that his or her opponent did in the preceding round

It turns out that variants of tit-for-tat are very effective in repeated play of prisoners' dilemma–type games. If the other player makes a cooperative move (in the gas station example, setting high prices), then you respond with a cooperative move (also raising your prices). If the other player defects with a noncooperative move (cutting prices), you respond with a noncooperative move (also cutting prices). Two players who are both playing tit-for-tat can quickly find their way toward lasting cooperation.

Note that there is no need to enter into public commitment strategies or explicit agreements for players in a repeated-play game to achieve cooperation. For example, prices of gas in our two-station town could remain high indefinitely through nothing more than the rational game-playing of the two players. Indeed, explicit agreements to keep prices high would be illegal (collusion), and public commitments to keep prices high would not go down well with consumers. So instead, companies sometimes find subtle ways to reassure their competitors that they are committed to a tit-for-tat strategy, thereby reducing the risk that the competitor will threaten the equilibrium by lowering prices. See the Real Life box "What do price-matching guarantees guarantee?" to read about one common arrangement.

Real Life

What do price-matching guarantees guarantee?

Some companies advertise that if you can find a lower price anywhere else, they will match it. The implication is that they are confident they have the lowest prices in town. However, the real game going on here may be more subtle, and not necessarily a good one for customers. In fact, game theory suggests that price-matching guarantees guarantee higher, not lower, prices.

(continued)

As of the writing of this book, the competing home-improvement giants Home Depot and Lowes had nearly identical price-matching policies. The two stores promised not only to match a competitor's advertised price, but to beat it by 10 percent. Paradoxically, these guarantees meant that neither firm had an incentive to lower prices. In fact, price-matching policies send a clear and public signal that firms are committed to a tit-for-tat strategy.

Imagine, for example, that both firms are offering the same lawnmower for $300. What happens if Lowes decides to cut the price to $250? Home Depot's price-matching offer means that customers can get the lawnmower at Home Depot for $25 less (the $250 price, less an extra 10 percent), or $225. As a result, Lowes has little to gain by lowering prices. The same logic applies to Home Depot.

We don't know of an economic study of prices at Home Depot and Lowes relative to their costs. But the example gives us insight into a surprising outcome that can happen with price-matching policies: Game theory shows us that guaranteeing a *lower price* does not necessarily guarantee *low prices*. Because explicitly cooperating to fix prices is illegal, a firm's best option is to engage in a tit-for-tat strategy. By creating and publicizing a legally binding price-match policy, the firm creates a credible threat that it will follow a tit-for-tat strategy. As a result, prices can stay high, benefiting both firms at the customers' expense.

Tit-for-tat is an extremely powerful idea. Why doesn't it also ensure that political campaigns are clean, with each campaign repeatedly rewarding the other for running only positive ads by running only positive ads itself? There are a couple of reasons. One is that unlike selling gas, election campaigns do not go on indefinitely—as election day draws closer, the game becomes more like a one-off game, increasing the incentive to defect. Another reason is that the players in the election game are primarily concerned with doing better *relative* to the other player (getting more votes than the opponent). Gas stations, in contrast, are more interested in their *absolute* payoffs (making as much profit as possible).

Even though tit-for-tat may not work in every situation, it represents an incredibly effective tool for dealing with many situations. In fact, a professor of political science, Robert Axelrod, held a tournament in which dozens of computer programs based on different strategies were run against each other. His aim was to find which strategy gave the largest payoff in a repeated prisoners' dilemma game. Out of 14 competing strategies, the most successful entry, submitted by mathematician Anatol Rapoport, was tit-for-tat.

The From Another Angle box "Tit-for-tat and human emotions" describes the theory that many human emotions evolved from the tit-for-tat games played by our ancient ancestors.

From Another Angle
Tit-for-tat and human emotions

Why do we feel emotions such as sympathy, gratitude, vengeance, guilt, and forgiveness? Evolutionary biologists such as Robert Trivers, who developed the theory of reciprocal altruism, speculate that we evolved these emotions to help us achieve cooperation by playing the tit-for-tat strategy in "games" that helped our ancestors to survive.

Imagine that you are a hunter-gatherer in a prehistoric society. One day you are successful, bringing back more food than you can eat, while your neighbor returns with nothing. You could be cooperative (sharing food with your neighbor) or noncooperative (gorging on all the food yourself). The next day, perhaps your neighbor has success and you don't, and she has to make the same decision. In a situation like this, both you and your neighbor will do better if you can sustain cooperation (sharing food and both eating well every day) rather than being noncooperative (alternately starving and gorging).

What is required to achieve sustained cooperation? First, you need to feel *sympathetic* enough to give your unlucky and hungry neighbor some food. Then your neighbor needs to feel *gratitude,* prompting her to repay your favor and give you food the next day. If your neighbor one day defects with a noncooperative move, refusing to share her food with you, you need an emotion such as *vengeance* to prompt you to punish her by not sharing your food with her the next day. And if your neighbor subsequently feels *guilty* and shares with you the day after, you need an emotion such as *forgiveness* to get you back into the mutual sharing routine.

Of course, nobody knows for sure why humans have the capacity to experience the emotions that we do. But it is interesting that so many of our emotions are just what is required to help us intuitively play a tit-for-tat-type strategy in repeated-play prisoners' dilemma games.

✓CONCEPT CHECK

☐ How does a tit-for-tat strategy help players to achieve cooperation? **[LO 9.6]**

Sequential Games

So far, we've analyzed games in which players make decisions simultaneously. In games like the prisoners' dilemma and rock-paper-scissors, each player decides which strategy to adopt before knowing what the other player will do. In many real-world situations, however, one person or company has to make a decision before the other. These are called *sequential games* because the players move sequentially rather than simultaneously.

Think forward, work backward

LO 9.7 Explain how backward induction can be used to make decisions.

In sequential games, an especially important part of strategic behavior is to "think forward, work backward":

- First you have to *think forward:* What are all the possible outcomes of the situation you are considering? Which of them do you prefer?
- Then you have to *work backward:* What choice would you need to make to achieve your preferred outcome?

This process of analyzing a problem in reverse—starting with the last choice, then the second-to-last choice, and so on, to determine the optimal strategy—is called **backward induction**. It's probably something you do naturally all the time without even realizing it.

To take a simple example, suppose you're trying to choose your courses for next semester. There are so many options—what should you do? First, think forward: Let's say you aspire to become a Pulitzer Prize–winning journalist. Now work backward: What do you need to do to win the Pulitzer? You need to get a job at a top newspaper. How do you get a job at a top newspaper? You need a graduate degree in journalism. How do you get into a graduate course in journalism? You need an undergraduate degree majoring in English or Communications. This requires that you take prerequisite courses in nonfiction writing. Therefore, you should take introductory nonfiction writing this semester.

This line of reasoning is an example of backward induction: Start with the outcome you want, then work backward in time to determine each choice you must make to achieve that outcome.

backward induction
the process of analyzing a problem in reverse, starting with the last choice, then the second-to-last choice, and so on, to determine the optimal strategy

Deterring market entry: A sequential game

LO 9.8 Use a decision tree to solve a sequential game.

Backward induction can be an especially useful process in sequential games, when your aspirations are affected by decisions other players will make in response to a decision of your own. This is especially true in business; many firms have to make strategic decisions in sequential "games." One example involves entry into a market. Imagine that McDonald's Corporation is considering opening a restaurant in a small town that currently has no fast-food outlet. Also imagine that McDonald's will consider only locations where it expects to get at least a 10 percent rate of return on the investment because the company knows it could get 10 percent by investing the money elsewhere instead.

The company is trying to decide whether to buy land in two possible locations: It could buy in the center of town, where real estate is expensive but access for customers is more convenient. Or it could buy on the outskirts of town, where land is cheaper, but customers will have to drive out of their way to get there.

The company's calculations (which are hypothetical in this example) show that a new McDonald's on the outskirts of town will generate a 20 percent return. A new McDonald's at the central location will generate a 15 percent return. If the company stopped its analysis at this point, it would build on the outskirts.

Thinking strategically, however, McDonald's will take into account the possibility that Burger King could also be considering moving into the same town. McDonald's calculations show that the locations of the restaurants matter if there are two competing fast-food restaurants:

- If there is a fast-food restaurant at the central location, most customers won't bother driving to the restaurant on the outskirts. The restaurant in the center of town will do much better, earning a 12 percent rate of return, whereas the one on the outskirts will earn only a 2 percent rate of return.
- If there are two restaurants competing on the outskirts, each will earn an 8 percent rate of return.
- If there are two restaurants competing at the central location, each will earn a 4 percent rate of return.

What should McDonald's do, given the uncertainty about whether Burger King will enter the market?

- If McDonald's builds on the outskirts, it can expect Burger King to open in the central location, attracted by a 12 percent return. This would reduce McDonald's rate of return to only 2 percent.
- But if McDonald's builds in the central location, it can confidently predict that Burger King will not enter the market at all. With a McDonald's already existing in the central location, Burger King would receive a return of only 4 percent if it also built in the central location, or 2 percent if it built on the outskirts. It's likely that Burger King would rather invest its money for a 10 percent return elsewhere and not build at all.

We can analyze the decision McDonald's is facing using a chart called a *decision tree,* shown in Figure 9-7. Since McDonald's is ready to make a decision about entering this market, it has the first move in this game. The first decision node (on the left side of the figure) shows its choice to build on the outskirts or in the center of town. Whichever choice McDonald's makes, Burger King can then decide whether to build on the outskirts, in the center, or not at all—a decision represented at the second level of the tree (the two boxes in the center).

We can use backward induction to determine the best course of action for McDonald's. First we consider Burger King's decision: Starting on the right side of the tree, we can see that Burger

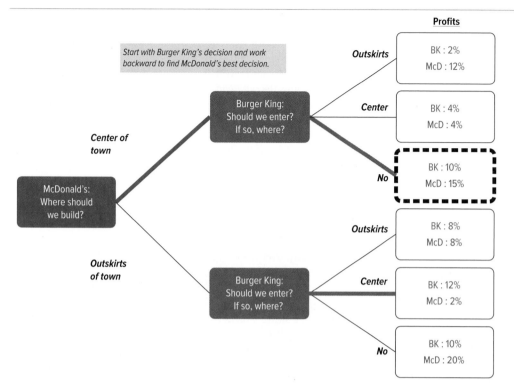

FIGURE 9-7

Decision tree for market entry

The right column shows the six potential outcomes of McDonald's and Burger King's decisions. Starting with Burger King's choices, we can narrow these six potential outcomes to two by identifying Burger King's preferred choice in each circumstance. These are the two possible outcomes that McDonald's will face, depending on what choice it makes in the first stage of the game. Then we can identify which of these outcomes McDonald's prefers.

King will build in the center if McDonald's builds on the outskirts. (See the heavy line pointing to the "Center" option.) But if McDonald's builds in the center, Burger King will not enter the market at all.

So, the decision tree reveals that McDonald's is not facing a choice between a 15 percent return in the central location or a 20 percent return on the outskirts, as we might first have thought. Instead, the choice is between a 15 percent return in the central location or a 2 percent return on the outskirts. Even though building in the center isn't the best choice for McDonald's in the absence of competition, it *is* the best *strategic* decision because it deters competitors from entering the market.

Using strategic thinking and backward induction can even win you $1 million—if you're a contestant on the television show *Survivor*. To see how, read the What Do You Think? box "Surviving with strategic thinking."

What Do You Think?

Surviving with strategic thinking

The first season of the successful reality television show *Survivor* provides a great example of strategic thinking in a sequential game. In the final episode, three contestants remain, but only one will win $1 million. There are two rounds to pass before winning: a challenge and a vote.

(continued)

In the challenge, the three contestants compete to see who can stand on a stump in the water the longest. Whoever wins the challenge automatically proceeds to the next round. Also, that person gets to choose which of the two remaining contestants proceeds (and thus which one gets eliminated). The two contestants who move on to the next round are subjected to a vote by the last nine ousted contestants. Whoever wins the vote wins the $1 million.

In the first season, the remaining three contestants were Richard, Rudy, and Kelly. Rudy was quite popular among the other contestants. Kelly and Richard both knew that if Rudy made it to the final two, he would likely win. However, Richard and Rudy had previously made an agreement to protect each other. Richard knew that if he (Richard) won the challenge, he would face a tough decision:

- If he chose Kelly to go with him to the final stage, he would be breaking his pact with Rudy, which would certainly cost him Rudy's vote.
- If he chose Rudy to go with him to the final stage, he would almost definitely lose due to Rudy's popularity with the voting contestants.

However, Richard knew that if Kelly won the challenge, she would very likely choose to bring Richard with her to the final stage. Kelly would prefer to compete for votes against Richard since Rudy was so popular. Richard also knew that if Rudy won, he would likely bring Richard, keeping their pact—although Rudy would most certainly win the vote. One extra fact is helpful here: Kelly had already won a string of endurance challenges. All bets were on Kelly to beat Rudy in yet another endurance challenge.

So what did Richard do? He used backward induction and jumped off the wood stump before the other two fell. He purposefully lost the challenge because it was his best strategy to win round two. And it worked: Kelly beat Rudy and chose to go to the final stage with Richard. Because the pact hadn't (technically) been broken, Richard retained Rudy's vote and won the $1 million by a 5-4 vote.

WHAT DO YOU THINK?

1. What would you have done in this situation if you were Kelly?
2. What would you have done if you were Rudy?
3. Did either Kelly or Rudy also have a good reason to jump off early?

First-mover advantage in sequential games

LO 9.9 Define first-mover advantage and identify it in practice.

In the market-entry game, first-mover McDonald's ends up with a 15 percent return, while latecomer Burger King is forced to invest elsewhere at a 10 percent return. If Burger King had gotten to town first, it could have put itself in McDonald's situation, building in the center of town and deterring McDonald's from entering the market. In this game, whoever gets to town first gets a higher return; the company that arrives second settles for less. This is a game with a **first-mover advantage**, in which the player who chooses first gets a higher payoff than those who follow.

First-mover advantage can be extremely important in one-round sequential games. Consider a bargaining game in which a company is negotiating with its employees' labor union over wages. Effectively, the two parties are bargaining over the division of the *surplus* created by their decision to trade wages for labor. (Remember that in this context *surplus* refers to the benefits people get from transactions.) Let's say this negotiation is a one-round sequential game: If the company

first-mover advantage
benefit enjoyed by the player who chooses first and, as a result, gets a higher payoff than those who follow

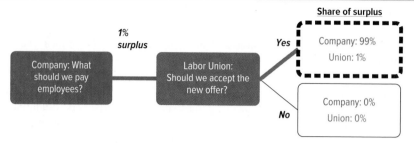

FIGURE 9-8

Decision tree for the ultimatum game

This decision tree shows the straightforward outcome when there is a very strong first-mover advantage, as seen in the ultimatum game. The company makes a "take it or leave it" offer, and the union will always accept an offer that is greater than zero. The 1% of surplus it gains may be low, but receiving nothing would be even worse.

is the first mover, it could offer just 1 percent of the surplus, and the union would have to make a choice. The union could accept the offer, or reject it by going on strike and shutting down production. That choice leaves both the company and the union with zero surplus. Calculating that 1 percent is better than nothing, the union would begrudgingly accept the offer. The decision tree in Figure 9-8 represents this calculation.

However, if the *union* had the first move, it could demand 99 percent of the surplus. It could assume that the company would rather pay that amount than risk its employees going on strike (during which the company would make no money at all). This is an example of what economists call an *ultimatum game:* One player makes an offer and the other player has the simple choice of whether to accept or reject. Of course, this is not a realistic representation of how union bargaining usually works. There are often multiple rounds of offers and counteroffers. As we will see in the next section, the ability to make counteroffers—that is, to turn a one-round game into a multiround game—dramatically changes things.

Repeated sequential games

LO 9.10 Explain why patient players have more bargaining power in repeated games.

We've seen that repeated play changes the nature of a simultaneous game such as the prisoners' dilemma by allowing cooperation to be sustained. Repeated play can also change the outcome in *sequential* games by reducing the first-mover advantage.

The ability to make counteroffers transforms bargaining from a game in which first-mover advantage trumps everything to a game in which patience is the winning strategy. Why? In almost all cases, the value of a given sum in the future is less than the value of that same sum now. Bargaining takes time; for every round of bargaining that takes place before the players reach agreement, the value of the surplus they are splitting goes down. In wage negotiations between a company and a labor union, we can think of this reduction in value as the productive time that is lost while negotiations take place. In these situations, the more-patient player—the one who places more value on money in the future relative to money in the present—has an advantage. The player who is willing to hold out longer has more bargaining power, and so receives a better payoff.

In the real world most wage negotiations don't drag on for years (although some do). If each player knows how patient the other is, the two sides don't need to play all the rounds. Instead, the company can simply offer the split that *would eventually occur* if the two sides played all the rounds. In that case, the surplus will be divided in proportion to each player's patience.

Commitment in sequential games

> **LO 9.11** Explain how a commitment strategy can allow players to achieve their goals by limiting their options.

Recall that in a commitment strategy, players agree to submit to a penalty in the future if they defect from a given strategy. In simultaneous games such as the prisoners' dilemma, making a credible commitment can change the payoffs and influence the strategy of the other players. We will see that the same is true in sequential games. Consider an example from military strategy, in which a general used a commitment strategy to improve his chances of victory—paradoxically, by limiting his own options.

In the early sixteenth century, the Spanish conquistador Hernán Cortés arrived on the coast of Mexico intending to claim the land for the king of Spain. The land was held by the powerful Aztec empire, a formidable fighting force. Figure 9-9 shows a decision tree for this game. Each opponent can choose to advance or retreat, and the Aztecs—deciding how to respond to Cortés's arrival—get the first move:

- If the Aztecs retreat, they know that Cortés will advance and take their land.
- If the Aztecs advance, then Cortés will have two choices: retreat and survive, or advance and fight to the death.

No matter how brave and committed Cortés claims his soldiers to be, the Aztecs expect that if the Spanish soldiers are faced with the prospect of a fight to the death, they would rather retreat to the safety of their boats. So the Aztecs will decide to advance. If both players behave rationally, the result of this game will be that Cortés retreats.

Anticipating the Aztecs' calculations, Cortés makes a drastic move, though: He burns his own ships, cutting off any possibility of retreat by fearful soldiers. Figure 9-10 shows how this bold move changes the decision tree. Under the new scenario, the Aztecs now know that if they attack, Cortés will have no choice but to fight to the death. The Aztecs decide *they* would prefer to retreat and live rather than to advance and risk death.

By committing to reduce his options, Cortés forces a change in his opponents' strategy. That commitment results in a payoff that would otherwise be out of reach for Cortés. This famous

FIGURE 9-9

Decision tree for Cortés and the Aztecs

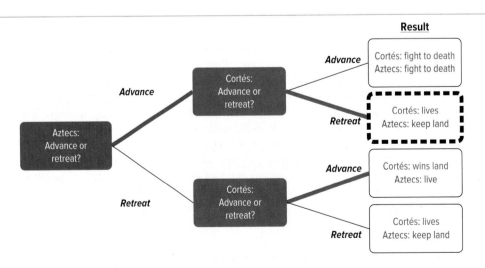

The Aztecs know that if they retreat, Cortés will advance and take their land. But if they advance, they can guess that Cortés will rather retreat and keep his troops alive. Knowing this, the Aztecs will advance to protect their land, expecting Cortés to retreat.

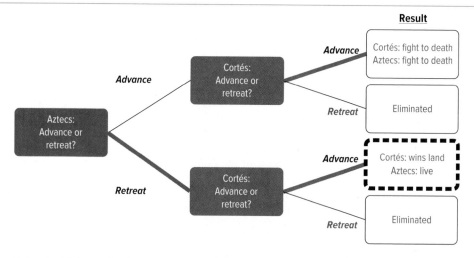

FIGURE 9-10
**Decision tree with
burning boats**

By burning his boats, Cortés removes the possibility of retreat. The Aztecs know that whatever they do, the Spanish troops have no option but to advance. Given this knowledge, the Aztecs prefer to retreat and cede their land to Cortés rather than fight to the death.

historical example of a commitment strategy is sometimes referred to as "burning your boats." For other applications of commitment strategies, see the Real Life box "Dr. Strangelove, or how we learned to love the commitment device."

Real Life

Dr. Strangelove, or how we learned to love the commitment device

Consider the game of "chicken," in which two car drivers head directly toward each other at great speed. If neither swerves, they will have a head-on collision. But that requires nerves of steel, to say the least. Usually, one person loses his courage and swerves out of the way of the other car, losing the game and becoming the "chicken." Clearly, this is a game in which one slight strategic miscalculation—both waiting one beat too long to swerve—could lead to things going very wrong indeed.

The game of chicken has been used to understand why, during the Cold War, the United States and the Soviet Union built up huge stockpiles of nuclear weapons. Their strategy, sometimes referred to as mutually assured destruction, was for each to amass enough deadly warheads to destroy the other. Military and political strategists assumed that if one country attacked, the other would counterattack with even greater force. This would end up being mutually suicidal, like a head-on car crash on a global scale. Given this threat of mutual destruction, the strategists reasoned, neither country would risk an attack on the other, no matter how bad relations got between them. This is very much like both drivers being certain that when the collision is imminent, the *other* driver is sure to swerve. Many people living during the Cold War did not find this logic reassuring.

How do you win a game of chicken? You could take a lesson from Cortés, the Spanish general who burned his boats after landing in Mexico. By throwing your steering wheel out of the window in full view of the other driver, you are signaling your commitment to the strategy of continuing to drive in a straight line. The other player now knows you will not back down, and so faces the choice of losing by swerving or causing a head-on collision.

(continued)

Such a commitment strategy in a nuclear context was comically dramatized in the classic 1964 movie *Dr. Strangelove,* which imagined the Soviet Union building a "doomsday" device. This device would automatically launch an all-out attack on the United States if any nuclear warhead exploded on Soviet territory. The United States would then know for certain that the Soviets would destroy the world if attacked, which in theory should guarantee that the Soviets would never be attacked. If you have seen the movie, you will know that the story ends with the world engulfed in mushroom clouds. In the end, the doomsday device assured, rather than prevented, mutual destruction.

In real life, nobody has yet invented a doomsday device, and the fear of nuclear war has receded since the Cold War. But a legacy of the Cold War is that there are still more than enough nuclear warheads in existence to destroy the world many times over. The major nuclear powers have struggled to come to an agreement that would reduce their nuclear stockpiles. That means there is always the possibility of a new arms race—and another game of nuclear chicken.

Source: http://www.thenation.com/article/dr-strangelove.

✓CONCEPT CHECK

☐ How can backward induction help you decide what courses to take next semester? **[LO 9.7]**

☐ Why does the possibility of Burger King's entry into the same town change McDonald's strategy? **[LO 9.8]**

☐ Why would Burger King have been better off if it had been the first chain to build a restaurant in the town? **[LO 9.9]**

☐ How can reducing your choices lead to a better outcome in a sequential game? **[LO 9.10]**

☐ Why does repeated play dilute the first-mover advantage in a bargaining game? **[LO 9.11]**

Conclusion

This chapter introduced the concept of strategic games. Many real-life situations can be analyzed as if they were strategic games, with associated rules, strategies, and potential payoffs.

Game theory can explain the logic behind outcomes that might not seem intuitive at first. Sometimes, for example, both players in a simultaneous game may choose to behave in a way that makes both worse off. When games are played in turns rather than simultaneously, the first mover's decision can dictate the outcome of the entire game. With repeated play, however, the first mover's advantage weakens. Players who can communicate with each other and agree on a strategy can often secure a better outcome than if they acted alone. Such agreements may break down if one side tries to get ahead by defecting.

Backward induction is another useful analytical tool; it allows you to break down your decisions and predict how they will affect others' decisions and shape the final payoff.

When trying to solve a real-life problem, whether societal, personal, or business, it helps to think through these strategic issues. Doing so can help you see how to "play" the game given the rules and constraints. It also can help you see how to *change* the rules and constraints, if possible, to help get to a better outcome.

Much of the analysis in this chapter involved one player guessing what the other will do and acting accordingly. In the next chapter, we'll see that knowing what one player is planning to do isn't always easy, and that a lack of information can have real economic consequences.

Key Terms

Summary

LO 9.1 Understand strategic behavior and describe the components of a strategic game.

If people make the necessary choices to achieve a goal by anticipating the interaction between their own and others' decisions, we say they are *behaving strategically.* Economists use the term *game* to describe a situation that requires those involved to think strategically. Games have *rules,* which define the actions players are allowed to take; *strategies,* or plans of action that players can follow to achieve a desired goal; and *payoffs,* the rewards that come from taking particular actions.

LO 9.2 Explain why noncooperation is always the outcome in the prisoners' dilemma.

The *prisoners' dilemma* is a situation in which two people can find cooperation difficult even when it is mutually beneficial. Each player has a choice to cooperate or not to cooperate. Each prefers mutual cooperation to mutual noncooperation, but noncooperation is the best choice because its payoff is higher no matter what strategy other players choose. In this game, pursuing your own self-interest leaves everyone worse off.

LO 9.3 Identify whether or not a player has a dominant strategy in a one-time game.

When a strategy is the best one to follow no matter what strategy other players choose, it is called a *dominant strategy.* We saw this intuitively worked through in the previous section. However, not all games feature a dominant strategy; in some games there is no single strategy that will work best for you.

LO 9.4 Identify whether or not a Nash equilibrium will be reached in a one-time game.

When all players choose the best strategy they can, given the choices of all other players, those players have reached a *Nash equilibrium.* Players who have reached a Nash equilibrium have no reason to regret their own

decision. This doesn't necessarily mean that an equilibrium outcome to a game is a good one; we can see both negative-negative and positive-positive outcomes in equilibrium. The only condition is that there is no incentive to switch from one decision to another.

LO 9.5 Explain how a commitment strategy can be used to achieve cooperation in a one-time game.

In the prisoners' dilemma, the players of the game would be better off if they could cooperate and make a deal beforehand not to confess. However, even if you know your accomplice will not confess, you are still better off confessing. To solve this problem, players may sometimes reach a mutually beneficial equilibrium by pursuing a *commitment strategy,* in which they agree to submit to a penalty if they defect from the equilibrium.

LO 9.6 Explain how repeated play can enable cooperation.

In a *repeated game,* players can penalize each other for defecting in one round by punishing each other in the next round. As a result, players can sometimes achieve a mutually beneficial equilibrium, even when they couldn't do so in a single game.

A common strategy in repeated games is *tit-for-tat,* in which a player takes the same action as his or her opponent in the previous round. Anyone who is playing against a person with a tit-for-tat strategy has a strong incentive to cooperate because defecting would push him or her into a less profitable equilibrium in every future round of the game.

LO 9.7 Explain how backward induction can be used to make decisions.

Backward induction is the process of analyzing a problem in reverse—starting with the last choice, then the second-to-last choice, and so on—in order to determine an optimal strategy. This problem-solving tool can be used to choose between options with different consequences down the road: You first choose the goal you are trying to reach and then determine the steps you must take to reach it.

LO 9.8 Use a decision tree to solve a sequential game.

In many situations, one person or company must make a decision before the other one. These situations can be represented as games in which players move sequentially rather than simultaneously. Because the payoff each achieves still depends on the other's decision, the player who moves first must anticipate the decision the next player will make in response. These decisions can be diagrammed as the nodes in a *decision tree,* which branch off into the choices or payoffs that follow from each option. Backward induction can be used to analyze decision trees and determine the best course of action at each stage of the game.

LO 9.9 Define first-mover advantage and identify it in practice.

In a game with *first-mover advantage,* the player who moves first gets a higher payoff than those who follow. The ultimate example of a first-mover advantage is a one-round bargaining game in which the person who makes the first offer gets virtually everything. The ability to bargain over multiple rounds of offers and counteroffers dilutes the first-mover advantage.

LO 9.10 Explain why patient players have more bargaining power in repeated games.

The ability to make counteroffers transforms bargaining from a game in which first-mover advantage trumps everything into a game of patience. Because bargaining takes time, in every round of bargaining that takes place before the players reach agreement, the value of the payoff they are splitting goes down. Thus, the more-patient player (the one who places more value on money in the future relative to money in the present) has an advantage over the less-patient player. In the end, the surplus will be divided in proportion to the patience of each player.

LO 9.11 Explain how a commitment strategy can allow players to achieve their goals by limiting their options.

In a sequential game, limiting your own choices can change your opponent's behavior. For example, following a commitment strategy, such as cutting off the option for retreat, turns a noncredible threat into a credible one, changing the payoffs associated with an opponent's options.

Review Questions

1. Taking an exam can be considered a game. Describe a rule, a strategy, and payoff for this game. **[LO 9.1]**

2. Why is strategic behavior required to win a presidential election? Describe some of the rules, strategies, and payoffs that define this game in the real world. **[LO 9.1]**

3. Felix and Sam are roommates. They both want the dishes to be washed, but each would prefer that the other person do it. Use the decision matrix in Figure 9Q-1 to explain why Felix and Sam are likely to end up with a sink full of dirty dishes. Their preferences are ranked from 1 (lowest) to 4 (highest). **[LO 9.2]**

4. Two neighbors share a pond they have stocked with catfish. They have agreed upon the amount of fishing each can do in order for the stock of catfish to replenish itself. If one neighbor increases the amount he fishes a little bit, the catfish stock could still replenish itself. If both neighbors increase their fishing, the stock will not be sustainable. Both neighbors would like to cheat and increase the amount they fish but want the other neighbor to stick to the agreement. **[LO 9.2]**

   a. What is the noncooperative outcome, and why does it occur?

   b. What is the cooperative outcome, and how could the neighbors achieve this outcome?

5. You have been texting with your friends trying to make plans for this evening. Your best friend Jocelyn is not sure if she will finish her homework in time to come out, but if she does, she wants to go to a new restaurant on the north end of town that you've both been wanting to try. Another group of friends is going to a restaurant on the south end of town, but you've already been to this restaurant and it was only okay. No one is returning your calls, but you need to get on the subway and head into

FIGURE 9Q-1

town if you want to do anything this evening. You have to decide whether to head north or south. Do you have a dominant strategy? Explain why or why not. **[LO 9.3]**

6. You have just played rock, paper, scissors with your friend. You chose scissors and he chose paper, so you won. Is this a Nash equilibrium? Explain why or why not. **[LO 9.4]**

7. Two firms each have the option of polluting during production or cleaning up their production process such that they don't pollute. Of course, polluting is cheaper than not polluting. The payoffs for each of the choice combinations are shown in the decision matrix in Figure 9Q-2. The government would like to stop pollution by making it illegal and charging a fine if a firm is found polluting. How large does the fine need to be to keep a firm from polluting? **[LO 9.5]**

8. Explain how you could use a tit-for-tat strategy to motivate your roommate to do his share of the cleaning. **[LO 9.6]**

9. Toni and Kala are new coworkers. They make a plan to go out together every Thursday night. On their first Thursday night out, Toni buys a pitcher of beer and shares it with Kala. Kala is excited to discover that her Thursday night outings will include free beer as well as a way to have fun with her new coworker. Explain why Kala is likely to be disappointed. **[LO 9.6]**

10. Suppose your goal is to be promoted at your job. Use backward induction to determine what you should do to work toward that goal right now, and describe each step in your logic. **[LO 9.7]**

11. You are playing a game with a friend. It's your move, but you don't have a dominant strategy. Your payoff depends on what your friend does *after* your move. You consider flipping a coin to decide what to do. You are about to reach for a coin, but then you realize that your friend has a dominant strategy. Explain how using backward induction (rather than a coin toss) will now determine your next move. **[LO 9.7]**

12. Melissa let Jill cheat off of her during a history exam last week. Now Melissa is threatening to tell on Jill unless Jill pays her $50. Use the decision tree in Figure 9Q-3 to explain whether Jill will pay Melissa to keep her quiet. **[LO 9.8]**

13. Nicolas has asked for a raise. His boss must decide whether to approve his request. If Nicolas doesn't get the raise, he will have to decide whether to stay at his job or quit. Construct a decision tree for these sequential decisions and choose a payoff structure where Nicolas has a dominant strategy to stay at his job even without getting the raise. **[LO 9.8]**

14. Job offers could be considered a one-round bargaining game with a first-mover advantage: The company offers you a job at a certain salary, and you can take it or leave it. Explain why the company might not capture all the surplus in this game, even if you can't make a counteroffer. **[LO 9.9]**

15. Muriel likes her job, but her boss gives lousy bonuses. Muriel was recently offered a new job with better rewards, and her friend wants to know if she intends to take it. "It depends on whether the bonus this year is generous. Let's wait and see. We'll find out next week." Explain why Muriel is likely to be accepting the new job. How could she improve her strategy if she wants to stay at her current job and be better rewarded? **[LO 9.9]**

16. Suppose you are moving out of the country and need to sell your car fast. Explain why you are likely to get lower offers from used-car dealers if they find out that you are moving away soon. **[LO 9.10]**

17. Hal is negotiating his salary for a job offer. Hal's potential employer moves first by making an offer. Hal knows he will accept the offer but asks for a couple of weeks to

FIGURE 9Q-2

	Firm B	
	Pollute	**Don't Pollute**
Firm A — Pollute	$75,000 / $75,000	$25,000 / $90,000
Firm A — Don't Pollute	$90,000 / $25,000	$25,000 / $25,000

FIGURE 9Q-3

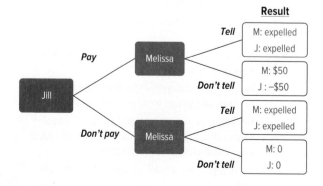

FIGURE 9Q-4

	Gas Station B	
	Lower price	**Higher price**
Gas Station A / **Lower price**	$35,000 \ $35,000	$65,000 \ $125,000
Gas Station A / **Higher price**	$125,000 \ $65,000	$95,000 \ $95,000

FIGURE 9P-1

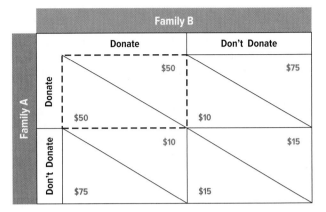

think it over. If the offer was acceptable to Hal, why did he do this? **[LO 9.10]**

18. Many warrior cultures have codes of conduct that make retreat from battle and other cowardly behaviors extremely dishonorable. Warriors are expected to die bravely in battle rather than surrender; if they do retreat, they face an enormous social stigma. Paradoxically, these codes could help warriors to win their battles. Explain. **[LO 9.11]**

19. A town's two gas stations are each considering lowering prices to attract more sales. How this affects the profits for each gas station depends on whether the other station also lowers prices. The decision matrix in Figure 9Q-4 shows the payoffs, depending on what each player decides to do.

    Suppose both gas stations lower their prices, and they find themselves in the worst-case scenario in which both have also lowered their profits. Now suppose gas station A announces in an advertisement that it is committed to keeping the new low prices. Why would gas station A do this? What outcome would you expect? **[LO 9.11]**

Problems and Applications

1. Say whether each of the following is a rule, a strategy, or a payoff. **[LO 9.1]**
   a. In chess, when you capture your opponent's king, you win the game.
   b. In Monopoly, players frequently mortgage their existing properties to raise cash to buy new ones.
   c. In chess, the rook piece can move any number of spaces directly forward, backward, or to either side, but it cannot move diagonally.
   d. In rock-paper-scissors, you might always play rock.

2. Sharon is going to an auction. Say whether each of the following is a rule, a strategy, or a payoff. **[LO 9.1]**
   a. Bids must increase in increments of $20.
   b. The highest bid wins the item being auctioned.
   c. Sharon waits until the bidding is just about to close before she enters a bid.
   d. The money raised from the auction goes to charity.

3. Two families are trying to decide whether to donate to a fund to build a public park. The payoffs are shown in Figure 9P-1. **[LO 9.2]**
   a. What is the mutually beneficial outcome?
   b. Acting in their best interests, what strategy will each family choose?
   c. Explain why this game is or is not an example of a prisoners' dilemma.

4. In Figure 9P-2, what is the dominant strategy for Player A? What is the dominant strategy for Player B? **[LO 9.3]**

FIGURE 9P-2

	Player B	
	Strategy 1	**Strategy 2**
Player A / **Strategy 1**	−2 \ −2	−3 \ 1
Player A / **Strategy 2**	1 \ −3	0 \ 0

FIGURE 9P-3

		Gas Station B	
		Lower price	**Higher price**
Gas Station A — Higher price	$35,000 \ $35,000		$65,000 \ $125,000
Gas Station A — Lower price	$125,000 \ $65,000		$95,000 \ $95,000

5. A town's two gas stations are each considering lowering prices to attract more sales. How this affects the profits for each gas station depends on whether the other also lowers prices. The decision matrix in Figure 9P-3 shows the payoffs, depending on what each player decides to do. Identify any Nash equilibria. **[LO 9.4]**

6. Consider again the two families trying to decide whether to donate to a fund to build a public park. The payoffs are shown in Figure 9P-1. **[LO 9.4, LO 9.5]**

   a. What is the Nash equilibrium?

   b. Suppose Family A agrees to match the donation of Family B. Under these new circumstances, what strategy will each family choose?

7. In which of the following situations, *a* or *b,* is a tit-for-tat strategy more likely to be successful at maintaining cooperation? **[LO 9.6]**

   a. An agreement of mutual support between players on a reality television show, in which the relatively worst-off player is eliminated every episode.

   b. A peace treaty between neighboring countries.

8. Which of the following are examples of tit-for-tat strategies? **[LO 9.6]**

   a. A friend forgets to send you a birthday card this year, so you decide not to send one to her on her next birthday.

   b. Your friend let you borrow her class notes last week, so you decide to skip class again this week.

   c. You and your roommate take turns buying toilet paper, milk, and other shared items.

   d. Your book club chooses a book you don't want to read, so you decide not to go this month.

9. Using backward induction in Figure 9P-4, decide which classes a hypothetical college student should take her freshman and sophomore years, assuming that she wants to be an economics major. **[LO 9.7]**

FIGURE 9P-4

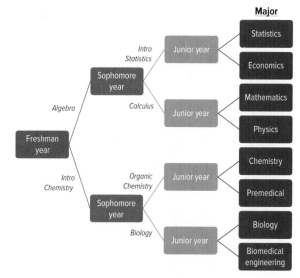

10. You need to travel from Minneapolis to Copenhagen; it's now Tuesday morning. You know you need to arrive in Copenhagen no later than 4 p.m. on Wednesday. Using backward induction in Table 9P-1, choose your travel itinerary. Enter the flight numbers for each leg of your trip. **[LO 9.7]**

TABLE 9P-1

Flight Number	Departure	Arrival
13	Minneapolis 5:45pm	Chicago 7:15pm
456	Minneapolis 7:00pm	Chicago 8:35pm
1252	Minneapolis 3:45pm	New York 6:15pm
368	Minneapolis 5:50pm	New York 8:20pm
8120	Chicago 5:20pm	London 7:30am
905	Chicago 6:00pm	London 8:05am
1644	Chicago 7:10pm	London 9:45am
2004	New York 8:05pm	London 9:30am
1968	New York 10:30pm	London 11:45am
44	New York 11:10pm	London 12:30pm
952	London 9:00am	Copenhagen 11:55am
803	London 11:15am	Copenhagen 2:25pm
15	London 1:45pm	Copenhagen 4:55pm
681	London 3:05pm	Copenhagen 6:00pm

FIGURE 9P-5

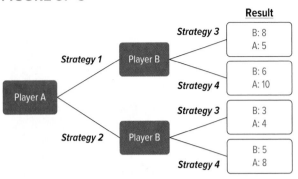

FIGURE 9P-7

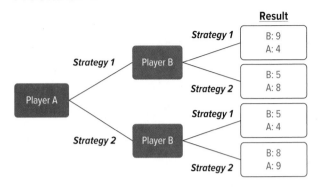

11. In the sequential game shown in Figure 9P-5, what choice should Player A make now to achieve the highest payoff at the end of the game? **[LO 9.8]**

12. Company A is considering whether to invest in infrastructure that will allow it to expand into a new market. Company B is considering whether to enter the market. Assume the companies know each other's payoffs. Using Figure 9P-6, choose the outcome that will occur from the list below. **[LO 9.8]**

    a. A invest, B enter.

    b. A invest, B don't enter.

    c. A don't invest, B enter.

    d. A don't invest, B don't enter.

13. In the sequential game shown in Figure 9P-7, does Player A have a first-mover advantage? **[LO 9.9]**

14. Which of the following are examples of first-mover advantage? **[LO 9.9]**

    a. You make an offer on a house. The seller can only accept or reject the offer.

    b. You and your roommate are dividing chores. The chores are written on slips of paper and drawn from a hat. You get to draw first.

    c. You are first in line to buy a raffle ticket.

    d. You can take vacation whenever you like, as long as no other employees are also scheduled to take vacation. You submit your vacation requests first this year.

15. Which player is likely to have higher bargaining power: a city government responding to angry citizens' demands that the trash be collected regularly or the sanitation workers' union? Explain your answer. **[LO 9.10]**

16. Which player is likely to have higher bargaining power: a large, established company shopping around for a new parts supplier or a start-up company trying to sell its parts? Explain your answer. **[LO 9.10]**

17. Figure 9P-8 shows a sequential game in which one player decides whether to injure another player. The injured player can then choose whether to sue, which involves costly legal fees. **[LO 9.11]**

    a. What is the predicted outcome in this "game"?

    b. The injured party threatens to always sue when injured. Is this a credible threat? What is the predicted outcome if the injured party has threatened to always sue when injured?

    c. What is the predicted outcome if the injured party has made a binding commitment to always sue when injured?

FIGURE 9P-6

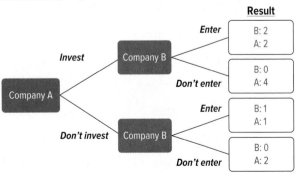

FIGURE 9P-8

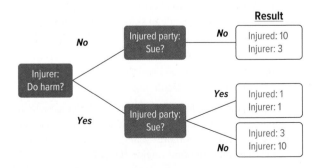

18. Two companies are considering whether to enter a new market. The decision matrix in Figure 9P-9 shows each company's payoff, depending on whether one, both, or neither enters the market. Company A is in Costa Rica. Company B is in Nicaragua. **[LO 9.11]**

    a. If company A enters, what should company B do?

    b. If company B enters, what should company A do?

    c. Suppose the Nicaraguan government releases a press statement that it will cover any profit losses for Company B. How much will this policy cost the Nicaraguan government?

FIGURE 9P-9

	Company B (Nicaragua)	
	Enter	**Not Enter**
Company A (Costa Rica) — **Enter**	−$3M / −$1M	$2M / $0
Company A (Costa Rica) — **Not Enter**	$0 / $3M	$0 / $0

Information

A SOLUTION FOR STUDENT LOANS?

In the 1970s, administrators at Yale University thought they had come up with a student loan program that solved many of the problems faced by students trying to pay for an education. Here's how it worked: Students could choose to join a plan through which, instead of paying back individual loans, they would owe a small percentage of their income every year after graduation. They would stop owing payments when the debt for their *entire graduating class* was paid off.

The idea was to help students who wanted to go into public-service careers afford to do so. The university realized that these students had a harder time paying off individual loans than did students who went into better-paying careers. Under their new plan, graduates with low incomes would pay only a small amount; those with higher incomes would make up the difference. University administrators figured that every class would have some captains of industry and some social workers, teachers, nonprofit staff, writers, and artists. By pooling everyone's debt, things would even out. The investment bankers and corporate lawyers would hardly miss the extra money they had to pay; teachers and artists would benefit tremendously from their lower monthly payments.

Good idea? If you said yes, you wouldn't be the only one to think so. The plan was supported by Yale economist James Tobin, who subsequently won a Nobel Prize. It drew on an idea put forward earlier by Milton Friedman, a University of Chicago economist (and another Nobel winner). Unfortunately, almost 30 years later, not a single graduating class had succeeded in paying off its collective debt. The program was deemed a total flop, and the university was pressured into canceling much of the debt.

Mandel Ngan/AFP/Getty Images

What went wrong? There were two problems. The first was that the program was optional: Students could choose to opt out and pay off their debt individually in the usual way. Administrators had assumed that a representative cross-section of students would want to participate in the program. They overlooked the fact that many students have a fairly good sense of whether their incomes after college are likely to be high or low. Those who are drawn to banking or medicine can expect to earn a lot of money; those called to teaching or preaching can expect to earn less. To a student expecting to earn a low income, the program looked like a great deal—pay only what you can afford. For a student expecting a higher income, the prospect wasn't so attractive: She'd likely end up paying off not only her own loan, but also those of her less-wealthy peers. Not surprisingly, then, many students who anticipated a higher income chose *not* to join the program. The planned pooling of big and small contributions did not take place.

As if this wasn't bad enough, a second problem soon became apparent: The university could not automatically collect payments from alumni's paychecks. It had to rely on program participants to feel so good about their alma mater that they would willingly report their income and pay what they owed. You may not be surprised to hear that this did not work out so well. Not all participants held up their end of the deal. The university had to try to hunt down its alumni, find out how much money they had made, and force them to pay. It was not well-equipped to do this.

These two problems have a common theme—an imbalance of information. When students were deciding whether to join the program, they knew how likely it was that they would become investment bankers, but the university didn't. (Even if the university had known about students' career intentions, that wouldn't have forced the future investment bankers to participate. Alarm bells might have rung had the university noticed that the program was disproportionately packed with education and art majors, but no finance majors.) Then, as the program participants graduated and started work, the university couldn't know how much they were earning and if they were underpaying on what they owed. The problems caused by the missing information weren't just flukes or the result of lax enforcement; they were inherent in the program's design.

234

Up to this point in the book, we have mostly assumed that economic decision makers are fully informed when they make decisions. We will see in this chapter that imbalances in information can cause problems in all kinds of transactions—between lenders and borrowers, buyers and sellers, and employers and employees. We'll see that when the parties to a deal have access to different information, markets are often inefficient; sometimes they even fall apart entirely. We'll also explore some ways that people try to find out or share information that isn't immediately observable, so they can make better decisions in the face of limited information.

Information: Knowledge Is Power

Do you want to buy a fabulous MP3 player? Only $20! A fantastic bargain! Now that you've given us $20, we regret to inform you that the player holds only 10 songs. Also, it's broken. Sorry about that. And no, you can't have your money back.

Up to now, when we have asked questions like, "How much would you be willing to pay for an MP3 player?" we have assumed that you know exactly what you will be getting for your money. In general, to make rational economic choices, people need to know what they are choosing between. When people are fully informed about the choices that they and other relevant economic actors face, we say they have **complete information**.

Unfortunately, people rarely have perfectly complete information. Often, they have *good enough* information to make acceptable choices. But in many cases, people are truly underinformed in ways that matter. You've probably seen people around you make decisions about which they were underinformed—decisions they later came to regret. Maybe they bought products that proved to be shoddy, lent money to an acquaintance who turned out to be a deadbeat, or moved to a new apartment with terrible plumbing or a leaky roof.

Of course, some choices are genuinely risky. When you invest in stocks or real estate, you can't have perfectly complete information about how your investment will perform. Despite this, markets can still work well. For example, let's say you are buying annual insurance against the possibility of flood damage to your house. Neither you nor the insurance company can have perfect information about exactly how much heavy rainfall there is likely to be in the next 12 months, but there still can be a market for flood insurance that works well enough for both you and the insurance company. In this chapter, we distinguish decisions that involve risk-taking from situations in which some people have better information than others and can use it to their advantage.

> **complete information**
> state of being fully informed about the choices that relevant economic actors face

Information asymmetry

LO 10.1 Explain why information asymmetry matters for economic decision making.

Problems are likely to arise when one person knows more than another, a situation that is called **information asymmetry**. Let's consider the example of taking your car to a mechanic. The mechanic knows a great deal about the condition of your car, whereas you probably know very little. He could tell you that the entire brake system needs to be replaced, and you'd probably pay for it without ever knowing if he was telling the truth.

To see why such information asymmetries create problems, consider *the wants and constraints of those involved:*

- You want your car fixed at the lowest possible price. You are constrained by your ignorance of exactly how your car functions or why it broke down.

> **information asymmetry**
> a condition in which one participant in a transaction knows more than another participant

- The mechanic wants to make as much money as possible. He is constrained only by his moral scruples and concern about possible damage to his reputation and his business if he turns out to have underestimated your knowledge of the workings of brake systems.

When one person knows much more than the other, that person can achieve what he wants at the other's expense—in this case, the mechanic may succeed in making more money by charging you for repairs that your car doesn't really require.

Note that this is a problem only because your wants (spend as little as possible) are opposed to the mechanic's (charge as much as possible). If both parties' incentives are *aligned,* then the information asymmetry doesn't matter. If a mechanically minded friend is fixing your car as a favor, you both want the repair to cost as little as possible. It doesn't matter that you know less than your friend about cars.

Here, we'll discuss two important types of information asymmetry—*adverse selection* and *moral hazard.* These asymmetries are common problems for the insurance industry, and we will see that they plague other markets, too.

Adverse selection and the lemons problem

LO 10.2 Explain how adverse selection is caused by asymmetric information.

As we saw in the chapter-opening example of the student loan program at Yale, rational, utility-maximizing people choose to take part in transactions from which they expect to benefit; likewise, they choose not to take part in transactions from which they do not expect to benefit.

When there are particular types of information asymmetries, the problem of *adverse selection* can result. **Adverse selection** occurs when buyers and sellers have different information about the quality of a good or the riskiness of a situation, and this asymmetric information results in failure to complete transactions that would have been possible if both sides had the same information. In Yale's student loan program, only the students who will have trouble paying off their loans (the "adverse" types) will opt into the program. But because only the bad types opt in, the loans don't get paid off.

One well-known example of adverse selection is the "lemons" problem in the used-car market. A lemon is a car that breaks down again and again. There is information asymmetry in the used-car market because sellers of used cars know a lot more about the true characteristics of their cars than potential buyers do. A test drive won't necessarily reveal how long the car will run before it breaks down. Buyers of used cars are well aware that they are on the wrong end of this asymmetry: They are always suspicious that a used car could be a lemon. They won't pay as much for a lemon as they would if they could be certain the car was in perfect shape. That means sellers of used cars that *are* in perfect shape will be underpaid.

Meanwhile, sellers of lemons will still be paid more than their cars are worth. To see why this is true, suppose the used-car market consists of just two types of cars: lemons and high-quality cars (we'll call them "plums"). If buyers could tell which is which, they would establish one price for plums and another, lower price for lemons. But if buyers can't differentiate between plums and lemons, they will have to offer an average price that reflects the likelihood of getting one or the other. That price will be lower than they'd pay for a guaranteed plum (because there is a chance they might get a lemon); it will be higher than they'd pay for a guaranteed lemon (because there is a chance they might get a plum).

If you know the car you own is a lemon, you'll be attracted by the prospect of selling it at a high price. But if you know the car you own is a plum, you won't want to sell for less than it's worth. Sellers of lemons will be willing market participants; sellers of plums will be less willing. Over time, the result will be more lemons and fewer plums on the market. As buyers start to notice they are increasingly likely to get a lemon, they will offer even lower prices, making it even less attractive for plum sellers to enter the market. A vicious cycle ensues, in which the

adverse selection
a state that occurs when buyers and sellers have different information about the quality of a good or the riskiness of a situation, and this asymmetric information results in failure to complete transactions that would have been possible if both sides had the same information.

selection of cars on the market becomes more and more adverse from the buyer's perspective. This explains why a barely used car that works perfectly is worth a lot less than exactly the same car offered new at a dealership—the buyer of the slightly used car doesn't know whether or not to trust the seller.

Another common example of adverse selection occurs in insurance markets because of the information asymmetry between insurance companies and their customers. At any given price, drivers who know they are careless will be more eager than careful drivers to buy auto insurance; they know they will be more likely to make claims. The selection of customers is adverse from the insurance company's perspective.

To see how this problem might play out in a similar way to the lemons problem, ask, *How does the insurance company respond to this situation?* The company sets premiums according to the average risk of policyholders; as more risky drivers take out insurance, the average risk increases and so must the premiums. In turn, consumers who know they are careful drivers will respond to higher premiums by becoming even less interested in buying insurance. The average risk goes up again, so premiums must go up again: Just as in the lemons example, there is a vicious cycle. (As we'll explain later in the chapter, there is a solution to the adverse-selection problem in car insurance: mandated participation.)

Even in a best-case scenario, adverse selection reduces the efficiency of markets because some transactions that would make both sides better off fail to take place, and surplus is lost. To see why, suppose I would be willing to accept $8,000 for my used car, which I know is a plum (a good car), and you would be willing to pay $10,000 for a *guaranteed* plum. If you could be certain that my car was a plum, we could agree to trade for $9,000; each of us would enjoy $1,000 worth of surplus. But because you face the risk that my car is a lemon (a bad car), you are understandably not willing to pay $9,000. What if the car turns out to be worth only $5,000? You would have paid $4,000 too much. Given the possibility that the car might be either a plum or a lemon, you might be willing to pay only $7,000 for the used car. At that price, the deal does not take place, and we both lose out.

In a worst-case scenario, the vicious cycle caused by adverse selection can cause markets to fall apart entirely (i.e., create a market failure). That's what happened with the student loan–pooling program in the chapter-opening example. In our used-car example, it would be profitable for owners of lemons to sell their cars at a price of $7,000, but it would not be profitable for owners of plums to sell their cars for $7,000. Thus, owners of plums would not be willing to sell their used cars. The used-car market in that price range would be comprised of only lemons.

You might be wondering: If adverse selection is such a problem with used cars, then how does the used-car market continue to exist? As we will discuss later, there are some solutions to mitigate adverse selection. In the case of used cars, companies such as Carfax provide potential buyers with much more information about a used car than they could obtain on their own. This decreases the degree of information asymmetry, reduces adverse selection, and enables the market to exist.

Principal–agent problems and moral hazard

LO 10.3 Explain how moral hazard is caused by asymmetric information.

Information asymmetries can also cause problems *after* selection has occurred and the two parties have entered into an agreement. This type of problem often arises when one person entrusts a task to another person. In what is called a *principal–agent problem,* a person called a **principal** entrusts someone else, called the **agent**, with a task.

The most basic example of a principal–agent problem caused by asymmetric information is the relationship between an employer (the principal) and an employee (the agent). The asymmetry exists because each employee knows how hard he or she works, but the employer does not.

principal
a person who entrusts someone with a task

agent
a person who carries out a task on someone else's behalf

Because the principal usually cannot monitor what the agent is doing all the time, the agent may be tempted to put less effort into the task than the principal would want.

In short, employees have an incentive to slack off when the boss isn't watching. Why not play games online or take a few extra coffee breaks, if no one is any the wiser? The tendency for people to behave in a riskier way or to renege on contracts when they do not face the full consequences of their actions is called **moral hazard**. With moral hazard, people engage in behavior that is considered undesirable by the person who bears the cost of the behavior.

Moral hazard can be avoided by correcting the information asymmetry through better monitoring. If the boss were able to see how much effort employees were really putting in, she could adjust their incentives to maintain steady effort. What would happen if you were inclined to play games online at work but knew someone was closely monitoring your workplace computer activity, and your wages could be docked or you could lose your job if you were caught? That knowledge would probably increase your workplace productivity significantly.

It is not always possible to correct such an information asymmetry, however. Not all types of jobs allow bosses to monitor employees closely enough to avoid moral hazard. The same is true of insurance markets, in which moral hazard is a common problem. For instance, if your car is insured against theft, you might not be as careful to park in a safe place and double-check that the door is locked; you know the insurance company would cover almost all of the cost if the car were stolen. Ironically, then, having insurance against car theft may actually make it more likely that a car will be stolen, driving up the cost to the insurance company. There is no way your insurance company can monitor where you tend to park and how careful you are about locking your doors.

There are sometimes other ingenious ways insurance companies can avoid moral hazard, such as the crop insurance described in the Real Life box "The weather can't cheat."

moral hazard
the tendency for people to behave in a riskier way or to renege on contracts when they do not face the full consequences of their actions

Real Life

The weather can't cheat

Hanumanthu, a 36-year-old farmer, lived with his mother, wife, and two children in Anantapur, India. Like a third of the world's population, they depended on agriculture for a living, growing their own crops on a small plot of land.

The year 2009 was a bad one for Hanumanthu and his family. When a prolonged drought caused their crops to fail, they did not have savings to fall back on. Hanumanthu had to borrow from the village moneylender just to cover the cost of food. As his debt grew bigger and bigger, the moneylender began harassing him to repay the loan.

This whole situation could have been helped if farmers like Hanumanthu had insurance. Their livelihoods are certainly risky; even one bad harvest can be devastating. In early attempts to offer insurance to farmers, insurers compensated farmers for low crop yields. If a farmer's fields yielded less than a certain amount of food, the insurance company would reimburse him for the difference.

This system turned out to be prone to moral hazard. Because farmers knew they could get money if their crops failed, they had less incentive to invest time and effort in farming. They might be less diligent in weeding or might skimp on expensive fertilizer. Insurers had no way to monitor the farmers to make sure they were putting in the required effort. As a result, agricultural losses actually increased with the introduction of insurance, and so did insurers' costs.

More recently, insurers have been trying a new idea: They are selling insurance that protects farmers against low rainfall levels, rather than low crop yields. The advantage of such an approach is that farmers can't control the rainfall. As long as rainfall patterns are highly correlated with crop yields, insurance will offer them protection against crop failures that are truly accidental. Insurers will not be stuck with the bill if a farmer's crop fails simply because he didn't weed or plant on time.

With rainfall insurance, farmers become less vulnerable, but they still have an incentive to invest time and effort in their fields and maximize their productivity, avoiding the pitfalls of moral hazard.

Source: E-Pao, http://www.e-pao.net/GP.asp?src=6..171109.nov09.

Moral hazard and adverse selection—avoiding confusion

Sometimes people confuse adverse selection with moral hazard because they often occur together. Careless drivers are more likely to buy auto insurance voluntarily (adverse selection); drivers with auto insurance may be more likely to be careless (moral hazard). To clarify, remember that:

- Adverse selection relates to *unobserved characteristics* of people or goods. It occurs *before* the parties have entered into an agreement.
- Moral hazard is about *actions* and occurs *after* the parties have voluntarily entered into an agreement.

Although adverse selection and moral hazard can be found at different stages of the same transaction, such as auto insurance, it is possible to have one without the other.

To see how, think back to our chapter-opening example of the student loan program, which involved both problems. Imagine first that the student loan–pooling scheme had been mandatory. That would have eliminated the problem of adverse selection: Students who anticipated high earnings would not have been able to opt out. But it would have left the problem of moral hazard because it would still have been possible for all participants to evade payment.

Now consider an alternative scenario, in which participation remained optional, but the IRS agreed to help by reporting income to the university so that the university could effectively collect against its alumni with higher incomes. This plan would have lessened the moral hazard problem, but not the adverse selection. (For the record: This alternative scenario is totally hypothetical—the IRS is not legally allowed to engage in the activity described in the scenario.)

The rest of this chapter will focus on ways in which the problems arising from information asymmetries can be corrected.

✓CONCEPT CHECK

- ☐ Why is information asymmetry not a problem if both parties to an agreement want the same thing? **[LO 10.1]**
- ☐ How is the lemons problem caused by the buyer's inability to identify the true quality of a used car? **[LO 10.2]**
- ☐ How can better monitoring solve moral hazard problems? **[LO 10.3]**

Solving Information Problems

Before we look at ways to solve information problems, we should point out that they are not always worth solving. Sometimes, remaining uninformed is optimal. Why? Because the cost of acquiring information would be prohibitive. When you pay a mechanic for car repairs that you don't fully understand, for example, it's not as if you *couldn't* learn how brake systems work if you really wanted to. Or you could hire another mechanic to review the assessment and confirm the repairs are needed. You don't do either because it would take you a lot of time and effort to do those things. The trade-off isn't worth it. It's as if you've asked yourself, *What's the opportunity cost of acquiring more information?* For most of us, the opportunity cost of acquiring mechanical expertise is probably significantly higher than the occasional cost of unnecessary repairs.

Often, however, it *is* worth the effort to solve problems caused by information asymmetry. In this section, we'll consider some approaches that can be taken by those directly involved in a transaction: screening, signaling, building a reputation, and using statistical discrimination. Finally, we'll also consider two ways in which governments can get involved.

Screening

LO 10.4 Differentiate between screening and signaling and describe some applications of each.

If you know you are on the wrong end of an information asymmetry, you could always try asking the other party for the information you want. Rather than simply hoping they tell you the truth, you could also look for clever ways to put them in a situation that forces them to reveal, perhaps without even realizing it, the information they know and you don't. Taking action to reveal private information about someone else is called **screening**. In this context, *private* doesn't necessarily mean personal or embarrassing; it simply means that the information is not public, or available to everyone.

screening
taking action to reveal private information about someone else

Interviewing candidates for a job is a classic use of screening to improve hiring decisions. Employers may simply ask questions about your education, experience, and skills, and hope you're telling the truth. But because candidates have an incentive to hide negative information, many employers also use more proactive screening methods. One method is to ask for references. An applicant who cannot easily provide good references is revealing a piece of private information that any employer wants to have when hiring. Another is requiring applicants to perform certain tests of their skills, or perhaps even to take a drug test. If the applicant fails the tests, or refuses to take them, this also reveals useful private information.

Ever wonder why auto insurance companies offer different deductibles? (*Deductibles* are amounts a policyholder must pay out of pocket before an insurance company settles a claim.) Offering different deductibles is not just a matter of offering different products to suit different customer needs. Instead, it's a device to force the more accident-prone drivers to reveal themselves. Reckless drivers know that their cars are likely to be involved in accidents more often than usual. A driver who expects to have frequent accidents would not choose a high-deductible plan; it could end up being very expensive. A cautious driver, however, would be willing to carry a high deductible; after all, he doesn't anticipate having frequent accidents. Offering different deductibles screens out the reckless drivers. Such screening allows the insurance company to offer lower monthly premiums to cautious customers, thus helping to avoid the problem of adverse selection.

This is, of course, not the only way insurance companies try to solve the problem of asymmetric information. In fact, solving this problem is so important to the insurance industry, many people make a career out of it, as described in the Where Can It Take You? box "Risk management."

Signaling

Screening is useful when trying to correct information asymmetry by uncovering private information that people would rather not share. Sometimes, though, the party with more information would be all too happy to share it. For instance, if I am selling a used car I know is in excellent

Where Can It Take You?
Risk management

How can you pay less for car insurance? Getting good grades in school is a first step. Being female, over 25 years old, or married also helps. When you buy auto insurance, the agent will ask you questions about all these factors and will set the price of your policy accordingly.

What do any of these characteristics have to do with driving? Who decided that these factors should determine the cost of your insurance? Insurance rates are developed by people who specialize in risk management. An entire profession, in fact, is devoted to assessing risk in different industries and situations. In the insurance business, it's called *underwriting;* in general, it's called *actuarial science.*

Actuaries are the people who figure out what kind of information a company needs to assess the risks it faces. We've seen that the information asymmetries that separate insurance providers and policyholders are huge. Policyholders have an incentive to hide information that might raise their premiums. Also, factors that might make certain policyholders more costly to the insurer—a tendency toward road rage, or terrible parallel-parking skills—can be difficult for insurers to observe.

To solve these information problems, underwriters identify correlations between the risks the company faces and characteristics that can be easily observed in policyholders. Examples are age, gender, and diligence in schoolwork. Based on that information, insurers then create categories of riskiness. Those categories are designed to accurately predict a policyholder's cost to the company and to guard against adverse selection.

In 2015, CareerCast.com (a career guidance website), ranked the actuary position as the best overall job in the United States, based on salary, opportunities for advancement, job satisfaction, environment, and hiring outlook. Actuaries must be good at math and be willing to acquire a series of professional certifications—and they must understand correlation and causation really well.

Source: http://www.careercast.com/jobs-rated/best-jobs-2015.

condition, I would be delighted to share this knowledge with you, the potential buyer. Both of us would prefer to eliminate the information asymmetry that afflicts us. The problem is that we lack a *credible* way to share information. After all, somebody selling a lemon also will insist that her car is top quality. Knowing this, you would have no reason to believe me.

How does the seller of a good used car prove to potential buyers that it's not a lemon, so he can ask a higher price? One way to credibly signal that a car is not a lemon is to certify it through a brand dealership. The dealership inspects the car for defects and, if it passes muster, offers it for sale with a certificate of quality and a warranty. The certificate reassures the buyer that the car is a good one and enables the seller to receive a higher price. This solution corrects an inefficiency in the market, allowing more transactions that are valuable to both buyers and sellers to take place.

When people take action, on purpose or not, to reveal their own private information, they are **signaling**. Signaling happens in many situations; you may even be doing it by taking an economics course. The signaling theory of education argues that a college degree is like a certificate of quality for used cars: It credibly signals to potential employers that you are intelligent,

signaling
taking action to reveal one's own private information

"YESTERDAY was tie-down, sleeves-up...
today is tie-up, sleeves-down!"

Signals can be positive or
negative. Here, one worker
is signalling being out of
touch with the group norm.
*Cartoon © Chris Wildt.
Sourced from www.
CartoonStock.com.*

hardworking, and able to complete assignments. That's why many employers prefer candidates with college degrees, even if what they learned in school has little relevance to the job in question.

The key to a successful positive signal is that it is not easily faked. For a signal to be credible, it must carry some sort of mechanism or cost that makes it inaccessible or unappealing to those it is meant to exclude. In the case of a used-car certificate, an unbiased third party checks the car. Sellers of lemons will not apply. In the case of a college degree, both admissions screening and tuition costs discourage applicants who are not sufficiently talented and hardworking. In theory, the more selective the admissions process and the costlier the tuition, the stronger the signal a college degree sends to potential employers.

Signals can be negative or positive. For example, dressing badly may be a negative signal, whereas dressing sharply may be a positive one. Personal appearance is so important a signal, in fact, that it motivated one woman to create a new charity; see the Real Life box "Dress for success."

REAL LIFE

Dress for success

Personal appearance is an important way to signal otherwise hidden information. Wearing a T-shirt with the name of your favorite band signals to everyone you meet that you like a particular kind of music. You could make some new friends by wearing it. Wearing that same T-shirt to a job interview, however, signals more about your lack of professionalism than about your musical preferences.

Of course, a person who wears a T-shirt to a job interview could be more qualified than a candidate who wears a suit. But the one wearing the suit has made an effort to appear professional, signaling a familiarity with common office practices that could indicate she is likely to be a productive employee. Even with a superior resume, the T-shirt-wearing candidate's unprofessional appearance could cost him the job.

The answer to this signaling problem might seem simple: If you are serious about getting a good office job, get yourself a suit. Unfortunately, for some people purchasing a new suit before getting a job is financially impossible. A disadvantaged person who has successfully completed a job-training program, for example, might be unable to afford a new suit.

Nancy Lublin, founder of the nonprofit organization Dress for Success, recognized this problem. Her organization provides women in need with clothing that will help them signal their professionalism during a job interview. Women are referred to Dress for Success by other social service programs. More than 100 Dress for Success affiliates now help women to correct asymmetric-information problems by providing professional-looking clothes to wear for job interviews.

Source: http://www.dressforsuccess.org/whatwedo.aspx.

Reputation

LO 10.5 Explain how reputations can help to solve information problems.

So far we have focused on asymmetric-information problems affecting one-time interactions, such as a one-off private used-car trade. Often, however, interactions occur over and over, like the repeated games in Chapter 9, "Game Theory and Strategic Thinking." Used-car dealers, for example, sell used cars every day. This repetition can enable a new solution to the information problem, as people develop a reputation for trustworthiness (or lack thereof).

Consider a mechanic who routinely charges customers for unnecessary repairs. Once in a while, one of those customers will call on a friend who understands car repairs for a second opinion, and the mechanic will get caught overcharging. The mechanic thus risks developing a bad reputation. This risk creates an incentive for the more-informed party (in this case, the car mechanic) not to take unfair advantage of the information asymmetry. *What's the opportunity cost* of squeezing an unfair advantage out of a deal? If no one will ever find out, the answer is probably "nothing." With your reputation on the line, however, the opportunity cost is the loss of valuable business in the future.

Have you ever hesitated about buying something from eBay, but then been reassured by noticing that the seller has a good user-feedback score? If so, you will understand the power of reputation to overcome the problem of asymmetric information. A good reputation can be viewed as a special form of signaling. Just like getting a college degree, building a good reputation can be a costly and time-consuming business.

Statistical discrimination

LO 10.6 Explain how statistical discrimination might be used to solve information problems.

When you don't have time to become fully informed about a specific new situation, you may find yourself relying on a rule of thumb. Suppose you're choosing between having dinner at a Mexican restaurant or the burger place next to it. You know nothing about these two restaurants, and you're too hungry to stop and ask the opinions of locals or search for reviews online. You remember hearing, though, that this neighborhood is known for great Mexican food. It makes sense to choose the Mexican restaurant. Of course, you may be unlucky and find that this *particular* Mexican restaurant happens to be terrible. Using a generalization here is perfectly rational, though: If the neighborhood has a reputation for great Mexican food, you have a reasonably good chance that this particular Mexican restaurant will, in fact, be great.

Filling gaps in your information by generalizing based on observable characteristics is called **statistical discrimination**. It's something most of us do all the time. Suppose you are choosing among three movies: an action movie starring Liam Neeson, a romance starring Ryan Gosling, or a psychological drama starring Jennifer Lawrence. You may know little about the particular movies but still be able to tell which you are likely to enjoy most, based on knowing which type of movie you typically like best, or which actor or actress you like the most. You've filled the gaps in your information by generalizing from what you already know.

To return to the lemons problem, you may prefer to buy one particular used car over another because you know that, in general, cars of that brand tend to age well. As with the Mexican restaurant, you may be unlucky—the particular car you buy may turn out to be a lemon. Likewise with the movie, your favorite genre or movie star does, on occasion, let you down. But generalizing in this way is a rational response to being on the wrong end of an information asymmetry.

However, statistical discrimination can be a controversial way to tackle information problems. It can often be far less benign than choosing between restaurants, movies, or used cars. The problem is that we can generalize about any observable characteristic—not just genre of food or movie or brand of car, but also a person's race, age, gender, or religion. Saying that statistical discrimination can be *rational* doesn't mean that it is always admirable, ethical, or even legal. Rational statistical discrimination can limit the opportunities of individuals just because they happen to belong to a certain group of people. See the What Do You Think? box "From spray paint to auto insurance" for some examples.

statistical discrimination
distinguishing between choices by generalizing based on observable characteristics in order to fill in missing information

What Do You Think?

From spray paint to auto insurance

In 2007, New York City banned the sale of spray paint to anyone under the age of 21. (The ban was later overturned by an appeals court.) The rationale for the ban? Vandals who use spray paint to deface property with graffiti are statistically more likely to be under age 21.

This ban was a response to an information problem: If the city knew which individuals wanted spray paint to deface property, it could simply ban its sale to those individuals. The city didn't have this information, of course. Instead, it used a rule of thumb, banning the sale of spray paint to a *category* of people statistically more likely to harbor these intentions. If you were a law-abiding 19-year-old who wanted to buy spray paint for a school art project, you might have been pretty annoyed about this law.

Statistical discrimination can also be far more intrusive than an inability to purchase spray paint. Put yourself in the place of a successful young black male who owns a nice-looking car and keeps getting pulled over by police. Or imagine being a bearded Muslim who often gets singled out in airports for extra security checks. Both instances of statistical discrimination are highly controversial. Some examples of statistical discrimination are so controversial, they have been banned altogether. For example, young women are statistically more likely than other employees to leave their jobs to start a family. But any employer who cites this as a reason for preferring to hire a man risks getting sued for gender discrimination.

Yet other examples of age- and gender-based statistical discrimination are hardly objected to at all. We have come across one such example already in this chapter: the cost of auto insurance. If you are an extremely careful driver who happens to be young and male, you will be charged more for your car insurance because *other* young men are statistically more likely to drive recklessly and cause accidents.

Why do we accept age- and gender-based discrimination in the auto-insurance market, but not in the jobs market? Is it any less unfair to charge young men more for their car insurance than to ban teenagers from buying spray paint?

WHAT DO YOU THINK?

1. Is banning the sale of graffiti-related materials to young people an acceptable or unfair form of statistical discrimination?
2. Should statistical discrimination be used as a basis for legislation?
3. Police are sometimes accused of stopping members of some ethnic or racial groups more than others. Is racial profiling by police ever justifiable?

Source: Maeve Reston, "To fight graffiti, L.A. Council may restrict spraypaint sales," *Los Angeles Times,* July 6, 2009, http://latimesblogs.latimes.com/lanow/2009/07/la-council-weighs-getting-tougher-on-graffiti-outlawing-spray-can-sales-to-minors.html.

Regulation and education

LO 10.7 Discuss the uses and limitations of education and regulation in overcoming information asymmetry problems.

When parties to a transaction can't resolve information asymmetry problems on their own and those problems have a negative effect on sufficiently large numbers of people, the government will sometimes step in.

Governments can help to solve information asymmetry problems in two ways. One is to provide the missing information to the less-informed party, or require the more-informed party to reveal it. For example, almost every packaged-food item you can buy in the United States lists its ingredients and nutritional content. This is the result of Food and Drug Administration (FDA) regulations that force food producers to divulge otherwise-private information. These regulations correct an information asymmetry that is important (consumers want to know what they're eating) and hard to solve without government intervention.

Disclosure laws sound like a good thing, but they don't always work well. Sometimes they can replace the problem of consumers having too little information with the opposite problem—information overload. Thanks to disclosure laws, everything from cell phone plans to prescription drugs and home mortgages comes with page after page of rules, disclaimers, and technical information. Not surprisingly, many consumers don't bother to read the fine print. Instead, they base decisions on a salesperson's explanation. In the early 2000s, laws requiring banks and mortgage brokers to disclose the terms of home loans failed to prevent many Americans from entering into irresponsible mortgage agreements. In many cases, borrowers didn't read or understand the information the companies had been forced to disclose.

In Chapter 23, "Public Policy and Choice Architecture," we'll see how some organizations work to frame people's options in these situations of information overload. Their goal is to try to simplify the choices people face and help them make better decisions.

The second way governments can use public regulation to tackle information problems is to *mandate participation* in a market or program. Mandates prevent markets from failing because of adverse selection. Governments choose this option when the functioning of those markets is thought to be in the public interest. For example, we have seen how adverse selection drives up the price of auto insurance. Careful drivers might conclude that insurance is too expensive to be worth it. Those decisions could set off the vicious cycle we discussed earlier: Only reckless drivers want insurance, so premiums have to rise higher and higher, eventually leading the market to collapse.

But governments want drivers to be able to compensate innocent victims if they cause a road accident. So most states require *all* drivers to buy at least a minimum level of insurance to cover liability to third parties. This mandated participation solves the adverse-selection problem, but not the moral-hazard problem: Drivers with insurance are still more likely to drive carelessly.

One effect of the government mandating participation in the auto-insurance market is to keep premiums lower than they would be if careful drivers had a choice to opt out. This reasoning leads some policy-makers to suggest that mandatory health insurance coverage would help to reduce the cost of health care. The idea is that mandating coverage would overcome adverse selection in the market for health insurance. The downside is that mandating coverage could undermine people's freedom to choose their own insurance status.

✓CONCEPT CHECK

1. What is the difference between screening and signaling? **[LO 10.4]**
2. Why does a seller with a good reputation face a different opportunity cost for offering poor-quality goods than a seller with no reputation to lose? **[LO 10.5]**
3. What concept uses observable qualities in order to fill in missing information when making a decision? **[LO 10.6]**
4. How can too much fine print undermine the goals of a public-disclosure law? **[LO 10.7]**

Conclusion

People make decisions based on what they know, but sometimes they don't have enough information to make good decisions. One of the key assumptions behind perfect markets is that individuals have perfect information. When this is not true, individuals are not necessarily able to make decisions that set marginal benefits equal to marginal costs.

We've seen in this chapter that in many situations information asymmetry can allow one person to take advantage of another. In other cases, markets may fall apart because people are afraid to trade with one another. Problems like adverse selection and moral hazard can derail what appear to be clever programs or business models.

Screening and signaling, if used correctly, can help to correct these inefficiencies and increase surplus. Statistical discrimination can also be helpful, but it can have unintended downsides. Sometimes government may step in to correct information problems that affect large numbers of people. The success of government regulation, however, depends on whether or not people understand and are motivated to use the information made available to them.

Key Terms

complete information, p. 235

information asymmetry, p. 235

adverse selection, p. 236

principal, p. 237

agent, p. 237

moral hazard, p. 238

screening, p. 240

signaling, p. 241

statistical discrimination, p. 243

Summary

LO 10.1 Explain why information asymmetry matters for economic decision making.

Information asymmetry means that one person knows more than another. Asymmetric information creates problems because it allows a person who is more informed to achieve goals at the expense of a person who is less informed. If the incentives of both parties are aligned, then the information asymmetry doesn't matter.

LO 10.2 Explain how adverse selection is caused by asymmetric information.

Adverse selection occurs when buyers and sellers have different information about the quality of a good or the riskiness of a situation. As a result, some buyers and sellers fail to complete transactions that would have been possible if both sides had the same information. Adverse selection relates to unobserved characteristics of people or goods, and it occurs before the two parties have entered into an agreement.

LO 10.3 Explain how moral hazard is caused by asymmetric information.

Moral hazard occurs when people behave in a riskier way or renege on a contract because they do not have to face the full consequences of their actions. In contrast to adverse selection, moral hazard has to do with actions, and it happens *after* the two parties have entered into an agreement. It generally occurs when a principal entrusts an agent with a task but cannot observe the agent's actions, as in the employer–employee relationship.

LO 10.4 Differentiate between screening and signaling and describe some applications of each.

Screening is a method for correcting information asymmetries that involves taking action to reveal private information about someone else. Common examples include interviewing job candidates and checking references when hiring, or offering insurance products that appeal to people with different characteristics. Screening works best when there is a way to ensure that the information received is credible, since people have an incentive to keep their private information private.

Signaling is a method for correcting information asymmetries that involves taking action to reveal one's own private information. Common examples include certifying a used car, getting an advanced degree, and dressing for success. Signaling is useful in cases in which the more informed party would prefer to eliminate the information asymmetry. For a signal to be credible, it must carry some cost or mechanism that makes it inaccessible or unappealing to those it is meant to exclude; otherwise everyone will use the signal and it will lose its meaning.

LO 10.5 Explain how reputations can help to solve information problems.

The potential to develop a reputation creates an incentive for the more-informed party to an exchange to behave in a way that is fair and favorable toward the less-informed party. Because hidden information often reveals itself over time, people who consistently take advantage of a less-informed party will develop a bad reputation, and customers will begin to avoid doing business with them.

A good reputation is a signal that a business or person has treated partners well in the past.

LO 10.6 Explain how statistical discrimination might be used to solve information problems.

Statistical discrimination is a method of distinguishing between choices by generalizing based on observable characteristics in order to fill in missing information. When specific information is missing, rules of thumb and inferences based on statistical averages can serve as rational decision-making tools. However, statistical averages are not necessarily accurate, nor are inferences made using statistical discrimination, even if they are the best option when full information is unavailable.

LO 10.7 Discuss the uses and limitations of education and regulation in overcoming information asymmetry problems.

When an information problem is pervasive and has a pronounced negative effect on society, government will sometimes step in to provide the missing information or require that others reveal private information. The effectiveness of these interventions depends on how well the government's requirements are enforced and how well people understand the information they receive. In a few cases, government may mandate participation in a market or program to counter a severe adverse selection problem.

Review Questions

1. Return to the description of the student loan program that opened the chapter. Suppose that all students at the university are perfectly altruistic and share the university's goal of reducing debt for graduates with low incomes. Would information asymmetry cause a problem in this situation? Why or why not? **[LO 10.1]**

2. Suppose you are in the market to purchase your first home. You found a house you like in your price range and are buying directly from the previous owner. Describe an information asymmetry in this situation. Explain who is likely to benefit from this information imbalance. **[LO 10.1]**

3. A club charges a flat fee for an open bar (all-you-can-drink). Describe the adverse-selection problem. **[LO 10.2]**

4. A course description posted during the registration period notes that homework is graded *complete* or *incomplete* rather than being corrected by the instructor. Describe the adverse-selection problem. **[LO 10.2]**

5. A club charges a flat fee for an open bar (all-you-can-drink). Describe the moral-hazard problem. **[LO 10.3]**

6. Imagine that you own a bagel shop, which you visit once a day. According to company policy, employees are supposed to pay for all the bagels they eat. Why is moral hazard likely to be a problem in this situation, and what could you do to prevent it? **[LO 10.3]**

7. The college admissions process involves both screening and signaling. Give an example of each. Who is doing the screening? Who is doing the signaling? **[LO 10.4]**

8. Explain why joining a fraternity or sorority might include elaborate or difficult rituals. **[LO 10.4]**

9. Walter wants to signal his devotion to Emily. He has $75 and is considering a bracelet for Emily or a tattoo for himself of her name. Which is the more effective signal? **[LO 10.4]**

10. Advertising often features testimonials from satisfied customers, who happily describe the characteristics of the goods or services they received. Why do advertisers use this technique rather than a direct description of the goods or services? **[LO 10.5]**

11. Two instructors are offering elective courses this semester. One instructor has been teaching at the university for several years. The other instructor is new. For which instructor will teaching evaluations be the most important this semester? Explain why. **[LO 10.5]**

12. Consider the market for life insurance. Give an example of statistical discrimination an insurer might use to set premiums. **[LO 10.6]**

13. Consider the market for auto insurance. Explain why insurers ask student drivers about their grades. **[LO 10.6]**

14. Suppose the government is thinking of requiring pharmaceutical companies to print the exact chemical formulas of medications on the label, so consumers will know exactly what they are ingesting. Is the new disclosure rule likely to benefit the average consumer? Explain your reasoning. **[LO 10.7]**

15. Some people have argued that mandatory health insurance could reduce health-care costs. Explain this argument. What problem would mandatory coverage not solve that could undermine cost savings? **[LO 10.7]**

Problems and Applications

1. In which of the following situations is an information asymmetry likely to cause problems? **[LO 10.1]**

    a. Cab drivers know the shortest route to any destination better than their passengers do.

    b. Managers can't always supervise members of their sales staff who work on commission. (That is, staff members receive a percentage of the total value of the sales they make.)

2. In which of the following situations is an information asymmetry likely to cause problems? **[LO 10.1]**

 a. Parents know more than their children about how to write a good college application.

 b. People who book hotel rooms online know less about the quality of the room they are reserving than the hotel's management.

3. Which of the following situations are likely to involve adverse selection? **[LO 10.2]**

 a. After receiving an emergency call during class, a professor leaves students unsupervised for the rest of the period.

 b. A course has a reputation for being an easy A, even though after the term begins, students realize that it isn't.

 c. A course is a requirement for physics majors but an elective for biology majors.

4. In which of the following situations is adverse selection *not* a concern? **[LO 10.2]**

 a. A company offers employees the opportunity to purchase group health insurance.

 b. A company requires employees to purchase group health insurance.

 c. The health insurance plan does not include dental care.

5. There is a town with exactly 1,000 residents. 75% of the residents make healthy choices, and 25% of the residents consistently make unhealthy choices, but the health insurance company in town cannot tell who is health and who is unhealthy. A healthy person has an average of $600 in medical expenses each year and is willing to pay $800 for insurance. An unhealthy person has an average of $1,600 in medical expenses each year and is willing to pay $2,000 for insurance. The health insurance provider can offer insurance at only one price. **[LO 10.2]**

 a. In equilibrium, what is the minimum price of insurance?

 b. In equilibrium, who will buy insurance?

6. Which of the following situations are likely to involve moral hazard? **[LO 10.3]**

 a. After receiving an emergency call during class, a professor leaves students unsupervised for the rest of the period.

 b. A course has a reputation for being an easy A, even though after the term begins, students realize that it isn't.

 c. A course is a requirement for physics majors but an elective for biology majors.

7. In which of the following government policies is moral hazard not a concern? **[LO 10.3]**

 a. Government provides disaster relief for homeowners who lose their homes in a flood.

 b. Government provides unemployment insurance when workers are laid off.

 c. Government raises taxes to pay for social services.

 d. Government requires hospitals to treat anyone who comes to the emergency room, regardless of insurance status.

8. Say whether each of the following situations involves screening or signaling. **[LO 10.4]**

 a. Auto shops and motels advertise that they are AAA-approved.

 b. Employers check interviewees' Facebook or MySpace profiles before hiring one of them.

 c. Applicants must pass an exam before becoming eligible for a civil service position.

 d. People wear expensive clothing with large brand names or logos.

9. Jane uses an online dating service. For each of the following activities, say whether Jane is screening or signaling. **[LO 10.4]**

 a. Jane views profiles of only nonsmokers.

 b. Jane describes her volunteer activities in her profile.

 c. Jane lists museums and foreign films among her interests.

 d. Jane looks for matches who live within 25 miles of her address.

10. Consider the effect of reputation and say whether you are likely to be treated better in scenario *a* or scenario *b*. **[LO 10.5]**

 a. You tell an auto mechanic that you have just moved to town.

 b. You tell an auto mechanic that you are moving out of town.

11. Consider the effect of reputation and say whether you are likely to be treated better in scenario *a* or scenario *b*. **[LO 10.5]**

 a. You are purchasing your car from an individual who advertised it on craigslist.

 b. You are purchasing your car from a local dealership.

12. In college admissions, which of the following are examples of statistical discrimination? Choose all that apply. **[LO 10.6]**

a. A college has minimum required scores on standardized tests.

b. A college is an all-women's school.

c. A college uses high-school GPA to rank students for scholarship offers.

d. A college requires three letters of recommendation.

13. In a market for car insurance, which of the following are examples of statistical discrimination? Choose all that apply. **[LO 10.6]**

a. Premiums are adjusted based on the zip code of the insured.

b. Premiums are adjusted based on the color of the car.

c. Premiums are adjusted based on the driving record of the insured.

d. Premiums are adjusted based on the model of the car.

14. Say which public regulation approach is likely to be more effective in providing information to consumers of pharmaceuticals. **[LO 10.7]**

a. Requiring pharmaceutical companies to list major side effects of their medications in television advertisements.

b. Requiring pharmaceutical companies to post online the full text of research results from medical testing done during the development of new drugs.

15. Say which public regulation approach is likely to be more effective in providing information to consumers of restaurant meals. **[LO 10.7]**

a. Filing a notice at city hall when a restaurant fails a health and sanitation inspection.

b. Posting a public notice on the door of a restaurant that fails a health and sanitation inspection.

Time and Uncertainty

11

Learning Objectives

LO 11.1   Explain why money is worth more now than in the future, and how the interest rate represents this relationship.

LO 11.2   Calculate compounding over time with a given interest rate.

LO 11.3   Calculate the present value of a future sum.

LO 11.4   Evaluate the costs and benefits of a choice using expected value.

LO 11.5   Explain the behavior of individuals who are risk-averse or risk-seeking.

LO 11.6   Explain how risk aversion makes a market for insurance possible.

LO 11.7   Explain the importance of pooling and diversification for managing risk.

LO 11.8   Describe the challenges that adverse selection and moral hazard pose for insurance.

IS COLLEGE WORTH IT?

As the 2012 presidential campaign swung into gear, Republican Mitt Romney and Democrat Barack Obama agreed on one thing: the interest rate on federal student loans should be frozen at 3.4 percent per year.[1] Both candidates seemed to feel that the government should limit the financial burden associated with the choice to attend college.

For most students, college loans are not just political talking points. The total amount of student loan debt has now climbed to about $1.2 trillion dollars; about 40 million Americans have at least one outstanding student loan.[2] Because you pay a future fee (called *interest*) to borrow the money, you eventually pay back a lot more than the amount you borrowed. Is it worth it? In 2014, just over half of recent college graduates were working at a job that didn't require a college degree.[3]

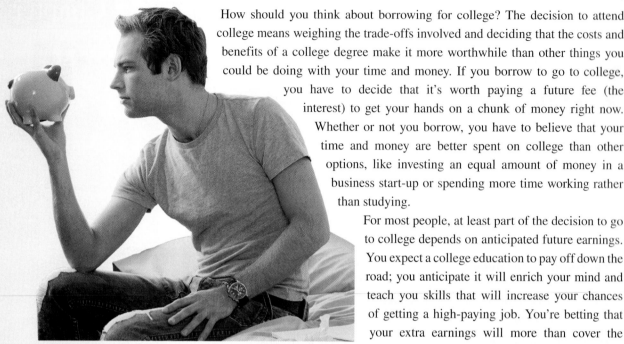

How should you think about borrowing for college? The decision to attend college means weighing the trade-offs involved and deciding that the costs and benefits of a college degree make it more worthwhile than other things you could be doing with your time and money. If you borrow to go to college, you have to decide that it's worth paying a future fee (the interest) to get your hands on a chunk of money right now. Whether or not you borrow, you have to believe that your time and money are better spent on college than other options, like investing an equal amount of money in a business start-up or spending more time working rather than studying.

For most people, at least part of the decision to go to college depends on anticipated future earnings. You expect a college education to pay off down the road; you anticipate it will enrich your mind and teach you skills that will increase your chances of getting a high-paying job. You're betting that your extra earnings will more than cover the interest costs of your loan. You also are betting that those earnings will be greater than what you could have accrued by investing borrowed money somewhere else and starting to work right away instead. For most people these are good bets. But there's always uncertainty, especially when the economy is shaky. Economics provides a way to think about choices like this, which have uncertain future costs and benefits.

Image Source/Getty Images

When you make decisions that require you to weigh uncertain future costs and benefits, you face two complications. The first is that you can't directly compare costs and benefits that show up now (such as college tuition) with those that show up in the future (such as higher salaries) because the value of money changes over time. In this chapter, we'll show how to use interest rates to make these comparisons accurately.

The second complication is that the future is uncertain. For instance, there is always the possibility that you might *not* end up earning more, despite your college degree. In the following section we look at how to account for risk when making decisions about the future. In the final part of the chapter, we'll see how some risks can be managed through diversifying and pooling.

You can put the ideas in this chapter to work to understand many important life decisions: whether to take out a loan to buy a house or a car or to start a business; whether to purchase insurance against car accidents or theft, or to provide for your children if you get too sick to work; and whether you should invest in some opportunity or other—the stock market, real estate, retirement funds—in the hope of getting income in the future.

Value over Time

In previous chapters we've talked about making decisions by weighing the benefits and opportunity cost of each option. Conveniently, many decisions involve immediate trade-offs—that is, costs and benefits that occur at the same time: You give the barista your money, and in return you get handed a coffee, right away.

In this chapter, we'll apply the question *What are the trade-offs?* to a trickier set of decisions—those that involve costs that occur at one time and benefits that occur at another time.

Timing matters

LO 11.1 Explain why money is worth more now than in the future, and how the interest rate represents this relationship.

Why does it matter if the costs and benefits of a choice occur at different times? Consider the following scenario: You have won first prize in a competition. Congratulations! For your prize, you can choose one of the following options.

Option A: You can have $100,000 now.

Option B: You can have $100,000 ten years from now.

Which would you choose? We're guessing you'd take option A. If you take the $100,000 now, you can do fun or useful things with it right away—like pay for your college education, treat yourself to a brand new car, or donate tens of thousands of insecticide-treated bednets to help people living in malarial areas of Africa stay healthy. Why would you wait 10 years to do any of these things?

Even if you don't intend to do anything with the money right away, you're still better off taking option A—you can always just save it while you think about what to do with it. Pretty much everyone would rather have money now than the same amount of money later. Conversely, most people prefer *costs* that are delayed to those they have to bear immediately. That's why so many people buy things on credit.

These preferences—for immediate benefits and delayed costs—are another way of saying that money is worth more to us *now* than in the future. Because this is so, we cannot simply equate costs and benefits that occur at different times. To be able to weigh trade-offs that happen over time, we need a way of reflecting the changing value of money over time.

Interest rates

How *much* more is money worth now than in the future? Suppose that the prize options for winning the competition change to:

Option A: You can have $100,000 now.

Option B: You can have $1,000,000 ten years from now.

Which would you choose? Tempting as it would be to take $100,000 now, we bet most people would probably be willing to wait 10 years to get their hands on a million dollars.

Now ask yourself this: How much would we have to offer to convince you to take option B over option A? $105,000? $200,000? $350,000? $500,000? Not everyone will have the same answer. It depends on how much more it is worth to you to have money now, rather than 10 years from now. If you strongly prefer to have cash in hand, then we'd have to offer you a lot more money in the future in order to convince you to wait. If you're more patient, we wouldn't have to offer you so much.

Where do these individual preferences come from? Think about this question in terms of opportunity cost. *What is the opportunity cost* of waiting until the future to get your money? It's the value of whatever you could otherwise have done with the money in the meantime.

interest rate
the price of money, typically expressed as a percentage per dollar per unit of time; for savers, it is the price received for letting a bank use money for a specified period of time; for borrowers, it is the price of using money for a specified period of time

When a bank lends you money to attend college, for example, it passes up the opportunity to do something else productive with that money instead. Thus, if you want the bank to give you money now, you have to agree to pay something extra when you repay the loan in the future. The opportunity cost to the bank of lending you money is represented by the **interest rate** it charges you on the loan—the price of borrowing money for a specified period of time, expressed as a percentage per dollar borrowed and per unit of time. The interest rate tells us how much more the money is worth to the bank today than in the future. Different banks may offer loans at different interest rates, depending on how strongly they prefer to have cash in hand.

POTENTIALLY CONFUSING

In the real world, interest rates also reflect the risk that a borrower will default on a loan and the risk of inflation. For the sake of simplicity, we are ignoring inflation and are assuming that all loans are certain to be paid back. This enables us to zero in on what interest rates fundamentally represent: the *opportunity cost* of having to wait to get your money.

On the flip-side, when you save money at a bank, the bank usually pays you interest on your deposit. In essence, the bank is borrowing money from you, the depositor. You, too, have an opportunity cost—the value of whatever else you could have done with that money instead of depositing it with the bank. Again, for each individual this will be different. Some will be happy to deposit money at 1 percent interest; others would prefer to do something else with their money unless they are offered at least 5 percent. Interest rates are an important concept in macroeconomics as well as microeconomics, and we'll return to them in greater detail later in the book. For now, we'll focus on why they matter for individual decision making.

Typically, the interest rate is expressed as a percentage of the sum of money in question, over a specified time period—usually one year. For instance, if the interest rate on a loan of $1,000 is 5 percent per year, it means that after one year the borrower will owe the original $1,000 plus 5 percent of $1,000 in interest:

$$\$1,000 + (\$1,000 \times 5\%) = \$1,000 \times 1.05 = \$1,050$$

The general formula for the value of a loan of amount X at the end of one period of time with an interest rate r is:

EQUATION 11-1   Value of a loan with interest $= (X \times 1) + (X \times r) = X \times (1 + r)$

An alternate way to think of interest is as a cost per unit, just like other prices. An annual interest rate of 5 percent is the same thing as saying that the price of borrowing money is $0.05 per year for every dollar you owe. Interest is a price per dollar, *per unit of time:*

EQUATION 11-2   Interest rate: $r = \dfrac{\text{Price per } \$}{\text{Time}}$

Compounding

LO 11.2 Calculate compounding over time with a given interest rate.

An annual interest rate of 5 percent tells us that the cost of borrowing $1,000 for one year is $50. So what's the cost of borrowing $1,000 for two years, or five years, or 10 years?

Unfortunately, it's not as simple as just $50 a year. That's because interest also accumulates on interest, not just on the original sum. Let's say you deposit $1,000 in a bank account that offers 5 percent interest. (Remember, when you put your money in a bank account that pays interest, the bank is effectively borrowing the money from you.) After one year, you have $1,050. Then, in the second year, you earn 5 percent interest *on $1,050* (not the original $1,000). The interest in year 2 is $52.50. After two years you have $1,102.50, not $1,100.

$$\text{1st year:} \quad \$1,000 \times 1.05 \quad = \$1,050.00$$
$$\text{2nd year:} \quad \$1,050 \times 1.05 \quad = \$1,102.50$$
$$= \$1,000 \times (1.05)^2 = \$1,102.50$$

This process of accumulation, as interest is paid on interest that has already been earned, is called **compounding**.

It was relatively easy to find the amount after two years of compounded interest: We knew the amount after one year and just multiplied that amount by the 5 percent interest rate. But beyond year 2, it's far simpler to use a formula than to do year-by-year calculations. With compounding, the general formula for finding the future value of an initial deposit (*PV*) over a time period of *n* years at interest rate *r* is:

compounding
the process of accumulation that results from the additional interest paid on previously earned interest

EQUATION 11-3   Future value of a sum $= FV = PV \times (1 + r)^n$

Over time, compounding can have a big effect. If you were expecting your initial $1,000 deposit to grow by a steady $50 per year, then after 20 years you would expect to have $2,000 in the bank. But thanks to compounding, your 5 percent interest earnings help you accumulate $1,000 \times (1.05)^{20} = \$2,653.29$.

Compounding is welcome news for investors because it means your money grows at a greater rate than you might have expected. Instead of taking 20 years to double your money, as it would if your $1,000 grew by just $50 a year, it takes just a little over 14 years for your deposit to double in value at an interest rate of 5 percent.

As nice as compounding is for savers, it can be dangerous territory for borrowers. This is especially true when interest rates are much higher than 5 percent, as they often are for credit cards and personal loans. While federally guaranteed student loans currently top out at 6.8 percent per year, private student loans can cost as much as 18 percent. If you don't keep up with payments on your loans, unpaid interest incurs *more interest* due to compounding, and debts can rapidly spiral out of control.

For discussion of the use of compounding techniques to calculate the growth of an investment over time, see Appendix F, "Math Essentials: Compounding," which follows this chapter.

Present value

LO 11.3 Calculate the present value of a future sum.

The decision to go to college means accepting immediate costs—such as tuition, room and board, and time spent studying rather than earning a salary—in return for the anticipated benefit of earning higher salaries down the road. Knowing that interest rates represent the opportunity cost of delaying benefits, we can come closer to answering the question with which we started this chapter: How can you know whether the delayed benefits of college will outweigh the immediate costs?

Economists use interest rates to compare the present value and future value of a sum. Earlier, we asked how much you'd have to be offered before you'd prefer to wait 10 years than to have $100,000 right now. Let's say you think you could invest the money for an 8 percent annual return. We can calculate that the future value of $100,000 in 10 years with an 8 percent interest rate is $100,000 \times (1.08)^{10} = \$215,892.50$.

present value

how much a certain amount of money that will be obtained in the future is worth today

If we know the future value, we can also rearrange this equation to calculate **present value**. Present value is how much a certain amount of money that will be obtained in the future is worth today. So if you knew that an investment was going to pay you $215,892.50 in 10 years, and you knew that the interest rate over that time would be 8 percent, then you could calculate the present value of that investment as $215,892.50 ÷ $(1.08)^{10}$ = $100,000.

More generally, if r is the annual interest rate, then the formula for calculating the present value of a sum FV received in n years at interest rate r is as follows:

EQUATION 11-4 $$\text{Present value of a sum} = PV = \frac{FV}{(1+r)^n}$$

Notice that this formula is simply another way of writing Equation 11-3. The relationship between present value and future value is always given by the interest rate and the time period:

- If you know the present value, you can multiply by the compound interest rate to find the future value.
- If you know the future value, you can divide by the compound interest rate to find the present value.

Present value translates future costs or benefits into the equivalent amount of cash in hand today. That information enables us to compare the future amounts directly with the immediate amounts.

It's surprising to learn that many people earn a million dollars over a lifetime of work. (However, at $8 an hour, you'd have to work about 16 hours a day for over 30 years.)

Let's go back to your college-loan decision. Say you expect that if you *don't* have a college degree, you'll earn a total career income of $1.2 million. (That amount equates to an average of $40,000 a year over 30 years.) If you *do* have a degree, you expect to earn an extra $20,000 a year, raising your total career income to $1.8 million. So if you go to college, you expect to have earned an extra $600,000 after working for 30 years ($20,000 × 30).

What is that future $600,000 worth in today's money? Let's say that your first job starts five years from now and that you expect to be able to invest your money at a 5 percent interest rate. We can calculate the present value of your first year of earning by entering these values into Equation 11-4:

$$PV = \frac{\$20,000}{(1.05)^5} = \$15,670.52$$

Note that $n = 5$ because you do not receive your first payment of $20,000 until five years from now (when you start your job). The way to interpret this present value is to say you could invest $15,670.52 today at an annual compounding interest rate of 5 percent, and it would yield $20,000 in five years.

Bizarro

The following calculation shows that the present value of the entire extra $600,000 you earn by going to college is equivalent to having $252,939 in hand right now:[4]

$$\frac{\$20,000}{(1.05)^5} + \frac{\$20,000}{(1.05)^6} + \frac{\$20,000}{(1.05)^7} + \ldots + \frac{\$20,000}{(1.05)^{34}}$$

In the above calculation, the first term is the present value of the first $20,000 payment. The second term is the present value of the second $20,000 payment, received six years from today. Similarly, we calculate the present value of the $20,000 received each year for all 30 years, with the last payment received at $n = 34$.

According to the calculation, as long as you are paying less than $252,939 to attend college, then the future benefit will exceed the present cost. In fact, a more realistic version of this calculation would show college in an even more favorable light since you don't have to pay all the tuition money at once. This is just an example, of course. With your own predictions about your likely earnings (based on your expected career, where you're going to live, and other relevant variables), you can calculate a comparison that's tailor-made for your own situation.

Knowing how to translate between present and future values can be useful in many other decisions when the benefits and opportunity cost occur at different times. For example:

- If you want a certain level of income when you retire, how much should you save into your retirement fund now?
- If you run a business, what value of future sales would be needed to make it worthwhile to invest in a new piece of machinery?

You can compare these kinds of costs and benefits as long as you know three of the four variables in Equations 11-3 and 11-4: time period, interest rate, and either the present or future value of the costs and benefits.

✓ CONCEPT CHECK

- ☐ What does the interest rate on a loan represent to the lender? **[LO 11.1]**
- ☐ What is the "rule of 70"? **[LO 11.2]**
- ☐ What two factors determine the relationship between a future sum of money and its present value? **[LO 11.3]**

Risk and Uncertainty

If you are the worrying sort, you may have noticed a limitation of, or problem with, our analysis of the costs and benefits of college. What happens if your income doesn't increase as much as you expect it to as a result of attending college?

Just as in this example, some of the most important life decisions you will face involve weighing uncertain future costs and benefits against today's costs and benefits. We can make educated guesses about what will happen in the future, but there is always the chance that these guesses will turn out to be wrong. The changing value of money over time is only one challenge when making decisions about the future; risk is another.

What is risk?

Risk exists when the costs or benefits of an event or choice are uncertain. Everything in life involves some uncertainty. When you fly, there might be a delay that means missing an important connection. When you buy a used car, it might turn out to need expensive repairs. When you invest in a company, its stock price could tumble. When you invest in a college education, you might graduate just as the economy is tanking and well-paying jobs are hard to find. Evaluating risk requires that we think about different possible outcomes and accept that our best guess about future costs and benefits could be wrong.

risk
exists when the costs or benefits of an event or choice are uncertain

POTENTIALLY CONFUSING

Although they may seem like similar ideas, some economists often distinguish between *risk* and *uncertainty*. They use *risk* to refer to situations in which the probabilities that different outcomes will happen *are known*. We know, for example, that a coin has a 50 percent chance of coming up heads when it's flipped. Making a bet on a coin flip thus entails risk. Or consider airline safety: Although you may not want to look at

(continued)

the numbers (they are actually quite reassuring), the Federal Aviation Administration collects extensive statistics on the safety of airplanes; anyone can make a reasonable guess of the chance of the next flight crashing.

Those examples contrast with situations of *uncertainty,* in which the probabilities are *not known,* and may not even be measurable. The decision to go to college, for example, involves uncertainties about your future earnings and happiness in different kinds of careers. Even the best economists can't accurately predict what the health of the economy will be 10 or 20 years down the road.

The distinction may matter when you take courses focused on risk and uncertainty. But in the rest of the chapter, we'll use the terms *risk* and *uncertainty* interchangeably to refer to choices for which the probabilities of the event occurring are known.

Expected value

LO 11.4 Evaluate the costs and benefits of a choice using expected value.

Even when we can't know for *certain* how something will turn out, we can often say something about the *likelihood* that it will turn out one way versus another. If we can estimate how likely different outcomes are, and the financial implications of each outcome, then we can come up with a single cost or benefit figure that takes risk into account. That figure is called **expected value**. Expected value is the average of each possible outcome of a future event, weighted by its probability of occurring.

expected value
the average of each possible outcome of a future event, weighted by its probability of occurring

We can use expected value to make the analysis of the benefits of a college education a bit more realistic. In reality, of course, you could follow countless possible career paths. But for the sake of simplicity, let's say there are just two possibilities open to you *without* a college degree. Without a college degree, you have:

- A 50 percent chance of a career in which you make $1.5 million over 30 years ($50,000 a year).
- A 50 percent chance of making $900,000 over 30 years ($30,000 a year).

Then suppose that getting a college degree opens up a new range of job options. *With* a college degree, you have:

- A 50 percent chance of making $2.4 million.
- A 25 percent chance of making $1.5 million.
- A 25 percent chance of making $900,000.

Table 11-1 shows these possibilities.

We can't know for sure which of these possible career paths will come true. But since we know the probability of each, we can measure the expected value of your future income with and without college. The general formula for the expected value of a decision is found by multiplying

TABLE 11-1
Probability of outcomes

Lifetime earnings by education level	$0.9 million	$1.5 million	$2.4 million
No college degree	50%	50%	0%
College degree	25%	25%	50%

each possible outcome of an event (which we will call S) by the probability P of it occurring, and then adding together each of these terms for n different outcomes:

EQUATION 11-5   Expected value $= EV = (P_1 \times S_1) + (P_2 \times S_2) + \ldots + (P_n \times S_n)$

Using this formula, the expected value of your income without a college degree is:

$$EV = (50\% \times \$1,500,000) + (50\% \times \$900,000) = \$1,200,000$$

Applying the same method to find the expected value of your income with a college degree, you get:

$$EV = (25\% \times \$1,500,000) + (25\% \times \$900,000) + (50\% \times \$2,400,000)$$
$$= \$1,800,000$$

Unlike our earlier estimates, these figures incorporate the risk that your income might actually be lower with a college degree than it would have been without. It's always a possibility—you might get unlucky. But since you cannot know ahead of time whether you will be lucky or not, you can still make a choice based on your *expected* income, which is $600,000 higher with a degree.

Expected value can be a useful tool for making decisions whenever future outcomes are uncertain. For example, when investing in a retirement fund, you won't know for certain how quickly that fund will grow, but calculating an expected value can help you to decide how much you need to be saving. When choosing between different options, though, you won't necessarily always want to choose the option with the highest expected value. As we will see, you will also want to consider the worst-case outcome for each option and decide whether the risk of the worst-case outcome is unacceptably high.

Propensity for risk

> **LO 11.5** Explain the behavior of individuals who are risk-averse or risk-seeking.

Some things are riskier than others. There's a very low risk of injury when playing golf, for example, and a more significant risk when skiing. Similarly, some things that you can do with your money involve a higher risk of loss than others. Putting your money in a savings account or in government bonds carries a very low risk of loss; investing in a start-up company or playing the stock market usually carries a much higher risk.

People have different levels of willingness to engage in risky activities. Those who generally have low willingness to take on risk are said to be **risk-averse**. Those who enjoy a higher level of risk are **risk-seeking**. These attitudes toward risk are an aspect of an individual's preferences—as is a preference for a certain ice-cream flavor or a preference to spend your spare income on clothes or concerts.

Although individuals have varying tastes for taking on financial risks, economists believe that people are generally risk-averse in the following sense: When faced with two options with equal expected value, they will prefer the one with lower risk. Let's say we run a competition, and you're the winner. As a prize, we offer you these options:

Option A: We flip a coin. If it comes up heads, your prize is $100,001. If it's tails, your prize is $99,999.

Option B: We flip a coin. If it comes up heads, your prize is $200,000. If it's tails, you get nothing at all.

Both options have an expected value of $100,000. (Write out this calculation using Equation 11.5 to make sure.) When economists say

risk-averse
having a low willingness to take on situations with risk; when faced with two options with equal expected value, the one with lower risk is preferred

risk-seeking
having a high willingness to take on situations with risk; when faced with two options with equal expected value, the one with higher risk is preferred

Different individuals have different preferences for risk.
© Mark Anderson. www. Andertoons.com

© MARK ANDERSON, WWW.ANDERTOONS.COM

"OK, I'm going to say you're *quite risk averse*."

that people are generally risk-averse, it implies that most people prefer option A, even though both options have the same expected value. That is, people generally would prefer to forgo something in order to reduce the risk of a large loss. This is exactly why people buy insurance. (Clearly, though, not *everyone* would choose option A. If that was the case, nobody would ever go to a casino and take big chances by piling their bets on red or black on the roulette wheel.)

To put it another way, the *expected value* of option B would have to be greater before most people would accept the risk of winning nothing. If you chose option A, ask yourself *how much* would the value in option B have to rise to tempt you to switch to B? Perhaps to $250,000? (The expected value of option B would then rise to $125,000.) How about $1,000,000 (for an expected value of $500,000 for option B)? The answer depends on your personal taste for risk, and it will differ for each individual.

Although it may seem unlikely (alas) that you will ever win such a prize in a competition, this trade-off between risk and expected value is exactly the kind of choice you have to make whenever you think about investing money in stocks, retirement funds, bonds, or real estate.

✓**CONCEPT CHECK**

☐ How is the expected value of a future event calculated? **[LO 11.4]**
☐ Why do economists say that people tend to be risk-averse? **[LO 11.5]**

Insurance and Managing Risk

People cope with uncertainty about the future in many ways. One approach is to simply avoid taking greater risks than are strictly necessary. If you don't want to risk hurting yourself while skiing, then don't go skiing! But some risks in life are unavoidable, and some risky activities—like skiing—are avoidable but fun. So people have also developed ways to *manage* the risks they face in their lives.

The market for insurance

LO 11.6 Explain how risk aversion makes a market for insurance possible.

One common way to manage risk is to buy insurance. An *insurance policy* is a product that lets people pay to reduce uncertainty in some aspect of their lives. For instance, if you enjoy skiing, you can buy insurance to cover the cost of being airlifted to a hospital if you break your leg in a fall on the slopes. Insurance products usually involve paying a regular fee in return for an agreement that the insurance company will cover any unpredictable costs that arise.

You've probably encountered many types of insurance associated with common risks that people face in life. There is auto insurance to manage the risk of having your car damaged or causing damage to someone else. Medical insurance manages the risk of becoming ill or injured. Homeowner's or renter's insurance manages the risk of having your belongings destroyed or stolen. Companies that provide these insurance products collect a fee—called a *premium*—in return for covering the costs that clients would otherwise have to pay if they experienced any of these unfortunate events.

In general, the amount people pay for insurance is higher than its *expected value*. For instance, suppose that you pay $1,000 per year for auto insurance. Suppose also that in any given year there is a 1.5 percent likelihood that you will get into an accident that costs $10,000 and a 0.2 percent likelihood of an accident that costs $200,000. If we assume that your insurance policy would cover the full cost of these accidents, then the expected value of coverage in any given year is $550:

$$EV = (1.5\% \times \$10,000) + (0.2\% \times \$200,000)$$
$$= (0.015 \times \$10,000) + (0.002 \times \$200,000) = \$150 + \$400 = \$550$$

Does paying $1,000 for something with a $550 expected value make people suckers? Not at all. Because most people are risk-averse, they are willing to incur the added cost. In the auto insurance example, the $450 buys peace of mind: That amount represents the utility that comes from knowing that if you do get into an expensive auto accident, you will not be ruined by the costs.

The reason people are generally willing to pay for insurance is that, with insurance, the upward limit of their liability in case of an unfortunate event is usually much lower than the actual cost. Without insurance, most people would have trouble finding enough money to replace their homes and all of their possessions following, say, a fire, or to cover the cost of long-term hospital care if they fell very ill. Insurance allows people to feel confident that if they are suddenly faced with these huge expenses, they won't face bankruptcy or be unable to pay for the services they need.

In fact, if the expected value of insurance policies were equal to the premiums paid, insurance companies would not stay in business very long: The insurers would be paying out approximately the same amount they received in premiums, with nothing left over. The industry exists only because it can make a profit from the extra amount that people are willing to pay for the service of managing risk.

Pooling and diversifying risk

LO 11.7 Explain the importance of pooling and diversification for managing risk.

Insurance does not reduce the risks inherent in life. Having car insurance will not make you less likely to be in an accident. (As we will see in the next section, it may actually make accidents *more* likely.) Instead, insurance works because it reallocates the costs of such an event, sparing any individual from taking the full hit. This reallocation occurs through two mechanisms.

The first mechanism for reallocating risk is called pooling. **Risk pooling** occurs when people organize themselves in a group to collectively absorb the cost of the risk faced by each individual. This is the foundational principle that makes insurance companies work. The company is able to easily absorb the cost of one person's emergency because, at any given time, it will have many other clients who are paying their premiums and not making claims.

risk pooling
organizing people into a group to collectively absorb the risk faced by each individual

Suppose, for example, a company has 1,000,000 clients. Putting aside the question of the company's profits, this is equivalent to every client agreeing that he or she will pay $\frac{1}{1,000,000}$ of the cost of catastrophes that happen to other clients. In return, all clients have the assurance that they won't have to pay $\frac{999,999}{1,000,000}$ of the cost if a catastrophe happens to them. Pooling doesn't reduce the risk of catastrophes happening; it just reallocates the costs when they do.

An example of risk pooling comes from the method used by the United Kingdom and other countries to pay for student loans. Rather than making individual students responsible for the costs of their education, all students get their loans from a government-backed company. That company must be repaid only if students earn enough money out of college to do so. You can read about the merits and problems of this system in the What Do You Think? box "Who should bear the risk that a college degree doesn't pay off?"

 ## What Do You Think?
Who should bear the risk that a college degree doesn't pay off?

Suppose you could buy insurance against the possibility that, despite your college degree, you will never get a high-paying job: If your salary never rises above a certain level, the insurance company will pay off the loan you took out to go to college. Would you be interested in buying such an insurance product?

Actually, this is exactly the kind of student loan system in place in some countries, such as the United Kingdom. Students borrow from a government-backed company and repay their

(continued)

loans only once they start earning above a certain amount. If their earnings never reach that level, the loan is eventually written off.

Supporters of this system say it encourages more young people to go to college. Nobody needs to fear that by getting an education, they will incur debts that they will struggle to pay off. Critics point out that taxpayers—including people who never went to college—end up subsidizing graduates who fail to get high-paying jobs.

Some people have proposed replacing this system with a "graduate tax." Under this proposal, college education would be free; it would be paid for by levying an additional income tax on all college graduates earning above a certain sum. Instead of asking all taxpayers to foot the bill for college, only people who attend college would be on the hook.

Effectively, this is a debate about who should bear the risk that a college education doesn't pay off. In the UK, it's currently the taxpayers. Under the graduate-tax proposal, the risk would be pooled among everyone who attends college. In the United States, the responsibility usually falls on the individual student or student's family. Should others be required to pay for the education of people who decide to be social workers or poets? On the other hand, does society as a whole lose something by discouraging students from pursuing their passions for social services or the arts?

WHAT DO YOU THINK?

1. Who should bear the costs of a college education for those people who do not earn enough money to pay back their loans?
2. Should the tuition for those who go into certain majors or professions be forgiven? If you think so, how should we choose which majors or professions should be chosen for this type of program?

diversification

the process by which risks are shared across many different assets or people, reducing the impact of any particular risk on any one individual

The second mechanism for managing risk is diversification. Risk **diversification** refers to the process by which risks are shared across many different assets or people, reducing the impact of any particular risk on any one individual. Diversification is about not putting all your eggs in one basket, and it can be practiced by individuals or firms. For instance, if you invest all of your money in one company, you are completely dependent on that company's fortunes. If it goes bankrupt, so will you. Instead, many people choose to diversify by investing smaller amounts in many companies. If one company fails, they will lose some money, but not all of it. Like pooling your risks, diversifying your risks does not change the likelihood that bad things will happen. It just means that you're not going to be completely ruined by a single unfortunate event.

Suppose you are considering investing $500 in shares of stocks. Stock X is priced at $10 per share, so you can purchase 50 shares. There is a 20 percent chance that, in the future, the price of X will fall to $2. If it does, the value of your 50 shares would be $100. But there is also an 80 percent chance that, in the future, the price of X will increase to $20. If that happens, the value of your shares would be $1,000. Thus, the expected value of your 50 shares in the future is $820:

$$EV = (0.20 \times \$100) + (0.80 \times \$1,000) = \$820$$

We can see these values in panel A of Figure 11-1. Now suppose there is a second stock available, stock Y. Stock Y is also initially priced at $10 per share and also faces the possibility of either falling to $2 per share or rising to $20 per share. However, the prices of stock X and stock Y do not necessarily rise and fall together:

- There is a 4 percent chance that the prices of both stocks will fall to $2 per share.
- There is a 16 percent chance that the price of X will rise while the price of Y falls.
- There is a 16 percent chance that the price of X will fall while the price of Y rises.
- There is a 64 percent chance that the prices of both stocks will rise to $20.

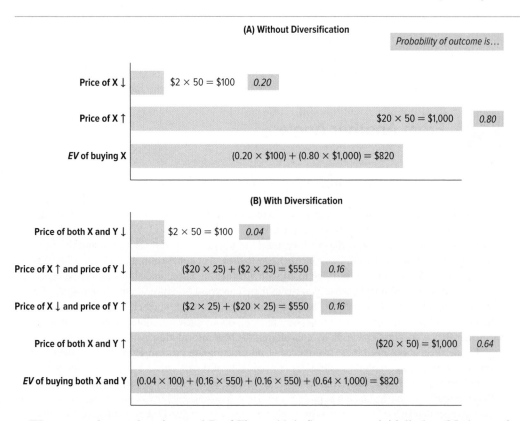

FIGURE 11-1

Expected value of stock purchases with and without diversification

We can see these values in panel B of Figure 11-1. Suppose you initially buy 25 shares of X and 25 shares of Y. We can again calculate the expected value of your shares in the future:

$$EV = (0.04 \times \$100) + (0.16 \times \$550) + (0.16 \times \$550) + (0.64 \times \$1,000) = \$820$$

Notice that the expected value of your shares in the future is the same whether you purchase 50 shares of only X or if you purchase 25 shares of X and 25 shares of Y. However, purchasing 25 shares of X and 25 shares of Y carries much less risk:

- There is only a 4 percent chance of ending up with $100. (In contrast, purchasing only shares of X means a 20 percent chance of having only $100 in the future.)
- Furthermore, because there is only a 4 percent chance of losing money, there is a 96 percent chance that you will have *more* money in the future than you have now.
- The potential gains from buying shares of both X and Y (64 percent) are slightly smaller than if you bought only shares of X (80 percent). However, the risk of losing any money at all is much smaller under diversification.

The key to diversification is that the risks should be as unrelated as possible. For instance, suppose an insurance company sells only one type of insurance—home insurance against earthquakes in San Francisco. This would not be a sensible way for homeowners in San Francisco to pool their risks: If one client's home is destroyed by an earthquake, that same earthquake is likely to destroy many other clients' homes as well. The insurance company could face *all* of its clients making claims at once, and would go bankrupt. In other words, the risk of earthquake damage to one home in San Francisco is *highly correlated* with the risk of earthquake damage to other homes in San Francisco. (Remember that *positive correlation* means things tend to occur together.)

To avoid this problem, the insurance company will diversify. In addition to home insurance in San Francisco, it might choose also to sell, say, car insurance in New Jersey and hurricane insurance in Florida. Earthquakes, car crashes, and hurricanes in different parts of the country are *uncorrelated:* None is more or less likely to occur if one of the others occurs. The insurance company has diversified its risk by selling different products in different places. If it has to pay out after an earthquake in San Francisco, those costs will be covered by the premiums it continues to collect in other places.

These days, you're offered insurance quite often, whether on a new tennis racquet or a cell phone. At the time of the purchase, you have no idea whether it's a good idea to buy it or not. If the cell phone breaks, the insurance is totally worth it; if the phone lasts for years, you didn't need insurance at all. As the From Another Angle box "Hindsight is 20/20" describes, though, it's not best to look at a decision to buy insurance many years after the fact.

From Another Angle
Hindsight is 20/20

Say you bought an extended warranty that guarantees the replacement of your washing machine if it breaks, and then the washing machine actually does break. You might feel quite pleased with yourself. Now imagine that after living in the Mississippi delta and paying flood insurance for 20 years, you move away without having experienced a single flood. You might feel like you threw away your money. Was the washing machine warranty the right decision and the flood insurance the wrong decision? Don't be too hasty to draw that conclusion. In both cases, the way things actually turned out has nothing to do with whether the initial decision was a good one.

Decisions that seem right when you make them can seem horribly wrong in retrospect. It's tempting to think that you need the benefit of hindsight to judge whether a decision about the future was right. But that's the wrong way to think about such decisions. You have to judge whether they were right or wrong by considering the best information available *at the time.*

In decisions about insurance, two pieces of information are crucial: How likely is the event you're insuring against and how catastrophic would it be if it happened? The Mississippi delta is quite likely to flood, and recovering from flood damage can be ruinously expensive. So, buying flood insurance in this instance was probably the right decision, even if you didn't end up using it. On the other hand, flood insurance is probably not such a smart purchase if you live on the top of a hill in Denver—flood damage would be just as ruinously costly, but the likelihood is minuscule.

How about the washing machine? Suppose it costs $450, and the salesperson offers you insurance at $12.50 a month. This comes to $150 a year, so if the washing machine works well for at least three years—which is quite likely—you've already saved enough to buy a new one. If you're unlucky and it does break down before then, it wouldn't be a disaster: It would be annoying to have to fork out $450 for another washing machine, but it probably wouldn't bankrupt you. Unless you're extremely risk-averse, refusing the insurance at that price is the right decision—even if it turns out that the washing machine then breaks down in its second year.

After the fact, the uncertainty about the future that drove you to buy insurance has been resolved. But that doesn't mean that you should second-guess your decisions. If your hilltop Denver home suffers damage in a flash-flood, you're an unlucky person—but you didn't necessarily make the wrong decision about whether or not to buy flood insurance.

Problems with insurance

adverse selection
a state that occurs when buyers and sellers have different information about the quality of a good or the riskiness of a situation, and this asymmetric information results in failure to complete transactions that would have been possible if both sides had the same information.

LO 11.8 Describe the challenges that adverse selection and moral hazard pose for insurance.

Pooling and diversifying are common ways of managing risk. For example, when U.S. insurance companies insure individuals, they typically offer insurance to all employees of a particular business. In this way, they pool their risk over a large group of workers so they aren't insuring only the workers most prone to illness. In addition to mitigating risk, most insurance markets also face problems with information asymmetry. This leads to two main problems with insurance: adverse selection and moral hazard. Although we discussed these ideas at length in Chapter 10, "Information," they are particularly crucial for thinking about insurance and risk management.

The first problem insurance companies face is **adverse selection**. This concept describes a state that occurs when buyers and sellers have different information about the quality of a good or the riskiness of a situation, and this asymmetric information results in failure to complete transactions that would have been possible if both sides had the same information. In the context of insurance, adverse selection refers to the tendency for people with higher risk to be drawn toward insurance. For example, in car insurance, the hidden information is that insurers don't know who the bad drivers are, and the unattractive good is an insurance policy on a reckless driver. If you know you're a terrible driver, you'll try to buy as much car insurance as you can. If you smoke, eat mostly fast food, and do not exercise, you might be an enthusiastic customer for health insurance, and so on.

If insurance companies knew everything about their clients, adverse selection would not be a problem. The insurers would simply charge higher premiums to higher-risk clients. Insurance companies can and do ask potential clients seemingly endless questions about their driving records, smoking habits, and so on. But the clients still often know much more about their relevant risk factors than the insurance company. The result is that insurers have a hard time accurately assessing how risky a particular customer will be and charging the right price. To cover their costs, insurance companies usually end up charging higher prices to *all* customers. That decision can make insurance a much less good deal for low-risk individuals. If not kept in check, adverse selection can make it hard for less-risky individuals to find an insurance contract that's worth buying.

The second problem insurance companies face is **moral hazard**—the tendency for people to behave in a riskier way or to renege on contracts when they do not face the full consequences of their actions. If your car is insured against theft, for example, you may be more relaxed about parking it in an unsafe-looking neighborhood. This problem is especially acute with medical insurance: People who know that their medical costs are covered may demand treatments and tests that they would never purchase if they had to pay for them on their own. In these cases, insurance can actually *increase* the expected cost of risks, as discussed in the What Do You Think? box "Should health insurance include preventive care?"

moral hazard
the tendency for people to behave in a riskier way or to renege on contracts when they do not face the full consequences of their actions

What Do You Think?

Should health insurance include preventive care?

One of the highest-profile political debates in America is about how to rein in the steadily increasing costs of medical care. Skyrocketing medical expenditures have been attributed to many factors, including the increased prevalence of obesity, an aging population, and steadily rising malpractice liabilities for doctors.

One strategy that many have suggested to rein in costs is to increase the incentives for people to seek preventive care. Following the passage of the Affordable Care Act of 2010, most health plans in the United States cover preventive care at no out-of-pocket cost to the patient. Examples of covered preventive care include screening for high blood pressure, screening for several types of cancers, and screening for diabetes. With many diseases—including cancer and diabetes, two of the costliest to treat—spending money on early detection and preventive care can prevent much higher costs from being incurred down the road. Preventive care can also reduce the suffering that comes with chronic illness.

On the other hand, moral hazard comes into play. If people with medical insurance are entitled to preventive care, they may demand all kinds of expensive tests and preventive treatments that they don't need. Some people worry that this increase in spending might negate the benefit of future savings.

WHAT DO YOU THINK?

1. Should government policy encourage insurance companies to cover preventive care?
2. Should insurance companies be able to choose which procedures they cover?
3. If you were asked to be a judge in a decision on this matter, what additional information would you need to answer this important question?

✓CONCEPT CHECK

☐ Why are people often willing to pay more for insurance than the expected value of the coverage? **[LO 11.6]**

☐ What's the difference between risk pooling and risk diversification? **[LO 11.7]**

☐ Why can moral hazard increase the costs of insurance coverage? **[LO 11.8]**

Conclusion

Some of life's most important decisions involve weighing uncertain *future* costs and benefits against costs and benefits *today*. In this chapter, we looked at tools that can help with these decisions. Interest rates enable you to compare apples to apples when you think about costs and benefits that occur at different times. Expected value can help you think about what is the best option given uncertainty. Managing risk through pooling or diversification can allow you to avoid bearing the full cost of a worst-case scenario if it happens.

Key Terms

interest rate, p. 254

compounding, p. 255

present value, p. 256

risk, p. 257

expected value, p. 258

risk-averse, p. 259

risk-seeking, p. 259

risk pooling, p. 261

diversification, p. 262

adverse selection, p. 264

moral hazard, p. 265

Summary

LO 11.1 Explain why money is worth more now than in the future, and how the interest rate represents this relationship.

Money is worth more in the present than in the future because it can be immediately spent or invested in productive opportunities. The interest rate is the cost of borrowing money for a certain unit of time. It is usually expressed as a percentage per time period. The interest rate is the amount needed to compensate the lender for the opportunity cost of loaning out money—in other words, the amount of money the lender could have earned from investing in something else if he or she weren't lending it.

LO 11.2 Calculate compounding over time with a given interest rate.

Compounding is the process of accumulation that results from the additional interest paid on previously earned interest. With compound interest, the amount of interest earned increases each period, since interest payments earned in the past themselves accumulate interest in future periods. We calculate the future value of a sum of money, including compound interest, as $FV = PV \times (1 + r)^n$.

LO 11.3 Calculate the present value of a future sum.

Present value refers to how much a certain amount of money in the future is worth today. It can be calculated by rearranging the formula for the future value of a sum, to $PV = \frac{FV}{(1 + r)^n}$. Translating cost or benefits that occur at different times into their present value gives you a common unit of value, allowing you to compare apples to apples.

LO 11.4 Evaluate the costs and benefits of a choice using expected value.

Risk exists with uncertainty about the future—the possibility that things won't turn out as you expect. In order to understand the likely value of a choice with multiple possible outcomes, we calculate its expected value. *Expected value* is the average of all possible future values, weighted by their probability of occurring. Expected value allows us to account for risk when comparing options.

LO 11.5 Explain the behavior of individuals who are risk-averse or risk-seeking.

People have varying degrees of willingness to take on risk. Those who have a low willingness to take on risk are *risk-averse;* those who have a high willingness to take on risk are *risk-seeking.* People are generally risk-averse in the limited sense that when two choices have the same expected value, they will prefer the less-risky one. People generally would prefer to gain a smaller amount than to risk losing everything. The loss of utility caused by losing a large sum is greater than the benefit of gaining the same amount.

LO 11.6 Explain how risk aversion makes a market for insurance possible.

Insurance is a common strategy for managing risk. An insurance policy lets people pay to reduce uncertainty in some aspect of their lives. Such products usually involve paying a regular fee (premium) in return for an agreement that someone else will cover any unpredictable costs that arise. Insurance does not reduce the risk of something bad happening; it simply guarantees that the cost of the event to the insured person will be low. Risk aversion makes a market for insurance profitable: People are willing to pay to shield themselves from the cost of bad things happening, above and beyond the actual expected cost of those things.

LO 11.7 Explain the importance of pooling and diversification for managing risk.

Risk pooling is a strategy for managing risk that involves many people organizing themselves in a group in order to collectively absorb the cost of the risk faced by each individual. Risk pooling doesn't decrease the risk that a bad event will occur; it only reduces the cost to a particular individual in the event that it does occur.

Diversification is another strategy for managing risk that involves replacing large risks with smaller, unrelated ones. That way, the cost of failure for any one investment is not so great, and the chance of many different investments all failing together is small, so the risk of losing a large amount is reduced. Like pooling, diversification does not change the likelihood that bad things will happen; it just reduces the costs associated with any single event.

LO 11.8 Describe the challenges that adverse selection and moral hazard pose for insurance.

One challenge faced by insurance schemes is *adverse selection*—the tendency for people with higher risk to be drawn toward insurance. If insurance companies were able to accurately identify risky clients, adverse selection would not be a problem; insurers would simply charge more for higher-risk clients. But clients often know much more about their relevant risk factors than the insurance company does.

Moral hazard is another challenge for insurance companies. *Moral hazard* means that people will behave in a riskier way when they know that their risks are covered by insurance.

Review Questions

1. Anna is indifferent between receiving $200 today and $230 in a month. What does this imply about her opportunity cost in the coming month? How much interest would Anna need to charge to lend $200 for the month in order to break even? **[LO 11.1]**

2. Colton has a choice between $100 today and $150 in three months. Farah has a choice between $100 today and $125 in three months. Colton chooses $100 today. Farah chooses $125 in three months. Explain why Farah is the one who delays payment even though Colton stands to earn more by waiting. **[LO 11.1]**

3. Suppose your aunt invests $2,000 for you. You are not allowed to have the money until the original amount doubles. Your aunt's investment earns 10 percent, compounded annually. Give a rough estimate of how long it will take before you can access the money your aunt invested for you. **[LO 11.2]**

4. You are considering taking out a two-year loan of $1,000 from a bank, on which you can pay either compound yearly interest of 1 percent or a flat rate of 2 percent for the whole two-year period. Which option is a better deal, and why? **[LO 11.2]**

5. Suppose you know that an investment will earn a positive return in the future. Why is it important to know the present value of the investment? **[LO 11.3]**

6. Suppose you are selling a piece of furniture to a friend who can't afford to pay you upfront but offers to pay you in monthly installments for the next year. What information do you need to calculate the present value of this offer? (*Hint:* Think about the formula for present value.) **[LO 11.3]**

7. A pharmaceutical company is considering investing in the development of a new drug. The company stands to make a lot of profit if the drug is successful. However, there is some risk that the drug will not be approved by government regulators. If this happens, the company will lose its entire investment. Advise the company how to take this risk into account as managers evaluate whether to invest. **[LO 11.4]**

8. You have a big exam tomorrow. You were planning to study tonight, but your friend has tickets to a concert and has invited you to join her. You would be willing to accept a B on the exam in order to go to the concert. You estimate that if you don't study, you have a

35 percent chance of scoring a 90, a 35 percent chance of scoring an 80 (the score required to earn a B), a 25 percent chance of earning a 75, and a 5 percent chance of earning a 60. Will you go to the concert? Explain why or why not. **[LO 11.4]**

9. Many individuals prefer to have insurance (health insurance, car insurance, etc.) rather than not, even if the expected value of their wealth is higher without insurance. What does this imply about their willingness to take on risk? **[LO 11.5]**

10. Lenders tend to offer lower interest rates to borrowers with high credit scores and higher interest rates to borrowers with low credit scores. What does this imply about lenders' willingness to take on risk? **[LO 11.5]**

11. Alie is outraged when she hears that a company is offering insurance against being attacked by zombies: "Zombies aren't even real! This company is just taking advantage of people." Without acknowledging the possible existence of zombies, provide an alternative perspective on the insurance company's ethics. **[LO 11.6]**

12. Julia pays $1,200 for an insurance policy with an expected value of $1,000. Explain why this is a rational choice for Julia. **[LO 11.6]**

13. Suppose that the crop yield of corn farmers in Iowa depends solely on rainfall levels. Also suppose that every part of the state gets approximately the same amount of rain as every other part in any given year. Will the corn farmers of Iowa be able to effectively use pooling to reduce their exposure to risk? Why or why not? **[LO 11.7]**

14. An insurance company that faces fierce competition from other providers is considering a strategy to sell more policies by simplifying its portfolio and becoming the expert in flood insurance for the state. The company managers reason, "Everyone buys flood insurance in this state, so let's focus our efforts on becoming the preferred provider." Evaluate this strategy. **[LO 11.7]**

15. Suppose the economy is suffering and many people are afraid they will be laid off from their jobs. Workers would like to protect against this risk with insurance. Identify and explain two problems that prevent insurance companies from offering layoff insurance. **[LO 11.8]**

16. BackPedal is a bike-rental shop that rents bicycles, helmets, and other gear by the day. **[LO 11.8]**

    a. BackPedal offers an optional helmet rental for $10/day with the rental of a bicycle. To his surprise, the store manager has noticed that cycling accidents are higher among customers who rent helmets than those who do not. Explain this phenomenon using economic concepts. Assume that customers who do not rent helmets also do not own helmets.

    b. BackPedal is considering offering helmets for free with a bike rental. Explain how this new policy will affect the issues you identified in part *a.*

Problems and Applications

1. Your bank offers 3 percent annual interest on savings deposits. If you deposit $560 today, how much interest will you have earned at the end of one year? **[LO 11.1]**

2. You have $350, which a friend would like to borrow. If you don't lend it to your friend, you could invest it in an opportunity that would pay out $392 at the end of the year. What annual interest rate should your friend offer you to make you indifferent between these two options? **[LO 11.1]**

3. If you deposit $500 in a savings account that offers 3 percent interest, compounded annually, and you don't withdraw any money, how much money should you expect to have in the account at the end of three years? **[LO 11.2]**

4. Suppose you run up a debt of $300 on a credit card that charges an annual rate of 12 percent, compounded annually. How much will you owe at the end of two years? Assume no additional charges or payments are made. **[LO 11.2]**

5. Your savings account currently has a balance of $32,300. You opened the savings account two years ago and have not added to the initial amount you deposited. If your savings have been earning an annual interest rate of 2 percent, compounded annually, what was the amount of your original deposit? **[LO 11.3]**

6. You run a business and are considering offering a new service. If you offer the new service, you expect it to generate $60,000 in profits each year for your business over the next two years. In order to offer the new service, you will need to take out a loan for new equipment. Assume a 5 percent annual interest rate. **[LO 11.3]**

7. You are driving home from work and get stuck in a traffic jam. You are considering turning off from your usual route home and taking a longer route that might have less traffic. However, you know that there is some chance that the traffic on your usual, shorter route will clear up. Based on Table 11P-1, calculate the expected value (in minutes until you arrive home) of each option. **[LO 11.4]**

8. Books for Kids is a not-for-profit organization that runs after-school reading programs in four school districts. Books for Kids is planning a fund-raiser to buy new books. Last time it held a fund-raiser, donors were allowed to specify which district program they wanted to receive their donation. Table 11P-2 shows

TABLE 11P-1

	Light traffic	Moderate traffic	Heavy traffic
Probability of encountering on Route 1	30%	20%	50%
Duration of drive on Route 1	10 minutes	30 minutes	60 minutes
Probability of encountering on Route 2	50%	50%	0%
Duration of drive on Route 2	20 minutes	40 minutes	80 minutes

TABLE 11P-2

	Average donation ($)	Percent of donations (%)
Northwest district	25	15
Southeast district	50	30
West district	15	20
South district	12	35

the average donations and the percent of all donations that went to each district. Using the last fund-raiser as a projection, what is the expected value of the average donation across all four programs? **[LO 11.4]**

9. Cora had two options when buying car insurance. The expected value of her wealth would be higher with Option A, but Cora chose option B. From the list below, what can we assume about these policies and Cora's willingness to take on risk? Check all that apply. **[LO 11.5]**

   a. Option B was riskier.

   b. Option A was riskier.

   c. Cora is risk-seeking.

   d. Cora is risk-averse.

10. Consider the following scenarios. For each scenario, determine whether a risk averse person will definitely choose Option A, definitely choose Option B, be indifferent between Options A and B, or might choose either Option A or B, **[LO 11.5]**

    a. *Option A:* There is a 50% chance of winning $1,000 and a 50% chance of winning $0. *Option B:* There is a 100% chance of receiving $500.

    b. *Option A:* There is a 40% chance of winning $90 and a 60% chance of winning $110. *Option B:* There is a 100% chance of winning $90.

    c. *Option A:* There is a 50% chance of winning $0 and a 50% chance of winning $100. *Option B:* There is a 50% chance of winning $20 and a 50% chance of winning $60.

11. Suppose you own a beach house on a coast that has a small chance of encountering a hurricane each year. There is a 1% chance that there will be a hurricane this year that would completely destroy your $350,000 home. (Assume that this home is the only store of wealth that you have.) An insurance company has offered you insurance that would reimburse you the entire value of your home in the event of a hurricane. The premium for this insurance is $4,000. **[LO 11.6]**

    a. What is the expected value of your wealth if you do not purchase insurance?

    b. What is the expected value of your wealth if you purchase the insurance at a $4,000 premium?

    c. Will a risk-averse person choose to purchase insurance?

    d. Will a risk-seeking person choose to purchase insurance?

    e. What would the premium have to be to make a risk-neutral person indifferent between buying the insurance and not buying the insurance?

    f. If the insurance company offered the premium you found in part (e), would a risk-averse person purchase insurance?

12. You are considering buying one of two types of health insurance. You guess that in the next year there is a 1 percent chance of serious illness that will cost you $67,500 in health care; a 9 percent chance of a moderate illness that will cost you $2,500; and a 90 percent chance of regular health care needs that will cost you $500. One type of health insurance is emergency-only coverage; it will cover your expenses for serious illness but not moderate illness or regular care. The other type covers moderate illness and regular expenses, but its payout is capped, so it will not cover the cost of a serious illness. **[LO 11.6]**

    a. What is the expected value of payouts from the emergency-only insurance?

    b. What is the expected value of payouts from the capped-coverage insurance?

    c. Which option is a more risk-averse person likely to choose?

13. For each of the following scenarios, say whether *pooling* or *diversification* is a more promising risk-mitigation strategy. **[LO 11.7]**

a. Employees of a company who invest their savings in that company's stocks.

b. Families who are worried about losing their possessions if their houses burn down.

c. Neighboring farmers who grow the same crop, which is prone to failure in dry years.

14. You have two possessions you would like to insure against theft or damage: your new bicycle, which cost you $800, and a painting you inherited, which has been appraised at $55,000. The painting is more valuable, but your bicycle must be kept outdoors and is in much greater danger of being stolen or damaged. You can afford to insure only one item. Which should you choose? Why? **[LO 11.7]**

15. Farmer Tom is trying to decide what to produce on his farm in the upcoming season. In the past, he has usually grown Crop A. If he grows Crop A, there is a 70% chance that his crop will yield $15,000 in profit and a 30% chance that he will earn zero profit. **[LO 11.7]**

a. What is the expected value of his profit if he grows only Crop A?

b. Now Farmer Tom considers dividing his land between two crops: Crop A and Crop B. There is a 5% chance that both crops will fail, and Tom will earn zero profit. The is a 25% chance that only one crop will grow, and Tom will earn $6,000 in profit. There is a 60% chance that both crops will grow, and Tom will earn $15,000 in profit. What is the expected value of his profit if he grows both crops?

c. Which option would a risk-averse farmer choose?

d. Which option would a risk-seeking farmer choose?

e. Which option would a risk-neutral farmer choose?

16. Say whether each of the following scenarios describes an insurance problem caused by *adverse selection* or by *moral hazard*. **[LO 11.8]**

a. People who have homeowners insurance are less likely than others to replace the batteries in their smoke detectors.

b. People who enjoy dangerous hobbies are more likely than others to buy life insurance.

c. People whose parents died young are more likely than others to seek out health insurance with better coverage.

d. People who have liability coverage on their car insurance take less care than others to avoid accidents.

17. As part of the Affordable Care Act of 2010, all individuals in the U.S. are now required to have health insurance. Do economists expect mandatory health insurance to reduce adverse selection, moral hazard, both, or neither? **[LO 11.8]**

Endnotes

1. B. Greene, "Obama, Romney agree on extending student loan interest rate cut," *U.S. News and World Report,* April 23, 2012, http://www.usnews.com/news/articles/2012/04/23/obama-romney-agree-on-extending-stafford-interest-rate-cut.

2. K. Holland, "The high economic and social costs of student loan debt," June 15, 2015, http://www.cnbc.com/2015/06/15/the-high-economic-and-social-costs-of-student-loan-debt.html.

3. J. Weiner, "Why Sally can't get a good job with her college degree," September 5, 2014, https://www.washingtonpost.com/blogs/she-the-people/wp/2014/09/05/why-sally-cant-get-a-good-job-with-her-college-degree/.

4. The reason the superscripts in the denominators in the computation begin with 5 is that in the example, you don't start earning your salary until year 5—that is, after college is over.

Math Essentials: Compounding

Learning Objective

LO F.1   Use compounding to calculate the present and future value of money.

In Chapter 11, "Time and Uncertainty," you learned how to compute the future value of money using compound interest. Compounding occurs because the interest your money earns in one time period itself earns interest in the next time period. Multiplying a single investment by an interest rate is simple enough, but calculating the growth of an investment over time is more complicated because the base keeps changing. In every period, we have to multiply the interest rate by the initial investment *plus* any interest earned in earlier time periods. This appendix will walk you through the act of compounding.

Compounding and Future Value

LO F.1 Use compounding to calculate the present and future value of money.

Let's say that you invest $100 right now at an interest rate of 10 percent. You plan to withdraw your money in 4 years, and the interest compounds annually. What will be the value of your investment in 4 years?

Let's first calculate the value year by year, accounting for the compounding interest. This calculation is essentially calculating percentage change. The 10 percent in interest represents how much the original amount you invest will change in one time period (in this case, one year).

Year 1:	$100.00 + ($100.00 × 0.10) = $110.00
Year 2:	$110.00 + ($110.00 × 0.10) = $121.00
Year 3:	$121.00 + ($121.00 × 0.10) = $133.10
Year 4:	$133.10 + ($133.10 × 0.10) = $143.41

Notice that each year we incorporate the interest earned in the previous year into the base investment for the next year. In other words, we multiply the interest rate not by the initial investment, but by the initial investment *plus* any previously earned interest.

Instead of these year-by-year calculations, we can use a formula. The general formula for computing the future value of money using compounding is:

EQUATION F-1 $$\text{Future value} = FV = PV \times (1 + r)^n$$

where *PV* is the amount (present value) of the initial investment, *FV* is the future value of the investment, *r* is the interest rate, and *n* is the number of time periods between now and the future.

Let's try the problem again using the formula for compound interest. First, remember the order of operations:

PEMDAS

P: *P*arentheses, from the innermost outward

E: *E*xponents

MD: *M*ultiplication and *D*ivision from left to right

AS: *A*ddition and *S*ubtraction from left to right

Therefore, we plug in your initial investment of $100 for *PV*1 and the time period of 4 years for *n*, and solve for *FV* in the following order. (*Hint:* You might want a calculator for this.)

$$FV = PV \times (1 + r)^n$$
$$FV = 100 \times (1 + 0.1)^4$$
$$FV = 100 \times (1.1)^4 \qquad \text{(Remember to } \textit{start with the operations inside the parentheses.)}$$
$$FV = 100 \times 1.4641 \qquad \text{(Now you } \textit{apply the exponent.)}$$
$$FV = \$146.41$$

After 4 years, your investment of $100 will be worth $146.41.

Let's see how the problem changes when we change the interest rate. This time, let's calculate the future value of your $100 investment if the interest rate is 5 percent. We will still invest for 4 years with interest compounded annually.

Year 1: $100.00 + ($100.00 × 0.05) = $105.00
Year 2: $105.00 + ($105.00 × 0.05) = $110.25
Year 3: $110.25 + ($110.25 × 0.05) = $115.76
Year 4: $115.76 + ($115.76 × 0.05) = $121.55

Now, let's do the problem again using the formula.

$$FV = 100 \times (1 + 0.05)^4$$
$$FV = 100 \times (1.05)^4$$
$$FV = 100 \times 1.2155$$
$$FV = \$121.55$$

After 4 years, your investment of $100 is worth $121.55.

This same method can be used to calculate the value of a borrowed sum of money, as well as an invested one. Instead of an initial investment, we can plug in the initial amount borrowed. The interest rate is the rate at which the debt increases, rather than the rate at which your investment grows; otherwise the calculations are exactly the same.

Suppose you borrow $1,000 at a monthly interest rate of 10 percent, and wait for 5 months to pay it off. Let's assume that interest is compounded monthly. How will your debt accumulate each month?

Month 1: $1,000.00 + ($1,000.00 × 0.10) = $1,100.00
Month 2: $1,100.00 + ($1,100.00 × 0.10) = $1,210.00
Month 3: $1,210.00 + ($1,210.00 × 0.10) = $1,331.00
Month 4: $1,331.00 + ($1,331.00 × 0.10) = $1,464.10
Month 5: $1,464.10 + ($1,464.10 × 0.10) = $1,610.51

Let's do the problem again using the formula.

$$FV = 1,000 \times (1 + 0.1)^5$$
$$FV = 1,000 \times (1.1)^5$$
$$FV = 1,000 \times 1.61051$$
$$FV = \$1,610.51$$

After 5 months, you will owe $1,610.51, or more than one-and-a-half times your initial debt.

The rule of 70

You've now seen how to calculate compounded amounts over time. There's also a quick and easy tool for estimating the effects of compounding over time. Called the "rule of 70," it states that the amount of time it will take an investment to double in value is roughly 70 time periods divided by the interest rate per period. Therefore, if you are earning 5 percent interest per year on your savings account, it will take about $70 \div 5 = 14$ years for the value of your account to double.

This is only a rough estimate—if you do the math precisely, you will find that after 14 years your money would not quite have doubled yet. (In the case of a $1,000 deposit, for instance: $1,000 \times (1.05)^{14} = \$1,979.93$.) The rule of 70 is less precise when applied to higher rates of interest. But it works pretty well for most interest rates you're realistically likely to encounter, so many businesspeople use it to make quick mental calculations. For example, if you are considering investing in a business that earns 10 percent profit per year, and you will reinvest all of your profits at the end of each year, it will take about $70 \div 10 = 7$ years for your investment to double in value.

The rule of 70 can also be applied to other rates of accumulation. For instance, economists can use the same rule to estimate how many years it will take for a country's national wealth to double. We could say, for instance, that if China and Brazil continue to grow at current rates, China's income will quadruple in the time it takes Brazil's to double.

Are you wondering where the rule of 70 comes from? We'll spare you the full mathematical proof, but the short answer is that it's related to the natural logarithm of 2, which is 0.693147. That means it really should be the rule of 69.3147—but that wouldn't be quite so quick and easy.

Problems and Applications

1. If you invest $250 at an annually compounded interest rate of 10 percent, how much will you have in 3 years? **[LO F.1]**

2. Suppose you invest $500 at an annually compounded interest rate of 3 percent. **[LO F.1]**
   a. How much will you have in 10 years?
   b. How much will you have in 20 years?
   c. How much will you have in 50 years?

3. Suppose you borrow $50 from a payday lender, who charges a monthly interest rate of 5 percent, compounded monthly. **[LO F.1]**
   a. If you pay back the loan in one month, how much will you owe?
   b. If you pay back the loan in one year, how much will you owe?
   c. If the interest rate is raised to 6 percent rather than 5 percent, how much *more* will you owe if you wait for a year to pay off the debt?

Part Four

Firm Decisions

The six chapters in Part 4 will introduce you to . . .

the choices and decisions that companies make. Every day, about 120 million Americans get up and go to work in over 6 million different offices, stores, factories, and other businesses.[1] These 6 million firms are diverse in what they do and how they do it, but there are important common threads: Most firms focus on meeting customers' needs while managing employees and physical resources. While doing that, they're usually working hard to keep up with the competition.

A lot of tough choices have to be made along the way. Imagine being a CEO at a large firm and having to decide which product to invest in, where to locate a new factory, which employees to hire, or whether to cut prices after the competition drops theirs. The next chapters explain how firms—big and small—make these kinds of choices.

We begin in Chapter 12, "The Costs of Production," with a simple look at revenues and costs. Understanding the form that costs take can give insight into the choices the firm faces. The types of costs a business has to pay drive its decisions about how much to produce to maximize profits. Those costs also drive decisions about when to stay in business or shut down.

Firms also have to know about the competition they face in the market. Some markets are a fierce battleground, with many companies trying to sell the exact same thing. Other markets have only a few companies. Still other markets are dominated by one firm that faces no competition at all. Chapters 13, 14, and 15 ("Perfect Competition," "Monopoly," and "Monopolistic Competition and Oligopoly") describe the features of these different kinds of markets, and how firms behave in each.

Regardless of what they are selling, businesses need to pay for inputs like raw materials, equipment, and workers to produce goods or services. These are called the *factors of production,* and they are the focus of Chapter 16, "The Factors of Production." Thinking about the markets for factors of production can explain why some professions earn more than others. Those markets also can explain how businesses make decisions about how much to produce and what inputs to use.

Chapter 17, "International Trade," describes what happens when businesses go global. International trade connects American consumers and businesses to people and producers all over the world. In this chapter, we take a look at why certain goods are made in one country and shipped to another. We also consider how globalization, trade, and government policies affect the well-being of workers and consumers in different countries.

Endnote

1. Data on firms and employment are from U.S. Bureau of the Census, Statistics of U.S. Business for 2009, http://www.census.gov/econ/susb/.

The Costs of Production

WHAT ARE YOU PAYING FOR IN THAT PRESCRIPTION?

Lipitor®, a cholesterol-lowering drug produced by U.S. pharmaceutical titan Pfizer, earned the company nearly $13 billion in 2006. The drug reduces the chance of heart attacks and strokes, and in 2006 over 45 million Americans were taking a daily pill.[1] Back then, Lipitor sold for around $2.70 per pill. The cost of producing each pill (which includes the raw materials, the packaging, wages for factory labor, and so on) was generally about a dime.[2] Such big markups make drugs very profitable for pharmaceutical companies. For a decade, sales of Lipitor alone accounted for about a quarter of Pfizer's revenue.[3] That was great news for Pfizer, but customers were paying $2.70 for something that cost almost nothing to produce. It would be easy for customers to feel ripped off. But were they?

Answering that question correctly is critical for policy-makers. They have to make decisions that balance the benefits of affordable medicine for consumers with giving pharmaceutical companies the incentive to invent new lifesaving drugs. If we consider only the raw materials and factory labor that go into a pill, we won't get an accurate picture of the real costs involved. The chemical formula for Lipitor didn't fall out of the sky. Pfizer's research and development department designed, refined, and tested Lipitor over many years.

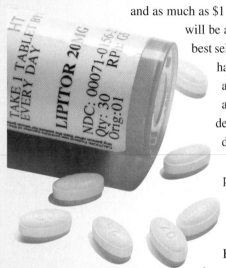

© Greg Wright/Alamy

That's an expensive business. Some estimates suggest that companies often spend a decade and as much as $1 billion on research to develop a new drug. Only a few of the developed drugs will be approved for sale. Only a few of those that are approved for sale will become best sellers like Lipitor. In fact, a research and development (R&D) manager at Pfizer has said that his team might develop 5,000 chemical compounds in a year, and have only a half dozen of them make it to the clinical trials that precede approval for use.[4] Pfizer needs its sales revenue to recover not only the costs of developing Lipitor, but also the ongoing costs of developing all those drugs that don't make it to market.

When we think about why drug companies charge such a high price for their products, we have to consider the cost of running a research and development department. This cost remains the same, however many pills Pfizer happens to produce in any given year. Whether it produces 10 thousand Lipitor pills or 10 billion makes no difference to the costs of running an R&D facility. Economists call this kind of cost—one that remains the same, regardless of how much is produced—a *fixed* cost. In contrast, costs that depend on the level of production—such as the raw materials for the pills and the factory labor required to make them—are *variable* costs.

We'll see in this chapter that the difference between fixed and variable costs explains a lot about the way firms behave, in the pharmaceutical industry and beyond. We'll discuss different ways of measuring costs, revenue, and profits, and how they influence production decisions. We'll dig into the details that determine the supply curve we studied in earlier chapters. Understanding the details of cost and profit is critical to running a business, or deciding whether to invest in one.

What do you pay for when buying a pill like Lipitor? The tools developed in this chapter will allow us to tackle this question. We'll also see how a rigorous understanding of the costs that firms face has helped create incentives to tackle some of the world's biggest diseases.

The Building Blocks of Business: Revenues, Costs, and Profits

In business, people frequently say, "It's all about the bottom line." What they mean is that making a profit is the central goal of a business. (The origin of the term "bottom line" is from accounting—profit is shown on the last line of a company's income statement.) Everything that happens—management, engineering, marketing—is in some way directed toward generating as large a profit as possible.

Economists also assume that a firm's goal is to maximize profits. The profit motive is central to understanding firm behavior, just as the quest for utility is the driving force behind *individual* decision making. When we ask, *What are a firm's wants?* the answer is that it wants to maximize its profits.

You've probably run into some businesses that have, or claim to have, additional goals. Some businesses refer to their "double bottom line" or "triple bottom line." What they are saying is that they value not only dollars but also social or environmental impacts. But even a business that would sacrifice some profit to achieve social and environmental goals still has to make a profit to survive. On the whole, the profit motive does a good job of explaining the behavior of most firms.

Profit is revenue minus costs

LO 12.1 Define total revenue, total cost, and profit.

To define profit, we have to start with two other economic concepts that may be familiar—revenue and cost:

- The amount that a firm receives from the sale of goods and services is its **total revenue**. (As discussed in Chapter 4, "Elasticity" total revenue is calculated as the quantity sold multiplied by the price received for each unit.)
- The amount that a firm pays for all of the inputs that go into producing goods and services is its **total cost**. Total cost includes both *one-time expenses* (like buying a machine) and *ongoing expenses* (like rent, employee salaries, raw materials, and advertising). In other words, total cost is anything and everything that the company expends to make its products.

Together, revenue and cost determine how much profit a firm makes. In the simplest terms, **profit** is the difference between total revenue and total cost, as shown in Equation 12-1.

EQUATION 12-1
$$\text{Profit} = \text{Total revenue} - \text{Total cost}$$

Unfortunately, measuring profit for a real firm is rarely so simple. To see the complexity, let's break things down into the two parts, revenue and cost.

Revenue is relatively straightforward to measure. As Equation 12-2 shows, it's equal to the quantity of each product the firm sells multiplied by the price at which it's sold.

EQUATION 12-2
$$\text{Revenue} = \text{Quantity} \times \text{Price}$$

Suppose, for simplicity's sake, that Pfizer makes only one drug, Lipitor. Imagine that it sells 5 billion pills of Lipitor at \$2.70 each. Using Equation 12-2, we can calculate the firm's total revenue:

$$\text{Revenue} = 5 \text{ billion} \times \$2.70 = \$13.5 \text{ billion}$$

Of course, very few companies sell only one product. When multiple products are involved, revenue equals quantity times price for *all* of the products a firm sells, as Equation 12-2a shows:

EQUATION 12-2A
$$\text{Revenue} = \text{Quantity} \times \text{Price}$$
$$= (Q_1 \times P_1) + (Q_2 \times P_2) + \ldots + (Q_n \times P_n)$$

Suppose, now, that Pfizer sells two drugs—Lipitor and an arthritis medication called Celebrex®. Imagine that it sells 5 billion pills of Lipitor at \$2.70 each and 2 billion pills of Celebrex at \$1.25 each. We can calculate the firm's total revenue using Equation 12-2a:

$$\text{Revenue} = (5 \text{ billion} \times \$2.70) + (2 \text{ billion} \times \$1.25)$$
$$= \$13.5 \text{ billion} + \$2.5 \text{ billion} = \$16 \text{ billion}$$

total revenue
the amount that a firm receives from the sale of goods and services; calculated as the quantity sold multiplied by the price paid for each unit

total cost
the amount that a firm pays for all of the inputs that go into producing goods and services

profit
the difference between total revenue and total cost

Revenue calculations are generally quite simple. *Cost* is the tricky factor when thinking about profits. We'll see in the next few sections of the chapter that measuring different types of costs—particularly opportunity costs—is complicated. The ability to measure costs accurately, though, makes a big difference for important decisions about production.

Fixed and variable costs

LO 12.2 Explain the difference between fixed and variable costs, and give examples of each.

fixed costs
costs that do not depend on the quantity of output produced

The first complicating factor in calculating costs is the distinction between fixed and variable costs. As noted in the chapter introduction, **fixed costs** are those that don't depend on the quantity of output produced. For Pfizer, running a research and development department is a fixed cost; it would be incurred whether any given drug sells well or not.

Sometimes a fixed cost is a one-time, upfront payment that has to be made before production can even begin. If you are opening a take-out pizza place, for example, you will have to incur the one-time, upfront fixed cost of buying an oven before you can produce your first pizza. Fixed costs can also be ongoing: If you lease a corner shop for your business, you have to pay the cost of the lease every month, however many pizzas you produce and sell.

variable costs
costs that depend on the quantity of output produced

Variable costs, on the other hand, depend on the quantity of output produced. These costs include the raw materials that go into production, as well as many types of labor costs. A drug company's variable costs would include the chemicals that go into pills, packaging materials, and wages of employees in the factories that make and package the pills. A pizza firm's variable costs would include pizza dough and toppings, cardboard take-away containers, and the wages of employees. In order to produce more pills or more pizzas, these firms would have to buy more raw materials and hire more employees, adding to their total variable costs.

If a firm produces nothing—if it stops production—then its variable cost is zero. But it is still stuck with its fixed costs. If Pfizer has developed a pill that isn't approved for sale by the Food and Drug Administration, the variable cost associated with the pill is zero. But the company has already incurred the fixed cost of research; that cost is the same whether or not the pill is approved and mass-produced. If a pizza firm decides to stop making pizzas, it no longer has to pay employees or buy ingredients. But it will still be obliged to pay for its space until the lease expires.

A firm's total cost is the combination of all of its fixed and variable costs. Table 12-1 shows how a hypothetical pharmaceutical company's total cost varies as its output increases. As the

TABLE 12-1

A firm's total costs

As the number of pills produced increases, so do the variable costs. The fixed costs, however, remain the same even when the number of pills produced is very large. Combining the fixed and variable costs will give us the total costs.

Quantity of pills (millions)	Fixed costs ($)	Variable costs ($)	Total costs ($)
0	1,000,000	0	1,000,000
10	1,000,000	100,000	1,100,000
20	1,000,000	200,000	1,200,000
30	1,000,000	300,000	1,300,000
40	1,000,000	400,000	1,400,000
50	1,000,000	500,000	1,500,000
60	1,000,000	600,000	1,600,000
70	1,000,000	700,000	1,700,000
80	1,000,000	800,000	1,800,000

names suggest, the firm's fixed cost is constant as quantity increases; variable cost rises with each additional unit produced.

Although we have so far been talking about variable and fixed costs in the business sense, these costs also factor into more personal decisions. For a different take on the importance of fixed versus variable costs, look at the From Another Angle box "The 'production' of kids."

From Another Angle
The "production" of kids

Raising children is expensive, but many of the costs are incurred only once. Such one-time costs include buying a changing table, spending time to find a pediatrician, and toddler-proofing the house. People pay these costs regardless of whether they have one child or five. The money and time spent on prenatal classes or how-to books about being a parent are also costs that parents probably don't need to pay again for a second child. Some of the clothes bought for the first baby can be passed down to later kids. Toys and books purchased for the first child can be put into service again.

These can all be thought of as the fixed costs of having children. If raising children involves big fixed costs, the first child will be very expensive. Each child after that incurs only variable costs to the parents. These variable costs include the additional food the next kid eats, medical expenses, soccer-league fees, education costs, and so on. Since the fixed costs are already paid, having multiple kids is cheaper *per child* than having just one. In *A Treatise on the Family,* the Nobel Prize–winning economist Gary Becker argued that we can use economics to understand the "production" of children.

Of course, we don't mean to suggest that parents consider only dollars and cents when contemplating how many children to have. There are other questions, such as whether your existing children might appreciate another sibling, or whether you could cope with another child. Nonetheless, for all but the wealthiest parents, dollars and cents certainly come into the equation when deciding on the optimal size of a family.

Pfizer wouldn't develop a drug to produce only one pill. A take-out restaurant owner wouldn't buy a pizza oven to produce only one pizza. Likewise, some parents say to themselves that once they have one child, they ought to have more. After all, the fixed costs of the lifestyle change, shareable clothes and toys, and many other costs have all been incurred. Additional children cost less than the first one, but there's a good chance that they'll give you as much joy.

Source: Gary Becker, *A Treatise on the Family* (Cambridge, MA: Harvard University Press, 1988).

Explicit and implicit costs

LO 12.3 Explain the difference between explicit and implicit costs, and give examples of each.

In Chapter 1, "Economics and Life," we saw that true costs are *opportunity costs,* or the value to you of what you have to give up in order to get something. When economists think about a firm's costs, therefore, they are thinking about everything the firm gives up in order to produce output. A firm's opportunity cost of operations has two components: *explicit costs* and *implicit costs.*

Explicit costs are costs that require a firm to spend money. They include just about everything we typically think of as a cost, including both fixed and variable costs. Rent on a building, employee salaries, materials, and machines—all of these require the firm to pay someone else in order to acquire them.

Implicit costs, in contrast, are costs that represent forgone opportunities. These are opportunities that *could have* generated revenue *if* the firm had invested its resources in another way.

explicit costs
costs that require a firm to spend money

implicit costs
costs that represent forgone opportunities

Let's look at an example in order to understand the difference:

- Suppose Pfizer *rents* a warehouse for $4,000 a month and stores boxes of pills in it before they are shipped out to pharmacies around the country. This is an *explicit cost:* The firm has to pay cash to someone for the use of the warehouse.
- If, however, Pfizer *owns* the warehouse and uses it for the same purpose, it pays nothing. Pfizer incurs zero dollars in explicit costs.
- Does that mean that using the warehouse costs nothing? No—that warehouse could instead be rented out to another company for $4,000 per month. Pfizer *could have earned* $4,000 by renting out the warehouse to someone else rather than storing pills in it. The choice to not earn money in another way is an *implicit cost.*

Once we account for implicit costs, storing pills costs Pfizer $4,000, regardless of whether it owns the warehouse or not.

One particularly notable type of cost faced by nearly all firms is the opportunity cost of the money invested in starting up the business. Suppose you need $100,000 of startup capital to get your take-out pizza place up and running. You have a few options for obtaining the startup capital:

- You can borrow the $100,000 from a bank. If you do, you will need to pay total interest of 10 percent on the loan. This would be an *explicit* cost of $10,000.
- But what if you already have $100,000 invested in your savings account? If you use that money as your start-up capital, there is no *explicit* cost; that is, you don't have to pay anyone else. But there is an *implicit* cost: You are giving up whatever interest you could have earned by leaving the money in your savings account or whatever you could have earned by investing it elsewhere.

You can see that any input used in a business—warehouses, equipment, cash—could alternatively be used to generate income some other way. To properly account for the total costs incurred by a firm, we have to think about the opportunity cost of using each of these inputs. As we are about to see, the distinction between explicit and implicit costs can have a huge impact on how we calculate a company's profits.

Economic and accounting profit

> **LO 12.4** Calculate economic and accounting profit, and explain the importance of the difference.

accounting profit
total revenue minus
explicit costs

Usually, when a company reports its profits, what you see is its **accounting profit**. This is total revenue minus explicit costs, as shown in Equation 12-3.

EQUATION 12-3   Accounting profit = Total revenue − Explicit costs

Thinking only about explicit costs will mislead us about how well a business is really doing, though. To get a clearer picture, we need to talk about a firm's **economic profit**—total revenue minus all opportunity costs, both explicit and implicit—as shown in Equation 12-4.

economic profit
total revenue minus
opportunity costs, explicit
and implicit

EQUATION 12-4   Economic profit = Total revenue − Explicit costs − Implicit costs

To see why the difference matters, follow the arguments in Figure 12-1. If the CEO listens to the advice of Executive A, then the firm will have an *accounting profit* to report to investors in the company. But if she expects the investors to be happy, she will be in for an unpleasant surprise: Investors are more interested in *economic profit.* Because the shareholders are also aware of current interest rates, they will realize, like Executive B, that the company could make more money by investing in another business opportunity instead.

FIGURE 12-1

Defining profit in a business decision   The definition of profit makes a difference. Even when the *accounting profit* for an investment may be large, the *economic profit* could be small or even negative.

Exactostock/SuperStock

CEO: We have the opportunity to buy a new manufacturing facility. Is this a smart move for our company?

Executive A: The new facility would cost $6 million to buy and $4 million to operate over the next decade, for a total cost of $10 million. The medicines we could produce there would bring in revenue of $13 million. We could make $3 million in profits. *Buy the factory!*

Executive B: But you're forgetting about all of the other things we could do with $10 million. By my calculations, we could earn $6 million in interest over the next 10 years if we invested the money. That means that the true cost of buying the facility is $16 million, and revenue would be only $13 million. *If we bought the factory, we could lose $3 million!*

Knowing the distinction between economic and accounting profits is a sink-or-swim issue for most firms. However, there are some exceptions, as discussed in the From Another Angle box "Beyond the bottom line."

From Another Angle

Beyond the bottom line

Husk Power Systems uses innovative technology to generate electricity from the husks left over when rice is processed. The company aims to sell that electricity to a market of around 350 million people in remote villages in rice-growing regions of India—people who are not connected to the regional power grid. As well as having their lives improved by getting a reliable electricity supply, the villagers can use a by-product of the technology—ash—as fertilizer to improve their next crop of rice.

Husk Power Systems, started by a group of MBA graduates from the University of Virginia, is an example of a social enterprise. It seeks to turn a profit but is also motivated by serving a social goal. The influential thinker C. K. Prahalad famously argued that some of the best untapped business opportunities lie in serving the billions of extremely poor people at the "bottom of the pyramid." When social enterprises turn an economic profit by finding these opportunities, then even investors who couldn't care less about its social goals take notice.

For many social enterprises, however, this is not the case. They may turn an *accounting* profit, but not an *economic* profit. Investors who are purely focused on economic profit will not invest in such businesses; they could make more money elsewhere. If Husk Power Systems

(continued)

finds itself in this position, it will rely for its survival on finding a different type of investors. It will need investors who are willing to accept a lower return on their investment because they feel good about making life better for rice-growing Indian villagers and for helping an environmental cause.

Investors in social enterprises still want to make a profit. But when we think clearly about the difference between accounting profit and economic profit, the distinction between social enterprises and charity becomes blurred. By investing in a firm that is producing lower returns than they could get elsewhere, investors are effectively losing money. Social enterprises that are not making economic profits therefore rely on the philanthropic tendencies of their investors, just as much as any charity.

Sources: http://acumen.org/investment/husk-power-systems; C. K. Prahalad, *The Fortune at the Bottom of the Pyramid: Eradicating Poverty through Profits* (Upper Saddle River, NJ: Pearson, 2006); and Jonathan Morduch, "Not so fast: The realities of impact investing," *Americas Quarterly,* Fall 2011.

✓CONCEPT CHECK

- ☐ How do you calculate the revenue of a firm that produces only one good? **[LO 12.1]**
- ☐ When a firm doubles its output, how much do its fixed costs increase? **[LO 12.2]**
- ☐ When a restaurant owner works in his own restaurant waiting tables, what is the implicit cost he incurs? **[LO 12.3]**
- ☐ What is the difference between accounting profit and economic profit? **[LO 12.4]**

Production Functions

Firms create value by bringing together different ingredients to create a good or service that consumers want. The ingredients that go into the production process—raw materials, labor, machines, time, ideas—are the *inputs*. The goods and services that are produced are the *outputs*. The relationship between the quantity of inputs and the quantity of outputs is called a **production function**.

production function
the relationship between quantity of inputs and the resulting quantity of outputs

Marginal product

LO 12.5 Define marginal product, and show why there is diminishing marginal product.

The production process itself can be thought of as a sort of recipe that combines certain amounts of inputs, in a certain way, to achieve the desired output. The analogy with cooking is not exact, however. If you've ever followed a recipe, you'll know that what matters are the *ratios* of ingredients. If the recipe serves four and you're cooking for eight, you can generally just double the amount of all ingredients. This simple scaling up or down doesn't usually work for firms. Sometimes, a firm can *more than* double its outputs by doubling its inputs. Sometimes, it has to more than double its inputs to double its outputs.

To see why, let's consider your new take-out pizza firm. For simplicity, we'll focus on just one of the inputs—labor. If you start out with only yourself working there, you won't be able to make many pizzas. You'll constantly have to break off to prep more ingredients, take orders, and handle payments from customers. If you employ a second worker to help with these jobs, doubling your labor input, you will probably be able to much more than double your pizza production; the two of you will waste less time switching between tasks. Adding a third worker might lead to an even bigger jump in productivity: One of you spends all your time dealing with customers, one focuses exclusively on prepping ingredients, and one does nothing but make pizzas.

There comes a point, however, when the opposite applies. Suppose you now have five workers. What happens if you employ another five? The kitchen gets overcrowded and people get in each other's way. You have to spend a lot more time watching over your new employees; you need to make sure they're keeping up your high standards, check that orders don't get misplaced, and see that employees are not slacking off. You'll end up producing more pizzas with 10 workers than you did with five—but probably fewer than twice as many.

The increase in the number of pizzas that can be produced by hiring an additional employee is called the marginal product of that employee. In general, the **marginal product** of any input into the production process is the increase in output that is generated by an additional unit of input.

Table 12-2 shows how this might work in a take-out pizza place. It shows the *marginal product of labor*—the increase in output that is generated by adding more workers. On your own, let's say you are able to produce 50 pizzas. Hiring another employee enables you to jump to 150 pizzas—a *marginal product* of 100 additional pizzas. Adding a third worker increases production to 330 pizzas—a marginal product of 180.

From the third worker on, however, each additional employee increases production by slightly less. When you have nine employees, adding a tenth increases production by only 40 pizzas. This illustrates a common principle of production, called **diminishing marginal product**. This principle states that, holding other inputs constant, the marginal product of a particular input decreases as the quantity of that input increases.

We can represent the production function visually on a graph like the one shown in Figure 12-2. This graph plots the data from the first two columns in Table 12-2. The number of employees appears on the *x*-axis, and the quantity of pizzas produced on the *y*-axis. Marginal product is represented by the slope of the total production curve. At low levels of output, the curve becomes steeper as workers are added. This shows that marginal product initially increases. But then the principle of diminishing marginal product kicks in and the slope of the curve gradually flattens out.

marginal product
the increase in output that is generated by an additional unit of input

diminishing marginal product
a principle stating that the marginal product of an input decreases as the quantity of the input increases

TABLE 12-2

Total production and marginal product

In this pizza business, the first few workers have an increasing marginal product. Soon, however, each additional worker contributes less to total production, reflected by decreasing marginal product.

Labor (employees)	Total production (pizzas)	Marginal product of labor (pizzas)
0	0	–
1	50	50
2	150	100
3	330	180
4	500	170
5	630	130
6	730	100
7	810	80
8	875	65
9	925	50
10	965	40

FIGURE 12-2
Production function

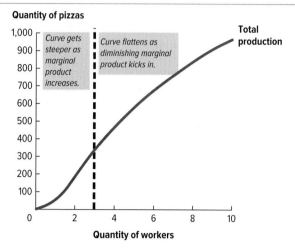

The graph of the production function shows
that marginal product increases with the first
few workers hired, but then begins to decrease.
When output is very low, each additional worker
has a higher marginal product than the previous
one, represented by the increasing slope of the
total production curve. As more workers are
added, marginal product starts to diminish,
represented by the flattening out of the curve.

Another way to visualize diminishing marginal product is to graph the number of pizzas each
additional employee adds. Figure 12-3 shows that the marginal product curve initially increases
as the first few workers are added; it then trends downward.

FIGURE 12-3
**Average and marginal
product**

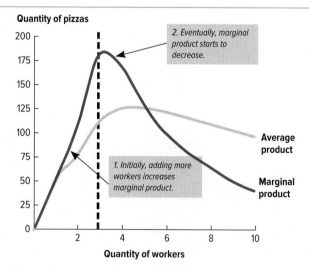

As the first few workers are added, marginal
product increases. As the quantity of workers
continues to increase, however, the principle of
diminishing marginal product kicks in. When the
marginal product curve crosses the average
product curve, average product also starts to
decrease.

Figure 12-3 also shows *average product*—the number of pizzas produced per worker, on average. Average product is calculated by dividing total production by the number of workers. When a new employee's marginal product is greater than the existing average product, the average increases. As soon as a new worker's marginal product is less than the existing average, the average number of pizzas per worker starts to fall.

Thinking about marginal product connects us to an important aspect of rational decision making first discussed in Chapter 1, "Economics and Life." We noted that people engage in marginal decision making; they weigh trade-offs, rather than seeing choices as all-or-nothing. We'll see in the coming chapters that firms also make production decisions "on the margin." That is, they compare the marginal product of an input to its marginal cost when deciding whether to employ an additional worker or build another factory.

✓ CONCEPT CHECK

☐ Suppose that an accounting firm with 10 employees hires another accountant. By doing so, it goes from serving 30 customers each week to serving 32 customers each week. What is the marginal product of labor for the new accountant? **[LO 12.5]**

☐ Why might marginal product be increasing at lower levels of output and decreasing at higher levels of output? **[LO 12.5]**

Cost Curves

We've just taken a careful look at the production side of a firm. Firms decide how much of each input to use. These decisions, quite directly, determine the quantity of outputs the firm will produce.

Costs of inputs also matter, of course. When a firm increases its output by adjusting its use of inputs, it incurs the costs associated with that decision. In general, the cost of an input won't change simply because you've reached the point of diminishing marginal product in your firm. Your tenth employee costs as much in wages as your first, even if he adds less to your production.

In this section, we'll take a close look at how companies use the concepts of total, average, and marginal costs.

Total, average, and marginal costs

LO 12.6 Define and graph total cost, average costs, and marginal cost.

Suppose you own a pizza parlor; how will you decide how many pizzas to produce? Remember that firms want to maximize profits. We have already seen how firms measure their revenue. We will now look at how costs change as firms change their production quantity.

Total and average costs

Let's assume that every additional employee costs the same, regardless of how many more pizzas they help you make. Say that wages are $200 per worker. Assume that the cost of your workers is the only variable cost. There are also fixed costs—ones you would have to pay regardless of how many pizzas you make. For simplicity's sake, we'll consider just one fixed cost: the lease on your premises. We'll say this is $300.

As defined earlier in the chapter, total cost represents all the inputs a firm uses in production. These inputs consist of fixed costs plus variable costs, as Equation 12-5 shows.

EQUATION 12-5   Total cost = Fixed costs + Variable costs

In our pizza example, if you have one worker, then your total costs are $300 (fixed) + $200 (variable) = $500. If you have two workers, they are $300 + ($200 + $200) = $700. And so on. You can see these data in Table 12-3.

In the example just above, we assumed simple numbers for the calculation. In a real-life situation, or a more complicated example, the numbers might not be so simple. In that case, it's useful to be able to use averages for the cost inputs:

average fixed cost (AFC)
fixed cost divided by the quantity of output

- **Average fixed cost (AFC)** is fixed cost divided by the quantity of output.
- **Average variable cost (AVC)** is variable cost divided by the quantity of output.
- **Average total cost (ATC)** is total cost divided by the quantity of output.

average variable cost (AVC)
variable cost divided by the quantity of output

Equations 12-6, 12-7, and 12-8 show that for each type of average cost, we simply divide the cost by the quantity of the output. In our example, that quantity is the number of pizzas produced.

EQUATION 12-6
$$\text{Average fixed cost (AFC)} = \frac{\text{Fixed cost}}{\text{Quantity}}$$

average total cost (ATC)
total cost divided by the quantity of output

EQUATION 12-7
$$\text{Average variable cost (AVC)} = \frac{\text{Variable cost}}{\text{Quantity}}$$

EQUATION 12-8
$$\text{Average total cost (ATC)} = \frac{\text{Total cost}}{\text{Quantity}}$$

Table 12-3 shows the average fixed cost, average variable cost, and average total cost for our pizza example, along with a lot of other data. Let's visualize each measure in turn, with the help of some graphs.

TABLE 12-3 Costs of production

Fixed costs have to be paid, however many pizzas you produce. Pizza production depends only on your variable costs—the cost of labor. Total cost is the sum of fixed and variable costs. The marginal cost of producing one extra pizza is calculated by dividing the increase in variable cost by the increase in number of pizzas produced.

Labor (workers)	Total production (pizzas)	Marginal product (pizzas)	Fixed costs ($)	Average fixed costs ($/pizza)	Variable costs ($)	Average variable costs ($/pizza)	Total cost ($)	Average total cost ($/pizza)	Marginal cost ($/pizza)
0	0	–	300	–	0	–	300	–	–
1	50	50	300	6.00	200	4.00	500	10.00	4.00
2	150	100	300	2.00	400	2.67	700	4.67	2.00
3	330	180	300	0.91	600	1.82	900	2.73	1.11
4	500	170	300	0.60	800	1.60	1,100	2.20	1.18
5	630	130	300	0.48	1,000	1.59	1,300	2.06	1.54
6	730	100	300	0.41	1,200	1.64	1,500	2.05	2.00
7	810	80	300	0.37	1,400	1.73	1,700	2.10	2.50
8	875	65	300	0.34	1,600	1.83	1,900	2.17	3.08
9	925	55	300	0.32	1,800	1.95	2,100	2.27	4.00
10	965	45	300	0.31	2,000	2.07	2,300	2.38	5.00

FIGURE 12-4

The total cost curve

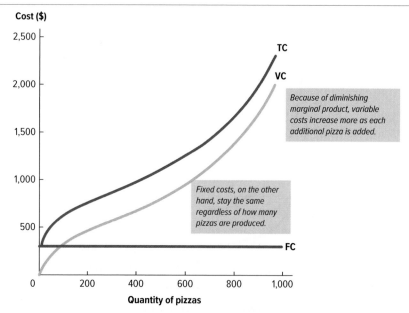

The increasing slope of the total cost curve reflects the principle of diminishing marginal product: Each additional worker costs the same as the previous worker but adds fewer additional pizzas to production. Fixed costs, of course, stay the same regardless of how many pizzas are produced. The total cost curve is the sum of variable and fixed costs.

We'll start by graphing total cost; see Figure 12-4. The fixed cost of the lease, of course, stays constant at $300, regardless of how many pizzas you produce. Looking at variable costs, notice that while the variable costs appear to increase at a constant rate in Table 12-3, this is misleading. Each *worker* costs an additional $200, but the cost to produce *each pizza* is changing. The second worker is more productive than the first. You pay $200 for the first 50 pizzas. But for your next $200 paid, your employee produces 100 pizzas.

Reflecting the increasing marginal product of the first few employees, the variable cost (VC) curve initially becomes less steep. As the principle of diminishing marginal product kicks in, we see the variable cost curve in Figure 12-4 getting gradually steeper. As workers become less productive, the firm must pay the same amount of money ($200) for fewer pizzas. In other words, each pizza is becoming more costly to produce. You can see that each additional unit of output along the *x*-axis requires a bigger change in cost on the *y*-axis than the one before it. This pattern of increasing marginal cost is the inevitable result of diminishing marginal product: As the productivity of each unit of input decreases, it costs more to get another unit of output.

Next, let's see what happens when we graph the average cost curves, as shown in Figure 12-5. The first thing to note is that the average fixed cost (AFC) curve trends downward. The reason is that the fixed costs remain the same as quantity produced increases; as fixed costs are averaged over more units of production, the fixed cost per unit of production must decrease.

Next, note that the average variable cost (AVC) curve is U-shaped. It initially slopes downward because the first few employees have an increasing marginal product. For the first worker, the average variable cost of one pizza is $200 ÷ 50 = 4. When a second, more productive worker is added, the average variable cost of one pizza declines to $400 ÷ 150 = $2.67. After the fifth worker, AVC trends upward.

What you really want to know for your pizza business are your costs *per pizza*. If you know the cost per pizza, then you can calculate the profit for each pizza by subtracting the cost per

FIGURE 12-5
Average cost curves

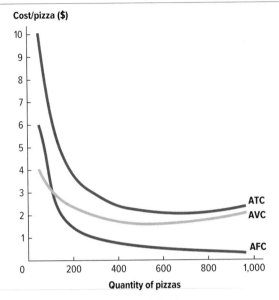

This figure shows the key features of average cost curves. Average fixed cost (the red line) always decreases as output increases because the same cost is spread out over more units of output. Average variable cost (the pink line) at first decreases and then increases, reflecting the marginal product of inputs. Average total cost (the purple line) is simply what you get when you add these two together. It's also U-shaped as the increases in average variable cost are weighed against the decreases in average fixed cost.

pizza from the price received for each pizza. To find the cost per pizza, you have to account for both fixed and variable costs, which takes us to the average total cost (ATC) curve.

As you can see in Figure 12-5, the ATC curve is also U-shaped, though less noticeably so than the AVC curve. The reason is that the increases in AVC are, for a while, cancelled out by the decreases in AFC. Looking back at the data in Table 12-3, we can see that average *variable* costs are lowest (at $1.59 per pizza) with five employees. But average *total* costs are lowest (at $2.05 per pizza) with six employees. This difference is due to the effect of adding average fixed costs. In going from five employees to six, average fixed costs *de*creased more than average variable costs *in*creased. The result is that, on net, the pizzas are cheaper to make with six employees. This shows that it would be a mistake to look only at average variable cost when considering how many workers to employ.

Marginal cost

Another important component of production and hiring decisions is *marginal cost*. Because firms make decisions on the margin, they can ask what *additional cost* they will incur by producing one additional unit of output. This is the **marginal cost (MC)** of that unit. In other words, it is the variable cost of producing the *next unit* of output.

We calculate the marginal cost of production by dividing the change in total cost by the change in the quantity of output, as Equation 12-9 shows.

marginal cost (MC)
the additional cost incurred by a firm when it produces one additional unit of output

EQUATION 12-9

$$\text{Marginal cost} = \frac{\text{Change in total cost}}{\text{Change in quantity}}$$

$$MC = \frac{\Delta \text{ total cost}}{\Delta \text{ quantity}}$$

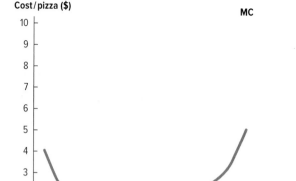

FIGURE 12-6
The marginal cost curve

The marginal cost curve has the inverse shape of the marginal product curve. This is because every additional unit of input costs the same, regardless of the contribution it makes to production. As marginal product initially increases, so marginal cost initially decreases; as the principle of diminishing marginal product kicks in, the marginal cost curve increases.

As we can see from Figure 12-6, the marginal cost curve is also U-shaped. Like AVC, this U-shape is a result of increasing and then decreasing marginal product of labor: Marginal cost initially decreases (as marginal product increases) and then increases (as marginal product decreases). Reading the data in Table 12-3, we can see that the second worker produced an additional 100 pizzas for a cost of $200 ($700 − $500). Thus, the marginal cost of each additional pizza for the second worker is $200 ÷ 100 = $2.00. Employing a third worker would yield an additional 180 pizzas, but the additional variable cost remains $200. Thus, the marginal cost of each additional pizza for the third worker is only $200 ÷ 180 = $1.11.

So, marginal cost initially decreases. As the data table shows, marginal cost decreases for the pizza business up through the addition of the fourth worker. Eventually, though, marginal cost increases (because marginal product decreases): With the fifth worker, marginal cost begins to increase. At that point, the MC curve in Figure 12-6 begins to slope upward. Notice in Table 12-3 that the marginal cost per pizza for the ninth worker is $4.00, and adding a tenth worker leads to a marginal cost of $5.00 per pizza. Such information is important as firms make production and hiring decisions. If your pizzas sell for $4.50, for example, you shouldn't employ that tenth worker.

Finally, let's plot the marginal cost curve on the same graph as the ATC curve, as shown in Figure 12-7. Notice that the *marginal cost (MC) curve intersects the lowest point of the ATC curve.* Here's why:

- If the marginal cost of increasing production by one unit is *less* than your current average total cost, then producing that extra unit will *decrease* your average cost. For example, if the average total cost of producing pizzas is currently $2.20 and the marginal cost of one additional pizza is $1.54, then producing one more pizza will clearly bring the average below $2.20 per pizza. This can be seen in Table 12-3 when production increases from 500 to 630.
- If, on the other hand, the marginal cost of increasing production by one unit is *more* than your current average total cost, then producing that extra unit will *increase* your average cost. Notice that for all quantities above 730, the marginal cost is above average total cost. As a result, average total cost is pulled upward.

FIGURE 12-7

**Marginal and average
cost curves**

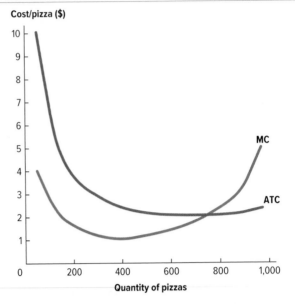

When the marginal cost of producing another pizza
is less than the average total cost, producing that
extra pizza will decrease the average total cost.
When the marginal cost of producing another pizza
is more than the average total cost, producing that
extra pizza will increase the average total cost.
Therefore the marginal cost curve intersects the
average total cost curve at its lowest point.

The concepts of marginal cost and average total cost are fundamentally important to decisions about production, as we will see in the next few chapters. To help review, Table 12-4 summarizes the various types of costs.

TABLE 12-4

Costs in general

Cost	Description	Calculation
Total cost (TC)	The amount that a firm pays for all of the inputs (fixed and variable) that go into producing goods and services	TC = FC + VC
Fixed costs (FC)	Costs that don't depend on the quantity of output produced	—
Variable costs (VC)	Costs that depend on the quantity of output produced	—
Explicit costs	Costs that require a firm to spend money	—
Implicit costs	Costs that represent forgone opportunities	—
Average fixed costs (AFC)	Fixed costs divided by the quantity of output	AFC = FC ÷ Q
Average variable costs (AVC)	Variable costs divided by the quantity of output	AVC = VC ÷ Q
Average total costs (ATC)	Total costs divided by the quantity of output	ATC = TC ÷ Q
Marginal cost (MC)	The additional cost incurred by a firm when it produces one additional unit of output	MC = ΔTC ÷ ΔQ

□ What is the difference between average total cost and marginal cost? **[LO 12.6]**

□ Why does marginal cost usually increase as output increases? Under what circumstances might marginal cost decrease? **[LO 12.6]**

□ Why does the marginal cost curve intersect the average total cost curve at its lowest point? **[LO 12.6]**

Production in the Short Run and the Long Run

In Chapters 3 and 4 ("Markets" and "Elasticity"), we noted that supply is more flexible over longer periods of time. The commonsense explanation behind this fact is that some things just take time to do. For a firm to adjust its production, it may have to build new factories, purchase new properties, or hire more employees. These activities don't happen overnight. The differences between the costs that firms face in the short run and the long run reflect this need for production adjustment time.

Costs in the long run

LO 12.7 Explain why firms face different costs in the long run than in the short run.

Which costs are "fixed" depends on what timescale you're thinking in. Consider a take-out pizza firm's lease of its premises. If the firm decides to make fewer pizzas this month, it is still committed to pay the monthly cost of its lease. When the lease expires, the firm could decide to move to smaller, cheaper premises. The cost of the lease is fixed in the *short run* (whatever the length of the lease is), but not fixed in the *long run*.

We have used factory laborers and pizza take-out workers as examples of variable costs. These kinds of employees tend to operate on flexible-shift systems, working as much as—and often no more than—required. The period of notice to terminate employment tends to be short and new workers don't need much training. In contrast, none of these things are true of research scientists. In the short run, therefore, it's pretty easy for Pfizer to reduce or increase the number of workers in its factories. But reducing or increasing the size of its R&D department is something it can do only in the long run.

How long is the long run? Economists don't think of the long run as being a certain number of days or months or years. Instead, it refers to however long it would take for a firm to vary all of its costs, if it wanted to. So, the definition of long run depends on the type of firm and type of production. For a take-out pizza firm, the long run is probably not very long. The lease on its premises may run for a year, for example. Costs that are fixed when the firm plans for a month ahead will become variable when the firm plans for a year ahead. That may not be true for a firm such as Pfizer, which may need to make operational decisions over time spans of 5 or 10 years. It takes time to build new research laboratories, factories, or warehouses, or to decommission old ones.

The cost curves we have been considering so far in this chapter are short-run cost curves. We'll now turn our attention to what cost curves look like in the long run, when all costs are considered variable.

Economies and diseconomies of scale

LO 12.8 Understand what economies and diseconomies of scale are and their implications for production decisions.

Remember why the ATC curve is U-shaped? Initially, additional inputs have an increasing marginal product, which results in decreasing average total cost. Sooner or later, the principle of diminishing returns kicks in. Then marginal product decreases and average total cost starts to increase.

Something similar happens in the long run, too. When firms plan for the long run, they consider the *scale* at which they want to operate: Should they move to bigger or smaller premises? Should they build more factories, or close some down? *Economies of scale, diseconomies of scale,* and *constant returns to scale* describe the relationship between the quantity of output and average total cost.

Initially, a small firm may find that increasing the quantity of output enables it to lower its average total cost. When this happens, we say the firm is facing **economies of scale**. For example, if you own 10 pizza places rather than one, you may be able to negotiate bulk-purchase discounts on ingredients. The company that prints your menus will charge less per menu to print 10 times as many. You'll pay only slightly more for hosting your website, even though it's handling 10 times as much traffic.

However, bigger isn't always better. There may come a point at which increasing scale leads to *higher* average total cost. Imagine running a chain of tens of thousands of pizza places, spread across dozens of countries. It might be such a logistical nightmare to keep the spending under control that your average total cost would be higher than when you had fewer outlets in fewer countries. When a firm is in a position in which increasing its quantity of output starts to raise its average total cost, economists say it is facing **diseconomies of scale**.

In between these extremes, there may also be various quantities of output at which a firm can operate without experiencing higher or lower average total cost. In that situation, we say the firm is facing **constant returns to scale**.

Figure 12-8 illustrates the idea of economies and diseconomies of scale on a long-run ATC curve. It shows the three possibilities relating to quantity of output and average total cost:

- When a firm could achieve economies of scale by expanding, its long-run ATC curve slopes down. This shows that ATC decreases as output increases.

economies of scale
returns that occur when an increase in the quantity of output decreases average total cost

diseconomies of scale
returns that occur when an increase in the quantity of output increases average total cost

constant returns to scale
returns that occur when average total cost does not depend on the quantity of output

FIGURE 12-8
Economies and diseconomies of scale

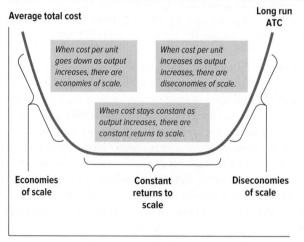

When a firm could achieve economies of scale by expanding, its long-run ATC curve slopes down, showing decreasing ATC as output increases. When it would face diseconomies of scale by expanding, the curve slopes up, showing rising ATC as output increases. The long-run ATC curve is flat in the middle, representing the various levels of output at which the firm achieves constant returns to scale.

- When a firm would face diseconomies of scale by expanding, the curve slopes up. This shows that ATC increases as output increases.
- Often, the long-run ATC curve is shown with a flat portion in the middle. That flat portion represents constant returns to scale—the different levels of output the firm achieves without increasing ATC.

The Real Life box "Walmart and economies of scale" describes how one company has taken advantage of economies of scale.

Real Life

Walmart and economies of scale

More than 100 million Americans shop at Walmart each week. They buy everything from car parts to groceries to prescription drugs to money transfers. Walmart started as a single discount store in northwest Arkansas. It has increased its output by adding more stores—some 5,200 stores across the United States, with a total of 11,500 stores in 11 countries around the world.

Walmart's success largely comes from its ability to offer a huge variety of products at low prices. Having so many stores means Walmart can guarantee huge purchases to vendors. As a result, it can negotiate low wholesale prices, thus lowering its average total cost—an example of an economy of scale. Smaller stores simply can't match Walmart's bargaining power.

However, Walmart has also overcome some issues that could easily have led to diseconomies of scale. With increased size come increased logistical problems. One such problem is how to manage inventory across thousands of stores. Buying 10 million items cheaply from a wholesale supplier may not be so cost-efficient if those items are sitting in a warehouse in Oregon when a store runs out of stock in Georgia. Walmart minimized this problem through technological innovation that lowered costs: It invested in a sophisticated computerized inventory system. The system tracks inventories and helps to ensure that stores are stocked with the products they need.

Sources: Walmart corporate website, http://corporate.walmart.com/newsroom/company-facts.

A firm's long-run ATC curve covers a much greater range of output than its short-run ATC curve. In the short run, all firms are stuck on a smaller cost curve; they are constrained by the limited capacity of their fixed inputs. The long-run cost curve can be thought of as consisting of points on various short-run ATCs faced by firms of various sizes, operating at different scales. By increasing or decreasing their scale, firms can move along the long-run ATC curve from one short-run ATC curve to another. Figure 12-9 shows this idea. Effectively, when a firm moves along the long-run cost curve, it does so by choosing to move to the short-run cost curve that would be associated with a larger or smaller firm.

When a firm cannot lower its average total cost by either increasing or decreasing its scale, it is said to be operating at an **efficient scale**. At that scale, it is producing the quantity of output at which average total cost is minimized. People sometimes say that a particular industry has "large economies of scale." By this, they mean that some characteristic of that industry gives an advantage to larger firms. The pharmaceutical industry is a good example: Firms such as Pfizer need to be large to sustain the research and development budget necessary to develop enough new drugs to have a chance of some of them becoming bestsellers.

This brings us back to the question with which we started the chapter: Is Pfizer ripping off customers by charging $2.70 for a cholesterol-lowering pill that costs next to nothing to manufacture? For a discussion, see the What Do You Think? box "The profit motive and 'orphan' drugs."

efficient scale
the quantity of output at which average total cost is minimized

FIGURE 12-9
Average total cost in the long run

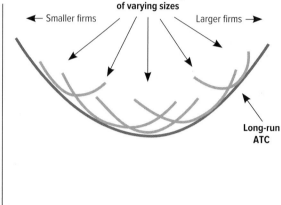

Short-run ATC curves cover a smaller range of output than the long-run ATC curve. The scale of the firm limits how high production can rise in the short run. The long-run cost curve can be thought of as consisting of points on various short-run ATCs faced by firms of various sizes. By increasing or decreasing their scale, firms can move along the long-run ATC curve from one short-run ATC curve to another.

What Do You Think?

The profit motive and "orphan" drugs

Pharmaceutical companies such as Pfizer spend many billions of dollars each year on the fixed costs of research and development (R&D). In 2015, Pfizer's R&D budget was about $7.7 billion, for example. Much of this money is "wasted," in the sense that most of the drugs created turn out to be useless. But it's only by experimenting with so many drugs that these companies have any chance of finding ones that are useful. The only way they can afford to spend so much on the fixed costs of R&D is by charging vastly more for the successful drugs, such as Lipitor, than the pills themselves cost to manufacture.

Lipitor and other drugs are simply chemical formulas. Once research finds that a particular chemical formula is useful in lowering cholesterol, other companies could manufacture exactly equivalent pills, known as "generics." Competitors can sell generics at a profit by charging just a few cents. The lower price would enable far more people to afford and benefit from the drugs. But it would deprive Pfizer of the money to spend on R&D in the hope of developing yet more new treatments.

Most governments think it's a good thing to give drug companies incentives to develop new treatments. As a result, they protect the chemical formulas with patents. However, most governments also feel uncomfortable about people being charged very large amounts for effective treatments. So patents on drugs are issued for a limited period of time. The patent on Lipitor, for example, ran for 15 years. Any company that made a generic version of Lipitor while it was under patent protection would have been breaking the law. The patent expired in 2011, allowing generic-drug manufacturers to enter the market and undercut Pfizer's prices. This system means that drug companies have a limited initial period to make enough profits on their best-selling drugs to cover their ongoing R&D costs.

An amazing variety of medicines have been developed under this profit-driven model. Recently, the U.S. government even approved a prescription treatment to lengthen and darken eyelashes. This is where some people start to question the system. Many fatal diseases still await a cure, and many of them receive nowhere near the amount of R&D investment that would be required to develop a vaccine or treatment. For instance, malaria and pneumococcal disease affect 1 billion people in low-income countries each year. Yet they receive little attention from drug developers.

The drugs that receive little research attention and yet could cure diseases are often referred to as "orphan" drugs because no one is willing to take ownership of their development. Drug companies don't research these treatments because they don't expect to make enough profit from finding a cure. If the disease is rare, then too few people would buy the cure. If the people who suffer from it are poor, then they would not be able to afford the high prices that would need to be charged to recoup the R&D costs. That's why drug companies produce drugs that cure less-severe ailments that people are willing to pay to treat, such as dissatisfaction with their eyelash length.

Some say this result indicates the market system is working exactly as it should. It is allocating scarce resources to goods for which there is the most demand. Others think it is immoral that the system prioritizes research into "trivial" diseases over finding cures for major killers.

One approach to solving the problem of orphan diseases is called *advanced market commitment* (AMC). In this approach, a government or private charity promises to purchase a minimum quantity of a drug, once developed, to treat an orphan disease. The thinking is that this commitment delivers a similar incentive for research as firms would face if the disease afflicted large numbers of wealthy patients. For some background on the use of AMCs, look at the Gates Foundation's efforts: http://www.gatesfoundation.org/vaccines/Pages/advanced-market-commitments-vaccines.aspx.

WHAT DO YOU THINK?

1. Should pharmaceutical companies and their stockholders feel morally obligated to work on "orphan" drugs?
2. Should governments step in and pay companies to undertake research in an advanced market commitment? Should the responsibility rest with private charity?

Sources: http://www.nytimes.com/2012/05/02/business/pfizer-profit-declines-19-after-loss-of-lipitor-patent.html; http://www.statista.com/statistics/267810/expenditure-on-research-and-development-at-pfizer-since-2006/; http://www.pfizer.com/system/files/presentation/2015_Pfizer_Financial_Report.pdf.

✓ CONCEPT CHECK

☐ Why do most fixed costs become variable costs in the long run? **[LO 12.7]**

☐ What does it imply about the shape of the average total cost curve if a firm faces constant returns to scale? **[LO 12.8]**

Conclusion

In this chapter, we've explored the costs that all firms face when they produce goods or services. Understanding the relationship between inputs, outputs, and costs is crucial because costs, along with the firm's revenues, determine profits. The pursuit of profits, of course, drives every firm's decision-making process, including how much to produce and whether to stay in business.

Over the next few chapters, we'll continue to dig into the details of firm behavior that determine the market supply curve. Hold onto your understanding of production functions, different types of costs, and ways of calculating profits. We'll build on them as we continue to describe firm choices and market structures.

Key Terms

Summary

LO 12.1 Define total revenue, total cost, and profit.

The amount that a firm pays for all of the inputs that go into producing goods and services is its *total cost.* The amount that a firm receives from the sale of goods and services is its *total revenue. Profit* is the difference between cost and revenues.

LO 12.2 Explain the difference between fixed and variable costs, and give examples of each.

Fixed costs are costs that don't depend on the quantity of output produced. Often, a fixed cost is a one-time, upfront payment that has to be made before production can begin. Examples are buying a factory or hiring researchers to develop a new product. *Variable costs* are costs that depend on the quantity of output produced. Examples are the cost of raw materials and, often, workers' salaries.

LO 12.3 Explain the difference between explicit and implicit costs, and give examples of each.

Explicit costs are those that require a firm to spend money, such as paying for rent on a building, employee salaries, materials, and machines. *Implicit costs* are costs that represent forgone opportunities. They do not require a firm to spend money or take on obligations. Instead, they could have generated revenue if the firm had invested its resources in another way, such as investing money instead of spending or renting out factory space instead of producing goods

LO 12.4 Calculate economic and accounting profit, and explain the importance of the difference.

Economists think about costs as opportunity costs, and therefore they consider both explicit and implicit costs

when calculating profit. A firm's *economic profit* is total revenue minus explicit costs minus implicit costs. In contrast, accountants deal strictly with costs that involve an outlay of money. A firm's *accounting profit* is total revenue minus explicit costs. Because economic profit subtracts explicit *and* implicit costs from revenue, it is generally smaller than accounting profit.

LO 12.5 Define marginal product, and show why there is diminishing marginal product.

The ingredients that go into the production process—raw materials, labor, machines, time, ideas—are inputs. The goods and services produced are outputs. This relationship between the quantity of inputs and the quantity of outputs is called a *production function.*

The *marginal product* of any input into the production process is the increase in output generated by an additional unit of the input. In many cases, the marginal product of an input decreases as the quantity of the input increases, a principle called *diminishing marginal product.*

LO 12.6 Define and graph total cost, average costs, and marginal cost.

Total cost is the sum of fixed costs and variable costs. Average cost is calculated by dividing cost by the total quantity of output produced. The basic measure of average cost is *average total cost (ATC);* it is equal to total cost divided by the quantity of output. We can also use *average fixed cost (AFC)* or *average variable cost (AVC),* which are equal to fixed or variable costs, respectively, divided by quantity of output.

The *marginal cost (MC)* of production is calculated by dividing the change in total cost by the change in the quantity of output. In other words, it is the variable cost of producing the *next unit* of output.

LO 12.7 Explain why firms face different costs in the long run than in the short run.

Firms are able to adjust their property and production processes over time. Thus, costs that are fixed in the short run can become variable in the long run. A firm's long-run cost curves reflect the increased flexibility of fixed costs. In the long run, a small firm can expand its production capacity to look like that of a larger firm by changing the quantity of inputs that were fixed in the short run.

LO 12.8 Understand what economies and diseconomies of scale are and their implications for production decisions.

The average total cost curve is U-shaped. At levels of output where the curve slopes downward (i.e., ATC is decreasing as output increases), a firm faces *economies of scale*. At levels of output where the ATC slopes upward, a firm faces *diseconomies of scale*. When average total cost does not depend on the quantity of output—as in the flat middle section of the long-run curve—a firm faces *constant returns to scale*. A firm faces an incentive to increase or decrease its production to reach its *efficient scale*, the quantity of output at which average total cost is minimized.

Review Questions

1. Economists assume that firms have a goal to maximize profits. Is this a reasonable assumption for not-for-profit organizations? **[LO 12.1]**

2. Suppose you are evaluating the profit earned by a pharmaceutical company that produces three different medicines. What information will help you determine the company's revenue? What information will help you determine the company's total cost? **[LO 12.1]**

3. Suppose that a pharmaceutical company's costs include researchers' salaries, chemicals, warehouses, and paper and plastic packaging. Which of these costs do you expect to be fixed in the short run, and which variable? **[LO 12.2]**

4. Dustin is planning to open a catering business. Give examples of a one-time fixed cost, an ongoing fixed cost, and a variable cost his new catering business might incur. **[LO 12.2]**

5. A shopkeeper explains to you that she keeps down the cost of running her business because her husband works in the shop for free. Is her worker really free? Explain why or why not. **[LO 12.3]**

6. Dustin is planning to open a catering business. Give examples of an explicit cost and an implicit cost his new catering business might incur. **[LO 12.3]**

7. Imagine you're in a meeting with the owner of a restaurant, who is trying to decide whether to keep his restaurant open or to invest his time and money in another way. Explain to him the difference between accounting and economic profit, and why it should matter for his decision. **[LO 12.4]**

8. Explain why self-employed business owners frequently overestimate their profit levels. **[LO 12.4]**

9. Imagine a restaurant in which tables are spread over a large area, and there is only one waitperson. Explain to the manager why there might be increasing marginal product of labor associated with hiring a second waitperson. **[LO 12.5]**

10. If a firm experiences diminishing marginal product, does this mean that total output decreases? Explain. **[LO 12.5]**

11. A firm is trying to decide whether it could earn higher profits by increasing its output. Explain to the firm's manager why she needs to consider the marginal cost and the marginal revenue of the next unit of output to make this decision, rather than average costs. **[LO 12.6]**

12. A firm's output and total costs are given in Table 12Q-1. Going from a quantity of 3 to a quantity of 4, is marginal product increasing or decreasing? How can you tell? **[LO 12.6]**

13. Explain the statement, "In the long run, there are no fixed costs." **[LO 12.7]**

14. Suppose that a pharmaceutical company wants to grow in size but is constrained in the short run by its production capacity. Describe some steps that it can take in the long run to overcome these constraints. **[LO 12.7]**

15. Explain why an industry experiencing constant returns to scale is "just the right size." **[LO 12.8]**

16. Explain why the pharmaceutical industry is characterized by large economies of scale. **[LO 12.8]**

TABLE 12Q-1

Quantity	Total cost ($)
0	40
1	64
2	86
3	111
4	139
5	169

Problems and Applications

1. A hair salon offers three services: haircuts, color treatment, and styling. The salon charges $40 for a cut, $65 for color, and $30 for styling. Last month, the salon sold 68 haircuts, 34 color treatments, and 22 styling sessions. If the salon's costs for the month totaled $2,843, what was its profit? **[LO 12.1]**

2. Lisa is a self-employed physical therapist who works from a rented space. Lisa charges $250 for a therapy session. She incurred the following costs last month: space and equipment rental, $1,200; wages, $3,500; materials, $1,800. If Lisa's profit last month was $2,000, how many clients did she see? **[LO 12.1]**

3. Kat runs a cake shop. Her monthly expenses are listed below. For each cost, indicate whether the cost is a fixed cost or a variable cost of producing cakes in the short run. **[LO 12.2]**
    a. Ingredients (flour, butter, sugar).
    b. Bakers (cooks).
    c. Rent.
    d. Payments for equipment (ovens).
    e. Interest payments for borrowed capital.

4. An auto-repair shop faces the following weekly costs: rent, $500; labor, $400 per worker; parts and supplies, $30 per repair. Each worker can repair three cars per week. **[LO 12.2]**
    a. Fill in the costs in Table 12P-1.
    b. What are the total costs if the shop repairs 15 cars in a week?
    c. What are the total costs if the shop repairs 0 cars in a week?

5. Paola is thinking of opening her own business. For each of the production inputs listed below, indicate whether the input incurs an implicit cost, explicit cost, or no cost. **[LO 12.3]**
    a. Rent.
    b. Wages.
    c. Owned equipment.

6. Paola is thinking of opening her own business. For each of the production inputs listed below, indicate whether the input incurs an implicit cost, explicit cost, or no cost. **[LO 12.3]**
    a. Borrowed capital.
    b. Investment from savings.
    c. Donated supplies.

7. Keri owns a landscaping business. For each of Keri's inputs given in the list below, indicate whether the associated cost is fixed or variable, whether it is explicit or implicit, and whether the cost affects accounting profit only, economic profit only, or both. **[LO 12.2, 12.3, 12.4]**
    a. Landscapers.
    b. Plants taken from her home garden.
    c. Truck rental.
    d. Owned lawn mowers.

8. Last year, Jarod left a job that pays $60,000 to run his own bike-repair shop. Jarod's shop charges $65 for a repair, and last year the shop performed 3,000 repairs. Jarod's production costs for the year included rent, wages, and equipment. Jarod spent $50,000 on rent and $100,000 on wages for his employees. Jarod keeps whatever profit the shop earns but does not pay himself an official wage. Jarod used $20,000 of his savings to buy a machine for the business. His savings were earning an annual interest rate of 5 percent. **[LO 12.4]**
    a. What is Jarod's annual accounting profit?
    b. What is Jarod's annual economic profit?

9. If adding an additional input does not produce additional output, what is the slope of the production function at this point? **[LO 12.5]**

10. Webby Inc. is a web development company. Webby's monthly production function for developing websites is given in Table 12P-2. **[LO 12.5]**
    a. Fill in the marginal product column.
    b. After which programmer does marginal product diminish?

11. Webby Inc. is a web development company. Webby's monthly production function for developing websites is given in Table 12P-3. Webby pays $4,000 a month in rent for office space and equipment. It pays each programmer $2,000 a month. There are no other production costs. Fill in the table of production costs. **[LO 12.6]**

12. A firm's output, variable costs, and total costs are given in Table 12P-4. **[LO 12.6]**
    a. Calculate marginal cost using the formula given in the chapter,
    $$\frac{\Delta \text{ total cost}}{\Delta \text{ quantity}}.$$
    b. Calculate $\dfrac{\Delta \text{ variable cost}}{\Delta \text{ quantity}}$.

13. The dean of a college faces the following costs: graders, faculty, classroom space, and chalk. Of these costs, which are likely to be variable in the long run? **[LO 12.7]**

TABLE 12P-1

Quantity of repairs	Fixed costs ($)	Variable costs ($)	Total costs ($)
0			
3			
6			
9			
12			
15			
18			
21			
24			

TABLE 12P-2

Programmers	Websites	Marginal product
0	0	
1	2	
2	6	
3	14	
4	20	
5	24	
6	26	

TABLE 12P-3

Programmers	Websites	VC ($)	TC ($)	AFC ($)	AVC ($)	ATC ($)	MC ($)
0	0						
1	2						
2	6						
3	14						
4	20						
5	24						
6	26						

TABLE 12P-4

Quantity	Variable cost ($)	Total cost ($)
0	0	100
10	50	150
20	80	180
30	120	220
40	180	280
50	260	360

14. In the pet industry, would you expect the long run to be longer for a pet store or a veterinary clinic? **[LO 12.7]**

15. Consider a firm that increases its inputs by 15 percent. For each scenario, state whether the firm experiences economies of scale, diseconomies of scale, or constant returns to scale. **[LO 12.8]**

    a. Outputs increase 15 percent.

    b. Outputs increase by less than 15 percent.

    c. Outputs increase by greater than 15 percent.

16. A firm's long-run total costs are given in Table 12P-5. **[LO 12.8]**

    a. Fill in the long-run average total cost column.

    b. Over what production range does this firm experience economies of scale?

    c. Over what production range does this firm experience constant returns to scale?

    d. Over what production range does this firm experience diseconomies of scale?

Endnotes

1. http://www.forbes.com/sites/matthewherper/2011/04/19/americas-most-popular-drugs/

2. http://usatoday30.usatoday.com/money/industries/health/treatments/story/2011-11-29/Pfizer-maneuvers-to-protect-Lipitor-from-generics/51475288/1.

3. http://www.nytimes.com/2011/11/30/health/generic-lipitor-sets-off-an-aggressive-push-by-pfizer.html?ref=lipitordrug.

4. Bruce Roth, in http://money.cnn.com/magazines/fortune/fortune_archive/2003/01/20/335643/index.htm.

TABLE 12P-5

Output	Long-run total costs ($)	Long-run average total cost ($)
0	18	
1	24	
2	28	
3	30	
4	34	
5	40	
6	48	
7	63	
8	80	

Perfect Competition

TRAINSIDE VARIETY

When we think about markets in action, one image that comes to mind is the bustling trading floor of the New York Stock Exchange. But let's travel for a moment to an interesting market scene that's much farther away. Imagine sitting on a long-distance train in West Africa, on a journey from Yaoundé in the south of Cameroon to Maroua in the north. Every now and then, the train grinds to a halt near a town. Not many passengers get on or off—most are simply going from one of these big cities to the other. This journey takes many, many hours, and there is no restaurant car on board the train. The travelers need food and drink, and at each stop local merchants rush toward the train, offering refreshments for sale.

There is a limited range of goods being offered. Some vendors are selling bunches of small, ripe bananas. Some sell bags of oranges, partially skinned so you can crush them in

© Tommy Trenchard/Alamy

your hand and sip the juice. Others offer bags of peanuts, which have been soaked in salty water and dried in the sun. You will be able to find corn on the cob or plantain (a less-sweet kind of banana), roasted over an open fire. Vendors jostle for position along the train as passengers take turns to hang out of the window, peruse the choice of snacks, and hand down money to the vendors.

You won't see much bargaining going on. Everyone seems to know and accept the prices as given. After all, if a vendor tries to charge more than the going rate for a roasted plantain, a passenger has many other vendors to choose from. And if a passenger tries to pay less for a roasted plantain, vendors can easily sell to someone else. Eventually, all the passengers have bought the snacks they want, the train rolls off again, and the local merchants head back home and wait for the next train to come by with a new batch of customers.

For reasons we will explain in this chapter, this scene is probably about as close as you will come in the real world to observing a situation that economists call *perfect competition*. Like many of the concepts we've explored in this book, a *perfectly competitive market* is a simplified model that is rarely an exact fit with messy reality. It nonetheless tells us a lot about how the real world works. It also represents one of the miracles of economics: how well-functioning markets can deliver goods and services at wide scale and at low prices—with price signals determining the appropriate supply and demand, and without the government ever stepping in.

In this chapter, we'll describe the behavior of firms in a perfectly competitive market. We'll investigate how firms in such markets make decisions about what quantity of output to produce and when to stop producing altogether. We'll see that although firms are driven to seek profits, in the long run we can expect that firms in a perfectly competitive market *won't* earn *economic* profits. Understanding the decisions made by firms takes us behind the market supply curve we've used in previous chapters, to analyze the forces that shape it in the short run and in the long run.

In showing how competition works, we'll also see why it can bring benefits to consumers. The forces of competition help make millions of products and services available and affordable to billions of people, just as competition makes cheap, refreshing snacks available to passengers on a long train journey.

A Competitive Market

In this chapter, we'll discuss how firms make production decisions. Before we can begin this analysis, we have to break down one of the most important and powerful assumptions frequently made by economists: that firms are operating in competitive markets. We can analyze the importance of competitive markets through the lens of the first economists' question, *What are firms' wants and constraints?* In the previous chapter we identified what firms *want:* to maximize their profits. Participation in a competitive market, however, places some very specific *constraints* on their ability to achieve this goal, as we're about to see.

Characteristics of a competitive market

> **LO 13.1** Describe the characteristics of a perfectly competitive market.

We touched on the idea of a **competitive market** in Chapter 3, "Markets," where we discussed its four defining characteristics:

1. Buyers and sellers can't affect prices—the going price is the going price.
2. Goods are standardized.
3. Buyers and sellers have full information.
4. There are no transaction costs.

competitive market
a market in which fully informed, price-taking buyers and sellers easily trade a standardized good or service

Many markets have some degree of competitiveness but don't meet all four characteristics. Economists use the idea of *perfectly competitive markets* to refer to an idealized model of market competition in which all four characteristics hold true.

Let's briefly review the four main characteristics of a perfectly competitive market. We'll then add a fifth characteristic that is nonessential but important in defining competitive markets.

Individuals can't affect the going price

If you were the only seller of roasted plantains to a train full of hungry passengers, you'd be in a pretty good position: You could charge a very high price, knowing that some people would be hungry enough to pay it. Similarly, if you were the only passenger on a train and were facing dozens of roasted plantain sellers, you'd be in a great position: You could offer a very low price, confident that some seller would be desperate enough to sell you a plantain.

Most sellers and buyers in most markets are not in the happy position of being able to set their own price. Instead, most face some degree of competition. Nonetheless, they may still have some ability to decide what price to set. Say you're the only plantain seller at this train stop, but passengers know there will be many more at the next stop in half an hour's time. You may be able to charge a little bit of a premium to very hungry passengers who can't wait that long, but the presence of competition constrains your ability to charge what you like.

The first main characteristic of a *perfectly* competitive market is that buyers and sellers have *so much* competition, they have *no ability at all* to set their own price. As explained in Chapter 3, "Markets," a buyer or seller who cannot affect the market price is a *price taker*. Usually this implies that the market contains a large number of buyers and sellers. In such markets, the decisions of individual participants are so small relative to the total size of the market that they can't affect market prices. Instead, buyers and sellers have to accept the going rate. In a perfectly competitive market, buyers and sellers are price takers, who must "take" (accept) the prevailing price as they find it. The opposite of being a price taker is having **market power**, or the ability to noticeably affect market prices.

market power
the ability to noticeably affect market prices

Goods and services are standardized

The second main characteristic of a *perfectly* competitive market is that the goods and services being traded are standardized. When goods are standardized, they are interchangeable. Buyers have no reason to prefer those sold by one producer over those sold by another, provided that

they are the same price. This means that producers have to sell at the market price. They'd lose all of their business if they charged more, and they have no incentive to charge less.

Standardized goods are usually not the case in real life. Typically, goods are differentiated by quality, brand name, or characteristics that appeal to different tastes. Imagine the American equivalent of the Cameroonian train stop: turning off the interstate for a burger. Do you go to McDonald's or Burger King? Your choice is probably not determined solely by the price of the burgers, but also by your knowledge of whether you happen to prefer one over the other: A McDonald's burger is similar to a Burger King burger, but they are not the same. McDonald's fries are similar to Burger King's, but they not the same.

When goods are not standardized, producers will be able to charge different prices. Sellers of roasted plantains to Cameroonian train passengers, though, are not in this position. There are no brand names here—one roasted plantain is the same as any other. The good is standardized, thus meeting the second defining characteristic of a perfectly competitive market.

What markets, other than plantains for Cameroonian train passengers, sell standardized goods? Many natural resources, such as metals and lumber, can be considered standardized goods. At the same price, buyers don't care whether their gold comes from a mine in the United States or Uzbekistan, or whether their crude oil comes from a well in the Saudi Arabian desert or tar sands in Canada. As long as it meets certain defined characteristics, then gold is gold, and crude oil is crude oil. Standardized goods like this are often referred to as *commodities*.

Market participants have full information

The third main characteristic of a *perfectly* competitive market is that all market participants, buyers and sellers, have full information. One implication of goods being standardized is that everyone knows exactly what is being traded; there are *no information asymmetries* in a perfectly competitive market.

In the Cameroonian market for plantains, buyers have all the information they need to make the best decision possible. They know what price each seller is charging, and they can see the quality of the plantains for themselves. Sellers also have all the information they need to conduct transactions. In other types of markets, some sellers may have more information than others, giving them an advantage. But in perfectly competitive markets, all sellers are able to obtain all important information.

For one illustration of the importance of information in keeping markets competitive, see the Real Life box "Bazaar competition."

Real Life
Bazaar competition

Bazaars are often the most vibrant and colorful places in towns and cities around the world. International travelers are sometimes surprised to see massive bazaars that specialize in one very specific type of product, such as fruit, flowers, furniture, or fabric. In many cities, there are huge markets where hundreds and even thousands of vendors all sell exactly the same goods for exactly the same prices.

This tendency may seem perplexing. We sometimes see something similar in the United States: All the auto dealers in town may locate on the same road, for example. Doing so increases their chances of attracting potential customers who want to test-drive different brands of cars. But having a Honda dealership next to a Ford dealership next to a Chevrolet dealership is not the same as having a hundred small shops all selling the *exact same thing,* for the *exact same price.* To find a different product, you will have to go to a different bazaar.

Wouldn't it be easier for consumers to have a single location where they could go to buy all the different things they need, like the typical American mall or shopping center? And wouldn't sellers find it easier to operate in a location where they were the *only* ones selling their particular type of goods, rather than facing so much competition?

Perhaps we can answer these questions by considering that the bazaar may be an ancient way of ensuring healthy market competition. In the days before you could search Google to see how much different sellers are charging for a particular good, the vast majority of people had no way to know the price of something without going to the shop to ask. Moreover, just getting to a market can require a significant time investment. Therefore, if there is only one shop selling a good in a particular location, customers will be stuck buying whatever they can find there. Knowing this, the shopkeeper has a strong incentive to increase prices.

As a consumer, would you shop at the store located all by itself, or the one next to a hundred other identical stores? If they all sell standardized goods, you should feel confident that competition among the hundred stores will bring down the price as far as possible. Shop owners, in turn, know that customers will prefer to shop in a location where competition flourishes. Thus, it makes sense for stores to locate next to the hundred other stores selling the exact same things.

In short, bazaars aren't so bizarre—they're an old fashioned way of ensuring that competition works.

Source: John McMillan, *Reinventing the Bazaar: A Natural History of Markets* (New York: W.W. Norton, 2002).

No transaction costs

The fourth main characteristic of a *perfectly* competitive market is that the buyers and sellers face very low or zero transaction costs. This means buyers and sellers do not incur costs (or they incur very little cost) in making an exchange of goods in a perfectly competitive market.

In the Cameroonian market for plantains, sellers can easily sell their plantains to customers. Similarly, consumers can easily purchase the plantains. Neither buyers nor sellers must pay for the right to exchange the plantains. Furthermore, the buyers and sellers are all quite near each other geographically. Together, all these things mean that there are approximately zero transaction costs in the Cameroonian market for plantains. (We say "approximately zero" because, naturally, there are some tiny costs. For example, it does take a few seconds to make a trade, and maybe one has to walk a block.) The lack of transaction costs in perfectly competitive markets is very important because this helps allow for free entry and exit, which we discuss below.

Firms can freely enter and exit

The four characteristics described above are sufficient to define a perfectly competitive market. But another characteristic of perfectly competitive markets is important to understanding the way such markets function in the long run: Firms are able to freely enter and exit the market. This means that new firms can be created and begin producing goods and services if they want to, and existing firms can decide to shut down if they want to do so.

The extent to which firms can freely enter and exit explains some differences among markets. It helps us see why the market for roasted plantains at train stations comes close to a perfectly competitive market, but the market for, say, crude oil does not. It's pretty easy to set up as a plantain roaster. All you need is charcoal, a grill, and some plantains. It's a lot more difficult to set up as an oil producer. You need all kinds of expensive machinery and expertise. These entry requirements make it relatively easy for existing producers of oil to collude with each other to keep prices artificially high—causing the oil market to fail the "price-taking" requirement of perfect competition. It would be difficult for sellers of roasted plantains to do the same. New firms would enter the plantain market and undercut the colluders' prices.

In general, free entry into a market keeps existing firms on their toes. It can help drive innovation, cost-cutting, and quality improvements, as firms respond to the entry of new competitors. If entry and exit are costly, because of transactions costs, information gaps, or perhaps regulatory action, firms may collude, which would lead to a less than perfectly competitive market.

Remember that in real life, few markets meet all the assumptions of perfect competition. Nonetheless, perfect competition is a useful beginning assumption; it provides a base for describing interactions between buyers and sellers and plays a significant role in most markets. We'll work with this simplification for now, but keep in mind that the picture will become more complicated as we continue.

Revenues in a perfectly competitive market

> **LO 13.2** Calculate average, marginal, and total revenue.

The characteristics of perfect competition lead to a less-than-obvious conclusion: *In a perfectly competitive market, producers are able to sell as much as they want without affecting the market price.* This conclusion follows from two of the characteristics of a perfectly competitive market: (1) that individual buyers and sellers are price takers and (2) that consumers are indifferent between the standardized goods sold by different producers.

These two very important assumptions mean that when firms make decisions about the quantity they will produce, they don't have to worry about

1. whether their actions will cause the market price to rise or fall or
2. whether they will find buyers.

Therefore, as we analyze the revenue that firms can expect to bring in, we can assume that firms in a competitive market will be able to sell *any quantity of output at the market price.*

But remember, this doesn't mean that firms will *want* to sell an ever-increasing amount of their product. We learned in Chapter 12, "The Costs of Production," that as the quantity produced increases, average total cost first decreases but eventually increases. Because costs are not constant, firms want to find and produce at the level of output that maximizes profits.

POTENTIALLY CONFUSING

How can every firm in a competitive market sell as much as it wants? If every firm produced more and more, wouldn't the quantity for sale outstrip the quantity demanded, pushing the price down?

In theory, yes. But there are two reasons why this doesn't interfere with our conclusion. First, firms will not want to produce an infinite quantity. Remember the principle of diminishing marginal product (from Chapter 12, "The Costs of Production"): As firms produce more, their costs tend to go up. As we'll see later in this chapter, that means there will come a point for every firm at which it doesn't want to produce any more.

Second, remember that we are thinking about decisions made by individual firms. By definition, in a perfectly competitive market, each individual firm is so small relative to the size of the whole market that an increase in its output causes a negligibly small increase in the total quantity supplied. Any *individual* firm's choice about the quantity to produce has such a tiny effect on the total quantity supplied to the market that the change in price is essentially zero.

Let's imagine that you live in a Cameroonian town and you are setting up a plantain-roasting enterprise to cater to passing train travelers. What can we say about your firm's revenue? In Chapter 12, "The Costs of Production," we talked about *total revenue:* the price that a firm receives for each good, multiplied by the quantity of that good it sells, as seen in Equation 13-1. In this case, the firm sells only one good: roasted plantains. Its total revenue is therefore equal to the price of roasted plantains times the quantity it sells.

EQUATION 13-1 $$\text{Total revenue} = P \times Q$$

For instance, if the price is 1,000 CFA francs (the Cameroonian currency) per bunch of plantains, and the firm produces 5 bunches of roasted plantains, its total revenue will be 5,000 CFA francs.

Table 13-1 shows revenue for a firm in a competitive market—in this case, the plantain firm. The third column in the table shows *total revenue* at various quantities. Because the firm is a price taker in a competitive market, price remains the same regardless of the quantity that the firm produces (as shown in column 2). So, if the firm triples the quantity it produces, from 1 bunch of plantains to 3 bunches of plantains, revenue also triples from 1,000 CFA francs to 3,000 CFA francs.

TABLE 13-1

Revenue of a firm in a competitive market

The price received per bunch remains constant because the firm is a price taker in a competitive market.

(1)	(2)	(3)	(4)	(5)
Quantity of plantains (bunches)	Price (CFA francs)	Total revenue (CFA francs)	Average revenue (CFA francs/bunch of plantains)	Marginal revenue (CFA francs)
1	1,000	1,000	1,000	1,000
2	1,000	2,000	1,000	1,000
3	1,000	3,000	1,000	1,000
4	1,000	4,000	1,000	1,000
5	1,000	5,000	1,000	1,000

average revenue
revenue generated per
product, calculated as
total revenue divided by
the quantity sold

Besides total revenue, we also need to consider two other measures of revenue: average revenue and marginal revenue. **Average revenue** is the revenue generated per unit; it is calculated as total revenue divided by the quantity sold, or

EQUATION 13-2 $\text{Average revenue} = \dfrac{\text{Total revenue}}{\text{Quantity sold}} = \dfrac{P \times Q}{Q} = P$

In other words, *for any firm selling one product, average revenue is equal to the price of the good.*

marginal revenue
the revenue generated
by selling an additional
unit of a good

Marginal revenue is the revenue generated by selling an additional unit of a good. It is calculated as the change in total revenue divided by the change in quantity sold, or

EQUATION 13-3 $\text{Marginal revenue} = \dfrac{\text{Change in total revenue}}{\text{Change in quantity sold}}$

In our example, when the quantity sold increases by 1 unit, what happens? The change in total revenue increases by the market price of that unit ($1,000 CFA francs). Thus, one unit of the good always generates revenue of $1 \times P = P$. So, *for a firm in a competitive market, marginal revenue is equal to the price of the good.* (If the market were not competitive, however, producing an additional unit of a good might affect the market price.)

But, wait, did we just say that average revenue is equal to the price of the good *and* that marginal revenue is equal to the price of the good? Yes—that's right: *For firms in a perfectly competitive market, average revenue and marginal revenue both equal price.*

We can check these equalities in Table 13-1 by calculating average and marginal revenue directly from quantity and price. Average revenue, shown in column 4, is equal to the value in column 3 (total revenue) divided by the value in column 1 (quantity). Marginal revenue, shown in column 5, is calculated by subtracting total revenue in one row from total revenue in the next row, as quantity increases. We can confirm that at any quantity, average and marginal revenue are both equal to price for this price-taking firm in a competitive market.

✓ CONCEPT CHECK

☐ What are the four defining characteristics of a competitive market? What is the fifth non-essential characteristic? **[LO 13.1]**

☐ What happens to the market price when a producer in a competitive market increases its output? **[LO 13.1]**

☐ What is the relationship between marginal revenue and price in a competitive market? **[LO 13.2]**

Profits and Production Decisions

The quest for profits is the most important driving force behind firms' behavior. In our analysis of competitive markets, this assumption allows us to predict how much firms will choose to produce under different circumstances. In the following section, we'll draw on our discussion from Chapter 12, "The Costs of Production," and combine it with an understanding of revenues in competitive markets.

Deciding how much to produce

LO 13.3 Find a firm's optimal quantity of output.

A plantain-roasting enterprise, like all firms, is trying to maximize its profits. Because it is a price taker in a competitive market, it cannot affect the price it receives for the roasted plantains it sells. We'll assume that the markets for its production inputs—raw plantains, charcoal, and labor—are perfectly competitive, too. At any given quantity, therefore, the firm's revenue and cost per plantain are determined by factors outside of its control.

The only choice that such a company can make to affect its profits is to decide the *quantity* of roasted plantains to produce. It is tempting to assume that since the firm can sell any quantity it wants without driving down prices, the firm should simply produce as much as possible to maximize its revenues. However, profits depend not just on revenues; costs also matter.

Table 13-2 shows (in columns 2, 3, and 4) total revenue, total cost, and the resulting profit (revenue minus cost) at each quantity of plantains that the firm might produce. It's important to realize that total cost includes both fixed and variable costs. In this case, fixed costs include the cost of the cooking equipment and monthly rent for workspace.

The firm looks at the total revenue, total cost, and profit and sees that it can maximize profit by producing either 3 or 4 bunches of plantains each day. At either of those quantities, profit will be 400 CFA francs. That's useful: We now know that to maximize profit, we want to produce more than 2 bunches but not as many as 5. Can we determine whether 3 or 4 is the optimal quantity?

We have already seen (in Table 13-1) that marginal revenue stays the same in a perfectly competitive market. Column 5 of Table 13-2 shows the marginal revenue for the plantain-roasting business. Costs matter too: As column 6 shows, the marginal cost of the first bunch is 500 CFA francs, which increases for each bunch thereafter. We can see the effect of total cost in two places in the table:

- Given that marginal revenue for the first bunch is 1,000 CFA francs and marginal cost is 500 CFA francs, producing the first bunch must increase profit by 500 CFA francs. We see this reflected in column 7.
- We also see this profit reflected in column 4, where profit increased from −700 to −200 CFA francs.

? POTENTIALLY CONFUSING

In case you are wondering: Yes, it's still correct to say that "profit increased" when the amount of profit is a negative amount—such as when the amount in the profit column changed from −700 to −200 CFA francs. Another way to say this same thing would be to say that the "loss decreased" from −700 to −200 CFA francs. No matter which phrasing you use, the business is coming closer to the point at which it can cover its costs and have some CFA francs in hand by the end of the business day.

TABLE 13-2

Revenue, cost, and profit

As revenues increase, costs do as well. The relationship between revenues and costs determines where profits are maximized.

(1)	(2)	(3)	(4)	(5)	(6)	(7)
Quantity of plantains (bunches)	Total revenue (CFA francs)	Total cost (CFA francs)	Profit (CFA francs) [cols. (2) − (3)]	Marginal revenue (CFA francs)	Marginal cost (CFA francs)	Marginal profit (CFA francs) [cols. (5) − (6)]
0	0	700	−700	—	—	—
1	1,000	1,200	−200	1,000	500	500
2	2,000	1,800	200	1,000	600	400
3	3,000	2,600	400	1,000	800	200
4	**4,000**	**3,600**	**400**	**1,000**	**1,000**	**0**
5	5,000	4,800	200	1,000	1,200	−200

As long as marginal revenue is greater than marginal cost, production of an additional unit will increase profits. When marginal revenue stays the same but marginal cost increases, this very important fact follows: *A firm should continue to increase production for as long as marginal cost is less than marginal revenue; it should stop increasing production as soon as the two are equal.*

To see how this fact can help decide how many plantains to roast, look at column 7 in Table 13-2, which shows marginal profit (marginal revenue minus marginal cost). We can confirm the decision the firm made earlier (solely on the basis of profit maximization) to increase output from 2 bunches to 3 bunches of roasted plantains:

- At an output of 2 bunches, marginal revenue is 1,000 CFA francs, marginal cost is 600 francs, and so the marginal profit is 400 francs.
- At an output of 3 bunches, marginal revenue is 1,000 CFA francs, marginal cost is 800 francs, and so the marginal profit is 200 francs.

It makes sense to increase production from 2 to 3 bunches because roasting an additional bunch will still yield positive marginal profit. This confirms the earlier decision.

What happens when the firm is producing 4 bunches of plantains? Should it increase production to 5 bunches? Marginal cost in this case is 1,200 francs, but marginal revenue remains at 1,000 francs, so the marginal profit is −200 francs. The firm would lose 200 francs of profit by producing the extra plantains, so it should stick with 4 bunches.

These calculations lead us to a decision rule for deciding how much to produce: *The profit-maximizing quantity is the one at which the marginal revenue of the last unit was exactly equal to the marginal cost.* In Table 13-2, we find this amount at 4 bunches of plantains. If the firm produced any more than this amount, its profits would start to go down.

Figure 13-1 shows this idea graphically by plotting the values from Table 13-2 in graph form. As we discussed in Chapter 12, "The Costs of Production," the marginal cost (MC) curve slopes upward because marginal cost increases with quantity. A horizontal line at the price level represents marginal revenue (MR). The point at which the marginal revenue curve intersects the marginal cost curve shows the profit-maximizing quantity at which to produce.

FIGURE 13-1

Choosing the optimal production quantity

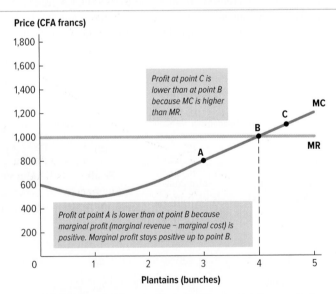

The profit-maximizing quantity is the one at which the marginal revenue of the last unit was exactly equal to its marginal cost. As long as marginal revenue remains larger than marginal cost, the firm increases its total profits by producing another unit. When marginal cost exceeds marginal revenue, however, the change in profits from producing another unit is negative.

TABLE 13-3

Revenue, cost, and profit when price falls to 800 CFA francs

When price decreases, this firm no longer earns a profit, however many bunches of plantains it sells.

(1)	(2)	(3)	(4)	(5)	(6)	(7)
Quantity of plantains (bunches)	Total revenue (CFA francs)	Total cost (CFA francs)	Profit (CFA francs) [cols. (2) − (3)]	Marginal revenue (CFA francs)	Marginal cost (CFA francs)	Marginal profit (CFA francs) [cols. (5) − (6)]
0	0	700	−700	—	—	—
1	800	1,200	−400	800	500	300
2	1,600	1,800	−200	800	600	200
3	2,400	2,600	−200	800	800	0
4	3,200	3,600	−400	800	1,000	−200
5	4,000	4,800	−800	800	1,200	−400

A change in the going price could change a firm's decision about how much to produce. To see why, imagine that something happens to cause the market price of plantains to drop to 800 CFA francs; let's say a rumor spreads that roasted plantains are bad for your health, making train travelers less willing to buy them. Table 13-3 shows what happens to profits at the new market price. After the change in price, the firm finds that marginal revenue equals marginal cost at a production quantity of 3 rather than 4 bunches. But the drop in price means that the business loses money at every level of production.

Despite the effect that the change in price has on profit, we can still find the optimal production level. How? By finding the quantity where marginal revenue equals marginal cost. As you can see in Table 13-3, the firm's losses are smallest when the firm cuts production from the previously optimal level of 4 bunches of plantains (at a market price of 1,000 CFA francs) to only 3 bunches (at a price of 800).

You might be wondering at this point why the firm is producing at all if it loses money at every level of production. Wouldn't it be better to earn zero dollars than to lose money? Of course it would be, but firms are sometimes unable to quickly exit a market. For example, a firm that rents a space might have to continue paying rent for the remainder of its lease. Even if production drops to zero, the fixed costs remain for some time. As we discuss below, when firms are making negative profits, they must make a decision about what to do during the time that they still owe fixed costs. Should the firm produce zero and lose all of its fixed costs? Or should the firm produce some amount and try to recoup a portion of its fixed costs?

Deciding when to operate

LO 13.4 Describe a firm's decision to shut down or to exit the market, and explain the difference between these choices.

The most extreme choice that a firm can make about how much to produce is to produce nothing at all. Look again at Figure 13-1 and imagine what happens when the market price decreases. The horizontal MR line falls lower on the graph, intersecting the MC curve at lower and lower quantities. We have already seen from Table 13-3 that a price decrease lowers the profit-maximizing quantity. How low would the market price have to fall before the firm decided to produce nothing?

Let's draw the MC curve again, this time adding the AVC and ATC curves. Remember (from Chapter 12, "The Costs of Production") that the MC curve intersects both AVC and ATC at their lowest points. Remember, too, that the difference between a firm's variable and total costs is its *fixed costs*. The firm has to pay those costs regardless of how much it produces, and even if it produces nothing at all. For a plantain-roasting enterprise, fixed costs might include the purchase of roasting equipment and the lease of a place in which to set up the equipment. Variable costs— the costs that vary according to output—would include charcoal, raw plantains, and labor.

We know that in a perfectly competitive market, the market price is the same thing as the firm's average revenue. As long as average revenue (that is, the market price) remains above average total cost, total revenue will be higher than total cost, and the firm will be making positive profits. Mathematically, this leads to a new equation for calculating profits, shown in Equation 13-4:

EQUATION 13-4   Profit = (Average revenue – ATC) × Q

Because average revenue is equal to the price for a competitive firm, we can rewrite this in another way, to get Equation 13-4a:

EQUATION 13-4A   Profit = (Price – ATC) × Q

Notice that Equation 13-4 implies that as long as the price (or average revenue) is above average total cost, the firm is making positive profits. But if the market price falls below the bottom of the firm's ATC curve, there is no level of output at which the firm can make a profit. It's bound to make a loss. Does that mean it should stop production?

The obvious answer is yes—at that point, the firm *wants* to exit the market. However, the decision is complicated by the fact that a firm is likely *unable* to exit the market immediately. Because of this, the answer to whether the firm will stop production depends on a concept introduced in Chapter 12, "The Costs of Production"—whether we are thinking in the *short run* or the *long run*.

Short-Run Decisions

When a firm *shuts down* production, it stops producing for some interval of time, until market conditions change. (The concept of shutting down is a temporary decision; it does not mean closing the business entirely.) Shutting down avoids incurring *variable* costs because the quantity produced is zero.

In the short run, however, the firm is stuck with its *fixed* costs; they do not decrease when quantity falls to zero. A cost that has already been incurred and cannot be refunded or recovered is a *sunk cost*. Fixed costs like land or large machinery are usually sunk costs in the short run. They have to be paid regardless of how much the firm produces, or whether it produces anything at all. *Fixed costs are therefore irrelevant in deciding whether to shut down production in the short run.*

The decision to stop producing depends entirely on the variable costs of production. If the market price is lower than ATC but higher than AVC, the firm should still continue to produce in the short run. Doing so yields more revenue than variable cost. To make this idea concrete, look again at Table 13-3. The firm would lose 700 CFA francs if it shut down production and produced a quantity of zero, as seen in column 4. Those 700 CFA francs lost are the fixed cost incurred before producing even 1 bunch of roasted plantains. However, the firm will lose only 200 CFA francs if it produces 3 bunches of plantains, again shown by column 4. (That's the *smallest loss* it can incur given the fixed and variable costs at the market price of 800 per bunch.) Thus, the firm should continue to produce 3 bunches of plantains as long as it is required to pay its fixed costs.

To generalize, the profit-maximization rule remains the same for firms whose price is below average total cost but above average variable cost: *The profit-maximizing (or, in this case, the loss-minimizing) level of production is the quantity at which the market price intersects the marginal cost curve.* The firm will be losing money at that point, but it will lose less money than if it did not produce at all.

However, if the market price drops *below* the bottom of the AVC curve, it makes sense for the firm to stop production in the short run. As well as having to pay its fixed costs, the firm will be losing additional money for every unit it produces. The loss-minimizing level of production is zero. At that level, losses due to fixed costs are unavoidable. But at least the firm won't lose even more money by roasting more plantains, each of which costs more to produce than the revenue it brings in.

In Table 13-4, we see what happens if the price drops to 400 CFA francs. As was the case at the price of 800 CFA francs, the firm loses 700 CFA francs if it stops production. But now the price is so low that the losses increase with each unit of production. Thus, *the profit-maximizing (or loss-minimizing) level of production when price is below average variable cost is to produce nothing.*

We can state the short-run shutdown rule as follows:

EQUATION 13-5   Shut down if P < AVC

Above average variable cost, a firm's short-run supply curve is the same as its marginal cost curve, as shown in Figure 13-2. At each price, the firm will supply the profit-maximizing quantity. The profit-maximizing quantity is the one at which marginal cost equals marginal revenue. Since marginal revenue is the same as price in a perfectly competitive market, we can take a shortcut to finding the point at which to shut down production by simply reading the quantity corresponding to each price along the marginal cost curve. Below the shutdown price, however, the firm will not want to produce at all.

Long-Run Decisions

We've seen that in the *short run,* fixed costs may lead a firm to shut down production until market conditions change. When the firm makes *long-run* decisions, the reasoning is different: In the long run, all costs become variable. Leases can expire and not be renewed; machinery can be sold. It is only in the long run that firms are able to make the decision to completely exit the market.

TABLE 13-4

Revenue, cost, and profit when price falls to 400 CFA francs

When price decreases still further, this firm no longer earns a profit, however many bunches of plantains it sells.

(1)	(2)	(3)	(4)	(5)	(6)	(7)
Quantity of plantains (bunches)	Total revenue (CFA francs)	Total cost (CFA francs)	Profit (CFA francs) [cols. (2) − (3)]	Marginal revenue (CFA francs)	Marginal cost (CFA francs)	Marginal profit (CFA francs) [cols. (5) − (6)]
0	0	700	−700	—	—	—
1	400	1,200	−800	400	500	−100
2	800	1,800	−1,000	400	600	−200
3	1,200	2,600	−1,400	400	800	−400
4	1,600	3,600	−2,000	400	1,000	−600
5	2,000	4,800	−2,800	400	1,200	−800

FIGURE 13-2

The short-run supply curve and the shutdown rule

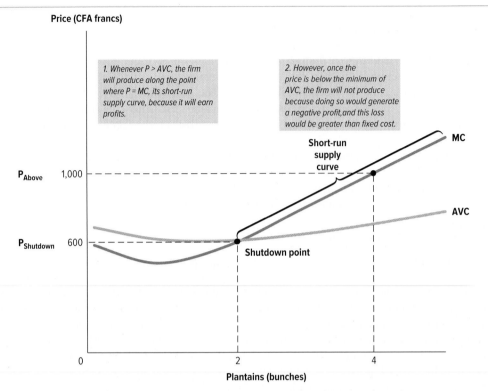

1. Whenever P > AVC, the firm will produce along the point where P = MC, its short-run supply curve, because it will earn profits.

2. However, once the price is below the minimum of AVC, the firm will not produce because doing so would generate a negative profit, and this loss would be greater than fixed cost.

The section of the marginal cost curve that is above AVC describes the firm's short-run supply curve. At any price above that point, the firm will produce the quantity where price intersects the MC curve. At prices below the minimum of AVC, the firm produces nothing because it would generate a negative profit.

? POTENTIALLY CONFUSING

The terms *shut down* and *exit* seem very similar, but to economists, each means very specific things.

- The decision to *shut down* is a decision that is made only in the *short run*. A firm that shuts down in the short run is still technically in the market, but it is not producing any units of product. The firm is still responsible for paying any fixed costs that it owes.

- The decision to *exit* is a decision that can be made only in the *long run*. When a firm exits, it closes its doors, cancels all contracts, and is no longer in the market at all. Keep in mind that any firm that shuts down in the short run will also be exiting in the long run if it believes prices will continue to be low in the future. Additionally, even if a firm continues to produce in the short run, it will still exit in the long run if the price it can charge is less than its average total cost (that is, if the firm is making negative profits).

When deciding whether to exit in the long run, the firm should consider whether average revenue is greater than average *total* cost. If the market price is less than the lowest point on the ATC curve, the firm should make a long-run decision to exit the market for good. Keep in mind

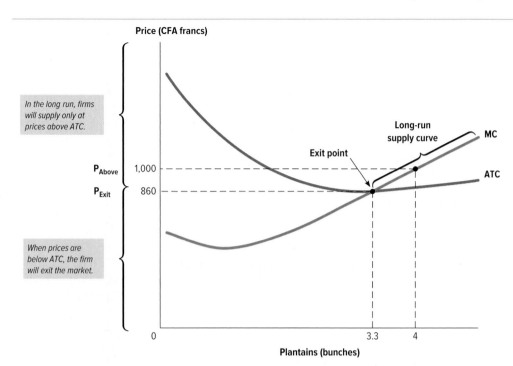

FIGURE 13-3

The long-run supply curve and the exit rule

Price (CFA francs)

In the long run, firms will supply only at prices above ATC.

Long-run supply curve

MC

Exit point

P_{Above} 1,000

ATC

P_{Exit} 860

When prices are below ATC, the firm will exit the market.

0   3.3   4

Plantains (bunches)

In the long run, a firm can avoid not only the variable costs of production, but also fixed costs, by exiting the market. If price is less than average total cost, the firm should exit the market. Conversely, if price is more than average total cost, a firm should enter the market.

that firms making negative profits will always *want* to exit the market. In the short run, they are *unable* to exit. In the long run, they *are* able to do so. We can state the exit rule as:

EQUATION 13-6   Exit if P < ATC

Figure 13-3, which shows the firm's long-run supply curve, illustrates the exit rule. At prices above average total cost, the firm will produce at the point where price intersects marginal cost. At prices below average total cost, the firm will choose to produce nothing and will exit the market.

In making the long-run decision, the firm will consider whether the market price is likely to remain low *in the long run*. If it believes that the market price has fallen only in the short run, and will increase again in the long run, then it would not make sense to exit the market permanently. This reasoning explains why a firm might decide to halt production temporarily in the short run when price dips below AVC but might not make the long-run decision to exit the market permanently. The firm could stop its variable costs (lay off workers, buy no more raw materials) but keep open the possibility of restarting production by retaining its machinery and premises, in the hope that the price goes back up again.

✓ CONCEPT CHECK

☐ What is the relationship between cost and revenue at the profit-maximizing quantity of output? **[LO 13.3]**

☐ How do sunk costs affect a firm's decision to shut down? **[LO 13.4]**

☐ When should a firm exit the market in the long run? **[LO 13.4]**

Behind the Supply Curve

So far in this text, we've used the supply curve to describe the relationship between price and the quantity supplied on a market level. So far in this chapter, we've seen how an individual firm's costs determine its decisions about how much it is willing to supply at a given price. It's time to connect the two. By doing so, we will see how the supply curve *for the market* reflects the sum of the choices of many individual suppliers, each willing to produce a certain quantity of a good at each price. We've seen that firms think differently about their production decisions in the short run and the long run. The choices of individual firms also generate differences between market supply curves in the short run and the long run.

Short-run supply

LO 13.5 Draw a short-run supply curve for a competitive market with identical firms.

In the short run, we assume that the number of firms in the market is fixed. The total quantity of a good that is supplied at a given price is therefore the sum of the quantities that each individual producer is willing to supply. To simplify things a bit, let's assume that each plantain-roasting firm currently in the market has the same cost structure. Each has the same resources, same technology, and so on, such that each is willing to supply the same quantity at a given price as all of the others.

Panel A of Figure 13-4 shows the supply curve for one of these roasted-plantain firms. (Note that it's the same short-run supply curve we established in Figure 13-2: It is the firm's MC curve at points after it intersects the AVC curve.) Now suppose that there are 100 producers currently operating in the roasted-plantain market, each with the same individual supply curve. The total

---

FIGURE 13-4

Firm and market supply curves

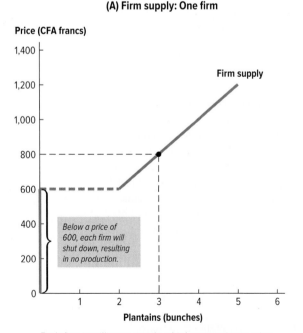

(A) Firm supply: One firm

Each firm is willing to supply a higher quantity as price increases. Price equals MR, and the optimal quantity at any price is where MR equals MC. Each optimal quantity-price pair adds a point on the supply curve.

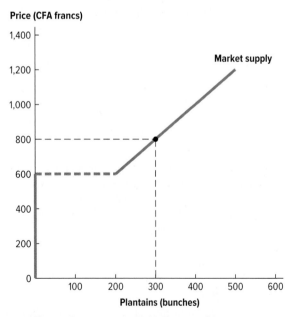

(B) Market supply: 100 firms

The total quantity supplied is the sum of the quantity that each firm supplies. If there are 100 identical firms in the market, the market supply at any price is 100 times the quantity supplied by each firm.

quantity supplied—the market supply—is simply the sum of the quantities that each firm supplies. Panel B of Figure 13-4 shows the market supply curve. At every price level, the total quantity supplied in the market is 100 times the quantity supplied by each firm.

Long-run supply

LO 13.6 Draw a long-run supply curve for a competitive market with identical firms, and describe its implications for profit-seeking firms.

The key difference between supply in the short run and supply in the long run is that we assume that firms are able to enter and exit the market in the long run. The number of firms is not fixed; it changes in response to changing circumstances. In general, the circumstances that make firms decide to exit or enter are as follows:

- We've already seen what makes a firm decide to *exit* the market—price falling below the lowest point on the ATC curve. At that point, the firm would be operating at a loss.
- Conversely, a firm would want to *enter* the market if it sees it could produce at a level of ATC that is below the market price. In other words, new firms will enter a market if the existing firms are making a profit.

Let's look more deeply at the effect on the long-run supply curve of those two decisions.

Effects of market entry on the long-run supply curve

The existence of economic profits in a market signals that there is money to be made. *How will others respond* to this signal? They will enter the market to take advantage of the profit-making opportunity. If firms supplying roasted plantains to Cameroonian train travelers are making more money than firms supplying salted peanuts or candied oranges, what would be likely to happen? We can expect orange-candying firms and peanut-salting firms to switch their resources toward roasting plantains instead, if the costs of doing so are not very large.

But as more firms enter the roasted-plantain market, what happens? Remember from Chapter 3, "Markets," that the number of firms in the market is one of the nonprice determinants of supply: More firms means an increase in supply, and the whole market supply curve shifts to the right. As supply increases and demand stays constant, the market equilibrium moves to a lower price and higher quantity.

What does the new equilibrium imply for the profits made by firms in the market? Remember that profits are revenues minus costs. As the equilibrium market price falls, revenues fall—and so do profits. As long as *economic* profit is positive, however, more firms still have an incentive to enter the market to take advantage of them.

? POTENTIALLY CONFUSING

At this point we need to remember the difference between *accounting profit* and *economic profit.* When calculating economic profit, total costs *include opportunity costs,* such as the money a firm could have made if it had invested its resources in other business opportunities.

Accounting profit = Total revenue − Explicit costs

Economic profit = Total revenue − Explicit costs − Implicit costs

When a firm is making zero *economic* profit, the firm is still likely earning positive *accounting* profit. Thus, when we say that the price in the long run is such that firms earn zero economic profit, we don't mean that firms are earning no money. Instead, we simply mean that a firm is earning just as much money as it could be earning in its next-best opportunity.

In the long run, as long as *economic* profit is positive, new firms have an incentive to enter the market. As new firms enter the market, the market supply curve shifts to the right; the new market equilibrium is found at a higher quantity and a lower price. Eventually, the price will be so low that economic profits are reduced to zero—in other words, $P = ATC$. At this point, firms are indifferent between the roasted-plantain market and other business opportunities; they no longer have an incentive to enter the market.

Effects of market exit on the long-run supply curve

Now that we understand why firms might enter a market, let's consider why firms decide to make the opposite decision—to exit a market. If price falls below ATC, a firm may still be making an accounting profit. But at that point the firm is making negative economic profit. It could be making more money by pursuing other opportunities. It thus has an incentive to exit the market and invest its resources elsewhere.

What happens when some firms exit the market? The market supply curve shifts to the left; the new market equilibrium is found at a lower quantity and a higher price. As price increases, profits also increase. The process continues until economic profits are zero. At that point, no more firms exit the market; they are indifferent between the roasted-plantain market and other business opportunities.

Understanding the process of market entry and exit leads us to several conclusions. In the long run in a perfectly competitive market: (1) Firms earn zero economic profits. (2) Firms operate at an efficient scale. (3) Supply is perfectly elastic (in theory). Let's consider each.

Firms earn zero economic profit

This first conclusion might sound surprising: *In the long run, firms in a perfectly competitive market earn zero economic profit.* This doesn't mean that a business is not earning *accounting* profit. It simply means that the firm could not earn greater accounting profit by choosing to operate in a different market instead.

Remember, though, that *perfectly* competitive markets do not often exist in the real world. In the next section, we'll see why this first conclusion rarely holds in reality.

Firms operate at an efficient scale

The second conclusion about firms in competitive markets is less counterintuitive than the first, but powerful nonetheless: *In the long run, firms in a competitive market operate at an efficient scale.* Remember from Chapter 12, "The Costs of Production," that a firm's *efficient scale* is the quantity that minimizes average total cost in the long run.

To reach this conclusion, we need to bring together three pieces of information discussed earlier. First, remember that a firm's optimal production is the point at which price (that is, marginal revenue) equals marginal cost. Second, remember that the marginal cost curve intersects the average total cost curve at its lowest point. Third, we just established that *in the long run, economic profits are zero*, meaning that price is equal to average total cost. In equation format, these three rules for *long-run outcomes* are:

EQUATION 13-7

(1)   P = MR = MC at the profit-maximizing quantity

(2) MC = ATC at the minimum of ATC (at its lowest point)

(3)   P = ATC in the long run

These identities tell us that, *in the long run,*

EQUATION 13-7A $P = MC = ATC$

The intersection of all three lines takes place at only one point, as shown in Figure 13-5. As we know, MC = ATC at the minimum of ATC. When a firm produces at a point that satisfies this condition, it is therefore necessarily producing the quantity that minimizes average total cost in the long run. In other words, it is operating at its *efficient scale*.

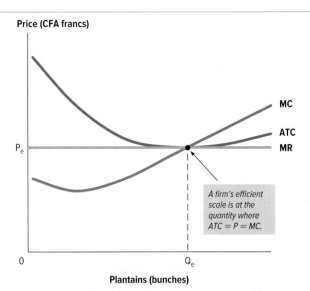

FIGURE 13-5

Firms operate at efficient scale in the long run

Price (CFA francs)

MC

ATC

MR

P_e

A firm's efficient scale is at the quantity where ATC = P = MC.

0   Q_e

Plantains (bunches)

In the long run, firms in a competitive market operate at an efficient scale. A firm's efficient scale is the quantity that minimizes average total cost, which occurs where P = MC = ATC.

Supply is perfectly elastic

Our third conclusion about competitive markets in the long run follows directly from the first two. We have established that economic profits are zero. In order for this to be true, price must be equal to the minimum of ATC.

If anything causes the market equilibrium to move away from this price, the resulting positive or negative profits will cause firms to enter or exit the market. Such entry and exit will increase or decrease the quantity supplied, until price returns to the level that yields zero economic profits. Thus, in the long run, price is the same at any quantity. This causes the supply curve to be horizontal, as shown in Figure 13-6.

Remember from Chapter 4, "Elasticity," that a horizontal supply curve is *perfectly elastic*—producers will supply any quantity at the market price. In theory, therefore, in a competitive market, the price of a good should never change in the long run.

Why the long-run market supply curve shouldn't slope upward, but does

LO 13.7 Explain why a long-run supply curve can slope upward.

How important was our previous assumption that the price of a good or service never changes and that all firms face identical costs? It certainly enabled us to build a tidy theory. But that theory makes a few predictions that don't quite match what we actually observe to be true. Here, we'll add a few nuances to the model just discussed. You will see why price doesn't stay perfectly constant in the long run and what the effect of that fact is on the long-run market supply curve.

The main tweak to the model from the previous section removes the assumption that all firms have the same cost structure. In the real world, this is hardly ever true: Some firms are simply more efficient than others at converting inputs into outputs. It would not be realistic to expect new entrants to an industry to achieve the same low costs as firms that have built up expertise over the years. The newer firms with higher costs will enter only markets with higher prices.

FIGURE 13-6

Perfectly elastic long-run supply curve

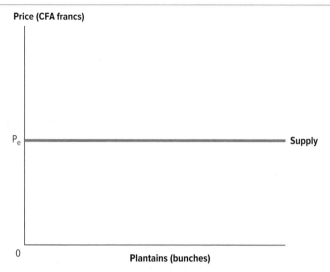

If anything causes the market to move away from the minimum-of-ATC price, the resulting positive or negative profits will cause firms to enter or exit the market, increasing or decreasing the quantity supplied until it returns to the equilibrium price. Thus, in the long run, price is the same at any quantity, and the supply curve is horizontal.

In practice, therefore, the long-run supply curve will slope upward. Why? Because price has to rise to entice new firms to enter and increase the total quantity supplied.

In reality, price is equal to the minimum of ATC for only the least-efficient firm in the market, not for every firm currently in the market. Dropping the simplifying assumption that every firm's costs are the same also overturns the surprising conclusion we came to in the last section—that firms in a perfectly competitive market earn zero economic profit. Instead, the *last firm* to enter the market earns zero economic profit because its ATC is equal to price. But more efficient firms, with lower ATC, are able to earn positive economic profit.

Even if every firm in a market has the same ATC, there is a second reason why prices will still change in the long run. Over time, average total cost itself may change. Innovative firms are always searching for better production processes and new technologies that enable them to produce goods at lower cost. For example, imagine that a new form of efficient barbecue enables plantains to be roasted using half the amount of charcoal. This innovation will reduce the variable costs of plantain-roasting firms. It will lower both the MC and the ATC curves as shown in Figure 13-7. This change, in turn, will increase profits. You can guess what will happen next: Increased profits will incentivize new firms to enter the market, which will increase the quantity supplied, which will drive down price.

For a real-world example of technological innovation driving down costs in the long run, see the Real Life box "How Ford changed the world."

Real Life

How Ford changed the world

The market for cars is not perfectly competitive; brands and styles of cars differ, so the goods are not standardized. But we can use aspects of our perfect-competition model to see how the technological innovation behind the Model T allowed Ford to lower its costs and increase its profits.

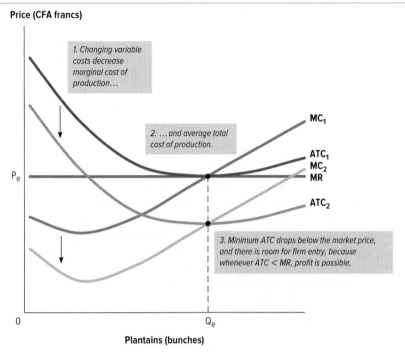

FIGURE 13-7

Market entry due to changing production costs

Price (CFA francs)

1. *Changing variable costs decrease marginal cost of production…*

2. *…and average total cost of production.*

MC₁

ATC₁
MC₂
MR

ATC₂

Pₑ

3. *Minimum ATC drops below the market price, and there is room for firm entry, because whenever ATC < MR, profit is possible.*

0   Qₑ

Plantains (bunches)

As technology and production processes improve, ATC can decrease. Since price must be equal to the minimum of ATC in the long run, price will fall as production costs fall.

About 100 years ago, the Ford Company's pioneering use of the factory assembly line revolutionized the automobile industry. On an assembly line, each worker specializes in one small step of production, such as tightening a single bolt or welding a particular piece. The goods under production move along the line; a worker at each station completes a single step, until the product is finished. An assembly line allows each worker to learn one task very well—to specialize.

In the early 1900s, Ford pioneered the use of assembly lines to produce its flagship automobile, the Model T. Ford spent seven years tweaking its production process to be as efficient as possible. The result was that Ford was able to produce the Model T at a dramatically lower cost than competitors' cars and to sell it at a lower price, thereby reaching a much larger market. Ford's technological innovation in the production process enabled the company to quickly become the dominant auto producer in the world.

Ford's competitors had no choice but to adopt the assembly line to stay competitive. By 1930, over 250 auto manufacturers that did not adopt the assembly line had gone bankrupt. Ford's surviving competitors, who adopted the assembly line themselves, were able to compete with Ford on price, creating incentives for further innovation.

The net result of this competition and innovation was that cars became cheap enough for middle-class consumers—a development that radically changed the social and geographic landscape of America.

Responding to shifts in demand

LO 13.8 Calculate the effect of a shift in demand on a market in long-run equilibrium.

We have seen why the long-run supply curve will not be perfectly elastic in practice. However, we'll return to the simplified model of a perfectly elastic long-run supply curve for the final section of this chapter. This model can still tell us something about how a shift in demand affects the equilibrium of a perfectly competitive market in the long run. Although we rarely see *perfect* competition in the real world, the simplified model is helpful to understand what happens in theory. Knowing that, we are able to understand in later chapters why it matters when reality diverges from the model.

Suppose, for instance, that there is a shift in demand for roasted plantains among Cameroonian train travelers. What might cause such a shift in demand? One possibility is a change in the price of a substitute good—for instance, roasted corn. Suppose there is a poor harvest of corn this year, increasing its price. Faced with more expensive corn, travelers in general will become more interested in buying plantain instead. This will shift the demand curve for plantain to the right. *How will the market respond to this shift?*

Panel A of Figure 13-8 shows the market for roasted plantains before the demand curve shifts. Notice that it shows both the short-run supply curve, which slopes upward, and the long-run supply curve, which—in theory at least—is horizontal in a perfectly competitive market.

With the increased price of corn, the short-run demand curve for plantains shifts to the right, from D_1 to D_2, as shown in panel B. The equilibrium point slides up the short-run supply curve—a higher quantity of roasted plantains is traded, at a higher price.

This higher price means that plantain-roasting firms are making economic profit. That economic profit creates an incentive for more firms to enter the market. As more firms enter the market, the short-run supply curve shifts to the right, from S_1 to S_2, as shown in panel C. The market equilibrium price slides down the new demand curve until it reaches the long-run supply curve. At that point, plantain-roasting firms are no longer making economic profit, so no new firms enter the market.

In the long run, then, the end result of the demand curve shifting to the right is to increase the quantity traded—but without any change in the price, which remains at the minimum level of average total cost.

FIGURE 13-8

Responding to shifts in demand

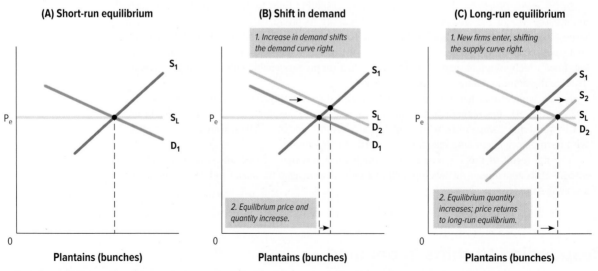

Initially, equilibrium price and quantity in a market fall at the intersection of the demand curve and the long-run supply curve (panel A). When an external change in market conditions increases demand, the price and quantity move away from the long-run equilibrium in the short term (panel B). In the long run, however, market entry increases supply, pushing price back down to the long-run equilibrium level (panel C).

CONCEPT CHECK

☐ What induces new firms to enter a market? **[LO 13.6]**

☐ Why do firms operate at their efficient scale in the long run in a perfectly competitive market? **[LO 13.6]**

☐ Why can the long-run supply curve slope upward if firms don't have identical cost structures? **[LO 13.7]**

☐ What happens to the equilibrium price and quantity supplied in a perfectly competitive market if the market demand curve shifts to the right? **[LO 13.8]**

Conclusion

In this chapter, we dug into the wants and constraints that drive firm behavior in competitive markets. Firms will choose to produce a quantity that maximizes their profits. In the short run, they will shut down if their revenues don't cover their *variable* costs of production. In the long run, they will exit the market if their revenues don't cover their *total* costs of production.

This analysis leads to some surprising conclusions about *long-run* supply in competitive markets: Firms earn zero economic profit; they operate at their efficient scale; and long-run supply is, in theory, perfectly elastic. Firms are able to enter and exit the market freely to adjust the quantity supplied at a given price.

These choices by firms benefit consumers by keeping prices low and ensuring that supply is responsive to needs. As we have noted, however, real-world markets are not guaranteed to be perfectly competitive. Firms may wield market power, or offer products that are not perfectly standardized. There may be barriers that prevent firms from freely entering or exiting the market. Understanding what perfect competition looks like, we can now spend the next few chapters looking at how firms behave when we relax the assumptions of perfect competition.

Key Terms

competitive market, p. 301

market power, p. 301

average revenue, p. 306

marginal revenue, p. 306

Summary

LO 13.1 Describe the characteristics of a perfectly competitive market.

A perfectly competitive market has four main, defining characteristics and one that is nonessential but important. The first main characteristic of a perfectly competitive market is that it contains a large number of buyers and sellers. The second is that sellers offer standardized goods; buyers have no reason to prefer one producer over another at a given price. The third is that buyers and sellers have perfect information. The fourth is that there are approximately zero transaction costs. Finally, firms in competitive markets are usually able to enter and exit the market freely.

LO 13.2 Calculate average, marginal, and total revenue.

Total revenue is equal to the quantity of each good that is sold, multiplied by its price. *Average revenue* is total revenue divided by the quantity sold. In other words, average revenue is equal to the price of the good. *Marginal revenue* is the revenue generated by selling an additional unit of a good. For a firm in a competitive market, marginal revenue is also equal to the price of the good.

LO 13.3 Find a firm's optimal quantity of output.

The profit-maximizing quantity is the one at which the marginal revenue of the last unit is exactly equal to the marginal cost. Another way of putting this is that it's the quantity at which the marginal cost (MC) curve intersects the marginal revenue (MR) curve. Producing any more or less would decrease profits.

LO 13.4 Describe a firm's decision to shut down or to exit the market, and explain the difference between these choices.

There are two ways that a firm can choose to produce nothing. First, it can *shut down* its operations temporarily, producing a quantity of zero, but leaving open the possibility of restarting production in the future. Second, it can *exit* the market—a permanent decision in which it chooses to produce nothing in the present or in the future.

The two decisions have different decision rules: If average revenue is less than the average variable cost of production (if P < AVC), then the firm should shut down in the short run. In the long run, if price is less than average total cost (if P < ATC), the firm should exit the market. (It's important to remember that firms cannot exit the market in the short run due to fixed costs.)

LO 13.5 Draw a short-run supply curve for a competitive market with identical firms.

In the short run, we assume that the number of firms in the market is fixed. The total quantity of goods that are supplied at a given price is therefore simply the sum of the quantity that each existing individual producer is willing to supply.

LO 13.6 Draw a long-run supply curve for a competitive market with identical firms, and describe its implications for profit-seeking firms.

The key difference between supply in the short run and supply in the long run is that we assume that firms are able to enter and exit the market in the long run. Thus, if economic profits are nonzero, firms will be induced to enter or exit the market, driving supply up or down until profits are zero.

This leads us to three conclusions about competitive markets in the long run: Firms earn zero economic profits, firms operate at their efficient scale, and supply is perfectly elastic.

LO 13.7 Explain why a long-run supply curve can slope upward.

The assumption of perfectly elastic supply is based on the idea that in the long run, price must equal the minimum of average total cost. Over time, however, average total cost itself may change. New production processes and technologies enable firms to produce goods at lower cost. Also, if firms face different costs of production due to scarce resources or skills, prices will have to be higher at higher quantities to induce higher-cost firms to enter the market.

LO 13.8 Calculate the effect of a shift in demand on a market in long-run equilibrium.

In the short run, firms in a competitive market respond to a shift in demand (in the way described in Chapter 3, "Markets"). If demand increases, price increases and quantity supplied increases. However, this pushes firms that are already in the market to earn a positive economic profit and operate at a size larger than their efficient scale. In the long run, other firms respond to the opportunity to earn economic profit by entering the market, which pushes price back down to its long-run equilibrium level.

Review Questions

1. You stop by a crafts fair and you notice consumers haggling with vendors over prices. What does this tell you about the competitiveness of this market? Suppose you plan to go to a farmers' market next. Do you expect to find more or less haggling at this market than you did at the crafts fair? Why? **[LO 13.1]**

2. In the market for gold jewelry (unlike the market for gold ore), products come in a range of designs, styles, and levels of quality. Which of the characteristics of a competitive market is violated in the jewelry market? What does this imply for consumers' willingness to buy from different producers? **[LO 13.1]**

3. Suppose that the manager of a donut shop tells you that he sold 220 donuts today, for a total revenue of $220 and average revenue of $0.90. What's wrong with this story? **[LO 13.2]**

4. Suppose an individual firm is one of many firms in a perfectly competitive market. Explain why this means the firm's marginal revenue will be equal to the market price. **[LO 13.2]**

5. The manager of the donut shop tells you that he sells donuts for $1 each, and that if he were to make additional donuts, based on his current level of output, it would cost him $0.80 per donut. Do you recommend that the manager increase or decrease the number of donuts he makes? **[LO 13.3]**

6. Suppose a firm is operating in a competitive market and is maximizing profit by producing at the point where marginal revenue = marginal cost. Now suppose that consumer wealth decreases in this market (and the good is a normal good). What might you expect to happen to the profit-maximizing output quantity for the firm? **[LO 13.3]**

7. A restaurant owner is trying to decide whether to stay open at lunchtime. She has far fewer customers at lunch than at dinner, and the revenue she brings in barely covers her expenses to buy food and pay the staff. What do you recommend that she do? Explain your reasoning to her. **[LO 13.4]**

8. In what ways are profit-maximizing and loss-minimizing the same? In what ways are they different? **[LO 13.4]**

9. Suppose that the profit-maximizing quantity of output for a firm in the competitive textile industry is 1 million yards of cloth. If this firm is representative of others in the industry, how can you describe total supply in the market, with respect to the number of firms? **[LO 13.5]**

10. What would you expect to happen to market supply if variable costs decreased for individual firms in the market? **[LO 13.5]**

11. Suppose that the airline industry is in long-run equilibrium when the price of gasoline increases, raising the cost of operating airplanes. In the long run, what do you expect to happen to the number of airlines in business? Why? **[LO 13.6]**

12. The firm in Figure 13Q-1 represents the cost structure for all firms in the industry. Describe the steps that will lead to long-run equilibrium in this market. **[LO 13.6]**

13. Corn farmers in Iowa are producers in a highly competitive global market for corn. They also have some of the most fertile, productive land in the entire world. Could Iowa's farmers be earning a positive economic profit in the long run? Why or why not? **[LO 13.7]**

14. Suppose that firms in an industry have identical cost structures and the industry is in long-run equilibrium. Explain how the profit motive could lead to *lower* market prices. **[LO 13.7]**

15. A market is in long-run equilibrium and firms in this market have identical cost structures. Suppose demand in this market decreases. Describe what happens to the profit-maximizing output quantity for individual firms as the market leaves and then returns to long-run equilibrium. **[LO 13.8]**

16. A market is in long-run equilibrium and firms in this market have identical cost structures. Suppose demand in this market decreases. Describe what happens to the market quantity as the market leaves and then returns to long-run equilibrium. **[LO 13.8]**

Problems and Applications

1. Suppose the market for bottled water and the market for soft drinks both have large numbers of buyers and sellers. Which of these markets is likely to be more competitive? **[LO 13.1]**

2. Suppose the market for steel and the market for cars both have large numbers of buyers and sellers. Which market is likely to be affected by information asymmetries? **[LO 13.1]**

3. Select all that apply. In a perfectly competitive market, MR equals: **[LO 13.2]**
   a. Price
   b. Average revenue
   c. Total revenue
   d. $\dfrac{\Delta \text{ in total revenue}}{\Delta \text{ in quantity}}$

4. Darla sells roses in a competitive market where the price of a rose is $5. Use this information to fill out the revenue columns in Table 13P-1. **[LO 13.2]**

FIGURE 13Q-1

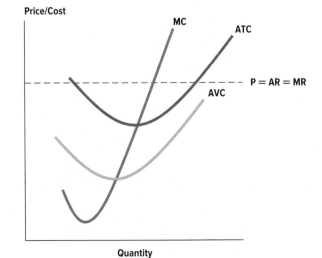

TABLE 13P-1

Quantity of roses	Total revenue ($)	Average revenue ($)	Marginal revenue ($)
1			
2			
3			
4			
5			

TABLE 13P-2

Quantity of beef (lb.)	Total revenue ($)	Total cost ($)	Profit ($)	Marginal revenue ($)	Marginal cost ($)	Marginal profit ($)
0	0	4		—	—	—
1	5	6				
2	10	9				
3	15	14				
4	20	22				

FIGURE 13P-1

FIGURE 13P-2

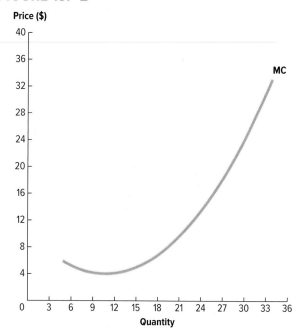

5. Paulina sells beef in a competitive market where the price is $5 per pound. Her total revenue and total costs are given in Table 13P-2. **[LO 13.3]**

    a. Fill out the table.

    b. At what quantity does marginal revenue equal marginal cost?

    c. What is the profit-maximizing quantity?

6. On Figure 13P-1, show the profit-maximizing quantity when price is P_1. Label this point Q_{max1}. Show the profit-maximizing quantity when price is P_2. Label this point Q_{max2}. **[LO 13.3]**

7. Figure 13P-2 shows the marginal cost curve for a firm in a competitive market. The market price is $24. Plot this firm's profit-maximizing price and quantity. **[LO 13.3]**

8. The data in Table 13P-3 are the monthly average variable costs (AVC), average total costs (ATC), and marginal costs (MC) for Alpacky, a typical alpaca

wool manufacturing firm in Peru. The alpaca wool industry is competitive. **[LO 13.4]**

    For each market price given below, give the profit-maximizing output quantity and state whether Alpacky's profits are positive, negative, or zero. Also state whether Alpacky should produce or shut down in the short run.

	Price	Q_{max}	Profit (+,−, 0)	Produce in SR? (Y/N)
a.	$22.00	_____	_____	_____
b.	$18.00	_____	_____	_____
c.	$16.00	_____	_____	_____

TABLE 13P-3

Output (units of wool)	AVC ($)	ATC ($)	MC ($)
0	–	–	–
1	20.00	30.00	20.00
2	17.00	22.00	14.00
3	16.70	20.00	16.00
4	17.00	19.50	18.00
5	18.00	20.00	22.00
6	22.33	24.00	44.00

FIGURE 13P-4

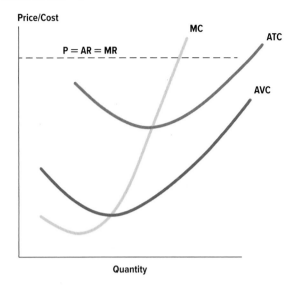

Price/Cost

9. The marginal costs, average variable costs (AVC), and average total costs (ATC) for a firm are shown in Figure 13P-3. In the figure, mark the quantity the firm will choose to produce in the short run given this cost structure and the market price. Does the firm earn positive or negative profits? Graph the area that defines the firm's profit (or loss) at this rate of output. **[LO 13.4]**

10. The marginal costs, average variable costs (AVC), and average total costs (ATC) for a firm are shown in Figure 13P-4. In the figure, mark the quantity the firm will choose to produce in the short run given this cost structure and the market price. Does the firm earn positive or negative profits? Graph the area that defines the firm's profit (or loss) at this rate of output. **[LO 13.4]**

11. The cost curves for an individual firm are given in Figure 13P-5. **[LO 13.4]**
    a. In panel A of Figure 13P-5, highlight the firm's short-run supply curve.
    b. In panel B of Figure 13P-5, highlight the firm's long-run supply curve.

12. Suppose the quantity of apples supplied in your market is 2,400. If there are 60 apple producers, each with identical cost structures, how many apples does each producer supply to the market? **[LO 13.5]**

13. Suppose an industry consists of many firms with identical cost structures, represented by the "typical individual firm" in panel A of Figure 13P-6. Price is P_1. With the aid of panel A, draw the short-run market supply curve in panel B and show the firm and market output quantities at the equilibrium price in each panel. Label the firm output q_1 and the market output Q_1. **[LO 13.5]**

14. The monthly average variable costs, average total costs, and marginal costs for Alpacky, a typical alpaca wool manufacturing firm in Peru, are shown in Table 13P-3. All firms in the industry share the same costs as Alpacky, and the industry is in long-run equilibrium. What is the market price? **[LO 13.6]**

15. The industry in Figure 13P-7 consists of many firms with identical cost structures, and the industry experiences constant returns to scale. **[LO 13.6]**
    a. Draw the short-run market supply curve.
    b. Draw the long-run market supply curve.

FIGURE 13P-3

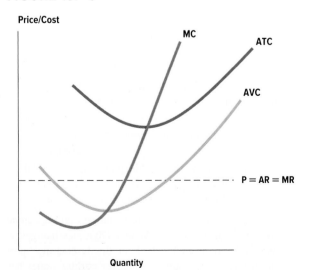

Price/Cost

FIGURE 13P-5

(A)

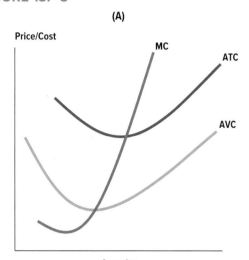

(B)

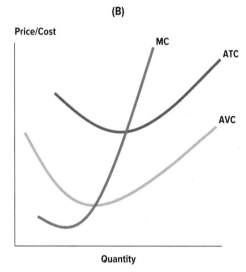

FIGURE 13P-7

(A) Typical individual firm

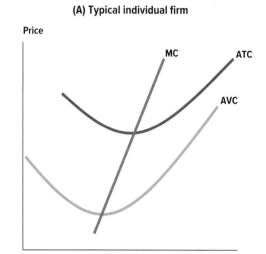

(B) Market

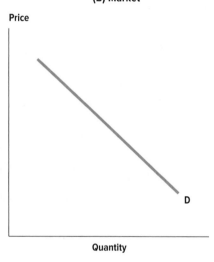

FIGURE 13P-6

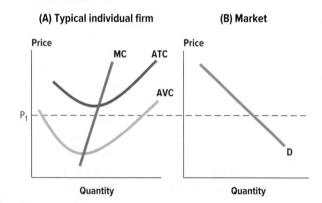

16. A firm's costs are represented in Table 13P-4. Suppose the price in the market is $110. **[LO 13.7]**

    a. Suppose all firms in the market have identical cost structures. Is the market in long-run equilibrium—yes, no, or can't determine?

    b. Suppose the firms in the market may have different cost structures. Is the market in long-run equilibrium—yes, no, or can't determine?

17. Curling is a sport that involves sliding a granite stone over a patch of ice. The Winter Olympics has generated a lot of excitement about the fascinating sport of curling. As a result, demand for curling stones has

TABLE 13P-4

Quantity	VC ($)	MC ($)	AVC ($)	TC ($)	ATC ($)
0	0	—	—	1,000	—
10	500	50	50	1,500	150
20	900	40	45	1,900	95
30	1,700	80	57	2,700	90
40	4,400	270	110	5,400	135
50	8,000	360	160	9,000	180
60	14,000	600	233	15,000	250

FIGURE 13P-8

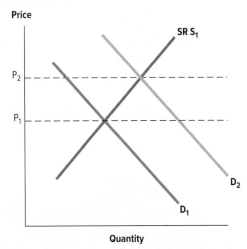

increased. Curling stones are made from blue Trefor granite. There are limited deposits of blue Trefor, and other types of granite are poor substitutes. If the increase in demand for curling stones persists, do you expect the long-run equilibrium price to increase, decrease, or stay the same? **[LO 13.7]**

18. The industry in Figure 13P-8 consists of many firms with identical cost structures, and the industry experiences constant returns to scale. Consider a change in demand from D_1 to D_2, which increases price from P_1 to P_2 in the short run. **[LO 13.8]**

   a. Draw the new short-run supply curve that will occur in response to the increase in demand and increase in price.

   b. Draw the long-run supply curve.

19. Suppose the market for gourmet chocolate is in long-run equilibrium and an economic downturn has reduced consumer discretionary incomes. Assume chocolate is a normal good and the chocolate producers have identical cost structures. **[LO 13.8]**

   a. What will happen to demand—shift right, shift left, no shift?

   b. What will happen to profits for chocolate producers in the short run—increase, decrease, or no change?

   c. What will happen to the short-run supply curve—increase, decrease, or no change?

   d. What will happen to the long-run supply curve—increase, decrease, or no change?

Monopoly

Learning Objectives

LO 14.1 List four barriers to entry into monopoly markets.

LO 14.2 Explain why a monopolist is constrained by demand.

LO 14.3 Calculate the profit-maximizing production price and quantity for a monopolist.

LO 14.4 Calculate the loss in total social welfare associated with a monopoly.

LO 14.5 Describe the pros and cons of common public policy responses to monopoly.

LO 14.6 Explain why a firm has an incentive to use price discrimination when possible.

DIAMONDS WEREN'T ALWAYS FOREVER

Diamonds are, perhaps, the ultimate symbol of luxury. For reasons we will discover in this chapter, they have become nearly synonymous with romantic commitment. More than 80 percent of brides-to-be in the United States receive a diamond engagement ring, at an average cost of more than $3,000. Across society, diamonds are also synonymous with conspicuous consumption. From swanky New York society to Los Angeles hip-hop stars, people use diamond jewelry to display wealth and status.

Why do diamonds carry such social cachet? They're expensive. People wearing diamonds show that they can afford the best. And why are diamonds expensive? You might assume it's because they are scarce and therefore precious. As it turns out, diamonds are not so rare. Tens of thousands of pounds of diamonds are produced every year.

Why, then, do we pay so much for diamonds? The answer lies in the story of one of the most successful companies of all time: De Beers. For more than a century, De Beers used aggressive business tactics to control almost all of the international market for diamonds. It also used ingenious marketing methods to boost demand for its product. By controlling the production and sale of most of the world's diamonds, De Beers became the opposite of a price-taking firm in a competitive market: It had so much market power that it was effectively able to set the market price of diamonds. It did so by choosing the quantity it released into the market at any given time.

The story of De Beers starts in the 1870s, when diamonds were truly rare. Just a few diamonds were found every year, scooped out of riverbeds and jungles in India and Brazil. They were expensive; only the truly elite could afford diamond jewelry. Then, British miners discovered enormous deposits of high-quality diamonds in South Africa.[1] This must have seemed like a fabulous opportunity to make huge amounts of money. But there was also a danger: If companies flooded the market with diamonds, the quantity supplied would shoot up and the price would be forced down. Soon it would no longer be so exclusive and prestigious to own a diamond, reducing people's willingness to pay for them. This change in preferences would shift demand, which would result in even lower prices. People would buy a lot of diamonds—but the sellers wouldn't make as much money.

A businessman named Cecil Rhodes joined with other mine owners to form a single corporation, De Beers. By controlling all of the newly discovered diamond mines—and almost all of the world's diamond production—De Beers ensured that smaller amounts of diamonds came onto the market, keeping prices high. In this way, De Beers made much more money than it would have if it had produced lots of diamonds but sold them at vastly lower prices.

In this chapter we'll see how monopolists such as De Beers calculate the optimal quantity and price to maximize their profits. We'll also see that a monopolist profits from its control of the market, but consumers lose—and, in general, total surplus decreases. For these reasons, governments usually try to limit monopoly power, using a range of policies that we'll discuss. Even the mighty De Beers has been unable to resist these pressures. It now controls only about 40 percent of the world diamond market—still a huge share, but a far cry from its heyday.[2]

This look at monopolies takes us away from the model of perfect competition. In looking beyond markets with lots of firms competing against each other, we start to see the range and diversity of markets that make up the economy.

Why Do Monopolies Exist?

Most firms face some degree of competition. In Chapter 13, "Perfect Competition," we considered what would happen if a firm faced so much competition that it had no choice but to accept the going market price for its products. In this chapter, we'll ask what happens if a firm faces *no competition at all* and is therefore able to have total control over how much it charges for its products.

monopoly
a firm that is the only producer of a good or service with no close substitutes

Economists call such a firm a **monopoly**. The word *monopoly* comes from a root meaning *single seller,* and it describes a firm that is the only producer of a good or service that has no close substitutes. A firm is a *perfect monopoly* if it controls 100 percent of the market in a product. Firms can still have a large degree of *monopoly power* if they control slightly less than 100 percent of the market. For example, throughout the twentieth century, De Beers controlled 80 to 90 percent of the diamond market. It wasn't a perfect monopoly, but it wielded so much monopoly power that it was almost totally able to exert control over diamond prices.

The *lack of a close substitute* for a product is an essential part of the definition of monopoly. For example, if you are a monopoly seller of water, you can pretty much set your own price and people have no choice but to pay it. Water has no close substitutes. If you are a monopoly seller of orange juice, you don't have the same power. If you set your price too high, people will buy apple juice instead.

One of the keys to De Beers's success is that it persuaded many people that diamonds are a good with no close substitutes. This is quite an impressive feat. After all, when it comes down to it, a diamond is simply a sparkly stone that looks nice in jewelry. It ought to have some close substitutes, such as rubies, sapphires, and emeralds (and also synthetic diamonds, which are practically indistinguishable from ones dug out of the ground). If De Beers ensures that the price of diamonds is high, why don't people buy these other stones instead? The answer is that De Beers has marketed diamonds very cleverly. The famous phrase "A diamond is forever" was the invention of a De Beers advertising campaign that ran in the United States from 1938 to the late 1950s. Within one generation, De Beers created the idea that the diamond is the recognized symbol of betrothal. Pursuing the same strategy in Japan, it advertised diamonds as representing modern, Western style. Between 1967 and 1981, the number of Japanese brides wearing diamond engagement rings went from 5 percent to 60 percent.[3]

Many women nowadays would feel disappointed if they received an engagement ring containing another kind of stone or an artificial diamond. Diamonds are truly beautiful, but the strength of our preference for them reflects decades of clever marketing by the people at De Beers.

Barriers to entry

LO 14.1 List four barriers to entry into monopoly markets.

It's easy to see why any firm would love to be a monopoly. But we can also see how the forces of competition are usually stacked against any one firm gaining that much market power. After all, when a firm charges high prices in a competitive market, some other enterprising firm will generally come along charging a lower price. In a monopoly situation such as the diamond market, other firms could make profits by entering the market and undercutting the monopolist's high prices. So we have to ask, *why isn't someone, or everyone, already doing it?*

The key characteristic of a monopoly market is that there are barriers that prevent firms other than the monopolist from entering the market. The barriers allow the monopolist to set prices and quantities without fear of being undercut by competitors. *Barriers to entry* contradict the *free entry and exit* feature that characterizes perfectly competitive markets.

Barriers to entry take four main forms: scarce resources, economies of scale, government intervention, and aggressive business tactics on the part of market-leading firms.

Scarce resources
The most straightforward cause of barriers to entry is scarcity in some key resource or input to the production process. This was the case, at first, in the diamond market. Diamonds come out of the ground in only a limited number of places, after all. If a firm owns all the diamond mines (as De Beers effectively did in the 1870s), it has control of the production process. A new firm cannot simply enter the market without somehow gaining control of a mine.

Economies of scale
In Chapter 13, "Perfect Competition," we discussed the idea of *economies of scale*—instances when, as a firm produces more output, its average total cost goes down. In some industries, the required infrastructure is costly and creates a barrier to entry. In these cases, economies of scale

are so powerful that competition between two or more firms simply doesn't make much sense. Replicating the required infrastructure would raise fixed cost too much to be viable.

Imagine what would be needed to create competition in the electricity-supply industry, for example: Multiple firms would have to build power plants and huge systems of distribution poles and wires, just to serve the same area. Building such a system would be prohibitively expensive for a new firm. The electric industry has high fixed costs relative to the variable cost of supplying another unit of electricity. The firm that can sell the most electricity can spread its fixed costs more widely. By doing so, the firm can achieve a lower cost per unit than a firm with the same fixed costs but lower output. The result is that one big firm can have a large cost advantage in providing all of the electricity for a given region.

natural monopoly
a market in which a single firm can produce, at a lower cost than multiple firms, the entire quantity of output demanded

Electricity supply is an example of a **natural monopoly**. This is a market in which a single firm can produce, at a lower cost than multiple firms, the entire quantity of output demanded. Drinking-water supply and natural gas are other examples of natural monopolies; these depend on a network of pipes that would be immensely expensive for new market entrants to duplicate. Yet another example is public transport: Imagine trying to enter the railways business by constructing new sets of tracks between major cities.

The term *natural monopoly* comes from the fact that, paradoxically, monopoly can be the "natural" outcome of competitive forces. An electricity supplier or a railway company doesn't have to worry about new firms entering the market to compete. Other firms have no incentive to enter because they would face higher costs of production than the monopoly. Thus, high fixed costs create an effective barrier to entry.

Governments often get involved in natural monopolies to try to protect the public from abuse of monopolistic power. We'll see how later in the chapter.

Government intervention

Government intervention is another barrier to entry. Governments may create or sustain monopolies where they would not otherwise exist. In many U.S. states, for example, the government has created a monopoly on the sale of alcoholic beverages. In Iran, an elite branch of the army called the Revolutionary Guard Corps controls the construction industry as well as the oil and gas industries. Governments usually say they are creating monopolies in the public interest. In some cases, though, critics wonder if the real reason is to use monopoly power to benefit insiders.

Sometimes governments create monopoly power for state-owned firms. They can do this through a legal prohibition on other firms entering the market, or by subsidizing a state-owned enterprise so heavily that private companies effectively cannot compete. (Not all state-owned enterprises are monopolies, though. For instance, some governments own airlines that compete against privately owned airlines.)

Governments can also create or support private monopolies through regulation of intellectual property rights. Consider that governments grant patents and copyrights to people who invent or create something; these grants give their holders the exclusive right to produce and sell their creations for a given period of time. For example, a patent on a particular drug forbids the use of that chemical formula by other manufacturers. The patent allows the pharmaceutical company that holds it to act temporarily as a monopolist in the market for that particular drug. The patent-holder can raise prices and earn higher profits. When the patent expires, government protection of the monopoly ends; competitors can then drive down prices by producing a generic version of the same drug.

Creative works like art, movies, and music are also frequently protected by intellectual property laws. Copyright laws, for example, make it illegal to distribute unauthorized copies of movies. By granting copyright protection, governments give movie-making companies a legal monopoly over selling downloads of the movies they make. The result is that downloads of movies are more expensive than they would be if anyone could legally copy the movie and sell it.

Creating monopolies through intellectual property protection has costs and benefits for society:

- On the plus side, protection of intellectual property gives firms an incentive to invest in research and creative activities that lead to products that enrich people's lives. Movie companies wouldn't spend millions of dollars on special effects if anyone could legally copy the download of the finished movie and sell it at any price.

- On the negative side, as we will see later in this chapter, monopolies drive down consumer surplus by setting higher prices than would be charged in a competitive market. In most cases, they reduce total surplus.

Whether the social costs outweigh the social benefits is hotly debated and likely depends on the scenario at hand.

Aggressive tactics

A fourth barrier to entry is aggressive business tactics. As the chapter-opening story described, the limited number of diamond mines in the world was not the only explanation for how De Beers managed to exert monopoly power over the diamond industry for so long. As new deposits of diamonds were found by other companies in other countries, De Beers had to constantly protect its monopoly power from the forces of competition.

How could De Beers prevent new companies from undercutting its prices? It employed a number of tactics: It offered to buy up the companies that discovered new sources of diamonds. It entered into exclusive agreements with diamond-producing countries. And it was not afraid to employ aggressive methods of persuasion. De Beers punished anyone who did business with independent diamond producers. The punishment it meted out could be deadly for a smaller player in the diamond market.

For example, in the 1970s, Israeli diamond merchants began amassing stockpiles of diamonds as a safe way to store their wealth. De Beers didn't like this. It feared that the price of diamonds might collapse if the Israeli merchants chose to sell their stockpiles all at once. De Beers sent a representative to tell the Israeli merchants to stop stockpiling gems. If they did not do so, De Beers threatened to bar them from its "sightings," its exclusive invitation-only diamond sales. Many of the diamond merchants resisted, before eventually giving in. Those who resisted paid a high price for their rebellion: The Israeli diamond industry suffered so badly that a quarter of its employees lost their jobs.[4]

A more recent example of a company accused of employing aggressive tactics to gain or maintain monopoly power in local markets is Walmart. The company has been sued on several occasions for *predatory pricing*—that is, temporarily slashing prices until rival local stores are forced out of business.[5] Predatory pricing is a way for a large company, which can sustain short-term losses, to force smaller rivals out of the market. By doing so it can create monopoly power, which then enables the company to dictate its own prices.

Not all tactics to maintain monopoly power are so unwelcome to smaller competitors, however. For example, although Google controls around four-fifths of the world's Internet searches,[6] it knows that a new company with a better search algorithm could overtake it. It tries to preserve its dominant position by buying promising-looking inventions in search technology. Many web entrepreneurs set up in business actively hoping that one of the giants of the industry—Google, Facebook, Microsoft, or Apple—will come along with a lucrative offer to buy them out.

✓CONCEPT CHECK

- ☐ How do scarce resources create barriers to entry? **[LO 14.1]**
- ☐ How do economies of scale create barriers to entry? **[LO 14.1]**
- ☐ How do government policies create barriers to entry? **[LO 14.1]**
- ☐ How do aggressive tactics create barriers to entry? **[LO 14.1]**

How Monopolies Work

We have to begin our analysis of a monopoly's behavior by understanding its *wants and constraints.* Just like any other firm, a monopoly *wants* to maximize its profits. As we saw in Chapter 13, "Perfect Competition," a firm in a perfectly competitive market is constrained by the fact that its production decisions cannot affect the prevailing market price. A monopoly does not face this constraint—but it *is* constrained by the market demand curve. In this section, we'll first see why this constraint exists and then how the monopolist makes production choices to maximize profits.

Monopolists and the demand curve

LO 14.2 Explain why a monopolist is constrained by demand.

In a perfectly competitive market, the demand curve *for the market as a whole* slopes downward, reflecting the inverse relationship between price and quantity (as price decreases, quantity demanded increases). However, in a perfectly competitive market, each *individual firm* effectively faces a horizontal demand curve. This is because each firm is assumed to be too small for its production decisions to affect the market price. It can sell as much as it wants at the market price. But if it tries to charge more, it will be undercut by competitors and won't be able to sell anything. We can depict this graphically with a horizontal line, as in panel A of Figure 14-1, which shows a horizontal demand curve for roasted plantains. (As discussed in Chapter 13, "Perfect Competition," the market for roasted plantains has many buyers and sellers, none of which can affect the price of plantains.) Panel A shows the demand faced by a seller of roasted plantains in a perfectly competitive market where the market price is 1,000 CFA francs.

To compare the demand curves in perfectly competitive and monopolistic markets, let's turn our attention from the plaintain-roasting business to violet diamonds. Violet diamonds are the rarest of colored diamonds. Each year, only a select few are mined from the Argyle diamond mine in Australia. The monopolist can choose to sell at any price it wants without fear of being

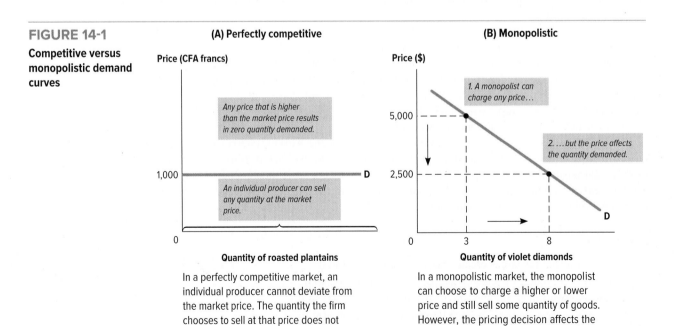

FIGURE 14-1

Competitive versus monopolistic demand curves

(A) Perfectly competitive

Price (CFA francs)

Any price that is higher than the market price results in zero quantity demanded.

1,000   D

An individual producer can sell any quantity at the market price.

0

Quantity of roasted plantains

In a perfectly competitive market, an individual producer cannot deviate from the market price. The quantity the firm chooses to sell at that price does not affect the quantity demanded.

(B) Monopolistic

Price ($)

1. A monopolist can charge any price…

5,000

2. …but the price affects the quantity demanded.

2,500

D

0   3   8

Quantity of violet diamonds

In a monopolistic market, the monopolist can choose to charge a higher or lower price and still sell some quantity of goods. However, the pricing decision affects the quantity demanded.

undercut because there are no other firms to do the undercutting. However, it is still constrained by market demand. What, then, is the shape of the monopolist's demand curve?

As the *only* producer in the market, a monopolist faces the demand curve for the entire market, and this demand curve is downward-sloping. The demand curve faced by the monopoly seller of violet diamonds is shown in panel B of Figure 14-1. Naturally, the monopolist would love to sell a huge quantity of goods at a high price. But *how would consumers respond to a high price?* The law of demand says that, all else equal, quantity demanded falls as price rises. If the monopolist wishes to increase its price, it must accept that the increase in price will result in a decrease in quantity demanded. The monopolist may choose any price-quantity combination on the demand curve; it is unable to choose points that are not on the curve. (It can't force customers to buy more or less than the quantity they demand at any given price.) The monopolist can choose to sell at a high price of $5,000 per diamond, but at that price it will sell only a small quantity—three diamonds. Or it can choose to sell five more diamonds, reaching a total of eight, but only by lowering its price to $2,500 per diamond.

De Beers recognized the fact that its sales were limited by demand. That's why it went beyond controlling the supply side of the market and invested heavily in shifting the demand curve outward through the marketing methods we discussed earlier. Only by increasing demand would it be able to sell a higher quantity of diamonds at a higher price.

POTENTIALLY CONFUSING

Sometimes in this chapter we'll refer to a monopoly "picking a price." At other times, we'll say that it controls the quantity of goods available for sale. It's important to understand that these two decisions are equivalent. Each possible price corresponds to one specific quantity on the demand curve, and vice versa. So:

- The monopoly can control the market by setting a price and allowing customers to buy the quantity they demand at that price.
- Or it can control the market by restricting the quantity supplied and allowing prices to adjust so that the quantity demanded meets the quantity supplied.

Thus, the resulting price-quantity combination is the same, regardless of whether the monopoly picks a price or a quantity to supply.

Monopoly revenue

LO 14.3 Calculate the profit-maximizing production price and quantity for a monopolist.

The first step in understanding a monopolist's quest for profits is to map out the revenues it can bring in. Suppose that De Beers can choose the price of the diamonds it offers for sale in the United States. To simplify our model, let's assume for now that De Beers sells diamonds of uniform size (one-carat violet diamonds) and quality. What revenue can it expect to bring in at each possible price?

Column 1 of Table 14-1 shows the range of prices De Beers is considering. Because it is constrained by demand, DeBeers has to accept the quantity that American consumers are willing to buy at a given price. Column 2 shows the quantity of diamonds demanded at various prices. When price is high, consumers demand a small quantity of diamonds. For example, if De Beers chooses to charge $6,000 per diamond, only one person would purchase a diamond. As price decreases, consumers demand higher and higher quantities. At a price of $1,500, consumers will purchase 10 violet diamonds. If we were to graph the price and corresponding quantity sold from the first two columns of the table, we would have the market demand curve (which can be seen in panel B of Figure 14-1).

TABLE 14-1   Monopolist's revenue

The price a monopolist chooses to charge affects the quantity demanded, and therefore total revenue.

(1)	(2)	(3)	(4)	(5)
Price ($/diamond)	Quantity sold (Violet diamonds)	Total revenue ($)	Marginal revenue ($)	Average revenue ($/diamond)
6,500	0	0		—
			6,000	
6,000	1	6,000		6,000
			5,000	
5,500	2	11,000		5,500
			4,000	
5,000	3	15,000		5,000
			3,000	
4,500	4	18,000		4,500
			2,000	
4,000	5	20,000		4,000
			1,000	
3,500	6	21,000		3,500
			0	
3,000	7	21,000		3,000
			−1,000	
2,500	8	20,000		2,500
			−2,000	
2,000	9	18,000		2,000
			−3,000	
1,500	10	15,000		1,500

The *total revenue* that De Beers could earn at each price is simply price times quantity sold, which is the amount shown in column 3. As price increases and quantity sold decreases, total revenue first rises, and then falls. Remember (from Chapter 4, "Elasticity") that total revenue increases on sections of the demand curve where demand is price-elastic; it decreases on sections of the curve where demand is price-inelastic.

Average revenue, shown in column 5, is the revenue De Beers receives per diamond sold. It is calculated by dividing total revenue by quantity sold. This is simply a rearrangement of the equation that total revenue is quantity times price. Thus, just as in a competitive market, average revenue is equal to price.

Marginal revenue is the revenue generated by selling each additional unit. We calculate marginal revenue by taking total revenue at a certain quantity and subtracting the total revenue when quantity is one unit lower. For instance, based on Table 14-1, total revenue from five diamonds is $20,000, and total revenue from four diamonds is $18,000. So, the marginal revenue in the interval between four and five diamonds is $20,000 − $18,000 = $2,000.

Unlike a firm in a competitive market, a monopolist's marginal revenue is not equal to price. In a competitive market, a firm can sell as much as it wants without changing the market price. The additional revenue brought in by one unit is always simply the price of that unit. Thus, in a competitive market, marginal revenue is equal to price. In a market dominated by a monopoly, however, the monopoly's choice to produce an additional unit drives down the market price and thus drives down marginal revenue. Because of this effect, producing an additional unit of output has two separate effects on a monopolist's total revenue:

1. *Quantity effect:* The increase in total revenue due to the money brought in by the sale of additional units.

2. *Price effect:* The decrease in total revenue that occurs because the increase in quantity requires a lower price.

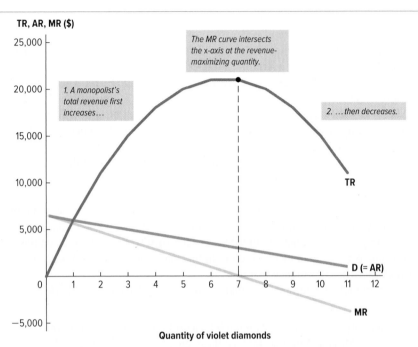

FIGURE 14-2

Monopolist's total, average, and marginal revenue

As the monopolist increases the price, total revenue (TR) first increases and then decreases. Total revenue is maximized when marginal revenue (MR—the lightest green line) equals zero. The demand curve (which equals average revenue, or price) is always above the marginal revenue curve because each additional unit sold brings less revenue than the prior unit.

Depending on which of these effects is larger, total revenue might increase or decrease when De Beers increases the quantity of diamonds it sells. If there were no price effect (as in a perfectly competitive market), then marginal revenue would be determined solely by the quantity effect; it would be equal to price. But the price effect always works in the *opposite direction* of the quantity effect—it decreases revenue. Thus, *marginal revenue in a monopoly market is always less than the price.*

Figure 14-2 shows hypothetical values for De Beers's total and marginal revenue at various prices in the U.S. market for violet diamonds. Because the demand curve is downward-sloping, the monopolist must decrease its price if it wishes to sell more diamonds. The marginal revenue curve lies below the demand curve because marginal revenue is always less than price.

Table 14-1 and Figure 14-2 show that marginal revenue can sometimes be negative. This occurs in our example at quantities above the quantity at which the marginal revenue curve crosses the *x*-axis in Figure 14-2.

What does it mean when marginal revenue drops below zero in Figure 14-2? Think back to the price effect: Negative marginal revenue means that the price effect has become bigger than the quantity effect. At that point, each additional unit of output *decreases* total revenue. Thus, *the point at which the MR curve crosses the* x*-axis represents the revenue-maximizing quantity.* In our example, total revenue is maximized in the interval between 6 and 7.

Revenue is important, but as we know, what firms really care about is maximizing profit. So how do monopolists go about maximizing their profit?

Maximizing profits by picking price and quantity sold

De Beers exerted control over the diamond market through the quantity of diamonds it released for sale at any given time. The company held back stockpiles of diamonds worth billions of dollars for years at a time to maintain this control.

The purpose of this stockpiling was to ensure that the quantity of diamonds for sale was always the quantity that maximized De Beers's profits. How can a monopolist choose the price-quantity combination that maximizes its profits? Perhaps surprisingly, it can approach this problem in exactly the same way that a firm in a competitive market would.

Figure 14-3 shows hypothetical cost and revenue curves for De Beers. The general appearance of these curves should be familiar from Chapter 13, "Perfect Competition." The only relevant difference between the curves for a monopoly and the equivalent ones for a firm in a competitive market is that marginal and average revenue slope downward for the monopolist. (In a competitive market, those curves are horizontal at the market-price level.) Just as in a competitive market, the profit-maximizing quantity of output for a monopoly is *the point at which the marginal revenue curve intersects the marginal cost curve.* Why is this so?

Remember that the contribution of each additional unit of output to a firm's profit is the difference between marginal revenue and marginal cost. If the marginal revenue of a unit of output is higher than its marginal cost, then producing the unit brings in more money in sales than it costs the firm to produce it. Thus, it contributes to the firm's profit. What if, on the other hand, marginal revenue is lower than marginal cost? In that case, the unit costs more to produce than it brings in, and the firm loses money by producing it.

The same marginal decision-making analysis we used in Chapter 13, "Perfect Competition," applies here:

- At any quantity of output *less than* the intersection of the marginal revenue and marginal cost curves, MR is higher than MC. At these quantities, De Beers could earn more profits by offering an additional diamond for sale.

- At any quantity of output *greater than* the intersection, the company loses profits on each additional diamond it offers for sale. At these quantities, De Beers could earn more profits by offering fewer diamonds for sale.

FIGURE 14-3

Monopolist's cost curves

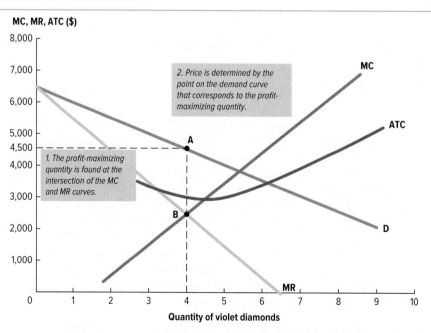

A monopolist can choose both the quantity and the price at which to produce. To maximize profit, the monopolist will always produce that quantity at which marginal cost equals marginal revenue. It then sets the price based on the demand for that quantity.

Therefore, De Beers should increase the quantity of output up to the point where it can no longer earn more profits by increasing output. That point is where MR = MC, shown as point B in Figure 14-3. It should then stop producing output, before it starts losing money.

There is an important difference between a firm in a competitive market that produces at the point where MR = MC and a monopoly that does the same thing:

- In a competitive market, marginal revenue is equal to price.
- For a monopolist, price is greater than marginal revenue; therefore, price is also greater than marginal cost at the optimal production point. The profit-maximizing price for a monopolist is the price on the demand curve that corresponds to the profit-maximizing quantity of output. This is shown as point A in Figure 14-3.

This fact—that a monopoly's profit-maximizing price is higher than its marginal costs—is key to understanding how monopolies are able to earn positive economic profits in the long run. Remember that a firm in a competitive market produces at the point where P = MC = ATC in the long run. If price is higher than MC, other firms will enter the market, increasing supply and driving down the price until profits are zero and there is no longer an incentive for more firms to enter. In a monopoly market, however, other firms can't enter the market; they face the barriers to entry that allowed the firm to become a monopolist in the first place. The result is that a monopolist is able to maintain a price higher than average total cost (ATC).

Remember that the formula for calculating profit is:

$$\text{Profit} = (P - ATC) \times Q$$

So, if price is greater than ATC, profits will be positive, even in the long run.

We can observe this same fact graphically, as shown in Figure 14-4. De Beers's profit is equal to the area of the shaded box, defined as follows:

- The box's length is equal to the profit-maximizing quantity of output.

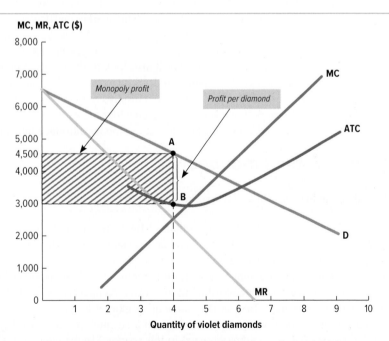

FIGURE 14-4

Monopoly profit

The monopolist sets the price at point A on the demand curve, which corresponds to the profit-maximizing quantity. The monopolist's profit equals the difference between the price and the average total cost (point B), multiplied by the quantity sold. Put another way, Profit = (P − ATC) × Q, or the area of the shaded box.

- The box's height is the distance between the profit-maximizing price and average total cost. We can also think of that amount—the difference between A and B in the figure, which is $1,500—as the profit earned on the average diamond sold.

This analysis shows us why De Beers had such a strong incentive to maintain its monopoly power. The fact that there were no other diamond producers to enter the market and drive down the price of diamonds gave De Beers the ability to maintain a price higher than its costs. This market power in turn allowed it to earn economic profits in the long run.

✓CONCEPT CHECK

- ☐ Why can't a monopoly choose to sell at any price-quantity combination it wants? **[LO 14.2]**
- ☐ Why is marginal revenue lower than price for a monopoly? **[LO 14.3]**
- ☐ Why are monopolies able to earn positive economic profits in the long run? **[LO 14.3]**

Problems with Monopoly and Public Policy Solutions

Since 2000, De Beers's grip on the diamond industry has lessened: Its market share has dropped from more than 80 percent of the world diamond trade to near 40 percent. This is partly due to large-scale mining of diamonds in Canada and Russia, outside of De Beers's range of control. It is also due in part to increased pressure from governments and diamond consumers to stop De Beers from exercising its monopoly power. Following a series of lawsuits in the United States and Europe, De Beers was banned from operating in certain countries and forced to pay large fees or change its practices in others.[7] Until 2004, De Beers executives weren't even allowed to travel to the United States on business.

Monopolies are great for the monopolist, and not so great for everyone else. In the De Beers example, consumers get fewer diamonds at a higher price. This market inefficiency reduces total surplus. In this section, we'll see how the existence of monopolies has *welfare costs*, which are the loss of well-being of market participants as measured by changes in consumer surplus or producer surplus—specifically, deadweight loss. We'll also look at the range of public policies governments use to try to discourage monopolies and mitigate their effect on consumers. As we'll see, these policy responses are imperfect, and often highly controversial. Before we weigh the costs and benefits of different policy responses, let's consider the welfare costs of monopoly power. In other words, how much deadweight loss does a monopoly introduce into a market?

The welfare costs of monopoly

LO 14.4 Calculate the loss in total social welfare associated with a monopoly.

Why do policy-makers get riled up about monopolies? Because a monopoly's ability to keep quantity low and prices high hurts society in general and consumers in particular. Let's dig back into the monopolist's production decision to show why this is so.

Figure 14-5 shows the market demand curve for diamonds, as well as hypothetical marginal revenue and marginal cost curves, for two different markets: a competitive market (panel A) and a monopoly (panel B). Let's look, first, at the competitive market in panel A. The equilibrium price and quantity in a competitive market maximize total surplus. In other words, *the market is efficient.* What is the efficient production level in this market? Remember from Chapter 13, "Perfect Competition," that a competitive firm's supply curve is equivalent to the section of the marginal cost curve that lies above average total cost. In the competitive market, the *efficient quantity lies at the intersection of supply (marginal cost) and demand,* at point C in panel A. What would happen at other quantities?

- At any higher quantity, total surplus is reduced because the increase in consumer surplus is less than the decrease in producer surplus.

- At any lower quantity, total surplus is also reduced—the decrease in consumer surplus is greater than the increase in producer surplus.

A monopoly, however, will produce the quantity where marginal revenue intersects marginal cost, at point B in panel B of Figure 14-5. This quantity is lower than the efficient quantity that would prevail in a competitive market, which tells us that total surplus is not maximized. It also tells us that producer surplus is higher than the level in a competitive market, and consumer surplus is lower. Panel B represents the loss of total surplus as a deadweight loss (exactly as we did in Chapter 5, "Efficiency," when discussing the welfare cost of taxes). To see a list of the main differences between perfectly competitive markets and monopoly markets, see Table 14-2.

It's important to remember that this description of the costs of monopoly is a positive statement—a statement about how things *are*. That is different from a normative judgment—a statement about how things *should* be. There can be cases in which people believe that the advantages to maintaining a particular monopoly outweigh the total welfare costs due to lost surplus. This is similar to the feeling many people have that it is worth accepting some deadweight loss from taxes in order to achieve goals such as providing benefits to the poor or supporting military or police forces. There is no principle that tells us that maximizing efficiency trumps other goals.

However, voters and policy-makers in many countries have made the normative judgment that monopolies are usually a bad thing. This isn't so surprising: Maximizing total surplus means that society's resources are being used efficiently, and few people are excited to provide

FIGURE 14-5

Deadweight loss in a monopoly market

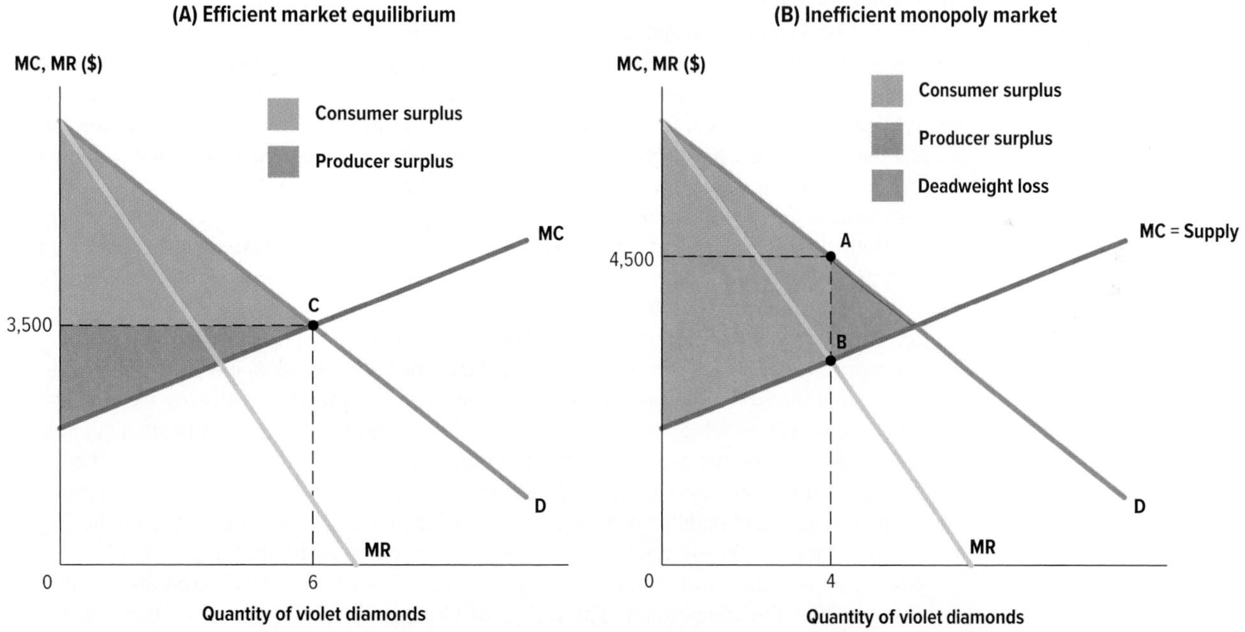

(A) Efficient market equilibrium

(B) Inefficient monopoly market

A competitive market produces the equilibrium price and quantity (point C) where price equals marginal cost. When the market is in equilibrium, total surplus is maximized, and there is no deadweight loss.

A monopoly market produces the quantity at which marginal revenue equals marginal cost (point B). Quantity is lower than the market equilibrium quantity, and price is higher than the competitive price. As a result, consumer surplus is smaller than in the competitive case. Fewer trades take place, and society suffers a deadweight loss.

TABLE 14-2

Comparing the characteristics of market models

Characteristic	Perfect competition	Monopoly
How many firms?	Many firms	One firm
Price taker or price maker?	Price taker	Price maker
Marginal revenue?	MR = Price	MR < Price
Profit-maximizing quantity occurs where?	MR = MC	MR = MC
Can earn economic profits in the short run?	Yes	Yes
Can earn economic profits in the long run?	No	Yes
Quantity is efficient?	Yes	No

extra profits to monopolies. After all, voters are more likely to be consumers than owners of monopolies.

This does not mean that monopolists are always wealthy, large-scale enterprises. For an example of a monopolist toward whom we might feel more than usually sympathetic, check out the From Another Angle box "Poor monopolists."

From Another Angle

Poor monopolists

When Muhammad Yunus won the Nobel Peace Prize in 2006, the Grameen Bank became a household name around the world. The bank is credited with bringing access to financial services to millions of rural Bangladeshis. It is less widely known that Grameen was also the first to bring access to phones within reach of the same population.

Grameen used an ingenious business model to accomplish this, in a country known for its strained rural infrastructure and limited resources. The bank recruited long-standing clients to act as local phone operators. It loaned them the $420 necessary to start a small phone kiosk and trained them to operate it as a business. Grameen also sold the operators discounted telephone airtime on credit, which the operators in turn sold to villagers.

The demand for phone services in Bangladeshi villages was tremendous, and the phone kiosks flourished. Farmers and traders used the phones to manage business orders and keep track of prices in local markets. Families used the phones to stay in touch with relatives who had left home to find work in the city.

Because Grameen's operators were the first to bring phone services to rural villages, they had no competitors. Grameen initially established a single phone-kiosk operator in each village. By doing so, it inadvertently created a local monopoly in this previously missing market. This turned out to be a huge windfall for the operators; they were able to earn profits often amounting to double or triple the average Bangladeshi income. Needless to say, this new stream of income enabled the operators to pay off their loans in record time. Recognizing the demand for phone services, and perhaps that the new rural telecom market would benefit from healthy competition, Grameen began establishing multiple operators in each village.

When you hear the word "monopolist," you might think of a massive corporation getting rich by quashing the competition. The reality of Grameen phone operators couldn't be further from this stereotype. The phone operators were indeed monopolists, but they were also impoverished villagers, just trying to improve their families' lives. Remember—there's nothing inherently evil about monopoly. The important thing is to weigh the social welfare benefits that accrue to monopolists against the efficiency losses to the rest of society.

Source: http://www.grameentelecom.net.bd/about.html.

Public policy responses

> **LO 14.5** Describe the pros and cons of common public policy responses to monopoly.

Policy-makers have developed a range of policy responses to monopolies. These tools aim to break up existing monopolies, prevent new ones from forming, and ease the effect of monopoly power on consumers. Each comes with costs as well as benefits. Some economists argue that the best response is often to do nothing at all. As we discuss each type of policy, keep a critical eye on its pros and its cons.

Antitrust laws

The regulation of monopolies has been a high-profile political issue in America for quite a while. In the late nineteenth century, massive corporations called "trusts" were beginning to dominate entire industries. To check their growing power, Congress passed the Sherman Antitrust Act in 1890. The act requires the federal government to investigate and prosecute corporations that engage in anti-competitive practices. Included in such practices are price fixing and bid rigging. The early twentieth century was also a period of major antitrust activity in the United States. President Theodore Roosevelt, in particular, became known as a "trustbuster." Using the Sherman Act, he vigorously prosecuted corporations that used monopolistic practices to stifle competition. Over the years, the government has used the Sherman Act to break up monopolies in various industries, including railroads, oil, aluminum, tobacco, and telecommunications.

The Sherman Act still has an impact. As recently as the late 1990s, it was uncommon to use an Internet browser other than Microsoft's Internet Explorer. In 1999, the U.S. government sued Microsoft for anti-competitive behavior. The suit alleged that by bundling Internet Explorer with Microsoft Windows, the company was unfairly pushing competing web browsers out of the market. (Microsoft eventually reached a settlement with the government and agreed to stop certain business practices perceived to be anti-competitive.) Today, there are lots of Internet browsers, including Chrome, Firefox, Safari, and improved versions of Internet Explorer.

For another case concerning an area in which the antitrust law has not yet had much impact, read the Real Life box "Rockers vs. Ticketmaster."

Real Life

Rockers vs. Ticketmaster

Anyone who has been to a major concert or show in the United States has probably experienced the hefty fees and charges that come with buying a ticket through Ticketmaster. These fees can add up to between 20 and 40 percent of the face value of the tickets themselves.

Ticketmaster is a dominant player in the lucrative U.S. primary-ticket-sales business. For context, Ticketmaster has signed deals with a number of NHL and NBA teams to sell event tickets only through its site. Many of the nation's leading concert and theater venues have similar agreements. These exclusive agreements are a crucial element of Ticketmaster's business strategy. Because of them, competitors have difficulty gaining a foothold in the market. Many feel that Ticketmaster has thus become a de facto monopoly in the market for tickets.

This has infuriated many musicians who want to keep prices of tickets low for their fans' sake. Two groups have even pursued lawsuits against Ticketmaster. In 1994, Pearl Jam complained to the U.S. Justice Department about Ticketmaster's allegedly monopolistic practices and high markups. The group's lawsuit was unsuccessful. In 2003, jam band String Cheese Incident sued Ticketmaster. The suit alleged that the exclusive agreements with venues were

(continued)

monopolistic and violated the Sherman Antitrust Act. This case settled out of court, and the results were not publicly disclosed.

The power of Ticketmaster may not last long, though. A slew of new sites that sell concert tickets online, including Eventbrite, Etix, and Ticketfly, are growing steadily in the primary-ticket-sales market. While Ticketmaster is still the official ticketing partner for the NBA, several teams now have their own ticketing partners. For instance, StubHub became the official ticketing partner for the Philadelphia 76ers in February 2016, cutting directly into Ticketmaster's market share. Since competitors can offer cheaper booking fees for bands and ticket prices for fans, they may prove to be a win for everyone—except, of course, Ticketmaster.

Sources: http://www.rollingstone.com/music/news/string-cheese-incident-eliminate-service-charges-for-summer-tour-20120302; http://latimesblogs.latimes.com/music_blog/2010/08/ticketmaster-a-new-era-of-transparancy-or-smoke-mirrors-.html; http://www.nba.com/sixers/news/sixers-stubhub-launch-revolutionary-new-ticketing-platform.

The U.S. government has also used the Sherman Antitrust Act and its partner, the Clayton Antitrust Act of 1914, to prevent monopolies from forming in the first place. The Justice Department can block two firms from merging if the merger would result in a company with too much market power. A few examples include a proposed merger between office-supply giants Office Depot and Staples, which the Justice Department blocked in 1997; a failed AT&T merger with T-Mobile in 2011; and a merger between Comcast and Time Warner Cable that was blocked by the Justice Department in 2015.[8]

However, in recent years the government has only infrequently used the power to block mergers. More often, the government investigates a potential merger and allows it to go forward. For instance, in 2012, United Airlines merged with Continental Airlines to become the then-largest airline in the world. Then, in 2013, the merger of US Airways and American Airlines created a new global number one.[9] These mergers occurred with the full blessing of the Justice Department, which determined that there was sufficient pressure from other airlines to maintain competition. Further, the mergers were seen as actually generating benefits for customers due to cost savings in airport operations and the organization of plane fleets.

People sometimes criticize antitrust actions as being politically motivated or causing more inefficiency than they create. How could antitrust action cause inefficiency in the market? It could accidentally break up a natural monopoly. Or it could break a large company into several firms that operate at a smaller-than-efficient scale. Different regulators handle these decisions differently. For instance, Microsoft still faced antitrust lawsuits in Europe long after it settled its case in the United States.

Public ownership

Natural monopolies pose a particular problem for policy-makers. On the one hand, the monopolist is able to achieve lower costs of production than multiple competing producers would. Often, the marginal cost for a natural monopolist is very low and constant. For example, the cost to an Internet supplier of providing one more megabyte of data is very small. But the fixed costs of entering the market and becoming an Internet provider are very high. This barrier to entry makes an Internet provider a natural monopoly.

Because of the high fixed costs of entry but the low marginal costs of production, a natural monopoly is often perceived as less harmful than other monopolies. However, even a natural monopoly chooses to produce at the profit-maximizing quantity where MR = MR; this results in a price that is higher than marginal cost, causing deadweight loss.

One possible solution is for governments to run natural monopolies as public agencies. Examples of public ownership of natural monopolies include the U.S. Postal Service to deliver mail and Amtrak to provide train services. The rationale behind public ownership of natural monopolies is that governments are supposed to serve the public interest rather than maximize profit. They could choose to provide broader service than a private monopolist might. For example, a government-supported monopoly might deliver mail to any postal address in the country; a private monopolist might prefer not to deliver to remote addresses that are more expensive to reach.

Figure 14-6 shows the MC and ATC curves for a natural monopoly. Panel A shows an example of how a publicly owned monopoly could set prices lower than an unregulated monopolist would. In this case, the regulated government-monopoly price is higher than average total cost but is lower than the price that an unregulated "private monopoly" would set. Even though price is lower than it would be if the monopoly were unregulated, there is still some deadweight loss, as shown in the figure.

Panel B of Figure 14-6 shows how governments often regulate prices for a natural monopoly in order to diminish deadweight loss. Recall that in a competitive market, where deadweight loss is zero, firms produce at the point where P = MC. However, a natural monopoly is defined by the fact that ATC falls as quantity increases, which means that MC must be below ATC at all possible quantities. As a result, a natural monopolist that sets price equal to marginal cost will incur losses, as shown in panel B.

However, public ownership of a natural monopoly has its problems. Politicians may feel pressure to lower prices even further, below the level they would be in a competitive market. As we saw in Chapter 5, "Efficiency," doing so will create shortages and people will demand more than it makes sense for the producer to supply at that price. Publicly owned companies may also make business decisions—such as where to locate or what types of products to offer—on the basis of political concerns.

FIGURE 14-6

Price regulation of a natural monopoly

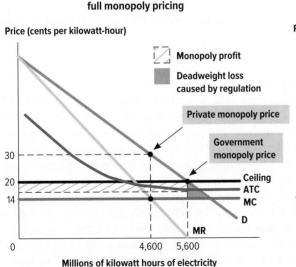

(A) Price ceiling above MC but below full monopoly pricing

When the price ceiling (20 cents) is set above the natural monopoly's average total cost, the firm will produce at the point where the price intersects the average revenue curve (which is identical to the demand curve) to maximize its profit. Some deadweight loss remains.

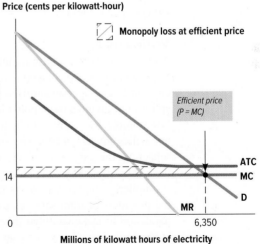

(B) Price ceiling at efficient price

In a competitive market, there is no deadweight loss, and the efficient price occurs at the point where P = MC. A publicly owned natural monopoly producing at this point loses money.

Perhaps the most significant problem of public ownership of a natural monopoly relates to the profit motive. The loss of the profit motive could reduce the publicly owned monopolist's motivation to improve efficiency and to provide better service or lower costs. After all, there is no rule stating that all monopolies must make a profit. (Amtrak reported an operating loss of over $306 million in fiscal year 2015, and USPS reported a profit in the first quarter of 2016 for the first time since 2011.[10]) If an inefficient public monopoly cannot provide a service at a price that sufficient numbers of people are willing to pay, it can remain in operation by covering its losses with revenue from taxes.

These concerns explain why public ownership of monopolies has become much less common. Since the 1980s, especially in Europe, many government-operated agencies such as state airlines, telecoms, and utilities have been privatized (that is, sold to private companies) and regulated instead.

Regulation

If policy-makers don't want to go all the way to public ownership, one common intermediate step is to regulate the behavior of natural monopolies. Such regulation takes the form of controls on the prices natural monopolies are allowed to charge. This is frequently the case in utility markets. For instance, many governments allow private monopolies to exist in the supply of electricity, tap water, or natural gas but cap the price these companies can charge.

In theory, such controls could have the same effect as public ownership: By capping the price at ATC, regulators can force natural monopolies to earn zero economic profits. Doing so reduces deadweight loss as much as possible without causing the firm to incur losses and exit the market.

Unfortunately, things are rarely so simple in practice: Firms have an incentive to avoid giving regulators useful information about their true costs of production. Lack of information makes it difficult for regulators to determine the appropriate price level. Also, the idea behind privatizing natural monopolies relates to incentives: A private firm should be more motivated than a public one to increase its profits by innovating and reducing costs, and those savings should result in lower prices for consumers. But if the regulator sets a price so low that *all* of the cost savings go to consumers, the firm will have no incentive to reduce costs. If the regulator sets the price at a level insufficient to cover the monopolist's costs, it could even drive the firm out of business.

Vertical splits

Another common response to natural monopolies is to look for ways to split an industry "vertically" and introduce competition into parts of it. A "vertical" split divides the original firm into companies that operate at different points in the production process. (In contrast, a "horizontal" split would divide a monopolist into multiple companies that compete to sell the same product.) For example, the supply of electricity is a natural monopoly, but the generation of electricity is not. Policy-makers in countries such as New Zealand have split the electricity industry vertically, separating the generation of electricity from supply. Firms compete to generate electricity, but then all use the same wires to supply the electricity to people's homes and businesses.

Similarly, countries such as the UK have split the railway industry vertically. Several competing providers of train services run their trains on the same sets of tracks. This requires active regulation to make sure that different companies do not try to run trains in different directions at the same time. Critics also say that the system enables the operators of train services and the monopoly that manages the tracks to blame each other for delays.

No response

Looking at the pros and cons of various interventions in monopoly markets, some economists conclude that the best response to a monopoly is sometimes no response at all. When might the right solution be to do nothing? Doing nothing might be preferable if regulation is too difficult to create or manage effectively. If government interventions in the market are subject to corruption or political mishandling, it might be better not to act. This view doesn't deny that monopoly power causes inefficiency. Instead, it simply holds that sometimes the problems caused by intervention might be worse.

✓CONCEPT CHECK

☐ Why does monopoly cause deadweight loss? **[LO 14.4]**

☐ What are some of the potential problems with public ownership of monopolies? **[LO 14.5]**

Market Power and Price Discrimination

In any market, some consumers typically would be willing to pay more for the good than the market price. When they buy at a price lower than their willingness to pay, they enjoy consumer surplus. If you were a firm, wouldn't you like to be able to charge different individuals different prices for the same good? You could charge a higher price to customers with higher willingness to pay, transforming their consumer surplus into your producer surplus. The more monopoly power a firm has, the more able it is to do exactly this.

What is price discrimination?

price discrimination
the practice of charging customers different prices for the same good

LO 14.6 Explain why a firm has an incentive to use price discrimination when possible.

The practice of charging customers different prices for the same good is called **price discrimination**. It involves "discriminating" between customers on the basis of their willingness to pay. Examples of price discrimination are all around us. Have you ever used your student ID card to claim discounts on public transport or theater tickets? That's an example of price discrimination. You are getting exactly the same product as people who are being charged full price, but you receive a discount because companies assume that for many goods, on average, students have lower willingness to pay.

Price discrimination in action: Tourists who don't read Spanish pay extra.
© The McGraw-Hill Companies, Inc./Mark Dierker, photographer.

How can a firm charge different customers different amounts for the same good? In a perfectly competitive market, it couldn't. Remember that firms in a perfectly competitive market sell at a price equal to their average total cost, and earn zero economic profit. They couldn't afford to offer discounted prices to students; doing so would result in *negative* profit. Nor could they choose to charge nonstudents a higher price because those customers would simply go to a competing firm instead.

As we move away from the model of perfect competition, price discrimination becomes possible. Whenever firms gain a degree of market power, they look for ways to exploit customers' varied willingness to pay. Consider why clothing stores hold periodic sales, for example. It enables them to charge two different prices: They charge one price to consumers who are willing to pay more to get the item when it first hits the market. They charge a lower price to those who don't mind waiting until the sales are on. Similarly, theaters tend to charge lower prices for matinee showings: They attract the cash-poor and time-rich during the day; people with busy work schedules will generally be both more willing and able to pay the higher prices charged for an evening showing.

The more monopoly power a firm has, the more it is able to price-discriminate. For example, college students are often pleasantly surprised to find that they can buy computer software through their colleges for significantly lower

FIGURE 14-7

Demand for Microsoft Office®

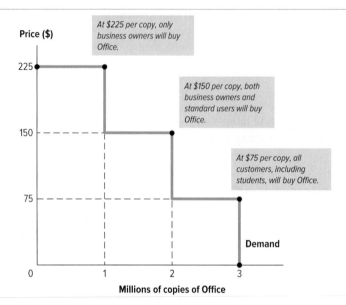

This simplified demand curve shows the demand for Office in a perfectly segmented market. In this example, all members of each group have the same willingness to pay: All business owners will pay $225 or less; all standard users will pay $150 or less; and all students will pay only $75 or less.

prices than they could in a store or online. (Take a look at your school's information technology website. We bet you'll find discounts.) The Microsoft Office® suite of programs, such as Word®, Excel®, and PowerPoint®, often sells for half as much when bought through a university.

While Microsoft Office does have substitutes, such as the open source OpenOffice suite, for many people these are not close enough substitutes. These free products cannot handle the full range of Office functions; if you are sharing documents with other people who all use Microsoft Office, then you also need to own Microsoft Office.

Microsoft can use its monopoly power to exploit differences in the willingness to pay of different groups. For simplicity, suppose Microsoft knows that there are three groups of potential Office customers:

- students, who are willing to pay $75
- standard computer users, who are willing to pay $150
- people who use their computers to run their businesses, who are willing to pay $225

And say there are 1 million potential customers in each group, as shown in the stylized demand curve in Figure 14-7. There is a limit to the quantity Microsoft can sell at any given price.

Of course, in reality, there is variation in people's willingness to pay within these groups. For example, some students are willing to pay more than $75, and some less. But for the sake of simplicity, let's assume for now that all students, all standard users, and all business users are the same. Let's also assume that there is a fixed cost of $50 million to produce Office (for instance, to pay for research and development) and that the variable cost of production is essentially zero. (Zero isn't too far from reality—making a copy of software doesn't cost very much.) With no variable cost, the profit that Microsoft earns is simply total revenue minus fixed costs. (Note, too, that if variable costs are zero, marginal costs also are zero.)

What price should Microsoft set for Office? If it chooses $75, all 3 million potential customers will buy a copy of Office, and the company will earn:

$$\text{Profit} = \text{Total revenue (TR)} - \text{Fixed costs (FC)}$$
$$= (3 \text{ million} \times \$75) - \$50 \text{ million}$$
$$= \$225 \text{ million} - \$50 \text{ million}$$
$$= \$175 \text{ million}$$

What if Microsoft chooses to charge $150? As the calculations in Table 14-3 show, only 2 million customers will buy at the higher price. In that case, the company will earn $250 million in profits. If it charges $225 per copy of Office, only 1 million business customers will choose to buy, and Microsoft will earn $175 million in profits.

If Microsoft can pick only one price, it should pick $150 to maximize its profits. However, by charging $150, Microsoft loses the business of students, who have a lower willingness to pay. It also misses out on the extra $75 that business customers would have been willing to pay. Microsoft does best if it can find a way to charge these three groups the exact price they are willing to pay. Then, its profits are:

$$\text{Profit} = \text{TR} - \text{FC}$$
$$= [(1 \text{ million} \times \$225) + (1 \text{ million} \times \$150) + (1 \text{ million} \times \$75)] - \$50 \text{ million}$$
$$= \$450 \text{ million} - \$50 \text{ million}$$
$$= \$400 \text{ million}$$

Microsoft can earn an additional $150 million [($400 − $250) × 1 million copies] in profits if it can charge students less and businesses more. We can see why any firm with market power would want to price-discriminate. As a student, this is good news for you too (at least if you're facing monopoly pricing).

Perfect price discrimination

Dividing a firm's customers into just three categories—students, business owners, and others—is a blunt way of discriminating among them. In reality, there are not just three types of customer—there are millions, all with their own individual willingness to pay. What if Microsoft was able to price-discriminate more accurately by charging every individual customer a price exactly equal to her willingness to pay?

Figure 14-8 shows a smooth demand curve representing the varied willingness to pay of many individuals (rather than just three clusters of customers). Panel A shows what happens if Microsoft does not price-discriminate—if it charges just one price, $150, for Office. Its profit is represented by the green-shaded area. The gold-shaded area represents the consumer surplus enjoyed by customers who would have been willing to purchase for more than $150. The gray area shows deadweight loss. That represents the mutually beneficial trades that could have taken place but did not. These are customers who would have been willing to purchase Office for a price between $150 and zero.

Now look at panel B, which shows what happens when Microsoft price-discriminates among the three categories of customer. The size of the blue-shaded area, representing Microsoft's

TABLE 14-3   Profit without price discrimination

If Microsoft can charge only one price for Office, the best option is to choose $150, which will maximize profit at $250 million. That option, however, will exclude students, who are unwilling to pay more than $75.

Price ($)	Number of copies	Total revenue ($)	Fixed cost ($)	Profit ($)
75	3,000,000	225,000,000	50,000,000	175,000,000
150	2,000,000	300,000,000	50,000,000	250,000,000
225	1,000,000	225,000,000	50,000,000	175,000,000

FIGURE 14-8   Price discrimination

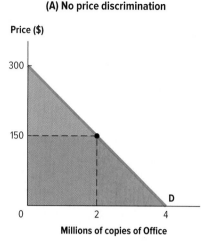

(A) No price discrimination

With no price discrimination, Microsoft charges one price, $150, to all customers.

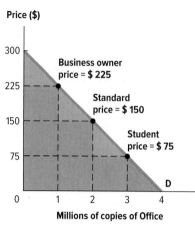

(B) Imperfect price discrimination

With imperfect or tiered price discrimination, Microsoft can earn a profit on sales to both students and other buyers. Because not all students have the same willingness to pay, however, some mutually beneficial trades (represented by the gray-shaded area) don't take place.

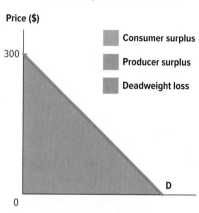

(C) Perfect price discrimination

If Microsoft could charge each customer his or her exact willingness to pay, the company would profit on all exchanges, eliminating both the deadweight loss and the consumer surplus shown in panel A.

profits (producer surplus), has increased. At the same time, consumer surplus has decreased for the group of customers who were willing to pay over $150. Customers who were willing to pay between $75 and $150, however, now enjoy some consumer surplus. Finally, deadweight loss has been reduced to only those mutually beneficial trades that could have taken place between $75 and zero but did not.

Panel C shows what would happen if Microsoft were able to price-discriminate perfectly—if it could find each customer's willingness to pay. The area representing Microsoft's profits becomes even bigger. There is no consumer surplus at all any more. The consumer surplus that previously existed has all been transformed into producer surplus. Neither is there any deadweight loss. Instead, all possible mutually beneficial trades take place—meaning the market is *efficient*.

The more perfectly a company is able to price-discriminate, the more profit it makes, and the more efficiently the market works. Remember that efficiency doesn't say anything about the distribution of surplus—including whether it goes to consumers or producers—but only whether total surplus is maximized.

So why doesn't a monopoly charge every individual a different price? There are some obvious problems with this idea, as we will see.

Price discrimination in the real world

The first problem with price discrimination in the real world is defining categories of customers. Microsoft's price-discrimination strategy would not work very well if anyone could simply say, "I'm a student," and be charged the lower price. The company needs some way to verify who is a student. To get around this problem, Microsoft enters into agreements with colleges, which take responsibility for identifying who is a student. In general, students have to go through their colleges' websites and enter their student ID number or other verification to purchase software at the discount price. Similarly, if you turn up at the box office of a theater asking to purchase a ticket with a student discount, the cashier will ask for your student ID card.

The second problem facing the firm that tries to price-discriminate is that many products can easily be resold. If someone you know is about to pay $150 for Microsoft Office, some people might be tempted to buy student versions at a low price and illicitly resell them at a higher price. To prevent this, there needs to be some way of punishing people who cheat the system. Hence, Microsoft can use legal enforcement against anyone who uses a student version of Office for his or her business. Similarly, theaters need some way to stop students from bulk-buying tickets and selling them to nonstudents. They may, for instance, demand to see a student ID before allowing entrance into a theater with a student ticket.

Many goods do not lend themselves to this kind of tracking as easily as software or theater tickets. Imagine if Apple sold iPhones to customers under age 18 for a 50 percent discount. This might seem like a neat way to increase its profits, if there are lots of under-18s who would love to buy an iPhone but cannot afford to pay full price. However, high school students would have a thriving business buying up the iPhones at the local Apple store and reselling them to older buyers for a profit. No one over 18 would buy their iPhones directly from Apple, which therefore has no incentive to offer different prices.

For a firm that wants to practice *perfect* price discrimination, the challenges are even more forbidding. It would need to be able to read the minds of each individual customer and form an accurate impression of how much that customer would be willing to pay. Much as Microsoft would love to be able to read the minds of potential purchasers and charge them exactly what they'd be willing to pay, the task is essentially impossible.

Still, some practitioners of price discrimination are adept at sizing up their customers before quoting a price. See the From Another Angle box "Rickshaw rides: Price discrimination and asymmetric information."

From Another Angle

Rickshaw rides: Price discrimination and asymmetric information

Tourist regions charge visitors notoriously inflated prices. Taxi and rickshaw drivers in India are especially famous for charging foreign-looking, wealthy-looking, and clueless-looking passengers significantly higher fares than they would charge to locals. This practice is the root of countless confrontations in which rickshaw drivers and foreign tourists try to bargain over fares, generally in a mix of broken English and improvised sign language. What are the economic forces underlying this common scene?

One explanation is that tourists are the victims of a severe information asymmetry. Tourists often don't know how far their destination is and have no idea about the standard "local" rate for going there. Since drivers invariably know more than tourists about the "fair price" of fares, they are able to exploit this information asymmetry to boost their earnings.

Another factor contributing to the difference in the prices paid by locals and tourists is their differing willingness to pay. Tourists from wealthier countries are generally willing to pay more than most Indians would for the same goods and services. Someone from New York City might consider 100 rupees (about $2) for a rickshaw ride across Delhi to be an incredible bargain (a similar ride in a New York taxi could cost $25), even if 100 rupees is more than twice what locals pay.

But why doesn't competition between drivers push fares back down to competitive levels? Remember, price discrimination works only for producers with market power. One individual rickshaw driver may not have much sway in the market, but the rickshaw drivers in a particular location often operate like a cartel. Rather than competing, they have standing agreements not to undercut one another on price.

However, the days of frustrated tourists might be numbered. More and more cities across India are requiring rickshaws to start using the mortal enemy of price-discriminating drivers everywhere: the fare meter.

✓ CONCEPT CHECK

☐ Why do firms have an incentive to price-discriminate? **[LO 14.6]**

☐ Name several practical barriers to perfect price discrimination. **[LO 14.6]**

Conclusion

Monopolies can use their market power to hold price above the level that would prevail in a competitive market. By doing so, they turn consumer surplus into positive economic profits and reduce total social welfare. This poses a tricky problem for policy-makers, who want to regulate or break up monopolies to increase social welfare. Practically speaking, it can be difficult to accomplish this goal without causing more inefficiency. Policies designed to address the problems associated with monopolies run the risk of setting prices at the wrong level or raising costs by breaking up a natural monopoly.

This difficult situation is complicated further by the fact that few firms are truly perfect monopolies. Instead, many markets include firms with some degree of market power, ranging on the spectrum from perfect monopoly to perfect competition. We can call markets in this range "imperfectly competitive." It turns out that small differences in the structure of imperfectly competitive markets can make big differences in how firms behave; those differences can give policy-makers headaches. In the next chapter, we'll take a close look at two specific varieties of imperfect competition.

Key Terms

monopoly, p. 330   natural monopoly, p. 332   price discrimination, p. 347

Summary

LO 14.1 List four barriers to entry into monopoly markets.

The key characteristic of a monopoly market is that there are barriers that prevent firms other than the monopolist from entering the market. Barriers to entry take four main forms: scarce resources, economies of scale, government intervention, and aggressive business tactics on the part of market-leading firms.

Scarcity in some key resource or input into the production process means that firms may have difficulty accessing the resources they need to enter the market. When there are large economies of scale in a market, firms have no incentive to enter; they would face higher costs of production than the monopoly. Some monopolies are created or sustained by the power of government, through public ownership or protection of intellectual property. Finally, some monopolies use their size and various aggressive tactics to keep smaller firms from getting a toehold in the market.

LO 14.2 Explain why a monopolist is constrained by demand.

As the only firm in the market, a monopoly is constrained in the price-quantity combinations it can sell by the market demand curve. All else equal, quantity demanded falls as price rises. The monopoly can choose any price-quantity combination on the demand curve, but it is unable to choose points that are not on the curve because it can't force customers to buy more or less than they demand at any given price.

LO 14.3 Calculate the profit-maximizing production price and quantity for a monopolist.

A monopoly chooses the profit-maximizing quantity the same way a firm in a competitive market would: by producing at the quantity for which marginal revenue is equal to marginal cost. Price is the price that corresponds to that quantity on the demand curve. Unlike a firm in a competitive market, however, the monopoly price is higher than marginal revenue, and therefore also higher than marginal cost at the profit-maximizing point. This means that a monopoly earns positive economic profits.

LO 14.4 Calculate the loss in total social welfare associated with a monopoly.

The equilibrium price and quantity in a competitive market maximize total surplus. A monopoly's profit-maximizing quantity, however, is lower than the efficient quantity that would prevail in a competitive market. This tells us that total surplus is not maximized, and that producer surplus is higher than competitive levels, while consumer surplus is lower. The deadweight loss caused by a monopoly is equal to total surplus under perfect competition minus total surplus under a monopoly.

LO 14.5 Describe the pros and cons of common public policy responses to monopoly.

Policy-makers have developed a range of policy tools aimed at breaking up existing monopolies, preventing new ones from forming, and mitigating the effect of monopoly power on consumers. Antitrust laws allow the government to sue firms that engage in anti-competitive practices and to block mergers that would result in too much market power. Public ownership of natural monopolies maintains the cost advantages of economies of scale but removes the profit motive that might drive quality improvements and cost reductions. Price regulation may also preserve the cost advantages of natural monopoly while holding down price, but it is practically difficult to set price at the right level. In some cases, doing nothing may actually be the best policy response to monopoly.

LO 14.6 Explain why a firm has an incentive to use price discrimination when possible.

Price discrimination is the practice of charging customers different prices for the same good. Price discrimination allows a firm to charge each customer a price closer to his willingness to pay, turning consumer surplus into producer surplus and increasing the firm's profits.

Review Questions

1. If competition places discipline on costs, motivating firms to innovate and find more cost-effective ways to produce, explain why in some markets a single firm without competitors will produce at a lower cost than if the firm faced competition. **[LO 14.1]**

2. Suppose a city has a chain of fitness centers (gyms) all owned by the same company, Fit Fun. A new company is considering opening a gym in the city. Give an example of an aggressive tactic Fit Fun might take to maintain its monopoly. **[LO 14.1]**

3. Suppose that De Beers and the local water utility are both monopolists, in the markets for diamond jewelry and water, respectively. If both monopolies decided to raise prices 15 percent, which monopoly would be more likely to see its total revenue decrease? Why? **[LO 14.2]**

4. Suppose that a producer in a previously competitive market is granted the sole right to produce in the market. Given that demand in the market is unchanged, but now all consumers must purchase from the same producer, why might the new monopolist produce less than the quantity that was produced when the market was competitive? **[LO 14.2]**

5. Suppose that an inventor discovers a new chemical compound that can change the color of people's eyes with no negative side effects. Since she holds a patent on this chemical, she has a monopoly over the sale of the new eye-color treatment. However, she's an inventor, not a businessperson. Explain to her how she should set the price for the eye-color treatment in order to maximize her profits. **[LO 14.3]**

6. Suppose a monopolist has to purchase new equipment and his fixed costs increase. Explain what will happen to the monopolist's profit-maximizing output quantity and the monopolist's profits. **[LO 14.3]**

7. Until the 1980s, AT&T held a monopoly over the national market for phone services. Suppose that AT&T argued that it was a natural monopoly because the fixed cost of creating a nationwide phone network generated huge economies of scale, and that there was therefore no welfare loss associated with its monopoly. Counter this argument by explaining how even a natural monopoly causes deadweight loss. **[LO 14.4]**

8. Suppose you are advising a mayoral candidate in your town. The candidate's platform includes strong opposition to monopoly suppliers because consumer welfare is compromised by monopoly pricing. Present your candidate with an alternative view about why it may make sense to tolerate the existence of some monopoly firms. **[LO 14.4]**

9. Suppose that your state is considering a law that would force all monopolies to charge no more than their average total costs of production. Explain to your legislator the pros and cons of this approach. **[LO 14.5]**

10. Suppose that your state is considering a law that would force all monopolies to charge the efficient price that would prevail if the market were competitive. Explain to your legislator why the state will have to subsidize natural monopolies if this law goes into effect. **[LO 14.5]**

11. Suppose a small town has one theater for live performances and several restaurants, including one Indian restaurant. Will it be easier for the theater or for the Indian restaurant to price discriminate? **[LO 14.6]**

12. Suppose a museum charges different entrance fees for children, students, adults, and seniors, but these groups all pay the same amount for souvenirs at the gift shop. Explain why the museum price discriminates on admission but not souvenirs. **[LO 14.6]**

Problems and Applications

1. The U.S. Postal Services maintains a monopoly on mail delivery in part through its exclusive right to access customer mailboxes. Which barrier to entry best describes this situation: scarce resources, economies of scale, government intervention, or aggressive tactics? [LO 14.1]

2. Which (if any) of the following scenarios is the result of a natural monopoly? [LO 14.1]
   a. Patent holders of genetically modified seeds are permitted to sue farmers who save seeds from one planting season to the next.
   b. Doctors in the United States are prohibited from practicing without a medical license.
   c. There is one train operator with service from Baltimore to Philadelphia.
   d. Coal is used as the primary energy in a country with abundant coal deposits.

3. Due to arduous certification requirements, Nature's Crunch is currently the only certified organic produce grower in a region that produces lots of nonorganic produce alternatives. From a profit-maximizing perspective, would it be better for Nature's Crunch to lobby the government to relax organic certification requirements or to require grocery stores to clearly label its produce as organic? [LO 14.2]

4. Nature's Crunch is currently the only certified organic produce grower in a region that produces lots of nonorganic produce alternatives. To be certified organic, a producer cannot use chemical pesticides. Which of the following scenarios would increase Nature's Crunch's profits? Check all that apply. [LO 14.2]
   a. A tomato blight affecting chemically treated plants.
   b. An increase in the cost of chemical pesticides.
   c. A new report about the environmental dangers of chemically treated plants.
   d. Income tax cuts for all consumers.
   e. A new report showing that there is no nutritional difference between organic and nonorganic produce.

5. Table 14P-1 presents the demand schedule and marginal costs facing a monopolist producer. [LO 14.3]
   a. Fill in the total revenue and marginal revenue columns.
   b. What is the profit-maximizing level of output?
   c. What price will the monopolist charge for the quantity in part *b*?

6. Table 14P-2 presents the demand schedule and marginal costs facing a monopolist producer. [LO 14.3]

TABLE 14P-1

Q	P ($)	TR ($)	MR ($)	MC ($)
0	10			−
1	9			2
2	8			2
3	7			2
4	6			2
5	5			2
6	4			2
7	3			2
8	2			2
9	1			2
10	0			2

TABLE 14P-2

Q	P ($)	TR ($)	MR ($)	MC ($)
0	8			−
1	7			1
2	6			2
3	5			3
4	4			4
5	3			5
6	2			6
7	1			7
8	0			8

   a. Fill in the total revenue and marginal revenue columns.
   b. What is the profit-maximizing level of output?
   c. What price will the monopolist charge for the quantity in part *b?*

7. Figure 14P-1 presents the demand curve, marginal revenue, and marginal costs facing a monopolist producer. [LO 14.3, 14.4]

FIGURE 14P-1

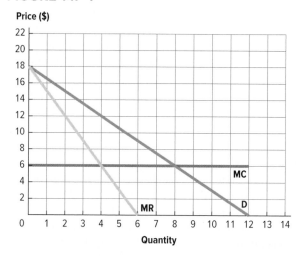

FIGURE 14P-2

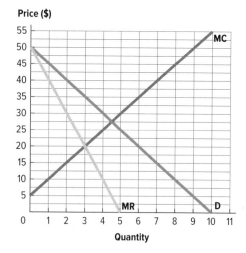

a. What is the profit-maximizing level of output?

b. What price will the monopolist charge for the quantity in part *a?*

c. Plot the profit-maximizing price and quantity from parts *a* and *b* on the graph.

d. What are the efficiency costs (deadweight loss) of monopoly output/pricing? Provide a numerical answer and illustrate this area on the graph.

e. What is consumer surplus under monopoly output/pricing? Illustrate this area on the graph.

8. Figure 14P-2 presents the demand curve, marginal revenue, and marginal costs facing a monopolist producer. **[LO 14.3, 14.4]**

   a. What is the profit-maximizing level of output?

   b. What price will the monopolist charge for the quantity in part *a?*

   c. What are the efficiency costs (deadweight loss) of monopoly output/pricing? Provide a numerical answer and illustrate this area on the graph.

   d. What is consumer surplus under monopoly output/pricing? Illustrate this area on the graph.

   e. What is the loss of consumer surplus under monopoly outcomes versus efficient outcomes? Provide a numerical answer.

9. Figure 14P-3 presents the demand curve, marginal revenue, marginal costs, and average total costs facing a monopolist producer. **[LO 14.5]**

   a. Plot the profit-maximizing price and quantity on the graph.

   b. Under monopoly pricing, are profits positive, negative, or zero?

FIGURE 14P-3

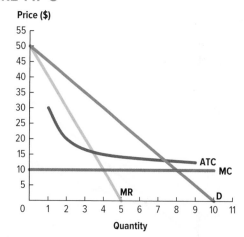

c. Draw the deadweight loss under monopoly pricing.

d. If government mandates P = ATC, are profits positive, negative, or zero? Compared to monopoly pricing, is deadweight loss smaller, larger, or the same size?

e. If government mandates efficient pricing, are profits positive, negative, or zero? Compared to monopoly pricing, is deadweight loss under efficient pricing smaller, larger, or the same size? Compared to a mandate where P = ATC, is deadweight loss under efficient pricing smaller, larger, or the same size?

f. Is this a natural monopoly?

10. Use Figure 14P-4 to answer the following questions. **[LO 14.5]**

    a. If this monopolist were regulated, would it prefer average total cost pricing (P = ATC) or efficient pricing?

    b. Is this a natural monopoly?

11. Suppose a monopolist discovers a way to perfectly price-discriminate. What is consumer surplus under this scenario? What are the efficiency costs? **[LO 14.6]**

12. Suppose there are three types of consumers who attend concerts at your university's performing arts center: students, staff, and faculty. Each of these groups has a different willingness to pay for tickets; within each group, willingness to pay is identical. There is a fixed cost of $1,000 to put on a concert, but there are essentially no variable costs. **[LO 14.6]**

    For each concert:

- There are 140 students willing to pay $20.
- There are 200 staff members willing to pay $35.
- There are 100 faculty members willing to pay $50.

FIGURE 14P-4

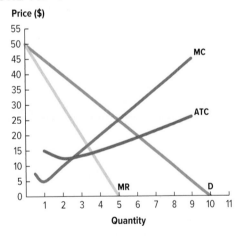

a. If the performing arts center can charge only one price, what price should it charge?

b. What are profits at this price?

c. If the performing arts center can price discriminate and charge two prices, one for students and another for faculty/staff, what are its profits?

d. If the performing arts center can perfectly price discriminate and charge students, staff, and faculty three separate prices, what are its profits?

Endnotes

1. http://www.theatlantic.com/magazine/archive/1982/02/have-you-ever-tried-to-sell-a-diamond/304575/.

2. http://www.nytimes.com/2008/08/09/business/worldbusiness/09nocera.html?_r=2&ref=business.

3. http://www.theatlantic.com/magazine/archive/1982/02/have-you-ever-tried-to-sell-a-diamond/304575/.

4. http://www.theatlantic.com/magazine/archive/1982/02/have-you-ever-tried-to-sell-a-diamond/304575/.

5. https://ilsr.org/walmart-charged-predatory-pricing/; https://ilsr.org/mexico-investigates-walmart-antitrust-violations/.

6. http://www.statista.com/statistics/216573/worldwide-market-share-of-search-engines/.

7. http://www.diamonds.net/News/NewsItem.aspx?ArticleID=38343.

8. http://www.forbes.com/sites/greatspeculations/2015/04/28/comcast-twc-merger-called-off-where-do-these-companies-stand-now/#6ce5fa9d7114.

9. https://www.washingtonpost.com/business/the-last-days-of-us-airways/2015/09/25/f5530686-60a6-11e5-8e9e-dce8a2a2a679_story.html.

10. https://www.amtrak.com/ccurl/998/601/Amtrak-National-Fact-Sheet-FY2015.pdf; http://www.govexec.com/management/2016/02/usps-records-first-profit-five-years-obama-calls-shedding-12k-postal-jobs/125825/.

Monopolistic Competition and Oligopoly

Learning Objectives

LO 15.1 Name the defining features of oligopoly and monopolistic competition.

LO 15.2 Calculate the profit-maximizing price and quantity for a monopolistically competitive firm in the short run.

LO 15.3 Describe a monopolistically competitive market in the long run.

LO 15.4 Analyze the welfare costs of monopolistic competition.

LO 15.5 Explain how product differentiation motivates advertising and branding.

LO 15.6 Describe the strategic production decision of firms in an oligopoly.

LO 15.7 Explain how basic tenets of game theory apply to an oligopoly's incentive to compete or collude.

LO 15.8 Compare the welfare of producers, consumers, and society as a whole in an oligopoly to monopoly and perfect competition.

WHICH ONE OF THESE IS JUST LIKE THE OTHERS?

What do the musicians Avicii, Katy Perry, and Kanye West have in common? We'll give you a hint. It's the same thing that Avenged Sevenfold has in common with Death Cab for Cutie and Dean Martin, and that Shakira shares with the winner of the 2016 Nobel Prize for Literature, Bob Dylan.

Each of these groups of artists is on one of the three major recording labels that together account for more than 60 percent of the U.S. music market. These three labels—Universal Music Group (Universal), Sony Music Entertainment (Sony), and Warner Music Group (Warner)—each controls between 10 and 30 percent of the market.[1] If you want to be a successful recording artist, you'll have a much better chance with one of them on your side.

That wasn't always the case, though. In the 1950s and 1960s, many stars were able to make their names with small record labels. An Alabama radio host named Sam Phillips started Sun Records out of a cheap storefront in Memphis. He promptly signed then-unknown artists Elvis Presley,

© Prince Williams/WireImage/Getty Images

Johnny Cash, and B.B. King. A Ford assembly-line worker, Berry Gordy, formed Motown Records in Detroit with a tiny family loan, and made stars of artists including Marvin Gaye and Stevie Wonder.[2] In the last decade, as the Internet has revolutionized music distribution, new ways have opened up again for musicians to market themselves independently of the three major labels. But it's still not as common for an artist to break through on a small label today as it was in the early days of rock and roll (although this is changing, as social media and sites like YouTube have made it cheaper for musicians to self-publish).

In previous chapters, we described two extreme market structures: monopoly and perfect competition. In this chapter, we'll see why neither of those two models describes the music industry—both past and present. Instead, the music industry is a market that is somewhat competitive, but not perfectly competitive. Such a market structure is quite common in the real world.

In particular, we'll discuss two types of market structures that are *imperfectly competitive:* monopolistic competition and oligopoly. These market structures aren't mutually exclusive. As we'll see, many industries, including the music industry, display characteristics of both.

Understanding market structure is key to running a successful business. A business owner needs to know the type of market in which she is engaged in order to know how much freedom she has to set prices, or how much attention to pay to the behavior of other firms. Her business strategy may differ greatly depending on how much competition she faces and of what sort. Understanding market structure can also be valuable in making good choices as a consumer or policy-maker. It can help us to interpret a firm's choice to advertise, for example, or to decide when we should favor regulators stepping in to address "anti-competitive" business practices. The concepts that we explore in this chapter will help us understand choices faced by businesses, consumers, and policy-makers.

What Sort of Market?

What sort of market is the music industry? That's the 5-billion-dollar question for everyone from record-label executives to retailers to antitrust lawyers at the Department of Justice. In answering it, we'll focus on the two characteristics that define a range of market structures: number of firms and product variety.

Let's start by looking at the number of firms. Figure 15-1 shows that the music industry is dominated by three labels; no single one of them is big enough to dominate the industry in the

FIGURE 15-1   **Market share in the music business**

The music industry is dominated by three big firms. Their record sales represent over 60 percent of the market. They are so big that their behavior affects the entire market for music.

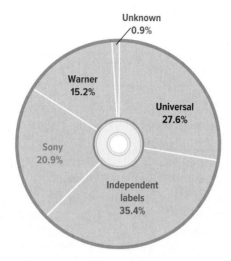

way that De Beers dominated the diamond market in the twentieth century. This tells us the music industry is not a monopoly.

It's also not perfectly competitive. That's not simply because the market is dominated by a few large firms. It's also because it encompasses a wide variety of products. Even if there were thousands of small record labels competing, the market would not be perfectly competitive because music is not a standardized product. There are many similarities between, say, a Kanye West track and a music file by The Shins: They're both digitized versions of music, using data-compression technology with a common digital encoding format. Both emit sounds of instruments and voices when played. They're similar enough that it makes sense for us to think of them both as products of the same industry, the music industry. But they are certainly not a standardized product—at least, not to fans of either artist.

These two features of the music industry—a small number of large firms and product variety—are the defining features of two market structures that lie between the extreme models of monopoly and perfect competition. Both of those market structures—oligopoly and monopolistic competition—are common in the real world. While many industries display features of both models, understanding each model separately allows us to make powerful predictions about how firms will behave.

Oligopoly and monopolistic competition

LO 15.1 Name the defining features of oligopoly and monopolistic competition.

Oligopoly describes a market with only a few firms. (The word itself is derived from the Greek words for "few sellers.") These companies sell a product or service that may or may not be completely standardized but is similar enough that the firms are in competition. Examples of oligopolies are wireless network providers (the U.S. market is dominated by four companies— Verizon, AT&T, Sprint, and T-Mobile) and fast-food burgers (think McDonald's, Burger King, and Wendy's).

One of the defining features of an oligopoly is that strategic interactions between a firm and its rivals have a major impact on its success. In particular, we'll see that the price and quantity set by an individual firm affect the other firms' profits. This stands in contrast to firms in perfectly competitive markets or monopolists: In a perfectly competitive market, other firms' actions

oligopoly
a market with only a few firms, which sell a similar good or service

cannot affect the market. If you are a true monopolist, there *are* no other firms (unless another firm is trying to create a product that can substitute for yours).

If you are in charge of a company in an oligopoly, though, it is a vital part of your job to keep an eye on competitors. The shareholders of Wendy's would not be impressed if the CEO had no idea that McDonald's had just introduced a new kind of burger or that Burger King was offering promotional discounts on sodas.

Oligopolies are also characterized by the existence of some barriers to entry. Remember that barriers to entry enable monopolies to exist. You couldn't set up in the diamond business to challenge De Beers without discovering a new source of diamonds. In perfect competition, by contrast, we assume there are *no* barriers to entry—it's easy for new firms to enter the market. Oligopoly is somewhere in the middle. It would be possible to set up as a wireless carrier but expensive to construct the infrastructure. It would be possible to break into the national burger chain market but tough to overcome established brand loyalties.

monopolistic competition

a market with many firms that sell goods and services that are similar, but slightly different

Monopolistic competition describes a market with *many* firms that sell goods and services that are similar, but slightly different. Remember that a feature of perfect competition is that consumers are indifferent between the products of competing firms. A feature of monopoly is that the product has no close substitutes. Between these two extremes are markets in which products have substitutes that are close but not perfect. Consumers might be willing to pay a bit extra, but if the price differential is too large, they will choose a substitute product instead.

Although the name *monopolistic competition* sounds like a contradiction in terms, it expresses the idea that firms in such a market have a kind of monopoly but in a limited sense. For example, in the 1950s Sun Records had a monopoly on selling Elvis records. If you wanted an Elvis record, you had no choice but to buy it from Sun. Devoted fans of Elvis might be willing to pay more for an Elvis record than for records by other artists. Thus, Sun had some power to set its own price, but not much. If Sun raised the price of Elvis records too high, most people would prefer to save their money or to buy records by other artists instead.

Monopolistic competition describes a great many real-world markets. For example, General Mills, the parent company of Häagen-Dazs, has a monopoly on selling Häagen-Dazs brand ice cream, but not a monopoly on ice cream in general. If you especially like Häagen-Dazs, you might be willing to pay a bit extra for it. But if the price differential becomes too great, you'll switch to another brand, such as Ben & Jerry's. Similarly, you might be willing to pay a little more for a meal at your favorite restaurant, but if the price is too high, you'd be happy to settle for your second favorite.

Oligopoly and monopolistic competition are often found together, as in the music industry. In short:

- Oligopoly is about the *number of firms.*
- Monopolistic competition is about *variety of products.*

Record companies are oligopolists: There are only a few record companies, each has market power, and the basic service they provide (access and distribution of music) is roughly the same. Individual musicians are monopolistic competitors: They have a monopoly over their own music but must also compete with other musicians. Each musician, of course, is different, providing his or her own unique product.

The fact that the "music" industry can be described in both of these two ways makes it more complicated to analyze. However, there are markets that are distinctly oligopoly markets and those that are distinctly described as monopolistic competition. Oligopolies can exist when products are standardized; monopolistic competition can exist when there are many small firms. To keep things clean, we will now explore the two market structures separately.

✓CONCEPT CHECK

☐ What is the difference between oligopoly and monopolistic competition? **[LO 15.1]**

Monopolistic Competition

Remember that under the model of perfect competition, firms do not make economic profits. It's not surprising, then, that firms would rather be operating under conditions of monopolistic competition, where they *can* make economic profits.

How do monopolistically competitive firms make economic profits? By making a product that consumers perceive to be different from the products of their competitors. In other words, firms must offer goods that are similar to competitors' products but more attractive in some ways. This process is called **product differentiation**. It is an essential part of the strategy of many businesses.

Sometimes product differentiation is accomplished through genuine innovation. The many record labels operating in the 1950s music business are an example. They competed to discover and shape new, exciting, *different* performers who could attract a following of loyal fans. The more enthusiastic Elvis fans were, the less interchangeable they considered Elvis's records to be with those of other artists. The less interchangeable the records, the more Sun could charge without fear of losing sales. The founder of Sun Records discovered a wealth of previously overlooked talent in and around Memphis: He was happy to work with black musicians who were otherwise excluded from white-dominated parts of the music business in that era of segregation. In doing so, he helped to create rock and roll—not only recognizing talent, but shaping it into something new.

Regardless of whether genuine innovation is involved, firms have an interest in persuading customers that their products are unique. This is the role of advertising and branding. Even when a firm's product is not really very different from other products on the market, it may be possible to convince customers that the product *is* different, and thereby persuade them to pay more for a particular brand. We'll return to these issues later in the chapter.

product differentiation
the creation of products that are similar to competitors' products but more attractive in some ways

Monopolistic competition in the short run

LO 15.2 Calculate the profit-maximizing price and quantity for a monopolistically competitive firm in the short run.

Product differentiation enables firms in monopolistically competitive markets to produce a good for which there are no exact substitutes. In the short run, this allows a firm to behave like a monopolist. In the long run, as we will see, the situation is different. This difference between the short and long run is the key to understanding monopolistic competition.

First, we'll look at the short run, when monopolistically competitive firms can behave like monopolists. Figure 15-2 shows these short-run production choices:

1. Firms face a downward-sloping demand curve. Just like a monopolist, a monopolistically competitive firm cannot adjust its price without causing a change in the quantity consumers demand.

2. Assuming that production involves both fixed and marginal costs, firms face a U-shaped average total cost (ATC) curve.

3. The profit-maximizing production quantity is at the point where the marginal revenue (MR) curve intersects the marginal cost (MC) curve. The profit-maximizing price is determined by the point on the demand curve that corresponds to this quantity.

In summary, a monopolistically competitive firm can behave just like a monopolist in the short run: It will produce at the point where marginal revenue equals marginal cost and then charge a higher price according to the demand curve. In doing this, the firm can earn positive economic profits in the short run.

FIGURE 15-2

Monopolistic competition in the short run

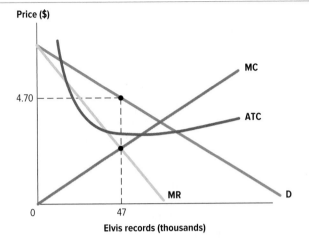

In the short run in a monopolistically competitive market, Elvis's label will produce records up to the point where marginal revenue is equal to marginal cost, and charge the corresponding price on the demand curve. At this point, we find the profit-maximizing quantity and price.

? POTENTIALLY CONFUSING

Sun Records was a small player in a very competitive music market. So why wasn't it a price taker, facing a horizontal demand curve, as a small firm in a perfectly competitive market would be? Why did it face a downward-sloping demand curve in the short run?

The key here is how we define the scope of the market. Sun Records was small relative to the market for *records*. But it was large—in fact, a monopolist—in the market for *Elvis records*. Consumers who wanted Elvis records could buy them only from Sun. Because Sun was not a price taker in the market for Elvis records, it faced a downward-sloping demand curve.

The steepness of the demand curve is determined in part by the degree of substitutability between Elvis records and other records:

- What if buyers see the records as very close substitutes? In that case, if Sun raises the price even a little bit, people will switch to other artists. The demand curve will be quite flat.
- What if, on the other hand, fans are very loyal to Elvis? In that case, most won't stop buying Elvis records even when prices go up, and the demand curve will be steeper.

In other words, the less-differentiated the products are, the closer each firm's demand curve is to the horizontal curve faced by perfectly competitive firms. By differentiating their products more—for example, finding a very distinctive artist such as Elvis and building a loyal following of devoted fans—firms can increase the steepness of the demand curve they face in the short run.

Monopolistic competition in the long run

LO 15.3 Describe a monopolistically competitive market in the long run.

For all of their similarities in the short run, the monopolistically competitive firm faces one huge problem that the monopolist does not: Other firms can enter the market. When existing firms are making positive economic profits, other firms have an incentive to enter the market.

Of course, it's not always possible for other firms to enter the market and produce *exactly* the same product. There's only one Elvis, after all, and he belonged to Sun Records. What other firms *can* do is look for artists who are *like* Elvis, and whose records will therefore be seen by music lovers as close substitutes for Elvis records.

This explains why, in music and in many other industries, products tend to come in waves. A new musical performer with an original style comes along and makes a splash; other record labels rush to sign artists who have a similar style. A trendy high-fashion label produces a new range of clothing; other fashion labels rush to produce clothes that look similar. Apple releases the iPad, and other companies rush to produce touchscreen tablet computers. And so on.

What effect does the entry of more firms have on the demand faced by each existing firm? Remember from Chapter 3, "Markets," that availability of substitute goods is one of the determinants of demand. More firms making more products that are similar to the original product means that consumers have a wider range of substitutes. With more product options from which consumers can choose, demand for the original product decreases at every price. The demand curve faced by the original firm shifts to the left.

As long as firms currently in the market are earning profits, more firms will enter the market with products that are close substitutes. As a result, the demand curve will continue to shift to the left. This process will continue until the point when potential firms no longer have an incentive to enter the market. When does that happen? At the point when existing firms are *no longer earning economic profits.*

The opposite logic holds if firms in the market are losing money in the short run: Firms will have an incentive to exit the market when they are earning negative profits. These exits will drive up demand for the existing firms and shift the demand curves they face to the right. This process will continue until, in the long run, firms are breaking even and no longer have an incentive to exit. You may have noticed something like this happening in the music industry: Sometimes so many performers are releasing similar-sounding music, the market niche becomes oversaturated.

In the long run, firms in a monopolistically competitive market face the same profit situation as firms in a perfectly competitive market: Profits are driven to zero. Remember from earlier chapters that zero profit means that total revenue is exactly equal to total cost. In per-unit terms, zero profit means that price is equal to average total cost (ATC). Figure 15-3 shows this situation; in the long run, the ATC curve is *tangent to* the demand curve at exactly one point, where ATC = Price.

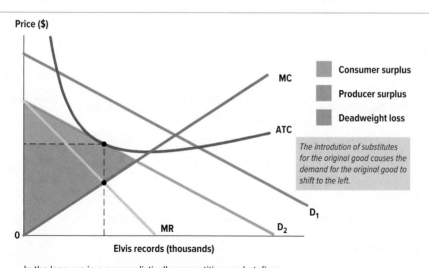

Price ($)

Consumer surplus

Producer surplus

Deadweight loss

The introdution of substitutes for the original good causes the demand for the original good to shift to the left.

MC

ATC

D₁

MR   D₂

0

Elvis records (thousands)

FIGURE 15-3

Monopolistic competition in the long run

In the long run in a monopolistically competitive market, firms will enter the market, driving down demand until all market participants earn zero economic profits. Elvis's label will produce records up to the point where marginal cost equals marginal revenue. Because profits are zero, this is the same as the quantity at which the average total cost curve is tangent to the demand curve.

Note that for the monopolistically competitive firm, ATC touches the demand curve at the same quantity where MR intersects MC. This graphic relationship is equivalent to saying that profits are zero. If ATC is not exactly tangent to the demand curve at the profit-maximizing quantity, then profits will be positive or negative, depending on the location of ATC and the demand curve:

- If the ATC is above the demand curve, this would mean that costs were higher than price, and firms would lose money and exit the market.
- If, on the other hand, ATC hit the demand curve at multiple places, costs would be below price and firms would earn profits. This situation would induce firms to enter the market.

This process of entry and exit, which moves the demand curve left or right, continues until ATC touches the demand curve at the quantity where MR intersects MC.

In the long run, monopolistic competition has some features in common with monopoly, and others in common with perfect competition. Table 15-1 summarizes some of those features. Just like a *monopoly,* a monopolistically competitive firm faces a downward-sloping demand curve. Such a curve means that marginal revenue is less than price; this in turn means that marginal cost is also less than price at the profit-maximizing quantity. But, like a firm in a *perfectly competitive* market, a monopolistically competitive firm earns zero economic profits in the long run.

These differences have two important implications:

1. **Monopolistically competitive firms operate at smaller-than-efficient scale.** As we've just described, the optimal production point for a monopolistically competitive firm in the long run will be where the ATC curve touches the demand curve. Because the demand curve is downward-sloping, this will always be on the decreasing section of the ATC curve, as panel A of Figure 15-4 shows. This contrasts with the situation in a perfectly competitive market, in which firms' optimal production is at the lowest point on the ATC curve, as shown in panel B.

   When firms produce the quantity that minimizes average total cost (as in a perfectly competitive market), we say they are operating at their *efficient scale.* In contrast, a monopolistically competitive firm maximizes profits by operating at a smaller scale than the efficient one. Another way of saying this is that the firm has *excess capacity.*

2. **Monopolistically competitive firms want to sell more.** For a firm in a perfectly competitive market, price is equal to marginal cost. If the firm sold an additional unit at that price, marginal cost would rise above price, and profit would fall.

TABLE 15-1

Comparing the Characteristics of Market Models

Characteristic	Perfect competition	Monopoly	Monopolistic competition
How many firms?	Many firms	One firm	Many firms
Price taker or price maker?	Price taker	Price maker	Price maker
Marginal revenue?	MR = Price	MR < Price	MR < Price
Profit-maximizing quantity occurs where?	MR = MC	MR = MC	MR = MC
Can earn economic profits in the short run?	Yes	Yes	Yes
Can earn economic profits in the long run?	No	Yes	No
Quantity is efficient?	Yes	No	No

FIGURE 15-4

Monopolistic competition versus perfect competition in the long run

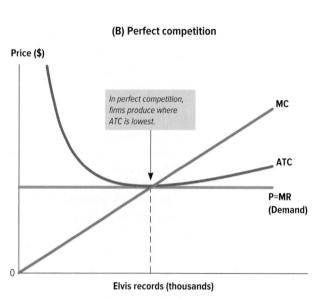
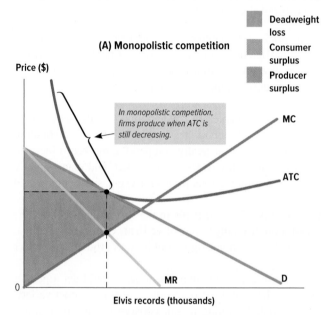
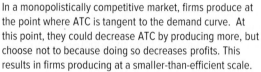

In a monopolistically competitive market, firms produce at the point where ATC is tangent to the demand curve. At this point, they could decrease ATC by producing more, but choose not to because doing so decreases profits. This results in firms producing at a smaller-than-efficient scale.

In a perfectly competitive market, firms produce at the quantity that minimizes ATC. This is the efficient choice since they cannot produce more or less without increasing costs.

In contrast, a monopolistically competitive firm sells at a price that is equal to average total cost, but higher than marginal cost. (Look again at panel A of Figure 15-4.) If the firm was able to sell an additional unit without lowering the price, that unit would generate more revenue than cost, and so increase the firm's profits. In other words, when we depart from the model of perfect competition, firms have an incentive to engage in tactics for bringing in more customers, such as advertising and brand promotion.

The need for continual innovation

Our analysis of monopolistic competition in the long run has another interesting implication. Ask yourself: How will firms respond to competitors entering the market with closer and closer substitutes for existing products? Clearly, existing firms will want to step up their own attempts to differentiate their product. Only by constantly finding new ways to be different is it possible for a monopolistically competitive firm to generate profits in the long run.

The need for continual innovation explains why record labels are constantly on the lookout for new talent. It explains why firms in so many industries put so much effort into launching new products and finding new ways to advertise their products. If they don't, their competitors will catch up, and their economic profits will disappear. A truly innovative firm that manages to stay one step ahead of its competitors can continue to earn economic profits by always offering something slightly different.

For this reason, economists usually believe that competition encourages innovation. In contrast, a monopolist has far less incentive to innovate because there is no danger of customers switching to a firm with newer and better products.

The welfare costs of monopolistic competition

LO 15.4 Analyze the welfare costs of monopolistic competition.

Like any deviation from the equilibrium price and quantity that would prevail under perfect competition, monopolistic competition is inefficient. Firms maximize profits at a price that is higher than marginal cost, and the quantity bought and sold is smaller than it would be under perfect competition. This means that there is deadweight loss—the market does not maximize total surplus.

Can anything be done about this problem? In Chapter 14, "Monopoly," we discussed ways that policy-makers try to address the welfare costs of monopolies, and noted that it is difficult to do so successfully. Unfortunately, regulating a monopolistically competitive market to increase efficiency is even harder. By definition, there are many firms in the market, and many slightly different products. Trying to assess firms' costs and regulate prices for every single one would be a gargantuan task.

Instead, the government could set a single price for all firms in the market and then let the natural forces of competition take over. Monopolistically competitive firms earn zero economic profits. With a regulated price, those firms that could not figure out how to produce at a lower cost would be forced to leave the market.

Such regulation would come with a definite cost. Although consumers would get a greater quantity of similar products at a lower price, they would also lose out on some product variety. Instead of dozens or hundreds of similar products aiming to suit consumers' different tastes, everyone would have to make do with fewer options. How would you feel if instead of having five options for fast food in town, you had only three, but the burgers were a little bit cheaper?

Most governments are not too bothered about the welfare loss from monopolistic competition. Even if they could do something about it, it's not obvious whether consumers would appreciate having lower prices if it's at the expense of having many products to choose from.

Product differentiation, advertising, and branding

LO 15.5 Explain how product differentiation motivates advertising and branding.

We've seen that product differentiation enables firms to keep making economic profits in the short run. Firms therefore have an incentive to persuade customers that their products cannot easily be substituted with a rival product. They can do this either by making products truly different or by convincing consumers that they are different. Advertising is one strategy employed by firms to inform customers about—or convince them of—the differences between products.

Whether advertising is a good or bad thing is a subject for debate. On the one hand, advertising can convey useful information to consumers. You may learn about a new product or technology from an ad, or find out where something you want is sold, or when it is on sale, or what styles or flavors are available. In general, advertising provides this information in a pleasant, easy-to-understand format, free of cost and inconvenience. You don't need to trudge from store to store to find out where the sales are, or search online every day to see whether that new movie has been released yet. Instead, companies will spend money to hand you all of this information.

If we believe that the main effect of advertising is to provide useful information about products and prices, then advertising serves a valuable purpose. More information will increase competition in a marketplace. Consumers will learn when a firm is offering a cheaper product that is a close substitute for higher-priced competitors. This will drive prices down, bringing the market closer to the model of perfect competition.

On the other hand, advertising rarely consists of a bullet-pointed list of straightforward facts. Instead, advertisers go to great lengths to make viewers feel good about the thing being advertised. Ads portray beautiful people having a fabulous time, or heart-warming family moments, or adrenaline-inducing stunts and special effects. Often, this portrayal has little or nothing to do with the product being advertised. Instead, it is intended to make us associate a particular image or emotion with that product. The image of happy lovers embracing in a romantic location doesn't tell us anything about the unique qualities of a particular company's jewelry. It may, though, create a strong mental association between falling in love and receiving a new pair of earrings. For evidence that this kind of advertising can and does work, see the Real Life box "What really sells loans?"

Real Life

What really sells loans?

Ads often aim to make the viewer feel good and to associate feeling good with the product. For example, an ad might try to associate a new car with shots of long sunny adventures with attractive friends. But how much of a difference does this really make? Don't potential customers just see through these ads?

Could emotions really matter as much as something economically important, such as the price of the good? Several economists (including one of the authors of this book) designed a study to answer this question in the context of advertising for consumer loans. In the experiment, a lender in South Africa sent ads by mail to tens of thousands of prior clients. The ads varied in the interest rate at which the loan was offered, as well as the appearance and content of the mailer. Different mailers included different combinations of features: an image of an attractive woman, a list of possible uses for the loan, information on interest rates, or a promotional raffle for a cell phone.

Not surprisingly, customers were more likely to take out a loan in response to mailers advertising lower interest rates. But they were also more likely to borrow if there was an attractive woman's picture on the ad. In fact, putting an attractive woman's picture on the mailer increased demand to the same degree as reducing the interest rate by 25 percent!

Of course, if you had asked loan customers directly whether they would rather have a 25 percent cheaper loan or look briefly at a picture of an attractive woman, most would likely have opted for the cheaper loan. The fact that their responses to the mailer told a different story demonstrates that economic information is only one input into people's decision making when faced with cleverly designed advertising.

Source: Marianne Bertrand, Dean Karlan, Sendhil Mullainathan, Eldar Shafir, and Jonathan Zinman, "What's Advertising Content Worth? Evidence from a Consumer Credit Marketing Field Experiment," *Quarterly Journal of Economics* 125, no. 1 (2010), pp. 263–306.

What if we believe that the main effect of advertising is not to convey useful information but to persuade customers that products are more different than they truly are? In this view, advertising decreases consumers' willingness to substitute between similar products. The result is that firms can charge a higher markup over marginal cost. This in turn drives prices up throughout the market.

So which *is* the main effect of advertising? There's no simple answer. Whether advertising serves mainly to provide useful information or to trigger gut-level reactions probably varies across markets. Sometimes, however, we can get a clue as to which effect is stronger from the reaction of producers when lawmakers consider banning advertising. (They have proposed such bans for tobacco, prescription drugs, alcohol, legal services, and even cosmetic surgery.) If producers object strongly to a ban on advertising, it is probably because they believe advertising persuades customers that products are more different than they really are. Producers' silence in the face of bans, or even in support of them, may indicate that advertising in this industry serves mostly to inform consumers and promote competition—something that existing firms won't want to see happen.

Advertising as a signal

It's often hard to tell what real information about a product we're supposed to get from an ad. Why should we believe an actor who is well paid to say that a particular cellular network is faster than another? What does GEICO Insurance's green animated gecko know about car insurance? Sometimes, though, advertising may contain useful information for customers, even if it's not stated explicitly.

Think about the problem of *asymmetric information* (discussed in Chapter 10, "Information"). Firms know more about the true quality of their products than consumers do. Consumers would like to find the best products, and the firms who make the best products would like to make themselves known to customers. But consumers can't trust a firm that simply *says* it has high-quality products. Every firm, whether it produces high-quality or low-quality products, has an incentive to claim that its products are the best. The high-quality firms need a way to credibly signal the quality of their products. Advertising fits the bill because advertising costs money.

Let's think, from a firm's perspective, about the choice to advertise. Suppose that a music label has signed a brilliant new artist and is sure people will love his first album if they hear it. The company calculates that if it spends a large amount of money on a high-profile TV advertising campaign, lots of people will buy the album; they will like it so much they will tell their friends and will buy concert tickets, fan merchandise, and the artist's future albums. What are the possible outcomes?

- If the company is right about the new artist, the label will end up making $10 million in profits.
- If the company is wrong, and people don't like the album, the firm won't recover the cost of the money it spends on advertising—and will lose $5 million.

The advertising expenditure will be a great investment for the label if the quality of the product is good, and a terrible investment if the quality is bad.

On the other hand, what does this decision look like if the label is not so confident about the quality of the new album? If the firm doesn't promote the album, there's still a chance that people who buy it will love it and tell their friends. But the sales will be much lower than if there was a huge ad campaign behind it. What are the possible outcomes if the label does not advertise the album?

- If people like the unadvertised album, the label makes $2 million.
- If the people who buy the unadvertised album don't like it, the label will lose some money it spent producing the music, but only $50,000.

If the label is not so confident in the quality of the album, then it makes sense *not* to advertise. If people don't like it, at least the label will lose much less money than it would have if it had advertised it. The choice to advertise or not advertise is illustrated in the decision tree in Figure 15-5.

Now let's think from a *consumer's perspective* about the firm's choice to advertise. Consumers can observe only the final outcome—whether the firm chooses to advertise or not—and not the true quality of the product. However, consumers can view the advertising as a credible signal. If they see that a music label is spending a lot of money on high-profile TV advertising for a new singer's album, they can reasonably conclude that the label is very confident that people will like the album.

It may be perfectly reasonable, therefore, for consumers to try a product based on advertising. The important factor for consumers in assessing the usefulness of advertising as a signal is not the ad's content, but *how much it cost*. The more expensive the advertising is, the more consumers can assume the firm is confident that it has a good product that will earn repeat business from satisfied customers.

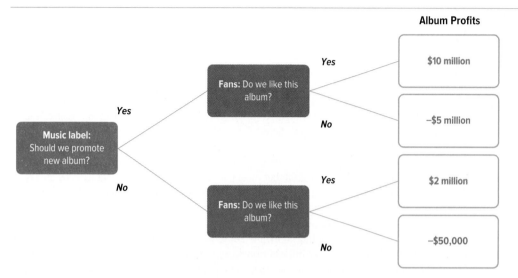

Album Profits

FIGURE 15-5

Advertising as a signal of quality   If the music label suspects fans will not like the album, it will actually lose money by advertising. Because rational music companies will choose to advertise an album only if they know it is good, consumers can use promotion efforts as a signal of album quality.

Branding

In 2009, two kitchen workers employed by Domino's Pizza uploaded videos to YouTube showing themselves contaminating food in various ways—we'll spare you the details—before allegedly giving the food to customers. (When the story was made public, the makers of the videos insisted it was a prank and that none of the food had ever been served.) The employees responsible were immediately fired, but the damage to Domino's image had been done. Consumer surveys completed after the story broke showed a marked downturn in perception of the Domino's *brand* (the combination of characteristics that identify and differentiate a particular company or product). Consumer perceptions moved from positive to negative in a matter of days. It needed quick action and some savvy public relations work for Domino's to help its brand recover.[3]

This story illustrates why it may be rational for consumers to think of a strong brand as being an implicit guarantee of a product's quality. Firms with no reputation to protect may not be too concerned with the repercussions of selling a bad-quality product. But just one unfortunate incident can undo years of careful thought and hard work that a firm such as Domino's put into building a strong brand. Because consumers know that firms stand to lose when their brand's reputation is damaged, they can conclude that firms with strong brands probably have strong quality control in all locations and levels of the company.

For this reason, a brand may also convey useful information in a confusing situation. A traveler in a strange city may have little information about the quality of food and drink available in local stores. If she sees a Starbucks, however, she can assume with confidence that she will be able to buy a familiar drink of predictable quality. The local tea shop might actually be better than Starbucks, but the traveler doesn't know that. She may rationally choose to go for the known quantity of the Starbucks brand, rather than take a risk on the local competition.

It isn't always rational to rely on brand names to make decisions, however. Brands may also perpetuate false perceptions of quality or product differences. For instance, brand-name pharmaceuticals often command much higher prices than their generic counterparts, despite the fact that the two are made with identical active ingredients and have the same medical effect. In such cases, strong brands can even form a *barrier to entry* in a market, moving it toward a structure of oligopoly in which a few leading players have a significant amount of market power. Before we look at how oligopolies work, see the From Another Angle box "Coke, Pepsi, and the not-so-secret formula" for an illustration of just how important it can be for firms to use branding to differentiate their products.

From Another Angle

Coke, Pepsi, and the not-so-secret formula

In its advertising, Coca-Cola makes a big deal about its "secret formula." When two employees tried to sell the company's confidential recipe to Pepsi in 2007, you might think Pepsi would have jumped at the chance to learn how its rival makes its product. In fact, Pepsi not only refused to buy the information, it participated in an FBI operation that led to the arrest of the would-be informants. What was going on here?

The market for colas can be described as monopolistically competitive: Each company tries to increase the size and loyalty of its customer base by emphasizing the differentiation of its product. Many blind taste tests have found that most people—even those who claim to be ardent fans of one brand or the other—can't distinguish between them when they don't know which they're drinking. So this seems to be a clear example of an industry in which advertising mainly serves to persuade people that products are more different than they really are.

Consider for a moment what would happen if Pepsi were to buy Coke's secret formula and publish it for the world to see. That information would make it easier for new companies to enter the cola market; they could advertise that their products are exactly identical to Coke. What would happen then? The entrance of new companies with undifferentiated products would bring the market closer to the model of perfect competition. The result would be to push down the price of Coke. This would be a disaster for Coke—but it would be bad news for Pepsi, too. The new colas would be close substitutes for Pepsi; some Pepsi customers would probably switch to the new wave of cheaper, undifferentiated colas. Under this scenario, Pepsi loses customers, and profits.

Why, then, didn't Pepsi buy the recipe, keep it secret, and use it to make its own cola taste exactly like Coke? After all, Coke has 49 percent of the market to Pepsi's 21 percent as of 2015, so Coca-Cola must be doing something right. The problem for Pepsi was that since Coke has an established brand, Coke customers would have no reason to switch to Pepsi for the same taste at the same price. Pepsi would have to reduce its price to attract Coke customers to switch, and it would meanwhile lose the ability to charge a premium to the loyal 21 percent who actually claim to prefer the taste of Pepsi. If Pepsi made the move, it would not be able to earn as much economic profit.

Pepsi did the right thing in an ethical sense. But we also see why Pepsi's move may have been smart from an economic angle too. Pepsi's profit-maximizing decision was to ignore the chance to learn Coke's secret formula, and continue to differentiate its own product instead.

Sources: http://www.nytimes.com/ref/business/20070527_COKE_GRAPHIC.html; http://freakonomics.blogs.nytimes.com/2006/07/07/how-much-would-pepsi-pay-to-get-cokes-secret-formula/; http://www.statista.com/statistics/387318/market-share-of-leading-carbonated-beverage-companies-worldwide/.

✓CONCEPT CHECK

☐ How does product differentiation allow monopolistically competitive firms to gain market power? **[LO 15.2]**

☐ How does the short run differ from the long run in a monopolistically competitive market? **[LO 15.2]**

☐ Why are monopolistically competitive firms always willing to increase the quantity they sell? **[LO 15.3]**

☐ Why is it difficult to regulate a monopolistically competitive market to increase efficiency? **[LO 15.4]**

☐ Why might it be rational for a consumer to make purchasing decisions based on advertising? **[LO 15.5]**

☐ Why do firms want to develop their brands? **[LO 15.5]**

Oligopoly

Suppose you're an executive at Universal Music Group. Your day-to-day decisions hinge on how to make your company as profitable as possible. You have a lot to think about: Which new artists should we sign? How should we advertise upcoming releases? How much can we charge for CDs and legitimate downloads without driving customers into illegal downloading? What should we do to get more radio play for our latest singles?

One common thread runs through these decisions: You know your competition. You know you're playing to win against Sony and Warner. You know their executives, their catalogs of artists, and at least a bit about their distribution and advertising deals. You probably also have some idea of what new releases they have coming in the pipeline. You might keep an eye on smaller, independent companies too, but your real preoccupation is with the other major players. In other words, you're playing in a game with two very identifiable competitors.

This situation contrasts sharply with the situation in a perfectly competitive market. As a price-taking firm in a perfectly competitive market, you'd be competing against dozens, hundreds, or even thousands of other firms. You probably wouldn't know the managers at those firms, and it wouldn't matter. Making business decisions with the intent of beating out any one of them would be pointless since all of the other firms would simply move in to fill the gap.

The fact that firms in an oligopoly market compete against a few identifiable rivals with market power drives our analysis. Firms in a perfectly competitive market have only one choice—what quantity to produce given the market price. Oligopolists, on the other hand, make *strategic* decisions about price and quantity that take into account the expected choices of their competitors. As we analyze oligopolies, we'll draw on our discussion of *game theory* from Chapter 9, "Game Theory and Strategic Thinking."

Oligopolies in competition

LO 15.6 Describe the strategic production decision of firms in an oligopoly.

Let's begin our analysis of oligopoly with a pared-down example from the music industry. For the sake of simplicity, suppose that there are only two big labels—Universal and Warner—rather than three. (Technically, an oligopoly with two firms is known as a *duopoly*.) Also suppose that music is a standardized good, so that consumers are indifferent between buying music released by Universal and music released by Warner. (Although we discussed earlier in the chapter why this is not entirely true, it's a reasonable simplification to clarify our analysis of oligopoly.) Each label has such a large stable of artists that fans of any particular musical genre will be likely to find close substitutes for their tastes between the two rival labels.

Figure 15-6 shows the market demand schedule for albums, and the corresponding demand and marginal revenue curves, for this two-company market. As we'd expect, the number of albums demanded increases as the price decreases. The third column of the table in panel A shows total revenue at each price-quantity combination. Remember that the quantity in the first column represents the total quantity demanded *in the whole market,* so column 3 shows the combined revenue of the two firms. Suppose that each firm pays a fixed cost of $100 million to sign artists and record albums. Let's also assume, for the sake of simplicity, that the marginal cost of producing each new album is zero.

Remember from Chapter 13, "Perfect Competition," that for perfectly competitive firms, marginal revenue is the same as price. The profit-maximizing quantity of output occurs where marginal revenue equals marginal cost. As a result, price is driven down until it equals marginal cost. Since we're assuming the marginal cost of production is zero, the market equilibrium under perfect competition would be 140 million albums at a price of zero. (Of course, in the long run, albums couldn't remain free because music labels would not be covering their fixed costs; firms

FIGURE 15-6

Demand for albums

(A) Demand and revenue schedule

Albums (millions)	Price ($)	Revenue (millions of $)
40	20	800
50	18	900
60	16	960
70	14	980
80	12	960
90	10	900
100	8	800
110	6	660
120	4	480
130	2	260
140	0	0

Market equilibrium for a monopoly ← 70 | 14 | 980

Market equilibrium for perfect competition ← 140 | 0 | 0

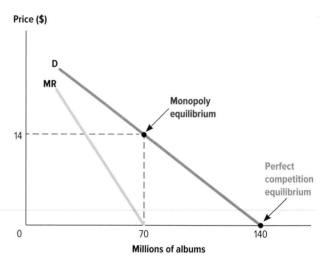

(B) Demand and marginal revenue curve

If albums were produced by a monopoly, the firm would produce the profit-maximizing quantity. In perfect competition, price would be driven down to marginal cost, which in this case is zero.

would exit the market until the price rose to a level where fixed costs were covered.) This is just another way of saying something we know already: In the model of perfect competition, no firm makes an economic profit.

In contrast, what if the market were a monopoly? We know from Chapter 14, "Monopoly," that the monopolist faces a downward-sloping marginal revenue curve. The monopolist maximizes profits by producing the quantity where marginal revenue equals marginal cost and then charging a higher price according to the demand curve. Looking at the table, we can see this point would be 70 million albums at a price of $14. The monopolist's profit would be $880 million, which is its total revenue of $980 million minus its fixed cost of $100 million.

What happens when there are *two* firms in the market—Universal and Warner? Since the monopoly production choice maximizes profits, the best the two firms could do would be to agree to act like a joint monopolist. If each produced 35 million albums, total quantity sold would equal 70 million, and the two labels could each earn profits of $390 million:

$$TR - TC$$
$$(35 \text{ million} \times \$14) - \$100 \text{ million} = \$390 \text{ million}$$

Sounds great, right? But let's say that Warner has a wily CEO who decides to produce another 5 million albums without letting the CEO of Universal know about her plan. The total quantity of CDs sold on the market goes up to 75 million, which pushes the price down to $13. However, rather than splitting production equally, Warner is now selling 40 million albums while Universal continues to produce 35 million. As a result, Warner's profits go up to $420 million; Universal's profits are reduced by $35 million because each of the 35 million albums it sells is now going for one dollar less than it was before:

Warner's profits = (40 million × \$13) − \$100 million = \$420 million
Universal's profits = (35 million × \$13) − \$100 million = \$355 million

The CEO of Universal won't be happy. What happens if he responds by sneaking an extra 5 million albums onto the market himself? The total quantity sold will be 80 million, which pushes the price down even further to \$12. Now, each firm is selling 40 million albums, rather than 35 million, for a price that is \$2 less per album:

Profits for each of two firms = (40 million × \$12) − \$100 million = \$380 million

Universal has gained some ground by retaliating, though each label is worse off than it was when it agreed to cooperate by producing 35 million albums each. This logic continues to drive quantity sold up and price down: Now Warner's CEO decides to produce 45 million albums, which would drive price down to \$11 and increase her firm's profits to \$395 million. However, the Universal CEO responds with the same decision, and each firm actually sells 45 million albums at a price of \$10 each, for a lower profit of \$350 million. Competition between oligopolists drives price and profits down to below the monopoly level, just as perfect competition does.

However, unlike perfect competition, oligopolistic competition does not necessarily drive profits all the way down to the efficient level. Remember from Chapter 14, "Monopoly," that monopolists considering whether to produce an additional unit of output need to weigh two effects:

- *Quantity effect:* The increase in total revenue due to the money brought in by the sale of additional units.
- *Price effect:* The decrease in total revenue that occurs because the increase in quantity will push the market price down.

The oligopolist also needs to weigh the quantity and price effects. In an oligopoly:

- When the quantity effect outweighs the price effect, an increase in output will raise a firm's profit level. In this case, profit-maximizing firms will increase their output.
- But when the price effect outweighs the quantity effect, the firm has no incentive to increase output.

For example, consider the next quantity decision faced by Warner's CEO. If she produces another 5 million albums, she'll still make only \$350 million in profits (50 million × \$9 = 45 million × \$10). The quantity effect (selling an extra 5 million units) is exactly canceled out by the price effect (the price is \$1 lower). She has no incentive to increase production.

Universal faces the same decision. Thus, we can predict that both companies will choose to stay at a production level of 45 million albums. The market equilibrium in this competitive duopoly is 90 million albums at a price of \$10.

In reality, of course, there aren't just two big firms in the music business; there are three. But the principle remains exactly the same. Let's work through the example using three firms: Suppose we begin again with the total profit-maximizing monopoly quantity—70 million albums at a price of \$14 each—with output divided equally among the three firms. Each firm produces 23.3 million albums and brings in \$326 million in revenue, minus its fixed costs of \$100 million, for profit of \$226 million.

$$TR - TC$$
$$(23.3 \text{ million} \times \$14) - \$100 \text{ million} = \$226 \text{ million}$$

But each firm has an incentive to raise its own profit if it can, even if it means decreasing the profits of other firms and of the market as a whole. As long as the quantity effect is greater than the price effect, each firm will keep increasing its output.

Now that there are three firms rather than two in the market, the quantity effect for each firm is larger:

- Consider the price and quantity effects for a market split between only two firms. If the two firms are each producing 35 million albums, increasing production by 5 million albums increases an individual firm's output by 5/35 = 14 percent, but it increases total market production by only 5/70 = 7 percent. When market quantity increases from 70 to 75, price falls from $14 to $13. This is a 1/14 = 7 percent decrease in price. Thus, to the individual firm, the quantity effect (14 percent) outweighs the price effect (7 percent).

- Now consider the price and quantity effects for a market split between *three* firms. If the three firms are splitting the total quantity of 70 and are each producing 22.3 million albums, increasing production by 5 million albums increases an individual firm's output by 5/23.3 = 21.5 percent, but it increases total market production by only 5/70 = 7 percent. When market quantity increases from 70 to 75, price falls from $14 to $13. This is a 1/14 = 7 percent decrease in price. Thus, to the individual firm, the quantity effect (21.5 percent) outweighs the price effect (7 percent).

The smaller the increase in total quantity, the smaller the downward effect on market price. Thus, each firm will increase its quantity by more before the quantity effect becomes equal to the price effect. In the three-firm market, the equilibrium quantity for each firm will be 35 million albums. This makes the total market equilibrium quantity 105 million albums and pushes the equilibrium price down to $7. As the number of firms grows larger and larger, the oligopoly market becomes more competitive, and the equilibrium quantity comes closer to the competitive market equilibrium. This effect can be seen in Figure 15-7.

Whatever the number of firms in the market, an oligopolist will continue to increase output up to the quantity at which the positive quantity effect of an additional unit on profits is exactly equal to the negative price effect.

Analyzing an oligopolist's production decision in terms of the price and quantity effects highlights an important general idea: An oligopolist's production decision affects not only its own profits, but those of other firms as well. The profit-raising quantity effect is felt only by the individual firm that decides to produce more; the profit-lowering price effect also affects all other firms in the market. A decision that increases profits for an individual firm lowers combined profits for the market as a whole.

FIGURE 15-7

Demand for albums in different markets

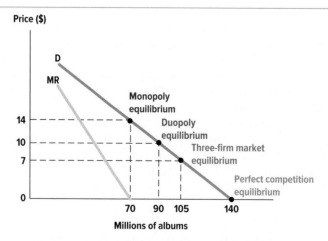

When there is only one firm in the market, the total market quantity is 70 million albums. when two firms split the market, total quantity grows to 90 million, and when three firms split the market total quantity is 105 million. As more firms are added to the market, it moves closer to the efficient quantity.

This is an example of a general economic truth: When an individual (person or firm) reaps all of the benefits and all of the costs of a decision, he (or it) will rationally make an optimal choice. But when a decision imposes costs or benefits on others, an individual's rational choice will not necessarily be optimal for the group. In the case of oligopoly, other firms have to bear the costs of one firm's rational decision to increase output. We'll return to this topic in much more detail in later chapters when we talk about externalities and public goods.

Compete or collude? Using game theory to analyze oligopolies

LO 15.7 Explain how basic tenets of game theory apply to an oligopoly's incentive to compete or collude.

You don't get to be CEO of Warner or Universal if you don't understand how an oligopoly works. You can bet these are smart people who know they are engaged in a strategic "game" in which one's outcomes depend on another's choices. Often, oligopolies face a *prisoners' dilemma,* a situation in which two people (or two firms) make rational choices that lead to a less-than-ideal result for both. (You can review the classic prisoners' dilemma in Chapter 9, "Game Theory and Strategic Thinking.")

The best outcome of the strategic "game" in our two-firm music industry example would be for both firms to produce 35 million albums. However, both firms have an incentive to increase production to 45 million albums. But when both firms produce 45 million albums, they end up worse off than they would have been had each produced only 35 million albums. Thus, the firms act rationally, but then end up worse off.

In our example, the firms have two options: to compete with each other or to join forces and act like a monopolist. The act of working together to make decisions about price and quantity is called **collusion**. As we have seen, when Warner and Universal choose to compete with each other, they end up producing 45 million albums each and making profits of $350 million. If they agree to collude, they will each produce 35 million albums and make $390 million in profits. If collusion can enable firms to earn higher profits, *why isn't everyone doing it?*

When Universal's CEO decides how many albums to produce, he will think strategically and ask himself what Warner's CEO is thinking. What if Universal's CEO thinks that Warner will produce 35 million albums? Look at the payoff matrix in Figure 15-8. Reading across the top row of the matrix, we see that if Warner produces 35 million albums, Universal can make

collusion
the act of working together to make decisions about price and quantity

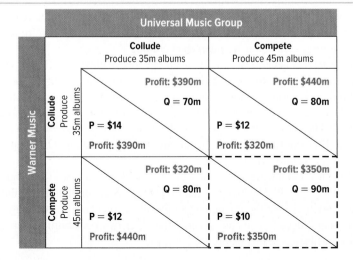

FIGURE 15-8

Oligopoly production as the prisoners' dilemma

Record labels' decision to collude can be modeled as a game called the prisoners' dilemma. Although both firms would be better off if they could agree to collude and produce a lower quantity, each has an incentive to defect from this agreement and earn more profits.

$390 million if it also produces 35 million albums. Alternatively, Universal can make $440 million if it produces 45 million albums when Warner is producing 35 million albums. The right choice for Universal is clear: produce 45 million albums if it believes Warner will produce only 35 million albums.

But what if Universal's CEO thinks that Warner will produce 45 million albums? Reading across the bottom row in Figure 15-8, we see that if Universal makes 35 million albums, it will earn $320 million. Alternatively, if it produces 45 million albums, it will earn $350 million. Again, Universal's choice is clear: produce 45 million albums if it believes that Warner will produce 45 million albums.

Putting this together, we can see that if Universal's CEO believes Warner will produce 35 million albums, Universal should produce 45 million albums. If Universal's CEO believes Warner will produce 45 million albums, Universal should produce 45 million albums. Looking at his options, the CEO of Universal will conclude that *no matter what Warner decides to do,* Universal should compete and produce 45 million albums. When one strategy is always the best for a player to choose, regardless of what other players do, we call it a **dominant strategy**. In this example, competition (rather than collusion) is a dominant strategy for Universal.

Now, consider the decision from Warner's point of view. If Warner expects Universal to produce the lower, "collusion" quantity, Warner can earn $50 million more in profit by competing than by colluding. (How do we know? Compare Warner's profit in the top left square of Figure 15-8 to those in the bottom left square.) If Warner expects Universal to produce the higher, "competitive" quantity, Warner still earns more profit by competing than by sincerely sticking to the collusion agreement. (Compare the $350 million of the bottom right square to the $320 million of the top right square.) We can conclude that Warner also has a dominant strategy in this game: Choosing to compete is always better for Warner *no matter what Universal chooses to do.*

Looking at the strategic decision illustrated in Figure 15-8, two things stand out. First, as we've already calculated, both firms do worse when they both choose to compete with each other than when they both choose to collude. By competing, they drive quantity sold above the profit-maximizing monopoly level that would be achieved by collusion.

Second, each firm has an incentive to renege on a collusion deal and compete, regardless of what the other firm does. In other words, both firms have a dominant strategy, and that strategy is to compete. As a result, both firms will choose to compete rather than collude, producing 45 million albums and making only $350 million in profits.

Oligopolies and Nash equilibriums

When all players in a game have a dominant strategy, the result is called a **Nash equilibrium**. It is an outcome in which all players choose the best strategy they can, given the choices of all other players. A Nash equilibrium is significant because when it is reached, no one has an incentive to break the equilibrium by changing his strategy. (A Nash equilibrium can be reached even when firms don't have a dominant strategy, but in the music industry example we're using, each does have a dominant strategy—to compete rather than collude.)

Not all games have a Nash equilibrium. Consider a soccer player kicking a penalty kick. He can either kick the soccer ball to the left side of the goal or to the right side of the goal. The goalie faces a similar decision; he can either defend the left side of the goal or the right side of the goal. If the player kicks the ball to the right and the goalie also defends that side of the goal, the kick is blocked. The goalie is happy with his decision, but the kicker wishes he had kicked a different direction. If he could do it again, he has an *incentive to switch his behavior.* Thus, they have not reached a Nash equilibrium.

Similarly, if the kicker kicks the ball to the right but the goalie defends the opposite side of the goal, the kicker scores a point. The kicker is happy with his decision, but the goalie would prefer to change his strategy. Because the goalie has an incentive to change his strategy, this situation is also not a Nash equilibrium. You can consider the other two possibilities, and you'll see that there is no Nash equilibrium in this game.

dominant strategy
a strategy that is the best one for a player to follow no matter what strategy other players choose

Nash equilibrium
an equilibrium reached when all players choose the best strategy they can, given the choices of all other players. It is a situation wherein, given the consequences, the player has no regrets about his or her decision.

HINT

There are three important things to remember about a Nash equilibrium:

- If all players have a dominant strategy, then playing the dominant strategy results in a Nash equilibrium.
- If not all players have a dominant strategy, then a Nash equilibrium may or may not exist.
- Not all games have a Nash equilibrium.

In a Nash equilibrium, no player has an incentive to break the equilibrium by changing his or her strategy. In a prisoners' dilemma, this means that the players are stuck in a less-than-ideal outcome. In our oligopoly example, each firm would prefer that they *both* choose to collude. But Warner cannot force Universal to collude; similarly, Universal cannot force Warner to collude. Thus, once in the Nash equilibrium, there is no way for either firm to change its own strategy in a way that increases its profit.

However, as described in Chapter 9, "Game Theory and Strategic Thinking," there *is* a way out of this dilemma for the two CEOs. The key is to remember that many decisions are made not once, but over and over again between the same set of firms. Universal and Warner are not playing this game just once; the game will be repeated many times.

Once the Universal CEO considers that the interaction is a "repeated game," his incentives change. If he reneges on the deal while the CEO of Warner keeps her word, he will gain $50 million in profit for this year. But he will be sure that Warner will retaliate *next year* by going back to the competitive production levels. He therefore knows Universal will lose $40 million in profit *every year thereafter;* the firm will earn $350 million in the competitive equilibrium rather than $390 million in the collusion equilibrium. With *future* profits in mind, both companies may take an initial chance that the other will hold up its end of an initial agreement to collude. If both stand firm, they may keep cooperating, each producing 35 million albums, year after year.

This sort of strategy is often the glue that holds firms together in a **cartel**—a number of firms that collude to make collective production decisions about quantities or prices. A well-known cartel is the Organization of the Petroleum Exporting Countries (OPEC). Member countries agree to limit the amount of petroleum they produce in order to manipulate the market price and maximize their profits. Each member country knows it is in its *long-term* interest to collude rather than compete. That knowledge is enough to keep OPEC together. Interest in future profits dissuades any individual country from chasing short-term profits by producing more oil in any given year. Although OPEC does not control all of the global supply of oil, it is a powerful force in global oil prices.

cartel
a number of firms that collude to make collective production decisions about quantities or prices

If cartels are so advantageous for firms operating in an oligopoly, why don't we see more of them? There's a pretty straightforward reason: They're usually illegal. No international court has the power to force OPEC to stop colluding in the global oil market. Most countries, however, do have laws against firms making agreements about prices or quantities. If firms are caught circumventing those laws, they can be fined and punished.

Oligopoly and public policy

LO 15.8 Compare the welfare of producers, consumers, and society as a whole in an oligopoly to monopoly and perfect competition.

We saw in Chapter 14, "Monopoly," that the United States has strict laws prohibiting "anti-competitive" behavior. It is even illegal for an oligopolist to *offer* to collude, regardless of whether the collusion actually happens. The reason lawmakers are so concerned about collusion, of course, is that while it's good for the oligopolists, it's bad for the rest of us. In our hypothetical example, when Warner and Universal are colluding, the price of albums is $14. When they are competing, the price is only $10. The music-buying public is better off if Warner and Universal compete rather than collude.

Remember that in a monopoly, there is deadweight loss—a welfare loss caused by the transactions that did not take place because the market equilibrium was at a higher price and lower quantity than would be efficient. Figure 15-9 compares the producer surplus, consumer surplus, and deadweight loss under varying amounts of competition. Note that the last two graphs—collusion and monopoly—are identical. Because the market outcomes in a competitive oligopoly are between those of a monopoly and a perfectly competitive market, deadweight loss still exists, but it is lower than when there is collusion.

It's no wonder governments are so keen to prevent firms from colluding, and no wonder firms are so keen to collude without being caught. In 1960, for example, the U.S. government reviewed its annual records for bids it had received when it invited companies to supply certain types of heavy machinery. Government agencies discovered that 47 manufacturers had submitted *identical* bids for the previous three years of bidding. This showed that the manufacturers were secretly colluding on their bids. They were taking turns to submit the lowest bid, at a price that would be much higher than if they were actually competing. It is estimated that the cartel, until it was broken up, cost U.S. taxpayers $175 million each year.

FIGURE 15-9

Deadweight loss under varying amounts of competition

Perfect competition represents one end of the deadweight loss spectrum, and collusion/monopoly represents the other. A competitive oligopoly falls somewhere in between. There is less deadweight loss than in the case of collusion or monopoly, but it does not eliminate deadweight loss in the way that perfect competition does.

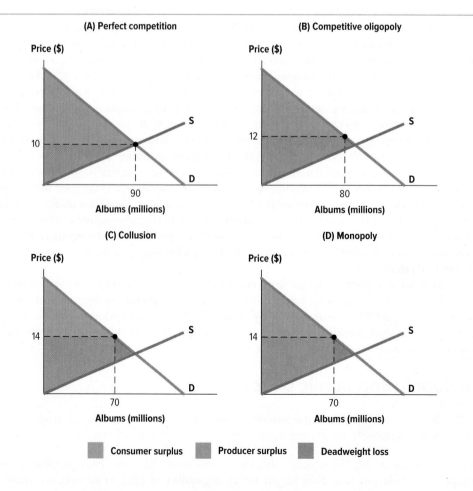

✓ CONCEPT CHECK

☐ Why is the equilibrium in an oligopolistic market less efficient than a competitive market? **[LO 15.6]**

☐ Why would two companies in an oligopoly benefit from colluding? **[LO 15.7]**

☐ Why would it be difficult for companies to collude, even if doing so were legal? **[LO 15.7]**

☐ Why are firms more easily able to collude in a repeated game than in a game played just once? **[LO 15.7]**

☐ What happens to deadweight loss as the number of firms in an oligopolistic market increases? **[LO 15.8]**

Conclusion

In previous chapters, we've explored two opposite ends of the spectrum of market structures: perfect competition and monopoly. In this chapter, we've moved to the gray area in between, learning about imperfect competition and the characteristics of industries that fall into the categories of monopolistic competition and oligopoly. Knowing about these market structures helps business owners make optimal decisions about production and pricing. Such knowledge also helps consumers make sense of firms' behavior and the abundance of advertising they see in the real world.

Market structure can tell us a lot about how firms make decisions, but there are still a number of other factors that we haven't explored yet. Up until now, we've focused on the amount of any given good that firms choose to produce. In the next chapter, we'll see how markets for the factors of production play an important role in *how* firms choose to produce goods.

Key Terms

oligopoly, p. 359

monopolistic competition, p. 360

product differentiation, p. 361

collusion, p. 375

dominant strategy, p. 376

Nash equilibrium, p. 376

cartel, p. 377

Summary

LO 15.1 Name the defining features of oligopoly and monopolistic competition.

Most markets in the real world don't fit perfectly into any one model of market structure. It can, though, be useful to categorize markets in terms of the number of firms and product variety. *Oligopoly* describes a market with only a few firms that sell a similar good or service. In this setting, firms tend to know their competition and each firm has some price-setting power, but no one has total market control. *Monopolistic competition,* in contrast, describes a market with many firms that sell goods and services that are similar, but slightly different. These firms are not

necessarily price takers, but they still face competition in the long run.

LO 15.2 Calculate the profit-maximizing price and quantity for a monopolistically competitive firm in the short run.

In the short run, monopolistically competitive firms behave just like monopolists. They face a downward-sloping demand curve and cannot change price without causing a change in the quantity consumers demand. The profit-maximizing production quantity is at the point where the marginal revenue (MR) curve intersects the marginal cost (MC) curve. The profit-maximizing price is determined by the point on the demand curve that corresponds to this quantity.

LO 15.3 Describe a monopolistically competitive market in the long run.

In the long run, monopolistic competition has some features in common with monopoly and other features in common with perfect competition. Just like a monopoly, a monopolistically competitive firm faces a downward-sloping demand curve, which means that marginal revenue is less than price. This in turn means that marginal cost is also less than price. Like a firm in a perfectly competitive market, however, a monopolistically competitive firm earns zero economic profit in the long run.

LO 15.4 Analyze the welfare costs of monopolistic competition.

Like any deviation from the equilibrium price and quantity that would prevail under perfect competition, monopolistic competition is inefficient. Because firms maximize profit at a price that is higher than marginal cost, some mutually beneficial trades never occur. This means that there is deadweight loss—the market does not maximize total surplus. However, regulating monopolistically competitive markets to increase efficiency is difficult, and usually comes at the expense of product variety.

LO 15.5 Explain how product differentiation motivates advertising and branding.

Producers invest in advertising to convince consumers that their products are different from other similar products. The less substitutable a good seems with other goods, the less likely consumers are to switch to other products if the price increases. Thus, producers have an incentive to differentiate their products—either by making them truly different or by convincing consumers that they are different. Through advertising and branding, firms either explicitly give the desired information to the consumer or signal the quality of their products.

LO 15.6 Describe the strategic production decision of firms in an oligopoly.

Oligopolists make strategic decisions about price and quantity that take into account the expected choices of their competitors. Unlike price-taking firms in a competitive market, an oligopolist produces a quantity that affects the market price. The increase in total revenue due to the money brought in by the sale of additional units of output is called the *quantity effect*. The decrease in total revenue that occurs because the increase in quantity will push the market price down is called the *price effect*.

Typically, an oligopolistic firm will increase output until the positive quantity effect outweighs the negative price effect.

LO 15.7 Explain how basic tenets of game theory apply to an oligopoly's incentive to compete or collude.

An oligopolist has an incentive to produce more output than is profit maximizing for the market as a whole, driving down price and imposing costs on its competitors. By colluding, firms can maximize industry profits by producing the equivalent monopoly quantity and splitting revenues. However, each firm involved always has an incentive to renege on the agreement since a firm could earn higher profits by competing.

An outcome in which all players choose the best strategy they can, given the choices of all other players, is called a *Nash equilibrium*. If all players in a game have a dominant strategy, then a Nash equilibrium will occur when they play their dominant strategies. However, a Nash equilibrium can also arise even if no players have a dominant strategy. When a Nash equilibrium is reached, no one has an incentive to break the equilibrium by changing his strategy. However, if firms recognize their production decisions as a repeated game, with *future* profits in mind, a firm may take an initial chance that the other firm will hold up its end of an initial agreement to collude. This sort of strategy often holds firms together in a cartel.

LO 15.8 Compare the welfare of producers, consumers, and society as a whole in an oligopoly to monopoly and perfect competition.

The competitive equilibrium in an oligopoly leads to a quantity and price that are somewhere between the outcomes of a perfectly competitive market and those of a monopoly. Because the equilibrium is not the same as in a competitive market, oligopoly results in some deadweight loss and increases producer surplus at the expense of consumer surplus. When oligopolists collude, the equilibrium looks like a monopoly outcome and results in even higher deadweight loss and higher producer surplus.

Review Questions

1. Explain why an oligopolist (with few competitors) pays more attention to what its competitors are doing than a producer in a competitive market (with many competitors) does. **[LO 15.1]**

2. If a market has few barriers to entry and many firms, how might firms still have positive economic profit? Describe a strategy a firm in this type of market might use to maintain economic profits. **[LO 15.1]**

3. McDonald's, Burger King, and Wendy's all produce hamburgers, among other things. However, if you prefer burgers from McDonald's, you might consider other burgers an imperfect substitute. With this in mind, how would you expect McDonald's to set its prices in the short run? Describe the relationship between price, marginal revenue, and marginal cost. **[LO 15.2]**

4. Consider Jimmy Choo designer shoes. In what way does Jimmy Choo face many competitors? In what way does Jimmy Choo face no competitors? **[LO 15.2]**

5. Restaurants offer related but differentiated products to their consumers. In the long run, new restaurants enter the market and imitate the cuisine and atmosphere of successful competitors. How would you expect a restaurant to set its prices in the long run? Describe the relationship between price and average total cost. Does a restaurant earn economic profits? **[LO 15.3]**

6. In both perfectly competitive and monopolistically competitive markets, when firms are making positive economic profits, other firms will enter until price equals ATC and profits are zero. Despite these similarities, in a perfectly competitive market total surplus is maximized, while in a monopolistically competitive market surplus is not maximized. Explain this difference. **[LO 15.3]**

7. Suppose a perfectly competitive market for hot-dog stands in New York City becomes monopolistically competitive when gourmet, discount, and ethnic hot-dog retailers show up, making each cart slightly different. If hot dogs from different stands are now imperfect substitutes and there are numerous carts in the city, compare the producer and consumer surplus and total social welfare before and after the change. **[LO 15.4]**

8. Given that the market for smartphones is inefficient, explain why consumers of smartphones might not want the price to be regulated. **[LO 15.4]**

9. Imagine that you have a program on your cell phone that allows you to walk up to any item in the supermarket and have your phone recognize it and display all the necessary information about the product. The program tells you where and how it is made, and when it is predicted to go on sale next. Does a firm selling goods in this setting need to advertise? Why or why not? **[LO 15.5]**

10. Why might the cost of advertising be relevant to a consumer's decision about which brand of a product to purchase? **[LO 15.5]**

11. Suppose that the market for e-readers is an oligopoly controlled by Amazon, Barnes and Noble, Sony, and Apple. Barnes and Noble is considering increasing its output. How would this affect the market price? How would it affect the profits of each company? **[LO 15.6]**

12. Compare the efficiency of perfectly competitive markets, monopoly markets, and oligopoly markets. Explain why the same profit-maximizing behavior for the individual firm leads to different levels of efficiency in these three types of markets. **[LO 15.6]**

13. The Organization of the Petroleum Exporting Countries (OPEC) is a cartel of 12 countries that controls roughly two-thirds of the world's oil production. The cartel gives countries quotas for production. Why might a country be tempted to produce above quota for a year? How do you think other OPEC countries might respond if it did so? **[LO 15.7]**

14. Isabella runs an IT solutions business for her college peers and has only one competitor, Franco. Isabella and Franco have decided to collude and provide monopoly-level output. Given that they are both freshmen and intend to run their businesses for the next three years, is this agreement sustainable? Would your answer change if Franco knew he planned to transfer to another college next year? **[LO 15.7]**

15. The U.S. Postal Service (USPS) has a government monopoly on home mail delivery, but several private companies, such as FedEx, UPS, and DHL, compete with the USPS for other types of delivery service. Describe the differences in producer and consumer surplus, and in overall social welfare, that would occur in each of the following scenarios. **[LO 15.8]**

    a. The USPS has a monopoly on every type of mail or package.

    b. Consumers are allowed to choose between USPS, UPS, FedEx, and DHL for home mail delivery.

    c. There are an infinite number of local and national mail providers.

16. Explain why government is usually more concerned about regulating an oligopoly than a monopolistically competitive market. **[LO 15.8]**

Problems and Applications

1. Identify whether each of the following markets has few or many producers, and uniform or differentiated products. Which market is an oligopoly? Which market is monopolistically competitive? **[LO 15.1]**

    a. College education.

    b. Retail gas market.

2. Match the statement about goods sold in a market with the market type. **[LO 15.1]**

    a. There are imperfect substitutes for the goods.

    b. There are no substitutes for the goods.

    c. The goods may or may not be standardized.

3. Interscope sells the music of Lady Gaga, who promotes a unique public image and fashion style. Given her huge success, it is likely that by the end of the coming year, multiple performers will be imitating or borrowing heavily from her style. Suppose the current period's supply and demand for Lady Gaga MP3s is given in Figure 15P-1. **[LO 15.2, 15.3]**
    a. Identify the profit-maximizing price and quantity for Lady Gaga MP3s on the graph. What are the values for the profit-maximizing price and quantity in the short run?
    b. In the long run, what happens to the demand curve?
    c. In the long run, what happens to the profit-maximizing price?

4. Figure 15P-2 shows the monopolistically competitive market for smartphones. **[LO 15.3]**
    a. Plot the profit-maximizing price and quantity on the graph. Is this producer earning positive or negative profits in the short run?
    b. In the long run, will supply or demand for this producer's good be affected? Will economic profits increase or decrease for this producer?

5. Figure 15P-3 shows a monopolistically competitive market for a fictional brand of shampoo called SqueakyKleen. **[LO 15.4]**
    a. What are the price and quantity of SqueakyKleen in the short run?
    b. What are the efficient price and quantity of SqueakyKleen?
    c. Draw the deadweight loss.

6. The marginal costs (MC), average variable costs (AVC), and average total costs (ATC) for a monopolistically competitive firm are shown in Figure 15P-4. **[LO 15.4]**
    a. Plot the profit-maximizing price and quantity on the graph.
    b. Is this firm earning zero, positive, or negative profits? Why?
    c. Is this firm in a long-run equilibrium?

7. For which good would you expect deadweight loss to be smaller relative to the total surplus in its market: Burger King hamburgers or Lady Gaga MP3s? Explain your answer. **[LO 15.4]**

8. For which product would you expect producers to have a stronger reaction to a ban on advertising: music artists or fast-food burgers? Explain your answer. **[LO 15.5]**

FIGURE 15P-1

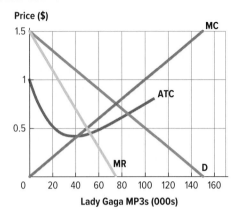

FIGURE 15P-2

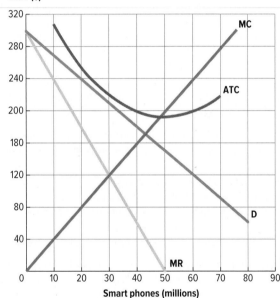

FIGURE 15P-3

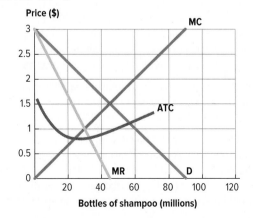

FIGURE 15P-4

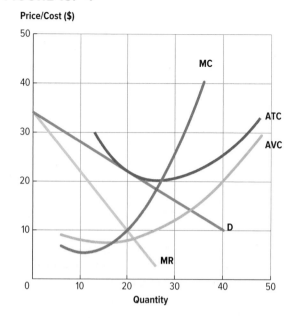

Price/Cost ($)

FIGURE 15P-5

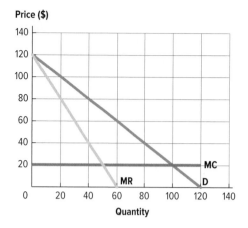

Price ($)

9. Suppose you manage a firm in a monopolistically competitive market. Which of the following strategies will do a better job of helping you maintain economic profits: obtaining a celebrity endorsement for your product or supporting the entry of firms that will compete directly with your biggest rival? Explain your answer. **[LO 15.5]**

10. Table 15P-1 shows the monthly demand schedule for a good in a duopoly market. The two producers in this

TABLE 15P-1

Quantity	Price ($)	Total revenue ($)	Marginal revenue ($)
0	40	0	—
200	35	7,000	35
400	30	12,000	25
600	25	15,000	15
800	20	16,000	5
1,000	15	15,000	−5
1,200	10	12,000	−15
1,400	5	7,000	−25
1,600	0	0	−35

market each faces $5,000 of fixed costs per month. There are no marginal costs. **[LO 15.6]**

   a. What is the monthly profit for each duopolist if they evenly split the quantity a monopolist would produce?

   b. Suppose duopolist A decides to increase production by 200 units. How much will each duopolist produce and what price will they charge? How much profit will each duopolist earn?

11. Figure 15P-5 shows the monthly demand curve for a good in a duopoly market. There are no fixed costs. **[LO 15.6]**

   a. What is the monthly profit for each duopolist if they evenly split the quantity a monopolist would produce?

   b. What is the deadweight loss if the duopolists evenly split the quantity a monopolist would produce?

   c. What is the monthly profit for duopolist A and duopolist B if duopolist A decides to increase production by 10 units?

   d. What is the deadweight loss if duopolist A increases production by 10 units?

12. Oil Giant and Local Oil are the only two producers in a market, as shown in Figure 15P-6. They have an agreement to restrict oil output in order to keep prices high. **[LO 15.7]**

   a. What is the dominant strategy for each player?

   b. If this game is played once, what is the Nash equilibrium?

   c. Now suppose that both players know that the game will be played multiple times. What outcome would we expect?

FIGURE 15P-6

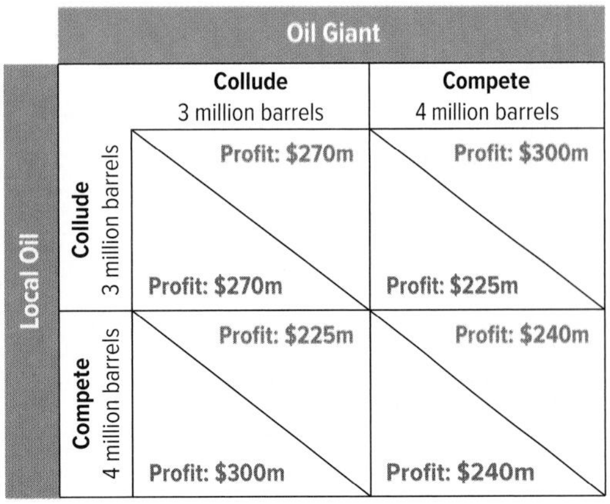

FIGURE 15P-7

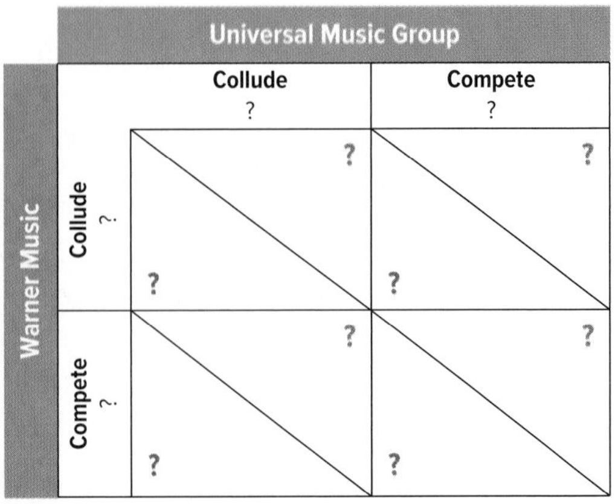

13. Suppose Warner Music and Universal Music are in a duopoly and currently limit themselves to 10 new artists per year. One artist sells 2 million songs at $1.25 per song. However, each label is capable of signing 20 artists per year. If one label increases the number of artists to 20 and the other stays the same, the price per song drops to $0.75, and each artist sells 3 million songs. If both labels increase the number of artists to 20, the price per song drops to $0.30, and each artist sells 4 million songs. **[LO 15.7]**

   a. Fill in the revenue payoffs for each scenario in Figure 15P-7.

   b. If this game is played once, how many artists will each producer sign, and what will be the price of a song?

   c. If this game is played every year, how many artists will each producer sign, and what will be the price of a song?

14. Suppose a new product is developed and is supplied by a monopolist with a patent. Compared with the monopoly outcome, indicate whether consumer surplus, producer surplus, and total surplus increase, decrease, or remain the same under the following scenarios. **[LO 15.8]**

   a. Another producer creates a similar product and colludes with the original producer.

   b. Another producer creates a similar product and competes with the original producer.

   c. The patent expires.

15. For which of the following markets would there be a greater increase in total welfare if government were able to intervene and regulate prices: OPEC or the music industry? Explain your answer. **[LO 15.8]**

Endnotes

1. http://www.musicbusinessworldwide.com/independent-label-us-market-share-trounces-universal-sony-warner/

2. http://www.peterjalexander.com/images/Market_Structure_and_Product_Variety.PDF; http://www.jstor.org/stable/2096413?seq=1#page_scan_tab_contents.

3. http://query.nytimes.com/gst/fullpage.html?res=9A04E4DD173FF935A25757C0A96F9C8B63&ref=dominos-pizza-inc.

The Factors of Production

Learning Objectives

LO 16.1 Describe how factors of production contribute to output.

LO 16.2 Graph the demand curve for a factor of production and explain its relationship to marginal productivity.

LO 16.3 Graph the supply curve for a factor of production and explain what determines the supply of labor.

LO 16.4 Explain how to find the equilibrium price and quantity for a factor of production.

LO 16.5 Use graphs to demonstrate the effect of a shift in labor supply or labor demand and describe what causes these curves to shift.

LO 16.6 Explain the importance of human capital in the labor market.

LO 16.7 Describe the similarities and differences between the markets for land and capital and the market for labor.

LO 16.8 Describe two reasons why a wage might rise above the market equilibrium and how this affects the labor market.

LO 16.9 Describe several causes of imperfectly competitive labor markets and their effect on workers and employers.

THE FIELDS OF CALIFORNIA

In 2016, baseball pitcher Clayton Kershaw earned a base salary of $32 million a year, plus another $2.5 million in signing bonus, playing for the Los Angeles Dodgers. The contract he signed with the Dodgers in 2014 guarantees him $215 million over seven years. At the same time, another group of workers were also engaged in tough, physical work—but they earned a lot less money. California's tens of thousands of agricultural workers earned an average annual salary of just over $34,000 in 2015.[1]

Of course, there are many, many differences between baseball and farm work. On a superficial level, though, baseball players have something in common with farm laborers. They are both

© Harry How/Getty Images

mostly young men in their 20s and 30s, many of whom were born outside the United States. They do hard, physical, seasonal work, and they train on the job rather than in school.[2]

So, why does Clayton Kershaw make almost 1,000 times more money than someone who prunes orange trees or picks tomatoes? For that matter, why does Kershaw make so much more than other Major League Baseball players? (Don't feel too sorry for the others; their average salary is still over $4 million a year.) Why do baseball players make more than other professional athletes, whose average salary is about $105,000?[3]

We suspect that you intuitively know the answer to these questions. When he signed his huge contract with the Dodgers, Clayton Kershaw was one of the top pitchers in baseball. Of course he gets paid a lot! Not just anyone can do what he does. The same thing goes for professional baseball players in general. If there are only a thousand people in the entire country who have a particular skill, they can demand a lot of money to do what *only* they can do.

Furthermore, Americans like to watch baseball, and they're willing to pay to see it played well. We like tomatoes and oranges too, but if farm workers earned millions of dollars a year, consumers would have to be willing to pay a lot more for dinner. Similarly, the very best professional racquetball player in California makes far less money than Clayton Kershaw. That happens not necessarily because he is less skilled or because there is a larger supply of great racquetball players, but because sports fans simply aren't willing to pay as much to watch racquetball.

The economic reasoning behind this intuition is that labor—whether slugging, pitching, fielding, or harvesting—is an ingredient in producing a good that consumers want, such as a baseball game or a tomato. The labor that goes into producing these goods is bought and sold in a way that is tied to the market for the goods themselves. The price that workers are paid depends both on the number of people who are able to supply that type of labor and on the demand for the goods that are produced with it.

In this chapter we'll discuss the markets for *factors of production*. Economists usually lump the factors of production into three categories: labor, land, and capital. We'll see how prices in the markets for factors of production are determined by markets for consumer goods as well as by public policy. Seeing how supply and demand govern factor markets enables us to understand how firms make decisions about how much of which factors to use. This choice is important for any business owner: Is it worth buying a new machine or hiring another employee? How can you know?

Understanding factor markets—particularly labor markets—is also a key to explaining people's income. We'll describe how ownership of different factors of production affects income and why people earn different amounts. This chapter is thus a building block for understanding income inequality. Since the majority of people make their living primarily by selling their labor, we'll focus on understanding the differences between the wages people earn. What differentiates Clayton Kershaw from a farm worker, a professional racquetball player, a plumber, or you? This chapter will leave you with tools for understanding labor markets as a worker, a boss, or a voter.

The Factors of Production: Land, Labor, and Capital

LO 16.1 Describe how factors of production contribute to output.

When you buy a ticket to a baseball game, what are you really paying for? A baseball game requires the time and skills of players and of managers, umpires, coaches, ticket collectors, food vendors, and janitors. It also requires a ballpark and a parking lot, training facilities, loudspeakers, jumbo screens, balls and gloves, and other equipment.

The ingredients that go into making a baseball game, or a tomato, or any other good or service, are called **factors of production**. We can think about three different types of factors—labor, land, and capital:

- *Labor* is the time employees spend working.
- *Land* is the place where employees work.
- **Capital** refers to manufactured goods that are used to produce new goods. The capital needed to produce a baseball game includes equipment like bats, lights, uniforms, and video screens. The capital needed to produce a tomato includes seeds, fertilizer, irrigation equipment, and trucks to transport harvested tomatoes.

factors of production
the ingredients that go into making a good or service

capital
manufactured goods that are used to produce new goods

Factors of production are bought and sold in markets, in much the same way as the goods they go into producing. The sellers in factor markets are people who own the factors of production. The buyers are firms that want to use the factors to produce goods and services. The price of each factor is determined by supply and demand.

In this section, we'll describe the production decisions that drive factor markets and make them slightly different from other markets. We'll see how factor markets are tied to markets for consumer goods, and how each factor's contribution to production is measured. These are tools that you will need in order to figure out how businesses make production decisions, and, ultimately, to see why baseball players are paid more than farm workers.

Derived demand

How does a firm decide how much of each factor of production it wants to use? The Los Angeles Dodgers wanted—and were willing to pay for—Kershaw's labor because it would help them win baseball games. That, in turn, would raise the value of tickets and broadcast rights to baseball games, which are then supplied to fans. The demand for baseball players is "derived" from a team's choice to supply games; that demand depends on how much individual players contribute to the value of the end product.

Likewise, consider a farmer who wants to produce tomatoes: He will need to decide whether to buy a field that could be used to grow tomatoes, how many workers to employ to pick tomatoes, or whether to invest in new irrigation equipment. As he makes such decisions, he will consider the market for tomatoes. Farmers' demand for good tomato-growing land, tomato pickers, and irrigation equipment is *derived from* the market for tomatoes. If consumers want more tomatoes, demand for the factors of production that go into tomatoes will increase. If they want fewer tomatoes, demand for those factors of production will decrease. For this reason, the demand for factors of production is referred to as *derived demand.*

Marginal productivity

marginal product
the increase in output that is generated by an additional unit of input

In Chapter 12, "The Costs of Production," we discussed *production functions,* which describe the relationship between the quantity of inputs a firm uses and the resulting quantity of outputs. For example, a farm that hires more workers can produce more tomatoes. The increase in output that is generated by an additional unit of input is called **marginal product**.

Graphically, we can think of the marginal product of a factor as the slope of the total production curve, with output measured on the *y*-axis and the quantity of the input measured on the *x*-axis. Figure 16-1 shows the marginal product of labor in tomato production. The change in the quantity of tomatoes produced due to hiring one additional worker is the *marginal product of labor* for that worker. Marginal product also applies to the other factors of production: land and capital.

Recall that inputs usually have diminishing marginal productivity. In other words, for a given amount of land, the 10th farm worker will generally contribute less to a farm's output than the first worker. This fact will become important as we describe the demand for labor.

Picking the right combination of inputs

In some cases, firms can choose what combination of factors to use, substituting one for another. For instance, picking tomatoes can be done either by hand or by machine. A farmer can choose to hire many workers and buy no machinery, or hire fewer workers and buy more machinery. (Note that this trade-off doesn't work for all goods: You can't choose to produce a baseball game by having fewer players and more bats.)

FIGURE 16-1

Marginal product of labor

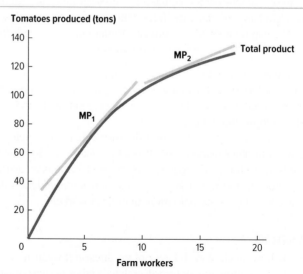

The more workers a farm employs, the more tomatoes the farm can harvest. Hiring an additional farm worker adds fewer tomatoes to the harvest than were added with the previous worker. As the number of workers increases, total production increases, but the marginal product of labor diminishes.

A profit-seeking firm will choose the combination of inputs that *maximizes profit,* based on the local price of each factor of production. The price of farm machinery is similar all over the world, but the cost of farm labor varies more widely. In poorer economies, labor is usually cheap, so farmers tend to hire lots of workers and buy fewer machines. In rich countries, labor costs more, so farmers tend to hire fewer workers and buy more machines. Another way of saying this is that farming tends to be *labor-intensive* in poor countries and *capital-intensive* in rich countries.

✓CONCEPT CHECK

- ☐ Give examples of each of the factors of production that are used in an auto repair shop. **[LO 16.1]**
- ☐ What is labor demand "derived" from? **[LO 16.1]**
- ☐ What is the relationship between a worker's marginal product and a firm's total output? **[LO 16.1]**

Labor Markets and Wages

We now have some concepts to use when thinking about the markets for factors of production. We'll use them to take a closer look at the markets for labor and capital. Before we start, though, there are a couple of things to mention, which will help as you learn about the market for labor.

First, remember that individuals who work are the "suppliers" of labor. Firms that produce goods using those workers are the "buyers" of labor. This is the reverse of the usual market situation, in which we think of firms as suppliers and individual people as buyers.

Second, the wage that workers earn is the "price" of labor. We rarely use the word *price* when talking about people and their skills. But wages play exactly the same role in labor markets as prices do in markets for goods and services. In the labor market, the terms *wage* and *price* mean exactly the same thing: Wages are simply the price of labor.

We'll start by considering the demand for labor.

Demand for labor

> **LO 16.2** Graph the demand curve for a factor of production and explain its relationship to marginal productivity.

Let's consider how a tomato farmer decides how many workers to employ. For simplicity, we'll assume that the tomato farm is a profit-maximizing firm in a competitive market. That makes sense when there are many different tomato farms, each a price taker in the market for selling tomatoes and in the market for hiring farm workers. Let's also assume for now that all farm workers are equally productive.

What determines the number of workers the farm hires? Consider the owner's *wants and constraints*. The owner wants to maximize the farm's profit. Remember that a firm in a competitive market maximizes profits by producing the quantity at which the revenue it earns from the last unit is equal to the cost of producing that unit. So, a tomato farm wants to produce tomatoes up to the point where the marginal revenue from the last ton is equal to the marginal cost of producing that ton.

Since the farm is a price taker in a competitive market, the farmer cannot control the going price of tomatoes. Nor can he control the going wage of tomato pickers. Both of those factors— prices of goods and workers' wages—affect how much profit the farmer will make. Therefore, maximizing profit boils down to making the right choice about the quantity to produce.

If we leave land, tractors, and other inputs fixed at a certain level, the farm's output will be determined by the number of workers hired and each worker's marginal productivity. Table 16-1 shows relevant data for a single hypothetical farm. For any number of workers (in column 1), the table tells us the quantity of tomatoes produced (column 3) and the marginal cost of hiring the last worker (in column 6). That marginal cost of the last worker is the worker's annual wage; in this example, it is $20,000 for each worker.

Each worker hired adds something to total production—that worker's *marginal product of labor (MPL)*. In other words, the MPL is the quantity of additional output generated by the worker (shown in column 2). You can see that the marginal product of labor diminishes with each added worker. The first group of workers is able to harvest lots of tomatoes. As more and more workers come to the farm, they start to get in each other's way, and marginal productivity decreases.

The question of how much labor a firm will hire comes down to whether added workers are going to generate more revenue than what it costs to pay them. Therefore, we want to find the *marginal revenue* associated with each worker. If the worker brings in more revenue than it costs to pay him or her, the worker should be hired.

value of the marginal product
the increase in revenue generated by the last unit of an input; calculated as the output generated by an input (marginal product) times the unit price of the output

To find the marginal revenue of an additional worker, we multiply the worker's marginal product of labor (shown in column 2) by the market price of tomatoes (column 4). In doing so, we translate the worker's marginal product into a dollar value (as shown in column 5 of the table). This is shown in Equation 16-1.

EQUATION 16-1   Value of marginal product (VMP) = Marginal product × Price of output

We call this increase in revenue the **value of the marginal product**. It is calculated as the output generated by an additional unit of input times the price of the output. (The VMP is also

TABLE 16-1

Labor productivity and cost

(1) **# of workers (L)**	(2) **Marginal product of labor***	(3) **Tomatoes produced (Y)**	(4) **Price ($) of tomatoes (P)**	(5) **Value ($) of marginal product†**	(6) **Annual wage ($) (W)**	(7) **Marginal profit ($)††**
0	0 tons/worker	0 tons	2,000 per ton	0	20,000	—
1	15	15	2,000	30,000	20,000	10,000
2	14	29	2,000	28,000	20,000	8,000
3	13	42	2,000	26,000	20,000	6,000
4	12	54	2,000	24,000	20,000	4,000
5	11	65	2,000	22,000	20,000	2,000
6	10	75	2,000	20,000	20,000	0
7	9	84	2,000	18,000	20,000	−2,000
8	8	92	2,000	16,000	20,000	−4,000
9	7	99	2,000	14,000	20,000	−6,000

* Marginal product of labor (MPL) = Change in Y/Change in L
† Value of marginal product of labor (VMPL) = MPL × P
†† Marginal profit = VMPL − W

sometimes referred to as the *marginal revenue product.*) For example, the marginal product of the eighth worker hired by the farm is 8 tons of tomatoes, and the going price for tomatoes is $2,000 per ton. The value of the marginal product of the eighth worker would be $8 \times \$2,000 = \$16,000$.

For a competitive firm, the price of the output is always going to be the same. This implies that the value of the marginal product decreases for each additional worker. Why? Because the price of the output stays constant while the marginal product of labor decreases.

We stated earlier that maximizing profit boils down to making the right choice about the quantity to produce. At what number of workers will that occur for the tomato farmer? Column 7 shows the *marginal profit* for each number of workers; that amount is calculated as the value of the marginal product minus the annual wage for each worker. As you can see in the table, hiring three workers definitely makes sense for the farm. The third worker produces $26,000 of tomatoes but costs the farmer only $20,000. Therefore, hiring the third worker yields a marginal profit (column 7) of $6,000. Hiring the next two workers also makes sense for the farm: Each adds more revenue than what he or she is paid in wages.

When should the farmer stop hiring workers? A competitive firm should keep hiring as long as the value of the marginal product is greater than or equal to the marginal cost of the worker (the worker's wage). In our example, the tomato farmer should hire the sixth worker, whose VMP is $20,000. The farmer should not hire the seventh worker, though. That worker adds only $18,000—an amount less than the extra cost of her $20,000 wage.

Figure 16-2 shows in graph form the relationship between the value of the marginal product and the number of farm workers hired. The table in panel A shows the values of the marginal product for each worker, taken from Table 16-1. Panel B plots these numbers onto a graph. You can see that the curve formed by plotting the value of the marginal product for workers is downward-sloping, due to the diminishing marginal product of each additional worker.

What is the profit-maximizing quantity of labor that the farmer decides to hire? We find the answer by seeing where the value of the marginal product of labor intersects the market-wage level. At that point, the value of the last worker's marginal product is greater than or equal to marginal profit.

Note that at any given wage, there is only one profit-maximizing quantity of labor. As wages rise or fall, firms adjust the quantity of labor they demand. We can plot this profit-maximizing

(A) Value of the marginal product

Labor (# workers)	VMPL ($)
1	30,000
2	28,000
3	26,000
4	24,000
5	22,000
6	20,000
7	18,000
8	16,000
9	14,000

(B) VMPL equals labor demand

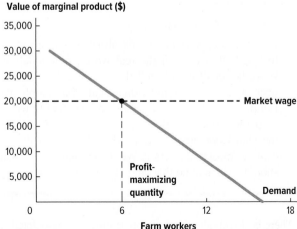

FIGURE 16-2
Value of the marginal product and the demand curve for labor

The value of the marginal product of labor decreases with the number of workers hired. The quantity of labor demanded at any given wage is the quantity at which the value of the marginal product of labor equals the wage. The result is a downward-sloping demand curve, with the quantity of labor demanded increasing as the wage decreases.

quantity for a variety of wages and generate a whole demand curve. This demand curve is the same as the value of the marginal product (VMP) curve: At each point along the demand curve, the wage is equal to the VMP of the last worker hired and therefore corresponds to a point on the VMP curve.

The curve shown in Figure 16-2 is just one demand curve—the demand curve for the tomato farmer. It's straightforward, though, to find the labor demand curve for the entire tomato market: Add up the quantities of labor demanded by all firms in the market, just as we did with the demand for consumer goods in Chapter 3, "Markets."

Supply of labor

LO 16.3 Graph the supply curve for a factor of production and explain what determines the supply of labor.

As in all markets, the demand for labor tells only half the story. Ultimately, the equilibrium quantity and wage are determined by the interaction of demand and supply. The supply of labor is more complicated than the supply of most goods and services but is still driven by a basic trade-off between the costs and benefits of supplying labor to firms.

Consider the choice made by an individual worker—say, a farm worker in California—who is deciding how many hours to work each week. The main benefit of working is earning a certain wage for every hour of work. Workers can choose to work more in order to earn more money, or they could choose to work less in order to have more time off.

Now, what about the cost side of the trade-off? The "cost" to an individual of supplying her labor is more difficult to calculate than the benefit. Because the worker doesn't need to buy any inputs to "produce" an hour of labor, we can't directly compare the worker's cost of supplying labor to a firm's cost of production.

Instead, we need to *think about the opportunity cost* of supplying another hour of labor. If you work an extra hour, you give up the chance to spend that hour doing something else—such as going for a run, checking Instagram, or doing your laundry. Economists usually categorize all nonwork activities under the term *leisure.* Although they may not seem relaxing or fun, doing chores around the house or errands in town are usually classified as leisure. The cost of working is therefore the forgone opportunity to enjoy leisure.

POTENTIALLY CONFUSING

For simplicity's sake, we talk about people deciding to supply their labor from hour to hour. Of course, in the real world, individuals usually can't set their own hours. A worker can't usually tell the boss that he wants to work 39 or 41 hours this week instead of 40. For an individual, real labor-supply decisions are often whether to work full time, part time, or not at all, and whether to work overtime or take a second job.

It turns out, though, that over an extended period and a large group of workers, the *total* labor supply is quite flexible, and analyzing changes in average hours in fact captures most of the action. We'll continue to talk about workers choosing hours, but you should keep in mind that labor-supply decisions can involve a broader range of choices.

There is also another kind of opportunity cost associated with the choice to work for a particular employer. A person who decides to work an extra hour on a farm gives up the opportunity to spend that hour working at another paying job—say, as a construction worker or bartender. The worker has to decide whether the opportunity cost of *not* working that other job outweighs the benefits of more farm work. In making that decision, he or she will have to consider not only the wages each

FIGURE 16-3
Supply of labor

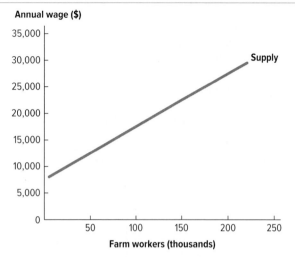

A producer will generally supply more of a good or service as its price rises. The same rule applies to workers who supply their labor, yielding the familiar upward-sloping supply curve.

other job offers but also any other perks of each job. Workers value many benefits like health insurance, a pleasant work environment, and the chance to learn new skills.

The decision to supply another hour of labor depends on the trade-off between the benefits of an hour of work (the wage plus any other perks) and the opportunity cost (lost time for leisure or other kinds of work). If the benefits outweigh the costs, we would expect a person to work an additional hour. This logic holds up to the point where the benefit of another hour of work exactly equals the opportunity cost. At that point, the worker becomes indifferent between spending the next hour on work or leisure.

What happens to the quantity of labor supplied if wages go up? In most markets, when price increases, so does quantity supplied. It makes sense then that when higher wages are being offered, the benefits of work go up, people will want to work more, and the quantity of labor supplied will increase. This relationship is shown in the labor-supply curve drawn in Figure 16-3. The market labor-supply curve would be formed by adding up all of the individual labor-supply curves.

The price and income effects

One important feature of the labor-supply curve, however, makes it different from other supply curves. Although higher wages generally increase the quantity of labor supplied, this is not always true. A higher wage increases the benefit of an additional hour of work, but it also, less obviously, increases the *opportunity cost* of working.

To see why, we have to go back to the individual decision to supply labor. The key to figuring out why opportunity costs increase is the fact that leisure is usually more enjoyable when we have money to spend. If your wages go up, you have more money, so you might prefer to spend that extra hour using some of that money to enjoy your leisure time. Indeed, if you are now getting paid more per hour, you might decide that you'd rather work *fewer* hours. If this is the case, a wage increase might actually *reduce* the supply of labor.

Economists have two terms to describe the competing incentives that influence a worker's response to a change in the wage:

- The *price effect* describes the increase in labor supply in response to the higher wage that can be earned for each hour of work.

- The *income effect* describes the decrease in labor supply due to the greater demand for leisure caused by a higher income.

We can see in Figure 16-4 the influence of the income and price effects on labor supply decisions. (This analysis is similar to that of the income and substitution effects we saw in Chapter 7, "Consumer Behavior," when considering purchasing decisions under a budget constraint.) In this case, workers are constrained by the amount of time they have available. There are 8,760 hours in a (non-leap) year. Assuming that workers will spend some portion of that time sleeping and eating, let's say there are roughly 5,000 hours available for work per year.

FIGURE 16-4

Income and price effects of a wage increase

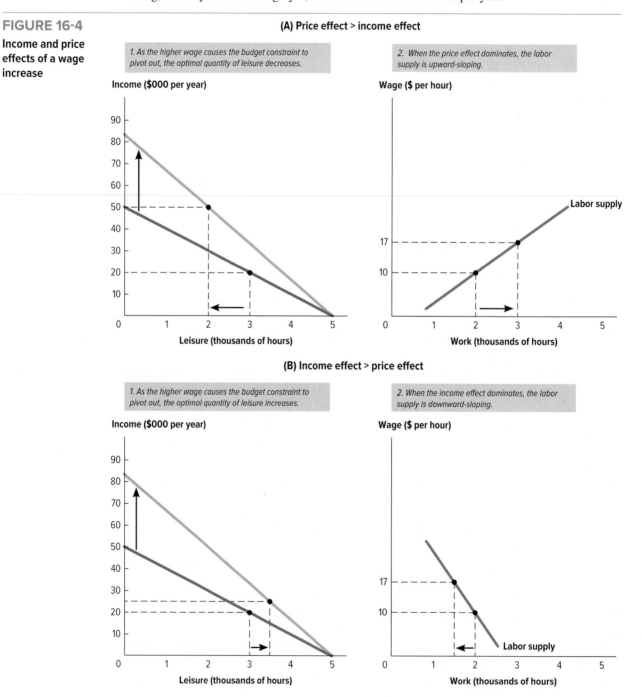

(A) Price effect > income effect

1. As the higher wage causes the budget constraint to pivot out, the optimal quantity of leisure decreases.

2. When the price effect dominates, the labor supply is upward-sloping.

(B) Income effect > price effect

1. As the higher wage causes the budget constraint to pivot out, the optimal quantity of leisure increases.

2. When the income effect dominates, the labor supply is downward-sloping.

The price effect causes labor supply to increase in response to a wage increase. The income effect causes labor supply to decrease in response to the same change. Whether total labor supply goes up or down depends on which effect dominates.

Time translates into income through work and wages. At an initial wage rate of $10 per hour, a worker faces a budget constraint represented by the darker line in the left graphs of Figure 16-4:

- He can choose to work zero hours, earn nothing, and have 5,000 hours of leisure a year.
- He can choose to work 5,000 hours, earn $50,000, and have no leisure time.
- He could choose any point in between.

Suppose that based on personal preferences, an individual chooses to work 2,000 hours, earn $20,000, and have 3,000 hours of leisure. Now, let's say the wage increases from $10 an hour to $17 an hour (quite a raise!). When the wage increases, the budget line pivots outward. Now, the worker's choice is on the lighter line in the left graphs (which runs between no income with 5,000 hours of leisure and $85,000 with no leisure time per week).

The left graph in panel A of Figure 16-4 shows how a worker reacts to this wage increase when the *price effect* is bigger than the income effect. This worker responds to the new budget constraint by choosing to increase his hours worked from 2,000 to 3,000 hours (thus losing 1,000 hours of leisure). He earns $51,000 and has only 2,000 hours of leisure. Here, an increase in the wage has caused an increase in the amount of labor supplied. The right graph in panel A translates the leisure chosen on the left into a labor supply curve. That curve shows the hours of labor the worker supplies at any given wage rate. The fact that the price effect outweighs the income effect is reflected in the upward-sloping labor supply curve.

The left graph in panel B shows what happens when the *income effect* is bigger than the price effect. This worker responds to the same wage increase by decreasing his hours worked from 2,000 to 1,500 hours (thus gaining 500 hours of leisure). He earns $25,500 and has 3,500 hours of leisure time. Here, an increase in the wage has caused the worker to supply 500 *fewer* hours of labor. When the income effect outweighs the price effect, the labor supply curve slopes downward, as the right graph in panel B shows.

Either of these two situations is a rational response, depending on whether the individual in question gets more utility from additional leisure or additional money. These preferences determine the relative sizes of the price and income effects.

Which of these effects dominates in the real world? In most cases, the price effect will outweigh the income effect. In general, people respond to higher wages by wanting to work more. So, for the rest of this chapter, we will use the usual upward-sloping supply curve for labor, indicating that the quantity of labor supplied increases as the wage increases.

Reaching equilibrium

LO 16.4 Explain how to find the equilibrium price and quantity for a factor of production.

A worker deciding how many hours to work can be represented with an individual labor-supply curve. A farm choosing the profit-maximizing number of employees can be represented with a firm-level demand curve. In order to see how the labor market works as a whole, however, we need to add up all the supply curves of individual workers and the demand curves of individual firms to find *market-level* supply and demand.

The process for identifying the equilibrium wage and quantity in the labor market should look very familiar. As in all competitive markets, the equilibrium is found at the point where the supply and demand curves intersect. Figure 16-5 shows the equilibrium in a market for tomato-farm workers in California. At this point, the quantity of labor supplied equals the quantity demanded by tomato farmers in California at the market wage. Farm workers get $20,000 per year, and farmers hire 125,000 workers.

The labor market reaches equilibrium through the same process as any other market, assuming that both wages and the quantity of labor can adjust freely in response to incentives. For instance, suppose the wage for farm workers is $11.50 per hour (roughly $23,000 per year, at

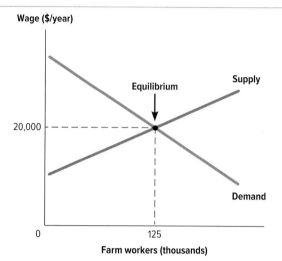

FIGURE 16-5

Labor market equilibrium

In a competitive labor market, the price of labor (that is, the wage) is determined by the intersection of the supply and demand curves for labor. Here, the labor market reaches equilibrium at a wage of $20,000 per year. At that point 125,000 workers are hired.

40 hours of work per week for 50 weeks per year). At that price, given the value of the marginal product of labor, farmers want to hire 100,000 workers.

However, 163,500 workers want to work at that wage, given their opportunity cost of labor. Because the quantity of labor supplied is greater than the quantity demanded, the market is out of balance. Some workers who want to work will be left without a job, or at least with fewer working hours than they want. In other words, at that price there is a surplus of farm labor.

If you were a farm owner, *how would you respond to this situation?* Knowing that there are plenty of underemployed and willing workers out there, you might offer a lower wage—say, $10 per hour instead of $11.50. If you can get the work done at a lower cost, you probably won't complain. When the wage falls from $11.50 to $10 per hour, the quantity of workers demanded by farm owners will increase.

At the lower wage, what happens to the number of workers? Some workers will be willing to work for $10 per hour. Others will find that the opportunity cost of work outweighs the benefits. The latter group will be unwilling to work for $10. Thus, the quantity of labor supplied will decrease, while the quantity demanded will increase, bringing the market into equilibrium.

If wages drop below the market equilibrium level, the opposite will happen: Farmers will demand more labor than workers are willing to supply. Farmers will have to offer higher wages to attract the workers they need, increasing the quantity of labor supplied and decreasing the quantity demanded. This process will continue until the wage brings the supply of labor into balance with demand.

Shifts in labor supply and labor demand

LO 16.5 Use graphs to demonstrate the effect of a shift in labor supply or labor demand and describe what causes these curves to shift.

Just as in the supply and demand model in Chapter 3, "Markets," the supply and demand curves for labor can shift right or left with changes in nonprice determinants. In the labor market, such factors include technology, labor market regulations, and other external forces.

Determinants of labor demand

In thinking about the underlying determinants of the labor demand curve, the key is to remember that *labor demand is determined by the value of the marginal product of labor.* As a result:

- Any event that increases the value of the marginal product will increase demand, shifting the labor demand curve right.
- Any event that decreases the value of the marginal product will decrease demand, shifting the labor demand curve left.

In general, many shifts in the labor demand curve can be traced to three determinants: supply of other factors of production, technology, and output prices. Table 16-2 summarizes the effects of such changes.

We can see an example of a shift in labor demand resulting from technology by assuming that the tomato farm decides to invest in more farm machinery. Adding machinery can vastly improve the productivity of a small group of farm workers. However, with the added machinery, the marginal product of labor diminishes very quickly. Once you have the few workers you need to operate the machines, adding more workers adds little to the quantity harvested.

POTENTIALLY CONFUSING

Popular opinion holds that technology displaces workers. This is sometimes true, as with farm machinery. However, it is not always true. Consider the effect of the Internet on research assistants' productivity. In pre-Internet days, when a professor asked an assistant to find some data, it took days of digging at the library. Now, it takes minutes on a search engine. You might assume that when the Internet came along, professors could employ fewer research assistants to do the same amount of work, just as farm machinery enables farmers to employ fewer workers to harvest the same amount of crops.

But another dynamic is at work. In the days before the Internet, a professor would have had to really need some data before she paid a research assistant to search for it. With the Internet, a professor can ask for data just on the chance that it might be interesting. As a result, professors' appetite for data has increased, and the demand for more research assistant labor has remained the same, or even increased.

TABLE 16-2

Nonprice determinants of labor demand

Factors that shift labor demand	Effects on marginal product and labor demand
Technology	When technology changes are *labor-augmenting:* The MPL increases and labor demand also increases (shifts right). When technology changes are *labor-saving:* The MPL decreases and labor demand also decreases (shifts left).
Supply of other factors	If the supply of other factors causes the MPL to increase, labor demand increases (shifts right). If the supply of other factors causes the MPL to decrease, labor demand decreases (shifts left).
Output prices	If output prices decrease, the value of the marginal product of labor (VMPL) decreases and labor demand also decreases (shifts left). If output prices increase, the value of the marginal product of labor (VMPL) increases and labor demand also increases (shifts right).

Such a reduction in the marginal product of labor would decrease the quantity of labor demanded at any given wage, shifting the entire demand curve to the left. As Figure 16-6 shows, the equilibrium point slides down the supply curve to a new equilibrium point (E_3 in the figure) at a lower quantity and a lower wage. Note that at the new equilibrium point, there are fewer total farm workers and a lower equilibrium wage.

Determinants of labor supply

In thinking about the underlying determinants of labor supply, the key is to remember that at any given wage, *labor supply is determined by the number of workers and the opportunity cost of providing their labor.* As a result:

- Changes that increase the opportunity cost of work or decrease the number of workers will decrease the labor supply, shifting the supply curve left.
- Changes that decrease the opportunity cost of work or increase the number of workers will increase the labor supply, shifting the supply curve right.

The determinants of labor supply include culture, population, and other opportunities. Table 16-3 summarizes the effects of such changes.

We can see an example of a shift in labor supply by looking at changes in the population of workers. Many of California's farm workers (most, by some accounts) are in the United States illegally. Occasionally the authorities implement a crackdown on illegal immigration, increasing the strictness of border controls with Mexico. We can think of this as an external change that decreases the supply of workers at any given wage level. To see why, we first need to ask, *How should we expect Mexican prospective farm workers to respond to stricter border controls?* The greater chance of getting caught at the border and being deported, after a dangerous and expensive trip, decreases the expected value of supplying their labor to California's farmers. Faced with this choice, some workers will stay home. Others will make the trip but will be turned back at the border.

FIGURE 16-6

Decrease in the demand for labor

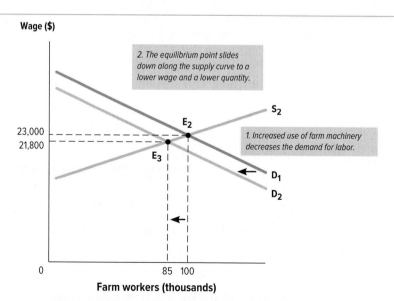

When increased use of farm machinery decreases the marginal product of labor, the labor demand curve shifts left. The equilibrium number of workers falls from 100,000 to 85,000, and the equilibrium wage falls from $23,000 to $21,800.

TABLE 16-3

Nonprice determinants of labor supply

Factors that shift labor supply	Effect on labor supply
Population	When there are more potential workers (as a result of demographic changes and/or immigration), labor supply increases (shifts right).
Culture	When cultural attitudes view work favorably, labor supply increases (shifts right). When cultural attitudes view work unfavorably, labor supply decreases (shifts left).
Other opportunities	When the next-best opportunity available to workers offers better benefits, the labor supply will move toward that better opportunity, whether that increases or decreases supply. *Examples:* Better wages in retail or service jobs might lead workers to supply less labor to farms, decreasing the labor supply for farms but increasing the labor supply for retail and service jobs. A decrease in the cost of higher education might lead workers to go back to school, decreasing the labor supply.

Thus, stricter border controls will cause the total supply of labor to be lower at any given wage than it was under more lax enforcement. We can represent this decrease in the supply of labor by shifting the entire supply curve to the left, as shown in Figure 16-7. The equilibrium point slides up along the demand curve, from E_1 to E_2 in the figure. At that new equilibrium point, the quantity of labor supplied is lower and wages are higher.

In the early 2000s, California cracked down on illegal immigration, but wages of California farm workers did not rise during this period—at least, no more than wages on average rose throughout the country. Why not? Do these real-world data mean our model is wrong? Not necessarily. There could have been another factor at work, shifting the demand curve to the right at

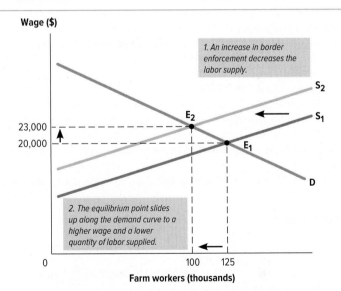

FIGURE 16-7
Decrease in the labor supply

When an external change in border controls causes a change in workers' trade-offs, the labor supply curve shifts. In this case, stricter controls shift the curve to the left, decreasing the equilibrium number of farm workers supplied from 125,000 to 100,000 and increasing the equilibrium wage from $20,000 to $23,000.

the same time. For instance, consider *how farm owners might respond* to an illegal immigration crackdown that was causing an increase in wages. As we saw earlier, firms can sometimes substitute one factor of production for another. Faced with a higher cost of labor, farmers might have decided they could maximize profits by employing fewer workers and investing in more farm machinery instead.

That's what one farmer in Arizona did when he couldn't find enough workers to pick his jalapeño peppers—he aimed to cut the number of laborers he needed by 90 percent and hire machinists instead. Between 2007 and 2012, Arizona's population of undocumented workers dropped by 40 percent. And between 2010 and 2014, wages for Arizona farm workers rose approximately 15 percent.[4] For a more nuanced discussion of the economic effects of immigration, read the What Do You Think? box "Should the United States be a country of immigrants?"

What Do You Think?

Should the United States be a country of immigrants?

The economy of the United States—arguably, more than any other economy in the world—has been shaped by huge waves of workers emigrating from other countries (see Figure 16-8).

German farmers settled the Midwest in the 1850s. Chinese workers built the transcontinental railroad in the 1880s. Immigrants from southern and eastern Europe powered northeastern factories during the early decades of the twentieth century.

However, millions more are turned away. To work legally in the United States, noncitizens need a permit called a visa. Unless you have rare and valuable skills—such as being a top baseball player, scientist, or doctor—you won't be guaranteed to get one. Faced with this difficulty, many people try to enter the country and work without a visa. An estimated 10.9 million people are working in the United States today without one.

Immigration stirs powerful feelings. Arguments stem from disagreements about whether immigration is economically good or bad for those already in the country. Often, immigrants are willing to work for less money than native-born workers. This is good for businesses, which can hire cheaper labor, and for consumers, who can purchase goods and services at lower cost as a result. Economists usually argue that immigration promotes efficiency and economic growth by allowing resources (in this case, people and skills) to go where they will be most productive. Therefore, most economists believe that in the long run immigration creates new jobs. However, this is not much consolation to a local worker who has lost his job and now needs to look for a new one—perhaps in another industry or another part of the country.

The problem is complicated because these disagreements are driven not just by economic concerns, but also by cultural and philosophical attitudes. Some believe that it's worth paying higher prices so that more Americans can get jobs at a slightly higher wage. Others wonder whether it is fair to withhold the ladder of opportunity that the ancestors of current citizens may have climbed up.

As long as the United States continues to be a land of opportunity, attracting immigrants from around the world, this debate will surely continue.

WHAT DO YOU THINK?

1. Does the government have a responsibility to address the negative effects of immigration on native-born workers who are affected by it?
2. Should everyone who wants to work in the United States be legally allowed to do so? Where should the line be drawn, and why?

Sources: http://www.usafis.org/green_card/prev_years.asp; http://www.dhs.gov/files/statistics/publications/LPR09.shtm. http://www.pewresearch.org/fact-tank/2015/11/19/5-facts-about-illegal-immigration-in-the-u-s/; https://www.washingtonpost.com/news/federal-eye/wp/2016/01/20/u-s-illegal-immigrant-population-falls-below-11-million-continuing-nearly-decade-long-decline-report-says/.

FIGURE 16-8

U.S. immigration, 1820–2013

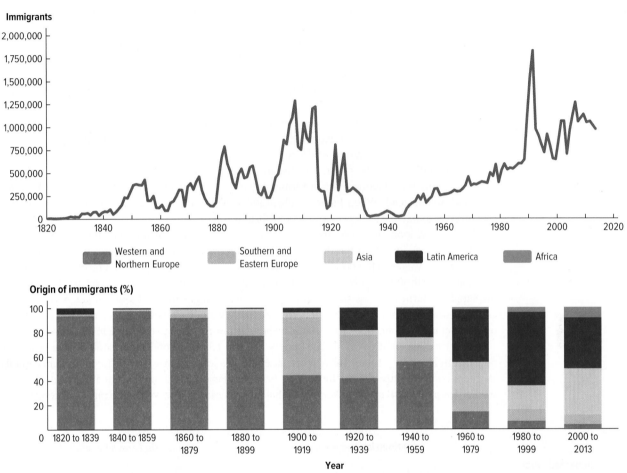

Source: http://www.migrationpolicy.org/programs/data-hub/us-immigration-trends#history; U.S. Department of Homeland Security; http://www.dhs.gov/files/statistics/publications/LPR08.shtm.

What's missing? Human capital

LO 16.6 Explain the importance of human capital in the labor market.

There is not a single market with a single equilibrium for all labor in an economy. Baseball players are not paid the same wage as farm workers, after all. But even within specific markets, like the market for baseball players, workers are not paid the same wage. Clayton Kershaw, the baseball player from the chapter opening story, earns about 11 times the salary of Kenta Maeda, another starting pitcher for the same team.

What causes this difference? It's the idea of **human capital**, the set of skills, knowledge, experience, and talent that determine the productivity of workers. In taking courses at school, you are acquiring human capital. Human capital determines the productivity of workers.

Human capital is so crucial in determining how labor markets work that economists sometimes consider it the fourth, and possibly the most important, factor of production. Workers differ from one another, and are paid differently, because they have different amounts and types of human capital that allow them to be more or less productive than other workers at various tasks.

human capital
the set of skills, knowledge, experience, and talent that determine the productivity of workers

Is the difference between a highly paid player such as Clayton Kershaw and other "less productive" players due more to natural talent, personal characteristics, hard work, or experience? The truth is, it's hard to say. Human capital can encompass all of these considerations.

Some types of human capital make workers more productive at a wide variety of jobs—for instance, having a strong work ethic, being good with numbers, or having a knack for getting along with people. Other types of human capital are specific to a particular job or task. For instance, going to medical school won't necessarily make you a better plumber, painter, or computer technician. Top professional athletes often find that their human capital is not easy to transfer: They may be amazingly good as a player but hopeless as a coach, manager, or television personality.

Human capital also allows us to understand that what we call the labor market is actually a collection of many different, interconnected labor markets for workers with similar skills. The more similar the skills required to do any two jobs, the more workers and employers can substitute one skill set for the other, and the more connected the two labor markets will be. For example, many farm laborers in California may have the human capital required to work in the hotel industry instead. When labor is substitutable between two markets, we should expect the two markets to pay the same or similar equilibrium wage.

To see why, look at Figure 16-9. Suppose that an increase in the demand for hotel rooms in California has increased the demand for hotel workers, as shown in panel A. The increased demand raises wages in the hotel industry. If hotel work is paying better than farm work, workers who can do both jobs will be inclined to work at hotels. Their move into hotel work decreases the supply of farm labor, as shown in panel B, raising wages in that labor market. Workers will continue moving from farms to hotels as long as they can earn better wages by switching from one market to the other. The process stops when farm wages rise to the same level as hotel wages.

In contrast, ups and downs in the supply of farm labor or hotel labor should have no effect on Clayton Kershaw's salary for playing baseball. His job requires very different human capital. Workers compete only against those who have similar or substitutable human capital. When a worker has a rare skill or talent, supply in that labor market is low. When the rare skill contributes

FIGURE 16-9

Interconnected labor markets

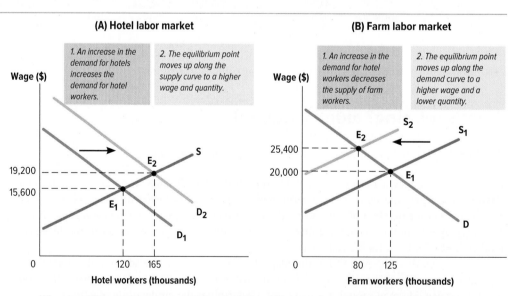

When two different jobs require workers with similar skill sets, a change in the demand for labor in one industry can affect the supply of labor in another. When the demand for hotel workers increases, as shown in panel A, workers who might have been indifferent between farm work and hotel work will shift toward hotel work. Their move to a different labor market will decrease the number of farm workers, shifting the farm labor supply curve left, as shown in panel B.

to the production of something that consumers value highly, like pitching scoreless innings, the value of the marginal product is high. Low supply and high demand leads to the equilibrium outcome we see in the Major League Baseball labor market: few workers and high wages.

✓ CONCEPT CHECK

☐ What is the relationship between the value of the marginal product of labor, the wage, and the demand for labor? **[LO 16.2]**

☐ Under what circumstances might an increase in the wage decrease the labor supply? **[LO 16.3]**

☐ What happens to the equilibrium wage and quantity of labor when the demand for labor increases, holding all else equal? **[LO 16.4]**

☐ Which way does the labor supply curve shift after a population increase, holding all else equal? **[LO 16.5]**

☐ What are some ways that people can acquire human capital? **[LO 16.6]**

Land and Capital

We now turn from labor to the other two main factors of production: land and capital. If you were a farmer, would you be willing to pay as much for an acre of land in California's Sonoran Desert as you would for an acre of land in California's super-fertile Central Valley? If you owned a baseball team, would you pay as much for a stadium located 50 miles outside the city as you would for one in the heart of downtown? In both cases, one type of land has greater marginal productivity than the other. We can expect producers to pay more for land with higher productivity.

As these scenarios suggest, we can think about the markets for land and capital in a way that is very similar to our analysis of labor markets—with some differences. In this section, we'll examine a few features of the markets for land and capital that make them unique. We'll also look at how ownership of the different factors of production determines a person's income.

Capitalists: Who are they?

Capital is a tricky concept. Sometimes the word *capital* can mean physical capital, such as machinery. At other times it can mean financial capital, as in "She needs some start-up capital for her new business." Then, of course, there's human capital, which we discussed earlier.

These uses of the term are related. The reason the word *capital* sometimes refers to financial assets is that money can be invested in a business, which then uses the money to buy physical capital. Thus, a "capitalist" is someone who *owns physical capital.* Sometimes that ownership is direct, as in ownership of a factory. Often it is indirect, as in ownership of shares of stock, which represent partial ownership of a company and its physical capital.

In general, when people talk about investing, they mean that they have lent their money to someone who will use it to buy physical capital. Thus, anyone who puts money into the stock market, holds bonds or stocks, or opens a retirement account owns capital. This actually represents a sizable share of the population—by this definition, in the United States, just over half of Americans qualify as "capitalists."[5]

Markets for land and capital

LO 16.7 Describe the similarities and differences between the markets for land and capital and the market for labor.

Before we say anything else about the markets for land and capital, we should note one important difference from labor markets: When a firm wants to use land or capital, it has two choices—to buy or rent. When we talk about the price of land or capital, then, we need to distinguish between the rental price and the purchase price:

rental price
the price paid to use a factor of production for a certain period or task

purchase price
the price paid to gain permanent ownership of a factor of production

- The **rental price** is what a producer pays to use a factor of production for a certain period or task.
- The **purchase price** is what a producer pays to gain permanent ownership of a factor of production.

The rental price and the purchase price are both important concepts for understanding markets for land and capital.

Rental markets

The rental prices of land and capital are determined in the same way as the wage in a labor market:

- When Walmart hires a full-time cashier, Walmart is actually "renting" the cashier's labor for 40 hours a week.
- Walmart also is renting when it leases a new building or borrows money.
- When Walmart borrows money, the rental price of capital is the interest it pays on loans.

As with labor, the demand for land or capital is determined by the value of the marginal product (VMP) of each unit. No firm will rent land or machinery that contributes less to the firm's output than its rental cost.

On the other side of the market, the quantity of land or capital supplied depends on the other opportunities available for using them. The market equilibrium price and quantity in the rental market are determined by the intersection of supply and demand, just as in any other market.

economic rent
the gains that workers and owners of capital receive from supplying their labor or machinery in factor markets

In the markets for factors of production, economists use the phrase **economic rent** to describe the gains that workers and owners of capital receive from supplying their labor or machinery in factor markets. In the rental markets shown in Figure 16-10, the area above the supply curve but below the equilibrium rental price is economic rent. It represents the rental price of a factor of production minus the cost of supplying it. If Clayton Kershaw is willing to play baseball for $28 million, the $4 million difference between this willingness to play and his actual salary of $32 million is economic rent earned by Kershaw.

FIGURE 16-10

Economic rent in rental markets for land and capital

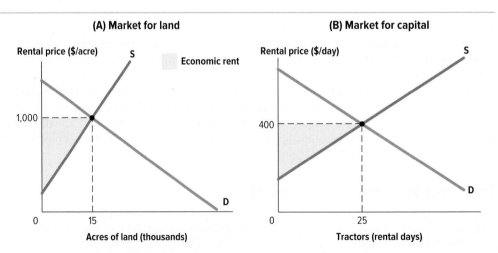

Just as in the labor market, the rental markets for land and capital reach an equilibrium price and quantity at the point where the supply curve intersects the demand curve. The area above the supply curve and below the equilibrium rental price is called *economic rent*.

The shaded area in Figure 16-10 may seem familiar to you: In Chapter 3, "Markets" (and elsewhere), we identified this as *producer surplus*. The concept is the same, but in the markets for factors of production, we use the term *economic rent*. Later, we'll discuss what role these gains (as part of something called the factor distribution of income) play in the economy.

POTENTIALLY CONFUSING

Be careful not to confuse the term *economic rent* with the everyday usage of *rent*. The everyday use has a related but more general meaning: the money paid to landlords for the privilege of using their land or capital.

Purchase markets

Renting land or capital allows a firm to use it for a certain period without worrying about its long-term value. In contrast, buying land or capital requires potential owners to think about an asset's long-run productivity.

To determine the price they should pay for land or capital, potential buyers must forecast what its marginal product is likely to be over time. They can then assess the value of the expected future flows of income in order to compare them to the cost of the asset. (We explored the relevant tools in Chapter 11, "Time and Uncertainty.") Smart sellers will make similar calculations in order to calculate their own notion of a reasonable price.

The factor distribution of income

Most people own at least one factor of production. If you can work, you own your own labor, which you can rent to producers for a wage. Many people also own some capital or land. Ownership of these productive resources determines your income, which in turn determines your ability to consume goods and services. Who owns what, and how much income they receive from it, are therefore crucial questions.

Economists refer to the pattern of income that people derive from different factors of production as the *factor distribution of income*. In other words, the factor distribution of income shows how much income people get from labor compared to land and capital. Figure 16-11 shows the U.S. factor distribution of income. In the United States, the majority of income—about

FIGURE 16-11

The factor distribution of income   In the United States, the majority of income comes from compensation for labor. Corporate profits, interest, and rent all go to owners of physical capital, while proprietor income goes to individual business owners for both the labor and capital put into their businesses.

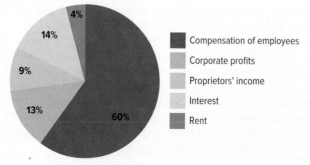

Source: Bureau of Economic Analysis, National Income and Product Accounts.

60 percent—comes from labor (shown in the figure as "compensation of employees"). Corporate profits, interest, and rent all go to owners of physical capital (including those who own physical capital by owning shares of stock). Proprietor income represents both the labor and capital factors that proprietors put into their businesses. Perhaps surprisingly, the factor distribution of income hasn't changed much in the last century, despite enormous changes in the economy and technology.

Big inequalities in earnings from the factors of production can sometimes seem unfair. Writing in the nineteenth century as new factories were transforming the economic landscape of Europe, Karl Marx unleashed his fury at the fact that workers earned so little relative to factory owners. To Marx, the owners of capital exploited those who earned their income through labor, and he urged workers to revolt against the capitalist system. Marx's ideas inspired some of the biggest political upheavals of the last two centuries, including revolutions in Europe, Russia, and China fought in the name of giving more power to workers. In each case, though, capitalism eventually returned as the dominant economic system.

The triumph of capitalism doesn't mean that all policy debates have ended. Marx's judgment was *normative*. His ideas differ from the *factual* analysis in this chapter of how income is determined in an efficient, competitive market—by the productivity of the land, labor, or capital that people own. That productivity, in turn, is defined by how much consumers will pay for the output the factors produce. Our aim is to describe how competitive factor markets allocate resources. Our analysis does not imply whether the existing factor distribution of income is, or is not, *fair* in a broader sense. You have to draw on your own values to answer for yourself whether it is right or wrong that Clayton Kershaw and other professional athletes earn far more than a farm worker, or why owners of certain types of capital earn more than others.

For one example of a debate on the question of how productivity is rewarded, see the What Do You Think? box "Work, wages, and social value."

What Do You Think?
Work, wages, and social value

In most professions, people are comfortable with the idea that workers are paid according to their productivity. For example, we tend to accept that exceptionally talented professional baseball (and football, basketball, and hockey) players will earn more than their teammates, that lawyers who regularly win tough cases will charge more than other lawyers, and that salespeople who bring in lots of revenue to a firm will be rewarded accordingly. In general, we see higher pay as both a reward and an incentive for higher productivity.

In some professions, however, pay for performance may seem out of keeping with the nature of the work. For example, the idea that a pastor should be paid for each new member she brings into a congregation might strike some people as odd. That's not to say it doesn't happen, though. Looking at records from United Methodist churches in Oklahoma, researchers at the University of North Carolina found that, on average, pastors received a pay increase equal to 3 percent of the revenues generated by the new members they brought into the church. That is comparable to how much of the salary of Fortune 500 CEOs depends on their own company performance—although the typical pastor's salary is much lower.

Debates over performance pay are especially heated when it comes to teachers. Almost everywhere in the United States, teachers earn a salary that depends mainly on their years of experience. Proponents of performance pay say that teachers should be compensated largely in proportion to the results their students achieve, as measured through standardized tests. They argue that such a system rewards good teachers and encourages them to work hard. Opponents say that performance pay encourages teachers to focus too much on test scores, distracting them from teaching deeper concepts and helping struggling students.

A related debate focuses on the salaries of workers in nonprofit organizations, especially those that assist the poor. Some people argue that rewarding good performance with high salaries attracts the best workers; those workers make nonprofits more effective at doing good for those in need of help. Opponents counter that it is inappropriate for workers in nonprofits to earn so much more than those they serve, and that the resulting income gap can make it difficult for nonprofit workers to understand their clients' situation.

WHAT DO YOU THINK?

1. Do you think that people should accept performance pay in some professions but not in others?
2. Would performance pay for teachers be less controversial if it were easier to get a more complete picture of performance, in such areas as helping students develop rounded personalities and inspiring learning?
3. Would stronger financial incentives change the fundamental nature of social professions such as teaching and preaching? Might that be a good thing? What might be lost?

Source: http://www.slate.com/id/2258794/.

✓CONCEPT CHECK

☐ What is the difference between the rental price and the purchase price of capital? **[LO 16.7]**
☐ How is physical capital related to financial capital? **[LO 16.7]**

Real-World Labor Markets

We've now looked at the main factors of production—labor, land, and capital, as well as human capital. For the rest of the chapter, we'll return to labor, to see how the real world looks in relation to the model of perfectly competitive labor markets we outlined above. One important dimension we consider here is the role of government policy. Another is the power of bosses or unions to influence market outcomes. Still another dimension is created by changes in population size. The simple model of perfect competition in labor markets provides an important benchmark, and here we enrich the picture to describe realities that you'll probably encounter throughout your working life.

Minimum wages and efficiency wages

LO 16.8 Describe two reasons why a wage might rise above the market equilibrium and how this affects the labor market.

The model of labor supply and demand we outlined earlier in this chapter does a good job of explaining the most important determinants of wages. It gives a reasonably accurate picture of many labor markets. However, two notable exceptions to the model—minimum wages and efficiency wages—can push wage rates above the market equilibrium point.

In the United States, the federal government requires that all employers pay all workers a wage that is at or above a certain minimum rate (as of March 2016, $7.25 per hour). Some state governments impose higher minimum wages (as of March 2016, up to $10 per hour in the state of California).[6] Minimum wages are a controversial topic. Supporters usually argue that a minimum wage is needed to protect low-paid workers from greedy employers and to guarantee workers an acceptable standard of living. Opponents see a minimum wage as a form of government interference in the free market; they contend that it raises the cost of doing business, causing unemployment in the process. As economic analysts, how can we weigh these opposing claims?

FIGURE 16-12

The minimum wage

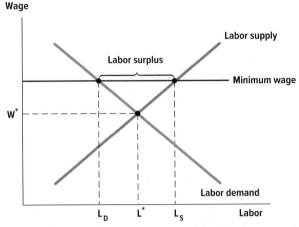

When people are willing to supply more labor than firms are willing to hire, the labor market has a surplus of workers, which is also known as unemployment.

First, we need to separate positive arguments from normative arguments. Let's start by asking what effect we would expect a minimum-wage law to have on the labor market. Minimum-wage laws are examples of price floors, discussed in Chapter 6, "Government Intervention." Imposing a price floor causes the quantity demanded to decrease and the quantity supplied to increase, compared with equilibrium levels. In other words, more people are willing to work than there are jobs available, causing unemployment. This situation is shown in Figure 16-12. Imposing a price floor is good news for the people who keep their jobs, and bad news for the people who were employed at the equilibrium wage but are not employed after the minimum wage is imposed.

However, this analysis assumes that the labor market is perfectly efficient. If the market is already inefficient and the minimum wage is below the equilibrium level, the effect of a minimum wage might not be to cause unemployment. The minimum wage might instead transfer surplus from employers to workers.

The evidence on how minimum wage laws affect the real world is mixed. In some cases, a minimum wage causes some unemployment. In others, the biggest impact is on *who* is employed. Since higher-skilled workers become cheaper relative to low-skilled workers when the minimum wage increases, employers might hire more skilled and experienced workers, and fewer young and unskilled workers. Whether or not you think that result is a good one is a normative question, which we will leave to your own judgment.

Another reason that wages might rise above market equilibrium is that some employers may voluntarily choose to pay workers more, to increase their productivity. Economists call this arrangement an **efficiency wage**. There are two ways in which an efficiency wage might increase workers' productivity. First, earning more than the market wage gives workers an incentive to stay with the firm. Thus, the firm gets to hold onto experienced, well-trained workers, rather than repeatedly having to spend time and resources to train new employees.

The second reason is an extension of the first. If workers have a lot to lose by leaving the firm, they will work hard to avoid getting fired. Efficiency wages make sense when a boss cannot constantly supervise workers—say, a shop owner who visits only a couple of times a week. If a salesperson at the shop receives the market wage, she may take the risk of slacking off since if she's caught, she can hope to get another job at an equivalent wage. But if the salesperson receives a wage sufficiently larger than the going market rate, even the small probability that the boss might catch her slacking off carries a higher potential cost. She'd be fired from an especially rewarding job.

In the end, workers respond to incentives, and when it becomes more costly to leave or get fired from a job, employees are going to work harder to stay. This is good for both sides.

efficiency wage
a wage that is deliberately set above the market rate to increase worker productivity

While businesses get more productive workers, employees also get a higher wage. This is why efficiency wages have been used from the first assembly line (Henry Ford offered his workers double the going wage in 1914) to the market for high-powered lawyers today.

That said, efficiency wages are a great deal only for workers who get them. The use of efficiency wages creates unemployment by keeping wages above the equilibrium wage level, similar to the way minimum wage laws can create unemployment. If you have a well-paying job, you'll be happy. But if you're unemployed and struggling to find a job, you will probably view the existence of efficiency wages with a wary eye.

Company towns, unions, and labor laws

LO 16.9 Describe several causes of imperfectly competitive labor markets and their effect on workers and employers.

Just as the markets for goods and services aren't always perfectly competitive, neither are labor markets. In some real-world labor markets, *employers* have market power, pushing wages down to capture more surplus. In other labor markets, *workers* have market power, pushing wages up. In addition, government regulation of the workplace can impose costs or friction on a market.

Let's first consider the scenario in which employers have market power. Normally, we would call a firm with market power a monopolist or an oligopolist. But because firms are the buyers in this situation (remember, they are buying labor in the labor market), we need a new term. A market in which there is only one buyer but many sellers is called a **monopsony**. Whereas a monopolist can maintain a price *higher* than the price in a competitive market, a monopsonistic employer can push wages (that is, the price of labor) *lower* than the competitive level.

monopsony
a market in which there is only one buyer but many sellers

Sometimes, a firm that is the largest employer in a region, or one of only a few major employers, can gain market power. Historically, such situations arose when a town sprang up around the worksite for a major company. These "company towns" were common in Appalachia, where coal mines or steel plants were the main source of jobs. Often, the company literally owned everything in town, including the grocery store. More recent, less extreme examples include Detroit, with its reliance on the success of the Big Three car companies, and Redmond, Washington, home to Microsoft.

Workers also can gain market power. When they do, they can push wages higher than the market equilibrium. Gaining market power requires that workers join together to make a collective decision about when to supply their labor, much like a cartel in the market for commodities. Labor unions are the usual mechanism for organizing workers in this way. To raise wages (or improve nonwage benefits) and capture some surplus for workers, unions must have a monopoly or near-monopoly on labor in a particular market. Otherwise, competition for jobs will push wages back down to the market equilibrium level, just as in a competitive market for goods.

The importance of union monopoly was demonstrated during the 1987 NFL strike. When the football players in the league went on strike, owners simply found replacement players to take their place. Although fans weren't entirely convinced by teams made up of replacement players, the games were still aired on TV; teams and owners still made money. The striking NFL players realized that they did not have monopoly power and that the league could move on without them. That realization helped convince them to end the strike.

In general, the larger the membership of a union, the more power it has. For this reason, unions often span multiple labor markets. The AFL-CIO, the largest union organization in the United States, is a confederation of unions that represents 12.5 million workers, ranging from pilots and bricklayers to actors and police officers. Other large union federations include AFGE (American Federation of Government Employees), the union that represents government workers, and the NEA (National Education Association), which represents workers in many different parts of the education sector.

FIGURE 16-13

Major labor laws of the twentieth century

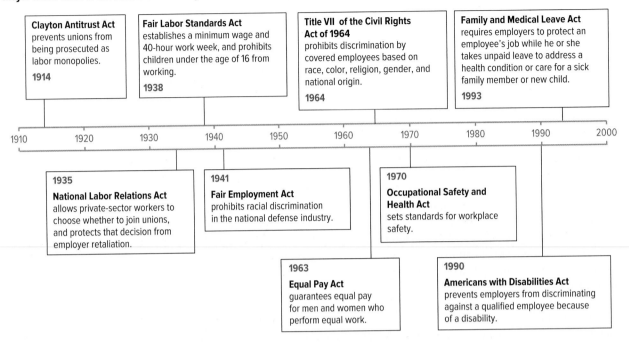

Sources: http://www.bls.gov/opub/mlr/2015/article/labor-law-highlights-1915-2015.htm; http://library.gsu.edu/search-collections/special-collections-archives/southern-labor-archives/.

Finally, government intervention in the labor market can cause wages and employment to move away from the market equilibrium, much as in the markets for goods and services. We have already discussed the minimum wage. Other types of regulation, summarized in Figure 16-13, can also affect the labor market. Regulations such as standards to ensure that workers won't be injured at work are relatively uncontroversial. But they do impose some costs, moving away from the efficient equilibrium.

Changing demographics

Earlier in this chapter, we saw how immigration can affect the labor market. Rising or falling birth rates also have a profound effect on the overall supply of labor and economic growth. Countries with a declining population may have too few workers to power production and too few consumers to drive a healthy demand for goods and services.

Excessive population growth is a concern as well. Overpopulation can strain the environment and limit the government's ability to pay for education and other services. High birth rates can also make it harder for parents to invest as much as they would like in their children's development and education. This lack of investment ends up reducing the human capital (and therefore the productivity) of the future labor force.

When growing populations suddenly start to slow down, the result is often that a small number of workers ends up supporting a lot of elderly dependents. The United States has found itself in this situation, as birth rates have fallen and medical advances enable people to live longer: In 1940, 160 working people were paying into the Social Security program for every retiree who received benefits. In 2015, just a little less than three working people were paying into the system for every retiree.[7] A wave of workers from the baby boom generation are reaching retirement age, and the following generations that will be entering the workforce to support them are far smaller.

Because of the serious effects of population growth on the economy, many governments have enacted policies to encourage or discourage childbearing. For a discussion of the pros and cons of such policies, see the What Do You Think? box "Population policy and the wealth of nations."

What Do You Think?

Population policy and the wealth of nations

When you look at a newborn baby, the child's future contribution to the economy probably is not the first thing that comes to mind. But today's birth rates determine the size of the future labor force, so many countries have adopted policies to encourage or discourage births.

Many European countries have negative population growth rates; each year more people die than babies are born. This drives European governments to encourage couples to have more children by subsidizing day care, granting generous parental leave from work, and offering tax credits for children.

China faced the opposite problem: a population explosion that threatened to outstrip the country's ability to feed and house all its citizens. From 1979 to the end of 2015, China enforced a one-child policy. Under that policy, those who lived in urban areas faced heavy fees if they chose to bear more than one child. (Effective January 1, 2016, China changed to a two-child policy.)

The one-child policy was controversial, but there's little argument about its contribution to curbing the country's population growth. In 1950, the average Chinese woman had six children; under the one-child policy, the average was just under two. The country's income has grown more than 2,000 percent in two generations. Some attribute China's incredible economic growth, in part, to its population policy (because the population policy may have led to higher investments in human capital of children, and also allowed parents to work more).

Population policies can have some serious side effects. In China and India, local government officials have reportedly used harsh means to lower birth rates, such as intimidation and forced sterilization. In places where having sons is culturally important, some women have sex-selective abortions or even practice female infanticide to ensure that their child will be male. Opponents of China's one-child policy pointed to a growing gender imbalance: By 2020, men will outnumber women in China by an estimated 24 million. Defenders of the law, on the other hand, argue that it allowed China to avoid the worst strains of overpopulation and encouraged families to invest fully in children's education.

WHAT DO YOU THINK?

1. Is it right for the government to discourage or encourage couples to bear children for economic reasons? How would you weigh the importance of lifting people out of poverty against the right to privacy and self-determination?
2. If the government is going to play a role in influencing population growth, what sort of policy might be appropriate? What kind of policy would cross the line?
3. What alternative to the one-child policy might China have had? What kind of policy would you propose for a country that has serious concerns about the economic effects of overpopulation?

Sources: http://data.un.org/Data.aspx?q=china&d=PopDiv&f=variableID%3A54%3BcrID%3A156%2C948; http://news.bbc.co.uk/2/hi/8451289.stm.

✓CONCEPT CHECK

☐ Why might an employer choose to pay an efficiency wage? **[LO 16.8]**

☐ What would you expect to happen to wages in a monopsonistic labor market? **[LO 16.9]**

☐ If birth rates go up, what happens to the size of the labor force in the future? **[LO 16.9]**

Conclusion

Why do some people earn more than others? That is one of the most fundamental questions in economics and politics. When markets are competitive, everyone earns income in proportion to the productivity of the factors of production they control. For most people, that means their income is based on their own productivity as workers. That's usually closely tied to the skills, education, and other talents that determine our human capital. For farmers, the productivity of land matters as well. For investors, income is determined by the productivity of their financial capital. Competitive markets have the remarkable ability to reward work according to what is contributed to the economy.

We've seen that we can use the familiar tools of supply and demand to put prices on the factors of production. We also examined how business owners decide how much of each factor to use in producing goods and services. Their choice is driven by both the marginal productivity and the price of each factor. In future chapters we'll return to the markets for land, labor, and capital, to see what happens when we add public policy and collective decision making to the picture.

Key Terms

factors of production, p. 387

capital, p. 387

marginal product, p. 388

value of the marginal product, p. 390

human capital, p. 401

rental price, p. 404

purchase price, p. 404

economic rent, p. 404

efficiency wage, p. 408

monopsony, p. 409

Summary

LO 16.1 Describe how factors of production contribute to output.

The ingredients that are used to make a good or service are called factors of production. We can divide factors of production into three major categories: land, labor, and capital (a previously produced good that can be used to produce a new good). Factors of production are rented, bought, and sold in markets, at prices and in quantities that are determined by supply and demand. Firms choose to produce using the combination of factors that will maximize their profit.

LO 16.2 Graph the demand curve for a factor of production and explain its relationship to marginal productivity.

The demand for factors of production is determined by their contribution to the value of a firm's output. We can use the marginal product of labor (or land or capital) to measure the increase in output gained by using one more unit of a factor of production. Thus, the value of the marginal product of labor is the revenue that is generated by an additional worker. Firms will hire workers up to the point where the wage equals the value of the marginal product of labor (where marginal revenue equals marginal cost).

If we graph the value of the marginal product against the number of workers, we get a downward-sloping relationship that is the same as the demand curve for labor.

LO 16.3 Graph the supply curve for a factor of production and explain what determines the supply of labor.

The supply of a factor of production is driven by the opportunity cost of using that factor in a given market. The opportunity cost of supplying labor in a particular labor market is the time you would otherwise have spent on leisure or working at another job.

An increase in wages has two effects on the labor supply, a price effect and an income effect. The price effect causes the quantity of labor supplied to increase, all else held equal. The income effect decreases the labor supply, as workers demand more leisure time. In general, the price effect outweighs the income effect, which means that the labor supply curve slopes upward.

LO 16.4 Explain how to find the equilibrium price and quantity for a factor of production.

Factor markets reach equilibrium at the point where the demand curve intersects the supply curve, and the quantity demanded equals the quantity supplied at a given price or wage.

> **LO 16.5** Use graphs to demonstrate the effect of a shift in labor supply or labor demand and describe what causes these curves to shift.

If the underlying determinants of supply or demand change, the equilibrium point can shift. The determinants of labor demand include anything that affects the value of the marginal product, including the supply of other factors, changes in technology, and output prices. The determinants of labor supply include culture, population, and the availability of other opportunities.

> **LO 16.6** Explain the importance of human capital in the labor market.

In addition to the three primary factors of production, economists note a fourth critically important factor, human capital. Human capital is the set of skills, knowledge, experience, and talent that goes into the work people do. Workers differ from one another because they have different amounts and types of human capital to offer, which allow them to be more or less productive than others at different tasks. Some types of human capital make workers more productive at a wide range of jobs; others relate to very specific tasks. Differences in human capital are a key determinant of wages, and therefore of differences in people's incomes.

> **LO 16.7** Describe the similarities and differences between the markets for land and capital and the market for labor.

The markets for land and capital are similar to markets for labor, with the major difference being that land and capital can be purchased as well as rented. The rental price is what a producer pays to use a factor for a certain period or task; the purchase price is what a producer pays to gain permanent ownership. The word *capital* is often used loosely to refer to financial capital as well as physical capital. When people invest money in the stock market or a company, they are using financial capital to purchase a share of the company's physical capital.

> **LO 16.8** Describe two reasons why a wage might rise above the market equilibrium and how this affects the labor market.

There are two common reasons for a wage to rise above the market equilibrium: minimum wages and efficiency wages. A minimum wage is a price floor on the price of labor. In an efficient labor market, a price floor causes excess supply and unemployment. An efficiency wage is

an above-market equilibrium wage that an employer voluntarily pays to employees to increase their productivity.

> **LO 16.9** Describe several causes of imperfectly competitive labor markets and their effect on workers and employers.

Just as the markets for goods and services are not always perfectly competitive, neither are labor markets. When a labor market has only one employer but many workers, the employer is called a monopsonist. A monopsonist has the market power to push wages below market equilibrium. Workers can also gain market power, by banding together to make joint labor supply decisions and push their wages above equilibrium. Through regulations, government can also impose costs on labor markets.

Review Questions

1. Consider the factors of production that go into a fast-food restaurant. Give an example of land, labor, and capital. **[LO 16.1]**

2. Suppose an auto manufacturer has one factory in the United States and one in Mexico. The auto manufacturer produces the same number of cars and the same models in each factory but hires more workers in Mexico than in the United States. Give an explanation for the discrepancy in the amount of labor hired in each location. **[LO 16.1]**

3. Suppose you run a flower-delivery business and employ college students to drive the vans and make deliveries. You are considering hiring an additional worker. What information would you need to know to decide whether doing so would increase or decrease your profit? **[LO 16.2]**

4. Christina runs an IT consulting firm in a competitive market. She recently determined that hiring an additional consultant would mean that she would be able to serve five more clients per week. Assuming her goal is to maximize her profits, explain why Christina did not hire another consultant. **[LO 16.2]**

5. Suppose your retired grandmother has complained of boredom and is considering taking a part-time job. Use the concept of opportunity cost to advise your grandmother how to decide whether to take the job. **[LO 16.3]**

6. Jackie and Samia are both nurses at the same hospital. Jackie and Samia have the same duties, experience, and performance reviews. Give an example that explains why Samia makes more than Jackie for the same job. **[LO 16.3]**

7. Suppose BMW runs a great ad campaign that increases demand and drives up the price of BMWs. What do you expect will happen to the demand for the labor in

auto-manufacturing plants? Explain how the equilibrium price and quantity of labor will change. **[LO 16.4]**

8. Suppose a cafe owner wants to switch to automatic espresso machines instead of paying baristas to pack the coffee grounds by hand. The machines are twice as effective as a human; the fixed cost per machine equals the yearly wage of one employee. Explain how the equilibrium price and quantity of labor will change. **[LO 16.4]**

9. Leo runs a bicycle repair shop. He recently examined information on wage and employment levels and noted that he employs the same number of workers today that he employed in 2012. However, wages (controlling for inflation) increased quite substantially between 2012 and 2016. Assume the supply of labor remained constant over this time period. Give two possible explanations for why Leo's workers are paid more in 2016. **[LO 16.5]**

10. Consider a labor market that traditionally discriminates against hiring women. Suppose a new law effectively prohibits this practice. What would you expect to happen to the wages of men in this industry? **[LO 16.5]**

11. Suppose your friend wants to become a doctor. Describe some of the human capital required to achieve this goal. **[LO 16.6]**

12. Madison has a full-time job, but she is considering going back to school for a master's degree. Describe how Madison might decide whether or not to continue her education. **[LO 16.6]**

13. Ariel is shopping for a space to open a new restaurant. She has two options in her target neighborhood. One space is available for lease and the other for purchase. How would you advise Ariel to think through her choice of restaurant location? What factors should she consider? **[LO 16.7]**

14. Suppose you have inherited a few acres of land from a relative and you are considering what to do with your inheritance. A farmer with land next to yours offers to buy your acres so he can expand his grazing area. How will you decide whether to sell your land to the farmer? What factors should you consider? **[LO 16.7]**

15. Large telecom companies like AT&T routinely send repair technicians to customers' homes. Although they are skilled laborers, they must usually train on the job, so it takes some time for them to reach a high standard of quality. In addition, their work cannot be constantly supervised. Explain why an efficiency wage could help telecom companies to increase the productivity of repair techs. **[LO 16.8]**

16. The Coalition of Immokalee Workers (CIW) claims that the going wage for farm labor is exploitative. The CIW supports a minimum wage for farm workers. Explain how the minimum wage would affect a farm's hiring

decision. Are farm workers better off under this policy? **[LO 16.8]**

17. Suppose a new law passes requiring farms to provide health benefits to farm labor. Assume that workers value having health benefits. When the new law goes into effect, what will happen to the wage for farm labor at equilibrium? Now suppose farm workers place no value on health benefits. How does this affect your answer? **[LO 16.9]**

18. Suppose a group of high school friends work at the same fast-food restaurant. They all dislike the manager because she doesn't allow them to swap shifts with one another whenever someone has a big exam to study for or a date. One of the friends suggests that they all agree to walk out if the manager doesn't change her policy. Explain whether the manager will change her policy to avoid a walkout. **[LO 16.9]**

Problems and Applications

1. Recently, some college alumni started a moving service for students living on campus. They have three employees and are debating hiring a fourth. The hourly wage for an employee is $18 per hour. An average moving job takes three hours. The company currently does three moving jobs per week, but with one more employee, the company could manage five jobs per week. The company charges $80 for a moving job. **[LO 16.1, 16.2]**

   a. What would be the new employee's marginal product of labor?

   b. What is the value of that marginal product?

   c. Should the moving service hire a fourth worker?

2. Fresh Veggie is one of many small farms in Florida operating in a perfectly competitive market. Farm labor is also perfectly competitive, and Fresh Veggie can hire as many workers as it wants for $20 a day. The daily productivity of a tomato picker is given in Table 16P-1. If a bushel of tomatoes sells for $5, how many workers will Fresh Veggie hire? **[LO 16.1, 16.2]**

3. Dustin's labor supply curve is graphed in Figure 16P-1. **[LO 16.3]**

   a. Consider a wage increase from $5 to $6. For Dustin, does the price effect or income effect dominate his labor supply decision?

   b. Consider a wage increase from $7 to $8. For Dustin, does the price effect or income effect dominate his labor supply decision?

4. Sasha has 60 hours a week she can work or have leisure. Wages are $8/hour. **[LO 16.3]**

   a. Graph Sasha's budget constraint for income and leisure.

TABLE 16P-1

Labor	Bushels of tomatoes	MP of Labor	VMPL
0	0	—	—
1	12		
2	22		
3	30		
4	35		
5	38		
6	40		

TABLE 16P-2

Hourly wage ($)	Labor hours demanded	Labor hours supplied
24	0	600
22	50	550
20	100	500
18	150	450
16	200	400
14	250	350
12	300	300
10	350	250
8	400	200

FIGURE 16P-1

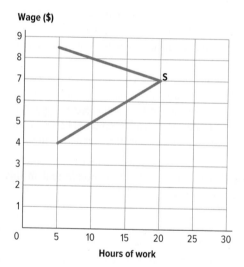

TABLE 16P-3

Wage ($)	Quantity supplied	Quantity demanded
3	2,000	5,000
4	3,000	4,500
5	4,000	4,000
6	5,000	3,500
7	6,000	3,000
8	7,000	2,500
9	8,000	2,000

b. Suppose wages increase to $10/hour. Graph Sasha's new budget constraint.

c. When wages increase from $8/hour to $10/hour, Sasha's leisure time decreases from 20 hours to 15 hours. Does her labor supply curve slope upward or downward over this wage increase?

5. Suppose you run a business that specializes in producing graphic T-shirts, using labor as an input. Based on Table 16P-2, graph the labor supply and demand curves and identify the market equilibrium wage and quantity of labor hours. **[LO 16.4]**

6. Based on Table 16P-3, indicate what would happen in this labor market at various wage rates by selecting one of the three choices shown for each item. **[LO 16.4]**

a. At $8/hour: excess labor supply; excess labor demand; or equilibrium.

b. At $3/hour: excess labor supply; excess labor demand; or equilibrium.

c. At $5/hour: excess labor supply; excess labor demand; or equilibrium.

7. Identify which way the labor supply curve would shift under the following scenarios. **[LO 16.5]**

a. A country experiences a huge influx of immigrants who are skilled in the textile industry.

b. Wages increase in an industry that requires similar job skills.

c. New machines require additional maintenance over time, so that the marginal productivity of labor rises.

FIGURE 16P-2

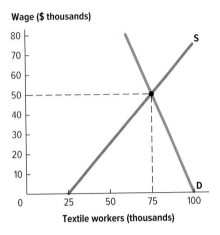

Wage ($ thousands)

Textile workers (thousands)

8. Figure 16P-2 shows the supply and demand for labor in the textile industry. In each of the following scenarios, identify the direction of the shift in either the supply or demand curve and state whether the resulting equilibrium wage and quantity *increase* or *decrease*. **[LO 16.5]**

    a. What are the original equilibrium wage and quantity?

    b. Immigration and layoffs from other jobs increase the population of textile workers.

    c. A new technology for making self-printed T-shirts reduces the marginal product of labor for textile workers.

9. Figure 16P-3 shows the supply and demand for labor in the hybrid automobile industry. In each of the following scenarios, identify the direction of the shift in either the supply or demand curve, and state whether the resulting equilibrium wage and quantity *increase* or *decrease*. **[LO 16.5]**

    a. A new tool is invented that increases each worker's marginal product.

    b. The demand for hybrid cars increases.

10. Suppose that fast-food chains start using healthier ingredients, increasing the demand for fast food and therefore for food-service workers, as shown in Figure 16P-4. **[LO 16.6]**

    a. What are the new equilibrium wage and quantity of labor in the fast-food industry?

    b. Assume that the skills required of a sales clerk at a retail store are similar to those required of workers at a fast-food restaurant. If workers are completely indifferent between fast-food jobs and retail-sales jobs, what will be the wages for sales clerks?

11. Suppose a town's largest employers are its auto manufacturing plant and its airplane manufacturing plant. Airplane manufacturing jobs require familiarity with a technology that is not currently used in auto manufacturing. Assume workers are indifferent between the two types of manufacturing work. **[LO 16.6]**

    a. All else equal, which plant will pay its workers more?

    b. Suppose the auto industry adopts the same technology used by airplane manufacturers and trains its current workers in this technology. What will happen to the pay differential between auto manufacturing and airplane manufacturing work?

12. Figure 16P-5 shows a local labor market for landscapers. What is the value of economic rent in this labor market? **[LO 16.7]**

FIGURE 16P-3

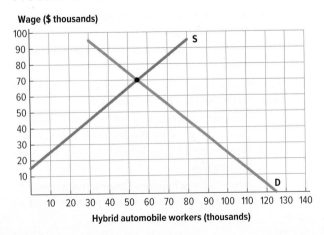

Wage ($ thousands)

Hybrid automobile workers (thousands)

FIGURE 16P-4

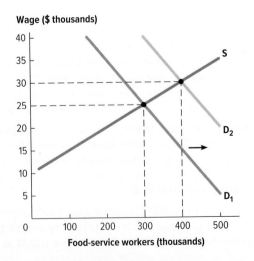

Wage ($ thousands)

Food-service workers (thousands)

FIGURE 16P-5

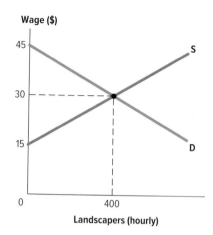

Wage ($)

Landscapers (hourly)

FIGURE 16P-6

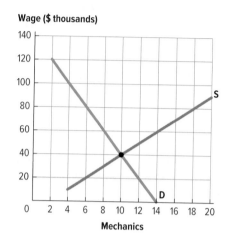

Wage ($ thousands)

Mechanics

13. Match the following aspects of factor markets with the corresponding characteristics. **[LO 16.7]**

   a. analogous to producer surplus
   b. affected by an asset's long-run productivity
   c. interest paid on loans
   d. determined by ownership of factors of production
   e. determined by the value of marginal product

   __Demand for factors of production
   __Economic rent
   __Purchase markets for factors of production
   __Rental price of capital
   __Income

FIGURE 16P-7

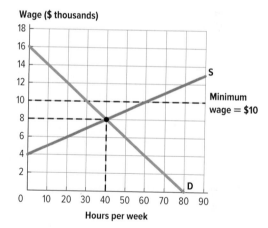

Wage ($ thousands)

Hours per week

14. Figure 16P-6 shows a local labor market for mechanics. What are the quantity supplied and quantity demanded when the minimum wage is each of the following? **[LO 16.8]**

   a. $40,000.
   b. $20,000.
   c. $60,000.

15. The market for grocery-store baggers is a competitive labor market, as shown in Figure 16P-7. Suppose a new federal law raises the minimum wage to $10 per hour. **[LO 16.8]**

   a. What is the equilibrium wage rate prior to the law being enacted?
   b. What are total labor earnings at the equilibrium wage?

   c. How much labor is being hired at the minimum wage?
   d. What are total labor earnings with enactment of the minimum wage?

16. Imagine that, faced with budget shortfalls, a government changes its current policy of granting tax credits based on family size to a flat rate tax credit for a family with one or more children. **[LO 16.9]**

   a. Over time, what will happen to the average age in the population?
   b. Over time, what will happen to the size of the workforce?

17. In each scenario, will wages rise above the market equilibrium or fall below it? **[LO 16.9]**

    a. All but one of the factories in a town go out of business.

    b. All the software engineers in Silicon Valley organize into a union and go on strike.

    c. A major grocery store chain buys out all the other stores in the city.

Endnotes

1. http://www.spotrac.com/mlb/los-angeles-dodgers/clayton-kershaw/; http://www.bls.gov/oes/current/oes452099.htm.

2. http://www.ers.usda.gov/topics/farm-economy/farm-labor.aspx.

3. http://www.bls.gov/oes/current/oes272021.htm.

4. http://www.wsj.com/articles/the-thorny-economics-of-illegal-immigration-1454984443.

5. http://www.statista.com/statistics/270034/percentage-of-us-adults-to-have-money-invested-in-the-stock-market/.

6. http://www.paywizard.org/main/salary/minimum-wage.

7. https://www.ssa.gov/news/press/basicfact.html.

International Trade

Learning Objectives

LO 17.1 Define comparative advantage and list some root causes of comparative advantage on a national level.

LO 17.2 Determine whether a country will become a net-importer or net-exporter of a good when it moves from autarky to free trade.

LO 17.3 Calculate the change in surplus and the distribution of benefits within a market when a country opens up to trade.

LO 17.4 Identify when and how an economy's trade policies affect world supply of and world demand for a good.

LO 17.5 Explain the effect of a tariff on quantity, price, and the distribution of surplus.

LO 17.6 Explain the effect of an import quota on quantity, price, and the distribution of surplus.

LO 17.7 Describe the effects of trade on the factor distribution of income.

LO 17.8 Discuss the challenges of establishing environmental or labor standards in international markets.

MADE IN LESOTHO

Around the year 2000, a tiny country in southern Africa called Lesotho suddenly developed a flourishing business making T-shirts and jeans for companies including Walmart, Old Navy, Levi Strauss, and Kmart. Lesotho is home to around 2 million citizens—smaller than the city of Houston, Texas. It doesn't grow cotton—a crop you might have expected in a country with a T-shirt and jeans industry. In fact, it doesn't grow much of anything; the mountainous country's lowest point is 4,593 feet above sea level. Common ways of earning a living in Lesotho include herding goats and working in diamond mines. It's a difficult place to get goods into or out of: It's landlocked, meaning it has no seaport, and it also lacks a major airport. All in all, Lesotho seems like a strange place in which to suddenly find a garment-export industry. Stranger yet, many of the factories that sprang up were owned by firms based in Taiwan.

Why did Taiwanese businesses go to Lesotho to make clothing to be sold thousands of miles away in the United States? What changed in 2000 that caused this unexpected trade pattern to flourish?

In this chapter, we pick up on the story told in Chapter 2, "Specialization and Exchange," of how clothing production has moved around the world over the last 200 years, following the path of cheap labor. When we left the story, Bangladesh was one of the world's largest clothing makers; many consumers in the United States were wearing shirts made in Bangladeshi factories. Bangladesh's success in making clothing—as well as Lesotho's sudden emergence as a garment manufacturer—is made possible only by a crucial fact: Americans can buy clothing made in Bangladesh and Lesotho. That seems obvious, but the ability to buy goods from across the world is a relatively new development. Before the vast improvements in transportation over the last century, it was hard to reach far-off trading partners, let alone bring large quantities of goods back home.

Modern transportation and communication technology have made international trade much easier. But trade has also been shaped by a complex web of international agreements. For example, for most of the last 40 years, international trade in textiles and clothing was strictly regulated. The Multifibre Arrangement (MFA)—actually a whole group of separate treaties between individual countries—set limits on how much of what type of clothing could be traded between which countries, often on a level of detail that seems ridiculous in retrospect. How many pairs of cotton socks were Bangladeshi firms allowed to sell to American consumers? How many wool sweaters? The MFA had an answer, and it was not "as many cotton socks and wool sweaters as Americans want to buy." In other words, there was some trade in clothing between the United States and Bangladesh, but it was not unrestricted *free* trade. Similar restrictions applied to most of the major clothing-producing countries in the world.

At the same time, the United States made other treaties that exempted some countries from the limits set by the Multifibre Arrangement. Free-trade agreements with Mexico and Central American countries overrode the restrictions on clothing trade. So did the African Growth and Opportunity Act (AGOA) of 2000, which granted preferential trading-partner status to some very poor countries in Africa—including Lesotho. Taiwanese clothing companies quickly figured out that the MFA meant they couldn't sell T-shirts and jeans to American consumers if they made them in factories in Taiwan. But under AGOA they *could* reach those consumers by building factories in Lesotho. So they did.

© Feng Yu/Alamy

This garbled combination of trade policies didn't last long. By 2005, the restrictions set by the Multifibre Arrangement had been gradually phased out, freeing up trade in clothing and textiles. What effect did it have on consumers? How about the effect on workers in Asia and the United States—and in tiny Lesotho? As we'll see later in the chapter, that was good news for Asian suppliers and bad news for Lesotho.[1]

In this chapter, we'll see how trade affects prices, workers, and consumers in different countries. We'll also see how trade provides enormous benefits to some countries and industries, but creates losers too. For a business owner, navigating this web successfully can be the difference between riches and bankruptcy. As workers and consumers, the wages we get and the prices we pay are deeply affected by trade, sometimes in ways that are hard to see at first.

Why Trade? A Review

Trade between most countries isn't free. Before we consider why not, let's briefly review why countries would want to trade in the first place. We can draw on some basic concepts from Chapter 2, "Specialization and Exchange," to predict where different goods will be made when markets function smoothly and what the advantages of trade will be.

Comparative advantage

LO 17.1 Define comparative advantage and list some root causes of comparative advantage on a national level.

The United States imports clothing from all over Asia, and especially from Bangladesh. What does that fact tell us? Most obviously, it tells us that both Bangladeshi firms and American consumers have something to gain from this trade. As we know, voluntary exchanges generate surplus, leaving both participants better off than they were before. This is as true when firms or countries trade as it is when individuals do.

It also tells us that Bangladesh must have some advantage over the United States when it comes to producing clothes. If it did not, then the United States would produce its own. What kind of advantage? It might mean that Bangladeshi firms are simply more productive than those in the United States. If that were true, we would say that Bangladesh has an *absolute* advantage at clothing production. *Absolute advantage* is the ability to produce more of a good than others with a given amount of resources—for instance, to produce more T-shirts with the same number of workers.

But remember that absolute advantage does not determine who produces what. Comparative advantage does. *Comparative advantage* is the ability to produce a good or service at a lower opportunity cost than others can. The fact that companies in Bangladesh sell clothing to the United States doesn't necessarily tell us that Bangladesh is more productive at making clothes, but it definitely tells us that Bangladesh's opportunity cost of making a shirt is lower than that of the United States. (For a review of absolute versus comparative advantage, look back at the "Absolute and Comparative Advantage" section in Chapter 2, "Specialization and Exchange.")

Gains from trade

If U.S. workers are at least as productive as Bangladeshi workers at making shirts, why do U.S. firms import shirts made in Bangladesh? Simply put, *both* countries can gain when each specializes in producing the good for which it has a comparative advantage. The two can then trade to get the combination of goods that people in each country want to consume. The increase in welfare in both countries that results from specialization and trade is called, straightforwardly enough, the *gains from trade*.

To see the gains from trade in action, let's compare total production and consumption with and without trade, as shown in Table 17-1. We've made up numbers to keep the example simple,

TABLE 17-1

Hypothetical global production and consumption with and without trade

	Country	Wheat produced (billions)	T-shirts produced (billions)	Wheat consumed (billions)	T-shirts consumed (billions)
Without trade	United States	1.0	0.30	1.0	0.30
	Bangladesh	0.7	0.05	0.7	0.05
	Total	**1.7**	**0.35**	**1.7**	**0.35**
With trade	United States	2.0	0.0	1.2	0.3
	Bangladesh	0.0	0.5	0.8	0.2
	Total	**2.0**	**0.5**	**2.0**	**0.5**

but they capture the spirit of the real situation. For simplicity, we'll assume that only two goods are produced by the United States and Bangladesh: wheat and T-shirts. Let's look at what would happen, in this example, with and without trade.

Without trade, each country has to produce the combination of wheat and shirts that its people actually want to consume. This means that:

- The United States will produce 300 million shirts and 1 billion bushels of wheat.
- Bangladesh will produce 50 million shirts and 700 million bushels of wheat.

Total global production is thus 350 million shirts and 1.7 billion bushels of wheat.

When trade is possible, each country can produce the goods that it has a comparative advantage at producing, rather than the exact combination of goods its consumers want. In our simple story, that means the United States will specialize in growing wheat and Bangladesh will specialize in making shirts. Under the trade scenario:

- The United States will produce 2 billion bushels of wheat.
- Bangladesh will produce 500 million T-shirts.

The result is that global production is higher: With trade, there are 150 million more shirts and 300 million more bushels of wheat than there were before.

With trade, both countries can consume more than they were able to before, and the two countries can split this bonus in a way that makes both better off. Notice that in Table 17-1, both countries have higher consumption of both goods after specialization and trade. (To review the calculation of production specialization, look back at Chapter 2, "Specialization and Exchange," especially Table 2-1.)

The roots of comparative advantage

The media often describe countries trading as national entities, just as we have done above with the United States and Bangladesh. (For example: "The United States will specialize in growing wheat, and Bangladesh will specialize in making shirts.") From such wording, you might get the impression that trade requires *governments* to get together, employ an economic superplanner to crunch the numbers, and agree on who is going to specialize in what. But that's not the case at all. The reality is that the day-to-day business of trade is carried out almost entirely by firms and individuals in individual countries, not by governments.

How does a factory in Atlanta, Georgia, know what its comparative advantage is relative to a factory in Dhaka, the capital of Bangladesh? This is a case of the "invisible hand" at work.

But the working of the invisible hand doesn't mean that the right decision about what to produce and who to trade with happens *automatically*. If you own a factory, it's up to you to research the cost of inputs such as labor and raw materials, and the sale prices of different goods you could produce, and calculate the most profitable option. If you get it right, you'll make profits. If you get it wrong, you'll go out of business.

Meanwhile, factory owners in Dhaka and everywhere else in the world are all doing the same kind of research and calculations. When everyone *responds* to the profit motives they face as individual producers, they gravitate toward producing the products in which they have a comparative advantage, and the gains from trade fall into place.

Let's get a little more concrete. We discussed in the previous chapter how the prices of *factors of production* are determined. For instance, you might want to hire workers to sew shirts in your factory in Georgia, but those workers can also choose to supply their labor to a company that makes car parts. If the workers are more productive at making car parts than shirts, the car-parts factory will be willing to offer them a higher wage. This decreases the supply of labor for making shirts, which, in turn, pushes up the wage for shirt-makers.

Now suppose that workers in Dhaka don't have such good alternatives to shirt-making. They are willing to work in a shirt factory for lower wages, so firms in Dhaka have a lower cost of producing shirts. That lower cost, in turn, makes firms in Dhaka willing to offer shirts at a lower price on the world market.

In this way, the price of each factor of production incorporates the opportunity cost of using that factor to produce other goods. You, as a would-be shirt-producer in the United States, consider the prices of all the factors of production for shirts, and the price you could get for shirts on the world market. When you compare the costs to the market price, you conclude that your factory won't be able to break even selling shirts at this lower price. This is the market telling you that your factory in Georgia doesn't have a comparative advantage at producing shirts, and you should make something else instead.

To put it another way, only a firm with a comparative advantage at producing shirts—that is, the lowest opportunity cost of production—will be able to make shirts profitably. Simply by responding to the prices of inputs and outputs and choosing to produce the good that earns it the highest profits, each firm ends up producing the good in which it has a comparative advantage.

So far, so good. But what *causes* firms in one country to have a lower opportunity cost of production for sewing shirts versus making car parts versus programming computers or anything else? Economists look to several national characteristics that affect the cost of producing goods in a particular country: natural resources and climate, endowment of factors of production, and technology.

Natural resources and climate

Why does Hawaii have a comparative advantage over Russia in growing pineapples? There's a simple reason—it's warm in Hawaii and often cold in Russia. Diversity in climate and natural resources is an important determinant of comparative advantage. Certain parts of California and France, for instance, have a complex combination of soil and weather that allows them to grow grapes that make world-class wine.

Climate and geography may also affect the costs of transporting goods to other places once they are produced. For instance, a country with great seaports will be able to trade different goods than will a landlocked country far from major consumer markets, such as Lesotho.

Factor endowment

The relative abundance of different factors of production makes some countries better suited to produce certain goods. For instance:

- A country with a lot of land relative to its population, such as New Zealand or Argentina, may have a comparative advantage in *land-intensive* activities such as grazing cattle or sheep.

- A country with plenty of capital and little land, such as Hong Kong or Japan, might do well with more *capital-intensive* activities such as producing high-tech electronics, providing financial services, or doing biomedical research.
- A country with plenty of cheap labor, such as Bangladesh or Lesotho, will do well with *labor-intensive* activities such as clothing manufacturing, which requires relatively little capital or technology.

Factor endowment helps to explain the story we told in Chapter 2, "Specialization and Exchange," about how clothing production has moved around the world over the last few centuries. It has followed the path of cheap labor from country to country. As workforces became more educated in countries that were early leaders in the textile industry, cheap labor became less abundant relative to skilled labor and capital. As a result, comparative advantage shifted toward countries with more cheap labor relative to the other factors of production.

Technology

Lastly, technology can have an effect on comparative advantage. Over time, technology tends to spread from country to country, equalizing opportunity costs. However, at any given time, technology or production processes developed in a particular country may give that country a temporary comparative advantage. We saw in Chapter 2, "Specialization and Exchange," that the invention of the power loom initially gave Great Britain an advantage at clothing production. However, the new technology quickly spread to the United States, erasing that advantage.

Incomplete specialization

In our analysis of international trade we have talked about comparative advantage at the country level. But, of course, not everyone in a country has the same job. Not all Americans grow wheat, not all Bangladeshis make shirts, not all New Zealanders graze sheep, and so on. If there are big gains to be had from specialization and trade, *why doesn't every country produce just one good?*

The answer has two parts. First, no national economy is a perfectly free market, and neither is trade between national economies. As we will discuss later in the chapter, specialization is often limited by trade agreements. These agreements are dependent on noneconomic considerations such as national security, tradition, and not-so-rational politicking. Those restrictions and political concerns put limits on how much specialization we can expect.

Second, even if trade were perfectly free, nations would not specialize completely. Within each country there are differences in the natural resources, climate, and relative factor endowment of different areas. For example:

- It makes sense to produce wine in California, but not in Alaska due to its cold climate.
- The opportunity cost of making cars may be low in Alabama but high in downtown Manhattan, where space for factories is hard to find.
- Land is fertile for growing wheat in much of Iowa, but not in much of Nevada.

We can talk *in general* about Bangladesh having a comparative advantage in producing shirts and the United States in growing wheat. But in a super-fertile wheat-growing region of Bangladesh, the opportunity cost of growing wheat is lower than making shirts. It would make sense for Bangladesh to grow wheat in that region and import from the United States the rest of the wheat it needs.

In other words, the opportunity costs are not always constant. If the United States was producing only wheat, some farmers would probably have to work on land that isn't well-suited to producing wheat. In particular, it's very hard to grow wheat in an urban area. So in urban areas, the opportunity cost of producing wheat might be very high. Thus, the United States will produce a different good that is not wheat in areas where the opportunity cost of wheat production is very high. Because the United States is a very large country, opportunity costs vary by location, and it produces many different types of goods.

✓CONCEPT CHECK

☐ What is the difference between absolute and comparative advantage? Which one determines what goods countries specialize in producing? **[LO 17.1]**

☐ What are the major characteristics that determine comparative advantage? **[LO 17.1]**

From Autarky to Free Trade

Free, unrestricted exchanges between individual buyers and sellers maximize surplus, producing benefits for both parties. Similarly, free trade between countries maximizes surplus, producing benefits for both parties.

But simply saying "the United States gains from trade" glosses over the fact that the United States consists of many different industries, firms, and individual people. In reality, some of these will gain and some will lose from trade. However, the *total gains* will be higher than *total losses*. In order to understand the effects of trade on a more detailed level, and to see who exactly gains in what way, we need to dig deeper.

Let's start by imagining a world without any trade at all. Countries in this imaginary world neither import nor export:

- **Imports** are goods and services that are produced in other countries and consumed domestically.

- **Exports** are goods and services that are produced domestically and consumed in other countries.

We call an economy that is self-contained and does not engage in any trade with outsiders an **autarky**. Suppose that the U.S. economy is an autarky, meaning there are no imports or exports. Under autarky, nothing produced outside the country is sold inside, and nothing produced inside the country is sold outside.

What would the market for shirts in the United States look like without any trade? We can describe the domestic market with the same supply and demand curves that we've used in previous chapters. The supply curve shown in Figure 17-1 includes only *domestic* clothing manufacturers. The demand curve includes only *domestic* consumers. This situation without any trade allows us to determine the price and quantity of shirts sold in the country by finding the intersection of the supply and demand curves, just as we've done all along. U.S. consumers and producers will buy and sell 300 million shirts per year at a price of $25.

imports
goods and services that are produced in other countries and consumed domestically

exports
goods and services that are produced domestically and consumed in other countries

autarky
an economy that is self-contained and does not engage in trade with outsiders

FIGURE 17-1
Domestic supply and demand for shirts in an autarky

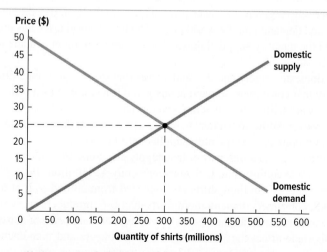

Under autarky, the domestic price and quantity of shirts are determined by the intersection of the domestic supply and domestic demand curves.

Becoming a net-importer

LO 17.2 Determine whether a country will become a net-importer or net-exporter of a good when it moves from autarky to free trade.

LO 17.3 Calculate the change in surplus and the distribution of benefits within a market when a country opens up to trade.

In our imaginary scenario, the United States is not trading with other countries, but let's suppose that all other countries have free trade in clothing. This means that outside the United States, shirts are being bought and sold at a *world price,* which is not necessarily the same as the U.S. price (which, remember, is $25). In fact, let's say that the world price of shirts is only $15.

POTENTIALLY CONFUSING

In reality, there is not a *single* world price for shirts. A shirt costs less in rural Mexico than it does in New York City for a variety of reasons. However, the idea of a world price in an international market with free trade is a useful simplification that lets us describe a complicated situation. It's analogous to the market price in any other sort of market with free exchanges—any seller who tries to sell at a higher price will simply lose all of his customers to other sellers.

If you are a U.S. company trying to sell your product, you can usefully think of the world price as the amount you could get for it by exporting to a wholesaler outside of the United States.

What happens in our autarky example if the U.S. government decides to free up trade in clothing—to allow unrestricted imports and exports? The domestic price of shirts is $25, the world price is $15, and all of a sudden, shirts can be freely traded across U.S. borders. Now, U.S. consumers have no reason to pay more than $15 for a domestically produced shirt. They can instead simply buy a shirt imported from abroad.

What happens then? The market price for shirts within the United States falls to $15. At the lower price of $15, more U.S. buyers want to buy shirts. However, fewer U.S. producers are willing to produce shirts, given the lower price. Figure 17-2 illustrates the interaction between domestic supply and demand and the world price. The lower world price has pushed the quantity demanded up and the quantity supplied down. The gap between them is made up by shirts being *imported* from abroad.

Note that the domestic supply and demand curves themselves have not shifted. Trade doesn't affect the quantity that consumers demand at any given price, nor does it affect the quantity that domestic producers are willing to sell at any given price.

Trade does, however, allow consumers to buy at a price where domestic demand doesn't equal domestic supply. Of course, total quantity supplied still has to equal total quantity demanded at the equilibrium price—it's just that part of that supply can come from international producers.

In the new free-trade equilibrium, U.S. consumers buy 420 million shirts, U.S. producers sell 180 million shirts, and 240 million shirts are imported from abroad—all at a price of $15 per shirt. Because U.S. consumers demand more shirts than U.S. producers are willing to supply, the U.S. will have to import the difference—thus becoming a *net-importer* of shirts.

How does this trade affect the welfare of U.S. shirt buyers and manufacturers? Who gains from free trade and who loses? Figure 17-3 shows how consumer and producer surplus in the market for shirts change when the United States goes from autarky to free trade. Panel A shows the surplus under autarky and panel B shows what happens to the surplus after trade.

FIGURE 17-2
Becoming a net-importer

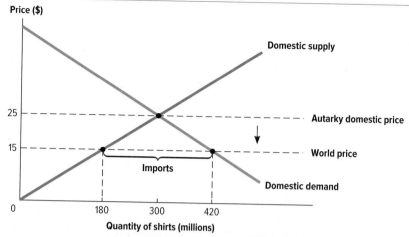

When a country opens its market to trade and the *world price is lower than the domestic price*, the domestic price will fall to meet the world price. At the lower price, domestic quantity demanded increases, but domestic quantity supplied decreases. Imports will make up the difference between the quantities domestically supplied and demanded at the world price.

FIGURE 17-3

Welfare effects of becoming a net-importer

(A) Surplus under autarky

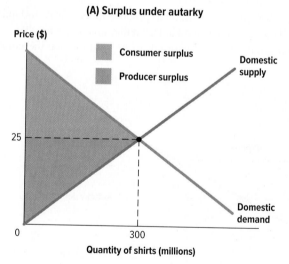

Under autarky, consumers receive the top (gold) shaded area as surplus, while producers receive the bottom (blue) shaded area.

(B) Surplus after trade

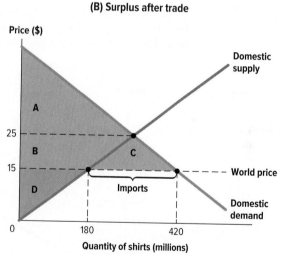

When a country opens up to trade and becomes a net-importer of shirts, consumer surplus in the shirt market increases, while producer surplus decreases. In panel B, consumer surplus increases by the area B + C. Producer surplus decreases by the area B. Total surplus now equals A + B + C + D. The net increase in surplus is area C.

Notice that areas A, B, and D are surplus for somebody, both before and after trade:

• Area A is consumer surplus in both scenarios.
• Area D is producer surplus in both scenarios.

- Area B represents surplus that was enjoyed by U.S. producers before trade and is enjoyed by U.S. consumers after trade; that is, it is surplus that transitioned from producers to consumers.

Area C, however, is *new* surplus created by trade: It arises as trade enables consumers to buy more shirts at the lower world price. Overall, free trade increases *total* surplus by area C. In this example, we can say that overall the United States has gained from trade. But that doesn't mean everyone in the United States is better off. Shirt consumers have gained a lot from trade, but shirt producers have lost out.

Becoming a net-exporter

Do producers always lose and consumers always win with free trade? That's the result only when the world price is *lower* than the domestic price. The opposite happens when the world price is *higher* than the domestic price. Let's look at what happens when the United States opens itself up to international trade in a good for which the world price is higher than the domestic price—say, wheat.

Figure 17-4 shows the domestic supply and demand curves for wheat in the United States. As with shirts, before trade restrictions are lifted, we can find the domestic price and quantity of wheat at the intersection of the supply and demand curves. Let's suppose U.S. consumers buy 60 million tons of wheat at a price of $200 per ton, but in the rest of the world, a ton of wheat sells for $260.

How will U.S. wheat producers *respond* to this difference in prices when trade opens up? Because they can sell as much wheat as they want to foreign consumers at $260, U.S. wheat producers have no incentive to sell it at a lower price in the United States. Therefore, if U.S. consumers want to buy wheat, they will have to pay $260, too.

At the world price of $260 per ton, U.S. farmers are willing to produce more wheat—80 million tons. However, given the higher price, U.S. consumers demand a smaller quantity, only 40 million tons. The gap between the two—40 million tons—is exported, to be sold outside the country.

FIGURE 17-4

Becoming a net-exporter

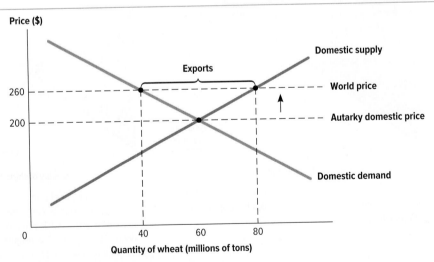

When a country opens its market to trade and the *world price is higher than the domestic price*, the domestic price will rise to meet the world price. At the higher price, domestic quantity supplied increases, but domestic quantity demanded decreases. Excess supply is exported to make up the difference between the quantities domestically supplied and demanded at the world price.

FIGURE 17-5

Welfare effects of becoming a net-exporter

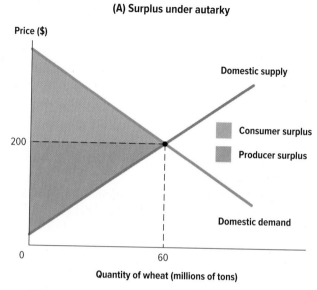

(A) Surplus under autarky

Without trade, consumers receive the top (gold) shaded area as surplus, while producers receive the bottom (blue) shaded area.

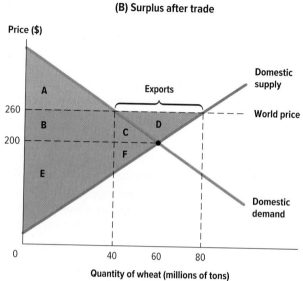

(B) Surplus after trade

When a country opens up to trade and becomes a net-exporter of wheat, consumer surplus in the wheat market decreases, while producer surplus increases. In panel B, producer surplus increases by the area B + C + D. Consumer surplus decreases by the area B + C. Total surplus now equals A + B + C + D + E + F. The net increase in surplus is area D.

In this new equilibrium, the price of wheat is higher. Because U.S. consumers demand less wheat than U.S. producers are willing to supply, the U.S. will have to export the difference—thus becoming a *net-exporter* of wheat.

How does becoming a net-exporter of wheat affect the welfare of U.S. consumers and producers? Figure 17-5 shows how consumer and producer surplus in the wheat market change when the United States goes from autarky to free trade. Panel A shows the surplus under autarky and panel B shows what happens to the surplus after trade.

Again, notice that areas A, B, C, E, and F were surplus for somebody both before and after trade:

- Area A is consumer surplus in both scenarios.
- Area E + F is producer surplus in both scenarios.
- Area B + C represents surplus that was enjoyed by U.S. consumers before trade and is enjoyed by U.S. producers after trade; that is, it is surplus that transitioned from consumers to producers.

Area D, however, is *new* surplus created by trade: It is gained by producers because trade enables them to sell more wheat at a higher price.

On net, total surplus increases by the area of D. That means that the post-trade equilibrium is more efficient than the pre-trade (autarky) equilibrium. In this example, we can say that overall the United States has gained from trade. But not everyone in the United States is better off: Wheat producers have gained from trade, but wheat consumers have lost out.

Big economy, small economy

LO 17.4 Identify when and how an economy's trade policies affect world supply of and world demand for a good.

If you were paying very close attention in Chapter 3, "Markets," when we discussed the external factors that determine demand and supply, you might remember discussion of the nonprice factors that can determine the quantity of goods demanded or supplied. If you did remember that discussion as you read this chapter, then you might have come up with some questions about our analysis of what happens when we move from autarky to trade. Specifically:

- An increase in the number of buyers is one of the external factors that can move a demand curve to the right. If you remembered that, then you might have wondered, "Wouldn't free trade cause an increase in the world demand for shirts, as U.S. consumers join the world market, pushing the world price up?"
- On the supply side, an increase in the number of sellers is one of the external factors that can move a supply curve to the right. If you remembered that, then you might have wondered, "Wouldn't free trade cause an increase in the world supply of wheat as U.S. wheat farmers join the world market, pushing the world price down?"

These are good questions, and the answer to both is: It depends how big the United States is relative to the total size of the world market. What do we mean by "big" in this context? To use the terminology of competitive markets, we assumed in our examples above that the United States is a *price taker* in the world market. That is, the decisions of its citizens about what quantity to produce or consume have no effect on the world price. Remember that buyers and sellers are *price takers* if they are too small, relative to the total size of the market, to have enough market power to influence the price.

In other words, for the United States to be a price taker in the global market for some good, the quantity it produces and consumes must be very small relative to the total amount of that good bought and sold worldwide. In some markets, the United States is probably small enough to be considered a price taker. Consider, for instance, the market for lychee—a tasty fruit that is very popular in Asia. Not many people eat lychee in the United States, and almost nobody grows lychee. Imagine that the U.S. government had banned the import and export of lychee, and then decided to end the ban and allow international trade. Would that change have much effect on the world price of lychee? Probably not because the quantity of lychee produced and consumed in the United States is very small compared with the total quantity sold globally.

In a lot of markets, however, the United States is definitely a big economy. (In fact, in overall terms, it is the biggest economy in the world.) If the United States decided to stop trading shirts or wheat, this decision almost certainly *would* affect the world price. Why? Because the quantity of these goods that the United States produces and consumes is *not* negligible relative to the total quantity sold worldwide.

This means we need to add a level of nuance to our analysis. Figure 17-6 shows supply and demand in the *world* market for shirts. (Be careful not to confuse the *world-market* supply and demand curves with the *domestic-market* supply and demand curves, shown in Figures 17-1, 17-2 and 17-3.) When the United States moves from autarky to free trade, the world demand curve shifts to the right because U.S. shirt consumers have entered the market. The world supply curve also moves a bit to the right because U.S. shirt producers have also entered the world market.

To find the new equilibrium in the world market, we need to see where the new supply and demand curves intersect. On net, because demand has increased by more than supply, we can see that the effect of the United States joining the market is that the world price of shirts increases from $15 to $17.

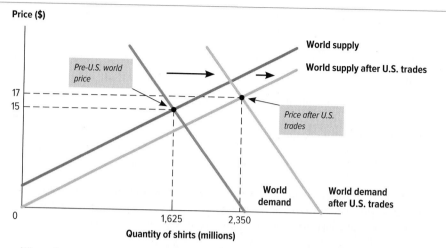

FIGURE 17-6

Impact of a big economy on the world price

When a large economy such as the United States enters the world market for shirts, it will influence both world supply and demand for that good. Because the United States is a net-importer of shirts at the world price, the shift in world demand is greater than the shift in world supply. The result is an increase in both world price and quantity of shirts.

What does this mean for U.S. shirt producers and consumers? Figure 17-7 shows what happens when the U.S. decision to move from autarky to free trade increases the world price (now that we are considering the size of the U.S. market). The bottom line is the same as before: The price of shirts in the United States goes down, and the country as a whole is better off, but U.S. shirt producers lose out.

FIGURE 17-7

From autarky to trade in a big economy

(A) Before market entry

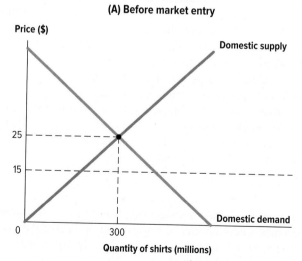

Under autarky, the United States produces 300 million T-shirts at a price of $25

(B) After market entry

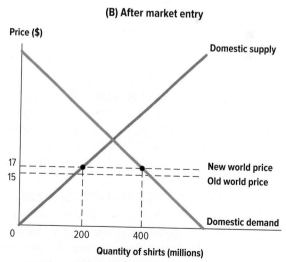

If the United States enters the world market as a large economy, it pushes the world price up from $15 to $17. The U.S. domestic price still drops relative to autarky, but by less than it would have if the United States was a price taker with no effect on the world market.

Compared with the graph in Figure 17-3, though, we can see that the quantity imported is slightly smaller than it would be if the United States were a price taker on the world market. The overall gain in surplus for the United States is smaller, and U.S. shirt producers are hurt a bit less.

Now that we've added this nuance to the analysis, we can see that the U.S. move from autarky to free trade also affects shirt producers and consumers outside the United States:

- Because the U.S. entry into the world market has increased the price of shirts, consumers in the rest of the world have to pay $17 instead of $15 for their shirts. That change reduces the surplus they enjoy.
- Foreign shirt producers, on the other hand, enjoy higher surplus due to the higher price and greater quantity they sell.

If we were to perform the same analysis for wheat, we would find that the effect of the U.S. entry into the world market would be to reduce the world price of wheat. That would be good news for foreign wheat consumers and bad news for foreign wheat producers.

✓ CONCEPT CHECK

☐ What is autarky? **[LO 17.2]**

☐ If the domestic price of a good is below the world price when it opens up to trade, will it become a net-importer or net-exporter of that good? **[LO 17.2]**

☐ When a country becomes a net-importer of a good, what happens to domestic consumer surplus? **[LO 17.3]**

☐ When a country becomes a net-exporter of a good, what happens to domestic producer surplus? **[LO 17.3]**

☐ When a large economy moves from restricted to unrestricted trade, what happens to world supply and world demand? **[LO 17.4]**

Restrictions on Trade

Even from our simple analysis so far, we can see how proposals to impose or lift restrictions on trade will be viewed very differently by different groups of people. A proposal for the United States to move from autarky to free trade would be opposed by U.S. shirt producers and foreign wheat farmers. But it would be welcomed by U.S. wheat farmers and foreign shirt producers. Americans who eat a lot of wheat-based food wouldn't like it, nor would foreign shirt-buyers. But Americans who buy lots of shirts would be happy, as would wheat-loving foreigners.

The big debates about international trade get more complicated because the questions are rarely about whether to completely forbid trade or to completely open it up to free global exchange. Instead, significant quantities of goods and services flow between countries, but much of that flow is heavily regulated. Understanding how prices and quantities will be affected by trade, and who wins and who loses, requires understanding trade restrictions.

Why restrict trade?

We saw in the previous section that trade is efficiency-enhancing: It *increases total surplus* regardless of whether the country becomes a net-importer or net-exporter of a particular good. Yet all countries restrict trade to some extent, and some restrict it quite heavily. Given that trade increases total welfare, why would anyone want to restrict it?

Some trade restrictions are based on global politics (as we'll discuss in the next section). But much of the rationale for restricting trade has to do with protecting those who lose surplus, or are perceived to lose surplus, as a result of free trade. For this reason, laws limiting trade are often referred to as *trade protection,* and a preference for policies that place limits on trade is called

protectionism. In contrast, policies and actions that reduce trade restrictions and promote free trade are often referred to as **trade liberalization**.

In this section, we'll examine two common tools for restricting international trade—tariffs and quotas—and see how they affect the distribution of surplus within a country.

Tariffs

LO 17.5 Explain the effect of a tariff on quantity, price, and the distribution of surplus.

A **tariff** is a tax that applies only to imported goods. Just like any other tax, a tariff causes deadweight loss and is inefficient. It also raises public funds, but that is not usually its aim. Typically, the most important goal of a tariff is to protect the interests of domestic producers.

In 2002, for example, the United States imposed a tariff of up to 30 percent on the sale price of imported steel for a three-year period. The rationale behind the tariff was explicitly to benefit the domestic steel industry. When then-president George W. Bush announced the new tariff, he described it as:

> . . . temporary safeguards to help give America's steel industry and its workers the chance to adapt to the large influx of foreign steel. This relief will help steel workers, communities that depend on steel, and the steel industry adjust without harming our economy.[2]

Did the steel tariff accomplish this goal? Let's take a look. The price of a ton of steel in early 2002 was around $250. With a 30 percent tariff, foreign firms selling steel in the United States had to pay $75 to the government for the privilege of importing each ton of steel.[3]

How should we expect foreign steel producers to have responded to this new cost? They would no longer sell steel in the United States for any price lower than $325 per ton—the world price of $250 plus the $75 tariff. If they sold for less than $325 per ton in the United States, they would still have to pay the $75 tariff and the difference would be their revenue. But why accept less revenue per ton when they could sell as much as they wanted for $250 per ton in other countries?

And how should we expect domestic steel producers to have responded? Assuming that $325 is still lower than the domestic price that would prevail under autarky, they would have had no reason to sell for less than $325 either, even though they were not subject to the tariff.

The tariff thus had exactly the same effect on the U.S. steel market as an increase in the world price to $325 per ton, as shown in Figure 17-8. The new, higher price pushed domestic producers up along the supply curve. They were still not willing to produce as much as consumers wanted to buy at that price, but they were willing to produce more than they were at a price of $250 per ton. The difference between the quantity supplied and the quantity demanded was still made up by imports, but that difference was smaller than it was before the tariff.

As a result of the tariff, domestic steel producers enjoyed an increase in surplus. That, after all, was what President Bush said he wanted it to achieve. Figure 17-9 shows the surplus before the tariff (in panel A) and after imposition of the tariff (in panel B):

- The amount producers gained in surplus from selling a larger quantity at a higher price is shown in area C. Notice that this gain in producer surplus comes at the expense of a loss in surplus for domestic consumers of steel, such as the U.S. auto and construction industries.
- Domestic steel consumers lost the surplus represented by area C to producers, but they also lost areas D, E, and F.
- Part of the loss in consumer surplus was converted into revenue for the government, which collects tariff payments on imports—shown as area E.
- The rest of the lost consumer surplus—areas D and F—became deadweight loss.

protectionism
a preference for policies that limit trade

trade liberalization
policies and actions that reduce trade restrictions

tariff
a tax on imported goods

FIGURE 17-8

Effect of a tariff on
imported steel

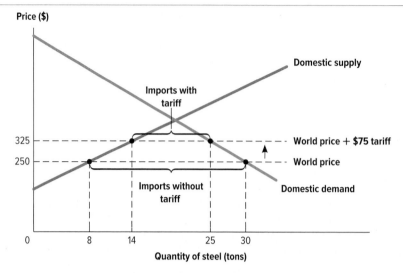

The world price before the tariff is $250. With a $75 tariff, the effective
world price increases to $325. The higher price increases domestic
supply, while it decreases domestic demand. As a result, the quantity
of imports also decreases.

FIGURE 17-9

Domestic welfare effects of a tariff

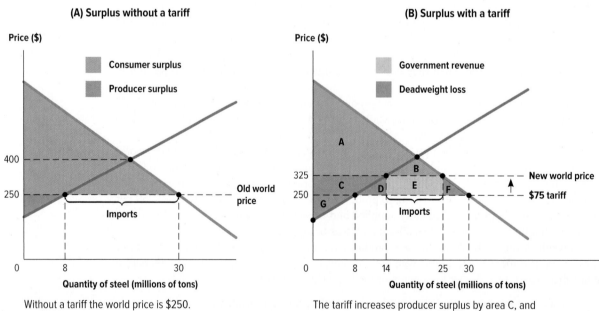

(A) Surplus without a tariff

Without a tariff the world price is $250.
Consumers demand 30 million tons of steel
and domestic producers are willing to sell
8 million tons.

(B) Surplus with a tariff

The tariff increases producer surplus by area C, and
decreases consumer surplus by area C + D + E + F.
Area E is the government revenue from the imposed tariff,
while area D + F is the deadweight loss. Note that the loss
of consumer surplus is greater than the sum of producer
surplus and government revenue gains.

In other words, the combined benefits that the tariff brought to steel producers and the U.S. government were outweighed by the loss in surplus suffered by domestic steel consumers.

We can see, then, that the steel tariff did not *exactly* achieve its goal of helping the domestic
steel industry "without harming our economy." In the end, was imposing the tariff the right

decision? That depends on how highly you value the benefit to the U.S. steel-production industry versus the loss to steel consumers, like the auto and construction industries.

In any case, the steel tariff didn't last long. In 2003, the World Trade Organization ruled that the tariffs were illegal, and President Bush withdrew them. We'll say more about the role of the World Trade Organization later in this chapter.

Quotas

LO 17.6 Explain the effect of an import quota on quantity, price, and the distribution of surplus.

The Multifibre Arrangement (MFA), which regulated trade of clothing items from the 1970s to 2005, used another type of trade restriction—the quota. An **import quota** is a limit on the amount of a particular good that can be imported. Under the MFA, different countries were subject to different quotas for different kinds of clothing goods. For instance, China could sell only so many cotton shirts in the United States, Pakistan could sell only so many, and Bangladesh, and so on.

import quota
a limit on the amount of a particular good that can be imported

Let's start with a simple example of a quota: a cap on the total number of pairs of blue jeans that can be imported into the United States. (For now, don't worry about how this quota is allocated between countries that produce jeans—we'll come back to that in a moment.) Figure 17-10 shows that under free trade, at the world price of $25 per pair, domestic jeans producers are willing to supply 500 million pairs of jeans. At that price, American consumers demand 1,350 million pairs of jeans. The difference—850 million pairs of jeans—is imported.

But what happens if a quota is imposed, limiting the total number of imported jeans to 500 million? The domestic price of jeans has to rise from $25 per pair to $32 per pair. That change in price shrinks the gap between domestic supply and domestic demand down to the 500 million limit imposed by the quota.

Notice that the effect of the quota is very similar to the effect of a tariff. The domestic (U.S.) price increases over the world price. As a result, domestic quantity demanded decreases, domestic

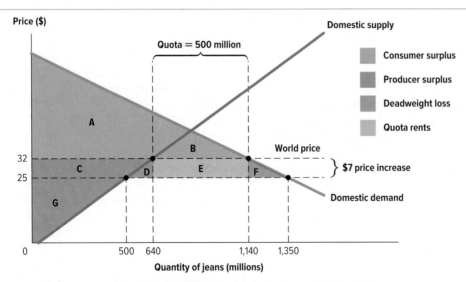

FIGURE 17-10
Domestic welfare effects of a quota

At the pre-quota price of $25, the gap between domestic demand (1,350 million) and supply (500 million) is met by an imported quantity of 850 million jeans. With an import quota of 500 million jeans, imports can't make up the full gap, pushing the domestic world price up to $32. As a result, producer surplus increases by area C, and consumer surplus decreases by area C + D + E + F. Area E is the quota rent gained by whoever holds the rights to import, while area D + F is the deadweight loss.

quantity supplied increases, and the quantity of imports falls. Domestic producers gain surplus from selling a higher quantity at a higher price. But domestic consumers lose even more surplus from buying a lower quantity at a higher price, resulting in deadweight loss (areas D and F).

However, there is an important distinction between the impact of tariffs and that of quotas—who *benefits* from the difference between the value of jeans in the United States and their value on the world market:

- Under a tariff, the U.S. government collects tax revenue equal to the quantity of imports multiplied by the difference between the domestic price and the world price.

- Under a quota, this value goes to whoever holds the rights to import. For instance, under a quota, if the U.S. government gives the government of Bangladesh the rights to import jeans into the United States, Bangladesh can then choose to sell those rights or hand them out to favored firms. Thus, the value of tax revenue under a tariff turns into profits earned by *foreign* firms or governments. These are called **quota rents**.

quota rents
profits earned by foreign firms or governments under a quota

Who will be granted the right to import how much of what goods into which countries is among the thorny issues trade negotiators grapple with when deciding on the details of trade treaties.

Selective exemptions from quotas and tariffs

Sometimes, wealthy countries may try to help poorer countries by agreeing to exempt them from quotas. Remember from the beginning of the chapter that tiny Lesotho was one of the countries exempted from most of the quotas and tariffs on clothing imported into the United States, under a policy called the African Growth and Opportunity Act (AGOA). Should we expect this approach to succeed in doing good for Lesotho?

Lesotho has a higher opportunity cost of producing blue jeans than big clothing manufacturers such as China and Bangladesh. (We know this because if it weren't true, Lesotho would have been producing and exporting clothing even before AGOA.) If there were no quotas, we would not expect Lesotho to produce any jeans at all.

However, as we have seen, the effect of quotas is to drive up prices. The quotas in the Multifibre Arrangement drove up prices so much that the benefits of making jeans in Lesotho started to outweigh the opportunity cost. Companies in Taiwan were not allowed to export as many jeans to the United States from Taiwan, so they started to build factories in Lesotho, from which they could export as many jeans as they liked. Quotas were bad for U.S. consumers and Taiwanese producers. But quotas were great for manufacturers and workers in countries such as Lesotho that were suddenly able to compete on the world market due to their preferential trade status.

The flip-side of this story is that when the United States began to peel back its trade restrictions on clothing, Lesotho once again faced competition from big, low-cost producers in Asia. By the time the Multifibre Arrangement was phased out in 2005, almost 70 percent of Lesotho's economy was based on exported clothing and textiles; the country as a whole took a big hit from falling prices and rising competition. Moving away from the Multifibre Arrangement toward free trade was efficient and increased total surplus in the world as a whole. It was great news for U.S. consumers and Taiwanese producers, for a start. But it was not universally beneficial. Trade policies—whether free trade or restricted—always generate both winners and losers, and one of the losers in this case was Lesotho.

✓CONCEPT CHECK

- ☐ How does a tariff on an imported good affect surplus for domestic producers of that good? **[LO 17.5]**
- ☐ How does a quota on an imported good affect surplus for domestic consumers of that good? **[LO 17.6]**
- ☐ In what way are tariff revenues and quota rents similar? **[LO 17.6]**

Trade Agreements

We've described what happens when a closed economy opens up to trade and what happens when a tariff or quota is imposed or lifted. Now we can talk more about *why* these things happen.

We've touched on reasons why U.S. politicians might want to protect domestic steel producers by imposing tariffs, or help impoverished African economies by exempting them from quotas. In this section, we'll dig deeper into how such decisions often are motivated by political and moral ideas, and see how economic analysis can be harnessed to understand their implications.

International labor and capital

LO 17.7 Describe the effects of trade on the factor distribution of income.

Political battles between free-traders and protectionists have always been fierce, and they continue to be so today. In the United States, protectionists accuse free-traders of shipping overseas the jobs of hard-working Americans. Free-traders accuse protectionists of giving handouts to big corporations at the expense of American consumers. Why are voters and politicians unable to agree on what is best?

Although the country as a whole gains from liberalizing trade, we've seen that certain segments of the population will lose out. As a general rule, free trade increases demand for factors of production that are domestically abundant. Free trade also decreases the supply of factors that are domestically scarce. In other words, free trade acts to equalize the supply of and demand for factors of production across countries. In turn, factor prices (such as wages) then start to converge across countries. The result:

- The owners of domestically scarce factors of production lose due to increased competition.
- The owners of domestically abundant factors gain from increased demand.

As we discussed in the previous chapter, people earn income from ownership of the factors of production. Changes in factor prices as a result of international trade have a big effect on the distribution of income within a country.

Let's consider two examples of how trade has tipped the balance between owners of scarce and abundant factors of production: Bangladesh and the United States.

Bangladesh is a small country in terms of land area, but a big one in terms of population. Imagine an area the size of Illinois or Iowa, with a population equal to half of the entire United States. In the days before there was much international trade, land owners in Bangladesh benefited greatly from their control over that scarce resource, using cheap labor that was in plentiful supply. In other words, land was scarce in relation to labor.

As the country became more and more connected to international markets through trade, textile firms seeking cheap labor moved in. Bangladeshis began to earn enough from textile work to be able to import food from countries where land is less scarce. As a result, the price of labor has risen, and the price of land has fallen. The relative incomes of the owners of labor and land have changed accordingly.

In the United States, a more subtle change in the factor distribution of income has taken place. With its tech-savvy, highly educated population, the United States has a relative abundance of high-skilled labor—scientists, financial managers, engineers, and so on. In comparison with other

The rapid growth of exports from countries like China and Bangladesh opens new opportunities—and some new debates.
© *Imaginechina/AP Images*

countries, the United States doesn't have so many low-skilled workers. When the country didn't engage in much trade, this was good for the low-skilled workers. They represented a scarce resource relative to high-skilled workers, which drove up the wages of low-skilled workers. In the 1950s, for instance, the United States was a great place to be a factory worker.

As trade has increased astronomically in recent decades, however, the balance of high-skilled and low-skilled workers has tipped. Many economists believe that this change explains part of the increase in income inequality that has occurred in the United States in recent decades. High-skilled workers are earning more as a result of the increased demand for their labor due to free trade, while low-skilled workers are earning less.

You can see why certain people in both Bangladesh and America would be upset about trade. Of course, as we have seen, trade increases efficiency and total surplus. We can therefore expect economies to grow as a result of trade—and when economies grow, they usually create jobs. Americans whose jobs have been lost to freer trade should, in theory, be able to find new jobs, given time. Nonetheless, for someone who has spent 10 or 20 years doing a particular job, the idea of moving and retraining for a different type of work is understandably daunting or unappealing.

Does this mean that we should impose trade restrictions to protect the owners of scarce factors of production, such as American factory workers? Remember that any move to liberalize or restrict trade creates losers as well as winners. In this case, the losers would be American shareholders, American consumers, and Bangladeshi factory workers—and the economy as a whole would shrink. Arguments over trade policy are never just about protecting people in your own country from foreign competition. They're also debates about the distribution of benefits within each country.

The WTO and trade mediation

Have you heard about the great Franco-American cheese war of 2009? Probably not. No shots were fired and, as far as we know, no one was physically hurt. Nonetheless, the great cheese war is an example of how trade restrictions can spiral out of control.

Paradoxically, the cheese war actually began with beef. The European Union (EU) banned imports of beef containing artificial hormones, which includes most beef raised in the United States. Not surprisingly, the United States was opposed to this trade restriction. What measures can a country take when it doesn't like another country's trade restrictions? It can appeal to the **World Trade Organization (WTO)**, an international organization designed to monitor and enforce trade agreements, while also promoting free trade. Although the WTO doesn't have an army or the power to enforce its decisions, many countries have voluntarily joined and agreed in principle to liberalize their trade policies and abide by the WTO's decisions.

Acting like a judge, the WTO reviewed the evidence and the law in the beef-imports dispute. The WTO's rules allow such trade restrictions, but only if they protect public health and safety. The United States argued that there was no legitimate evidence that artificial beef hormones pose a health risk and that the EU's ban was therefore illegitimate. In 2008, the WTO ruled in favor of the United States. Although it usually abides by WTO decisions, in this case the EU felt so strongly about the issue that it refused to lift the ban.

In response, the United States slapped a 300 percent tariff on imports of French Roquefort cheese.[4] In response to that response, the French parliament debated imposing heavy import tariffs on Coca-Cola products from the United States. This tit-for-tat exchange was eventually ended, as trade negotiators reached a deal: The United States agreed to the EU keeping its ban on hormone-treated beef, and in return the EU agreed to import more nontreated beef from the United States.

These retaliatory measures were largely symbolic—the United States is not a major buyer of Roquefort. Yet they show what can happen when countries fail to reach agreement on trade restrictions. Most national leaders understand enough about economics to know that trade barriers are usually mutually harmful (at least in the sense of decreasing total surplus). But when

World Trade Organization (WTO) an international organization designed to monitor and enforce trade agreements, while also promoting free trade

political power is at stake, it can be easy to get stuck in a bad pattern, imposing trade restrictions on one another in retaliation. The WTO was founded explicitly to *prevent* such trade wars from escalating.

Labor and environmental standards

LO 17.8 Discuss the challenges of establishing environmental or labor standards in international markets.

Europe's resistance to artificial beef hormones is an example of a wider problem. Each country has its own set of laws and policies governing the economy. These include safety policies, labor standards, environmental regulations, taxes, laws about corporate finance and governance, and much more. Inconveniently, they vary hugely among countries, which can be a source of friction in international trade.

For example, many clothes sold in the United States are produced in ways that would be illegal in the United States. Some of the clothes you're wearing now were probably made in a country where children work in factories, where the minimum wage is tiny or nonexistent, or where leftover chemicals and fabric dyes get dumped into the drinking water. Although these circumstances might seem unacceptable to American consumers, "unacceptable" is always in the eye of the beholder. European consumers, for instance, are often outraged by the sale of genetically modified food products, which are completely legal and relatively uncontroversial in the United States. (If you ate bread today, we bet that it was made from genetically modified grains.)

The problem of inconsistent standards can be approached in two main ways: policy-makers making explicit laws about imports and consumers making voluntary purchasing decisions.

Import standards

One solution that some countries have used to address the problem of differing labor or environmental standards is simply to impose standards on imported goods. There are two main channels for this sort of policy: (1) *blanket standards* imposed on *all* imports or (2) *import standards* on *specific countries.*

Blanket standards on imports usually address issues affecting consumers, rather than workers in the countries where production takes place. In the United States, for instance, imported food products must meet certain standards to protect the health of U.S. consumers. Imports of products that violate domestic copyright or patent laws—such as pirated movies or music—are also restricted.

Import standards on specific countries are less common. Such standards typically address production issues in the country of origin, such as labor or environmental conditions. When used, they are integrated into individual trade agreements with those countries.

An example is the North American Agreement on Labor Cooperation (NAALC)—part of the North American Free Trade Agreement (NAFTA) among the United States, Canada, and Mexico. NAALC expresses the agreement of the three countries to work in the long term toward a set of labor standards. The standards address various issues: the elimination of child labor, prevention of workplace injuries, enforcement of minimum wages, and equal pay for men and women, among others. NAALC does not, however, require each country to maintain the same standards on these issues; for instance, there is no expectation that the minimum wage in Mexico will be the same as the minimum wage in the United States. Instead, it requires only that each country enforce its own existing labor laws. Furthermore, the ability of each country to enforce compliance on the other two is quite limited.

In cases where the goal of regulation is to solve an international problem, such as pollution, legislating on a country-by-country basis may even worsen the problem. To see how this might happen, read the From Another Angle box, "Are environmental regulations bad for the environment?"

From Another Angle

Are environmental regulations bad for the environment?

Do national environmental regulations improve the quality of the environment worldwide? The answer seems obvious: How could laws limiting pollution *not* reduce pollution? It *is* possible, however, that regulations in one country might *increase* worldwide pollution by pushing polluting industries into countries without regulation. This idea is called *pollution displacement.*

When a firm decides where to operate, it considers the costs of production it will face in each country. These costs include many factors such as local wages and rents. They also include the cost of complying with regulations. In a country with strict environmental standards, companies have to pay for things like clean technologies, safe disposal of waste material, and so on. All else equal, the cost of production will be higher in countries with stricter environmental regulations. That fact gives firms an incentive to move to countries with less regulation and lower costs.

Of course, all else is never exactly equal. For example, Canada has relatively strict environmental standards regulating companies that cut down trees. The standards seek to limit clear-cutting and protect streams and wildlife habitats. In contrast, Indonesia has far fewer such regulations. If you were a logging company deciding where to locate a new operation, would the obvious choice be Indonesia? Not necessarily. There are counterbalancing advantages to doing business in Canada: a more highly skilled labor force and better transportation infrastructure. Taking all things into consideration, a logging company may decide that the benefits of working in Canada outweigh the costs.

Now, imagine that the Canadian parliament passes a new law imposing even stricter environmental regulations on the logging industry. This increases the cost of doing business in Canada so much that logging companies decide to move to Indonesia. With less logging taking place in Canada, and more in Indonesia, the net result could be an *increase* in the worldwide negative environmental impact of logging.

Something similar can happen even if companies don't move their production to countries with looser regulations: Companies already operating in those countries can supply the world market at cheaper prices and gain market share. Either way, the result is the same—imposing tighter national environmental regulations leads to more of the good being produced in countries where less-stringent regulations are in place. On net, that might increase the total amount of pollution worldwide.

Thankfully, this doesn't often happen. For example, in the United States, the Clean Air Act of 1990 restricted emissions of sulfur dioxide, a common by-product of coal-fired power plants, yet virtually no power generation moved offshore. Why? It's difficult and expensive to import power generated overseas, so there is a huge cost advantage to generating power close to where it will be consumed. In cases like this, environmental regulations do have their intended effect.

Fair(ly) free trade

What if there are no regulations that set standards for imported goods? Individual consumers can still make choices about what they are and are not willing to buy. The *fair trade movement* attempts to inform and influence consumers' choices. It certifies and labels goods whose production meets certain standards; these include paying workers minimum wages, ensuring safe working conditions, and not causing undue harm to the environment.

Because production that meets fair-trade standards usually costs more, fair-trade-certified products cost more too. Individual consumers decide whether it is worth it to them to pay more for products that are produced in a certain way.

The fact that some consumers are willing to pay more for fair-trade goods means it is a way for producers to differentiate their products. Since the end of the Multifibre Arrangement in 2005 opened up Lesotho's garment industry to low-cost competition from Asia, one of the ways it has tried to preserve the industry is by raising standards in its factories and marketing itself as a source of fair-trade clothing.

Sometimes activist groups try to change industrywide standards by influencing individual buying decisions. For instance, in the 1990s, activists encouraged consumers to boycott Nike products; they highlighted the poor working conditions in Nike's factories around the world. This pressure did seem to make a difference; Nike started imposing higher standards, and by 2005 activists were applauding its efforts. In 2012, activists pressured Apple into conducting audits of Chinese factories where iPads and other popular electronics are assembled after exposés reported dangerous working conditions.

The fair-trade movement offers consumers the opportunity to buy goods that meet certain standards. Consumers can decide whether fair-trade products, such as the bananas being harvested here, are worth the added cost.
© Simon Rawles/Getty Images/The Image Bank

Embargoes: Trade as foreign policy

Sometimes the motivations behind trade restrictions are not ultimately economic at all. Instead, countries may use trade as a tool for foreign policy. Because trade increases surplus and allows a country to access goods that it cannot manufacture itself, restricting the ability to trade can be seen as a form of punishment. The restriction or prohibition of trade in order to put political pressure on a country is an **embargo**.

For example, when North Korea tested a nuclear device in the spring of 2009, the U.N. Security Council passed a resolution that banned any other country from trading any sort of weapons with North Korea. Such trade restrictions can be an alternative to using military force against a country. A similar embargo is currently in place restricting trade in military goods or nuclear materials with Iran.[5]

In other cases, the goods and services covered by an embargo are not intrinsically dangerous. Between the Gulf War in 1990 and the U.S.-led invasion in 2003, the United Nations imposed a very broad embargo on Iraq. It prohibited trade of "any commodities or products" except medical supplies and food under certain conditions. Why did the United Nations want to stop ordinary Iraqis from having cars and shirts and other consumer goods? It hoped the Iraqi people would be so annoyed about the lack of goods that the Iraqi government would fear a popular uprising and would change its policies. For a similar example, read the What Do You Think? box "Lift the embargo on Cuba?"

embargo
a restriction or prohibition of trade in order to put political pressure on a country

What Do You Think?
Lift the embargo on Cuba?

In 1960, shortly after Fidel Castro came to power, the United States imposed an economic embargo on Cuba. In addition to prohibiting almost all trade with Cuba, the embargo also restricted travel to Cuba for U.S. citizens. The Cuban economy is estimated to have lost $685 million per year as a result of the embargo.

(continued)

Supporters believe that the embargo is the only effective tool the United States has to encourage political change in Cuba without direct military invasion. They believe that depriving Cuban citizens of the opportunity to trade will someday encourage them to rise up against the Castro regime. The Cuban American National Foundation goes so far as to argue that lifting the embargo "would be tantamount to sentencing the Cuban people to the continuation of the deprivation of economic, civil and human freedoms."

Opponents argue that the embargo has failed to motivate any change in the Cuban government since 1960. They believe that free trade and travel would nurture closer relationships between Cubans and Americans, which might be a more effective political tool than the embargo. They also emphasize that the economic costs of the embargo are not limited to Cuba: The U.S. Chamber of Commerce estimates that the embargo costs the U.S. economy $1.2 billion per year.

In recent years, parts of the embargo have been relaxed. Since 2000, the United States has allowed sale of agricultural goods and medicine for humanitarian purposes. In 2009, the United States loosened restrictions on Cuban-Americans who want to travel to or send money back to Cuba; Cuba was allowed to reenter the Organization of American States. In 2016, President Obama lifted travel restrictions to Cuba for "educational travel" and became the first U.S. president to visit Cuba since 1928. Obama and Castro both called for the removal of the embargo. In October 2016, President Obama lifted part of the embargo, allowing U.S. citizens to buy Cuban cigars and rum for personal use.

WHAT DO YOU THINK?

1. An embargo is designed to put pressure on a foreign government by causing hardship to its citizens. How should the future value of achieving political objectives be weighed against the cost of current hardship for citizens?
2. Is the embargo against Cuba an effective way for the United States to pursue its foreign policy objectives?

Sources: http://www.canf.org; http://www.dollarsandsense.org/archives/2009/0309pepper.html; http://www.usnews.com/news/articles/2016-03-15/obama-administration-relaxes-travel-financial-restrictions-on-cuba; http://www.usnews.com/news/articles/2016-03-21/obama-castro-call-for-trade-embargo-on-cuba-to-be-lifted.

✓CONCEPT CHECK

☐ What happens to the price of domestically scarce factors of production when a country opens up to trade? What happens to the price of domestically abundant factors of production? **[LO 17.7]**

☐ What does the WTO do? **[LO 17.7]**

☐ What is the purpose of an embargo? **[LO 17.8]**

Conclusion

The chapter has taken a close look at one of the most powerful economic insights: There can be big gains from specialization and exchange. This is true for countries as well as individual people and companies.

Even though the total gains from trade are usually positive on a national level, the distribution of those gains to different people and industries matters a lot in the real world. There are usually winners and losers from trade, especially in the short run. The hope is that opening up to trade eventually makes everyone better off, but getting to that point requires responsive political solutions.

Trade restrictions such as tariffs and quotas are used in varying degrees by every country in the world to protect some groups and industries from international competition. Some domestic policies, such as environmental and labor standards, can also affect trade.

Because trade takes place across countries, the role of public policy in shaping international trade is more obvious than in most of the domestic topics we've covered so far. In upcoming chapters, we'll tackle other ways that public policy drives the economy, on both the domestic and international levels.

Key Terms

imports, p. 425

exports, p. 425

autarky, p. 425

protectionism, p. 433

trade liberalization, p. 433

tariff, p. 433

import quota, p. 435

quota rents, p. 436

World Trade Organization (WTO), p. 438

embargo, p. 441

Summary

LO 17.1 Define comparative advantage and list some root causes of comparative advantage on a national level.

Comparative advantage is the ability to produce a good or service at a lower opportunity cost than others can. Absolute advantage is the ability to produce more of a good than others can with a given amount of resources. It is comparative advantage, rather than absolute advantage, that determines which countries produce which goods for trade.

The most efficient economic arrangement is one in which each country specializes in the good for which it has a comparative advantage and trades with others. Characteristics such as climate, natural resources, factor endowment, and technology determine which goods and services a country will have a comparative advantage at producing. Because features like climate, population, and technology are not uniform throughout an entire country, incomplete specialization, in which a country produces some of many different kinds of goods, can also be efficient.

LO 17.2 Determine whether a country will become a net-importer or net-exporter of a good when it moves from autarky to free trade.

When a country moves from autarky (a self-contained economy that does not trade with others) to trade, the difference between the world price and the domestic price of a good determines whether the country becomes a net-importer or net-exporter. If the world price is lower than the domestic price, the domestic price will drop when the country opens to trade. In that case, domestic supply

will no longer be sufficient to meet domestic demand at the lower price. Imported goods will make up the difference, and the country will become a net-importer. If the world price is higher than the domestic price, the domestic price will rise when the country opens up to trade. Domestic supply will outstrip domestic demand at the higher price, and the country will export the excess supply, becoming a net-exporter.

LO 17.3 Calculate the change in surplus and the distribution of benefits within a market when a country opens up to trade.

When markets function well, total surplus increases when a country opens up to trade. The domestic distribution of surplus depends on whether the country becomes a net-importer or net-exporter of the good being traded. In net-importing countries, consumers gain surplus from buying a larger quantity at a lower price; producers lose surplus from selling less at a lower price. When a country becomes a net-exporter, consumers lose surplus from buying a smaller quantity at a higher price; producers gain surplus. In both cases, total surplus increases, making trade more efficient than autarky.

LO 17.4 Identify when and how an economy's trade policies affect world supply of and world demand for a good.

Our previous examples hold only if the economy in question is a *price taker*; that is, the decisions of its citizens about what quantity to produce or consume have no effect on the world price. But if we are dealing with a "big" economy, its decisions *would* affect the world price. In this case, the economy's move from autarky to free trade would shift the world demand curve to the right (because more consumers have entered the world market) and also shift the world supply curve to the right (because more producers have entered the world market).

LO 17.5 Explain the effect of a tariff on quantity, price, and the distribution of surplus.

In order to raise public funds and redistribute surplus toward domestic producers, governments use import tariffs. A tariff is a tax on imports, and like any tax, it causes inefficiency and deadweight loss. A tariff raises the domestic price of a good, causing a reduction in the quantity demanded, an increase in the quantity supplied domestically, and a reduction in the quantity imported. Domestic producers will enjoy an increase in surplus as a result of selling more at a higher price, and government will receive tax revenue. However, domestic consumers lose surplus as a result of buying less at a higher price, and total surplus decreases.

LO 17.6 Explain the effect of an import quota on quantity, price, and the distribution of surplus.

Import quotas limit the amount of a particular good that can be imported. The effect of the quota on domestic price and quantity is similar to the effect of a tariff: Domestic price increases, quantity sold decreases, and the quantity imported decreases. Domestic producers gain surplus from selling at a higher price; domestic consumers lose surplus from buying a lower quantity at a higher price. Some surplus goes to whoever holds the rights to import, called quota rents.

LO 17.7 Describe the effects of trade on the factor distribution of income.

International trade equalizes the supply and demand of factors of production across countries. In general, trade increases demand for factors that are domestically abundant, and it increases the supply of factors that are domestically scarce. As a result, the price of domestically scarce factors will typically drop due to increased foreign competition, and the owners of these factors lose surplus. In contrast, the price of domestically abundant factors increases due to increased demand, and owners will gain surplus.

LO 17.8 Discuss the challenges of establishing environmental or labor standards in international markets.

Each country has its own set of laws and policies governing the economy. These regulations vary among countries, which can be a source of friction when economic activity takes place across national boundaries. Policymakers and consumers approach the problem of inconsistent standards in several ways, ranging from explicit laws about imports to voluntary purchasing decisions by consumers.

Review Questions

1. Why might a country that is more productive in producing wheat than its trading partners end up importing wheat? **[LO 17.1]**

2. Imagine two nations with similar landmasses and levels of wealth that do not specialize in the same industries. What characteristics might drive differences in their comparative advantages? **[LO 17.1]**

3. Producing socks is labor-intensive, while producing satellites is capital-intensive. If India has abundant labor and the United States has abundant capital, which good will the U.S. export? Is trade beneficial to textile laborers in the United States? **[LO 17.2]**

4. Suppose Egypt wants to open its trade borders to the world market for natural gas. What will determine whether Egypt becomes a net-exporter or net-importer of natural gas? If Egypt becomes a net-exporter, will domestic supply be equal to, less than, or greater than domestic demand? **[LO 17.2]**

5. If Argentina becomes a net-exporter of beef after trade barriers are removed, how does total welfare in Argentina change compared with autarky? Are Argentine cattle ranchers better or worse off? What about Argentine consumers? **[LO 17.3]**

6. Suppose a country opens its trade borders and becomes a net-exporter of beef. Is it better for domestic consumers of beef if the country is a large player on the world market or a small player? **[LO 17.3]**

7. Suppose the United States wants to open its trade borders to the world market for coffee. What will determine whether the world price for coffee is affected? **[LO 17.4]**

8. Suppose that Japan is a net exporter of automobiles. If a large country like the United States moves from autarky to free trade in automobiles, how will the price of automobiles sold in Japan change? How will the amount of automobiles exported change? **[LO 17.4]**

9. Suppose Mexico wants to protect its domestic automobile industry from U.S. and Japanese competition. How will a tariff on imported cars help it to accomplish this task? How does the tariff affect domestic producer and consumer surplus? **[LO 17.5]**

10. Refer back to Figure 17-9. Explain why area D is a deadweight loss. What about area F? **[LO 17.5]**

11. Imagine Mexico is considering using an import quota rather than a tariff to protect its domestic automobile industry. How does the outcome differ from that of a tariff? [**LO 17.6**]

12. Explain how lifting an import quota on other countries will affect an exporting country that had been exempted from the quota restriction. [**LO 17.6**]

13. Labor is relatively abundant in Mexico compared with arable land. Explain who wins and who loses in Mexico as a result of the North American Free Trade Agreement (NAFTA), which liberalized trade between the United States, Canada, and Mexico. [**LO 17.7**]

14. If capital is domestically scarce in a country, do you expect owners of capital in that country to be free-traders or protectionists? Why? [**LO 17.7**]

15. Suppose Great Britain wants to take a stance on labor standards for imports. The prime minister imposes a blanket standard that requires all imports to meet certain labor standards. Who will benefit from this policy? What are the drawbacks for Great Britain and countries that export to Great Britain? [**LO 17.8**]

16. Suppose the United States imposes a trade embargo on North Korea in order to exert political pressure on the government. Consider how the embargo will affect U.S. producers. Under what conditions would they support the embargo? Why might they oppose it? [**LO 17.8**]

Problems and Applications

1. If a country has relatively abundant unskilled labor, with scarce land and capital, it is more likely to have a comparative advantage in which of the following industries? Check all that apply. [**LO 17.1**]

    a. Food service.

    b. Textiles.

    c. Agriculture.

    d. Financial services.

2. Suppose Ghana discovers it has lost its comparative advantage in the production of maize. Which of the following could explain the loss of comparative advantage? Check all that apply. [**LO 17.1**]

    a. Maize-processing technology developed in Ghana spreads to other maize-producing countries.

    b. Decline in global demand for maize.

    c. Immigration of cheap labor into Ghana.

    d. Growth of low-skill service jobs in Ghana.

3. Calculate the following values using Figure 17P-1, which shows domestic supply and demand for steel in the United States under autarky. [**LO 17.2**]

FIGURE 17P-1

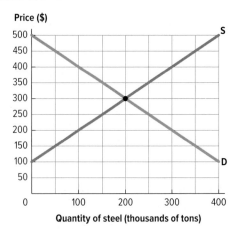

a. What are the equilibrium price and quantity of steel under autarky?

b. Suppose the United States allows trade, and the post-trade domestic quantity supplied is 150 thousand tons of steel. What are the domestic quantity demanded and the new world price?

c. Is the United States a net-exporter or net-importer of steel?

d. What quantity of steel is imported/exported?

4. Table 17P-1 shows the domestic supply and demand schedule for rice in Thailand. [**LO 17.2**]

    a. In autarky, what are the domestic quantity supplied and price?

TABLE 17P-1

Price of rice ($/kg)	Quantity demanded (millions of kg)	Quantity supplied (millions of kg)
3.50	2,100	3,300
3.25	2,150	3,200
3.00	2,200	3,100
2.75	2,250	3,000
2.50	2,300	2,900
1.25	2,350	2,800
1.00	2,400	2,700
0.75	2,450	2,600
0.50	2,500	2,500
0.25	2,550	2,400

b. The world price of rice is $1.25 per kilogram. If Thailand opens up to trade in rice, what will be the new domestic price of rice? (*Hint:* You can assume Thailand is a small producer of rice relative to the world market.)

c. What quantity of rice will be supplied by domestic producers?

d. What quantity of rice will be demanded by domestic consumers?

e. How much rice will Thailand import or export?

5. Guatemala represents a small part of the world poultry market. Based on Figure 17P-2, answer the following. **[LO 17.3]**

a. Calculate producer and consumer surplus in autarky.

b. Assume that the world price of poultry is $0.30/kg. If Guatemala opens to trade, what are the domestic quantity consumed and produced? Plot these quantities on the graph. What is the quantity of imports?

c. Calculate the post-trade producer and consumer surplus, and plot these areas on the graph. Who is better off after trade: producers or consumers?

6. Guatemala represents a small part of the world poultry market, and is fully open to trade. Assume the world price of poultry is $0.30/kg. Suppose a $0.10/kg tariff is imposed on poultry imports. Based on Figure 17P-2, answer the following questions. **[LO 17.3, 17.5]**

a. What are the quantity of poultry consumed and produced in Guatemala under the tariff? Plot these quantities on the graph. What is the quantity of imports?

b. Now suppose the tariff is eliminated and instead the world price of chicken feed increases significantly. This causes the world price of poultry to rise from $0.30/kg to $0.40/kg. How much poultry is now bought and sold in Guatemala? What is the quantity of imports?

c. Compare the efficiency of the two situations. Calculate the deadweight loss under the tariff. Calculate the deadweight loss resulting from the higher price of chicken feed.

7. Suppose the United States is initially an autarky. Figure 17P-3 shows the domestic market for paper. When the U.S. does not allow trade, the world price is $0.30. When the United States does allow trade, the world price falls to $0.20.

Based on the figure, which of the following statements is correct? **[LO 17.4]**

a. The increase in world demand for paper was larger than the increase in world supply of paper.

b. The decrease in world demand for paper was larger than the increase in world supply of paper.

c. The increase in world supply of paper was larger than the increase in world demand for paper.

d. The decrease in world supply of paper was larger than the increase in world demand for paper.

8. The world wheat market is shown in Figure 17P-4. **[LO 17.4]**

a. What is the initial world price?

b. Suppose a large country like the United States has been an autarky but is now going to allow free trade. Draw the effect the entrance of the United States into the world market has on the world supply and world demand curves.

c. How will the world price be affected by the entrance of the United States into the world market?

FIGURE 17P-2

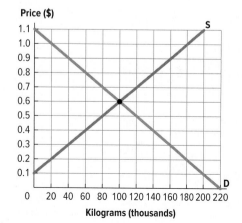

FIGURE 17P-3

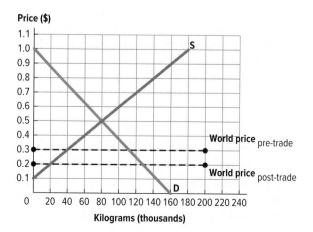

FIGURE 17P-4

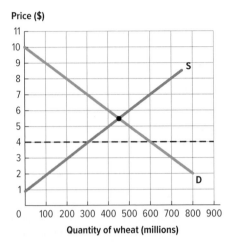

Price ($)

Quantity of wheat (millions)

9. The U.S. wheat market is shown in Figure 17P-5. Suppose the United States wants to protect its wheat industry by imposing a tariff of $1/bushel on foreign wheat, which currently sells at the world price of $4/bushel. **[LO 17.6]**

   a. Graph consumer and producer surplus after the $1/bushel tariff is imposed.

   b. How much revenue does the U.S. government collect from the tariff?

   c. Graph the deadweight loss associated with the tariff below the equilibrium quantity. Then graph the deadweight loss associated with the tariff above the equilibrium quantity.

10. The U.S. wheat market is shown in Figure 17P-5. **[LO 17.6]**

    a. When the world price is $4/bushel, will the United States import or export wheat? How many bushels?

b. How many bushels of wheat should be allowed under an import quota in order to increase the domestic price from $4 to $5 per bushel?

c. Graph the domestic producer surplus increase as a result of this quota.

d. Graph the deadweight loss associated with the quota below the equilibrium quantity. Then graph the deadweight loss associated with the quota above the equilibrium quantity.

11. Suppose a country imposes a tariff on coffee imports. Using the diagram of supply and demand in Figure 17P-6, identify the correct shaded areas as follows. **[LO 17.3, 17.5, 17.6]**

    a. In autarky, which area(s) comprise domestic consumer surplus? Which area(s) comprise domestic producer surplus?

    b. When the country opens up to trade, which area(s) do consumers gain as surplus? Which area(s) do producers lose?

    c. After trade, if an import tariff is imposed, which area(s) do domestic producers gain as surplus? Which do domestic consumers lose?

    d. With the tariff, which area is government revenue?

    e. Which area(s) represent deadweight loss as a result of the tariff?

    f. If the country uses an import quota instead of a tariff, what is the quota quantity if the quota price is $7?

FIGURE 17P-5

Price ($)

Quantity of wheat (millions)

FIGURE 17P-6

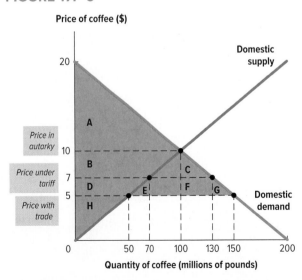

Price of coffee ($)

Quantity of coffee (millions of pounds)

12. Suppose a country where capital is scarce and most of the industry is labor-intensive with low-skilled labor moves from autarky to free trade. Which of the following do you expect to happen? Check all that apply. **[LO 17.7]**

    a. Owners of capital become wealthier.

    b. Wages for labor increase.

    c. The returns to capital (surplus) decrease.

13. Suppose two countries are considering a new agricultural trade agreement with each other. Country A has abundant low-skilled labor and scarce land. Country B has abundant arable land but little population. In which country do land owners support a trade agreement? In which country do workers support a trade agreement? **[LO 17.7]**

14. Suppose a country has abundant capital but scarce labor. Which group would be more harmed by a trade embargo: owners of capital or laborers? **[LO 17.7, 17.8]**

15. Which of the following policies is likely to cause more pollution displacement: imposing environmental standards on domestic production or a blanket environmental standard on all imports? **[LO 17.8]**

Endnotes

1. http://www.economist.com/node/9516043?story_id=9516043.

2. http://georgewbush-whitehouse.archives.gov/news/releases/2002/03/20020305-6.html.

3. http://www.fas.org/sgp/crs/misc/RL32333.pdf.

4. http://www.telegraph.co.uk/news/worldnews/europe/france/4306018/France-targets-Coca-Cola-in-escalating-cheese-wars.html.

5. http://www.telegraph.co.uk/news/worldnews/middleeast/iran/11739214/A-summary-of-the-Iran-nuclear-deal.html.

Part Five

Public Economics

The six chapters in Part 5 will introduce you to . . .

how microeconomics might help solve important policy problems, including questions about technological innovation, the environment, inequality, and social security.

Until now, our analysis has focused on buyers and sellers in a particular market, but sometimes others have a particular stake in the outcomes. Many people bear the cost when a polluting factory emits smoke that contributes to climate change. Or, to take a positive example, your classmates benefit when you get a flu shot that helps prevent the spread of flu on campus. Chapter 18, "Externalities," deals with these kinds of costs and benefits, known as externalities. Externalities cause some goods and services to be overdemanded or oversupplied ("too much") or similarly underdemanded or undersupplied ("too little"), relative to what might be efficient for society. This kind of inefficiency is an example of market failure.

Chapter 19, "Public Goods and Common Resources," describes two special types of goods that are undersupplied or overdemanded in free markets: public goods and common resource goods. Public goods like national defense tend to be underprovided if left to the free market. Common resources suffer from the opposite problem: Individuals or firms will tend to use more of a common resource than is optimal socially. Overfishing in a lake is a classic example: Everyone would be better off if each person fished less in order to protect the long-term viability of the fish stock, but no individual has an incentive to cut back. We'll discuss how taxes, subsidies, and quotas might be used to get incentives right.

Few people love paying taxes, but most accept that taxes generate the revenue required by governments to build parks and highways, hire teachers and police officers, and provide other basic services for citizens. Chapter 20, "Taxation and the Public Budget," describes the role of taxes, the burden they place on taxpayers, and how some types of taxes can target certain problems better than others.

Chapter 21, "Poverty, Inequality, and Discrimination," analyzes facts and policies related to poverty and income inequality. We examine why some families are poorer and some are richer, and we describe what new research suggests about reducing income gaps. At the end of the chapter, we look at insights from economics into the problem of discrimination.

No matter what the particular topic is, making policy choices involves both economics and politics. With that in mind, Chapter 22, "Political Choices," looks at the political system through an economic lens. We show how economic analysis provides insight into fundamental political questions like why people vote, how politicians become corrupt, and how the president can influence the economy.

Chapter 23, "Public Policy and Choice Architecture," describes a new set of ideas that are shaping policy discussions. The idea of "choice architecture" builds on the simple insight that how you frame a choice can shape the decision that's made. We show how policy-makers are using "nudges" designed to help people achieve goals like saving for retirement and conserving energy.

Together, these chapters show how microeconomics gives us insight and potential solutions to solve policy problems, big and small.

Externalities

THE COSTS OF CAR CULTURE

California's culture centers around cars. In 1904, Los Angeles was home to just 1,600 cars. (Back then, the speed limit was 6 miles per hour downtown.) Today, nearly 35 million vehicles drive on the state's roads. Californians drive from the state's beaches to its mountains, and everywhere in between.[1]

But all of that driving has a downside as well. Los Angeles is notorious for its gridlocked freeways full of commuters. It's also one of the smoggiest cities in the country. If you're stuck in L.A. traffic, you won't need much persuading that the presence of all those other cars on the road is imposing a cost on you. (Of course, *your* presence on the road is also contributing to congestion that imposes a cost on everyone else.) Likewise, if you're an L.A. resident breathing in exhaust fumes every day, you're paying a price for the city's car culture.

In previous chapters, we saw that when people make individual decisions to maximize their own welfare or well-being, competitive markets are typically efficient. Or, as some economists would say, the magic of the invisible hand maximizes total surplus. That's an important result, but it is true only when one person's choice does not affect the well-being of others. In many cases, that's a fair assumption. There are some situations, however—such as driving on congested highways—in which one person's decision has real implications for others.

GABRIEL BOUYS/AFP/Getty Images

In this chapter, we'll look at transactions that affect people other than the buyers and sellers directly involved. We'll see that in these cases, markets may no longer work efficiently. That is, *markets fail to maximize total surplus when individual choices impose uncompensated costs or benefits on others.*

We'll also look at some ways in which we can try to correct these market failures and restore efficiency. California's gasoline taxes—about 40 cents per gallon, among the highest of any state—are one example.[2] As we will see, such taxes are partly an attempt to force drivers to consider the costs they impose on others when they get behind the wheel. There is much debate over the right way to design policies to control congestion and pollution. Yet most economists agree that controlling pollution is an area in which government should be part of the solution. In this chapter, we'll see how government intervention, taxes, and other regulations might actually *increase* efficiency in the presence of externalities, by changing prices to reflect the true cost of individuals' decisions. That's right—in the presence of certain types of market failure, taxes can make everyone better off.

What Are Externalities?

Think about the decision to drive a car. Although you probably don't make a conscious calculation every time you sit in the driver's seat, there is an underlying *trade-off* that you consider, at least subconsciously. On the one hand, you get the benefit of driving: getting from one place to another quickly and easily. On the other hand, you incur the costs of driving: paying for gasoline and some wear and tear on the car, and maybe also toll fees and the cost of parking.

When you make the decision to purchase or drive a car you are considering only your private costs and private benefits. We can model these decisions using supply and demand curves for a market with only private costs and private benefits, as shown in Figure 18-1, which illustrates the market for gasoline. The price and quantity at which buyers and sellers trade goods and services reflect their *private* costs and benefits. Recall the discussion from Chapter 5, "Efficiency," to see this relationship.

Now let's consider other types of costs that you might not typically think about. Every mile you drive burns gasoline, which emits pollutants into the air. If you're the only one on the road, the costs are negligible. When there are lots of drivers, the costs add up. The pollutants have two kinds of costs, one local and one global:

- Locally, if pollution levels get high, they can create regional smog and health problems. The situation in and around Los Angeles, California, is an example.
- Globally, the cost of burning gas comes from the production of carbon dioxide. Carbon dioxide is a greenhouse gas, which traps heat from the sun in the atmosphere and contributes to global warming, the gradual warming of the earth's atmosphere. Rising temperatures contribute to higher sea levels and melting of glaciers and ice caps, as well as changed precipitation patterns around the world.[3] Although global temperatures have fluctuated throughout history, most scientists today agree that human production of greenhouse gases contributes to climate change.

FIGURE 18-1

Market with only private costs and private benefits   In a market with only private costs and benefits associated with the transaction, the market will reach an equilibrium at the intersection of supply and demand. The equilibrium quantity of gasoline traded will set marginal benefit equal to marginal cost for the last unit traded.

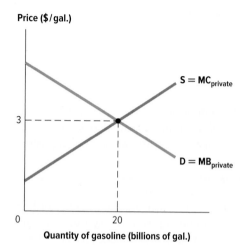

Do you consider these costs every time you weigh whether to go somewhere in your car? We don't know many people who do. The pollution caused by burning gasoline imposes costs on people *other than* the driver. In the case of vehicle emissions, any single driver has a tiny impact on the costs borne by others, so they're often easily ignored. The problem is that millions of small external costs, incurred every day, can add up to create big concerns.

So, let's imagine that drivers *did* take into account these kinds of costs, on top of the costs to themselves. Then their cost-benefit trade-offs would shift slightly, and they would, on net, drive a bit less since total costs of driving would now be higher compared to just private costs. This suggests that failure to recognize the external costs is causing people to drive more than is optimal from the perspective of society as a whole.

Similarly, when you purchase a new car, you are buying a car that had to be manufactured. That manufacturing process emitted carbon dioxide (among other potential emissions).[4] If buyers considered all the costs associated with manufacturing a new car, their trade-offs would change by a small amount and likely fewer people would buy a car.

These kinds of issues are common in economics. We'll see that expanding upon the basic supply and demand framework shown in Figure 18-1 gives us a simple way to think about these external costs and benefits.

External costs and benefits

LO 18.1 Explain how external costs and benefits affect the trade-offs faced by economic decision makers.

To think clearly about the issues of external costs and benefits, we need to introduce some new terminology. In the car example, when we've talked about costs, we've been talking about costs borne by a driver herself—such as gasoline, wear and tear on a car, road tolls, and parking fees. To be specific, we call costs that fall directly on an economic decision maker **private costs**. But we've seen that there are other costs as well, such as the cost of pollution. Individual drivers don't personally bear all—or even most—of the costs of the pollution they produce. Pollution, and any

private costs
costs that fall directly on an economic decision maker

external costs

costs imposed without compensation on someone other than the person who caused them

social cost

the entire cost of a decision, including both private costs and any external costs

other uncompensated costs that are imposed on someone other than the person who caused them, are called **external costs**.

When we add private costs to external costs, we call the sum **social cost**. For example, suppose you decide to host a noisy party. The *private costs* might include food, drink, and any cleanup costs the next day. The *external costs* would include annoyance felt by neighbors who can't sleep or study because of the noise your party is creating; your neighbors are not compensated for the discomfort caused by your party. The *social cost* would be the sum of these two types of costs.

HINT

Why don't we call the sum of private costs plus external costs "total cost" instead of *social cost*? Because *total cost* is the term used to describe costs of production. Also, the term *social cost* helps make it clear that we are thinking about this idea from society's perspective.

---

private benefits

benefits that accrue directly to the decision maker

external benefits

benefits that accrue without compensation to someone other than the person who caused it

social benefit

the entire benefits of a decision, including both private benefits and external benefits

externality

a cost or benefit imposed without compensation on someone other than the person who caused it

There also are lots of situations in which a person's behavior helps, rather than hurts, others. Imagine that you have decided to tidy up your messy front yard and paint your house. Clearly, you benefit from this decision: You have the aesthetic pleasure of a tidy yard and a prettier house, and the value of your property might even increase. These are benefits that accrue directly to the decision maker. We call them (as you might have guessed) **private benefits**. Your neighbors, too, benefit from your decision to fix up your house. They get the pleasure of living in a nicer-looking neighborhood, and the value of their properties may also increase a bit—all at no cost to them. Benefits that accrue without compensation to someone other than the person who caused them are called **external benefits**.

When we add private benefits to external benefits, we call the sum **social benefit**. As another example, suppose you decide to get vaccinated against the flu and to wash your hands frequently. The private benefit is that you are less likely to get the flu. The external benefit is that you are less likely to transmit the flu to other people. The social benefit is the sum of these two effects—the overall reduction in likelihood of the flu spreading, both to yourself and to others.

We use the term **externality** to refer to an external cost or an external benefit. We typically call an external cost a *negative externality* and an external benefit a *positive externality*. Externalities are an incredibly important concept in economics. They are one of the most common causes of market failure. From this point on, we will use the terms learned in this section to distinguish between choices that are optimal from the perspective of an *individual decision maker* (those based only on private costs and private benefits) and choices that are optimal from the perspective of *society as a whole* (those that account for social costs and social benefits).

The size of the external cost or benefit caused by a particular action may vary based on location, timing, quantity, or many other factors. For instance, driving during the middle of the day in the summer usually contributes more to smog than driving at night or driving during winter (because sunlight is a key ingredient in the formation of smog). Painting the one run-down house in a nice neighborhood is likely to boost neighbors' property values more than painting one house in a neighborhood full of run-down homes. However, for the sake of simplicity, in this chapter we mostly assume that externalities involve a *constant, predictable* external cost or benefit.

network externality

the effect that an additional user of a good or participant in an activity has on the value of that good or activity for others

Finally, there is one special type of externality that doesn't neatly fit into the categories we just laid out. A **network externality** is the effect that an additional user of a good or participant in an activity has on the value of that good or activity for others. Network externalities imply that people can help or harm others simply by virtue of their participation in a group. Network externalities can be positive or negative.

We've already described one example of a negative network externality—driving in L.A. rush hour. Every additional person who decides to use the L.A. road network imposes a *negative network externality* on other road users. You may have also experienced negative network externalities on wireless Internet networks, when each additional user draws down bandwidth, slowing the connection for other users.

Positive network externalities are frequently associated with technology, especially communication technology. An important historical example is the telephone. Telephones, like most communication devices, are useful only if other people have them too. In the early days, when very few people had telephones, having one let you contact only a limited number of people. Now, most people have phones, and in seconds you can reach people across town or across the world. The more common telephones became, the more people they allowed you to contact, and the more useful they got. Each person who joined the telephone network made telephones more useful for everyone else—a positive network externality. For a more recent example, Facebook is a perfect example of a service that has positive network externalities: The more of your friends who are on it, the more you benefit from being on it yourself.

Negative externalities and the problem of "too much"

LO 18.2 Calculate the effect of a negative externality on market price and quantity.

We can separate externalities by whether they impose an external cost or an external benefit on a third party. A positive externality is one that creates a benefit for a third party and a negative externality is one that imposes a cost on a third party. We can also think about when the externality occurs: during the production or the consumption of the good or service. An externality that occurs when a good or service is being produced is a **production externality**. An externality that occurs when a good or service is being consumed is a **consumption externality**.

In this section, we will look at negative production and consumption externalities.

production externality
an externality that occurs when a good or service is being produced

consumption externality
an externality that occurs when a good or service is being consumed

Negative production externality

A *negative production externality* is an external cost that occurs when a good or service is being produced. For example: When a car company considers whether to make a new car, it takes into account how much the car costs to manufacture by adding up the cost of labor and the cost of material. But without regulations or taxes, the company does not have to take into account any external, third-party costs that are generated by the manufacturing process, such as pollution. Society as a whole incurs those negative production costs. From the perspective of the car company, the car seems "cheaper" to manufacture than it seems to society as a whole. The private cost to the car company is less than the cost to society as a whole.

Imagine that car sales are completely unregulated in California. At any given price, there are some suppliers who consider that price to be greater than the costs of producing the car and thus are willing to sell the car at that price. This relationship between price and quantity supplied is the car company's supply curve in the market.

To add in the external cost associated with car production, we need to quantify how much damage is being imposed on everyone each time a car is manufactured. This external cost represents the size of the negative production externality. Because the negative production externality adds an external cost to society, we show this externality using the supply side of the market, as seen in Figure 18-2.

What are the equilibrium price and quantity of cars traded in an unregulated market? It occurs where the private supply curve ($S = MC_{private}$) and the market demand curve ($D = MB_{private}$) intersect.

But when the negative external cost is accounted for by producers, we see that the efficient quantity of new cars produced falls (to the point where social cost and the market demand

FIGURE 18-2

Market with a negative production externality   At the private equilibrium, 10 million cars are manufactured at a price of $20,000 each. At the private equilibrium the market creates a deadweight loss by not accounting for the external costs. Once those external costs associated with car manufacturing are accounted for, the efficient equilibrium falls to 8 million cars, while the efficient price rises to $22,000.

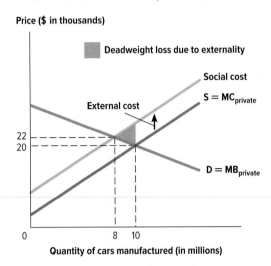

curve intersect). As a result, the efficient price for a new car rises. The true, or social, cost of manufacturing a car is higher than the private cost. The socially efficient equilibrium in the market reflects the external costs in addition to the benefits and costs to the buyers and sellers.

The cost to society of manufacturing too many cars is shown via the deadweight loss triangle in Figure 18-2. For every car manufactured beyond the socially efficient quantity (at 8 million), the cost to society is more than the benefit to buyers from acquiring the car. Remember from Chapter 5, "Efficiency," that producing where marginal costs exceed marginal benefits creates a deadweight loss to society. This deadweight loss reduces economic surplus to society. The negative production externality results in "too much" car production.

Negative consumption externality

A *negative consumption externality* is a third-party cost that occurs when a good or service is being consumed. As an example, let's consider cars again, and this time think about how much someone drives. (Naturally, this logic also applies to the decision to buy a car at all versus using public transportation, biking, or walking.) Because air pollution and environmental damage are external costs, the costs of driving a car look smaller from the perspective of an individual driver than from the perspective of society as a whole. Because drivers don't take the external cost into account, they will decide to drive more than they would if they themselves had to bear the full cost of driving (which mostly includes the cost caused by any pollution, and which people may value differently depending on their views).

Why is that a problem? It means people drive "too much"—that is, more than they would if they faced the social costs of their actions. Where there are externalities, the free market no longer allocates resources in a way that maximizes total surplus for society as a whole.

Just like in the case of a negative production externality, buyers and sellers in the market don't consider the external costs, and the market outcome occurs at "too much production." Every gallon of gas consumed beyond the efficient quantity costs society more than buyers value the gasoline, thus producing a deadweight loss and decreasing overall economic surplus. The negative consumption externality results in "too much" gasoline production.

Positive externalities and the problem of "too little"

> **LO 18.3** Calculate the effect of a positive externality on market price and quantity.

Externalities can also occur when a third-party *benefit* is created. These are *positive* externalities. As was the case for negative externalities, there can be positive production and positive consumption externalities. We'll look at both types of positive externalities in this section.

It is tempting to think that a positive externality must be a good thing. A negative externality decreases surplus, so a positive externality must do the opposite, right? Sadly, that is not the case. A positive externality also pushes quantity away from the efficient equilibrium level, reducing total surplus.

Positive consumption externality

A *positive consumption externality* is a third-party benefit that occurs when a good or service is being consumed. Consider the decision to paint the outside of your house. A homeowner will paint her house if the private benefits (such as increased property value, a nicer-looking home) outweigh the private costs (such as the time and money required to paint the house or pay someone else to do it). But this personal decision doesn't take into account benefits that accrue to neighbors, who also enjoy increased property values and a tidier-looking neighborhood. As a result, houses get painted "too little"—that is, less than the amount that would maximize total surplus, once we also consider the surplus of people other than the homeowner and house painter.

Maintaining the outside of one's house creates both private benefits for the homeowner and external, social benefits for the neighborhood.
Jupiterimages/Getty Images/Brand X Picture

Although the external benefits of house painting probably vary a lot, let's make a rough estimate. Suppose that the external benefits are worth $500 per paint job. In other words, $500 is the combined amount your neighbors would be willing to pay to *avoid* having your shabby-looking house lowering the tone of the neighborhood. Let's imagine that somehow it were possible to turn the external benefit into private benefit—by some magic, every time a homeowner paints her house, $500 is transferred from her neighbors' bank accounts into her own.

If this $500 transfer happened, the homeowner's trade-off would look different: The benefits of painting would increase and the costs would stay the same. How would she *respond* to this change? We can represent the difference between the private trade-off and the social trade-off (including the external benefit) by adding the external benefits to the private benefit or demand curve, creating a new social benefit curve. At any given market price, homeowners will behave as if the price were reduced by the amount of the external benefit.

Because the positive consumption externality adds an external benefit to society, we show this externality using the demand side of the market. We can show the case of painting our homeowner's house by modeling the social benefit curve $500 above the private demand curve, as shown in Figure 18-3.

We can find the equilibrium price and quantity of painted houses in an unregulated market by looking at the intersection of the private supply curve ($S = MC_{private}$) and private demand curve ($D = MB_{private}$). In the unregulated market, 300 houses get painted. When the external benefit is accounted for, we see that the efficient quantity of painted houses increases to 360 houses. The social demand (social benefit) curve intersects the private supply curve at a higher quantity. This means that the social benefit of painting your house is higher than the private benefit. The socially efficient equilibrium in the market incorporates the external benefits in addition to the benefits that accrue to the buyers and sellers.

FIGURE 18-3

Market with a positive consumption externality   At the private equilibrium, 300 houses are painted at a price of $1,500 each. At the private equilibrium, the market creates a deadweight loss by underproducing house painting and not accounting for the external benefits. Once the external benefits associated with painting your house are accounted for, the efficient equilibrium rises to 360 houses, while the efficient price rises to $1,750.

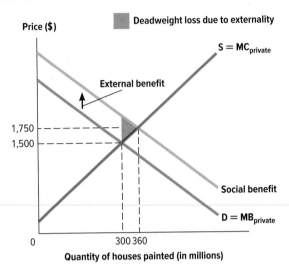

Here again, the net cost to society is shown in Figure 18-3 via the deadweight loss triangle. For every house painted below the efficient quantity, it would benefit society more than it costs the seller, thus producing a deadweight loss and decreasing overall economic surplus. Again, recall the discussion of deadweight loss from Chapter 5, "Efficiency." Underproducing a good or service will reduce economic surplus and generate a deadweight loss. The positive consumption externality results in "too little" house painting.

Positive production externality

A *positive production externality* is a third-party benefit that occurs when a good or service is being produced. Consider a power company producing electricity. We often think of power plants as creating negative externalities (along with lots of private benefits, of course). But along the coast of Florida, power plants produce an unexpected positive externality. Power plants in Florida use ocean water in their cooling systems, drawing in the cold water and then releasing the warmed water back into the ocean. This warmed water turns out to be an ideal manatee habitat. Warm water emissions from Florida power plants have allowed the manatee population to increase from fewer than 1,000 manatees in 1967 to over 6,300 manatees in 2016.[5]

The increased number of manatees (and habitats for them) is an external benefit to a power plant's decision to produce electricity. In an unregulated market, the power plant will not consider the effects on the manatee population when making production decisions. But if regulations force the power plant to improve the manatee habitat, then the question to be considered is how much power the plant should produce. To consider how much power to produce, we need to measure the value to society of the manatee habitat. We can then use this value to measure the positive production externality of the Florida power plants.

In the same way we might measure how much people would pay to avoid pollution, we can measure how much people would pay to preserve manatee populations. If, hypothetically, the value of supporting the manatee population is $1 per kilowatt hour of electricity produced by the power plant, we can find the social benefit of the electricity production. The social benefit is then worth the private benefit plus the $1 per kilowatt hour of external benefits.

The manatee population along the coast of Florida has flourished due to warm water being released by nearby power plants.
© *James R.D. Scott/Getty Images RF*

But in an unregulated market, power plants and consumers do not consider the external benefit when making the production decision, and the market will produce "too little." Just as we saw with our positive consumption example, producing an amount of output different from the socially efficient quantity produces a deadweight loss. In this case, the market is underproducing electricity by failing to take into account the full social benefits of the activity. For every kilowatt hour of electricity not produced between the market equilibrium and the socially efficient equilibrium, society is missing out on a net benefit. This underproduction produces a deadweight loss and decreases overall economic surplus. The positive production externality results in "too little" electricity production.

✓ CONCEPT CHECK

- ☐ What is the difference between a positive and negative externality? **[LO 18.1]**
- ☐ How is a network externality different from other externalities? **[LO 18.1]**
- ☐ How does a negative externality affect the supply curve? How does this change the equilibrium price and quantity relative to the same market in which the externality is faced? **[LO 18.2]**
- ☐ How does a positive externality affect the demand curve? How does this change the equilibrium price and quantity relative to the same market without the externality? **[LO 18.3]**
- ☐ Does an externality cause total surplus to increase or decrease? **[LO 18.2, 18.3]**

Private Solutions to Externalities

LO 18.4 Describe how individuals could reach a private solution to an externality and explain why this doesn't always occur.

We've learned that externalities reduce total surplus by creating a deadweight loss for society. In theory, however, it is possible to address this problem by transforming external costs and benefits into private costs and benefits. Efficiency could be restored if drivers give money to pollution sufferers or if neighbors join together to subsidize the painting of rundown houses on their block. Under certain circumstances, private individuals may be able to deal with externalities, restoring efficiency to the market on their own. This section details the conditions necessary for private solutions to externalities to be successful and discusses why it is often the case that those necessary conditions don't exist in the market.

Suppose a friend is enjoying her lunch, but her tuna sandwich is giving off a really strong odor. Unless you like the smell of tuna, she would be causing a negative externality by eating the tuna in front of you. What can you do? You could ask her to eat it later, but she might object. If you felt strongly enough, you could consider paying her to not eat the sandwich. In practice, that would probably seem weird, but in principle it's a legitimate option for eliminating the external-ity. After all, not every conflict involving externalities requires a regulatory solution. Sometimes, people can find solutions to conflicts surrounding externalities on their own.

A basic idea in economics is that individuals will pursue mutually beneficial trades. No mutu-ally beneficial trade should go unexploited because someone always has something to gain from pursuing it. The result is that when we add up all of the actions of self-interested individu-als, every opportunity to gain surplus should have been exploited, and total surplus should be maximized.

But we've just seen that an externality reduces surplus. Therefore—somewhere, somehow—there are mutually beneficial trades *waiting to be exploited.* For instance, the Californians who bear the cost of air pollution lose more surplus than is gained by drivers who don't have to pay for it. Here's a crazy idea: Why don't those who suffer from pollution *pay* drivers to drive less? Since there is surplus to be gained from decreasing the quantity of gas burned, a mutually ben-eficial trade exists. If a given reduction in driving would cause drivers to lose $9.4 billion in surplus and other Californians to gain $10 billion in surplus, why don't those other Californians agree to pay drivers, say, $9.7 billion to drive less? Both groups will be better off. The quantity of driving—and, hence, of pollution—would fall to the efficient equilibrium level, and total surplus in society as a whole would be maximized.

The idea that individuals can reach an efficient equilibrium through private trades, even in the presence of an externality, is called the **Coase theorem.** The Coase theorem is named for econo-mist Ronald Coase, a British economist whose work focused on property rights and transaction costs. He won the Nobel Prize in Economics in 1991.[6] A couple of key assumptions must hold for the Coase theorem to work:

1. People can make enforceable agreements (also known as contracts) to pay one another.
2. There are no transaction costs in coordinating and enforcing agreements.

The trouble is that these two assumptions almost never hold true. What kind of elaborate organization would be required to bring together all 39 million citizens of California, get each of them to agree to pay the amount that avoiding pollution is worth to them personally, redis-tribute that money to drivers who agreed to drive less, and then monitor those drivers to make sure they actually followed through? Whew! The costs of coordination and enforcement would surely be much higher than the surplus lost to the externality. It wouldn't be worth the effort to even try.

The idea of having people in California pay drivers to reduce their driving illustrates a second drawback of the Coase theorem. The private solution yields an *efficient* outcome—the surplus-maximizing quantity of gas is bought and sold. But the distribution of that surplus (who gets the benefit of the surplus) is often quite different from solutions reached through government intervention:

- In the private solution, the *citizens of California* have to pay drivers not to drive. The citi-zens are still better off paying the drivers (since pollution decreases), but they are not as well off as they would be if drivers had to pay for the right to pollute.
- In a solution reached by government intervention (for example, adding a tax to the market and using the revenue to compensate pollution sufferers), it is likely that the *drivers* would have to pay all California citizens $1 per gallon to compensate for pollution.

Coase theorem

the idea that even in the presence of an externality, individuals can reach an efficient equilibrium through private trades, assuming zero transaction costs

Notice that either solution is efficient, but the assumptions about what is "fair" and who has the "rights" to do what are different:

- In one case (the private solution), it's assumed that drivers have a right to pollute and have to be paid not to.
- In the other case (the government intervention), it's assumed citizens have a right to live free of pollution and have to be paid to accept pollution.

The Coase theorem reminds us that efficiency is all about maximizing total surplus. It says nothing about achieving a "fair" distribution of that surplus. Whoever starts with the property rights, if the conditions of the Coase theorem hold, should not affect who ends up with them. But it does affect who pays whom to compensate for trading the rights.

But what happens when property rights are unclear and transacting is not costless? See the What Do You Think? box "Reclining transactions" for an interesting debate regarding the transaction of reclining your airline seat.

What Do You Think?
Reclining transactions

On a recent United Airlines flight from New Jersey to Denver, two passengers seated near each other got into such an intense fight that the pilot had to divert the plane to Chicago. The passengers were arguing over whether the one in the front seat could recline his seat. If they had thought like economists, they might have averted the conflict.

This is a simple example of a consumption externality. If the person in the front seat "consumes" the reclining function of the seat, this has a negative impact on the person in the back seat. If the person in the back seat "consumes" the space in front of him (i.e., prevents the person in the front seat from reclining), this has a negative impact on the person in front.

How might an economist approach this problem? Simple:

- First, we must understand who starts with the *property right*. Does the person in front have the right to recline "his" chair? Or does the person behind have the right to fly without the passenger in front leaning back into "his" space?
- Next, we should give the two passengers an opportunity to make a trade in which the party with the property right could sell it to the other.

This logic is essentially the Coase theorem: The efficient solution can be found, as long as parties can easily transact with each other.

This situation is not merely hypothetical. Economist Erik Snowberg likes to recline his seat when flying. If the passenger seated behind Snowberg asks him not to recline, Snowberg politely asks that passenger, "How much is it worth to you for me not to recline my seat?" So far, nobody has offered Snowberg more than $5. He values reclining his seat more than $5, so he has yet to accept an offer. But by monetizing the transaction, Snowberg has avoided conflicts (or befuddled people into silence).

Why is this solution not more common? There are two complicating factors.

- First, the property rights need to be clearly assigned. In this case, consumers sign a contract with the airline when they buy plane tickets. This contract gives them the right to use their chair and its functions (one of which is to recline), subject to safety rules. But not everyone knows this. When you don't know who is holding the rights—in this case, that passengers have the right to recline their own seats—it's hard even to consider, much less complete, a trade.
- Second, the Coase theorem requires that transacting is costless. In the case of the airline seat, social norms make it awkward for many to shift the conversation to "How much can I pay you not to put your seat back?" Not everybody is willing to start up a negotiation with a stranger

(continued)

or to put a price on something that's not commonly assigned a value. Because of social norms, transaction costs may not be zero. (Feeling weird and awkward counts as a transaction cost!) Some individuals, like Erik Snowberg, may find it easy to start a negotiation, and for these people, the transaction costs are near zero. But for others, the perceived personal costs of opening negotiation may be high enough that they are not willing to speak up.

Still, think about how a market for seatback space could benefit both parties: The business traveler in back who wants to open her large laptop to make last-minute changes to a presentation might be more than willing to offer a few dollars to the teenager in front, who in turn might be thrilled to have some extra money to spend when the plane lands. So, the next time you're on a plane and the person sitting in front of you starts to reach for the recline button, perhaps think about what it's worth to you and make an offer.

WHAT DO YOU THINK?

1. Would a world with more bargaining be a better one?
2. Could you imagine bargaining with a stranger on an airplane over reclining your seat? Why or why not?
3. Can you think of another way to solve this problem?

Source: "United Flight Diverts over 'Knee Defender' Fight," *USA Today*, August 26, 2014; United Airlines' aircraft seating FAQs: https://www.united.com/web/en-US/content/help/seating.aspx.

In practice, deciding who pays whom, in order to solve the externality problem, is often less a question of economics than of politics, law, and philosophy. Even when it would make people better off to pay someone else to do, or stop doing, something that affects them, they often feel it is not "fair" or "just" to do so. For example, the 2000 movie *Erin Brockovich* is based on the true story of a woman who discovered that a big company was polluting the groundwater in her community, allegedly causing high rates of cancer and other health conditions. She started a legal campaign to force the company to stop polluting and compensate the families. Can you imagine if Erin Brockovich instead organized her community under the Coase theorem to *pay the company* to stop polluting? We very much doubt that moviegoers would have found it such a heartwarming, feel-good story.

Given the challenges described above, people usually care not only about reaching an efficient equilibrium, but also about how we get there and who benefits. If you go knocking on your neighbors' doors to explain positive externalities and propose that they contribute toward the cost of painting your house, you'll probably get doors slammed in your face. For a somewhat unlikely application of the Coase theorem, look at the From Another Angle box "Does no-fault divorce law increase the divorce rate?"

From Another Angle

Does no-fault divorce law increase the divorce rate?

In 1969, California became the first state in the country to legalize "no-fault" divorce. Prior to no-fault laws, a divorce could be granted only if a person showed that his or her spouse was "at fault" for committing some wrongdoing, such as adultery, abandonment, or abuse. If both partners wanted out, they could agree to lie in court, pretending that one of them was at fault. But if only one partner wanted out, he or she was stuck. Under no-fault divorce laws, either partner could obtain a divorce, without agreement or having to show evidence of wrongdoing.

Should we expect this change in the law to increase the divorce rate? At first glance, the answer might be yes: Before, it was extremely difficult to get divorced if your partner didn't agree. After, it is relatively easy. However, the Coase theorem gives us a different perspective. It predicts that the number of divorces will stay the same, but the *distribution of surplus between marriage partners* will change.

To see how this works, imagine a situation in which one partner wants to get divorced and the other doesn't. Under the old law, the partner who wanted the divorce would have to make concessions to persuade his or her spouse to lie in court—say, offering more alimony or greater visitation rights to the children. The partner who wanted to stay married needed to offer no concessions at all.

Once no-fault divorce came in, this situation was reversed: The partner who wanted to stay married would have to offer something that would improve the value of the marriage to the partner who wanted out. For example, maybe he or she would offer to dramatically change behavior or make amends for a serious failing. The Coase theorem predicts that roughly the same number of couples will eventually agree to divorce or stay married under no-fault divorce law as before—but the partner who wanted out will now get the better end of the bargain. The partner who wants to keep the marriage together will make the concessions.

As it happens, divorce rates *didn't* go up much after no-fault laws. A short flurry of divorces was followed by a return to pre-no-fault levels. In this instance at least, the Coase theorem made the right prediction.

Source: J. Wolfers, "Did Unilateral Divorce Laws Raise Divorce Rates? A Reconciliation and New Results," *American Economic Review* 96, no. 5 (2006).

✓ CONCEPT CHECK

☐ What conditions are required in order for people to be able to privately solve externalities under the Coase theorem? **[LO 18.4]**

Public Solutions to Externalities

Because of the cost and difficulty of designing and coordinating private solutions, people often turn to public policy for solutions to externalities. The most common public policy remedies to externality problems involve taxes and subsidies or quotas and tradable allowances.

It sounds relatively straightforward to impose a tax on a good that creates a negative externality, right? However, solutions to the externality problems are often easier to describe than to implement. External costs and benefits can be diffuse, complex, and hard to control. Solutions must try to ensure that economic decision makers experience costs and benefits that are *equal in value* to the true social costs and benefits of their choices. If everyone affected has to be involved in the process, that could mean coordinating across millions—or even billions—of people. This is a tricky problem to solve, even for the most committed policy-makers.

We will also see that there can be a tension between efficiency and fairness in finding solutions to externalities. Saying a market "works efficiently" means only that it maximizes surplus. Increasing surplus *for society* may decrease surplus for some groups while increasing it for other groups. Thus, efficiency doesn't say anything at all about the *distribution* of that surplus—who gets the benefits of the surplus. For example, if people who commute are poorer than those who live downtown, transferring surplus from "polluters" to "nonpolluters" means transferring from poor to wealthy. Also, some technically sound solutions might seem unfair (like rewarding people for *not* polluting, rather than taxing people who do pollute) and thus also might not get far in the political arena.

In this section we will look at public solutions to externalities in detail and discuss the successes and challenges of such solutions.

Taxes and subsidies

LO 18.5 Show how a tax or subsidy can be used to counteract an externality and discuss the pros and cons of such solutions.

At points in the chapter, we've said that the most basic public policy remedy to an externality problem involves counterbalancing the externality with a tax or a subsidy. Here, we look more deeply at two options: countering a negative externality with a tax and countering a positive externality with a subsidy.

Countering a negative externality with a tax

Let's return to the negative externality of producing a car. Imagine that the city government in Los Angeles decides to solve the problem of too much car production by taxing car manufacturers at a rate of $4,000 per car. The city then will use that money to compensate those affected by any environmental damage created.

Pigovian tax
a tax meant to counterbalance a negative externality

A tax meant to counter the effect of a negative externality is called a **Pigovian tax**, named for economist Arthur Pigou. Pigou was an English economist at the University of Cambridge; his work focused primarily on welfare economics.[7] Other Pigovian taxes include so-called sin taxes on alcohol and cigarettes as well as carbon taxes.

As panel A of Figure 18-4 shows, the effect of a negative externality is that the supply curve ($S = MC_{private}$) is lower than it would be if producers had to account for social costs. The effect of a Pigovian tax—like the effect of any tax—is that it *increases the effective price* that is paid for a good. As shown in panel B of Figure 18-4, this creates a new supply curve ($S + tax$) above

---

FIGURE 18-4

A tax counteracts the effect of a negative externality

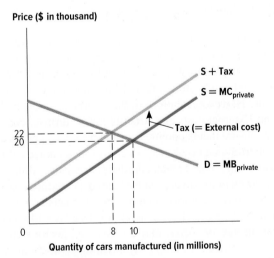

(A) The effect of a negative externality

(B) The effect of a Pigovian tax

Under a negative externality, the private supply curve is below the social marginal cost curve by the amount of the external cost. This causes the equilibrium quantity to be higher than the efficient level.

A Pigovian tax counteracts a negative externality. If the tax is set equal to the external cost, the tax raises the private marginal cost to the social marginal cost, and the resulting equilibrium quantity is efficient.

the private supply curve (S = MC$_{private}$). If the supply curve (S + tax) is pushed up far enough, it will move the equilibrium quantity back to the efficient level—that is, the level at which the market maximizes total surplus.

With a production tax, car manufacturers face the full social costs of producing the car, represented by the new supply curve (social cost). When a production tax is introduced, the equilibrium point moves up along the demand curve to its intersection with the social supply curve, resulting in a higher price–lower quantity combination. The example demonstrates a very important conclusion: *If manufacturers had to pay the full cost of producing vehicles, including the external cost of pollution, they would choose to produce fewer vehicles.*

However, Pigovian taxes are not a perfect solution to externalities. There are two problems. The first is setting the tax at the right level. As we have seen, it is not always easy to put an exact dollar-and-cents value on external costs. In our example, we estimated the external cost associated with producing a car to be $4,000, so we chose an optimal Pigovian tax of $4,000 per vehicle. What will happen if the estimate is wrong?

- If the estimate is too low, then the tax is set too low. In that case, the market will move closer to the efficient equilibrium, but it will remain somewhat inefficient.

- If our estimate is too high, then the tax is set too high. In that case, the market will overshoot—the new equilibrium quantity will be inefficient because it is too low, rather than too high.

The second problem with Pigovian taxes involves *distribution of the surplus.* Taxes are effective at transferring surplus away from consumers and producers and toward the government. But there is no guarantee that the government can or will then do anything to help the people who are bearing the external cost. The revenue collected from a Pigovian tax is sometimes used as compensation, but often it is not.

Yet, whether or not the revenue is redistributed to address the impacts of climate change, the tax still maximizes total surplus *in society as a whole* by moving the car market to the efficient equilibrium. Remember, the *distribution* of surplus is an entirely separate question from maximizing total surplus.

Capturing a positive externality with a subsidy

Just as a tax can counterbalance an external cost, a subsidy can help consumers or producers capture the benefits of positive externalities. If the government calculates that painting houses creates $500 worth of external benefits for neighbors, it might offer $500 subsidies to people who want to paint their houses.

As panel A of Figure 18-5 shows, the effect of a positive externality is that the demand curve (D = MB$_{private}$) is lower than it would be if consumers accounted for social benefits. The effect of a subsidy is that it *decreases the effective price* that is paid for a good by the buyer. As shown in panel B of Figure 18-5, this creates a new demand curve (D + subsidy) above the private demand curve (D = MB$_{private}$). If the demand curve (D + subsidy) is pushed up far enough, it will move the equilibrium quantity up to the efficient level—that is, the level at which the market maximizes total surplus.

Remember that, as with a Pigovian tax, using a subsidy to increase efficiency does not necessarily equal fairness. Such a subsidy would maximize total surplus in society. But the *distribution of that surplus* depends on where the government gets the money to pay for the subsidies. It might seem more "fair" if the subsidies were paid for out of property taxes because property owners have the most to gain from nicer neighborhoods. But even if the money was collected from general taxation, total surplus would still be maximized.

Public policies that use subsidies to solve externality problems are sometimes less noticeable than taxes. Once you begin to look for them, you'll see they are extremely widespread. One example that's a lot less trivial than painting houses is elementary and secondary education. If parents had to pay to send their children to school, many might decide the trade-off wasn't worth

FIGURE 18-5

A subsidy counteracts the effect of a positive externality

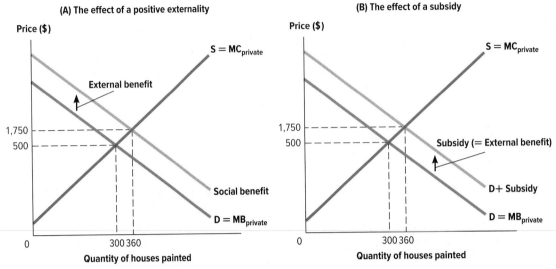

(A) The effect of a positive externality

Price ($)

S = MC$_{private}$

External benefit

1,750

500

Social benefit

D = MB$_{private}$

0   300 360
Quantity of houses painted

Under a positive externality, the private demand curve is below the social marginal benefit curve by the amount of the external benefit. This causes the equilibrium quantity to be lower than the efficient level.

(B) The effect of a subsidy

Price ($)

S = MC$_{private}$

1,750

500

Subsidy (= External benefit)

D + Subsidy

D = MB$_{private}$

0   300 360
Quantity of houses painted

A subsidy counteracts a positive externality. If the subsidy is set equal to the external benefit, the subsidy raises the private marginal benefit to the social marginal benefit, and the resulting equilibrium quantity is efficient.

it; more kids might drop out before finishing high school. Yet educating children has all sorts of external benefits: With education, children are more likely to become economically productive members of society and engaged citizens. That's why most governments offer public schools, which subsidize the cost of education.

You may also have seen how universities often subsidize small services in the campus community. Examples include free immunization shots to keep students from passing the flu around and antivirus software to keep viruses and malware out of the university computer network. In both of these cases, the thinking is that if it were left entirely to the market, students would consume "too little" of these goods or services. That is, fewer students would pay for immunizations and antivirus software than the amount that would maximize total surplus on the campus as a whole.

As with taxes, solving a positive externality through subsidies requires quantifying the external cost or benefit accurately. What will happen if the estimate is wrong?

- If the subsidy is set too low—say, a $50 subsidy for painting your house—then the number of houses painted will remain inefficiently low.
- If the subsidy is set too high—say, a $5,000 subsidy—then total surplus will not be maximized either. The increase in social benefits from the additional house painting will be less than the cost of the subsidy.

Other policy options: Quotas and tradable allowances

LO 18.6 Show how quantity regulations and tradable allowances can be used to counteract an externality and discuss the pros and cons of such solutions.

Another set of policy options is to set regulations or quotas on the amount of a good or service that can be produced or consumed. Sometimes these quotas can be designed to be traded among interested parties.

Quotas

If we know the socially optimal quantity of something—for instance, how much pollution we are willing to tolerate—why not simply regulate quantity (set a *quota*) rather than impose taxes? For example, California could calculate the efficient quantity of car manufacturing and limit each producer's production to its share of that amount. This approach would reduce car production by the same amount as a tax and also would reduce pollution by the same amount.

However, perhaps surprisingly, limiting total consumption to the efficient quantity *does not* make the market efficient. The real magic of the invisible hand in a market is not just that it pushes price and quantity to the efficient level. Rather, it does so by allocating resources to those with the greatest willingness to pay for them. Maximizing surplus depends not only on how many cars are manufactured but also on *who* manufactures them. Some car manufacturers will find it easy to reduce emissions. Others may use old technology and find it difficult to reduce their emissions. A tax allows the market to sort itself out in this way; a quota does not.

Tradable allowances

You may have spotted an obvious way to improve a quota system. The fact that different manufacturers have a different ability to reduce emissions implies that there is a missed opportunity for a mutually beneficial trade: A high-emissions manufacturer could pay a low-emissions manufacturer some amount in exchange for the rights to emit one more ton of carbon. In that trade, both would end up better off.

Why not set a quota but then allow firms to buy and sell their quota allowances? This solution allows policy-makers to choose a quantity rather than set a tax rate, while still ensuring that the quota is allocated to the people with the highest willingness to pay. A production or consumption quota that can be bought and sold is called a **tradable allowance**.

Just as with a quota, a system of tradable allowances will result in the efficient quantity of a good being bought and sold (as long as the total quota is set at the right quantity, of course). Like a tax, tradable allowances maximize surplus. There is one important difference, though, between a Pigovian tax and a tradable allowance:

tradable allowance
a production or consumption quota that can be bought and sold

- The Pigovian tax results in revenue collected by the *government*.
- In contrast, the tradable allowance creates a market in which quota rights are bought and sold among *private parties*.

The government could collect revenue by selling the initial quotas. But in cases where such programs have been implemented, they are more commonly allocated for free to consumers or producers, who then trade among themselves.

For more on the recent policy debate over whether to institute a carbon tax or a system of tradable carbon allowances in the United States, read the Real Life box "The fight over cap-and-trade legislation."

Real Life

The fight over cap-and-trade legislation

Pollution and greenhouse gases can be reduced by simple steps such as car-pooling and replacing incandescent light bulbs with energy-efficient ones. But, scientists argue, reductions of the scale that would be needed to slow climate change require more dramatic steps. In order to stabilize global temperatures at 3.5 degrees above pre-industrial levels, carbon in the atmosphere would have to fall to 50 to 85 percent of year-2000 levels. The big target is reductions in the emissions from the burning of fossil fuels by factories and drivers.

(continued)

In practical terms, this reduction could be accomplished in two major ways. The first, a tax on carbon, is the method favored by many economists. Most proposals put to Congress in 2009 called for a "starter" flat-tax amount—generally around $15 per ton of carbon released into the atmosphere. (A $15 per ton tax would equate to about 4 cents per gallon of gas.) Every year thereafter, the carbon tax would increase by $10, up to a final tax amount of about $100 per ton.

However, Lester Brown, director of the Earth Policy Institute, says that a tax of that magnitude wouldn't go nearly far enough to fight global warming. Instead, he recommends a much larger tax, which would start at $20 per ton and would increase to $240 per ton. Economists argue that these taxes should be applied "upstream," meaning that rather than sending factories and drivers a bill based on how much carbon they released in a year, the tax would be applied when fossil fuels are produced or imported. This tax would cause the quantity of fossil fuels demanded to drop. With factories, businesses, and everyday drivers consuming less fossil fuel, carbon-dioxide emissions would drop as well. The government would collect any revenue generated by the tax.

The alternative solution is to create a market for tradable carbon allowances—often called "cap-and-trade." It would set a *cap*—the maximum amount of carbon emissions to be allowed over the course of a year. Firms would be given allowances (permits) to emit a certain amount of carbon that they could trade or sell. In 2009, the Waxman-Markey climate change bill proposed cap-and-trade as a way to reach the ambitious goal of cutting carbon emissions by 86 percent by 2050, measured against 2005 levels.

How would it achieve that goal? In the early years, the cap would be set very close to the current level of carbon emissions. Over time, the cap would be reduced until the desired goal is met.

Then comes the "trade" part: "Clean" firms that are able to achieve low carbon emissions at low cost can sell their permits to companies that find it harder or more expensive to reduce their emissions. If many firms find it expensive to decrease their emissions, demand for carbon permits would go up, and the price of the permits will increase. As new, clean technologies are invented and adopted, the cost of reducing emissions would go down, causing reductions in the demand for and price of carbon permits.

Cap-and-trade programs can be designed so the permits are auctioned off to firms at the beginning of the program; the revenue from the auction goes to the government. In the Waxman-Markey bill, however, over 85 percent of the carbon allowances were to be given away to firms for free. Since these permits are highly valuable, those who were lucky enough to receive the permits would essentially be getting a windfall profit, courtesy of the government.

Putting aside the question of who collects revenue, economists usually will tell you that the two proposed solutions—a tax on carbon or a cap-and-trade market—actually produce quite similar outcomes. Both impose a cost on consumers: They raise the cost of producing goods, driving up prices that consumers pay. Food, for example, has to be transported from farms to stores by trucks and boats that emit carbon. Thus, higher carbon prices also increase the price of food at the supermarket. Critics worry that the higher prices could slow the economy and increase unemployment.

Of course, economists are not the people with the final say over public policy. After barely surviving a vote in the House of Representatives, the Waxman-Markey legislation died in the Senate in 2009 and was never implemented. (A carbon tax doesn't exist yet either in the United States.) However, in 2011 California introduced the nation's first state-administered cap-and-trade program of carbon emissions and Oregon and Washington are exploring programs to follow suit. Starting in 2013, many California industries faced an enforceable cap on the amount of carbon they can emit.

A 2014 report by the World Bank found 39 examples of real-world polices addressing carbon pricing. For example, in addition to California's cap-and-trade program, China has recently implemented several pilot tradable emissions programs and new carbon taxes have been introduced in Mexico and France.

Sources: http://www.time.com/time/health/article/0,8599,1700189,00.html; http://www.carbontax.org/bills/; http://www.arb.ca.gov/cc/capandtrade/capandtrade.htm; http://ntl.bts.gov/lib/32000/32700/32779/DOT_Climate_Change_Report_-_April_2010_-_Volume_1_and_2.pdf; http://www.worldbank.org/en/news/feature/2014/05/28/state-trends-report-tracks-global-growth-carbon-pricing.

Targeting externalities with public policy

When economists propose taxes or tradable allowances as a way to tackle externalities, they try to propose taxes based on the externality itself, rather than on the action that generates it. But this is often quite hard to do. In this chapter, we've talked a lot about gas taxes, which are targeted at a good that generates pollution, rather than at pollution itself. Ideally, environmental policy would target the end product—carbon emissions—directly. That way, the policy would apply to all the thousands of different activities that generate an external cost through carbon emissions—from raising livestock, to operating a power plant, to lighting a wood fire in a fireplace. However, measuring emissions from all these different sources is extremely difficult, logistically speaking. Taxing gasoline, rather than pollution, is a second-best solution; the first-best solution may simply be unattainable.

Because of the difficulty of measuring pollution directly, many policies do target individual goods and processes. For instance:

- Cars are generally required to have catalytic converters, which reduce emissions of nitrous oxides, carbon monoxide, and unburnt hydrocarbons.
- Governments often subsidize recyling or energy-saving appliances and light bulbs.
- Local governments ban wood fires during smoggy times of the year or when dry conditions make fires especially dangerous.

The downside of targeting individual activities is that such policies risk misaligning the incentives that consumers and producers face with the goal of minimizing the externality.

For example, in 1975 the U.S. government imposed fuel-efficiency standards, called the *CAFE standards,* on cars. The goal was to reduce pollution. But the regulations were designed in such a way that "light trucks" were subject to looser standards than cars. The result? Auto manufacturers started producing cars that were big and heavy enough to be classed as a light truck; those vehicles didn't have to meet the standards for cars. Average fuel efficiency of cars actually *fell* rather than increased. The CAFE standards were updated in 2012 with new regulations requiring automakers to raise the *average* fuel efficiency to 54.5 miles per gallon for cars and light trucks by 2025. The impacts of this policy are still uncertain.[8]

A policy that directly targets pollution encourages the development of cleaner technology and processes; it doesn't give clever companies the chance to find ways around the policy. In fact, such policies give consumers and producers an incentive to find new ways of doing things that *don't* generate pollution. They want to avoid having to pay a tax or pay for the rights to an allowance—and that desire aligns their incentives with the end goal of the policy.

✓ CONCEPT CHECK

- ☐ Are subsidies used to correct for positive or negative externalities? **[LO 18.5]**
- ☐ Which is a more efficient way of correcting a negative externality—a quota or a tax? **[LO 18.6]**
- ☐ What is the difference between a normal quota and a tradable quota? Which is more efficient and why? **[LO 18.6]**

Conclusion

Typically, we rely on the invisible hand of markets to maximize total surplus by allocating the right quantity of goods to the right people. But what happens when one person's choices impose costs or benefits on others? Free-market outcomes can be less than ideal. They sometimes result in too much or too little of the good or activity in question.

As the examples in this chapter show, positive or negative externalities (for both production and consumption) are a common part of economic life. They're the context for discussions of issues like climate change, pollution, blighted neighborhoods, and education policy. Sometimes, individuals can find private solutions, by paying others to do (or to not do) things that affect them. However, the difficulty of coordinating or enforcing these private agreements often overwhelms the benefits.

In these cases, we've seen that government policies like taxes and subsidies can actually *increase* efficiency, even though we typically think of taxes as creating distortions. This is because taxes and subsidies can counterbalance an externality by forcing buyers or sellers to take into account the value of the external cost or benefit. At first glance, quotas look like a simple way to counter the "too much" problem of negative externalities, but they fail to maximize surplus unless people are allowed to buy and sell the quotas.

In the next chapter, we'll examine other challenges that are closely related to the idea of externalities. When goods are collectively owned, individuals have limited incentive to take into account the impact of their actions on the publicly held resources. As we are about to see, the resulting market failures and corresponding policy solutions look very similar to those we've discussed in this chapter.

Key Terms

private costs, p. 453

external costs, p. 454

social cost, p. 454

private benefits, p. 454

external benefits, p. 454

social benefit, p. 454

externality, p. 454

network externality, p. 454

production externality, p. 455

consumption externality, p. 455

Coase theorem, p. 460

Pigovian tax, p. 464

tradable allowance, p. 467

Summary

LO 18.1 Explain how external costs and benefits affect the trade-offs faced by economic decision makers.

Any cost that is imposed without compensation on someone other than the person who caused it is an *external cost*. A benefit that accrues without compensation to someone other than the person who caused it is called an *external benefit*. External costs and benefits are collectively referred to as *externalities,* and we call the former *negative externalities* and the latter *positive externalities.* Costs and benefits that fall directly on an economic decision maker are *private costs/benefits,* while the total cost of the decision including any externalities is referred to as the *social cost/benefit.*

LO 18.2 Calculate the effect of a negative externality on market price and quantity.

A negative externality makes the private cost of a decision lower than the social cost, which causes the individuals who bear only the private cost to demand or supply an inefficiently high quantity at any given price. In the presence of a negative externality (production or consumption), the market equilibrium yields a higher quantity than the efficient level, failing to maximize total surplus. The market price is too low relative to the social cost. The loss of surplus falls on those outside the market who bear the external cost of the decision.

LO 18.3 Calculate the effect of a positive externality on market price and quantity.

A positive externality makes the private benefit of a decision lower than the social benefit, which causes individuals who enjoy only the private benefit to demand or supply an inefficiently low quantity at any given price. In the presence of a positive externality (production or consumption), the market equilibrium yields a lower quantity than the efficient level, failing to maximize total surplus. The market price is too low relative to social benefit. The loss of surplus falls on those outside the market who would gain from a larger quantity transacted.

LO 18.4 Describe how individuals could reach a private solution to an externality and explain why this doesn't always occur.

The idea that individuals reach an efficient equilibrium through private trades, even in the presence of an externality, is called the *Coase theorem.* Because an externality fails to maximize surplus, in theory, everyone could be made better off if those who are burdened with external costs or benefits pay others to buy or sell the efficient quantity. The theorem makes two big assumptions, however: that people can make enforceable agreements and that there are no costs involved in the transaction.

> **LO 18.5** Show how a tax or subsidy can be used to counteract an externality and discuss the pros and cons of such solutions.

A tax meant to counterbalance the effect of a negative externality is known as a *Pigovian tax.* In order to exactly counterbalance a negative externality, policy-makers want to set the tax equal to the value of the external cost, thus reducing the equilibrium quantity. Similarly, a subsidy can counterbalance a positive externality by moving the equilibrium to a higher quantity. When the tax or subsidy is set at the right level, the externality is exactly counterbalanced, and the market becomes efficient.

> **LO 18.6** Show how quantity regulations and tradable allowances can be used to counteract an externality and discuss the pros and cons of such solutions.

Setting a quota (a quantity regulation) to counteract inefficiently high consumption due to a negative externality can bring quantity down to the efficient level, but it does not actually maximize surplus. Maximizing surplus and achieving efficiency depends not only on how much of a good is bought and sold, but also on *who* buys and sells it.

A production or consumption quota that can be bought and sold is called a *tradable allowance.* Just as with a quota, a system of tradable allowances will result in the efficient quantity of a good being bought and sold, as long as the total number of allowances is set at the right quantity. Like a tax, however, tradable allowances maximize surplus by allocating sales to those with the highest willingness to pay. The government can collect revenue by selling the initial quotas, but more often, they are allocated for free to consumers or producers, who then trade among themselves.

Review Questions

1. Describe an externality not listed in the chapter. Is it positive or negative? Who is the economic decision maker, and who bears the external cost or benefit? **[LO 18.1]**

2. Consider the decision to adopt a dog. Describe a private cost, a private benefit, an external cost, and an external benefit that might result from your decision to adopt a dog. **[LO 18.1]**

3. What are the private costs and benefits associated with smoking cigarettes? What are the external costs? If smokers paid the social cost of cigarettes, what would happen to the quantity demanded? **[LO 18.2]**

4. When U.S. farmers in the Southwest irrigate their land, salt in the ground soil leaks into the Colorado River. The Colorado River has become so salty that Mexican farmers further down the river cannot irrigate their own land, and Mexican crops have suffered. Explain why this situation constitutes a negative production externality, how it leads to too much irrigation, and what it would mean for U.S. farmers to face the externality. **[LO 18.2]**

5. If education has private benefits to an individual as well as external benefits to society, explain why a less-than-optimal amount of education occurs. **[LO 18.3]**

6. Hand washing has external health benefits, helping prevent the spread of communicable diseases. If a program were somehow devised so that people got paid a small reward every time they washed their hands, how would it affect the number of people who are sick at any given time? **[LO 18.3]**

7. Jimi loves turning up his electric guitar amp all the way, but his next-door neighbor hates listening to him. How might Jimi and his neighbor reach a private solution to their problem? Describe potential problems that might make it hard for a private solution to occur. **[LO 18.4]**

8. Felix and Oscar are roommates. Oscar is messy, and Felix is planning to move out unless they can come to an agreement. For the roommates to reach a private solution, does it matter whether Oscar compensates Felix for being messy or Felix pays Oscar to clean up? **[LO 18.4]**

9. Suppose that you are an economic-policy advisor. Environmental groups are pressuring you to implement the highest-possible carbon tax, while industry groups are pressuring you to implement no carbon tax at all. Both argue that their position makes more sense economically. Explain to them what the most-efficient tax level will be and why there are costs to setting the tax too high or too low. **[LO 18.5]**

10. In what circumstances will a tax make a market less efficient? In what circumstances will a tax make a market more efficient? **[LO 18.5]**

11. The city of Seattle limits each household to one can of free garbage collection per week. There are fees for any extra garbage collected from the curb. Is this policy the most efficient way of reducing waste? Why or why not? **[LO 18.6]**

12. Suppose an environmental impact study shows that the coral reef near Port Douglas, Australia, can sustain 20 scuba diving tours per week. Explain why a quota might have an advantage over a tax in this situation. **[LO 18.6]**

13. The city of Seattle limits each household to one can of free garbage collection per week. There are fees for any extra garbage collected from the curb. Suppose that a neighborhood group in Seattle organizes a group of families so that those who plan to go over their one-can garbage quota can find households that are under their quota and pay them to put out the extra trash. Does this change the efficiency of the policy? **[LO 18.6]**

14. Suppose the government is considering two policies to limit factory air pollution: taxing all producers, or providing each producer with an allotment of tradable permits. If both policies lead to the same amount of pollution reduction, why might producers prefer the tradable-permit option? **[LO 18.6]**

Problems and Applications

1. State whether each of the following primarily causes an external cost or an external benefit. **[LO 18.1]**

    a. Fishing at a popular lakeside vacation spot.

    b. Buying a fax machine.

    c. Conducting research to find an AIDS vaccine.

    d. Occupying a seat on a bench in a crowded park.

    e. Littering.

    f. Spaying or neutering your pet.

2. You are considering whether to enter a holiday lights display contest that pays $1,000 to the winner. State whether each of the following constitutes private costs, private benefits, external costs, or external benefits. Check all that apply. **[LO 18.1]**

    a. Increased traffic congestion.

    b. Neighbors have difficulty parking on your street.

    c. Increased electric bill from the holiday lights.

    d. Winning the holiday lights display contest.

3. Figure 18P-1 shows the demand curve for a U.S. farmer for irrigating his land. It costs the farmer $100 per acre to irrigate the land. Each acre of land irrigation generates salty runoff that winds up in the Colorado River. It costs $50 to desalinate this river water so Mexican farmers can irrigate their crops. **[LO 18.2]**

    a. Draw the marginal private cost of irrigation on the graph.

    b. Draw the marginal social cost of irrigation on the graph.

    c. How many acres will the U.S. farmer irrigate?

    d. What is the efficient level of irrigation?

4. The weekly supply and demand for packs of cigarettes in the United States is given in Figure 18P-2. **[LO 18.2]**

    a. Suppose cigarette smoking causes a $6/pack external cost on nonsmokers. Draw the social

FIGURE 18P-1

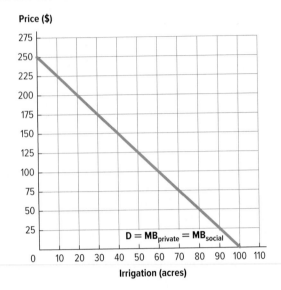

FIGURE 18P-2

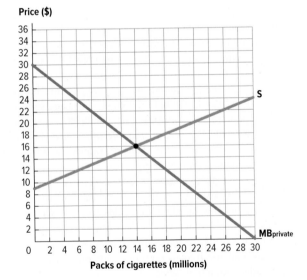

benefit curve that accounts for the external cost associated with smoking.

    b. Assuming the externality associated with smoking is not faced by consumers, how many packs of cigarettes are consumed per week?

    c. What is the efficient number of cigarette packs?

5. Figure 18P-3 shows supply and demand for first-aid training, based on private costs and benefits. **[LO 18.3]**

    a. Suppose that the external benefit from first-aid training is worth $6. Graph the social benefit

FIGURE 18P-3

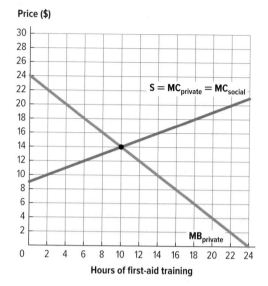

Price ($)

Hours of first-aid training

FIGURE 18P-4

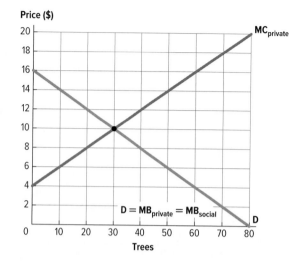

Price ($)

Trees

curve for first-aid training that accounts for the external benefit.

b. Ignoring the social benefits of training, how many hours of first-aid training will occur?

c. What is the socially optimal quantity of first-aid training?

d. What is the deadweight loss to society when consumers are unable to capture the $6 external benefit they provide from first-aid training? Graph the deadweight loss.

6. Figure 18P-4 shows supply and demand for planting trees, based on private costs and benefits. Trees sequester carbon, meaning that they help counteract pollutants that contribute to climate change. **[LO 18.3]**

a. Suppose that the carbon sequestration that results from planting a tree is worth $4. Graph the social cost curve for tree planting that accounts for the positive externality of trees.

b. Ignoring the positive externality, how many trees will be planted?

c. What is the socially optimal quantity of trees?

d. What is the deadweight loss that occurs when suppliers are unable to capture the $4 external benefit they provide from planting trees? Graph the deadweight loss.

7. Your neighbor never mows her lawn. You don't have any legal right to force her to mow, but the mess in her front yard is making your neighborhood unsightly and reducing the value of your house. The reduction in the value of your house is $5,000, and the value of her time to mow the lawn once a week is $1,000. Suppose you offer her a deal in which you pay her $3,000 to mow. How does this deal affect surplus? **[LO 18.4]**

a. The deal increases only your surplus.

b. The deal increases only your neighbor's surplus.

c. The deal increases both your surplus and your neighbor's.

d. The deal increases your surplus but decreases your neighbor's.

e. The deal increases your neighbor's surplus but decreases yours.

f. The deal does not affect surplus.

8. Johnston Forest in Rhode Island has a cave that houses thousands of fruit bats. Bat droppings are highly acidic and have ruined the paint on many cars. The flying radius of the Johnston Forest bats encompasses two towns, Johnston and Foster. The residents of Johnston collectively value bat removal at $400,000. Foster residents collectively value bat removal at $500,000. Pest control experts estimate that the cost of bat removal would be $450,000. Which of the following scenarios would lead to removal of the bats? Check all that apply. **[LO 18.4]**

a. Foster pays Johnston $50,000 to contribute to bat removal.

b. Foster and Johnston evenly split the cost of bat removal.

c. Johnston contributes nothing toward bat removal.

9. The local government has decided that because children's health has large external benefits, it will offer a subsidy to help families pay for visits to the pediatrician. However, the government isn't sure at what level to set the subsidy. Figure 18P-5 shows the current

FIGURE 18P-5

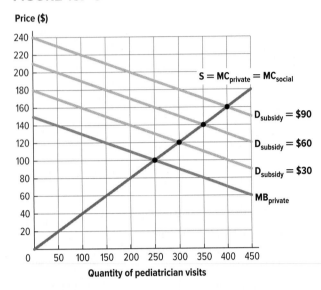

Price ($)

Quantity of pediatrician visits

S = MC$_{private}$ = MC$_{social}$

D$_{subsidy}$ = $90

D$_{subsidy}$ = $60

D$_{subsidy}$ = $30

MB$_{private}$

FIGURE 18P-6

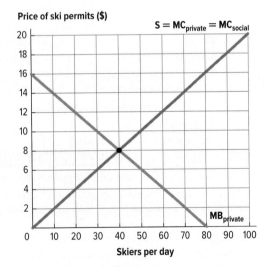

Price of ski permits ($)

S = MC$_{private}$ = MC$_{social}$

MB$_{private}$

Skiers per day

demand curve for pediatricians' visits (MB$_{private}$) and three alternative subsidies, represented by curves D$_{subsidy=\$30}$, D$_{subsidy=\$60}$, and D$_{subsidy=\$90}$. **[LO 18.5]**

    a. Assume that the correct level of subsidy is $60. What is the socially optimal level of pediatrician visits?

    b. Compared to the efficient outcome, graph the deadweight loss that would result from subsidies of $30 or $90.

10. Figure 18P-6 shows the daily market for water skiing permits on El Dorado Lake. Suppose each skier (each permit) causes $4 of damage to the lake. **[LO 18.5]**

    a. Draw the social benefit curve that accounts for the external cost of skiers, and draw the

deadweight loss that occurs at the market equilibrium. What is the socially optimal level of water skiing? Calculate the deadweight loss if there is no government intervention in this market.

    b. Suppose the government imposes an $8 tax on buyers of ski permits. Draw the after-tax demand curve. Is this tax too high or too low? Draw the deadweight loss associated with this tax.

    c. Compared to no intervention, how does the tax affect total surplus?

11. Suppose certain fireworks are legal in a residential area on the Fourth of July. The fireworks have been approved for safety, but they do cause noise pollution so their use must be limited. Jenny and Salo like to purchase fireworks for their families; Table 18P-1 shows each individual's willingness-to-pay for fireworks. The price of fireworks is $2 per firework. **[LO 18.6]**

    a. If a quota of 30 fireworks per person is imposed, what is each individual's willingness-to-pay for their last firework?

    b. If the government wants no more than 60 fireworks total to be purchased, what amount of tax should be imposed? How many fireworks will Jenny and Salo purchase under this tax?

12. Many municipalities are concerned about the environmental impact of plastic bags, which often end up as litter, clogging drains and hanging from tree branches. A town is considering whether to impose a tax on plastic

TABLE 18P-1

Willingness to pay ($)	Q Jenny	Q Salo
10	0	0
9	10	5
8	20	10
7	30	15
6	40	20
5	50	25
4	60	30
3	70	35
2	80	40
1	90	45
0	100	50

FIGURE 18P-7

(A) Quota

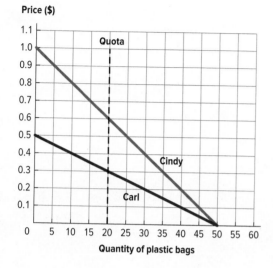

Quantity of plastic bags

(B) Tax

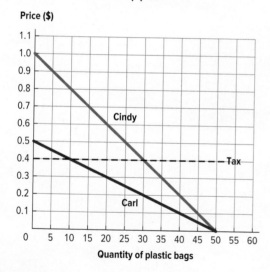

Quantity of plastic bags

bags to be collected at the store, or a per person quota. Cindy and Carl are two average citizens who both use plastic bags when they go grocery shopping. Plastic bags are currently free when they shop. Figure 18P-7 shows each individual's demand curve for plastic bags. **[LO 18.6]**

a. Under the quota, what is each individual's willingness-to-pay for the last bag used?

b. How many bags will each shopper use under the tax? What is each individual's willingness-to-pay for the last bag used under the tax?

c. Would you recommend that the town adopt a plastic-bag quota or tax?

Endnotes

1. http://www.laalmanac.com/transport/tr10.htm; https://www.dmv.ca.gov/portal/wcm/connect/5aa16cd3-39a5-402f-9453-0d353706cc9a/official.pdf?MOD=AJPERES.

2. http://www.usatoday.com/story/money/2016/02/06/24-7-wallst-state-gas-tax-oil/79834368.

3. National Research Council, *Advancing the Science of Climate Change* (Washington, DC: The National Academies Press, 2010).

4. http://www.theguardian.com/environment/green-living-blog/2010/sep/23/carbon-footprint-new-car.

5. http://www.eenews.net/stories/1060031090.

6. https://coase.org/aboutronaldcoase.htm.

7. https://www.britannica.com/biography/Arthur-Cecil-Pigou.

8. http://www.nhtsa.gov/About+NHTSA/Press+Releases/2012/Obama+Administration+Finalizes+Historic+54.5+mpg+Fuel+Efficiency+Standards.

Public Goods and Common Resources

A NEW TRAGEDY OF THE COMMONS

In 1910, there were roughly 300,000 rhinoceroses roaming the savannas of East Africa. A century later, rhino populations are dwindling in alarming numbers: There are no more than 5,500 black rhinos on the African continent, with several other species near extinction.[1] A growing human population encroaching on the rhinos' habitat is part of the explanation. The bigger cause of the rhinos' downfall has been their own value to hunters.

In the early 1900s, thousands of big-game hunters traveled from Europe and America to shoot rhinos for sport, including U.S. president Theodore Roosevelt. These days, it's mostly illegal to hunt rhinos, but a flourishing illegal trade in ivory from rhino horns continues. In parts of Asia, ivory is an ingredient in traditional medicines and is worth more per ounce than gold. As a result, some species of rhino—such as the northern white—are on the verge of extinction.

Why are poachers killing rhinos so fast that they're becoming extinct? As soon as they become extinct, after all, that's the end of the profits for poachers. Wouldn't poachers want to carefully manage the rhino population so that it can produce ivory for many years to come? The problem, as we'll see in this chapter, is that the rhinos don't "belong" to anyone in particular. As a result, no one has a big enough financial incentive to maintain their value. Instead, everyone wants to get in quickly and take what they can before the rhinos are gone.

Ingo Arndt/Getty Images/Minden Pictures

The near-extinction of black rhinos in Africa isn't just a problem for biologists and nature-lovers; it's also an example of an important type of economic inefficiency. Not all goods are allocated efficiently by competitive markets, and in this chapter, we'll discuss two major types of goods that are subject to market failure. The first category is *public goods,* such as national defense, public health, roads, education, and research. Public goods could end up *undersupplied* if left to competitive markets. The second category is *common resources* such as rhinos and other wildlife. As the rhino example shows, common resources could end up *overconsumed* and depleted if left to competitive markets.

In both cases, we'll see that the root of the problem is the difficulty of forcing people who consume the goods to pay for what they take. Both the problems this causes and the corresponding solutions are related to the concept of external costs and external benefits we discussed in the previous chapter.

In the end, rhinos aren't doomed. Some policies for protecting common resources and providing public goods are extremely effective. As a result, the population of white rhinos in southern Africa has taken the opposite path from that of the black rhinos. Although there were only 50 remaining white rhinos in the wild in the early 1900s, there are now approximately 20,000. What made this difference? Paradoxically, part of the solution was to encourage people to hunt rhinos—but only on their own private land. The government of South Africa also established well-protected national parks.[2] In this chapter, we'll see why these and other examples of government action and thoughtfully designed public policies can go a long way toward allocating both public goods and common resources more efficiently.

Characteristics of Goods

LO 19.1 Define different types of goods in terms of rivalry and excludability.

What types of goods tend to go the way of the rhino, suffering from overuse? River water, but not orange juice. Fish in the sea, but not chickens on the farm. Computers at the public library, but not personal laptops. What is the common thread?

The first thing to notice is that river water, fish in the sea, and public-library computers are not usually owned by a private individual. Instead, they are *held collectively* by a community or country.

We can go further and specify two important characteristics that determine how goods are used and whether they are allocated efficiently by markets:

- When a good is **excludable**, sellers can prevent its use by those who have not paid for it.
- When a good is **rival in consumption** (or just **rival**), one person's consumption prevents or decreases others' ability to consume it.

Most of the goods we've discussed in this book are **private goods**, which are *both* excludable and rival in consumption. Many goods, however, lack one or both of these characteristics. Before describing these types of goods, we'll explore the ideas of excludability and "rivalness" a bit further.

excludable
a characteristic of a good or service that allows owners to prevent its use by people who have not paid for it

rival in consumption (rival)
the characteristic of a good for which one person's consumption prevents or decreases others' ability to consume it

private goods
goods that are both excludable and rival

Excludable goods

Excludability matters because it allows owners to set an enforceable price on a good. If you can't prevent people from consuming something, then they have little reason to pay for using it.

For instance, street lights are a nonexcludable good. Once they are put up in a neighborhood, everyone who comes through gets the benefit, regardless of whether they've paid to put up the lights. How would you prevent the person who didn't pay from getting the benefit of the lamps? Have a police officer standing by to make him wear special dark sunglasses? Make him close his eyes? Wall off the neighborhood? Most of the time, it's hard to imagine that you could allow some people but not others to enjoy the benefit of street lights.

Excludability can be a matter of degree, though. Take roads: It *is* possible to make bridges, tunnels, and major highways excludable by setting up toll booths at every entrance. For most roads, though, this is not a practical option. You can't have a toll booth at the end of every small street. (Although with new technological advances, we are starting to see strategies approaching this. For example, in London driving in the city center incurs congestion charges during peak times; cameras set up throughout the city help enforce these payments.)

Rival-in-consumption goods

Rivalry has to do with whether one person's consumption of a good prevents or decreases others' ability to consume it. Most goods are rival goods. Some particularly obvious examples:

- Rhino horns: When someone shoots a rhino and cuts off its horn, the next person to come along can't also use the rhino for that purpose.
- Fish: Once a fish is caught by one fishing boat, it's no longer out in the water to be caught by the next boat.
- Jeans: If one person is wearing a pair of jeans, someone else cannot also be wearing that same exact pair of jeans.
- Food: After you eat your lunch, nobody else can eat that same exact plate of food.

So, what types of goods are *nonrival*? Here are some examples:

- Streetlights: Two people walking down a lit-up street are able to enjoy the light just as much as one person. (This is a good that is both nonexcludable and nonrival.)
- A song on the radio: One person listening doesn't "use it up" and doesn't prevent others from listening as well.

In general, knowledge and technology are nonrival because once something has been thought up or invented, everyone can take advantage of it.

Often, rivalry is a matter of degree. Again, think of roads. A rarely used country road is probably not rival in consumption. If one more person drives on the road, it has a negligible effect on the ability of other drivers to use it. A heavily congested highway, however, has elements of a rival good. Every car that gets on the highway increases the amount of traffic, slowing down other cars and reducing the value of the highway for other drivers.

Sunlight is a public good—both nonrival and nonexcludable.

The same applies to streetlights: One other person walking along will likely not get in your way. But if 100 people are crowded onto the sidewalk, and you're trying to use the streetlight to find something you dropped, you might have trouble. But this is an extreme situation; for the most part we think of streetlights as nonrival goods.

FIGURE 19-1
Four categories of goods

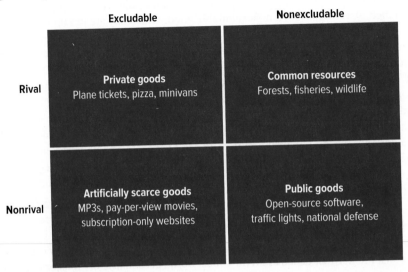

Four categories of goods

Whether a good is excludable and rival in consumption has important implications for how it is allocated through a market system. By combining the concepts of excludability and rivalry, we can define four categories of goods, as shown in Figure 19-1.

public good
a good that is neither excludable nor rival

common resource
a good that is not excludable but is rival

- *Private goods* are goods that are both excludable and rival. They are usually allocated efficiently by competitive markets, as we've discussed throughout the book.
- **Public goods** are the opposite of private goods, as the name suggests. They are neither excludable nor rival.
- **Common resources** are not excludable but are rival.
- *Artificially scarce goods* are excludable but not rival.

We won't discuss the economic issues surrounding artificially scarce goods in this chapter; we have discussed them already in Chapter 14, "Monopoly," and Chapter 15, "Monopolistic Competition and Oligopoly." Essentially, the markets for artificially scarce goods function just like the markets for private goods, and it is the lack of close substitute for a good that makes it artificially scarce. This scarcity allows the sellers of these goods some power to charge a price above what is possible in a perfectly competitive market. The remainder of the chapter will focus on public goods and common resources.

✓ CONCEPT CHECK

- ☐ What does it mean for a good to be excludable? **[LO 19.1]**
- ☐ What does it mean for a good to be rival in consumption? **[LO 19.1]**
- ☐ What is the difference between public goods and common resources? **[LO 19.1]**

Public Goods

Markets work well for allocating private goods efficiently. They do not always work so well for allocating public goods and common resources. The reason is that the price charged by competitive firms does not capture the true costs and benefits of consumption. In this way, the problems with public goods and common resources are closely tied to the problems of externalities discussed in the previous chapter.

Although public goods and common resources are both inefficiently allocated, the problem with public goods is fundamentally different from the problem with common resources. For public goods, that problem is called the *free-rider problem.*

The free-rider problem

LO 19.2 Describe the free-rider problem and its consequences.

Think about a public bus. It costs something to run the bus along its route—to pay the driver, buy gasoline, make repairs, and so on. To support these costs, the bus driver charges riders a fare as they enter the bus. But suppose someone decides he doesn't want to pay the fare and slips in the back door when the driver's not looking? This person gets to ride the bus for free. In fact, we might even call him a "free rider."

If this free rider is alone, then no great harm is done. He takes up a seat on the bus but doesn't fundamentally detract anything from others. Also, there are still enough paying riders to cover the cost of operating the bus.

However, imagine a bus with a back door that is always open. Riders can choose to get on through the front door and pay the fare, or they can choose the back door and not pay anything. Under these circumstances, we'll likely see a lot of free riders. As more people choose to ride for free, the city will have less revenue to cover the costs of operating buses. If too many people ride for free, the city will no longer be able to afford to run as many buses as before. The reduced bus services don't reflect reduced demand or a lower value to riders, though. There are still many people who have a willingness to pay that is at least as high as the price of a bus ticket, but no individual person has an incentive to *voluntarily* pay the fare.

In technical terms, the **free-rider problem** we've just described is caused by nonexcludability leading to *undersupply* of a public good. When a good is not easily excludable, what people pay for it will not necessarily reflect the real value they place on it. After all, even if you value the bus ride highly and would willingly pay for a ticket if you had to, you might still hop on for free if given the chance. The problem is that when a good is nonexcludable, it is difficult for firms to make any profit from the production and sale of the good. If firms cannot earn a profit, there is no incentive to produce the good. As a result, the good will be undersupplied (as compared to the efficient quantity).

free-rider problem
a problem that occurs when the nonexcludability of a public good leads to undersupply

Note that the free-rider problem *does not* have to do with whether nonpaying riders are taking up seats on the bus. Imagine a bus that could fit an infinite number of riders: Seats would not be in short supply, but not enough riders would pay the fare to cover the cost of running the bus. Even J. K. Rowling's Knight Bus, which can defy the laws of physics, charges Harry Potter 11 sickles to ride.

Since public goods are, by definition, nonexcludable, the free-rider problem occurs with *all public goods*. Public transportation is the classic example for which the problem is named, but there are many other cases in which people metaphorically "ride" for free. All sorts of services end up undersupplied as a result:

- Imagine a public bathroom with a sign reading, "Please clean the sink when you're finished." How many people would do that? Surely not everyone, even if everyone places some value on having a clean public bathroom.

- Or suppose if, after a big snowfall, everyone was expected to get a shovel and clear part of the road. If everyone pitched in, the road would get cleared in no time. But this is not usually what happens.

If given the opportunity, people will free-ride: They will walk out of the bathroom without cleaning up, and they will choose not to go outside to shovel the road.

One way to think about the free-rider problem is that free riders enjoy positive externalities from others' choices to pay for bus rides, clean public bathrooms, or shovel roads. As we saw in Chapter 18, "Externalities," when positive externalities exist, the equilibrium quantity of the good or service is less than the level that would maximize total surplus in society as a whole. The result is that public transportation, clean public bathrooms, and clear roads after a snowstorm are *undersupplied* if left solely to the market.

Some important public goods are more abstract than buses or bathrooms. Health, cleanliness, general knowledge, and safety are all public goods that have a huge impact on everyday life. Consider an example from public health: If 99 percent of the population is vaccinated against a disease—such as polio or smallpox—the remaining 1 percent can probably remain unvaccinated without fear of getting sick.

But if everyone tried to be a free rider by remaining unvaccinated, the risk of disease would quickly increase. It's not possible to exclude the unvaccinated from the benefits of living around others who are vaccinated. When there are too many free riders and an undersupply of vaccination, the result is that everyone is more likely to get sick. Similarly, an army, police force, and "neighborhood watch" are all ways of providing public safety. It is not possible to easily exclude free-riding residents who don't contribute from enjoying the benefits.

One of the most abstract public goods is general knowledge or information. For a case in which the free-rider problems surrounding these public goods seem to have been overcome to everyone's benefit, look at the From Another Angle box "Why does Wikipedia work?"

From Another Angle
Why does Wikipedia work?

In 2001, Jimmy Wales and Larry Sanger launched Wikipedia, a free online encyclopedia generated entirely by voluntary contributions from users. Contributors are unpaid and unsupervised. Anyone can edit Wikipedia, and anyone can choose to read articles without making a contribution. In other words, Wikipedia is a classic public good. It is nonexcludable because anyone can use it for free. It is nonrival because, generally speaking, one person reading a web page doesn't diminish others' ability to do so.

Given what we know about public goods, it's easy to think of ways that Wikipedia might have failed. At best, we might expect articles to be undersupplied. After all, how many people will want to spend their time writing encyclopedia articles for free? At worst, we can imagine contributors filling Wikipedia with self-serving or misleading information. Stephen Colbert, formerly the host of the satiric news-commentary show *The Colbert Report,* was once banned from Wikipedia for asking his viewers to edit the page on elephants to say that their population had tripled in three months. Colbert's point, of course, was that "facts" on Wikipedia are sometimes subject to the whims and biases of contributors.

In Wikipedia's early days, it seemed as if these predictions might cripple the project. Articles were short, riddled with errors, and much more likely to be about *Star Trek* than Friedrich Nietzsche. Fifteen years later, however, Wikipedia has 5.1 million articles—more than 40 times the number in the online version of *Encyclopedia Britannica.* A spot-check of 45 articles on general science topics found that Wikipedia is just as accurate as traditional peer-reviewed encyclopedias. How does Wikipedia overcome the problems of undersupply and misuse that generally plague public goods?

To rephrase the question: What sort of benefits could outweigh the costs of time and effort involved in editing Wikipedia? When asked directly in a survey, the vast majority of contributors listed altruistic-sounding reasons, such as: to "fix an error" or "contribute to the share of knowledge." Only 2 percent of all contributors listed fame or recognition as a motivation for editing. We might be somewhat skeptical about this modesty, though. After all, many contributors register a user name and page that provides a history of their edits for others to view.

Whatever the exact motivation of contributors, Wikipedia is designed in a way that is conducive to overcoming the challenges it faces as a public good. Since the costs of contributing are relatively low (just click "edit," type the changes, and click "submit"), it is easy to correct abuses. As a result, fewer than 5,000 dedicated editors (those who make over 100 edits a month) in the English version at last count do a remarkably good job of correcting incidences of vandalism and misuse. In addition, the project capitalizes on the idea that sharing knowledge is good for society. This motivates users to contribute and police one another on their own.

As Wikipedia and other free, open-source resources become more prominent, economists are adapting their ideas about the provision of public goods, and the motivations that drive people to contribute to them.

Sources: Denise Anthony et al., "Reputation and Reliability in Collective Goods: The Case of the Online Encyclopedia Wikipedia," *Rationality and Society* 21, no. 3 (2009), pp. 283–306; https://en.wikipedia.org/wiki/Wikipedia:About.

Solutions to the free-rider problem

LO 19.3 Explain how and when problems with public goods can be effectively solved by social norms, government provision, and expansion of property rights.

The free-rider problem leads to a market failure: Markets typically undersupply public goods. Fortunately, this undersupply problem can be solved in a variety of ways:

- Change social norms relating to the good or service.
- Make somebody responsible for the provision of a certain quantity of the good or service (such as municipal snow plowing on public roads).
- Make the good or service more excludable by assigning property rights (such as the pay-per-use public toilets found in some big cities).

The many possible solutions generally fall under three categories: social norms, government provision, and private property rights. We'll consider each of these solutions in this section, starting with social norms.

Social norms

For some public goods, society tries to get people to act in the interest of society by shifting social norms. For example, campaigns to shame those who try to sneak on the back of the bus or suggested donations at a museum's entrance may change people's opinions on what is individually optimal.

The free-rider problem is a problem of *trade-offs*—people are able to enjoy the benefits of something without paying the corresponding costs. Strong social norms can help rebalance the trade-off by imposing "costs" on people who litter, sneak through the back door of the bus, fail to do their bit of snow shoveling, and so on. Remember, costs don't have to be financial. Social disapproval, guilt, or conflict with those in your community can also be costs.

Suggested-donation boxes attempt to change social norms in order to address the free-rider problem which leads to the under-supply of public goods.
© *Matthew Ferris/Alamy*

As you would expect, social disapproval carries a higher cost in places where you know the people around you, care about their opinions, and expect to interact with them again in the future. For example, we might expect social norms to be more effective at deterring free riders on a small-town bus system than on the subway in New York City.

While changing social norms works for some public goods, in other cases, the government tries to fix the market failure through regulation or direct government provision.

Government provision

Local governments usually repair roads. Why doesn't the private sector do it instead?
© Laramie Boomerang, Andy Carpenean/AP Images

To combat the undersupply of public goods, the more typical solution is for the government to step in and provide a good directly. In the United States and many other wealthy countries, we see government provision of public goods everywhere: in national defense, transportation systems, education and research, parks, safety, and much more.

Well-intentioned people can argue about when it makes sense for government to provide these services directly and when it should contract with a private company to provide them or force individuals to pay a private provider. Whichever method a government chooses to supply a public good, two common issues arise: First, what is the right amount of the public good to supply? Second, who will pay for it?

In a functioning market, people will buy a good up to the point where the marginal benefit they enjoy from the last unit is equal to the marginal cost of that unit. If the marginal benefit were greater than the cost, they could increase their utility by buying more. If the cost were greater than the marginal benefit, they could increase their utility by buying less. This same analysis applies to public goods: If the government is supplying a public good, such as road maintenance, *the efficient quantity is the one at which the marginal social benefit equals the cost.*

What is the marginal social benefit of a public good? Each individual who uses the road network gains some marginal benefit from increased road maintenance (more potholes filled, more frequent repaving). When roads are in good repair, everyone who uses them enjoys the benefits. Therefore, the marginal social benefit is actually the sum of the marginal benefit gained by each individual user. The government should calculate the cost of increased road maintenance, add up the marginal benefit to every user, and supply the quantity of road maintenance at which the two are equal.

Unfortunately, this cost-benefit analysis is simpler in theory than it is in practice. How can the government find out the true value that each citizen places on an additional unit of road maintenance? You might think one way would be to simply ask everyone how much they value well-maintained roads. Unfortunately, each individual has an incentive to overstate the marginal benefit he will receive because he expects the government to pay for it. Since no individual driver pays the cost, each might as well petition for perfectly maintained roads. This is another example of individually rational behavior being socially inefficient.

In reality, governments try to conduct a cost-benefit analysis when deciding how much of a public good to supply, whether it is road maintenance, schools, the military, or cancer research. This means making a best guess at what the marginal social benefit of an additional unit will be. Sometimes economic research can help with this problem. It can, for example, attempt to quantify the diffuse benefits that people get from better schools, reduced disease, or safer neighborhoods. But we usually have to accept that our best guess will be an imperfect one.

The second issue is figuring out how to pay for government provision of public goods. Determining who will pay depends in part on how easy it is to exclude people who don't pay. In some cases, it is possible to make the good excludable: The government can use its power to monitor use and enforce payments among those who actually use them. Examples are the tolls that drivers pay to use toll roads, the fares that riders pay on buses and trains, and the tuition that students pay at public universities.

In other cases, it is either difficult or undesirable to charge user fees. For services that are "used" by almost all citizens—sewer systems, police and fire protection, and military defense—it may be more costly to try to exclude nonusers than it is worth. Instead, these services are usually funded through general tax revenue, usually in a way that is not directly connected to the services themselves (as we'll see in Chapter 20, "Taxation and the Public Budget").

Assigning property rights

The defining characteristics of a *public good* are nonexcludability and nonrivalry. *Private goods* are both excludable and rival. Thus, one solution to the free-rider problem is to make a public good more like a private good. This can be achieved by making a public good excludable.

As discussed above, one way to make a good more excludable is to use the government to monitor use and enforce payments. Another way to achieve excludability is to give individuals or firms the right to use or sell a public good, by assigning property rights.

For public goods like knowledge and ideas, a public good can be made excludable through patents and copyrights. Without patent or copyright protection, the profits from a new idea could be claimed by anyone, not just the inventor of a new idea. As we saw with the example of Pfizer's drug Lipitor in Chapter 12, "The Costs of Production," the idea behind intellectual property rights is to assure corporations that others will not be able to free-ride on their innovations. Such protection increases their incentives to undertake research that will create new knowledge. Giving firms an incentive to conduct research solves the undersupply problem.

✓ CONCEPT CHECK

- ☐ How does the free-rider problem affect the supply of public goods? What is the resulting effect on equilibrium quantity? **[LO 19.2]**
- ☐ How can social norms change the trade-offs faced by potential free riders? **[LO 19.3]**

Common Resources

Like public goods, common resources are inefficiently allocated. However, public goods and common resources suffer from different problems:

- The problem with public goods is that they are undersupplied.
- In contrast, the problem with common resources is that they are overconsumed.

This overconsumption problem is called the *tragedy of the commons*.

The tragedy of the commons

LO 19.4 Describe the tragedy of the commons and its consequences.

Remember that public goods are nonrival—they are not used up when people consume them. As we have seen, rhinos are not a public good because they *are* rival—if someone shoots a rhino, it is definitely *not* there for the next person to enjoy.

Usually, when you consume a rival good, you have to compensate the person who owns it. When you want to eat chicken, you pay the grocery store, or the restaurant, or the chicken farmer.

But historically, before land was divided into private pieces, when you hunted a wild animal such as a rhino, buffalo, or elephant, you didn't have to pay anyone. No one owned the wildlife, so no one could force you to pay. In other words, wildlife was typically rival. It also was not excludable—it was a common resource that anyone could hunt.

Common resources are goods that are not excludable but are rival. Nonexcludability causes people to demand a higher quantity than they would if they had to pay for what they consumed. Because a common resource is also rival, it gets "used up" every time someone accesses it. Demand for common resources is characterized by inefficiently high demand and dwindling quantity. This combination leads to what is often called the **tragedy of the commons**—the depletion of a common resource due to individually rational but collectively inefficient overconsumption. Notice the contrast between the free-rider problem and the tragedy of the commons:

- The free-rider problem is triggered by nonexcludability alone.
- The tragedy of the commons arises from the combination of rivalry and nonexcludability.

tragedy of the commons
the depletion of a common resource due to individually rational but collectively inefficient overconsumption

How can equilibrium quantity be both individually rational and collectively inefficient? Let's start with the *individually rational* part: Think about the consumption decision from the perspective of a rhino hunter. On the benefit side, he gets the high value of rhino ivory on the black market. On the cost side, he faces the cost of hunting equipment, the time spent hunting rhinos, and the risk of getting in trouble with the law. He does not, however, have to pay anyone for the rhino horn he takes. As a result, hunters will hunt more than they would if they had to pay someone for the rhino horn.

Why is this *collectively inefficient*? Because we don't typically think of rhinos as having market value, it may be difficult to see that unrestricted hunting does not maximize total surplus. However, using a common resource imposes a negative externality on others: When the rhino population is depleted through poaching, the people of Africa lose a key part of the local ecosystem. Anyone who wants to go on safari to see rhinos will lose surplus. So too will local communities that get a boost from safari tourism. Lastly, if rhinos go extinct, there is a loss to the world's biodiversity.

Applying the reasoning we used in the previous chapter, if rhino hunters could be forced to consider the external costs of their activities, their demand curve would shift downward. The equilibrium quantity of rhinos poached would fall to the efficient level—the level that would maximize surplus in society as a whole.

Solutions to the tragedy of the commons

LO 19.5 Explain how and when problems with common resources can be effectively solved by social norms, government regulation, and expansion of property rights.

We've seen that overdemand for common resources leads to an inefficient quantity of production and consumption. In other words, common resources are subject to market failures. There are many possible solutions, which generally fall under three categories: social norms, government regulation, and private property rights.

As we discuss each solution, think about how it changes the *trade-off* between costs and benefits that people face when supplying or consuming a common resource. We'll see that the range of solutions to the tragedy of the commons is related to externalities.

Social norms
Dirty public spaces arise because littering is easy. Littering saves you the trouble of finding a garbage can and is very unlikely to incur any real punishment or cost. There is little incentive to take into account the negative externality imposed on others. In spite of this potential problem, lots of public spaces manage to stay clean and pleasant and relatively free of litter. How does this happen?

Sometimes, especially in big cities, public spaces stay clean because the government pays janitors or public works employees to clean them. But there are many public spaces, especially in close-knit neighborhoods, that stay clean through a simpler mechanism: the expectations and potential disapproval of the community. If you don't litter, we're guessing that it's *not* primarily because you're afraid of being caught and fined by the police. Rather, it's simply because you've learned that it's not a *nice* thing to do.

Some specific "design principles" make informal, community-based solutions to common-resource problems more effective. These principles include

- Clear distinctions between who is and is not allowed to access the resource.
- The participation of resource users in setting the rules for use.
- The ability of users to monitor one another.

Elinor Ostrom won the 2009 Nobel Prize in economics for her research showing that unregulated, commonly held property is frequently managed better than standard theory would lead us to expect—due to strong local organizations and social norms.[3] Ostrom began by observing that groundwater was managed by informal associations in southern California. She moved on to studying other cases where resource management didn't fit neatly into either the market or the government realms, from irrigation systems in Nepal to Maasai pastureland in Kenya. In her research, Ostrom showed that social norms can sometimes be powerful enough for commonly held property to be managed extremely well.[4]

Government regulation: Bans and quotas

What happens when informal institutions and rules are not enough? The management of common resources is one case in which government regulation can be productive and efficiency enhancing. The reason for this is simple: Often, government bodies have the power to impose limits on how much of a resource is consumed when individuals and informal associations do not. Have a problem with keeping public spaces clean? Make littering illegal. Worried about rhinos and other endangered species becoming extinct? Make hunting them illegal, or impose a quota on how many rhinos each poacher is legally allowed to hunt.

Of course, littering usually is illegal, and bans or quotas apply to hunters in many countries. Yet the problems persist, so clearly implementing bans and quotas is not a perfect solution. To see why, we have to understand that making something illegal is simply one way of changing the *trade-offs* that people face, by creating costs for breaking the ban or exceeding the quotas. The cost that rule-breakers expect to face depends both on the punishment associated with rule breaking *and* on the likelihood of being caught and punished. If the punishment is not severe, or the likelihood of getting caught is low, the cost may not be high enough to change the trade-off.

Bans and quotas therefore often fail in situations where it is difficult or costly for authorities to monitor and punish rule-breakers. For instance, poor countries find it difficult to enforce laws against poaching and habitat destruction. Most governments in East Africa, for instance, typically lack the funds to hire enough park rangers, build enough fences, and take other measures needed to fully protect wildlife. Bans on poaching rhinos thus have limited impact.

In contrast, the United States and other wealthy countries tend to have relatively well-funded, well-policed national parks and conservation areas. Bans and quotas in these areas effectively protect endangered species. More than 90 percent of species listed as endangered in the United States have increased or stabilized populations since being declared endangered.[5] Similarly, South Africa has several large and well-managed national parks that protect rhinos and elephants effectively. As a result, the ban on hunting rhinos has proved to be effective.

In countries that have the resources to enforce them, bans or quotas that limit the use of common resources are straightforward public-policy approaches to solving the problem of overuse. Especially when the optimal quantity of consumption is zero—for instance, with an endangered species on the brink of extinction—it may be the best approach.

In conservation, tough moral and practical questions come into play. In particular, policy-makers argue over both the principle and the pragmatism of setting total bans on use of endangered species and habitats versus allowing people to earn money from limited use. For a deeper consideration of these questions, read the What Do You Think? box "Should conservationists be principled or pragmatic?"

What Do You Think?

Should conservationists be principled or pragmatic?

Can you put a dollar value on the existence of tigers? How about elephants? How about the Devil's Hole pupfish, a tiny fish less than one-inch long that is native to a single pool in a limestone cavern in Death Valley National Park in California? What about unique habitats such as the Grand Canyon or the Amazon rain forest? How much would you be willing to pay to preserve these natural wonders?

Some conservationists argue, on principle, against efforts to place a monetary value on the existence of beautiful, unique creatures and landscapes. Such things are beyond value, they argue, and even trying to put a price tag on them demeans and undermines conservation efforts.

Other conservationists feel that putting a price on endangered land and animals is the only practical way to save them in the long run. When something has no monetary value, they argue, no one has an incentive to protect and sustain it. Saying that something is "beyond" financial value sounds great, but functionally, they argue, it is the same as saying that it has *zero* financial value.

Those who take the latter approach promote programs that allow people to earn money from controlled use of endangered resources. These pragmatists favor use of private incentives to improve excludability and conservation. They point out that locals often face a steep opportunity cost of conserving land or endangered species by forgoing hunting, farming, or logging.

A prime example of this pragmatic strategy is ecotourism. It offers locals an alternative way to earn money by showing interesting flora or fauna to travelers, and it gives them an incentive to conserve natural areas.

In a related strategy, some nonprofit groups in the United States are paying ranchers and other landowners to set aside parts of their land. These agreements—known as *easements*—allow landowners to enter voluntarily into legal contracts that restrict what they can do with their land. For instance, a conservation group might pay someone who owns sensitive marsh-land in a suburban area to agree not to build on that land. The owner earns money from leaving the land undeveloped. Similar ideas are being tried in East Africa: Conservation groups directly pay locals to maintain endangered plants and habitats, and governments give locals the rights to earn money through tourism or controlled hunting or harvesting.

Even conservationists who believe it is possible to put a price on conservation, though, sometimes criticize such pragmatic approaches. Their concerns relate to difficulties in monitoring and enforcement. The United States may have a well-functioning legal system, but many endangered species and landscapes are located in countries that do not. Without effective monitoring mechanisms, it can be difficult to distinguish legitimate activities from illegitimate activities. An outright ban may therefore be easier to enforce.

WHAT DO YOU THINK?

1. Should we try to put a dollar value on the existence of endangered species? If so, how could we go about calculating it?
2. If the existence of a place or species is a public good, how could we get individuals to contribute the real value they put on it, rather than free riding?
3. Is it always better to hold a hard line and stick to a pure preservation, zero-use approach to avoiding the tragedy of the commons? Or are there situations in which limited-use approaches are more likely to succeed?

Property rights: Privatization

Common resources are not allocated efficiently by markets, but private goods are. Wouldn't the most convenient solution be to turn everything into a private good? In some cases, the answer is, yes!

The classic case of turning a common resource into a private good is the one that gave the "tragedy of the commons" problem its name. Hundreds of years ago, most villages in Europe and America had town "commons"—open, grassy areas in the middle of town that were used by everyone and owned by no one. Farmers could graze their livestock on the common. You know the end of this story: The town common was a common resource, and each farmer had an incentive to graze more and more animals. Individual farmers had no incentive to limit their own usage in order to preserve the value of the common for everyone. The grazing land was ruined, and everyone was left worse off.

In the end, the solution to this original tragedy of the commons was surprisingly simple. The first step was to institute rules about who got to graze where and when. The ultimate step was to break up the town common into private lots. Each farmer had to graze his livestock on his own land. In New England, many towns still have a small "green," which is the descendant of the town common, but you are unlikely to see sheep or cows grazing there. When each farmer had to bear all the costs and all the benefits of his choices about how many animals to graze, each made the most efficient decision for his own land. Privatization solved the nonexcludability problem.

One policy credited with contributing to rhinos' recovery in South Africa allowed farmers to own wild animals on their land. Landowners are eligible for tax breaks if they keep and protect endangered species (such as rhinos). They also can earn money by selling the animals or admitting tourists to see them. This law essentially "privatizes" rhinos and other large animals like elephants; it allows individuals to capture the benefits of protecting the animals. This policy gives people an incentive to keep out poachers and increase the population of rhinos.

Increasingly, many governments are taking this sort of combined public-private approach to wildlife and other resource management. The privatization aspect helps introduce excludability and assign responsibility for costs and benefits; the public aspect helps counteract remaining externalities.

Assigning property rights over common resources is often far from simple, though. Especially in cases in which many people are already using a resource, it can be very difficult to decide who owns what. Not surprisingly, no one wants to be the person who has to reduce her consumption.

Property rights: Tradable allowances

One common way that governments can institute private property rights is through the use of tradable allowances or permits. Remember that quotas can control total quantity, but they don't necessarily allocate supplies in the most efficient way. They can result in undesirable side-effects, such as damaging extraction methods or rushes to get as much of a resource as possible before hitting the quota.

The method of using tradable allowances works the same way for solving a common-resource problem as it does for solving an externality problem: A cap is set on the total quantity of the resource that can be used, and shares of that total are allocated to individuals or firms. After the initial allocation, people can buy and sell their shares. Trading ensures that the resource is allocated to those with the highest willingness to pay, while still limiting overall quantity to an efficient level. The people who own shares now have private property rights—and an incentive, as owners, to make sure that the common resource does not get overused.

This may sound familiar. In Chapter 18, "Externalities," we discussed tradable allowances and permits as a way to tackle negative externalities. Since the depletion of common resources imposes a negative externality, tradable permits are also useful in allocating common resources.

The use of tradable permits is part of an ongoing battle to protect the world's fisheries from overuse. The story of how these allowances have been used in the United States is told in the Real Life box "North American fisheries learn from failure."

Real Life

North American fisheries learn from failure

Visitors to Maine in the 1600s gave accounts of cod so plentiful the fish could be scooped out of the sea in baskets. The incredible bounty of the Grand Banks and Georges Bank fisheries supported coastal communities from Newfoundland to Massachusetts for hundreds of years. But in the mid-twentieth century, fishing technology began to change dramatically. Small fishing vessels gave way to huge ships that could carry 8 million pounds of fish and drag nets large enough to ensnare a jumbo jet. These technologies allowed fish to be harvested faster than ever before—at rates much faster than the fish could reproduce.

Since cod were a valuable and unregulated common resource, free for the taking, there was an incentive to catch as many cod as possible before they disappeared. That approach made sense for individuals, but not for the fishing community as a whole. It's individually rational but collectively inefficient.

Authorities tried to solve the problem by instituting a quota, but they made two errors. First, worried that sharp reductions in the amount of cod that could be harvested would hurt the small towns whose economies relied on fishing, regulators set the quota far too high.

Second, the quota covered the total catch rather than individual fishing operations. That meant each fisherman still had an incentive to catch as many fish as possible as quickly as possible, before the total quota was met. The result was an annual "fishing derby," in which boats stuffed with gear had only a few days to pull in their catch for the whole year. Fishermen got injured, and the sudden glut of cod that hit fish houses in the days after the derby meant that fishermen received low prices for their catch.

None of these plans worked, and so the Canadian government placed a *total* ban on all fishing in the Grand Banks. As a result, 20,000 people lost their jobs. The economies of small towns all along the coast suffered.

Fortunately, younger fisheries in North America have learned from the disaster that occurred on the Grand Banks. In 1995, the harvest of Pacific halibut was put under an Individual Fishing Quota program—a tradable allowance system. Under it and many programs like it (often called "catch-shares"), a limit is set on the total catch; a share of that total is given to an individual fisherman, community, or fishing association. Every year, regulators adjust the total allowable catch. They allocate shares accordingly, with a goal to carefully manage the fish population.

Catch-shares allow permit holders to fish whenever and however they find most convenient and profitable. Most importantly, the shares are completely transferable and can be freely bought and sold. This feature creates a market for permits. That market ensures that fishers harvest an environmentally sustainable quantity in the most efficient manner. This system should sound familiar: It's exactly the same as a cap-and-trade approach to carbon emissions.

Based on the success of early catch-shares programs, all U.S. Pacific Ocean fisheries adopted the practice in 2008. The success of these efforts stands in stark contrast to the overall health of the world's fisheries. Scientists estimate that if current practices continue, by 2048 we may have few commercially viable fisheries.

Sources: http://www.edf.org/page.cfm?tagID=3332; http://www.nefsc.noaa.gov/history/stories/groundfish/grndfsh1.html; http://hmapcoml.org/publications/.

There is a whole field dedicated to the study of the economics of the environment. Appropriately named *environmental economics,* this field applies many of the tools you have learned so far in this course to problems that were once thought to be the responsibility of government officials and environmentalists. If this is something that interests you, you may want to see if your school offers a class in environmental or resource economics.

✓ CONCEPT CHECK

☐ How does the tragedy of the commons affect the demand for common resources? What is the resulting effect on equilibrium quantity? **[LO 19.4]**

☐ Why is a tradable quota more efficient than a traditional quota? **[LO 19.5]**

☐ How can turning a common resource into private property solve the tragedy of the commons? **[LO 19.5]**

Conclusion

Public goods and common resources are a significant source of market failure. Generally speaking, unregulated public goods will encounter the free-rider problem, in which nonexcludability leads to undersupply. On the other hand, unregulated common-resource goods will fall prey to the tragedy of the commons, which occurs when nonexcludability and rivalry combine to cause overconsumption and depletion of the resource.

These challenges can be overcome through a variety of solutions. In some cases, strong social norms or local organizations can improve excludability and increase the cost of free riding or overconsumption enough to avoid market failure. In other cases, government can step in, enforcing bans or quotas to limit the use of a common resource. Sometimes, it makes sense for government to simply provide a public good to counteract undersupply.

In general, limits like bans and quotas work only when they are backed by sufficiently strong monitoring and enforcement. In places where this is not the case, privatization or combined public-private solutions can harness individual incentives to manage use and improve excludability. In the next chapter, we'll look into the practical details of how governments fund the provision of public goods and other services.

Key Terms

excludable, p. 478

rival in consumption (rival), p. 478

private good, p. 478

public good, p. 480

common resource, p. 480

free-rider problem, p. 481

tragedy of the commons, p. 486

Summary

LO 19.1 Define different types of goods in terms of rivalry and excludability.

When a good is *excludable,* those who haven't paid for it can be prevented from using it. When a good is *rival,* one person's consumption prevents or decreases others' ability to consume it. Most of the goods discussed in this book are private goods, which are both excludable and rival.

Public goods are the opposite of private goods: They are neither excludable nor rival. Common resources are rival, but not excludable. Artificially scarce goods are excludable, but not rival.

LO 19.2 Describe the free-rider problem and its consequences.

The free-rider problem is caused by nonexcludability leading to undersupply of a public good. When a good is not easily excludable, individuals have no incentive to pay for it. Therefore, supplying a public good involves a significant positive externality to free riders who receive the benefits without paying for them. The result is undersupply of a good.

LO 19.3 Explain how and when problems with public goods can be effectively solved by social norms, government provision, and expansion of property rights.

Strong social norms can help rebalance the trade-offs involved in consuming public goods by imposing social costs on those who break the "rules" of good behavior. Imposing costs on free riding can help bring the quantity consumed closer to the efficient level.

Another way to solve the undersupply problem inherent in public goods is for the government to directly provide the public goods, or to force individuals to pay a private provider. Just as in a functioning market, the government must find the efficient quantity at which the marginal social benefit equals the cost. Oftentimes, governments must guess at what the marginal social benefit of an additional unit will be, and they must also solve the issue of figuring out who will pay for the supply of the public good.

Alternatively, the government can make the public good more like a private good by giving some individuals or firms the right to produce and sell a good; this often is accomplished through patents and copyrights.

LO 19.4 Describe the tragedy of the commons and its consequences.

A tragedy of the commons is the depletion of a common resource due to individually rational but collectively inefficient overconsumption. The ability to access the benefits of a common resource without paying any costs increases demand. Because the resource is rival in consumption, it imposes a negative externality on those whose ability to consume the resource is reduced.

LO 19.5 Explain how and when problems with common resources can be effectively solved by social norms, government regulation, and expansion of property rights.

Strong social norms can help rebalance the trade-offs involved in consuming common resources by imposing social costs on those who break the "rules" of good behavior. Imposing costs on overconsumption can help bring the quantity consumed closer to the efficient level.

Often, government bodies have the power to solve the nonexcludability problem, while individuals do not. Banning or limiting use of common resources is a straightforward public-policy approach to solving the problem of overuse. However, such bans and limits often fail in situations where it is difficult or costly for authorities to monitor and punish rule breakers, and it is not necessarily efficient.

Sometimes the best way to solve the tragedy of the commons is to convert a common resource into a private good. Privatization works when it is possible to divide up a resource and make it excludable by giving a private owner control over its use. The owner has the right incentives to ensure an efficient level of use—bearing all of the costs and reaping all of the benefits. Another common way that governments can institute private property rights is through the use of tradable allowances or permits. Tradable allowances create a market for the rights to consume a common resource, ensuring that it is allocated to those with the highest willingness to pay.

Review Questions

1. Popular software can cost thousands of dollars even though the marginal cost of producing another copy on CD or via download is near zero. What kind of good are these programs? **[LO 19.1]**

2. Suppose a popular band decides to hold a free concert in its hometown. Admission is available on a first-come, first-served basis. Is the concert a public good? **[LO 19.1]**

3. A talented musician plays for tips on the street but never seems to make very much money. Explain why his tip jar is never very full. **[LO 19.2, 19.4]**

4. Suppose a community garden in your neighborhood has both individually owned plots and a large, common plot. If soil and sunlight conditions are the same everywhere in the garden, explain why tomatoes grown in individually owned plots are so much better than tomatoes grown in the common plot. **[LO 19.2, 19.4]**

5. Why is it difficult for private markets to provide the optimal quantity of a public good? Why is it difficult for government to provide the optimal quantity of a public good? **[LO 19.3]**

6. Consider a fund-raising campaign for your school's library. What is the free-rider problem in this situation? How might publicly listing the names of donors to the library fund affect this problem? **[LO 19.3]**

7. Aquifers are underground sources of clean water that stretch over thousands of square miles. People who own land over the aquifer are free to take as much as they want. What is likely to happen to water supplies in an aquifer? Is this efficient? **[LO 19.4]**

8. Which do you expect to be more sustainable: grazing on public land or grazing on privately owned pastures? Why? **[LO 19.4]**

9. Even though many school zones don't have much traffic and aren't regularly monitored by the police for speed, most drivers are very careful to drive at or below speed limits when near schools. Why might this be the case even in the absence of strong government intervention? **[LO 19.3, 19.5]**

10. Consider a proposal to privatize street lighting. Would this be feasible? Why or why not? Does street lighting suffer from a tragedy of the commons problem? **[LO 19.3, 19.5]**

11. The government of India has made killing Bengal tigers illegal, but poaching of the endangered animal continues. List some possible reasons that the ban hasn't been very successful, and suggest an alternative approach. **[LO 19.5]**

12. The U.S. government is concerned about the huge numbers of people converging on Yellowstone Park every year. Government officials are worried that the park might be getting overused and the natural beauty will be ruined as a result. Suppose someone suggests dividing the park into private lots and selling it to individuals. How might this solution address the tragedy of the commons that is occurring? **[LO 19.5]**

Problems and Applications

1. Identify whether each of the following goods is usually excludable or nonexcludable. **[LO 19.1]**
   a. AM/FM radio.
   b. A round of golf on a course.
   c. Street art.
   d. A museum exhibition.
   e. Toll roads.

2. Identify whether each of the following goods is rival or nonrival. **[LO 19.1]**
   a. Cable TV.
   b. A pair of jeans.
   c. Street signs.
   d. Attending a baseball game.

3. Consider community safety or defense, meaning freedom from crime and threats, to answer the following questions. **[LO 19.2]**
   a. What sort of good is community safety?
   b. If you lived in a place with no government-funded police force, would you expect community safety to be *oversupplied* or *undersupplied*?

   c. Suppose that some neighbors get together and organize a block watch group. What term do economists use to describe someone who lives in the neighborhood but chooses not to volunteer as part of the block watch?

4. From the list below, which of the following do you expect to suffer from a free-rider problem? Check all that apply. **[LO 19.2]**
   a. Pay-what-you-can yoga classes.
   b. Unlimited yoga classes with monthly membership dues.
   c. Fund-raiser for public television.
   d. Neighborhood park cleanup day.
   e. Housecleaning business operating in your neighborhood.
   f. Suggested museum-admission donation.

5. Which of the following subway announcements are attempts to establish or enforce a social norm? **[LO 19.3]**
   a. "Loud music and phone conversations are discourteous to fellow riders. Please keep the noise down."
   b. "If you see something, say something."
   c. "Please watch your step as you exit. Be careful of the gap between the train and the platform edge."
   d. "Please be patient and allow others to exit the train before you attempt to enter."
   e. "The train is being held at the station due to traffic ahead. We apologize for the inconvenience."

6. Would you expect tourists or locals to be more likely to give up their seat on a bus to an elderly person? **[LO 19.3]**

7. Consider the following government-provided goods. Which of these goods necessarily require funding via general taxation (as opposed to direct user fees)? **[LO 19.3]**
   a. Street lights.
   b. A park.
   c. A fireworks display.
   d. Public radio.
   e. A library.

8. In much of the United States and Canada, logging takes place in both privately owned and government-owned forests. **[LO 19.4]**
   a. Are privately owned forests excludable? Are they rival? What type of good are they?
   b. Suppose that anyone is legally allowed to enter a government-owned forest and start logging. What type of good are these forests?

c. Do you expect the rate of logging in government-owned forests to be faster, slower, or equal to the efficient level?

9. Suppose that the government decides to start regulating use of its forests, charging anyone who wants to log. Which of the following ways of calculating the price to charge for each acre will lead to an efficient quantity of logging? **[LO 19.4]**

 a. The sum of the marginal social value of each acre to all logging companies.

 b. The average price citizens say they would be willing to pay for an acre.

 c. The external cost that logging an acre imposes on all citizens.

10. Determine whether each of the following policy interventions is designed to increase supply or decrease demand for a public good or common resource. **[LO 19.3, 19.5]**

 a. A city government increases the frequency of street sweeping.

 b. London begins charging a toll to all vehicles that drive within the city limits.

 c. A gated community passes a bylaw requiring all homeowners to mow their lawns once a week during the summer.

 d. The National Park Service increases the cost of a pass to enter the Everglades.

11. Public-opinion polls in a small city have revealed that citizens want more resources spent on public safety, an annual fireworks display, and more community swimming pools. Which of these three citizen requests could be privatized by assigning property rights? **[LO 19.5]**

12. For each of the following examples, state which of these approaches is being taken to manage a common resource or supply a public good: social norms, quota, tradable allowance, government provision, or property rights. **[LO 19.3, 19.5]**

 a. A nonprofit organization spray-paints signs on storm drains reminding everyone that it "drains to the ocean" with a picture of a fish.

 b. A city starts a free program that collects recyclable glass, paper, and plastic from residents' doorsteps.

 c. In England, municipal-waste authorities are given a percentage of an overall limit that can be put in the landfill each year. These percentages can be traded among municipalities.

 d. American bison, which once roamed freely across the Great Plains, are now raised on ranches for commercial purposes.

13. There is a road between the suburbs and downtown. The road becomes congested at rush hour. As long as fewer than 100 people use the road at rush hour, the trip takes 30 minutes. When the 101st person enters the road, everyone has to slow down and the trip now takes 31 minutes. People value their time at $6 per hour (i.e., $0.10 per minute) and so a 30 minute trip costs $3. **[LO 19.5]**

 a. What is the private cost of one of the 100 individuals using the road? What is the total private cost of 100 people using the road? What is the total social cost of 100 people using the road?

 b. What is the total social cost of 101 people using the road? What is the private cost of using the road for the 101st individual? What is the external social cost of the 101st person using the road?

Endnotes

1. https://www.savetherhino.org/rhino_info/rhino_population_figures.

2. http://www.economist.com/node/16941705?story_id$16941705.

3. http://www.nobelprize.org/nobel_prizes/economic-sciences/laureates/2009/ostrom_lecture.pdf.

4. Elinor Ostrom, *Governing the Commons: The Evolution of Institutions for Common Action* (New York: Cambridge University Press, 1990).

5. http://esasuccess.org/report_2012.html#.UA8e_WHOwro.

Taxation and the Public Budget

HAPPY TO PAY TAXES?

Lawn signs are a common sight during election season. With bright colors and catchy slogans, they try to draw the attention of passersby to the name of a favored political candidate. In 2003, however, a new and unusual sign appeared on the lawns of some Minnesota voters. In place of a politician's name, the bright orange signs simply read, "Happy to pay for a better Minnesota."

The Minnesota couple behind the "happy to pay" campaign told reporters that they weren't promoting any particular candidate or party. They simply wanted to share their opinion that a tax increase was not necessarily a bad thing. In their view, a tax increase would allow Minnesota to have a balanced budget *and* maintain public services.[1]

The "happy to pay" campaign raised eyebrows because it bucked the usual trend of voters demanding lower taxes. Sometimes, as with the "Tea Party" movement that swept U.S. politics in 2009–2010, voters demand cuts in *both* government programs *and* taxes. Other voters express a desire for functional roads, good schools, and other services, while also wanting lower taxes.

Governments can, and often do, borrow money, rather than raise taxes, to pay for public spending. But the borrowed money comes due eventually. Sooner or later, somehow or other, government will always need to collect tax revenues to pay for what it spends.

Each time you vote, whether for your mayor or a national candidate, you're likely to face choices between candidates with different views on taxes. In this chapter we describe general principles of taxation and spending that can help you disentangle the debates. In earlier chapters we saw that when externalities exist, taxes can correct market failures, and thus increase total surplus. But we also saw that when markets are already efficient, taxes reduce total surplus.

Here we investigate the effects of a variety of taxes: how much money they raise, how much inefficiency they cause, and who bears the burden. We'll explore arguments for and against each kind of taxation, and give you the tools to weigh the issues and make informed choices when casting your vote.

© *Daily News/Joe Imel/
AP Images*

Why Tax?

> **LO 20.1** Describe the major public policy goals of taxation.

Taxpayers often dread April 15th—the day when federal income tax returns are due. Unlike the "happy to pay" tax supporters in Minnesota, many citizens grumble about the bite that taxes take out of their paychecks. Why do voters continue to support governments that tax them? What's the gain that balances the pain? We saw in earlier chapters that taxes do two things: raise revenue and change the behavior of buyers and sellers.

- **Raising revenue:** The most obvious use of taxes is to raise public revenue. This revenue allows governments to provide goods and services to citizens, from national defense to highway building. Many tax-funded programs, such as public schools and roads, are intended to increase surplus and stimulate economic growth. Others are intended to provide basic human needs such as food, health care, or housing to people in need. People may disagree about which services should be funded through tax dollars, but most agree that at least some services are necessary.

- **Changing behavior:** Taxes change behavior because they alter the incentives faced by market participants. Taxes drive a wedge between the price paid by buyers and the price received by sellers. That wedge results in a lower equilibrium quantity of the good or service being consumed. In some cases, this effect on incentives is just a side effect of a tax designed to raise revenue; in others, it is the explicit purpose of the policy. Taxes on alcohol, tobacco, and gasoline are examples of policies *designed* partly to reduce demand.

Figure 20-1 summarizes these two effects of taxes.

We saw in Chapter 18, "Externalities," that when a market involves negative externalities, such as air pollution, the effect of a tax can be to *increase* total surplus in society as a whole by moving the market to a lower equilibrium quantity.

However, we also saw in Chapter 6, "Government Intervention," that when a tax is implemented in an already-efficient market, it causes *deadweight loss*. Deadweight loss is usually considered a *cost of taxation*. Sometimes, though, even when markets are functioning efficiently, governments use taxes to discourage certain purchases. For a discussion of whether such taxes increase or decrease total surplus, see the From Another Angle box, "Love the sinner, love the sin tax."

FIGURE 20-1

A tax raises revenue and changes behavior

Price

Price paid by consumers

Tax

Price received by sellers

S

1. Raises revenue…

D_1

2. …and changes behavior.

D_2

Quantity

A tax shrinks the market, moving equilibrium to a lower quantity and driving a wedge between the price paid by buyers and the price received by sellers. A tax also raises revenue, equal to the tax rate multiplied by the quantity traded under the new equilibrium.

From Another Angle

Love the sinner, love the sin tax

Any teacher, preacher, parent, or politician will tell you that people don't always know what's best for them. However, economists usually start from the premise that *what people do* tells us what maximizes their utility. This idea underlies the concept of revealed preference we saw in Chapter 7, "Consumer Behavior." For instance, if smokers choose to smoke and drinkers choose to drink, that tells us something about their true preferences. Despite these revealed preferences, many people advocate for taxes on alcohol and tobacco. To make the point, these policies are sometimes called "sin taxes."

The potential motivations behind sin taxes are numerous:

- Some favor sin taxes to combat negative externalities—the costs to others associated with breathing secondhand smoke or encountering drunk drivers on the road.
- Some voters support sin taxes simply because they disapprove of smoking and drinking. These advocates for sin taxes believe that reducing smoking or drinking through taxes accomplishes a moral goal.

Economists add another layer to the analysis. They argue that we should also take into account the well-being of smokers and drinkers—and not in the direction you might think. Even if a community is better off with less tobacco and alcohol use, smokers and drinkers are made worse off by having to pay more in taxes. The right policy then depends on the relative size of the cost to smokers and drinkers versus the size of the benefit to the broader community.

Behavioral economics has brought a more nuanced perspective to the economic analysis of sin taxes. Behavioral economists point out that smoking and drinking are not like other economic activities. Some people *want* to stop smoking and drinking (or at least cut back) but have a tough time following through, due to problems with self-control or addiction. Under these circumstances, revealed preference doesn't tell the whole story about what people really want. That's why new research on cigarette taxes suggests that economics *can* explain how, under certain circumstances, a sin tax could make "sinners" better off as well.

(continued)

Economists Jonathan Gruber and Sendhil Mullainathan looked at how the self-reported happiness of people in the United States and Canada changed as cigarette taxes rose. They found that increases in cigarette taxes actually made people who were likely to smoke happier. Why? The research suggests that sin taxes can act as a sort of commitment device for people who truly want to change their behavior but have problems with self-control. Making cigarettes more expensive provides a disincentive to smoke, which helps motivate people struggling against temptation.

As economists gain a better understanding of behavioral and psychological responses to public policy, we are learning more about the nuances and versatility of taxes. It turns out that some of the people who thought that they'd lose through sin taxes turn out to be winners.

Source: Jonathan Gruber and Sendhil Mullainathan, "Do cigarette taxes make smokers happier?," *Advances in Economic Policy and Analysis* 5, no. 1 (2005).

Throughout the chapter, keep in mind the two goals of taxation: raising revenue and changing behavior. People may disagree about when it is appropriate to use taxes to accomplish them, but the goals provide a starting point for discussion about the costs and benefits of taxation.

Even when people have agreed on a goal, some types of taxes may be more effective than others in achieving it. In this chapter, we will evaluate the effects and side effects of different methods of taxation. As a voter, you can combine this factual understanding of taxes with your moral or political beliefs about which public services should be funded and what types of behavior ought to be discouraged.

✓CONCEPT CHECK

☐ Does a tax increase or decrease the quantity of the taxed good that is consumed? **[LO 20.1]**

☐ Why does a tax in an efficient market decrease total surplus, while a tax in a market with a negative externality increases total surplus? **[LO 20.1]**

Principles of Taxation

If you live in the United States, your state constitution (unless you live in Vermont) requires that the state budget be balanced. So, if your governor has ambitious ideas to offer new state services, keep in mind that the legislature and governor almost surely have to raise fees or taxes to make it happen. Even if your governor is working to reduce taxes, he or she has to decide which kinds of taxes to cut and how fast. The economic question is how to tax in a way that keeps the economy healthiest.

Not all taxes are alike, and there are different ways to design a tax to raise a certain amount of revenue. In this section, we focus on understanding how to analyze the impact of different types of taxes. Three concepts are particularly useful in evaluating the costs and benefits of alternative types of taxes: *efficiency, revenue,* and *incidence.* We'll discuss each of these concepts as a framework for evaluating the costs and benefits of a particular tax.

Efficiency: How much (extra) will the tax cost?

LO 20.2 Explain how deadweight loss and administrative costs contribute to the inefficiency of a tax.

When considering the costs and benefits of a tax, it is tempting to assume that the cost is the amount that taxpayers have to pay and the benefit is whatever services are provided using those funds. However, we know from the analysis of taxes in earlier chapters that it's not quite that simple. Taxes cause changes in economic behavior, potentially shifting supply and demand away from their optimal levels. We need to take that into account. In addition, collecting taxes takes up resources in itself.

Just because a tax creates inefficiency does not necessarily mean that the tax is bad. While the tax itself may create an inefficiency, the revenue it generates may be used to fix another one. The net effect of the tax is specific to each tax and to each use of government proceeds from the tax. Here we will discuss two types of inefficiencies that taxes can create:

- The first kind of inefficiency we consider is one we have described already: *deadweight loss.* This is the difference between the loss of surplus to taxpayers and the tax revenue collected.
- The second form of inefficiency is *administrative burden,* which comes from the costs involved in collecting the tax.

We'll discuss these two costs and how to calculate their size.

Deadweight loss

Remember from Chapter 6, "Government Intervention," that a tax in an efficient market decreases total surplus. This loss of surplus is called **deadweight loss**. It occurs because the quantity of a good that is bought and sold is below the market equilibrium quantity.

deadweight loss
a loss of total surplus that occurs because the quantity of a good that is bought and sold is below the market equilibrium quantity

It's important to distinguish deadweight loss from the total amount of surplus lost to those in the market as the result of a tax. The surplus that is lost to buyers and sellers but converted into tax revenue is not considered a cost because the tax revenue funds public services. Those services provide surplus to citizens who benefit from them. Sometimes these are the same people who paid the taxes, and sometimes not. The value of that surplus may be *transferred* to someone else through government policies, but *it is not lost.*

In contrast, deadweight loss is value that simply *disappears* as the result of a tax. Neither buyers nor sellers nor recipients of government services benefit from it. It is lost altogether.

Let's briefly review how to calculate the value of deadweight loss that results from a tax in an efficient market—say, the market for jeans. Suppose that the market equilibrium for jeans is 4 million pairs at a price of $50 per pair. For the sake of simplicity, let's imagine that the sales tax on clothes is a flat dollar amount (rather than a percent of the sale price). Figure 20-2 demonstrates the effect of a $20 per pair tax on jeans. (We admit that's a pretty large tax, but it helps clarify the example.)

What happens? The tax causes the demand curve to shift down by the amount of the tax. The reason: The effective price paid by consumers is now $20 higher at any given market price. Thus, the amount consumers are willing to pay to suppliers (before the tax) is $20 less. The tax drives a wedge between the price received by sellers (the market price—in this case, $40) and the price paid by buyers (the market price plus the $20 tax—in this case, $60). The shift in the demand curve causes the equilibrium point to slide down the supply curve to a lower market (pre-tax) price and a lower quantity. Under the tax, 1 million fewer pairs of jeans are sold. The consumer and producer surplus that is no longer generated by those sales is deadweight loss.

How much deadweight loss a tax causes depends on how *responsive* buyers and sellers are to a price change. In other words, the size of deadweight loss is determined by the price elasticity of supply and demand: The more price-elastic the demand or supply curve, the larger the drop in equilibrium quantity caused by a given increase in price, and the larger the deadweight loss will be.

Figure 20-3 shows graphically that the area of the triangle representing deadweight loss is larger in a market with higher price elasticity of demand, given a tax of the same size. This leads to a general principle of taxation: Deadweight loss is minimized when a tax is levied on something for which people are *not likely to change their behavior much in response to a price change.*

FIGURE 20-2

A tax causes deadweight loss

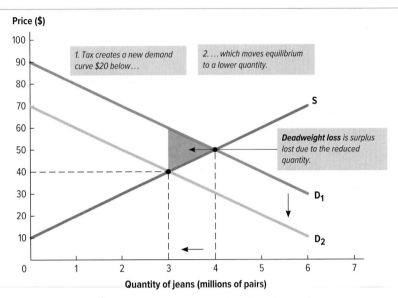

A tax of $20 on jeans adds a new demand curve, sliding the equilibrium point along the supply curve from 4 million to 3 million pairs. The surplus lost to people who would have bought and sold those 1 million pairs of jeans but no longer do so under the tax is deadweight loss.

FIGURE 20-3

Deadweight loss increases with price elasticity

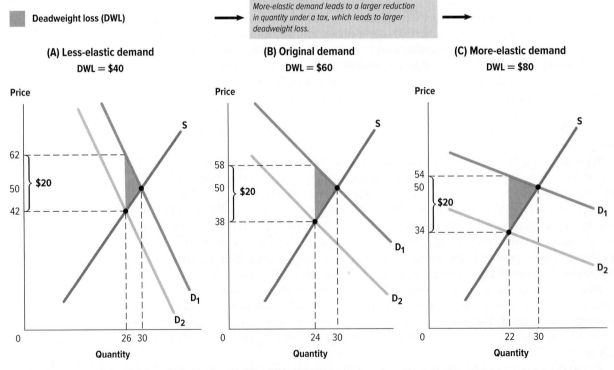

With less-price-elastic demand, a $20 tax decreases equilibrium quantity from 30 to 26. The total value of the deadweight loss is $40.

Originally, a $20 tax decreases equilibrium quantity from 30 to 24. The total value of the deadweight loss is $60.

With more-price-elastic demand, the same tax causes a larger decrease in quantity (from 30 to 22) and more deadweight loss (a total value of $80).

It is worth bearing in mind that this discussion also applies to the markets for factors of production. In general, a tax discourages people from engaging in whatever behavior is taxed. For example, a tax on income discourages people from working extra hours. How much inefficiency is caused by income tax, and how much revenue is raised by it, depends on *how price-sensitive* people are. In other words, how much will workers reduce the quantity of labor they supply in response to a tax on wages? (Not surprisingly, policy-makers are particularly interested in the answer to this question.)

If deadweight loss is minimized when we tax activities that people will continue to do anyway, why not push this idea to its logical conclusion and simply tax people for existing? This idea—of taxing everyone the same amount, regardless of their economic behavior—is called a **lump-sum tax**, or **head tax**. To understand why a lump-sum tax is very efficient, think about *how taxpayers will respond* to the tax. If everyone is required to pay $1,000 to the government each year no matter what they do, or how much they earn, or what they buy, there is no incentive to change such behaviors.

If our only goal in implementing a tax was to maximize efficiency and minimize deadweight loss, a head tax might be the way to go. But while head taxes may be highly efficient, many people do not think it's fair to have everyone, both rich and poor, pay the exact same dollar amount in taxes. A lump-sum tax also reduces the total amount of revenue that can be raised because the size of the tax is limited by the poorest citizens' ability to pay. For these reasons, we rarely see lump-sum taxes.

> **lump-sum tax (head tax)**
> a tax that charges the same amount to each taxpayer, regardless of their economic behavior or circumstances

Administrative burden

Administering and collecting taxes carries costs. Someone has to create procedures for collecting revenues, enforcing tax payments, and handling the collected funds. These logistical costs associated with implementing a tax are called the **administrative burden**. It includes the time and money spent by the government agencies that track and follow up on tax bills. It also includes taxpayers' time and expense of filing their returns and hiring accountants and lawyers to give them tax advice. For instance, in 2015 the federal government spent $13.26 billion to run the Internal Revenue Service (IRS), the government agency tasked with collecting around $3.18 trillion (or $3,180 billion) in tax revenue.[2] Administrative burden is the second form of tax inefficiency.

> **administrative burden**
> the logistical costs associated with implementing a tax

In general, the more complex the tax, the higher the administrative burden will be. Consider, for instance, the difference between the federal income tax and a local sales tax:

- The federal income tax requires people to fill out pages and pages of forms, calculate types of income from different sources, and account for deductions and exclusions. Record-keeping takes time and sometimes involves hiring an accountant or tax preparer. On the government side, the income tax involves an entire government agency devoted to calculating and processing tax returns and tracking down people who fail to pay.

- In contrast, a sales tax, while certainly not costless, is much easier to process. Merchants calculate and collect the tax with each purchase, and they send this tax revenue to the local government. The sales tax doesn't require as much extra time or effort to process. If maximizing efficiency was our only goal, simpler taxes would certainly be more efficient than more complicated ones.

Revenue: How much money will the tax raise?

> **LO 20.3** Calculate the effect of a tax increase on revenue, taking into account price and quantity effects.

Calculating the revenue raised by a tax is simple: Multiply the tax rate per unit by the number of units of the thing being taxed:

EQUATION 20-1   Tax revenue = Tax per unit × Number of units

If it's a tax on a toll road, for example, multiply the fee per car by the number of cars. If it's a general sales tax, then you multiply the tax per dollar of sales by the number of dollars in sales. If it's an income tax, multiply the tax per dollar of income by the number of dollars of income.

The catch is to not forget that the tax shrinks the market before you get to collect revenue. Remember that when you tax something, you get less of it. So, don't multiply the tax rate by the *pre-tax* quantity of units. Instead, you have to figure out how taxpayers will *respond* to the tax and predict the *post-tax* quantity.

Look again at Figure 20-3. It shows that the rectangle representing tax revenue is smaller in the market with more-price-elastic demand (panel C) because the equilibrium quantity shrinks further (from 30 to 22). All else equal, imposing taxes in markets where demand and supply are price-inelastic not only causes less inefficiency but also raises more revenue. This may be another reason—beyond negative externalities and "sin"—why governments like to tax cigarettes and alcohol: The demand for these goods is highly price-inelastic. This inelastic demand ensures that the tax collects a large amount of revenue. In New York State, a $1.60 tax on cigarettes imposed in 2010 raised over $500 million.

To see why it is so important to understand elasticity, suppose that you are a state legislator considering whether to increase a gasoline tax from $1 per gallon to $2. You know that 5 million gallons of gasoline are currently sold in your state every day. The current tax brings in $5 million in tax revenue. If you raise the tax by a dollar, can you expect to bring in *another* $5 million of revenue? No—remember that the tax will increase the price of gasoline; the higher price will drive down demand, reducing the equilibrium quantity bought and sold. In an extreme case, the net effect of a tax increase could even be to *reduce* total tax revenue. For example, if the tax increase reduces the equilibrium quantity to 2 million gallons, your $2 gas tax would bring in only $4 million in revenue.

In other words, we have to consider two opposing effects of a tax increase:

- Raising taxes means that the government gets more revenue per units sold—the *price effect.*
- But the higher tax rate causes fewer units to be sold—the *quantity effect.*

This idea, shown in Figure 20-4, is parallel to the discussion in Chapter 4, "Elasticity," of the relationship between price elasticity and revenue for a private firm.

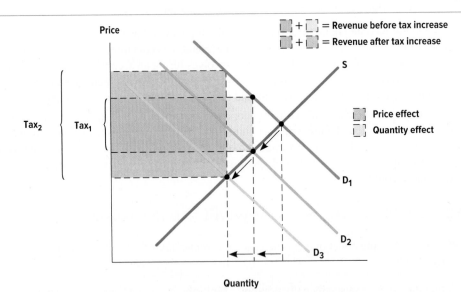

FIGURE 20-4

Raising taxes has both price and quantity effects on revenue

An increase in the tax rate increases the amount of revenue earned per unit, but the higher "price" of taxes means that quantity decreases. The net effect on revenue depends on whether the quantity effect outweighs the price effect.

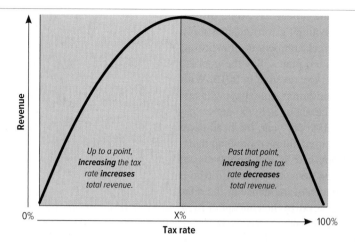

FIGURE 20-5

Raising taxes first increases and then decreases revenue

In the beginning, raising the tax rate increases revenue. After a certain point, further increases in the tax rate decrease the amount of revenue collected. At this point, maximum revenue is collected.

We can generalize this point to see that raising taxes has diminishing returns to revenue, as shown in Figure 20-5:

- As tax rates get higher, we can expect revenue to increase at a slower and slower rate. This occurs as the quantity effect catches up with the price effect.

- At some point, taxes can get so high that the quantity effect dominates. At that point, raising taxes reduces total revenue.

The point at which the revenue-maximizing tax level is reached depends on the elasticity of supply and demand: The more elastic, the quicker the revenue-maximizing point will be reached.

After the revenue-maximizing point, *lowering* taxes *increases* total revenue. The graph shown in Figure 20-5 is sometimes referred to as the *Laffer curve,* after economics professor Arthur Laffer. As an advisor to President Ronald Reagan in the 1980s, Laffer argued that U.S. tax rates had become so high (especially on the wealthiest Americans, who paid 70 percent of their income in taxes in 1980) that Reagan could achieve a politician's dream: He could lower tax rates and simultaneously increase government revenue. Reagan took this advice and signed large-scale tax cuts into law in 1981.

The idea that people change their behavior in response to taxes is uncontroversial among economists. But the question about *how much* and *in what ways* they change their behavior is the subject of much research. Most of that research suggests that the elasticity of the labor supply with respect to taxes is very low for most people. In contrast to Laffer's prediction, people hardly increase the amount they work when tax rates fall. However, research shows that people *do* rearrange their income from different sources to reduce their tax burden, especially higher-income people who face the highest tax rates. In the end, we can't say for sure at what point the Laffer curve reaches its maximum. Estimates range from 40 percent to near 80 percent. This may seem high, but remember, what we're considering here is the tax rate that maximizes the government's revenues, not the level that is "best" for the economy.

As we'll discuss later in the chapter, knowing the price and quantity effects of taxation is critical when weighing political arguments about who should be taxed and by how much.

Incidence: Who ultimately pays the tax?

LO 20.4 Identify proportional, progressive, and regressive taxes.

We have seen that a head tax would theoretically be more efficient than other types of taxes. That's because a head tax is levied equally on everyone, no matter how much they earn or what they buy. As a result, a head tax won't distort economic behavior and thus it minimizes dead-weight loss. So, why don't governments simply collect all of their tax revenue using a head tax?

Let's use some real numbers to draw a rough sketch of what a head-tax-only system would look like in the United States. Say the goal is to collect $3.25 trillion in taxes—which was the approximate federal tax revenue in 2015. With approximately 54 percent of America's population (which is 175 million people) paying taxes in the country, to raise the needed amount, a head tax would have to be about $18,500 per taxpayer. Given that roughly 40 percent of Americans earn less than $25,000 per year, the head tax would be a very big percentage of many people's income. For many, it would be more than their actual income.[3]

The larger lesson here is that policy-makers—and taxpayers, of course—are concerned not only with what a tax does, but also with who pays it. In Chapter 6, "Government Intervention," we introduced the idea of incidence as the relative burden of an excise tax on buyers versus sellers. We can now generalize the concept of **incidence** as a description of who bears the burden of any sort of tax. This means not just buyers and sellers, but also old people or young people, rich people or poor people, and so on.

In Chapter 6, "Government Intervention," we also described an important insight that's not immediately obvious. We observed that the burden a tax places on buyers versus sellers is independent of which side is charged for the tax. This idea says that the *statutory incidence* of the tax (that is, who is legally obligated to pay the tax to the government) has no effect on the *economic incidence* of the tax (that is, who actually loses surplus as a result of the tax). Instead, the side of the market that is more inelastic—the side that responds less to changes in prices—will bear more of the tax burden. This means that policy-makers do not have much power in shifting the tax burden between buyers and sellers.

The distinction between statutory and economic incidence is important. For instance, the statutory incidence of a sales tax may fall entirely on consumers; they're the ones actually paying the tax at the cash register. But if consumers respond by buying less, the tax will clearly also affect the stores where they shop. If the stores respond by reducing prices, the stores are effectively sharing part of the tax burden. The economic incidence of the tax thus falls in part on the stores, even though they don't literally pay the tax.

Similarly, an income tax that employees are legally obliged to pay will also affect the corporations that employ them. If the tax reduces employees' willingness to supply labor at any given price level, corporations may have to raise wages in response in order to attract workers. The higher wages could lead corporations to reduce the dividends they pay to shareholders. Or corporations might increase the prices charged to customers. Both would represent a loss of surplus. In short, the people who pay the tax can be very different from those who ultimately feel the pinch.

We generally assume that policy-makers do not have the power to redistribute the tax burden between consumers and producers. But they *do* have the ability to affect the relative economic incidence of the tax burden on the rich and the poor. Economists and policy-makers classify taxes in one of three categories: proportional, regressive, or progressive.

Proportional taxation

A tax that is **proportional** takes the same *percentage* of income (as opposed to the same dollar amount) from all taxpayers. In other words, people are taxed *in proportion* to their income. In a political context, a proportional income tax is sometimes called a "flat tax."

Under a 25 percent flat tax on income, for instance, someone with an income of $20,000 would pay the same *proportion* of his or her income as someone with an income of $200,000. The absolute amount paid by each of the two taxpayers would be $5,000 (0.25 × $20,000) versus $50,000 (0.25 × $200,000), as shown in panel A of Figure 20-6.

Progressive taxation

The current income tax in the United States is not a proportional tax—instead, it is **progressive**. A tax is considered progressive if people with low incomes owe not only a smaller absolute amount but also a smaller *percentage* of their income than high-income people.

incidence
a description of who bears the burden of a tax

proportional/flat tax
a tax that takes the same percentage of income from all taxpayers

progressive tax
a tax that charges low-income people a smaller percentage of their income than high-income people

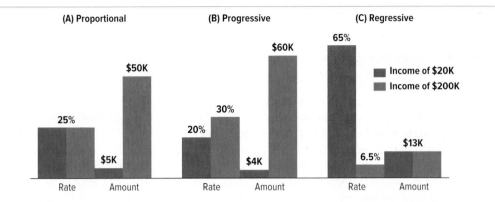

FIGURE 20-6

Proportional, progressive, and regressive taxes

Under a proportional tax, everyone pays the same percentage of their income in taxes. With a progressive tax, lower incomes are taxed less both as a percentage of their incomes and in total amount paid. A regressive tax charges the poor a higher percentage of their income than the rich, even though everyone is taxed the same dollar amount.

The U.S. personal income tax has different "brackets" for people with different levels of income; the percentage of income owed increases with each bracket. Panel B of Figure 20-6 shows an example of a progressive income tax: The person earning $20,000 pays at a 20 percent tax rate—for an absolute amount of $4,000 (0.20 × $20,000). The person earning $200,000 pays at a 30 percent tax rate—for an absolute amount of $60,000 (0.30 × $200,000).

Regressive taxation

The final category of tax incidence is regressive. A **regressive tax** is levied in such a way that low-income taxpayers pay a greater proportion of their income toward taxes than do high-income taxpayers. Most countries avoid explicitly regressive income taxes. That is, they structure their tax systems so that people in lower brackets do not pay a higher percentage of income in taxes.

However, other taxes can still be regressive. The lump-sum tax is an example, as shown in panel C of Figure 20-6. Assume that both taxpayers must pay the same absolute lump-sum tax of $13,000. That amount equates to a much higher proportion of the poorer taxpayer's income— 65 percent ($13,000 ÷ $20,000) compared with only 6.5 percent ($13,000 ÷ $200,000) for the high earner.

As we consider different types of taxes, it is important to keep in mind the relationship between efficiency and incidence. For example, some politicians propose replacing all *income* taxes with a single *sales* tax. The beauty of the idea is that it would be much simpler and more efficient than the current system. On the other hand, it would be regressive: On average, people with lower incomes spend a higher proportion of their income, rather than saving or investing it. Thus, a higher proportion of their income would be affected by a sales tax. In contrast, an income tax system like the one currently in place is more progressive, but is also probably less efficient due to the higher administrative burden and incentive effect on richer households.

We can see some of the challenges faced by politicians and economists as they try to find taxes that are fair and efficient and that raise enough money. Finding a tax system that pleases everyone is seldom possible. As a voter you can expect to have to weigh both *positive* judgments about the efficiency of a proposed tax and *normative* judgments about the "fairness" of its incidence.

regressive tax
a tax that charges low-income people a larger percentage of their income than it charges high-income people

✓CONCEPT CHECK

- ☐ Which is likely to be more efficient: a tax on a good with highly price-elastic demand or a tax on a good with inelastic demand? **[LO 20.2]**
- ☐ What is the difference between the price effect and the quantity effect of a tax increase on tax revenue? **[LO 20.3]**
- ☐ Is a tax that charges $100 to every citizen for garbage collection regressive, proportional, or progressive? **[LO 20.4]**

A Taxonomy of Taxes

LO 20.5 Describe the sources of tax revenue in the United States, and discuss the role played by different types of taxes.

So far, we've mentioned several types of taxes without going into much detail on how and why they are levied. In this section, we'll explain the important features of different kinds of taxes. We'll focus on the revenue, efficiency, and incidence of each tax.

Let's start first with an overview of U.S. government tax revenue. The federal government calculates taxes by *fiscal year,* which begins in October of one calendar year and runs through September of the following year. In fiscal year 2015 (that is, October 2014 through September 2015), the federal government collected $3.18 trillion in revenue. Where does all this tax money come from? Figure 20-7 lists the various categories of taxes and the percentage of total tax revenue that they contribute. Approximately 90 percent of tax revenue comes from three sources:

- Personal income taxes account for 46 percent of total tax revenue.
- Payroll taxes account for 34 percent of total tax revenue.
- Corporate income taxes account for 11 percent of total tax revenue.

In this section, we'll discuss each of these three major federal taxes, as well as other, smaller ones. States also levy taxes, but because state-level taxes vary a lot, we'll focus mainly on federal taxes. (In many states, sales taxes provide the most revenue, followed by a personal income tax if the state has one.)

Personal income tax

income tax
a tax charged on the earnings of individuals and corporations

An **income tax** is exactly what it sounds like: a tax charged on the earnings of individuals and corporations. The largest source of income for most people is wages earned at work. Other sources may include income from interest in savings accounts, rental income from properties you own, investment income, or even lottery and game-show winnings.

The higher your income, the higher your income tax "bracket." Each bracket is taxed at a different tax rate, and those in higher tax brackets pay a higher percentage of their income.

FIGURE 20-7

Federal tax receipts in the United States

The U.S. government earns most of its revenue from individual income taxes and payroll taxes (social insurance and retirement contributions). The vast majority of social insurance and retirement contributions come from Medicare and Social Security payments.

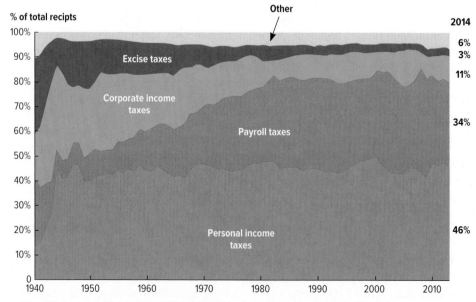

Source: Office of Management and Budget, Historical Tables, Table 2.1: https://www.whitehouse.gov/omb/budget/historicals.

The relationship between tax rates and brackets is somewhat complicated—not every dollar is treated equally. Instead, the tax rate corresponding to each tax bracket is a **marginal tax rate**, or the tax rate charged on the last dollar a taxpayer earns.

marginal tax rate
the tax rate charged on the last dollar a taxpayer earns

To see how this works, let's look at an example. Table 20-1 illustrates the tax brackets for a single person for the tax year 2017. The lowest tax bracket applies to incomes from $1 to $9,325 and has a marginal rate of 10 percent. The second bracket applies to incomes from $9,326 to $37,950 and has a marginal rate of 15 percent.

Let's say that you are a single person who earned $50,000 in 2017. How much federal income tax would you owe? On the first $9,325, you would owe 10 percent, or $932.50. On the income above $9,325 but below $37,950 ($37,950 − $9,325 = $28,625), you would owe 15%, or $4,293.75. On the remaining income over $37,950 ($50,000 − $37,950 = $12,050), you would owe 25 percent, or $3,012.50. In calculating the amount of personal income tax you owe, you would round the amounts to the nearest dollar:

$$\begin{aligned} \$\ 9{,}325 \times 0.10 &= \$\ \ \ 933 \\ +28{,}625 \times 0.15 &= \ \ 4{,}924 \\ +12{,}050 \times 0.25 &= \underline{\ \ 3{,}013} \\ \text{Total tax} &= \$8{,}240 \end{aligned}$$

Your *marginal* tax rate is 25 percent—that's the rate you pay on the last dollar you earned. But notice that your *average* tax rate is only 16.5 percent:

$$\frac{\$8{,}240}{\$50{,}000} = 16.5\%$$

Note that if you earn any amount less than $9,325, your average tax rate is 10 percent. Once you earn above that amount, the more you earn, the higher your average tax rate will be. In other words, the American individual income tax is *progressive:* The more people earn, the higher the percentage of their total income they pay.

Economists debate the extent to which income taxes discourage people from supplying their labor. One argument in favor of a progressive income tax rests on the idea that the supply of labor becomes more price-inelastic as people earn more. In other words, high earners tend to be highly educated people in jobs they like for reasons beyond the paycheck. They tend to be motivated by enjoyment of their work and the social status of their positions, not just the salary. If this is the case, we could expect that increasing the marginal tax rates on high earners would not cause them to work significantly fewer hours. Thus, progressive tax rates should bring in tax revenue without causing much deadweight loss. Note that this is a *positive* argument about the efficiency of progressive income tax rates (not a *normative* or philosophical one).

Single Tax Bracket ($)	Marginal Tax Rate (%)
1–9,325	10.0
9,326–37,950	15.0
37,951–91,900	25.0
91,901–191,650	28.0
191,651–416,700	33.0
416,701–418,400	35.0
418,401+	39.6

TABLE 20-1

U.S. personal income tax brackets in 2017

Source: www.irs.gov/pub/irs-drop/rp-16-55.pdf.

Many countries around the world also use a progressive income tax system. However, the marginal tax rates can vary a great deal across countries. Table 20-2 shows the top marginal tax rate for several different countries. This table also shows how high one's income must be before one faces the highest marginal tax rate. Notice that in Sweden, The Netherlands, and Belgium the top marginal tax rate is higher than in the United States *and* more individuals face the top marginal rate in those countries than in the United States (because the highest rate kicks in at a lower income). Both the tax rate as well as the income threshold required to meet this rate can affect a tax system's progressivity.

Many complicating factors can make the amount you owe in income taxes different from what would be suggested by your tax bracket alone. For instance, people who live in a household with a spouse or dependent children or a disabled relative will be charged less for the same level of income. Certain types of expenses, such as charitable donations, college tuition, and business expenses can be "deducted" from your taxable income. In reality, therefore, you might earn $50,000, but your *adjusted (or taxable) income* would probably be lower than that.

It might be useful to say a few words about the mechanics of tax collection: In the United States, the federal government withholds federal personal income tax from your paycheck based on your *expected* annual income. (You'll see later that income from certain sources is subject to additional or lower taxes.) Many states also withhold a state personal income tax, also based on your *expected* annual income. When you file taxes for the year, you report your *actual* earnings:

- If actual earnings are lower than the expected earnings, you overpaid the amount you owe. The government returns some of the taxes it withheld: You get a tax refund.
- If actual earnings are higher than expected earnings, you have to write a check to the government for the additional money you owe.

Withholding income taxes from your paycheck makes collecting the taxes easier. People don't have to remember to put the money aside. Imagine if the government didn't withhold money for taxes, and people had not put money aside for the eventual tax bill. April 15th would come around and many would find themselves unable to pay their tax bill.

Although the personal income tax doesn't generally distinguish between income from different sources, there is one important exception: capital gains. People often buy real estate, shares on the stock market, or other financial assets as investments. They hope, eventually, to earn a "return" by selling those capital assets at a higher price in the future. While they own these assets, they may earn income from them—dividends on shares or rent on real estate—that is taxed as normal income. However, the profit earned by buying investments and selling them

TABLE 20-2

International comparison of tax rates, tax year 2015

Country	Top marginal tax rate (%)	Income threshold for top marginal tax rate (USD)
Sweden	57.0	88,180
The Netherlands	52.0	74,870
Belgium	50.0	42,550
Israel	48.0	215,770
Germany	47.5	282,570
Japan	45.0	360,000
United States	39.6	415,050
New Zealand	33.0	50,000

at a higher price is called a *capital gain*. Capital gains are taxed separately from other types of income, under the appropriately named **capital gains tax**.

capital gains tax
a tax on income earned by buying investments and selling them at a higher price

Taxes on capital gains in the United States are somewhat complicated and the subject of much debate. The relevant fact, however, is that income from capital gains is taxed at a lower rate than most other income. Congress lowered the tax on long-term capital gains in 2003 and raised it again in 2013. The intent of the lower rate was to give individuals and corporations greater incentives to invest in capital and, by doing so, to encourage entrepreneurship. Critics contend that because higher-income people earn more through capital gains, the benefits of this tax cut go mostly to the wealthy.

The tax law has special provisions meant to reward some kinds of investment. For instance, assets that are owned for longer than one year are taxed at a lower rate than those held for a short time. Also, the sale of a house that was used as a primary residence is taxed at a lower rate than other real estate.

Payroll tax

In the United States (and many other countries), specific programs are funded by taxing payroll; this type of tax is thus often referred to as a **payroll tax**. Payroll taxes are different from income taxes (although the taxation may feel the same). In the United States, payroll taxes are charged and accumulated to pay for Social Security and Medicare. Payroll taxes are charged to both employees and employers, each paying half. The employee's portion shows up on your paystub as *FICA withholding* (FICA stands for Federal Insurance Contribution Act). Your employer withholds that amount and sends it to the federal government on your behalf. (This is in addition to the amount held for personal taxes discussed above.)

payroll tax
a tax on the wages paid to an employee

Employers pay their half of payroll taxes directly to the government when they send the employee's amount. (Of course, you know that statutory incidence is not the same as economic incidence. The evidence suggests that most of the burden of payroll tax ultimately falls on employees, in the form of lower wages.) If you are self-employed, you pay both parts of the tax (the employee and the employer parts), typically by sending a check every three months. As Figure 20-7 showed, FICA makes up a huge portion of federal government revenue.

The payroll tax in the United States is different from the personal income tax in several critical ways. The most important difference is that the U.S. payroll tax is tied directly to specific government programs. Income taxes go into general government revenue, to be allocated through the public budget. FICA is a direct contribution to Social Security and Medicare, programs that provide income and medical benefits to retired people. Since people who pay FICA during their working years are eligible for Social Security and Medicare benefits when they retire, the payroll tax is sort of like forced saving for retirement.

However, the connection between what you pay and what you later receive in Social Security and Medicare benefits is indirect. The government doesn't just hold your money until you retire and then pay it back to you. Instead, the Social Security system is based on a pay-as-you-go model, under which people who are currently working pay taxes that are then spent to provide benefits for people who are currently retired. The benefits that the elderly receive are determined through a complex formula based on earnings (and therefore FICA tax payments) during their working years. When you retire, your benefits will be paid for by the next generation. As the number of retired people relative to the number of working people grows, this system has run into problems, which we discuss later in the chapter.

Two more differences between the U.S. payroll tax and personal income tax are important. First, the payroll tax is charged only on "earned" income, such as wages or income from self-employment. Thus, the payroll tax is not paid on other sources of income such as investments or gifts. Because people with higher overall income also tend to receive a higher percentage of income from these other sources, they end up paying less in payroll taxes as a percentage of their total income.

Second, the Social Security component of the payroll tax applies only to income up to $127,200 in 2017 (the cap typically increases a little bit each year). People who make more than $127,200 pay, in payroll tax, a lower percentage of their total earnings the more they earn. Thus, households with higher income typically pay less in payroll tax as a percentage of their income.[4]

These two factors imply that the payroll tax is a regressive tax, but this is not inherent to the nature of a payroll tax. One could design a payroll tax that has no cap, or one that charges higher marginal rates for people with higher wages. The benefits people receive from Social Security are progressive: Those who had higher income during their working years receive higher benefits in absolute dollar amounts, but lower benefits as a percentage of their earnings.

Corporate income tax

Like individuals, corporations also pay taxes, the most prominent of which is the *corporate income tax*. In the United States, the corporate income tax is progressive: Smaller corporations (or those that earn less income) pay a lower percentage of their income than do larger corporations (or those that earn more income). The federal corporate income tax starts out at a rate of 15 percent for the smallest companies. It tops out at a marginal rate of 35 percent for companies with income over $18 million. Most states, although not all, also charge a corporate income tax; most top out with the highest bracket somewhere between 4 and 12 percent.[5]

Although it is corporations that are legally responsible for paying the corporate income tax, the burden of the tax could be borne in varying degrees by shareholders (through lower dividends), employees (through lower wages), or customers (through higher prices).

Other taxes

sales tax
a tax that is charged on the value of a good or service being purchased

Even if you've yet to pay income tax, it's a safe bet that you have often paid sales tax. **Sales tax** is charged based on the value of a good or service being purchased. Many states have a general sales tax but exempt certain classes of items considered to be necessities, such as food or clothing. Often, states also charge separate sales taxes, called **excise taxes**, that are targeted at specific goods, such as gasoline or cigarettes.

excise tax
a sales tax on a specific good or service

In the United States, there is no *federal* sales tax, but sales taxes are a major source of revenue for state governments. In fact, in 2009 sales taxes made up almost half of state tax revenue, with about two-thirds of that generated by general sales taxes and one-third by excise taxes on goods such as alcohol, insurance premiums, gasoline, and cigarettes. This average conceals wide variation across states. For instance, California's sales tax is the highest at 7.5 percent, while five states—Alaska, Delaware, Montana, New Hampshire, and Oregon—have no sales tax at all. Although there is no federal sales tax at this time, every so often politicians propose a form of national sales tax, called a *value-added tax (VAT)*. There are, as with any tax, arguments pro and con that have to do with tax incidence. The European Union has a VAT; so far, the United States does not.

property tax
a tax on the estimated value of a home or other property

For many people, a house is the most valuable item they own. **Property tax** is a tax on the estimated value of a home or any property owned by a taxpayer. Property taxes are an important source of revenue for local governments in many parts of the country. For instance, property taxes often fund public schools. The local taxing authority assesses property values every few years and charges a fraction of the value as the tax. (Property taxes are not collected at the federal or state levels in the United States.)

The categories we've just discussed cover the major types of taxes and bring in the majority of federal and state government revenue. There are also many minor taxes, which make up only a small part of the federal budget but sometimes pack an outsized political punch. These include taxes on certain types of imports, taxes on large financial gifts (unless they are donations to a recognized nonprofit group), and taxes on money and assets that are left to heirs when you die. This last tax—the *estate tax,* also sometimes known as the inheritance or "death" tax—has been a particularly divisive issue in recent years. Read up on it in the What Do You Think? box, "Death, taxes, and 'death taxes.'"

What Do You Think?

Death, taxes, and "death taxes"

Taxes are the subject of many heated political arguments. In this chapter, we've focused primarily on facts about taxes and how to analyze them. But although people frequently disagree about the correct answers to *positive* analyses of taxes, debates over taxation are just as often driven by underlying *normative* disagreements. One of the most politically divisive arguments over U.S. tax policy has centered on the estate tax. This tax is charged when a person dies and passes money or assets on to his or her heirs. Opponents of the estate tax sometimes refer to it as the "death tax."

Here's how the estate tax works: After a person dies, his or her estate is valued, and the value determines the tax rate. No tax is due if the value of the estate is less than a certain sum—$5.45 million in 2015. For estates worth more than that, marginal rates start at 10 percent and increase to 40 percent. There are exemptions for widows and widowers and for people in specific circumstances, such as inheriting family-owned farms. Only a very small number of wealthy people pay the tax at all. Estimates by the Center for Budget and Policy Priorities, for example, suggest that approximately 2 out of every 1,000 estates face the estate tax.

So, why the big fuss about a tax that affects only a tiny minority of Americans? One possibility is confusion caused by the success of its opponents in popularizing the term "death tax." After all, everyone dies, so you might assume that everyone must be subject to a "death tax," right? There is, in fact, some evidence that such confusion exists: One survey found that almost half of the voters surveyed wrongly thought that the estate tax applied to "most" American families. If it were popularly referred to as, say, the "inherited-wealth tax" instead, such popular confusion might be reduced.

Beyond this possibility, the estate tax hits a nerve because it addresses underlying political and moral disagreements over the role of taxes in redistributing wealth. Opponents argue that people should have a right to do what they want with their money. That includes saving it and passing it on to their children. The estate tax, some argue, is an unfair double tax. First, people are taxed when they earn their income, and then they're taxed again when they give it away at the end of life. (Of course, if the estate tax is a double tax, then we are all being taxed four or five times already: Payroll taxes, income taxes, sales taxes, excise taxes, and property taxes all cut into our earnings at some point.)

Supporters of the estate tax, including the billionaire Warren Buffett, counter that it's healthier for the economy and society to give each generation incentives to work their way up on their own merits, rather than living off inherited wealth.

WHAT DO YOU THINK?

1. Which of the arguments—for or against the estate tax—do you find more convincing? Should there be any limits on people's ability to pass down wealth across generations?
2. If you were in charge, what, if anything, would you change about the estate tax? Would you abolish it? Would you make it even more progressive by increasing the marginal rates or lowering the exemptions?

Sources: http://www.nytimes.com/2010/12/18/your-money/taxes/18wealth.html; http://www.irs.gov/businesses/small/article/0,,id=98968,00.html; http://home.gwu.edu/~jsides/estatetax.pdf; http://www.forbes.com/sites/ashleaebeling/2015/10/22/irs-announces-2016-estate-and-gift-tax-limits-the-10-9-million-tax-break/#4b4fbbb86a7c.

✓CONCEPT CHECK

☐ Why is there a difference between the marginal tax rate associated with an income tax bracket and the average tax rate that people in that bracket end up paying? **[LO 20.5]**

☐ Why is FICA a regressive tax? **[LO 20.5]**

☐ What is the difference between a general sales tax and an excise tax? **[LO 20.5]**

The Public Budget

> **LO 20.6** Discuss the important features of the public budget and the relationship between revenues and expenditures.

The U.S. federal government collected almost $3.2 trillion in revenue in 2015. That's a big sum of money—so big that it's a bit difficult to visualize what it means in real terms. There are a number of ways to consider tax revenue that make it easier to grasp. In our flat-tax thought experiment earlier in the chapter, we estimated total tax revenue as an average amount paid per taxpayer—approximately $18,500.

Another, more common approach is to look at tax revenue in comparison to the size of the total economy. The *gross domestic product (GDP)* is one way to measure the size of a country's economy. It is the sum of the market values of all final goods and services produced within a country in a given period of time. Total federal tax revenue in the United States for 2014 was approximately 11.7 percent of the country's GDP.[6]

Comparing the quantity of tax revenue collected in other countries to tax receipts in the United States is another way to better understand the quantity of taxes collected by the federal government. As Figure 20-8 shows, low-income countries tend to collect less in taxes as a percentage of GDP. High-income countries, especially those with extensive government-provided social benefits, tend to collect taxes that represent a greater share of their GDP. (The United States is an extreme exception to this rule.) Norway, for example, collects taxes equal to over 50 percent of its GDP. In contrast, the taxes collected by the government of Guatemala represent only 12 percent of the country's total GDP.

Expenditures

The relationship between public revenue and public expenditure is messy. On one hand, spending eventually has to be covered by revenue. Even the government can't go on forever spending more than it earns. On the other hand, most public spending is not tied directly to government

---

FIGURE 20-8

Taxes around the world

Looking at tax revenue as a percentage of GDP is one way to compare taxes across countries. Wealthy countries that provide many social services to their citizens tend to collect a greater share of GDP in taxes in order to pay for those services. (Data for the United States excludes contributions for Social Security and similar social programs. If these data were included, the U.S. figure would rise to about 22 percent of GDP.)

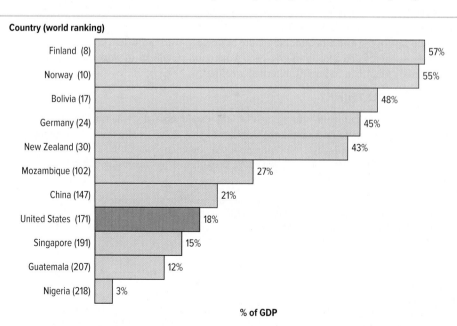

Country (world ranking)

Country	% of GDP
Finland (8)	57%
Norway (10)	55%
Bolivia (17)	48%
Germany (24)	45%
New Zealand (30)	43%
Mozambique (102)	27%
China (147)	21%
United States (171)	18%
Singapore (191)	15%
Guatemala (207)	12%
Nigeria (218)	3%

% of GDP

Source: Estimated percentage of 2015 GDP, for 219 countries: https://www.cia.gov/library/publications/the-world-factbook/rankorder/2221rank.html; https://www.cia.gov/library/publications/resources/the-world-factbook/fields/2221.html.

revenue, let alone to particular taxes. Revenue collected at a certain time or place can be stockpiled or moved around to pay for expenditures in a different time or place. Or, more commonly, governments borrow against future revenue to finance spending today.

Figure 20-9 shows how the U.S. government spends tax revenue:

- Social Security is the largest percentage of government spending for a stand-alone program. This program is funded by proceeds from the payroll tax and provides income to people aged 62 years and older (although only people who wait until age 66 to receive Social Security will receive the full percentage of benefits).
- In recent years, the amount of spending on health expenditures has grown substantially, making it currently the second-largest category of outlays.
- National defense represents the third-largest category of government expenditures.
- The fourth-largest category of expenditure includes programs to support people with low income, such as welfare, public and subsidized housing, and food stamps.

One interesting feature of federal government spending in the United States is that little of it is discretionary. **Discretionary spending** involves public expenditures that have to be approved each year, such as the military, public construction and road building, and scientific and medical research.

discretionary spending
public expenditures that have to be approved each year

FIGURE 20-9

Federal government spending in the United States

The allocation of the U.S. budget has shifted in response to national events. During World War II, national defense took priority. In recent years, as the U.S. population ages, health and social security have risen.

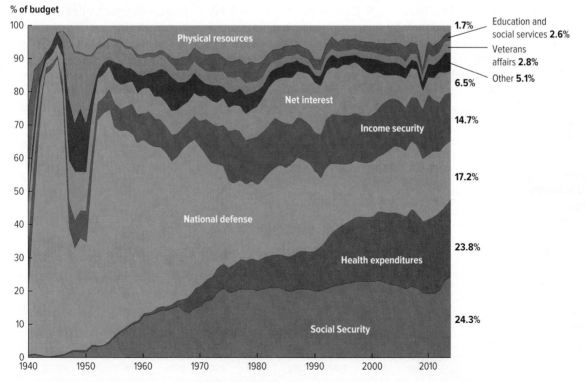

Source: Budget of the U.S. Government, Historical Tables, FY 2016, https://www.whitehouse.gov/sites/default/files/omb/budget/fy2016/assets/hist.pdf.

In contrast, the vast majority of federal expenditures are *nondiscretionary.* Such spending goes toward programs for which spending is mandated and regulated by permanent laws. Social Security, Medicare, and welfare programs are all examples of nondiscretionary spending called **entitlement spending.** Under these spending programs, people are "entitled" to benefits by virtue of age, income, or some other factor. Spending on entitlement programs automatically rises and falls with the number of people who are eligible according to the legal criteria. Therefore, expenditures on these programs cannot be decreased without changing the eligibility requirements and benefits set in the laws on which the programs are based.

You may be surprised by some of the things that are *not* included in Figure 20-9. Many of the public services that touch people's daily lives in the most noticeable ways are funded by state and local budgets:

- Public education is largely (although not entirely) supported at the state and local levels.
- Services such as police and fire protection, motor vehicle registration, and garbage collection also come out of state or local budgets.
- Many of the most visible federally funded services—such as subsidized student loans and national parks—actually make up a very small proportion of the federal budget.

entitlement spending

public expenditure that "entitles" people to benefits by virtue of age, income, or some other factor

Balancing the budget

In many years, the federal government spends more than it brings in. When a government spends more than it earns in revenue, we say that it has a **budget deficit.** When it earns more than it spends, we say it has a **budget surplus.**

Deficits and surpluses are commonly calculated as a percentage of national GDP. So, if the federal government brings in $3.25 trillion in tax revenues and spends $3.69 trillion, as it did in 2015, the budget deficit *in absolute terms* is $0.44 trillion. The budget deficit is usually stated as a *percentage relative to GDP.* For example, the 2015 deficit was approximately 2.44 percent of GDP ($0.44 trillion ÷ U.S. GDP of $18 trillion = 2.44%).[7] Historically, the United States has gone back and forth between surplus and deficit, as shown in Figure 20-10.

You may notice that there have been a lot more deficits than surpluses in recent years. Many people are concerned about the growing debt—for the same reasons you'd be worried about a family sinking deeper and deeper into debt. Debts have to be paid at some point, and the longer you stay in debt, the more you owe in interest. For this reason, some people favor balanced budget laws, which require the government to spend no more than it owes in any given year. In fact,

budget deficit

an amount of money a government spends beyond the revenue it brings in

budget surplus

an amount of revenue a government brings in beyond what it spends

---

FIGURE 20-10

Surpluses and deficits in recent U.S. history

For most of the past three decades, the U.S. government has run a budget deficit. Although deficits have not been correlated with recession historically, the most recent large budget deficit occurred during a deep recession.

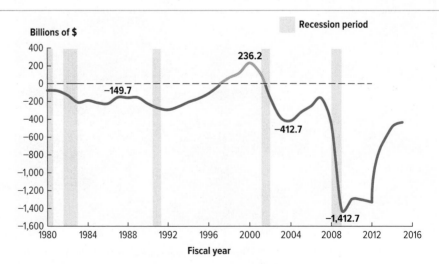

Source: *Office of Budget and Management,* https://www.whitehouse.gov/omb/budget/Historicals table 1.3, column D.

most state governments have a balanced budget requirement of some sort, although some are stricter than others.

On the surface, balancing the budget seems like an unarguably great idea. It forces policy-makers to adopt responsible spending policies that prevent the government from going into debt over the long run. So *why don't all governments balance the budget every year?*

In practice, it can be difficult to balance a public budget every year. Even with the best planning, it is unlikely that revenues will exactly equal planned expenditures in any given year. For instance, think about what happens during an unexpected economic downturn. If people lose their jobs and companies earn lower profits, the government gets less individual and corporate income tax revenue than it was expecting. It also may collect less sales tax revenue as people cut back on purchases. At the same time, it has to increase its spending on entitlement programs as people's incomes decrease and more qualify for unemployment benefits or food stamps. This means that balancing the budget in a year when the economy is doing poorly would require deep cuts in discretionary spending. Some economists argue that, by contrast, discretionary public spending should be *increased* during a downturn, to help stimulate the economy back to growth.

For these reasons, many economists argue that governments should not try to balance the budget every year. Instead, they advocate that public budgets be balanced *over the business cycle.* In brief, the idea is that governments should run surpluses when the economy is doing well and allow deficits when the economy is doing poorly—striking a balance in the long run. In other words, they should behave like a responsible family that saves up when times are good so they can spend down their savings when times are bad.

Sounds sensible, right? Unfortunately, policy-makers are under just as much pressure from voters and lobbyists to spend when the economy is doing well as when it's doing poorly. The result is that the government sometimes gets stuck in patterns of unsustainable spending. For an important case in point, see the Real Life box, "The insecure future of Social Security."

Real Life

The insecure future of Social Security

Most Americans get their paychecks only after part of their earnings have been taxed to pay for Social Security and Medicare. These two programs provide pension and medical insurance benefits to retired and disabled people and their families. Social Security is a hugely popular program. Without it, half of all Americans over the age of 66 would fall below the poverty line.

So far, the Social Security system has worked well, but recent demographic shifts are creating challenges. The system is funded through a pay-as-you-go strategy: Current workers' taxes fund benefits for current retirees. The strategy works well when there are a lot of people of working age relative to the number of retirees. The trouble is that over the last half century, Americans began to live much longer and have fewer children. As a result, the number of working-age people relative to retired people has decreased. In 1950, there were 16 workers for every retiree. By 2035, there will be only two.

This means that Social Security has to support more and more retirees with tax revenue from fewer and fewer workers. As Figure 20-11 shows, the outlay for Social Security is projected to increase over the coming decades, while the revenues stay steady. The figure also shows that in past decades, revenues have exceeded outlays. The good news is that this money is being saved up in the Social Security Trust Fund. The bad news is that this fund is projected to run dry by 2034—well before most of today's college students reach retirement age.

Many proposals have been floated to fix the Social Security problem. Some solutions focus on reining in spending by making retirement benefits less generous—for example, by raising

(continued)

the retirement age. When the retirement age is increased, presumably people would work and pay into the system for longer. When the Social Security Act was first implemented, the full retirement age was 65, and was so for many years. However, the 1983 amendment raised the retirement age to 66 for people born after 1938 and to 67 for people born after 1959. This move is projected to save the system an average of $30,000 per worker.

Other proposed solutions focus on increasing tax revenues. As of 2016, the Social Security payroll tax applies only to earnings up to $118,500. Anything you earn beyond that cap isn't taxed for Social Security. (It is, of course, taxed as part of your personal income tax.) So one idea is to eliminate the Social Security cap. Doing so would effectively increase the payroll taxes paid by high-income workers.

Another option would be to increase the rate of payroll taxes that fund Social Security for all workers (currently 12.4 percent of earnings, split equally between employers and employees).

Because Social Security is an entitlement program, with benefits defined and mandated by law, making changes requires action by Congress. Neither raising taxes nor dropping benefits is popular with constituents, so legislators have been slow to act. This no doubt will remain a hot debate for years to come.

Sources: http://www.ssa.gov/pressoffice/basicfact.htm; http://www.msnbc.msn.com/id/41293592/ns/ politics-more_politics/; http://www.cbo.gov/doc.cfm?index=11943&zzz=41347; http://www.gallup.com/ poll/141611/americans-look-wealthy-help-save-social-security.aspx; https://www.irs.gov/taxtopics/tc751.html, https://www.ssa.gov/history/1983amend.html, https://www.cbo.gov/publication/51047; https://www.ssa.gov/ oact/trsum/.

FIGURE 20-11

The future of Social Security

Presently, the revenue stream for Social Security is greater than the outlays paid in benefits. Funds can be withdrawn from the Social Security Trust Fund to make up the difference between revenue and outlays for several more decades, but the trust fund is projected to run out in 2034.

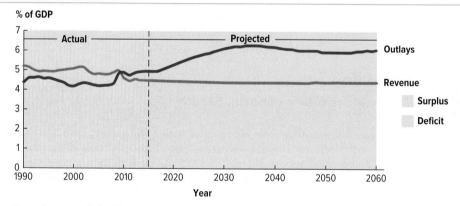

Source: Congressional Budget Office, https://www.cbo.gov/publication/51047.

✓CONCEPT CHECK

☐ What is the difference among discretionary, nondiscretionary, and entitlement spending in the public budget? **[LO 20.6]**

☐ Why is maintaining a balanced budget every year more difficult than it might at first seem? **[LO 20.6]**

Conclusion

The fine points of tax law are complex, but the basics are fairly straightforward. The ideas and evidence in this chapter show what's at stake in political debates. Understanding the implications of taxes can also help you make better personal financial choices.

When it comes to taxes, economists focus on trade-offs between revenue, efficiency, and incidence. In other words, we're concerned with how much money is raised, how costly it is to raise it, and who ultimately shoulders the burden. We've seen why governments need to balance revenues and expenditures in the long run, but also why they might not want to do so in the short run.

Public support for taxation depends on whether citizens like how governments spend their tax dollars. If voters think that governments misuse money or spend too much, they'll want to reduce taxes. When voters think that governments are helping to create stronger communities and better opportunities for citizens, they won't mind the tax bite as much. We'll dig deeper into some of these questions in the next chapter, as we address issues around poverty, inequality, and the uses of public funds.

Key Terms

deadweight loss, p. 499

lump-sum tax (head tax), p. 501

administrative burden, p. 501

incidence, p. 504

proportional/flat tax, p. 504

progressive tax, p. 504

regressive tax, p. 505

income tax, p. 506

marginal tax rate, p. 507

capital gains tax, p. 509

payroll tax, p. 509

sales tax, p. 510

excise tax, p. 510

property tax, p. 510

discretionary spending, p. 513

entitlement spending, p. 514

budget deficit, p. 514

budget surplus, p. 514

Summary

LO 20.1 Describe the major public policy goals of taxation.

The most important goal of taxation is to raise public revenue. This allows governments to provide goods and services such as education, highways, and national defense. A second use of taxation is to change the behavior of market participants by driving a wedge between the prices faced by buyers and sellers. This function of a tax can counterbalance a negative externality, bringing consumption down to an efficient level. Taxes may also be used to discourage specific behaviors, such as smoking or drinking, for reasons that are not necessarily related to negative externalities.

LO 20.2 Explain how deadweight loss and administrative costs contribute to the inefficiency of a tax.

There are two sources of inefficiency associated with taxation: administrative burden and deadweight loss. Administrative burden includes the time and money spent by the government to collect and monitor tax payments, as well as the time and money spent by individuals on filing tax returns or hiring accountants.

Deadweight loss is the reduction in total surplus that results from the decrease in the number of trades that occur due to the tax.

LO 20.3 Calculate the effect of a tax increase on revenue, taking into account price and quantity effects.

Two forces are at play in the relationship between tax rates and revenue. Raising taxes means that the government gets more revenue per units sold, which increases total revenue. But the shrinking effect of a higher tax rate causes fewer units to be sold, which decreases total revenue. In other words, a change in the tax rate has both a *price effect* (the government collects more tax for every unit) and a *quantity effect* (the government collects taxes on fewer units). Raising taxes has diminishing returns to revenue because the quantity effect gradually overtakes the price effect. At some point, taxes can be so high that the price effect dominates, and raising taxes actually reduces total revenue.

LO 20.4 Identify proportional, progressive, and regressive taxes.

Incidence describes who bears the burden of paying a tax. Incidence can describe whether the tax burden falls on buyers or sellers but also on how much is paid by the rich versus the poor. *Proportional* taxes take the same percentage of income from everyone. *Progressive* taxes take a higher percentage of income from those with higher income. *Regressive* taxes do the opposite, charging a higher percentage of income to those with lower income. The economic incidence of the tax describes who ultimately bears the burden of the tax and is not necessarily the same as the statutory incidence of the tax, which describes who is legally obligated to pay it.

> **LO 20.5** Describe the sources of tax revenue in the United States, and discuss the role played by different types of taxes.

The vast majority of tax revenue the United States collects comes from personal income and payroll taxes; a significant minority comes from the corporate income tax.

Personal income taxes are charged on income from all sources, with increasing marginal rates for higher income levels. Payroll taxes are charged at a flat rate on earned income and are tied directly to Social Security and Medicare expenditures. The personal income tax and corporate income tax are progressive; the payroll tax is generally considered to be regressive. In contrast to the federal government, many state governments bring in most of their revenue through general sales and excise taxes.

> **LO 20.6** Discuss the important features of the public budget and the relationship between revenues and expenditures.

The United States takes in tax revenue equal to about 15 percent of its GDP. However, spending is not tied directly to government revenue. Revenue collected at a certain time and place can pay for expenditures in a different time or place, and the federal government can and does borrow money to pay for current expenses. The majority of federal government spending goes to nondiscretionary budget items. These include entitlement programs like Social Security and Medicare, for which benefits are mandated by law. Both tax revenue and spending fluctuate from year to year as the economy goes up and down, resulting in budget deficits or surpluses.

Review Questions

1. Both a payroll tax and an excise tax on alcohol raise revenue and, respectively, shrink the markets for labor and alcohol. Although both have some functions in common, governments may have different goals when levying them. What goals do you think motivate a payroll tax? What goals motivate an alcohol tax? **[LO 20.1]**

2. The demand for cigarettes, which create negative externalities through secondhand smoke, is often relatively inelastic. That is, when the price of cigarettes changes, the quantity demanded changes by a smaller portion. Using this fact, explain to what extent you think a tax on cigarettes would fulfill each of the goals of taxation. **[LO 20.1]**

3. Which would you expect to be less efficient, a flat tax on all income or a property tax (charged based on the assessed value of real estate)? Explain why, in terms of both deadweight loss and administrative costs. **[LO 20.2]**

4. A local government is considering ways to raise taxes to pay for making sidewalks. One prominent citizen suggests taxing people based on how much they walk on the sidewalk, measured in yards each day. Explain why, despite its apparent fairness, this tax is likely very inefficient. **[LO 20.2]**

5. In an election debate, two candidates for governor are debating about whether to raise the general sales tax from 5 to 7 percent. One argues that this would increase tax revenues, enabling the state to maintain essential services. The other argues that the tax would hurt retailers and consumers, and would actually slow down the economy so much that it would decrease tax revenues too. Restate these candidates' positions in economic terminology and explain what assumptions they must be making in order to justify their different positions, in terms of price and quantity effects. **[LO 20.3]**

6. Explain, with reference to the price and quantity effects, why all else equal, taxing several goods at a modest rate is better than taxing one good at a very high rate. **[LO 20.3]**

7. People with low income spend more, as a share of their overall income, on food and clothing than wealthier people. As a result, they tend to spend a higher proportion of their income relative to people with high income. Given this trend, explain how a general sales tax of 8 percent could be regressive. Now, suppose that food and children's clothing are exempted from the sales tax. Is this likely to make the tax more or less regressive? **[LO 20.4]**

8. Suppose you turn on the television to find an ad by a local politician accusing car dealers of making too much money off consumers. As a remedy for this abuse, the official proposes to tax the dealers at a higher rate and reward car buyers with the proceeds of the tax. Drawing on the idea of economic incidence and administrative cost, explain why this tax may not benefit consumers after all. **[LO 20.4]**

9. Your friend Edgar has just finished his first year working full time and comes home beaming with an envelope from the IRS, which has sent him a check for $650 after he sent in his tax forms. Explain to Edgar why this does not mean that he didn't pay taxes. **[LO 20.5]**

10. Explain why most people's marginal tax rate is higher than their average tax rate. Is a system in which average tax rates are higher than marginal tax rates regressive, proportional, or progressive? **[LO 20.5]**

11. A challenger presidential candidate vows to cut entitlement spending by 20 percent in the first few weeks that he is in office. Why is it unlikely the candidate could achieve this reduction? **[LO 20.6]**

12. When the federal government borrows money, it can fund higher expenditures in the short term but incurs a debt that accrues interest and has to be paid off in the long term. What does this imply about the trade-off between current and future taxes? How might this trade-off change if the overall size of the economy grows over time? **[LO 20.6]**

Problems and Applications

1. Consider each of the following tax policies. Decide for each whether the primary public policy goal is most likely raising revenue or changing behavior (with or without a market failure). **[LO 20.1]**

    a. Income tax.

    b. Cigarette tax.

    c. Payroll tax.

    d. Income tax exemption for charity donations.

2. Governments throughout history have levied some very interesting taxes. Each of the following taxes changed citizens' behavior. Determine whether it's likely that the tax also addressed a market failure. **[LO 20.1]**

    a. *The Hat Tax:* Adopted by the British government, requiring every hat to bear a stamp on the inside showing it was legal.

    b. *The "Flatulence Tax":* Proposed, but ultimately not adopted, in New Zealand to help reduce methane emissions from livestock.

    c. *The Window Tax:* Levied by English King William III on the number of windows in a house, which tended to be more numerous in wealthier homes.

    d. *The Cowardice Tax:* Introduced in medieval England and applied to people who refused to defend the country at the request of the king.

3. Suppose the government wants to levy a new excise tax. For each of the following goods, determine whether you would expect an excise tax to result in high or low deadweight loss. **[LO 20.2]**

    a. Alcohol.

    b. Milk.

    c. Diamonds.

    d. Tropical vacations.

    e. Socks.

4. Table 20P-1 shows supply and demand in the market for sub sandwiches in Wheretown, where the local government wants to raise revenue via a $1 tax on all sandwiches, collected from sandwich shops. **[LO 20.2]**

    a. Graph the initial supply and demand curves, before the tax. Then graph the after-tax supply curve. Before and after the tax: What is the equilibrium quantity? What is the equilibrium price? What price is paid by consumers? What price is received by suppliers?

    b. Calculate consumer and producer surplus before and after the tax.

    c. How much tax revenue does Wheretown receive? Draw this tax revenue on the graph.

    d. How much deadweight loss is caused by the tax?

TABLE 20P-1

Price of sub sandwich ($)	Quantity demanded	Quantity supplied
8.00	0	100
7.50	10	90
7.00	20	80
6.50	30	70
6.00	40	60
5.50	50	50
5.00	60	40
4.50	70	30
4.00	80	20
3.50	90	10
3.00	100	0
2.50	110	0
2.00	120	0

FIGURE 20P-1

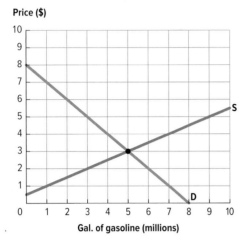

e. Suppose it costs Wheretown $35 to collect the tax revenue from sandwich shops. In the end, how much revenue from the sub tax is actually available to spend on public services?

5. Figure 20P-1 shows a hypothetical market for gasoline. **[LO 20.3]**

   a. Suppose an excise tax of $1.50 per gallon is levied on gasoline suppliers. Draw the after-tax supply curve. What price will consumers pay? What price will sellers receive?

   b. How much government revenue will result from the tax?

   c. Suppose the tax is raised to $3 per gallon. Draw the new after-tax supply curve. How much additional revenue will this raise compared to the $1.50 tax?

   d. Suppose the tax is raised again to $4.50 per gallon. Draw the new after-tax supply curve. Does this newest tax increase cause tax revenue to increase, decrease, or remain the same as compared to the $3 per gallon tax?

6. In each of the following examples, determine whether the price effect or the quantity effect dominates when the tax is applied. **[LO 20.3]**

   a. The government raises taxes on iPods from $10 per iPod to $20 per iPod. Prior to the tax increase, 10 million iPods were sold each year. The new equilibrium quantity is 9 million iPods.

   b. In response to concerns about chewing gum in schools, the government raises the tax on packs of gum from $0.20 per pack to $0.30 per pack. Before the tax increase, 50 million packs were sold each year. After the tax increase, 40 million packs are sold each year.

   c. Worried that Americans are addicted to coffee, the government raises the $0.05 tax on a cup of coffee to $0.10. Before the tax increase, 10 billion cups were sold each year. Afterward, 5 billion cups are sold each year.

7. Determine whether each of the following taxes is proportional, regressive, or progressive. **[LO 20.4]**

   a. An income tax of 25 percent on income from all sources.

   b. An income tax with three brackets and corresponding marginal tax rates: 10 percent for income up to $50,000; 20 percent for income up to $100,000; and 30 percent for income over $100,000.

   c. A fee of $500 per year for municipal services, charged to everyone who lives within the city limits.

   d. A capital gains tax that charges a flat rate of 40 percent, but only on capital gains over $1 million.

   e. A payroll tax of 10 percent on income under $200,000.

8. Table 20P-2 shows an income tax schedule for the imaginary country of Independence. Connor is a citizen of Independence who earns $95,000 per year at his job. Assume Connor is not eligible for any deductions or exemptions. **[LO 20.4, 20.5]**

   a. How much does Connor pay in income tax?

   b. What is Connor's marginal tax rate? What is his overall tax rate?

TABLE 20P-2

Taxable income ($)	Marginal tax rate (%)
0–5,000	5
5,001–15,000	7
15,001–30,000	9
30,001–50,000	11
50,001–75,000	13
75,001–100,000	15
100,001–130,000	20
130,001–175,000	21
175,001+	22

TABLE 20P-3

Category	Amount ($)
Income earned in wages	90,000
Income from capital gains	20,000
Spending on consumer goods subject to sales tax	10,000
Spending on charitable donations	3,000

TABLE 20P-4

Year	GDP ($)	Prior-year debt ($)	Current expenditures ($)	Tax revenue ($)
2013	8,500	5,100	1,200	950
2014	8,650		1,400	1,525
2015	9,000		1,800	1,500
2016	9,200		2,100	1,600

c. Connor isn't crazy about his job and wants to move to a job in a related industry that pays $100,000. How much will Connor have to pay in taxes in the new job?

d. Is the income tax in Independence regressive, proportional, or progressive?

9. Evangeline is a citizen of Independence, whose income and expenditures are shown in Table 20P-3. Table 20P-2 showed Independence's personal income tax schedule. In answering the following questions, you may assume the following. **[LO 20.5]**

1. All income other than capital gains falls under the personal income tax.

2. Deductible expenses are subtracted from income before income tax is calculated.

3. Charitable donations and money paid in payroll taxes are tax-deductible.

4. Payroll tax is 5 percent of earned income up to $50,000.

5. Capital gains tax is 3 percent on capital gains over $10,000.

6. Sales tax is 6 percent.

   a. How much does Evangeline pay in payroll taxes?

   b. How much does Evangeline pay in capital gains taxes?

   c. What is Evangeline's adjusted income subject to the personal income tax? How much does she pay in personal income tax?

   d. How much does Evangeline pay in sales taxes?

e. How much does Evangeline pay in taxes, in total? What percentage of her income does this represent?

10. Table 20P-4 shows an economy's GDP, current expenditures, and tax revenue for 2013–2016. **[LO 20.6]**

   a. Complete the table by filling in the prior-year debt for each year listed.

   b. For each year, is this economy experiencing a budget surplus or budget deficit?

   c. Debt is what percentage of GDP in 2013?

   d. Between 2013 and 2016, by what percentage has GDP changed? By what percentage has the debt changed? Is debt as a percentage of GDP growing, constant, or shrinking between 2013 and 2016?

11. Table 20P-5 shows an economy's GDP, population, debt, and GDP per capita for 2015 and 2016. **[LO 20.6]**

   a. Complete the table by filling in the debt per capita for both years.

   b. What is the percentage change from 2015 to 2016 in each of the following?

   1. GDP.

   2. Population.

   3. Debt.

   4. GDP per capita.

   5. Debt per capita.

   c. Which is growing faster—GDP per capita or debt per capita? Why?

TABLE 20P-5

Year	GDP (millions of $)	Population (millions)	Debt (millions of $)	GDP per capita ($)	Debt per capita ($)
2015	10,675,000	305.0	7,472,500	35,000	
2016	10,995,250	311.1	7,920,850	35,343	

Endnotes

1. http://news.minnesota.publicradio.org/features/2003/04/28_ helmsm_happytopay.

2. https://www.irs.gov/PUP/newsroom/IRS%20FY%20 2015%20Budget%20in%20Brief.pdf; https://www. nationalpriorities.org/budget-basics/federal-budget-101/ revenues/#endnotes.

3. http://www.usgovernmentrevenue.com/fed_revenue_ 2015USrn; https://www.ssa.gov/cgi-bin/netcomp .cgi?year=2014; http://www.marketwatch.com/story/45- of-americans-pay-no-federal-income-tax-2016-02-24.

4. Beginning in 2013, an additional Medicare tax of 0.9 percent applies for individual wages of more than $200,000 ($250,000 for married couples filing jointly).

5. http://rsmus.com/pdf/2015_taxrate_card.pdf; http://taxfoundation.org/article/ state-corporate-income-tax-rates-and-brackets-2016.

6. http://data.worldbank.org/indicator/GC.TAX.TOTL.GD.ZS.

7. https://www.cbo.gov/about/products/budget_economic_ data#2; http://www.cnsnews.com/news/article/terence- p-jeffrey/3248723000000-federal-taxes-set-record-fy- 2015-21833-worker-feds-0; http://www.cnsnews.com/ news/article/terence-p-jeffrey/3248723000000-federal- taxes-set-record-fy-2015-21833-worker-feds-0.

Poverty, Inequality, and Discrimination

Learning Objectives

LO 21.1 Understand how to measure poverty and describe the difference between absolute and relative measures of poverty.

LO 21.2 Understand why poverty persists.

LO 21.3 Explain and interpret different methods of measuring income inequality.

LO 21.4 Describe how income mobility differs from income equality.

LO 21.5 Identify the public policies that are used to reduce poverty and inequality and understand their goals.

LO 21.6 Explain the trade-off between equity and efficiency in poverty-reduction policy.

LO 21.7 Explain why economists differentiate between correlation and causation when studying discrimination and why markets do not always eliminate discrimination.

STRIKING IT RICHER

How rich is super-rich? In 1915—the era of the Rockefellers, Vanderbilts, and Carnegies, whose names are synonymous with extraordinary wealth—people worried that the wealthiest 1 percent of the population held 15 percent of the nation's income. Today, the richest 5 percent of the U.S. population holds almost *22 percent* of the income, and the richest 20 percent together earns over 51 percent. To be part of the richest 5 percent of the U.S. population in 2014, your family had to earn over $206,568. That's half of what an average Wall Street worker in New York City took home in 2014; it's almost the same as the annual wage a typical surgeon earns, and three times the average salary of elementary school teachers.[1]

While the rich have gotten richer, the poor have gotten richer too. Fifty years ago, almost a quarter of Americans lived in poverty. Over just a few decades, the national poverty rate fell by half. How can poverty be falling and inequality be rising at the same time? The answer is that the poor have gotten richer, but the rich have gotten richer at an even faster rate. Economic growth has increased incomes throughout the population, but a disproportionate amount has stayed with

the wealthy. Economist Emmanuel Saez, who has studied millions of U.S. tax returns, finds that between 1993 and 2010, the incomes of the richest 1 percent grew by 58 percent. The other 99 percent saw incomes grow by just 6.4 percent on average, and some incomes were flat or falling.[2]

Internationally, the picture looks similar. Hundreds of millions of people have been lifted out of poverty by economic growth in recent decades, but global inequality is also high. A lot of this has to do with differences between countries: Being born into a poorer family in the United States places you at about the same income level as the upper class in India or China.

Does inequality matter? The more equal a society is, the more that everyone will gain when the economy improves. But it doesn't necessarily follow that the most equal society is the best society, or even that it provides the most resources for its disadvantaged members. One view is that inequality gives people an incentive to work hard and take risks. In that view, work and risk-taking create jobs and contribute to economic growth that can benefit everyone, including the poorest.

Thinking about the "right" level of inequality is one of the hardest economic questions we face. Does success at the top trickle down to benefit the poor? To what extent do taxes and programs that equalize income also create a disincentive for hard work and entrepreneurship?

In this chapter, we will explore tough issues surrounding poverty and inequality—how they can be measured, how they affect people's lives and choices, and how governments design public policy in response. What can economics say about these big questions? We'll show examples of how innovative economic problem solving has provided new approaches to fighting poverty. We will also explore the economics of discrimination, an issue that is tied to longstanding patterns of poverty and inequality in many countries.

As we weigh ideas and evidence in this chapter, we ask you to remember the distinction between positive and normative analysis. We will use positive analysis to understand what poverty, inequality, and discrimination look like and how they affect the economy. That's a separate question from the big normative issue: Should governments try to reduce poverty, inequality, and discrimination in the name of social justice and fairness?

Poverty

Economics is the study of how people manage their resources. Poverty, which we can think about as a lack of material resources, is of particular interest to economists. Do people with few resources make different decisions than the wealthy? Do they approach those decisions in a different way? Why are they poor in the first place?

Of course, poverty is of concern for less-intellectual reasons as well. It can be upsetting to see people struggling to support themselves or even to stay alive. Without financial resources, it's difficult to access many of the basic goods that make life livable—food, shelter, health—and certainly those that make life comfortable. Economic thinking can suggest ways to make life better for those in need, both at home and around the world.

Several ideas will come up over and over again in this chapter:

- Is poverty a problem only when it represents an absolute deprivation, such as not having enough to eat?
- Or is poverty best defined in relative terms?
- Should people be considered to be "poor" when they have enough to live on, but still have much less than others in society?

Another theme to follow is that the causes of poverty may not always be obvious. For instance, around the world, being poor often comes along with having less education.

- Does a lack of education make people poor, or are poor people less able or willing to access education?

The patterns of poverty over decades or generations are also critical:

- How hard is it to start out poor and become rich, or vice versa?
- If your parents are poor, how does that affect you and your chances in life?

Keep these underlying questions in mind as we discuss the measurement of, causes of, and solutions to poverty.

Measuring poverty

LO 21.1 Understand how to measure poverty and describe the difference between absolute and relative measures of poverty.

At first glance, defining and measuring poverty might seem like a simple task. You know it when you see it, right? But there are important disagreements about how to measure poverty on a national level. As it turns out, different definitions of poverty paint different pictures of who is poor and how they live.

Absolute and relative measures

Imagine two families:

- One lives in the United States and has an income of $15,000 per year. This family of four lives in an apartment with running water, electricity, heat, and four rooms.

- The other family lives in India and earns $1,500 per year. This family of six lives in a one-room house with no water or electricity.

Both families earn less money than the majority of the people living in their countries. One, however, makes ten times as much money as the other. Which family is "poor"? Are both "poor"?

When defining poverty, the first important distinction to make is between absolute and relative measures. An **absolute poverty line** defines poverty as income below a certain amount, fixed at a given point in time. An absolute poverty line is usually set based on the cost of certain essential goods. In the United States, for instance, a married couple with two children who earns $23,263 per year is below the poverty line, which is $24,036 for a family of four. We can see this in Table 21-1. So the first family in our example above, the one from the United States, is indeed considered poor with earnings of $15,000.

In the United States, the official poverty line is an absolute poverty line based on the price of food. In the 1960s, officials calculated the cost of what they considered to be a reasonable diet for households of different sizes. They calculated that middle-class people at the time tended to spend about one-third of their income on food. So, they set the poverty line by taking the cost of food for a family of a given size and multiplying it by three. Recognizing that the price of food and other goods increases over time, the government adjusts the poverty line each year based on the *Consumer Price Index (CPI),* which we'll discuss at length in another chapter. The CPI measures increases in the price of a set of common consumer goods.

Critics of the U.S. definition of poverty note that it fails to account accurately for expenditures other than food. This is a real worry because most families devote a smaller share of their income to food than they did in the 1960s. If the price of food has gone down relative to the prices of other things such as rent, transportation, and utilities (including phone service), then basing the poverty level on the price of food will not account for those other necessary costs. Because of this change, a reasonable standard of living may now cost more than three times the price of food.

Critics also point out that the U.S. poverty definition does not account for regional differences in the cost of living. The federal government currently has only one "official" poverty line, even though the same income buys much more in some parts of the country than in others.

Recently, the U.S. government has begun to address these methodological challenges. In 2011, the Census Bureau introduced an "alternate" poverty measure. This alternate measure bases the poverty line on the prices of food, clothing, shelter, and utilities, and it adjusts for geographic differences in the cost of living. For now, it's helpful to track poverty as measured by both the official and the alternate measures.

A different approach to measuring poverty is based on a **relative poverty line**. Rather than measuring absolute deprivations, the relative poverty line defines poverty in relation to the income of the *rest* of the population. In the United Kingdom, for instance, the poverty line is set at 60 percent of the median income. The *median income* is the level earned by the household

absolute poverty line
a measure that defines poverty as income below a certain amount, fixed at a given point in time

relative poverty line
a measure that defines poverty in terms of the income of the rest of the population

TABLE 21-1

U.S. poverty line for different family sizes

Poverty lines are determined every year by the U.S. Census Bureau to measure the number of Americans living in poverty. Larger families need more money to keep themselves out of poverty.

Source: Family sizes with more than two people are families with two adults plus children. A full set of poverty lines is available at http://www.census.gov/hhes/www/poverty/data/threshld/index.html (2015).

Poverty line ($)	Family size
12,331	1
15,871	2
19,078	3
24,036	4
28,286	5
31,670	6
35,473	7

exactly in the middle of the national income distribution. (In other words, compared to that household, half of the population earns less and half earns more.)

The use of a relative poverty line can lead to some surprising patterns. Imagine that in the United Kingdom, for example, economic growth raises the incomes of poor households by 5 percent. This growth helps poor families, but it won't necessarily reduce the official **poverty rate**— the percentage of the population that falls below the absolute poverty line. In fact, the official poverty rate might even *rise* if the income of the median household grows faster than 5 percent.

Both absolute and relative poverty measures have merits:

poverty rate
the percentage of the population that falls below the absolute poverty line

- An absolute poverty line captures a family's ability to consume essential goods like food, shelter, and clothing. It defines as poor someone who can't afford basic necessities, regardless of how well off the rest of society is.

- In contrast, a relative poverty line captures the fact that people tend to measure themselves against the people around them, rather than against an absolute standard. (For a review of this idea, turn back to Chapter 7, "Consumer Behavior.") It defines poverty as not whether you're starving, but whether you're keeping up with the rest of society.

Thus, if someone is more concerned with inequality, the relative poverty line is more relevant. For someone more interested in the ability to buy a basic bundle of food, education, health care, and housing, the absolute poverty line will be more relevant. The difference in one's focus has important implications for policies that help the poor, specifically for deciding who should receive support and how much.

Who is poor?

We'll focus on the absolute poverty level of U.S. households, using the official federal poverty line. In 2014, 46.7 million people—14.8 percent of the population—lived under the official poverty line in the United States. This number was up from a near all-time low of 11.3 percent in 2000.[3]

Today, poverty in the United States looks remarkably different than it did when the government began tracking it in the late 1950s. As Figure 21-1 shows, almost a quarter of the population lived in poverty in 1959. That number plummeted throughout the 1960s and early 1970s. Since then, the poverty rate has fluctuated between 11 and 15 percent of the population.

What changed in the 1960s? One important factor was economic growth. Between 1959 and 1973, the total size of the U.S. economy grew at an average rate of 4.4 percent per year. (In contrast, it grew at an average rate of only 2.4 percent from 1974 to 2014.) Because the U.S. poverty line is an absolute measure rather than a relative one, the official U.S. poverty rate fell steadily when there was economic growth that raised the incomes of low-income families.

The development during the 1960s of new government programs to assist the poor also made a big difference. Between 1960 and 1995, for example, increases in Social Security benefits helped reduce the poverty rate among the elderly, from 35 percent down to 10 percent.[4]

Poverty rates may have improved for the elderly, but they remain high for other parts of the population. Table 21-2 shows that today black and Hispanic Americans have poverty rates twice as high as white Americans—roughly 25 percent versus 10 percent. Note, however, that there are more white people living in poverty *in total,* even though the poverty *rate* is lower, because there are more white people than black or Hispanic people in the United States. One other notable fact is that households headed by single women are especially likely to be poor.

Not all experiences of poverty are the same. The most fundamental distinction is between *chronic* and *transient* poverty. The difference between the two is essentially the difference between always being poor and being poor for a short time:

- *Chronic poverty* is usually defined as spending three or more years in poverty.
- *Transient poverty* is usually measured as a spell of poverty that lasts at least two consecutive months within a year.

FIGURE 21-1

U.S. poverty over time   Since the 1960s, the poverty rate has decreased by about 10 percent through economic growth and government assistance. After 1970, the poverty rate has largely fluctuated between 10 and 15 percent. Even though the U.S. population has nearly doubled since 1960, the number of people in poverty has increased by only a few million, and there are actually fewer children in poverty today than there were in 1960.

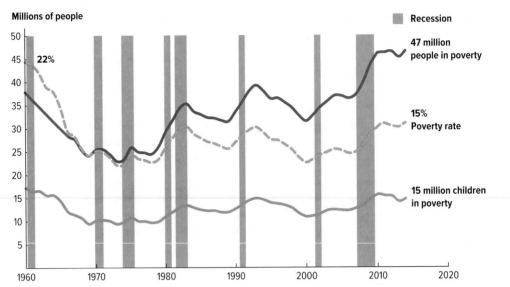

Source: U.S. Census Bureau, *Historical Povçerty Tables* (2014), Tables 1 and 11, https://www.census.gov/data/tables/time-series/demo/income-poverty/historical-poverty-people.html.

TABLE 21-2

The face of U.S. poverty (2014)

A diverse group of people live below the poverty line. Hispanics, blacks, single women, and children have the highest rates of poverty. Married families have the lowest poverty rates; single mothers have the highest. Nearly one-third of single mothers live in poverty.

Source: U.S. Census Bureau poverty data, 2014, Tables 3, 4, and 7.

Demographic	Number in poverty (millions)	Proportion of demographic in poverty (%)
White*	31.1	12.7
Black	10.7	26.2
Hispanic	13.1	23.6
Asian	2.1	12.0
Male	20.7	13.4
Female	25.9	16.1
Married	3.7	6.2
Single female	4.7	30.6
Single male	1.0	15.7
Under 18	15.5	21.1
18–64	26.5	13.5
Over 65	4.5	10.0

* White, non-Hispanic

Research suggests that only about 3 percent of people living under the poverty line in any given year are chronically poor. More than a quarter of the population experiences transient poverty at some point in their lives, perhaps due to losing a job or experiencing sickness or injury.[5]

The difference between transient and chronic poverty matters when evaluating anti-poverty policies. Later in the chapter we'll discuss programs like unemployment insurance, disability or health insurance, and job training. Those programs can be helpful in tackling transient poverty but are unlikely to make a big dent in chronic poverty. Addressing long-lasting poverty requires digging deeper to understand what causes a person to be poor over many years or a family to be poor over many generations.

Measuring international poverty

Measuring poverty on an international scale is similar to measuring it on a national one. The same concerns about differences in the cost of living and relative standards of wealth apply, only more so since these differences are much more dramatic on a global scale than a national one.

The most common international poverty measure is the number of people living on less than $1.90 per day. That's much lower than the official U.S. poverty line; still, according to most estimates, 896 million people lived on less than $1.90 per day in 2012, or roughly 13 percent of the world's population.[6] Over 77 percent of those (309 million) lived in South Asia, 388 million lived in sub-Saharan Africa, and nearly 147 million lived in East Asia and the Pacific.

As always, however, we have to be careful about the difference between the absolute numbers of people in poverty and the percentage of people in poverty (the poverty rate): Only about 7 percent of East Asians lived on less than $1.90 per day, compared to about 19 percent of South Asians and 43 percent of people living in sub-Saharan Africa. Figure 21-2 shows the *percentage* of the population living on less than $1.90 per day in each country.

FIGURE 21-2

Percentage of people living on less than $1.90 per day, by country   This map shows the percentage of people living on less than $1.90 per day, adjusted for purchasing power in each country. That level of income is the World Bank's measurement of extreme poverty. Most extreme poverty is clustered in sub-Saharan Africa. The majority of countries in the Northern Hemisphere have very low levels of poverty.

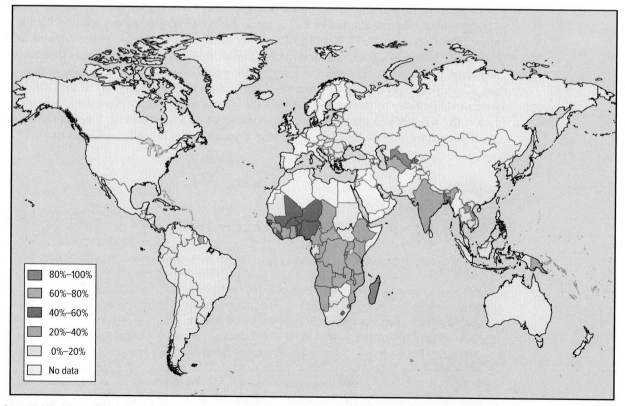

- 80%–100%
- 60%–80%
- 40%–60%
- 20%–40%
- 0%–20%
- No data

Source: World Bank Poverty & Equity Data (2014), Poverty headcount ratio, $1.90 per day, http://povertydata.worldbank.org/poverty/home.

**purchasing power
parity (PPP) index**
index that describes
the overall difference in
prices of goods between
countries

Calculating the $1.90 per person per day international poverty line involves a series of steps. Most importantly, poverty lines have to be adjusted to account for differences in prices across countries. Fortunately, there's a useful tool, called the **purchasing power parity (PPP) index**, to make those adjustments. It describes the overall difference in prices of goods between countries. With the index, you can translate the equivalent cost of a basket of goods in various countries.

To create the PPP index, economists collect data on prices in every country and develop an index that describes the overall difference in prices between countries. The aim is to capture the differences in prices among countries. For example, the PPP would show that most goods are cheaper in India than they are in the United States, cheaper in the United States than they are in Sweden, and so on. The process is not perfect since we don't all consume exactly the same things. (For example, Americans eat a lot of beef, while Indians eat relatively little beef.) Nevertheless, the PPP index captures key price differences.

Using the PPP index, the international poverty line is actually $1.90 per day at purchasing power parity. That means that in each country the poverty line is the amount that will allow you to buy a basket of goods equivalent to what $1.90 would buy in the United States. The $1.90 (PPP) per day line was chosen by averaging the national poverty lines of 15 poor countries. The idea is that this low poverty line represents *absolute* (not relative) poverty by some globally comparable standard. The $1.90 line is so low that it's not very relevant for the United States, but it gives a useful global snapshot.

Using the $1.90 standard, we can see significant changes in the pattern of global poverty over the last few decades. Overall, rapid economic growth has reduced the global poverty rate from 44 percent in 1981 to 12.7 percent in 2012. This change is a pretty incredible reduction. When we dig further, we see that the reduction in poverty has been heavily concentrated in China, whose poverty rate dropped from 88 percent in 1981 to 11.2 percent in 2010. South Asia and the Middle East saw significant reductions as well, and Latin America achieved smaller reductions. In contrast, the poverty rate in sub-Saharan Africa hardly changed at all in this period.[7]

To get a better picture, economists also use poverty lines higher than $1.90 per person per day—most often an alternative line is set at $3.10 per person per day. One of the little-appreciated facts about the $1.90 and $3.10 poverty lines is that they define poverty as measured by *average* income in a given year. It turns out, though, that most families' incomes fluctuate up and down around the average over the course of the year. No family with an average income of, say, $2 per person per day *literally* receives $2 per person each and every day. If they did, their lives would probably be much easier. Instead, the income earned in any given week depends on factors like whether jobs are available and the bounty of the recent harvest. You can read more about this challenge in the Real Life box "What if your $2 a day doesn't come every day?"

Real Life
What if your $2 a day doesn't come every day?

The World Bank estimates that about 13 percent of the planet lives on less than $1.90 a day per person. About 35 percent (more than 2 billion people!) live on less than $3.10 a day per person. It is hard to imagine what it must be like to live on so little, and it wouldn't be far-fetched to assume that the world's poor live in a never-ending scramble to meet daily needs. If so, saving and planning for the future would be impossible luxuries.

A group of researchers wanted to know if these assumptions were right. They spent a year getting to know families in India, South Africa, and Bangladesh. Spending time in rural villages and urban slums, they created a set of "financial diaries" for each family. These diaries tracked family expenses, income, and financial transactions. This project eventually came together in a book called *Portfolios of the Poor: How the World's Poor Lives on $2 per Day* (jointly written by one of the authors of this textbook).

The results were surprising; they showed that common assumptions can be quite wrong. By spending a whole year with these families, the researchers saw that the money problems of the poor are much more complicated than just having low incomes. In fact, the real challenge is uncertainty. The families' incomes rose and fell from season to season and even week to week, depending on the weather (for farmers) and whether they could find work and at what wages. It's crucial to remember that when we talk about living on $2 or $3 a day, that amount is an *average* over the year. In reality, incomes might be $5 one day and then $0.50 the next. There might be long periods with no income at all.

That finding helped to make sense of another surprising observation: Even the families living on less than $2 a day per person seldom consumed every penny of income as soon as it was earned. Instead, they saved money or used it to pay down loans. Even if families didn't have bank accounts, they took pains to hide savings at home or created informal "savings clubs" with their neighbors. On reflection, this makes perfect sense: When you live so close to the edge and don't know what next week will look like, having a financial cushion stashed away is critical.

Most fundamentally, the researchers saw that even the poorest households were managing their money actively. At any time, the families "had their eggs in several different baskets": A third of the families in Bangladesh used 10 or more different financial strategies over the year. In India, families started a new financial relationship, such as saving or borrowing, every two weeks on average. Rather than passively accepting their circumstances, most families patched together different solutions to try to improve their situations.

The problem was that those "solutions" often turned out to be unreliable, expensive, or imperfect. A neighbor might fail to pay back the money you lent her. A thief might steal savings kept in the house. A bank might charge high fees to take out a small loan.

The financial diaries project illuminated the hidden tragedy of poverty: The poor *want* to actively manage their money to guard against risks and hard times, but they lack reliable financial services to help them do so. In other words, they face a "poverty of tools," not just a poverty of incomes. Having better financial tools can begin to improve the lives of poor families, even if their incomes remain low.

Source: Daryl Collins, Jonathan Morduch, Orlanda Ruthven, and Stuart Rutherford, *Portfolios of the Poor: How the World's Poor Live on $2 a Day* (Princeton, NJ: Princeton University Press, 2009). Poverty data are from http://www.worldbank.org/en/topic/poverty/overview

Why are people poor?

LO 21.2 Understand why poverty persists.

Economists and policy-makers want to design policies that can attack poverty at its roots, rather than just deal with its consequences. To do so, we need to understand not only *who* is poor but also *why* they are poor.

Of course, the real world is an incredibly complex place and so the reasons for poverty are varied. Poverty can be a matter of bad circumstances, bad choices, bad luck, or a combination. But we know from observation that some common factors make falling into poverty more likely and climbing out of it harder.

Poverty from generation to generation

People who grow up in poor families are more likely to be poor themselves. One reason is straightforward: Poor parents tend to have limited money to bequeath to the next generation. Two other economic ideas—*human capital* and *social networks*—capture somewhat more subtle, but also critical, mechanisms.

Human capital is the set of skills, knowledge, experience, and talent that determine people's productivity as workers. Workers have different amounts and types of human capital that allow them

human capital
the set of skills, knowledge, experience, and talent that determine the productivity of workers

to be more or less productive at different tasks and therefore earn more or less money. You acquire human capital by getting a good education, being healthy, and gaining experience in jobs. You also benefit from watching and learning from your peers, your neighbors, and others around you.

You probably know (or know of) well-educated and successful professionals who came from humble backgrounds. But evidence shows that children in poor communities typically have reduced opportunities to acquire human capital, for many reasons. Think about all of the ways your skills and abilities are influenced by the environment in which you grew up. How good were the schools in your neighborhood? Did you have regular check-ups with a doctor? Was a family member able to help you with your homework? Were you actively encouraged to go to college? Can you afford to take unpaid internships to learn new skills rather than working during the summer?

As you can see, it is often difficult to tell cause from effect:

- Does low human capital cause poverty (because people with low human capital are less productive in jobs and therefore likely to earn less money)?
- Or does poverty cause low human capital (because growing up in a poor community can reduce access to education, health care, and informal learning opportunities)?

Likely, the causality runs both ways, creating a negative cycle of poverty and low human capital. To the extent that low human capital causes poverty, policies that break this cycle—such as improving schools, offering training in job skills, and providing health care—can help.

Family and community poverty may also pass from generation to generation through more subtle channels. Economic research shows that people at all income levels find jobs and other opportunities through their *social networks*. In this context, we don't mean social media networks like Facebook. Rather, we mean the real-world ways in which friends of your parents, neighbors, and others in your community can alert you to employment opportunities. The problem is that if the people around you are unemployed, or not employed in the kind of job you seek, how likely is it that they can help you find a job? If they don't have much money themselves, how can they help you finance a new business?

The Real Life box "Getting Out of the Neighborhood" describes a program that tried to help people break into new, higher-resource social networks by helping families move out of areas with high levels of poverty. The results are very interesting, and have strong implications for policy.

Real Life

Getting out of the neighborhood

Does growing up in public-housing projects limit the opportunities of those who live there? Public housing is intended to offer families a stable, affordable place to live. But might living in a community marked by high levels of poverty and unemployment in fact perpetuate poverty? Would residents of public housing be better off if they lived somewhere else?

To find out, economists teamed up with the U.S. Department of Housing and Urban Development on a program called Moving to Opportunity (MTO), which was implemented from 1994–1998. The program set up a lottery for housing benefits; residents of urban public housing in five U.S. cities were eligible to enter. Through the lottery, people were put into one of three groups:

- One group of people received a voucher that paid for a large part of rent and utilities in private housing; they had no restriction on where they could live.
- A second group received the same voucher, but residents were required to live in an area that had a poverty rate of less than 10 percent.
- A third group received no voucher, but residents were free to move or stay in public housing.

The design of the program allowed researchers to isolate the effects of moving to a new, less-poor neighborhood. They hypothesized that the new neighborhoods would offer better social networks for finding jobs, with cultures that would be more supportive of searching for and keeping jobs. They also expected that the new neighborhoods would pose fewer of the dangers and stresses that led to mental and physical health problems in public housing. Researchers expected increased income, employment, and health among people who moved into private housing in richer neighborhoods.

The short-term results, measured approximately two years after the vouchers had been handed out, didn't quite meet those lofty expectations. Adults who moved to better neighborhoods were not more likely to find jobs or earn more. On the plus side, however, people who moved with the help of the vouchers reported much better mental health. Overall, there was a 30 percent reduction in the risk of someone experiencing an episode of major depression in the short run. (This effect was larger than many of the most successful clinical treatments for depression.) As a result, the researchers theorized that on the whole, the change of zip code did not make adults who received the vouchers more likely to have a job, earn more income, or rely less on government assistance.

Why didn't the program work as expected for adults in the short run? One possibility is that social networks in the new neighborhoods didn't help people find jobs. While adults were not more likely to find jobs or earn more, even in the short run, their kids were far less likely to be delinquent or have behavior problems. Young women, in particular, became far more likely to graduate from high school.

The long-run results of this study are much rosier: Fifteen years later, economists Raj Chetty, Nathaniel Hendren, and Lawrence Katz examined the long-term differential effects of the MTO program on children and found substantial results. While the program had a slightly negative impact on adulthood outcomes for children who were over the age of 13, children who were younger than 13 when their families moved to a lower-poverty neighborhood saw improved outcomes in areas such as college attendance and income. The program significantly increased annual incomes for younger children by $1,624, but decreased incomes by $967 for older children (who were between the ages of 13–18 at the time of receiving the voucher), in comparison with those who didn't receive the voucher at all in the corresponding age groups.

Intuitively, this makes sense—younger children were able to make new friends, integrate into new social circles, and adopt new cultural attitudes more effectively than older children and adults. It could be that moving to a different environment at an older age, especially as an adolescent, had a disruptive effect on the individual's social networks and development. The longer the exposure to the new community, the better the results: College attendance rates and adult earnings both increased more for each year spent in the better-off neighborhood.

One of the major implications of these findings is that the MTO program should be targeted specifically to families with young children and should focus on helping them move to a lower-poverty neighborhood to facilitate better outcomes for their children.

Sources: http://www.huduser.org/Periodicals/CITYSCPE/VOL5NUM2/shroder.pdf; http://www.nber.org/mtopublic/481.pdf; http://www.nber.org/papers/w21156.pdf; http://users.nber.org/~kling/mto/mto_boston.pdf; Scott J. South, Dana L. Haynie, and Sunita Bose, "Student Mobility and School Dropout," *Social Science Research* 36, no. 1 (2007): 67–94.

Poverty creates poverty

You may have heard the saying, "the rich get richer and the poor get poorer." We've just described how difficulties in acquiring human capital or finding job opportunities might cause this to be true. But there can also be self-reinforcing mechanisms that make it hard for individuals to break out of poverty once they are already poor, regardless of family background. These mechanisms are called **poverty traps**, and they can help illuminate why the poor often stay poor.

Bad health is a straightforward example of a poverty trap. This trap is more relevant in very-low-income countries than it is in the United States. Suppose you live in a poor, rural area and you farm or work on other people's farms for your living. This is hard, physical work. For some reason—a bad harvest, low crop prices, illness, or injury—you may fall into poverty and not be

poverty trap
a self-reinforcing mechanism that causes the poor to stay poor

able to afford enough food to eat. Malnutrition makes your body weak and you are not able to do physical work as effectively. This in turn decreases your ability to earn income, which means you have less to eat, which makes you even weaker, and so on. The fact of being poor makes it hard to stay healthy and productive, and the resulting vicious cycle may be hard to escape.

There are also many poverty traps that affect people in rich countries. Suppose you lose your job, can't pay your rent, and suddenly become homeless. You want to apply for new jobs. What should you put down as your contact address? Where will you shower and change before interviews? This is the same sort of vicious cycle as malnutrition, although a nonphysical one: Not having a job to begin with actually makes it harder to find a job.

A different kind of poverty trap was presented in the beginning of this book. We discussed a case in which poor Bangladeshis with potentially profitable business opportunities were unable to borrow the money needed to take advantage of them. Banks would lend money only if the borrower could pledge a valuable asset as collateral (in case the investment turns out badly). The problem for poor borrowers is that they often lack the assets to pledge as collateral. So, even if they have great ideas, they can't get a loan to put their ideas into action. This poverty trap is called a **credit constraint**—the inability to get a loan even though a person expects to be able to repay the loan plus interest. Credit constraints are another way that poverty itself can make it harder to get ahead.

credit constraint
inability to get a loan even though a person expects to be able to repay the loan plus interest

Even in the United States, where the financial sector is much more developed, it can be difficult for people without collateral or with bad credit histories to get loans. Sometimes these potential borrowers are genuinely risky or have bad investment ideas. But even someone with a low-risk, profitable opportunity will have trouble getting a loan if he or she doesn't have the collateral or the credit history to back it up. As a result, credit constraints can limit the ability of talented but poor individuals to make profitable investments that will help them climb up the income ladder. Credit constraints are one reason why a lack of human capital isn't a simple problem to fix. A talented kid may not be able to borrow money to invest in education or internships, even if those opportunities would more than pay for themselves later in life in the form of better jobs and higher wages.

Poverty in the community

In some places in the world, there are opportunities to earn more money and live in greater comfort, even if they may be difficult to come by. In others, these opportunities may not exist, at least not for the majority of the population. What is it like to live in a society where a third or a half of the population is poor and most of the people you know struggle to find jobs?

Consider the difference, for instance, between having trouble paying your electric bill and living in a place where there is no electrical grid, even if you could afford it. Or what would it be like to search for a job in a place where very few formal jobs exist? What if you lived in a country where even if you had a good business idea, it takes two years and a fortune in bribes to get a business permit? This is the case in many developing countries around the world.

Even in wealthy countries, community-wide poverty creates problems beyond those faced by individuals. In these communities, transportation may be limited, jobs scarce, and schools below average. When most of the region is poor, it's hard for local governments to raise money through taxes; that makes it harder in turn for the region as a whole to invest in infrastructure, jobs, and schools. Long-term solutions to poverty must, then, involve ways to grow the economy and expand the range of opportunities available to the population.

✓CONCEPT CHECK

- ☐ What is the difference between an absolute and a relative poverty threshold? **[LO 21.1]**
- ☐ What is the international poverty line most commonly used, and why is it adjusted for purchasing power parity? **[LO 21.1]**
- ☐ What is a credit constraint, and how is it an example of a poverty trap? **[LO 21.2]**

Inequality

Poverty rates in the United States have changed little over the last few decades. However, income inequality has increased, mostly as a result of gains by the rich.

Does inequality matter? Some argue that overall economic growth is more important than the distribution of income. Those who hold this view note that if everyone is getting richer, the relative speed of these gains isn't as important. Others care about inequality for its own sake, believing that it is fundamentally unjust for some people to have so much when others have so little. The degree of inequality can be an important factor that signals or causes other things going on in the economy, such as the incentive people at the top have to work hard or the resources available to people at the bottom to invest in human capital.

In this section, we'll discuss how inequality can be measured and how it can relate to economic growth and stability. We'll also see some evidence of how unequal different countries actually are and how easy or difficult it is to go from being poor to rich or vice versa.

Measuring inequality

LO 21.3 Explain and interpret different methods of measuring income inequality.

Imagine that we could line up every adult in the United States in order of the amount of income they earn. We make their heights proportional to their incomes: People with average income are of average height, and the more money someone makes, the taller he or she is. Now, we ask them all to march down Main Street in that order, over the course of one hour. As bystanders watching this parade, what would we see?

The first marchers would be invisible, with their heads underground. These are people who own businesses or farms that are losing money. Then, we would see tiny people walking by, only inches high. These people earn very small amounts of money; they may be unemployed or on a small fixed income. As we pass the half-hour mark, halfway through the parade, the people going by are still only waist-high. These marchers in the middle represent minimum-wage workers, retail sales people, unskilled clerical workers, and the like. Even as skilled tradespeople and office workers start to stroll by, they are still below average size. Finally, at about 40 minutes, the people going by are of average adult height. In the parade's last 10 minutes, we start to see giants, more than 10 feet tall. These are specialist doctors, lawyers, scientists, and so on. Then, corporate executives go by, hundreds of feet tall. Next come movie stars and professional athletes, thousands of feet tall. In the last seconds of the parade, some of the richest people in the country go by (hello, Mark Zuckerberg, Bill Gates, and Warren Buffett), with their heads towering several *miles* above the ground.

This parade—first imagined by economist Jan Pen—is a visual representation of the income distribution in the United States.[8] It uses the marchers' heights as an analogy that allows us to visualize the relative income of people throughout the population. The parade image emphasizes some notable features of the income distribution: People of average height and income don't show up until well after halfway through the parade. The rich are *really* rich, compared not only with the poorest but even with highly paid professionals.

However visually striking the parade analogy may be, economists need more precise ways of summarizing the income distribution. The simplest method divides those marchers into five equally sized groups. We call each group a *quintile,* or 20 percent of the population. In a country of just over 300 million people, the approximate population of the United States, the first quintile is the 60 million poorest people, the second is the next 60 million, and so on, until the fifth quintile is the 60 million richest people.

We can use our quintiles to organize different types of statistics that describe income inequality. Table 21-3 shows two ways of looking at income inequality in the United States:

- First, we could find the *average income* within each quintile (column 2).

Quintile	Average pre-tax income ($)	Share of pre-tax income (%)
Lowest 20 percent	16,110	3.6
Second 20 percent	40,681	9.2
Third 20 percent	66,899	15.1
Fourth 20 percent	103,115	23.2
Highest 20 percent	217,021	48.9
Top 1 percent	1,260,508	21.2

- Second, we could add up everyone's income and find out what percentage of income earned in the whole country is earned by people within each quintile (column 3). If income were distributed completely equally—that is, if every person in the country made the same amount of money—each quintile representing 20 percent of the population would also earn 20 percent of the income.

Income is not distributed perfectly equally anywhere in the world, though. Thus, we always see that the top quintiles earn a disproportionately high share of income (more than 20 percent) and the lower quintiles earn a disproportionately low share (less than 20 percent). In the United States, the top 20 percent earns nearly 50 percent of total income, while the poorest 20 percent earns only 3.6 percent of total income.

If we want to compare income inequality across countries, income quintiles are less useful. Just as we need absolute and relative measures of poverty, we need measures of income inequality that allow us to compare the United States to other countries, like India. Households in India earn much less money in an absolute sense than households in the United States, so it doesn't make sense to compare the income quintiles in India to the U.S. income quintiles. Two measures of income inequality that do allow cross-country comparisons are the *Lorenz curve* and the *Gini coefficient*.

We can summarize income inequality visually, using a graph called the **Lorenz curve**. The Lorenz curve maps the percentage of the population against the cumulative percentage of income earned by those people. It shows the cumulative percentage of the population on the *y*-axis and the cumulative percentage of income those people earn on the *x*-axis.

The best way to understand the Lorenz curve is to see that if every person earned the exact same amount, the curve would be a straight, diagonal line with a slope of 1, as shown in panel A of Figure 21-3. That is, 20 percent of the population would earn 20 percent of the income, and 73 percent of the population would earn 73 percent of the income, and so on. However, if income is unequally distributed, the Lorenz curve will be bowed out in a U-shape: The poorest 1 percent of people will earn less than 1 percent of income, and the richest 1 percent will earn more than 1 percent of the income, as shown in panel B.

The Lorenz curve allows us to calculate an even more concise inequality metric—the **Gini coefficient**. The Gini coefficient describes inequality by putting a single number on the shape of the Lorenz curve. Specifically, the Gini coefficient is equal to the area between the Lorenz curve and the line of perfect equality (area A in Figure 21-4) divided by the total area under the line of perfect equality (area A plus area B in the figure). This calculation gives us a single number to describe income inequality.

Think about the two possible Gini coefficient extremes:

- If everyone earned the same amount and the income distribution were perfectly equal, the Gini coefficient would be zero: The Lorenz curve would *be* the line of perfect equality, and so the area between them would be 0.

- If one person earned all of the income and no one else earned anything, the Gini coefficient would be 1.

Lorenz curve
a graphic representation of income distribution that maps percentage of the population against cumulative percentage of income earned by those people

Gini coefficient
a single-number measure of income inequality; ranges from 0 to 1, with higher numbers meaning greater inequality

FIGURE 21-3

The Lorenz curve

(A) Perfectly equal income distribution

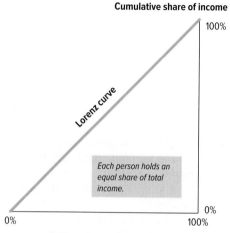

Cumulative share of income

100%

Lorenz curve

Each person holds an equal share of total income.

0%

0%   100%

Cumulative share of people

With a perfectly equal income distribution, each extra 1 percent of the population earns another 1 percent of income. In that case, the Lorenz curve forms at a 45-degree angle.

(B) Unequal income distribution

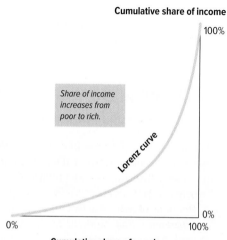

Cumulative share of income

100%

Share of income increases from poor to rich.

Lorenz curve

0%

0%   100%

Cumulative share of people

When income is not distributed equally, each extra percent of poorer segments of the population earn less than 1 percent of the total income. Among the richer part of the population, each extra 1 percent of the population adds more than 1 percent of their income. This distribution gives the Lorenz curve a concave shape.

FIGURE 21-4

The Gini coefficient

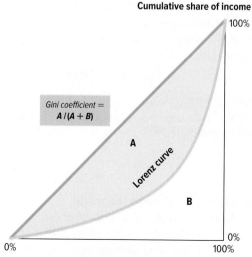

Cumulative share of income

100%

Gini coefficient = *A /(A + B)*

A

Lorenz curve

B

0%

0%   100%

Cumulative share of people

The Gini coefficient is calculated by measuring the area between the line of perfect equality and the Lorenz curve. This is represented by $A/(A + B)$. The greater the inequality, the deeper the U-shape in the Lorenz curve. The greater the area of A, the higher the Gini coefficient.

In reality, the distribution is always somewhere between these extremes. The closer the Gini coefficient is to 1, the more unequal the income distribution.

Now that we have a better sense of what inequality means and how to measure it, we can go back to the initial question: Does inequality matter? The popular media regularly present us with stories about the unbelievably large incomes of professional athletes, famous entertainers, and high-profile businesspeople, but most of the super-wealthy are people out of the public eye. This group has accrued massive wealth in the past few decades. Is that the sign of a strong economy or a sign of problems? To understand more, see the What Do You Think? box "The super-wealthy."

What Do You Think?
The super-wealthy

When people reap the rewards of their efforts, they are more likely to work hard and innovate. But when people are rewarded for their efforts, we typically end up with some inequality. From this angle, inequality is a by-product of a well-functioning market system, a system that ought to help everyone. Someone may get very rich by building a new website that millions use, but the millions of users also benefit by gaining access to the new website.

Guaranteeing all workers and entrepreneurs identical incomes would diminish incentives to work hard, innovate, and take risks. For example, without the chance to earn performance bonuses, engineers might not design the best new mobile app. Without the chance to earn billions of dollars, companies might not pursue the latest technologies or medical breakthroughs.

But can there ever be too much inequality? Wealth inequality is greater today than it has been for nearly a century. Historical data show that the increase in wealth inequality in the United States is almost entirely due to the growing fortunes of the top 0.1 percent of wealthiest people. In 2012, this group included a mere 160,000 individuals and families with net wealth over $20 million. That's not just the top 1 percent—*it's the top 10 percent of the top 1 percent.* This super-wealthy sliver now holds close to a quarter of all wealth in the United States. Almost half of the entire increase in U.S. wealth between 1986 and 2012 went to the top 0.1 percent alone.

WHAT DO YOU THINK?

1. Should these economic divides be embraced as part of the normal and desirable working of the economy? After all, the wealth has been accrued legally.

2. Can there be a level of inequality that is so high that citizens should be concerned? If so, are the most pressing concerns political, social, or economic?

3. What extra pieces of evidence would give a more informed view?

Source: Emmanuel Saez and Gabriel Zucman, "Wealth Inequality in the United States Since 1913: Evidence from Capitalized Income Tax Data," *Quarterly Journal of Economics* 131, no. 2 (2016,): 519–578, http://gabriel-zucman.eu/files/SaezZucman2016QJE.pdf.

Inequality in the United States and around the world

Now that we have some tools for measuring inequality, what can we say about how income distribution differs between countries and over time? Lorenz curves and Gini coefficients can be particularly helpful. For visualizing how inequality changes over time for a particular country, or how countries around the world differ, we use the Lorenz curve. For quantifying inequality differences, we use the Gini coefficient.

Most countries in the world have Gini coefficients ranging from 0.25 to 0.60. As you can see in Figure 21-5, there are significant geographic clusters. Most of Europe has relatively low inequality. Much of Latin America and southern Africa has relatively high inequality.

FIGURE 21-5

Gini coefficients around the world   The Gini coefficient is one way to measure inequality. Countries in Western Europe generally have low Gini coefficients and less income inequality. Countries in South America and southern Africa have much higher Gini coefficients.

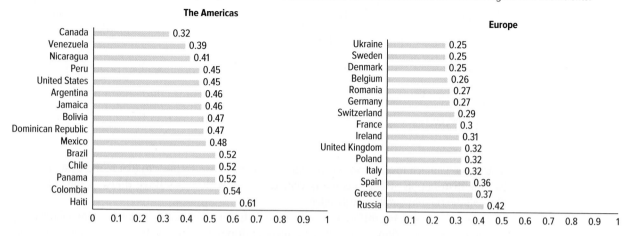

Source: Data gathered from the *CIA World Factbook*, https://www.cia.gov/library/publications/the-world-factbook/rankorder/2172rank.html.

The global pattern of inequality has been changing in recent decades:

- Inequality *between* countries, in terms of differences in their average national incomes, has been decreasing. Economic growth has lifted billions of people out of poverty, especially in China and India. Nonetheless, the poorest 5 percent of people in the United States are still richer on average than 70 percent of the rest of the world.

- Inequality *within* countries has largely been on the rise. This is true for both rich countries and poor ones, for countries with large amounts of growth and those that are barely growing at all.

For example, Gini coefficients in China have risen significantly since the 1980s as the country has experienced strong economic growth. In India and other Asian countries, though, which have experienced similar amounts of growth, income inequality has not changed much at all: Gini coefficients are essentially the same as they were three decades ago.

To paint a more specific picture of inequality within a sample of countries, Table 21-4 shows income distribution, measured in quintiles, in four countries. Here we can see how the United States compares with Sweden (a rich European country), Uganda (a poor African country), and Brazil (a middle-income Latin American country). Uganda's income *distribution* is the one the most similar to the United States, although, of course, the total *amount* of income being

TABLE 21-4

Income distribution comparison, four countries

The amount of income held by different levels of the population in various countries is one way to measure inequality. Among the countries in this table, Sweden is the most equal; Brazil is the most unequal.

Sources: World Bank WDI, Distribution of income or consumption: http://wdi.worldbank.org/table/2.9#. Figures are from the latest available data (U.S. 2013, Sweden 2012, Uganda 2012, and Brazil 2013).

	% of total national income			
	United States	**Sweden**	**Uganda**	**Brazil**
Top quintile	46.4	36.2	49.4	57.4
Fourth quintile	22.7	23.0	20.4	19.3
Middle quintile	15.4	17.8	14.0	12.4
Second quintile	10.3	14.3	10.1	7.6
Bottom quintile	5.1	8.7	6.1	3.3

distributed is much lower. *Average income* in Sweden is much closer to that in the United States. But the distribution of that income is very different, with nearly three times as much held by those in the bottom quintile in Sweden.

What causes such big differences in income distribution between countries? One factor is the extent to which governments redistribute income through the public budget. In many European countries, for instance, taxes on the rich are higher than in the United States; public services and income support to the poor are also higher. The result is that the after-tax income distribution is more equal than the income distribution before taxes were paid and public services provided.

Economists also attribute a large part of the increase in inequality within countries like the United States to something called *skill-biased technical change*. That's a mouthful, but what it means is straightforward: Over the last 50 years, the benefits of economic growth have increasingly been going to highly skilled workers with a lot of education. Then, add this technical change to increased trade between countries (which allows more manual and rote jobs to be done overseas in low-wage countries) and what do you get? People in rich countries are specializing more and more in high-tech, high-skill, high-education work, and they reap huge benefits. Those who are not in a position to take advantage of high-tech, high-skill, high-education work lose out, relatively speaking.

Inequality versus mobility

LO 21.4 Describe how income mobility differs from income equality.

How we feel about income inequality is often tied closely to assumptions about the equality of opportunity. Many people feel that if everyone has a fair chance to get ahead, then the fact that some people do get ahead and some don't, matters less.

One way to consider the relationship between inequality and opportunities is to look at **income mobility**—the ability to improve one's economic circumstances over time. Measuring income mobility tells us how likely a person is to end up rich if he or she starts out poor, or vice versa.

A standard way to measure mobility is to compare people's income to their parents' income. The idea is that if opportunities are truly equal, it should not matter much if your parents are rich or poor. Just as with poverty, we can measure income mobility in both absolute and relative terms:

income mobility
the ability to improve one's economic circumstances over time

- In *absolute* terms, we can look at whether a person's income is higher than her parents'.
- In *relative* terms, we can look at whether a person's income places her higher up in the income distribution than her parents.

Both measures are important. The United States has had high absolute mobility in the last century. This is not surprising considering it has had relatively high economic growth. Until recently, every generation has, on average, earned more and lived longer than their parents.

FIGURE 21-6

Income mobility in rich countries   This mobility measure shows the amount of intergenerational income elasticity (the relationship between parents' and children's incomes) for countries relative to the United States. Canada is, for example, 2.5 times more mobile than the United States. On the whole, Scandinavian countries and Canada have a high level of economic mobility; the United States and United Kingdom do not.

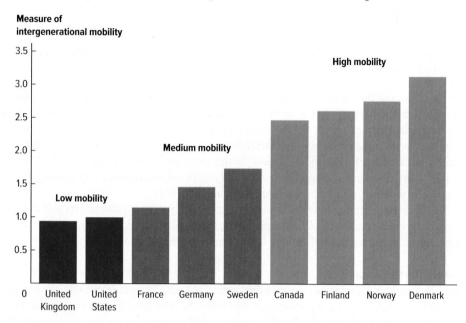

Sources: http://www.pewtrusts.org/~/media/legacy/uploadedfiles/wwwpewtrustsorg/reports/economic_mobility/emproadmappdf.pdf; http://www.brookings.edu/~/media/research/files/reports/2008/2/economic-mobility-sawhill/02_economic_mobility_sawhill_ch3.pdf.

In relative terms, however, the United States has much less income mobility. Almost half of those whose fathers were in the lowest income bracket end up in the lowest bracket themselves. Fewer than 1 in 10 makes the "rags to riches" jump to the highest quintile. (In contrast, "perfect" income mobility would imply that there is a 20 percent chance of ending up in each income quintile, regardless of one's parents' income.)

On the other end of the income distribution, it takes an average of six generations for the benefits of being born into a wealthy family to disappear. In other words, we have to go back six generations before your ancestors' place in the income distribution ceases to have any predictive power for what your own will be. In contrast, in Norway it takes only three generations. Figure 21-6 shows how relative mobility in the United States stacks up against that for a selection of other wealthy countries.

✓ CONCEPT CHECK

☐ What variables are on the *x*- and *y*-axes when we graph the Lorenz curve? **[LO 21.3]**

☐ What does it mean if a country's Gini coefficient is 0? What does it mean if the Gini coefficient is 1? **[LO 21.3]**

☐ What is income mobility? **[LO 21.4]**

Policies to Reduce Poverty and Inequality

Most governments, in both rich and poor countries, aim to limit poverty and inequality to some extent. Yet views differ about how to do so. It's also a difficult and controversial area of policymaking. Some people feel that taking from the rich to give to the poor is justice. Others feel it's theft. Some focus on equalizing opportunities rather than outcomes. Others focus on creating a safety net for people who lose their jobs or get sick. Even when people agree on policy goals, they may disagree about how to design the best policies to accomplish those goals. In this section, we'll discuss both motivations and design issues surrounding poverty-fighting policies.

Public policy goals

LO 21.5 Identify the public policies that are used to reduce poverty and inequality and understand their goals.

Before we talk about the "how" of policy-making, we have to talk about what policy-makers are trying to accomplish. Why might it be desirable to reduce poverty or inequality? Some people cite humanitarian reasons—concern for others suffering from hunger or homelessness. Some focus on the harm to the economy and social disadvantages that may result when much of the population lacks access to quality education, health care, and basic services like banking. Still others take a strictly pragmatic approach: A country with too much poverty or glaring inequalities is prone to violence, political unrest, or economic instability.

We can distinguish among three different types of public policy approaches related to poverty and inequality: economic development, safety nets, and redistribution. Knowing which goals are being pursued has important implications for designing public policies.

Economic development

Often, policy-makers look for investments that will spur future economic growth. We can group these policies under the category *economic development:* The goal is not only the immediate effect of the policy on poverty but also the growth it will produce for the entire economy. Common examples include public investments in education, job training, and infrastructure. These policies help reduce poverty indirectly, through increased economic growth and opportunities in the future.

Many of these policies serve dual goals—providing services in the short run and contributing to long-run growth. For instance:

- Education is considered an important good in itself. Most people want their children to have access to education for its own sake. However, from the perspective of the government, it is also a tool for economic development: Better-educated children grow up to be more productive workers who contribute to the economy and who are less likely to be poor and unemployed.

- Similarly, a plan to revitalize the downtown area of a struggling city may have dual goals: It may make living there more pleasant in the short run. The hope is also that it will attract businesses and new residents, improving the city's economy and reducing poverty in the long run.

Safety nets

Earlier in the chapter, we looked at the difference between transient and chronic poverty. Most people go through hard times at some point in their lives—an illness, a death in the family, the loss of a job, and so on. For those living close to the edge of poverty, one bad event can be enough to tip the scales.

social insurance
government programs under which people pay into a common pool and are eligible to draw on benefits under certain circumstances

Many policies are designed to protect against the temporary hard times that can lead to transient poverty. We can broadly categorize these as **social insurance** programs. Under these programs, people pay into a common pool and are in turn eligible to draw on benefits under certain circumstances. Important examples in the United States include unemployment insurance, Social Security, and Medicare.

Such programs are referred to as "social insurance" because, like private insurance programs, they pool risks across a large population. (For a more general discussion of insurance, turn back to Chapter 11, "Time and Uncertainty.") Unemployment insurance, for example, pools risk across the labor force. Since a large majority of people in the labor force have a job and pay taxes, the system is able to provide benefits for the minority who lose their jobs. The same is true for Social Security and Medicare, but the risks in these programs are spread across time. In both programs, benefits are provided by younger workers, who pay into the system under the promise that they'll get benefits when they retire.

One difference from private insurance programs is that social insurance programs usually serve everyone who meets baseline eligibility requirements. For instance, people who paid payroll taxes during their working years can draw on Social Security and Medicare when they retire or suffer a disability; those who live longer or have higher health care costs don't have to pay higher premiums in order to receive benefits.

Redistribution

Some policies explicitly seek to redistribute resources with the aim of alleviating the effects of poverty or income inequality. For instance:

- Homeless shelters and food banks don't have much to do with long-run economic development. Instead, they are meant to provide comfort and security to people who face an immediate lack of food and shelter.
- Similarly, government-subsidized housing, food stamps, Medicaid (health insurance for low-income households), and many other programs offer resources to the poor over the long term.

Most people see the primary purpose of such programs as using resources from society's wealthier members to ensure a basic minimum standard of living for its poorer members.

The welfare state

The term "welfare state" describes the idea that government has a responsibility to promote the economic well-being of its citizens. The basics of the welfare state in the United States started as part of the New Deal legislation that responded to the Great Depression in the 1930s. The government rolled out a variety of programs, including Social Security and the Civilian Conservation Corps, intended to help the growing number of poor and unemployed workers.

From those beginnings, the United States created a variety of programs to help guarantee a minimum standard of living for all. These programs range from food stamps that help the poor buy food to Head Start, an early-childhood education program. In this section, we discuss some of the more important economic welfare policies.

Progressive taxation

Governments can address poverty and inequality through both how public money is spent and how people are taxed. The design of the U.S. federal income tax system is *progressive*—the government charges lower tax rates to those with lower incomes. This design has the effect of reducing income inequality: Those with high income tend to pay a larger proportion of their income as taxes than those with low income. The result is that the after-tax gap between rich and poor is smaller than the pre-tax gap. As discussed in Chapter 20, "Taxation and the Public Budget," other types of taxation—such as sales and payroll taxes—can be *regressive*. The overall burden of federal taxation in the United States, though, is progressive.

One tax policy, the Earned Income Tax Credit (EITC), has a particularly large effect on the poor. The EITC is exactly what it sounds like: Those with low income are eligible for a tax credit, proportional to the amount of income they earn and the size of their families. The more the family earns, the higher the credit, which is then subtracted from the amount of federal tax owed. For those with very low incomes, the credit may be larger than the amount owed in taxes, in which case the balance is paid to the family as a tax "refund." The EITC is a way to encourage work while still providing income support to families with very low income.

Income support

Government programs that give money to the poor are commonly referred to as "welfare." In fact, there is no single program in the United States called "welfare." Rather, the term *welfare* is used to refer broadly to the various income-support programs for the poor run by each state. (Note that it differs from the term *welfare effects* that we first used in the context of deadweight loss calculations in Chapter 6, "Government Intervention.")

In 1996, Congress passed a law that greatly changed the role of the federal government in providing welfare. Until then, the federal government administered a program called Aid to Families with Dependent Children (AFDC). As the name suggests, this program gave money to poor households with children. To be eligible, the children had to be "deprived of parental support" in some way, usually by having a single or divorced parent. Each state set the level of income at which families of different sizes were eligible, as well as the amount of benefits received. Anyone who met the eligibility criteria was entitled to benefits. Under the program, each state received unlimited reimbursement from the federal government to cover the cost.

We can think of AFDC as an "unconditional" cash-transfer program; it provided financial support to any eligible person, without any restrictions on how the money could be used. In contrast, the program that replaced AFDC in 1996—called Temporary Assistance to Needy Families (TANF)—is a **conditional cash-transfer** program. Under this program, financial support is given only to people who engage in certain actions. The exact requirements vary from state to state. Generally, welfare recipients

conditional cash transfer
a program in which financial support is given only to people who engage in certain actions

- are eligible for benefits for a maximum of five years,
- must start working within two years of joining the program, and
- must work a minimum number of hours per week.

These conditions have shifted the nature of welfare away from a redistribution program toward a social insurance program. They are designed to help people through temporary hard times rather than provide long-term income support.

Conditional cash-transfer programs are an increasingly popular antipoverty strategy, both inside and outside the United States. Often, the conditions attached to financial transfers require recipients to invest in health and education for their children. Such conditional cash-transfer programs combine redistributive goals with economic-development goals.

In-kind transfers

in-kind transfer
a program that provides specific goods or services, rather than cash, directly to needy recipients

In contrast to cash-transfer programs, many government programs involve **in-kind transfers**. These programs provide goods or services, rather than cash, directly to needy individuals or households. In the United States, common in-kind transfers include public housing, free school lunches, and the medical treatment benefits provided by Medicaid. Often, in-kind transfers take the form of vouchers that are redeemable only for certain items. For example, the Supplemental Nutrition Assistance Program (SNAP, formerly known as the Food Stamp Program) provides vouchers that can be used to purchase only approved food items.

In-kind transfer programs are, by design, more restrictive than cash-transfer programs. When a poor household receives income support, it can use the money to buy whatever goods and services it wishes. When that same household receives an in-kind transfer, the choice of how to spend the money has already been made. If we believe that people make considered choices to maximize their own well-being, then in-kind transfers are inefficient. After all, cash provides recipients with the flexibility to choose the goods that will do them the most good. Why might a government prefer in-kind transfers? One reason is that it prevents recipients from spending cash on luxury items or on socially disapproved goods such as alcohol or drugs.

Social insurance

Social-insurance programs are designed to help people weather temporary bad periods. They also help people survive old age, disability, or other long-term conditions. As we noted above, in these programs, the government plays a role similar to that of a private insurance company: It collects contributions from working people in a common pool, defines the circumstances under which people are eligible to draw benefits, and administers and monitors the allocation of those benefits.

In the United States, the largest social insurance programs are

- *Social Security,* which provides pensions to retired and disabled people.
- *Medicare,* which provides medical insurance to retired and disabled people.
- *Unemployment insurance,* which gives short-term income support to the unemployed.

Unemployment benefits are examples of social insurance in a straightforward sense. If you lose your job or have an injury or medical condition that prevents you from working, the government will step in to provide a small stipend to help cover everyday living expenses.

Retirement benefits are less like private insurance (which is generally used to protect against unexpected events) and more like a collective saving program. Nevertheless, because there is an uncertainty about the circumstances the elderly face—when they will retire, what medical problems they will face, how high the cost of living will be, and how long they will need to live on retirement income—retirement benefits are widely seen as an example of social insurance. They play an important role in reducing poverty among the elderly, as we showed earlier in the chapter.

Trade-offs between equity and efficiency

LO 21.6 Explain the trade-off between equity and efficiency in poverty-reduction policy.

All of the programs we just discussed are paid for by taxes. This is true for programs that target everyone, such as Social Security and public schools, and for programs that target the poor, such Medicaid and food stamps. Of course, the amount of money required for each program can vary dramatically. Figure 21-7 shows the annual spending on several different types of welfare programs in the United States. As we saw in Chapter 20, "Taxation and the Public Budget," higher

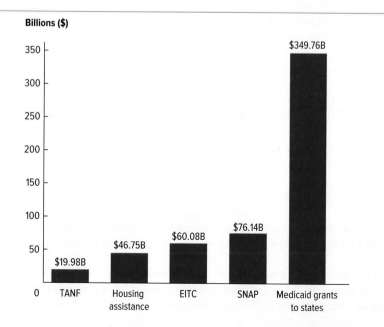

Billions ($)

FIGURE 21-7

Federal expenditure on welfare programs

This figure shows federal expenditure on large welfare programs in the United States in 2015.

Source: Office of Budget and Management, Historical Tables, Table 11.3, https://www.whitehouse.gov/omb/budget/historicals.

taxes often mean larger deadweight loss. Pursuing equity—that is, greater income equality—thus means accepting some inefficiency due to increased taxation.

means-tested
the characteristic of a program that defines eligibility for benefits based on recipients' income

While all taxes typically create some distortions, welfare programs that are *means-tested* can be problematic when not designed carefully. **Means-tested** programs define eligibility for benefits based on recipients' income. The goal of means-testing is to target resources toward those who need them the most. Often, means-testing is more complex than a simple eligible/not-eligible distinction. For instance, under the EITC described earlier, the size of the credit at first increases with earned income at very low income levels; it then begins to decrease as income rises past the poverty line. The thinking is that a family with income *just* under the poverty threshold requires less support to access basic goods and services than a family very far below the line.

But means-testing can create perverse incentives. Imagine a simple means-test: If your income is under the poverty line, you are eligible for a cash transfer of $5,000 per year; if your income is over the poverty line, you are not. Now imagine you are working part time and living just under the poverty line. Your boss offers you the opportunity to pick up an extra five hours of work each week. Here's the choice you face:

- If you accept the added hours, your income will increase by $3,000 over the course of the year.
- That $3,000 more in pay will push you over the poverty line.
- As a result, you will lose your government transfer of $5,000. On net, you will end up $2,000 poorer.

How would you respond to this situation? Would you accept the extra hours? Unless there is some sort of extra benefit we're not considering (gaining experience or favor with your boss that will improve your job opportunities down the road, for example), most people would say no to working longer hours for lower income.

It is possible to fix this sort of perverse incentive by designing more nuanced means-tests. For instance, a program could phase out benefits as income increases (like the EITC) rather than use a strict cutoff. That way, there will be no point at which a large amount of benefits are lost from a small increase in income. In general, the more narrowly targeted support is to those with low income, the greater the potential inefficiency caused. These examples show why economists often see a trade-off between equity and efficiency in poverty policy.

This is not to say that poverty policy is always inefficient. Some policies, like those that alleviate credit constraints or those that promote equal opportunities, can improve both equity and efficiency. In this case, a market failure is being solved, so there is no trade-off. But understanding the potential for trade-offs and unintended consequences is an important consideration when designing poverty policy.

✓CONCEPT CHECK

- ☐ What is social insurance? **[LO 21.5]**
- ☐ What's the difference between a conditional and an unconditional cash-transfer program? **[LO 21.5]**
- ☐ What is means-testing? **[LO 21.6]**

Discrimination

LO 21.7 Explain why economists differentiate between correlation and causation when studying discrimination and why markets do not always eliminate discrimination.

You may be wondering why we discuss discrimination in this chapter. In many ways it's a separate topic from poverty and income inequality. Not everyone who is poor is discriminated against, and not everyone who is discriminated against is poor. We chose to discuss these topics in the same chapter because, historically, they have often gone hand in hand. It's important to understand when discrimination, poverty, and inequality are connected; when they are not; and how to tell the difference.

Economists think about **discrimination** as the practice of making choices using generalizations based on observable characteristics like race, gender, or age. But people can also discriminate based on ethnic origin, appearance, sexual orientation, what type of music you listen to, or any other observable characteristic that allows them to generalize about what type of person you might be. In Chapter 10, "Information," we said that discrimination can be a useful tool for making decisions when we don't have access to full information. In common language, however, when people say "discrimination," they usually mean "unfair or illegal discrimination."

Economists recognize that *statistical discrimination*—making a choice based on the difference in average characteristics between two groups—can sometimes be rational. For instance, imagine that an employer has to make a quick decision on which of two candidates to employ, a younger candidate versus an older one. She decides to hire the younger one as she believes that the younger candidate would be healthier and miss work less frequently. When forced to make a decision without full information, the employer is making a *rational guess* based on her knowledge of the average differences between middle-aged people and young people. It's an understandable strategy if she doesn't have good information about the health of the two candidates as individuals, but that doesn't make it fair or efficient for society. (In fact, making a hiring decision based on a worker's age or health is oftentimes illegal.)

Society loses when talented individuals who face discrimination are discouraged from acquiring the skills, education, and positions that they otherwise might get. In short, statistical discrimination can be rational for an individual employer, but that doesn't necessarily make it right, socially efficient, or even legal.

discrimination
making choices by using generalizations based on people's observable characteristics like race, gender, and age

Measuring discrimination in the labor market

There's little doubt that discrimination has played a major role in U.S. history. Does it still matter today? It's surprisingly hard to say how big an effect discrimination now has on people's economic opportunities and success.

We can start to answer this question by looking at the outcomes achieved by people in different demographic groups. Table 21-5 shows that average income for adults still varies widely across gender and racial groups. It's possible that these differences are due to discrimination in the labor market, but there are also plenty of other possible explanations. For instance, historically more men have had college degrees than women (though by 2015 women had caught up to men).[9] To the extent that being more educated is a signal or a cause of higher productivity as a worker, this could explain higher male wages. Similarly, women are more likely than men to choose to leave the labor force when they have children, and therefore have less work experience on average.

Group	Male ($)	Female ($)
Asian	40,901	25,391
White	37,574	22,479
All	36,302	22,240
Black	26,569	20,966
Hispanic	26,675	17,585

TABLE 21-5

Income by race and gender in the United States

Median personal income distribution varies by race and gender in the United States.

Source: *U.S. Census Bureau*, 2014 data, Table P2: Race and Hispanic Origin of People by Median Income and Sex, https://www.census.gov/data/tables/time-series/demo/income-poverty/historical-income-people.html,

We should be careful about confusing *correlation* with *causation*. In this case, income is *correlated* with race and gender. That doesn't necessarily mean that discrimination based on race and gender is *causing* the difference in wages. To draw on a concept from all the way back in Chapter 1, "Economics and Life," it's possible that *omitted variables* are causing the correlation. Other factors that are related to both earnings and race or gender but that we are not observing could include education, work experience, and choice of occupation.

It's also important to remember that we don't know what might be causing differences in those other factors. Suppose that a large part of the difference in wages between men and women can be explained by differences in occupational choice. For instance, men are more likely to be doctors and women are more likely to be nurses.[10] Since doctors earn more on average than nurses, the gender difference in occupational choices contributes to the difference in earnings between men and women. This doesn't tell us *why* women are more likely to be nurses—maybe it's a response to social pressures, or a need for flexibility in work hours, or maybe it has to do with differences in how girls and boys are brought up. These explanations may also be partly a function of a kind of discrimination.

To read about an innovative way researchers tested one of the factors that could be causing a discrepancy in wages in the labor market, read the Real Life box "Are Emily and Greg more employable than Lakisha and Jamal?"

Real Life

Are Emily and Greg more employable than Lakisha and Jamal?

Many companies go out of their way to advertise their support for diversity in the workplace or to note they are an "equal opportunity employer." Title VII of the Civil Rights Act of 1964 made it unlawful to discriminate on the basis of race, color, religion, gender, or national origin when hiring employees. Yet in spite of the good intentions of many companies and legal prohibitions against racial discrimination in the workplace, people of different races still have very different rates of employment and levels of earnings. How much of this, if any, is due to lingering discrimination by employers?

To answer this question, economists Marianne Bertrand and Sendhil Mullainathan conducted a study to test for racial discrimination in the job-application process. They created resumes for fictitious applicants and sent the resumes in response to help-wanted ads. Some resumes represented a fake applicant with a "white-sounding" name, such as Emily Walsh or Greg Baker. Others were given traditionally "black-sounding" names like Lakisha Washington or Jamal Jones. Aside from the difference in names, the actual qualifications and job experience were the same on average across "white" and "black" resumes.

The researchers found that "white" names—with otherwise-identical qualifications—were 50 percent more likely to receive callbacks in response to a job application. On average, Emily and Greg had to send out 10 resumes in order to receive a response from an employer. Lakisha and Jamal had to send out 15.

Furthermore, resumes with "black" names got less benefit from increased qualifications. An "Emily" resume with more education or job experience got 27 percent more callbacks than an "Emily" with a lower-quality resume. In contrast, resumes with "black" names and higher qualifications got only 8 percent more callbacks than those with lower qualifications. In other words, applicants with "black-sounding" names received fewer rewards in their job search for the same increase in accomplishments.

From the perspective of real young people of different races, this gap presents very different incentives to invest time and money in education and skill-building.

Sources: http://www.eeoc.gov/laws/statutes/titlevii.cfm; Title VII of the 1964 Civil Rights Act; http://www2.econ.iastate.edu/classes/econ321/orazem/bertrand_emily.pdf.

Do free markets reduce discrimination?

How does the idea of discrimination fit into a model of efficient, well-functioning markets? Under some conditions, markets may help to eliminate discrimination. For instance, imagine a shop owner who has a unique prejudice against people over six feet tall. He refuses to hire tall employees or to serve tall customers. Since no one else in the market has this strange bias against tall people, the shop owner's competitors will take advantage of his discrimination: They will hire good workers who happen to be tall and will get business from the tall customers he refuses to serve. If the market is competitive, the discriminatory shop owner will get pushed out of the market; his competitors will benefit from his inefficient choices.

Under other circumstances, however, discrimination can be consistent with an efficient market. For much of the twentieth century, for instance, shopkeepers who discriminated against black customers were the norm rather than the exception. As long as their competitors and their white customers agreed with and supported this discrimination, it was unfortunately often in their interest to maintain it. For instance, a shopkeeper in the 1940s who allowed black people to sit at the same counter as white people risked losing business from prejudiced white customers. In situations where businesses discriminate in response to the preferences of consumers, discrimination is consistent with efficient markets—which, of course, doesn't make it morally right or acceptable.

Long-term effects of discrimination

Even though the passage of the Civil Rights Act in 1964 made many forms of discrimination illegal, it couldn't undo the effects of discrimination that took place in earlier decades. Discrimination can have long-lasting effects on people and markets, even after the active discrimination itself ends.

We noted earlier that differences in educational attainment explain part of the difference in earnings between racial groups. We have to ask ourselves: Why do people of different races have more or less education on average? Although there are many complicated social, cultural, and economic reasons, some part of it is certainly the lingering result of discrimination decades ago.

On the most basic level, a black person who was born in the United States in the 1940s probably completed most of his or her education in segregated schools. But the lingering effects of historical discrimination can affect new generations, even if they didn't grow up under discriminatory policies. One important example is segregated communities. Earlier in the chapter, we discussed the idea that people's chances in life are affected by the human capital of those around them. Imagine that, at one time, people of a certain race, national origin, or religion experienced discrimination that made it harder for them to get a good education or acquire job experience or productive skills. Even after that active discrimination ends, imagine that they still tend to cluster together in neighborhoods. The kids who grow up in these neighborhoods are surrounded by adults who have low education or job experience, affecting the development of the kids' human capital.

Correcting such lingering effects of discrimination is one reason often put forward for "affirmative action" programs that ensure people of other races gain access in college admissions or hiring decisions, as described in the What Do You Think? box "Affirmative action in college admissions."

What Do You Think?
Affirmative action in college admissions

In 1961, President John F. Kennedy required government contractors to "take affirmative action to ensure that applicants are employed [. . .] without regard to their race, creed, color, or national origin." That original use of the term "affirmative action" meant taking steps to avoid racial discrimination. Over time, the term evolved to refer to the general practice of giving preference to members of underrepresented groups.

(continued)

One of the most hotly debated areas of affirmative-action policy is in university admissions. Since the 1970s, many universities have practiced "positive discrimination" to increase the number of women and racial minorities they admit. Early on, many of these policies took the form of specific racial quotas, such as reserving 15 percent of available spots for nonwhite students. The Supreme Court ruled quotas unconstitutional (in the 1978 case *Regents of the University of California v. Bakke*) but allowed less-explicit forms of racial affirmative action. In a hard-fought case involving the University of Michigan (*Gratz v. Bollinger* in 2003), the Court ruled that considering race as a "plus" in a multifactor admissions decision is acceptable if it helps achieve diversity among students. However, the Court noted that it viewed this as a short-term solution that would be unnecessary in 25 years.

Proponents of affirmative action in university admissions commonly base their support on one of two ideas:

- First, having a diverse student body is inherently valuable and serves educational purposes.
- Second, "positive discrimination" is a temporary measure to counteract the lingering, intergenerational effects of historical "negative discrimination."

Opponents often argue that there is no such thing as "positive discrimination." They feel that preference on the basis of race is simply wrong, regardless of who is harmed or helped by it. "Two wrongs don't make a right," they say.

Still others argue that if affirmative action is intended to address historical disadvantages, it should take a wider view than race. For example, who has been more disadvantaged by his family background: the son of a poor white coal miner or the son of a wealthy black neurosurgeon?

WHAT DO YOU THINK?

1. In what ways, if any, do you think that students applying to U.S. colleges today might be affected by past racial and gender discrimination? Think about human capital investments, social networks, and economic mobility.
2. If some students are adversely affected by historical discrimination, are college admissions an effective way to correct that disadvantage before graduates enter the labor market? How should we think about the benefits and costs of such a policy, including the opportunity cost? Can actions be taken to counter these disadvantages elsewhere in society or the economy?

✓ CONCEPT CHECK

☐ How do economists define discrimination? **[LO 21.7]**
☐ Why don't differences in income between demographic groups necessarily imply discrimination? **[LO 21.7]**

Conclusion

Understanding the roots of poverty, inequality, and discrimination matters for economists and policy-makers alike. From an intellectual perspective, these topics push us to understand how markets and institutions really work. They also take us below the surface of statistics such as average income and GDP to understand who gets how much and why. From the perspective of a policy-maker or a concerned citizen, they may raise challenging economic and social issues. What does a fair society look like? How much poverty is acceptable? Does equality of opportunity matter more than the distribution of income itself?

We've seen in this chapter that even the measurement of poverty, inequality, mobility, and discrimination can be tricky. We have to decide whether we care more about absolute or relative measures, adjust for differences across regions, and pick out the causal factors we care about. In the next chapter, we turn to the question of how these and other policy issues are dealt with in the political world. We'll see that arriving at policy choices is even more complicated than simply finding the facts and establishing goals. The workings of the political system itself have a huge influence on the shape of the economic policies that are created.

Key Terms

absolute poverty line, p. 526

relative poverty line, p. 526

poverty rate, p. 527

purchasing power parity (PPP) index, p. 530

human capital, p. 531

poverty trap, p. 533

credit constraint, p. 534

Lorenz curve, p. 536

Gini coefficient, p. 536

income mobility, p. 540

social insurance, p. 542

conditional cash transfer, p. 544

in-kind transfer, p. 544

means-tested, p. 546

discrimination, p. 547

Summary

LO 21.1 Understand how to measure poverty and describe the difference between absolute and relative measures of poverty.

An absolute poverty line defines poverty as income below a certain amount. The poverty line is fixed at a certain dollar amount at a given point in time; it is usually set based on the cost of certain essential goods. In contrast, a relative poverty line defines poverty in terms of the income of the rest of the population. The official U.S. poverty line is an absolute amount based on the price of food in the 1960s; poverty rates in the United States have fluctuated between 10 and 15 percent of the population in recent decades. The most commonly used international poverty measure is also an absolute poverty line, $1.90 per person per day at purchasing parity. According to this metric, roughly one-quarter of the world's population lives in poverty.

Absolute poverty lines measure people's access to concrete goods and services; relative poverty lines do a better job of capturing the importance of economic conditions relative to those of others.

LO 21.2 Understand why poverty persists.

There are some common factors that help explain why poverty continues to exist. We tend to see poverty continue from generation to generation, although we cannot say for sure whether this is because low human capital causes poverty or because poverty causes low human capital. There are also poverty traps that tend to make the poor stay poor—things like poor health, credit constraints, and imperfect markets for making investments. And for some societies, community-wide problems hinder the poor—problems such as drought and war.

LO 21.3 Explain and interpret different methods of measuring income inequality.

Income inequality is commonly summarized by measuring the average income in each quintile of the population, or the percentage of total income held by people in each quintile. We can also represent income inequality using a graph called the Lorenz curve. It maps the cumulative percent of the population against the cumulative percent of income those people earn. The Gini coefficient summarizes inequality in a single number by dividing the area between the Lorenz curve and the line of perfect equality by the total area under the line of perfect equality.

LO 21.4 Describe how income mobility differs from income equality.

Income mobility is the ability to improve your economic circumstances over time. Measuring income mobility in a country tells us how likely you are to end up rich if you start out poor, or vice versa. We can measure income mobility in both absolute and relative terms. In absolute terms, we can look at whether a person's income is higher than her parents'. In relative terms, we can look at whether a person's income places her higher up in the income distribution than her parents.

LO 21.5 Identify the public policies that are used to reduce poverty and inequality and understand their goals.

Four main policies are used to reduce poverty and inequality. Progressive taxation reduces inequality, as it taxes the rich at a higher rate than the poor, narrowing the gap between these two groups. Income support comes in two forms, conditional cash transfers and direct cash transfers. In both, families receive cash from the government. In-kind transfers give goods and services (most commonly, food stamps and housing vouchers) to the poor instead of cash. Social insurance programs, including Social Security and Medicare, pool risks across the population by providing income support and health care, respectively, for the elderly.

LO 21.6 Explain the trade-off between equity and efficiency in poverty-reduction policy.

Means-tested programs define eligibility for benefits based on recipients' income. Often, means-testing involves not just a simple eligible/not-eligible distinction, but also a determination of how much recipients are eligible to receive. However, anytime benefits decrease as income increases, the motivation to earn additional income is reduced. There is no way to prevent everyone from falling through the cracks without loss of efficiency. Thus, economists see a trade-off between equity and efficiency in poverty policy. Trade-offs are also created due to the inefficiencies created by taxes levied to pay for anti-poverty programs.

LO 21.7 Explain why economists differentiate between correlation and causation when studying discrimination and why markets do not always eliminate discrimination.

Income for adults varies widely by race and gender in the United States. These differences could be the result of discrimination in the labor market. They also could be the result of other factors that are related to both earnings and race or gender, such as education, work experience, and choice of occupation. It is difficult to distinguish the causal effect of discrimination from these other unobserved factors.

Under some conditions, markets may help to eliminate discrimination. When consumer preferences are not in agreement with the discrimination (or when the discrimination is irrelevant to consumers' preferences), markets will cause those who discriminate to lose profitable opportunities. However, when consumer preferences support discrimination, discrimination and efficient markets can coexist.

Review Questions

1. In season three of the TV show *The West Wing*, the federal government considers redefining the national poverty measure in a way that would classify an additional 4 million people as poor. The president worries that his administration will be criticized for leading the country into greater poverty. Explain whether this change would have reflected a shift in an absolute measure of poverty or a relative measure of poverty, or whether it cannot be known. Finally, explain why, all else equal, the president is not responsible for causing greater poverty. **[LO 21.1]**

2. Poverty in Decilia is measured relatively, with people in the bottom 10 percent of the income distribution being defined as poor. Suppose a politician in Decilia promises to halve the poverty rate in five years. Explain why this could never be achieved given the poverty statistic Decilia uses. Propose an alternative measure of poverty that would allow the politician to achieve that goal. **[LO 21.1]**

3. Explain why it might be difficult for low income individuals to receive a college education and why the government may need to subsidize student loans for a college education. **[LO 21.2]**

4. Some people argue that unpaid internships should be illegal. In what ways is an unpaid internship part of a poverty trap? **[LO 21.2]**

5. Is it possible for two countries to have the same Gini coefficient but different distributions of income? Explain how you came to your conclusion. **[LO 21.3]**

6. Explain why it's possible for income inequality to decrease globally while increasing in every country at the same time. **[LO 21.3]**

7. In which of the following countries is income mobility likely higher? Explain your answer. **[LO 21.4]**

    a. A country with a poverty rate of 25 percent, of which 80 percent represents chronic poverty.

    b. A country with a poverty rate of 30 percent, of which 20 percent represents chronic poverty.

8. Suppose there is an economy where 80 percent of people earn more than their parents and 40 percent end up in a different income quintile than their parents. What measure of the income distribution does the first statistic tell you about? What about the second? **[LO 21.4]**

9. In March 2010, President Barack Obama signed into law the Patient Protection and Affordable Care Act, which required insurance companies to accept patients with preexisting conditions. Classify this provision into one of the approaches to alleviating poverty discussed in the chapter and explain your reasoning. **[LO 21.5]**

10. If unconditional cash transfers have the same effect as conditional cash transfers, which one allows the government to alleviate poverty more effectively? In answering the question, draw on your knowledge of administrative costs. **[LO 21.5]**

11. John Rawls is a philosopher famous for his "maximin" principle, which states that society should maximize

the position of the people with the minimum amount of goods, and not focus only on the level of inequality. For instance, Rawls would favor a society in which the bottom 10 percent earn $30,000 per year and the top 10 percent earn $2 million over a society in which the bottom 10 percent earn $28,000 per year and the top 10 percent earn $40,000 per year. Drawing on the trade-off between equity and efficiency, explain whether Rawls would favor (a) redistribution that limits growth but creates equality or (b) economic development that encourages growth but creates inequality. **[LO 21.6]**

12. Your professor has decided that, from now on, students who receive less than a 60 percent grade on any exam will be eligible to go to a review session. If they attend the session, they will receive an extra 10 percent on their grade. You see a problem with this policy, and instead propose to your professor that people who go to the review session should receive 50 percent of the difference between their grade and 60 percent. Explain why this situation represents a trade-off between equity and efficiency. **[LO 21.6]**

13. Is it possible that even though men make more than women in a particular industry, there could be gender discrimination *against* men in that industry? If no, explain why not. If yes, explain why and give an example. **[LO 21.7]**

14. For each of the scenarios below, determine whether you think it is likely that an employer could be discriminating against a person because of his or her age. Explain why or why not. **[LO 21.7]**

    a. A young lawyer who just finished work on a multimillion-dollar development deal downtown is hired by an economic development firm in lieu of an older lawyer who works on litigation.

    b. A large retail outlet hires an 80-year-old woman to greet customers instead of a 30-year-old woman who has been greeting customers in other stores for a decade.

    c. The owner of a local, hip smoothie bar in a university town just fired a graduate student who had worked at the bar for three years and instead hired a college sophomore.

15. Jackie Robinson broke baseball's color barrier in 1947, which precipitated integration in all major league teams after 12 years. Explain why the market might have acted to eliminate discrimination in this example. **[LO 21.7]**

16. Some economists have studied the effects of "lookism," or discrimination based on how attractive a person is. Give an example of a case in which the market might encourage lookism and an example of a case in which the market might combat lookism. **[LO 21.7]**

Problems and Applications

1. Table 21P-1 shows a data set that contains the annual income of 20 households, each with a household size of four people. **[LO 21.1]**

    a. What percent of these households are below the national poverty line of $18,250 for a household of four people?

    b. What is the average income of the bottom 20 percent of the households?

2. Table 21P-2 shows the incomes of 10 households in two different years, 2020 and 2021. Assume that the government is considering two different measures of poverty, an absolute level of below $10,000 and a relative measure of being in the bottom 40 percent of income earners. **[LO 21.1]**

    a. What is the poverty rate using the *absolute* measure of poverty in 2020? In 2021? Does it go up, down, or stay the same between the two years?

    b. What is the poverty rate using the *relative* measure of poverty in 2020? In 2021? Does it go up, down, or stay the same between the two years?

    c. Which yields a higher rate, the absolute measure of poverty or the relative measure of poverty in 2020? In 2021?

    d. Now assume that the government decides to index the poverty rate to inflation. Suppose inflation was 5 percent from 2020 to 2021. Now

TABLE 21P-1

Income of households 1–10 ($)	Income of households 11–20 ($)
30,000	10,000
11,000	41,000
88,000	21,500
17,000	78,000
21,000	25,000
75,000	13,000
24,000	103,000
81,000	149,000
52,000	76,000
44,000	27,000

TABLE 21P-2

Household	Income in 2020 ($)	Income in 2021 ($)
1	20,000	20,050
2	8,000	9,000
3	13,000	13,000
4	33,000	34,000
5	2,000	2,500
6	7,500	8,000
7	9,050	10,100
8	80,000	85,000
9	40,000	42,000
10	3,000	3,100

what is the poverty rate according to the absolute measure in 2021? Is it higher than the relative rate in 2021?

3. In the United States, public schools are often funded by property taxes levied on the property in surrounding areas. Which of the following statements explains how this can result in a poverty trap? Select all that apply. [LO 21.2]

a. Individuals must buy a higher-priced home in order to attend a school that receives more property taxes.
b. Renters do not have to pay property taxes.
c. Schools in areas with cheaper housing will receive less funding.
d. Low-income families are able to receive the same quality schooling for less money.

4. Table 21P-3 shows the incomes of 10 households in two different years, 2020 and 2030. Each household makes a choice in 2020 about how many years of education they will acquire. Suppose each year of education costs $2,000 and households can acquire a maximum of six years of education. For the sake of simplicity, suppose that there is no risk in education. Each year of education will increase your 2030 income by $3,000. Otherwise, your 2030 income will be the same as your 2020 income. Finally, suppose you need at least $2,000 to survive. [LO 21.2]

a. Fill in the three remaining columns in the table.
b. What is the percentage of total societal income held by the lowest quintile in 2020?
c. What is the percentage of total societal income held by the lowest quintile in 2030?
d. How is this an example of a poverty trap?

5. Using the data for income distribution found in Table 21-4, determine the following. (The data are provided by the World Bank.) [LO 21.3]

a. Does Sweden or Brazil have a higher Gini coefficient?

TABLE 21P-3

Household	Income in 2020 ($)	Income quintile in 2020	Income in 2030 ($)	Income quintile in 2030
1	20,000			
2	8,000			
3	13,000			
4	33,000			
5	2,000			
6	7,500			
7	9,050			
8	80,000			
9	40,000			
10	3,000			

TABLE 21P-4

Country	Gini coefficient	% of income held by bottom 10%	% of income held by top 10%
Argentina	0.42	1.6	30.6
Chile	0.51	1.7	41.5
El Salvador	0.44	2.1	34.4
Honduras	0.54	1.0	41.5
Panama	0.52	1.1	40.0
Paraguay	0.48	1.5	37.6
Uruguay	0.42	1.9	31.0

   b. From the bottom quintile to the middle quintile, is the Lorenz curve for Brazil above or below Sweden's?

6. Look at the various measures of poverty in 2013 for several countries in Table 21P-4. (The data are provided by the World Bank.) **[LO 21.3]**

   a. Rank the countries from the country with the highest inequality to the lowest using the Gini coefficient. (Higher Gini coefficients represent higher inequality.)

   b. Rank the countries from the country with the highest inequality to the lowest using the ratio of the top decile to the bottom decile.

   c. Rank the countries from the country with the highest inequality to the lowest inequality using the share of total income held by the top 10 percent.

7. Determine whether each of the scenarios is possible. **[LO 21.4]**

   a. A poverty rate based on a relative measure is high, income mobility is low, and there is perfect income equality.

   b. A poverty rate based on an absolute measure is high, income mobility is zero, and there is perfect income equality.

   c. A poverty rate based on an absolute measure is high, income mobility is high, and there is high income equality.

   d. There is no poverty based on a relative measure, income mobility is high, and there is perfect income equality.

8. The left column of Table 21P-5 shows the income data for 10 people at age 40. The right column shows the income for one of their children at the same age (adjusted for inflation). **[LO 21.4]**

TABLE 21P-5

Income for 1st generation (at age 40) ($)	Income for 2nd generation (at age 40) ($)
800	2,225
9,120	2,105
12,830	1,380
1,275	1,140
6,260	10,200
1,600	11,880
4,150	1,250
2,200	15,000
975	420
3,590	5,630

   a. How many people in the second generation are in a higher income quintile than their parents?

   b. How many people in the second generation are in a lower income quintile than their parents?

   c. How many people are in the highest income quintile who had parents who were in the lowest quintile?

9. Classify the following social policies based on the approach taken to alleviating poverty: economic development, safety nets, or redistribution. **[LO 21.5]**

   a. The government of Zimbabwe reorganizes property rights, giving traditionally marginalized black Zimbabweans access to land owned by white Zimbabweans.

b. As part of a package called the GI Bill, the United States offered to pay the college tuition of newly returned veterans of World War II.

c. The government of Chile privatizes its social security system. The new system sets up private accounts that require contributions of at least 10 percent of income. This money is invested by private actors and then returned to each person at retirement.

10. Imagine a person who makes $400 per week working 40 hours per week for 50 weeks of the year. She is currently eligible for a welfare program, available to people with income below $21,000, which gives her $800 a year. No such program is available to people with income above $21,000 per year. Her boss offers her a promotion that would increase her wage by 25 cents per hour. **[LO 21.5]**

a. What is her total income before the promotion?

b. What is her total income if she accepts the promotion?

c. Should she accept the promotion if she wants to have higher income?

11. President Joe Nositall just published a report for his country, laying out various scenarios for the economy in the next year. Table 21P-6 shows his report, with various levels of GDP growth, income equality, and tax rates. **[LO 21.6]**

a. Rank the scenarios from the most equal to the most unequal income distribution (defined as the average income of the top decile of earners divided by the average income of the bottom decile of earners).

b. Rank each scenario in terms of the level of GDP growth between 2017 and 2018.

c. Between which scenarios is there no trade-off between GDP growth and income equality?

12. Which of the following are means-tested programs? **[LO 21.6]**

a. A local public university starts to give financial aid to individuals who score above the 98th percentile on the SAT.

b. The United Kingdom decides to start giving out pension benefits based on individuals' prior amount of savings.

c. A government decides to give tax credits to anyone who purchases computers made domestically.

d. Canada begins to pay half of the cost of public transportation for people who do not own a car.

13. Table 21P-7 shows hypothetical salaries for three pairs of men and women who share the same position. It also shows the average increase in income associated with having certain qualities as a worker; assume these represent the only qualities that are relevant for doing the job well. Using these averages, determine for each male-female pair (A, B, and C) whether there is gender discrimination. If so, say who it is against and how large the gap is in dollar terms. **[LO 21.7]**

14. Working women in the United States earn only three-quarters of what men earn. Consider each of the following explanations for this statistic, and say whether each *could be true* or *must not be true* in order to explain this fact. **[LO 21.7]**

a. Women choose lower-paying professions (e.g., becoming a nurse rather than a doctor).

b. Women are discriminated against when being considered for promotions or raises.

c. Women are more educated and have more work experience than men, on average.

d. Women are discriminated against in the hiring process.

e. Women benefit from affirmative action in the hiring process.

TABLE 21P-6

Scenario	GDP in 2017 (trillions of $)	Average tax rate (%)	Average total income for the bottom 10% of earners ($)	Average total income for the top 10% of earners ($)	GDP in 2018 (trillions of $)
A	14.1	16	25,000	100,000	14.6
B	13.0	40	35,000	80,000	13.2
C	16.5	30	27,000	90,000	17.2
D	18.0	45	40,000	95,000	18.1

TABLE 21P-7

Industry-average compensation	Gender	Years of schooling	Years of experience	Salary ($)
		$1,000 per year of schooling	$2,000 per year of experience	A base salary of $50,000
A	Male	5	10	75,000
	Female	3	8	69,000
B	Male	0	5	60,000
	Female	2	7	70,000
C	Male	3	5	63,000
	Female	3	7	63,000

15. Are the workings of the free market likely to encourage or discourage discrimination in the following examples? **[LO 21.7]**

    a. The musical director of a symphony orchestra that records but never performs in front of an audience refuses to hire female musicians.

    b. In apartheid South Africa (where racial discrimination was legal and popular among white voters for many decades), a white business owner refuses to hire black candidates to work in management positions dealing with white customers.

    c. In a Martian culture in which blue hair is considered the most beautiful, a Martian modeling agency preferentially hires blue-haired models.

16. Consider Table 21P-8, which shows several different types of goods sold in a hypothetical town. Imagine a new competitor enters who refuses to discriminate between locals and foreigners in hiring employees. Determine whether the new competitor will do well in the town, given market conditions for each market (pajama pants, bow ties, and yo-yos). **[LO 21.7]**

TABLE 21P-8

Good	% of customers who will buy the good only from companies that hire only locals	% of stores that hire only local employees
Pajama pants	50	70
Bow ties	70	50
Yo-yos	10	5

Endnotes

1. Report on earnings on Wall Street: http://www.businessinsider.com/wall-street-pay-hit-a-new-record-2015-10; May 2015 National Occupational Employment and Wage Estimates (Bureau of Labor Statistics, U.S. Department of Labor): http://www.bls.gov/oes/current/oes_nat.htm.

2. Data on the income of the top 1 percent is from Emmanuel Saez, *"Striking It Richer: The Evolution of Top Incomes in the United States* (Updated with 2009 and 2010 estimates)," University of California, Berkeley, March 2, 2012, http://elsa.berkeley.edu/~saez/saez-UStopincomes-2010.pdf.

3. http://www.census.gov/hhes/www/poverty/about/overview/index.html.

4. http://www.nber.org/aginghealth/summer04/w10466.html.

5. http://www.census.gov/prod/2010pubs/p60-238.pdf; http://www.irp.wisc.edu/publications/focus/pdfs/foc262g.pdf.

6. http://www.worldbank.org/en/topic/poverty/overview.

7. http://www.worldbank.org/en/topic/poverty/overview.

8. http://www.theatlantic.com/magazine/archive/2006/09/the-height-of-inequality/5089/.

9. http://www.census.gov/content/dam/Census/library/publications/2016/demo/p20-578.pdf.

10. http://kff.org/other/state-indicator/physicians-by-gender.

Political Choices

Learning Objectives

LO 22.1 Explain the predictions and assumptions of the median-voter theorem.

LO 22.2 List the characteristics of an "ideal" voting system and identify which criteria are met by real systems.

LO 22.3 Discuss problems with the idea of the "rational voter" and define the idea of rational ignorance.

LO 22.4 Explain the persistence of policies that provide concentrated benefits to a few while imposing diffuse costs on the majority.

LO 22.5 Explain why corruption and rent-seeking can persist in a democratic system.

LO 22.6 List three major features of political structure and identify how they can affect policy choices.

GLOBAL WARMING HOT POTATO

Since the turn of the 21st century, debate over climate change has been a fixture of American politics. Scientists and economists have been drawn into this debate to provide their expert opinions on the factual questions involved. Economists aren't well suited to weigh in on the earth-science side of the issue, but the question of how to tackle negative externalities is a familiar economic problem.

Two economic solutions to counter the externalities associated with carbon emissions have been widely debated. The first is a carbon tax levied on businesses, which provides an incentive to reduce emissions. The second approach is a "cap-and-trade" policy that grants businesses the right to emit a certain amount of carbon and then allows them to buy or sell those allowances as needed. Both policies would reduce the total quantity of pollution by raising the price of burning carbon-based fuels.

However, both proposals died in Congress. Why? It is possible for reasonable and informed people to disagree about the merits of a carbon tax versus a cap-and-trade policy, and, indeed, about the necessity of either. But the failure of the proposals appeared to have little to do with science and a lot to do with old-fashioned politics.

Most economists, regardless of political philosophy, believe that a carbon tax is a simpler and more transparent and efficient solution than cap-and-trade. But many policy-makers viewed backing any sort of "tax" as political suicide. Some policy-makers and electric companies instead favored a cap-and-trade proposal that granted companies some free carbon allowances. In the end, however, politicians rejected even the cap-and-trade proposal, worried that the resulting increase in consumer heating and gas prices would anger voters.[1]

In the previous few chapters, we've seen how government action can correct market failures and increase total surplus. The fight over a carbon tax versus cap-and-trade is just one illustration of how difficult it can be to translate economic theory into government action. Students of economics, therefore, have an interest in understanding how policy is formed through the political process. Economics is, after all, the study of how resources are managed, and governments play a major role in resource allocation.

The most basic economic model for understanding electoral politics starts from standard assumptions of economics—that people are rational and fully informed. The model assumes that voters have preferences regarding policy, have full information about candidates, and vote for the one whose policy platform most nearly resembles their preferences. Once those candidates are in office, the expectation is that they will simply implement the platforms on which they were elected. In this way, rational voters directly determine the shape of public policy.

You may have noticed, however, that the real world is much more complicated. Voters are not necessarily well informed, politicians often pursue their own interests rather than those of voters, and small groups with large stakes in a policy proposal (such as electric companies in the case of a carbon tax) can have a big influence on the outcome.

To help account for these real-world observations, in this chapter we'll build an economic model of political choices. We'll talk about why it's not so simple to arrive at policy conclusions by just adding up the votes. We'll question the assumptions that voters are rational and informed and that they vote according to their preferences. We'll look at post-election policy choices and talk about why voter preferences won't necessarily translate directly into policy. Finally, we'll see how political structure affects policy outcomes; we will zoom in on some specific features of the U.S. political structure that affect the national economy.

The Economics of Elections

To start, imagine that the typical voter has clear opinions on a broad range of policy issues and knows the positions held by every candidate in every election. To assess the realism of this assumption, take a quick quiz: Do you know your senators' and representative's positions on the death penalty or taxes? Very few of us, sometimes including politicians themselves, can actually answer questions like these with confidence.

Even if these assumptions held true, how do you think that elections would play out? We'll start by thinking about a simplified model, and then get more realistic in two important ways.

Stick to the middle: Median-voter theorem

LO 22.1 Explain the predictions and assumptions of the median-voter theorem.

Does it ever seem to you that political candidates in the United States become more moderate once nominated by their party, before the general election? That even though they might stake out extreme positions in primary debates, for the general election they start to shift their rhetoric, to appeal to more people "in the middle"? If so, a basic theory of political decision making in economics can help explain why.

Imagine a one-dimensional policy question, such as how much money to spend on the military. Now, suppose that all voters have a preference along this one dimension (more spending or less spending on the military). Each person will vote for the politician whose policy platform is closer to his or her own preferences. To simplify the math, let's also imagine there are only seven voters. (You can think of each of the seven as representing one-seventh of all the real voters.) In this simple model, how should two candidates running for election choose their policy positions?

Suppose the two candidates start by saying what they really think. One candidate, Mr. Dove, advocates relatively low military spending. As shown in panel A of Figure 22-1, his position falls between the beliefs of the third and fourth voters. The other candidate, Ms. Hawk, favors very high military spending. Her position falls at the other end of the scale. The result? Ms. Hawk will get only two of the seven votes; the other five voters are closer to Mr. Dove's position.

Now suppose you are employed by Ms. Hawk's campaign. What would you advise? If she moves her position toward the center (in other words, toward lower proposed military spending), she can steal voters #4 and #5 from Mr. Dove and win the election, as panel B shows. How can Mr. Dove *respond* to this strategy to regain the lead? He can also move toward the center, recapturing the vote of voter #4, as shown in panel C.

If we take this electoral game to its logical conclusion, the only way for either candidate to maximize votes is to take the exact same position as voter #4—the median, or middle, voter. If either candidate moves away from this position, he or she loses the middle voter and thus loses the election. So, regardless of what they really think, if the candidates want to maximize their chances of winning, we would expect both candidates to end up advocating the *exact same position.*

FIGURE 22-1

Candidates win by catering to the median voter

(A) An extreme position loses the election: Seven voters are ranked on a one-dimensional scale. Each voter votes for the candidate who is closest to his own preferences. Opinion polls show that, by taking an extreme position, Ms. Hawk is set to attract the votes of only two out of seven voters.

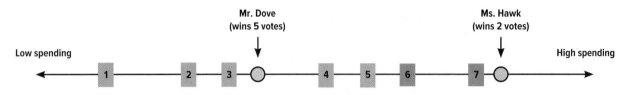

(B) Moving to the center wins more votes: Ms. Hawk looks at the polls and decides to moderate her position. New opinion polls show she will now win the election with four votes, against three for Mr. Dove.

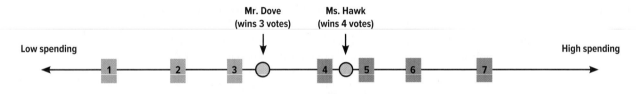

(C) Candidates end up catering to the median voter: Mr. Dove now looks at the opinion polls and decides to moderate his position, too. By moving closer to the median voter, he now wins 4-3. This process of moderating positions continues until both candidates are advocating the position held by the median voter.

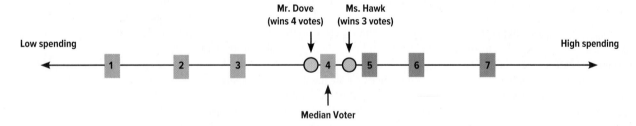

median-voter theorem
a model stating that under certain conditions, politicians maximize their votes by taking the policy position preferred by the median voter

This simple model is called the **median-voter theorem**. It suggests that politicians maximize their votes by taking the policy position preferred by the median voter, under certain conditions. The conditions are:

- There is a single, one-dimensional policy question (such as more or less spending).
- Voters always vote for the candidate whose position is closest to their own.
- There are only two candidates.
- A candidate wins by majority vote.

Note that under this model, the chosen policy will be the one preferred by the *median* voter, rather than the average voter or the largest number of voters. We can imagine a situation, for instance, in which

- Three voters want zero spending on the military.
- Three voters want to spend 50 percent of the budget.
- Only one voter wants to spend 20 percent.

Median-voter theorem says that military spending will end up being 20 percent of the budget (which is the middle ground), even though only one voter actually preferred that solution.

Of course, real elections aren't this simple. Many policy issues are not one-dimensional. (You may care about the level of military spending but also how that money gets spent—for example, whether on fighter jets versus higher salaries for the troops.) Also, voters usually care about more than just one policy issue. Nonetheless, the median-voter theorem offers a powerful explanation for the observation that candidates in a two-party system often take similar policy positions, regardless of their political party. It also casts light on why we often see presidential candidates change their positions over the course of a campaign. They may advocate relatively extreme positions during party primary elections, and then adopt more moderate positions in the general election: In the primary, the goal is to appeal to the median *of voters in their own party*. In the general election, they want to appeal to the median *of all voters.*

The elusive perfect voting system

LO 22.2 List the characteristics of an "ideal" voting system and identify which criteria are met by real systems.

Now, let's get more realistic. What happens if voters care about more than one policy (say, military policy *and* the budget deficit), or if they have more than two candidates to consider? Once voting becomes more complicated, the way in which votes are cast becomes important.

How do we take the preferences of all voters and add them up in a fair and consistent way, so that the opinion held by the most voters carries the day? Imagine that voters were directly voting on the issues, rather than for a candidate. In his book *Social Choice and Individual Values,* economist Kenneth Arrow proposed four criteria for an "ideal" voting system:

1. **Unanimity.** If everyone in the group prefers option X to option Y, then X beats Y. In other words, if every voter would rather spend more on education than on national parks, then the ideal voting system would be structured so that education spending wins.

2. **No dictator.** There is no person who has the power to single-handedly enact his or her own preferences. A voting system would not be ideal if someone has the power to put all funds into national parks, even if most would rather spend the money on schools.

3. **Transitivity.** If option X beats Y, and Y beats Z, then transitivity says that X also beats Z. In other words, if voters would rather spend on schools than parks, and they would rather spend on parks than alternative energy, then any voting system that could result in alternative energy winning out over schools would not be considered ideal.

4. **Independence of irrelevant alternatives.** If a group is voting on option X versus option Y, this decision should not depend on any information or preference about another unconnected option, Z. In other words, whether or not spending on alternative energy also happens to be an option shouldn't affect whether voters prefer spending on schools versus parks.

These all sound reasonable enough. You might think it should be straightforward enough to create a voting system that meets these four criteria. To see why it isn't, let's look at how a couple of existing voting systems measure up.

First-past-the-post

In most elections in the United States (and in many other countries), the voting system is simple:

- All candidates go up against each other at once.
- Each voter can choose one and only one candidate.
- The candidate who receives the most votes wins.

This voting system is often referred to as *first-past-the-post*, or *plurality voting*.

First-past-the-post has merits, notably simplicity. Voters have to think about only one thing—which candidate is their favorite—and then check the box next to that candidate's name.

But plurality voting is not an ideal system: It fails the "independence of irrelevant alternatives" criterion, also known as the "third-party problem." In most national elections in the United States, the major candidates represent the two major parties: the Republican Party and the Democratic Party. Every once in a while, which of them wins depends on whether an additional candidate from a minor "third party" is also on the ballot.

Consider the 2000 presidential election between Governor George W. Bush and Vice President Al Gore. Consumer advocate Ralph Nader also ran, as the candidate of the Green Party. In total, Nader received less than 3 percent of the vote, yet many commentators believe Nader's presence on the ballot swung the election for Bush over Gore in a tight race.

It turned out that the election hinged on the workings of the Electoral College system, and Florida was the deciding state in that election: Whoever won the popular vote in Florida won the presidency. Panel A of Figure 22-2 shows a theoretical distribution of voters' preferences between the two major-party candidates in Florida. If the choice is between only these two, our theoretical figures show that Gore will win Florida and the election 51 percent to 49 percent.

What happens when we add Nader into the mix, in panel B? Notice that Nader's presence doesn't change any voters' preferences between Bush and Gore. Any Floridian who wants Bush over Gore or vice versa still feels the same way. But because in this example the 3 percent of voters who now vote for Nader would have favored Gore, the effect is that Gore's share drops to 48 percent, and Bush now wins Florida, and the election, by 49 percent to 48 percent. The addition of an "irrelevant alternative"—Nader—flips the outcome of the election. Plurality voting fails one of the ideal voting-system criteria.

FIGURE 22-2

The third-party-candidate problem

(A) 2000 election with two parties		(B) A third party changes the election outcome	
Preference	Percent of voters	Percent of voters	Preference
1. Gore **2.** Bush	51%	3%	**1.** Nader **2.** Gore **3.** Bush
		48%	**1.** Gore **2.** Nader **3.** Bush
1. Bush **2.** Gore	49%	49%	**1.** Bush **2.** Gore **3.** Nader

Gore wins   Bush wins

With only two parties in the election, Gore is the first preference of a larger share of voters than Bush. This means that Gore wins the election.

If Nader enters the race, some of the people who previously voted for Gore switch their votes. Although voters' preferences between Gore and Bush are the same, Bush now is the first preference of the largest share of voters, and wins the election.

Condorcet paradox

How might we avoid the third-party problem? One possible answer could be to use a system called *pair-wise majority voting.* It gets its name because options are taken in pairs, and the majority vote wins. When all options have been put to a "head-to-head" match between a pair of opponents, you might expect the most popular option to win. Likewise, we might expect the best tennis player to win a tournament consisting of a series of head-to-head matches.

To see how this might work, imagine that in the 2000 election, voters had first been asked to choose between Bush and Nader. It turns out that more voters would prefer Bush to be president, so Bush wins round one. He then goes on to face Gore in round two. More voters prefer Gore, so Gore becomes president. This result holds true regardless of the order of the vote. Gore would defeat both Bush and Nader in any round in which they were pitted against each other.

However, it turns out that this system fails another of our criteria—transitivity. To see why, imagine a city council with three members, voting on how to spend the city's construction budget for public buildings. The council has three choices: a new jail, a new city hall, or a new library. Each council member has his or her own order of preference, as shown in panel A of Figure 22-3.

If the council members take a simple vote, the result is a three-way tie. Suppose that they instead decide to use pair-wise majority voting to narrow their choices. They decide to vote first on the jail versus the city hall. As shown in panel B of Figure 22-3, under the first election order, the jail wins this matchup, with two votes to one for the city hall. As the winner of the first round, the jail goes up against the library and loses, with one vote for the jail versus two for the library. Therefore, the council decides to build the library. Tie broken, right?

Not so fast. What if the council changes the order in which they vote on each pair? Let's look at panel B again, this time with the second election order presented. Suppose they vote first on

FIGURE 22-3

Condorcet voting paradox

(A) Preferences of 3 city council members

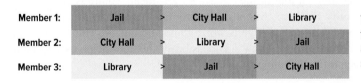

This table shows the ordered preferences of three city council members who are choosing among three different projects on which to spend the city's construction budget.

(B) Election outcomes depend on the order in which options are considered

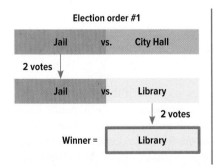
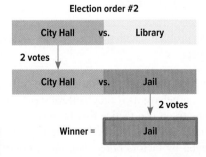
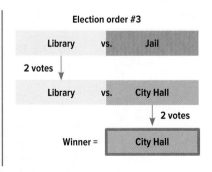

When pairs of the three construction options are considered in different orders, the ultimate outcome of the vote changes. This chart shows that any of the three buildings can be chosen depending on the order of votes. As a result, the person who "sets the agenda" by choosing the order in which options are considered has the power to affect the outcome.

the city hall versus the library, and then the library versus the jail. In this case, the city hall beats the library in the first round, and the jail beats the city hall in the second round; the jail ends up as the overall winner. Furthermore, we can look at the third election order and see that if the council starts with the library versus the jail, and then votes on the library versus city hall, the city hall wins.

In other words, it's possible for *any* of the three building plans to be chosen, depending on the order in which they vote on the pairs. Even though each individual's preferences are transitive, this method of aggregating the group's preferences is not transitive. (Remember that transitivity means that if an option X is preferred to another option Y, and Y to a third option Z, then X must be preferred to Z.) This is called the **Condorcet paradox**.

When voting systems fall short of the ideal by violating the principle of transitivity, the power to set the agenda is sometimes crucial in shaping the final outcomes. The person who decides on the order in which issues are brought to a vote for the city council, for example, wields considerable power.

Arrow's impossibility theorem

We've looked at two ways of holding elections. There are many more possible systems, devised over the years by political scientists, social scientists, and economists. Here are several, for example:

- Variations on first-past-the-post, such as holding a runoff between the top two candidates.
- "Instant-runoff" systems, in which voters rank all of the candidates by *order* of preference rather than casting a vote for their single most preferred candidate.
- "Approval voting," in which voters can vote for multiple candidates.
- The Borda count, commonly used to rank sports teams in national polls.

We won't go into detail about each. Each has its merits, but each also has some problem that causes it to fall short of the ideal.

In fact, in *Social Choice and Individual Values,* economist Kenneth Arrow proved that no voting system can aggregate the preferences of voters (assuming they are choosing among three or more options) while meeting all four of the criteria for an "ideal" voting system. This idea is called **Arrow's impossibility theorem**. Although the proof of Arrow's theorem is well beyond the scope of this book, his takeaway message is worth remembering: No voting process is perfect, but some are better than others. Arrow's impossibility theorem helps us understand the trade-offs we face between different voting systems.

Political participation and the myth of the "rational voter"

LO 22.3 Discuss problems with the idea of the "rational voter" and define the idea of rational ignorance.

So far, we've assumed that voters are rational and fully informed. What if they're not?

Politicians do not behave as if they believe most voters are influenced only by policy issues. Instead, politicians often use tactics that have little to do with policy positions—handshaking, baby-kissing, mudslinging, eating food at state fairs, and so on. Research demonstrates that elections can be swayed by factors *other than the rational policy considerations* of well-informed voters. See the Real Life box "Face value—May the best-looking politician win" for more about these factors.

Condorcet paradox
a situation in which the preferences of each individual member of a group are transitive, but the collective preferences of the group are not

Arrow's impossibility theorem
a theorem showing that no voting system can aggregate the preferences of voters over three or more options while satisfying the criteria of an ideal voting system

Real Life

Face value—May the best-looking politician win

The opening debate of the 1960 election was the first presidential debate ever to be aired on television. Before then, debates had been broadcast only on radio. One of the candidates, Senator John F. Kennedy, understood the difference. He arrived looking tanned, fresh, and well rested. His opponent, Vice President Richard Nixon, did not. Nixon was out campaigning until just hours before the debate. He arrived tired and unshaven, refused the attention of make-up artists, and went on the air looking pale and sweaty and sporting a five o'clock shadow. Supposedly, his own mother called him after the debate to ask if he was sick.

This dramatic difference in appearance had a remarkable influence on voters: Those who had watched the debate on television overwhelmingly reported that Kennedy had won the debate. Those who listened on the radio—and therefore only heard the candidates but didn't see them—thought Nixon carried the day. The television opinion won out, and shortly after the debates, John F. Kennedy pulled ahead in polling and eventually won the election.

If voters were rational and based their voting decisions purely on the policy statements of the candidates, these results would be hard to explain. No one seriously thought that Nixon was too sick to function as president. Nor is a tan usually considered to be a meaningful indicator of political ability. But looks are an important part of electoral politics.

This finding has been backed up by formal studies around the world. In a study of Australian elections, attractive candidates consistently did about 1.5 to 2 percent better in the vote than plainer-looking competitors. Studies of Finnish national elections and German state-level elections found similar results.

Why does physical appearance influence voters? One explanation is the *halo effect.* The halo effect is a psychological bias in which the perception of one trait in a person is influenced by the perception of their other traits. This means, for instance, that voters might assume that more-attractive candidates are also more intelligent or more competent.

Research has found appearance to be more influential in "low information" elections, in which voters know little about the candidates. The halo effect fades as voters gain more substantive information about the people they are evaluating.

Sources: http://people.anu.edu.au/andrew.leigh/pdf/BeautifulPoliticians.pdf; http://courses.washington.edu/pbaf-hall/514/514%20Readings/todorov%20science.pdf; http://www.ifo.de/portal/page/portal/DocBase_Content/WP/WP-CESifo_Working_Papers/wp-cesifo-2007/wp-cesifo-2007-05/cesifo1_wp2002.pdf.

Let's not be too hard on voters for not being fully informed. After all, it takes time to learn about the issues and the candidates, and that time could be spent doing something else. The trade-off may simply not be worth it. Economists call this idea **rational ignorance**. It means choosing to remain ignorant when the opportunity costs of gathering information outweigh the benefits. We saw in Chapter 19, "Public Goods and Common Resources," that what is individually rational is not necessarily *socially optimal.* If we think of good governance as a public good created by well-informed voters, we can predict that it will be undersupplied.

rational ignorance
choosing to remain ignorant when the opportunity costs of gathering information outweigh the benefits

Even voting *itself* is not costless. The time you spend getting to a polling place, waiting in line, and marking your ballot could be spent on other things. What are the benefits of voting that outweigh these opportunity costs? The most obvious answer is to influence the outcome of the election and have your preferences represented in government.

However, the odds of one vote actually making the difference in any given election are extremely low. In all of the U.S. congressional elections in the past 100 years, only one has been decided by one vote. In over 40,000 elections for state legislators, with 1 billion votes cast, only seven have been decided by a single vote. In the end, only 1 out of 100,000 votes cast in U.S. elections was pivotal in changing the outcome of an election.[2] In other words, your vote has a 99.999 percent chance of being pointless. Would a rational person find a better use for his or her time?

Research has shown that voters are, indeed, more likely to turn out in elections with small electorates and when the election is likely to be very competitive. These results suggest that the likelihood of casting a pivotal vote may influence the choice to show up to vote. However, by looking at voting only in terms of time costs and likelihood of casting the pivotal ballot, we may be missing the point. Perhaps voters gain "expressive benefits" from voting. In other words, they get utility from participating in a civic event, regardless of whether their votes are likely to be decisive. Alternatively, voters may altruistically decide to contribute to the democratic process by voting, even when it is not personally beneficial to do so.

Another theory suggests that people may vote partly in response to social pressure to "do their duty" as citizens. For example, when Switzerland—which has famously high levels of voting—started allowing people to mail in their ballots rather than go to a polling place, voting decreased in small towns. On the face of it, this is a baffling result. Mail-in ballots, after all, represent a significant reduction in the time costs associated with voting. One explanation is that people in small Swiss communities went out to vote because they wanted to be seen carrying out their civic duty. Once voting wasn't visible to the rest of the community, people had less incentive to do it at all.[3] The social benefit of voting may be the idea behind the "I voted" stickers that some polling places hand out.

✓ CONCEPT CHECK

- ☐ Can the median-voter theorem be applied to multidimensional policy questions? **[LO 22.1]**
- ☐ What does it mean for a voting system to satisfy the independence of irrelevant alternatives? **[LO 22.2]**
- ☐ Why might it be rational for voters to remain uninformed? **[LO 22.3]**

The Economics of Policy-Making

Now that we've looked at who gets elected, we'll turn to how policies get made. In this section we'll see why a minority of voters who feel strongly about an issue can often win out over a larger group with a different opinion. We'll also look at how the interests and incentives of policy-makers help predict their behavior.

Diffuse costs, concentrated benefits

LO 22.4 Explain the persistence of policies that provide concentrated benefits to a few while imposing diffuse costs on the majority.

In Chapter 19, "Public Goods and Common Resources," we saw that markets won't necessarily allocate public goods (like national parks and police protection) efficiently. The problem is that people are often reluctant to voluntarily pay for goods and services that provide benefits for everyone, including those who don't pay. This is the "free-rider" problem, and it happens when people think, "Why pay if I don't have to?" If enough people think like that, valuable goods and services are undersupplied because everyone hopes that someone else will pay for them.

The same idea can apply to political advocacy and engagement. Inefficiencies can happen when people think, "Why get personally involved if I can spare myself the hassle but still benefit from the solutions that others create?" The problem is that the best ideas might not win out if lots of people fail to lend their support.

We refer to situations in which individuals need to act collectively to reach solutions that will make everyone better off as **collective-action problems**. In these situations, a group of people stand to gain from an action that is not rational for any of the members to undertake individually.

However, engaging in collective action has costs. It takes time and money to organize a group or a campaign and to get the attention of lots of busy people. As a rule, the larger the group that needs to be organized, the more difficult and costly it is to coordinate successful collective action. Even if the total benefit to coordinating is big, each individual member may stand to gain only a small amount.

Combining these two ideas, we find that organizing larger groups often involves higher costs and lower benefits per person. The likelihood of successful collective action can therefore be lower for large groups. This leads to an interesting prediction: If two groups disagree about a policy, a smaller group that experiences higher benefits per person can be the one more likely to get its way.

Imagine, for instance, there is a national park where private companies run tour buses. Many people who visit the park find the tour buses to be disruptive and also harmful to the wildlife. Some organize a campaign to tighten regulations on tours in the park. Alarmed by this proposal, the tour-bus companies work together to contest the proposed new regulations. Whichever group is more effective in organizing and influencing the opinion of park management will get its way.

We can imagine that there are only a few owners of tour-bus companies. It will be easy for them to coordinate. We can also imagine that each one gains a lot from unrestricted use of the park. Thus, all of the tour-bus owners will be willing to devote a lot of resources to fighting the proposals.

What about the organizing efforts of the park visitors? Even if restricting bus use would deliver higher *total* benefits to the many people who visit the park occasionally, those benefits are much lower *per person*. The park visitors may be willing to sign a petition or write an e-mail, but most will not feel strongly enough to fight as determinedly as the tour-bus operators.

There are collective-action differences:

- The benefits of pro-bus policy are *concentrated* for tour-bus company owners.
- The costs of anti-bus policy are *diffuse* for private park users.

From this difference, we can predict that the tour-bus owners will care more and will likely get their way.

The theory that groups with concentrated benefits tend to win out in policy battles over those with diffuse costs has many applications. Economists use it to explain the persistence of policies that don't appear to be in the interest of the majority of voters. For instance, observers are sometimes puzzled by the staying power of large farm subsidies and trade protections for agricultural goods. These policies push up the costs of food and taxes for the majority of voters. Why don't voters elect officials who will end these policies?

One theory is that the typical voter experiences only small costs—a few extra cents in the price of milk and sugar, a few dollars in taxes. At the same time, a small number of commercial farms and agricultural businesses experience high benefits. The members of the small group find it easier and individually worthwhile to organize themselves for lobbying and public relations efforts to capture those large benefits. Organizing a whole nation of voters for a comparable effort to fight the small increase in the price of groceries would be extremely difficult.

collective-action problem
a situation in which a group of people stands to gain from an action that it is not rational for any of the members to undertake individually

Corruption and rent-seeking

LO 22.5 Explain why corruption and rent-seeking can persist in a democratic system.

An economic analysis of politics needs to account for the fact that policy-makers have their own interests, biases, and priorities. In other words, they have their own *wants and constraints*.

Of course, we would like to think that all policy-makers *want* to do what their best judgment tells them is in the public good. But some may, instead, *want* to promote their own personal gain or that of their friends and family. In such cases, they will be constrained only by the capacity of their opponents and of watchdog organizations to find out what they are doing and make voters care about it. At its extreme, the use of the powers of government by public officials to achieve personal gains is *corruption.*

More generally, government can create waste and inefficiency by contributing to **rent-seeking**. Rent-seeking is the act of pursuing privileges that increase the surplus of a person or group without increasing total surplus. Often, this activity involves lobbying by groups that receive exclusive benefits or contracts to keep others from getting access. On the flip side, it can involve lobbying by those who don't yet have access to such benefits but want to have it.

rent-seeking
the act of pursuing privileges that increase the surplus of a person or group without increasing total surplus

Some lobbying shapes trade regulations—say, domestic-steel producers trying to keep imports out. Others shape licensing policy—for instance, protecting doctors who want to strictly limit who gets to call themselves a doctor. Big campaign contributions usually come alongside the lobbying efforts, all in an attempt to get extra clout for groups that benefit from particular regulations and licenses. Such rent-seeking and lobbying are perfectly legal, but can be wasteful.

Why doesn't the process of electing officials prevent rent-seeking and corruption? If a politician starts making policies that hurt his constituents or promote himself at their expense, why doesn't he get kicked out of office by angry voters in the next election? Why don't corrupt bureaucrats always get fired? The reality is that it is costly to acquire information about what public officials are and should be doing. What voter has time to study public expenditures looking for corrupt behavior? How many voters care enough to analyze whether a particular firm wins a government contract because it is the most qualified or because it is owned by the mayor's buddy?

Of course, political opponents have every incentive to dig up dirt on incumbents before an election and to inform voters about anything bad they find. But such revelations can get lost in the noise of campaigning. Also, voters might not be sure that the opponents will end up being more trustworthy than the incumbents. The news media—blogs, television, radio, newspapers—can play an important role in uncovering corruption. But even in a relatively free society, the media may face mixed incentives: Reporters rely to some extent on public officials' willingness to give them information about what's happening in government. If reporters blow the whistle on minor offenses, they may suddenly find that their sources are no longer so friendly.

Bureaucratic capture is a specific avenue through which corruption and rent-seeking can occur. This involves filling government positions with people who have close ties to the group they are supposed to regulate. Of course, there are sensible reasons for appointing people with practical experience in a certain area of policy. But having close ties between regulators and those they are regulating can introduce biases or personal sympathies. In the aftermath of the 2008 financial crisis, for instance, some questioned the effectiveness of the Securities and Exchange Commission's (SEC) supervision of capital markets. Critics accused the SEC of failing to enforce regulations that might have mitigated the crisis. They say this was because the SEC was staffed by people with close ties to the financial industry.

Corruption goes one step further than the types of rent-seeking described above. Since it is illegal, corruption is by nature hidden. As a result, it can be difficult to find out how much of it really goes on. It also can be difficult to determine what methods are most effective at reducing it. This is why attempts to reform government actions believed to be corrupt center on *transparency.* The more the public knows about the actions of government, the theory goes, the more they will be able to see and oust corrupt actions and politicians.

The issues surrounding corruption may go beyond transparency, though. In the Real Life box "Monitoring corruption in Indonesia," we discuss a unique attempt at measuring and reducing corruption.

Real Life

Monitoring corruption in Indonesia

For decades, Indonesia was ruled by Suharto, a dictator who presided over an incredibly corrupt political regime. Transparency International, an international watchdog organization, cited Suharto as the most corrupt ruler of the 20th century. Even though he was overthrown in 1998, a deep tradition of corruption still exists in Indonesia at all levels of government. As the world's fourth most populous country seeks to improve its democratic system and tackle poverty, ensuring that government uses public funds for their intended purpose is a pressing question.

The National Program for Community Empowerment (formerly known as the Kecamatan Development Project) is a large public works program in Indonesia. It provides money to rural villages, which then decide how to spend the money. Often, villages choose to pave dirt roads, but road-building projects are regarded as especially prone to corruption. How might misuse of funds be minimized so that villages can put every dollar to productive use? One possibility is to make projects subject to audits by government officials. Another is to force local planners to account for their spending at open community meetings. Which, if either, method will more successfully reduce corruption?

Economist Ben Olken attempted to answer this question. His idea was to get an objective estimate of what a road-paving project *should* cost. He then would compare that cost to what was actually spent. The comparison would give him a reasonable measure of the degree of waste and corruption. Olken employed a team of engineers to estimate the true cost of paving a road in different villages. Then, he randomly selected villages that were building roads to receive different types of project oversight: Some were told they would be audited, others participated in efforts to increase involvement in community meetings, and others had no oversight.

Olken found that over a quarter of the funds went missing—but that telling villages that they would be subject to a government audit reduced missing amounts by almost a third. Since the audits cost less than the average reduction in missing funds, Olken found that the effort of auditing every single project would be cost-effective.

Increasing community involvement, on the other hand, had less effect on corruption. The program *was* successful at getting more villagers to attend community meetings. But more involvement had no average impact on overall levels of missing funds. There was one specific and interesting exception: The only area of spending where misuse of funds was reduced by increased community involvement was labor costs. This was a factor that villagers, as the people being employed to work on roads, had the most direct interest in controlling. Otherwise, citizens appeared to have little leverage over their leaders to make them toe the line.

Sources: Ben Olken, "Monitoring Corruption: Evidence from a Field Experiment in Indonesia,"*Journal of Political Economy* 115, no. 2 (2007): 200–249; http://news.bbc.co.uk/2/hi/3567745.stm; http://www.nytimes.com/2008/01/28/world/asia/28suharto.html?pagewanted=1.

The system matters: How political structure affects outcomes

LO 22.6 List three major features of political structure and identify how they can affect policy choices.

During the eighteenth century, the Polish legislature used the *liberum veto* (Latin for "I freely forbid"). At any time, a member of parliament had the right to shout *Nie pozwala!* ("I do not allow"). This move forced an end to the current session and voided any legislation that had been passed. The intent was to make sure that there was complete consensus about new laws.[4]

As you might expect, the system often led to chaos. Eventually, foreign powers took advantage of this system and bribed Polish legislators to oppose unwanted legislation with a cry of *Nie pozwala,* grinding the Polish political system to a halt. Not surprisingly, the *liberum veto* went out of fashion. Still, the lesson remains relevant: The rules of the game can have a big effect on outcomes.

There are too many aspects of political structure to discuss all of them here. (We'll leave that to political science professors.) There are, though, three worth singling out: the number of political parties, term limits, and increasing the right to vote. These three have a particularly big impact on how voters' preferences are translated into policy choices.

Number of political parties

The first is the number of viable political parties. Few countries—with the exception of single-party dictatorships—have explicit requirements about the number of parties. In general, first-past-the-post voting, like that used in the United States, leads to a two-party system. Since candidates have to obtain a plurality of votes to win an election, a third party could consistently win 20 percent of the votes and still win zero elections. As a result, if smaller parties want to have a say in policy-making, they have an incentive to consolidate with larger ones. Doing so will increase their chance of gaining enough vote share to win elections and have a say in policy-making.

In contrast, many countries use a *proportional-representation* system. In such systems, a party that receives 20 percent of the votes nationwide will receive about 20 percent of the seats in the legislature. Under such a system, small parties can carve out niches. From these, they are able to influence policy-making by forming coalitions with others after being elected.

Compared to proportional-representation systems, two-party systems are thought to lead to more centrist politics. (Remember the median-voter theorem.) In addition, since both parties have to represent large portions of the population, they sometimes lead to unwieldy combinations of policies within one platform. For instance, supporters of lower government spending often vote Republican. But these voters may have a wide range of opinions about social issues. As a result, people with different policy preferences may have to make compromises when voting. If, for instance, you support both low taxes and gay marriage, you might have to decide which of those issues is more important to you when choosing which party will get your vote.

Proportional-representation systems, on the other hand, are thought to bring more diverse views into the policy process and offer a wider variety of platforms among which voters can choose. One criticism of this system, however, is that small extremist parties can wield disproportionate power. When a big party doesn't get an outright majority, it has to ask small parties to join with it in a governing coalition in order to form a majority. In bargaining for political support, the smaller party will often insist that some of its policies be enacted, even if those policies don't represent the preferences of most people.

Term limits

A second feature of political structure that's worth mentioning is *term limits*. Term limits prevent officials from holding office for longer than a certain amount of time. For instance, U.S. presidents can't be elected to office more than twice or hold office for more than 10 years. These laws are typically thought to discourage corruption by ensuring that one person isn't allowed to hold onto power for too long.

However, some have speculated that the opposite might be true under certain circumstances. Politicians who know they will be out of office at the end of their term, regardless of their behavior, have less of an incentive for good behavior.

In Brazil, for example, mayors are limited to two terms. While first-term mayors who are up for reelection have an interest to stay relatively clean, mayors who know they will be out of office at the end of their term regardless of their behavior have less of an incentive to do so. A recent study by two economists found that misappropriation of funds was 27 percent lower among mayors who had to face reelection than among second-termers.[5] If this is right, then getting rid of term limits could reduce losses due to corruption by $160 million, equal to about half of the amount spent on *Bolsa Familia,* Brazil's largest social program to help poor families.

Increased enfranchisement

The final important part of political structure comes from *enfranchisement,* or who has the right to vote. In the past, voting systems in most countries required that you both be male and hold property in order to vote. Historically, controlling who was able to vote was an important tool for those who wanted to keep other groups out of power, especially women, ethnic and religious minorities, and the poor. Even when the right to vote is universal, poll taxes, literacy requirements, or other such obstacles to voting can keep the poor or uneducated from being able to vote. Rules like these resulted in political systems that represented the interests of those who could vote at the expense of others.

But voters can also be disenfranchised by circumstance. Voters who cannot get to the polls or who cannot read the ballots when they get there are, for all intents and purposes, disenfranchised as well. For an example of how a simple change can promote enfranchisement, see the Real Life box "Enfranchising the poor helps the poor."

Real Life

Enfranchising the poor helps the poor

It stands to reason that politicians are more interested in helping people who are likely to vote. But in most of the world, the poor are much *less likely* to vote than the wealthy. The result is that politicians may be less concerned with catering to the needs and interests of the poor.

Brazil first approached this problem with a straightforward solution: The government simply required all citizens to vote. Unfortunately, 23 percent of the population could not read or write. They struggled to understand the paper ballots, which often contained thousands of eligible candidates. As a result, about a quarter of all ballots were filled out incorrectly and thus disqualified. In effect, many of the poorest voters were still disenfranchised, even when they had voted.

Next, officials in Brazil looked for ways to make voting easier for the illiterate poor. They created electronic voting machines that closely resembled the interface of a telephone. Each candidate has a number; before confirming their votes, voters are presented with the name and pictures of the candidate corresponding to the number code they put into the machine.

The introduction of this new technology increased the number of votes cast correctly by 11 percent. This change was particularly pronounced in poorer districts and in the votes for parties that are traditionally supported by the poor. Millions of poor people whose votes would previously not have been counted were suddenly enfranchised in fact as well as in theory.

How did this sudden enfranchisement affect policies? Since the poor were able to vote for the politicians they wanted, they were able to put officials in office who worked to implement policies that helped them. Research by Thomas Fujiwara shows that shortly after the electronic voting machines went into use, the amount of state budgets spent on public health increased by 50 percent. Fujiwara shows that this increase in spending on public health translated into improved health outcomes, such as improved birth weight of infants.

Brazil's experience shows that enfranchising the poor doesn't always need complex government initiatives or changes to the political structure. A simple change in technology can be all it takes.

Source: Thomas Fujiwara, "Voting Technology, Political Responsiveness, and Infant Health: Evidence from Brazil," *Econometrica* 83, no. 2 (March 2015), http://www.princeton.edu/~fujiwara/papers/elecvote_site.pdf.

☐ Given the same amount of total benefits, why is it harder for a large group to overcome a collective-action problem than a small one? **[LO 22.4]**

☐ How does rent-seeking differ from corruption? **[LO 22.5]**

☐ Why is it difficult for small third parties to survive under a first-past-the-post voting system? **[LO 22.6]**

Conclusion

As students of economics, we are interested in how policy is formed—both for its own sake as an important realm of human decision making and for the effect it has on the economy. In this chapter, we began with a simplified model of political choices: Voters are fully informed and rational, they pick the candidate that best fits their views, and that candidate then faithfully carries out the policy platform on which he or she was elected.

We then moved to a more nuanced model of political choices. First, we saw that even if voters are informed and rational, aggregating their opinions through elections is not as simple as just tallying the votes. In fact, no process exists that can meet even a fairly basic set of criteria we'd hope for in an ideal voting system.

Second, we questioned just how rational and informed voters really are—and whether a rational person would even choose to vote. Then, we looked at government officials as fallible humans with their own biases and interests. Many of these biases are shaped by the rules of the political system, and we showed how these rules affect policy outcomes.

In the next chapter, we'll take a look at how policy-makers can influence outcomes, sometimes without even changing the underlying policies. Sometimes the way policies are presented can lead to important changes in the choices people make, on topics as important as retirement savings and as simple as what to eat for breakfast.

Key Terms

median-voter theorem, p. 562

Condorcet paradox, p. 566

Arrow's impossibility theorem, p. 566

rational ignorance, p. 567

collective-action problem, p. 569

rent-seeking, p. 570

Summary

LO 22.1 Explain the predictions and assumptions of the median-voter theorem.

The median-voter theorem suggests that politicians maximize their votes by taking the policy position preferred by the median voter. The theorem relies on several assumptions: that there is a one-dimensional policy question, voters always vote for the candidate whose position is closest to their own, there are only two candidates, and the winner is determined by majority vote. Given these conditions, the median-voter theorem suggests that candidates in a two-party system should take similar policy positions in order to maximize their chances of winning. Second, it predicts that the chosen policy will be the one preferred by the median voter, rather than the average

voter or the largest number of voters. The median-voter theorem falls apart when voters care about multiple issues or issues that can't be measured on a single spectrum.

LO 22.2 List the characteristics of an "ideal" voting system, and identify which criteria are met by real systems.

Arrow's impossibility theorem states that no system can aggregate the preferences of voters among three or more discrete options while satisfying four basic criteria for an ideal voting system: unanimity, transitivity, irrelevance of independent alternatives, and no dictator. The plurality system used in the United States, for example, violates the independence of irrelevant alternatives; the presence of a third-party candidate can alter the outcomes of an election between the two leading candidates. Pair-wise majority voting violates the principle of transitivity, which causes the ultimate outcome of an election to depend on the order in which the choices are considered.

> **LO 22.3** Discuss problems with the idea of the "rational voter" and define the idea of rational ignorance.

The simplest economic models of political decision making treat voters as fully informed, rational agents. However, voting incurs costs, in both time spent to inform oneself about policy issues and time spent actually casting a ballot. The likelihood that any one vote changes the outcome of an election is very low; the benefits of voting are low as well. We should not be surprised if many people choose to go to the polls ill-informed, or not to vote at all. Uninformed voting is an example of rational ignorance, when the costs of gathering information outweigh the benefits. Since people are not typically perfectly rational, we should expect voters to sometimes be biased and influenced by less-than-rational factors when choosing candidates.

> **LO 22.4** Explain the persistence of policies that provide concentrated benefits to a few while imposing diffuse costs on the majority.

Often, government is the coordinating force that allows people to work together to overcome the free-rider problem or the tragedy of the commons. These are collective-action problems, in which a group of people stands to gain from an action that it is not rational for any of the group members to undertake individually. Collective action is easier when the benefits are concentrated among members of a small group and is harder when the benefits are spread out over a large group because the cost of organizing is higher with a lower potential gain for each participant. As a result, when two groups stand to benefit from contradictory policy choices, we should expect the one that experiences more concentrated costs or benefits to prevail. The theory that groups that experience concentrated benefits tend to win out over those with diffuse costs in policy battles is often used to explain the persistence of policies that don't appear to be in the interest of the majority of voters.

> **LO 22.5** Explain why corruption and rent-seeking can persist in a democratic system.

Corruption is the use by public officials of the powers of their position to achieve personal gains. Rent-seeking is the act of pursuing arrangements that increase one's own surplus without increasing total surplus. It can encompass corruption by politicians but also actions by any political actors to shape policy to their own benefit. In a simplistic model of politics, we might expect that the process of electing officials would prevent rent-seeking and corruption. But voters have trouble tracking all of the details of policies and the actions of elected officials. This lack of transparency may make it difficult for them to monitor and punish corruption in reality. Bureaucratic capture is a specific avenue through which corruption and rent-seeking can occur. Through it, government positions are filled by people with close ties to the industry or other group that they are intended to regulate.

> **LO 22.6** List three major features of political structure and identify how they can affect policy choices.

Certain features of political structures can affect voters' preferences and thus policy choices. Three major features are the number of political parties, term limits, and increasing the right to vote. First, countries vary widely with respect to the number of political parties. Few countries have explicit requirements about the number of political parties. Some implement a proportional-representation system, thought to offer more diverse views, whereas others hold two-party systems, thought to lead to more centrist politics. Second, term limits are meant to discourage corruption by ensuring one person can't hold power for too long, although in some cases they may remove the incentive for good behavior. Third, controlling who is able or likely to vote keeps certain groups out of power and results in political systems that represent the interests of those who do vote. Voters who do not vote due either to law or the costs of voting can become disenfranchised.

Review Questions

1. Assume there's an election coming up in which voters need to decide between two candidates on the question of taxes. Polls indicate the attitudes about taxes among likely voters as shown in Table 22Q-1. Candidate A proposes a 20 percent tax, and Candidate B, a 15 percent tax. According to the median-voter theorem, which candidate will win? **[LO 22.1]**

2. Suppose we are trying to predict the positions that three candidates will take on who should be eligible for public-housing subsidies (e.g., poor families, the elderly, poor families with children, and so on). Can we use the median-voter theorem to analyze this problem? Explain why or why not, based on which of the assumptions of the median-voter theorem are met by this situation. **[LO 22.1]**

TABLE 22Q-1

Level of taxation (%)	Percent of voters in favor (%)
No taxes	10
10	20
20	40
25	30

3. In researching a voting system, you discover that it obeys three of the four criteria of an ideal voting system: transitivity, irrelevance of independent alternatives, and unanimity. With this information, what else do you know about this system? How can you be sure? **[LO 22.2]**

4. Every year the residents of a historical town gather to determine how much to spend on their park, 10 percent or 15 percent of the budget. If everyone votes for the same percentage, they will spend that amount, unless the year before everyone voted for the opposite percentage, in which case they spend the average of the two. What characteristic of the ideal voting system is violated in this example? **[LO 22.2]**

5. Compare a national presidential election that receives around-the-clock media coverage with an obscure local race for a state house seat. Which imposes higher costs on people seeking to become informed voters, and why? Which carries higher benefits to voting, and why? **[LO 22.3]**

6. Explain whether you think the following changes in a voting system would increase or decrease the number of votes cast. **[LO 22.3]**

   a. Before casting their ballot, voters are required to watch a 30-minute video with facts about the issues at hand, greatly increasing the information they have about the issues.

   b. A new cellphone app allows you to vote by sending a text to your local Board of Elections.

   c. After voting, voters can elect to receive a small pin that allows everyone to know that they voted.

7. Chapter 17, "International Trade," discussed the trade restrictions that limit imports of clothing into the United States and Europe from certain clothing-manufacturing companies. Explain why a policy like this might persist even if it was unpopular with the majority of voters. **[LO 22.4]**

8. As part of a plan to subsidize avocado production, farmers suggest that the costs of a subsidy should be paid by grocery-store owners (who will presumably benefit from higher sales of avocados). Are there concentrated benefits in this situation? Are there diffuse costs? Is there a collective-action problem? Explain your answer. **[LO 22.4]**

9. Do collective-action problems contribute to or discourage rent-seeking? Explain your answer. **[LO 22.5]**

10. Explain why having a minimum voting age may cause rent-seeking. **[LO 22.5]**

11. Explain why voters are more likely to share beliefs with candidates in a proportional-representation system than a two-party system. **[LO 22.6]**

12. Explain why political candidates in the United States often have unusual and also persistent combinations of policy preferences. (For example, a candidate that is against abortion is usually also against gun control and prefers lower taxes.) **[LO 22.6]**

Problems and Applications

1. Suppose that two candidates in a local election are trying to develop their policy positions regarding how much their town should spend on education. The numbers break down as shown in Table 22P-1.

   According to the median-voter theorem, how much will the town spend on education? **[LO 22.1]**

2. A football team is voting for a captain based on how many times the captain would have the team practice per week. Table 22P-2 shows the number of team members in favor of various numbers of practices per week. **[LO 22.1]**

   a. If the team is choosing between three captains—Buck, Jim, and Brian—can we use the median-voter theorem?

TABLE 22P-1

Percent of budget to spend on education (%)	Number of voters in favor
1	40
5	80
9	110
13	150
17	220
21	180
25	90

TABLE 22P-2

Number of practices per week	Team members in favor
2	10
4	11
6	10
8	10

b. Assume that at the last minute, Buck decides to withdraw from the race. Can we use the median-voter theorem for the race as it stands now?

c. If you can use the median-voter theorem to predict the result without Buck, how many times will the team practice? If you cannot use the theorem, what two answers can you rule out?

d. Assume that two more players join the team before the vote. They both prefer to practice 10 times a week. If you can use the median-voter theorem to predict the result without Buck, how many times will the team practice? If you cannot use the theorem, what two answers can you rule out?

3. Three friends are trying to decide where to go to dinner. There are four restaurants nearby: Thai, Italian, Tex-Mex, and sushi. Assume the friends have the following preferences: **[LO 22.2]**

   Gabe: Thai > Italian > Sushi > Tex-Mex
   Arnold: Italian > Tex-Mex > Sushi > Thai
   Julie: Sushi > Tex-Mex > Thai > Italian

   a. The friends decide to hold a majority vote that pits the Thai place against the Italian; the winner of that vote against the Tex-Mex; and then the next winner against the sushi. Which restaurant do they end up going to?

   b. If they vote on sushi versus Tex-Mex, the winner against Italian, and then the winner against Thai, which restaurant will they choose?

   c. Which of the criteria for an ideal voting system is violated in this example?

4. In a runoff election, if no candidate receives a majority of votes in the first round of voting, the top two candidates face each other in a second round. Let's say that people voting on Candidates A, B, C, and D in a runoff election have the following preferences. **[LO 22.2]**

   12 voters: A > B > C > D
   8 voters: C > B > D > A
   10 voters: D > B > C > A
   4 voters: B > D > A > C

a. Does anyone receive an outright majority in the first round? If so, which candidate? If not, which two candidates move on to the second round, and which of them wins?

b. Suppose Candidate A drops out of the race. Does any candidate now receive an outright majority in the first round? If so, which candidate? If not, which two candidates move on to the second round, and which of them wins?

c. Does this situation violate the independence of irrelevant alternatives?

5. According to the rational voter theory, will the following increase or decrease voter turnout? **[LO 22.3]**

   a. Electronic voting machines make the process of casting a ballot faster and less complicated.

   b. 24-hour news networks emphasize how close they expect the election to be, with only a few thousand votes deciding the outcome.

   c. The number of polling stations increases.

   d. Pollsters predict a landslide victory for the incumbent candidate a few days before the election.

6. Determine whether each of the following represents rational ignorance. **[LO 22.3]**

   a. Doug doesn't know the return on his retirement account in the last quarter or the types of investments that comprise the account.

   b. Sally doesn't know about a new provision in nuclear energy regulation, which is decided by a national panel overseen by nuclear physicists.

   c. Jim doesn't know whether to support new requirements for licensing among city contractors.

   d. Tom doesn't know the average price of a parking ticket, despite parking on the street every day.

7. For each of the following, state who benefits and who bears the costs, and whether the costs and benefits are concentrated or diffuse. Based on this assessment, predict which side is likely to get its way. **[LO 22.4]**

   a. A rubber producer lobbies the government to prohibit the import of cheaper foreign rubber, driving up the cost of consumer goods.

   b. The government increases federal gas taxes by 1 cent per gallon to finance building high-speed train routes between major East Coast cities.

8. For each of the following conditions, determine whether a collective-action problem exists. **[LO 22.4]**

   a. Diffuse benefits, diffuse costs.

   b. Diffuse benefits, concentrated costs.

   c. Concentrated benefits, diffuse costs.

   d. Concentrated benefits, concentrated costs.

9. Decide which of these labels best fits each of the following situations: *rent-seeking, corruption,* or *bureaucratic capture.* (If more than one is potentially applicable, pick the one that is the most narrowly tailored to the scenario.) **[LO 22.5]**

   a. A contract manager at a government department is bribed to ensure that his friend's company gets a construction contract even though it was not the lowest bidder.

   b. A senior-citizens group lobbies the city government to spend more on special public-transit shuttles for the elderly.

   c. The president appoints a former head of an investment bank to the Securities and Exchange Commission (which oversees capital markets and enforces financial regulations).

   d. The head of a local teachers' union offers support to a political candidate in exchange for her promise to spend more of the state budget on teacher salaries.

10. Determine whether each of the following shifts is likely to increase or decrease the prevalence of rent-seeking. **[LO 22.5]**

    a. The spread of smartphones enables more widespread access to information.

    b. Judges strike down a law that forces politicians to report when they receive a gift worth over $500.

    c. Congress passes a law requiring lobbyists to spend at least two years in another unrelated position before getting hired in government to regulate the industries they were advocating for as lobbyists.

11. Suppose that political candidates in an election are trying to develop their policy positions regarding how high to set the top marginal tax rate. The numbers break down as shown in Table 22P-3.

    If the political system is a two-party system, will a candidate who believes the top marginal tax rate should be 30 percent be more likely to announce support for a marginal tax rate below 30 percent, above 30 percent, or exactly 30 percent? **[LO 22.6]**

12. Suppose that a country currently does not allow its political leaders to be in office for more than one term. The country is considering moving from a policy of no reelection to allowing one reelection (i.e., two terms in office). Figure 22P-1 shows a governor's options while serving as governor. She can either act honestly or dishonestly. If she acts honestly, the voters will vote to reelect her. If she acts dishonestly, the voters will not

TABLE 22P-3

Top marginal tax rate (%)	Number of voters in favor
5	60
10	70
15	110
20	170
25	200
30	110
35	90

FIGURE 22P-1

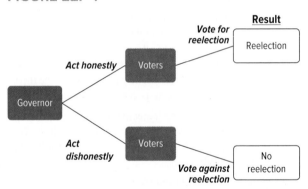

vote for her reelection. Assume that the governor would prefer to be reelected. How will moving from a policy of no reelection to allowing one reelection affect the governor's honesty in her first (and potentially second) terms? **[LO 22.6]**

Endnotes

1. http://www.washingtonpost.com/wp-dyn/content/article/2007/03/31/AR2007033101040.html.

2. http://www.nytimes.com/2005/11/06/magazine/why-vote.html; http://mondrian.die.udec.cl/~mmedina/Desvarios/Files/Mulligan-PivotalVote.pdf.

3. http://www.nytimes.com/2005/11/06/magazine/why-vote.html; http://papers.ssrn.com/sol3/papers.cfm?abstract_id=917770.

4. http://www.britannica.com/topic/liberum-veto.

5. http://eml.berkeley.edu/~ffinan/Finan_Termlimits.pdf.

Public Policy and Choice Architecture

Learning Objectives

LO 23.1 Define choice architecture and identify how nudges can influence individual decision making.

LO 23.2 Explain several ways in which human decision making does not conform to the model of full information and rational choices.

LO 23.3 Explain how demand for commitment devices can be rational.

LO 23.4 Explain how information, when presented well, can help people make decisions that are good for them.

LO 23.5 Describe how default rules affect people's choices and the implications for policy.

LO 23.6 Describe how framing affects the way people process information and its implications for policy.

SAVING MORE FOR TOMORROW

Many Americans save little for retirement outside of the "forced" savings of contributions to Social Security made through payroll taxes. Taken alone, this fact isn't necessarily puzzling; maybe most people don't want to save more than that. What makes it strange, though, is that most Americans *say* that they want to be saving more.

If people want to save more, why don't they do it? Typically, economists assume that people make rational, purposeful decisions about saving. They save up when income is high and spend down savings when income is low or gone, such as in retirement. Based on the idea of *revealed preference,* economists often infer that whatever choices people are making must be "right" for them and their situations in life. If someone occasionally doesn't save as much as planned one month, we assume that he or she will simply adjust to put a little more in the bank in the future. Over the long term, we expect to see people's actions matching up with their intentions.

But suppose that some people are consistently letting current temptations get in the way of long-term saving goals. They're not just miscalculating for a month here and there, but are saving

© The McGraw-Hill Companies, Inc./Mark Dierker, photographer.

much less than they'd like to over years and years. They may find themselves with less than they want to have in the bank to support their kids' education or to live on in retirement. Can anything be done, in their moments of reflection and planning, to help them make decisions they would feel better about? Economists Shlomo Benartzi and Richard Thaler designed a program to help people overcome their own limitations and save more.[1]

This approach, called Save More Tomorrow (or SMarT™), offers employees the option to commit a fraction of future pay raises to a tax-free retirement savings account. Benartzi and Thaler realized that most of us dislike the feeling of giving up what we already have—such as having to accept a cut in our current pay in order to save more. By tying increases in saving to *future* pay raises, SMarT helps people save without feeling they are "giving up" something in order to save more. (To be as flexible as possible, the program allows people to change their minds later on and, if they want, back out of their commitment and lower their saving rate back down.)

If people are already making optimal choices about saving, then a program like SMarT will have no effect. But it turns out that people who participated in SMarT almost quadrupled their saving rate over a few years. That rate went from 3.5 percent of income to 13.6 percent. This increase suggests that people really *were* saving less than they wanted to but needed a little nudge to get them on track.

SMarT is designed to help employees overcome at least two different types of mental barriers to saving:

- First, SMarT takes advantage of a *status-quo bias:* We often are reluctant to make active decisions to change something, even if it is fairly easy to do so. SMarT is designed so that an increase in future savings occurs if the participant takes *no action.* If you want to change your mind about the amount committed to future savings, you can do so easily. It turns out, though, that with saving as the default option, people are more likely to go through with it.

- Second, SMarT can overcome *time inconsistency:* Many people are unwilling to forgo current consumption to save now but *are* willing to cut back future consumption to save for the even farther-off future. Why? Saving more right now means giving up things that are immediately tempting to us. It's often hard to do that. Saving *later* doesn't feel as painful right now, so we are more willing to agree to do it. However, if one must wait until the future to make the saving decision, then you might find yourself unwilling to save when the future finally arrives. By committing *now* to saving in the future, you can maintain the saving decision that you want.

The SMarT program shows that simply changing the way we present options can affect people's behavior and help them overcome mental biases and avoid regret. Thaler and his collaborator Cass Sunstein have come up with a term for this idea: *choice architecture.* When we think critically about how to design the environment in which people make choices, we are engaging in *choice architecture.* In their book *Nudge: Improving Decisions About Health, Wealth, and Happiness,*

Thaler and Sunstein promote the idea that the structure of policies and products affects the outcomes of individuals' decisions. They argue that it is possible to design policies and products in a way that gently "nudges" people toward choices that will make them happier in the long run.

What makes people happier in the long run can be hotly debated. Thaler and Sunstein don't want to dictate what people should do. Instead, they want to make it easier to make better choices, while leaving people free to make those choices themselves. Even if a policy-maker does not want to engage in "nudging," he or she still has to choose how to present choices to people. Each presentation approach will lead to certain predictable choices. So the mantra of Thaler and Sunstein is to recognize this responsibility and nudge toward good outcomes.

In this chapter, we'll describe how choice architecture works. We'll start by describing some of the psychological biases that can shape economic choices. Then we'll explore how policy-makers, private companies, and choice architects of all sorts are putting the ideas into action to help guide people toward decisions that they say they want to make.

Choice Architecture and Nudges

Sometimes people do things that they themselves would agree are not the right decisions. They might *say* they want to save money but never get around to opening a savings account. They might agree that they'd be better off dieting, but they keep eating junk food.

We first approached this idea in Chapter 8, "Behavioral Economics: A Closer Look at Decision Making." Here, we'll apply some of the insights of behavioral economics to see how policy-makers can design products and policies that nudge people toward making better decisions.

Why nudge?

LO 23.1 Define choice architecture and identify how nudges can influence individual decision making.

A growing pile of evidence indicates that people's decisions can be influenced by how options are presented to them. **Choice architecture**—the organization of the context and process in which people make decisions—can alter actual decisions and thus the ultimate outcomes. Choice architecture focuses on such factors as the timing of choices and how different options are described.

"Choice architects" are people who are in a position to shape the decision-making environment. Because they can influence the outcomes of people's choices, we have to ask how they ought to exercise this influence. As Uncle Ben told Peter Parker (aka Spiderman), "with great power comes great responsibility." Some might say choice architects should aim to use their power as lightly as possible, by being "neutral."

On closer inspection, though, it's not clear what a neutral policy means in most situations. For instance, research shows that supermarket shoppers are more likely to purchase items placed in noticeable locations, such as at eye level on the shelf. No matter how you arrange things, some products are going to be located at eye level and others aren't. There's no such thing as "neutral" shelving. But we *can* make a choice about which items end up at eye level. This is where the power of choice architecture comes into play.

choice architecture
the organization of the context and process in which people make decisions

If policy can't be neutral, what should it be? For the supermarket manager, the answer is easy enough. She wants to put at eye-level items that will maximize profits. What if the choice architect has in mind goals other than maximizing profit? In that case, the decision is a tougher one:

- Should choice architects aim to encourage choices that *they* think will be better for society?
- Or should they try to push people toward things that *people themselves* would agree are better for them?

In this chapter, we focus mainly on describing *how* policy can influence people's decisions. We leave open the question of the appropriate use of these tools.

Thaler and Sunstein use the term **nudge** to describe an implementation of choice architecture that alters people's behavior in a deliberate and predictable way without changing economic incentives much.[2] In other words, a nudge is a gentle push in a particular direction, but anyone who wants to go in a different direction is still able to do so. The SMarT program, for example, nudges people toward higher saving, but people still have the freedom to change their minds and lower their saving rate. In the grocery store, placing an item at eye level nudges shoppers toward selecting it, but they can still choose items from higher or lower shelves instead.

Nudges can sometimes accomplish public policy goals in a less expensive and coercive way than more traditional methods. Why set tough quotas, crank up taxes, or make something illegal if you can nudge people in the socially desired direction? Below, we'll see numerous examples of successful, cost-effective nudges. These nudges help people make the choices that they would actually prefer to make for themselves. Most importantly, unlike strict rules, they still preserve freedom of choice for others who don't want to go in the direction they're being nudged in. Read the Real Life box "Committing to fertilizer" for one example of a nudge from the developing world.

nudge

an implementation of choice architecture that alters people's behavior in a deliberate and predictable way without changing economic incentives much

Real Life

Committing to fertilizer

In Western Kenya, many people make a living by growing crops. However, the soil is very poor. As a result, these subsistence farmers typically earn the equivalent of a dollar a day. By applying small amounts of fertilizer to the top of the soil, farmers can increase their harvest by 48 percent. The return on this investment is well worth the cost of the fertilizer, and farmers are well aware of these benefits. But still, 55 percent of farmers in this region have never used fertilizer. Why?

There's an obvious answer: Maybe the farmers can't afford it. This explanation has led to a traditional policy response: huge subsidies on fertilizer. Zambia, another East African country, dedicates 2 percent of its entire public budget to such subsidies.

However, economists Esther Duflo, Michael Kremer, and Jonathan Robinson wondered if there might be another explanation. When they asked the farmers, most said that they *intended* to use fertilizer and that they earned enough *at harvest time* to be able to afford it. But when the time came to plant their crops, money was tight again, so they decided to forgo fertilizer. Much like people who intend to save more for retirement but find it hard to consume less now to do so, Kenyan farmers had trouble saving after the harvest to pay for fertilizer at planting time.

In response to this problem, the three economists, working with nonprofit organization Innovations for Poverty Action, created a nudge to help farmers follow through on their intention to use fertilizer. The nudge worked by offering farmers the chance to buy fertilizer at different times during the year. Field workers sold vouchers that let farmers pay in months when they had surpluses, with a guarantee that fertilizer would be delivered to them at the next planting season.

Sure enough, when the workers visited farmers shortly after a harvest, fertilizer purchases increased by 60 percent. The fertilizer vouchers enabled the farmers to *commit* to use fertilizer by paying for it when they had money available. Of course, they could have saved the money for those three months, but without the commitment, that often didn't happen.

The evidence suggests that timing was everything. When farmers were allowed to pay for the vouchers just a few days after the initial sales visit—as opposed to having to pay during the sales visit—the percentage of those who purchased fertilizer fell by over half. Farmers who were offered vouchers later in the off-season were also much less likely to buy fertilizer—even when the price was reduced by 50 percent.

The findings suggest an alternative to expensive government subsidies to increase fertilizer usage. More broadly, they also show that choice architecture—in this case, altering the *timing* of the farmers' decision about fertilizer purchases—can make a real difference even to people who are among the poorest in the world. The farmers already knew it was in their best interests to buy fertilizer. All they needed was a nudge.

Sources: Esther Duflo, Michael Kremer, and Jonathan Robinson, "Nudging Farmers to Use Fertilizer: Theory and Experimental Evidence from Kenya."*American Economic Review* 101, no. 6 (2011): 2350–90, DOI:10.1257/aer.101.6.2350.

What is a "bad" choice?

When we talk about a "mistake" or a "bad choice" in this chapter, we're not imposing our own views about the merits of a choice in question. Instead, we're defining "mistake" from the perspective of the person doing the choosing. A mistake is a choice that the chooser later regrets.

It's worth a short side trip to consider how economists think about good and bad choices. Economics allows for the idea that people have diverse preferences. As a result, it's difficult to say what constitutes a good choice for others. For some, the frustration of sticking to a diet is worth the weight loss. For others, it might not be. As a rule, economics assumes that people weigh trade-offs and make choices that maximize their utility. In a traditional economic view (as seen in the idea of *revealed preference* described in Chapter 7, "Consumer Behavior"), there is no such thing as a "bad" choice. That's because we assume, by definition, that people choose what is best for themselves.

Consider a person who runs up huge debts by taking out expensive loans. A psychologist might conclude that he is a compulsive shopper with a self-control problem. But economists usually start with the assumption that the shopper's decision can be explained by his preferences. If he has a strong preference for current consumption, for example, then he is rationally maximizing his utility by taking on heavy future repayment obligations to buy more stuff now.

This traditional economic approach is at the core of this book for good reason. For one thing, it's based on a reasonable simplifying assumption: People do tend to *try* to act in their own self-interest. It also gives people the benefit of the doubt that they often know what's best for themselves, at least better than others do. However, studying behavioral economics, choice architecture, and nudges allows us to integrate some lessons from psychology into this core economic approach—that we can go beyond the simplifying assumption that people *always* make the choices that are best for themselves.

However, this leaves us in a tough spot. When people make choices that look funny to others, is it simply because they have different preferences? Or are they actually making mistakes? A behavioral economics approach suggests that it could be either. Who gets to decide what constitutes a "bad" choice? Friends? Neighbors? Parents? Policy-makers? How and when should their opinions be put into action? Answering these questions could take up entire textbooks, and we don't attempt to address them here. Instead, we use the words "bad choice" and "mistake" only when *the decision makers themselves* would later agree that they have made a bad choice or mistake.

Mistakes people make

LO 23.2 Explain several ways in which human decision making does not conform to the model of full information and rational choices.

Once we accept that people try to maximize their well-being but sometimes make mistakes, we start to find that those mistakes happen in common and predictable ways. Here, we consider some important categories of biases in human decision making. In the next section, we'll see more examples of how choice architects can put these insights to work.

Temptation

In Chapter 8, "Behavioral Economics: A Closer Look at Decision Making," we talked about how people struggle with temptation and procrastination. How can we as economists and policy-makers understand people who say they want one thing—to save money, or stay on a diet, or quit smoking—but then do something else? Our economic model described temptation as sort of split-personality problem: We have one set of preferences about what to do today and another about what to do in the future.

time inconsistency
a situation in which we change our minds about what we want simply because of the timing of the decision

We use the term **time inconsistency** to describe a situation in which we change our minds about what we want simply because of the timing of the decision. People's preferences about the present are inconsistent with their preferences about the future, simply because the future choices are more distant. Note that it's not time inconsistency if your preferences are different because the circumstances are different in some important way. For instance:

- If you want to eat junk food now because you're on vacation and you will start a diet next week when the vacation is over, that's not time-inconsistent.

- When you want to start your diet one week from today, but when that time comes, you want to start it in yet one more week, and so on, it *is* time-inconsistent. In this case, your preferences changed simply because time passed.

As we saw in the chapter-opening story, time inconsistency is one of the common biases that the SMarT program helps to tackle. Sometimes temptation is just temptation, and we might rationally choose to give in to the temptation. But sometimes recognizing time inconsistency in temptations can help people avoid undesirable choices. When we recognize the problem, we can use appropriate solutions. As we saw in Chapter 8, "Behavioral Economics: A Closer Look at Decision Making," a common solution to time inconsistency is a commitment device. If you can commit your future self to making the decision you want, then it is impossible to give in to the temptation of changing your behavior in the future.

Limited processing power

We learned in Chapter 22, "Political Choices," why it can be rational to choose to not be fully informed about a political issue. We used the term *rational ignorance* to explain that people might choose to remain ignorant when the opportunity costs of gathering information outweigh the benefits. For example, you would probably do a bit of comparative shopping before buying a new computer, but few people become world experts on computing technology. Is it possible that you're making the wrong decision about which machine is best for you? Sure. But is it really worth spending a whole year researching computers in order to be more sure that you're picking the exactly right model? Probably not. Think about all of the other things you could be doing during that year that are worth more to you than the risk of having a less-than-ideal computer.

Sometimes, though, our ignorance isn't so carefully considered, and the consequences of bad choices are big. We might simply get overwhelmed by the complicated information involved in a choice. For example, the question of how much you should be saving at any given time in your life to achieve a comfortable retirement is challenging to answer, even for economics professors.

Psychological research shows that choices that involve processing lots of complicated information are, unsurprisingly, likely to turn out worse than those involving simple information.

Practice can make perfect, even when making hard decisions. But unfortunately, lots of important choices in life don't come with practice rounds. Familiar choices—like what to eat for dinner—are easy. They are easier than choices that we make only infrequently, such as choosing between different types of surgery or how to invest retirement funds. In part, this is because we have all eaten enough dinners to understand the utility we are likely to get from different choices. We're more likely to make mistakes with situations we face infrequently, such as how to invest our retirement funds, how different types of surgery are likely to affect us five years down the road, or which college we should go to.

Avoiding mistakes when making infrequent decisions is especially hard when it's not clear how to translate available information into something personally meaningful. When deciding which college to go to, you may have been bombarded with statistics and stories—average SAT scores, how many students graduate on time, professor-to-student ratios, and so on. This information was useful to you only insofar as you could translate it into a prediction for how enjoyable and productive your life as a student at that college would be. This problem gets even worse in situations where you're not sure what will ultimately matter to you. If you've never been to college before, how can you know whether you care about how big your classes will be?

Reluctance to change

People go with the flow. They tend to stick with the current situation over other options, even when it is cheap to switch. Economists call this **status-quo bias**. It is one of the common mistakes we saw in the chapter-opening story about SMarT.

In the arena of decision making, status-quo bias means that the "default" option—the one that will automatically take place if the chooser fails to make an active decision—has a lot of power. For an example of status-quo bias at work, consider what happens when you sign up for a free trial of an online product. Most of the time, if you don't go back and cancel, you'll be signed up for the full program automatically at the end of the free trial. Many of us plan to cancel but then just forget and end up paying for something we didn't really want.

An interesting twist on status-quo bias is the **endowment effect**. This is the tendency to place a higher value on something you already own simply because you own it. In a well-known experiment, psychologist Daniel Kahneman and economists Jack Knetsch and Richard Thaler doled out plain coffee mugs to one group of people. They then asked another group that didn't get mugs how much they'd be willing to pay to get one. (Everyone could see the mug and assess its quality.) They also asked students with mugs how much they'd have to be paid to give up their mugs. If the students had similar tastes on average (which is reasonable to assume, given that they were randomly split into groups), we'd expect that the values for the mugs would be roughly the same. But in the experiment, students who had been given mugs placed a higher value on them than students who hadn't—more than twice as much, in fact.[3] This experiment was cited by the Nobel Committee when awarding Daniel Kahneman the Nobel Memorial Prize in Economic Sciences in 2002.

The endowment effect is related to **loss aversion**, a general tendency for people to put more effort into avoiding losses than achieving gains. Loss aversion is not to be confused with *risk aversion,* which we described in Chapter 11, "Time and Uncertainty." Risk aversion is about preferring certain outcomes over uncertain ones. Instead, the insight behind loss aversion is that people will typically put out more effort to avoid losing $100 than they would to gain $100.

Framing matters

Choice architects know that whether something *feels* like a loss or gain often depends on how it is *framed.* For instance, suppose you are a shopkeeper who charges a slightly higher price for credit-card transactions than for cash purchases. We could describe this price difference in two ways:

- As a "discount" for paying in cash.
- As a "fee" for paying with a credit card.

status-quo bias
the tendency to stick with the current situation over other options, even when it is cheap to switch

endowment effect
the tendency of people to place more value on something simply because they own it

loss aversion
the tendency for people to put more effort into avoiding losses than achieving gains

Evidence shows that people care more about avoiding a fee than they care about getting a discount. So as a shopkeeper, you can expect a greater tilt toward cash-paying when you advertise a "credit-card fee" than if you advertise an equivalent "discount" for paying cash.

There are many other situations in which people respond to the way choices are framed. This is true even when that framing does not change the substance of the available options. Imagine you're deciding which of two universities to attend:

- University A sends you a brochure saying, "Within three months after graduation, 80 percent of our students have found jobs!"
- University B's brochure says, "Three months after graduation, 20 percent of our students have failed to find jobs."

Which school do you want to choose?

As we're sure you noticed, universities A and B actually have identical job-placement rates—but university A clearly has a better public relations department. On a purely rational level, a reader should see that 80 percent of graduates from both schools have jobs and 20 percent don't. But our subconscious processing system interprets the information differently. We respond better to the positive framing (emphasizing the successful graduates) than to the negative (emphasizing the failures).

✓ CONCEPT CHECK

☐ Does a nudge force people to make a better choice? **[LO 23.1]**
☐ Explain how time inconsistency accounts for procrastination. **[LO 23.2]**
☐ What is the endowment effect? **[LO 23.2]**

Tools of Choice Architecture

In this section we explore techniques that choice architects use to structure the decisions that people face. Remember that we're discussing methods—not necessarily endorsing the outcomes.

Commitment devices

> **LO 23.3** Explain how demand for commitment devices can be rational.

In a simple world, we usually assume that having more options is a good thing. Typically, there is no cost to ignoring options you don't like. In the best-case scenario, you gain new, good options. In the worst-case scenario, you ignore all the new, bad options and are in the exact same spot you were before.

However, understanding time inconsistency shows us why someone might rationally want to limit her own options. Assume you want to start a diet in a week, but you know that your future self will be tempted to keep putting off the diet. You don't quite trust yourself to make the right choice. So, you might want to take actions now to make sure there won't be any junk food in the house next week. By limiting your food options, you make it harder for your future self to make bad choices.

In Chapter 8, "Behavioral Economics: A Closer Look at Decision Making," we saw some examples of tools that allow people to voluntarily restrict later choices so they can make better decisions in the future: setting personal deadlines for long-term assignments, signing up for a savings account that requires regular deposits, or installing a browser extension that limits your access to time-sink websites.

These voluntary mechanisms are **commitment devices**. They allow people to voluntarily restrict their choices in order to make it easier to stick to plans. Some commitment devices are

commitment device
a mechanism that allows people to voluntarily restrict their choices in order to make it easier to stick to plans

completely informal—such as not buying junk food this week so that you won't have ready access to it next week when you intend to start your diet. Other commitment devices are formal policies and products. For instance, salaried workers can sign up to have their employers automatically deduct pension contributions from future paychecks.

Commitment devices are an example of using choice architecture to help people overcome temptation. Some commitment devices have strong commitments that are hard to get out of. Other devices have weak commitments that are easier to change. Neither is inherently better than the other. Specific people and situations call for different types of commitment. SMarT is a weak commitment device; it commits you to a savings plan, but it's easy to reverse the decision later. One way of understanding the economic insight behind commitment devices is to think about them as methods either to increase the price of your vices or to lower the price of your virtues.

There are three important rules in creating good commitment devices:

1. Make goals realistic.
2. Be specific about what you will do and how you will do it.
3. Set the right stakes, whether financial or peer pressure, that will keep you on track to fulfill your goal.

Information campaigns and disclosure rules

LO 23.4 Explain how information, when presented well, can help people make decisions that are good for them.

Because choices are hard and people have limited processing capacity, we often rely on rules of thumb. Rules of thumb help us translate complicated information into a simpler and more familiar framework. A rule of thumb is an example of a **heuristic**—a mental shortcut that helps us make decisions (sometimes in good ways, but sometimes not). Some such rules of thumb can be entirely personal. For example, one person we know always goes with the spicier option when facing unknown food choices in a new restaurant.

heuristic
a mental shortcut for making decisions (sometimes in good ways, but sometimes not)

Another popular heuristic is *anchoring*—estimating unknown quantities by starting from a known "anchor" point. Suppose you were asked to estimate the cost of a flight from Omaha to New Orleans for Thanksgiving vacation. You might start by thinking of a figure you happen to know that is somewhat related—say, the cost of a flight from Chicago to Houston. You then would do something to that figure—say, add a bit because you're not sure how far apart Omaha and New Orleans actually are and you know that flights are generally more expensive around Thanksgiving. It's a rough way of making a guess, but you'll probably be closer than someone who has no idea what any plane tickets cost, and so has no anchor point.

However, research shows that people also tend to latch onto any nearby number as an anchor point, without even realizing it. Suppose we asked, "Guess how much an Omaha to New Orleans flight costs. Is it more than $200?" You might think, "Surely it's got to be more than that . . . say, $300?" But if we asked, "Guess how much an Omaha to New Orleans flight costs. Is it less than $600?" you might think, "Gee, that does sound like a lot. . . . Is it $500, perhaps?" The question hasn't changed, but suggesting an anchor has changed your guess.

Anchoring can bias choices in some predictable ways. Think of how charities solicit donations. Nonprofits often send fund-raising requests in the mail, with suggestions of amounts to contribute. People who get a solicitation with boxes suggesting donations of $50, $100, or $500 will tend to give more than if the boxes suggested $1, $5, or $10—even though the donors are also given the option to write in any amount they want instead of checking a box. A clever choice architect at a charitable organization can nudge people to give more simply by suggesting different amounts on a web page or a mail flyer. (Of course, there is a balance to be struck. If you set the anchor points too high, you risk scaring people away from donating at all.)

The newest EPA stickers (bottom sticker) give estimated annual fuel costs in comparison to the average new vehicle, plus emission ratings, to nudge consumers toward vehicles that have better fuel efficiency.
Source: www.epa.gov/fueleconomy

Choice architects can also affect the choices that people make by nudging them toward the use of specific choices in particular situations. For example, the Environmental Protection Agency (EPA) has for decades required car manufacturers to use a standard-format sticker disclosing the city and highway gas mileage of each car model. However, the average person may not be able to translate gas mileage into facts that really matter to them: How much might I spend on gas each year? How much gas will I need to drive 100 miles? Recognizing the importance of translating this into helpful information, the EPA updated the formatting of the stickers to try to help people make better choices.

Can presenting information differently also help people stay out of debt? In the 2007–2009 recession, for example, many families got into trouble from having run up too much debt on their credit cards. The federal government already required lenders to disclose detailed information about fees, interest rates, and so on. But many people do not read in detail, or do not understand, the lengthy sections of small print on the credit-card application and monthly statements.

Recognizing this problem, Congress passed the Credit Card Accountability, Responsibility, and Disclosure Act (CARD Act), which went into effect in 2010.[4] It requires credit-card bills to state the interest rate and other terms of the card. It also requires them to translate that information in ways that customers will understand. For example, all credit-card bills must now tell you how long it will take to pay off the full balance if you pay only the minimum amount. They also must tell you how much you would have to pay each month to pay off your balance within three years.

Even more than credit-card companies, "payday lenders" are often accused of not providing the information that would help their clients make informed choices about whether to use their services. Payday lenders provide high-fee, high-interest, short-term loans meant to help people pay for expenses until their next paycheck arrives. If these loans aren't paid off quickly, the costs add up fast.

Default rules

> **LO 23.5** Describe how default rules affect people's choices and the implications for policy.

Earlier we noted that people tend to stick with the current or starting option in many choice situations. Even if they're completely free to change things, they often don't. If your employer starts you off with a basic retirement plan, for example, you're more likely to stick with it than you would be to choose it yourself from a whole set of options. We call this starting option a **default rule**; it defines what will automatically occur if someone fails to make an active decision otherwise.

default rule
a rule defining what will automatically occur if a chooser fails to make an active decision otherwise

For example, many workers have retirement savings accounts called 401(k) accounts. As part of an employment-benefits package, some employers offer to match their employees' contributions to the accounts. Commonly, companies will add an amount equal to half of what an employee adds, up to some percent of their salary. It's usually a good deal: The matching contribution from the company is "free money" for the employee, who can defer paying taxes on it until he or she withdraws from the account later in a career or at retirement. However, signing up for a 401(k) retirement account usually requires filling out some paperwork, and a large fraction of people who are eligible for such a plan simply fail to enroll. At many companies, the default rule for a 401(k) account is "no contribution," and lots of people stick with this default.

Choice architects suggest a simple solution: Change the default option so that all new employees are automatically enrolled. Those who don't want to put money into a 401(k) account can still opt out. Those who do want to put money into a 401(k) won't have to bother filling out forms, and they also will capture the employer's matching contribution.

The idea of changing behavior by changing default rules has been applied in unexpected places. For an example, see the Real Life box "Who doesn't want to be an organ donor?"

Real Life

Who doesn't want to be an organ donor?

Over 120,000 people in the United States are currently waiting to receive a donated organ, like a healthy kidney or lung. Many transplants do take place (about 30,000 each year), but about 8,000 people die each year while waiting for an organ. On the face of things, it's hard to see why there is such a mismatch between supply and demand. The vast majority of Americans say they support organ donation. Since many people die with healthy organs every year, the supply of organs for transplants should be plentiful. But it's not.

A big part of the reason lies in how people are asked about organ donation. The rules governing organ donation differ from state to state. In most cases, when people receive or renew their driver's licenses, they are asked if they would like to be a donor. In other words, people have to actively opt in to being an organ donor; the default is to *not* be a donor. The result is that about 51 percent of adults are registered donors, in contrast with the 90 percent who say they support organ donation.

Some policy-makers have suggested a different system. Why not simply require people who *don't* want to be organ donors to opt out? This system, often called *presumed consent,* sets donation as the default option. We can see some startling differences in rates of organ donation between countries that do and do not have an opt-out system:

- Germany has an opt-in system, and only about 12 percent of its population registers to donate.
- Germany's neighbor Austria has an opt-out system, and 99 percent of the population is registered to donate.
- In Belgium, kidney donation doubled within three years after presumed-consent legislation passed.

Researchers have found similar results in studies in the United States. They divided people into two groups. Each group was told to imagine they had moved to a different state and needed to make a decision about whether to be an organ donor. The default rule changed behaviors:

- For one group, the default was to *not* be an organ donor. Only 50 percent stayed with that default.
- For the other group, the default was to be a donor. Over 80 percent of people in this group stayed with the default.

A simple change of the default rule was enough to cause a 30-percentage-point difference in the number of (hypothetical) registered donors. Even without changing the default rule, subtle differences in the way people are asked about organ donation are correlated with big differences in outcomes. In the states with the highest donation rates, at the time when you receive or renew your driver's license, employees of the Department of Motor Vehicles are required to ask whether you want to be an organ donor. In the states with the lowest rates, applicants have to volunteer that they want to be an organ donor or find a checkbox deep in the driver's license renewal forms.

When it comes to figuring out who wants to be an organ donor, the answer depends on how you ask the question.

Sources: http://www.econlib.org/library/Columns/y2009/Tabarroklifesaving.html; http://optn.transplant.hrsa. gov/; http://nudges.org/2010/10/10/how-required-choice-for-organ-donation-actually-works-in-practice/; http:// www.dangoldstein.com/papers/DefaultsScience.pdf; http://www.hks.harvard.edu/fs/aabadie/pconsent.pdf; https://donatelife.net/statistics/.

Framing choices

LO 23.6 Describe how framing affects the way people process information and its implications for policy.

We have seen already in this chapter some examples of how the *framing* of choices can affect people's decisions. In fact, marketers in private companies knew this long before behavioral economists started talking about "nudges" and "choice architecture." As we saw in Chapter 15, "Monopolistic Competition and Oligopoly," advertisers know that *framing* a product matters: Associating the product with young, beautiful people partying on a tropical island will cause more people to buy it, even if the product has nothing to do with being young, beautiful, or on a tropical island. The ways that framing can be used to influence people's choices are diverse. Here we'll look at two that are particularly relevant for public policy-makers: social norms and loss aversion.

If you were a policy-maker in charge of persuading people to pay their taxes, how would you go about it? You could run a campaign informing them about fines for nonpayment. But it turns out there's an even more powerful way to persuade them: Inform them that almost everyone else pays their taxes. Researchers have found that when you frame choices in terms of *social norms—* that is, what others do—people tend to go along with the majority. Most of us don't like to feel that we are outliers.

Pressure to conform to social norms can be a double-edged sword for choice architects, though. If you were charged with increasing voter turnout among the young, you might want to raise awareness of the problem by talking about how "only about 20 percent of young people voted in the last election." Unfortunately, this approach might actually make the problem worse. Hearing this, young people may conclude, "So it's no big deal if I don't vote—no one else is doing it either."

We have already seen a couple of examples of how choice architects can use the idea of loss aversion: the SMarT program's tying of saving to future pay raises and the difference between a "cash discount" and a "credit-card fee."

Some creative researchers wrestled with framing decisions as they tried to harness the power of social norms to reduce home-energy consumption. The results, described in the From Another Angle box "Turn down the AC for a smiley face," might surprise you.

From Another Angle
Turn down the AC for a smiley face

Americans spend a lot on energy to heat and cool their homes. This isn't necessarily a "bad" choice. Still, many people say they want to use less energy, and energy companies have tried many techniques to encourage them to follow through. They may increase prices during periods of peak energy use or ask people to commit to reducing their consumption. One study found that simply asking people to set goals for their own energy use caused a reduction of 4 to 7.5 percent. Providing people with feedback on how well they did increased the reduction to 12 percent.

A group of researchers wondered if there might be an easier, cheaper way. What if we harnessed the power of social norms to frame people's choice about how high to crank up the air conditioning? What if we simply tell people if they're using more electricity than their neighbors?

One such experiment was conducted in San Marco, California. Hundreds of households received notices telling them how much energy they had consumed in the past two weeks relative to the average energy consumption in their neighborhood. Sure enough, in response to this information, households that had been consuming more than average reduced their usage. Unfortunately, though, households that discovered they had been consuming less than average actually *increased* their usage! In other words, both high- and low-use consumers moved toward the middle, an outcome that researchers refer to as the "boomerang effect." Maybe customers who discovered they were low-use felt able to indulge themselves a bit more by turning up the AC. Or maybe people simply like to do whatever everyone else is doing, for better or worse.

This was a head-scratcher. How could the energy company nudge high-use customers to use less electricity without inadvertently also nudging low-use customers to use more? The answer turned out to be very, very easy: The researchers added a smiley face to the notice for households consuming less than average. It added a frowny face for households consuming more than average. The reduction by high-use customers increased, and the boomerang effect among low-use customers disappeared.

While people's most basic impulse is to be average, you can overcome that impulse. You just have to find a way of signaling to them that it's good to be better than average.

Sources: Hunt Allcott, "Social Norms and Energy Conservation,"*Journal of Public Economics* (2011), DOI:10.1016/ j.jpubeco.2011.03.003; P. W. Schultz, J. Nolan, R. Cialdini, N. Goldstein, and V. Griskevicius, "The Constructive, Destructive, and Reconstructive Power of Social Norms,"*Psychological Science* 18 (2007): 429–434.

✓ CONCEPT CHECK

☐ How can a commitment device help overcome time-inconsistent preferences? **[LO 23.3]**

☐ What is a heuristic? **[LO 23.4]**

☐ Why does status-quo bias imply that default rules are important? **[LO 23.5]**

☐ How do choice architects use social norms to frame choices? **[LO 23.6]**

Conclusion

Advertisers know that sales depend on more than delivering an appealing economic proposition. Clinching the deal often depends on hitting the right psychological buttons. Recently economists have also started bringing psychology into their problem-solving approach, and it's delivering practical ways to help people make choices that they are less likely to regret.

Choices are often influenced by the way that options are presented. Almost any presentation subtly pushes people toward one option or another, so it's difficult for choice frameworks to be truly neutral. In this chapter, we described how "choice architects" can present options in a way that helps people overcome biases and voluntarily make choices they are happier with.

We've walked through some of the tools that choice architects can use to "nudge" people toward better decisions. Often, these nudges are simple and inexpensive: changing the wording or increasing the clarity of information provided to people, redefining default options, or offering people ways to commit to a desired course of action. Used thoughtfully, nudges can help companies earn more profit and can help policy-makers achieve economic and social goals. One of the most striking lessons from behavioral economics is that small changes in choice architecture can sometimes lead to big changes in behavior.

Key Terms

choice architecture, p. 581

nudge, p. 582

time inconsistency, p. 584

status-quo bias, p. 585

endowment effect, p. 585

loss aversion, p. 585

commitment device, p. 586

heuristic, p. 587

default rule, p. 588

Summary

LO 23.1 Define choice architecture and identify how nudges can influence individual decision making.

Choice architecture is the design of the environment in which people make decisions. It matters because evidence shows that people's decisions are influenced by the way in which options are presented to them. Although the idea that people are rational utility-maximizers is a useful simplifying assumption, we know that people also make mistakes in their efforts to increase their own well-being. They choose options that they themselves would agree were not the right ones to pick. A nudge is an aspect of choice architecture that affects people's behavior without coercing them or fundamentally changing the economic incentives they face. Nudges can be used to help people bypass their own shortcomings to make better choices.

LO 23.2 Explain several ways in which human decision making does not conform to the model of full information and rational choices.

People make mistakes in some common and predictable ways. Time inconsistency—a situation when we change our minds about what we want simply because of the timing of the decision—helps us explain procrastination and temptation. People also have limited ability to process information. They are more likely to make mistakes when the decisions they face are complicated or unfamiliar, or for which the relationship between available information and the outcomes that actually matter is unclear.

In general, people have trouble with change, tending to prefer the status quo, avoiding losses, and ascribing more value to things they own than things they don't. Finally, decisions are influenced by the way in which options are presented, including minor details like phrasing.

LO 23.3 Explain how demand for commitment devices can be rational.

Commitment devices are strategies and tools that allow people to commit to make good choices in the future by voluntarily restricting their own options. If a person is

aware of her own time inconsistency, she might prefer to have fewer options to choose from (or to make bad options more expensive); these strategies might help reduce the chance that she'll give in to temptation in the future. As a result, allowing people to voluntarily opt in to a commitment device can actually help them increase their own well-being.

LO 23.4 Explain how information, when presented well, can help people make decisions that are good for them.

People often rely on mental shortcuts to help them make decisions. This suggests that information presented well, and at the right time, can help people make good decisions. Realizing this, choice architects try to figure out what information people need to make good decisions and give that information to them in a usable and timely way. Such efforts are often called *nudges*.

LO 23.5 Describe how default rules affect people's choices and the implications for policy.

People tend to stick with what they're given—whether that is a mug or a default option for investing their retirement funds. This fact means that default rules in products and policies, which define the option that will automatically occur if someone fails to make an active decision, have a power to influence people's choices. Default rules can nudge people toward particular outcomes.

LO 23.6 Describe how framing affects the way people process information and its implications for policy.

People respond to the way in which the choices are framed, even when that framing does not change the substance of the options available to them. Choice architects can encourage people to make certain choices through the context or way in which they present information. For instance, people are more likely to do something if they think everyone around them is also doing it; giving people information on how they compare to their peers can encourage or discourage behaviors.

Review Questions

1. Is instituting a $200 fine for anyone caught littering a nudge? Why or why not? **[LO 23.1]**

2. Suppose two parents present their 16-year-old with a list of the cars that they will allow him to buy. If the parents decide to add another vehicle to the list, is that affecting the choice architecture for their son? Why or why not? **[LO 23.1]**

3. Suppose you have plans to save 5 percent of your salary next year. Then your company goes bankrupt, your pay gets slashed by 30 percent, and you end up not saving at all. Is this an example of time inconsistency? Why or why not? **[LO 23.2]**

4. With his first paycheck, Steve decides to buy a car. After spending hours researching the many specifications each car has—from gas mileage to horsepower—he decides to give up trying to find the perfect car based on these metrics and buys the best-looking one on the first lot he visits. Explain one aspect of bounded rationality discussed in the text that this example exhibits. **[LO 23.2]**

5. At the website stickK.com (started by one of the authors of this book), you can sign up for a contract in which you promise to meet certain weight-loss targets each week and forfeit money that you put up as stakes if you fail to meet those targets. Describe why a rational person might be willing to pay money if he does not lose weight, and how this constitutes a commitment strategy. **[LO 23.3]**

6. One contributor to the rational demand for commitment devices is the time-inconsistency problem. Explain how limited processing capacity might also contribute to the demand. **[LO 23.3]**

7. Suppose you need to estimate the cost of your textbooks for the upcoming semester. What would be a good "anchor" to use in your estimate? **[LO 23.4]**

8. Jaelyn sees a sweater that she likes in a store. The price is $22. Jaelyn wouldn't usually purchase the sweater at this price, but then she notices a sign that says the sweater is marked down from $44 and decides to buy the sweater. Is Jaelyn's decision an example of a commitment device, the endowment effect, a nudge, or anchoring bias? Explain. **[LO 23.4]**

9. Many online subscription services have "automatic renewal" policies, in which they will automatically bill you for another year's subscription when your current one runs out. Why is this default rule a savvy business strategy on the part of the online company? **[LO 23.5]**

10. Explain the psychological bias that causes people's decisions to be affected by default rules or the endowment effect. **[LO 23.5]**

11. Imagine a public service announcement on television that is intended to scare kids away from using drugs. A big focus of the PSA is that a *lot* of teens are already on drugs. The directors of the PSA intend this statement to emphasize the size of the problem. Explain why this strategy for framing the anti-drugs message to teenagers could backfire. **[LO 23.6]**

12. Suppose you're trying to get your friends to go to dinner with you. Which of the following statements is more likely to convince your friends to go out to dinner? **[LO23.6]**
   Statement 1: "The dinner would only cost $5 more than the food we would make ourselves."
   Statement 2: "Dinner at our favorite restaurant will cost $5 less than a meal at every other restaurant around town."

Problems and Applications

1. In each of the following scenarios, determine whether the change in people's behavior is the result of a nudge or a substantive change in economic incentives. **[LO 23.1]**

   a. A country with a low birth rate decides to offer free public child care for kids under the age of five.

   b. A nonprofit organization runs a highly publicized campaign offering teenage girls a very small symbolic reward (say, $5) for each week that they stay in school, come to support group meetings, and avoid pregnancy.

   c. A country with a rapidly growing population levies steep fines on any family that has more than two children.

   d. A government agency runs an ad on television informing women about low-cost birth-control options.

2. Determine whether each of the following changes represents a shift in the choice architecture of a decision. **[LO 23.1]**

   a. After presenting the dessert menu to patrons, the waiter at a restaurant mentions that there's an additional option for dessert not on the menu.

   b. A restaurant presents dessert menus to patrons before they have eaten.

   c. A waiter shows patrons a menu without prices.

   d. A waiter asks patrons whether they would like to order more fries after telling the couple that the plate of fries is very small.

3. Label each of the following examples as a case of *time inconsistency, limited processing capacity, status-quo bias,* or *framing.* **[LO 23.2]**

   a. A person buys a nice bottle of wine for $50 and leaves it in the pantry for 20 years. At that point, the wine has aged and the value has appreciated to $250. Although he would never be willing to buy a bottle of the same wine for $250, the person plans to drink his old bottle rather than sell it.

b. Every night, a person sets her alarm for 7 a.m. the next morning, and every morning, she hits the snooze button at least four times.

c. People who are told the survival rate for a surgical procedure are more likely to undergo it than people who are told the death rate (even though the death rate is actually the same in both cases).

4. Determine whether each of the following represents loss aversion. **[LO 23.2]**

a. Nearing retirement, an investor chooses investments with lower return and lower risk because she wants to make sure she has a certain amount of money available in five years.

b. A gambler refuses to play a game in which if heads shows up after a coin toss he will win $40, but if tails shows up he will lose $50.

c. Offered a brand-new blanket that is twice as comfortable and cute as her old one—the only two criteria she cares about in a blanket—a toddler refuses to give up her old blanket.

The following information applies to Problems 5, 6, and 7:
Clocky™ is an alarm clock that rolls off your bedside table and runs away when you hit the snooze button. When the alarm goes off again, Clocky will be hiding somewhere on the opposite side of your bedroom so that you are forced to get out of bed to turn off the alarm.

5. Clocky is a commitment device to help overcome time inconsistency. Which of the following are the time periods over which someone might have inconsistent preferences and need Clocky's help? **[LO 23.3]**

a. Between the time the person hits the snooze button and the time the alarm goes off again.

b. Between the time the person sets the alarm the previous night and the time the alarm goes off.

c. Between the time the person actually gets out of bed one morning and the time he sets his alarm for the next morning.

6. Which of the following are relevant areas of preference inconsistency that Clocky is able to help with? **[LO 23.3]**

a. The optimal volume for an alarm.

b. What time to go to bed at night.

c. What time to wake up in the morning.

d. Whether an alarm should be placed on the bedside table or across the room.

7. How much should someone with time-inconsistent preferences be willing to pay for Clocky? **[LO 23.3]**

a. Nothing because a regular alarm will work just as well.

b. Something because Clocky increases his utility by getting him up at the right time.

c. You'd have to pay him to use Clocky because his utility is decreased by having to get out of bed and search around to shut off the alarm.

8. Which of the following is not a strictly rational reason for someone to be interested in a commitment device? **[LO 23.3]**

a. The device can eliminate the time-inconsistency problem.

b. By making the decision to restrict choices now, the person saves future effort in deciding among more, but undesirable, choices.

c. Restricting choice now eliminates the possibility of considering other, potentially better choices that can't be foreseen right now.

d. The device helps the person make the choice that she wants to make right now but might not make in the future.

9. When it comes to making decisions, which of the following statements are true? Select all that apply. **[LO 23.4]**

a. Individuals will make the same choices no matter how information is presented.

b. Anchoring is always helpful when making decisions.

c. Anchoring can mislead individuals into making suboptimal choices.

d. Anchoring can help individuals make better decisions.

10. Suppose you want to buy your significant other tickets to see his or her favorite musical on Broadway in New York City, but you have never purchased tickets to a Broadway musical before and don't know how much they cost. What would be a good "anchor" to use in your estimate? **[LO 23.4]**

a. The cost of movie tickets.

b. The cost of the soundtrack to the musical.

c. The cost of tickets to a musical performed by your local community theater group.

d. The cost of tickets to a Broadway production touring in your hometown.

11. Which of the following are true statements about default rules? (You can choose more than one.) **[LO 23.5]**

a. Defaults have staying power because opting out of them is typically very costly, requiring people to hire lawyers or prove to authorities that they have sufficient reason for choosing another option.

b. The more difficult it is to opt out of the default option, the more likely people are to stick with it.

c. One reason default options might have staying power is that people often equate "default option" with "recommended option."

d. Default rules work to influence choices only if people are aware of the default option.

12. In which of the following examples would we see the influence of a default option? (You can choose more than one.) **[LO 23.5]**

   a. A doctor recommends continuing treatment, but the ultimate decision of whether to continue treatment is left up to the patient.

   b. A website automatically checks the option "share my activity with my friends on Facebook" when users sign up.

   c. Pets from an animal shelter are automatically spayed or neutered unless the owner would prefer them not to be.

   d. A mobile phone user has to enter a choice at start-up between installing a special feature or not. The user is informed that most people choose to install the special feature.

13. A group of people is offered two scenarios and asked which they would prefer: (A) a 3 percent wage decrease in a world with no inflation or (B) a 3 percent wage increase in a world with 6 percent inflation. **[LO 23.6]**

   a. What is the increase or decrease in the real wage in option A? What about in option B?

   b. Knowing what you know about framing and loss aversion, which option do you expect more people to prefer?

   c. In light of your answer to b, if you were an employer trying to cut real labor costs, would you prefer to have some inflation or no inflation in the economy?

14. Choose the statement that people are more likely to choose based on the framing of the choice. **[LO 23.6]**

   a. Stock investment:
      i. Invest in a stock with low uncertainty of return.
      ii. Invest in a stock with high certainty of return.

   b. Car purchase:
      i. Buy a car that costs $20,000, which is $5,000 cheaper than the next level for that maker.
      ii. Buy a car that costs $20,000, which is $5,000 more expensive than the lower level for that maker.

   c. Movie choice:
      i. Go to the movie to which 100 out of 150 people give a five-star rating.
      ii. Go to the move to which 50 out of 150 people give less than a five-star rating.

   d. Choice of college class:
      i. Take a class in which 50 percent of students get an A.
      ii. Take a class in which 50 percent of students don't get an A.

Endnotes

1. http://www.anderson.ucla.edu/faculty/shlomo.benartzi/smartjpe226.pdf.

2. Cass Sunstein and Richard Thaler, *Nudge* (New Haven: Yale University Press, 2008).

3. https://www.princeton.edu/~kahneman/docs/Publications/Anomalies_DK_JLK_RHT_1991.pdf.

4. http://bucks.blogs.nytimes.com/2010/02/22/what-the-credit-card-act-means-for-you/?_r=0.

Part Six

The Data of Macroeconomics

The two chapters in Part 6 will introduce you to . . .

the topic of macroeconomics and two important macroeconomic concepts: gross domestic product and consumer prices.

How well off do you think you will be in 10 years? In 20 years? Your answers probably depend on choices that you may already be considering—especially choices about where to live, family plans, and your career.

Of course, your future financial position will also depend on forces outside of your control. Some of those forces will be economic, like how many jobs are available, how housing prices change, and how fast prices rise over time. These forces are the focus of macroeconomics, the study of how billions of daily decisions made by individuals add up to shape the overall economy. It's the study of economic growth, inflation, booms and busts, and unemployment.

Chapter 24, "Measuring GDP," covers the calculation of gross domestic product (GDP), the most useful metric of macroeconomics, which sums up the amount of economic activity in a country. It's the first number economists look at when tracking overall economic growth and the ups and downs of the economy.

Chapter 25, "The Cost of Living," covers another important part of macroeconomic record-keeping: consumer prices. A century ago, a bottle of Coke cost a nickel and and a brand-new car could be purchased for hundreds of dollars. Both items cost a lot more today, but that doesn't mean that we're worse off—our incomes have risen along with prices. As you'll see, accounting for consumer prices gives an important part of the macro picture.

As we progress through the study of macroeconomics, the concepts of GDP and changing price levels will come up over and over again; they are useful tools for answering questions about the health and direction of the economy. These two chapters offer insight into forces that will affect your job and income, as well as the wealth and well-being of the whole country.

Measuring GDP

Learning Objectives

LO 24.1 Understand the importance of using the market value of final goods and services to calculate GDP and explain why each component of GDP is important.

LO 24.2 Explain the equivalence of the expenditure and income approaches to valuing an economy.

LO 24.3 Explain the three approaches that are used to calculate GDP and summarize the categories of spending that are included in the expenditure approach.

LO 24.4 Explain the difference between real and nominal GDP.

LO 24.5 Calculate the GDP deflator.

LO 24.6 Use GDP per capita to compare economies and calculate the real GDP annual growth rate.

LO 24.7 Discuss some limitations to GDP, including its measurement of home production, the underground economy, environmental degradation, and well-being.

IT'S MORE THAN COUNTING PEANUTS

If we made a list of the economic changes that are most dramatically reshaping the world, the rapid growth of China's economy would likely top it. In 1978, when China's leaders moved to open up its economic system, it was the world's 15th-largest economy. The size of China's economy doubled. Then it doubled, and doubled, and doubled again. By 2011, China's economy clocked in at about $6 trillion, passing Japan's to become the second-largest economy in the world. Rapid economic growth can create jobs, reduce poverty, and improve standards of living. In China, the fraction of the population living below the international poverty line ($1.90 per person per day) fell from 88 percent in 1981 to 6.5 percent in 2012.[1]

Economic growth has increased living standards all over the world in recent decades, although typically in less dramatic fashion than in China. The health of the national economy has a powerful effect on everyday life in any country. When the economy is doing well, jobs are plentiful and most people can live well and securely. When the economy does poorly, jobs are

© The McGraw-Hill Companies, Inc./Elite Images

scarce, businesses close down, and people struggle. It's no wonder that politicians spend a lot of energy debating the best plan to expand the economy. Over the next few chapters, we'll discuss many of the ideas and terms used in those debates.

But, first, we need to answer a basic question: How do we measure the "size" of an economy? If we can answer that, we can compare China's economy to economies of other nations. We also can determine whether an economy is growing or not over time. What does it really *mean* to say that China has a $6 trillion economy?

The answers to these questions require some careful accounting. As a start, think about just one of the many transactions that take place in the U.S. economy. Say you bought a jar of peanut butter when you went to the grocery store. Although you may not have thought beyond your next peanut butter and jelly sandwich, your purchase contributed to the size of the economy.

Consider some of the things that happened before that jar of peanut butter made it into your shopping cart: A farmer grew the peanuts, perhaps on a small farm in Georgia. The farmer sold his peanuts to a wholesaler in Atlanta. The wholesaler then sold the peanuts to a peanut butter factory in Ohio, which combined the peanuts with other ingredients to produce a jar of peanut butter. The factory then sold that jar to a grocery store chain, which delivered it to your neighborhood store.

Many people were employed to produce that peanut butter: farmers, accountants, truck drivers, custodians, and grocery-store cashiers. Many firms earned profits from the jar of peanut butter, too: the peanut farm, the wholesaler, the factory, the shipping company, and your local store. Clearly, the activities that went into making and buying the jar of peanut butter added value to the economy. Can we measure how much?

The peanuts passed through many stages: from seed, to harvested nut, to peanut butter, to a jar on the grocery store shelf. At each stage, the peanuts were sold as an *output* of one firm and purchased as an *input* by another firm. Should we add up all of these sales individually to calculate the value the jar of peanut butter added to the economy? No—if we did that, we'd be overcounting the value of the peanuts. All of the sales were just steps toward one end product: your peanut butter. How then *do* we calculate the total value of your jar of peanut butter to the economy?

This is the problem that economists faced in the 1920s and 1930s when they first attempted to calculate the value of the U.S. economy. How can you add up all economic activity to arrive at an overall value for the economy, *without double-counting* items that are resold more than once before they reach the consumer?

The solution is a system called *national income accounting,* created by Nobel Prize winners Simon Kuznets and Richard Stone. In this chapter, we'll see how to use this system to calculate the value of a national economy. We'll see why it's so useful to measure a country's total output and also why gross domestic product (GDP), the most commonly used measure, has some limitations. In later chapters, we'll put these ideas to work to explain economic growth, unemployment, and economic booms and slowdowns.

Valuing an Economy

Economics has traditionally been divided into two broad fields, microeconomics and macroeconomics. *Microeconomics* is the study of how individuals and firms manage resources. In microeconomics, we zero in on a single person's budget, or one firm's cost of production, or the price of a particular good.

Macroeconomics, on the other hand, is the study of the economy on a broad scale, focusing on issues such as economic growth, unemployment, and inflation. In macroeconomics, we talk about consumption, production, and prices in the *aggregate,* on a national level, and we look at the effects of those aggregate forces on the whole economy.

Compared to microeconomics, the concepts of macroeconomics may seem distant from decisions we make and challenges we face. But macroeconomic issues can have profound impacts on our daily lives. Everyone tends to do better when there are steady economic growth, stable prices, and low unemployment. On the flip side, long periods of stagnation, inflation, and high unemployment can do great damage to families and communities.

At the start of the chapter, we introduced one of the most important macroeconomic issues of our time: the incredible growth of the Chinese economy. Thinking about the Chinese economy raises some questions:

- How do we know how big the Chinese economy is?
- How do we know that it is larger than Japan's but smaller than the United States's?
- What does it mean to say that the size of China's economy doubled?

To talk about these critical issues, we need a tool for measuring the "size" or "value" of a national economy. Based on the kind of questions that metric lets us answer, you can see why it is one of the most important and commonly used data points in macroeconomics. It gives us a sense of the well-being of the average person in a country. It also allows us to gauge the direction an economy is headed, by looking at changes over time.

The most commonly used metric for measuring the value of a national economy is **gross domestic product**, or **GDP**. Gross domestic product is the sum of the market values of all final goods and services produced within a country in a given period of time. That's a mouthful of a definition. Before we look at how economists calculate GDP, let's unpack the component parts of the definition.

Unpacking the definition of GDP

LO 24.1 Understand the importance of using the market value of final goods and services to calculate GDP and explain why each component of GDP is important.

The definition of GDP has four important pieces:

- the *market value*
- of *final goods and services*
- produced *within a country*
- in a *given period of time.*

Let's take each piece one at a time and explain its importance.

macroeconomics
the study of the economy as a whole, and how policy-makers manage the growth and behavior of the overall economy

gross domestic product (GDP)
the sum of the market values of all final goods and services produced within a country in a given period of time

Market values

If we measured the output of economies by simply listing every single good and service, we wouldn't learn much—680 million jars of peanut butter, 103 million copies of Microsoft Word, 421 million haircuts, and so on. The list would go on for thousands of pages. It wouldn't be very interesting. Nor would it be useful for comparing the overall size of national economies, which tend to make different things. For example, how would we compare the U.S. economy, which produces lots of peanut butter, with the Mexican economy, which produces lots of tortillas?

Clearly, we need to translate the production of peanut butter, tortillas, software, haircuts, and all the other goods and services into a common unit so we can add them up. That common unit is their *market value*—which in the United States is measured in dollars. So we know from this part of the definition that GDP is going to be a number measured in the local currency.

Final goods and services

Consider the 800 or so peanuts that end up in your jar of peanut butter. Suppose our Georgia peanut farmer sells them to the Atlanta wholesaler for 12 cents. The wholesaler sells them to the Ohio peanut butter factory for 24 cents. The peanut butter factory sells the jar of peanut butter to the grocery store for $1.85. Finally, the grocery store sells it to you for $3.40 in an 18-ounce jar. How much does this process contribute to GDP?

If we simply add up all the transactions, we might think that the jar of peanut butter contributed $5.61 to GDP ($0.12 + $0.24 + $1.85 + $3.40). But, if that were true, producing the jar of peanut butter would contribute more to GDP than its final selling price. That can't be right. If it were, we could grow the economy just by trading the same jar of peanut butter for the same dollar, over and over again, and adding up each "transaction."

The problem here is that by adding each of the transactions, we are double-counting, giving us too big a total. To avoid double-counting, we should ignore the price of *intermediate* goods and services—that is, goods and services used only to produce something else, like the raw peanuts that were sold to the peanut butter factory.

Instead, we want to count only expenditures on *final goods and services*—those that get sold to the consumer. In this case, the only final good was the jar of peanut butter you bought at the store. Its price was $3.40—so that is how much your purchase contributed to GDP.

Inge van Mill/Hollandse Hoogte/Redux

Produced within a country

The goods and services that count toward GDP are defined in terms of the *location of production,* not the citizenship of the producer. So:

- If a U.S. company owns a factory in Mexico, the value of the goods produced in that factory will count toward Mexican GDP, not U.S. GDP.
- A U.S. citizen working in France will contribute to French GDP.
- Likewise, a French or Mexican citizen working in the United States will contribute to U.S. GDP.

What if we want to measure the value of what is produced by all U.S. companies regardless of their location? In this case, we use a different metric, called **gross national product (GNP)**. GNP is the sum of the market values of all final goods and services produced and capital owned *by the permanent residents* of a country in a given period of time. GNP measures those market values no matter where in the world the production occurs. It is similar to GDP except that it

1. includes *worldwide* income earned by a country's enterprises and permanent residents and
2. excludes production by foreign nationals working domestically.

gross national product (GNP)

the sum of the market values of all final goods and services produced and capital owned by the permanent residents of a country in a given period of time

Given period of time

In theory, we could calculate the output of the economy over any time period—a day, a month, a year. When you hear people talking about GDP, they're often referring to an annual figure. However, a year is a long time to wait for an update on how the economy is doing, so GDP is usually calculated on a *quarterly* basis—that is, four times a year.

Typically, what we really want to know is an estimate of annual GDP, using the most recent quarterly information. We can't just multiply this quarter's GDP by four, however, because the economy seldom rolls along at the same pace all year. For instance, December usually has more economic activity than other months due to people buying presents and traveling. Therefore, we need to adjust quarterly GDP estimates to account for these seasonal patterns. That's why quarterly GDP is typically shown as a *seasonally adjusted estimate at an annual rate.* By taking account of predictable seasonal patterns, we can have a good guess at what annual GDP will be if the economy continues at its current pace.

Production equals expenditure equals income

LO 24.2 Explain the equivalence of the expenditure and income approaches to valuing an economy.

Now that we have defined the term *gross domestic product,* how do we go about measuring it? First of all, let's zero in on what we really mean when we talk about the size of an economy: the amount of "stuff" people in the economy are making.

Economists refer to this "stuff" as either *output* or *production,* and it includes both goods and services. Indeed, about three-quarters of U.S. output is services, not goods. As we've seen, though, there's not much point in simply listing thousands of pages of goods and services. So how do we put a dollar value on it? There are three ways of approaching this problem. We'll look at the first two ways briefly here (and then look at all three in the next section). The first is called the *expenditure approach.* The second is called the *income approach.*

The market value of a good or service is the price at which it is bought and sold. If we add up all the money people spend buying final goods and services—being careful to omit spending on intermediate goods so as not to double-count—the sum will be the market value of all output sold in the economy. In other words, we can use the expenditure approach to measure total output by *measuring total expenditure.*

Every transaction, of course, has not only a buyer who spends on a good or service but also a seller who earns income from the sale. Thus, expenditures by one person translate directly into *income* for someone else. So, we can also measure production using the income approach by *adding up everyone's income.* This may sound familiar if you remember the *circular flow model* of the economy that was presented in Chapter 1, "Economics and Life," and is repeated here in Figure 24-1.

Households buy things from firms in the market for goods and services. Firms then use some of the money they earn in revenue to pay wages to workers and rent to landowners in the market for the factors of production. In each of these transactions, expenditures by one party are income for another.

The circular flow model is a major simplification of the economy. (We're ignoring, for now, the money paid in taxes or the money that is saved instead of spent, for example.) Yet it shows that we should get to the same figure for GDP regardless of whether we measure expenditure or income in an economy:

National production = National expenditure = National income

This equality is a crucial idea in the study of macroeconomics.

FIGURE 24-1
Circular flow diagram

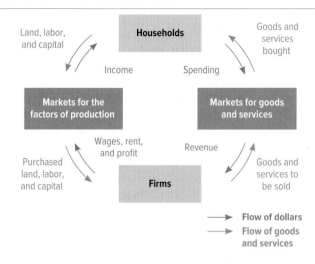

✓ CONCEPT CHECK

☐ Why are only final goods and services counted under GDP? Why are sales of used goods not counted? **[LO 24.1]**

☐ Why is total income in a country equal to total expenditures on goods produced in that country? **[LO 24.2]**

Approaches to Measuring GDP

LO 24.3 Explain the three approaches that are used to calculate GDP and summarize the categories of spending that are included in the expenditure approach.

We just saw that national production equals national expenditure equals national income. The equality of production, expenditure, and income would hold true in a literal, straightforward way if we lived in a *closed economy*—an economy in which all goods were produced and sold domestically and everything was consumed as soon as it was made. The actual economy is more complicated, but the basic equality still holds—as long as we're a little more careful about how we define each part.

One complication is international trade. Once we start to consider imports and exports, we see that expenditure in one country can translate into income in *another* country. Also, what happens when goods are produced but not sold? In this section, we will consider three approaches to measuring GDP—the expenditure approach, the income approach, and the value-added approach. Looking at the different approaches, we will see how economists deal with the complications of international trade and unsold inventories.

Why are there three approaches—and how do you know when to use one instead of another? It turns out that all three approaches end up with the same GDP number, but each provides a slightly different picture of how the different pieces make up the big picture. You'll understand the details after reading the next three sections. For now, it's enough to give this broad overview of the differences:

- The *expenditure approach* highlights the importance of consumer spending versus government purchases.

- The *income approach* emphasizes information about the relative importance of different factors of production.
- The *value-added approach* is especially useful for tracking how goods are sold and resold.

Many countries use all three approaches to calculate GDP so that policy-makers and researchers can get a full picture of economic activity.

The expenditure approach

To measure output using the *expenditure method*, we start by breaking down expenditure into categories. We don't want to double-count, so we *don't* include intermediate products, like raw peanuts and the labor of peanut factory workers, which firms buy only to transform into final goods and services. But we *do* include the following:

- *Final goods and services.* Most final goods and services are bought by people who intend to *consume* them, such as a family buying groceries or clothes or haircuts.
- *Goods bought as investment.* Firms buy some goods as an *investment* in future production, such as a farmer buying a new tractor to help him grow peanuts or a peanut butter factory buying new peanut-grinding machinery. The reason we count these is that the tractor and the machinery are not "used up" in producing a jar of peanut butter in the same way that raw peanuts are.
- *Government purchases.* We also want to count *government* purchases, which includes everything from fighter planes, to asphalt for road repair, to those plastic bins that go through the scanner at airport security checkpoints.
- *Net exports (exports minus imports).* If we're interested in the output of the U.S. economy, then clearly we want to count goods and services produced in the United States and bought by foreigners, which are called *exports.* But we *don't* want to count expenditures by Americans on items produced outside of the United States, which are called *imports.* For that reason, we subtract the amount of imports from the amount of exports and use the result—*net exports*—to calculate expenditures.

To find total expenditure we add together these four categories: consumption, investment, government purchases, and net exports. Let's look at each in more detail.

Consumption

The first category, **consumption**, measures spending on goods and services by private individuals and households. It includes almost anything you'd buy for yourself, from basic, nondurable goods (like food and clothing), to durable goods (like computers and cars), to services (like tutoring and plumbing). If you pay rent or college tuition, those expenses are also included in consumption.

Note that what is consumed has to be *new.* This requirement avoids the illogical conclusion that we could grow the economy simply by reselling the same jar of peanut butter over and over again. If you buy a used camera on eBay, for example, the camera itself is not counted toward the size of the economy; the original purchase of the camera was already recorded in GDP when it was sold new. However, the fee the seller pays to eBay *is* counted as consumption and so is the price the seller pays FedEx to deliver the camera to you.

consumption
spending on goods and services by private individuals and households

Investment

The second category, **investment**, includes spending on productive inputs, such as factories, machinery, and inventories. That means goods bought by people or firms who plan to use those purchases to produce other goods and services in the future, rather than consuming them. It includes *capital goods,* which are items like machines or tools that will be used for production

investment
spending on productive inputs, such as factories, machinery, and inventories

of other goods or services. It also includes buildings and structures, like warehouses, that will be involved in providing goods and services.

It's worth noting that newly built houses are also counted as investment. In contrast, if you rent a house, the expenditure falls under consumption. Why the difference? A newly built house will provide a place to live (or to rent out) now and for years to come, just as a newly built factory will generate output now and in future years. But when you *rent* a house, you are paying its owner for the service of letting you live there. You are consuming "place-to-live" services, but you're not making an investment because the house belongs to someone else and won't generate future revenues for you.

Again, note that investment goods are counted only if they are *new*. We don't count buying an existing factory or secondhand tools as investment. Nor do we count an individual's purchase of an existing house. The services of the Realtor selling you the house, though, would be counted toward consumption.

? POTENTIALLY CONFUSING

You may have heard people talk about their "investments"—stocks, bonds, mutual funds, and other products bought and sold in the financial markets. While it may seem as if these financial products should be counted under the "I" (investment) term in GDP, *they do not get counted as a part of GDP.* There are two reasons for that:

- First, if you buy a share of General Motors stock through the New York Stock Exchange, your money does not go to General Motors. Instead, you are buying stock from some other investor who has decided to sell her stock in General Motors. (We'll cover how economists think about buying stocks and making other financial "investments" in Chapter 31, "The Basics of Finance.")
- Second, including stock purchases in GDP calculations would be another type of double-counting. If we added to GDP every time someone bought shares, we could make the economy seem to be growing simply by having people resell the same shares over and over again—just like selling the same jar of peanut butter multiple times.

Finally, our definition of investment also includes a less-obvious type of "purchase": spending on inventories. When we equated production, income, and expenditure, we raised the question of how to deal with goods that are produced but not sold. **Inventory** is the answer: It's the stock of goods that a company produces now but keeps to sell at a future time. If Ford manufactures a car this year, but the car sits on the lot until next year, the car becomes part of Ford's inventory. If Apple makes a batch of iPhones but keeps them in a warehouse until it's time to release the new model for public sale, they become part of Apple's inventory.

inventory
the stock of goods that a company produces now but does not sell immediately

When a good is added to a company's inventory, we treat it as if the *producing company* has "bought" it to keep in stock for the future. The value of that "sale" is included in our calculation of investment for the year. What happens next year when a consumer buys the new-model iPhone? We don't want to count the same iPhone toward GDP in two different years. So, its value will be subtracted from Apple's inventory at the same time as it is counted as consumption. These two transactions cancel out, meaning the purchase results in no net increase in GDP.

Government purchases

government purchases
spending on goods and services by all levels of government

The next category of spending, **government purchases**, represents goods and services bought by all levels of government. This includes both

- "Consumption"-type purchases of goods (for instance, buying new bulbs to go in street-lights) and services (buying the labor of government workers who repair streetlights).

- "Investment"-type purchases (for instance, buying a truck that government workers will use to repair streetlights in the future).

In fact, the technical name for this category of spending is "government consumption expenditures and gross investment." We'll stick with the term *government purchases* because it's less of a mouthful.

However, one important category of government spending does *not* count as a government purchase: spending that simply *transfers* resources to individuals, through Social Security or similar programs. The Social Security payment to an elderly person from the government does not count toward government purchases. When that person spends money from his Social Security check to buy groceries, the spending will then be counted as private consumption.

Net exports

The three categories of spending we've considered—consumption, investment, and government purchases—include spending on goods and services produced abroad as well as those produced domestically. Let's think about the GDP of the United States. Our calculation of consumption will include instances when people in the United States buy goods made abroad—say, a sweater imported from Scotland. If we're trying to measure the value of the goods produced *within the United States,* we don't want to count this spending. On the flip side, we don't want to miss spending by people in other countries on goods or services made in the United States and exported for sale abroad.

These two forces work in opposite directions: Domestic spending on imports should get subtracted from our GDP calculations, while international spending on exports should get added. We can simplify these international transactions by combining exports and imports into one term, called **net exports** or **NX**. Net exports represent the value of goods and services produced domestically and consumed abroad minus the value of goods and services produced abroad and consumed domestically. If exports are higher than imports, NX will be positive. If imports are higher than exports, NX will be negative. Figure 24-2 shows how we can think about the role of net exports using a visual tool.

net exports (NX) exports minus imports; the value of goods and services produced domestically and consumed abroad minus the value of goods and services produced abroad and consumed domestically

FIGURE 24-2

Adding up expenditures when there are imports and exports   Everything that is produced domestically is added to GDP, whether it is purchased for consumption, for investment, by the government, or by people abroad (exports). Goods that are produced internationally but bought domestically, otherwise known as imports, are subtracted from GDP because they represent expenditures leaving the country. Transactions between foreign producers and foreign buyers do not involve domestic production or expenditure and therefore do not figure into GDP calculations.

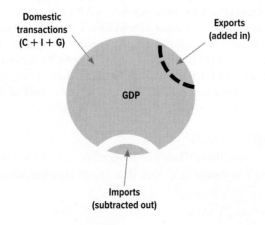

FIGURE 24-3

U.S. GDP breakdown   This figure shows the *expenditure method* of calculating GDP, which adds together consumption, investment, government purchases, and net exports (exports minus imports). In the United States, imports are currently higher than exports, so the value of net exports is negative and is subtracted from the total.

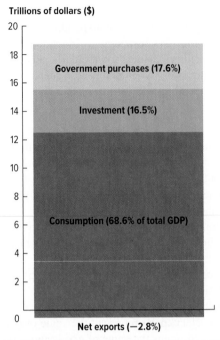

Sources: Bureau of Economic Analysis, Table 1.10, Gross Domestic Income by Type of Income (percent of GDP, 2016), and Table 1.1.5, Gross Domestic Product (USD, 2016), http://www.bea.gov/iTable/iTable.cfm?ReqID=9&step=1#reqid=9&step=1&isuri=1.

Summing spending categories

When we add together spending in all four categories—consumption, investment, government purchases, and net exports—the total will be equal to expenditures on all goods and services produced in a country. As we learned in the previous section, the total of those national expenditures is equal to the value of national production. This equation is represented as follows.

EQUATION 24-1 $$\text{Expenditure} = C + I + G + NX = \text{Production}$$

As you can see in Figure 24-3, consumption is by far the largest single category of expenditure in the United States, but investment and government purchases are also significant. We can also see that U.S. residents *buy* more goods from abroad than they *sell* to people abroad. That's why the value for net exports is a negative number, −2.8 percent of total 2016 GDP. In other words, in 2016 U.S. consumers spent more abroad than U.S. producers earned from foreigners buying U.S.-made goods, and the size of that difference was equal to 2.8 percent of GDP. If exports had been higher than imports, this number would have been positive.

Figuring out what goes into GDP and what isn't counted in the expenditure method takes a little practice. To help you keep track, Table 24-1 summarizes some of the examples presented in this chapter.

The income approach

A different way to think about the value of a national economy is to add up the *income earned by everyone in the country*. The income approach thus brings together information on the different factors of production.

TABLE 24-1

Is it GDP?

Situation	GDP Category	Why?
Buying a new digital camera	Consumption	Purchasing a *new* good or service always counts toward GDP.
Buying a used camera on eBay	Not counted	As a used good, the camera does not count toward GDP as it was already counted when new. The fees paid to eBay for selling the camera count as consumption, though.
Buying a new house	Investment	Since the house can increase or fall in value, it makes sense to think of it as an investment.
Renting an apartment	Consumption	You are paying the owner of the house for a service, so it is counted as consumption.
Apple makes a new batch of iPhones but doesn't sell them until next year	Investment	Counted as a part of investment as Apple is holding these phones as a part of its inventory.
Buying shares of General Motors stock	Not counted	Shares of stock are a transfer of money from one owner of the stock to another. Including stocks would cause a double-counting problem.
TSA buys plastic bins for airport security	Government spending	Any consumption or investment purchases made by the government are counted in GDP as government spending.
Babysitting for your neighbor	Not counted	In principle, it should be included in GDP, but such income is often not reported to the IRS, and thus it can't be included in official statistics.

To value an economy using the income approach, we add up

- wages earned by workers,
- interest earned on capital investments,
- rents earned on land and property, and
- profits earned by firms (plus a couple of additional technical adjustments).

These cover all the types of income earned by people in a country. National income can be shown in an equation as:

EQUATION 24-2   Income = Wages + Interest + Rental income + Profits

This *income approach* will give us the same result as the expenditure approach in an economy without any imports and exports. Why? Because in every transaction, there is not only a buyer who spends but also a seller who earns the same amount in income. If you spend $20 on gasoline, that same $20 is both expenditure to you and income to the owner of the gas station. The expenditure approach added up everything on one side of this transaction. Now, the income approach adds up everything on the *other side* of the transaction, which comes out to the same amount.

What happens with foreign trade? When goods produced in the United States are exported, that's expenditure by other countries and income for the United States. When people in the United States spend money on goods made in another country, that's expenditure in the United States and income for the other country.

The "value-added" approach

Finally, we come to the third approach that economists sometimes use to measure economic output: the *value-added approach.* We have seen that the expenditure approach solves the double-counting problem by considering only transactions that represent final, and not intermediate, goods and services. For example, we count a consumer's purchase of a jar of peanut butter from a store but not a peanut butter factory's purchase of peanuts from a peanut wholesaler. What if, instead, we looked at *all* transactions, but counted only the *value they add* to the economy?

To see the reasoning behind this approach, let's stick with peanut butter. At each stage of the peanut butter production process, let's look at the difference between the sale value of the product and the value of the inputs that went into it. This difference represents the "value added" at that stage of production. For instance:

- The farmer *adds value* to the economy by taking seeds, land, and water and growing peanuts. Just for simplicity, imagine the farmer didn't pay anything for his inputs. The value added to the economy is the $0.12 the farmer gets from selling his peanuts to the wholesaler, minus the value of the inputs, which we are imagining to be zero.
- If the wholesaler buys those $0.12 in peanuts and sells them to a peanut butter factory for $0.24, then the wholesaler has added $0.12 ($0.24 − $0.12) in value to the economy by helping to link up farmers and factories.
- The peanut butter factory adds value by pressing the peanuts into butter and putting it into jars. If the factory is able to get $1.85 per jar, it has added $1.61 ($1.85 − $0.24) in value to the economy.
- The grocery store adds value by transporting jars to a convenient location in your neighborhood, where clerks are on hand to allow you to purchase it for the final price of $3.40 per jar, a value added of $1.55 ($3.40 − $1.85).

To see the final value added, simply sum up the value added at each stage of the process: $0.12 + $0.12 + $1.61 + $1.55 = $3.40. You'll notice that this is the same as the final price of the peanut butter in the store—the amount that is counted in the expenditure method. The value-added approach is an alternative, and equally valid, way of avoiding the problem of double-counting the peanuts. It lets us break down the total value paid and see how much value was created at each step of the production process.

The value-added approach is especially useful when thinking about services involved in the resale of existing goods. We've already seen, for example, that resale of used cameras, existing houses, and shares of company stock do not count toward GDP—but the related services provided by eBay, Realtors, and stockbrokers do. Added value helps us to think about why this is so. A stockbroker adds value by handling the paperwork associated with purchasing shares of stock. A Realtor adds value by publicizing the fact that a house is for sale, showing potential purchasers around, and helping negotiate a sale. eBay adds value by connecting buyers with sellers.

In general, any intermediary involved in the sale of used goods adds value by sourcing those goods and making them available for sale in a convenient way.

✓CONCEPT CHECK

- ☐ What is the difference between consumption spending and investment spending? **[LO 24.3]**
- ☐ Under which category of expenditure do inventories fall? **[LO 24.3]**
- ☐ Does the sale of intermediate goods count toward GDP in the expenditure approach? **[LO 24.3]**
- ☐ How do the expenditure approach and income approach capture two sides of the same transactions? **[LO 24.3]**
- ☐ How do GDP calculations account for the value added in the sale of an existing house by a realtor? **[LO 24.3]**

Using GDP to Compare Economies

U.S. GDP increased from $12.5 trillion in 2005 to over $18 trillion in 2016. Does this mean that people in the United States produced more goods and services in 2016 than in 2005? Or does it mean that we just paid more for the same things because prices were higher? GDP is a function of both the quantity of goods and services produced (output) and their market value (prices).

Often, an increase in GDP is the result of growth in *both* components—an increase in output *and* an increase in prices. If we want to use GDP to compare the health of a national economy over time or to compare economies of different countries, we need to know how much of the growth to attribute to each factor.

Real versus nominal GDP

LO 24.4 Explain the difference between real and nominal GDP.

GDP enables us to track changes in the value of output over time. But if you compare levels of just GDP in different years, you can't be sure whether differences are due to changes in production or prices, or both. To zero in on changes in production, we need a new measure. We use the term *real GDP* to refer to GDP measurement that focuses *solely on output,* controlling for price changes. Formally, **real GDP** is calculated based on goods and services valued at *constant prices.* Those constant prices are given for a specific year. We might, for example, measure real GDP by valuing output in 2016 at the prices that prevailed in 2010.

If we report GDP *without controlling for price changes,* we are talking about *nominal GDP.* **Nominal GDP** is calculated based on goods and services valued at *current prices* (current at the time they are produced). Thus, in nominal GDP measurement, output for 2016 would be valued in 2016 prices.

real GDP
GDP calculation in which goods and services are valued at constant prices

nominal GDP
GDP calculation in which goods and services are valued at current prices

Calculating nominal and real GDP

To see the difference between real and nominal GDP measures in practice, let's imagine an economy with only two goods: pizza and spaghetti. For ease of discussion, let's call this fictional economy "Pizzetta."

Suppose that in 2013, Pizzetta produced 5 million pizzas at a price of $10 each and 20 million plates of spaghetti at a price of $8. Table 24-2 shows this output. In 2014, the number of pizzas and plates of spaghetti increased to 6 million and 22 million, respectively; prices stayed the same. In 2015, Pizzetta produced the same number of pizzas and plates of spaghetti, but prices increased. In 2016, both quantity and prices increased.

In order to calculate nominal GDP, we simply multiply the quantity of each good produced in a given year by its price in that year, as shown in column 6 of Table 24-2. We can see that Pizzetta's nominal GDP increased between 2013 and 2014 and again in 2015 and 2016.

What doesn't nominal GDP tell us? If we looked just at nominal GDP, we couldn't tell the cause of the increase. We wouldn't see that in 2014 the increase was due to larger output, or that in 2015 the increase was due only to an increase in prices with no increase in output. Looking at real GDP helps us see the different causes of the changes in GDP in the two years.

To calculate real GDP (GDP valued at constant prices), we have to choose a *base year.* In the base year, nominal GDP and real GDP are equal. In every other year, we multiply the quantity of a good produced in that year by its price in the base year. In essence, we are holding prices constant while allowing quantities to rise and fall. This method isolates increases in output from increases in prices.

Looking at the Pizzetta example, suppose we pick 2013 as our base year. We can see in Table 24-2 that in 2014, the increase in real GDP is actually the same as the increase in nominal

TABLE 24-2

Calculating real versus nominal GDP growth

Nominal GDP is the sum of the market values of all final goods and services, which we calculate by multiplying the quantity of each output by its market price in the current year. To calculate *real GDP,* we want to value those goods and services at their prices in the base year. When prices stay the same, nominal GDP and real GDP increase at the same rate. If prices rise, nominal GDP will be higher than real GDP.

(1)	(2)	(3)	(4)	(5)	(6)	(7)	(8)
Year	Pizzas (millions)	Price of pizza ($)	Spaghetti (millions)	Price of spaghetti ($)	Nominal GDP (millions of $)	Real GDP in 2010 prices (millions of $)	What's happening
2013 (base year)	5	10	20	8	(5 × $10) + (20 × $8) = **$210**	(5 × $10) + (20 × $8) = **$210**	In the base year, nominal GDP and real GDP are equal by definition.
2014	6	10	22	8	(6 × $10) + (22 × $8) = **$236**	(6 × $10) + (22 × $8) = **$236**	When output rises and prices stay constant, nominal and real GDP rise at the same rate.
2015	6	12	22	10	(6 × $12) + (22 × $10) = **$292**	(6 × $10) + (22 × $8) = **$236**	When prices rise and output stays constant, nominal GDP rises, but real GDP does not.
2016	7	13	25	11	(7 × $13) + (25 × $11) = **$366**	(7 × $10) + (25 × $8) = **$270**	When both output and prices rise, nominal and real GDP rise at different rates.

GDP ($236 million). That makes sense: Prices didn't change between the two years, so base-year prices are the same as current-year prices.

Between 2014 and 2015, however, the difference between nominal and real GDP shows up. Nominal GDP increases because prices increased. (Prices of pizza and spaghetti increased by $2 each.) But real GDP stays constant because output stayed constant.

Between 2015 and 2016, both nominal *and* real GDP increase because both prices *and* output increased. However, the increase in real GDP ($34 million) is smaller than the increase in nominal GDP ($74 million). What does that tell us? It indicates that only $34 million of the $74 million growth in nominal GDP is due to rising output; the rest is due to rising prices.

In summary:

- Real GDP isolates changes in an economy's output.
- Nominal GDP encompasses changes in both output and prices.

As a result, because economists and policy-makers are often most interested in changes in output, they typically use real GDP numbers as a reference point. When economists and policy-makers do want to focus on changes in prices, they turn to another measure—the GDP deflator.

The GDP deflator

LO 24.5 Calculate the GDP deflator.

We just saw that the difference between nominal and real GDP is the difference between current prices and base-year prices. If we want to know about how prices have changed, we *could* directly compare the price of each good in the current and base years. But that would be much like listing every good and service instead of reporting total GDP: It's not incorrect, but it's long and boring and doesn't do much to summarize what's going on in the economy as a whole. The GDP deflator is one way of summarizing how prices have changed across the entire economy.

The **GDP deflator** is a measure of the overall change in prices in an economy, using the ratio between real and nominal GDP. To compute the index, we first need to have measures of nominal GDP and real GDP from the current year. Then, we calculate the GDP deflator as follows:

GDP deflator

a measure of the overall change in prices in an economy, using the ratio between real and nominal GDP

EQUATION 24-3
$$\text{GDP deflator} = \frac{\text{Nominal GDP}}{\text{Real GDP}} \times 100$$

The GDP deflator equation gives us the ratio between the base-year value of current output (the real GDP number) and the current-year value of current output (the nominal GDP number). The equation has three direct implications:

- In the base year, the GDP deflator is always equal to 100 because current prices *are* base-year prices. Thus, in the base year, nominal GDP equals real GDP.
- If prices have risen such that nominal GDP is now higher than real GDP, the deflator will be greater than 100. So, for example, if the GDP deflator is 115 in a given year, we infer that the overall price level is 15 percent higher than it was in the base year.
- If prices have fallen such that nominal GDP is now lower than real GDP, the deflator will be less than 100. Similarly, if we are looking at a year before the base year, when prices were lower, the deflator will be less than 100.

Table 24-3 shows the GDP deflator for the imaginary country Pizzetta in 2013–2016.

The GDP deflator gets its name from its relationship to inflation. *Inflation* is an idea we'll discuss at length in future chapters; in fact, Chapter 33, "Inflation," is entirely devoted to the topic. For now, it's enough to note that inflation describes how fast the overall level of prices is changing. Inflation is defined in terms of a year-to-year increase in prices, rather than an increase over a base year.

Year	Nominal GDP (millions of $)	Real GDP (millions of $)	Deflator	Inflation
2013	210	210	$\frac{\$210}{\$210} \times 100 = \mathbf{100}$	—
2014	236	236	$\frac{\$236}{\$236} \times 100 = \mathbf{100}$	$(100 - 100)/100 = 0\%$
2015	292	236	$\frac{\$292}{\$236} \times 100 = \mathbf{124}$	$(124 - 100)/100 = 24\%$
2016	366	270	$\frac{\$366}{\$270} \times 100 = \mathbf{136}$	$(136 - 124)/124 = 9.7\%$

TABLE 24-3
Calculating the GDP deflator and inflation rates

Using the values of nominal and real GDP, we can calculate the GDP deflator, a measure of price changes over time. It is set to 100 for a base year; as prices increase, the value of the deflator increases as well. With the GDP deflator we can calculate inflation, the percentage change of prices.

We can calculate inflation by looking at the increase in the GDP deflator between any two years using the equation below:

EQUATION 24-4 $$\text{Inflation rate} = \left[\frac{\text{Deflator}_{\text{Year 2}} - \text{Deflator}_{\text{Year 1}}}{\text{Deflator}_{\text{Year 1}}}\right] \times 100$$

For instance, as shown in Table 24-3, the inflation rate in Pizzetta between 2015 and 2016 is:

$$\text{Inflation rate} = \left[\frac{\text{Deflator}_{2016} - \text{Deflator}_{2015}}{\text{Deflator}_{2015}}\right] \times 100$$

$$= \frac{136 - 124}{124} \times 100$$

$$= 9.7\%$$

The GDP deflator is one simple way of measuring changes in the price level. It allows us to "deflate" nominal GDP by controlling for price changes. In official government statistics, the GDP deflator is actually calculated using a somewhat more elaborate method called a *chain-weighted index.* The basic intuition is the same as the simpler approach we've described here.[2] We'll return to the idea of changes in the overall price level in Chapter 25, "The Cost of Living."

Using GDP to assess economic health

LO 24.6 Use GDP per capita to compare economies and calculate the real GDP annual growth rate.

How do we use GDP to compare economies? We could, of course, simply look at the GDPs of two countries side by side to see their relative sizes. High GDP means a big economy. Figure 24-4 shows the GDPs of a number of countries around the world. As you can see, the United States has the largest economy by far, followed by China.

However, if what we really want to know is the income of an *average individual* in these countries, GDP will paint a misleading picture. The reason is that the populations of the countries are quite different sizes. China's GDP is just over one-third as high as that of the United States, but its population is more than four times as large. India has just under four times as many people as the United States but only one-tenth the GDP. The total income earned in China and India is spread across far more people, so the average person has a lower income. Meanwhile, Norway has a much smaller economy than the United States, but because its population is also much smaller, the average Norwegian is actually richer than the average American. To compare average income across countries, we need to know GDP per capita.

GDP per capita

GDP per capita
a country's GDP divided by its population

If we want get an idea of how much is produced *per person* in a country, we need to divide GDP by population size. This measure is called **GDP per capita**. ("Per capita" simply means per person.) Figure 24-5 shows GDP per capita in each country in the world. When we compare this map to Figure 24-4, the most noticeable pattern is that the wealthy but small countries of Europe and the Middle East rise to the top, while populous countries like China, Brazil, and India move down.

GDP per capita is a useful measure. Knowing, for example, that GDP per capita in Switzerland is $58,087 while in Haiti it is only $1,750 suggests a lot about differences in life in these two countries.

FIGURE 24-4

GDP around the world (2016)

The top 10 countries in terms of overall nominal GDP include rich countries—with both large populations (the United States) and small (the United Kingdom)—as well as some poorer countries with large populations (China and India).

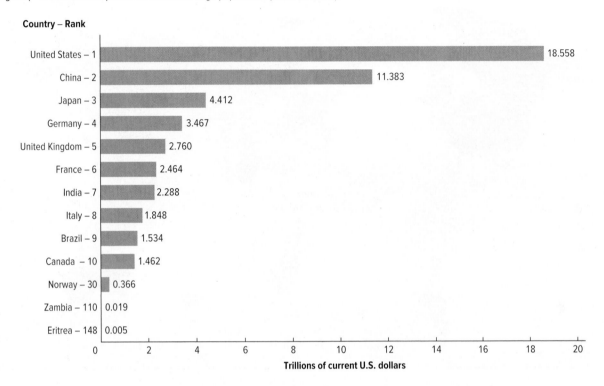

However, GDP per capita doesn't tell us everything. First, it is a measure of *average* income; it doesn't tell us anything about how that income is distributed. A country with deep poverty and a rich elite could have higher GDP per capita than a country where everyone has a moderate standard of living.

Second, it doesn't tell us what you can buy with a given amount of money in that country. The same goods might be more expensive in some countries than in others. For instance, GDP per capita in the United States and Hong Kong are both about $58,000, but many goods and services are more expensive in Hong Kong than in the United States. A dollar in Hong Kong won't buy you as much as it would in the United States. When we account for this difference in the cost of living, the real value of GDP per capita in Hong Kong falls to about $52,000, which is *lower* than in the United States.[3]

Conversely, many poor countries are cheaper to live in than rich ones. This doesn't mean that every single thing costs less but that, overall, the cost of living is lower. Looking at GDP per capita without accounting for differences in the cost of living makes poor countries look even poorer than they really are. In the United States or Hong Kong, for example, it would be almost impossible to survive on an income of $3,000 per year. In parts of Tanzania or Bangladesh, on the other hand, it would buy you a decent basic lifestyle. We will return to the subject of how to account for these differences in price levels in the next chapter. For now, just remember that GDP per capita is only a start in understanding people's real ability to consume goods and services.

FIGURE 24-5
Global GDP per capita (in 2015 U.S. dollars)

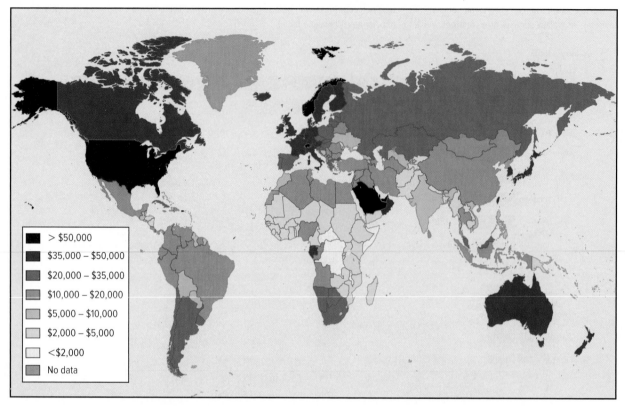

■	> $50,000
■	$35,000 – $50,000
■	$20,000 – $35,000
■	$10,000 – $20,000
■	$5,000 – $10,000
■	$2,000 – $5,000
□	<$2,000
■	No data

Source:Ali Zifan, via Wikimedia Commons, https://commons.wikimedia.org/wiki/File:Countries_by_GDP_(PPP)_Per_Capita_in_2015.svg. Uses IMF data.

GDP growth rates

One of the most common uses of GDP is to track changes in an economy over time. We usually talk about changes in GDP in terms of the *growth rate*. This is often measured as the percent change in real GDP from one time period to the next, typically annually or quarterly at an annual rate:

EQUATION 24-5
$$\text{GDP growth rate} = \left[\frac{\text{GDP in Year 2} - \text{GDP in Year 1}}{\text{GDP in Year 1}}\right] \times 100$$

For instance, if U.S. real GDP grew from $14 trillion in one year to $14.5 trillion (in constant dollars) the next, the annual growth rate would be:

$$\text{GDP growth rate} = \left[\frac{\$14.5 \text{ trillion} - \$14 \text{ trillion}}{\$14 \text{ trillion}}\right] \times 100 = 3.6\%$$

If the economy shrinks, the growth rate will be negative. For instance, the U.S. economy shrunk between 2008 and 2009, with a negative annual real GDP growth rate of −2.4 percent.

We can think about GDP growth rates in several ways. Let's think first about how economic growth changes year to year for the same country. A shrinking economy is a big deal. It means that people are actually producing less than they did the year before.

We have special terms for a period in which the economy contracts:

- A **recession** is a period of significant decline in economic activity. There is no hard-and-fast rule about what constitutes a "significant decline," but a recession is usually marked by falling GDP, rising unemployment, and an increased number of bankruptcies.

- A **depression** is a severe or extended recession. Again, there is no hard-and-fast rule about when a recession becomes a depression.

An old joke, heard from both Harry Truman and Ronald Reagan, says that a recession is when your neighbor loses his job; a depression is when you lose yours.

In the United States, a recession or depression is considered "official" when a committee of economists at an organization called the National Bureau of Economic Research (NBER) calls it one. The country often feels the effects of a recession long before they register in government statistics: People start losing their jobs and businesses experience falling sales. In the 2008 recession, for instance, the news media were using the word "recession" for almost a year before the NBER confirmed it.

Recessions are actually not as uncommon as you might think. Figure 24-6 shows that there were eight periods of recession in the United States in the 56 years between 1960 and 2016. You can also see that, overall, U.S. real GDP grew significantly and quite steadily over this same period. The 1990s and early 2000s were particularly recession-free decades, with only two brief and relatively mild dips in GDP. The 2008 recession involved a much deeper dip in GDP and lasted much longer.

Another way we can look at economic growth is to compare how fast different countries are growing. High growth rates are not necessarily associated with high total GDP or high GDP per capita, as Figure 24-7 shows. We can see that real GDP growth in the world's rich countries, such as the United States and Europe, has been relatively slow in recent years (albeit from a much higher starting level). Much more rapid growth has occurred in middle-income and poorer countries, led by China and followed by South Asia and East Africa.

FIGURE 24-6

U.S. real GDP over time   Real GDP has been steadily rising since 1960, and has more than quadrupled in value over the past 56 years. The gray bars show recessions, when economic activity slows.

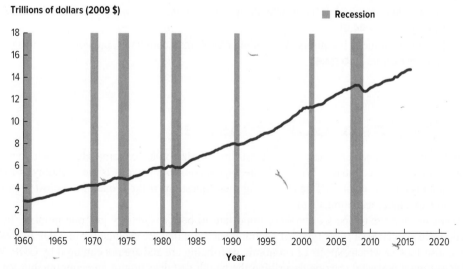

Sources: Federal Reserve Bank of St. Louis, **https://research.stlouisfed.org/fred2/series/GDPC1#** (quarterly real GDP); and NBER, **http://www.nber.org/cycles/cyclesmain.html**(recession dates).

FIGURE 24-7

Global real GDP growth rates (2014)   In contrast with the map of overall income, poorer countries grew faster than more developed countries, on average.

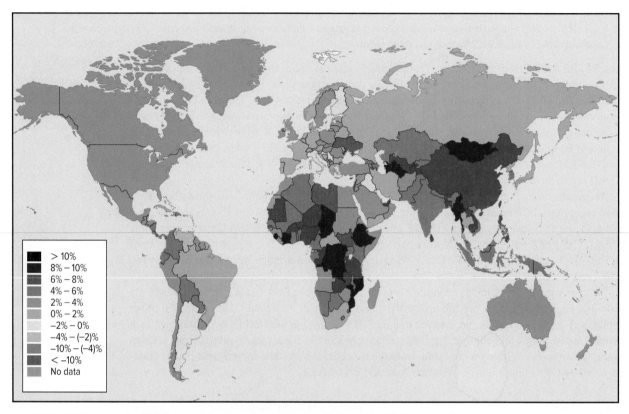

Source: Ali Zifan, via Wikimedia Commons, **http://www.statsilk.com/maps/world-stats-open-data.** Uses The World Factbook data.

✓ CONCEPT CHECK

☐ What is the difference between real and nominal GDP? **[LO 24.4]**

☐ To calculate the GDP deflator, why do we divide nominal GDP by real GDP from the *same* year? **[LO 24.5]**

☐ What does it mean if country A has higher GDP than country B, but country B has higher GDP per capita? **[LO 24.6]**

Limitations of GDP Measures

GDP is a powerful and versatile way of measuring the size of an economy. How much do people produce in different countries? What is the average income per person? Is the economy growing? How quickly? The uses of GDP in answering these questions make it one of the most important measures in a macroeconomist's toolbox.

However, we can't expect *everything* important to be measured by just one number. In this section, we'll talk about some types of economic activity that are excluded from GDP by design. We'll also look at which aspects of economic well-being are and are not captured by GDP. With GDP, we get a powerful start on describing the health and direction of an economy, but we can get an even richer picture by supplementing it with other metrics.

Data challenges

LO 24.7 Discuss some limitations to GDP, including its measurement of home production, the underground economy, environmental degradation, and well-being.

When critics argue that we should look beyond GDP, they point out that GDP calculations leave out some important types of economic activity. GDP measures the market value of final goods and services, but it doesn't include anything that is not traded in a market or that isn't reported to the government. That means that three major categories of economic activity are not counted as part of GDP: home production, the underground economy, and nonmarket externalities such as environmental degradation.

Home production

Goods and services that are both produced and consumed within one household are called *home production*. In general, home production goods and services are not included in GDP:

- If you eat out, your meal is part of GDP. If you eat at home, it's not.
- If you hire a cleaning service to clean your home, that's part of GDP. If you clean your own home, it's not.

Similarly, the same goods might or might not be part of GDP, depending on whether you sell them or consume them yourself:

- If you grow vegetables in your garden and sell them at a farmers' market, that's part of GDP. If you eat them yourself, it's not.
- If your grandmother knits a sweater and gives it to you for your birthday, that's not part of GDP. If your grandmother sells her knitting on eBay or Etsy, it is.

Home production is a major component of economic activity in most places. Because of that, it can change how one country compares to another. In relatively poor countries, many people grow their own food on small farms and may make their own tools and clothes. In these instances, the official GDP measure may be missing a significant percentage of real production. Even in wealthy countries, much of the value of caretaking work—raising children or caring for elderly parents—is uncounted.

Some economists have made efforts to quantify the value of this work. For more detail, read the From Another Angle box "Valuing homemakers."

From Another Angle
Valuing homemakers

If you were to compare the GDP growth of the United States and Germany between the 1970s and the 1990s, you'd find that the U.S. economy grew more than Germany's. Does this mean that life got better in the United States during that period relative to life in Germany? Estimates of home production cast an interesting light on this question.

One major difference between the United States and Germany over those three decades is the change in the number of people in the workforce. In the 1970s, comparable proportions of Germans and Americans were in paid employment; by the 1990s, a higher proportion of Americans had jobs. This difference can be largely explained by the rising rate of female participation in the U.S. labor force. A larger workforce makes for a larger GDP.

(continued)

But the larger GDP does not necessarily mean that the United States is better off. The women who stayed at home in the 1970s weren't sitting around doing nothing. They were running households and raising families, growing and making goods for home consumption, doing volunteer work in their communities, and so on. Although these are valuable activities, a mother or father who stays home to look after children and bake cookies contributes nothing to GDP. But when she or he goes out to work, hires someone to look after the children, and buys cookies at the store, that adds to GDP.

Therefore, we can't automatically conclude from the rise in U.S. GDP relative to Germany's that more goods and services were being produced in the United States in the 1990s. Could it be that some goods and services simply moved from the uncounted area of home production to the documented area of GDP?

Studies suggest this may, in fact, be the case. When you add up paid work, home production, and volunteer work, Americans and Germans put in about the same number of hours per week, but workers in Germany spend 5.3 hours less on paid work and 6 hours more on household production than do Americans. Estimating home production suggests that a lower German employment rate does not necessarily imply lower overall production or a lower standard of living.

Consideration of home production can also change the way we view recessions. U.S. GDP dropped in 2008, but home production went up. Feeling a financial squeeze, people substituted home-cooked meals for restaurant meals, planted vegetable gardens, and did their own repairs rather than hire someone. When the economy was doing well, people's choices suggest that they preferred to hire others to do these tasks. So the recession clearly reduced people's well-being. But economist Nancy Folbre, who has led efforts to quantify the value of home production, argues that it might not have reduced well-being by nearly as much as official GDP statistics suggest.

Sources: http://economix.blogs.nytimes.com/2009/05/04/including-home-production-gdp-might-not-look-so-bad; http://www.nber.org/papers/w8797.pdf; http://scholar.harvard.edu/files/alesina/files/work_and_leisure_in_the_u.s._and_europe.pdf.

The underground economy

Many goods and services are sold below the radar, outside of official records. These transactions make up the *underground economy*.

On the extreme end, there is trade in goods and services that are themselves illegal—banned drugs, restricted weapons, endangered animals and plants, and so on. Sales of illegal goods and services are part of what is called the *black market*. Because black-market transactions are illegal, they are, of course, not reported to the government or tax authorities. As a result, they don't show up in government statistics, and they don't get counted as part of the official GDP. In principle, though, black-market activities belong in the GDP calculation.

At the less-extreme end are economic transactions that are otherwise legal but are sometimes not reported to the government. Failure to report can be either accidental or deliberate (to avoid paying taxes). For instance, were you ever hired to mow a neighbor's lawn, or babysit, or run errands for a few bucks when you were in high school? If you didn't report those amounts to the IRS,[4] you were participating in what's known as the *gray market*—so called because it sits somewhere between the black market and the documented economy.

Gray-market transactions aren't counted in GDP for the same reason that black-market transactions aren't counted: If it's not reported, it doesn't show up in government statistics. And, if it doesn't show up in government statistics, it can't be counted in GDP.

Even though black- and gray-market transactions don't get reported, researchers try to quantify them to get a sense of what's missing in our GDP calculations. It turns out that the underground economy accounts for a significant portion of the total economy in many countries. On average across the world, the underground economy is worth about one-third of GDP. This average hides wide variations, though:

- In the United States, for example, the underground economy has been valued at only around 7 or 8 percent of GDP.

- It is estimated at more than half of GDP in Nigeria and more than two-thirds in some Latin American countries.[5]

The typical explanation for this pattern reflects the cost of doing business legally. In some countries you have to pay extremely high taxes or pay bribes to officials to cut through bureaucratic red tape. When the cost of doing business legally is high, people are much more likely to conduct their business through other channels. In such countries, GDP may significantly underestimate the true size of the economy. In the case of Nigeria, it would mean increasing the official GDP figure by 50 percent.[6]

Environmental externalities

Suppose an electricity company causes air pollution by burning coal. The electricity generated ends up being counted in GDP. It may appear in the price paid by households for their electricity. Or it may be wrapped up in the price of goods and services that other firms make using the electricity as an input.

Some economists feel that GDP, as a metric, is missing the costs associated with pollution. They argue that we need to account for the *negative externalities* of economic activities. In a sense, we can think of the value of negative externalities as *negative output*. They are final "goods" that do harm to people, and therefore have negative value, but don't otherwise get counted in production or expenditure measures.

Increasingly, those who deal with economic statistics are trying to incorporate the value of negative externalities into GDP. Some countries have tried to calculate **green GDP**. This alternative measure of GDP subtracts the environmental costs of production from the positive outputs normally counted in GDP.

In some countries that are growing rapidly, such as China and India, there are few regulations to guard against environmental degradation. When the Chinese government attempted to calculate green GDP in 2007, it came up with some shocking results. Once adjusted for pollution, the soaring GDP growth rates in many provinces in China dropped to almost zero. This was such an inconvenient finding that the government abandoned the green-GDP project.[7]

The Chinese government is not alone in its concerns about the political implications of GDP measures. For more about the intersection of politics and national accounting, read the From Another Angle box "The politics of green GDP."

green GDP
an alternative measure of GDP that subtracts the environmental costs of production from the positive outputs normally counted in GDP

From Another Angle
The politics of green GDP

Since GDP is widely viewed as the measure of the overall health of the economy, politicians have an incentive to make GDP numbers look as strong as possible. Strong numbers help their reelection chances. As a result, the question of what is the best way to measure the economy isn't left to number-crunching economists—it can also be deeply political.

A perfect example of this is green GDP. Recognizing that GDP may not capture the negative externalities of environmental production, officials in the U.S. Bureau of Economic Analysis (BEA) started to work on how to calculate a more "complete" measure of economic activity.

(continued)

This idea started off with the typical GDP equation: C + I + G + NX. What made the new GDP calculation "green" was that it would weigh the value of this production against its overall environmental costs. Included in those costs would be the consumption of nonrenewable resources—such as pumping oil and mining coal—and some of the costs from pollution.

You may have noticed that we don't see this figure reported in the news. Why not? The BEA needed funding to continue the project, which needed the approval of Congress. The National Academy of Science supported the proposal, but members of Congress nixed it. It seems they were worried that measuring green GDP might suggest the economy was shrinking rather than growing, and that industry—which has powerful lobbies—would get the blame.

By contrast, a similar French effort had top-level support. Former President Nicolas Sarkozy recruited several prominent economists—including two Nobel laureates, Amartya Sen and Joseph Stiglitz—to serve on the grandly named "Commission on the Measurement of Economic and Social Progress."

The commission published a 300-page report in September 2009 outlining 12 recommendations. These included measures of the state of health, education, the environment, and income inequality that could be used to build a more inclusive measure of overall well-being. This measure was never officially calculated. We can guess roughly what it might show by seeing how France scored in other, already-crafted measures such as the Better Life Index from the OECD (Organisation for Economic Co-operation and Development): France ranked 18th among 34 OECD member countries. That ranking is seven positions *lower* than how France stood when the same countries were ranked by the size of their GDP per capita.

If President Sarkozy had been hoping for a new metric that would make the French feel good about their country on the world stage, then this type of calculation would have fallen far short. As we have seen, the traditional measurement of GDP is more than just a metric favored by economists—it can be quite useful for politicians as well.

Sources: http://www.oecdbetterlifeindex.org/; http://www.nytimes.com/2010/05/16/magazine/16GDP-t .html?pagewanted=all; http://www.insee.fr/fr/publications-et-services/default.asp?page=dossiers_web/stiglitz/ documents-commission.htm.

GDP vs. well-being

GDP tells us a lot about the living standards in a country, but it can't tell us everything. Suppose you are offered the chance to live in a country that you know nothing about. You could quickly learn more by finding out the country's average income as measured by its GDP per capita. Which data would you turn to next to find out about the quality of life there? Quality of life is a nuanced idea, and it's hard to capture perfectly with any number. However, metrics like infant or child mortality (how many babies and children die), literacy rates (how many people can read), and life expectancy (how long people live) can give us a fuller picture of the well-being of a country's inhabitants.

You might assume that countries with high GDP per capita are likely to do well on these other metrics. The wealthier a country is, the more easily it can afford good health care and education for its people. Broadly speaking, you would be right. As Table 24-4 shows, GDP per capita *is* highly correlated with these quality-of-life measures. However, the correlation is not perfect: Look at Equatorial Guinea in Africa. Countries that are much poorer than Equatorial Guinea— such as Brazil, Bulgaria, and China—nonetheless seem to do a much better job of caring for the health of their children and elderly.

There are good reasons to expect that GDP per capita might not perfectly correlate with people's well-being. Let's take an obvious example: Equatorial Guinea is relatively rich on average (thanks to having important oil reserves), but its income is distributed very unequally. While the

TABLE 24-4 GDP compared with other measures of well-being

While GDP is commonly used to measure average income in a country, it can't capture all aspects of quality of life. Overall, metrics of well-being and quality of life like infant mortality, literacy, and life expectancy are correlated with GDP per capita, but in extreme cases, like that of Equatorial Guinea, they can diverge dramatically.

Country	GDP per capita (Current U.S. $)	Literacy rate (% of population over 15)	Life expectancy at birth (Years)	Child mortality (Deaths per 1,000 under age 5)	Life Satisfaction Index (0 to 10)
Norway	97,299	[No data]	82	3	7.5
United States	54,629	[No data]	79	7	7.1
Equatorial Guinea	18,918	95.3	58	94	[No data]
Brazil	11,726	92.6	74	16	6.9
Bulgaria	7,851	98.4	75	10	4.2
China	7,590	96.4	76	11	5.1
Mali	704	38.7	58	115	3.9

Sources: World Bank WDI, 2014, http://data.worldbank.org/indicator (GDP per capita, Life expectancy, Child mortality); CIA World Factbook, 2015 https://www.cia.gov/library/publications/the-world-factbook/fields/2103.html (Literacy Rate); World Happiness Report 2015 http://worldhappiness.report/wp-content/uploads/sites/2/2015/04/WHR15.pdf (Life Satisfaction Index);

country's elite are rich, more than three out of four citizens live on under $2 a day.[8] In this sense, pursuing GDP growth as the highest priority can be in opposition to improving quality of life in other ways, at least in the short term.

If what we care about is not so much the output of an economy but the happiness of the people who comprise it, can we measure happiness directly? Economists and others are trying to do this in a systematic way. These efforts are recent, and nobody is suggesting that such measures replace GDP. One of the measures they've developed is the Life Satisfaction Index. (See the final column in Table 24-4.) It suggests that the correlation between GDP per capita and happiness is, indeed, far from perfect. For example, people in Bulgaria seem to be less happy than we might expect from their average income; people in Mali seem to be happier. For more on measuring happiness, read the Real Life box "Can money buy you happiness?"

Real Life

Can money buy you happiness?

Everyone has heard the saying, "Money can't buy you happiness." But is that actually true? The answer turns out to depend on how much money and how you define happiness.

First, how can we tell whether someone is happy? Researchers have generally relied on just asking people how they feel. Studies show consistently that people who are married tend to be happier, as do people who are religious and people who are in good health. Income seems to matter a lot, too.

However, we need to remember the difference between *causation* and *correlation.* The fact that wealth and life satisfaction are correlated doesn't mean that having more money *causes* happiness. In fact, when you look at the same country over time, people don't necessarily get happier as the country they live in gets richer.

(continued)

For instance, the United States has a much higher GDP per capita now than it did 50 years ago, but researchers have found that Americans are not noticeably happier than they were 50 years ago. One possible explanation for this puzzle is that people naturally tend to compare their lifestyles and material wealth to those of their peers, rather than to their parents or grandparents.

How about the relationship between money and happiness for individuals within a country? Research in the United States has found that there *is* a correlation between happiness and money—up to a point. That point happens to be an income level of about $75,000 per year. Below that income level, more money appears to be related to higher levels of happiness on average. Above that income level, it's much less clear—whether money buys happiness seems to depend on the way in which you ask people if they're happy.

Typically, researchers use two distinct methods. One is to ask something like, "How satisfied are you with your life as a whole these days?" This measure, usually called *life satisfaction,* continues to rise with income. In other words, someone earning $750,000 is likely to tell a researcher that she is more satisfied than someone earning $75,000.

The other method is to ask people about the emotions they felt *on the previous day.* For example, did you feel happiness yesterday? Enjoyment? Anger? Stress? Worry? Here, we find that overall someone earning $75,000 is more likely to have experienced positive emotions than someone earning $25,000. But despite what you would think, someone earning $750,000 did not report more positive emotions, and less negativity, than someone earning $75,000. Although money doesn't always buy happiness, it seems to help up to a certain point.

Sources: Angus Deaton, "Income, Health, and Well-Being around the World: Evidence from the Gallup World Poll," *Journal of Economic Perspectives* 22, no. 2 (2008), pp. 53–72; http://economix.blogs.nytimes .com/2009/03/10/the-happiest-states-of-america/; http://www.princeton.edu/~deaton/downloads/deaton_kahneman_high_income_improves_evaluation_August2010.pdf.

✓ CONCEPT CHECK

- ☐ What is home production? **[LO 24.7]**
- ☐ Why might GDP fall if environmental damages caused by production were taken into account? **[LO 24.7]**
- ☐ What supplemental metrics are commonly used to measure quality of life alongside GDP per capita? **[LO 24.7]**

Conclusion

GDP is a powerful and versatile metric. There are good reasons that it is one of the most commonly used tools in macroeconomics. It gives a simple measure of the size of an economy and the average income of its participants. It also allows us to make comparisons over time or across countries. The system of national income accounts gives us a picture of how output, expenditure, and income are linked, and a framework for adding up the billions of daily transactions that occur in an economy.

Comparing nominal and real GDP allows us to disentangle the role of increasing prices versus increasing output in a growing economy. The GDP deflator and the inflation rate track changes in overall price levels over time—which, as we'll see in the next chapter, is a major task in macroeconomics.

GDP per capita gives us a sense of the average income within a country, although it doesn't tell us about the distribution of income or quality of life. Finally, calculating real GDP growth rates shows us in which direction the economy is moving, and is an important indicator of recession or depression.

In the next chapter, we'll dig deeper into the tools that economists use to measure price changes and the cost of living. When we combine these tools with GDP, we have a menu of macroeconomic metrics that will allow us to describe and analyze national and international economies.

Key Terms

macroeconomics, p. 601

gross domestic product (GDP), p. 601

gross national product (GNP), p. 602

consumption, p. 605

investment, p. 605

inventory, p. 606

government purchases, p. 606

net exports (NX), p. 607

real GDP, p. 611

nominal GDP, p. 611

GDP deflator, p. 613

GDP per capita, p. 614

recession, p. 617

depression, p. 617

green GDP, p. 621

Summary

LO 24.1 Understand the importance of using the market value of final goods and services to calculate GDP and explain why each component of GDP is important.

Most goods and services go through several production steps and may pass through multiple firms before ending up in the hands of the consumer. However, when calculating GDP, we should consider only the value of the final good or service, in order to avoid double-counting. The value added by each step of the production process will be included in the price of the final product.

The most commonly used variable for measuring the value of a national economy is gross domestic product, or GDP. GDP is the sum of the market values of all final goods and services produced within a country in a given period of time. The goods and services that count toward GDP are defined in terms of the location of production, not the citizenship of the producer. GDP is usually calculated on both annual and quarterly (three-month) bases; only new goods and services being produced within that time period are counted. Quarterly GDP estimates are typically given as a seasonally adjusted annual rate, which projects what annual GDP will be based on the current quarter's output if the economy continues to follow expected seasonal patterns.

LO 24.2 Explain the equivalence of the expenditure and income approaches to valuing an economy.

Economists can think about the size of a national economy in three different ways: how much is produced (output), how much is spent (expenditure), and how much income is earned (income). All three of these methods add up to the same thing. Total output is the *value* of the things produced in an economy in dollar terms, which is

the same as the price for which those outputs sell, which is the same as what people spent to buy those outputs. Therefore, the value of output is equal to expenditures. Every transaction has both a buyer and a seller, so expenditures by one person translate directly into income for someone else; therefore, income equals expenditure.

LO 24.3 Explain the three approaches that are used to calculate GDP and summarize the categories of spending that are included in the expenditure approach.

The *expenditure* approach of calculating the size of an economy involves adding up all spending on goods and services produced in an economy and subtracting spending on imports. We can break expenditures into four categories: *Consumption* (C) measures spending on goods and services to be consumed by private individuals and families. *Investment* (I) includes any goods that are bought in order to produce other goods and services in the future. *Government purchases* (G) are goods and services bought by all levels of government, for either consumption or investment. Finally, *net exports* (NX) are foreign spending on domestically produced goods and services minus domestic spending on foreign-produced goods and services. The sum of these categories and the equivalence of income (Y) and expenditure gives us the equation $Y = C + I + G + NX$.

The *income* approach adds up the income earned by everyone in a country—including wages (earned by workers), interest (earned on capital investments), rental income (earned on land and property), and profits (earned by firms).

The *value-added* approach accounts for the value that is added at each stage of production in the economy. This approach allows economists to investigate the contribution of each transaction in the economy to overall GDP.

It also solves the double-counting problem because only part of the value of each transaction is registered, and it does not register the total price of intermediate goods and services.

Many countries use all three approaches to calculate GDP so that policy-makers and researchers can get a full picture of economic activity.

> **LO 24.4** Explain the difference between real and nominal GDP.

GDP is a function of both the quantity of goods and services produced (output) and their market value (prices); an increase in GDP can result from growth in either or both components. To isolate the role of growing output, we can control for price changes. *Real GDP* is calculated based on goods and services valued at constant prices. *Nominal GDP* is calculated based on goods and services valued at current prices.

> **LO 24.5** Calculate the GDP deflator.

One way to measure price changes is by calculating the GDP deflator. The GDP deflator summarizes the overall increase in prices in an economy using the ratio between real and nominal GDP in a given year. If prices have risen such that nominal GDP is now higher than real GDP, the deflator will be greater than 100. If prices have fallen such that nominal GDP is now lower than real GDP, the deflator will be less than 100. The GDP deflator allows us to "deflate" nominal GDP by controlling for price changes.

> **LO 24.6** Use GDP per capita to compare economies and calculate the real GDP annual growth rate.

GDP per capita is total GDP divided by the population of a country. It tells us the average income or productivity per person in the economy. To track changes in an economy over time, we can calculate the real GDP growth rate, measured as the percent change in real GDP from one time period to the next, typically annually or quarterly at an annual rate. When the economy shrinks, the growth rate is negative and is one of the major indicators used to determine whether the economy is in a recession or depression.

> **LO 24.7** Discuss some limitations to GDP, including its measurement of home production, the underground economy, environmental degradation, and well-being.

GDP is a rough measure of the average standard of living in a country, but it does not tell us about the distribution of wealth. Furthermore, three important segments of the economy are not included in GDP by design:

home production (goods and services that are produced and consumed within a household), the underground economy (illegal transactions, or legal transactions that simply aren't reported to the government), and externalities (such as pollution) that are not fully accounted for in regular production or consumption measures. Higher GDP is often associated with other indicators of higher well-being, such as health, education, and life satisfaction, but does not guarantee those things.

Review Questions

1. U.S. car dealers sell both used cars and new cars each year. However, only the sales of the new cars count toward GDP. Why does the sale of used cars not count? **[LO 24.1]**

2. There is an old saying, "You can't compare apples and oranges." When economists calculate GDP, are they able to compare apples and oranges? Explain. **[LO 24.1]**

3. When Americans buy goods produced in Canada, Canadians earn income from American expenditures. Does the value of this Canadian output and American expenditure get counted under the GDP of Canada or the United States? Why? **[LO 24.2]**

4. Economists sometimes describe the economy as having a "circular flow." In the most basic form of the circular flow model, companies hire workers and pay them wages. Workers then use these wages to buy goods and services from companies. How does the circular flow model explain the equivalence of the expenditure and income methods of valuing an economy? **[LO 24.2]**

5. In 2011, the average baseball player earned $3 million per year. Suppose that these baseball players spend all of their income on goods and services each year, and they save nothing. Argue why the sum of the incomes of all baseball players must equal the sum of expenditures made by the baseball players. **[LO 24.2]**

6. Determine whether each of the following counts as consumption, investment, government purchases, net exports, or none of these, under the expenditure approach to calculating GDP. Explain your answer. **[LO 24.3]**
   a. The construction of a court house.
   b. A taxicab ride.
   c. The purchase of a taxicab by a taxicab company.
   d. A student buying a textbook.
   e. The trading of municipal bonds (a type of financial investment offered by city or state governments).
   f. A company's purchase of foreign minerals.

7. If car companies produce a lot of cars this year but hold the new models back in warehouses until they release

them in the new-model year, will this year's GDP be higher, lower, or the same as it would have been if the cars had been sold right away? Why? Does the choice to reserve the cars for a year change which category of expenditures they fall under? **[LO 24.3]**

8. The value-added method involves taking the cost of intermediate outputs (i.e., outputs that will in turn be used in the production of another good) and subtracting that cost from the value of the good being produced. In this way, only the value that is added at each step (the sale value minus the cost of the goods that went into producing it) is summed up. Explain why this method gives us the same result as the standard method of counting only the value of final goods and services. **[LO 24.3]**

9. Imagine a painter is trying to determine the value she adds when she paints a picture. Assume that after spending $200 on materials, she sells one copy of her painting for $500. She then spends $50 to make 10 copies of her painting, each of which sells for $100. What is the value added of her painting? What if a company then spends $10 per copy to sell 100 more copies, each for $50? What is the value the painter adds then? If it's unknown how many copies the painting will sell in the future, can we today determine the value added? Why or why not? **[LO 24.3]**

10. In a press conference, the president of a small country displays a chart showing that GDP has risen by 10 percent every year for five years. He argues that this growth shows the brilliance of his economic policy. However, his chart uses nominal GDP numbers. What might be wrong with this chart? If you were a reporter at the press conference, what questions could you ask to get a more accurate picture of the country's economic growth? **[LO 24.4]**

11. Suppose that the GDP deflator grew by 10 percent from last year to this year. That is, the inflation rate this year was 10 percent. In words, what does this mean happened in the economy? What does this inflation rate imply about the growth rate in real GDP? **[LO 24.5]**

12. An inexperienced researcher wants to examine the average standard of living in two countries. In order to do so, he compares the GDPs in those two countries. What are two reasons why this comparison does not lead to an accurate measure of the countries' average standards of living? **[LO 24.4, 24.6]**

13. In 2010, according to the International Monetary Fund, India had the world's 10th-highest nominal GDP, the 135th-highest nominal GDP per capita, and the 5th-highest real GDP growth rate. What does each of these indicators tell us about the Indian economy and how life in India compares to life in other countries? **[LO 24.6]**

14. China is a rapidly growing country. It has high levels of bureaucracy and business regulation, low levels of environmental regulation, and a strong tradition of entrepreneurship. Discuss several reasons why official GDP estimates in China might miss significant portions of the country's economic activity. **[LO 24.7]**

15. Suppose a college student is texting while driving and gets into a car accident causing $2,000 worth of damage to her car. Assuming the student repairs her car, does GDP rise, fall, or stay constant with this accident? What does your answer suggest about using GDP as a measure of well-being? **[LO 24.7]**

Problems and Applications

1. Suppose a gold miner finds a gold nugget and sells the nugget to a mining company for $500. The mining company melts down the gold, purifies it, and sells it to a jewelry maker for $1,000. The jewelry maker fashions the gold into a necklace that it sells to a department store for $1,500. Finally, the department store sells the necklace to a customer for $2,000. How much has GDP increased as a result of these transactions? **[LO 24.1, 24.3]**

2. Table 24P-1 shows the price of inputs and the price of outputs at each step in the production process of making a shirt. Assume that each of these steps takes place within the country. **[LO 24.1, 24.3]**

   a. What is the total contribution of this shirt to GDP, using the standard expenditure method?

   b. If we use a value-added method (i.e., summing the value added by producers at each step of the production process, equal to the value of output minus the price of inputs), what is the contribution of this shirt to GDP?

   c. If we mistakenly added the price of both intermediate and final outputs without adjusting for value added, what would we find that this shirt contributes to GDP? By how much does this overestimate the true contribution?

3. The U.S. government gives income support to many families living in poverty. How does each of the following aspects of this policy contribute to GDP? **[LO 24.2]**

TABLE 24P-1

	Cotton farmer ($)	Fabric maker ($)	Sewing and printing ($)
Inputs	0	1.10	3.50
Value of output	1.10	3.50	18.00

a. Does this government's expenditure on income support count as part of GDP? If so, in which category of expenditure does it fall?

b. When the families buy groceries with the money they've received, does this expenditure count as part of GDP? If so, in which category does it fall?

c. If the families buy new houses with the money they've received, does this count as part of GDP? If so, in which category does it fall?

4. Given the following information about each economy, either calculate the missing variable or determine that it cannot be calculated. **[LO 24.2, 24.3]**

    a. If C = $20.1 billion, I = $3.5 billion, G = $5.2 billion, and NX = −$1 billion, what is total income?

    b. If total income is $1 trillion, G = $0.3 trillion, and C = $0.5 trillion, what is I?

    c. If total expenditure is $675 billion, C = $433 billion, I = $105 billion, and G = $75 billion, what is NX? How much are exports? How much are imports?

5. Using Table 24P-2, calculate the following. **[LO 24.2, 24.3]**

    a. Total gross domestic product and GDP per person.

    b. Consumption, investment, government purchases, and net exports, each as a percentage of total GDP.

    c. Consumption, investment, government purchases, and net exports per person.

6. Determine which category each of the following economic activities falls under: consumption (C), investment (I), government purchases (G), net exports (NX), or not included in GDP. **[LO 24.3]**

    a. The mayor of Chicago authorizes the construction of a new stadium using public funds.

    b. A student pays rent on her apartment.

    c. Parents pay college tuition for their son.

TABLE 24P-2

Sector	Value (millions)
Consumption	$770,000
Investment	$165,000
Government spending	$220,000
Net exports	−$ 55,000
Population	50

d. Someone buys a new Toyota car produced in Japan.

e. Someone buys a used Toyota car.

f. Someone buys a new General Motors car produced in the United States.

g. A family buys a house in a newly-constructed housing development.

h. The U.S. Army pays its soldiers.

i. A Brazilian driver buys a Ford car produced in the United States.

j. The Department of Motor Vehicles buys a new machine for printing drivers' licenses.

k. An apple picked in Washington in October is bought at a grocery store in Mississippi in December.

l. Hewlett-Packard produces a computer and sends it to a warehouse in another state for sale next year.

7. Table 24P-3 shows economic activity for a very tiny country. Using the expenditure approach, determine the following. **[LO 24.3]**

    a. Consumption.

    b. Investment.

TABLE 24P-3

Activity	Total value (thousands of $)
Families buy groceries	600
Electronics company sells HD projectors to households	100
Personal trainer gives Zumba class	5
Custard stand sells pistachio ice cream	2
Police department buys new cars	500
Mayor leads creation of new education budget	300
Elevator construction company builds new factory	600
Local businessperson purchases corn from Mexico	400
Sports-gear company sells hockey gloves to Canadian team	200
Bike store sells used carbon-fiber bikes	200
Local stockbroker executes trades for clients	2,000

TABLE 24P-4

Category	Value (billions of $)
Wages	8.3
Interest	0.7
Total business expenditures	21.0
Total business revenues	30.0

c. Government purchases.

d. Net exports.

e. GDP.

8. During the recent recession sparked by financial crisis, the U.S. economy suffered tremendously. Suppose that, due to the recession, the U.S. GDP dropped from $14 trillion to $12.5 trillion. This decline in GDP was due to a drop in consumption of $1 trillion and a drop in investment of $500 billion. The U.S. government, under the current president, responded to this recession by increasing government purchases. **[LO 24.3]**

   a. Suppose that government spending had no impact on consumption, investment, or net exports. If the current presidential administration wanted to bring GDP back up to $14 trillion, how much would government spending have to rise?

   b. Many economists believe that an increase in government spending doesn't just directly increase GDP, but that it also leads to an increase in consumption. If government spending rises by $1 trillion, how much would consumption have to rise in order to bring GDP back to $14 trillion?

9. Assume Table 24P-4 summarizes the income of Paraguay. **[LO 24.3]**

   a. Calculate profits.

   b. Calculate the GDP of Paraguay using the income approach.

c. What would GDP be if you were to use the value-added approach?

d. What would GDP be if you were to use the expenditure approach?

10. Table 24P-5 provides information about the cost of inputs and the value of output for the production of a road bike. Note there are four different stages of production. **[LO 24.3]**

   a. What value is added by the supplier of the raw materials?

   b. What value is added by the tire maker?

   c. What value is added by the maker of the frame and components?

   d. What value is added by the bike mechanic?

   e. What value is added by the bike store?

   f. What is the total contribution of the bike to GDP?

11. Imagine that the United States produces only three goods: apples, bananas, and carrots. The quantities produced and the prices of the three goods are listed in Table 24P-6. **[LO 24.4]**

   a. Calculate the GDP of the United States in this three-goods version of its economy.

   b. Suppose that a drought hits the state of Washington. This drought causes the quantity of apples produced to fall to 2. Assuming that all prices remain constant, calculate the new U.S. GDP.

   c. Assume, once again, that the quantities produced and the prices of the three goods are as listed in Table 24P-6. Now, given this situation, carrot sellers decide that the price of carrots is too low, so they agree to raise the price. What must be the new price of carrots if the U.S. GDP is $60?

TABLE 24P-6

Goods	Quantities produced	Prices ($)
Apples	5	2.00
Bananas	10	1.00
Carrots	20	1.50

TABLE 24P-5

Raw materials	Manufacturing	Construction	Sale by the retailer
• Rubber for one tire ($20) • Aluminum for the frame ($80) • Other component materials ($70)	• Tire maker sells tires for $30 each • Frame maker sells bike frame and components for a total of $250	• Bike mechanic puts everything together and sells the bike for $350	• Retailer sells the bike for $500

12. Based on Table 24P-7, calculate nominal GDP, real GDP, the GDP deflator, and the inflation rate in each year, and fill in the missing parts of the table. Use 2014 as the base year. **[LO 24.4, 24.5]**

13. Suppose that the British economy produces two goods: laptops and books. The quantity produced and the prices of these items for 2015 and 2016 are shown in Table 24P-8. **[LO 24.4, 24.5]**

    a. Let's assume that the base year was 2015, so that real GDP in 2015 equals nominal GDP in 2015. If the real GDP in Britain was $15,000 in 2015, what was the price of books?

    b. Using your answer from part *a,* if the growth rate in nominal GDP was 10 percent, how many books must have been produced in 2016?

    c. Using your answers from parts *a* and *b,* what is the real GDP in 2016? What was the growth rate in real GDP between 2015 and 2016?

14. Based on Table 24P-9, calculate nominal GDP per capita in 2015 and 2016, and the real GDP growth rate between the two years. Which countries look like they experienced recession in 2015–2016? **[LO 24.6]**

TABLE 24P-7

Year	Quantity of oranges	Price of orange ($)	Quantity of beach balls	Price of beach ball ($)	Nominal GDP ($)	Real GDP ($)	GDP deflator	Inflation rate (%)
2014	500	1.00	850	5.00				
2015	600	1.50	900	7.50				
2016	750	1.65	1,000	8.25				

TABLE 24P-8

Year	Quantities produced	Price ($)
2015	Laptops = 50 Books = 1,000	Laptops = 200 Books = ?
2016	Laptops = 100 Books = ?	Laptops = $150 Books = 10

TABLE 24P-9

	2015			2016		
	Nominal GDP (billions of $)	Real GDP (billions of $)	Population	Nominal GDP (billions of $)	Real GDP (billions of $)	Population
Argentina	328.03	383.48	39,746,000	310.17	386.68	40,134,000
Egypt	162.44	123.21	75,200,000	188.61	128.97	76,800,000
Germany	3,651.62	2,100.54	82,013,000	3,338.68	2,002.46	81,767,000
Ghana	28.53	11.27	22,532,000	26	11.8	23,108,000
United States	14,319	13,228.65	304,718,000	14,119	12,880.53	307,374,000

15. Table 24P-10 describes the real GDP and population of a fictional country in 2015 and 2016. **[LO 24.6]**

    a. What is the real GDP per capita in 2015 and 2016?
    b. What is the growth rate in real GDP?
    c. What is the growth rate in population?
    d. What is the growth rate in real GDP per capita?

16. Table 24P-11 shows data on population and expenditures in five countries, as well as the value of home production, the underground economy, and environmental externalities in each. **[LO 24.6, 24.7]**

    a. Calculate GDP and GDP per capita in each country.
    b. Calculate the size of home production, the underground economy, and environmental externalities in each country as a percentage of GDP.
    c. Calculate total and per capita "GDP-plus" in each country by including the value of home production, the underground economy, and environmental externalities.

TABLE 24P-10

Year	Real GDP (billions of $)	Population (millions)
2015	10	1.0
2016	12	1.1

    d. Rank countries by total and per capita GDP, and again by total and per capita "GDP-plus." Compare the two lists. Are the biggest and the smallest economies the same or different?

17. Suppose a parent was earning $20,000 per year working at a local firm. The parent then decides to quit his job in order to care for his child, who was being watched by a babysitter for $10,000 per year. Does GDP rise, fall, or stay constant with this action, and how much does GDP change (if at all)? **[LO 24.7]**

TABLE 24P-11

Country	C ($)	I ($)	G ($)	Net exports ($)
Bohemia	9,800,000,000	230,000,000	950,000,000	−120,000,000
Silesia	450,000,000	78,000,000	100,000,000	13,000,000
Bavaria	2,125,000,000	319,000,000	597,000,000	134,000,000
Saxony	2,750,000,000	75,000,000	1,320,000,000	−45,000,000
Ottoman Empire	6,225,000,000	567,000,000	1,435,000,000	1,000,000

Country	Population	Home production ($)	Underground economy ($)	Environmental externalities ($)
Bohemia	1,200,000	1,250,000,000	5,770,000,000	−1,560,000,000
Silesia	160,000	75,000,000	128,000,000	−45,000,000
Bavaria	425,000	386,000,000	1,450,000,000	−523,000,000
Saxony	760,000	146,000,000	250,000,000	−820,000,000
Ottoman Empire	800,000	432,000,000	654,000,000	−396,300,000

Endnotes

1. http://databank.worldbank.org/data/reports.aspx?source=2&country=CHN&series=&period=, http://www.bjreview.com/Opinion/201510/t20151016_800040481.htm, and http://www.nytimes.com/2010/08/16/business/global/16yuan.html?_r=0.

2. To find out more about the chain-weighted index, see this explanation from the Federal Reserve: http://www.frbsf.org/publications/economics/letter/2002/el2002-22.pdf.

3. http://www.tradingeconomics.com/hong-kong/gdp-per-capita-ppp.

4. Below certain thresholds, some earnings from self-employment don't need to be reported, so failure to report isn't necessarily against the tax laws. In any case, if they're not reported, those activities are not captured in GDP calculations.

5. https://openknowledge.worldbank.org/bitstream/handle/10986/3928/WPS5356.pdf?sequence=1.

6. Ibid.

7. http://www.nytimes.com/2007/08/26/world/asia/26china.html?pagewanted=2.

8. http://data.worldbank.org/country/equatorial-guinea.

The Cost of Living

THANK YOU FOR NOT SMOKING

Tucked in among the signs and ads on commuter trains in Massachusetts is a small notice that says, "No smoking—General Laws Chapter 272, Sec 43A—Punishable by imprisonment for no more than 10 days or a fine of no more than one hundred dollars." It's the kind of sign that you'd glance at and quickly forget. But when you think about the crime and the two possible punishments (10 days in jail or paying $100 cash), it's a pretty imbalanced trade-off. Surely, most people would choose to pay $10 a day to avoid jail. What is the point of giving both options when one is clearly worse than the other?

To understand the reasoning behind the two punishments, it helps to know one fact: The no-smoking law was written in 1968. Back then, a Hershey Bar cost 5 cents and a box of cornflakes cost 29 cents. Today a box of cornflakes costs $3.79. Back then, it would take nearly eight days working at McDonald's to earn $100. Today it would take about two days at the current federal minimum wage of $7.25 per hour.

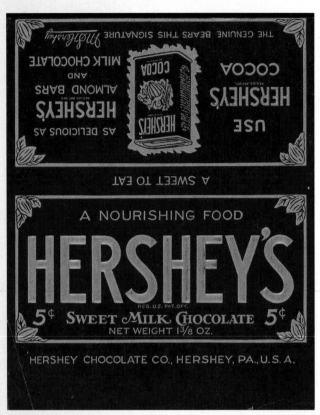

Courtesy of Hershey Community Archives, Hershey, PA

Clearly, prices and wages are much higher today than they were in 1968. When the fine was originally set, $100 went a long way. It also took a long time to earn. As prices increased over time, $100 bought less and less, and the opportunity cost of paying the $100 fine fell. In contrast, 10 days is still 10 days. As a result, what might have been a tough choice when the law was written—the fine or the jail time—now seems an easy trade-off.

The smoking fine draws our attention to an important idea: A dollar now is very different from a dollar in the past. More generally, it reminds us that a "dollar" is just a word or a piece of paper. What really matters is what we can buy with the dollar—and what we can buy with a dollar changes over time.

When we talk about what a dollar actually buys, we are talking about the *cost of living*. When we say the cost of living has gone up, we mean that, looking broadly over a range of goods and services, a dollar buys less today than it used to buy.

In this chapter we'll describe the most important measures of changing prices. In the first part of the chapter, you'll see how to measure changes of prices over time. In the second part, you will see why prices differ among countries and how to measure these differences. Along the way, you'll get a sense of how the cost of living factors into everything from how far your paycheck will stretch, to debates over the size of Social Security, to how many poor people live on the planet.

The Cost of Living

In Chapter 24, "Measuring GDP," we discussed how to measure output on a national level. Now we turn our attention to the second pillar of macroeconomic data: prices. Before, we calculated real GDP to see how output increases over time, independent of price changes. Now, we want to focus on the price changes themselves.

Measuring prices in a national economy helps us answer the question, "What's a dollar (or euro or yen or peso) worth?" This question is trickier than it might sound. What a dollar will buy you changes from year to year as the prices of goods rise or fall (but usually rise) over time. It also changes as you go from place to place. In general, a dollar will get you a lot more in Iowa City, Iowa, than in New York City, New York.

Of course, people earn more money now than they used to. And, on average, people earn more in New York City than they do in Iowa City. If higher income goes with higher prices, people's actual ability to consume the things they want may remain the same. The key to understanding the cost of living is to look at the full picture.

If all prices and incomes rose at the same rate everywhere in the world, tracking the cost of living would be a simple accounting question. What makes it an interesting and important macroeconomic topic is the fact that, in the real world, prices change at different speeds across time and place. Those differing speeds have effects on people's economic behavior. For example:

- At any given time, wages might be rising more slowly than the price of consumer goods. That difference effectively shrinks your ability to buy things.

- Or if you have $5,000 in student debt, rising price levels mean that the real value of that debt (in terms of the quantity of goods and services you have to give up in order to pay back the loan) is getting smaller over time.

- Or suppose you have competing job offers in New York City and Iowa City, Iowa. You will want to consider not only the salaries offered but also the costs of living in both places.

The cost of living can differ greatly, even for two cities in the same country, as shown in the Real Life box "The costs of living in New York City vs. Iowa City."

Real Life

The costs of living in New York City vs. Iowa City

"I want to wake up in that city that doesn't sleep," sang Frank Sinatra. "I want to be a part of it, New York, New York."

Waking up in the city that doesn't sleep isn't cheap, though. Today, New York City is the most expensive city in America. A simple one-bedroom apartment can cost thousands of dollars a month in rent. In fact, the median price of homes in Manhattan exceeds $485,000; the U.S. median is about $222,700. Other things are quite expensive as well. According to online price-tracker Numbeo, "cheap" eats in New York City will cost you about $18. A swankier three-course dinner is going to cost at least $80 per person.

Using the same price-tracker, we can compare the relative expense of living in different U.S. cities. It turns out that groceries in Manhattan cost 32 percent more on average than in Iowa City, and rent costs about 200 percent more. You can rent a one-bedroom apartment in Iowa City for about $600, less than you would pay for a walk-in-closet-sized apartment in Manhattan.

As you would expect, though, people also get paid more in New York City. The latest data from the U.S. Census show the median NYC household income is $52,737. Iowa City has a median income of $42,119. That's a difference in incomes of 20 percent.

The income difference is pretty substantial, but it's less than half of the difference in prices. In other words, the median household in Iowa City is substantially better off than the median household in New York City, at least in terms of the quantity of goods and services they can afford to buy.

Why, then, do people choose to live in New York City? Why doesn't everyone prefer to move to places like Iowa City? We can deduce that people who choose to live in Manhattan get some kind of additional utility from their choice, worth many thousands of dollars a year to them. But if living in a "city that doesn't sleep" isn't your thing, you're likely to find greater happiness—and cheaper meals—in another part of the country.

Sources: www.numbeo.com; http://www.bestplaces.net/col; http://www.dailymail.co.uk/news/article-2971028/Life-90-square-foot-box-Woman-s-apartment-takes-cramped-New-York-living-extreme-does-pay-750-West-Village.html; http://factfinder.census.gov/faces/nav/jsf/pages/index.xhtml.

As these examples show, changing price levels can have real effects on people's incentives and choices. They determine the relative value of your salary, of saving or borrowing, of living in one city or another, and a multitude of other decisions. When you add up all of these microeconomic choices, you can get big macroeconomic effects.

Measuring Price Changes over Time

What does it mean to track how "prices" change? After all, people buy many different goods and services, and each has its own price. For the things you routinely buy, some prices go up and some go down. Some prices move a lot, while some don't budge. For example:

- Perhaps your rent went up over the past year, but the price of gasoline held steady.
- Maybe it became cheaper to buy an older iPhone once the new iPhone came out.
- Maybe the price of clothing rose only slightly since last year, but cable bills went through the roof.

Some of these price changes will matter more to a given consumer than other price changes. The most important factors are how much the price changed (and in what direction) and whether the item is a big part of their total budget. A 10 percent increase in rent (often a big budget item) hurts much more than a 10 percent jump in the price of your favorite shampoo. Consumers can get a rough sense of how changes in prices affect them overall by:

- First considering how much of their spending goes to which items.
- Then using that knowledge to weigh the importance of individual price changes.

The same idea translates to thinking about changes in prices in the overall economy: The idea is to track how individual prices move over time, giving the most weight to the items that account for the biggest shares of a typical consumer's budget. That process can give a measure of how the *overall* cost of living has changed. The aim is a single number that summarizes changes in the prices of many goods, not just one at a time.

But how do we know which goods and services to look at in the first place? How do we weigh the importance of rent versus shampoo for the whole economy? The idea of a "market basket" gives us a method for comparing prices over time and locations.

The market basket

LO 25.1 Understand the importance of a market basket in tracking price changes.

When comparing the cost of living across time and place, we have to consider the prices of many different goods and services—housing, food, clothing, transportation, entertainment, and so on. To accomplish this, we construct something that looks like a really long shopping list, called a **market basket**. The list includes specific goods and services in fixed quantities that roughly correspond to a typical consumer's spending. (Who's a "typical" consumer? Good question. We'll come back to that later.)

market basket
a list of specific goods and services in fixed quantities

The goal of creating the market basket is to see how the cost of buying the goods and services on the list changes over time. By keeping goods and quantities constant, we can be sure that any change in the total cost of the basket is caused by a change in prices, rather than the type or amount of things being consumed.

To see how this method works, imagine that you noticed changes from last year to this year in the prices of four items you typically buy at the grocery store:

	Price last year ($)	Price this year ($)
Bread (per loaf)	3.00	3.15
Milk (per gallon)	2.50	2.55
Beef (per pound)	3.50	3.64
Carrots (per pound)	1.00	1.25

How much did the price of groceries increase since last year? It depends on which type of food you look at. The price of bread rose by 5 percent, milk by 2 percent, beef by 4 percent, and carrots by a whopping 25 percent.

Suppose we want to know how much the *overall cost of your groceries* rose—a very reasonable and practical question. To answer it, we have to know how much of each food you typically buy. For instance, if you typically buy a loaf of bread, a gallon of milk, three pounds of beef, and a pound of carrots, then:

> (*Remember:* The formula for calculating a percentage change is $\left[\frac{(X_2 - X_1)}{X_1}\right] \times 100$.)

$$\text{Cost last year} = (\$3.00 \times 1) + (\$2.50 \times 1) + (\$3.50 \times 3) + (\$1.00 \times 1) = \$17.00$$

$$\text{Cost this year} = (\$3.15 \times 1) + (\$2.55 \times 1) + (\$3.64 \times 3) + (\$1.25 \times 1) = \$17.87$$

$$\text{Price increase from last year to this year} = \left[\frac{(\$17.87 - \$17)}{\$17}\right] \times 100 = 5.1\%$$

This is the *basket approach*. It measures changes in the cost of your shopping basket, assuming that you buy the same items in the same quantities. This approach gives us a *single number* to measure how much your total costs rise over time.

Someone might ask, "Why not just average the increase in the price of each grocery item (bread, 5%; milk, 2%; beef, 4%; carrots, 25%)?" If we did that, we would get a completely different—and wrong!—answer:

$$= \frac{(5\% + 2\% + 4\% + 25\%)}{4}$$

$$= 9\% \text{ (Remember, *this answer is wrong!*)}$$

Why would this calculation be wrong? You don't spend nearly as much on carrots as you do on beef or milk or bread. Therefore, the relatively big increase in the price of carrots doesn't affect you as much as the average of the percentage increases would suggest. After all, we want a meaningful answer to the original question, "How much did the price of groceries increase since last year?" To get that answer, what we really want to know is how much more it will cost when you take your usual basket of groceries to the store checkout.

Of course, most people don't buy exactly the same thing all the time, especially when they see that prices are changing. In fact, we know that when prices rise, quantity demanded usually falls. In reality, you might decide to buy less beef and switch from carrots to potatoes. If we allowed your basket to change, though, we'd be capturing both the change in prices and the change in your behavior. To focus on the price change alone, we have to keep the basket fixed, even though we know that is not an entirely realistic simplification.

We'll come back to ways of dealing with this challenge later in the chapter. For now, the basket approach gives us a way to capture lots of different price changes in a single number that (approximately) represents the purchases of a typical consumer.

Consumer Price Index

LO 25.2 Calculate and use a price index to measure changes in the cost of living over time.

---

price index

a measure showing how much the cost of a market basket has risen or fallen relative to the cost in a base time period or location

Consumer Price Index (CPI)

a measure that tracks changes in the cost of a basket of goods and services purchased by a typical U.S. household

The basket approach allows us to track changes in the cost of living. To summarize these changes, we construct a **price index**. It measures how much the cost of a market basket has risen or fallen relative to the cost in a base time period or location.

The most commonly used index tool for tracking changes in the cost of living in the United States is the **Consumer Price Index**, or **CPI**. The CPI tracks changes in the cost of a basket of goods and services purchased by a typical U.S. household. It is calculated by the Bureau of Labor Statistics (BLS), a statistical agency in the U.S. federal government.

The method for calculating the CPI is relatively simple. First, the BLS comes up with a basket of goods and services purchased by a typical household. Then, every month it collects data on the prices of those goods and services in a variety of places around the country. Using these data, the BLS calculates the cost of buying that market basket.

The CPI measures the increase in the cost of the market basket relative to the cost in a given base year. For instance, suppose that the cost of the market basket was $40,000 in 2015 (the base year) and $40,400 in 2016. To find the index for 2016 relative to 2015, we use the following formula:

EQUATION 25-1

$$CPI = \frac{\text{Cost of desired-year basket in base-year prices}}{\text{Cost of base-year basket in base-year prices}} \times 100$$

$$= \left(\frac{\text{Basket}_{\text{desired-year}}}{\text{Basket}_{\text{base-year}}}\right) \times 100$$

$$= \left(\frac{\text{Basket}_{2016}}{\text{Basket}_{2015}}\right) \times 100$$

$$= \left(\frac{\$40{,}400}{\$40{,}000}\right) \times 100 = 101$$

In the base year, by definition, the index will always be 100. In future years:

- If the cost of the basket rises higher than the base-year cost, the index will be more than 100.
- If the cost of the basket falls below the base-year cost, the index will be less than 100.

In our example, with 2015 as the base year, the CPI increases from 100 to 101. This change implies a 1 percent increase in the basket of consumer goods. That 1 percent increase also means a 1 percent increase in the cost of living for a typical household.

The BLS's stated goal for the CPI is to answer the question, "What is the cost, at this month's market prices, of achieving the standard of living attained in the base period?" In other words, the CPI helps us understand how the cost of living today compares with the cost of living at some time in the past. In the (hypothetical) example above, the CPI tells us that the cost of living in 2016 was 1 percent higher than it was in 2015. As Figure 25-1 shows, the CPI has risen consistently over the last hundred years.

FIGURE 25-1

CPI from 1913 to 2015 Prices increased more dramatically in the second half of the last century than they did in the first half. Over the first 50 years, prices tripled. In 2015, prices were approximately eight times greater than they were in 1963.

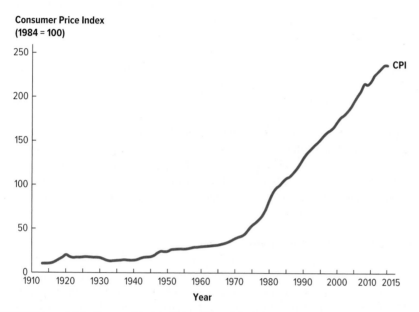

Source: http://inflationdata.com/Inflation/Consumer_Price_Index/HistoricalCPI.aspx?reloaded=true

 HINT

Figure 25-1 happens to use 1984 as the base year. In other words, the index for 1984 was 100, and the indexes for other years are numbers relative to 1984. An index of 105, for example, means prices were 5 percent higher than in 1984.

What would happen to the graph if a different base year had been chosen? The shape of the graph would be exactly the same, though the index numbers would be scaled to a different base year.

The challenges in measuring price changes

LO 25.3 Name the two main challenges the BLS faces when measuring price changes and outline how it responds to these challenges.

The idea behind the CPI is straightforward, but turning that idea into reality requires addressing two big challenges:

- The first is to figure out which goods should go into the market basket so that the CPI reflects the average purchases of the widest group of people.
- The second is how to measure changes over time. Take this simple question as an example: Is it a price increase if a computer costs 10 percent more but is also 10 percent faster?

In this section, we'll address both of these challenges in turn.

Which goods?

The first question is, *which goods* should go into the market basket to measure price changes? Your next-door neighbor may love carrots, and you may love beef. As a result, your grocery bills will probably look very different, and they will increase at different rates as the prices of carrots and beef change. There is no way to have a single number that perfectly describes changes in the cost of living for everyone because people buy different things. The best we can do is to come up with a basket that tries to represent a "typical" household.

Who is typical? The CPI is based on an average of the goods and services purchased by "urban consumers"—anyone living in a city of 2,500 or more. This accounts for 81 percent of the U.S. population; it includes people in all sorts of jobs as well as unemployed and retired people. It doesn't, however, include people living in rural areas, members of the military, or the "institutionalized" population (mostly people living in prisons or mental hospitals).

The CPI tries to balance out the consumption of different types of people in different life stages and situations. Rather than representing the exact consumption of any particular household, it is an average across a very large group of U.S. consumers. A particular family's cost of living might increase more or less than the CPI, depending on exactly how much of which things the family buys. Figure 25-2 shows the breakdown of spending in 2015 in the average urban-consumer household across eight major categories.

Changes over time: Substitution and innovation

Earlier, we noted that a price index like the CPI measures pure price changes only if the types and quantities of goods in the market basket remain constant. However, there is an accuracy trade-off involved: Keeping the basket fixed accurately isolates price changes from behavior changes. However, when real people's behavior has changed enough, keeping the basket fixed also means that it will no longer accurately represent the consumption of a typical household.

Price indexes have to deal with the fact that as tastes and prices change, households tend to buy different goods and services. There are two main reasons for changes in consumption patterns over time—substitution and innovation.

FIGURE 25-2

Spending by urban consumers represented in the CPI   This bar chart shows how much prices in certain sectors are weighted in the calculation of the Consumer Price Index. By far, the largest component of the Consumer Price Index is housing costs, at over 40 percent. The next two largest components are transportation, followed by food and beverage, which together make up about a third of the CPI. The rest of the categories together comprise the final quarter.

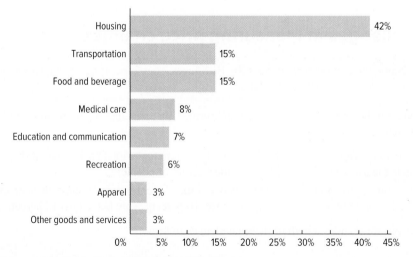

Source: U.S. Bureau of Labor Statistics, http://www.bls.gov/cpi/cpiri_2015.pdf

Substitution is the idea that people switch between similar goods and services when relative prices shift. For example:

- If the price of carrots goes up by 25 percent while the prices of other vegetables increase by a smaller amount, people will tend to buy fewer carrots and more other vegetables.
- If the price of going out to the movies goes up and the price of streaming video goes down, people will tend to watch more videos at home and fewer at the movie theater.

If the market basket doesn't reflect the fact that people buy less of particular goods as they get more expensive, it will overstate actual changes in the cost of living.

The second reason why the market basket has to change over time is *innovation:* As new goods and services become available, people change what they consume. When the CPI was first calculated during World War I, for example, it did not include refrigerators, washing machines, telephones, computers, and many other goods that almost all households today purchase at one time or another. Some of these things couldn't be bought at any price because they hadn't been invented. Others existed but hadn't made it into the general consumer market yet.

The BLS does occasionally update the basket used to calculate the CPI, to account for both substitution and new products. These updates undermine the idea of comparing a *constant* basket of goods and services. But the underlying aim is to capture the cost of achieving a certain *standard of living.* Creating a basket that balances these competing goals requires some tricky judgment calls.

Similar judgment calls are required when products get better. For example, cars today are far safer, are more reliable, and offer more features than did those in the 1950s. So if cars are more expensive now than they were in the 1950s, how do we tease apart the fact that the price of the basic product has increased from the fact that car quality is now higher? If a higher price represents higher quality, the true cost of living may not actually have increased.

Think about the reverse situation: Suppose that the price of a car stayed the same, but its features improved. We would say that the cost of living has fallen because you are able to achieve higher well-being for the same price. In the same sense, if the price of the car increases as its features improve, the cost of living may actually be constant, as you pay more but also achieve greater well-being.

The question is how we weigh the quality change against the price change. In trying to make these judgment calls, the BLS has to attempt something called *hedonic quality adjustment:* It tries to estimate what the price of the item would be *without* the improved features.

✓ CONCEPT CHECK

- ☐ What is the purpose of a market basket? **[LO 25.1]**
- ☐ What is a price index? **[LO 25.2]**
- ☐ Does the CPI show price changes for people living in rural areas? **[LO 25.3]**
- ☐ Name the two challenges that complicate the calculation of inflation. **[LO 25.3]**

Using Price Indexes

Now that we know how to measure price changes over time, what do we *do* with that knowledge? As we saw with GDP in Chapter 24, "Measuring GDP," many economic variables give an incomplete picture when expressed in nominal terms—that is, without accounting for price differences. To solve this problem, we can use price indexes to turn nominal variables into real ones.

Using price indexes, we can isolate changes in prices from changes in fundamentals like income and output and can express those changes in constant dollars relative to a base year. Those changes are captured in the **inflation rate**, which represents the size of the change in the overall price level. The inflation rate is one of the central concepts in macroeconomics. In this section we'll discuss how to calculate the inflation rate and how to use it.

inflation rate
the size of the change in the overall price level; the percent change in a price index such as the CPI from year to year

The inflation rate

LO 25.4 Calculate the inflation rate and recognize alternative measures.

The inflation rate is the percent change in the CPI from year to year, calculated as follows:

EQUATION 25-2
$$\text{Inflation rate} = \left[\frac{(\text{CPI}_{\text{year2}} - \text{CPI}_{\text{year1}})}{\text{CPI}_{\text{year1}}} \right] \times 100$$

Table 25-1 shows increases in the CPI from 2005 to 2015, using an average of prices in 1982–84 as the base period (when the CPI = 100). If we want to know how much prices have increased since the base period, the change in the CPI provides a direct answer. For instance, the 2005 CPI of 195.3 means that price levels in 2005 were 95.3 percent higher than they were in the base period, 1982–84.

When you read about inflation in the news, it is typically expressed as an increase over the *previous year.* For example, what if we want to compare 2006 to 2005, rather than to 1982–84? We can calculate the percent increase in prices from year to year as follows:

$$\text{Inflation rate}_{2006} = \left(\frac{\text{CPI}_{2006} - \text{CPI}_{2005}}{\text{CPI}_{2005}} \right) \times 100$$

$$= \left(\frac{201.6 - 195.3}{195.3} \right) \times 100 = 3.2\%$$

An inflation rate of 3.2 percent means that the overall price level increased at that rate between 2005 and 2006.

If you follow news reports on the economy, you may hear discussion of two different inflation measures:

- *Headline inflation* measures the changes in prices for the entire market basket of the average urban consumer. It's simply another term for inflation measured using the CPI.
- *Core inflation* measures price changes with food and energy costs taken out of the market basket.

TABLE 25-1

Calculating the inflation rate

To calculate the inflation rate, subtract the CPI of the previous year from the current year and then divide by the CPI of the previous year. In most years, prices have increased, but in 2009, there was negative inflation, or deflation.

Source: The base period (when the CPI = 100) is 1982–1984. U.S. Bureau of Labor Statistics and http://inflationdata.com/ Inflation/Consumer_Price_Index/ HistoricalCPI.aspx? reloaded=true.

Year	CPI	Calculation	Inflation rate(%)
2005	195.3	—	
2006	201.6	$\frac{201.6 - 195.3}{195.3} \times 100$	3.2
2007	207.3	$\frac{207.3 - 201.6}{201.6} \times 100$	2.8
2008	215.3	$\frac{215.3 - 207.3}{207.3} \times 100$	3.9
2009	214.5	$\frac{214.5 - 215.3}{215.3} \times 100$	−0.4
2010	218.1	$\frac{218.1 - 214.5}{214.5} \times 100$	1.7
2011	224.9	$\frac{224.9 - 218.1}{218.1} \times 100$	3.1
2012	229.6	$\frac{229.6 - 224.9}{224.9} \times 100$	2.1
2013	233.0	$\frac{233.0 - 229.6}{229.6} \times 100$	1.5
2014	236.7	$\frac{236.7 - 233.0}{233.0} \times 100$	1.6
2015	237.0	$\frac{237.0 - 236.7}{236.7} \times 100$	0.1

Why have two different measures? Compared to many goods, energy and food prices go up and down a lot. Because they might be very high or very low at the time the CPI is calculated, including them might over- or understate the real change in overall prices. On the other hand, most Americans spend a large part of their income on food and gas. Any basket that does not include these goods is missing a large part of the cost-of-living picture. Looking at both headline and core inflation can give us a more accurate sense of what's really happening in the economy.

Alternative inflation measures

The difference between headline and core inflation suggests a more general idea: We can measure inflation using *any* basket of goods or price index we want. The resulting measures of inflation will reflect changes in the prices of different sets of goods. The CPI focuses on prices *paid by consumers.*

What if we are more interested in the costs that businesses, rather than consumers, are facing? An alternative price index, the *Producer Price Index (PPI),* measures the prices of goods and services purchased *by firms.* The PPI includes things that are not part of the typical person's consumption basket, such as industrial machinery. Because increases in input prices eventually make it to consumers when they buy the final product, the PPI is considered a good predictor of *future* consumer prices. Regardless of whether we use the CPI or the PPI, inflation is measured as a *percent increase in the index from one year to the next.*

Another alternative is to calculate the inflation rate using the *GDP deflator,* as we did in Chapter 24, "Measuring GDP." The GDP deflator measures price changes for *everything produced in the country.* It doesn't, though, include goods produced abroad that might have a real effect on the typical household's cost of living, such as oil. Another key difference is that the GDP deflator is computed using the actual quantities that are produced in the economy each year, rather than using a "fixed" basket of goods.

All three measures of inflation—CPI, PPI, and GDP deflator—are useful; they simply measure different things. In practice, inflation rates calculated using the three methods track each other quite closely. Figure 25-3 shows inflation rates in the United States using each measure over the last 55 years.

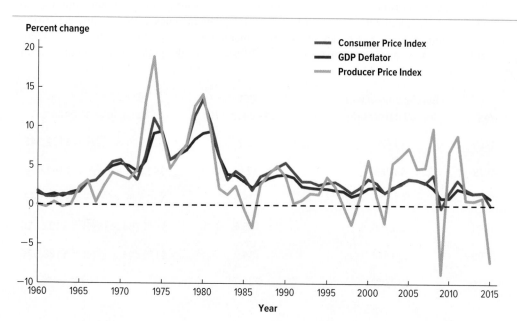

FIGURE 25-3

U.S. inflation rates, as measured by the CPI, PPI, and GDP deflator, 1960–2015

This graph shows the three main measures of inflation over the past 55 years. All three show similar trends in the rise and fall of prices. The Producer Price Index shows the most dramatic ups and downs, while the GDP deflator shows more restrained changes.

Source: U.S. Federal Reserve Bank of St. Louis—FRED, http://research.stlouisfed.org/fred2/.

Deflating nominal variables

LO 25.5 Use a price index to adjust nominal variables into real variables.

Often, we want to study how the real value of a variable, such as income, has changed over time. To do this, we can use the CPI (or another price index) to "deflate" the nominal variable and state it in constant, real terms.

You might be surprised, or even shocked, if your grandparents told you how much money they made in their younger days. For instance, in 1969, a salary of $20,520 would have allowed your grandparents to live a comfortable life, send their kids to college, and put away a little for retirement. When your grandparents retired 45 years later, in 2014, that income would have been below the federal poverty line for a family of four.

Suppose we want to know how much money your grandparents would have to earn now to have purchasing power equivalent to their income in 1969. To compare changes in purchasing power over time, we can translate nominal income in any past year into constant, real dollars. Equation 25-3 shows how any dollar amount from the past can be translated into its current value.

EQUATION 25-3 Value of year-X income in year-Y dollars

$$\text{Real value}_{\text{yearY}} = \text{Nominal value}_{\text{yearX}} \times \left(\frac{\text{CPI}_{\text{yearY}}}{\text{CPI}_{\text{yearX}}} \right)$$

Let's apply this equation to find the purchasing power of $20,520 in 2014 dollars. We multiply $20,520 by the ratio of the CPI in 2014 and 1969:

$$\text{Real value}_{2014} = \text{Nominal value}_{1969} \times \left(\frac{\text{CPI}_{2014}}{\text{CPI}_{1969}} \right)$$

$$= \$20{,}520 \times \left(\frac{236.7}{36.7} \right)$$

$$= \$132{,}346$$

What does this result mean? It means that in 2014 you would have needed $132,346 to buy the amount of goods and services your grandparents would have been able to buy with $20,520 in 1969. It turns out that they were doing pretty well, after all.

We can make this same calculation with any base year and any nominal variable. For instance, suppose we want to know how much of the increases in the incomes of the wealthy are attributable to inflation and how much they represent an increase in real wealth. The first two columns of Table 25-2 show average income for the top 20 percent of the population in nominal terms.

TABLE 25-2

Calculating the deflation of nominal variables

At first glance, the average income of those living in 1969 looks much lower than in 2014. When 1969 incomes are inflated so that the value of these dollars is the same between the two decades, the gap decreases.

Sources: Income data from the U.S. Census, https://www.census.gov/hhes/www/income/data/historical/families; CPI data from http://inflationdata.com/Inflation/Consumer_Price_Index/HistoricalCPI.aspx?reloaded=true.

Year	Average income of top 20 percent ($)	CPI (1982–84 = 100)	Value in 2014 dollars
1969	20,520	36.7	$20,520 \times \left(\frac{236.7}{36.7}\right)$ = **$132,346**
1979	43,265	72.6	$43,265 \times \left(\frac{236.7}{72.6}\right)$ = **$141,058**
1989	85,529	124.0	$85,529 \times \left(\frac{236.7}{124.0}\right)$ = **$163,263**
1999	135,250	166.6	$135,250 \times \left(\frac{236.7}{166.6}\right)$ = **$192,158**
2009	170,844	214.5	$170,844 \times \left(\frac{236.7}{214.5}\right)$ = **$188,526**
2014	217,021	236.7	217,021

The third column shows the CPI for each decade. The fourth column uses the CPI to translate income into a direct comparison of purchasing power in 2014 dollars. These data show that although the cost of living has increased, the income of the wealthiest 20 percent of Americans has increased faster. (How do we know that? We can see that real—inflation-adjusted—income of the group has grown steadily, except in 2009. So, income must have grown faster than prices. If they had grown at exactly the same rate, real income in 1969 would equal real income in 2014.) In other words, increased nominal incomes are partly due to inflation but also partly due to a real increase in purchasing power.

Inflation adjustment can make a huge difference in how we perceive things that happen *now* relative to things that happened *in the past,* as discussed in the From Another Angle box "The wealthiest American?"

From Another Angle
The wealthiest American?

Who would you say is the richest American in history? Bill Gates, maybe? Gates created the first computer operating system, which eventually bloomed into software giant Microsoft. At his wealthiest, he was worth over $101 billion—more dollars than any other individual in U.S. history. Whether that makes him the richest American, though, all depends on how you look at it.

Going backward through history, we find that the nominal wealth of the richest people in a generation keeps shrinking:

- At his death in 1937, John D. Rockefeller's wealth was a puny-sounding $1.4 billion.
- Cornelius Vanderbilt, famous for wealth gained through railroads and shipping, finished with a fortune of $100 million in 1877.
- John Jacob Astor, who had a virtual monopoly on the fur trade, had a final wealth of $20 million in 1848.

If all we did was consider *nominal* dollar amounts, Bill Gates looks vastly wealthier than all of them.

If we adjust those fortunes for inflation, we get a different picture. It's not exactly easy to compare the cost of living of today's multibillionaires with those of yesteryear. Technically, we'd need a constant basket of the kind of goods a typical multibillionaire might purchase. But we can't ask how much it might have cost Astor to buy a Bugatti sports car in 1848 or what Vanderbilt might have paid for a private jet in 1877. Those things didn't exist.

Still, some economists took a stab at translating the fortunes of history into constant 2006 dollars. The result?

- Rockefeller tops the inflation-adjusted list, by a lot. He would have been able to buy $305 billion worth of Cristal champagne and private Caribbean islands had he been alive in 2006.
- Not far behind, at $281 billion, is steel magnate Andrew Carnegie.
- Vanderbilt comes in third at $168 billion.
- Astor's $20 million in 1848 money would buy him $110 billion worth of luxury if he could have spent it in 2006.

As it turns out, Bill Gates doesn't tower over the super-rich from previous eras after all.

Sources: http://www.forbes.com/2007/09/14/richest-americans-alltime-biz_cx_pw_as_0914ialltime_slide_2. html; http://archive.fortune.com/magazines/fortune/fortune_archive/2007/03/05/8401299/index.htm.

Adjusting for inflation: Indexing

> **LO 25.6** Understand how indexing keeps the real value of a payment constant over time.

How can we be sure that wages will keep up with inflation? One fundamental theory in macroeconomics says that, with enough time, wages should naturally rise to offset the effects of inflation, so in the end inflation should not matter to people's well-being and their choices. However, most economists agree that there are times when some prices are changing so fast that the rest of the economy struggles to keep up.

If prices increase faster than wages, for instance, people will experience a drop in their standard of living. Everyone will face a very strong incentive to buy things *now* if they are afraid prices will be higher next week or next month. In that economic environment, inflation can distort economic choices. We'll talk a lot more about problems like these in later chapters, particularly in Chapter 33, "Inflation." For now, let's look at how *measuring* inflation can be an important step toward solving problems that inflation causes.

One very practical application of the CPI is to index payments to inflation. Ida May Fuller was the first-ever recipient of monthly Social Security benefits. When she retired in 1940, she received a check for $22.54. For the next decade, her benefits stayed constant, at $22.54 every month. By 1950, the real value of her Social Security check had fallen by almost half, due to inflation. In 1950, her $22.54 check could buy only $13.37 worth of goods and services, when translated into the purchasing power of 1940.

In the early years of Social Security, no accommodation was made for inflation. Retirees expected to receive the same nominal dollar amount monthly for the rest of their lives. In 1950, Congress looked at the problem faced by elderly people like Ms. Fuller. In signing the Social Security Act in 1935, President Franklin D. Roosevelt had expressed his intent that the law would "give some measure of protection to the average citizen . . . against poverty-ridden old age." With the real value of benefits dwindling every year as the cost of living rose, Social Security's success in protecting the elderly against poverty and hardship was limited. In response, Congress revised the law, to nearly double the value of monthly benefits.[1]

From 1950 to 1974, Congress amended the Social Security Act every few years. Each time, it increased the level of benefits in accord with the cost of living. However, these increases were sporadic and required a concerted effort on the part of lawmakers.

indexing
the practice of automatically increasing payments in proportion to the cost of living

Starting in 1975, Congress implemented a different solution: indexing. **Indexing** automatically increases payments in proportion to the cost of living. Such payments are said to be *indexed to inflation*. Congress indexed Social Security benefits directly to the CPI: If the CPI increases 5 percent, so does the nominal value of monthly benefits. As a result, the dollar amount of benefits has increased most years since 1975, keeping pace with changes in the cost of living.

Indexed payments are usually referred to as *cost-of-living adjustments*, or *COLAs*. In the United States, few salaries or income payments are indexed to inflation (except for those with union contracts, where they are more common). Social Security does have a COLA and affects millions of retirees. Indexing is much more common in other countries. In much of Europe, government employees' salaries receive automatic COLAs, as do retirees' pensions.

The reasoning behind indexing is straightforward: If you want the real value of a payment to stay constant over time, make the adjustment for inflation automatic. The alternative is to rewrite a law or a contract every year—a process that involves more work and less certainty.

However, indexing is not without controversy. To consider some reasons why COLAs can be a mixed blessing, read the What Do You Think? box "COLAs for better or worse."

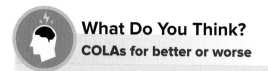

What Do You Think?
COLAs for better or worse

Cost-of-living adjustments (COLAs) provide increases in payments to offset inflation that occurred in the past year. Without an adjustment for the cost of living, what you could buy with a given wage or Social Security check would shrink steadily. Inflation would eat away at the value of these payments.

Traditionally, COLAs for the 59 million people who receive Social Security have been pegged to the *CPI-W*. This is a version of the Consumer Price Index that registers prices for urban and clerical workers. Some argue that the government should shift to a method more sensitive to the actual spending patterns of the elderly, who buy different things than urban and clerical workers. For example, in 2010 and 2011, retirees did not receive a COLA because the CPI-W stayed constant. However, health care costs increased by over 5 percent in both years. As a result, for the elderly the real value of Social Security payments fell.

One proposed alternative is a measure that uses a price basket geared to elderly consumers. In this alternative, for example, medical costs would represent 11 percent of the total, compared with 5 to 6 percent of the total in the traditional CPI-W.

There often are calls for COLAs to be applied to the minimum wage. Although the cost of living goes up every year, the federal minimum wage is not changed unless Congress decides to do so—which happens rarely. As you can see in Figure 25-4, increases in the minimum wage have not kept up with prices. The result is that the real value of the minimum wage has declined since the 1960s. Overall, the real value of the current minimum wage is about $3.00 per hour less than it was in 1968, although it is almost double the original minimum wage set in 1938.

(continued)

FIGURE 25-4

The real value of the minimum wage   Since the 1940s, the real value of the minimum wage has fluctuated as Congress has adjusted its nominal value to try to keep pace with inflation. Overall, the real value of the minimum wage climbed steadily between 1938 and the 1960s but has generally fallen since that time.

Source: https://www.dol.gov/featured/minimum-wage/chart1.

Some states, such as Washington, Vermont, and Colorado, have set a minimum wage above the federal level, which they adjust for inflation. While this ensures that the real value of the minimum wage stays the same in those states, opponents say that it's unwise to lose the flexibility to adjust the minimum wage as economic conditions change over time. When times are tough, requiring increases in the minimum wage could drive businesses to hire fewer workers.

WHAT DO YOU THINK?

1. Are COLAs an appropriate tool for Social Security? Are they appropriate for the minimum wage?
2. Returning to the chapter-opening example, should COLAs be used to determine fines for breaking laws like the no-smoking regulation on Massachusetts trains? How should the fines be calculated?

Source: http://www.nytimes.com/2011/03/27/opinion/27sun2.html?_r=1; https://www.ssa.gov/news/press/basicfact.html; http://oregonstate.edu/instruct/anth484/minwage.html.

✓ CONCEPT CHECK

☐ What is the role of the base period when measuring inflation? **[LO 25.4]**
☐ When is PPI, rather than CPI, the appropriate measure of inflation? **[LO 25.4]**
☐ How do differences between real and nominal variables reveal changes in prices over time? **[LO 25.5]**
☐ How does Social Security adjust payments based on changes to the cost of living? **[LO 25.6]**

Accounting for Price Differences across Places

So far, we've seen how to capture the fact that our grandparents paid less for a loaf of bread than we do today. Now, how do we capture the fact that a loaf of bread *today* costs less on average in Mexico than in the United States? Or, indeed, that a loaf of bread might cost less on average in Iowa City than in New York City? Just as we need to adjust economic variables for price changes over time, we sometimes need a tool that allows us to adjust for differences in prices across locations.

In Chapter 24, "Measuring GDP," we mentioned an idea called *purchasing power parity* that enables us to compare the true cost of living in various locations. Here, we explain how it works.

Purchasing power parity

LO 25.7 Explain what purchasing power parity is.

In theory, goods ought to cost the same everywhere, once they have been translated into a common currency using foreign exchange rates. To see why, imagine a pair of jeans that costs less in Mexico than in the United States. Given the difference in price, wouldn't entrepreneurs travel from the United States to Mexico, convert their dollars into pesos, buy the jeans, take them back to the United States, and sell them for a profit?

purchasing power parity (PPP) the theory that purchasing power in different countries should be the same when stated in a common currency

In principle, yes. These entrepreneurs will continue until the increased quantity of jeans supplied in the United States and the increased quantity demanded in Mexico cause the prices in the two countries to equalize. At that point, no one has an incentive to buy jeans abroad. The result is that purchasing power should theoretically be the same everywhere, when stated in a common currency. This idea is called **purchasing power parity (PPP)**.

In reality, PPP almost never holds exactly. Overall price levels are lower in Mexico. For most goods, $100 exchanged into pesos buys you more in Mexico than $100 would buy you in the United States. Why? There are three main factors: transaction costs, non-tradable goods and services, and trade restrictions. Let's briefly consider them.

- **Transaction costs:** One reason that PPP doesn't hold is transportation costs: It costs money to move goods from place to place. However, the difference in PPP is usually larger than what would be explained by transport costs alone; there are other transaction costs also. For example, it costs time and money to find sellers in another country. If the price difference is small and the costs of making transactions in another country are high, the *trade-off* involved may not be worth it. As a result, the entrepreneurs will decide not to bring in less-expensive jeans from Mexico.

- **Non-tradables:** Some goods and services just can't be taken from place to place very easily, or at all. For instance, you can't buy an apartment in Iowa City and transport it to Manhattan. You can't buy a pizza in Italy and transport it to North Dakota. (Well, you could, but it wouldn't be worth eating when you got it there.) You can't buy a haircut in India if you live in New Orleans. (Of course, you could fly to India to get your hair cut, but the transaction costs would be extremely high relative to the few dollars you'd save.) These types of goods and services are called *non-tradables*.

- **Trade restrictions:** Finally, international trade isn't free. There are often tariffs and trade restrictions that increase the cost or difficulty of making exchanges across national borders. Such restrictions discourage people from fully taking advantage of lower prices in other countries.

For these three reasons, we frequently see substantially different prices for individual goods and services, as well as different overall price levels, across countries or locations within a country. For example, the purchasing power of a dollar is higher in Mexico than in the United States and lower in Switzerland. If we want to compare incomes or costs across different countries, we're going to need to adjust nominal prices in different places. This is similar to what we do when comparing standards of living in different time periods. To compare prices in different places, economists have developed the idea of *purchasing power indexes*.

Purchasing power indexes

> **LO 25.8** Use a price index to calculate PPP-adjusted variables and compare the cost of living across different places.

Just as we can use a price index to account for changes in prices over time, we can also construct a price index that describes differences in prices across locations. The methodology is quite similar:

- First, we need to find a market basket of goods and services that we can compare across countries.
- Next, we measure the price of the goods in the basket in each country and calculate the overall cost of purchasing it in each country.
- Then, we build an index showing how much the basket costs in each country relative to some base.

For a simple example, let's think about the price of Big Macs around the world. The *Economist* magazine measures these prices in 120 countries in what it calls the Big Mac Index. The Big Mac isn't a basket that represents the full cost of living, of course. But it has the advantage of being similar in each country, due to McDonald's international production and sourcing policies. It also requires a variety of inputs, such as beef, bread, lettuce, labor, advertising, and real estate.

The Big Mac Index uses the United States as the base country and compares the cost of a Big Mac there to the cost in another country. In the United States, the price of a Big Mac in

January 2016 was \$4.93; in Mexico it was 49 pesos. Remember the theory of purchasing power parity—that purchasing power in different countries should be the same when stated in a common currency. If that theory holds true, Big Macs would have the same real price in the United States and Mexico. In that case, the exchange rate between dollars and pesos should be 9.93 pesos per dollar (49 pesos ÷ \$4.93).

In reality, the official exchange rate between pesos and dollars in January 2016 was 18.02 pesos per dollar. We can calculate the Big Mac Index by comparing the official exchange rate (18.02) to the exchange rate predicted by PPP (9.93):

$$\text{Big Mac Index for Mexico} = \frac{(9.93 - 18.02) \times 100}{18.02}$$

$$= \frac{-8.09 \times 100}{18.02} = -45\%$$

What does a negative Big Mac Index for Mexico tell us? It means that price levels in Mexico are lower than we'd expect if PPP held true. As a result, real purchasing power is higher in Mexico than it is in the United States. That is, if you exchange your dollars for pesos, they'll go further at a McDonald's in Mexico than one in the United States.

A positive Big Mac Index (as in expensive countries like Sweden and Switzerland) would imply that price levels are higher than predicted by PPP. Therefore, real purchasing power is lower in such places than in the United States.

Figure 25-5 shows how price levels differ across a number of countries, using the Big Mac Index and with the United States as the base level.

FIGURE 25-5

The Big Mac Index   The Big Mac Index is one way to measure differences in purchasing power across countries. According to the index, China and other countries in Asia, including Malaysia and Thailand, have a low cost of living. Rich countries generally have costs of living that are similar to that in the United States or even higher.

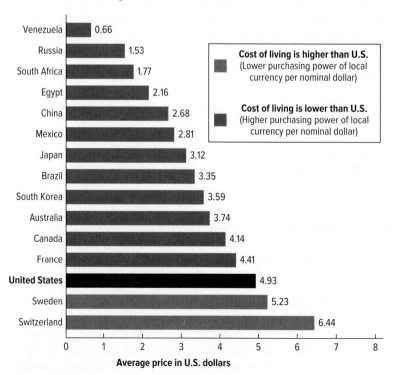

Source: Interactive data from *The Big Mac Index* © The Economist, http://www.economist.com/content/big-mac-index.

The Big Mac Index is a simple way of looking at price differences. The main measure actually used for international price comparisons is the World Bank's *International Comparison Program (ICP) index*. It uses a broad market basket that tries to represent the full cost of living across countries. The question is how to construct that market basket. People in different places consume different things depending on their culture, climate, religion, and so on. As a result, it's impossible to create a market basket that is "typical" everywhere. The methods behind the idea of PPP are still being improved, but for now, even imperfect PPP data are better than no data at all.

PPP-adjustment

Suppose that we are comparing GDP per capita around the world. What we want from this statistic is some sense of the differences in the average standard of living across countries. If the cost of living varies, the nominal level of GDP per capita will actually mean very different things in different countries.

PPP-adjustment involves recalculating economic statistics to account for differences in price levels across countries. When we do this, we say that we are calculating *PPP-adjusted* variables. PPP-adjustment using a price index is quite similar to adjusting for cost of living increases using a price index like the CPI.

PPP-adjustment
recalculating economic statistics to account for differences in price levels across countries

For example, let's calculate PPP-adjusted GDP per capita in the United States and Mexico. In 2014, nominal GDP per capita in the United States was $54,629; in Mexico it was $10,325.[2] The U.S. figure is about five times larger than that for Mexico. But because prices are generally lower in Mexico, we turn to data from the World Bank's International Comparison Program to account for differences in how much one's income can purchase in the two economies. According to the World Bank's PPP index, the purchasing power of a given amount of dollars was about 20.7 percent lower in the United States. In other words, on average, in Mexico goods and services cost about 20.7 percent less than they do in the United States. (Notice that this number differs from that found using the Big Mac Index. This is mainly because the PPP index considers much more than the price of Big Macs. Also, the PPP data are from 2014 and the Big Mac Index is from 2016.)

To find PPP-adjusted GDP per capita of any country relative to the United States, we can use Equation 25-4.

EQUATION 25-4 PPP-adjustment

$$\text{PPP-adjusted GDP} = \text{Nominal dollars}_{countryA} \times \left(\frac{1}{1 - \text{Price-level adjustment}_{countryA}} \right)$$

We can plug the numbers for Mexico into this equation:

$$\text{PPP-adjusted GDP} = \$10,325 \times \left(\frac{1}{1 - 0.207} \right)$$

$$= \$10,325 \times 1.2610 = \$13,019.83$$

If we look only at the nominal figure ($10,325), we might think that the average person in Mexico has a standard of living comparable to someone earning that amount in the United States. In reality, as the PPP-adjusted figure shows us, the average Mexican lives about as well as someone who earns $13,019 in the United States.

PPP-adjustment gives us a more realistic sense of differences in living standards around the world. In general, price levels are lower in poorer countries, so PPP-adjustment lets us see that poorer countries are not quite so poor as suggested by their nominal GDP per capita.

✓ CONCEPT CHECK

☐ How can transaction costs partially explain differences in purchasing power parity? **[LO 25.7]**
☐ What does the Big Mac Index show? **[LO 25.7]**
☐ Why do economists adjust international statistics based on purchasing power? **[LO 25.8]**

Conclusion

What can a dollar buy? The answer today is not the same as it will be next year, and it's not the same in New York City as it is in Iowa City. The result is that a nominal dollar amount in a particular time or place is just part of the answer. What we really care about is the *purchasing power* of that dollar amount. That's what determines how much you can buy at the store.

In this chapter, we've developed tools that allow us to track changes in the overall price level. These tools help us understand how the purchasing power of a dollar changes over time and across locations. Using the cost of a constant market basket allows us to construct a price index that shows relative price levels over time, such as the CPI. It also allows us to construct price indexes that show relative purchasing power in different places, such as the World Bank's International Comparison Program (ICP) index.

Using price indexes, we can adjust economic variables such as wages, income, GDP, and interest rates to see the difference between their nominal and real values. This lets us answer questions like "What would today's salaries have bought in our grandparents' time?" or "How rich are people in other countries relative to the United States?" It can also help us make better choices when deciding how to invest money, write contracts, or set up policies that account for the effects of inflation.

This chapter and the previous one have introduced the basic language and metrics of macroeconomics. We've discussed output and prices, and how to measure both the size of an economy and the cost of living there. In the next chapter, we'll move to another fundamental economic concern: how to maintain steady employment levels and avoid periods of high unemployment.

Key Terms

market basket, p. 636

price index, p. 638

Consumer Price Index (CPI), p. 638

inflation rate, p. 641

indexing, p. 646

purchasing power parity (PPP), p. 648

PPP-adjustment, p. 650

Summary

LO 25.1 Understand the importance of a market basket in tracking price changes.

To understand how the overall cost of living has increased, we need a way to measure the combined change in the prices of multiple goods, whose individual prices may be changing at different rates. To accomplish this, we can construct a market basket that includes specific goods and services in fixed quantities. By keeping goods and quantities constant, we can be sure that any change in the total cost of the basket is caused by a change in prices, rather than the type or amount of things being consumed.

LO 25.2 Calculate and use a price index to measure changes in the cost of living over time.

To summarize changes in price levels, we can construct a price index, which measures how much the cost of a market basket has risen or fallen relative to the cost in the base year or location. The most commonly used tool for measuring the cost of living in the United States is the Consumer

Price Index, or CPI. It tracks the cost of a basket of goods and services that is representative of the purchases of U.S. households. The price index in a given year is equal to the ratio of the cost of the market basket in that year to the cost in the base year, multiplied by 100. In the base year, the index will always be 100. In future years, if the price of the basket rises, the index will be more than 100. If the price of the basket falls below that in the base year, the index will be less than 100. An index of 120 implies a 20 percent increase in price levels over the base year.

LO 25.3 Name the two main challenges the BLS faces when measuring price changes and outline how it responds to these challenges.

The BLS faces two major challenges in constructing a basket: how to decide which consumption should be measured and how to account for changes in consumption over time. To deal with the first challenge, the CPI is based on an average of the goods and services purchased by "urban consumers," which ends up representing

81 percent of the U.S. population. It also presents two broad measures of this basket, headline inflation (another term for the CPI) and core inflation. Core inflation measures price changes for the CPI market basket, but with food and energy costs taken out. Removing those costs may miss a large part of the inflation picture.

The second challenge comes from changes to consumption and products over time. If the market basket doesn't change to reflect the substitutions consumers make as prices change, it will overstate the effect due to the rising prices. Finally, in trying to measure changes in the standard of living, economists need to tease out differences between mere changes in prices of products versus changes in quality as a result of innovation and technological advances.

LO 25.4 Calculate the inflation rate and recognize alternative measures.

The inflation rate describes the size of changes in the overall price level year to year. It is calculated by measuring the percent change in a price index from one year to the next. *Headline inflation* measures the changes in prices for the entire market basket of urban consumers. *Core inflation* measures price changes with food and energy taken out.

Inflation estimates based on the CPI measure price changes paid by consumers. Estimates based on the Producer Price Index (PPI) measure the prices of goods and services purchased by firms. Estimates based on the GDP deflator measure price changes for everything produced within a country (and thus exclude imports). Unlike the CPI and PPI, estimates based on the GDP deflator do not use a "fixed" basket of goods. In practice, inflation rates based on the CPI, PPI, and GDP deflator track each other quite closely.

LO 25.5 Use a price index to adjust nominal variables into real variables.

One of the most important applications of price indexes is the ability to be able to determine the purchasing power of money from a different time period. This gives the power to see the value of what a certain amount of dollars from the past could buy today, or how much a certain amount of dollars today would be worth in the past. To translate a nominal amount from year X into a constant, real amount in year Y, multiply the nominal value for year X times the ratio of the CPI of year Y divided by the CPI of year X.

LO 25.6 Understand how indexing keeps the real value of a payment constant over time.

Indexing is an important application of the need to adjust nominal values into their real purchasing power.

Recognizing that the purchasing power of money changes over time, payments and paychecks can be automatically indexed to inflation, so that their purchasing power stays equal even as prices change. Indexed payments are often referred to as cost-of-living adjustments.

LO 25.7 Explain what purchasing power parity is.

Purchasing power parity (PPP) is the idea that price levels in different countries should be the same, once they have been stated in a common currency. For a number of reasons—including transaction costs, non-tradable goods and services, and trade restrictions—PPP doesn't typically hold true; the real purchasing power of a dollar differs from place to place.

LO 25.8 Use a price index to calculate PPP-adjusted variables and compare the cost of living across different places.

When we recalculate economic variables to account for differences in purchasing power across countries, we say that we are calculating PPP-adjusted variables. To measure this difference in purchasing power, we can calculate a price index by comparing the cost of purchasing a market basket in each country. If the cost of living is lower than the base country, then PPP-adjusted GDP will be higher than nominal GDP. If the cost of living is higher than the base country, then PPP-adjusted GDP will be lower than nominal GDP.

Review Questions

1. If we want to measure changes in the cost of living, why don't we track differences in each household's *actual* expenditures from one year to the next, rather than the difference in the cost of a market basket? Offer several reasons why this method would fail to capture changes in the overall price level accurately. **[LO 25.1]**

2. There are many different types of market baskets that economists measure. For example, the market basket for consumers—called the Consumer Price Index—tracks the prices associated with the typical consumer's purchases of goods and services. The Producer Price Index tracks the prices of the goods and services purchased by firms. A third type of market basket is the Home Price Index, which tracks the value of residential housing. In what scenarios would each of these market baskets be useful? **[LO 25.1]**

3. Why is the list of the highest-grossing films of all time dominated by movies made within the last 10 years? (*Hint:* Did *Star Wars: The Force Awakens,* released in 2015, really sell considerably more movie tickets than the classic *Gone with the Wind,* or is something else going on?) **[LO 25.2]**

4. How would you use the concept of the Consumer Price Index to compare prices across different locations? **[LO 25.2]**

5. What types of goods and services would a basket measuring the inflation rate for farmers include? Why doesn't the BLS calculate the price levels for a market basket approximating the purchases of farmers? **[LO 25.3]**

6. Does the CPI represent the actual change in the cost of living for any given household? Explain why or why not. **[LO 25.3]**

7. Suppose wages rise in China, leading to an increase in the price of toys imported from China. How would this change affect the CPI, PPI, and the GDP deflator in the United States? **[LO 25.4]**

8. If the growth rate in nominal income is larger than the inflation rate (as measured by the change in the CPI or the GDP deflator), has the real value of income grown? **[LO 25.4]**

9. What is the better measure of inflation to determine how much should be paid to employees for cost-of-living adjustments: the Producer Price Index (PPI) or the CPI? Why? **[LO 25.5]**

10. Why are people unlikely to buy Big Macs in the places where they are relatively cheap according to purchasing power parity and sell them where they are relatively more expensive, in order to make a profit? **[LO 25.4, LO 25.6]**

11. In many poor countries, even middle-class families may have full-time servants, a luxury reserved for only the very wealthiest households in rich countries like the United States. How does the existence of low-cost domestic help affect PPP-adjusted GDP statistics in poor countries? **[LO 25.7, 25.8]**

12. Would Kentucky, a state with a very low cost of living, have a PPP-adjusted GDP higher or lower than its GDP calculated without PPP-adjustment? Why? **[LO 25.8]**

Problems and Applications

1. Subscribing to the theory that life is indeed a beach, the residents of La Playa spend all of their money on three things: Every year, they collectively buy 250 bathing suits, 600 tubes of sunscreen, and 400 beach

towels. Using the data in Table 25P-1, calculate the following. **[LO 25.1]**

   a. The total cost of this basket each year from 2013 through 2016.

   b. How much the price of this basket has changed from year to year in percentage terms.

2. Suppose a typical American consumer purchases three goods, creatively named good A, good B, and good C. The prices of these goods are listed in Table 25P-2. **[LO 25.1]**

   a. If the typical consumer purchases two units of each good, what was the percentage increase in the price paid by the consumer for this basket between 2015 and 2016?

   b. If the typical consumer purchases 10 units of good B and 2 units of both good A and good C, what was the percentage increase in the price paid by the consumer for this basket?

   c. Given your answers to parts a and b, what is the relationship between the market basket and the percentage price change?

3. Using the data in Table 25P-3, calculate the CPI and the inflation rate in each year, using 2010 as a base year. **[LO 25.2]**

4. Table 25P-4 lists the prices and quantities consumed of three different goods from 2014–2016. **[LO 25.2]**

   a. For 2014, 2015, and 2016, determine the amount that a typical consumer pays each year to purchase the quantities listed in the table.

   b. Using the amounts you found in part a, calculate the percentage change in the amount the consumer paid from 2014 to 2015, and from 2015 to 2016.

   c. Why is it problematic to use your answers to part b as a measure of inflation?

   d. Suppose we take 2014 as the base year, which implies that the market basket is fixed at the 2014 consumption levels. Using 2014 consumption levels, now find the rate of inflation from 2014 to 2015 and from 2015 to 2016. (*Hint:* First calculate the cost of the 2014 market basket using each year's prices and then find the percentage change in the cost of the basket.)

TABLE 25P-1

Item (amount purchased)	Price 2013 ($)	Price 2014 ($)	Price 2015 ($)	Price 2016 ($)
Bathing suits (250)	10.00	12.00	15.00	18.00
Sunscreen (600)	4.00	5.00	5.00	6.00
Beach towels (400)	5.00	5.50	7.00	9.00

TABLE 25P-2

Good	Price in 2015 ($)	Price in 2016 ($)
A	10	15
B	5	4
C	1	2

TABLE 25P-3

Year	Price of basket ($)	CPI	Inflation rate
2010	20,000	100	—
2011	21,500		
2012	22,800		
2013	26,150		
2014	28,825		
2015	32,700		

    e. Repeat the exercise from part *d*, now assuming that the base year is 2015.

    f. Why were your answers from parts *d* and *e* different?

5. Which of the following goods have likely required hedonic quality adjustment over time if they were included in the Consumer Price Index (CPI)? **[LO 25.3]**

    a. Laptop computers.

    b. Cellphones.

    c. Salt.

    d. Televisions.

    e. Housing.

    f. Tennis rackets.

6. Use Table 25P-5 to calculate core and headline inflation in each time frame relative to the base year, assuming that each category is weighted equally in the calculation of headline inflation. **[LO 25.2, 25.4]**

    a. 2012 to a base year.

    b. 2016 to a base year.

    c. 2012 to 2016.

7. Table 25P-6 shows the GDP deflator and the CPI over five recent years. By what percent did prices change between years for each measure? Calculate the annual inflation rate and then the inflation rate across the entire time period. **[LO 25.4]**

8. The median American household earned $9,387 in 1973 and $53,657 in 2014. During that time, though, the CPI rose from 44.4 to 236.7. **[LO 25.5]**

    a. Calculate the total growth rate in nominal median household income from 1973 to 2014.

    b. Calculate the total growth rate in real median household income from 1973 to 2014.

TABLE 25P-5

	Food and energy	Other goods and services
2012	120	102
2016	105	107

TABLE 25P-6

Year	GDP deflator	Change in GDP deflator	CPI	Change in CPI
2012	100		100	
2013	105		104	
2014	112		110	
2015	123		113	
2016	127		120	
2012–2016	—			

TABLE 25P-4

	2014		2015		2016	
Good	Price ($)	Quantity	Price ($)	Quantity	Price ($)	Quantity
A	10	10	15	8	20	5
B	5	18	3	30	4	25
C	1	10	2	5	5	10

9. Using Table 25P-7, find the real value of a $1,000 payment to be received each year given the following CPI values. Next, find the amount that this $1,000 should be adjusted to, in order to keep its real value at $1,000. **[LO 25.5, 25.6]**

10. Suppose General Electric paid its line workers $10 per hour in 2015 when the Consumer Price Index was 100. Suppose that deflation occurred and the aggregate price level fell to 80 in 2016. **[LO 25.5, 25.6]**

    a. What did GE need to pay its workers in 2016 in order to keep the real wage fixed?

    b. What did GE need to pay its workers in 2016 if it wanted to increase the real wage by 10 percent?

    c. If GE kept the wage fixed at $10 per hour in 2016, in real terms, what percentage increase in real wages did its workers get?

11. Suppose Table 25P-8 shows the prices of a tall Starbucks latte in countries around the world. Using the data, and the fact that a latte costs $3 in the United States, calculate how much a country's currency is under- or overvalued according to purchasing power. First, calculate the implied exchange rate for each country. Next, calculate the "latte index" for each country using the Big Mac index formula from the chapter. **[LO 25.7]**

TABLE 25P-7

Year	CPI	Real value of $1,000	Cost-of-living adjusted payment
2013	100	1,000	0
2014	103		
2015	105		
2016	110		

TABLE 25P-8

Country	Price	Official exchange rate
Thailand	60 baht	30 baht/dollar
Argentina	15 pesos	6 pesos/dollar
United Kingdom	2 pounds	0.5 pound/dollar
Japan	450 yen	80 yen/dollar

TABLE 25P-9

Office location	Salary ($)	CPI
Cleveland	80,000	100
Miami	120,000	155
New York City	150,000	210

TABLE 25P-10

Country	GDP ($)	Price level (%)
Ona	10,000	6
Rye	12,700	−27
Zolfo	14,100	−10
Avon	23,400	20

12. An employee asks her boss whether she can transfer offices so that she can work in a different part of the country. The boss responds positively and says that the employee can choose to work in Cleveland, Miami, or New York City. The boss then hands the employee a list, as shown in Table 25P-9, of the salaries that she would earn in the different cities and the average price levels in those same cities. **[LO 25.7, 25.8]**

    a. From a standpoint of maximizing the employee's consumption possibilities, which office should she choose?

    b. What would be the minimum salary in New York City the boss could offer the employee to make the employee indifferent between moving to Cleveland and to New York City?

13. Calculate the PPP-adjusted GDP for each of four countries, using the information found in Table 25P-10. **[LO 25.8]**

Endnotes

1. https://www.ssa.gov/history/briefhistory3.html.

2. http://data.worldbank.org/indicator/NY.GDP.PCAP.CD?order=wbapi_data_value_2014+wbapi_data_value+wbapi_data_value-last&sort=desc.

Part Seven

Labor Markets and Economic Growth

The two chapters in Part 7 will introduce you to . . .

labor markets and economic growth. As we explore labor markets, we turn to the forces that shape employment patterns in both the long run and the short run. Moving on to economic growth, we turn to the forces that determine why some countries are richer and others are poorer.

Chapter 26, "Unemployment and the Labor Market," discusses how the unemployment rate reflects the struggles of individuals looking for work and why it is considered to be an important barometer of the overall health of the economy. A strong economy has many benefits: Factories and business create new jobs, people find it relatively easier to get work, and unemployment is usually low. But when the economy falters, firms lay off workers to cut production and unemployment is high. Because it acts as a signal of the state of the economy, the unemployment rate is tracked closely from month to month and is influential in government policy and political debates.

Chapter 27, "Economic Growth," focuses on one of the great challenges in economics: How can policy and resources be combined to create healthy economic growth? Growth increases economic opportunities, creates a dynamic business environment, and generates new wealth that allows people to lead more comfortable, secure lives. In recent years, economic growth has lifted hundreds of millions of people around the world out of poverty. In the search for the combination of policies that will lead to economic growth, we look to success stories like the astounding advances in China in the last few decades, and we take cautionary lessons from countries that still search for ways to lift living standards.

Unemployment and the Labor Market

WHAT DOES IT MEAN TO BE UNEMPLOYED?

Rick Alexander is a master builder who spent three decades running a successful home-restoration business in Connecticut. When his elderly parents fell ill in 2008, he gave up his business and moved to Florida to help them. He thought it would be easy to find work—after all, he had a certified trade and many years of experience. He looked first for a job as a supervisor at construction sites but didn't find anything. Lowering his sights, he next looked for work at wholesalers and lumberyards, and then he applied for any job at hardware stores. Still, he experienced a constant stream of rejections. He tried to start his own business, but in the struggling housing market in Florida, he couldn't generate enough sales to make it profitable. Tired of the search, Rick Alexander gave up looking for work.[1]

Alexander's story is frustratingly common, especially during a recession. In tough times, jobs are hard to find. In October 2009, four months after the official end of the "Great Recession," the unemployment rate in the United States rose to close to 10 percent. Unemployment was even higher for certain groups of the population. For young men without a high-school degree, the unemployment rate was close to 30 percent.[2] Even many college graduates struggled to find work and ended up living back at home with their parents.

© Sean De Burca/Getty Images

Of course, unemployment exists even when the economy is not in a recession. The natural churning of the labor market causes people to be unemployed for short periods as they move between jobs. That churn is a normal part of economic life. Even when there's no recession, regional unemployment occurs as factories close and when the needs of local employers shift. Such unemployment is made worse when laid-off workers find that their skills no longer match the jobs that are available. Ironically, policies designed to protect workers—like minimum wage laws and unionization—also can lead to unemployment. Although they help existing workers, they often make it harder for those out of work to find jobs.

Some unemployment may be unavoidable, but too much of it can have serious consequences, both for the economy as a whole and on a personal level. One consequence of unemployment is that some of the productive potential of the economy—the time and skills of the unemployed—is not being put to use.

Another consequence is much more personal. Rick Alexander's story shows how prolonged unemployment can be one of the most difficult experiences that a person suffers. It creates uncertainty about the future and can bring on feelings of hopelessness, especially when trying to support oneself and one's family. Studies show that being unemployed is correlated with higher rates of depression and lower assessments of self-worth. Unemployment is an economic problem with potentially serious social and psychological consequences.

Being unemployed can take a mental toll, but the reality is that the difficulties of finding a job are in large part shaped by macroeconomic forces outside of an individual's control. What are these forces? Why does unemployment exist in the first place? These questions pose a puzzle for economists.

We start by assuming that a market reaches an equilibrium where quantity demanded is equal to quantity supplied at the prevailing price. Applying that idea to labor demand and labor supply, the fact that unemployment exists suggests that people want to supply more labor at the prevailing wage than firms are demanding. Why don't wages drop until unemployment is eliminated? In this chapter, we'll investigate the reasons why wages might not drop to an equilibrium level. We'll also see why some unemployment will exist even when the labor market is in equilibrium. As we distinguish between different sources of unemployment, we'll see the logic of different strategies to address the underlying problems.

Defining and Measuring Unemployment

LO 26.1 Explain how economists measure employment and unemployment.

Measuring unemployment turns out to be more complicated than simply counting those who aren't working. The chapter-opening story illustrates some of the complexity: On the one hand, we want to count Rick Alexander as unemployed when he's actively searching for a job. On the other hand, Alexander's retired parents don't have jobs, but they're not interested in getting them. How do we differentiate those two forms of being unemployed? And how do we represent the situation when someone like Alexander gets so discouraged that he stops looking for work? Defining unemployment in a clear and consistent way is an important step toward getting a handle on the underlying issues. In general, **unemployment** occurs when someone wants to work but cannot find a job.

People are unemployed for many reasons:

- Job seekers may be holding out for high salaries.
- Job seekers may lack relevant skills.
- Sometimes job seekers have the right skills and appropriate ambitions but still can't land a job in the current market.

unemployment
situation in which someone wants to work but cannot find a job in the current market

The government's definition of unemployment attempts to capture all of these situations. The Bureau of Labor Statistics, the government agency in charge of collecting employment statistics, defines unemployment in this way:

> Persons aged 16 years and older who had no employment during the reference week, were available for work, except for temporary illness, and had made specific efforts to find employment sometime during the 4-week period ending with the reference week.[3]

This definition means that the United States counts people as being unemployed *only if they meet three criteria:*

1. They didn't work at all in the prior week.
2. They were available to work if they had been offered a job.
3. They were making efforts to look for a job.

Measuring unemployment

In this section, we will put together all the pieces you need to understand the sort of unemployment figures you might see or hear in a news report or a Bureau of Labor Statistics (BLS) official report. These reports are extremely influential in the worlds of business and politics. Everyone wants to know what the latest information about unemployment says about the health of the economy.

First, we need to define some key groups of people. The *working-age population* is the civilian, noninstitutional population aged 16 and over. This category means all adults except those who are in the armed forces (such as soldiers) or who are inmates in an institution (such as prisons or mental facilities).

However, not everyone who is over 16 *wants to work*. In the official definition of unemployment, we want to count only those people who are "available for work" and "making specific efforts to find employment." That means we don't count as unemployed the following categories of people:

- Full-time students.
- Parents who are staying home to look after their children.
- People who cannot work because of a disability.
- People who have inherited wealth and choose to live off that wealth rather than work.
- Retirees. (Some countries define the "working-age population" as 16 to 64, but the BLS does not impose an upper age limit.)

When we want to refer to people of working age excluding those in the categories listed above (full-time students, stay-at-home parents, retirees, and so on), we instead talk about the *labor force.*

The **labor force** consists of people in the working-age population who are either currently working ("employed") or who would like to work and are actively trying to find a job ("unemployed"). That is,

labor force

people who are in the working-age population and are either employed or unemployed; people who are currently working or who are actively trying to find a job

EQUATION 26-1   Labor force = Employed + Unemployed

(The labor force does not include those people in the categories listed above who are in the working-age population but not wanting to work.)

The unemployment rate

unemployment rate

the number of unemployed people divided by the number of people in the labor force

We now have the numbers we need to define the **unemployment rate**, which is the number of unemployed people divided by the labor force:

EQUATION 26-2 $\text{Unemployment rate} = \dfrac{\text{Number of unemployed}}{\text{Labor force}} \times 100$

$$= \dfrac{\text{Unemployed}}{\text{Employed} + \text{Unemployed}} \times 100$$

Table 26-1 shows the official unemployment and employment numbers for the U.S. economy for December 2006 and December 2015. The first date, December 2006, is just before the start of a large economic downturn. The data for nine years later show the lingering effects that a deep recession can have on a labor market. Over this nine-year period, there was an increase in the number of unemployed people, from 6,762,000 to 7,904,000.

Table 26-1 also shows the number of people in the labor force. Dividing the number of unemployed by the size of the labor force gives us the unemployment rate at both dates:

Unemployment rate, December 2006:

$$\dfrac{6,762,000}{152,732,000} \times 100 = 4.4 \text{ percent}$$

Unemployment rate, December 2015:

$$\dfrac{7,904,000}{157,833,000} \times 100 = 5.0 \text{ percent}$$

TABLE 26-1

U.S. employment statistics

With increases in the working-age population and the number of people in the labor force, the overall number of people employed—as well as those unemployed—increased from 2006 to 2015.

Source: Bureau of Labor Statistics, Table A-1, Employment Status of the Civilian Population by Sex and Age, seasonally adjusted (accessed May 19, 2016), http://www.bls.gov/news.release/empsit.t01.htm#cps_empsit_a01.f1.

The December 2015 unemployment rate tells us that at the end of 2015, approximately 5 percent of Americans who wanted to work couldn't find work.

The unemployment rate describes what is going on in the national economy as a whole but doesn't tell us much about *who* is affected. In general, the unemployment rate varies greatly by educational status, gender, age, and race. On average, younger people have higher unemployment rates than older people, and people with less education are more likely to be unemployed than people with more education. Figure 26-1 shows some comparisons of unemployment among different types of people in the years 2003–2015.

Month	Working-age population (noninstitutionalized)	Labor force	Employed	Unemployed
December 2006	230,108,000	152,732,000	145,970,000	6,762,000
December 2015	251,936,000	157,833,000	149,929,000	7,904,000

FIGURE 26-1

Unemployment rates by demographic group

(A) Unemployment rate by sex

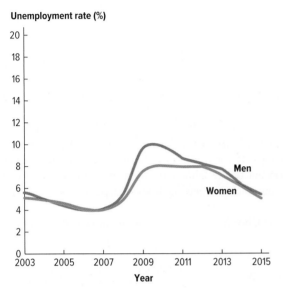

Until the start of the great recession, unemployment rates were the same for men and women. Afterwards, men were far more likely to be unemployed, although this has stabilized in recent years.

(B) Unemployment rate by age

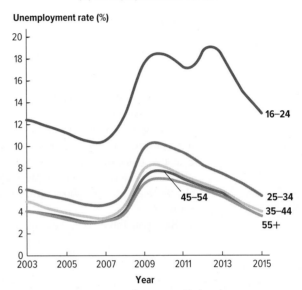

In general, younger people are more likely to be unemployed.

(C) Unemployment rate by race

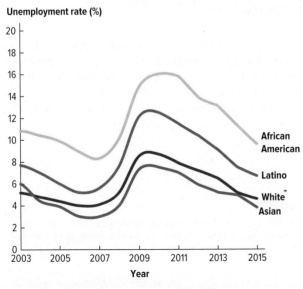

Although the overall trend is the same for all races, African Americans have a much higher rate of unemployment.

(D) Unemployment rate by education level

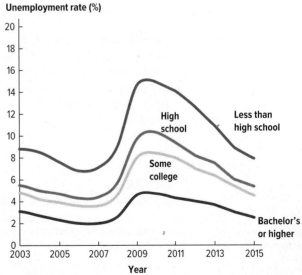

The more education a person has, the more likely he or she is to have a job.

Source: Bureau of Labor Statistics, Table A-2 Employment Status of the Civilian Population by Race, Age, and Sex (accessed April 16, 2013), http://www.bls.gov/cps/tables.htm.

The labor-force participation rate

We can also learn something interesting about the state of the economy by looking at the **labor-force participation rate**, which is the number of people in the labor force divided by the working-age population:

EQUATION 26-3

$$\text{Labor-force participation rate} = \frac{\text{Labor force}}{\text{Working-age population}} \times 100$$

This figure tells us what fraction of the population *wants* to be working, whether or not they actually have a job.

During recessions we usually see the labor-force participation rate fall. Some people who are unemployed eventually give up looking for work, like Rick Alexander in our chapter-opening example. Once these people stop actively looking for work, they are no longer considered part of the labor force. Other people may drop out of the labor force in a recession because they choose to go back to school, or take early retirement, or become homemakers instead of looking for work.

Based on Table 26-1, we can compute the labor-force participation rate in December 2006:

$$\frac{152,732,000}{230,108,000} \times 100 = 66.4 \text{ percent}$$

This means that 66.4 percent of the total working-age population was in the labor force in December 2006. In December 2015 the labor-force participation rate was:

$$\frac{157,833,000}{251,936,000} \times 100 = 62.6 \text{ percent}$$

Over the nine-year period, 3.8 percent of the working-age population stopped participating in the labor force. It is likely that at least some of these people would have been unemployed if they had stayed in the labor force. So the unemployment rate of 5 percent in December 2015 may understate the effect of the recession on employment.

Table 26-2 summarizes the two different measures of the U.S. labor market in 2006 and 2015.

TABLE 26-2

Employment in the United States, 2006 and 2015

The unemployment rate in 2015 was higher than in 2006, but the 2015 unemployment rate signaled a big improvement over conditions during the Great Recession (the unemployment rate had hit 10 percent in October 2009). At the same time, however, the percentage of the population participating in the labor force fell between 2006 and 2015.

	Unemployment rate (%)	Labor-force participation rate (%)
December 2006	4.4	66.4
December 2015	5.0	62.6
Change	+0.6	−3.8

Source: Bureau of Labor Statistics (accessed June 22, 2016), http://www.bls.gov/cps/tables.htm.

discouraged workers

people who have looked for work in the past year but have given up looking because of the condition of the labor market

underemployed

workers who are either working less than they would like to or are working in jobs below their skill level

Discouraged workers are not counted as unemployed.
© *Tony Biddle, Perfect World Design.*

? POTENTIALLY CONFUSING

When discussing unemployment, people often talk about *percentage point* changes—such as the unemployment rate increasing by 0.6 percentage *point,* from 4.4 percent to 5 percent. Sometimes people talk loosely about unemployment, referring to such a change as unemployment going up by "0.6 percent" rather than by "0.6 percentage point." There is a big difference, although people may guess what is meant by the loose talk.

If we want to, we could, of course, talk about changes in unemployment in terms of percent, rather than percentage points. For example, from 4.4 to 5 is an increase of 13 percent. That would be technically accurate, but you rarely hear economists talk this way.

Talking in percentage *points* makes a change easier to conceptualize: If you hear that the unemployment rate increased by "0.6 percentage point," for example, it means that 6 people out of every 1,000 in the labor force have lost their jobs.

On the other hand, if you hear that an economy's unemployment rate increased by "13 percent," you have no way of knowing how bad the change really is. Maybe the increase was from 1 percent unemployment to 1.13 percent, which would be considered a small change. Or maybe unemployment went from 10 percent to 11.3 percent, which would be considered a more substantial change.

This is why statisticians and economists report changes in percentage points, not percentages, when discussing unemployment.

Beyond the unemployment rate

People often use the unemployment rate to summarize the state of the labor market, but it has significant limitations. Most obviously, it doesn't include people like Rick Alexander, introduced at the start of the chapter. While Alexander was actively looking for work, he was counted as unemployed. Once he gave up hope of finding a job, he was deemed to have dropped out of the labor force and was no longer counted as unemployed.

This seems like a semantic trick. Why should we count Alexander as unemployed when he's feeling optimistic and spends his days sending out résumés, but not when he turns pessimistic and gives up the search? In fact, the Bureau of Labor Statistics (BLS) has a term for people like Alexander: **discouraged workers**. Discouraged workers are people who have looked for work in the past year but have given up looking because of the condition of the labor market. Thinking about discouraged workers gives a broader view of who is affected by a recession.

What about people who have part-time jobs but would like to work full time? Such people are defined as being **underemployed**. So are workers who are in jobs that are not suited to their skill level—for example, a law-school grad who can't get a job in law and reluctantly takes work as a barista at Starbucks. The BLS collects data on the first kind of underemployment (working fewer hours than you would like), but unfortunately not on the second kind (working in a job for which you are overqualified).

In fact, the BLS collects *six* different measures of unemployment, as shown in Table 26-3:

- The first two are "narrow" unemployment rates, counting only people who have been unemployed for a long time (U1) and those who have recently lost their jobs or done temporary work (U2).

TABLE 26-3

Six measures of unemployment

Total unemployment in an economy can be measured using narrower or broader definitions. The BLS reports six main measures, ranging from the narrowest (U1), which includes only those who are chronically unemployed, to the broadest (U6), which includes everyone from the chronically unemployed to those who are already working part time but want to be working full time. The "official" unemployment rate typically cited in the news media is U3.

Category of unemployment	Rate in December 2006 (%)	Rate in December 2015 (%)
U1: Long-time unemployed (more than 15 weeks)	1.4	2.1
U2: Job losers + those who completed temporary work	2.1	2.4
U3: Unemployed	4.4	5.0
U4: Unemployed + discouraged workers	4.6	5.4
U5: Unemployed, discouraged workers + marginally attached workers	5.2	6.1
U6: Unemployed, discouraged workers, marginally attached workers + underemployed	7.9	9.9

Source: BLS Table A-15, Alternative Measures of Unemployment and Underemployment, seasonally adjusted (accessed May 19, 2016), http://www.bls.gov/news.release/empsit.t15.htm.

- The "official" unemployment rate is the one shown in the table as U3.
- The fourth measure combines unemployed plus discouraged workers.
- The fifth measure adds "marginally attached" workers. These people are like discouraged workers in some respects—they would *like* to work, and they have looked for work at some point in the last year. But they don't meet the strict definition of unemployed because, for whatever reason, they haven't looked for a job in the last four weeks.
- The final definition, U6, includes underemployed people with part-time work who seek full-time jobs.

Adding extra dimensions to unemployment measures helps to paint a fuller picture of the labor market. Taking the broadest measure (U6)—which includes discouraged and marginally attached workers and the underemployed—almost 10 percent of the labor force was considered to not be working as much as they would like to in 2015, compared with under 8 percent in 2006.

The other notable change that occurred during the recession is the increasing percentage of people who were unemployed for a long stretch of time:

- In 2006, people unemployed for more than 15 weeks made up only 1.4 percent of the labor force, or approximately a third of all unemployed people.
- In 2015, this number rose to 2.1 percent of the labor force, or more than 40 percent of all unemployed people.

This change shows that unemployment during the recession wasn't just about short stints of joblessness between positions, but also about long-term inability to find work.

Where do the data come from?

The main source of information on unemployment in the United States is a household survey that asks people if they are working and how much they are earning. This survey, performed by the Bureau of Labor Statistics, is called the Current Population Survey. Every month, employees of the BLS survey about 60,000 households. It's not exact—it would be prohibitively expensive to survey every single U.S. household every month—but the sample size is big enough to give a reliable estimate for the economy as a whole.

The survey is collected year-round, allowing the BLS to analyze and adjust for changes in unemployment that are due to the season. If you're a trained ski instructor, for example, you'll more easily find work in February than in August. Farm workers and construction workers are also affected by seasonal changes. The BLS publishes statistics that are *seasonally adjusted* in order to help distinguish these expected seasonal patterns from deeper shifts in economic conditions. The data we show in the tables here are all seasonally adjusted.

✓ CONCEPT CHECK

☐ How is the labor-force participation rate calculated? **[LO 26.1]**
☐ Are discouraged workers counted as being unemployed? **[LO 26.1]**
☐ How is underemployment different from unemployment? **[LO 26.1]**

Equilibrium in the Labor Market

LO 26.2 Explain how wage rates above equilibrium cause unemployment.

The existence of *any* amount of unemployment is a bit of a puzzle. Labor is bought and sold in a market, just like other goods and services. There is demand for labor (from firms wanting to hire workers), a supply of labor (from individuals looking for jobs), and a price (called the wage). In most markets, we expect the price to adjust until the market reaches equilibrium, a point at which the quantity supplied equals the quantity demanded. The existence of unemployment suggests that this simplest of models can't fully explain what goes on in the labor market. In this section, we explore the predictions of the simple model. In the next section, we'll add nuance to show that unemployment can arise when the wage is held above the equilibrium level or when real-world frictions prevent labor supply or labor demand from adjusting perfectly to changes in the economy.

As in any other market, the labor market features a demand curve and a supply curve. The demand for labor comes from firms, who need labor to produce output. The **labor demand curve**, depicted in panel A of Figure 26-2, shows the relationship between the total quantity of

labor demand curve
a graph showing the relationship between the total quantity of labor demanded by all the firms in the economy and the wage rate

---

(A) Firms and the labor market	(B) Workers and the labor market	**FIGURE 26-2**

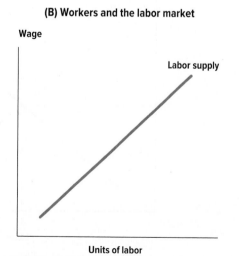

Labor demand and labor supply

As the price of labor, or the wage, decreases, the amount of labor demanded by firms increases. This relationship is shown by the curve above.

Conversely, as the wage rate increases, workers are increasingly willing to supply labor. This relationship is shown by the curve above.

labor demanded by all the firms in the economy and the wage rate. All things being equal, firms will want to hire more labor when wages are lower and less labor when wages are higher.

The supply of labor comes from people who are able to work and who choose to participate in the labor market. As we have seen, not everyone who could potentially work wants to work. Other things being equal, we expect that across the economy as a whole, people will be willing to supply more labor at higher wage rates and less labor at lower wage rates. The **labor supply curve**, pictured in panel B of Figure 26-2, shows the relationship between the total quantity of labor supplied in the economy and the wage rate.

labor supply curve
a graph showing the relationship between the total labor supplied in the economy and the wage rate

Together, the labor demand and labor supply curves describe the national labor market, as shown in Figure 26-3. As in any other market, equilibrium occurs at the intersection of the supply and demand curves. At the equilibrium wage, quantity demanded equals quantity supplied: Everyone who wants to work at prevailing wages and has the required skills is able to find a job.

Our definition of unemployment—people wanting to work but being unable to find a job at the prevailing wage—is easy to rephrase in the language of supply and demand. The quantity of labor supplied at the prevailing wage (people wanting to work at that wage) is greater than the quantity of labor demanded (jobs offered by firms wanting to hire at that wage). In other words, there is a *surplus* of labor.

Surplus arises in a market when the prevailing price is higher than the equilibrium price. (Look back to Chapter 6, "Government Intervention," if you need to confirm this statement.) Figure 26-4 shows how unemployment occurs when the wage rate is W_1—that is, higher than the equilibrium level of W^*. In this very simple model, unemployment is the gap between the number of people who want to work and the number of jobs offered at the prevailing wage. (However, we'll see in a minute that when a little nuance is added to the model, we can get unemployment even when the wage is not above the equilibrium level.)

Here's the puzzle: Why would wages remain above the equilibrium level? We know what *should* happen in a market when the price is too high: The price should fall until the market reaches equilibrium. Why don't firms offer lower wages, or unemployed people offer to work for lower wages, until the equilibrium wage is reached? In the next section we'll look at several reasons why this might not happen, as well as reasons unemployment occurs even at the equilibrium wage.

FIGURE 26-3

The labor market in equilibrium

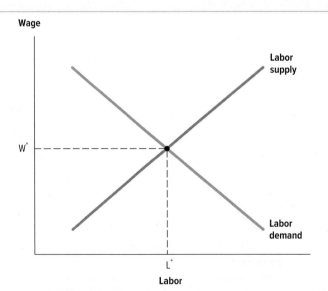

When the labor demand and labor supply curves are put together, this forms a labor market of people willing to buy and sell labor. Like any other market, where the two curves intersect, the market is at an equilibrium, with a stable wage (price) and amount of labor bought and sold.

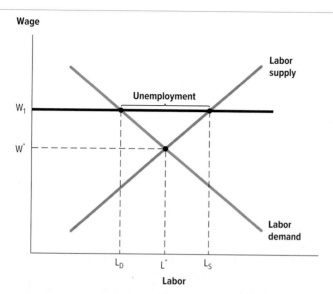

FIGURE 26-4
The labor market with unemployment

When people are willing to supply more labor than firms are willing to hire, the labor market has a surplus of workers, which is also known as unemployment.

✓CONCEPT CHECK

☐ What is the equilibrium price of labor also called? **[LO 26.2]**
☐ What two curves intersect at the labor market equilibrium? **[LO 26.2]**

Categories of Unemployment

To start understanding the causes of unemployment, it's helpful to separate out two categories of unemployment:

- First is unemployment explained by the *natural* rate of unemployment. This is the normal level of unemployment that persists in an economy in the long run.
- Second is *cyclical* unemployment, which describes short-term fluctuations around this long-run norm.

We'll see that some unemployment is an unavoidable part of a dynamic economy, but also that the amount of unemployment is affected by public policy.

Natural rate of unemployment

LO 26.3 Explain why there is a natural rate of unemployment in an economy.

The simplified model of the labor market described in Figure 26-3 suggests that we might reasonably expect to see *zero* unemployment when the market is in long-run equilibrium. The data in the first half of the chapter, however, showed that this is never the case (even when the economy is doing well, as it was around 2005).

Instead, all economies experience some level of unemployment, regardless of how well or badly the economy is doing in the short term. We refer to this normal level of unemployment that persists in an economy in the long run as the **natural rate of unemployment**. The natural rate of unemployment is also sometimes called the *equilibrium rate of unemployment*. Three contributors lead to the natural rate of unemployment: frictional, structural, and real-wage (classical) unemployment.

natural rate of unemployment
the normal level of unemployment that persists in an economy in the long run

Frictional unemployment

frictional unemployment
unemployment caused by workers who are changing location, job, or career

The first contributor to the natural rate of unemployment is **frictional unemployment**. It is unemployment caused by workers who are changing their location, job, or career. When people search for new jobs, it takes time to search for openings, submit applications, interview, move to a new city, and so on. How long it takes to make a job transition can depend on a lot of factors. These include things like:

- how well-informed workers are about job openings,
- how picky workers are about waiting to find the job that is the best possible match, and
- what resources workers can draw on to support them while they search.

Some amount of frictional unemployment is unavoidable—it's a natural and healthy part of life in a dynamic economy. Jobs in one company open up while others close, and ambitious workers leave their jobs to seek out better positions.

Structural unemployment

structural unemployment
unemployment that results from a mismatch between the skills workers can offer and the skills in demand

The second contributor to the natural rate of unemployment is **structural unemployment**. It is unemployment that results from a mismatch between the skills workers can offer and the skills that are in demand. Consumer preferences are constantly shifting, and new technologies are being invented all the time. As a result, skills that are in demand today may not be in demand next year.

If people could switch effortlessly from a job in a shrinking industry (like auto manufacturing) to one in a booming industry (like online services), then structural unemployment wouldn't exist. However, the reality is that people have educational qualifications, job experiences, and family and community ties that are hard to change in the short run. These qualifications and ties make them better suited for jobs in some sectors and locations than others. A changing economy can lead to a mismatch between the types of jobs that firms are offering and the types of jobs for which people are qualified.

For example, consider the job of travel agent. If you want to book a flight, you probably just go online, right? A couple of decades ago, you would have gone to a travel agent, who would have used a special database of routes and prices to propose an itinerary. The advent of websites such as Travelocity, Kayak, Priceline, and Expedia allows customers to do the travel agent's job for themselves easily and quickly. As a result, demand for the services of travel agents has plummeted; people who trained as travel agents lost their jobs and couldn't find new ones using the same knowledge and skills.

Some degree of structural unemployment is inevitable in an ever-changing economy, but governments can take steps to minimize it. One way is to provide information to unemployed people about which professions are experiencing rising demand for labor. Another way is to subsidize retraining programs for unemployed workers to learn new skills, improving their chances of finding work.

These programs can help, but the changes can take years. If you were a middle-aged, unemployed auto worker, could you imagine moving to a different part of the country to start a new career from scratch?

Real-wage (classical) unemployment

real-wage or classical unemployment
unemployment that results from wages being higher than the market-clearing level

The third contributor to the natural rate of unemployment is **real-wage** or **classical unemployment**. This idea captures the effect of wages remaining persistently above the market-clearing level. It's what we saw in Figure 26-4: Anything that acts like a price floor in the labor market will create surplus labor, which we call unemployment. Explanations include minimum wage laws, bargaining by unions, and strategic choices by employers to pay wages above the equilibrium rate. We'll explore each of these possible explanations later in the chapter.

The common thread in these three different contributors to the natural rate of unemployment is that they reflect underlying features of the economy. As you'd guess, the features can change over time, which can raise or lower the natural rate. For instance, a new policy dramatically raising the minimum wage by $10 an hour would surely raise the natural rate of unemployment. An educational system that retrains laid-off workers could lower the natural rate.

The natural rate of unemployment, however, doesn't go up and down with every boom and bust in the economy. Those short-term fluctuations in unemployment need a different explanation, which we turn to next.

Cyclical unemployment

LO 26.4 Explain why there is a cyclical component of unemployment.

The economy goes through ups and downs over time, which are reflected by changes in GDP growth. Economists call this pattern of ups and downs the *business cycle,* a topic we'll discuss further in Chapter 29, "Aggregate Demand and Aggregate Supply." The business cycle matters for unemployment because it affects the demand for labor:

- When the economy is going strong, demand for workers increases as firms expand their operations.
- When the economy slows down, demand for workers decreases as firms downsize.

Cyclical unemployment is unemployment caused by these short-term economic fluctuations. Because GDP growth tends to go in *cycles,* speeding up and slowing down in a regular pattern, we call the related unemployment *cyclical,* too.

Imagine the effect of an economic slowdown as a reduction in the total demand for labor at any wage. In other words, the labor demand curve shifts to the left. In the simple labor-market model, this change would cause the equilibrium to move down along the supply curve, reaching a new equilibrium at a lower quantity of labor and lower wage. Why don't wages simply fall during a cyclical slowdown, so that the market still clears and cyclical unemployment is zero? The typical explanation is that wages are "sticky" in the real world, meaning that they are slow to respond to shifts in the economy.

There are many possible reasons for wage stickiness: Some workers may be on contracts that are difficult to change, or employers may choose not to raise and lower wages all the time because it will upset workers and cause them to not work as hard. The degree of wage stickiness in the real world is a controversial topic, even among economists.

The result of wage stickiness is that actual wages are temporarily above the market-clearing level, which causes cyclical unemployment. When the economy swings back toward the boom part of the business cycle, labor demand will recover and cyclical unemployment will decrease.

Figure 26-5 shows the relationship between GDP and unemployment in the U.S. economy over the last 35 years. When growth goes down, unemployment tends to go up shortly after, and vice versa.

cyclical unemployment
unemployment caused by short-term economic fluctuations

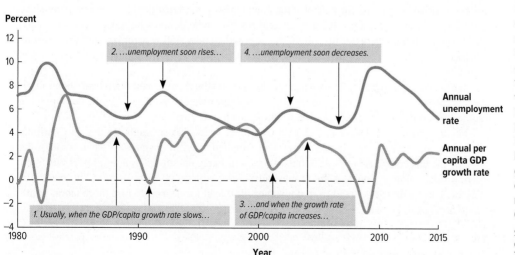

FIGURE 26-5

Cyclical unemployment in the United States   In general, unemployment tends to be higher when GDP growth is low, although this is not always true. Unemployment tends to lag behind overall GDP growth, meaning it will change soon after, but not at the same time as, GDP growth changes.

Source: BEA and BLS, accessed on the FRED (accessed on May 19 2016).

The slight delay, or time lag, makes unemployment what we call a *lagging* or *trailing* indicator. It takes time for changes in the economy to translate into changes in employment. Employers wait to see how bad a recession looks before making the difficult decision to lay off workers. They also wait to see how solid a recovery looks before committing to take on new employees. While playing wait-and-see, firms may first try to decrease or increase the hours of existing employees.

✓CONCEPT CHECK

☐ What is the natural rate of unemployment? **[LO 26.3]**

☐ Contrast frictional and structural unemployment. **[LO 26.3]**

☐ With what measure does cyclical unemployment tend to move? **[LO 26.4]**

Public Policies and Other Influences on Unemployment

Addressing issues relating to unemployment can be tough. Unemployment is an important indicator of the overall health of the economy. It is also a very personal issue for those who experience it. As a result, discussions about the causes of unemployment—particularly those that have implications for public policy—can get heated.

In this section, we'll break down some of the policies and other factors in the economy that can influence the level of unemployment. Before we get into the details, consider one example of a controversial unemployment-related debate: Do immigrants cause unemployment by taking jobs? See the From Another Angle box "Immigration's effects on the labor market" to see why economists generally disagree that this is the case.

From Another Angle

Immigration's effects on the labor market

Imagine an American worker—we'll call him John. John lives in Charlotte, North Carolina. He's 35 years old and works as a bus driver. Now, imagine a would-be immigrant—we'll call him José. José is a 35-year-old bus driver who lives in Lima, Peru; he makes about a quarter of what John earns.

José decides to move to Charlotte and knocks on the door of the local bus company. He offers to drive John's bus for half of what John earns. It's a great deal for the company since it will save money on wages. It's a great deal for José, who doubles his salary. Unfortunately, it's lousy for John, who loses his job unless he wants to take a 50 percent pay cut. (We assume that John's company doesn't have a union and that the company can hire and fire drivers when it wants.)

This is the kind of plausible scenario that lies behind the rhetoric you often hear about immigrants taking American jobs. It looks like a straightforward case, right? Well, no. Applying some economic logic, we can add important details to the story.

For a start, now that José is living in Charlotte, he is also spending money in Charlotte, increasing demand for the goods and services supplied by local businesses. Also, some of the money the bus company saves on John's wages will likely end up reflected in lower bus fares, saving riders money. Some of the money riders save will get spent elsewhere, in other businesses. This increased demand from consumers will lead local firms to hire more labor. That's good news for John, who is now looking for work.

Of course, this simplified example hides a good deal of complexity in the real-world effects of immigration on labor markets. Transition is painful, and businesses do not always have so much flexibility. And it's not easy for someone like John to get fired and then have to try to find a new job.

The point is that immigration can cause disruptions. But, over time, immigration also can expand the economy, rather than just steal jobs from current workers. The arrival of new workers increases the size of the labor force. It also contributes to economic growth by reducing the costs of production and increasing demand for goods and services. Immigration is a political hot potato for many reasons. Still, our simple example helps to illustrate why economists generally reject the simple assertion that immigration necessarily causes unemployment.

There are winners and losers, as immigrants tend to compete for some kinds of jobs more than others. Let's say there's an influx of new immigrants, many of whom want to find jobs as construction workers. How you see the situation depends on your personal situation. For example:

- It's bad news if you're an American looking for construction work: You face more competition for jobs, driving down wages.
- But it's good news if you're an American who runs a construction company: You now have more candidates to choose from, some of whom might be willing to accept a lower wage. You might earn higher profits, which you will then spend in other parts of the economy, creating demand for labor elsewhere.
- It's also good news if you're an American looking to buy or renovate a house or store, allowing you to get the same services at lower cost.

Rhetoric and emotion can get in the way of seeing the full picture. The political debate more readily focuses on immediate job losses, like the one suffered by John, the bus driver. And it's often hard to put numbers on society's longer-term gains, which tend to be diffuse. Economists see their role as trying to assess all of these trade-offs with as much balance as possible.

Source: Michael Clemens et al., "The Place Premium: Wage Differences for Identical Workers across the U.S. Border" (Center for Global Development Working Paper, 2008).

Factors that may stop wage rates from falling

LO 26.5 Identify factors that may stop wages from falling to the equilibrium level.

In the previous section, we noted that unemployment can be influenced by forces that prevent wages from falling to the market-clearing level, either in the long run (through the natural rate of unemployment) or in response to short-term economic fluctuations (though cyclical unemployment). Why don't wages fall so that everyone with the skills and desire gets a job? In this section we will look at three possible explanations:

- The government might prevent it, through minimum-wage legislation.
- Labor unions might prevent it, through bargaining backed by the threat to strike.
- Firms themselves might prevent it, by voluntarily choosing to pay higher wages than necessary.

Let's consider these three explanations in turn.

Minimum wage

A *minimum wage* is the lowest wage that a firm is legally allowed to pay its workers. In the United States, the federal minimum wage in 2016 was $7.25 per hour. Some states mandate a higher minimum wage. Individual cities, including Los Angeles, California, and Seattle, Washington, have passed laws to raise the minimum wage to $15 by 2020.[4]

The $7.25 per hour wage is approximately the wage that entry-level workers at a fast-food restaurant earn.[5] A worker who earns $7.25 an hour and works 40 hours a week earns just over $15,000 a year, before taxes. In 2016, that annual wage was not enough to keep a two-person household above the poverty line.

Supporters of minimum-wage legislation argue that workers deserve a basic standard of living. They say it is not fair to allow firms to pay workers a wage that would leave them struggling to escape poverty. But even those who support the idea of a higher minimum wage do not agree on the optimal level: $12 per hour? $15 per hour? Lower? Higher?

Opponents of minimum wage legislation point to graphs like the one we showed in Figure 26-4, which suggests that if the minimum wage is higher than the equilibrium wage, then we would expect unemployment to result. Of course, if the minimum wage is set at a level *below* the equilibrium wage, it will have no effect; this is called a *nonbinding* minimum wage.

Does a minimum wage cause unemployment? The question can't be resolved by a theoretical analysis alone. We need to look at data. Economists have found evidence both for and against the idea that a minimum wage causes unemployment:

- Evidence from fast-food restaurants in different U.S. states indicates that raising the state minimum wage did not cause fast-food chains to lay off employees. This implies that the real-world labor market does not work exactly like the model shown in Figure 26-4.

- In other cases, economists have found that minimum wages do appear to cause a small amount of unemployment or a change in *who* is employed, as firms substitute more skilled, older workers for unskilled, younger workers.

Another possibility some economists raise, given that the minimum wage applies only to people hired legally, is that it could drive jobs "under the table." That is, firms might respond to minimum-wage legislation by employing undocumented migrants at below-minimum wages or paying workers cash without telling the government.

Views on minimum wages vary greatly. If the minimum wage does indeed cause unemployment, people who can't find jobs will lose out, while people lucky enough to be in jobs will benefit. If it *doesn't* cause unemployment, then all workers will benefit, while firms lose out by making lower profits. The debate rages on.

Unions and bargaining

In 2007, television and screenplay writers went on strike. They picketed outside the major Hollywood studios and Broadway theaters, refusing to work until they were offered a bigger share of the profits from the shows they worked on. The writers' strike meant that production had to shut down for many TV shows; the writers gave up $285 million in lost wages. The strike was resolved after 100 days, with the writers gaining a pay increase and a bigger share of profits, especially from TV shows streamed over the Internet and mobile devices.

labor unions

groups of employees who join together to bargain with their employer(s) over salaries and work conditions

Strikes like this are made possible by the existence of labor unions. In this case the writers were part of a union called the Writers' Guild. **Labor unions** are groups of employees who join together to bargain with their employer(s) over salaries and working conditions.

Unions benefit their members by being able to bargain as a group. If just a few disgruntled writers had gone on strike, then other writers could easily have been brought in to cover for them. But if workers strike together, they can bring an industry to a halt. This threat enables workers to drive a harder bargain with employers on wages and working conditions, such as benefits like health insurance, pension plans, and vacation time.

In the United States, the power of unions is falling. In the 1950s, about one-third of U.S. workers were in unions. The proportion is far lower today: As of 2015, about 11.1 percent of all wage and salary workers, or just under 15 million Americans, are in unions. About 35 percent of these union members work for government entities.[6] In some countries independent unions are restricted or banned altogether.

What does the existence of labor unions mean for the labor market and for unemployment? If labor unions drive a hard enough bargain, wage rates can rise above the equilibrium level. Then, the effect of labor unions is the same as with the minimum wage. To the extent that the labor market behaves like any other market, when unions manage to negotiate higher wages for their members, employers will in theory respond by employing fewer people. That means that being in a union is good for its own members but can be harmful for the unemployed looking for work. There's some evidence, though, that the presence of unions pushes wages upward even for workers who are not in a union (if they work in a sector with a strong union presence). One reason is that employers with nonunion workers want to keep their employees happy enough that they do not feel the need to form a union.

Opinions about the role of unions on wages depend on whether you think that labor markets do a good job of determining fair wages, and how much weight you put on the well-being of unemployed people versus people with jobs.

Efficiency wages

Another reason why wages might be above the market-clearing level is that some firms may *want* to pay their workers more than the going wage. Why would they do this? There are two related reasons:

- First, paying a higher wage will make workers less likely to quit, saving the expense of advertising for, interviewing, and training new people.
- Second, workers are more likely to fear losing their jobs and might work harder to keep the jobs they have.

Thus, it could be efficient for a firm to pay workers more than the going wage rate, especially in sectors where skills are scarce and worker motivation really matters. The idea is to give positive incentives to maximize productivity: Job transitions, from one worker to another, harm productivity. Also, workers exerting more effort to keep their jobs obviously also improves productivity. Paying wages above market-clearing levels may simply be a smart decision by firms.

The idea of deliberately setting wages above the market rate in order to increase productivity is captured by the term **efficiency wages**. Henry Ford is famous for instituting an efficiency wage at the Ford car factories in Detroit. He doubled his workers' wages in 1914 in order to reduce costly turnover and absenteeism, a move that turned out to be quite profitable.

efficiency wages wages that are deliberately set above the market rate to increase productivity

How might efficiency wages prevent wages from falling in a recession? Imagine that you are running a firm with 10 employees, and a recession causes the wage rate for labor to drop by 10 percent. Which would you rather do: force all your employees to take a 10 percent pay cut or fire one employee?

You might calculate that the latter option is better. Sure, it would leave you with one fewer employee, but all nine remaining employees would be highly motivated to work hard and keep their jobs, knowing they are earning above the going rate. Among them, the nine employees may even end up producing more for the firm than 10 employees, disgruntled because of a pay cut, would have produced.

In addition, the fact that efficiency wages can create unemployment can strengthen their impact. When employers fire workers (rather than cut pay), the rising level of unemployment worsens the consequence of losing a job. When workers fear an extended period of unemployment (rather than just having to work at a lower wage), they are likely to push themselves that much harder.

There is little clear evidence so far about how much of unemployment can be explained by efficiency wages. Some economists think that it's a key feature of labor markets; others argue that simply raising wages is unlikely to increase productivity.

Recently economists have built on the efficiency-wage idea that workers' effort is also determined by whether wages are seen as being "fair." Needing to maintain "fair" wages might also limit employers' flexibility in cutting wages. The idea has support from laboratory-style economic experiments that explore made-up situations, and the idea awaits rigorous study in the real labor market.

Unemployment insurance

LO 26.6 Describe the challenges policy-makers face when designing unemployment insurance and understand how this and related policies can affect rates of unemployment.

unemployment insurance

money paid by the government to people who are unemployed

Frictional and structural unemployment are part of the normal working of the economy. Most economists, though, believe that some government policies can affect the level of these kinds of unemployment. One such policy is unemployment insurance. **Unemployment insurance** is money that is paid by the government to people who are unemployed. There are usually certain conditions that determine eligibility—such as actively looking for work and reporting work-related activities.

Unemployment insurance doesn't directly affect the wage rate, so it is not an explanation for why wages do not reach equilibrium. Rather, unemployment insurance can affect *how quickly* people find jobs. That factor will affect the natural rate of unemployment—that is, both frictional and structural unemployment. Unemployment insurance makes joblessness less painful by giving people income while they look for work.

The effect of unemployment insurance on unemployment is ambiguous:

- On one hand, if unemployment insurance is generous, then people might not look as hard for work. People may be more likely to take their time and wait for a better job, rather than accepting the first job offered. This suggests that unemployment insurance could increase the equilibrium level of unemployment.

- On the other hand, if people don't have to rush into taking the first job they're offered, they are more likely to find the right job for them. Having employers and employees "better matched" may mean that fewer people leave their jobs, which may reduce the level of frictional unemployment.

Which effect will be greater is up for debate. Also up for debate is the "right" level of unemployment insurance to offer if we want the two effects to balance out: We want to give people enough breathing space to find a suitable job, but not so much that they become unrealistic perfectionists.

The amount and duration of unemployment insurance vary widely across countries. In the United States, unemployment insurance is based on how much an individual earned over the previous year, up to a maximum level. The standard duration of unemployment benefits is 26 weeks. However, this time period can be extended in times of unusually high unemployment. For example, during the recession of 2008–2009, the maximum limit was extended to 99 weeks for most states.

What happens if you don't have a job when your unemployment insurance runs out? In the United States, people can move onto other government welfare programs such as food and housing assistance. In European countries, unemployment benefits typically last longer and replace a greater percentage of average work income.

Not all countries offer unemployment insurance. For more on how such countries help those who are out of work, see the Real Life box "Unemployment and developing countries."

Real Life

Unemployment and developing countries

Some developing countries have very high levels of unemployment. In South Africa, for example, more than 26 percent of the labor force is unemployed, even by the most narrowly defined measures. In developing countries, unemployment insurance is not the norm, and low-income countries must often devote government budgets to more pressing needs. Where does this leave the unemployed?

Governments in some low-income countries have implemented measures to help those without work. India, for example, has a program called the National Rural Employment Guarantee Act, which is meant to guarantee adults 100 days of work per year. The work usually is at the minimum wage on low-skilled projects such as building roads, but it's a job nonetheless. By December 2013, the program had provided work for adults from over 300 million households.

Two survival options for those without a job are much more common in low-income countries than in the United States. One is the *informal sector*. The informal sector provides jobs without formal contracts and legal protections. These jobs include street-sellers, maids, taxi drivers, weavers, and small-scale factory workers. The organization "Women in Informal Employment: Globalizing and Organizing" (WIEGO) has teamed up with the International Labor Organization to collect data about informal job activity. They estimate that, outside of agriculture, about one-half to three-quarters of workers in low-income economies are informally employed. If you include workers in agriculture (most of whom are farmers), the fraction can be as high as 90 percent, especially in South Asia and sub-Saharan Africa. The informal sector tends to offer lots of part-time, temporary jobs, and that makes it easier for people who lose one job to patch together income by taking other short-term jobs.

The other survival option is to rely on extended family. Studies like *Portfolios of the Poor: How the World's Poor Live on $2 a Day* (co-authored by one of the authors of this book) show that in Bangladesh and South Africa, where there is not much government support available, people in need often turn to their extended families in hard times.

In short, unemployment is a global problem—but like many problems, the solutions depend a lot on the resources available to address it within each country.

Sources: Government of India, Ministry of Rural Labor, Mahatma Gandhi National Rural Employment Guarantee Act, 2005: Report to the People, 2014, http://vikaspedia.in/agriculture/policies-and-schemes/nrega-report-to-people;Mari Megias, "Policy Matters: The Informal Economy," Harvard Kennedy School, 2012, http://www.hks.harvard.edu/news-events/news/articles/policy-matters-the-informal-economy;and Daryl Collins, Jonathan Morduch, Stuart Rutherford, and Orlanda Ruthven, *Portfolios of the Poor: How the World's Poor Live on $2 a Day* (Princeton, NJ: Princeton University Press, 2009).

Other factors: Taxes and worker rights

Unemployment insurance is just one policy we can expect to affect rates of unemployment. What are some others?

Taxes on wage income are important as well. We would expect, all else equal, that lower taxes would reduce unemployment. Why? The reasoning is that lower taxes give people more incentive to find a job, knowing they will keep more of the income they earn from the job. The magnitude of the impact taxes have on job-search effort, however, is inconclusive.

Another important factor is the ease with which employers can fire employees. In some countries, firing can be done on a whim, without explanation. In other countries, workers are legally protected, and employers have to prove they have a good reason. We would expect that policies to protect workers would lead to greater unemployment. Why? Because employers would be reluctant to hire people if they know that it will be difficult to get rid of them. A particular aspect of this debate is explored in the What Do You Think? box "Youth employees on trial."

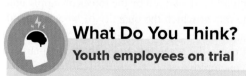

What Do You Think?
Youth employees on trial

When you start looking for your first professional job, you often hit a big challenge: Without work experience, it can be tough to find a job. But how do you get work experience without

(continued)

having a job? This is one reason why young people typically have a higher unemployment rate than older workers. If you look back at Figure 26-1, panel B, you'll see that youth unemployment peaked close to 20 percent during the recent recession, compared with around 7-10 percent for the whole population.

At the root of this issue lies a communication problem: Young people looking for their first job lack ways to credibly demonstrate to employers that they will be good employees. Why should employers take a chance on a young person who has no job experience, when they could instead choose to employ someone with proven skills in the workplace? Of course, a particular young person with no job experience might turn out to be a great employee. But until you've employed the person, you have no way of knowing that. And once you've employed someone, it can often be expensive, time-consuming, and even legally problematic to fire that person.

This is the thinking that led New Zealand to implement a policy allowing employers to fire new employees during their first 90 days at work—without the workers having any right to file legal action for unfair dismissal. Supporters of this policy say it helps young people to find jobs by removing some risk for the employer. The employer can test a new employee for 90 days and, if it doesn't work out, can simply offload him or her.

Not everyone is happy with the idea. Some critics argue that the trial period is a way for firms to exploit young people, employing them without the same benefits and protections that other workers take for granted. Some worry that firms might never actually hire *any* permanent workers, instead relying on constant turnover of employees under the trial period.

WHAT DO YOU THINK?

1. Is this policy a smart way to solve this information problem, or is it just a license to exploit young people?
2. What would keep employers from hiring and firing new workers every 90 days?

Source: New Zealand Institute of Economic Research, Inc., "90-Day Trial Periods Appear Successful—NZIER Insight 25," http://nzier.org.nz/publications/90-day-trial-periods-appear-successful-nzier-insight-25 (accessed November 28, 2012).

✔ CONCEPT CHECK

☐ Why do some governments set a minimum wage? **[LO 26.5]**
☐ Why would an employer pay an efficiency wage? **[LO 26.5]**
☐ What are the trade-offs in the effect of unemployment insurance? **[LO 26.6]**

Conclusion

Most of our adult lives are spent working, and finding a great job can be a key to happiness. At the same time, not being able to find the right job—or not being able to find any job at all—can be one of the toughest life experiences.

The labor market is in many ways like any other market. It's driven by the forces of supply and demand, and we can describe an equilibrium wage rate at which the quantity of labor supplied equals the quantity of labor demanded. But there are differences too: Minimum wages, bargaining by labor unions, and efficiency wages can all cause the wage rate to be above the market-clearing level for extended periods, which leads to unemployment.

We've discussed how the official unemployment rate is measured. Since the unemployment rate doesn't always give a full picture of labor-market conditions, economists and policy-makers often pore over other measures, such as the labor-force participation rate.

We've described the main reasons for unemployment. Frictional and structural unemployment occur naturally; they will exist in any labor market regardless of policy. They are caused by people switching between jobs or shifting from one sector to another.

Another type of unemployment, cyclical unemployment, mirrors the overall health of the economy and the business cycle. In boom times, jobs get created and cyclical unemployment is small. But jobs are lost when the economy weakens, and cyclical unemployment rises.

Economists debate how much the rules of the labor market affect the overall rate of unemployment. We've seen that labor-market policies often come with important trade-offs:

- Policy-makers have to decide how generous to make unemployment benefits. Providing more support for the unemployed may be desirable from a social perspective, but when benefits are *too* generous, incentives to actively search for a job are diminished.

- Similarly, raising minimum wages helps workers on the bottom rungs of the labor market, but raising minimum wages can also make it harder for unemployed workers to find jobs.

Unemployment is not something that occurs in isolation from the rest of the economy. In fact, one of the most powerful ways to reduce unemployment is to generate sustained economic growth in the overall economy. In the next chapter, we focus on this important economic challenge: How can policy and resources be combined to create healthy economic growth?

Key Terms

unemployment, p. 661

labor force, p. 662

unemployment rate, p. 662

labor-force participation rate, p. 664

discouraged workers, p. 665

underemployed, p. 665

labor demand curve, p. 667

labor supply curve, p. 668

natural rate of unemployment, p. 669

frictional unemployment, p. 670

structural unemployment, p. 670

real-wage or classical unemployment, p. 670

cyclical unemployment, p. 671

labor unions, p. 674

efficiency wages, p. 675

unemployment insurance, p. 676

Summary

LO 26.1 Explain how economists measure employment and unemployment.

To be considered unemployed, a person needs to meet three conditions: (1) be part of the working-age, civilian population; (2) not have worked in the previous week; and (3) be actively looking for work. Economists measure unemployment with the *unemployment rate*. This is the number of people who are unemployed, divided by the labor force.

The *labor force participation rate* is the fraction of the working age population that is working or looking for work. People who are not working but who are not actively looking for work—for example, students, homemakers, or *discouraged workers*—are not considered part of the labor force. Those, on the other hand, who are working jobs that don't utilize their skills or knowledge are considered to be *underemployed*.

LO 26.2 Explain how wage rates above equilibrium cause unemployment.

Like other markets, the labor market features a demand curve and a supply curve. The *total* demand for labor from all the firms in the economy is represented by the *labor demand curve*. On the whole, firms will want to hire more labor when wages are cheaper and less labor when wages are expensive, which means the labor demand curve slopes downward.

The total labor supply is represented by the *labor supply curve*. We would expect that people will be willing to supply more labor at higher wage rates and less labor at lower wage rates. This relationship gives the labor supply curve a positive slope.

Equilibrium in the market for labor is reached at the wage (price of labor) where the labor demand and labor supply curves meet. Unemployment results when the market wage rate remains above the market equilibrium; it is effectively a surplus of labor at the inflated wage rate.

LO 26.3 Explain why there is a natural rate of unemployment in an economy.

We think of the economy having a long-run natural level of unemployment. This *natural rate of unemployment* is the amount of unemployment that is unavoidable in a dynamic economy.

There are two reasons why we expect the economy to have some unemployment when everything else is normal: Some unemployment comes from *frictional* reasons, such as people changing jobs or locations. Some unemployment comes from *structural* reasons, such as government policies that affect how easily the wage rate can adjust. Structural unemployment also includes people who are unemployed because of technological development in the economy that results in a mismatch between the skills demanded by firms and the skills the labor force has.

LO 26.4 Explain why there is a cyclical component of unemployment.

There is also unemployment that is related to changes in GDP in the economy. When GDP is higher than normal, unemployment is lower than the equilibrium rate. When GDP is lower than normal, unemployment is above the equilibrium rate. This type of unemployment is called *cyclical unemployment.*

LO 26.5 Identify factors that may stop wages from falling to the equilibrium level.

Many factors affect the level of unemployment rate. Three reasons why the wage rate may not fully adjust to the equilibrium wage rate in the labor market are a minimum wage that is above the equilibrium wage rate, labor unions that negotiate a wage rate above the equilibrium wage rate, and *efficiency wages* (wages paid by firms, above the equilibrium wage rate).

LO 26.6 Describe the challenges policy-makers face when designing unemployment insurance and understand how this and related policies can affect rates of unemployment.

The design of the unemployment insurance programs is ultimately a balance of trade-offs. When benefits are not generous, losing a job can become a devastating financial hardship. When benefits are *too* generous, incentives to actively search for a job are diminished. In the United States, unemployment benefits last only a short time and pay only a fraction of people's average working wages, so as to minimize the incentive to shirk the job search.

Review Questions

1. During the 1960s societal norms regarding working women were changing, and many women who had been housewives began working outside the home. How would you expect this new norm to change the labor-force participation rate? What about the unemployment rate? **[LO 26.1]**

2. List at least five types of people who do not have paid jobs but would nevertheless *not* be considered unemployed. **[LO 26.1]**

3. Compare two countries, one that has unlimited unemployment insurance and one in which workers are eligible for 26 weeks of unemployment insurance. Explain one reason why the country with more unemployment insurance may have a higher equilibrium unemployment rate. **[LO 26.2]**

4. Suppose the president of a country comes to you to ask your advice. The country is currently at 8 percent unemployment, and the president wishes to reduce unemployment in the country to 3 percent. As an economist, you determine that the country's natural rate of unemployment is 5 percent. What advice would you give the president? **[LO 26.3]**

5. Innovation often requires "creative destruction," in which the new product or technology makes previous products or technologies obsolete. For example, when the personal computer was invented, typewriters became useless; hence, the personal computer "destroyed" the typewriter. This process of creative destruction often results in structural unemployment because workers who knew how to build and maintain the old products have skills that are no longer in demand. Do you think the government has a role in either limiting how often new products are created or in helping those workers who are displaced because of the new product? **[LO 26.3]**

6. Suppose the National Bureau of Economic Research (NBER) just came out with a report suggesting that the economy will soon dip into recession. How do you think the levels of frictional, structural, and cyclical unemployment will change as the recession begins? What will happen to the labor-force participation rate? **[LO 26.4]**

7. What happens to a country's levels of frictional, structural, and cyclical unemployment, as well as its labor-force participation rate, as a recession drags on for an extended period of time? **[LO 26.4]**

8. What happens to a country's levels of frictional, structural, and cyclical unemployment, as well as its labor-force participation rate, as a country begins to recover from a deep recession? **[LO 26.4]**

9. Give two reasons why it may be rational for a firm to offer wages above the minimum wage. **[LO 26.5]**

10. In France, labor laws typically made it very difficult or even illegal for firms to fire workers during economic downturns. How would these laws affect cyclical unemployment as well as frictional and structural unemployment? (Hint: Think about how these laws affect firms' decisions to hire workers in the first place.) **[LO 26.4, LO 26.5]**

11. Unemployment is often called a lagging or trailing indicator because unemployment tends to rise some time after the economy begins to slow down, and unemployment begins to fall again after the economy begins to rebound. In other words, unemployment trails GDP. Why do you think this might be the case? **[LO 26.5]**

12. The traditional goal of a government is to maximize its citizens' welfare. Given this goal, would you suggest getting rid of unemployment insurance? How would your answer change if the goal of the government is to maximize employment? **[LO 26.6]**

13. In the United States during regular economic times, the maximum length of time a worker can collect unemployment insurance is 26 weeks. During recessions, however, Congress often increases the length of time in which workers can collect benefits. During the recent financial crisis, workers could collect benefits for up to 99 weeks in some states. Comment on the advantages and disadvantages of this system. **[LO 26.6]**

Problems and Applications

1. For each of the following situations, is Rick Alexander (from the chapter-opening story) counted as employed, unemployed, or not in the labor force by the Bureau of Labor Statistics? **[LO 26.1]**

    a. Alexander is self-employed in his old job as a carpenter.

    b. Alexander moves to Florida and begins looking for work.

    c. Alexander feels discouraged looking for work and stops applying for jobs.

    d. Alexander starts looking for work again.

    e. Alexander starts work at a new job.

2. Consider the economy whose data appear in Table 26P-1. **[LO 26.1]**

    a. What is the unemployment rate?

    b. What is the labor-force participation rate?

TABLE 26P-1

Group of people	Number of people in group
Working-age population	100,000
Labor force	60,000
Unemployed	10,000

3. Table 26P-2 uses data for the year 2016, adjusted to be comparable to each other. All population values are in thousands.

    a. Fill in the blanks in the table. **[LO 26.1]**

    b. In part *a*, you should have found that the unemployment rates of the three countries differ significantly from one another. Suggest three possible reasons to explain why the countries might have different unemployment rates. **[LO 26.3, 26.4]**

4. Assume the equilibrium wage rate is $6. Draw a graph of the labor market to answer the following questions. **[LO 26.2]**

    a. When the government introduces a minimum wage of $5.50, does unemployment increase, decrease, or stay the same compared to unemployment at the equilibrium wage?

    b. When the government introduces a minimum wage of $6.50, does unemployment increase, decrease, or stay the same compared to unemployment at the equilibrium wage?

5. Assume that the labor demand equation for a fictional country is $L_d = 30 - w$, where w is the wage per hour worked and L_d is the number of workers demanded by firms. Assume also that the labor supply equation for that country is $L_s = 0.5(w)$, where L_s is the number of people willing to work. **[LO 26.2, 26.5]**

    a. Find the equilibrium wage and quantity of labor employed.

    b. At the equilibrium wage, how many people are unemployed?

    c. How would the number of unemployed change if the supply of workers increased?

6. Suppose a firm's labor demand equation is $L_d = 40 - 2(w)$ and the labor supply equation that it faces is $L_s = -20 + 3(w)$, where w is the wage per hour worked, L_d is the number of workers demanded by firms, and L_s is the number of people willing to work. **[LO 26.2, 26.5]**

    a. Find the equilibrium wage and quantity of labor employed.

TABLE 26P-2

Country	Working-age population	Labor force	Employed	Unemployed	Unemployment rate(%)	Labor-force participation rate (%)
Japan	110,849		64,460	2,160		
France		31,164		3,520		56.1
Germany	76,066	46,096			5.7	

b. The workers, thinking that their wages are too low, decide to strike. After tense negotiations, the firm decides to raise the wage by 50 percent. After the wage increase, how many people are unemployed?

7. Classify each of the following situations as either frictional, structural, or cyclical unemployment. **[LO 26.3, 26.4]**

   a. Maria has started looking for work after taking time off to have a baby.

   b. Juan left high school without graduating and can't find any jobs he is qualified for.

   c. Rohit had a job working on Wall Street but lost his job during the financial crisis.

   d. Adam has just arrived in a new city and is looking for work.

   e. Max wants to work as an air steward, but because the airline industry is heavily unionized there are very few jobs available.

   f. Jada has just lost her job in a web start-up that was affected by a downturn in the economy.

8. For each of the following situations, would the unemployment rate increase, decrease, or stay the same? **[LO 26.5]**

   a. A company begins paying efficiency wages above the equilibrium wage rate.

   b. The number of workers covered by union contracts falls.

   c. The government extends the duration of unemployment insurance.

9. Suppose a country has a 26-week limit on the duration that an unemployed person receives unemployment benefits. You collect some data and notice that workers in their 26th week of unemployment benefits somehow manage to find jobs at a much higher rate than other unemployed workers. What would this statistic tell you about the incentives involved with unemployment insurance? **[LO 26.6]**

10. Understanding that unemployment benefits give workers the incentive to not look for work until their benefits run out, suppose an economist suggested that instead of giving workers up to 26 weeks of unemployment benefits that end once the person finds work, a person who loses his or her job would just get a single big check for 26 weeks of benefits, regardless of how long the worker is unemployed. What are the advantages and disadvantages of this idea? **[LO 26.6]**

Endnotes

1. Rick Alexander's story is from Michael Luo, "Out of Work, and Too Down to Search On," *The New York Times*, September 7, 2009, p. A1, New York edition.

2. http://www.nytimes.com/2009/09/07/us/07worker. html?pagewanted=2.

3. Bureau of Labor Statistics: http://www.bls.gov/bls/ glossary.htm#U.

4. http://www.nelp.org/news-releases/14-cities-states-approved-15-minimum-wage-in-2015/.

5. http://www.payscale.com/research/us/ employer=mcdonald%27s_Corporation/Hourly_rate

6. Bureau of Labor Statistics, http://www.bls.gov/news. release/union2.nr0.htm, January 2016.

Economic Growth

Learning Objectives

LO 27.1 Calculate the growth rate of real GDP per capita, accounting for changes in price levels and population.

LO 27.2 Describe the relationship between productivity and growth and discuss the factors that determine productivity.

LO 27.3 Explain the difference between a country's level of income and its rate of growth.

LO 27.4 Use the growth accounting framework to describe how technology, labor, and capital contribute to economic growth.

LO 27.5 Assess the empirical evidence for and against convergence theory.

LO 27.6 Discuss policies that could promote growth and relate them to productivity.

LO 27.7 Explain how good governance and economic openness lay the foundation for growth.

WHY ECONOMIC GROWTH MATTERS

Between 2005 and 2015, a miracle occurred: Over 650 million people around the world rose out of poverty, cutting the number of the global poor by nearly half. These people moved from worrying about where their next meal was coming from to being able to worry instead about finding a better place to live or a more satisfying job.

What triggered this miracle? It wasn't a humanitarian intervention or massive government program. It was two little numbers: an annual (compounded) growth rate of average GDP per person of 8 percent for China and 5 percent for India.[1]

If you had traveled through those countries in recent years, you'd have found them buzzing with entrepreneurial spirit. Buildings and infrastructure sprouted like mushrooms. Highways roared with people and goods rushing between enormous cities. The bridge of new wealth connected millions of people to the Internet and a global consumer culture.

© Leung Cho Pan/Getty Images

High rates of economic growth have produced more than just tall buildings and smoother roads. The newly minted middle classes in China and India have cash to spend, buying the latest cell phones and flooding the roads with new cars. The middle class in China alone is bigger than the entire population of the United States. The bright lights of Shanghai and Mumbai also offer promise to millions of people who have migrated from poorer rural areas hoping to land jobs in factories or hotels, trading rural lifestyles for urban ones. Wages are rising, and poverty rates are plummeting.

It is easy to get excited by these transformations and to proclaim that we've found the solution to global poverty. But saying that economic growth is the solution to poverty is a bit like saying that brilliant medical research is the solution to curing diseases or that scoring lots of touchdowns is a good way to win a football game. Of course, it's important, but how do you make it happen? That's the hard part.

Leaders all over the world seek economic growth. It translates to wealthier, healthier, and better-educated citizens enjoying more comfortable lives. It also results in higher tax revenues for governments and enticing opportunities for investors. Sadly, we have no magic formula for economic growth. Decades of research have helped us see why some countries are rich and others poor. But history has also shown that it's not easy for policy-makers to translate this understanding into action.

The search for a recipe for economic growth captivates economists. It is simultaneously one of the most important and fascinating questions in economics, and one about which we're still learning. In this chapter, we will describe three aspects of the study of growth. First, we'll discuss how growth is measured and show the patterns that have emerged around the world in the last century. Second, we'll create a basic framework for understanding why growth happens, and how savings, capital, labor, and technology contribute to it. Finally, we'll dig into details on how public policy choices can affect growth.

Economic Growth through the Ages

Over the last 100 years, real GDP per capita in the United States has grown at an average rate of just about 2 percent per year. That might not sound so impressive compared to the 8 percent and 5 percent growth experienced, respectively, by China and India recently. In the context of history, however, it's revolutionary. In this section, we'll explore two reasons why this is so.

History of world growth

LO 27.1 Calculate the growth rate of real GDP per capita, accounting for changes in price levels and population.

Imagine you were living in 1800. Almost anywhere in the world at that time, income per person was not much different from what it had been a millennium earlier. The possibility of growth has always been around, of course, but very little of it actually happened until a century or two ago. Rapid economic growth is a modern phenomenon.

Look at Figure 27-1, which shows world population and income per person over the last 3,000 years. Historical records and archaeological evidence allow us to get a general sense of prices and standards of living in ancient days. Notice that for the first 2,800 of the last 3,000 years, very little was happening. The population was growing slowly, and the economy was growing just fast enough to keep up with the snail's pace of the population. The result was that real income per person barely changed at all.

Suddenly, in the 1800s, the nature of the global economy underwent a radical transformation. After staying about the same size for thousands of years, it started to grow. This growth was even more striking given that the world's population exploded at roughly the same time. The red line in Figure 27-1 shows real GDP per capita, calculated as if the entire world was one economy. The blue line shows world population growth. The figure shows that even though population grew at a historically fast pace in the twentieth century, real GDP per capita grew even faster.

FIGURE 27-1

History of world economic growth: Real GDP per capita, 1000 BC to AD 2000   For the first 2,800 years of this graph, real global GDP per capita was essentially constant. Then, in 1800, with the Industrial Revolution, incomes in Europe began to increase rapidly. In the last 50 years, real global GDP per capita quadrupled. Note that the numbers on the vertical axis refer to both real GDP per capita (calculated as if the entire world was one economy and deflated using PPP exchange rates) and to the number of people on earth—which rose to over 6 billion people (6,000 × 1 million) by 2000.

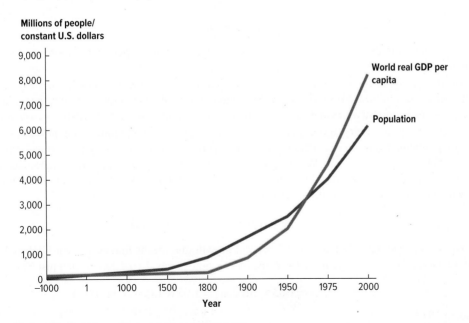

Source: http://www.j-bradford-delong.net/macro_online/ms/ch5/chapter_5.pdf.

The growth rate of real GDP per capita is typically the number we care about. It describes the change in actual purchasing power for each person. In order to get an accurate picture of the real GDP per capita growth rate, we need to subtract changes in both prices and population from the nominal GDP growth rate, as follows:

EQUATION 27-1

$$\text{Real GDP per capita growth rate} = \text{Nominal GDP growth rate} - \text{Inflation rate} -$$
$$\text{Population growth rate}$$

Just from glancing at Figure 27-1, you can see that the fast rise of GDP growth in the last few centuries means that nominal GDP must have grown much faster than inflation and population combined. As a result, the purchasing power of the average person in the world today is more than 30 times as high as it was 200 years ago. This represents a transformative change in the way people live. A growth rate like 2 percent may not sound revolutionary, but it is a big jump from what had been essentially zero growth for centuries before.

HINT

Growth rates usually compare the level of a variable in one year to its level the previous year (though growth rates can be calculated for other time frames too). To get a concrete sense of an annual growth rate, here's how to calculate the United States' real GDP per capita growth rate at the start of 2016: First, find the level of U.S. real GDP per capita in 2016 ($51,061 in January 2016) and the level in 2015 ($50,433 in January 2015).[2] Then subtract to find the absolute change, an increase of $628. The growth rate is then calculated as the absolute change between 2015 and 2016 expressed as a percentage of the level in 2015:

$$\left(\frac{\$628}{\$50,433}\right) \times 100 = 1.25 \text{ percent}$$

Compounding and the rule of 70

The second reason that the historical U.S. growth rate of 2 percent per year is more impressive than it sounds is that economic growth builds on itself over time. This process is the same as the *compounding of interest* in a savings account—earlier interest payments get added to the account and earn interest in turn. Similarly, a relatively modest annual growth rate can add up to a large change in the economy over time. In fact, real per capita GDP in the United States is *over seven times* what it was a century ago. Figure 27-2 shows this growth in real purchasing power.

Compounding results in total changes in GDP over time that are bigger than the annual growth rate would at first suggest. The key insight is that the base from which growth is measured gets bigger every year. To see how this works, let's call U.S. GDP in 1910 "Y." If the economy is growing at 2 percent per year, then in 1911, GDP will be:

$$\text{GDP}_{1911} = Y + (0.02 \times Y) = 1.02Y$$

To simplify the math, notice that a 2 percent growth rate means that every year GDP is 1.02 times GDP in the previous year. In 1912, the base is now larger, 1.02Y rather than just Y:

$$\text{GDP}_{1912} = 1.02 \times \text{GDP}_{1911} = 1.02 \times 1.02Y = (1.02)^2 Y$$

And, in 1913:

$$\text{GDP}_{1913} = 1.02 \times \text{GDP}_{1912} = 1.02 \times (1.02)^2 Y = (1.02)^3 Y$$

FIGURE 27-2

U.S. real GDP per capita, 1910–2015 (valued in 2009 dollars)   Since 1910, the trend of GDP has been overwhelmingly positive, with three exceptions. Two were caused by the Great Depression (in the early 1930s) and Great Recession (late 2007 to mid-2009). The other occurred toward the tail end of World War II (mid-1940s).

Sources: Louis Johnston and Samuel H. Williamson, "What Was the U.S. GDP Then?," *MeasuringWorth* (2016), https://www.measuringworth.com/usgdp12/.

Are you seeing the pattern? Because 1913 is three years after 1910, we find GDP in 1913 by multiplying the base 1910 GDP by one plus the growth rate three times—that is, by 1.02 to the power of three. If we generalize this formula, we can predict GDP per capita in any year, A. We start from year B and multiply by 1 plus the growth rate, as many times as there are years between B and A:

EQUATION 27-2 $\text{GDP}_{\text{yearA}} = \text{GDP}_{\text{yearB}} \times (1 + \text{Growth rate})^{(\text{yearA}-\text{yearB})}$

Let's apply this equation to the 105 years between 1910 and 2015. In 1910, real per capita GDP in the United States was roughly \$5,800 (valued in 2009 dollars). Plugging that amount for $\text{GDP}_{\text{yearB}}$ into Equation 27-2, we calculate that real GDP per capita in 2015 would have been roughly \$46,400 if the growth rate during that whole period had been a steady 2 percent per year:

$$\text{GDP per capita}_{2015} = \$5{,}800 \times (1 + 0.02)^{105} \approx \$46{,}400$$

It turns out that the actual real per capita GDP was \$50,970 at the start of 2015 (valued in 2009 dollars), so the approximation of steady 2 percent growth was low, but not far off.

A different way to calculate the implications of steady growth is to use the *rule of 70*. It states that the number of years it will take for income to double at a given annual growth rate is approximately equal to 70 divided by the annual growth rate:

EQUATION 27-3 $\text{Years until income doubles} = \dfrac{70}{\text{Annual growth rate}}$

Thinking of growth in terms of "years to doubling" makes it easier to appreciate how small differences in growth rates can add up to huge differences in income over time. What if the growth rate in the United States increased from around 2 percent to about 3.5 percent? That might not sound like a big difference, but consider:

- At a growth rate of 2 percent, income doubles every 35 years.
- At a growth rate of 3.5 percent, income doubles every 20 years instead of every 35.
- Over 100 years, income would have doubled five times instead of three.
- So, starting with $5,800 in 1910, instead of earning an average $46,400 by 2015 (at 2 percent growth per year), Americans would be earning an average of about $215,000—more than four times greater thanks to the 3.5 percent growth rate.

To see the effect that differences in growth rates can make, consider the incredible economic story of East Asia. Starting in 1960, four countries in Asia—Hong Kong, Singapore, Taiwan, and South Korea—managed growth rates of over 8 percent per year. That implies that real incomes doubled more than once every 10 years! In just 50 years, this impressive economic growth managed to vault many people in these countries out of poverty. For insight into the debate about why this "Asian miracle" hasn't happened elsewhere, see the Real Life box "What a difference 50 years makes."

Real Life

What a difference **50 years** makes: The story of Korea and Ghana

In 1960, Ghana and South Korea had similar levels of development. Both were quite poor, and most of their populations eked out livings on small farms. Ghana, however, had good prospects. Most economists thought it was poised to grow by at least 7 percent per year.

The consensus prediction for South Korea, on the other hand, was far less rosy. The first World Bank mission to the country called South Korea's growth plan "ridiculously optimistic"; it predicted sluggish growth.

Fast-forwarding 50 years, South Korea is now a major manufacturing force, making sophisticated, high-end electronics and cars. Its brands include Samsung, LG, Hyundai, and Kia. It is now a wealthy country, with a GDP per capita over $28,000.

Ghana's economy also grew, though much more slowly. But its population grew faster than South Korea's, so its average income per capita was actually *higher* in 1960 than in 2000. Today, Ghana is one of the richer countries in Africa, but it is much less well-off than South Korea. Ghana's GDP per capita in 2014 was a little over $1,400 per person. Over half of its workforce is still employed in the agricultural sector, either growing export crops such as cocoa or subsistence crops such as cassava and maize.

Why did Korea take off while Ghana failed to meet its early promise? The story is complicated, but an important part of it is that Ghana suffered years of political instability after 1960. Government intervention in the economy was heavy-handed and discouraged foreign trade.

South Korea, on the other hand, focused relentlessly on educating its citizens and encouraging people to save. The government gave firms generous incentives to export, including tax benefits and low-interest loans. South Korea's expanding manufacturing sector led it to an average growth rate of real GDP per capita of 5.4 percent in the half-century between 1961 and 2011.

The rule of 70 estimates that Korea doubled in size about every 13 years. Put another way, in the 50 years between 1961 and 2011, Korea doubled its income nearly four times. The result: The current generation of young adults in Korea have incomes that are about 13 times that of their grandparents, after adjusting for inflation.

Economists don't have a foolproof formula for creating growth miracles. But by studying how Korea grew and why Ghana didn't, we can get closer to a real understanding of economic growth.

Sources: http://siteresources.worldbank.org/DEC/Resources/84797-1275071905763/Lessons_from_Korea_Lim. pdf; http://countrystudies.us/south-korea/; http://www.nber.org/chapters/c8548.pdf; http://www.cimmyt.org/; http://economistsview.typepad.com/economistsview/2006/03/amartya_sen_dem.html; http://data.worldbank.org/ indicator/NY.GDP.PCAP.CD.

✓ CONCEPT CHECK

- ☐ What was the overall trend of economic growth in the world before 1800? **[LO 27.1]**
- ☐ What is the rule of 70? **[LO 27.1]**

Determinants of Productivity

Growth may seem like an abstract concept, but it has a big impact on people's standard of living. If you happen to have been born in the United States or South Korea, for instance, you likely enjoy a standard of living much higher than that of your grandparents and great-grandparents. You are probably taller, healthier, better-educated, and more widely traveled and have more luxury and comfort in your life. Other regions of the world have grown much more slowly or not at all. As a result, in those regions people live in ways relatively similar to earlier generations.

What determines the dramatic differences between countries and their growth paths over time? In this section, we will build a framework to understand factors that determine the level of income in a country and the rate at which it grows over time. With this framework, we will have a basis for discussing the historical circumstances and policy choices that cause some economies to grow and others to stagnate.

Productivity drives growth

Imagine a single household—say, a family that lives away from others, on a farm in a remote place. The only goods available to this family are things its members can produce. If the family wants food or clothes or toys or a house, it will have to grow or make them. Suppose some family members learn to sew more quickly; they will make clothes more quickly and have more time left over to make toys for their children. Or suppose they build a plow that allows them to plant vegetables more easily, freeing up time and energy to build an extra room in their house. The total amount of goods they produce will increase, and so will their standard of living.

In fact, the *only* way that the family can consume more and enjoy a higher standard of living is to increase the amount each person produces. We call that output **productivity**. Productivity can be measured in various ways, but it's typically measured as output per worker.

productivity
output produced per worker

From Chapter 24, "Measuring GDP," we know that *output per person on a country level* is the same thing as *GDP per capita*. Just like the farm family, we can think of a country as a self-contained economic unit: It can earn and consume only as much as it produces. Thus, a country's income—like that of the farm family—depends on how productive its workers are.

Of course, hardly any family or country today consumes exactly what it produces itself. Typically, both sell some of the goods and services they produce. They then use the money they earn to buy goods and services that others produce. Still, the underlying relationship holds: The more a country produces, the more it can consume. In the short term, it can temporarily push consumption higher than production by borrowing money. But in the long run, debts have to be paid, and the only way to get to consume more is by producing more.

As a result, the standard of living in a country is driven by the average productivity of its people. *Increases in productivity per person* lead to *increases in per capita income,* which we call *economic growth.* So now the question is: What makes a country's people more productive?

Components of productivity

LO 27.2 Describe the relationship between productivity and growth and discuss the factors that determine productivity.

To answer the question of what makes people more productive, we'll go back to the enterprising farm family. What determines how many vegetables they can grow in a year? The answer depends on several other questions: How skilled and experienced are they at farming? How fertile is their land, and what is the climate like? Do they have plows and fertilizer? Do they have state-of-the-art computerized irrigation systems, or do they depend on rainfall? Do they use the latest high-yield seed varieties?

Most of us are not farmers. But the factors that determine our productivity as workers fall into the same categories: *physical capital* (like plows and tractors), *human capital* (farming experience), *natural resources* (land quality and rainfall), and *technology* (high-tech tools and crop varieties). Let's walk through each determinant to see how it affects productivity.

Physical capital

physical capital
the stock of equipment and structures that allow for production of goods and services

Most types of production require tools, and better tools allow workers to be more productive. A farmer with a sturdy horse-drawn plow will outperform a farmer with a shovel but won't do as well as his neighbor with a tractor. These are examples of **physical capital**, the stock of equipment and structures that allow for the production of goods and services. Elsewhere in the economy, examples of physical capital include a manufacturer's factory and machines, a cellular network's towers and cables, and so on.

We calculate the amount of physical capital in an economy by adding up the value of all tools, equipment, and structures. Every year, some new physical capital is added through investment (farmers buy new tractors). Likewise, some old physical capital wears out or becomes obsolete (old tractors stop working). Taking into account both new investment and the retirement of older capital, we can tell how much physical capital has been added to the economy on net.

Where does the money for investment in physical capital come from? It largely comes from the savings of ordinary households. You put away money in the bank, and the bank then loans funds to farmers and factories and cellular networks so that they can purchase new equipment. Thus, the *level of savings* in an economy can be an important determinant of investment in capital, and through that mechanism, a determinant of future productivity. In countries with low levels of savings, firms have trouble finding the money they need to invest in their factories and businesses. We will look in more detail at the relationship between savings and investment in later chapters.

Human capital

human capital
the set of skills, knowledge, experience, and talent that determine the productivity of workers

Having new machines is usually a plus for productivity, but only if workers know how to use them. **Human capital** refers to the set of skills, knowledge, experience, and talent that determine the productivity of workers.

Education is one of the main ways that we think about people building human capital. By taking an economics course, you are learning things that will make you more productive in the workplace. Human capital can also be acquired through training or job experience.

Human capital contributes to growth because it helps workers in the economy produce more with the same amount of physical capital. In other words, people can work smarter. A large increase in human capital is one explanation for the growth in the U.S. economy over the last 100 years. A century ago, the average person in America completed only around 8 years of school; today, the average is more than 12 years of school. The average worker today knows more than the average worker at the start of the century and so will be more productive.

Countries with low levels of GDP per capita usually also have low levels of schooling. For example, the average person in Malawi or India has approximately 5 years of schooling. Helping people to invest in their human capital through better access to schools and job training is a priority for many developing countries.

Note that an individual's, or a nation's, human capital is not always improving—it can also become outdated or deteriorate. People who are unemployed for long periods of time can forget some of the skills that were valuable in the workplace, for instance.

Schools around the world aim to build human capital. Here, a school in Kenya shows attentive students in a jam-packed classroom. *Courtesy of Aude Guerrucci*

Natural resources

Natural resources are production inputs that come from the earth—lakes, mineral deposits, forests, and so on. Natural resources can be split into two categories: renewable or nonrenewable.

- *Renewable resources* can be replenished naturally over time. For instance, after cutting down a tree for lumber, you can plant another one to grow in its place. Likewise, when a hydroelectric plant harnesses the power of a river to generate electricity, it doesn't "use up" the river, which continues to flow. Of course, some things take longer to renew than others. The river renews immediately, but the trees take many years to replenish.

- Mineral deposits such as coal, oil, and gold, on the other hand, are *nonrenewable*. When you take them out of the ground and use them, they do not get replenished.

The availability of natural resources can account for some of the differences in economic development around the world. The United States has been blessed with a lot of fertile land, for example. Britain got a big boost from having easily accessible coal to power its manufacturing. But natural resources aren't everything. Japan and Switzerland are wealthy countries without an abundance of natural resources; Guinea and Kazakhstan are poor countries despite having many natural resources.

Technology

The word *technology* may conjure up the image of a sleek new consumer gadget. When we think of how technology contributes to productivity, though, we need to understand the term more broadly. Technology comes in all forms and sizes. It can be big developments such as the invention of the Internet or cell phones. It can also be seemingly small advances like a more efficient water pump for irrigating crops or an engine design that allows cars to travel further on the same amount of fuel.

Big or small, technology means that the same inputs will produce more outputs. In other words, countries with better technology will be able to produce more with the same amount of physical and human capital.

It is hard to overstate the importance of technology for understanding economic growth. Technology is fundamentally different from other factors of production, such as land, resources, capital, and labor. Whereas these other factors are in scarce supply and run into diminishing returns, technology can be shared relatively easily, with good ideas leading to even better ideas. A famous growth economist, Paul Romer of New York University, emphasized that ideas are like recipes: While the ingredients may be scarce, the instructions for combining the ingredients can be shared at low cost. Thus, if one country develops a better way to combine existing resources, that same idea can spread quickly to other countries and lead to faster economic growth worldwide.

One of the most striking examples of the power of technology is the transformation of agriculture in Asia starting in the 1960s. Scientists developed new varieties of seeds for crops like rice and wheat, which produced much higher yields than traditional seeds. These high-yielding seed varieties doubled the amount of food that could be produced on a plot of land. This "green revolution" not only erased the prospect of famine but also set the stage for the incredible overall growth that has occurred in Asia over the past five decades. We'll come back to this story later in the chapter.

Rates versus levels

LO 27.3 Explain the difference between a country's level of income and its rate of growth.

Imagine that you're driving a car and merging onto the highway, pressing the accelerator pedal to the floor. Your speedometer says you are doing 15 mph, then a second later 20 mph, then a second later 25 mph. Your *level* of speed is fairly low, but your *rate of change* is high. Now imagine you are on the highway and cruising at 55 mph. You are at a high *level* of speed, but the speed is constant—your *rate of change* is zero.

This analogy is useful for thinking about the differences between wealthy countries and fast-growing countries. Switzerland, for example, has high levels of physical and human capital and access to sophisticated technology. Consequently, it has high productivity and standards of living. Its current *rate* of growth is low, but it's starting from a high *level*. It's like the driver cruising along on the highway.

By contrast, China has lower *levels* of physical and human capital and less widespread access to the latest technologies. As a result, Chinese workers have lower productivity than Swiss workers, and GDP per capita in China is lower than in Switzerland. However, incomes are increasing very rapidly in China. They have not yet achieved the same level as Switzerland, but they are moving quickly in that direction. China is like the car merging onto the highway, not yet going as fast as the cars already on the highway, but with a high *rate of change*. Its level of speed is increasing all the time.

As we discuss policies that can influence future growth, the distinction between the *level of income* and the *rate of increase in income* is crucial. The factors that took a country to its current economic level may or may not be related to those that can lead to future growth. For instance, Kuwait has grown rapidly in the last few decades and enjoys high productivity and incomes. This growth was almost entirely due to its incredible natural endowment of oil. But Kuwait would be foolish to base its future economic growth strategy only on exploiting its oil reserves. The people of Kuwait might hope that there are untapped oil reservoirs hiding somewhere in the desert, but there's nothing they can do to make more oil than already exists.

The spread of technology is a key driver of economic growth and can speed up rates of convergence. This Bedouin youth talks on a mobile phone as he leads a camel in southern Iraq.
© *Essam Al-Sudanie/AFP/ Getty Images*

Similarly, we saw in Chapter 24, "Measuring GDP," that increasing participation of women in the labor market partially explained U.S. growth rates from the 1970s to the 1990s. But clearly, as with Kuwait's oil, it would not be sensible to think you can grow an economy forever by encouraging more and more stay-at-home parents to get jobs or current workers to work longer hours. Sooner or later there will be no stay-at-home parents left, and no more hours in the day for people to work overtime. Such one-time changes in the economy can cause growth spurts that lead to higher income *levels,* but they cannot sustain a higher *rate of change* over time.

In contrast, improvements in technology *can* sustain high rates of change. Sure, when an inventor creates a new gizmo, that invention is a one-time change. If technology stops improving, the economy won't continue to grow. But often, improvements in technology lead to *more* improvements in technology. For example, computing capacity has approximately doubled every two years since the invention of computers, a phenomenon called *Moore's law.* People are constantly finding better and more effective ways to do things, and as a result, their productivity is continuously increasing.

Accounting for growth

LO 27.4 Use the growth accounting framework to describe how technology, labor, and capital contribute to economic growth.

Now that we've seen the main ingredients of growth, it's natural to ask which ones are the most important. It turns out that we can decompose (separate) the growth rate of output per person into the contributions of capital, labor, and technology. When we describe the determinants of output, we often use a *production function,* an equation that captures the relationship between the quantity of inputs and the resulting quantity of outputs.

Here, instead, we want to capture the relationship between the *growth rate* of inputs and the resulting *growth rate* of outputs. Economists call this *growth accounting.* In particular, economists use an equation like this:

EQUATION 27-4 Growth accounting equation

$$g_Y = g_A + \alpha g_K + (1 - \alpha) g_L$$

where the *g*'s with subscripts denote the percentage change in the variable indicated by the subscript:

g_Y = the growth rate of output

g_A = the growth rate of technology

g_K = the growth rate of capital

g_L = the growth rate of labor

α = the share of GDP that is distributed to the owners of capital

$1 - \alpha$ = the share of output that is distributed to labor

The growth accounting equation tells us that the growth rate of GDP is equal to the growth rate of technology plus the growth rates of capital and labor, weighted by their shares of output.

An important aspect of growth accounting is that it offers a way to estimate the importance of technology in economic growth. Output, labor, and capital are relatively straightforward to define and measure. In contrast, technology is hard to measure. It can take the form of new innovations in information technology, better management practices, or simply reduced government distortions. Measuring technology directly would therefore be close to impossible.

Growth accounting, however, provides an *indirect* route to measuring technology. Since we can directly measure the growth of output, labor, and capital, and we also have a rough idea how large the capital and labor shares are, we can simply compute the growth of technology as a *residual* in the equation above. Indeed, this residual is exactly what macroeconomists have in mind when they talk about technology—it's the unexplained part of economic growth!

As an example of how growth accounting works in practice, let's consider China's growth experience from 1978 to 2004, an era that generated the highest sustained period of growth on record. China's GDP grew at an average annual rate of 9.3 percent; employment grew at around 2 percent; capital grew at about 10 percent.[3] The capital share of output in China was about

40 percent during this period, while the labor share was around 60 percent. Substituting these values into our growth accounting equation (Equation 27-4), we can solve for the implied growth rate of technology:

$$0.093 = g_A + (0.4 \times 0.10) + (0.6 \times 0.02)$$
$$g_A = 0.093 - (0.4 \times 0.10) - (0.6 \times 0.02) = 0.041$$

Thus, even though China experienced a rapid increase in its physical capital stock over the 30 years since the beginning of the reform era, just about half of the total growth in GDP came from "technology." The quotes around "technology" are there to remind you that technology includes all changes that lead the economy to use inputs more efficiently; this includes the effects of reduced government distortions, for example, as well as new management practices and modernized factories.

Convergence

LO 27.5 Assess the empirical evidence for and against convergence theory.

Are poor countries doomed to stay poor, like cars poking along forever at 10 or 20 mph? Or does the fact that a country now is poor just mean that we are seeing it early in the development process, like a car moving slowly but accelerating toward highway speed? Will China and other low-income but fast-growing countries eventually reach a similar level of wealth to the United States and Switzerland? If they do, will they keep accelerating forever, or will they eventually see their rates of growth slow and settle in on the highway alongside the world's rich countries?

One classic model of economic growth suggests the "settling in" story is the correct one. This model relates to the idea of *decreasing marginal returns* to factors of production: Countries that start with very little physical capital will get a higher return from adding a unit of capital than will a country that starts at a higher initial level. This leads to the general hypothesis that countries starting at low levels of income (which correspond to low levels of capital) will tend to grow at much faster rates than those starting with high levels of income. Each additional unit of capital provides larger gains when you're coming from behind.

convergence theory
the theory that countries that start out poor will initially grow faster than rich ones but will eventually converge to the same growth rate

This idea is called **convergence theory** (or the *catch-up effect*). It says that poor countries will grow faster than rich ones, until they catch up and all countries "converge" to the same growth rate. The theory predicts that even if countries differ in their rates of savings, population growth, and other features, they will still converge to the same *growth rate,* although not the same *level of income.* In other words, countries that start out poor should initially grow faster than ones that start out rich but will eventually slow to the same growth rate.

In some ways, convergence theory fits the evidence from the real world. Figure 27-3 shows the differences between growth rates in countries around the world from 1990 to 2010. Looking at the map, you'll see that:

- Richer countries have mostly been growing slowly.
- Most of the fastest growth rates are occurring in some of the poorest countries. (However, you can also see plenty of poor countries on the map that have not been growing quickly, especially in Africa.)

Many economists think convergence theory explains the incredible growth of the East Asian countries. Those countries experienced very high marginal returns as they began to accumulate physical and human capital. They also were well positioned to take advantage of technologies and capital flows from wealthier countries.

In other places, however, convergence is clearly not happening. Most African countries started at levels of physical and human capital as low as East Asia's half a century ago, but they have

FIGURE 27-3

World GDP per capita growth rates, 1990–2010[*]   Over these 20 years, there has been a wide disparity in the rate of economic growth. This growth has been strongest in Southeast Asia, while the rate of economic growth in most of Western Europe has been sluggish.

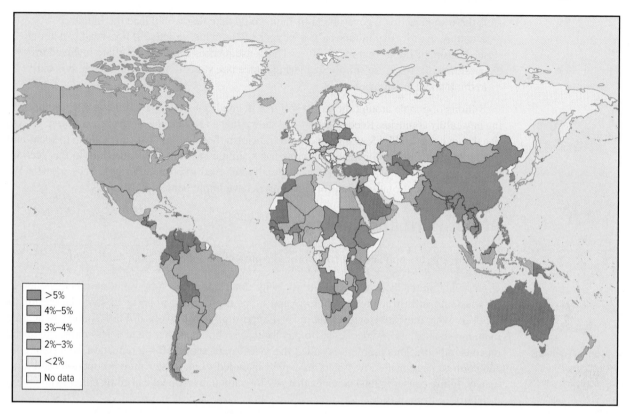

[*] In most of the former Soviet bloc, data start in 1991 after the fall of the USSR.
Source: World Bank, *World Development Indicators*, http://databank.worldbank.org/ddp/home.do.

not experienced the same growth spurt. In fact, many actually became poorer during the 1980s and early 1990s. Clearly, simply starting out poor is not a guarantee of achieving impressive growth rates.

The fact that the poorest regions of the world have tended to grow more slowly than the richest regions of the world suggests that world incomes have become more unequal over time. But that is true only if we take *countries* as our units of analysis. If we instead ignore countries and look at the distribution of *individual incomes* around the world, we arrive at a completely different picture of inequality. Because some of the fastest-growing countries in the world, such as China, India, and Indonesia, started out both relatively poor and populous, the world distribution of incomes has actually become more equal over time.[4]

To try to understand what allows some low-income countries to take off while others stagnate, we need to consider how public policy affects economic growth.

✓CONCEPT CHECK

☐ What are the main determinants of productivity? **[LO 27.2]**
☐ How are rates different from levels when talking about economic growth? **[LO 27.3]**
☐ How do economists measure the impact of technology on economic growth? **[LO 27.4]**
☐ What does convergence theory predict about growth rates? About income levels? **[LO 27.5]**

Growth and Public Policy

Nobel Prize winner Robert Lucas captured the fascination and sense of possibility that come with thinking about economic growth in this way:

> Is there some action a government of India could take that would lead the Indian economy to grow like Indonesia's or Egypt's? If so, what, exactly? If not, what is it about the "nature of India" that makes it so? The consequences for human welfare involved in questions like these are simply staggering: Once one starts to think about them, it is hard to think about anything else.[5]

Billions of people around the world still live in conditions that are unimaginable to those living in wealthy countries. Recent history has shown that a few decades of strong economic growth like that experienced by South Korea could transform their lives. What can be done to spark and sustain that growth? Unfortunately, no one has a simple answer to this question. In this section, we discuss some of the factors that are generally believed to promote or hold back growth. We also look at policy solutions that some countries have implemented successfully.

Investment and savings

> **LO 27.6** Discuss policies that could promote growth and relate them to productivity.

If physical capital increases productivity, why don't countries simply put as much money as possible into infrastructure, machinery, and other capital investments? In some cases, this is precisely what they do. However, there is an opportunity cost involved. For a country to acquire more physical capital, someone has to pay for it, which means that there is less money to spend on consumption. This problem is called the **investment trade-off**—a reduction in current consumption to pay for the investment in capital intended to increase future production (and, ultimately, future consumption). Savings that pay for capital investment can come either from within a country or from outside it.

investment trade-off
a reduction in current consumption to pay for investment in capital intended to increase future production

domestic savings
savings for capital investment that come from within a country; equal to domestic income minus consumption spending

Investment funds from within a country

Savings that come from within a country are called **domestic savings** and are equal to domestic income minus consumption spending. They can come from two sources:

- private households spending less than they earn or
- government revenues exceeding expenditures.

Savings rates vary enormously across countries, as Figure 27-4 shows. On one end of the spectrum, we have China, where the economy typically puts away a whopping 49 percent of GDP. In contrast, the United States saves just 18 percent, and households contribute a small share of that saving. In 2016, the U.S. household savings rate was just above 5 percent.[6]

Governments also can use tax revenues (or borrow money) to invest in physical capital. Governments often fund the underlying infrastructure that private companies rely on for their operations, such as roads, bridges, ports, and sewer systems. This infrastructure can have a major effect on growth. In many low-income countries, for example, even if farmers could grow more, it would be hard to get their goods to market because of poor roads. Many governments are currently investing heavily in communications infrastructure such as high-speed Internet, in the expectation that it will improve private companies' productivity.

foreign direct investment (FDI)
investment when a firm runs part of its operation abroad or owns all or part of another company abroad

Investment funds from outside a country

Funds for capital investment can also come from outside a country. **Foreign direct investment (FDI)** is investment that occurs when a firm runs part of its operation abroad or invests in another company abroad. For example, when Toyota operates a plant in the U.S. state of Georgia, the

FIGURE 27-4

Gross savings rates among countries in 2014.   Savings rates vary a lot around the world. For example, China saves a whopping 49 percent of GDP, India saves 31 percent, and the United States saves 18 percent. Gross savings are calculated as national income less total consumption plus net transfers.

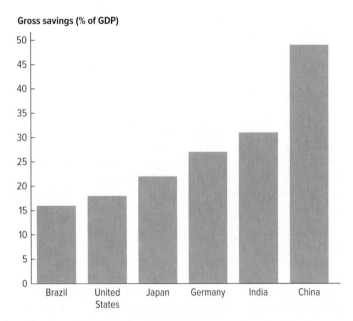

Gross savings (% of GDP)

Source: *World Bank Indicators*. http://data.worldbank.org/indicator/NY.GNS.ICTR.ZS.

Japanese firm owns the machinery and buildings, even though the production takes place in the United States. Similarly, factories owned by U.S. firms on the Mexican side of the United States–Mexico border are an important source of FDI in Mexico.

Many governments actively work to attract FDI, hoping it will build up their capital stock when domestic savings aren't sufficient. Another benefit of FDI is that when foreign companies invest in local firms, they can transfer human capital to local managers and workers. Perhaps managers from the foreign country travel to oversee the investment. In doing so, they can train local staff or set up more efficient procedures.

However, FDI has its critics. Foreign firms with money to invest often have numerous governments competing to attract the investment. The firm can drive a hard bargain, demanding special tax breaks or legal exemptions that governments cannot easily afford. The transfer of knowledge or technology may also not happen to the extent some would wish, if foreign managers oversee operations without training up local talent. As a result, some argue that a policy of attracting FDI might not ultimately be as beneficial as it first appears.

Education and health

In rich countries, we take free basic education for granted. In many countries, however, schools may be few and far between, charge unaffordable fees to students, or simply provide very low-quality education. One of the major efforts of the Sustainable Development Goals—a collection of targets set by the United Nations to tackle aspects of poverty in low-income countries by 2030—has been to push countries to provide free elementary school education.

Free availability of high-quality public education for all children is one of the most important ways a country can increase its stock of human capital. Education teaches skills such as literacy, basic math, and communication—all essential to perform more than the most elementary jobs. High-quality education also builds the pool of scientists, thinkers, and entrepreneurs who develop new technologies and business models.

Using public policy to promote health can also contribute to growth. Workers who are in good health will be more productive and less likely to miss work days. Some economic benefits of improved health are less visible, especially in low-income countries. For instance, health economists have found that reducing vitamin and mineral deficiencies such as anemia (the result of a diet with not enough iron in it) and parasites such as worms can improve people's mental and physical energy. Treatment for such health problems increases the ability to focus, making it easier for children to learn in school and for adults to do their best at work.

It's hard to accumulate greater levels of human capital when health problems and lack of educational opportunities combine. Most of us would agree that we are more productive when we're working with other highly educated workers. In some places, like California's Silicon Valley, this creates a positive feedback loop in productivity: Talented computer programmers and business managers can multiply their productivity by working with other talented programmers and managers. In low-income countries, however, this cycle can work in the opposite direction: The productivity of skilled workers can diminish due to the lower average levels of skill of their co-workers. Public policy can help to push a country out of this negative cycle by improving public health services and the quality of education.

Technological development

A lot of research and development takes place at private institutions—in firms, private laboratories, and so on. However, public policy can also encourage technological development—through the educational system, funding for research and study, and tax structures that encourage firms to develop and adopt new technologies. In the United States, just under 3 percent of GDP is spent on research and development. Less than a third of that amount is spent by the federal government to support universities and research institutes. Most research and development spending is done by business.[7]

You might be wondering why the government should be involved in research and development in areas other than military spending and public works. Recall that technology is fundamentally about ideas, which once created can be adopted at low cost by others. This means that there is a positive externality associated with innovation: Part of the benefit associated with a firm's investment in new ideas goes to competing firms. As a result, there is a "free-rider" problem associated with innovation.

The economy as a whole would be better off with more innovation. But firms underproduce innovation because they care only about the direct benefits of innovation for their own bottom line. They do not care about the indirect benefits to other firms in the economy. The tendency to underproduce innovation creates a reason for the government to keep supporting research and development.

Advancements in technology can be fantastic, but they can also be fickle. The "green revolution," which introduced new agricultural technologies, was a rousing success in Asia but has been more complicated in Africa. The Real Life box "Green revolutions in Asia and Africa" provides details of this story.

Real Life

Green revolutions in Asia and Africa

In 1961, India was at risk of famine. The population was booming, and no more farmland was available. How would everyone be fed? Incredibly, by 1985 the specter of famine had all but disappeared, not only in India but across Asia. In just 25 years, crop yields doubled, easily outpacing the growth of the population.

This transformation in agriculture, called the *green revolution,* was the result of painstaking research and development funded by private charities such as the Rockefeller Foundation. It resulted in new crop varieties, such as strain IR8, or "miracle rice," developed in 1968 by the International Rice Research Institute in the Philippines. "Miracle rice" required more intensive fertilizer and irrigation treatments than traditional varieties but produced about double the amount of rice per plant.

Unfortunately, the green revolution did not reach Africa. While climate, soil, and growing conditions are fairly similar across much of Asia, they vary widely in Africa. The high-yielding varieties of rice and wheat simply didn't grow as well there. A variety of rice that doubles yields in most Asian countries may wilt in the drier climate of Ethiopia or be swamped in the equatorial rains of the Congo.

African farmers today mostly still farm as their grandparents did, and as farmers in Asia did 50 years ago, with little fertilizer and limited tools. Growing enough food in Africa requires the agricultural sector to employ a large percentage of the labor force. Many economists believe that this difference partly explains why Asia's economies have grown more quickly than Africa's in the last half century: When you don't need as many workers to grow food, they can do something else instead, such as work in factories in the city.

The search is now on for ways to make the green revolution work in Africa. The Bill and Melinda Gates Foundation and the Rockefeller Foundation are funding a regional approach that tries to tailor plant varieties and practices to local conditions. This new work may not be as immediate or dramatic as the Asian green revolution, but it may lead to innovations that put ample food in every bowl—and help Africa along the path to greater prosperity.

Laying the groundwork: Good government, property rights, and economic openness

LO 27.7 Explain how good governance and economic openness lay the foundation for growth.

Imagine that you live in a country where, if someone steals your truck, there is nothing you can do about it. The police won't help you, unless you bribe them. Even if you could get police help, it might take five years and a lot of money to prosecute someone in court. Would you still buy a truck? You might, if you thought that the potential benefits were high enough to outweigh the risk of losing your investment. But you'd certainly be less inclined to invest in trucks and other expensive capital goods than you would if you thought that your property would be protected.

This is just one example of the ways in which enforceable laws and effective, trustworthy government services are critical to a well-functioning economy. Most countries have mechanisms to punish those who violate the property rights of others and to enforce contracts between buyers and sellers. Institutions like police forces, courts of law, and government bureaucracies are meant to protect property, settle disputes, and provide a predictable legal framework in which people can make plans and agreements. However, these institutions are more effective and reliable in some countries than in others.

Stability in leadership and institutions is important, as is effectiveness. Would you want to build an expensive new factory if you thought there was a good chance of new leaders coming to power who might seize it? Would you risk investing in a business if the tax policies or laws that determine its profitability change from month to month?

Many economists believe that good government has a major impact on economic growth. The degree of government effectiveness can help us understand why some economies have grown rapidly and others have stagnated. How to improve government is a tricky question, though. It is challenging to design effective policies to tackle corruption, make courts more efficient, limit the powers of politicians, and so on.

Government policy also determines how open a country will be to trade. Firms often argue that governments need to protect them from competition by placing tariffs on foreign goods. However, the "Asian miracle" countries succeeded by combining industrial policy with "outward-oriented" policies to gear their economies toward exporting goods. Later in the book, we'll discuss free trade and why most economists believe that there are important gains to keeping economies open.

The juggling act

As with many things in life, there are *trade-offs* between different ways of promoting growth through public policy. Most governments—especially those in poor countries—can't pay for education *and* health *and* highways *and* better police all at the same time. Unfortunately, this is a vicious cycle: The richer you are, the better able you are to pay for things that will help you be even richer in the future. The poorer you are, the less able you are to pay for the things that can make you richer.

Earlier in the chapter, we noted the trade-off between current consumption and investment in physical capital, human capital, and research that will contribute to growth and to higher future income. The poorer the country, the tougher this trade-off becomes. It's harder for people who live close to the edge on a dollar or two a day to save a given amount of money or pay more taxes than it would be for wealthier people. This logic leads to the vicious cycle described above. If you can't afford to pay for a good court system or to invest in a tractor or a computer, you will find it harder to climb out of poverty. This "poverty trap" is one of the main justifications for foreign aid that provides loans or funding for infrastructure and human capital development.

Why don't countries take one element at a time—for example, focusing limited resources first on infrastructure, and then on education or health, and so on? Unfortunately, it's not usually that simple. Growth often requires concurrent improvements in many aspects of the economy. For instance, translating new technology into growth often requires a population with sufficient human capital to take advantage of it, and sometimes specific infrastructure.

Imagine a country trying to build an Internet-based economy. This would be difficult, if not impossible, if much of the population can't read, or if the electrical grid experiences regular blackouts due to insufficient power generation. Harnessing the power of the Internet to promote commerce, and thus growth, would require simultaneous improvements in literacy, computer skills, the power grid, a trustworthy postal service, and payment mechanisms.

Another trade-off that governments face is how much to sacrifice their natural environment in pursuit of economic growth. The What Do You Think? box "Should poor countries be as earth-friendly as rich ones?" explores this particular trade-off.

What Do You Think?
Should poor countries be as earth-friendly as rich ones?

During the European Industrial Revolution, factories spewed pollution into the atmosphere as they rolled out a steady stream of textiles, steel, and other goods. Power plants fueled by dirty coal dotted cities throughout Western Europe and eventually the United States. Miners and factory workers alike often died of lung diseases and other health problems associated with dirty air and unsafe working conditions. After many years of unchecked pollution, conditions got so bad that London suffered from chronic smog that would settle over the city for days, blotting out the sun. In 1952, one particularly severe smog episode killed over 4,000 people. In retrospect, the environmental and health consequences of Europe's industrialization seem awful. At the time, though, they were simply part and parcel of a massive increase in wealth and economic power.

In the past 50 years, technologies have been developed that allow firms to produce goods and energy with far less pollution. Low-income countries today don't necessarily have to go through the same painful arc that marked earlier industrial transformations. Despite this, China's economic explosion has been accompanied by smog and the release of toxic chemicals into rivers. Occasionally, actual explosions at factories have killed thousands of people and filled the atmosphere with pollutants. Why haven't firms in China chosen to use the new, cleaner technology now available?

There are two reasons:

- Acquiring clean technologies is not always straightforward, due to stringent trade policies or intellectual property laws.
- Even when these technologies are accessible, they may be very expensive.

The reason factories and power plants in Europe and the United States are now relatively clean is not because the new technologies are always cheaper than the older, dirtier methods. Rather, it's often because governments in those countries have introduced strict regulations requiring firms to mitigate their environmental impact and protect the health and safety of their workers and neighbors.

The questions for China and other low-income countries are:

- Do we want to introduce strict environmental laws, forcing companies to use expensive clean technology?
- Or do we want to grow our economy as quickly as possible by using cheaper ways of doing things, even if they are environmentally damaging?

Many in richer countries feel that fast-growing countries such as India and China should have to protect the environment by using the cleaner technologies now available. They point out that production in low-income countries is releasing vast amounts of greenhouse gases, which affect other countries, too. For example, even though China's economy is barely a third the size of the U.S. economy, China is already the largest producer of carbon dioxide in the world. The effects, through climate change, could be disastrous all over the world.

Low-income countries, on the other hand, counter that being forced to use the cleaner technologies would make their goods more expensive and less competitive in the world market. They argue that developed countries created the problem of climate change by releasing greenhouse gases during their own industrial revolutions. It's not fair, they say, to expect poorer countries to pay the penance. It's also not clear what the more "humane" policy is: We've seen that economic growth can decrease poverty and alleviate suffering, and stricter regulations likely mean slower growth and slower poverty reduction.

To help solve this impasse, the United Nations has launched a "Green Climate Fund." Starting in 2020, the fund will distribute $100 billion per year to low-income countries, partly to help them acquire and pay for cleaner technologies. The fund may help countries avoid some of the pollution associated with economic growth, but probably won't solve the whole problem.

WHAT DO YOU THINK?

1. Should all countries be held to the same environmental standards?
2. Do rich countries have a responsibility to help poorer countries acquire cleaner technologies?
3. Is it worth implementing cleaner technologies if it means slower growth?

Sources: http://www.reuters.com/article/2011/04/15/us-climate-fund-idUSTRE73E3WG20110415; http://www.cnbc.com/id/43139649; http://news.bbc.co.uk/2/hi/uk_news/england/2545759.stm;http://www.nytimes.com/2010/07/29/world/asia/29china.html; http://www.law.duke.edu/journals/dltr/articles/2009dltr001.html.

✓ **CONCEPT CHECK**

☐ What determinant of economic growth is influenced by domestic saving? **[LO 27.6]**

☐ Why do police protection and efficient courts matter for economic growth? **[LO 27.7]**

Conclusion

Economic growth can make the rich richer. It also is a powerful way to make the poor richer too. In this chapter, we looked at how we define and measure economic growth and why growth is so important. Because of compounding, even a small increase in the growth rate will have a large impact on the level of income in the long run. A country that is growing at 3.5 percent, instead of 2 percent, will end up approximately four times richer after 100 years.

In order to grow, a country needs to be able to put together the ingredients:

- savings that can be invested into physical capital,
- healthy and skilled workers,
- appropriate technology, and
- supportive public policies and institutions.

All governments face tough trade-offs: How much should the country invest in health, education, and infrastructure? How can the government create a secure legal environment for people to invest? The goal is a positive cycle in which people gain human capital, invent better technology, become more productive at their jobs, get richer and be able to afford more physical capital, and so on.

This process is not easy, but it is important. If policy-makers, businesses, and workers come together effectively to build the right environment for investment, their contributions can deliver a foundation for the prosperity of future generations.

Key Terms

productivity, p. 689

physical capital, p. 690

human capital, p. 690

convergence theory, p. 694

investment trade-off, p. 696

domestic savings, p. 696

foreign direct investment (FDI), p. 696

Summary

LO 27.1 Calculate the growth rate of real GDP per capita, accounting for changes in price levels and population.

The fact that growth compounds over time makes it hard to tell just from looking at the annual growth rate what the total effect on incomes will be. GDP growth rates are often stated without taking population growth into account and sometimes without taking inflation into account. To find the rate of real GDP growth, take the nominal growth rate and subtract both population growth and inflation growth rates.

National economic growth builds on itself over time. The result is that a relatively modest annual growth rate, like 2 percent, actually adds up to quite a large total

growth rate over time. The rate at which GDP increases incomes can be found through the *rule of 70:* To find how long it takes incomes to double within a country, divide 70 by the rate of real GDP growth.

LO 27.2 Describe the relationship between productivity and growth and discuss the factors that determine productivity.

The only way that a country can consume more and enjoy a higher standard of living is to increase its *productivity*—the amount it produces per worker. Productivity can be measured for any unit of labor, whether that unit is an hour of time worked or how much one worker produces; it is typically measured as output per person. The factors that influence labor productivity are physical capital, human capital, technology, and natural resources.

LO 27.3 Explain the difference between a country's level of income and its rate of growth.

There are two important distinctions to make in terms of economic development. One is about the *level* of well-being. Countries like the United States or Switzerland that have very high amounts of physical and human capital are said to be at a high level of development. The other distinction is about the *rate* of economic growth. While the United States may have a high level of development, the rate of growth in U.S. GDP is not nearly as fast as China's. Level matters because it tells how wealthy a country currently is. Rates matter because they tell how quickly a country is increasing its wealth.

LO 27.4 Use the growth accounting framework to describe how technology, labor, and capital contribute to economic growth.

The growth accounting framework is a way to explain the growth rate of GDP as the sum of the growth rate of technology plus the growth rates of capital and labor, weighted by their shares of output. The framework helps us see how much of growth is due to using more inputs (capital and labor) versus using existing inputs more efficiently (via technology).

While labor and capital are relatively straightforward to measure, it's much harder to measure technology. Fortunately, the framework gives a way to estimate the importance of technology in economic growth by calculating it indirectly as a residual. The evidence shows that technology (defined broadly) is often extremely important in explaining growth.

LO 27.5 Assess the empirical evidence for and against convergence theory.

Convergence theory predicts that countries that are starting at lower levels of income will grow at a faster rate than those starting at higher levels, until they catch up and converge to the same growth rate.

In some ways, convergence theory fits evidence from the real world. The four East Asian countries that experienced incredible growth since the 1960s started from low levels of physical and human capital but were well positioned to take advantage of technologies and capital flows from wealthier countries. However, most African countries had similar or even lower levels of physical and human capital than did East Asia half a century ago but have not experienced high growth rates.

LO 27.6 Discuss policies that could promote growth and relate them to productivity.

Countries face an investment trade-off, in which they must reduce current consumption to pay for the capital investment needed to increase future production. Funds to pay for capital investment can come either from domestic savings or from foreign direct investment (FDI) from outside the country.

A variety of policies can promote economic growth. Education teaches skills such as literacy, basic math, and communication, which are essential to perform more than the most elementary jobs. Education is also a way to develop the training and skills that countries need to be able to undertake technological research and development. Public health systems can also contribute to growth by increasing the portion of the population that is fit, healthy, and able to work. Public policy can also encourage technological development through the education system, funding for research and study, and tax structures that encourage firms to develop and adopt new technologies.

LO 27.7 Explain how good governance and economic openness lay the foundation for growth.

Enforceable laws and effective, trustworthy government services are critical to a well-functioning economy. The most important is the provision of property rights, giving people the ability to have control over the resources they own. Most countries have institutions and infrastructure that are at least partially designed to protect these property rights. Courts enforce the contracts between buyers and sellers. They also are responsible, through the criminal justice system, for punishing people who are accused of violating the property rights of others.

Review Questions

1. Explain why inflation reduces the real value of nominal GDP per capita. **[LO 27.1]**

2. When policy-makers discuss policies that encourage long-run growth in per capita real GDP, they often mention policies aimed at reducing the growth rate in the population. If effective, why might these policies improve long-run growth? Also, what are the potential costs associated with these policies? **[LO 27.1]**

3. Does the rule of 70 predict greater increases in the amount of income for richer or poorer countries when both have the same growth rate? Why? **[LO 27.1, 27.3]**

4. Explain why many rich countries are able to continuously grow, even though they already have very high levels of physical and human capital. **[LO 27.2]**

5. At a young age, would you rather have a large level of savings or a pool of savings that was increasing at a faster rate? **[LO 27.3]**

6. If a country's labor and capital grow at the same rate, is this likely to have the same impact on the growth rate of output? Why or why not? **[LO 27.4]**

7. Measuring the growth in technology directly is almost impossible. How does the growth accounting equation allow economists to calculate an implied growth rate for technology? **[LO 27.4]**

8. Using the growth rates for countries found in Figure 27-3, is there evidence that poorer countries in Africa and Asia are converging to the level of income found in Western Europe? Why or why not? **[LO 27.5]**

9. Southern states in the United States are, on average, poorer than northern states. Southern states also have higher growth rates in real GDP per capita, on average, than northern states. Use these facts to draw a conclusion about whether the theory of convergence is correct. What other factors should be considered? **[LO 27.5]**

10. Many believe that technology is very costly to create but cheap to transfer. For example, think of the personal computer: The technology underpinning the personal computer took a generation of time and a ton of money to create. However, now that the personal computer has been created, it is easy for others to purchase and reap the benefits. Given this insight, what do you believe will be the growth implications for the United States (traditionally more apt to create new technology) and China (traditionally more apt to adopt technologies created elsewhere)? **[LO 27.5, 27.6]**

11. How might low rates of saving in the United States limit the accumulation of physical capital? **[LO 27.6]**

12. Realizing that poor countries must solve many problems at once has shifted donors away from the idea of giving multiple small payments to the idea of a "Big Push." This Big Push entails giving a very large sum of money that could be used to fix multiple problems at once. In fact, the amount of money required might be so large that other countries might be the only ones who could afford the donation. What are the trade-offs associated with this idea? **[LO 27.6]**

13. How is it possible that Switzerland, a landlocked country with almost no natural resources, is one of the richest countries in the world while the Democratic Republic of the Congo, a huge country with vast deposits of many strategically important minerals, is one of the poorest? **[LO 27.2, 27.6, 27.7]**

14. Why could a free press be important for economic growth? (Think about the connection between the press and government.) **[LO 27.7]**

Problems and Applications

1. Fill in the blanks in Table 27P-1. **[LO 27.1]**

2. Equation 27-1 states that Real GDP per capita growth rate = Nominal GDP per capita growth rate − Inflation rate − Population growth rate.

   This equation is an approximation of the exact rate of growth of GDP per capita, and so it results in some errors when calculating this rate. However, the simplified equation both is easy to use and results in small error terms when inflation, nominal GDP growth, and population growth are low, and so it is a useful approximation. Table 27P-2 lists a fictional country's nominal GDP, real GDP, GDP deflator, and population over two years. **[LO 27.1]**

   a. Use your knowledge from Chapter 25, "The Cost of Living," to verify that the real GDP figures in Table 27P-2 are accurate.

   b. Calculate this country's real GDP per capita for both 2015 and 2016.

   c. Calculate the growth rate in this country's real GDP per capita between 2015 and 2016.

   d. Calculate the growth rates in the nominal GDP, GDP deflator, and the population.

3. For each growth rate below, use the rule of 70 to calculate how long it will take incomes to double. **[LO 27.2]**

   a. 4 percent.

   b. 7 percent.

   c. 2.5 percent.

   d. 10 percent.

   e. 3 percent.

4. For each part below, determine whether the following actions will increase or decrease productivity, and name the component of productivity that each affects. **[LO 27.2]**

   a. The local government builds a new school.

   b. Teachers in the new school hold classes for young students.

   c. A manufacturer installs robots on its assembly line.

   d. A research team designs a more efficient system of irrigation.

   e. A soda company discovers a new source of underground water that can be used to make its products.

   f. A professor writes a new and improved economics textbook.

   g. A large number of people have less access to health care.

   h. A worker receives on-the-job training to be a mechanic.

TABLE 27P-1

Country	Nominal GDP growth (%)	Population growth (%)	Inflation (%)	Real GDP growth per capita (%)
Svea	5	3		−1
Bonifay	2	1	0	
Chaires		2	7	4
Drifton	5	0	−1	
Estiffanulga	7		3	3

TABLE 27P-2

Year	Nominal GDP ($)	GDP deflator	Real GDP ($)	Population
2015	1,000,000	1.00	1,000,000	1,000
2016	1,050,000	1.02	1,029,412	1,005

TABLE 27P-3

Country	GDP per capita 2010 ($)	GDP per capita 2015 ($)
Boliv	3,664	4,592
Chi	4,102	7,519
Ghala	2,007	2,615
Artinia	10,860	15,854
Plazi	8,603	11,239

TABLE 27P-4

Country	Income per capita ($)	Real per capita GDP growth rate (%)
Ansonia	5,000	7.0
Trumbull	7,500	4.5
Shelton	10,000	2.0

5. Which of the countries shown in Table 27P-3 had the highest level of per capita income in 2015? Which had the highest rate of income growth from 2010 to 2015? Do incomes in these countries appear to be converging? [LO 27.3, 27.5]

6. In 2015 the median household income in Louisiana was approximately $45,000 per year, while the income per household in Massachusetts was about $69,000. However, suppose the growth rate of per capita real GDP in Louisiana is higher than in Massachusetts (3 percent versus 2 percent). [LO 27.3, 27.5]

   a. From the perspective of trying to maximize your income per capita, which state will have higher increases in income over the next few years?

   b. From the perspective of trying to maximize your income per capita, which state will have higher increases in income in the long run?

7. Will the three countries in Table 27P-4 converge to the same level of economic development given enough time? [LO 27.3, 27.5]

8. Indicate whether each of the following statements is true or false and explain your answer. [LO 27.4]

   a. Country A's labor share is 60 percent, Country B's labor share is 70 percent, and labor is growing at a rate of 3 percent in both countries. All else the same, Country B has a higher growth rate of output.

   b. Country A's labor share is 40 percent, Country B's labor share is 70 percent, and labor is

   growing at a rate of 10 percent in country A and 6 percent in country B. All else the same, Country A has a higher growth rate of output.

   c. Labor is growing at a negative rate in country A and a positive rate in country B, so country B must have a higher growth rate of output.

   d. Labor and capital are both growing more quickly in Country A than in Country B, so Country A must have a higher growth rate of output.

9. Calculate the implied growth rate of technology in each scenario in Table 27P-5. Assume labor's share of output is 70 percent and capital's share of output is 30 percent. [LO 27.4]

TABLE 27P-5

Scenario	Growth Rate of Output (%)	Growth Rate of Labor (%)	Growth Rate of Capital (%)	Implied Growth Rate of Technology (%)
A	3.0	2	2	
B	4.2	3	3	
C	3.0	1	5	
D	4.2	1	4	

10. For each of the following examples, state whether this activity would likely hinder or promote economic growth, and name a component of productivity each produces or reduces. **[LO 27.2, 27.6]**

    a. Not requiring students to attend school.

    b. Granting patents on new inventions.

    c. Building a solid infrastructure system.

    d. Allowing local rivers and streams to become polluted.

11. Policy-makers in the U.S. government have long tried to write laws that encourage growth in per capita real GDP. These laws typically do one of three things, as listed below. For each of the three points, name a law or government program with that intention. **[LO 27.6]**

    a. They encourage firms to invest more in research and development in order to boost technology.

    b. They encourage individuals to save more in order to boost the physical capital stock.

    c. They encourage individuals to invest more in education in order to boost the stock of human capital.

12. Name the type of institution that is responsible for promoting a stable environment for the economy regarding each of the following situations. **[LO 27.7]**

    a. Someone steals your car, but is caught.

    b. You claim that your employer violated the terms of your employment contract.

Endnotes

1. Calculated using the series at http://data.worldbank.org/indicator/NY.GDP.PCAP.CD.

2. https://fred.stlouisfed.org/series/A939RX0Q048SBEA.

3. Barry Bosworth and Susan M. Collins, "Accounting for Growth: Comparing China and India," *Journal of Economic Perspectives* 22, no. 1 (Winter 2008): 45–66, https://www.aeaweb.org/articles?id=10.1257/jep.22.1.45.

4. Xavier Sala-i-Martin, "The World Distribution of Income: Falling Poverty and . . . Convergence, Period," *The Quarterly Journal of Economics* 121, no. 2 (2006): 351–97.

5. Robert Lucas, "On the Mechanics of Economic Development," *Journal of Monetary Economics* 22 (1988), p. 5.

6. http://www.tradingeconomics.com/united-states/personal-savings.

7. http://www.nytimes.com/2015/05/20/business/economy/american-innovation-rests-on-weak-foundation.html; http://www.aaas.org/page/historical-trends-federal-rd; data from World Bank and Bureau of Labor Statistics.

Part Eight

The Economy in the Short and Long Run

The three chapters in Part 8 will introduce you to . . .

a basic model of the entire economy. The preceding four chapters introduced the key economic concepts used to measure the health of the economy and how the economy changes over time. Now, we'll put the pieces together.

Chapter 28, "Aggregate Expenditure," focuses on the forces responsible for recessions and booms. The chapter develops a model of *aggregate expenditure,* which shows how an economy can get "stuck" producing below potential output. We build intuition without describing a complete model of the economy. To keep things simple, the chapter investigates what happens when the price level doesn't change in the short run.

Chapter 29, "Aggregate Demand and Aggregate Supply," introduces a more complete framework that describes the state of the national economy as a whole. All of the transactions in the economy—from the snack you bought on the way to class to the purchase of new computer servers by Amazon—can be represented by a single demand curve, called *aggregate demand.* On the other side, everything that firms produce is represented by a single supply curve, called *aggregate supply.* We can use these two curves, together, to investigate changes in the entire economy, through booms and busts. Aggregate demand and aggregate supply are the main concepts used in macroeconomics to provide fundamental insights into changes in the broader economy.

Using the aggregate demand/aggregate supply model, we can start to analyze how policy choices affect the national economy. Government decisions about taxes and spending make up *fiscal policy,* which is the focus of Chapter 30, "Fiscal Policy." The chapter compares the effects of taxes and government spending on the economy. It turns out that one dollar of government spending doesn't add just one dollar to overall GDP. Thanks to the effect of a multiplier, when the government spends money or changes taxes, the effect of the dollar gets magnified throughout the economy. If you understand the role of the multiplier, you're a long way toward understanding what policy can and can't do.

Chapter

28

Aggregate Expenditure

Learning Objectives

LO 28.1 Identify the factors that affect the consumption component of aggregate expenditure.

LO 28.2 Identify the factors that affect the investment component of aggregate expenditure.

LO 28.3 Identify the factors that affect the government spending component of aggregate expenditure.

LO 28.4 Identify the factors that affect the net exports component of aggregate expenditure.

LO 28.5 Describe autonomous expenditure and outline the simplifications made in the aggregate expenditure model.

LO 28.6 Describe the difference between planned and actual aggregate expenditure and show their relationship graphically.

LO 28.7 Show how to find equilibrium aggregate expenditure when given the relationship between planned aggregate expenditure and actual aggregate expenditure.

LO 28.8 Explain the importance of the aggregate expenditure equilibrium model to understanding the behavior of the economy.

LO 28.9 Illustrate how any initial change in aggregate expenditure can have a multiplier effect on the overall level of aggregate expenditure.

THE BIG CRASH

In the fall of 1929, a famous economist, Irving Fisher, remarked, "Stock prices have reached what looks like a permanently high plateau." Unfortunately, Fisher could not have been more wrong. Shortly after Fisher's optimistic prediction, stock prices in the United States started plummeting, bottoming out in July 1932 at a level 90 percent below the high of September 1929. Millions of Americans lost their investments. Worse yet, the stock market crash was followed by a devastating drop in output, employment, and prices in the United States and around the world, known as the Great Depression.

709

© General Photographic Agency/Stringer/Getty Images

Bill O'Reilly, a pundit on Fox News, recalls: "My parents were children during the Great Depression of the 1930's, and it scarred them. Especially my father, who saw destitution in his Brooklyn, New York, neighborhood: adults standing in so-called 'bread lines,' children begging in the streets."[1] The Great Depression started in 1929 and the worst part lasted through 1933, but it took over a decade for the economy to recover.

In contrast, the Great Recession of 2007–2009 was another sharp, global economic downturn, but it was shorter and less severe than what happened in the 1930s. As O'Reilly describes the biggest economic downturn since the Great Depression: "Fast forward to the severe recession of 2008, when millions of Americans lost jobs and equity in their homes. No bread lines, but much pain."[2]

Depressions and recessions are puzzling. People are *willing* to work at the prevailing wage, but they can't find a job. Firms can supply more output, but there simply isn't enough demand. Workers lose their jobs, machines run idle, inventories accumulate, and output falls sharply. A lot of people suffer.

It's no surprise that economists want to know why things go so wrong. More importantly, they want to know what policymakers can do to get an economy back on track. The classical economists of the day could not provide an answer—they assumed that markets would always reach equilibrium through increases or decreases in the relevant prices. They were like physicists who forgot to account for the role of friction in the mechanical transmission of energy.

In the 1930s, however, the British economist John Maynard Keynes (pronounced "canes") introduced price frictions into a model of the economy. That idea offered an explanation for downturns that focused on problems caused by declining aggregate demand, and it was revolutionary. Macroeconomists have now extended many of Keynes's original insights, and his basic ideas continue to help explain economic booms and busts in the United States and abroad.

In this chapter we'll use a simple model to explore Keynes's explanation for economic downturns. The model shows how it's possible for an economy to get stuck at a short-run level of output that lies below potential. In human terms, the model explains how widespread unemployment can persist, even when people are ready and willing to work. The model also points to practical solutions to help economies escape a recessionary rut.

The Components of Aggregate Expenditure

When economies face downturns, both spending and production fall. To understand that drop in spending, we need to start with the components of aggregate expenditure. Chapter 24, "Measuring GDP," showed that all activity in the economy can be summarized by gross domestic product (GDP), and one way of calculating GDP is by aggregating all expenditure in the economy. **Aggregate expenditure** can then be divided into four primary components of spending: consumption (C), investment (I), government spending (G), and net exports (NX).

If we use Y to denote aggregate expenditure, we can write the relationship simply as Y = C + I + G + NX. This tells us that everything that was produced must have been purchased by a combination of households, firms, the government, and foreigners. The equation is just an accounting identity. It doesn't depend on assumptions about the behavior of decision makers, and it can't tell us much about how the economy actually works.

To get further, we need to understand how the key players in the economy—especially households and firms—make decisions. With that knowledge, we can start to build a simple model of the economy. The model starts with a set of statements that we know to be true (like Y = C + I + G + NX). Then we'll use our understanding of economic relationships to make things more realistic. As Albert Einstein reportedly said, we're going to build a model that tries to "make things as simple as possible, but no simpler."

aggregate expenditure (Y)
the level of aggregate expenditure that consists of consumption, government spending, net exports, and actual investment by firms

Consumption

LO 28.1 Identify the factors that affect the consumption component of aggregate expenditure.

The starting point is *consumption.* Consumption makes up two-thirds to three-quarters of GDP in most countries. Because it accounts for such a large share, consumption accounts for much of the variation in aggregate economic activity.

You probably already understand the basics of consumption since you make consumption choices every day. You decide how much to spend on food, travel, entertainment, transportation, and housing. You also decide how much to save for later (that is, you choose how much *not* to consume now). Like most people making these choices, you likely consider four factors:

1. current income
2. wealth
3. expected future income
4. the interest rate on saving and borrowing

These basic factors are the building blocks of our model of consumption expenditures.

Current income

People who earn more tend to consume more. For example, most investment bankers live in nicer houses and drive fancier cars than college professors do. Of course, the exact relationship between earnings and consumption depends on the details: It matters whether your income will *always* be high or if it's likely to fall in the future. If you win the lottery this year, for example, you might save a big chunk of the winnings to spend later when your income goes back to normal. Alternatively, a young family may want to borrow to buy a house or car early on, especially if they expect that their future income will grow over time.

These details matter a lot when considering particular households. They matter much less when thinking about the *basic patterns* that hold across all households. When we think about households in general, we can streamline things by assuming that households simply consume a constant fraction of disposable income (income after taxes and transfers). This fraction is called

marginal propensity to consume (MPC)
the amount that consumption increases when after-tax income increases by $1

the **marginal propensity to consume**, abbreviated as MPC. If a household receives an extra $10,000 in disposable income, for example, and its marginal propensity to consume is 60 percent (MPC = 0.6), then the household will consume $6,000 (= 0.60 × $10,000) of the extra disposable income. The marginal propensity to consume plays a central role in the model of aggregate demand that we're developing.

Wealth

Wealth takes many forms. Examples of wealth include money held in savings and checking accounts; holdings of stocks, bonds, and mutual funds; and the value of houses. From those assets are subtracted the amount of any debt, such as credit card debt, mortgages (home loans), and student loans.

Wealthier households tend to spend more, so we assume that increased wealth leads to increased consumption (and decreased wealth leads to lower consumption). That should make sense. After all, higher-wealth households can afford to consume more for any given level of income. This is confirmed by the evidence: When the level of savings rises in an economy, aggregate consumption tends to rise as well. This occurs because households can dip into savings to fund consumption rather than being limited by their income. Indeed, changes in stock-market and housing wealth have driven some of the most dramatic movements in consumption in the past 20 years.

Often policymakers also want to know which households are likely to have a larger marginal propensity to consume. As we've noted, income and wealth matter. It is commonly assumed, for example, that poor households have a relatively high marginal propensity to consume out of income. Why? Because, by definition, poor households often do not have enough income. As a result, they are likely to spend a relatively big share of any income they receive. Recent research finds a surprising pattern: Some wealthy households also act like they're poor. To see why, read the Real Life box "The wealthy hand-to-mouth."

Real Life
The wealthy hand-to-mouth

The expression "living hand-to-mouth" means that you're spending all of your paycheck, with nothing left over to save. Not surprisingly, many poor families live hand-to-mouth. One implication is that, as a group, poor families have a high marginal propensity to consume out of disposable income.

But you don't have to *be* poor to *feel* poor. Economists from Princeton University and New York University found that some relatively wealthy people are living hand-to-mouth too. About a third of U.S. households are estimated to live hand-to-mouth, but only one-third of those are actually poor. The other two-thirds are relatively wealthy but still have to watch their budgets carefully.

These wealthy hand-to-mouth households are often young; many have assets that are tied up in forms that are hard to draw upon, such as a house or a retirement account, for example. As a result, they feel financially squeezed. They too have a high marginal propensity to consume out of disposable income.

This means that wealth alone is not a good predictor of the marginal propensity to consume—nor of how wealthy families feel. Figure 28-1 shows that the same pattern is even more pronounced in other countries. In each country, most people "living hand-to-mouth" are actually relatively wealthy.

FIGURE 28-1

Percentage of people living hand-to-mouth in various countries

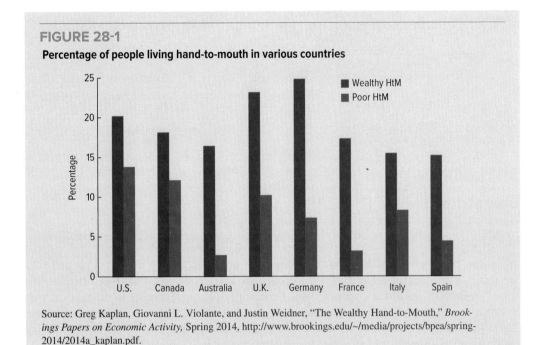

Source: Greg Kaplan, Giovanni L. Violante, and Justin Weidner, "The Wealthy Hand-to-Mouth," *Brookings Papers on Economic Activity,* Spring 2014, http://www.brookings.edu/~/media/projects/bpea/spring-2014/2014a_kaplan.pdf.

Expected future income

Most people try to keep their spending fairly steady even when their income rises and falls. (This is referred to as the desire to "smooth consumption" over time.) As a result, expected future income influences current consumption in much the same way that current income does:

- If you expect your income to rise in the future (specifically, expected future disposable income), you tend to be more willing to borrow or to dip into savings in order to fund a higher level of consumption today.

- Similarly, if you expect your income to be lower in the future, you tend to consume less now in order to save more for later.

As a result, there is a positive relationship between expected future income in an economy and current aggregate consumption.

The interest rate

The **interest rate** is also known as the price of money. For savers, it is the price received for letting a bank use money for a specified period of time. For borrowers, it is the price of using money for a specified period of time. Thus, the interest rate determines the financial return on saving and the cost of borrowing. The interest rate (specifically, the "real" interest rate, which is the interest rate adjusted for inflation) influences consumption:

- A higher interest rate generally encourages saving, which in turn decreases consumption.

- In the same way, a high interest rate discourages people from borrowing on credit cards and taking other loans to pay for purchases; this decreases consumption too.

Therefore, there is a negative relationship between the interest rate and consumption on an aggregate level.

Table 28-1 shows how increases in these determinants directly affect consumption. We can usually predict whether an increase in a determinant will increase or decrease consumption.

interest rate
the price of money, typically expressed as a percentage per dollar per unit of time; for savers, it is the price received for letting a bank use money for a specified period of time; for borrowers, it is the price of using money for a specified period of time

TABLE 28-1
Determinants of aggregate consumption

Increase in determinant	Effect on consumption (C)
Current income	Increase
Wealth	Increase
Expected future income	Increase
Interest rate	Decrease

Investment

LO 28.2 Identify the factors that affect the investment component of aggregate expenditure.

When you hear people talking about investing, they are often talking about buying and selling shares in the stock market. But when economists talk about investing, they often use the word "investment" in a more specific way. Economists use "investment" to refer to changes in capital—including changes in machines, structures, software, and even residential housing. The determinants of investment are thus the factors that change the benefits and costs of adding physical capital—specifically, expected profitability, the interest rate, and business taxes.

Expected profitability

Profit-maximizing firms, not surprisingly, make capital investments they think will increase profits. (And they avoid capital investments that they think will lose money.) When firms expect their projects will be profitable, they will invest more to grow their businesses. Therefore, there is a positive relationship between expected profitability and the current level of aggregate investment.

Not surprisingly, innovations that open up new spheres for profit usually spur high rates of investment in physical capital. For example, the information-technology boom of the 1990s was accompanied by a rapid increase in investment in the form of computer equipment and software.

The interest rate

One big way that businesses invest is by borrowing financial capital. The interest rate (again, the "real" interest rate, adjusted for inflation) can be thought of as the cost of borrowing. When the cost of borrowing decreases, the amount of borrowing increases. Therefore, there is a negative relationship between the interest rate and the amount of aggregate investment in an economy.

In fact, this relationship exists even if firms finance their investment by retaining earnings from their profits (rather than distributing them to shareholders). A lower interest rate reduces the returns that investors expect, which encourages firms to keep more funds for investment rather than distribute them.

In the same way, investment in housing is stimulated by a lower interest rate: When the interest rate is lower, it's less expensive for households to take out mortgages to fund home purchases. A lower interest rate generally results in an increase in mortgage borrowing.

(In practice, lenders may charge somewhat different interest rates, depending on the specific context. It's usually okay, though, to simplify by talking about "the interest rate," as a way to capture the role of interest rates in general.)

Business taxes

Business taxes reduce profits. Thus, when business taxes rise, firms have less incentive to invest. This dynamic creates a negative relationship between business taxes and aggregate investment in an economy.

Table 28-2 shows how increases in these determinants directly affect investment. We can usually predict whether an increase in a determinant will increase or decrease investment.

Increase in determinant	Effect on investment (I)
Interest rate	Decrease
Expected profitability	Increase
Business taxes	Decrease

Government spending

LO 28.3 Identify the factors that affect the government spending component of aggregate expenditure.

Government spending is not like the other components of aggregate expenditure. It is different because the government chooses how much to spend based on beliefs about what citizens need (roads, schools, and the like). The government may also choose spending levels as a way to stimulate or restrain the economy. (That is, government spending is a tool of fiscal policy.) Therefore, in the short run, government spending is not directly affected by standard macroeconomic factors such as aggregate income, wealth, and the interest rate, so we take government spending as given in our model of aggregate expenditure.

Note that transfer payments to individuals are not included in government spending. Transfer payments include spending on unemployment insurance and Social Security benefits—payments the government makes to households without receiving any goods or services in return. Those transfer payments are often negatively correlated with aggregate income. For instance, more people tend to qualify for unemployment benefits during recessions (a time when aggregate income is relatively low and unemployment rises).

Net exports

LO 28.4 Identify the factors that affect the net exports component of aggregate expenditure.

The *net exports* component of aggregate expenditure is exports (the value of goods and services sold to foreign consumers) minus imports (the value of goods and services purchased domestically from foreign producers). The factors that increase net exports, therefore, are forces that increase exports and decrease imports. These forces are domestic income, foreign income, exchange rates, tastes for foreign goods, and trade policies.

Domestic income
Domestic income is the income earned by those living within a country. As domestic income rises, so does consumption.

- An increase in consumption generally leads to an increase in purchases of imports (along with increased purchases of goods and services produced domestically).
- When imports increase, net exports decrease (because imports are subtracted out in the calculation of net exports).

Thus, domestic income and net exports are usually negatively related.

Foreign income
Foreign income is income earned by those living outside a country. We just saw that increases in domestic income tend to increase the consumption of imports. Similarly, increases in foreign income tend to increase exports: As income increases in a foreign economy, citizens there increase consumption of goods from outside. The result is increasing exports to the foreign economy. Therefore, foreign income and net exports are usually positively related.

TABLE 28-3
Determinants of net exports

Increase in determinant	Effect on net exports (NX)
Domestic income	Decrease
Foreign income	Increase
Exchange rates	Decrease
Tastes for foreign goods	Decrease
Trade policies	Depends

real exchange rate
the value of goods in one country expressed in terms of the same goods in another country

Exchange rates

Exchange rates—specifically, the **real exchange rate**—are discussed in detail in Chapter 35, "Open-Market Macroeconomics." For now, it is sufficient to keep in mind that the real exchange rate is the value of goods in one country expressed in terms of the same goods in another country. Real exchange rates represent conversions between the cost of foreign and domestic goods that incorporates both currency exchange rates (that is, nominal exchange rates) and differences in foreign versus domestic price levels.

When real exchange rates increase, domestic goods get more expensive relative to foreign goods. That usually leads to an increase in imports and a decrease in exports. Since imports are subtracted out when calculating net exports, real exchange rates are negatively associated with net exports.

Of course, an economy has many real exchange rates, one for each country that it does business with. Therefore, it is helpful to think of a change in real exchange rates as the direction that the overall set of exchange rates moves on average.

Tastes for foreign goods

When tastes for foreign goods increase (when people find foreign goods more attractive than they did previously), domestic consumption expenditure shifts toward consumption of imports. This shift increases imports and, as a result, decreases net exports. Therefore, tastes for foreign goods are negatively associated with the level of net exports.

Trade policies

In part, the effects of trade policies are reflected in exchange rates and other macroeconomic variables rather than influencing the level of net exports directly. That said, trade policies can be analyzed on a case-by-case basis to determine whether they have a direct effect on net exports as well.

Table 28-3 shows how increases in these determinants directly affect net exports. We can usually predict whether an increase in a determinant will increase or decrease net exports.

Table 28-4 summarizes the determinants of all the components of aggregate expenditure. It's important to keep in mind that these relationships hold "all else being equal." Also, you should recognize that changes in macroeconomic factors can have both direct and indirect effects. For example, an increase in interest rates affects consumption and investment directly and also affects consumption indirectly because higher interest rates affect levels of wealth and expected future income.

Autonomous expenditure and simplifying assumptions

autonomous expenditure
expenditure that is independent of the current level of aggregate income in the economy

LO 28.5 Describe autonomous expenditure and outline the simplifications made in the aggregate expenditure model.

In the analysis that follows, we distinguish between sources of expenditure that depend on income and those that do not. **Autonomous expenditure** is expenditure that is not affected by

TABLE 28-4

Summarizing all determinants of aggregate expenditure

This chart summarizes Tables 28-1 through 28-3. It shows at a glance how increases in the determinants of aggregate expenditure directly affect all components of aggregate expenditure. We can usually predict an increase or decrease.

Increase in determinant	Effect on C	Effect on I	Effect on G	Effect on NX	Effect on aggregate expenditure (Y)
Domestic income	Increase	—	—	Decrease	Generally increase
Wealth	Increase	—	—	—	Increase
Expected future income	Increase	—	—	—	Increase
Interest rate	Decrease	Decrease	—	—	Decrease
Expected profitability	—	Increase	—	—	Increase
Business taxes	—	Decrease	—	—	Decrease
Foreign income	—	—	—	Increase	Increase
Exchange rates	—	—	—	Decrease	Decrease
Tastes for foreign goods	—	—	—	Decrease	Decrease
Trade policies	—	—	—	Depends	Depends

the current level of income in the economy. In general, consumption expenditure changes when aggregate income changes. But there is also some baseline level of consumption that is insensitive to income. After all, households need to consume some basics (basic food and housing, for example) even if they have zero income. This "basics" part is autonomous expenditure. This distinction will become important when we start graphing changes in aggregate expenditure.

In the previous discussion, net exports are also a function of aggregate income, so it follows that net exports would not be classified as autonomous expenditure. To simplify things and focus on the most important macroeconomic relationships, however, we will treat net exports as autonomous expenditure.

✓CONCEPT CHECK

- ☐ What happens to the level of consumption in an economy when interest rates decrease? **[LO 28.1]**
- ☐ What happens to the level of (planned) investment in an economy when businesses become more cautious regarding future profitability? **[LO 28.2]**
- ☐ Suppose that business taxes decrease in an economy. Which components of aggregate expenditure are directly affected? **[LO 28.2]**
- ☐ What happens to the level of government spending in an economy when the level of wealth in an economy increases? **[LO 28.3]**
- ☐ What happens to the level of net exports in an economy when other countries experience rapid economic growth? **[LO 28.4]**
- ☐ In reality, do net exports count as autonomous expenditure? What about in our aggregate expenditure model? **[LO 28.5]**

Aggregate Expenditure Equilibrium and the Keynesian Cross

The Great Depression of the 1930s was the longest-lasting economic crisis in U.S. history, so it's not surprising that economists have spent a lot of time trying to understand it. Millions of families lost their wealth; almost half of U.S. banks failed. At the worst point, one in four workers was unemployed. As the U.S. economy reeled, other parts of the world suffered too. International trade fell by a third. Economists couldn't figure out how to help get people back to work, and the United States remained in a downturn through the 1930s.

In Britain, the economist John Maynard Keynes made the case that insufficient spending was the main culprit. He argued that low spending could explain how economies got stuck in a pattern of output and income below their long-run productive capacity—that is, below potential GDP. Attention then turned to the components of aggregate expenditure described in the previous section. The questions were: How can aggregate expenditure be increased? And what will be the effect on the economy and unemployment?

Keynes's insight has had a lasting influence on policymakers and economists. "Keynesian" ideas were widely discussed (and often debated) during the 2007−2009 economic crisis, for example. Governments around the world have used Keynesian solutions to stimulate economies that had fallen into deep recessions. In this section, we show the core of Keynes's insight.

Actual versus planned aggregate expenditure

LO 28.6 Describe the difference between planned and actual aggregate expenditure and show their relationship graphically.

Keynes's big insight was that firms don't always produce the most they *can* at a given price. Instead, they produce what they can *sell* at a given price. So when demand is weak and prices don't fall, firms end up producing only what is demanded. The problem is that the economy could be producing more if prices adjusted. Because prices fail to adjust, the economy can get stuck below potential output. The way to see this is by looking at firms' planned and actual aggregate expenditure.

Sometimes firms are hit by surprises. That creates a difference between their planned and actual levels of investment:

- *Planned investment* is the amount that firms actively decide to put into new capital resources and inventory accumulation. Planned investment can differ from actual investment because unexpected changes in demand can cause actual inventories to be higher or lower than expected.

- *Actual investment* is the amount of new capital investment and actual inventory changes. Changes in inventories are included in investment, so when firms draw down existing inventories, actual inventory investment is negative. And when firms accumulate inventories, actual inventory investment is positive.

Keynes recognized that the difference between planned and actual inventories is a measure of unexpected slackness in demand. If actual inventories exceed planned inventories, the firms' managers must have anticipated higher demand than actually materialized. In an effort to cut inventories back down to planned levels, firms should then cut production and slow orders from other suppliers. We can summarize their decisions in Table 28-5.

As the first relationship shows, ending up with more actual inventories than planned is a signal that demand is weaker than anticipated. Firms then adjust by reducing production.[3] Over time, firms adjust to macroeconomic conditions such that planned and actual inventories align exactly (and there is zero unplanned inventory expenditure).

TABLE 28-5

How actual and planned inventories affect production decisions

Inventory relationship	Production decision
If actual inventories > planned inventories	Reduce production
If actual inventories < planned inventories	Increase production
If actual inventories = planned inventories	Maintain current production

Putting the pieces together, we can decompose **planned aggregate expenditure (PAE)**—the level of aggregate expenditure that consists of consumption, planned investment, government spending, and net exports—into two parts: One part depends on income and the other part depends on all other factors (real interest rates, wealth, and taxes). We can express those two parts in equation format:

EQUATION 28-1 $$PAE = A + bY$$

where

A = a constant that represents the autonomous sources of spending—those that are not directly influenced by income,

b = a positive coefficient that relates spending to national income, and

Y = national income.

In this equation, A accounts for a diverse set of factors, including real interest rates, financial and housing wealth, government spending, export demand, and taxes. In some versions of the model, b will simply be equal to the marginal propensity to consume (MPC). In more realistic versions, b might also capture the impact of income on net exports or the tendency for taxes net of transfer payments to rise and fall with income.

Figure 28-2 is a graphic representation of the planned aggregate expenditure equation. The sloped line is the **planned aggregate expenditure curve**. The intercept of the line at the y-axis is the level of autonomous expenditures, A. The slope, b, is the response of planned aggregate expenditure to changes in income.

planned aggregate expenditure (PAE) the level of aggregate expenditure that consists of consumption, planned investment, government spending, and net exports

planned aggregate expenditure curve planned aggregate expenditure as a function of actual aggregate expenditure, holding all other factors constant

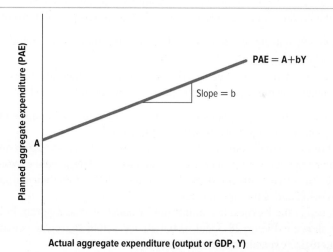

FIGURE 28-2

Planned aggregate expenditure This figure shows planned aggregate expenditure as a function of income.

POTENTIALLY CONFUSING

Aggregate expenditure. National income. National production. Total output. GDP. Y.
What's the difference among these terms? None. For our purposes in this chapter, they
are all the same.

In the "Production equals expenditure equals income" section of Chapter 24,
"Measuring GDP," we showed that these concepts are equivalent. We get the same
number for gross domestic product (GDP) whether we measure all the expenditure or
the income in an economy. We showed then that

$$\text{National production} = \text{National expenditure} = \text{National income}$$

This is an important simplification, but it is also potentially confusing because there are
many interchangeable terms. We have noted that national production and total output
refer to the same thing. Further, GDP = Y, and Y also refers to national income—which
is also aggregate expenditure, which is also national expenditure!

One important difference would arise if we consider international investment.
Then, the national income of the United States includes the income of U.S. companies
earned abroad (but it excludes earnings by foreign companies from sales in the United
States). We discuss the implications of this consideration in Chapter 35, "Open-Market
Macroeconomics."

In this chapter, however, we simplify by assuming that GDP = Y = National production
= Total output = National expenditure = Aggregate expenditure = National income. To
reduce confusion, we aim here to use Y (instead of GDP) and mainly discuss in terms of
changes in "aggregate expenditure." Just know that all of these terms refer to the same
thing.

Keynesian equilibrium

LO 28.7 Show how to find equilibrium aggregate expenditure when given the relationship
between planned aggregate expenditure and actual aggregate expenditure.

Given our description of planned aggregate expenditure (PAE), we are now ready to develop
Keynes's fundamental insight for how economies can get stuck producing less than potential
output. Keep in mind that the *only* difference between planned aggregate expenditure, PAE, and
actual output, Y, is the difference between planned and actual inventory investment.

Recall the production decisions relating to actual versus planned inventories:

- If actual inventories exceed planned inventories, then firms should cut production given
  the unexpected drop in demand.

- Conversely, when actual inventories fall short of planned inventories, firms get a signal
  that demand is higher than they expected; they should respond by increasing production.

Applying this mechanism to planned aggregate expenditure, we can see the effect our inventory
relationships have on output, as shown in Table 28-6.

Keynesian equilibrium
a situation in which
planned aggregate
expenditure is equal
to actual aggregate
expenditure

The last of these conditions characterizes what we call a **Keynesian equilibrium**—a situation
in which planned aggregate expenditure is equal to actual aggregate expenditure. It is an equilibrium in the sense that firms no longer have a desire to change their output in response to a gap
between planned and actual inventories.

We can depict the Keynesian equilibrium by adding to the diagram in Figure 28-2. The new
diagram is shown in Figure 28-3 and, as before, has actual aggregate expenditure on one axis and
planned aggregate expenditure on the other axis.

TABLE 28-6

How actual and planned inventories affect output

Inventory relationship	Implication	Effect on Y
If actual inventories > planned inventories	$Y > PAE$	Decrease in Y
If actual inventories < planned inventories	$Y < PAE$	Increase in Y
If actual inventories = planned inventories	$Y = PAE$	No change in Y

We can find the Keynesian equilibrium by drawing an additional 45-degree line representing all of the points where planned and actual aggregate expenditure are equal, or $PAE = Y$. Such a line represents all of the possible equilibrium points. To find the particular equilibrium that emerges, we look at where the two lines intersect. (In the new figure, the $PAE = A + bY$ line is labeled PAE_1.) The intersection of the new $PAE = Y$ line with the PAE_1 curve yields the unique equilibrium where planned aggregate expenditure is just equal to actual aggregate expenditure. We call this **equilibrium aggregate expenditure**.

In Figure 28-3, equilibrium aggregate expenditure is labeled as Y_1. As explained earlier:

- When planned aggregate expenditure (PAE_1) is higher than actual aggregate expenditure (given by the $PAE = Y$ line), firms are surprised by the lower-than-expected inventories, and they respond by increasing production over time. (You can think of unplanned inventory investment as the vertical distance between the $PAE = Y$ line and the planned aggregate expenditure line; just make sure that you get the sign right!) The increase in production in response to lower-than-expected inventory investment is indicated by the arrowheads to the left of Y_1 on the x-axis.
- When planned aggregate expenditure (PAE_1) is less than actual aggregate expenditure or output, firms are accumulating more inventory than planned, and they will decrease production in response. This is indicated by the arrowheads to the right of Y_1 on the x-axis.

These opposing forces, indicated by the two sets of arrowheads on the x-axis, drive the economy toward the steady state described earlier, which is the level of Y that brings planned and actual aggregate expenditure together.

equilibrium aggregate expenditure
the level of aggregate expenditure where unplanned investment is equal to zero, or, equivalently, where planned aggregate expenditure is equal to actual aggregate expenditure

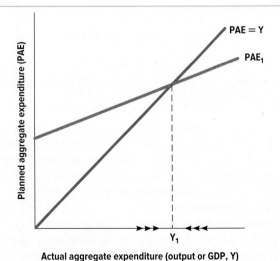

FIGURE 28-3

The equilibrium level of aggregate expenditure

FIGURE 28-4

Nonincome determinants and changes in aggregate expenditure equilibrium

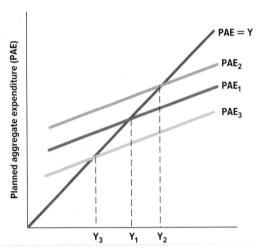

The equilibrium level of aggregate expenditure naturally depends on the levels of the nonincome determinants of the components of aggregate expenditure—interest rates, government spending, taxes, and so on:

- Economic environments that correspond to higher levels of planned aggregate expenditure (for a given level of Y) have PAE curves that are higher up on the expenditure diagram.
- Economic environments that correspond to lower levels of planned aggregate expenditure (for a given level of Y) have PAE curves that are lower on the expenditure diagram.

For example, in Figure 28-4, planned aggregate expenditure curve PAE_2 corresponds to an environment with lower interest rates, more business optimism, or some other feature that increases PAE relative to curve PAE_1. In the same way, the planned aggregate expenditure curve PAE_3 corresponds to an environment with less government spending, higher exchange rates, or some other feature that decreases PAE relative to curve PAE_1. Not surprisingly, higher PAE curves result in higher levels of equilibrium aggregate expenditure, and lower PAE curves result in lower levels of equilibrium aggregate expenditure.

Output gaps

recessionary output gap
an output gap that occurs when equilibrium aggregate expenditure is below the level needed for full employment

inflationary output gap
an output gap that occurs when equilibrium aggregate expenditure is above the level needed for full employment

LO 28.8 Explain the importance of the aggregate expenditure equilibrium model to understanding the behavior of the economy.

Crucially, the model provides an explanation for how an economy can get stuck at a level of aggregate expenditure that is either below or above the full-employment level of output.

A **recessionary output gap** occurs when equilibrium aggregate expenditure is below the level needed for full employment. Graphically, a recessionary output gap is shown by the length of the red arrow in Figure 28-5. (Full employment output is given by Y_{FE}.)

Equilibrium aggregate expenditure can also be above the level needed for full employment. In those cases, an **inflationary output gap** occurs when the current level of output is above the level corresponding to full employment. Graphically, an inflationary output gap is shown by the length of the red arrow in Figure 28-6. (Full employment output is given by Y_{FE}.)

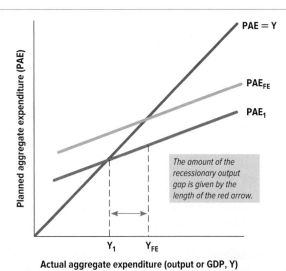

FIGURE 28-5

A recessionary output gap

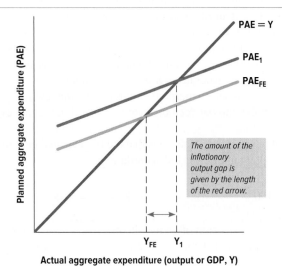

FIGURE 28-6

An inflationary output gap

The multiplier effect

LO 28.9 Illustrate how any initial change in aggregate expenditure can have a multiplier effect on the overall level of aggregate expenditure.

Another important insight that comes from the Keynesian model is that a change in autonomous expenditure (e.g., government spending) can have a *multiplier effect*. What does that mean? A **multiplier effect** is an increase in consumer spending that occurs when spending by one person causes others to spend more too, increasing the impact on the economy of the initial spending. The initial consumer spending ripples through the economy such that the overall change in output is larger than the initial change in expenditure.

To see the intuition behind the multiplier effect, consider what happens when you make a purchase: Let's say you hire a builder to construct a new deck for your backyard. The total bill is $5,000. This decision adds $5,000 to GDP, right? Yes, but that's not the end of the story.

Let's say that the builder decides to take her family on a two-week beach vacation, which she couldn't have afforded before you employed her to build your deck. The money she spends on her

multiplier effect
the increase in consumer spending that occurs when spending by one person causes others to spend more too, increasing the impact on the economy of the initial spending

vacation, including $3,000 on her family's hotel stay, also counts toward GDP. So, your decision to build a deck has added $8,000 to GDP, not $5,000. But that's still not the end of the story.

Thanks to the builder's stay at the hotel, the hotel owner feels able to buy a painting for the hotel lobby for $1,500. And so on. Your decision has sent ripples through the economy, increasing GDP by considerably more than the $5,000 you paid your builder. If you hadn't built the deck, none of this would have happened.

The multiplier effect arises because of an interaction between the consumers' response to changes in income and firms' reactions to the gap between planned and actual inventories. A positive marginal propensity to consume means that an initial change in government spending or consumption due to a change in taxes will have two effects: It will affect aggregate expenditure directly *and* it will start a cycle in which changes in expenditure cause changes in consumption, which in turn cause changes in expenditure, and so on. When this multiplier process finally comes to a halt, the economy has returned to a Keynesian equilibrium where unplanned aggregate expenditure is equal to zero, or, equivalently, where planned aggregate expenditure equals output.

Mathematically, with the help of a simple numerical example we can see how the multiplier effect works in our model. In particular, suppose that initially Y = PAE and then an increase in government expenditure causes PAE to increase above Y by $100. As a result, actual inventory investment is $100 less than planned inventory investment, and firms would respond by increasing output by $100. But the process doesn't stop there. Why? Because the increased output increases incomes by $100, and we know that b fraction of the increased incomes get spent, so that PAE is now $b \times \$100$ above Y. Firms again respond—this time by increasing output by $b \times \$100$. That increase then generates $b \times b \times \$100$ of additional consumption spending, so that firms once again find themselves increasing output, this time by $b \times b \times \$100$. This process continues, and eventually the gap between planned and actual aggregate expenditure shrinks to almost nothing.

The surprising result of the example above is that the final change in output will be larger than one-for-one. In the example, output changed according to:

$$\Delta Y = \$100 + b \times \$100 + b^2 \times \$100 + b^3 \times \$100 + \ldots = \$100 \times \left(1 + b + b^2 + b^3 + \ldots\right)$$

The sum in the parentheses is the sum of an infinite geometric series, which for $b < 1$ is simply equal to $1/(1 - b)$. Thus, the final change in output above is equal to

EQUATION 28-2
$$\Delta Y = \$100 \times \frac{1}{1 - b}$$

If, for example, $b = 0.8$, then $1 \div (1 - b) = 5$. So, the final change in output would be *five times* as large as the initial change in aggregate expenditure. The factor by which output increases in response to an initial change in aggregate expenditure is known as the **expenditure multiplier**.

expenditure multiplier
the factor by which output increases in response to an initial change in aggregate expenditure

The expenditure multiplier can also be seen graphically. The multiplier effect is illustrated by the fact that the distance between old and new equilibrium values of Y is greater than the distance between the corresponding old and new PAE curves. In Figure 28-7, the overall change in equilibrium aggregate expenditure is given by the length of the red horizontal arrow. Likewise, the initial change in planned aggregate expenditure is given by the length of the blue vertical arrow. The strength of the multiplier effect depends on the relative sizes of the two arrows.

The expenditure multiplier turns out to simply equal the length of the red horizontal arrow divided by the length of the blue vertical arrow. In the example given in the figure, the red arrow is longer than the blue arrow, implying an expenditure multiplier greater than 1.

The expenditure multiplier is a powerful idea in macroeconomics. As shown in the example above, the expenditure multiplier is critical in determining the impact of government spending on the economy. Knowing the size of the multiplier is important for economic policy. The

FIGURE 28-7

Overall change in equilibrium aggregate expenditure   The multiplier can be calculated as the length of the red horizontal arrow divided by the length of the blue vertical arrow. In the case drawn here, the multiplier is greater than 1.

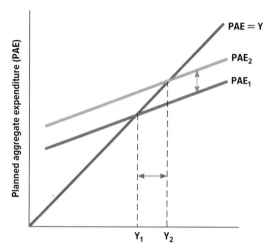

Actual aggregate expenditure (output or GDP, Y)

multiplier's size is an empirical matter, and it is a major subject of study. If the multiplier is large, even limited policy interventions can have big impacts.

The 2008 recession gives one example of how complex it can be to figure out how the multiplier effect works in the real world. Christina Romer of the University of California, who at the time was an economic advisor to the president, suggested a huge increase in government spending; other economists, such as Robert Barro at Harvard University, argued for tax cuts. The central focus of their debate was on the size of the multiplier for government spending. To see how this debate played out, read the Real Life box "The great 2009 multiplier debate."

Real Life

The great 2009 multiplier debate

Ask different economists about the size of the multipliers for government spending and tax cuts and you'll get different answers. Differing views on the size of the multipliers lead to disagreements between experts on how to design the best fiscal policy:

- On the optimistic end, the Congressional Budget Office predicted that the government-spending multiplier on "shovel-ready" projects in the 2009 stimulus bill, like building roads or schools, would be 1.5.
- More pessimistically, Robert Barro, an economist at Harvard University, argued that the government-spending multiplier was below 1. He thought that each dollar of government spending would add no more than 80 cents to GDP.

In the grand scheme of things, 1.5 may not sound that different from 0.8, but which figure you think is more accurate makes a huge difference to what economic impact you would expect from a policy to combat the recession. The difference in the expected impact of the 2009

(continued)

stimulus under a multiplier of 1.5 versus 0.8 is about $440 billion more in GDP increases and 4 million more jobs created.

Why is there such a large difference between different estimates of the multiplier? There are two big reasons. One is that the multiplier is determined by overall economic conditions. Suppose the government employs 100 workers to build a bridge at a time when the economy is doing pretty well and most of those 100 workers would have had little trouble finding other employment. In the worst case, the workers might actually get pulled into bridge-building from another, potentially higher-priority job. In that case, the impact of government spending on GDP would be much less than if those 100 workers had been sitting at home hoping for a job.

Second, economists hotly debate whether government spending has a positive or negative impact on private-sector investment. Some argue that stimulus spending will inspire confidence in the economy and encourage firms to invest more. This would increase GDP. Others counter that government borrowing may drive up interest rates. As the government increases its demand for money in order to finance its spending, all else equal, the cost of borrowing—i.e., the interest rate—will increase too. When faced with higher interest rates, firms may choose to invest less, decreasing GDP. This phenomenon is known as *crowding out*.

Taking these and other complicating factors into account, economists argue that different *kinds* of government spending and tax cuts will have different multipliers. Should the government invest in "shovel-ready" public works or put the money into widening the food stamp program? Would it be better to cut payroll taxes or corporate taxes? The answers to these questions lie in which programs have the highest multiplier.

Sources: https://www.cbo.gov/blog; http://online.wsj.com/article/SB123258618204604599.html.

✓ CONCEPT CHECK

☐ If planned and actual aggregate expenditure are always equal, what is the slope of the planned aggregate expenditure curve? **[LO 28.6]**

☐ What is the value of unplanned investment expenditure in an aggregate expenditure equilibrium? **[LO 28.7]**

☐ What important feature of the economy does the aggregate expenditure equilibrium analysis help to explain? **[LO 28.8]**

☐ Why can an increase in spending lead to a change in aggregate expenditure that is larger than the initial increase? **[LO 28.9]**

Conclusion

Keeping the economy running at capacity is one of the most important concerns of economics. A well-running economy doesn't just mean more production—it also generates income and jobs. But sometimes the economy fails to operate as well as it could. Our focus here has been on problems connected to aggregate demand.

In order to understand why aggregate demand and fiscal policy behave the way that they do, we developed a model of aggregate expenditure in the economy. We first outlined the drivers of aggregate expenditure and then used a simplified model to show how the drivers work. That helped show why even an economy with plentiful productive resources can still get stalled and not operate at its full potential.

The aggregate expenditure equilibrium model is the main building block for understanding the demand side of the macro economy. In the next chapter, we connect aggregate demand to aggregate supply to see a broader range of options available to policymakers.

Key Terms

Summary

LO 28.1 Identify the factors that affect the consumption component of aggregate expenditure.

Other than the price level, there are a number of factors that affect the current level of aggregate consumption in an economy. Current income and consumption are positively related through the marginal propensity to consume. The levels of wealth and consumption are positively related. Expected future income and consumption are positively related. Interest rates and consumption are negatively related.

LO 28.2 Identify the factors that affect the investment component of aggregate expenditure.

Other than the price level, there are a number of factors that affect the current level of planned investment in the economy. Expected future profitability and investment are positively related. Interest rates and investment are negatively related. The level of business taxes and investment are negatively related. There is a relationship between the levels of saving and investment in an economy, but there doesn't have to be perfect parity between the two when government budgets aren't balanced and international trade is present.

LO 28.3 Identify the factors that affect the government spending component of aggregate expenditure.

The level of government spending on goods and services in an economy is an explicit policy choice and therefore is not directly determined by macroeconomic factors. That said, macroeconomic factors may enter into the policy discussion in an indirect fashion.

LO 28.4 Identify the factors that affect the net exports component of aggregate expenditure.

Other than the price level, there are a number of factors that affect the current level of net exports in an economy.

Domestic income and net exports are negatively related. Foreign income and net exports are positively related. Exchange rates and net exports are negatively related. Tastes for foreign goods and net exports are negatively related. Trade policies can have an effect on net exports, but the analysis of the relationship must be done on a case-by-case basis since increases and decreases are not always well defined.

LO 28.5 Describe autonomous expenditure and outline the simplifications made in the aggregate expenditure model.

Autonomous aggregate expenditure refers to expenditure whose level is independent of the level of current income in the economy. For the purposes of the equilibrium aggregate expenditure analysis, we assume that all categories of expenditure other than consumption are autonomous.

LO 28.6 Describe the difference between planned and actual aggregate expenditure and show their relationship graphically.

Planned aggregate expenditure is the sum of consumption, planned investment, government spending, and net exports, where planned investment is the level of investment in productive capital and strategic inventory accumulation that firms choose before aggregate expenditure is realized. Actual aggregate expenditure, by definition, is equal to aggregate output and income, and it is the sum of consumption, actual investment, government spending, and net exports. Actual investment includes not only planned investment but also unexpected investment in the form of accumulation of unsold inventory or divestiture of existing inventory. Graphically, the relationship between actual and planned aggregate expenditure results in an upward-sloping curve with a slope equal to the marginal propensity to consume.

LO 28.7 Show how to find equilibrium aggregate expenditure when given the relationship between planned aggregate expenditure and actual aggregate expenditure.

The equilibrium aggregate expenditure can be found by calculating the level of unplanned investment for various levels of output and finding the level of output where unplanned investment is equal to zero. Graphically, the level of output where planned and actual aggregate expenditure are equal can be found by drawing a 45-degree line on the planned aggregate expenditure diagram and finding the point where this 45-degree line intersects the planned aggregate expenditure curve.

LO 28.8 Explain the importance of the aggregate expenditure equilibrium model to understanding the behavior of the economy.

The aggregate expenditure equilibrium model is important because it shows how an economy can persist at a level of output that deviates from full-employment potential GDP. Specifically, the model explains how recessionary expenditure gaps can occur where equilibrium aggregate expenditure is below what is needed to sustain potential GDP. In addition, the model explains how inflationary expenditure gaps can occur where equilibrium aggregate expenditure is larger than what is needed to sustain potential GDP. Lastly, the model explicitly shows how the different parts of the model come together to create the multiplier effect of initial changes in aggregate expenditure.

LO 28.9 Illustrate how any initial change in aggregate expenditure can have a multiplier effect on the overall level of aggregate expenditure.

The determinants of the components of aggregate expenditure show that there is a circular relationship between current income and current consumption: Current income is a determinant of current consumption, but current consumption is also a determinant of current income. Therefore, any initial change to a determinant of aggregate expenditure is going to flow through to this consumption/income cycle. The result is an overall impact that is larger than the initial change. This overall impact can't be infinitely large, however, since the effect of the initial change on aggregate expenditure gets smaller with each iteration of the cycle.

Review Questions

1. What effect does an increase in current income have on current consumption? What effect does an increase in expected future income have on current consumption? **[LO 28.1]**

2. What effect does an increase in the interest rate have on current consumption? What effect does an increase in wealth have on current consumption? **[LO 28.1]**

3. How does a change in expected profitability affect aggregate investment? How does a change in business taxes affect aggregate investment? **[LO 28.2]**

4. How does a change in the interest rate affect aggregate investment? What if firms prefer to pay for investment spending out of retained earnings? Does a change in the interest rate still affect aggregate investment? **[LO 28.2]**

5. Does the amount of government spending in an economy respond directly to changes in aggregate income, wealth, or interest rates? Does it respond indirectly to changes in these variables? **[LO 28.3]**

6. What are government transfer payments? Are they included as part of the government spending component of GDP? **[LO 28.3]**

7. What happens to the level of net exports in an economy when income in that economy increases? What happens to the level of net exports in an economy when income in other economies increases? **[LO 28.4]**

8. You read in the paper that the dollar has strengthened in value relative to the euro. How is this change in the exchange rate value of the dollar likely to affect exports to Europe and imports from Europe? **[LO 28.4]**

9. Which components of aggregate expenditure do not directly depend on current income? **[LO 28.5]**

10. The investment category of GDP measures three different types of expenditures. What are they? Why is planned investment sometimes different from actual investment? **[LO 28.6]**

11. What causes a movement along the planned aggregate expenditure curve? What causes the planned aggregate expenditure curve to shift? **[LO 28.6]**

12. In a Keynesian equilibrium will the economy always be producing at its level of potential output? Why or why not? **[LO 28.7]**

13. Suppose planned aggregate expenditure is greater than actual aggregate expenditure. In this case, what do you think will happen to output over time? **[LO 28.7]**

14. Suppose the economy is experiencing a recessionary output gap. What has happened to planned aggregate expenditure? What might have caused this change? **[LO 28.8]**

15. Suppose that an increase in business confidence increases investment expenditure by one million dollars. How do you expect this increase in investment expenditure to affect equilibrium output? Will equilibrium output increase by exactly one million, more than one million, or less than one million? **[LO 28.9]**

16. Define the relationship between the expenditure multiplier and the marginal propensity to consume. If the marginal propensity to consume increases, what happens to the expenditure multiplier? **[LO 28.9]**

Problems and Applications

1. "People who earn more income tend to have higher levels of consumption spending, so the value of their marginal propensity to consume must be greater than that of lower income people." Do you think this is a true statement? Why or why not? **[LO 28.1]**

2. Do you think there is a predictable relationship between the business cycle and aggregate investment spending? Why or why not? **[LO 28.2]**

3. "During a recession more people qualify for unemployment insurance. This will increase the government spending category of GDP and help reduce the severity of the recession." Do you agree with this statement? Why or why not? **[LO 28.3]**

4. "When one country in the world falls into a recession, this tends to cause other countries to also fall into a recession." Do you agree with this statement? Why or why not? **[LO 28.4]**

5. For each of the following shocks, identify what component(s) of planned aggregate expenditure is/are directly affected and in which direction. **[LO 28.1, 28.2, 28.3, 28.4]**
   a. Tax rates increase.
   b. China experiences an economic boom.
   c. People become more optimistic regarding their future prospects.
   d. Congress decides to increase funding for education.
   e. German fashion designs become popular among celebrities.

6. Which of the following would be classified as an autonomous change to planned aggregate expenditure? **[LO 28.5]**
   a. Interest rates in an economy decrease.
   b. Current income in an economy increases.
   c. Domestic goods become more expensive relative to foreign goods.
   d. Congress decides to undertake an infrastructure repair project.

7. Consider the planned expenditure curve in Figure 28P-1. What is the level of autonomous expenditure in this economy? **[LO 28.5, 28.6]**

8. Draw a planned aggregate expenditure curve as described in the chapter. Then show what happens to

FIGURE 28P-1

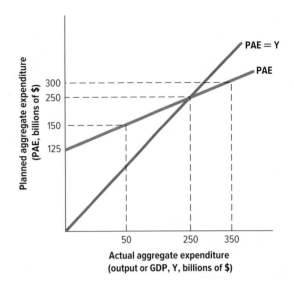

the planned aggregate expenditure curve in each of the following scenarios. **[LO 28.6]**
   a. Government spending increases.
   b. Business taxes increase.
   c. Aggregate income decreases.

9. Draw a planned aggregate expenditure curve for an economy where autonomous expenditure is $500 billion and the marginal propensity to consume is equal to 0.75. **[LO 28.6]**

10. Consider the data presented in Table 28P-1. **[LO 28.7]**
   a. What is the marginal propensity to consume for households in this economy?
   b. Based on the assumptions of our aggregate expenditure model, fill in the columns for planned investment, government spending, and net exports. What is this type of expenditure called?
   c. For each level of actual aggregate expenditure, calculate unplanned inventory investment.
   d. What is the equilibrium level of aggregate expenditure in this economy? How do you know?
   e. For each level of actual aggregate expenditure, label the future output tendency as "increase," "decrease," or "same" based on what you expect to happen to future output. What relationship does this categorization have to your answer in part *d*?

11. Suppose that an economy is at an aggregate expenditure equilibrium at an output level of $300 billion. **[LO 28.7]**

TABLE 28P-1

Actual aggregate expenditure or output (Y) (billions of $)	Consumption (C) (billions of $)	Planned investment (billions of $)	Government spending (G) (billions of $)	Net exports (NX) (billions of $)	Unplanned investment (inventory change) (billions of $)	Future output tendency
350	200	60	90	60		
400	220					
450	240					
500	260					
550	280					

TABLE 28P-2

Actual aggregate expenditure or output (Y) (billions of $)	Consumption (C) (billions of $)	Planned investment (billions of $)	Government spending (G) (billions of $)	Net exports (NX) (billions of $)	Unplanned investment (inventory change) (billions of $)
500	300	150	100	50	
600	350				
700	400				
800	450				
900	500				

a. Show this point on a planned versus actual aggregate expenditure graph.

b. Label a point on the planned aggregate expenditure curve where the economy will decrease its output next year. (To do this, pick a specific level of output that makes sense.)

c. Label a point on the planned aggregate expenditure curve where the economy will increase its output next year. (To do this, pick a specific level of output that makes sense.)

12. Consider the data presented in Table 28P-2. **[LO 28.7, 28.8]**

   a. For each level of actual aggregate expenditure, calculate unplanned inventory investment.

   b. What is the equilibrium level of aggregate expenditure in this economy? How do you know?

   c. Suppose that planned investment increases by $50 billion. What is the new equilibrium level of aggregate expenditure in this economy?

d. What is the marginal propensity to consume in this economy?

e. What is the expenditure multiplier in this economy?

13. Consider the graph in Figure 28P-2, where the full-employment level of output is given by Y_{FE} and is the equilibrium level of aggregate expenditure for curve PAE_1. **[LO 28.8]**

   a. Which planned aggregate expenditure curve will result in a recessionary output gap? Label the size of the recessionary output gap on the graph.

   b. Which planned aggregate expenditure curve will result in an inflationary output gap? Label the size of the inflationary output gap on the graph.

14. Consider the graph in Figure 28P-3. **[LO 28.9]**

   a. What is the expenditure multiplier in this economy?

   b. What is the marginal propensity to consume in this economy?

FIGURE 28P-2

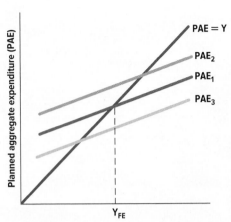

Actual aggregate expenditure (output or GDP, Y)

FIGURE 28P-3

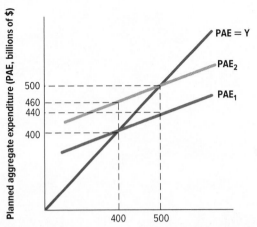

Actual aggregate expenditure (output or GDP, Y, billions of $)

15. In each of the following scenarios, describe and calculate the overall effect on aggregate expenditure. **[LO 28.9]**

   a. A recent stock market boom has increased household wealth by $20 billion, which increases consumption by $12 billion, and the marginal propensity to consume in the economy is equal to 0.6.

   b. Rising interest rates reduce domestic consumption by $4 billion and reduce investment by $7 billion, and the marginal propensity to consume in the economy is equal to 0.7.

Endnotes

1. Bill O'Reilly, "Welfare Nation," *Newsletter*, October 31, 2013, www.billoreilly.com/newslettercolumn?pid=41754.

2. Ibid.

3. When actual inventories are instead smaller than planned, it means that demand is stronger than anticipated. Then firms adjust by increasing production.

Math Essentials: Algebra and Aggregate Expenditure

Learning Objectives

LO G.1 Represent the components of planned aggregate expenditure algebraically and use these expressions to find equilibrium aggregate expenditure.

LO G.2 Illustrate the multiplier effect of aggregate expenditure using the algebraic form of the aggregate expenditure equilibrium.

In Chapter 28, "Aggregate Expenditure," we showed how to find the equilibrium level of aggregate expenditure by analyzing planned versus actual aggregate expenditure graphically. We can also solve for equilibrium aggregate expenditure algebraically if we make some assumptions about what functional form the components of aggregate expenditure take.

Using Algebra to Find Equilibrium Aggregate Expenditure

LO G.1 Represent the components of planned aggregate expenditure algebraically and use these expressions to find equilibrium aggregate expenditure.

The aggregate expenditure model that we developed in Chapter 28, "Aggregate Expenditure," implies that the functions for consumption, planned investment, government spending, and net exports depend on factors such as income, interest rates, and wealth. It is possible to include all of these factors in a model of the economy, but it helps to start by simplifying. We'll begin with a simplified model of the economy in which consumption depends only on disposable income plus a constant—the constant captures the roles of all other components of aggregate expenditure.

Consider a model economy, for example, represented by the following values for planned consumption, investment, government spending, net exports, and taxes net of transfers:

$$C = 0.75 \, (Y - T) + 30$$
$$I_{planned} = 50$$
$$G = 100$$
$$NX = 30$$
$$T = 100$$

(To be closer to reality, think of these numbers as representing billions of dollars.) Note that the expressions for planned investment, government spending, and net exports are constant values. The expression for consumption, on the other hand, has not only a constant component but also a component that depends on the level of current income in the economy.

We can now combine the expressions to find planned aggregate expenditure:

$$PAE = Y_{planned} = C + I_{planned} + G + NX = 0.75(Y - 100) + 30 + 50 + 100 + 30$$

$$PAE = 0.75Y + 135$$

As stated earlier, the equilibrium level of aggregate expenditure is the level where planned and actual aggregate expenditure are equal. In algebraic terms, the equilibrium condition translates to the following:

EQUATION G-1 $$PAE = Y$$

We can solve this equation for Y by plugging in the expression we found for planned aggregate expenditure:

$$0.75Y + 135 = Y$$
$$0.25Y = 135$$
$$Y = 540$$

Solving the equation tells us that the equilibrium level of aggregate expenditure in this economy is $540 billion.

We can generalize this analysis by separating the components of planned expenditure into those that depend on output, Y, and those that do not. Let A denote all of the components of planned expenditure that do not depend on output, and let b denote the slope of the planned expenditure function against output. (In the previous example, $A = 135$, and $b = 0.75$.) The Keynesian equilibrium requires that planned aggregate expenditure equals output, or:

EQUATION G-2 $$Y = PAE = A + bY$$

We can now find the equilibrium level of aggregate expenditure by performing the same steps as before:

$$Y = PAE = A + bY$$
$$Y - bY = A$$
$$Y(1 - b) = A$$
$$Y = \frac{A}{1 - b}$$

Using this expression, we can find the equilibrium level of aggregate expenditure by simply plugging in the relevant values for the constant components of aggregate expenditure and the slope coefficient on income in an economy.

Using algebra to derive the expenditure multiplier

LO G.2 Illustrate the multiplier effect of aggregate expenditure using the algebraic form of the aggregate expenditure equilibrium.

One of the main purposes of the equilibrium aggregate expenditure model is to determine the overall impact of an initial change in a component of aggregate expenditure. Therefore, it makes sense to extend our algebra to analyze this impact as well.

Writing our equilibrium aggregate expenditure expression in changes rather than levels form gives the following:

EQUATION G-3 $$\Delta Y = \frac{1}{1 - b} \Delta A$$

As before, a $1 change in autonomous expenditure results in a $1/(1 − b)$ change in equilibrium aggregate expenditure.

Continuing the model economy used above, we can analyze the impact of a $10 billion increase in government spending by plugging the relevant values into Equation G-3:

$$\Delta Y = \frac{1}{1 - 0.75} \times 10 = \frac{1}{0.25} \times 10 = 4 \times 10 = 40$$

Note that many of the terms in Equation G-3 drop out because all changes other than the change in G are equal to zero. In this case, equilibrium aggregate expenditure increases by $40 billion, from $540 billion to $580 billion.

What if we instead considered a $10 billion decrease in taxes? Will this increase output by the same amount as the $10 billion increase in government spending described above? The answer is no. Each $1 reduction of taxes increases disposable income by $1, but only 0.75 times (which is the marginal propensity to consume) that increase in disposable income gets spent. Thus, the change in A is not $10 billion, but $10 billion times 0.75, or $7.5 billion. The change in output is:

$$\Delta Y = \frac{0.75}{1 - 0.75} \times 10 = \frac{1}{0.25} \times 7.5 = 30$$

But notice that as long as you correctly compute the change in autonomous expenditure A, you will always be able to find the change in output as the change in A times the multiplier. This means that there is a reliable way to solve for both the equilibrium value of output and the change in output due to a change in one of the expenditure components in just two steps:

1. Figure out the slope coefficient on income, b. In simple versions of the model, it will just be the marginal propensity to consume (MPC). But in other versions, it might reflect the MPC as well as factors like the tendency to consume more imports when income rises.

2. Sum up all the other components of aggregate expenditure that do not depend on income, which yields A. The multiplier will always equal $1/(1 − b)$. The equilibrium level of output will always equal A times the multiplier. And the change in output due to a change in one of the components of expenditure will always equal the change in the component times the multiplier.

✓CONCEPT CHECK

☐ Based on the model assumptions, which components of aggregate expenditure are represented by constants? **[LO G.1]**

☐ Algebraically, what is the equilibrium condition for aggregate expenditure? When the economy has reached this equilibrium, is it necessarily the case that output has reached potential? Explain. **[LO G.1]**

☐ Why does a $1 decrease in taxes have a smaller expansionary impact on the economy than a $1 increase in government spending? **[LO G.2]**

☐ The model economy in this section assumed that taxes net of transfers were a lump sum, with $T = 100$. Suppose instead that taxes net of transfers depended on income, so that $T = 100 + 0.1Y$. Solve for the expenditure multiplier in this case and say whether it is larger, smaller, or the same as the original multiplier. Provide a brief intuition for your answer. **[LO G.2]**

Problems and Applications

1. Consider the following components of the aggregate expenditure equilibrium model:

    $$C = 0.6(Y - 200) + 150$$
    $$I_{planned} = 175$$
    $$G = 200$$
    $$NX = 50$$

    Assume all model parameters are in billions of dollars. **[LO G.1, LO G.2]**

    a. What is the marginal propensity to consume in this economy?

    b. What is the level of taxes in this economy? (You can assume that the functional forms above are consistent with those described earlier.)

    c. What is the equilibrium level of aggregate expenditure in this economy?

    Now suppose that planned investment decreases by $25 billion.

    d. Find the overall change in equilibrium aggregate expenditure that results from this initial change by finding the new level of equilibrium aggregate expenditure and comparing this new level to the initial level.

    e. Again, find the overall change in equilibrium aggregate expenditure that results from the initial change, but this time use the changes formulation of the equilibrium aggregate expenditure expression directly.

Aggregate Demand and Aggregate Supply

Learning Objectives

LO 29.1   Show how the aggregate expenditure equilibrium model can be used to trace out the aggregate demand curve and understand why the aggregate demand curve slopes downward.

LO 29.2   List factors that could cause the aggregate demand curve to shift.

LO 29.3   Explain how changes in government spending and taxes can have a multiplier effect on aggregate demand.

LO 29.4   Explain the difference between the short run and long run in the economy.

LO 29.5   Demonstrate a shift in the short-run aggregate supply curve and list factors that cause it to shift.

LO 29.6   Demonstrate a shift in the long-run aggregate supply curve and list factors that cause it to shift.

LO 29.7   Explain the short-run and long-run effects of a shift in aggregate demand.

LO 29.8   Explain the short-run and long-run effects of a shift in aggregate supply.

LO 29.9   Use the AD/AS framework to determine whether an observed change in output and prices was due to a demand shock or a supply shock.

LO 29.10   Describe the policy options the government can use to counteract supply and demand shocks.

"POP!" GOES THE BUBBLE

Home prices in the United States more than doubled between 2000 and 2007. Seeing that house prices were increasing, banks started making more mortgage loans, even to people who didn't earn enough to easily make their scheduled payments. The banks calculated that if these "subprime" customers got into trouble, the homes could be sold and the loans could be repaid from the profit.

© Ty Wright/Bloomberg via Getty Images

Homeowners started feeling flush as they saw the value of their homes increase, and they started to spend on other things—a new car, a new kitchen, a holiday shopping splurge. In short order, the economy was heating up.

Unfortunately, the housing boom turned out to be an example of what is called an *asset-price bubble.* Bubbles happen when people buy assets for no reason other than that they think the price will go up. There are, of course, good reasons why you might pay a lot for a house—say, if you're willing to pay to get a house you like in the location you want. But during the housing boom, many people were willing to pay hefty prices simply because they believed prices would keep going up and they'd be able to sell for a profit.

But—inevitably—housing prices stopped rising. Between the end of 2007 and the middle of 2009, house prices fell by 25 percent. Banks found that many customers couldn't afford to repay the money they'd borrowed to buy their houses. Suddenly, the "subprime" mortgages that banks had been so eager to approve became a massive burden. Worse still, in many cases the houses were now worth less than the amount the bank had loaned, so even foreclosing and taking possession of the house wouldn't fill the gap.

Facing huge losses, banks tightened down on credit of all sorts. Now, homebuyers weren't the only ones finding that loans were scarcer and more expensive than before—businesses also began to find borrowing more difficult. Homeowners who had been happily spending on other things, confident that they could afford it because their houses were growing in value, suddenly got cold feet and stopped buying. This double whammy—the loss of cheap lending and a sharp decrease in consumer spending—hit businesses hard. The result was that GDP fell, unemployment rose, and the economy entered the period that some call the Great Recession.

How can we explain what happened to the national economy during this turbulent period? What is the connection between home prices, consumer spending, business investment, and the overall health of the economy? In Chapter 28, "Aggregate Expenditure," we focused on issues specific to aggregate expenditure. In this chapter, we add more pieces. We will create a framework, called the *aggregate demand and aggregate supply model,* for understanding how the economy operates as a whole.

So far in this text we've looked at supply and demand in an individual market, for a particular good or service. As macroeconomists, however, we need to think about *all* the goods and services in the economy. The aggregate demand and aggregate supply model is a way of adding up everything, leading to an "equilibrium" that describes the state of the national economy. We will use this model to understand how three important macroeconomic variables—output, prices, and employment—are determined and how they affect each other.

This bird's-eye view lets us see the economy from the perspective of policy-makers and businesspeople, who need to consider macroeconomic shifts and frame strategies to respond to them. When President Barack Obama began the first term of his presidency in 2009, the economy was already in deep trouble. One of the first challenges he faced was figuring out how the government should respond. In this chapter and the next, we'll see which policies are available to a president and how they can affect the national economy.

Tying It All Together

In recent chapters, we've developed tools for measuring the major features of the macroeconomy: output (GDP), prices, and unemployment. We also investigated aggregate expenditure. But these aspects of the economy don't exist in isolation. Instead, they are different faces of one big, complex system. You probably have some intuitive sense of how they are tied together in determining the health of the economy. For instance, when we say the economy is "doing badly," most of us have a mental picture of both falling production *and* high unemployment. Similarly, you might associate crashing or skyrocketing prices of important goods, such as houses or gasoline, with economic troubles.

In this chapter, we're going to build an economic model under that intuition. The model shows how the condition of the economy—described in terms of GDP and overall price levels—is really an equilibrium outcome. That equilibrium equates the total demand for all goods and services with the total supply. In some superficial ways, this will look like a microeconomic model of demand and supply. In the *macroeconomic* model:

- *Price* is the overall price level, calculated as a weighted average of the prices of all goods and services.
- *Quantity* is represented by GDP, the measure of the value of all goods and services produced by the economy.

However, new forces come into play when we start to *aggregate* (add up) demand and supply across many different goods and services.

The model of aggregate demand and aggregate supply shows how output, prices, and employment are all tied together as part of a single economic equilibrium. This allows us to see what happens when an event like the popping of the housing bubble or a natural disaster hits the economy, and why it is likely to affect all three measures. Using the same tools, we can see how a change in government policy—perhaps intended to counteract the effects of the bubble or disaster—will operate on the same system.

Aggregate Demand

This section will develop a picture of the demand side of the macroeconomy. The term *aggregate demand* describes the total demand for all goods and services in the economy. That means adding up demand across all of the individual markets for goods and services.

It might seem strange to add up quantities of completely different items—literally, adding apples and oranges—but, fortunately, we've already developed a tool for dealing with that problem. In Chapter 24, "Measuring GDP," we introduced the concept of GDP, which adds up all the goods and services in the economy by translating them into a common unit: market value. Thus, *aggregate demand* measures the total quantity of goods and services demanded in the economy, in terms of their market value.

The aggregate demand curve

> **LO 29.1** Show how the aggregate expenditure equilibrium model can be used to trace out the aggregate demand curve and understand why the aggregate demand curve slopes downward.

aggregate demand curve

a curve that shows the relationship between the overall price level in the economy and total demand

The **aggregate demand curve** shows the relationship between the overall price level and the level of total demand in the economy. When we graph aggregate demand, the price level is shown on the vertical axis, and output (or, equivalently, aggregate expenditure, Y, or GDP) is on the horizontal axis.

> **HINT**
>
> Remember from Chapter 24, "Measuring GDP," that aggregate expenditure is equal to output, and that Y and GDP reflect the same quantity. In Chapter 28, "Aggregate Expenditure," we put aggregate expenditure on the horizontal (x) axis. Since in this chapter we will bring together aggregate demand and aggregate supply, we will most often label the horizontal axis as "output"—which is equivalent to aggregate expenditure.

The aggregate demand curve slopes downward, just like the demand curves for televisions, haircuts, and any other individual good or service. But the reason for the similarity is not as obvious as it might seem. Here's the difference:

- When we draw the downward-sloping demand curve for televisions, for example, we assume that the price of all other goods is held constant. Thus, the demand curve shows the change in the quantity of TVs that are demanded when *only* TV prices drop.
- With *aggregate* demand, though, we can't change the price of one good and hold the prices of all the other goods constant. By definition, aggregate demand represents *all* goods, so we're interested in what happens when the prices of *all* goods go up or down— as measured by the price index, or inflation level.

So *why* does the aggregate demand curve slope downward? In Chapter 28, "Aggregate Expenditure," we learned how each of the main components of output—consumption, investment, government spending, and net exports—are affected by important economic variables. Now let's examine how each component reacts to changes in the *overall price level* of the economy. Keep in mind that we are interested in how the *real* values of these variables change in response to the price level (so we do not have to worry about a mechanical relationship between the price level and the nominal values of the expenditure components).

How price level changes affect the components of output

First, let's consider consumption. In general, changes in the price level will change the real value of people's wealth and income. A rise in the overall price level means that a given number of dollars won't buy as much in terms of real goods and services. Thus, increases in the overall price level reduce people's wealth, in terms of real purchasing power. When people are less wealthy, they reduce their consumption, creating a negative relationship between the overall price level and consumption spending. This relationship, called the *wealth effect,* gives us one way to explain the downward-sloping aggregate demand curve. As prices rise, people feel less wealthy and want to spend less, leading to a smaller quantity of goods and services demanded in the aggregate.

There's one important caveat to note: If wages increase exactly as much as prices increase, the purchasing power of those wages will stay the same. Many employers have a standard practice of increasing wages along with inflation. In that case, the wealth effect won't come into play. But the same can't be said for wealth that you have stored as cash in your wallet, in non-interest-bearing checking accounts, and in other dollar-denominated assets, which won't necessarily increase along with inflation. So, even when wages keep pace with increasing price levels, most people will probably still experience some reduction in real wealth, causing consumption to fall.

Next, let's talk investment. When prices rise, the interest rate—roughly speaking, the price of borrowing—also tends to rise. Higher interest rates make it more expensive for firms to borrow, which means they invest less in new factories and working capital. (We'll come back to this idea in Chapter 31, "The Basics of Finance.") The increased borrowing costs create an indirect negative relationship between the price level and investment spending.

Shifting to the next component, much of government spending is independent of the price level. Even when prices rise and fall, the government still needs to spend roughly the same amount on Social Security checks and salaries for government employees. Thus, the government spending component does not contribute to the downward-sloping nature of the aggregate demand curve.

Finally, we consider net exports. When prices in the United States increase, U.S. goods become relatively more expensive than goods from other countries, assuming that price levels stay the same in the other countries. As a result, we would expect imports into the United States to increase and exports to decrease. This means that when the price level increases, net exports (exports minus imports) should decrease. This means there is a negative relationship between the price level and net exports.

Graphing changes in the price level

We can show the effects of price-level increases on our aggregate expenditure diagram in Figure 29-1. In this figure, P_1 is the lowest price, so P_2 represents a price increase from P_1, and P_3 represents a price increase from P_2. Each price increase is represented by a downward shift of the planned aggregate expenditure line. To understand why, keep in mind that the aggregate

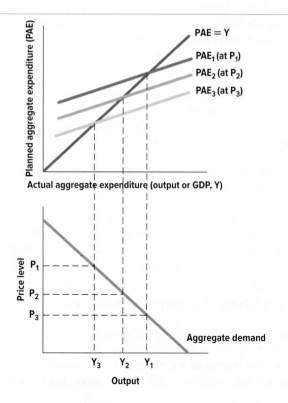

FIGURE 29-1

How price-driven shifts in planned aggregate expenditure trace out the aggregate demand curve

FIGURE 29-2

**The aggregate
demand curve**

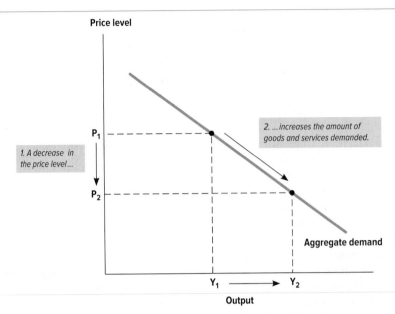

The aggregate demand curve shows the relationship
between the price level and the quantity of output
demanded by households, firms, the government, and
the rest of the world. This relationship shows that as
prices decrease, the quantity of aggregate output
demanded increases.

expenditure line gives planned aggregate expenditure as a function of Y. Therefore, a downward
shift represents a lower level of planned aggregate expenditure for each level of Y.

We can then use the equilibrium aggregate expenditure points to trace out the aggregate
demand curve. As shown in the figure, we can plot the (Y, P) pairs that correspond to the equilibrium aggregate expenditure levels and price levels for each of the aggregate expenditure curves.
We see, yet again, that the aggregate demand curve slopes downward.

What have we learned?

- There is a negative relationship between price level and national expenditure for three of
  the four expenditure components—C, I, and NX.
- There is no relationship between the price level and the fourth expenditure
  component—G.

When we put together this information, we get a negative overall relationship between the price
level and aggregate expenditure or GDP. In other words, we end up with a downward-sloping
aggregate demand curve, as shown in Figure 29-2.

Furthermore we have learned that every point along the aggregate demand curve corresponds
to an equilibrium in the aggregate expenditure model from Chapter 28, "Aggregate Expenditure."
One implication is that anything *other than a change in the price level itself* that leads to a different
equilibrium in the aggregate expenditure model will cause the aggregate demand curve to shift.

Shifting the aggregate demand curve

LO 29.2 List factors that could cause the aggregate demand curve to shift.

Price changes generate movements *along* the aggregate demand curve. We saw that when the
price level increases, for example, the wealth effect drives people to spend less, and overall

output falls. However, the entire aggregate demand curve can also *shift* in response to *nonprice changes* in any of the four components of aggregate demand—consumption, investment, government spending, and net exports. Such nonprice changes move the entire curve to the left or right, making aggregate demand lower or higher at any given price level.

Big changes to the national economy can sometimes be described as shifts in the aggregate demand curve. Consider, for instance, the story of the housing bubble. People felt confident when housing prices were rising steadily until late 2007. Homeowners could see the value of their houses increasing, which made them feel significantly wealthier and more optimistic. They started consuming more, which made all kinds of firms throughout the economy also feel good about their future prospects. They started investing more.

The total effect of this boost in consumer and company confidence was to shift the aggregate demand curve to the right. Because confidence was high, people and businesses were willing to spend and invest more, increasing aggregate demand at any price level, as shown in panel A of Figure 29-3.

Unfortunately, that increase in housing prices turned out to be a bubble, which popped in late 2007. House prices started to fall, and people became worried that they were not as wealthy as they thought they were. This concern reduced consumer confidence, and people bought less. In turn, managers of companies became worried that they would not sell as many goods and services in the future, so they became less willing to invest. Together, this drop in confidence throughout the economy shifted aggregate demand to the left, as shown in panel B of Figure 29-3.

Confidence is a fuzzy concept, but as the example of the housing bubble shows, it can be critical to both consumption and investment:

- If people feel positive about their prospects for future income, they will be more likely to consume more.

- On the other hand, if people feel worried about losing their jobs or paying higher prices in the future, they will probably start consuming less and saving more for a rainy day.

FIGURE 29-3

Shifts in the aggregate demand curve

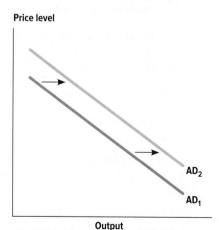

(A) A rightward shift of aggregate demand

When the aggregate demand curve shifts out (to the right) due to an overall increase in consumption, GDP is higher at every price level.

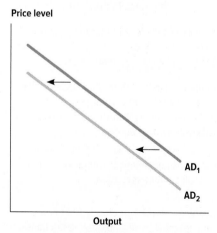

(B) A leftward shift of aggregate demand

When the aggregate demand curve shifts in (to the left), the opposite is true. At each price level, GDP is lower.

Much the same reasoning applies to firms:

- If businesses are optimistic about the direction of the economy, they will want to invest more in new factories, warehouses, and machinery.
- But if prospects for the economy start to look bleak, managers will be less interested in expanding and increasing capacity, and will invest less.

Increasing consumer and business confidence will therefore shift the aggregate demand curve to the right. Decreasing confidence shifts the curve to the left.

Some government policies, such as taxes and government spending, can also shift the aggregate demand curve:

- Cutting taxes on consumers is likely to increase consumption because people keep more of the money they earn and so are in effect wealthier. Increased consumption spending shifts the aggregate demand curve to the right.
- By the same logic, raising taxes can dampen the desire to spend by leaving consumers with less money. Higher taxes shift the aggregate demand curve to the left.

The government can also affect aggregate demand through its own spending:

- Government spending increases aggregate demand directly, through the "G" in the demand equation. (But as we'll see in detail in the next chapter, government spending can also have indirect effects on demand by encouraging more consumer spending.) In the face of a recession, government can increase spending in order to shift the aggregate demand to the right. For example, this strategy could mean the construction of federal highways, more spending for the military, or added spending for schools.
- If, instead, the government sharply cut its spending during a recession, it risks a decline in aggregate demand. In that case, the aggregate demand curve would shift to the left.

Table 29-1 shows examples of changes that can cause shifts in the aggregate demand curve. The middle column lists several factors that would increase aggregate demand, shifting the aggregate demand curve to the right. The right-hand column lists factors that would decrease aggregate demand, shifting the aggregate demand curve to the left.

TABLE 29-1

What causes the aggregate demand curve to shift?

Category	Increase (shift right)	Decrease (shift left)
Consumption	• High expectations about future income increase consumer spending. • Tax cuts increase consumer spending.	• Low expectations about future income lead to greater saving and less spending. • Higher interest rates discourage borrowing.
Investment	• Confidence in the future of the economy leads firms to expand their businesses. • A tax credit for small businesses inspires firms to buy new company cars.	• Firms cut back on spending in order to weather a recession. • Taxes on capital increase, leaving less money for investment.
Government spending	• Increase in government spending spurs spending after a recession.	• Decrease in government spending in response to concerns about increasing debt leads to less spending.
Net exports	• A new free trade agreement with Europe reduces most tariffs and other restrictions on U.S. goods. • Economic growth abroad in China increases demand for U.S. goods and services.	• Other countries increase their tariffs on U.S. goods, making the goods more expensive. • The dollar strengthens, making U.S. goods and services more expensive for international consumers, decreasing demand.

The multiplier and shifts in aggregate demand

LO 29.3 Explain how changes in government spending and taxes can have a multiplier effect on aggregate demand.

In Chapter 28, "Aggregate Expenditure," we saw that the *multiplier effect* means that each additional dollar of expenditure in the economy leads to more than one dollar of output. This principle has important consequences for economic policy.

Imagine that you're the president and you've just entered office. The economy is in a recession, and you are considering how to use economic policy to stimulate the economy and create jobs. Your economic advisors are divided over the best route to take:

- Some advise you to cut taxes. They reason that employees will take home more money and some of it will be spent, which will boost demand.

- Others advise you to increase government spending. Since millions are out of work, these advisors argue, the government should create jobs by spending on infrastructure projects. The income paid to newly employed workers will then flow into the economy as these workers in turn spend their new income on food, clothes, energy, and other things.

Both plans will stimulate the economy, but you want to ensure that you use government resources as efficiently as possible. Which policy gives you the "bigger bang" for the government's buck? First, let's consider the case of *stimulus spending,* as proposed by your second set of advisors. Suppose that government agencies buy new computers. Here's what happens:

- The government pays $500 million to the computer manufacturer. Immediately, this expenditure increases GDP by $500 million since government spending is one of the contributors to overall GDP.

- The computer manufacturer in turn uses the money to pay workers and make new capital investments, such as building a factory.

- The people employed to build the factory, in turn, spend money on goods and services elsewhere in the economy, and so on.

In the end, the $500 million injection of spending will increase GDP by $500 times the multiplier. In Chapter 28, "Aggregate Expenditure," we defined the expenditure multiplier as $1/(1 - b)$. If the marginal propensity to consume out of disposable income is 0.6, then $b = 0.6$ and the multiplier is $1/(1 - b) = 2.5$. Given a multiplier of 2.5, the stimulus spending would result in $500 million × 2.5 = $1,250 million in additional GDP.

Now imagine that, instead of spending that $500 million on new computers, the government decides to cut taxes by $500 million. The tax cut puts money in people's pockets, which they can use for consumption. The multiplier effect comes into play under this policy, too. This policy *seems* like it should have exactly the same impact as the direct increase in government spending, but that is not actually the case.

Again, the impact can be found by multiplying the initial spending increase by the expenditure multiplier. But note that in the case of the tax cut, the initial spending increase is not the full $500 million. Instead, because the marginal propensity to consume is less than 1, only a fraction, b, of the $500 million tax cut results in a first round of new consumption spending. Continuing to assume that $b = 0.6$, then the *initial* increase in aggregate expenditure with the tax cut is only $500 million × 0.6 = $300 million. This is less than the case of direct government spending, for which the entire $500 million was spent.

The tax cut still creates a multiplier effect, though. Because the expenditure multiplier is still 2.5, the total increase in output in the case of the tax cut would be $300 million × 2.5 = $750 million. More generally, each dollar *reduction* in lump-sum taxes will result in $b × 1/(1 - b)$ additional dollars of GDP.

Note that you do not need to memorize two different formulas for understanding the impact of government spending versus tax cuts. As long as you correctly compute the initial change in aggregate expenditure due to the policy, you still multiply that change by the same expenditure multiplier. The only difference with tax cuts is that the initial change in expenditures is smaller (in absolute value) than the full change in taxes.[1]

When the economy is slumping because consumer confidence is down, politicians often try to get things moving again by asking people to spend more. When times are good, though, they give very different advice, as seen in the From Another Angle box "Save . . . no, spend!"

From Another Angle

Save . . . no, spend!

When Barack Obama started his first term as president in January 2009, U.S. households were feeling the pinch. Worried about the future, they had cut back on their spending and started to save more. On an individual level, it's a good idea to save in times of economic trouble. Unfortunately, though, the overall health of the economy is tightly linked with how much people spend. In fact, over 70 percent of total GDP in the United States comes from consumption spending. That's why, in a speech to Congress in 2009, in the middle of the Great Recession, Obama noted that the best path to recovery was for everyone to spend a little more:

> That's what [the stimulus] is about. It's not about helping banks—it's about helping people. Because when credit is available again, that young family can finally buy a new home. And then some company will hire workers to build it. And then those workers will have money to spend, and if they can get a loan too, maybe they'll finally buy that car, or open their own business. Investors will return to the market, and American families will see their retirement secured once more. Slowly, but surely, confidence will return, and our economy will recover.

Just five years previously, U.S. consumers had heard a very different message. In a 2004 speech, Federal Reserve Board Vice Chairman Roger Ferguson called on households to stop spending so much and start saving more. He explained that this saving would mean banks had more funds to lend to U.S. companies:

> Probably nothing is more critical to the long-run well-being of the U.S. economy than ensuring high rates of productivity growth. Productivity growth requires adequate levels of investment. While foreign saving is currently a feasible source of investable resources, it would be more economically advantageous in the longer run if we could raise the amount of household and government savings and close the gap between domestic investment and national savings.

Why would policy-makers give totally different advice, just five years apart? The U.S. economy had changed sharply in the time between the two speeches. In 2004, the economy was doing well. U.S. firms were eager to invest, which meant borrowing money, but because U.S. households were saving so little, investment funds from domestic sources were scarce. The logic was that if households would save more, banks would have more money to loan out, and firms would be able to make more investments to improve their businesses.

By 2009, though, the economy was in a rough spot. Consumers weren't spending very much. This lack of spending meant that firms were no longer as interested in borrowing to invest. If households could be persuaded to spend more instead of saving, the AD curve would shift to the right. In 2009 the logic was that when firms saw that demand was increasing, they would want to employ more people and invest again. Consumer spending would kick-start economic recovery.

In both cases, the aim of the advice was to improve the health of the economy. When times are good, saving makes sense as a way to help firms make needed investments to secure the future. When times are bad, extra spending can help move the economy out of a rut and toward recovery.

Sources: http://www.federalreserve.gov/boarddocs/speeches/2004/20041006/default.htm; http://www.whitehouse.gov/the_press_office/Remarks-of-President-Barack-Obama-Address-to-Joint-Session-of-Congress/.

✓CONCEPT CHECK

- ☐ What four components of spending make up aggregate demand? **[LO 29.1]**
- ☐ Is the relationship between price level and aggregate demand generally positive or negative? **[LO 29.1]**
- ☐ Would the construction of a new interstate highway by the U.S. Department of Transportation shift aggregate demand to the left or right? **[LO 29.2]**
- ☐ Does a decrease in consumer spending after a tax increase shift aggregate demand to the left or right? **[LO 29.2]**
- ☐ Why does a tax cut have a different multiplier effect than an equally costly increase in public spending? **[LO 29.3]**

Aggregate Supply

Now that we've described the demand side of the economy, we'll turn to the other side. *Aggregate supply* is the sum total of the production of all the firms in the economy. Production occurs when factor inputs—technology, capital, and labor—are combined to produce output.

The **aggregate supply curve** shows the relationship between the overall price level in the economy and total production by firms (output). The aggregate supply curve is similar to a market supply curve, with two key differences:

aggregate supply curve
a curve that shows the relationship between the overall price level in the economy and total production by firms

1. The aggregate supply curve represents production in the economy *as a whole* rather than just one good or service.
2. At the macroeconomic level, there is a difference between how the economy operates in the short run and how the economy operates in the long run.

Because of the difference between the short run and the long run, there are actually *two* different aggregate supply curves:

- One describes aggregate supply in the long run; it is called the *long-run aggregate supply curve (LRAS)*.
- The second describes how firms decide how much to produce in the short run; it is called the *short-run aggregate supply curve (SRAS)*.

We'll look at both in this section.

The difference between short-run and long-run aggregate supply

LO 29.4 Explain the difference between the short run and long run in the economy.

In order to understand the two aggregate supply curves, we need to explore the difference between the short run and the long run in the economy.

Short-run aggregate supply

The *short run* refers to the hourly, daily, or weekly decisions that firms have to make. If you're running a fast-food burger joint, short-run decisions include choices about how much beef and lettuce you want to order for the week or how many hours you want each employee to work. In choosing these inputs, you are essentially deciding how much food you want to produce.

In the short run, the aggregate supply curve slopes upward, as Figure 29-4 shows. This means that as overall price levels increase, firms are willing to produce more. Why is this so? Because the prices of final goods and services—like burgers—tend to increase more quickly than the prices of inputs. (Below, we explain why.) So, the burger joint is able to increase revenues faster than the increases in its costs. As a result, it is willing to produce more.

Why do prices of final goods and services increase more quickly than inputs? The key idea is that when the price level increases, input prices don't all increase immediately. Instead, some prices are "sticky," meaning that they adjust slowly in response to changes in the economy. Wages are a prime example. To understand why sticky wages cause the short-run aggregate supply curve to slope upward, think about a sudden increase in the price level. Firms are going to earn more revenue because the prices of their products are higher. However, wages don't adjust right away. In the short run, the burger stand can make higher profits because revenues have increased but labor costs haven't. Because of the sticky wages, firms will be prepared to hire new workers and produce more output.

But why should input prices be sticky, yet the prices of final goods can change instantaneously? Contracts or informal practices make wages and the prices of other inputs sticky. For instance, many firms reevaluate wages only once a year. Unionized firms typically have formal labor contracts that often determine wage levels for several years at a time. If an employee wants higher wages or an employer wants to implement a pay cut, they will have to wait until the next period in which wages are adjusted or when the present contract expires. Often, raw materials are supplied on the same basis. For example, a fast-food chain might have a contract with a beef supplier setting out how much it will pay for beef over the coming year.

Although contracts are common for input prices, the prices of final goods are rarely dictated by contract. It's not likely, for example, that a fast-food stand would ever get its customers

FIGURE 29-4

The short-run aggregate supply curve

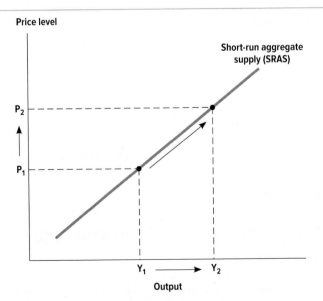

In the short run, the aggregate supply curve reacts to price changes. This means that firms are willing to change how much they supply based on price.

to agree to a long-term contract that specifies how many burgers and fries they'll buy over a year. Instead, customers grab a burger whenever they're hungry, paying the price on the current menu. To change the price, the fast-food stand simply changes its menu. Although changing final prices isn't always easy, in general, we assume that final prices can change far more easily than input prices.

Long-run aggregate supply

Now let's look at the long run. The first thing to know is that *the long run is not a set amount of time*, like one year, two years, or 10 years. Instead, it is however long it takes for prices of inputs—such as wages, rent, and raw materials—to *fully adjust to changes in economic conditions*. In the long run, a burger stand can renegotiate the rent on its building, hire new employees, and negotiate new wages.

The adjustment process between the short and long run in macroeconomics differs from the adjustment process studied in microeconomics. In microeconomics, we focus on individual markets, and the key adjustment problem is one of quantities. Some costs are "fixed" because the quantity of an input cannot be adjusted in the short run; others are "variable" costs because the quantity used can easily be adjusted in the short run. For example, back to the burger stand, basic equipment like deep fryers and heat lamps are fixed costs in the short run. In the long run, new equipment can be purchased and installed. In contrast, the amount of beef used is more likely to be a variable cost, increased or decreased as weekly burger sales dictate.

In macroeconomics, the focus is on how long it takes for *prices to adjust through the whole economy,* rather than the flexibility of *quantities* within an individual firm. What happens to the shape of the supply curve in the long run? Let's return to our example of the fast-food stand. In the short run, the burger stand's owners are making extra profits because revenues have risen but costs have not. That situation can't go on forever. Since goods are now more expensive, fry cooks and cashiers are going to ask for higher wages. Input prices, which have been under contract, will increase when the contracts are renegotiated.

Once these input prices adjust, the burger stand no longer makes higher profits. Its revenues may be higher, but its costs also are higher. As a result, profits go back to where they were before the price increase. *This same process happens throughout the economy.* Once wages and input costs adjust to the new price level, the economy will go back to where it started.

In the long run, when input prices can adjust, our model says that changes in the prices of goods and services paid by consumers have no effect on aggregate supply. The long-run aggregate supply curve is a vertical line, showing that the same amount of output is supplied at *any* price level. Figure 29-5 shows an example of a long-run aggregate supply curve.

If it's not prices, what does determine the quantity of output supplied in the long run? The long-run aggregate supply curve represents *potential output* in the economy—the level of output possible if the economy is operating at full capacity. It may help to think of the long-run aggregate supply curve as a production function. The production function shows how society's natural resources, labor, and capital can be combined to produce the greatest output.

Changes in the long-run aggregate supply curve happen because something changes in the way that society's resources create output. Maybe there has been a new technological invention or the discovery of new resources, like a new oil reserve. The process of steadily pushing the long-run aggregate supply curve to the right—that is, increasing potential output—is the main driver of economic growth.

The economy does not always produce its potential output. Sometimes less output is produced, and sometimes more:

- When output is higher than potential output, the economy is in a boom.
- When output is below potential, the economy is in a recession.

We call these fluctuations around the level of potential output the **business cycle**. Figure 29-6 shows the business cycle for the United States over the past 50 years.

business cycle
Fluctuations of output around the level of potential output in the economy

FIGURE 29-5

The long-run aggregate supply curve

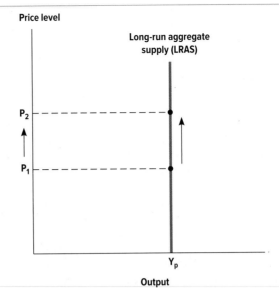

In the long run, the aggregate supply curve is fixed. Changes in the overall level of prices do not influence the level of output in the economy.

FIGURE 29-6

The business cycle

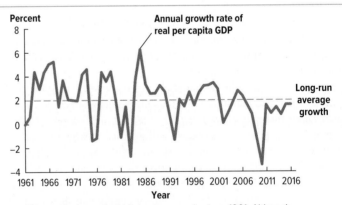

This graph shows the U.S. business cycle since 1961. Although the average real GDP per capita growth rate over this time is about 2 percent, the yearly average fluctuates quite a bit, with periods of expansion and recession.

Source: The World Bank Data, GDP per capita growth (annual %), http://data.worldbank.org/indicator/NY.GDP.PCAP.KD.ZG/countries.

You might be wondering: How can there ever be a boom? Using the model of aggregate demand and aggregate supply, how can short-run supply ever exceed the economy's level of potential output? It turns out that in the short run, production can be expanded beyond long-run potential by pressing all of the factors of production beyond their normal capacity. For instance, if firms ask workers to take on extra hours or run their factories around the clock, output can be temporarily pushed beyond the level of potential output.

To understand how this works, think about what happens at school during exam time. You may put in lots of extra hours to cram for a test. In doing so, you are operating beyond your long-run capacity for schoolwork. You may be able to study 18 hours a day for a few weeks before midterms, but that schedule is probably not sustainable over an entire semester. Cramming for exams racks up costs that wouldn't occur with a normal schedule. These include the stress that comes from worrying about final grades or the health costs of eating too much junk food, not getting enough exercise or sleep, and not having enough leisure time. Once exams are over, these costs will push you to return to a normal workload in the beginning of the next semester. In other words, you will go back to your potential output.

In the same way that you incur costs by operating above capacity during exam time, firms incur costs by operating beyond potential output in the aggregate supply and demand model. When the economy is below capacity, ramping up production is easy. Firms can hire workers who were unemployed and rent warehouses that were sitting empty. This isn't the case when the economy is operating at full capacity. Since wages and input prices are fixed in the short run, firms often have to pay current employees overtime to work longer hours, or hire workers who may not be fully qualified for the job.

Eventually, the intense demand for labor and capital when an economy is operating above capacity will drive prices upward. Hard-pressed workers will demand raises or leave to work for firms that are willing to pay them more money. As a result:

- input prices will increase,
- profits will shrink back to the original level, and
- supply will fall back to the long-run level.

The end result of this short-term boost in output is higher prices in the long run.

Shifts in the short-run aggregate supply curve

> **LO 29.5** Demonstrate a shift in the short-run aggregate supply curve and list factors that cause it to shift.

The short-run aggregate supply curve can shift—for example, if the costs of production change. Imagine that oil prices rise all of a sudden. Firms will feel the pinch. When oil prices rise, many firms will find that producing output is much more expensive. It's more costly for farmers to harvest and transport their crops, and transportation costs will make it more expensive to purchase the inputs that are needed for production. These changes shift the short-run aggregate supply (SRAS) curve to the left, as firms want to supply fewer goods at any given price level. Figure 29-7 shows this shift.

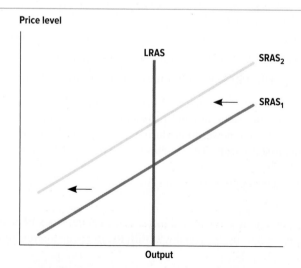

FIGURE 29-7

Shifts in the short-run aggregate supply curve

With an increase in the price of oil, prices increase for the same amount of production, so the aggregate supply curve shifts in (to the left).

POTENTIALLY CONFUSING

You may wonder at this point why a change in the world price of oil causes a shift of the SRAS instead of a movement along the curve. The reason has to do with the distinction between prices and costs. As oil prices rise, as we said, it's the increase in the *cost of inputs,* and therefore more costly production, that cause the SRAS to shift. An increase in the *cost of production* is different from an increase in the *price level:*

- An increase in the cost of production shifts the SRAS curve leftward, reducing the quantity of output produced at a given price level.
- In contrast, an increase in the price level itself—the weighted average of the prices of all goods and services we produce—would cause us to move from one point on the SRAS curve to another point on the same (unmoving) curve.

supply shocks

significant events that directly affect production and the aggregate supply curve in the short run

The short-run aggregate supply (SRAS) curve will also shift with other significant events that directly affect production—often called **supply shocks**. An example would be a major flood that disrupts the power grid and ruins crops.

Expectations about future input prices will also shift the SRAS. If firms *anticipate* that the price of oil, for example, is likely to increase, then suppliers will expect higher input costs in the future. This belief itself will reduce the quantity of goods supplied and shift the aggregate supply curve to the left.

Shifts in the long-run aggregate supply curve

LO 29.6 Demonstrate a shift in the long-run aggregate supply curve and list factors that cause it to shift.

In the long run, firms produce an amount dictated by available inputs, regardless of the overall price level. But that doesn't mean that the long-run aggregate supply curve never moves. Remember that the long-run aggregate supply (LRAS) curve is like a production function: A combination of land, technology, capital, and labor will produce a certain amount of output. Anything that affects the output possible using these factors will shift the LRAS curve, including new technologies, improved transportation systems, management innovations, and so on:

- The LRAS curve will shift to the right if the potential output of the economy expands.
- The LRAS curve will shift to the left if the economy loses productive capacity.

Consider the case of a new technology. When firms throughout the economy adopt a new technology, they can use the same amount of resources to produce more output than before. Historical examples include the power loom during the nineteenth-century Industrial Revolution and the Internet in the past 20 years. These innovations shift the LRAS curve out to the right, as illustrated in Figure 29-8.

The long-run aggregate supply curve also shifts with changes in the factors of production in the economy. For example:

- An increase in foreign investment will increase the capital stock of an economy. That will allow production to increase and will shift the long-run aggregate supply curve to the right.
- In contrast, if levels of investment are low and existing capital is not replaced as it wears out, we would see the opposite effect: Potential output decreases, and the long-run aggregate supply curve shifts to the left.

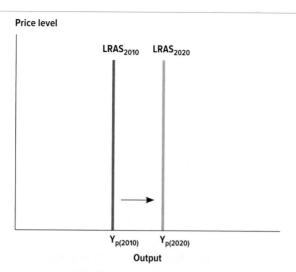

FIGURE 29-8

Shifts in the long-run aggregate supply curve

With an increase in technology, firms can produce more goods with the same amount of inputs. This shifts the long-run aggregate supply curve, the potential output of an economy, outward (to the right).

TABLE 29-2

What causes the LRAS curve to shift?

A variety of factors can shift the long-run aggregate supply curve by changing the potential output in an economy.

Factor	Increases LRAS	Decreases LRAS
Technology	Technological innovation allows for greater production using the same amount of inputs.	A new law stripping away intellectual property rights reduces the incentive to innovate.
Capital	Foreign investment in factories and machines increases available capital.	Depreciation and wear break down capital.
Labor	Immigration increases the available supply of labor.	Aging population takes workers out of the labor force.
Education	Universal primary education gives everyone a chance to go to school.	Reduction of federal college grants makes it more difficult for some to go to school.
Natural resources	New energy sources allow factories to produce more with the same inputs.	Climate change permanently reduces the amount of land that can be farmed.

Table 29-2 gives some examples of changes that will shift the long-run aggregate supply curve.

Do the LRAS and SRAS always shift together?

Do the long-run and short-run aggregate supply curves always shift together? No. On one hand, everything that shifts the LRAS curve will also shift the SRAS curve. The reason is that the available factors of production and technology that determine the position of the LRAS will also drive short-run supply. For instance, the spread of the Internet in the past 20 years shifted both the LRAS and the SRAS.

However, the opposite is not true. Not everything that shifts the SRAS curve will also shift the LRAS curve. Specifically, *changes in expectations* about future price levels *affect only the SRAS curve.*

Before we discuss why this is so, it's a good idea to remind ourselves that although this situation involves the price level, it shifts the aggregate supply curve (a change in aggregate supply) rather than causing a movement along the curve (a change in aggregate quantity supplied). Why? Because we are focusing on *expected* changes in prices, not *actual* changes in prices. There must be an *actual* change in those prices to cause a movement along a curve, whether in the short run or long run.

Expectations about prices, on the other hand, are just guesses about the future. These expectations affect firms' production plans. Firms don't want to be caught unaware by changes in their costs. When they expect prices to rise at some future point, they also expect that workers will demand higher wages in order to keep up with the higher cost of living. As a result, firms reduce production at any given current price level, shifting the SRAS curve to the left.

Why don't changes in expected prices shift the LRAS curve? We can look at this in two ways. The first comes from our definition of the LRAS—as a representation of the production function, located at the economy's potential output. The only things that can shift the LRAS are those factors that affect how we produce, such as the amount of labor, capital, natural resources such as land, and technology. Expected prices aren't included in the production function, so they cannot cause the LRAS to shift.

The second way to think about this is to consider our definition of the long run versus the short run. In the long run, expectations are fully incorporated into economic variables such as the price level. Since our expectations are fully accounted for, no shift occurs.

No matter how we look at it, while all other factors we mentioned shift the SRAS and LRAS curves in the same manner, *changes in expected prices shift only the SRAS curve:*

- In only the short run, an expected increase in prices shifts the SRAS curve leftward.
- In the long run, these expectations are incorporated into the LRAS curve, and so we see no change at all.

Changes in expected prices will not affect the LRAS curve if they do not affect the number of workers, the amount of capital, or the amount of land and technology in the economy. In the long run, prices will fully adjust to take into account any changes in policies or expectations.

✓ CONCEPT CHECK

- ☐ Why is the long-run aggregate supply curve vertical? **[LO 29.4]**
- ☐ What is the business cycle? **[LO 29.4]**
- ☐ Which way does the short-run aggregate supply curve shift when the cost of inputs decreases? **[LO 29.5]**
- ☐ Does the SRAS curve shift when the availability of land, labor, or capital decreases? If yes, in which direction does it shift? **[LO 29.5]**
- ☐ Does the LRAS curve shift when the availability of land, labor, or capital decreases? If yes, in which direction does it shift? **[LO 29.6]**
- ☐ How do changes in expected prices shift the SRAS? Why isn't the LRAS curve affected? **[LO 29.6]**

Economic Fluctuations

Now we have all the ingredients for a full model of the national economy: aggregate demand, short-run aggregate supply, and long-run aggregate supply. It's time to put them together.

Equilibrium in the national economy is the point at which aggregate demand equals aggregate supply. Short-run equilibrium is given by the intersection of the aggregate demand and short-run

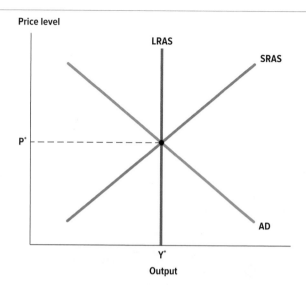

FIGURE 29-9
A model of the macroeconomy

$Q = GDP$

$PL =$

When the aggregate demand and supply curves are put together, we get a model of the entire economy. The intersection of these curves is the equilibrium, which represents a stable level of prices and output.

aggregate supply curves. In long-run equilibrium, the aggregate demand curve crosses the long-run aggregate supply and short-run aggregate supply curves *at the same point*. This means that prices are at expected levels and the short-run level of output is the same as long-run potential output. Figure 29-9 shows the macroeconomy in equilibrium: The intersection of the AD, LRAS, and SRAS curves gives the equilibrium price level and output.

A variety of shocks can push the economy out of long-run equilibrium. These shocks can shift either the aggregate demand curve or the short-run aggregate supply curve, causing the economy to shift away from potential output in the short run. In the long run, prices will adjust and the economy will return to its long-run equilibrium.

In reality, it's not always immediately clear whether a particular shock is shifting the aggregate demand or aggregate supply curve. In this section, we will show that supply-side shocks and demand-side shocks produce different implications for output and prices, which can help us to distinguish them.

Effects of a shift in aggregate demand

LO 29.7 Explain the short-run and long-run effects of a shift in aggregate demand.

Let's return to the example of the housing bubble. From 2000 to 2007, house prices were increasing, and people who owned homes felt that their wealth was increasing as well. Consumer confidence increased throughout the economy, and consumption rose. We saw earlier in the chapter that increased consumption shifts the aggregate demand curve to the right. How will an increase in consumption affect the economy in the short run and the long run?

Panel A of Figure 29-10 shows how the increase in consumption during a housing bubble affects the economy in the short run. When the AD curve shifts to the right, the short-run equilibrium moves from point E_1 (the intersection of the AD, LRAS, and SRAS curves) to point E_2 (the intersection of the new AD curve and the AS curve). Point E_2 shows the effect of the housing boom: Output was above the long-run potential level, and prices increased.

Point E_2 is an equilibrium point, but it is only a short-run equilibrium. How do we know this? *The long-run equilibrium is determined by the productive factors* in the economy, and this

FIGURE 29-10

The effect of an increase in aggregate demand

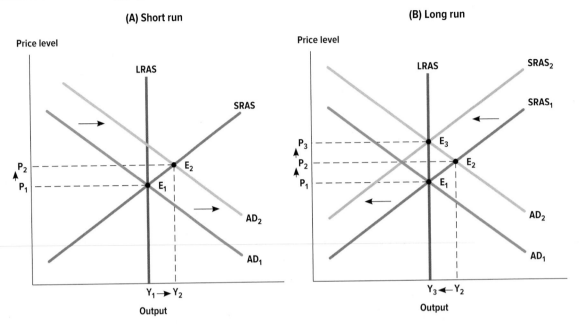

When people buy more as a result of increased consumer confidence, the aggregate demand curve shifts out. This results in a new short-run equilibrium at point E_2. At this new equilibrium, output and prices are higher.

As wages and prices increase due to the shift in aggregate demand, it becomes more costly to produce goods, so the short-run aggregate supply curve shifts to the left. This brings production back to its original level, but prices increase again.

increase in consumption didn't change any of the land, labor, or capital that was available for production. Therefore, we know that the LRAS curve hasn't moved.

How does the economy return to the long-run equilibrium? The SRAS curve has to shift again to restore the long-run equilibrium. As we'll see, this is where our model diverges from what actually happened during the housing boom. If the economy had come down naturally, wages and other resource prices would have started to increase gradually because of inflation, causing an increase in input costs for firms and therefore shifting aggregate supply. As contracts were negotiated and wages increased, the SRAS curve would have gradually shifted to the left until equilibrium was restored, as shown in panel B of Figure 29-10.

If you compare point E_1 to point E_3 in panel B of Figure 29-10—the movement from the initial long-run equilibrium to the new long-run equilibrium—you'll see that output didn't change, but the price level increased. So, the effects of an increase in consumption differ in the short and long runs:

- In the short run, absent any other changes, the effect of a shift in the AD curve due to an increase in consumer confidence will be to increase both prices and output.
- In the long run, the gains to output retreat, output returns to its former level, and the only change that is left is higher prices.

The economy is in an opposite situation when a negative shock shifts aggregate demand to the left, as shown in Figure 29-11. For example, suppose the economy is humming along at equilibrium. Then, all of a sudden, housing prices collapse. Consumer confidence falls, and consumption decreases, shifting the AD curve to the left.

In the short run, shown in panel A of Figure 29-11, output will be below the potential level of output. However, this change exerts downward pressure on prices. As prices adjust and inputs

FIGURE 29-11

The effect of a decrease in aggregate demand

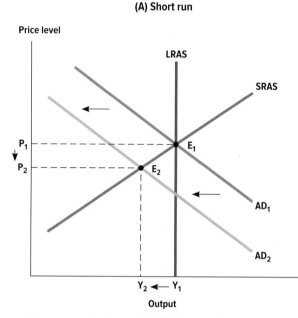

(A) Short run

When aggregate demand shifts in due to a decrease in aggregate demand, the new short-run equilibrium moves to point E_2. At point E_2 both prices and output are lower.

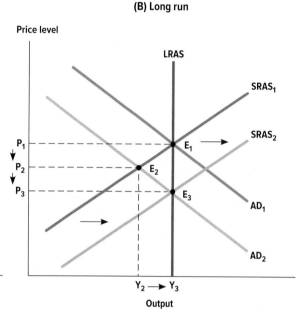

(B) Long run

Lower prices of inputs make it cheaper for firms to produce goods so the aggregate supply curve shifts out. This shift restores the economy to a long-run equilibrium with the same original level of output, but with lower prices.

get cheaper, firms will increase their output—shifting the SRAS curve to the right, as shown in panel B. The new long-run equilibrium will be at the original level of output, but with a lower price level (point E_3).

If you compare point E_1 to point E_3 in panel B of Figure 29-11—the movement from the initial long-run equilibrium to the new long-run equilibrium—you'll see that output didn't change, but the price level decreased. So, the effects of a decrease in consumption differ in the short and long runs:

- In the short run, absent any other changes, the effect of a shift in the AD curve due to a decrease in consumer confidence will be to decrease both prices and output.

- In the long run, as prices adjust and inputs get cheaper, output increases to its former level, and the only change that is left is lower prices.

Table 29-3 summarizes the effects of a change in aggregate demand in the short run and long run. The key is this: Demand-side shifts change only the price level in the long run, while output eventually returns to its long-run potential level.

TABLE 29-3

Changes in aggregate demand in the short run and the long run

The impacts of a shift in demand can be separated into two main paths. An increase in AD will increase both prices and output in the short run. In the long run, only prices will be higher as output slides back to the original equilibrium level. The opposite is true for a decrease in aggregate demand. ·

Shift	Example	Short run	Long run
Increase in AD	Increase in government spending: increases G	Output increases Price increases	Output unchanged Price increases
Decrease in AD	Reduction in consumer confidence: reduces C	Output decreases Price decreases	Output unchanged Price decreases

Effects of a shift in aggregate supply

LO 29.8 Explain the short-run and long-run effects of a shift in aggregate supply.

The other type of shocks the economy can face is shocks to the supply side. Supply-side shocks may be either temporary or permanent:

- When such changes are temporary, only the SRAS curve will shift.
- When the changes are permanent, both the LRAS curve and the SRAS curve will shift.

Temporary supply shocks

Let's first consider a temporary shock. Suppose there is a year-long drought in the Midwest and a lot of corn is damaged. This shock will shift the SRAS curve to the left, as shown in panel A of Figure 29-12. The economy will move from its long-run equilibrium at point E_1 to the new short-run equilibrium at point E_2. Prices will be higher and output will be lower. How does the economy adjust?

A situation in which output decreases while prices increase is often referred to as *stagflation*—economic stagnation coupled with high inflation. Adjustment from this short-run equilibrium is not easy. A drop in wages would help, but employees are usually reluctant to accept lower wages. We say that wages are generally "sticky downward," meaning that it takes a long time for them to fall. Sticky input prices contribute to keeping the economy in this undesirable equilibrium.

When the economy is producing at a level less than the potential output and wages are slow to fall, firms will lay off workers; unemployment will be higher than its natural rate. If the unemployment rate remains high, wages will eventually begin to fall. As labor becomes cheaper, the

FIGURE 29-12

The effect of a decrease in short-run supply: A drought in the Midwest

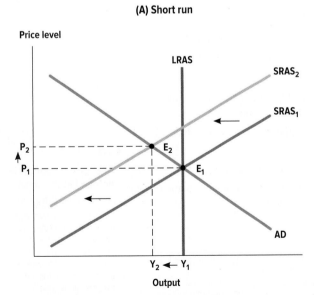

(A) Short run

A drought that destroys much of the corn crop will shift the short-run aggregate supply curve in. In the short run, prices will be higher, and output falls.

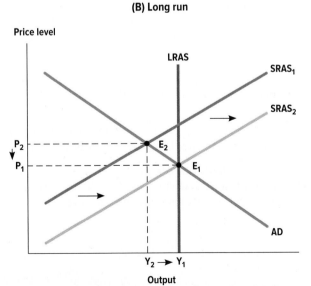

(B) Long run

As the rainfall returns and wages fall due to increased unemployment, the short-run aggregate supply curve will slide out. This means that prices and output return to their original levels.

costs of production for firms will decrease. The short-run aggregate supply curve shifts back to the right, as shown in panel B. Eventually, costs will decrease to the point where the SRAS is back to its original level, and the economy will be back at its old long-run equilibrium (point E_1). In the long run, both prices and output return to their initial level.

Permanent supply shocks

Now let's think about a permanent supply shock. Instead of just a short-term drought, imagine that cataclysmic climate change makes it impossible to grow corn or anything else with yields similar to what farmers now get in the Midwest. Since the Midwest is integral to U.S. food production, there simply isn't enough other land to make up the difference. With a loss of one of the factors of production (in this case, land), the LRAS curve will shift to the left, as in panel A of Figure 29-13.

This change has effects in the short run as well. Corn grown in the Midwest is important in the production of goods throughout the economy. Everything from the cereal you eat for breakfast to the gas you put in your car likely contains some corn or product derived from corn. The increase in food and other prices means that the costs of production will also rise, shifting the SRAS to the left. The SRAS curve may not shift immediately to the new long-run equilibrium point. In the short run, the equilibrium may move only to point E_2 in panel A of Figure 29-13.

As long as prices are above the long-run equilibrium level, the SRAS will continue to shift to the left, as shown in panel B. This process continues until the economy reaches a new long-run equilibrium (at point E_3), with higher prices and a lower level of potential output.

FIGURE 29-13

The effect of a decrease in long-run supply: Climate change

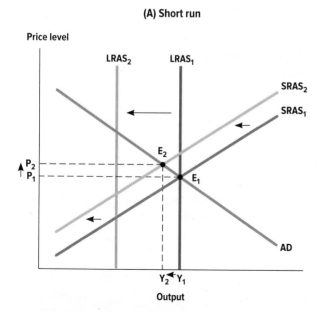

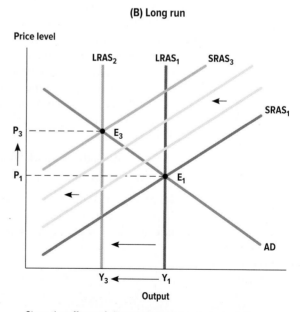

With climate change, the impact to the economy is initially similar to what occurs with a shock like a drought. The aggregate supply curve shifts in. At the new short-run equilibrium, point E_2, prices are higher and output falls.

Since the effects of climate change are permanent, the long-run supply curve shifts to the left. With continually increasing prices, the short-run aggregate supply curve will shift to the left until it reaches the new long-run equilibrium at point E_3. At this point, prices are much higher and output lower than the original equilibrium.

Comparing demand and supply shocks

LO 29.9 Use the AD/AS framework to determine whether an observed change in output and prices was due to a demand shock or a supply shock.

The AD/AS model is a powerful tool for understanding overall economic conditions and figuring out how to formulate policy response to shocks. Successful economic policy hinges on being able to tell the difference between a demand and a supply shock. If you apply a policy designed to fight the effects of one kind of shock and it turns out to be the other, you could potentially make things even worse.

This section describes the two main challenges that arise when using the AD/AS model to analyze events in the economy:

- If you see a specific shock, can you tell which side of the economy it is going to affect?
- If you see a change in the economy, can you work backward to figure out what type of shock might have caused it?

First, think through whom a shock will affect and what role they play in the economy. For example:

- Higher oil prices are going to affect businesses that use oil to produce goods. This means that an oil-price change will be a shock to the *supply side* of the economy. Because the shock has to do with prices rather than real factors of production, it will affect only the *short-run aggregate supply curve,* and not the long-run curve.
- In contrast, if you see a shock that affects consumers or government spending, it is likely to affect consumption. It therefore will act on the *demand side* of the economy.

Table 29-4 shows some examples of demand and supply shocks. For each shock, think about (1) which group of people the shock will affect, (2) whether it is a demand-side or a supply-side shock, and (3) whether it is a long-run or a short-run shock.

When thinking in the other direction—when working backward from effect on the economy to figuring out the cause—there are clear predictions about how different types of shocks will affect prices and output; these give clues about what the main shock must have been. For example, when output falls in the short run, the cause could be either a reduction in aggregate demand or a reduction in short-run aggregate supply.

The two cases are shown in Figure 29-14 (which actually recalls panels from Figure 29-11 and Figure 29-12). By comparing the two panels of Figure 29-14, we can see very different effects on prices:

- The demand-side shock will reduce prices (panel A).
- The supply-side shock will increase the price level (panel B).

So, an economy in which output has decreased and prices have decreased would suggest a decrease in demand. On the other hand, an economy in which output has decreased and prices have increased would suggest that there has been a supply-side shock.

TABLE 29-4

Comparing demand and supply shocks

The first task to determine how an event will affect the overall economy is to decide whether it is a demand or a supply shock. This means figuring out whom the shock most affects and what their role is in the economy.

Event	What kind of shock?
Temporary increase in the price of oil	Short-run supply shock
Technological innovation	Long-run supply shock
Drop in consumer confidence	Demand shock
Sudden increase in immigration	Long-run supply shock

FIGURE 29-14

Different short-run impacts of decreases in aggregate demand versus aggregate supply   When the economy experiences a decrease in aggregate demand, both prices and output decrease in the short run. But when the economy experiences a decrease in aggregate supply, prices rise and output falls in the short run.

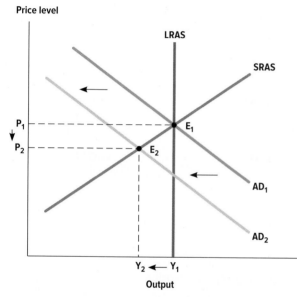

(A) Decrease in aggregate demand

When aggregate demand shifts in due to a decrease in aggregate demand, the new short-term equilibrium moves to point E_2. At point E_2 both prices and output are lower.

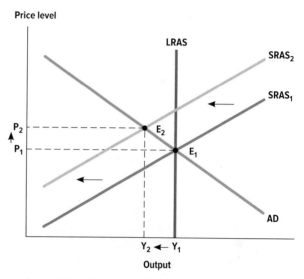

(B) Decrease in aggregate supply

A drought that destroys much of the corn crop will shift the short-run aggregate supply curve in. In the short run, prices will be higher, and output falls.

Sometimes, however, there can be a complex combination of overlapping shocks to untangle. For example, when the U.S. housing bubble popped in 2007, banks and other financial institutions faced large losses from the bad loans they had made. Their need to cover those losses and their growing pessimism about the economy made them less willing to lend to businesses. For firms, borrowing became harder and more expensive. The increase in the cost of doing business was a short-run supply-side shock; it shifted the short-run aggregate supply curve to the left. That was on top of the demand shock that happened when consumers reduced their spending after the housing bubble popped. The demand shock led to a further decrease in the level of output in the economy.

Demand-side and supply-side shocks can also differ in the long run:

- Demand-side shocks will cause a change to the price level in the long run since the short-run supply curve will shift in to restore the long-run equilibrium output.

- For a supply-side shock, there are no long-run changes to the price level. If the short-run supply curve initially shifts to the left, for example, prices will adjust to restore the long-run equilibrium.

We summarize the difference between supply-side and demand-side shocks in Table 29-5.

For an example of economic detective work to tease out whether shifts in supply or demand were responsible for observed effects in an economy, see the Real Life box "The Kobe earthquake and aggregate supply."

TABLE 29-5

Demand-side versus supply-side shocks

This table summarizes the impacts of a shock on the demand and supply sides of an economy. Each shock has a different effect on the economy in the long and short run.

Supply or demand?	Positive shock	Negative shock
Demand side	Short run: Output increases Price increases	Short run: Output decreases Price decreases
Demand side	Long run: No change in output Price increases	Long run: No change in output Price decreases
Temporary shock: Supply side	Short run: Output increases Price decreases	Short run: Output decreases Price increases
Temporary shock: Supply side	Long run: No change in output No change in price	Long run: No change in output No change in price
Permanent shock: Supply side	Long run: Output increases Price decreases	Long run: Output decreases Price increases

Real Life

The Kobe earthquake and aggregate supply

In January 1995, a large earthquake rocked the port city of Kobe, Japan. Many people lost their lives. Buildings and infrastructure were destroyed. The value of Japan's stock market dropped substantially. It was one of the most expensive natural disasters the world had ever seen, with a final damage bill equal to about 2.5 percent of Japan's GDP.

However, amazingly, only 15 months after the disaster, Japanese manufacturing was back to 96 percent of the pre-earthquake trend. How well can the aggregate supply and aggregate demand model explain the recovery of the Japanese economy?

George Horwich, an economist at Purdue, studied this question. The earthquake destroyed a large amount of capital, and so we would expect the short-run aggregate supply curve to shift to the left. This shift would push the price level higher and would reduce output, increasing unemployment. However, when Horwich looked at the data, he saw a different picture. Surprisingly, the price level was relatively stable, and employment was constant.

How can we match up those data with the predictions of the AD/AS model? There are two possibilities in Kobe: Either the aggregate supply curve shifted quickly back out again in the months after the earthquake or the aggregate demand curve shifted out.

We have a way to figure out what actually happened. If an increase in aggregate demand occurred, the price level would increase. But the data showed that the price level stayed constant, or even decreased. This suggests that there wasn't an aggregate demand response. Instead, Horwich argues, the aggregate supply curve shifted back out.

Although the damage in Kobe was significant, it seems that the Japanese economy was able to adjust to this very large shock in one part of the economy by rearranging how resources were used. In this process of adjustment, the aggregate supply curve shifted back out, returning the economy to its original position. The response to the Kobe earthquake tells us that the macro-economy can sometimes adjust surprisingly quickly, even after large supply-side shocks.

Source: George Horwich, "Economic Lessons of the Kobe Earthquake," *Economic Development and Cultural Change* 48, no. 3 (April 2000), pp. 521–542.

☐ Will a positive demand shock lead to increased or decreased output in short-run equilibrium? What about in long-run equilibrium? **[LO 29.7]**

☐ How do prices and output change with a leftward shift in aggregate supply? **[LO 29.8]**

☐ How do changes in the price level help distinguish between a demand-side shock to the economy and a supply-side shock? **[LO 29.9]**

The Role of Public Policy

LO 29.10 Describe the policy options the government can use to counteract supply and demand shocks.

It can take a long time for the economy to fully adjust to demand and supply shocks, and waiting for adjustments often isn't comfortable for people who experience changing prices and unemployment. When the economy hits a recession, voters often call upon politicians to "do something." We will examine the role of government in the economy in more detail when we look at fiscal policy and monetary policy in later chapters. For now, we will consider just one channel through which the government can try to boost the economy out of a recession: government spending.

Government spending to counter negative demand shocks

Imagine that things are going badly in the economy: Newspapers are full of stories about falling home prices, mass layoffs, and factory closings. With the steady beat of bad news, consumer confidence decreases and consumption falls. These changes cause the aggregate demand curve to shift to the left, shown in panel A of Figure 29-15. Output and the price level decrease.

The government can try to counter this negative demand shock by increasing government spending. As we have seen, the effect of an increase in government spending is to shift the aggregate demand curve to the right. For policy-makers, the goal is to counteract the negative shock to aggregate demand with a positive one, and restore the curve to its original position.

This is not so easy to do. In practice, it can be hard to gauge the overall effect of government spending on aggregate demand. Even worse, it's rare to perfectly design government policy so that spending occurs at just the right amount to restore aggregate demand to its original level. Panel B of Figure 29-15 shows a case in which the policy is partly, but not entirely, successful: The increase in government spending shifts the AD curve only part of the way back to its previous position.

What about the long run? We know that for any demand-side shock, there can't be an effect on long-run output. According to our model, if the government did nothing, then eventually prices would adjust downward until output rose to its previous level. This occurs through changes on the supply side, as cheaper prices reduce the costs of production, shifting the aggregate supply curve to the right.

If, instead of doing nothing, the government increases spending to stimulate the economy, the end result will be slightly different. In this example, government policy was only partly successful, so the economy still has to adjust before reaching long-run equilibrium. The process of adjustment is still the same as before, except that, now, SRAS doesn't have as far to go as it did when the government hadn't acted. In the end, the long-run effect of the government's increase in spending is that the previous level of output will be restored, but at a slightly higher price level than if the government hadn't acted, holding all else constant. The result is that with a given income or wealth, people can buy less. This trade-off between increasing the speed of adjustment and allowing higher prices is a genuine challenge the government faces in setting policies to fight downturns in the economy.

FIGURE 29-15

Government response to a negative demand shock: The housing crash

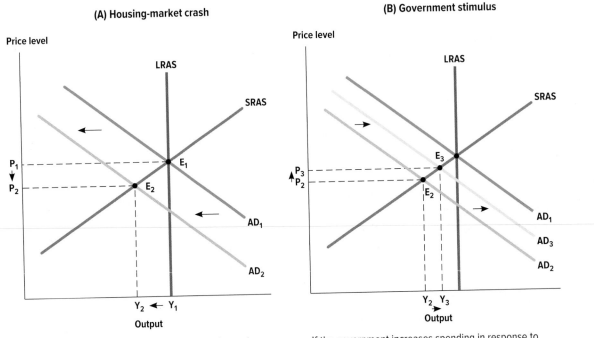

(A) Housing-market crash

In a crash of the housing market, aggregate demand drops sharply, shifting the curve in. The new short-term equilibrium has lower prices and output.

(B) Government stimulus

If the government increases spending in response to the housing crash, aggregate demand will shift back out. The new equilibrium is at a higher level of prices and output, but still below the levels under the long-run equilibrium.

Government spending to counter negative supply shocks

Now imagine a short-run supply-side shock: A terrible drought has reduced the corn harvest by 80 percent. The short-run aggregate supply curve has shifted to the left, as in panel A of Figure 29-16. The economy is now at point E_2: The level of output has fallen, and prices have risen.

In this case, policy-makers are in a bind. If they choose to do nothing, the economy will be stuck in a period of higher prices and lower output (stagflation). We'll talk more about the challenges of stagflation in Chapter 33, "Inflation." For now, imagine a period in which prices increase but with large amounts of unemployment and low output. It's a very hard situation to get out of. Remember that prices can be very sticky, especially when they have to adjust downward.

Instead of waiting for the aggregate supply curve to shift back out to the right, the government could choose to increase government spending in order to shift the aggregate demand curve. This action and effect are shown in panel B of Figure 29-16. With the shift in aggregate demand, the economy moves to a new short-run equilibrium at point E_3. While this shift solves the problem of low output and unemployment, it actually drives prices even higher.

In both examples, the long-run result of government intervention is higher prices at the same level of output. So, why would the government ever choose to intervene? One reason concerns the speed of the recovery. Without the increase in government spending, adjustment might have been a long and painful process. In addition, lower prices are not always a good thing. As we will see in Chapter 33, "Inflation," falling prices, called *deflation*, carry another set of challenges for the economy.

FIGURE 29-16

Government response to a negative supply shock: Extreme drought in the Midwest

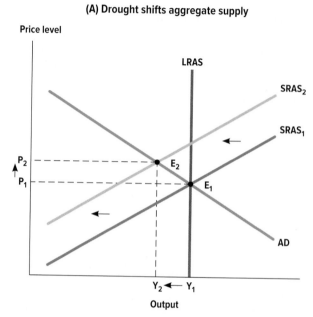

(A) Drought shifts aggregate supply

(B) Government response

Like before, a drought shifts the short-run aggregate supply curve in, which pushes the economy toward a new short-run equilibrium with higher prices and lower output.

In response to the drought, the government increases spending, which shifts the aggregate demand curve out. Instead of falling back to the original equilibrium, the new long-run equilibrium is at a higher prices level.

The bottom line is that government spending is a *short-term* policy action that is often applied to address short-term demand shocks. Government spending is less effective in countering negative supply shocks, but political pressures can sometimes drive government action even when it's not a great solution.

✓CONCEPT CHECK

☐ What is the long-term effect on prices and output when the government counters a negative demand shock with an increase in spending? **[LO 29.10]**

Conclusion

In this chapter, we created a model of the whole economy. This model is relatively simple, yet ambitious. It helps us to understand what drives key macroeconomics outcomes such as prices, unemployment, and GDP.

The aggregate demand and aggregate supply model breaks the economy down into two sides. The *demand side* is composed of all the components of expenditure in the economy: consumption, investment, government spending, and net exports. The aggregate demand curve identifies the relationship between overall price levels and aggregate demand in the economy. On the supply side of the economy, the aggregate supply curve identifies the relationship between overall price levels and total production in the economy.

In the short run the economy responds to changes in the price level by increasing or decreasing output, so the short-run aggregate supply curve is upward-sloping. In the long run, production is determined by the availability of inputs for production and the technology to convert inputs to outputs. In the long run, there is no relationship between the price level and output. The long-run equilibrium occurs at the intersection of the aggregate demand and long-run aggregate supply curves.

We used the model of aggregate demand and aggregate supply to understand the recession that engulfed the United States after the housing bubble popped in 2007, shifting the aggregate demand curve to the left. We also used it to understand the government's response, a stimulus package whose aim was to shift the aggregate demand curve back out and stimulate output and employment.

In the next chapter, we'll talk about policy responses to economic shocks in more depth and explore the different effects of spending versus taxes.

Key Terms

aggregate demand curve, p. 736

aggregate supply curve, p. 743

business cycle, p. 745

supply shocks, p. 748

Summary

LO 29.1 Show how the aggregate expenditure equilibrium model can be used to trace out the aggregate demand curve and understand why the aggregate demand curve slopes downward.

The aggregate demand and supply model captures the relationship between prices and output in the economy. It comprises two parts: the *aggregate demand* curve, which shows the relationship between the price level and total demand in the economy, and the *aggregate supply* curve, which shows the relationship between the price level and the total supply in the economy. The aggregate demand curve can be traced out by graphing how equilibrium planned aggregate expenditure changes as the price level changes. The aggregate demand curve is downward-sloping because consumption, investment, and net exports all decline when the price level rises.

LO 29.2 List factors that could cause the aggregate demand curve to shift.

Since the aggregate demand curve is derived from the definition of GDP—$Y = C + I + G + NX$—anything that affects any of the components of GDP will shift the aggregate demand curve. For example, if government spending increases, the aggregate demand curve will shift out; if net exports decrease, the aggregate demand curve will shift in. When the aggregate demand curve shifts, there will be a short-run change in output, but no long-run shift in output. The price level will change in both the short run and the long run.

LO 29.3 Explain how changes in government spending and taxes can have a multiplier effect on aggregate demand.

When the government increases spending, it sets into motion a series of additional rounds of expenditure in the economy. Each time aggregate expenditure increases, disposable incomes go up and households respond by spending more. The increased spending causes another round of increased aggregate expenditure, and the process continues. With taxes, the story is similar. A reduction in taxes increases disposable income, triggering a chain of higher spending, increased incomes, and further spending. There is, however, an important difference between the impact of taxes and government spending. Whereas government spending increases aggregate expenditure dollar-for-dollar in the first round of the multiplier process, a portion of the tax cut gets saved. Thus, the multiplier associated with a given dollar value of tax cuts will tend to be smaller than the multiplier associated with the same dollar increase in spending.

LO 29.4 Explain the difference between the short run and long run in the economy.

The aggregate supply curve is actually two different curves: a *long-run aggregate supply* (LRAS) curve and a *short-run aggregate supply* (SRAS) curve. The long-run aggregate supply curve shows what the economy can produce if all the factors of production are being utilized. This doesn't depend on prices, so the LRAS is vertical.

The SRAS is an upward-sloping curve between prices and output. There are factors that affect only the cost of production and do not change the amount of factors available for production. These changes will only shift the SRAS curve.

LO 29.5 Demonstrate a shift in the short-run aggregate supply curve and list factors that cause it to shift.

If the prices of *inputs* change, the entire aggregate supply curve will shift. Any change that makes production more expensive for firms will shift the supply curve in (to the left). Any change that makes production cheaper for producers will shift the aggregate supply curve out (to the right).

LO 29.6 Demonstrate a shift in the long-run aggregate supply curve and list factors that cause it to shift.

Anything that affects the output possible using these factors will shift the long-run aggregate supply curve. If the potential output of the economy expands, the long-run aggregate supply curve will shift out. If the production possibility frontier for the economy contracts, the long-run aggregate supply curve will shift in.

LO 29.7 Explain the short-run and long-run effects of a shift in aggregate demand.

When there is a positive shock in aggregate demand, prices and output increase in the short run. Eventually, input prices and wages catch up to the increase in the price level. The SRAS curve slowly adjusts to the right; in the end, this adjustment further increases prices while decreasing output. The final result is that output falls back to its original level, and prices are higher than they were originally. For a negative shock, the aggregate demand shifts to the left. Prices and output fall. The adjustment of the SRAS curve to the right brings output back to its original level, but prices fall even further.

LO 29.8 Explain the short-run and long-run effects of a shift in aggregate supply.

The aggregate supply curve is a relationship between total supply in the economy and price level. Anything that affects the factors of production or the level of technology will affect both the long-run aggregate supply curve and the short-run aggregate supply curve; this shift is a permanent supply shock. Anything that affects the prices of inputs or the costs of doing business will affect the short-run aggregate supply curve, but not the long-run aggregate supply curve; this shift is a temporary supply shock. When there is a temporary supply shock,

the price level and output change in the short run but not in the long run. For a permanent supply shock, both the price level and output change in the long run.

LO 29.9 Use the AD/AS framework to determine whether an observed change in output and prices was due to a demand shock or a supply shock.

In reality, we do not observe aggregate supply and demand curves shifting. Instead, what we see are changes in output and the price level. With the help of the AD/AS model, we can infer whether the changes in the economy were more likely to be caused by a shift in supply or demand and whether the shock was temporary or permanent. A situation where output falls and prices rise is likely due to a backward shift of the aggregate demand curve. If, however, output falls and prices rise, it's likely that the culprit is an upward shift in aggregate supply. Temporary shifts in demand and supply do not cause permanent changes in output and prices. Permanent shifts leave output unchanged, but they can lead to permanent changes in the price level. If, for instance, there is a permanent upward shift in the supply curve, long-run output will eventually return to potential, but prices will be permanently higher.

LO 29.10 Describe the policy options the government can use to counteract supply and demand shocks

---

Depending on the type of shock, the government can choose to increase or reduce government spending in response. The government often chooses to act because action is preferable to waiting for the economy to adjust after a shock. Shortfalls in aggregate demand can be corrected by increasing spending. The same is true of aggregate demand, although the government might want to be careful in this situation. Regardless of the shock, increases in government spending will produce higher prices in the long run.

Review Questions

1. Identify the four components of aggregate demand. Explain the relationship between aggregate demand and the price level. **[LO 29.1]**

2. The demand curves for individual goods are typically downward-sloping, due both to the substitution effect as well as to the income effect. Why does the substitution effect not affect the aggregate demand curve? **[LO 29.1]**

3. What is the relationship between the equilibrium level of aggregate expenditure in an economy and the aggregate demand curve? According to the aggregate expenditure equilibrium model, why does the aggregate demand curve slope downward? **[LO 29.1]**

4. What effect does rising business optimism and confidence have on the aggregate demand curve? What effect does falling optimism and confidence in business prospects have on the aggregate demand curve? [**LO 29.2**]

5. List several events that could cause a "demand-side" recession (i.e., a recession caused by a fall in aggregate demand). [**LO 29.2**]

6. Everything else equal, which will have a larger effect on aggregate demand and GDP: a $100 million reduction in taxes or a $100 million increase in government spending? Is everything else equal in practice? Why or why not? [**LO 29.3**]

7. Suppose the economy is in a recession and the president wants to stimulate production and create jobs. To do this, he has decided to increase government spending. Some of his economic advisors are suggesting the marginal propensity to consume (MPC) has a value of 0.9 and others are suggesting the value is 0.8. How will this difference in the value of the MPC affect the president's decision regarding the dollar amount of the increase in government spending? [**LO 29.3**]

8. Which typically can change faster: the components of aggregate demand or the components of aggregate supply? Explain. [**LO 29.4**]

9. Explain the difference between sticky wages and sticky prices. How do these two ideas explain the upward slope of the short-run aggregate supply curve? Why don't sticky wages or sticky prices affect the long-run aggregate supply curve? [**LO 29.4**]

10. List several events that could cause a "supply-side" recession (i.e., a recession caused by a fall in aggregate supply). [**LO 29.5**]

11. In the late 1990s, the United States experienced very high GDP growth, record low unemployment rates, and virtually nonexistent inflation. Based on the conclusions of the AD/AS model, what could explain this combination of good economic results? [**LO 29.5, 29.6**]

12. Why is long-run economic growth generally positive rather than negative? [**LO 29.6**]

13. Explain the mechanism through which the economy adjusts in the short run and the long run when consumer confidence falls. [**LO 29.7**]

14. Suppose a country is in the midst of an economic boom and is running large budget surpluses. The president suggests that due to the good economic conditions, the time is ripe for a large tax cut. What are the arguments for and against this position? [**LO 29.7, 29.10**]

15. Suppose a country is in the midst of a serious recession, with high unemployment and large government deficits. The president suggests that in times like this the

government has the obligation to "tighten its belt" and cut spending since so many families around the country have to do the same thing. Do you agree with the president? Why or why not? [**LO 29.7, 29.10**]

16. Using the aggregate demand and aggregate supply model, explain the difference between a one-year drought and permanent climate change. What happens to the price level and output in the short run and in the long run for each type of shock? [**LO 29.5, 29.6, 29.8**]

17. A government official observes that there has been a short-run increase in the price level. Is it possible for her to determine whether this was caused by a demand shock or a supply shock? Why or why not? [**LO 29.9**]

18. A government official observes that there has been a long-run increase in the price level but no change in the level of potential output. Is it possible for her to determine whether this was caused by a demand shock or a supply shock? Why or why not? [**LO 29.9**]

19. Why does the government have a harder time counteracting shifts in AS than in AD? [**LO 29.8, 29.10**]

20. Whenever AD or AS shifts, putting the economy out of long-run equilibrium, AS has a natural tendency to shift in such a way as to bring the economy back into long-run equilibrium. If the economy always eventually comes back to long-run equilibrium, why would the government ever try to implement policies to bring the economy into equilibrium through government means? [**LO 29.10**]

Problems and Applications

1. Is there a negative, positive, or no relationship between the price level and the following components of aggregate demand? [**LO 29.1**]
   a. Consumption.
   b. Investment.
   c. Government spending.
   d. Net exports.

2. If the government cuts taxes, what components of aggregate demand are affected? [**LO 29.1**]

3. Consider the planned aggregate expenditure lines in Figure 29P-1. [**LO 29.1**]
   a. Suppose that the planned aggregate expenditure lines correspond to price levels of 100, 110, and 120. Which line corresponds to which price level?
   b. Use the information in the expenditure diagram to trace out the aggregate demand curve for this economy.

4. For each of the following shocks, say whether it is a demand-side shock or a supply-side shock. [**LO 29.2, 29.5**]

FIGURE 29P-1

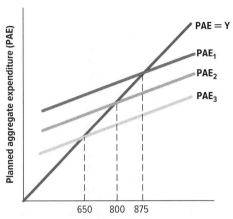

a. Consumer confidence falls.

b. Government spending increases.

c. The price of foreign goods increases.

d. The price of oil increases.

e. A cyclone destroys manufacturing plants.

5. In the late 1990s, the U.S. experienced a technology boom. In part the boom was due to a revolution in communication technology that resulted in a massive expansion of the Internet; in part the boom was due to households and firms purchasing new computer equipment in anticipation of Y2K. What two curves of the model would be affected by these events? **[LO 29.2, 29.5]**

6. Suppose the marginal propensity to consume (MPC) is either 0.75, 0.80, or 0.90. **[LO 29.3]**

    a. For each value of the MPC, calculate the expenditure multiplier, or the impact of a one-dollar increase in government spending on GDP.

    b. For each value of the MPC, calculate the impact on GDP of a $250 million increase in government spending.

    c. Explain the relationship between the MPC and the impact of a change in government spending on GDP.

7. Suppose the marginal propensity to consume (MPC) is either 0.75, 0.80, or 0.90. **[LO 29.3]**

    a. For each value of the MPC, calculate the impact of a one-dollar decrease in taxes on GDP.

    b. For each value of the MPC, calculate the impact on GDP of a $250 million decrease in taxes.

    c. Explain the relationship between the MPC and the impact of a change in taxes on GDP.

8. Say whether the following statements are true or false. **[LO 29.4]**

    a. In the long run, prices don't affect output.

    b. In the short run, prices may affect output.

9. Say whether the following statements are true or false. **[LO 29.4]**

    a. If the prices of all final goods and services are sticky, then the short-run aggregate supply (SRAS) curve is horizontal at the given price level.

    b. If the prices of inputs and wages are not fixed by contracts, and instead adjust more quickly to demand and supply shocks, then the SRAS curve is more vertical.

10. "Fracking" is a newly invented technology that allows drillers to extract significantly larger quantities of natural gas from existing deposits than was previously possible. How is this discovery likely to affect the economy? (*Hint:* Think about whether this will have a short-run or long-run effect.) **[LO 29.5, 29.6]**

11. Throughout the nineteenth and twentieth centuries, the U.S. economy experienced frequent ups and downs, but over the past 200 years, the real GDP in the United States rose from roughly $8.2 billion to over $16.1 *trillion,* an increase by a factor of nearly 2,000 times. This growth represents a change in which curve? **[LO 29.6]**

12. Suppose that a statement by the chair of the Federal Reserve Board about the state of the economy causes a loss of consumer confidence. What will be the long-run impact on the economy if the government allows the economy to adjust without a policy response? **[LO 29.7]**

    a. Output will fall below its initial level in the long run and the price level will decline.

    b. Output will return to its initial level in the long run, but the price level will be lower.

    c. Output will return to its initial level in the long run, but the price level will be higher.

    d. Output will rise above its initial level in the long run and the price level will rise.

13. For each of the following situations, use an AD/AS model to describe what happens to price levels and output in the United States in the short run. In each case, assume the economy starts in long- and short-run equilibrium, and describe the appropriate shifts in the AS or AD curves. **[LO 29.7, 29.8]**

    a. A stock market crash reduces people's wealth.

    b. The spread of democracy around the world increases consumer confidence in the United States.

    c. The European economy crashes.

d. The United States enters into an arms race with China, resulting in a significant increase in military spending.

e. A revolution in Iran results in a significant reduction in the world's supply of oil.

f. Terrorist activities temporarily halt the ability of Americans to engage in certain productive activities such as transportation and finance.

g. Intel develops a new computer chip that is faster and cheaper than previous chips.

h. A summer of perfect weather in the Midwest leads to record harvests of corn, wheat, and soybeans.

14. For each of the following scenarios, say whether the shock was a demand-side shock, a supply-side shock, or a combination of both shocks. **[LO 29.9]**

a. The price level and GDP both fell. GDP then increased, but the price level fell even further.

b. In the long run, the economy had the same level of output but a higher price level.

c. In the short run, the price level increased, but GDP fell.

d. In the long run, GDP increased, and the price level fell.

e. In the long run, GDP increased, and the price level was constant.

15. In 2009, during the height of the U.S. financial crisis, real GDP fell 3.5 percent, and the Consumer Price Index fell from 215.3 to 214.9. Was this recession likely caused by a shift in aggregate demand or aggregate supply? **[LO 29.9]**

16. In 1974, GDP fell by 0.6 percent, and inflation increased from 6.2 percent to 11.0 percent. Was this recession likely caused by a shift in aggregate demand or aggregate supply? **[LO 29.9]**

For questions 17–20, use an AD/AS model to answer the following questions. In each case assume the economy starts in long- and short-run equilibrium, and show the appropriate shifts in the AS or AD curves.

17. Suppose a stock market crash reduces people's wealth. **[LO 29.7, 29.8, 29.10]**

a. Show what happens to price levels and output in the United States in the short run.

b. Suppose the government takes no action to help the economy. What happens to price levels and output in the long run?

c. Suppose, instead, the government decides to take action to help the economy. What action(s) would you recommend? Why?

d. If the U.S. government makes the appropriate policy response, what happens to price levels and output in the long run?

18. Suppose the spread of democracy around the world increases consumer confidence in the United States. **[LO 29.7, 29.8, 29.10]**

a. Show what happens to price levels and output in the United States in the short run.

b. Suppose the government takes no action to help the economy. What happens to price levels and output in the long run?

c. Suppose, instead, the government decides to take action to help the economy. What action(s) would you recommend? Why?

d. If the U.S. government makes the appropriate policy response, what happens to price levels and output in the long run?

19. Suppose a revolution in Iran results in a significant reduction in the world's supply of oil. **[LO 29.7, 29.8, 29.10]**

a. Show what happens to price levels and output in the United States in the short run.

b. Suppose the government takes no action to help the economy. What happens to price levels and output in the long run?

c. Suppose, instead, the government decides to take action to help the economy. What action(s) would you recommend? Why?

d. If the U.S. government makes the appropriate policy response, what happens to price levels and output in the long run?

20. Suppose a summer of perfect weather in the Midwest leads to record harvests of corn, wheat, and soybeans. **[LO 29.7, 29.8, 29.10]**

a. What happens to price levels and output in the United States in the short run?

b. Suppose the government takes no action to help the economy. Show what happens to price levels and output in the long run.

c. If the U.S. government reacts to the record harvests by increasing taxes or decreasing spending, what happens to price levels and output in the long run?

d. What is the problem associated with the government reacting to the record harvests by increasing taxes or decreasing spending?

Endnotes

1. The impact of increasing government transfers to households can be analyzed similarly to the impact of a tax cut.

Fiscal Policy

Learning Objectives

LO 30.1 Explain the difference between contractionary fiscal policy and expansionary fiscal policy.

LO 30.2 Explain how fiscal policy can counteract short-run economic fluctuations.

LO 30.3 Identify the time lags that complicate the formulation of fiscal policy.

LO 30.4 Discuss how stabilizers can automatically adjust fiscal policy as the economy changes.

LO 30.5 Describe the theory and evidence about Ricardian equivalence and what it implies for the effectiveness of fiscal policy.

LO 30.6 Describe how revenue and spending determine a government budget and how the U.S. budget deficit occurs.

LO 30.7 Explain the difference between the government deficit and debt.

LO 30.8 Understand how Treasury securities work and why people value them.

LO 30.9 Identify the benefits and costs of government debt.

FROM HOUSING BUBBLE TO GREAT RECESSION

By 2008, the warning signs were everywhere: Unemployment was increasing. Business confidence was down. The economy was at the start of a recession. What, if anything, could the U.S. government do to give the economy a boost?

The two political parties had different answers: Democrats argued that increasing government spending would kick-start the economy. To that end, they advocated for construction projects and other public investments, with the intention of creating badly needed jobs. Republicans argued that since times were tough, the government should tighten its belt, as individuals do when they face money problems. Their favored solution was to lower taxes, allowing people to keep a larger share of their income, to encourage people to spend more, boosting demand.

© karen roach/Shutterstock

In the end, both sides got a little of what they wanted. One of the first acts of newly elected President Barack Obama was to sign the American Recovery and Reinvestment Act of 2009, more commonly known as the "stimulus plan." That plan included both tax cuts and a sizable increase in government spending. Its total cost was nearly $800 billion—slightly more than 5 percent of U.S. GDP.

Despite the big sum spent, the recovery was slow. When economists looked back four years later (at the end of 2012), the economy had still not fully recovered. In the meantime, millions of people had lost their jobs and homes, and many businesses had closed. Things looked better after another four years (at the end of 2016). While the unemployment rate had hit 10 percent at its peak in 2009, by 2016 the unemployment rate had fallen to about where it was before the recession, under 5 percent. The increased spending and decreased tax revenues, though, had put the U.S. government further into debt. By 2012, the dollar value of the debt had climbed past 100 percent of GDP. In 2016 the debt was 104 percent of GDP.[1]

So, was the stimulus plan a success? We can't judge this simply by looking at what happened before and after it was signed into law. Instead, we need to ask: What *would have* happened if the stimulus plan had *not* been enacted? Or what would have happened if the government had chosen an alternative balance of tax cuts and government spending? Would the level of unemployment and the health of the economy have been better, worse, or just the same?

To answer some of these questions, we'll create a framework for thinking about how taxation and government spending affect the national economy, based on the aggregate demand and supply model you saw in Chapter 29, "Aggregate Demand and Aggregate Supply." By the end of this chapter you should be able to discuss the pros and cons of different policies in terms of their effect on both short-run economic fluctuations and longer-run issues such as the national debt. These questions have been hotly debated since 2007, as policy-makers tried to steer the economy out of the Great Recession, and they continue to have critical implications for the national economy today.

Fiscal Policy

fiscal policy
government decisions about the level of taxation and public spending

Each February, the U.S. president and Congress begin the process of deciding how much to spend on the varied functions of the federal government: how much to spend on building bridges, supporting the military, investing in medical research, and so on. At the same time, Congress decides how much money should be collected in taxes to pay for all of these things. Government decisions about the level of taxation and public spending are called **fiscal policy**.

Expansionary or contractionary

LO 30.1 Explain the difference between contractionary fiscal policy and expansionary fiscal policy.

Fiscal policy is more than just simple budgeting. Choices about how much to spend, how to spend it, and how to raise the necessary funds can have dramatic impacts on the economy. Recall from Chapter 24, "Measuring GDP," that government spending is one of the components of GDP. It is also part of the way we calculate the demand side of the economy in the aggregate demand and aggregate supply model:

$$\text{Aggregate demand} = C + I + G + NX$$

Fiscal policy affects the economy by increasing or decreasing aggregate demand. As we saw in the previous chapter, shifts in the aggregate demand curve translate into higher or lower output and price levels throughout the economy. Fiscal policy affects aggregate demand through two channels: government spending and tax policy.

Government spending *directly* affects the "G" in the aggregate demand equation (above):

- An increase in government spending will generally shift the aggregate demand curve out (to the right).
- A decrease in government spending will shift the aggregate demand curve in (to the left).

Government spending can also have *indirect* effects on the "C" (consumption) and "I" (investment) components of aggregate demand. These effects come through mechanisms called the *multiplier effect* and *crowding out*.[2]

The second channel through which fiscal policy drives aggregate demand is tax policy. This effect acts on aggregate demand *directly* through consumption, or the "C" part of the aggregate demand equation. It can also indirectly affect the other components, such as investment. Before anyone gets a paycheck, the government takes some money in taxes. Consumption therefore depends not on total income but, rather, on *disposable income*—what's left after taxes. How much individuals consume is related to their incomes:

- If the tax rate increases, workers will take home less disposable income, and we can expect them to reduce their consumption. As a result, the aggregate demand curve will shift in (to the left).
- If, on the other hand, the tax rate decreases, workers take home more money and will consume more. The decrease in the tax rate will shift the aggregate demand curve out (to the right).

We differentiate two types of fiscal policy. The first aims to increase aggregate demand, and the second is used to decrease aggregate demand. The term **expansionary fiscal policy** describes the overall effect of decisions about government spending and taxation intended to increase aggregate demand. Increased government spending and lower taxes both have expansionary effects: They shift the aggregate demand curve to the right, as shown in panel A of Figure 30-1. In contrast, the term **contractionary fiscal policy** describes the overall effect of decisions about government spending and taxation intended to decrease aggregate demand. Decreased government spending and higher taxes both have contractionary effects, shifting the aggregate demand curve in to the left, as shown in panel B of Figure 30-1.

expansionary fiscal policy decisions about government spending and taxation intended to increase aggregate demand

contractionary fiscal policy decisions about government spending and taxation intended to decrease aggregate demand

FIGURE 30-1

Expansionary and contractionary fiscal policy

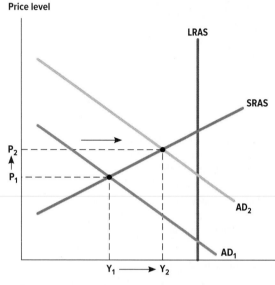

(A) Expansionary fiscal policy shifts the AD curve to the right

Increasing government spending and lowering taxes are fiscal policies with expansionary effects, shifting the aggregate demand curve out to the right from AD_1 to AD_2. This has the effect of increasing output and price levels.

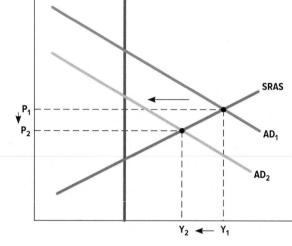

(B) Contractionary fiscal policy shifts the AD curve to the left

Decreasing government spending and raising taxes are fiscal policies with contractionary effects, shifting the aggregate demand curve in to the left from AD_1 to AD_2. This has the effect of decreasing output and price levels.

Policy response to short-run economic fluctuations

LO 30.2 Explain how fiscal policy can counteract short-run economic fluctuations.

One of the most important ways that policy-makers use fiscal policy is to try to smooth out fluctuations in the economy that might hurt consumers and businesses. In this section, we'll show how policy-makers use fiscal policy to counteract the effects of economic shocks through the aggregate supply and aggregate demand model.

In Chapter 29, "Aggregate Demand and Aggregate Supply," we saw how a shock like the collapse of the U.S. housing market in late 2007 can affect the national economy. The most immediate consequence of the steep drop in housing prices was that homeowners felt poorer. This response shifted the aggregate demand curve to the left. Panel A of Figure 30-2 shows the leftward shift of the aggregate demand curve, from AD_1 to AD_2. (If this figure looks familiar, it's because you saw a version of it before—as Figure 29-15, in a discussion of government response to a negative demand shock.) The decrease in aggregate demand caused the economy to produce below its level of potential output. The result was lower GDP (output) and higher unemployment, seen in panel A as a reduction in output from Y_1 to Y_2.

According to the AD/AS model, if nothing else happened, the economy would have automatically corrected itself—eventually. Wages would have fallen in response to unemployment, and lower production costs would bring other prices down. This response would cause the short-run aggregate supply curve to shift to the right until the economy returned to its original level of potential output level at Y_1. In the long run, output would have recovered to its previous level, with lower overall prices in the economy.

FIGURE 30-2

Effect of expansionary fiscal policy

(A) Initial market response to fall in AD

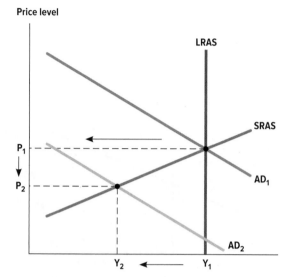

Initially, with a decrease in aggregate demand the AD curve shifts to the left. At the new equilibrium, prices and output are lower than before.

(B) Expansionary fiscal policy restores some AD

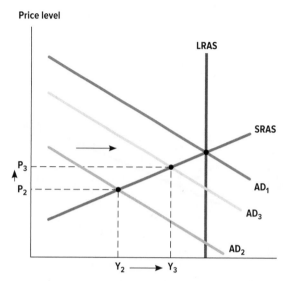

If the government decides to pursue expansionary fiscal policy, it will increase spending, which shifts the AD curve rightward (here, AD_2 to AD_3). The amount of the shift depends on the amount of spending. Here, the government's spending increases output and the price level, but not to their levels before the original fall in AD.

Why didn't lawmakers simply wait for this to happen? Because it could have been a painful and very slow process. The wage rate would have had to fall along with other prices; we saw in Chapter 26, "Unemployment and the Labor Market," some reasons why that might not happen quickly or easily.[3] When businesses fail and people lose their jobs, they want their government to do something about it. They don't want just to hear that the economy will work the problems out if they wait long enough. As economist John Maynard Keynes once said, "In the long run, we are all dead."

We'll show in this chapter that fiscal policy can have real effects on the economy even in the short run. Ideally, the government can counterbalance shocks like the collapse of the housing market, minimizing the damages to consumers and businesses without having to wait for the economy to correct itself in the long run. However, we'll also see that the government may not always be able to improve matters—it might even make things worse, for reasons we describe in the next section.

But if the government *is* going to act, for better or for worse, what should it do? Let's look at examples of both expansionary and contractionary policy responses.

Expansionary policy response

To counteract a decrease in aggregate demand like that caused by the 2007 housing-market collapse, the government can try to boost demand, either by spending more or taxing less. This kind of expansionary policy is often called "Keynesian," in recognition of John Maynard Keynes, who championed the strategy after the Great Depression of the 1930s.

The challenge is finding the dosage of fiscal policy that restores aggregate demand to its pre-recession level. As shown in panel B of Figure 30-2:

- A completely successful stimulus plan would shift the AD curve all the way back from AD_2 to its original position, AD_1.

FIGURE 30-3

Effect of contractionary fiscal policy

(A) Economy overheats from too much AD

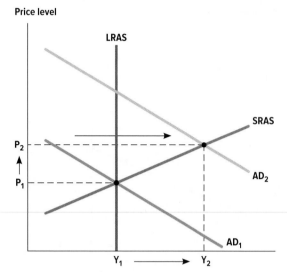

In an overheating economy, prices and output are above the long-run equilibrium in the economy.

(B) Contractionary fiscal policy lowers prices and output

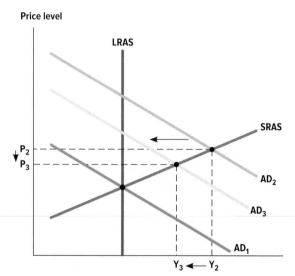

In order to slow down the economy, the government can cut spending or raise taxes, shifting the AD curve leftward. When this happens, prices and output fall, although the economy is still above long-run equilibrium.

- If the stimulus is only partly successful, then it would move the curve only part of the way back, from AD_2 to AD_3. Even a partially successful stimulus may be better than nothing since it pushes the economy toward a better outcome (and the economy can continue adjusting toward the long-run equilibrium over time).

Contractionary policy response

What should the government do when the economy is suffering from the opposite problem—that is, when the economy is growing too quickly? People are often happy when the economy is booming, but government policy-makers worry that big booms can get out of hand. Implementing contractionary fiscal policy to slow down the economy is a lot like shutting down a raging party because you are worried that the guests might regret their choices in the morning. It can be the smart thing to do, even though there will be plenty of grumbling.

A surge in aggregate demand—like that caused by the housing market boom of the early and mid-2000s—increases output and the price level, as shown in panel A of Figure 30-3. Contractionary fiscal policy slows down the economy by cutting government spending or increasing taxes, shifting the aggregate demand curve back in to the left, as shown in panel B of Figure 30-3.

Real-world challenges

LO 30.3 Identify the time lags that complicate the formulation of fiscal policy.

Fiscal policy can seem like a golden solution: Why should any government wait for the economy to correct itself in a slow and painful way when it can do the work much more quickly? The analysis so far suggests that fiscal policy is a potent tool. After all, we saw in Chapter 29, "Aggregate

Demand and Aggregate Supply," that increasing direct government spending has a larger multiplier effect on output than a similarly costly reduction in taxes net of transfers. Looking at the math alone, it seems that there's a strong case for tackling a recession through government spending instead of tax cuts.

Unfortunately, it's not so simple. The analysis rests on some big simplifying assumptions that do not always hold. In the real world, things are more complicated. For instance, we've assumed that government spending doesn't *crowd out* (i.e., reduce) private-sector spending. As we show in greater detail in Chapter 31, "The Basics of Finance," one common form of "crowding out" happens when the government has to borrow in order to finance the extra spending. The government's borrowing tends to push interest rates upward, which then can decrease investment by the private sector. The decrease in private investment undermines the positive impact of government spending.

Even without this kind of crowding out, fiscal policy can be hard to get right. Fiscal policy choices often amount to no more than educated guesses, made without the benefit of all the relevant information. Furthermore, time lags between when policies are chosen and when they are implemented mean that sometimes it is too late to do any good.

To see some of the difficulties of implementing fiscal policy, imagine that the economy is a bus. You're the driver and it's your job to prevent the bus from stalling if it comes to an uphill section of road or from running out of control if it comes to a downhill section. You can step on the gas (in terms of the economy, use expansionary fiscal policy). Or you can step on the brakes (use contractionary fiscal policy). Sounds easy enough, right?

Now imagine that the windshield is blacked out so you can't see the road ahead. In addition, the speedometer indicates how fast you were going three blocks ago rather than how fast you're going now. Even worse, imagine that the bus is run as a democracy, so you also have to get the agreement of a majority of the passengers before you can hit the brakes or the gas, and they typically argue the matter for at least four blocks. Finally, once you actually hit the brakes or gas, it takes six to 12 blocks for that action to take effect.

This is how policy-makers can feel when deciding about fiscal policy. Lags in the policy-making process come from three main sources:

1. Understanding what the current economic situation is. (*You can't see out of the front of the bus, and the speedometer is three blocks delayed.*)

2. The process of deciding on and passing legislation. (*If the president is the bus driver, lawmakers in Congress are the arguing passengers.*)

3. The time it takes for the policy to affect the economy. (*Once you push the gas or the brakes, it takes several blocks until the acceleration or braking engages.*)

Information lag

The first issue involves an *information lag*. It might seem pretty clear that the economy is in a recession or boom, just as it might seem pretty clear from looking out of the back window of a bus that you've started to go up or down a hill. But it can take a long time to collect data that tell policy-makers about GDP, unemployment, and inflation. GDP figures, for example, are released every three months, and they report on economic activity that was happening three or four weeks before. These early numbers aren't always accurate, so it may be six months or more before the true figures are known.

Three to six months is a short time to register a trend in the overall economy. You certainly don't want to be the one who raises the alarm about a huge mountain up ahead of the bus, only to find that it was actually a tiny hill. It took an entire year's worth of data to trigger the announcement by the National Bureau of Economic Research that the U.S. economy was in a recession in 2008. By then, the economy had lost over 1 million jobs.

Just as it takes time to find out how bad things are, it also takes time to find out if the economy has reached the end of a recession. There will be news reports of companies hiring more workers, but it can take months to discover if this has translated into real gains for the economy. In both cases, policy-makers have to make important decisions for the future, but they only know where the economy was a few months ago.

Formulation lag

The second issue is *formulation lag*—the time it takes to decide on and pass legislation. First, a policy needs to be drafted and proposed in Congress, where it becomes a bill. The bill is first debated in the House of Representatives. If at least half of the representatives approve it, it then moves to the Senate. If a majority of the 100 senators approve, the president can sign the bill into law, or veto it, in which case the whole process has to start again. The 535 members of Congress can take a while to make up their minds: It was clear in September 2008, with the collapse of the investment bank Lehman Brothers, that the economy was in real trouble. But the stimulus act wasn't passed until after President Obama and a new Congress had been inaugurated in January 2009.

Implementation lag

The last hurdle for fiscal policy is *implementation lag*. Even after a policy has been proposed and passed, it may take time for it to take effect. It takes time for funds to be disbursed, employees hired, and materials purchased. Even tax cuts can take some time to kick in. In 2008, the government sent U.S. taxpayers a tax rebate as part of a first response to the recession, but it took three months to print and mail the 130 million checks. Even after receiving the checks, it took time for people to spend the money.

These three lags in the policy process—information lag, formulation lag, and implementation lag—make conducting good fiscal policy a tough endeavor. In fact, the lags may be so large that by the time the policy takes effect, the economy might have corrected itself, making the policy unnecessary.[4] In the worst case, the economy might even have started to face the opposite problem, making the policy actively harmful—like slamming on the brake when it turns out the bus is just starting to go uphill, or stepping on the gas when it's now going downhill.

For a timeline of all the delays involved in the 2009 stimulus, see the Real Life box "A timeline of the 2009 stimulus plan."

Real Life

A timeline of the 2009 stimulus plan

The U.S. economy went into recession in 2007, prompting the government to approve a stimulus plan. By 2011, most of the stimulus money had been spent, but not all. Why the delay?

Let's start with the *information lag*. Although experts now concur that the U.S. economy entered into a recession in December 2007, this designation did not become official until a year later, in December 2008. The earliest major response to economic troubles was the Economic Stimulus Act of February 2008, passed under the administration of George W. Bush, which gave a one-time rebate to taxpayers.

However, many people were not convinced that there were serious weaknesses in the economy until September 2008, when the investment bank Lehman Brothers went bankrupt. This bankruptcy prompted an emergency bill creating the Troubled Asset Relief Program (TARP) in October 2008 to stabilize the financial system. Congress then began work on a broader stimulus bill that was intended to help "Main Street" through a combination of tax cuts and spending on projects that could jump-start the economy right away.

The *formulation lag* was actually fairly short, compared with the time it often takes for politicians to agree on legislation. The first version of the stimulus bill, known as the American Relief and Recovery Act (ARRA), was introduced to Congress in January 2009. The bill was passed by both the Senate and the House at the beginning of February. One of President Obama's first acts in the Oval Office was to sign the ARRA into law on February 17, a month after he was inaugurated.

Then *implementation lags* came into play. The stimulus bill appropriated $524 billion in stimulus spending and $288 billion in additional tax cuts. Tax cuts are relatively quick to implement, but public works projects like bridge building take time to set up: First you need to decide where to build the bridge, then you need an architect to design it, and so on.

By the second anniversary of ARRA being signed into law, in February 2011, less than two-thirds of the stimulus money set aside for "contracts, grants, and loans" had been paid out. It took until the end of 2013 for spending and tax cuts to top $800 billion.

Did the stimulus work, despite these delays? We can't know for sure what would have happened if the stimulus bill hadn't been passed. When the University of Chicago Booth School of Business surveyed leading economists, 80 percent felt that the stimulus had helped to reduce unemployment (4 percent disagreed). The Congressional Budget Office (CBO) gives a relatively optimistic review: It estimates that in 2010, GDP was 1.5 to 4.2 percent higher than it would have been without the stimulus. The CBO also estimates that in the same period unemployment fell by somewhere between 0.7 percent and 1.8 percent thanks to the stimulus.

Were these short-term gains worth the billions of dollars in costs? About that, only 46 percent of the economic experts in the University of Chicago survey said yes.

Sources: http://money.cnn.com/2011/02/17/news/economy/stimulus_bill/index.htm; http://money.cnn.com/ 2009/08/04/news/economy/stimulus_spending/index.htm; http://www.cbo.gov/ftpdocs/121xx/doc12185/ 05-25-ARRA.pdf; http://articles.washingtonpost.com/2012-06-06/business/35462388_1_stimulus-work-package-of-temporary-tax-tea-party-caucus.

Policy tools—discretionary and automatic

LO 30.4 Discuss how stabilizers can automatically adjust fiscal policy as the economy changes.

The 2009 stimulus bill is an example of targeted, or *discretionary,* fiscal policy. This is policy that the government actively *chooses* to adopt. Even if there had been no stimulus act at all, though, fiscal policy would still have had some effect on the economy due to already-existing taxes and spending policies. These taxes and government spending that affect fiscal policy without specific action from policy-makers are called **automatic stabilizers**. Let's look at how both taxes and government spending act as automatic stabilizers.

automatic stabilizers taxes and government spending that affect fiscal policy without specific action from policy-makers

Taxes as automatic stabilizers

The income tax system is designed so that people pay higher tax rates as their earnings rise. It turns out that this feature of the tax system creates automatic stabilizers.

Income tax laws require you to pay a given percentage on each portion of your income that falls between certain ranges (often called "tax brackets"). For example, in 2016 single Americans paid the following rates:

- 10 percent in taxes on the portion of their income from $0 to $9,225
- 15 percent from $9,226 to $37,450
- 25 percent from $37,451 to $90,750, and so forth.[5]

Discretionary fiscal policy via taxes usually requires policy-makers to deliberately *change tax rates* owed on income. For example, a discretionary fiscal policy decision in the case above (tax rates in 2016) could have been for policy-makers to decide to raise the tax rate from 25 percent of income between $37,451 and $90,750 to 27 percent.

Automatic stabilizers work differently from that kind of discretionary policy. Even when the schedule of tax rates is completely unchanged, people can end up paying a different proportion of their income as taxes simply because as their income changes, they face different tax obligations. For instance, if you earned $35,000 in 2016, the highest tax rate you faced was 15 percent. But if instead you got a raise to $45,000 in 2016, you would have had to pay a greater proportion of your income as taxes in 2016 (compared to the situation without a raise) because part of your income would now automatically be charged at 25 percent.

Changing the tax rates through discretionary policy allows for active management of the economy. But the effectiveness of such policy can be undermined by information, formulation, and implementation lags. Automatic stabilizers are not affected by those lags. In addition, automatic stabilizers work to push the economy in the same direction that correctly timed and correctly formulated discretionary policy would. For example:

- When the economy is booming, people earn more and move into higher income ranges, so they pay taxes at higher tax rates automatically—without any new intervention from policy-makers. When that happens, the increased taxes that people have to pay put a slight check on overall spending. This slight check cools down aggregate demand by taking away dollars that might have otherwise been spent—just as would happen if policy-makers had intentionally increased taxes as a contractionary fiscal policy.
- When the economy is in a recession, people earn less and so automatically end up paying lower tax rates as they move to lower income ranges. The reduced taxes put more money in people's pockets, encouraging spending. This spurs aggregate demand slightly, just as would happen if the government had intentionally decreased taxes to implement an expansionary fiscal policy.

Government spending as an automatic stabilizer

Some aspects of government spending also work as automatic stabilizers. Unemployment insurance benefits and welfare programs such as food assistance and Medicaid have set eligibility criteria based on low income or unemployment status. Their effects reflect the health of the economy:

- When the economy is booming, fewer people are eligible for these programs, so government spending on them falls. With reduced government spending, the aggregate demand curve shifts to the left. This has a contractionary effect similar to discretionary policy that lowers government spending, reducing aggregate demand.
- In a recession, more people qualify for unemployment insurance and food assistance, so spending on those programs automatically rises. With higher government spending, the aggregate demand curve shifts to the right. This has an expansionary effect similar to discretionary policy that raises government spending, increasing aggregate demand.

In sum, when the U.S. economy hits a recession, fiscal policy *automatically* becomes expansionary: Average tax rates go down and spending on welfare programs goes up. In a booming economy, fiscal policy *automatically* becomes contractionary: Tax rates rise and welfare payments fall. The kind of *discretionary* stimulus bill approved in 2009 comes on top of these automatic effects.

Limits of fiscal policy: The money must come from somewhere

LO 30.5 Describe the theory and evidence about Ricardian equivalence and what it implies for the effectiveness of fiscal policy

Politicians often cut taxes in response to recessions. The idea is that people will spend more money when they have more cash in their hands. That spending, in turn, will raise business profits, create jobs, and help the economy recover.

But it's not always so simple. Those tax cuts don't come for free. The government will eventually have to find a way to make up for the lost tax revenue. That means either cutting an equivalent amount of government spending or, more frequently, raising taxes in the future.

What happens if people see that today's tax cuts just mean higher taxes tomorrow? In that case, people won't want to spend as much from their tax cuts, and the stimulus strategy will be less effective. This idea is known as *Ricardian equivalence.* This theory predicts that if governments cut taxes but not spending, people will *not* change their behavior. Why not? Because people realize that the government will have to borrow money to cover the financial shortfall created by cutting taxes. They realize that at some point in the future, they—or their children or grandchildren—will eventually have to repay the extra government debt through future tax increases. In other words, taxpayers understand that the money to maintain government spending must come from somewhere.

Because taxpayers realize that the debt will eventually have to be repaid through future taxes, today's tax cut will feel more like a loan than a real windfall. According to the Ricardian equivalence theory, rational people should save what they receive rather than spend it today, in order to meet the financial obligation of future taxes. But if people save rather than spend, consumption does not increase, and the tax cut will be unsuccessful in increasing aggregate demand.

Of course, in reality, people may not be so rational and forward-looking. When they get a tax cut, they may go ahead and spend it (or part of it). If they do, Ricardian equivalence will fail to hold, and the fiscal policy *will* have the intended expansionary effect.

Nonetheless, the theory of Ricardian equivalence is a good reminder that people often respond to changes in government policy by adapting their behavior. Good policy has to take those responses and the unintended consequences that stem from them into account. In some cases, rational responses by individuals may be strong enough to make a well-intentioned policy fail. In practice, however, most people seem not to think about future tax increases when they open that envelope containing a tax rebate, as described in the Real Life box "Spending your stimulus check."

Real Life

Spending your stimulus check

In early 2008 it had become clear that the economy was ailing. President George W. Bush's administration took steps to address the problem with the Economic Stimulus Act, which sent taxpayers a "stimulus check"—a check that came in the mail, no strings attached, for the household to spend as it pleased. About 130 million households got checks, for a total of $100 billion across the nation. Individuals received between $300 and $600, and couples received twice that, plus $300 per child.

The government hoped that families would spend the checks, increasing consumption and shifting the aggregate demand curve to the right. But there was no requirement that people spend the money rather than just save it. In fact, the theory of Ricardian equivalence predicts that a rational family would save the rebate. This was the chance that the government took when sending out the stimulus checks.

What happened in practice? It turned out that families spent most of their windfall. They purchased cars and trucks and went back to the shopping mall. The average spending response amounted to between 50 and 90 percent of the value of the rebates. The increase in overall household spending did shift the aggregate demand curve to the right and helped stimulate the economy back toward its previous higher level of output.

(continued)

In short, people did not respond in the way predicted by Ricardian equivalence theory—they spent a good chunk of the rebate, although not all of it. The economy wasn't out of the woods yet, but the tax rebate served its intended purpose as an early counterstrike against the contractionary effects of the recession.

Sources: Jonathan Parker, Nicholas Souleles, David Johnson, and Robert McClelland, "Consumer Spending and the Economic Stimulus Payments of 2008," working paper, Kellogg School, Northwestern University, 2011, http://japarker.scripts.mit.edu/docs/PSJM2013.pdf; http://www.voxeu.org/index.php?q=node/1541.

Fiscal policy can be a powerful tool, enabling the government to counteract short-run fluctuations in the economy by increasing spending or cutting taxes. However, there is a catch: The government has to pay for all the roads and bridges and tax rebates somehow. Where does the money come from? It comes from taxpayers. If spending increases without a comparable increase in taxes, or if taxes are cut without a comparable decrease in spending, the government often goes into debt.

✓CONCEPT CHECK

- ☐ What are decisions about the level of government spending and taxation called? **[LO 30.1]**
- ☐ What type of fiscal policy increases aggregate demand? **[LO 30.2]**
- ☐ What are the three types of time lags involved in implementing fiscal policy? **[LO 30.3]**
- ☐ Are income taxes an example of discretionary or automatic fiscal policy? **[LO 30.4]**
- ☐ Why might citizens experience a tax cut more like a loan than a real windfall? And how would that affect fiscal policy? **[LO 30.5]**
- ☐ What does the evidence say about Ricardian equivalence? **[LO 30.5]**

The Government Budget

budget deficit
an amount of money a government spends beyond the revenue it brings in

budget surplus
an amount of revenue a government brings in beyond what it spends

We've seen why the government may want to influence the economy by changing the amount it spends or taxes. In practice this can require borrowing money. If spending is higher than revenue, which is the current situation in the United States and in most other countries, the government will have a **budget deficit**—an amount of money a government spends beyond the revenue it brings in. And although it happens more rarely at the federal level, it is also possible for the government to have a **budget surplus**—an amount of revenue a government brings in beyond what it spends.

When governments persist in running budget deficits year after year, the deficits can pile up over time. These accumulations are the *public debt*. In the remainder of this chapter, we'll discuss the government budget and the effect that public debt can have on the economy.

Revenue and spending

LO 30.6 Describe how revenue and spending determine a government budget and how the U.S. budget deficit occurs.

At a glance, how a government budget works is pretty simple: Money comes in as tax revenues and goes out through government purchases and transfer payments. (*Transfer payments* refer to payments from government accounts to individuals for programs, like Social Security, that do not involve a purchase of goods or services. As such, these payments are not reflected in GDP.) What's *not* simple about a government budget is the enormous amount of money involved.

Total U.S. government expenditure in 2016 was just under $3.7 trillion. The government took in, through tax revenue, approximately $3.2 trillion. The gap between revenue and spending—the budget deficit—was an incredible $439 billion.[6] The size of the deficit actually represents an improvement: In 2011, the U.S. government deficit was as high as $1.3 trillion. The last time the deficit had been that large as a percentage of GDP was during the run-up of spending on tanks and airplanes necessary to fight World War II.

It's important to keep in mind that government decisions about spending, income, and borrowing differ fundamentally from household decisions when it comes to recessions:

- When households face tough times, they usually think about belt-tightening and building up resources for a rainy day.
- When the government faces a downturn, it sometimes makes sense to *increase* spending and reduce taxes in order to stimulate aggregate demand.

Indeed, the government has a role in undoing the negative demand externality that occurs when households all "do the right things" for themselves (cut consumption), but which ends up reducing overall demand in the economy at a time when *greater* demand is in fact needed to help improve the economy.

The U.S. budget deficit

Figure 30-4 shows the U.S. budget deficit for the last 76 years. In almost every year since 1940 there has been a budget deficit. Deficits have been especially large in times of war, as government spending on the military increases. The amount of the budget deficit for 2015 was approximately $438 billion.

FIGURE 30-4

U.S. budget deficit since 1940   With the exception of World War II (the big upward spike in the 1940s comes from military spending), the U.S. budget was relatively balanced until about 1970. For a few decades afterward, there was a modest budget deficit. After a short period of surplus, the government again started running deficits due to tax cuts and, starting in 2008, efforts to spend the economy out of recession.

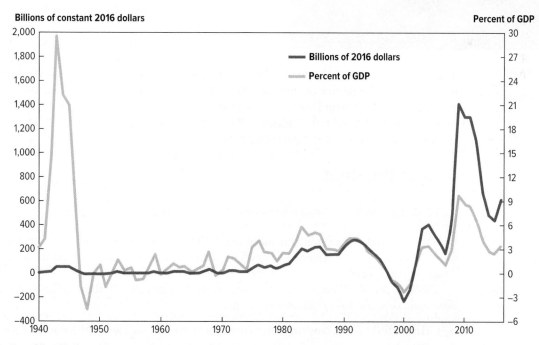

Source: White House Office of Budget and Management, Fiscal Year Budget Data, Tables 1.1 and 1.2, https://www.whitehouse.gov/omb/budget/Historicals.

Economists usually express the deficit as a *percentage of GDP* to emphasize the relationship between the deficit and the size of the economy. As Figure 30-4 also shows, during World War II, the deficit reached 30 percent of GDP. Much smaller spikes in spending corresponded with the 1990–1991 Gulf War and the period after September 11, 2001, when the wars in Iraq and Afghanistan were launched.

Spending increases can lead to larger deficits, but so can decreases in tax revenues. You may notice that the deficit was pretty high—on average 4 percent of GDP—during the 1980s, a time of economic growth and peace. This was due to changes on the revenue side of the government budget, as tax rates were lowered by President Ronald Reagan and the government took in less money. Recessions also tend to increase deficits, as can be seen in the sharp spike from 2007 onward. During a recession, government spending often increases as part of an expansionary fiscal policy, while revenues tend to decrease because people are earning and spending less.

✓CONCEPT CHECK

☐ What is the term for when the government collects more revenue than it spends? **[LO 30.6]**

☐ Name three reasons why the budget deficit might increase during a recession. **[LO 30.6]**

The Public Debt

Since this photo was taken at the Republican National Convention in August 2012, the U.S. national debt has crossed the $19 trillion threshold, with little sign of slowing.
© *DW labs Incorporated/ Shutterstock*

Just a few blocks from the flashy billboards and dazzling displays of Times Square in New York City is a far more humble digital counter that keeps tabs on the debt incurred by the U.S. federal government. Every time the government runs a deficit, the **public debt**—the total amount of money that a government owes at a point in time—increases.

In the rare years when the government runs a surplus, the debt decreases. When the public debt decreased at the end of the 1990s, the clock's owner had to shut down the clock temporarily because he hadn't programmed it to be able to count backwards.

The upward trend soon resumed. The next time the debt clock had to be shut down, the reason was to add another digit as the debt passed $9,999,999,999,999. In 2016, the clock had rolled past the $19 trillion mark and showed little sign of slowing. This $19 trillion was the equivalent of almost $60,000 of debt per citizen.[7] Seymour Durst, who put up the NYC debt clock, said, "It'll be up as long as the debt or [New York City] lasts," adding, "If it bothers people, then it's working."[8] How bothered *should* we be about the size of the public debt?

Size of the debt

LO 30.7 Explain the difference between the government deficit and debt.

public debt
the total amount of money that a government owes at a point in time; the cumulative sum of all deficits and surpluses

In 1792, Alexander Hamilton convinced the only two banks in the country to lend the newly formed United States of America $19,608.61. This is the first known entry on the ledger of the country's public debt.

Although people sometimes confuse the terms *debt* and *deficit,* they are different, and the distinction between them is an important one:

- The *deficit* tells us how much the government revenues fall short of spending *each year.*
- The *debt* is the *total* amount that the government owes.

FIGURE 30-5

U.S. government debt since 1940   The total amount of U.S. government debt was held below $1 trillion through 1980 due to low yearly deficits. Afterward, the debt began to increase dramatically. As a share of GDP, the total debt decreased after 1948. Then government debt started to increase as a share of GDP, especially in 2008 due to large deficits.

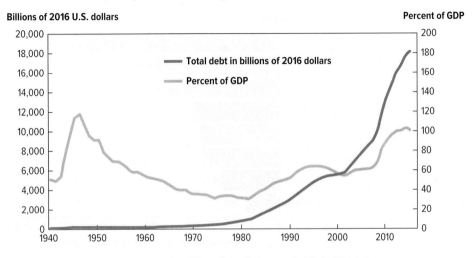

Source: White House Office of Management and Budget, Historical Tables, Table 7.1, https://www.whitehouse.gov/omb/budget/Historicals.

In other words, the debt is the cumulative sum of all deficits and surpluses.

Figure 30-5 shows the public debt since 1940, in real-dollar terms (green line) and as a share of GDP (peach line). This graph demonstrates the *cumulative effect* of the annual deficits depicted in Figure 30-4.

To see why it's useful to think of the public debt as a share of GDP, consider it in terms of personal finances. Which would you prefer:

- To be making $20,000 a year and owe $10,000 in debt?
- Or to be making $100,000 a year and owe $30,000 in debt?

In the second case, your debt is three times as large, but only 30 percent of your annual income. In the first case, your debt is smaller but amounts to 50 percent of your annual income. Even though you owe more in the second case, you'd be less worried about your ability to repay it.

Similar logic explains why debt as a share of GDP actually shrank between 1950 and 1980, even though in dollar terms the debt was going up: The economy grew quickly during these years, much faster than the growth in the debt. After 2009, in contrast, debt as a share of GDP increased quickly as the government spent money while the economy remained sluggish after the Great Recession.

Almost every country in the world has debt, some much more than the United States as a percentage of GDP. (Trivia: Only the nation of Brunei is debt-free, according to the International Monetary Fund.) Figure 30-6 shows the amount of debt owed by various countries. Four of them—Japan, Greece, Italy, and the United States—owe more than 100 percent of GDP.

How does the government go into debt?

LO 30.8 Understand how Treasury securities work and why people value them.

How exactly does government spending lead to debt? The process is more complicated than simply putting purchases on a charge card or getting a loan at a local bank. The government borrows money from people by selling **Treasury securities** (simply called "Treasuries" for short).

Treasury securities
debt-financing arrangements made by the U.S. government

FIGURE 30-6

Debt in various countries, 2013   There is a wide discrepancy in the amount of debt owed among countries. In 2013, Japan's debt was the highest in relation to GDP, at 242.6 percent of its GDP. Most countries have a level of debt that ranges between 20 and 80 percent of their GDP.

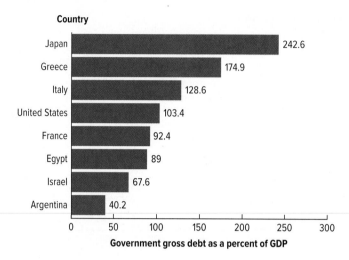

Source: International Monetary Fund, World Economic Outlook Database, http://www.imf.org/external/pubs/ft/weo/2015/01/weodata/index.aspx.

The details of Treasuries can be complex, but the basic idea is that the U.S. government accepts money from people with an obligation to pay them back by a certain date. Some Treasuries are short-term promises (the government will pay back the money after one month or one year); others operate on much longer time frames and don't get repaid for 30 years.

The shortest-term Treasury securities are *Treasury bills,* also known as *T-bills.* These are loans to the government that mature in less than a year. When you buy a T-bill, you're buying a promise that the government will pay you a set amount of money on a fixed date—for example, $1,000, three months from today. People bid for T-bills when they are issued, so depending on the state of the market for T-bills, you might pay, say, only $997 for this particular promise. The $3 difference is the equivalent of interest earned on a savings account. The return on these loans is usually quite low, but they are liquid (your money is tied up in the bond for less than a year). Most important, investors consider them to be very safe, and they thus appeal as a place to securely park money.

For longer-term investments, the government issues *Treasury notes* in 2-, 3-, 5-, 7-, and 10-year increments. When you purchase a Treasury note, every six months you receive an interest payment at a set rate. The return on 10-year Treasury notes is often cited as an indicator of the country's overall macroeconomic health. These notes pay more in interest than do T-bills, usually at a rate of about 3 percent for the 10-year note, since liquidity and interest paid are inversely related. (Chapter 31, "The Basics of Finance," addresses this relationship in more detail.) For those who are even more patient, the government offers its longest-term option: *Treasury bonds* mature in 30 years and pay a specified amount of interest every 6 months.

The big risk from investing in government securities is that inflation might eat away their value. For those worried about this risk, the Treasury offers *Treasury Inflation-Protected Securities (TIPS).* For TIPS, the original amount of the investment is pegged (tied) to changes in the overall Consumer Price Index (CPI), while the interest rate remains fixed. For example, if the original loan is for $10,000 with an interest rate of 3 percent, and inflation reaches 5 percent this year, the government would pay back slightly more than $10,800 ($10,000 plus the sum of the 3 percent interest rate and the 5 percent inflation rate). If the security were not inflation-protected, the government would pay back only $10,300.

FIGURE 30-7

The top seven foreign holders of U.S. debt, June 2015 In June 2015 the top seven holders of U.S. debt were Japan, China, banking centers (the Cayman Islands and Luxembourg), the United Kingdom, Canada, and Ireland. Due to the large export imbalance China and Japan have with the United States, together they hold just under a quarter of U.S. debt.

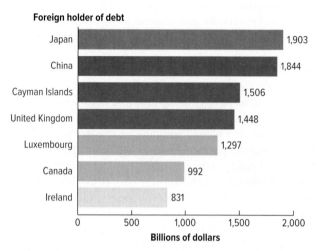

Source: U.S. Treasury, Report on Foreign Portfolio Holdings of U.S. Securities at End-June 2015, https://www.treasury.gov/press-center/press-releases/Pages/jl0469.aspx (June 2015).

Treasury securities are purchased as financial investments by individuals and by other governments and banks, both in the United States and abroad. Almost half of the privately held government debt is held by people who live outside the United States. Figure 30-7 shows the breakdown of U.S. debt holdings by country.

Why would people want to hold government debt? The main reason lies in the relative safety of the investment, especially when compared with other investments. When you invest in real estate, the housing market can crash. When you invest in a company's stock, the company can lose market value or go bankrupt. Governments can declare themselves bankrupt, too, and refuse to pay back money that people have loaned them. But investors generally believe that the odds of the U.S. government doing this are quite low, essentially zero. In the shakiest part of the Great Recession, investors flocked to short-term U.S. Treasuries to escape risks in the stock market and real estate market. Demand was so strong that for a while interest rates were negative, meaning that investors were willing to lose money in return for the safety of buying the debt of the United States.

Is government debt good or bad?

LO 30.9 Identify the benefits and costs of government debt.

In the summer of 2011, more than 100,000 people marched in the streets of Athens. They were protesting "austerity" measures that would cut government spending in the hope of taming Greece's astronomical debt burden. At 1.5 times the size of GDP, debt had become a serious drag on Greece's economy. (By 2015, Greece's debt had risen above 175 percent.)[9] However, most economists believe that *some debt* is necessary to the smooth functioning of government. What are the benefits and costs of government debt?

Benefits of government debt

There are two main benefits of government debt. The first is that it allows the government to be flexible when something unexpected happens. Hurricane Katrina, which devastated the Gulf

Coast in 2005, cost the U.S. government $105 billion, or almost 4 percent of government spending that year. If the choice is between borrowing to cover the costs of responding to an emergency or not responding at all, many people would say it's better to borrow.

The second benefit of debt is that it can pay for investments that will lead to economic growth and prosperity (and, presumably, higher tax revenues) in the long run. Just as you might decide to borrow to fund your college education because you expect it to lead to a better job and higher salary down the road, it can make sense for governments to borrow to invest in the education system or to construct roads and other infrastructure that will help the economy to grow more quickly.

Costs of government debt

On the other hand, there are both *direct* and *indirect* costs of government debt. The *direct cost* is the interest the government has to pay to the people it has borrowed from. Interest payments on the debt are substantial. In the past, interest payments on the U.S. debt have amounted to the fourth-largest budget expense, just behind spending on transfer payments (consisting of Social Security and means-tested transfer payments such as Medicare, the first- and third-largest budget categories, respectively) and defense (the second-largest budget category).

The direct cost of debt depends on the interest rate. If the interest rate increases, the government debt becomes more expensive to pay. The interest rate, in turn, depends on investors' confidence in the government's ability to pay back the debt. This can become a vicious cycle: If investors doubt that a government will be able to repay its debt, they will demand a higher interest rate before they are willing to lend to that government. That higher interest rate increases the burden of debt, making it even more doubtful whether the government can pay it back.

This self-reinforcing spiral of investor doubt and a higher interest rate has, in the past, forced defaults by some governments when they could no longer afford the direct costs. Although few people think there is a serious risk of this happening to the U.S. government, in 2011 the major rating agency Standard & Poor's downgraded its rating of U.S. debt from AAA to AA+. This downgrade implied some degree of doubt about whether U.S. politicians would be able to meaningfully tackle the tough choices required to shrink the ballooning amount of government debt.

There are also *indirect costs* of government debt. In some circumstances, government debt can distort the credit market and slow economic growth. We have already noted the possibility that government borrowing can *crowd out* private borrowing: When the government borrows money, it increases the demand for credit, and so increases the price of credit—the interest rate—in the wider economy. A higher interest rate increases the cost of borrowing for businesses that want to invest and for consumers who want to buy new homes or cars. (We describe this mechanism more extensively in Chapter 31, "The Basics of Finance.")

Finally, there is the question of who bears the burden of government debt. People today benefit when the government borrows to spend more on services or cut taxes, but people tomorrow will have to repay the loans. The costs of services are being kicked down the road to our children and grandchildren.

✓CONCEPT CHECK

☐ What is the difference between government debt and deficit? **[LO 30.7]**

☐ How do Treasury securities provide financing for the U.S. government's debt? **[LO 30.8]**

☐ What is one possible effect of government debt on the amount of private investment? **[LO 30.9]**

Conclusion

We started this chapter by looking at why the government might want to change fiscal policy to counteract economic fluctuations. When the economy is in a recession, expansionary fiscal policy—cutting taxes, increasing spending, or both, as with the 2009 stimulus plan—can increase aggregate demand and speed up recovery. Unemployment remained high even in the first years after the stimulus, but ultimately there is no way of knowing for certain whether it would have been even higher without it.

We also looked at how the government can borrow and how deficits lead to public debt. Debt adds to government flexibility, but it can be costly and slow down economic growth. It also raises questions about the fairness of expecting future generations to bear the burden of paying off the debt.

Governments have an alternative to fiscal policy when they want to influence the economy: monetary policy. Monetary policy works through the financial system, so before we get into monetary policy, we will cover the basics of finance in the next chapter.

Key Terms

fiscal policy, p. 768

expansionary fiscal policy, p. 769

contractionary fiscal policy, p. 769

automatic stabilizers, p. 775

budget deficit, p. 778

budget surplus, p. 778

public debt, p. 780

Treasury securities, p. 781

Summary

LO 30.1 Explain the difference between contractionary fiscal policy and expansionary fiscal policy.

Together, the level of taxation and government spending is called *fiscal policy*. We say that fiscal policy is either expansionary or contractionary.

Expansionary fiscal policy involves changes to fiscal policy that cause the aggregate demand curve to increase (shift out to the right). It is expansionary because it expands demand. Expansionary fiscal policy occurs because either government spending increases or the level of taxation decreases and is a response to recessionary conditions.

On the other hand, *contractionary* fiscal policy involves changes to fiscal policy that contract aggregate demand, causing the aggregate demand curve to decrease (shift in to the left). Contractionary fiscal policy occurs when government spending decreases or when taxation increases, and is a response to an overheating economy with the accompanying threat of excessive inflation.

LO 30.2 Explain how fiscal policy can counteract short-run economic fluctuations.

The government can use fiscal policy to counteract business-cycle fluctuations. When the economy is sluggish, the government can conduct expansionary fiscal policy to stimulate demand. This will lead to a faster recovery than without the fiscal policy. On the other hand, if the economy is overheating, the government can undertake contractionary fiscal policy to reduce

aggregate demand. This action also returns the economy closer to the long-run equilibrium level.

LO 30.3 Identify the time lags that complicate the formulation of fiscal policy.

Time lags can mean that sometimes a fiscal policy choice is too late to do any good. Time lags come in many forms. There are *information* lags (how long it takes to get the right information about the overall health of the economy), *formulation* lags (getting everyone to agree on the right policy), and *implementation* lags (how long it takes fiscal policy to have an effect on the economy).

LO 30.4 Discuss how stabilizers can automatically adjust fiscal policy as the economy changes.

To get around time lags, automatic stabilizers can affect fiscal policy without specific action from policy-makers. These features of government policy can automatically stimulate or slow the economy.

The tax system is designed so that people who earn more income should pay higher average tax rates. One consequence is that when the economy is booming, people move into higher income ranges, which means they automatically face higher tax rates. The automatically increased taxes have a contractionary effect by slightly checking overall spending and aggregate demand. When the economy is in a recession, people move to lower income ranges, which have lower tax rates. The automatically reduced taxes have an expansionary effect, encouraging spending and spurring aggregate demand.

Government spending can also work as an automatic stabilizer. When the economy is booming, fewer people are eligible for unemployment insurance benefits and welfare programs; government spending on those programs falls, reducing aggregate demand and having a contractionary effect. In a recession, more people are eligible for these programs and spending on them automatically rises, increasing aggregate demand and having an expansionary effect.

LO 30.5 Describe the theory and evidence about Ricardian equivalence and what it implies for the effectiveness of fiscal policy.

Ricardian equivalence predicts that if governments cut taxes but not public spending, people will recognize that the government will have to borrow money to cover the financial shortfall that's been created. People will then figure that, at some point in the future, taxes will have to go back up to repay the extra government debt incurred through tax cuts. Since people see that a tax cut today will just mean higher taxes in a few years (or maybe decades), they are reluctant to spend so freely after the tax cut. The theory says that, as a result, tax cuts will have no impact on spending: People will continue to save rather than spend, consumption will not increase, and the tax cut will be unsuccessful in changing aggregate demand.

Recent empirical evidence, however, shows that people do spend extra when taxes are cut, increasing aggregate demand. Ricardian equivalence is an important theoretical idea, but the data show it is not a good guide to predicting the actual effect of tax cuts.

LO 30.6 Describe how revenue and spending determine a government budget and how the U.S. budget deficit occurs.

The government budget includes all of the revenue it collects in taxes and all of the money it spends on government programs. When the government spends more than it collects in revenue, it runs a *deficit*. When it collects more revenue than it spends, it has a *surplus*. In most years, the government spends more than it collects in revenue. Deficits tend to increase during recessions and, more generally, when spending rises and tax revenues fall.

LO 30.7 Explain the difference between the government deficit and debt.

Deficits occur when annual spending is more than annual revenue. A surplus occurs when annual spending is less than annual revenue. The *public debt* is the total amount of money that the government has borrowed (but not yet repaid) over time. The debt and the deficit are closely related: The budget deficit tells us how much the government borrows each year, and the debt tells us the total that the government has borrowed and not paid back over time. In other words, the debt is the cumulative sum of all deficits and surpluses.

LO 30.8 Understand how Treasury securities work and why people value them.

The government borrows money from others by selling *Treasury securities,* which are debt-financing arrangements made by the United States with obligations to pay back the money over varying lengths of time (often for a year or less, but sometimes for as long as 30 years). Individuals, other governments, and banks, both abroad and in the United States, purchase Treasuries as financial investments. They are typically seen as relatively safe investments, and investors around the world flocked to these during the Great Recession and its aftermath.

LO 30.9 Identify the benefits and costs of government debt.

A deficit allows the government to spend more than its revenue. Allowing the government to run a deficit permits the government to respond to unexpected events and to undertake expansionary fiscal policy. However, there are also costs of running deficits. Interest needs to be paid on the debt, the government may not spend the money efficiently, and high government deficits may increase interest rates and thus reduce investment in the economy.

Review Questions

1. What is the best fiscal policy for a country suffering from high inflation? **[LO 30.1]**

2. If the government wants to reduce GDP by $500 million, should it increase or decrease its spending? Must it increase or decrease spending by exactly $500 million, some amount more than $500 million, or some amount less than $500 million? Would this be expansionary or contractionary fiscal policy? **[LO 30.1]**

3. President Obama said the following in November 2010 when announcing a two-year pay freeze for civilian federal employees: "After all, small businesses and families are tightening their belts. Their government should too." What do you think the intended effect of this policy would be, assuming the economy was in a recession at the time? Do you think it was the appropriate response? Why or why not? **[LO 30.2]**

4. If unemployment is high and spending is sluggish, what type of fiscal policy should be enacted? How would this be enacted via taxes? Via government spending?

What is the intended effect of this policy on aggregate demand? **[LO 30.2]**

5. "The problem with democracy," your friend tells you as you debate politics, "is the time it takes to get approval for every action the government takes. If the president didn't have to spend so much time arguing back and forth with Congress, policy wouldn't take so long to affect the economy." Is your friend right or wrong? What would your response be? **[LO 30.3]**

6. Explain the difference between tax rates and tax revenues, and how each is related to recession and policy enacted to counteract it. Do you expect to see tax rates rise or fall during recession? What about tax revenues? Explain your answer. **[LO 30.4]**

7. The government decides to reduce income taxes due to a recession in the economy over the past nine months. Will the reduction in income taxes boost spending in the economy? Why or why not? **[LO 30.5]**

8. Use the theory of Ricardian equivalence to explain why cutting taxes during a recession may not always be an effective expansionary fiscal policy. **[LO 30.5]**

9. Why have budget deficits been so high in the United States since 2007? **[LO 30.6]**

10. You hear on the nightly news that the president has vowed to decrease the nation's debt. "We'll have to buckle down and learn to do without, both the government and private citizens," he says. How can a nation lower its debt? How will the government and private citizens be affected? **[LO 30.6]**

11. A friend of yours looks at the state of the U.S. debt in 2011 and tells you, "Since the debt is so high, we must be running an incredibly large deficit every year." Is your friend's analysis valid? Why or why not? **[LO 30.7]**

12. Is it possible for a nation's government to run a budget deficit in some years but not have national debt? Explain your answer. **[LO 30.7]**

13. Explain the differences and similarities among Treasury bills, Treasury notes, and Treasury bonds. **[LO 30.8]**

14. Your friend thinks buying Treasury bills is riskier than leaving money in a savings account. You disagree. Who is right? **[LO 30.8]**

15. Taxpayers are clamoring for their government to be more responsible, and many strongly support a balanced-budget amendment. This would mean the country could no longer spend more than it takes in each year. Discuss the primary advantages and disadvantages of such a law. **[LO 30.9]**

16. Is government debt good or bad for the economy and the nation as a whole? Give one argument for each side of the debate. **[LO 30.9]**

Problems and Applications

1. Is each of the following policies an example of expansionary or contractionary fiscal policy? Explain your answers in terms of the effect on aggregate demand. **[LO 30.1]**

   a. The government slashes funding for the Environmental Protection Agency, without changing any other spending.

   b. The government raises taxes on households making more than $250,000.

   c. The government decides to fill gaps in Medicare by making it available to more people.

2. The economy is growing far too quickly, as high aggregate demand is causing inflation. What fiscal policy should be pursued in this instance—expansionary or contractionary? What will be the effect of the appropriate policy on aggregate demand? **[LO 30.1]**

3. Assuming that unemployment is high and spending is low, answer the following questions. **[LO 30.2]**

   a. Should the government pursue expansionary or contractionary fiscal policy?

   b. What will the appropriate policy do to the aggregate demand curve? Will the curve shift to the right or to the left?

   c. Through which component(s) of aggregate demand (C, I, G, or NX, or some combination of the preceding) will the change occur?

4. The diagram in Figure 30P-1 shows aggregate demand for New Caprica last year (AD$_1$) and this year (AD$_2$). If you were to advise the president of New Caprica on economic policy, how would you answer the following? **[LO 30.2]**

FIGURE 30P-1

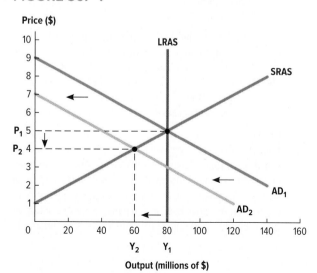

a. How large is current output? How large is potential output? What is the difference, if any, between the two?

b. Is New Caprica in a recession or a boom?

c. Given your findings, should the president enact expansionary or contractionary fiscal policy, or no policy at all?

d. In which direction would the aggregate demand curve shift if the president used contractionary fiscal policy?

5. "Our fiscal policy was unsuccessful," an economic analyst says, "due to partisan bickering in Congress that delayed the passing of the appropriate measures and our failure to realize we were headed into recession until it was too late." What type of lags is the analyst describing? **[LO 30.3]**

6. Assume that the government in some nation intended to respond to low employment via fiscal policy. What type of policy would this require? Assume that this policy ended up having an undesirable outcome. How could this happen in terms of formulation and implementation lags? **[LO 30.3]**

7. Brenda earns $62,000 a year and pays an average tax rate of 15 percent. **[LO 30.4]**

   a. Calculate Brenda's disposable income and the amount of tax she pays to the government.

   b. Suppose a recession hits the economy and Brenda's income falls to $50,000 per year due to the fact that she is earning a smaller annual bonus. If she now pays an average tax rate of 12 percent, what is her disposable income and the amount of tax she pays to the government?

   c. Calculate how much Brenda's annual salary and disposable income fell by due to the recession.

   d. Explain how income taxes are an automatic stabilizer in this example.

8. True or false? If the amount of time a person is eligible for unemployment compensation is reduced from 26 weeks to 4 weeks, people will have an incentive to quickly find a new job. This occurs because unemployment compensation is an important automatic stabilizer for the economy. **[LO 30.4]**

9. Consider three countries. The first country runs small budget surpluses each year. The other two countries run large budget deficits each year. In one of the deficit countries the national debt-to-GDP ratio has been steady, whereas in the other deficit country the national debt-to-GDP ratio has been rising. Suppose each of these countries decides to reduce income taxes. Is Ricardian equivalence likely to hold in all of these countries? Why or why not? **[LO 30.5]**

10. A country is in the midst of a recession with real GDP estimated to be $1.8 billion below potential GDP. The government's policy analysts believe the current value of the marginal propensity to consume (MPC) is 0.90. **[LO 30.5]**

    a. If the government wants real GDP to equal potential GDP, by how much should it increase government spending? Alternatively, by how much should it reduce taxes?

    b. Suppose that during the recession people have become less confident and decide they will spend only 50 percent of any additional income. In this case, if the government increases spending by the amount calculated in part *a*, will real GDP end up less than, greater than, or equal to potential GDP? By how much?

    c. With the same decrease in consumer spending described in part *b*, if the government decreases taxes by the amount calculated in part *a*, will real GDP end up less than, greater than, or equal to potential GDP? By how much?

    d. Why is it difficult for the government to predict exactly how a change in spending or taxes will affect GDP?

11. If in some year a nation's budget deficit is $9.56 trillion and government spending is $12.19 trillion, how much must it have earned in tax revenue this year? **[LO 30.6]**

12. "The government shouldn't borrow so much," your uncle claims. "Look at that national debt! It's no different from someone borrowing on credit cards they can't pay." **[LO 30.6]**

    a. Is your uncle right?

    b. How is government debt spending like someone borrowing on a credit card?

    c. How is government debt spending different from someone borrowing on a credit card?

13. Econo Nation started 2013 with no national budget debt or surplus. By the end of 2013, it had a budget surplus of $304 million; in 2014, it had a budget deficit of $452 million; in 2015 it had a budget surplus of $109 million, and the amount of its budget deficit or surplus in 2016 is unknown. If at the end of 2016 Econo Nation's national debt totaled $50 million, did it run a deficit or surplus in 2016? How much? **[LO 30.7]**

14. "Though the national debt has increased, don't worry," the president says in a televised speech. "We will not have to pay these funds back to bond buyers." How is

this possible? How must the government have financed its debt in this case? **[LO 30.7]**

15. You buy a Treasury note for $1,000. Every 6 months you receive a payment of $40. **[LO 30.8]**

    a. What is the annual rate of return?

    b. What would be the annual rate of return if the payment was instead $30?

    c. What would be the annual rate of return if the payment was instead $45?

16. Your friend believes buying Treasury bills or Treasury notes will offer protection against rising inflation in comparison to buying stocks or mutual funds, because the rate of return on the Treasury bills and notes is known at the time of purchase. Do you agree? Why or why not? **[LO 30.8]**

17. Which of the following are examples of the negative effects associated with government debt? **[LO 30.9]**

    a. Increased interest rates.

    b. Increased taxes or lower spending in the future.

    c. Increased investment in the economy.

18. If the government could borrow as much as it liked with a 0 percent interest rate, would the government debt be cost-free? Explain your answer. **[LO 30.9]**

Endnotes

1. http://data.bls.gov/timeseries/LNS14000000 and http://www.tradingeconomics.com/united-states/government-debt-to-gdp.

2. The multiplier effect is described in greater detail in Chapter 28, "Aggregate Expenditure," and Chapter 29, "Aggregate Demand and Aggregate Supply." Crowding out is described in greater detail in Chapter 31, "The Basics of Finance."

3. In Chapter 33, "Inflation," we will also see that there are other reasons to be concerned about *deflation,* or falling prices in an economy.

4. It turns out that many recessions last less than a year. The official length of the 2007–2009 recession was 14 months. Of course, it's impossible to know how long the recession would have lasted without the government's expansionary policy.

5. www.irs.gov.

6. https://www.cbo.gov/publication/51110.

7. http://www.brillig.com/debt_clock.

8. http://content.time.com/time/business/article/0,8599,1850269,00.html#ixzz1OtKQCoQM.

9. http://blogs.wsj.com/briefly/2015/07/03/greeces-debt-the-numbers.

Part Nine

The Financial System and Institutions

The four chapters in Part 9 will introduce you to . . .

the financial and monetary systems and the institutions that make them work. In Part 9, we'll discuss everything from the traders on Wall Street to the humble dollar bill in your wallet.

Chapter 31, "The Basics of Finance," runs through the basics of financial markets and describes the roles that individuals and institutions play in them—including everyone from a family buying a first house to the traders making million-dollar bets on Wall Street. Financial markets connect savers and borrowers, helping money flow to the parts of the economy where it is the most valuable at any given time and allowing people to manage their money over time and minimize the risks they face.

Chapter 32, "Money and the Monetary System," is all about money. Money helps the economy operate smoothly. As a medium of exchange, it enables you to buy a pack of gum, a car, or an entire tropical island. It is more than just bills and coins, though. In the United States, the Federal Reserve is the main institution responsible for creating and managing the overall money supply. This power gives it a unique ability to steer the economy through good times and bad.

Chapter 33, "Inflation," covers the delicate relationship between inflation and unemployment. Policy-makers at central banks, like the U.S. Federal Reserve, have the task of controlling fluctuations in the value of money. They can also use the tools of monetary policy to influence the overall level of unemployment. With this power comes great responsibility: Recent history is filled with examples of how countries have suffered from inflation and unemployment caused by poor monetary policy.

Although financial markets usually run smoothly, there are times when the system fails to efficiently manage risk and fund new ventures. Investigating how financial systems break down provides unique insights into how they actually work. In Chapter 34, "Financial Crisis," we'll pick through the details of the worst financial crisis for generations: the problems that followed the 2007 crash in the U.S. housing market, which plunged the U.S. economy and others around the world into deep recession.

The Basics of Finance

HENRY LEHMAN AND HIS BROTHERS

In 1844, Henry Lehman opened a dry-goods store in Montgomery, Alabama. At first, he sold groceries and basic supplies to local farmers. Soon, his brothers joined the firm, and the business began to expand. The Lehman brothers started acting as go-betweens for local planters, buying

© Nicholas Roberts/AFP/Getty Images

their cotton and then selling it in more distant markets. Business boomed, and they opened an office in New York City, adding coffee and other commodities to their cotton brokerage. With its southern roots, the company was hard hit by the U.S. Civil War. At the end of the war, it regrouped and soon had a contract with the state of Alabama to help manage its finances and debt payments. By the end of the nineteenth century, the Lehman Brothers brokerage house had become one of the largest and most powerful institutions on Wall Street.

Lehman Brothers survived the Civil War, the Great Depression, World War II, an ill-fated merger with a rival, and the September 11, 2001, destruction of its headquarters, located just across the street from the World Trade Center towers. Despite all of that, on September 15, 2008, Lehman Brothers declared bankruptcy. The failure of such a large, long-standing, reputable firm was almost unimaginable. Global markets panicked. How could such a seemingly sturdy organization, which less than a year earlier had earned record profits, suddenly go broke?

The story of Lehman's collapse, the housing market crash that led to it, and the financial-system implosion and Great Recession that followed is one of the most fascinating economic tales of our time. To understand these events, we have to begin with an understanding of the financial system itself.

Traditional markets in goods and services are relatively straightforward—they help to match prospective buyers with those willing to sell. In comparison, *financial markets* can seem abstract and remote. What do they do? What exactly are Wall Street firms selling and on whose behalf are they selling it? How did old-fashioned cotton brokers like the Lehman brothers end up on Wall Street? Why do we have a financial system?

In fact, the basic purpose of financial markets is similar to any other market—they match people who want money to spend now (buyers) with people who want to save their money for later (sellers). In doing so, they also help people manage their money over time and protect themselves against risk. The *financial system* brings together savers and borrowers in a set of interconnected markets in which people trade a variety of financial products.

The basic premise of a financial market is simple, but actual transactions can be quite complex. Financial markets offer a wide variety of financial products, targeted to people with different investment or saving needs. Just as wholesalers and grocery stores mediate between farmers and hungry consumers, there are many different firms and institutions that mediate between savers and borrowers in financial markets.

Businesses, governments, nongovernmental organizations, and individuals depend on the financial system to achieve their goals. The system helps people get the money they need, in the right amount, at the right time, with as little uncertainty as possible. If you have a savings account, checking account, credit card, student loan, home mortgage, or car loan, then you benefit from access to financial markets. People tend to take these services for granted. But the global disruptions surrounding the Lehman bankruptcy showed just how valuable a well-functioning financial system is, and how much it matters.

In this chapter, we'll start by looking at the role of *financial markets* and the value they provide to savers and borrowers. We build a simple model of the market in which savers and borrowers participate. Then we look at the *financial system* from three angles: the functions it serves, the players involved in it, and the assets they trade. Finally, we'll look at some general features of financial products, like risk and return.

The Role of Financial Markets

The high-tech, elaborate dealings we associate with Wall Street are a relatively recent phenomenon, but basic financial markets existed at least as far back as ancient Greece. Money-lenders, based in temples, accepted deposits, changed money for travelers, and (as their name implies) made loans. A person's show of wealth went from precious metals, which were weighed, to coins stamped by the nation-state, which were counted. Stock markets we would recognize today first appeared in the seventeenth century. Why have financial markets been such a natural and useful institution in different societies throughout history? What do they do?

What is a financial market?

> **LO 31.1** Define a financial market and describe the information asymmetry problems that can occur in them.

In a **financial market**, people trade future claims on funds or goods. These "claims" can take many different forms:

financial market
a market in which people trade future claims on funds or goods

- When you take out a loan, a bank gives you money now, in return for an agreement that you will repay the bank, with interest, in the future.
- When you buy stock in a company, you have a right to a share of any profits earned in the future.
- When you buy an insurance policy, you make regular premium payments, and the insurance company agrees to pay out, if and when something bad happens to you in the future.

We'll talk about the details of these and other types of financial assets later in the chapter. The important thing to notice, for now, is that they are all agreements that allow people to move funds around, *from one time, place, or situation to another.*

The key idea behind financial markets is that, at any given time, the people who have spare funds are not necessarily the same people who have the most valuable ways to spend those funds. Financial markets allow funding to flow to the places where it is most highly valued at the moment. A well-functioning market makes everyone better off, by matching buyers and sellers who both have something to gain from a trade. In financial markets:

- Buyers are people who want to spend money on something of value right now but don't have cash on hand. Among the buyers in financial markets are families buying new houses, students paying for college, corporations building new factories, entrepreneurs starting new ventures, and often the government when it needs to finance public spending.

- Sellers are people who have cash on hand and are willing to let others use it, for a price. Sellers in financial markets are individuals, corporations, and government entities willing to forgo some spending right now in return for repayment down the road.

Information asymmetries and financial markets

information asymmetry
a condition in which one participant in a transaction knows more than another participant

An **information asymmetry** arises when one participant in a transaction knows more than another participant. You may have already encountered examples of information asymmetries in microeconomics. For example, the people selling used cars often know more about the quality of the cars than the people buying them. People buying health insurance, on the other hand, usually know more about their own health issues than the companies selling insurance. And so on. But perhaps nowhere are information asymmetries more prevalent than in financial markets: The people seeking loans tend to know more about the potential uses (and misuses!) of the funds than the lenders.

Information asymmetries are so fundamental to financial markets that they have essentially determined the structure of modern financial systems, with banks, stock markets, bond markets, and regulatory agencies restricting the activities of both borrowers and lenders. To get a sense of why information asymmetries are so important in financial markets, let's consider the two classic problems that arise when parties have access to different amounts of information: adverse selection and moral hazard.

adverse selection
a state that occurs when buyers and sellers have different information about the quality of a good or the riskiness of a situation, and this asymmetric information results in failure to complete transactions that would have been possible if both sides had the same information.

Adverse selection refers to a state that occurs when buyers and sellers have different information about the quality of a good or the riskiness of a situation, and this asymmetric information results in failure to complete transactions that would have been possible if both sides had the same information. For example:

- Mortgage borrowers might know that the actual market value of their house is much lower than the public assessment.
- Executives of a company issuing *stock* (an asset that represents partial ownership in the company) might know that the company is much closer to bankruptcy (in which case the stockholders would receive nothing) than could be judged based on public information.

In either case, the problem that arises is that market participants cannot "separate the wheat from the chaff"—that is, they cannot separate the reliable borrowers from the reckless or the genuinely promising company from the frauds. Without tight regulation on the provision of public information, adverse selection would lead to sharp decreases in the market prices of company stock (since investors would worry about drawing a bad apple) and higher interest rates on bank loans.

moral hazard
the tendency for people to behave in a riskier way or to renege on contracts when they do not face the full consequences of their actions

Moral hazard refers to the tendency for people to behave in a riskier way or to renege on contracts when they do not face the full consequences of their actions. It's an asymmetric information problem that arises once a transaction takes place. Once drivers have purchased car insurance, for example, they face smaller (financial) consequences of getting in an accident. As a result, they might be more likely to speed or try to pass other cars in risky situations.

In the financial context, moral hazard arises in almost all transactions. For example:

- When a borrower has secured a loan, he might be tempted to make riskier investments than promised in the loan agreement. The upside of the investment belongs to the borrower, encouraging the greater risk, while the downside is borne by the lender.
- A company might believe that the government is likely to provide support in the event of a financial crisis. In this case, taxpayers are providing the company with implicit

insurance against catastrophic risk. The company (which might be a bank or financial firm) might then take advantage of this "insurance" by engaging in riskier practices.

Sometimes the consequences of these information asymmetries are so severe that financial transactions are impossible. But more often, the participants find ways to limit the problems. Financial innovators (like Muhammad Yunus, the microfinance pioneer from Bangladesh described in Chapter 1, "Economics and Life") have been creative in developing new ways of banking that help financial markets overcome moral hazard and adverse selection (and, in the process, have helped millions of people get better access to banks).

Functions of banks and financial markets

LO 31.2 Discuss the three main functions of financial markets.

These days, financial markets are extremely complicated—so complicated that when Lehman Brothers fell apart in 2008, very few people really had the full picture of what was going on. But the origins of financial markets are not so complicated. It starts with a bank, savers, and borrowers.

Imagine a world without banks. People face a problem: The times when you need to spend money almost never match up perfectly with the times when you earn money. This problem crops up in a lot of different ways. Some mistiming is long term, reflecting the cycle of your whole life:

- You might want to pay for a college degree or a house or a car early in life, before you've had a chance to do much earning.
- You might want to earn more than you spend during your working years and then live on the savings during retirement.

Other types of mistiming are shorter term:

- You might earn a paycheck once a month, but you want to buy things in various places and times throughout the month.
- If you run a business (such as a farm), your revenues might come in during one season (harvest) but most of your expenses come in another (planting).

A bank helps to solve these problems: It takes in savings from people who are earning more than they're spending at the moment. It gives out loans to people who currently want to spend more than they earn.

Why do we need banks for that? Why not just stuff cash under your pillow as you earn it and lend to or borrow from family and neighbors as needed? In fact, that *is* the old-fashioned way of managing money. Even today, billions of people around the world don't have good access to modern banks, and they still rely on those simple methods. But for those who have access to them, banks—and, more broadly, financial markets, of which banks are one example—serve three main functions.

Intermediating between savers and borrowers

The first function is that a bank acts as an *intermediary* between savers and borrowers. Without a bank, you'd have to make the rounds every time you need a loan, trying to cobble together bits and pieces of savings from the people you know. If they don't happen to have savings at the moment, you might just be out of luck. That sort of bad luck isn't unlikely if the people you know are similar to you in some way. If they are about your age or work in similar jobs or farm the same crops, then they're likely to be short on cash at the same times that you are.

A bank connects you to a much wider range of people who might have savings when you need to borrow. It also saves you (and them) the time and effort of managing dozens of small, person-to-person transactions. A bank is an easy, one-stop clearinghouse for everyone, whenever they need to save or to borrow.

Providing liquidity

Second, a bank makes it easier to have access to cash when and where you want it. In the old days, people had to have cash on hand to be able to buy something. They had to carry heavy gold or silver coins around, and worry about having them lost or stolen. What's more, it was risky to let others borrow or invest your coins (even beyond the risk of not being repaid) because the coins wouldn't be available if you needed them back in a hurry. For instance, if you made a loan to your neighbor and then your child got sick, you might have trouble getting your coins back right away to pay the doctor. It was safer to keep some coins around, doing nothing, just in case they were needed. A bank lets people enjoy the benefits of *liquidity*—having cash easily available when you want it—without the downsides of holding cash.

Some of the liquidity benefits are logistical. With banks and the tools they provide, like ATMs, checkbooks, debit accounts, and credit cards, it's simple and inexpensive to have access to cash when you want it. And you don't have to worry about protecting your cash when you don't need it. The real value is that you can deposit your savings at the bank and feel reasonably sure that you will be able to withdraw them if a need comes up.

This works because there are many depositors at the bank, and it's very, very unlikely that all of them will need to withdraw their savings at once. So, the bank can keep just a small amount of cash on hand and can loan out most of the deposits, to be put to use in productive investments. The borrowers pay the bank interest on the loans and the bank can pay savers interest on their deposits—all without losing the benefits of liquidity for individual savers.

Diversifying risk

Finally, banks help savers and borrowers to *diversify risk*. Suppose that in the pre-bank system you made a big loan to your cousin, who wanted to open a store. If the store did well, you'd get paid back and everything would be fine. But if the store went bankrupt—as small businesses often do—you might be financially ruined. When you borrow and save on a person-to-person level, there's no getting around the risk involved in having a lot of your eggs in one basket, even if everyone is well-intentioned and trustworthy.

In contrast, a bank spreads your eggs around to many different baskets. Because the bank has a big pool of borrowers, the risk of everyone failing to pay back their loans at once is very small. A few borrowers will default on their loans, but most will repay, and no individual saver will have to bear the full burden of a failed investment.

In fact, it's not only banks that provide these benefits. The whole financial system—made up of many institutions, including banks, insurance companies, investors, stock exchanges, and government agencies—is designed to *intermediate* between savers and borrowers, *provide liquidity,* and *diversify risk.* We'll come back to these ideas over and over again throughout the chapter. In the next section, we look at how these buyers and sellers come together in a simplified type of financial market we call the "market for loanable funds."

✓CONCEPT CHECK

- ☐ What is traded in a financial market? **[LO 31.1]**
- ☐ What are adverse selection and moral hazard, and how do they create problems in financial markets? **[LO 31.1]**
- ☐ What are the three main functions that banks, and the financial system in general, provide for savers and borrowers? **[LO 31.2]**

The Market for Loanable Funds: A Simplified Financial Market

Consider a whole country of people earning and spending. At any given time, some of them want to borrow and others want to save. How much do they want to borrow, and how much are they willing to save? If the amount people want to borrow is higher than the amount saved, what determines which loans get approved? Financial markets mediate the forces of supply and demand *by determining the price* at which the quantity of funds saved will be equal to the quantity invested.

Real-world financial markets involve many products, with different prices, targeted at different types of buyers and sellers. You can get the flavor of this variety just by browsing the business section of a newspaper or looking at the types of accounts and loans offered by any bank. We'll dig into some of this nuance later in the chapter. For now, let's simplify all saving and borrowing into one market, which we'll call the *market for loanable funds.*

Savings, investment, and the price of loanable funds

> **LO 31.3** Describe the market for loanable funds, including the price of loanable funds, and differentiate between savings and investment.

The **market for loanable funds** is a market in which savers, who have money to lend, supply funds to those who want to borrow for their investment spending needs. "Loanable funds" are the dollars that are on the table between them to be lent out and borrowed.

When talking about savings and investment, we have to be careful with terminology. Economists differentiate between savings and investment:

- **Savings** is the portion of income that is not immediately spent on consumption of goods and services.
- **Investment**, or, more properly, *investment spending,* refers to spending on productive inputs, such as factories, machinery, and inventories.

> ! **HINT**
> When people put money into a 401(k) account for retirement or purchase stocks, they often say they are "investing" the money. But to an economist, these are examples of *savings,* not investment.

---

market for loanable funds
a market in which savers supply funds to those who want to borrow

savings
the portion of income that is not immediately spent on consumption of goods and services

investment
spending on productive inputs, such as factories, machinery, and inventories

Using the economists' definitions of savings and investment, we can build a simple model of the market for loanable funds. The supply of loanable funds comes from savings; the demand for loanable funds comes from investment.

Just as in any market, savings (supply) and investment (demand) are brought into equilibrium at the price at which the quantity supplied and the quantity demanded are equal. For sellers and buyers in the market for loanable funds:

- Saving is like *selling the right to use your money* for a time. The quantity of savings that people are willing to supply will depend on the price they receive.
- Borrowing is like *buying the right to use someone else's money*. The quantity of investment funding that people demand also will depend on the price they receive.

interest rate
the price of money, typically expressed as a percentage per dollar per unit of time; for savers, it is the price received for letting a bank use money for a specified period of time; for borrowers, it is the price of using money for a specified period of time

For both savers and borrowers, the "price of money" is usually called the **interest rate**. It is typically expressed as a percentage per dollar per unit of time. Specifically:

- For savers, the interest rate is the price received for letting a bank use their money for a specified period of time.

- For borrowers, the interest rate is the price of borrowing money for a specified period of time. It is the price a lender charges a borrower for the use of funds until the loan is repaid. The interest rate determines the total amount that a borrower must pay back on a loan in addition to paying back the original amount borrowed (called the *principal*). For instance, if you take out a one-year loan of $1,000 with a 10 percent annual interest rate, you'll have to repay the $1,000 principal plus $100 ($1,000 × 0.10) in interest.[1]

Just as in any market, the intersection of the downward-sloping demand curve and the upward-sloping supply curve determines the equilibrium interest rate and quantity of loanable funds. The market for loanable funds is shown in Figure 31-1.

Why is the supply curve upward-sloping? This shape implies that the amount the population is willing to save increases as the interest rate increases. In markets for *goods and services,* the higher the price, the more people will find it profitable to supply the good. The relationship between price and quantity supplied in the market for *loanable funds* is essentially the same. The key is to realize that there is an opportunity cost of saving: Saving money means that you can't consume as much right now. People rationally calculate those trade-offs.

For example, if you save $100, you are trading off $100-worth of consumption now for the promise of getting some amount of money in the future. If the interest rate is zero, you will get just your $100 back. Some people will be willing to save even with zero interest—maybe they know they would rather consume $100 when they are retired than another $100 now. The higher the interest rate, the more people will find it worthwhile to delay their consumption in order to increase their future earnings. So, if you wouldn't save $100 in exchange for $101 a year from now, you might be willing to do it for $110. Even more people would save $100 if they were guaranteed to get $200 back in a year, and so on as the interest rate goes up.

FIGURE 31-1

The market for loanable funds

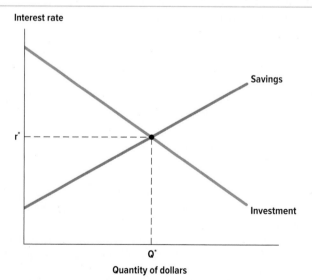

The typical market for loanable funds is at equilibrium at the point where the savings curve intersects the investment curve. From this point, one can determine the equilibrium interest rate (r*) and the amount of money traded in the market (Q*).

On the other side of the market for loanable funds, the demand curve is downward-sloping. This is because the cost of borrowing decreases as the interest rate decreases, making more and more investment opportunities worth the cost.

When deciding whether to borrow, firms or households that are contemplating an investment—say, building a factory or buying a new home—must first try to estimate the rate of return on that investment.[2] The *rate of return* describes the expected profit that the project will generate per dollar invested. The investment decision then becomes a matter of comparing benefits and costs:

- If the rate of return (the benefit of borrowing) is lower than the cost of borrowing, then the investor will lose money on net after paying back the loan. In that case, the investment probably isn't worth making.

- If the rate of return is above the interest rate, the investment will yield a profit, and it makes sense to borrow the money.

In the real world, there are a range of investment opportunities that offer different rates of return. As the interest rate rises, fewer and fewer of these opportunities will have a rate of return higher than the costs involved in borrowing, and so the quantity of loanable funds demanded will decrease. The result is the familiar downward-sloping demand curve.

Changes in the supply and demand for loanable funds

LO 31.4 List the factors that affect the supply and demand of loanable funds.

The underlying factors that determine how much people want to save and invest can change over time or differ from country to country. These determinants shift the supply and demand curves in the market for loanable funds, changing the quantity of funds supplied or demanded at any given interest rate. As a result, the equilibrium interest rate and quantity will change. In this section, we'll discuss some of the important underlying determinants of savings and investment.

Determinants of savings

Savings decisions reflect the *trade-off* people face between spending their income on consumption now and saving that money for later. The upward-sloping supply curve reflects the fact that as the interest rate increases, the value of saving relative to consuming increases. As the interest rate increases, people supply more savings.

However, factors other than the interest rate can also affect this choice. What are the underlying factors that determine how much people want to save at a given interest rate? Of course, many factors help determine individuals' choices about savings. In this chapter, however, we are concerned with factors that affect the economy on a macro level—issues that will cause the population of the country *as a whole* to want to save more or less. These factors can change over time within a country, but they can also help to explain differences across countries. The following are important factors that drive the supply of savings:

- **Wealth.** Studies show that richer households tend to save more of their income than others.

- **Current economic conditions.** When we think about how people's savings decisions respond to economic conditions, it's important to distinguish between *current* economic conditions and how current conditions might change expectations about the *future*. If expectations about the future don't change at all, then an economic downturn will generally decrease savings at a given interest rate. (That is, it will shift the supply curve for loanable funds to the left.) When times are bad and people lose jobs or have lower incomes, they will be less inclined to save and may even spend down past savings to pay for current expenses. In the recent recession, however, the savings rate actually went up. To explain this puzzle, we have to turn to . . .

- **Expectations about future economic conditions.** People often view a recession as a bad sign about how the economy will be doing in the future, as well as how it is doing at the moment. This expectation about the future can affect the savings rate: When people expect their income to be lower in the future, they will be more inclined to save, all else equal, to make sure that they have enough down the road.
- **Uncertainty.** When savers are uncertain about what the future holds, they are more likely to save extra as a precaution, just in case things turn out badly.
- **Borrowing constraints.** At any given interest rate, there will always be households and firms that would like to borrow at that interest rate but cannot. Banks and other lenders are typically willing to lend only to potential borrowers who have sufficient collateral (an asset that can be seized if the borrower is unable to pay) or sufficiently high expected incomes. When borrowing is difficult, households and firms are more likely to save to finance large purchases and investments. Borrowing constraints can change with loosening or tightening of regulations, changes in expectations about the future direction of incomes, and collateral values.
- **Social welfare policies.** Incentives to save at any given interest rate can be affected by public policies that determine the benefits people will receive if they lose their jobs, become sick or disabled, fall into poverty, or simply grow old. For instance, individuals in China may save more because they expect to bear more of the burden for their own health care and retirement costs in the future. In contrast, U.S. citizens expect to receive retirement benefits through Social Security and Medicare, reducing the need for some households to save. (Of course, tax contributions to Social Security could be thought of as forced saving for retirement—but that type of "saving" isn't counted in the savings rate.)
- **Culture.** Different cultures and traditions place varying weights on being frugal, showing your wealth through material goods, leaving an inheritance for future generations, and so on. These cultural expectations are difficult to quantify but at times help explain differing savings rates across countries.

A change in the underlying determinants of savings will shift the supply curve in the market for loanable funds. Imagine a change that makes people want to save less at any given interest rate. For instance, suppose people become more optimistic that the economy will be doing well over the next decade. Because they feel more confident that they will have jobs and earn plenty of money in the future, they become less concerned about saving now.

This change in expectations will shift the supply curve to the left, as shown in panel A of Figure 31-2. The equilibrium in the market for loanable funds moves up along the demand curve, to a new point with a higher interest rate and a lower quantity of funds saved and invested. In contrast, a change that increased the quantity people want to save at any given interest rate would shift the supply curve to the right, as shown in panel B of Figure 31-2. The new equilibrium would have a lower interest rate and a higher equilibrium quantity of funds saved and invested.

Diving further into the relationship between current economic conditions and expectations about future economic conditions, we can understand why average U.S. household savings rates *fell* dramatically when the economy was doing well through most of the 1980s, 1990s, and early 2000s, as shown in Figure 31-3. By 2005, households on average were hardly saving at all—the average savings rate was less than 2 percent.[3] Although we might think that good current conditions would make people willing to save more, it also made them optimistic about the future, which made them *less* inclined to save and more inclined to borrow. In addition, the strong economic times and housing boom meant that households saw an increase in their net worth, which further reduced saving. When the economy hit a big bump, the savings rate moved back up, starting in the depths of the financial crisis around 2008. This suggests that people took the recession as a negative sign about the future, and in response they saved more and borrowed less.

FIGURE 31-2

A change in the underlying determinants of saving shifts the supply curve for loanable funds

(A) Decrease in quantity of savings

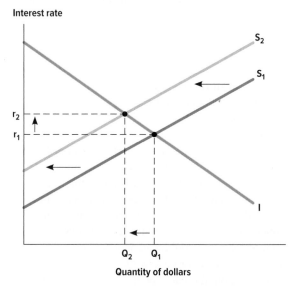

(B) Increase in quantity of savings

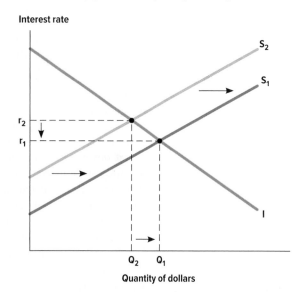

When the level of savings shifts dramatically to the left due to a change in one of the determinants of savings, the equilibrium interest rate is higher and the quantity of loanable funds in the market is lower.

When the level of savings shifts dramatically to the right due to a change in one of the determinants of savings, the equilibrium interest rate is lower and the quantity of loanable in the market is higher.

FIGURE 31-3

Savings rates in the United States since 1980   In the early 1980s, the savings rate in the United States was rather high, ranging from 8 to 10 percent. After this, the savings rate decreased steadily until it was about 2 percent in the mid-2000s. After the crash of the housing market in 2007, the savings rate jumped by about 5 percent.

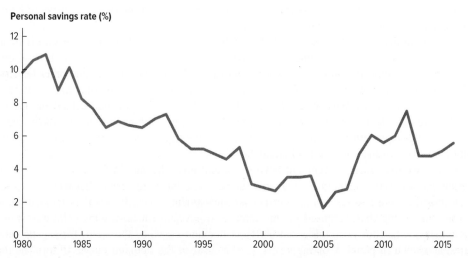

Source: Federal Reserve Bank of St. Louis, https://research.stlouisfed.org/fred2/series/PSAVERT#8eea7d87d8c09809d95.

Determinants of investment

Investment decisions are based on the *trade-off* between the potential profits that could be generated by an investment and the cost of borrowing money to finance that investment. The downward-sloping demand curve in the market for loanable funds reflects the fact that as the interest rate increases, fewer and fewer potential investments will generate returns high enough to make the cost of paying back a loan worthwhile.

Just as on the supply side of the market for loanable funds, there are other factors that affect the demand for loanable funds. What underlying factors determine how much people want to invest at a given interest rate? They include:

- **Expectations about future profitability and future economic conditions.** Apart from the interest rate, the primary factor affecting the demand for loanable funds is expectations about the future profitability of investments made today. This view about future profitability usually goes hand in hand with overall expectations about future economic conditions. For example, in 2006, just before the Great Recession, the economy was booming and consumer demand was high, due in part to the thriving housing market. A booming economy can make investors eager to borrow money because they expect ventures like new companies, products, shops, and real estate developments to earn large profits. This expectation shifts the demand curve to the right, as firms want to borrow more at any given interest rate. The opposite was true once the housing market soured in late 2007. Since consumer demand was weak throughout the economy, there was little incentive to take out a loan to expand production or start a new business.

- **Uncertainty.** When investors are uncertain about the likely path of the economy, the demand for loanable funds will fall. Uncertainty especially reduces demand when it's costly to change investment strategies once fresh information arrives.

- **Changes in the government's budget deficit.** When the government borrows more, it increases the demand for loanable funds. This is simply because the total demand for loanable funds consists of both public and private demand.

These factors change the set of investment opportunities in the economy, increasing or decreasing the number of investments that are worth making at any given interest rate. For example, a change that increases the value of potential investments throughout the economy will increase the quantity of loanable funds demanded at every interest rate, shifting the whole demand curve to the right, as shown in panel A of Figure 31-4. As a result, the equilibrium will move up along the supply curve to a new point with a higher interest rate and higher equilibrium quantity of funds saved and invested. On the other hand, if investors are uncertain about the path of the economy, their desire to borrow will decrease, and this will shift the demand curve for loanable funds to the left, as shown in panel B of Figure 31-4.

Investment decisions are also affected by external forces that determine the *supply* of loanable funds and the level of the interest rate. At any given interest rate, there will be households and firms that would like to borrow at that interest rate but cannot. Banks and other lenders are typically willing to lend only to potential borrowers who have sufficient collateral or sufficiently high expected incomes. We noted above that borrowing constraints can affect saving decisions; much more directly, borrowing constraints reduce the supply of loanable funds. Borrowing constraints can change with loosening or tightening of regulations, changes in expectations about the future direction of incomes, and collateral values.

Earlier we discussed government borrowing, and how changes in the government's budget deficit can affect the demand for loanable funds. Some have suggested that when the government borrows more, it can *crowd out* private investment. **Crowding out** is the reduction in private borrowing that is caused by an increase in government borrowing. The government's increased demand for borrowing can shift the demand curve to the right, forcing up interest rates, as shown in panel A of Figure 31-4. This shift in the demand curve, in turn, increases the cost of borrowing and so reduces private investment. This kind of crowding out of private

crowding out
the reduction in private borrowing caused by an increase in government borrowing

FIGURE 31-4

A change in the underlying determinants of investment opportunities shifts the demand curve for loanable funds

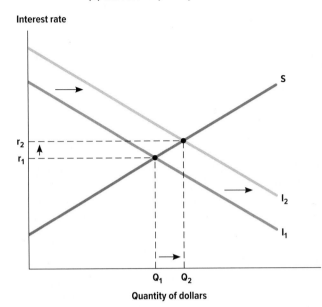

(A) Increase in quantity of investment

When the demand for investment increases, people are willing to invest more money at every interest rate. This takes the market for loanable funds to a new equilibrium, with higher rates and a greater quantity of loanable funds traded.

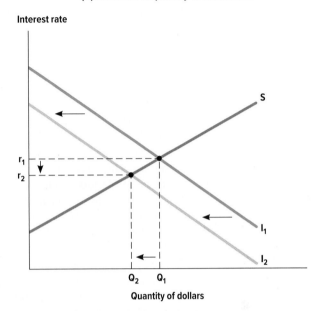

(B) Decrease in quantity of investment

A weak economy decreases the demand for loanable funds. At every interest rate, people are less interested in making investments, fearing such investments will not work out. At this new equilibrium, the interest rate is lower, and the quantity of loanable funds traded is lower.

investment is always a fear when the government intervenes in the market. Evidence from the Great Recession suggests that crowding out was minimal then, but it is always a possibility that policy-makers need to take seriously.

A price for every borrower: A more realistic look at interest rates

LO 31.5 Understand how interest rates on loans vary with the length of the loan and the riskiness of the transaction.

The simple model of the market for loanable funds illustrates the basic relationships between supply and demand in financial markets. In reality, however, *there is no such thing as a single interest rate* that is paid by all prospective borrowers. Different borrowers pay different interest rates:

- An individual may have to pay a higher interest rate to borrow money than an established company would. Almost everyone has to pay a higher rate than the U.S. government.
- Also, the same borrower may also pay different rates on different kinds of transactions. For example, the interest rate will be less on a mortgage than on a credit card for a given individual.

How is the interest rate for a particular loan determined? Two basic factors drive differences in interest rates: length of time and degree of risk.

The first factor is the *length of time* the borrower has to repay the loan. The reason for this is not immediately obvious. Isn't a lender already being compensated for lending over a longer period by earning interest over that longer period? Only partially. Think of it this way: Lenders want to be compensated for the *opportunity cost* of being unable to get their money back quickly. When they lend money for 20 years at a fixed interest rate, they've tied up their money for that length of time; they must pass up any better investment opportunities and interest rates that could emerge in those 20 years. Since there's more uncertainty about potential future investment opportunities over a longer period of time, lenders generally want a higher interest rate to compensate them for the added opportunity cost when loans stretch over a longer period.

The second factor that drives differences in interest rates is the *riskiness* of the transaction. To understand why, ask yourself a simple question: To whom would you rather loan money—a stranger on the street or the local bank? Regardless of your answer, you probably had a simple criterion for deciding: Who was more likely to pay you back?

default

the failure of a borrower to pay back a loan according to the agreed-upon terms

Lenders in the financial markets make this same calculation when they consider the likelihood that a borrower may default on a loan. A **default** happens when a borrower fails to pay back a loan according to the agreed-upon terms. If lenders think that a particular borrower might default, they will demand a higher interest rate to make it worth taking that risk.

Sometimes, loans are secured against an asset (called *collateral*), such as a house. If a borrower defaults on a mortgage loan, the lender takes ownership of the house as compensation for the loss. This explains why mortgages generally are made at a lower interest rate than credit card loans: If a mortgage borrower defaults, the lender can sell the house to get some money back (although usually not the full value of the loan). In contrast, credit cards aren't backed with valuable assets, so the lender's losses are higher if someone defaults.

risk-free rate

the interest rate at which one would lend if there were no risk of default; usually approximated by interest rates on U.S. government debt

The risk of a borrower defaulting on a loan is known as *credit risk*. It is measured against the **risk-free rate**—the interest rate at which one would lend if there were no risk of default. The risk-free rate is usually approximated by interest rates on U.S. government debt because the U.S. government is considered extremely unlikely to default. All other borrowers must pay higher rates to compensate lenders for the higher possibility that they will default.

The difference between the risk-free rate and the interest rate a particular investor has to pay is called the *credit spread* or *risk premium*. The difference can be quite large, both among investors and over time. The recession and financial crisis of 2007–2009, for example, caused credit spreads to rise dramatically, as borrowers of all kinds suddenly became more likely to default. Armed with data about the length of time of a loan and roughly how likely it is for the borrower to default, we can get an idea what price a particular borrower might face for a particular transaction in the market for loanable funds. In general, the longer the term of a loan and the more likely the risk of default, the higher above the risk-free rate will be the interest rate of that loan.

✓CONCEPT CHECK

- ☐ What is another name for the price of money in the market for loanable funds? **[LO 31.3]**
- ☐ What are factors that can cause the supply curve to shift right in the market for loanable funds? **[LO 31.4]**
- ☐ In the market for loanable funds, which factors can cause the demand curve to shift right? **[LO 31.4]**
- ☐ Describe the factors that explain why interest rates on loans to households and firms are not all the same. **[LO 31.5]**

The Modern Financial System

Now that we've covered the basic *theory* of financial markets, we'll turn our attention to some key *realities* of the modern financial system. We've already noted that the idea of a single market for loanable funds is an oversimplification. In reality, people and firms face different interest rates based on the length and riskiness of their loans. The institutions that make up the **financial system** bring together savers, borrowers, investors, and insurers in a set of interconnected markets where people trade financial products. This section takes a more nuanced look at the role the financial system plays in helping people manage their money and risk. It also defines some of the most important types of products that are traded in the financial system and identifies the people and institutions that trade them.

financial system
the group of institutions that bring together savers, borrowers, investors, and insurers in a set of interconnected markets where people trade financial products

Functions of the financial system

LO 31.6 Describe why it is important for the financial system to intermediate between buyers and sellers, provide liquidity, and diversify risk.

At the beginning of the chapter, we saw how financial markets—banks, in particular—can help to fill three basic roles in the economy: *intermediating* between savers and borrowers, providing *liquidity*, and *diversifying risk*. In this section, we expand on these ideas and show how the *financial system as a whole* contributes to achieving them.

Matching up buyers and sellers: Intermediation

Imagine you want to borrow to start a small business. How are you going to get enough money together? You could go to everyone you know and ask them to lend you whatever amount they can afford. This approach won't necessarily fund your business unless you happen to know a lot of people with spare cash sitting around. But even if you managed to pull it off, the process of arranging and keeping track of all of those loans would be incredibly time-consuming and complicated.

The existence of banks lowers the *transaction costs* of the borrowing process. When banks exist, there is only one person you need to persuade to lend you the entire sum of money—the bank loan officer. This saves you—and the friends and family you'd otherwise be pestering for loans—time and money by replacing a lot of small, informal transactions with one big, professionalized one.

Various institutions act as **financial intermediaries**—they channel funds from people who have them to people who want them. A bank is one kind of intermediary. A different kind of intermediary is a stock exchange, which matches people wanting to buy ownership shares of companies with people wanting to sell those shares. This intermediation reduces transaction costs, by centralizing information about share prices and providing a broad and dynamic marketplace for transactions. The financial system offers savers and borrowers a wide set of interconnected markets in which to find financial intermediaries.

financial intermediaries
institutions that channel funds from people who have them to people who want them

Providing liquidity

A second critical function of the financial system is to provide liquidity. Earlier in the chapter, we talked informally about why people value liquidity. Formally, **liquidity** is a measure of how easily a particular asset can be converted quickly to cash without much loss of value. We say that an asset is *liquid* if it can be sold for cash quickly without much loss of value and is *illiquid* if it can't.

Consider two types of assets that many people own: cars and houses. If you needed cash quickly, which would you sell? A car is relatively easy to sell quickly. You can simply drive into a car dealership and ask the dealer to make you a cash offer. You won't get the best possible price, of course—but you'll get much of what the car is worth, in cash, right away. The house, on the other hand, is much harder to sell. You can't walk into most real estate agencies and expect a cash offer on the spot. The real estate agent will instead help you find a buyer, which can take time,

liquidity
a measure of how easily a particular asset can be converted quickly to cash without much loss of value

Financial intermediaries, such as the Chicago Board of Trade shown here, centralize information about prices and provide a marketplace for transactions.
© *Tim Boyle/Bloomberg via Getty Images*

and even then there are still mountains of paperwork and things that could go wrong.

In other words, the car is a more liquid asset than the house. Why is there such a difference in liquidity? Houses are more difficult to value and legally complex to purchase. Before you decide how much to pay for a house, you should do a thorough check of every part of it—make sure it doesn't have a leaky roof and that there aren't plans to build a waste-processing facility nearby. Cars are much easier to value. An experienced dealer can accurately size up a car from a peek under the hood. That's why there are car dealers fulfilling the role of liquidity providers but few equivalents in the real estate market. A *liquidity provider* is someone who helps make a market more liquid by being always ready to buy or sell an asset.

Various players in the financial system are liquidity providers, helping ensure that markets are liquid. The very structure of financial assets such as stocks and bonds (as we'll define and discuss below) also serves to increase liquidity. If you want to sell a share of company stock or a government bond, there is almost always someone in the financial system willing to buy it from you. Often that someone is your bank or your broker; it may also be a mutual fund or simply a large financial investor. We sometimes call these people *market makers*—they, in effect, "make a market" by being always ready to buy or sell, just like the car dealer.

Liquidity is important because it affects people's willingness to save. Savers generally want to know that their money will be there for them when they need it. If markets were not liquid, you couldn't count on being able to sell your assets quickly in order to get your money back. As a result, you'd probably be extremely cautious about lending money out for investment in the first place. That reluctance would reduce the supply of loanable funds, which would drive up interest rates, reduce the amount of investment, and lead to slower growth in the economy.

Diversifying risk

The third major role played by the financial system is that it spreads risk. Imagine that, as a saver, you could lend your money directly only to other individuals or companies. If the borrower defaulted, you would lose everything. If you lend your money to a bank, however, you know that the bank will pool your money with that of other savers and make thousands of loans to different borrowers. Some of those borrowers will default, but the bank won't lose everything at once, and neither will its savers. The bank has *diversified* the risk. **Diversification** is the process by which risks are shared among many different assets or people, reducing the impact of a particular risk on any one individual. The financial system helps share risk even more broadly than an individual bank.

Diversification is critical for the functioning of the economy. People are more willing to save money, and entrepreneurs are more willing to start new ventures, if they don't have to worry too much about the risk of losing everything.

diversification
the process by which risks are shared across many different assets or people, reducing the impact of any particular risk on any one individual

Major financial assets

LO 31.7 Differentiate between debt and equity and define the major types of assets in each category.

How does the financial system fulfill its roles of intermediation, providing liquidity, and diversifying risk? It does so by creating financial assets that can be bought and sold within the financial markets. There are far more varieties of financial assets than we could possibly cover in this text; we'll focus on just the major ones: equity, debt, and derivatives.

Equity

When you own part of a company and share in its profits, we say that you *have equity* in that company. Financial assets that represent this partial ownership are called *equities.* A "stock"— the financial asset you probably hear the most about—is the common name for an equity asset. The news media report figures from the stock market every evening, such as the Dow Jones Industrial Average, the Standard & Poor's (S&P) 500, and the Nasdaq. There even are television networks dedicated to following every move of these indexes.

What exactly are stocks? A **stock** is a financial asset that represents partial ownership of a company. If a company has issued 100,000 shares of stock, then the owner of each share (called a *shareholder* or *stockholder*) owns 1/100,000 of the company.

Why do companies issue stock? For one thing, issuing stock allows a company to raise capital without borrowing. Imagine a store owner who wants to expand her business by opening a new store but needs money to do so. She has two choices:

- She could borrow money from the bank, but she'd have to pay interest and pay back the loan even if the new store fails.
- Alternatively, the store owner may choose to sell some equity in her company. People who buy the shares of stock will become part owners of her company. As part owners, they take on the risk of losing money if the new store fails, and they expect a percentage of the profits if it succeeds.

Stock is also a mechanism for turning an illiquid asset (ownership of a company) into a liquid one (a share that can be sold on the stock market). Ownership of an entire business is not easy to sell. Just like buying a house, there are many complicated things that a potential buyer will want to understand beforehand. On the other hand, stock can be easily bought and sold in small, standardized increments on the stock market. A privately held company is an illiquid asset. In contrast, stock in *public companies*—so called because anyone can buy a share—is a liquid asset.[4]

Stockholders, as partial owners, are usually entitled to vote on certain aspects of how the company is run. They elect the board of directors, for example. Stockholders also are entitled to receive a portion of the company's profits, proportional to the size of their ownership stake, in the form of dividends. A **dividend** is a payment made periodically, typically annually or quarterly, to all shareholders of a company.

Debt

The main alternative to equity is debt. The most basic and familiar type of debt is a loan. A **loan** is an agreement in which a lender gives money to a borrower in exchange for a promise to repay the amount loaned plus an agreed-upon amount of interest. Banks make loans to individuals to make purchases like houses and cars, and they lend to businesses that want to make investments.

Making a loan is generally both less risky and less potentially rewarding than buying stock:

- A borrower might default on a loan. People who have loaned money to a company that goes bankrupt do have some protection: They have the first legal claim on that company's assets and will be paid as much as possible before stockholders earn anything.
- Buying stock in a company comes with a higher risk of losing everything if the company fails. But if the company does very well and earns huge profits, stockholders are usually entitled to a share of those profits. With a loan, no matter how successful the company gets, the lender will never receive more than the amount specified in the original loan agreements.

Like any other financial asset, loans can be bought and sold. Imagine that a bank lends you money to buy a house. You sign a contract, and you have a legal obligation to pay the loan back

stock
a financial asset that represents partial ownership of a company

dividend
a payment made periodically, typically annually or quarterly, to all shareholders of a company

loan
an agreement in which a lender gives money to a borrower in exchange for a promise to repay the amount loaned plus an agreed-upon amount of interest

at a specified interest rate by a specified date. The bank could then sell that obligation to some-body else. The buyer of the loan would pay the bank for the right to collect the money from you, according to the terms of the loan deal.

To make loans more liquid, they can be standardized into a more easily tradable asset, called a *bond*. A **bond** represents a promise by the bond issuer to repay the loan, at a specified maturity date, and to pay periodic interest at a specific percentage rate. Because of the set interest rate, bonds are often referred to as *fixed-income securities*. The owner of the bond (bondholder) is legally entitled to receive scheduled interest payments (called *coupon* payments). These coupon payment are generally paid every three or six months.[5] The bond owner also receives a final pay-ment of the original loan amount for the bond (the *principal,* sometimes called the *face value,* of the bond) at the maturity date.

Bonds are issued in varying maturities. Corporate bonds typically have maturities of 10 to 30 years. Government bonds (issued by the U.S. Treasury, government agencies, and states and municipalities) generally range from one to 10 years. Governments and big companies often sell bonds as a way to borrow large sums of money, typically from a large number of lenders. Because bonds are standardized, it is easy for bondholders to sell them, making them a more liquid asset than regular loans.

Since a bond is essentially a loan, the basic risk-reward trade-off that applied to loans also applies to bonds: They are generally safer than stocks but also less rewarding. While returns can vary (and historical returns do not necessarily predict future returns), government bonds have historically averaged a real (inflation-adjusted) return of about 2 percent per year, while a broad index of stocks indicates a real return of nearly 7 percent per year over the same period.[6] Why might savers be interested in buying government bonds, with so much lower returns, instead of stocks? Because stocks are more risky. They can easily go down in value, whereas the govern-ment is very unlikely to default on a bond.

Wouldn't it be useful if there were a way to take nonstandard loans—say, loans to people to buy homes—and turn them into standardized, bond-like instruments that can be easily traded? It turns out there is such a process, called *securitization*. Securitization turns many loans into a single larger asset, thus reducing the risk to the lender of any individual borrower defaulting on the loan. Securitization became popular in the early 2000s. Financial assets of all types, from stu-dent loans to mortgage loans, were securitized to create liquid assets that would be appealing to a wide array of lenders. In Chapter 34, "Financial Crisis," we'll show how securitization played a starring role in the financial crisis that sparked the Great Recession and the fall of Lehman Brothers.

Despite its involvement in the financial crisis, debt is not bad when done right. As we've men-tioned, debt is behind many of the transactions we take for granted. When you're able to drive off the lot with a new car, or a firm is able to build a new factory, it's likely that debt helped make those investments possible.

Derivatives

Stocks, loans, and bonds are examples of financial contracts in which one person or firm agrees to pay another a certain amount, under certain circumstances. If you get creative, you can come up with much more complex arrangements, based on the same fundamental idea. For instance, you can create a contract based on the future value of particular assets or goods, like mortgages, stocks, or the price of oil.

Financial contracts based on the value of some other asset represent a special category of financial assets, called **derivatives**. A derivative is an asset whose value is based on (or "derived from"—hence the term *derivative*) the value of another asset, such as a home loan, stock, bond, or barrel of oil.

The best example of this type of arrangement is a *futures contract.* The buyer of a futures con-tract agrees to pay the seller a set amount today based on the expected future price of some asset. For example, through a futures contract you could sell all or part of your farm crop in advance at

---

bond

a form of debt that represents a promise by the bond issuer to repay the face value of the loan, at a specified maturity date, and to pay periodic interest at a specific percentage rate

derivative

an asset whose value is based on the value of another asset

a set price. If the crop ends up being worth more than the contract price, the person you sold the futures to will be able to sell it for a profit. If prices fall, the buyer of your crop will lose out, but you will still get the contract price. In effect, you have managed your risk by transferring both good and bad risks about the future price of the crop to your contract partner. In general, derivatives are meant to transfer risk to people who are more willing to bear it.

Major players in the financial system

LO 31.8 Name the main institutions in financial markets and describe the role that each plays.

So far, we've seen the functions of the financial system and the major assets that get traded. We'll now look at four key players without whom there couldn't be a well-functioning financial system: banks and other intermediaries, savers and their proxies, entrepreneurs and businesses, and speculators.

Banks and other financial intermediaries

We've already mentioned that banks play a crucial intermediary role. Digging deeper, we can divide banks into two categories: *commercial banks* and *investment banks.*

Commercial banks are probably what you think of when someone says "bank." When you make a deposit at a bank or get a mortgage or student loan from a bank, you are interacting with a commercial bank. As well as being an intermediary between savers and borrowers, commercial banks help to create liquidity. The loans they make are relatively illiquid assets, typically taking years to be repaid.

Most savers, however, don't want their money to be tied up for years. How can banks "lend long" (make loans of long duration) while also "borrowing short" (using the money gained from deposits to make loans that allow them to be ready to give depositors their money back at short notice)? Crucially, banks assume that not all depositors will try to get their money back at once, so they keep on hand only a fraction of all deposits. If too many depositors want their cash back at once, the bank would run out of funds—a potentially disastrous situation known as a bank run. (We'll further explore the topic of fractional lending in Chapter 32, "Money and the Monetary System.")

Investment banks are part of what is commonly referred to as "Wall Street"—banks like Goldman Sachs and the now-bankrupt Lehman Brothers. These banks don't take deposits and they don't make loans in the traditional sense. Instead, they provide liquidity to financial markets by acting as market makers. They help companies issue stocks and bonds by guaranteeing to buy any that remain unsold (a process known as *underwriting*).

Most banks are either a commercial bank or an investment bank, but not both at once. This fact is due to a law passed in the 1930s, the Glass-Steagall Act, which banned banks from taking on both roles. However, Congress repealed this law in 1999, and a few of the largest banks—such as JP Morgan Chase and Bank of America—have taken on both roles simultaneously.

Savers and their proxies

Most savers don't approach financial markets directly. Instead, they operate through a *proxy*—that is, they give their money to someone else to decide whom to lend it to. These proxies include banks, mutual funds, pension funds, and life insurance companies. According to the Federal Reserve, by 2016 U.S. mutual fund companies held $13 trillion in assets, while life insurance and private pension companies held $15 trillion in assets.[7] (Remember that in economic terminology, buying assets like stocks and bonds is a form of savings, not "investing.")

A **mutual fund** is a portfolio of stocks, bonds, and other assets managed by a professional who makes decisions on behalf of clients. Savers entrust their money to mutual funds to save themselves the hassle of researching the thousands of stocks and bonds they could buy; instead, they let a professional make the decisions.

mutual fund
a portfolio of stocks, bonds, and other assets managed by a professional who makes decisions on behalf of clients

There are many different types of mutual funds. Two popular types are specialized funds and index funds:

- Managers of *specialized funds* try to beat the performance of the market by researching specific companies and picking stocks they believe will earn higher returns than the market average.
- *Index funds* buy all the stocks represented in a broad market like the Standard & Poor's (S&P) 500, with the goal of mirroring the same average return as the market.

Mutual funds charge a fee for their services that can be as little as a tenth of a percent of assets (such as with a simple index fund) or as much as 3 or 4 percent (in the case of a fund that spends a lot on stock research).

Pension funds are also a major outlet for individual savings. Usually linked to one's employer, a **pension fund** is a professionally managed portfolio of assets intended to provide income to retirees. Two main categories of pension funds exist:

- *Defined-benefit* plans guarantee a fixed payout to employees who have met certain entry requirements, such as working a certain number of years with the company.
- *Defined-contribution* plans do not guarantee retirees a defined level of pension. Employees pay in a certain (defined) amount each year and their employers may match some portion of that contribution; the fund provides payouts that depend on how the stock market performs. The most common defined-contribution plan is the *401(k) plan,* in which contributions grow tax-deferred until they are withdrawn.

In the past, defined-benefit plans were the norm. Today, defined-contribution plans such as 401(k)s are much more common.

Life insurance policies are also a significant form of savings. The savings people put into these policies are called *premiums,* and as with mutual funds and pension funds, a professional decides how to use them in financial markets. Unlike mutual funds (from which you can take money out at any time) and pension funds (which you can access when you retire), life insurance policies pay out to your dependents only when you die.

These three proxies—mutual funds, pension funds, and life insurance policies—are by no means the only ways in which individuals can entrust their savings to a third-party manager. Other options include hedge funds, private-equity firms, and venture-capital funds. Still, surprisingly enough, the simplest approach may be the best, as outlined in the Real Life box "The incredible index fund."

pension fund

a professionally managed portfolio of assets intended to provide income to retirees

Real Life

The incredible index fund

Entire TV networks dedicate their efforts to reporting the rise and fall of asset prices, from stocks to the price of gold. Bookstores are filled with advice on playing the stock market. If you're lucky enough to have money to put in the stock market, how can you make sense of this noisy information and find a way to outperform the market?

Maybe you shouldn't even try. Many savers have embraced *index funds,* such as the pioneering Vanguard Index Fund. Index funds, now offered by a wide range of financial companies, attempt to replicate the exact movements of a given stock market index such as the S&P 500, which is comprised of stocks in 500 leading companies.

Index funds have a big advantage over traditional, actively managed mutual funds: They cost much less to maintain. One reason for their lower costs is that index funds don't need to employ highly paid asset managers to research which stocks have the highest probability of "beating the market." Instead, the goal is to simply mimic the market average.

A second benefit of index funds is that they minimize the capital gains taxes that are owed when stocks are bought or sold. This occurs because the stocks that comprise an index like the S&P 500 don't change much, so there is much less buying and selling of stocks.

Perhaps you've spotted the most common objection to index funds: Professional fund managers point out that since index funds attempt to duplicate the exact movements of what is essentially the *average* performance of the market, they can miss out on large returns earned by specific subsets of the market. In the dot-com boom during the late 1990s, for example, the returns for some mutual funds that specialized in up-and-coming technological firms far outstripped the returns for index funds.

Who's right? Over the five-year period after it was created, the Vanguard Index Fund beat the returns of over 90 percent of actively managed mutual funds.

Sources: Richard A. Ferri, *All about Index Funds: The Easy Way to Get Started,* 2nd ed. (New York: McGraw-Hill Education, 2007); http://www.fool.com/mutualfunds/indexfunds/indexfunds01.htm.

Entrepreneurs and businesses

Entrepreneurs and businesses also are major players in financial markets because they are often looking to borrow money to finance their latest ventures. Strictly speaking, these are the people who engage in economic investment, often with the advice of specialized investment banks that channel savers' money to them. Without these borrowers, much of the financial system would simply cease to exist.

Speculators

The last group of major players in the financial system is speculators, who play a unique and controversial role in the financial system. A *speculator* is anyone who buys and sells financial assets purely for financial gain. You may ask what's controversial about that—aren't the other three key players we've considered (intermediaries, savers, and entrepreneurs) also out for financial gain? Yes, but what sets speculators apart is that they are neither a "natural" buyer nor a seller but are willing to play either role in an effort to make a profit.

There is fierce debate over whether speculators are good for the health of the financial markets, as summarized in the What Do You Think? box "Are speculators a good influence on markets?"

What Do You Think?

Are speculators a good influence on markets?

From 2006 to 2008, prices of many staple commodities, such as wheat and corn, practically doubled. The sharp increase in food prices was caused in part by the combination of a decrease in supply due to poor harvests and an increase in demand from people actually intending to eat the food.

However, some say that this combination of events does not explain all of the increase in commodity prices. Instead, they say prices were pushed up by increased demand from speculators, who saw the opportunity to profit by buying food and then selling it again at a higher price. Pope Benedict XVI, former leader of the Catholic Church, gave voice to a number of critics when he asked, "How can we be silent before the fact that food has become an object of speculation, or tied to happenings in a financial market that, lacking any certain rules and devoid of moral principles, appears to be still rooted to the sole object of profit?"

(continued)

How might speculators defend themselves against such comments? The main argument in favor of speculators is their role in price discovery—that is, they help markets to find the "correct" price for an asset, reflecting all available information. What might the price of wheat be six months from now? Because speculators are trying to earn a profit, they will spend huge amounts of research energy on understanding every nuance of this kind of question. Their goal is to figure out if they should be buying or selling wheat futures at the current price. Many believe that this is a valuable service, saving wheat farmers, bakeries, and grocery stores from needing to do this research themselves. Instead, they can be confident that the market price already reflects the best information available.

Others believe, however, that speculation actually has the opposite effect. They say that it causes prices to swing wildly away from the "correct" levels. Such swings magnify small fluctuations in the market and create potentially destabilizing bubbles and busts. Consider the housing boom of 2000–2007, which was driven in part by speculators buying houses in expectation that the price of real estate would continue going up. Critics argue that something similar happened with the prices of corn and wheat: Speculators bid up the prices because they expected the price to continue to go up, creating a self-fulfilling prophecy.

This sounds like a puzzle. If speculators research the market thoroughly, wouldn't they realize that wheat was overpriced and want to sell, thereby returning wheat to its correct price? Some say that's what happens. Others believe that speculators might still want to buy overpriced wheat today, if they're confident that the wheat will be even more overpriced tomorrow, and that they'll be able to sell again for a profit before the inevitable crash comes. The "correct" price will be found in the end, but perhaps only after a period of hysteria and a lot of damage to consumers and savers.

WHAT DO YOU THINK?

1. What benefits can speculators provide through their participation in financial markets?
2. Do you think speculators' incentives to discover the "correct" price for a good are aligned with those of "natural" savers and borrowers like farmers and customers? Why might their incentives sometimes be different from those of other players in financial markets?
3. Do you agree with the Pope that there are moral issues that go beyond economics involved in speculation in food prices? Why or why not?

Source: http://www.nytimes.com/2008/04/10/opinion/10thu1.html.

✓CONCEPT CHECK

☐ Why is it important that the financial system provides liquidity? **[LO 31.6]**
☐ Which type of financial asset is included in the Dow Jones Industrial Average? **[LO 31.7]**
☐ Why would an investor wish to diversify his or her financial investments? **[LO 31.7]**
☐ What are the two different types of banks? **[LO 31.8]**
☐ What is a pension fund? **[LO 31.8]**

Valuing Assets

We've touched on one particular question a few times so far: *How do buyers and sellers in the market for financial assets reach agreement on the correct price?* We've already looked at how businesses balance the expected rate of return on an investment with the cost of borrowing. How do the suppliers of funds—that is, savers—decide whether to deposit money in a bank or to purchase stocks or bonds? And if they choose to purchase stocks or bonds, how do they decide what to buy? In this section, we'll explore some of the basic principles of *asset valuation,* which help savers make these decisions.

The trade-off between risk and return

LO 31.9 Explain the trade-off between risk and return in financial assets and describe how risk can be measured.

The basic trade-off in valuing any asset is between risk and return: If you face a high risk of losing your money, you're going to want the chance of a high return to make it worth taking that risk.

Figure 31-5 shows the historical risk and return profile for various major financial assets. As you can see:

- Cash and bond investments (both fixed-income and inflation-adjusted) are on the low-risk, low-return end of the spectrum.
- Stocks ("equities" of various types) are on the high end of the spectrum, both carrying a hefty amount of risk but generally also providing larger returns.

Different individuals have different appetites for risk: Some savers may prefer to keep their money in low-risk bonds. Speculators enjoy chasing high rewards at the risk of losing everything.

Diversification, market risk, and idiosyncratic risk

One way to manage risk is to hold assets like cash and fixed-income bonds that have low risk, but low return. Another way to manage risk but improve return is through diversification:

- If you put all your money in one company's stock and that company goes bankrupt, you've lost everything.
- If you buy stock in many companies, especially those in different industries, they're unlikely all to go bankrupt at the same time.

FIGURE 31-5

Risk and reward of various financial assets   There is clearly a strong correlation between the expected risk and expected return in financial assets. Assets such as cash and fixed-income bonds carry very low risk and reward. At the upper end of the scale, financial assets in developing countries carry a return that is high, but they also are quite risky.

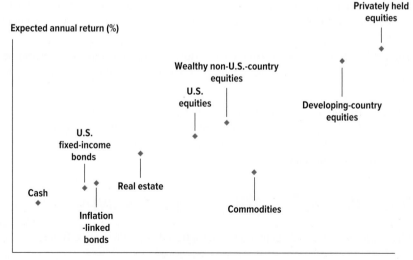

Source: http://www.nepc.com/writable/research_articles/file/2010_03_risk_parity.pdf/.

A *portfolio*—a collection or group of many different assets—will often have a higher return for a given level of risk than any individual asset could offer. To better understand how diversification works, let's look at two different types of risk that exist with financial assets.

First, **market risk**, also called *systemic risk,* refers to any risk that is broadly shared by the entire market or economy. An example would be the risk of unexpected inflation. Of course, some businesses will be more affected than others by unexpected inflation, but all businesses will face the consequences of the rising prices.

For this reason, market risk is harder to eliminate via diversification. For the case of unexpected inflation, one strategy to eliminate some of the risk is to buy inflation-linked bonds issued by the U.S. Treasury. The return to these bonds varies with inflation, so they hold their value even when prices rise without warning.

In contrast, **idiosyncratic risk** is unique to a particular company or asset. For example, the risk that a particular company will make a bad business decision, causing the value of its stock to fall, is idiosyncratic to that company. Idiosyncratic risks are the easiest to lower or even eliminate via diversification. If you buy stock in many different companies, it's unlikely that they're all going to fail at the same time.

A portfolio composed of many stocks succeeds in diversifying away idiosyncratic risks. As more stocks are added to the portfolio, idiosyncratic risk goes down without reducing the expected performance of the portfolio. Index funds are the natural extreme of diversifying to eliminate idiosyncratic risk: By investing in essentially all the stocks in the market, index funds achieve a very high level of diversification and face little to no idiosyncratic risk. A certain amount of market risk, just from having money in the financial market, remains in all portfolios and cannot be diversified away.

market (systemic) risk
any risk that is broadly shared by the entire market or economy; also called *systemic risk*

idiosyncratic risk
any risk that is unique to a particular company or asset

standard deviation
a measure of how spread out a set of numbers is

Measuring risk

How is risk measured? The most commonly used measure of risk in financial markets is a simple tool borrowed from statistics: the standard deviation. The **standard deviation** is a measure of how spread out a set of numbers is.

In financial markets, the simplest way to measure risk is to look at the standard deviation of an asset's return over time. That means that we keep track of how much money it makes each day or month or year, and then measure how widely these numbers differ from period to period. For example:

- The stock market has historically returned about 7 percent per year after inflation *on average,* but the actual returns in a *particular* year have ranged anywhere from −80 percent to +120 percent. A 20–30 percent increase or decrease in any given year would not be particularly surprising.
- Government bonds, on the other hand, have historically gained about 2–3 percent per year after inflation on average. Rarely have they experienced more than a 10 percent gain or loss.

In other words, government bonds have a much smaller standard deviation—meaning they have much less risk than the stock market. Those historical figures don't necessarily give a good prediction of average levels of future stock prices, but they do show the bigger point: Higher average returns usually come with substantially higher risk.

Predicting returns: The efficient-market hypothesis

LO 31.10 Give arguments for and against the assumption that markets are efficient.

Imagine you were asked to pick the stock most likely to go up in value over the next year. How would you do it? There are three basic approaches you could take.

The first approach is through *fundamental analysis,* which involves trying to predict how much profit a company will make in the future and using that as a basis for calculating how much the company is worth now. Fundamental analysis is a fancy way of describing extensive research on an individual company: poring over financial statements, studying how the company is run, understanding the industry the company is in and who its competitors are, and so on. Specialized investment funds often employ hundreds of analysts to do such research.

Once we have a prediction of future profits, we can use interest rates to translate between the *present value* and *future value* of money. If you estimate the future value of the profits the company will make, you can translate it into the company's **net present value** (often abbreviated as NPV). Net present value is a measure of the current value of a stream of cash flows expected in the future. This tells you the "correct" price of shares in the company.

The second approach is called *technical analysis.* It ignores any attempt to predict future profits or calculate NPV or indeed to learn anything whatsoever about the stock in question. Instead you analyze the *past* movements of a stock's price to try to predict future movements; you look for patterns in the data that could point to what's going to happen next. This method is usually done with the help of highly sophisticated computer software.

This is all pretty hard work. Is there an easier way? Well, yes. Here's the third approach: Make a list of all the stocks, pin it to a wall, and throw a dart at it. Wherever it lands, that's your choice. This doesn't sound like a great plan, does it? But if many academic researchers in the finance world are right, this approach is often just as good as either of the first two approaches, as well as being a whole lot cheaper, quicker, and simpler.

The idea underlying this third approach is called the **efficient-market hypothesis**. It states that market prices always incorporate *all available information,* and therefore they represent true value as correctly as is possible. Both fundamental and technical analysis are ways of trying to outsmart the market; they work only if you find a stock whose current price is either higher or lower than the "correct" price. The efficient-market hypothesis (EMH) implies that finding incorrectly priced stocks is impossible. If prices already represent the best-possible information about the true value of a stock, then all stocks are already correctly priced, and so there is no additional information you can use to predict which stocks will gain value.

The intuition behind this idea is pretty straightforward. Imagine that careful observers of the stock market have information that a particular company will announce high profits tomorrow. Such an announcement generally causes a stock's price to rise, so it makes sense to buy the stock today in the hope of selling at a profit tomorrow. The effect is to drive up the price of the stock today, until it reaches the price expected for tomorrow. The expectation of tomorrow's announcement is now *priced in.*

So what will happen to the stock's price tomorrow? According to the efficient-market hypothesis, the stock's expected movements might go in any direction—described as a *random walk.* Any attempt to predict the price of the stock tomorrow is foolish: If there were any credible information out there that suggested the stock would go up or down, then the stock would already have priced it in. This brings us back to our dart-throwing plan: If you can't possibly predict stock returns, you might as well just pin a list of stocks on the wall and throw darts at them.

Not surprisingly, the efficient-market hypothesis isn't popular with the Wall Street brokers and analysts who are paid handsomely for their attempts to pick winning stocks. They argue that some analysts simply have better information than others or at least a better ability to put together all the complex pieces.

However, the number of people who have consistently outsmarted the markets over a long period is vanishingly small. The efficient-market hypothesis is exactly the reason why we should not be surprised that index funds consistently outperform actively managed funds. Neither type of fund beats the market on average, but actively managed funds charge higher fees that erode their net rates of return.

One argument against the efficient-market hypothesis is that occasionally the same financial asset can be traded at different prices in different markets. That's evidence that the market isn't

net present value (NPV)
a measure of the current value of a stream of cash flows expected in the future

efficient-market hypothesis
the idea that market prices always incorporate all available information, and therefore represent true value as correctly as is possible

arbitrage

the process of taking advantage of market inefficiencies to earn profits

efficiently using all its information. If you can manage to simultaneously sell that asset in one place while buying it in another, you can make a risk-free profit. The process of taking advantage of market inefficiencies to earn profits is called **arbitrage**. Some fund managers specialize in scouring different markets in search of arbitrage opportunities. However, it takes a huge amount of effort to spot these opportunities, and if you get the timing even slightly wrong, you can end up losing a lot of money. Given what we know about risk and reward, though, if you get the timing right, you can reap big rewards.

Bubbles

According to the efficient-market view, markets are rational, in the sense that asset prices incorporate all relevant information at any given point in time. There are times, however, when asset prices rise far above historically justified levels and then subsequently collapse, a phenomenon known as a *bubble.*

One of the earliest examples of a bubble was the Dutch Tulip Mania of 1634–1637. At the top of that market, a single tulip sold for as much as a house. More recent examples include the stock-market boom in the 1920s, the Internet bubble in the late 1990s, and the housing bubble that ended with the onset of the global financial crisis of 2009. (See Chapter 34, "Financial Crisis," for further discussion of some famous bubbles.)

What exactly is a bubble? Robert Shiller, one of the leading scholars in behavioral finance and a Nobel laureate, described a bubble as:

> [a] situation in which news of price increases spurs investor enthusiasm, which spreads by psychological contagion from person to person, in the process amplifying stories that might justify the price increase. This attracts a larger and larger class of investors, who, despite doubts about the real value of the investment, are drawn to it partly through envy of others' successes and partly through a gambler's excitement.[8]

Thus, bubbles in asset prices can be seen as social epidemics, in which the excitement surrounding rapidly growing asset prices infects people with a "bug" to buy in the hope of selling at ever higher prices. Since this process can't continue indefinitely, bubbles will eventually pop and prices will plummet, often causing severe economic damage in the process.

✓CONCEPT CHECK

☐ What is the general relationship between risk and return in financial markets? **[LO 31.9]**
☐ How does idiosyncratic risk differ from market risk? **[LO 31.9]**
☐ Is a stock that has a net present value lower than the current market price a good buy? **[LO 31.9]**
☐ What is the prediction of the efficient-market hypothesis? **[LO 31.10]**
☐ Does the possibility for arbitrage suggest that a market is efficient? **[LO 31.10]**

A National Accounts Approach to Finance

LO 31.11 Describe why savings equals investment in a closed economy and how government spending and foreign capital flows affect the saving-investment relationship.

Earlier in the chapter, we showed that when the market for loanable funds is in equilibrium, savings (supply) must equal investment (demand). This applies the microeconomic logic of market equilibrium to the financial system. We also can approach the analysis from a purely macro-economic angle. By looking at savings and investment through the lens of the national income accounting method introduced in Chapter 24, "Measuring GDP," we can track the quantity of funds on a national level and separate out different sources of savings.

The savings-investment identity

Start by imagining a simplified economy with no government and no international trade. All transactions happen within the borders of the country, between its residents. How could the residents of our simple economy use the money they earn? They have only two possible uses for their income: They can *consume it* (spend it now) or they can *save it* (keep it for later). In other words, income is equal to the sum of consumption and savings:

EQUATION 31-1   Income = Consumption + Savings

In this simple economy, with no government or international trade, all savings are **private savings**—the savings of individuals or corporations within a country.

private savings
the savings of individuals or corporations within a country

Now, let's think about how people in this simple economy earn their income. Since there are no governments or foreign countries to interact with, they earn income only when other people in the country purchase goods or services from them. We can categorize all of these purchases as spending on *consumption* (things like meals, clothes, and cars) or as spending on *investment goods* (productive inputs like factories and machines). Income in the closed economy is equal to total spending, which is equal to consumption plus investment:

EQUATION 31-2   Income = Consumption + Investment

This result is related to the national accounts framework we developed in Chapter 24, "Measuring GDP."

Next, to relate savings to investment, we can put together Equations 31-1 and 31-2. Equation 31-1 says that consumption plus savings equals income. Equation 31-2 says that income also equals consumption plus investment. Putting the two together, we see that

Consumption + Savings = Income = Consumption + Investment

Since consumption appears on both sides of this equation, we can cancel it out and immediately see the *savings-investment identity:*

EQUATION 31-3   Savings = Investment

which is commonly written:

$$S = I$$

The savings-investment identity tells us that savings always equals investment in an economy with no government and no trade.

Private savings, public savings, and capital flows

Our simple economy is of course missing a large reality: government. When we add government to the picture, we also add taxes:

- If government takes in more through taxes than it spends, it can run budget surpluses. These government surpluses are another form of saving: The government receives income in the form of taxes and saves it by not spending it right away.

- On the other hand, if government runs a budget deficit (spending more than it takes in in taxes), it is *dissaving.* In that case, the government must borrow money from the rest of the economy in order to spend more than it collects in taxes.

public savings
the difference between government tax revenue and government spending

If we look at how much the government takes in through tax revenue and subtract what it spends, that difference is **public savings** . Mathematically, that's

EQUATION 31-4   Public savings = Taxes − Government spending

Adding public savings to private savings, we get **national savings**, which is the sum of the private savings of individuals and corporations plus the public savings of the government. When the government runs a deficit, national savings will be lower than private savings; the opposite is true when the government runs a surplus.

Now, there are *three* things that citizens of our simple economy could do with the income they earn: They can consume, save privately, or pay taxes to the government. We can show this by adding taxes to Equation 31-1:

EQUATION 31-5
$$\text{Income} = \text{Consumption} + \text{Private savings} + \text{Taxes}$$

There is also an additional way for citizens to earn income: They can sell goods and services to or receive benefits from the government. We can show this new income source as a variation on Equation 31-2.

EQUATION 31-6
$$\text{Income} = \text{Consumption} + \text{Investment} + \text{Government spending}$$

Just as we did before, we can put together these two ways of arriving at "income" (from Equations 31-5 and Equation 31-6):

$$\text{Income} = \text{Consumption} + \text{Private savings} + \text{Taxes} = \text{Consumption} + \\ \text{Investment} + \text{Government spending}$$

Canceling consumption from both sides, this reduces to

$$\text{Private savings} + \text{Taxes} = \text{Investment} + \text{Government spending}$$

Now, let's rearrange that equation to isolate investment:

EQUATION 31-7
$$\text{Investment} = \text{Private savings} + \text{Taxes} - \text{Government spending}$$

But we know (from Equation 31-4) that taxes minus government spending equals public savings. So, we can simplify further:

EQUATION 31-8
$$\text{Investment} = \text{Private savings} + \text{Public savings}$$

And we know that national savings equals private savings plus public savings. Therefore,

$$\text{Investment} = \text{National savings}$$

In other words, national savings are equal to the total investment in the economy.

Note that we are still assuming no international trade. The identity between national savings and investment holds only in a **closed economy**—an economy that does not interact with other countries' economies.

The final piece of real-world complexity we need to add to our model is opening it up to international interactions. This is called an **open economy**. When money is allowed to move freely across borders, two different types of international financial transactions can happen:

- A *capital outflow* occurs when the money saved *domestically* (within the home country) is invested in another country.
- Conversely, a *capital inflow* occurs when savings from another country finance domestic investment.

The difference between capital inflows and capital outflows is **net capital flow**. A net capital inflow occurs in countries where investment is higher than national savings. In the opposite case, when national savings are higher than domestic investment, there is a net capital outflow.

For an *open* economy, national savings can be more or less than investment. But for the *global economy as a whole,* savings must be equal to investment. This means that any excess savings in one country have to be soaked up as investment elsewhere. In the From Another Angle box "Savings glut?" we evaluate this possibility in practice.

From Another Angle

Savings glut?

As children, we were often reminded of the virtue of saving. Many of us dutifully put our allowances in piggy banks, looking forward to blowing it all on a bigger and better toy or treat down the road.

For the past decade, though, people in the United States haven't been saving much. The government has, for the most part, run large deficits. Households save only a small percentage of their income on average. Many actually spend more than they earn, financing the difference by credit cards and loans. In addition, the country has long been running a sizable *current-account deficit,* meaning that it imports far more than it exports. All of these patterns suggest that people in the United States are spending way too much.

But could the problem be that other countries are *saving* way too much? This hypothesis, called the *global savings glut,* ties recent U.S. economic ills to high savings rates in Asia and Latin America.

When economies are open to cross-border capital flows, savings no longer have to equal investment within a given country. It's possible for a nation to save more than its firms and individuals want to invest. When that happens, these excess funds end up searching for the best returns in other investments around the world. Most of these funds end up in the United States, largely because it is seen as a safe place to invest. In fact, economist Kenneth Rogoff estimated that in 2007, a full two-thirds of excess savings in the world ended up invested in the United States.

This represents a huge sum of money. In the years before the 2007 financial crisis, net capital inflows—the amount of money coming in minus the amount the United States invested around the world—were around 6 percent of U.S. GDP. Ben Bernanke, the Federal Reserve chair at the time, argued that this large inflow of money kept interest rates low, which translated to cheap borrowing for Americans. Cheap borrowing enabled the housing boom during the mid-2000s, when people borrowed heavily to buy houses they wouldn't have been able to afford at higher interest rates.

Could the U.S. housing bubble really have been caused in part by industrious savers in Asia and Latin America? It seems hard to believe, but it's possible that this played a role.

Sources: http://www.federalreserve.gov/newsevents/speech/bernanke20110218a.htm; Kenneth Rogoff, "Betting with the House's Money," *The Guardian,* February 7, 2007, http://www.guardian.co.uk/commentisfree/2007/feb/07/bettingwiththehousesmoney.

✓CONCEPT CHECK

- ☐ What are the components of national savings? **[LO 31.11]**
- ☐ What is it called when the amount of capital leaving a country is greater than the amount going in? **[LO 31.11]**

Conclusion

In this chapter we've explored the basic framework of financial markets and the financial system: how buyers find sellers, how interest rates set the price of borrowing and the return on lending, and how the various players interact. We've also learned about a few of the major financial-asset classes and explored some of the ways that investors attempt to evaluate the risk and return potential of their investments.

You've seen that financial markets mostly operate like other markets. However, financial markets can sometimes behave in mysterious and opaque ways. We'll see more examples in Chapter 34, "Financial Crisis."

Now that we've covered the basics of how financial markets and the financial system work, it's time to look at the bigger picture: how the financial system fits into the overall economy. In the next chapter, we'll look at the origins of money and how the modern financial system is responsible for both creating and destroying money. We'll also learn about the people who oversee much of the financial system, including influencing the money supply, and how their actions affect economic growth in ways both enormous and subtle.

Key Terms

financial market, p. 795

information assymetry, p. 796

adverse selection, p. 796

moral hazard, p. 796

market for loanable funds, p. 799

savings, p. 799

investment, p. 799

interest rate, p. 800

crowding out, p. 804

default, p. 806

risk-free rate, p. 806

financial system, p. 807

financial intermediaries, p. 807

liquidity, p. 807

diversification, p. 808

stock, p. 809

dividend, p. 809

loan, p. 809

bond, p. 810

derivative, p. 810

mutual fund, p. 811

pension fund, p. 812

market (systemic) risk, p. 816

idiosyncratic risk, p. 816

standard deviation, p. 816

net present value (NPV), p. 817

efficient-market hypothesis, p. 817

arbitrage, p. 818

private savings, p. 819

public savings, p. 819

national savings, p. 820

closed economy, p. 820

open economy, p. 820

net capital flow, p. 820

Summary

> **LO 31.1** Define a financial market and describe the information asymmetry problems that can occur in them.

A *financial market* is one in which people trade future claims on funds or goods. Financial markets help ensure that the world's wealth is channeled to the individuals and organizations that can most effectively take advantage of it. A well-functioning financial market matches buyers and sellers as efficiently and effectively as possible. In financial markets, buyers are people who want to spend money on something of value right now but don't have cash on hand. Sellers are people who have cash on hand and are willing to let others use it, for a price.

An *information asymmetry* arises when one participant in a transaction knows more than another participant. Adverse selection and moral hazard are two types of information asymmetry problems of financial markets.

Adverse selection refers to a state that occurs when buyers and sellers have different information about the quality of a good or the riskiness of a situation, and this asymmetric information results in failure to complete transactions that would have been possible if both sides had the same information. *Moral hazard* refers to people's tendency, after a transaction takes place, to behave in a riskier way or to renege on contracts when they do not face the full consequences of their actions.

> **LO 31.2** Discuss the three main functions of financial markets.

Financial markets—including banks, which are one example—serve three main functions. First, they act as *intermediaries,* bringing together savers and borrowers in an easy, one-stop clearinghouse. Second, they provide the benefits of *liquidity*—having cash easily available when you want it—without the downsides of holding cash. Third, they help savers to *diversify risk* by providing funds to a big pool of borrowers. No individual saver will bear the full burden of a failed loan or investment.

LO 31.3 Describe the market for loanable funds, including the price of loanable funds, and differentiate between savings and investment.

The market for loanable funds is a hypothetical marketplace that brings together everyone looking to lend money (savers) and everyone looking to borrow money (anyone with investment-spending needs). The market for loanable funds clears at a price where supply and demand meet. This price is known as the *interest rate*. A key determinant of the supply curve for loanable funds is how much people decide to save. Economists differentiate between savings and investment: *Savings* is the portion of income that is not immediately spent on consumption, whereas *investment* is spending on productive inputs.

LO 31.4 List the factors that affect the supply and demand of loanable funds.

Many factors influence the supply and demand curves for loanable funds. Factors that determine how much people save include wealth, current economic conditions, expectations about future economic conditions, borrowing constraints, social welfare policies, and culture. Factors that determine investment decisions include expectations about future profitability and future economic conditions, borrowing constraints, and crowding out (reduction in private borrowing that is caused by an increase in government borrowing).

LO 31.5 Understand how interest rates on loans vary with the length of the loan and the riskiness of the transaction.

Two basic factors drive differences in interest rates: length of time and degree of risk. Lenders generally want a higher interest rate to compensate for the added opportunity cost when loans stretch over a long period and for taking on additional risk. The interest rate at which one would lend if there were no risk of default is the *risk-free rate* (generally approximated by interest rates on U.S. government debt). In the market for loanable funds, loans with longer terms and higher risks of default will have interest rates further above the risk-free rate.

LO 31.6 Describe why it is important for the financial system to intermediate between buyers and sellers, provide liquidity, and diversify risk.

Financial systems provide features similar to financial markets: intermediating between savers and borrowers, providing liquidity, and diversifying risk. In financial systems, various institutions act as *financial intermediaries,* channeling funds from people who have them to people who want them. Intermediation in financial systems reduces transaction costs by centralizing information about prices and providing a broad and dynamic marketplace for transactions. Various players in the financial system are liquidity providers, helping ensure that markets are liquid. Some of these we even call *market makers* because they are always ready to buy or sell assets. The very structure of financial assets such as stocks and bonds also serves to increase liquidity. Liquidity is important because it affects people's willingness to save. Finally, the financial system spreads risk even more broadly than a financial market does: Savers can diversify into different savings products and across geographic areas; borrowers have access to loans from the funds provided by many more savers.

LO 31.7 Differentiate between debt and equity and define the major types of assets in each category.

The major types of financial assets are debt and equity. *Equity* is ownership in a company, and the most common form of such ownership is *stock*. As partial owners, stockholders are entitled to receive a portion of a company's profits, in the form of dividends, in proportion to the size of their ownership.

The most basic type of debt is a *loan. Loans* are an agreement between a lender and a borrower in which the lender lends money to the borrower in exchange for a promise to repay the amount loaned (the *principal* of the loan) plus an agreed-upon amount of interest. A *bond* is a loan that has been standardized into a more easily tradable and liquid asset. Bonds are a type of debt issued by corporations or governments as a way to borrow large sums of money. Stocks and bonds are liquid assets that are easily bought and sold in financial markets.

Financial contracts based on the value of some other asset represent a special category of financial assets, called *derivatives.* The best example of a derivative is a futures contract.

LO 31.8 Name the main institutions in financial markets and describe the role that each plays.

There are many different players in the financial market. There are banks, which can be divided into two categories: *commercial banks* and *investment banks.* When you make a deposit at a bank, or get a mortgage or student loan from a bank, you are interacting with a commercial bank. *Investment banks* focus on providing liquidity to the financial markets themselves, by acting as market makers, helping companies to issue stocks and bonds (a process known as *underwriting*).

Individual actors in the financial market have to operate through a *proxy*—they give their money to someone else to invest for them. These proxies include *mutual funds* (professionally managed portfolios of stocks and other assets), *pension funds* (professionally administered portfolios of assets intended to provide income to retirees), and life insurance policies (in which people pay *premiums* that pay out to dependents upon the death of the insured). Entrepreneurs and businesses are also major players in financial markets, as are speculators.

> **LO 31.9** Explain the trade-off between risk and return in financial assets and describe how risk can be measured.

In general, there is a direct relationship between risk and reward in the financial market. The riskier the investment, the higher its potential return. Typically, the investments with the lowest risk—and lowest return—are government bonds. Stocks are a considerably more risky investment, but also offer the possibility of higher returns. Two different types of risk exist for financial assets—*market risk* (risk that is broadly shared by the entire market) and *idiosyncratic risk* (risk unique to a particular asset or company). A *portfolio* of assets can help diversify away idiosyncratic risk; a certain amount of market risk remains in all portfolios.

In financial markets, the most commonly used method of measuring this risk is a simple tool borrowed from statistics: the standard deviation. The *standard deviation* is a measure of how far apart a set of numbers is in a distribution.

> **LO 31.10** Give arguments for and against the assumption that markets are efficient.

The efficient-market hypothesis holds that markets are *efficient*—that market prices incorporate all available information and, as a result, accurately predicting stock returns is impossible.

Supporters of the efficient-market hypothesis describe the expected movements of a stock as a *random walk,* a term from statistics that describes any variable (like the price of a stock) that moves in a completely unpredictable (random) way from one moment to the next. Those who argue against market efficiency suggest that some people simply have better information than others or a better ability to put all the complex pieces together to predict stock price. Occasionally markets have certain information inefficiencies that savvy investors, through *arbitrage,* can exploit to profit from the differences between prices in different markets.

> **LO 31.11** Describe why savings equals investment in a closed economy and how government spending and foreign capital flows affect the saving-investment relationship.

In a *closed economy,* one with no international trade, citizens can consume or save. The amount of savings within an economy is necessarily the amount of investment that can occur. Thus, savings and investment spending (the supply and demand of the financial markets) are always equal, a relationship called the *savings-investment identity.*

Review Questions

1. In financial markets, who are the sellers? Who are the buyers? **[LO 31.1]**

2. Identify the two types of information asymmetry defined in the chapter. What is the difference between them? **[LO 31.1]**

3. Explain why a country with poorly developed financial markets might have a hard time sustaining economic growth. **[LO 31.2]**

4. Is it savings or investment when Collins Inc. uses the proceeds from issuing bonds to purchase equipment needed to start a new product line? If Daisy buys some of the Collins Inc. bonds, is her purchase savings or investment? **[LO 31.3]**

5. When the real interest rate increases, what happens to the quantity of loanable funds supplied? What happens to the quantity of loanable funds demanded? **[LO 31.3]**

6. Why might a government want to encourage saving among its citizens? If the government enacts a successful policy aimed at encouraging saving, what would be the likely effect on the interest rate and the quantity of investment? **[LO 31.4]**

7. The government of a small country has enacted new regulations that make it more difficult to obtain a loan from a bank. How does this affect savings, investment, and the interest rate in the country? **[LO 31.4]**

8. Using the concept of default, explain why the interest rate on credit card debt is higher than the interest rate on a mortgage. **[LO 31.5]**

9. Your friend claims that there is no such thing as a risk-free interest rate because all loans are risky. Do you agree? Why or why not? **[LO 31.5]**

10. Is the stock exchange an example of a financial intermediary? Why or why not? **[LO 31.6]**

11. In a famous bet known as the Simon-Ehrlich wager, Paul Ehrlich bet that over the course of 10 years, the

prices of five commodities would be higher than they were at the start of the decade; Julian Simon believed the price of these goods would be lower. The loser had to pay the difference of the price from the starting point. What type of financial asset does this wager resemble? Why? **[LO 31.7]**

12. What is securitization? How did it contribute to the recent housing-market crisis? **[LO 31.7]**

13. How do economists generally define a bank? What kind of bank exemplifies this definition? Does an investment bank meet this definition? **[LO 31.8]**

14. What is an index fund, and why would a financial investor consider buying one? **[LO 31.8]**

15. Which is likely to have more risk, a government bond from a developing country or one from France? Which should have a higher return? **[LO 31.9]**

16. Define diversification and comment on how successful it is at managing market risk and idiosyncratic risk. **[LO 31.9]**

17. During the 1990s, securities related to technology and other dot-com firms experienced skyrocketing market prices, but around 2000 the market crashed. Was that crash an example that supports or offers evidence against the efficient-market hypothesis? **[LO 31.10]**

18. Describe the difference between fundamental analysis and technical analysis. Which, if any, does the efficient-market hypothesis suggest financial investors engage in? **[LO 31.10]**

19. Does the level of taxation in a closed economy have an impact on national savings? Explain. **[LO 31.11]**

20. Explain how a persistent government budget deficit can hurt a closed economy's ability to engage in economic investment. **[LO 31.11]**

Problems and Applications

1. For each scenario, indicate whether it is an example of moral hazard or adverse selection. **[LO 31.1]**

   a. You decide to buy a new car instead of a used car because you are worried about the quality of the used car.

   b. You sell your condominium because you fear there will be a large special assessment next year. There has been no official notice of an upcoming assessment.

   c. The owner of a company has just secured a new line of credit from the bank. He decides to change his business plan and open a second office in a foreign country.

   d. A firm that has purchased a large insurance policy becomes careless about setting the security alarm.

   e. A number of households find themselves owing more on their mortgages than their houses are currently worth. Some of them decide to abandon the house and walk away.

   f. The owners of a company suspect there will be more competition from foreign producers in upcoming years. They have just issued new shares of stock in their company.

2. The chapter discusses three main functions of a banking system. Classify each of the following by the function it best represents. **[LO 31.2]**

   a. Aaron can get cash out of the ATM at any time of day or night.

   b. Instead of lending all her savings out to one borrower, Barbara's bank makes the money in her savings account available to a variety of firms, with different characteristics and risk profiles, wishing to invest.

   c. When Charlie's car suddenly breaks down, he can quickly withdraw funds from his savings account to pay the mechanic and rent a car.

   d. Donna can get start-up funds for her new hair salon from a bank, instead of having to find people in her neighborhood willing to lend their extra money.

3. After graduating, you take an unusual job: consulting with the queen of a small, newly populated island in the middle of the sea. You've provided advice to her on matters related to government and the economy, and while she has taken your advice most of the time, she has so far turned down your suggestion to have a banking system. She claims that banks will make the economy more complicated and do little to make the lives of her subjects easier.

   Over the past several months, though, the queen has discussed with you several issues that have arisen in the newly formed economy. For each of the three quotes from the queen below, refer to one of the three functions of banks discussed in this chapter to explain how a banking system could help with the issue described. **[LO 31.2]**

   a. "When my subjects have money left over after spending, they want to keep it somewhere safe and earn some interest on it. But that's hard for most of them because they have no way of finding out who wants to borrow and whether it would be a good idea to lend to them."

   b. "My subjects are lucky that we have very little crime, so they can safely keep their extra money inside their houses and take only what cash they need for a day's spending. However, many of them have complained that if an emergency occurs when they're all the way on the other side of the island, they can't access their funds."

c. "Some of my subjects who are in the know about good borrowers have been making loans and earning interest. But lately there have been a couple of borrowers who defaulted on loans, and when they did, the lenders were totally out of luck. All that money just disappeared! And those bad experiences have made other potential lenders afraid, so that now borrowing and lending have dried up almost completely. If only there were some easy way for them to divide their savings among several different borrowers, they might feel safe enough to start lending again!"

4. Categorize each of the following as a type of savings or investment in the economic sense. **[LO 31.3]**

   a. You buy 100 shares of Apple Computer stock.

   b. You place part of your income in a mutual fund.

   c. A delivery service buys 1,000 new trucks.

   d. You put $1,000 in a certificate of deposit by giving money to the bank in exchange for a set amount of return.

5. Use the following words to fill in the blanks in the statements below about the market for loanable funds. *Choose from:* demanded, supplied; left, right; higher, lower. **[LO 31.4]**

   a. A change that makes people want to save less will shift the quantity of loanable funds ___ to the ___. The resulting new equilibrium in the market for loanable funds would be a ___ interest rate and a ___ quantity of funds saved and invested.

   b. A change that makes people want to save more will shift the quantity of loanable funds ___ to the ___. The resulting new equilibrium in the market for loanable funds would be a ___ interest rate and a ___ quantity of funds saved and invested.

   c. A change that makes people want to invest more will shift the quantity of loanable funds ___ to the ___. The resulting new equilibrium in the market for loanable funds would be a ___ interest rate and a ___ quantity of funds saved and invested.

   d. A change that makes people want to invest less will shift the quantity of loanable funds ___ to the ___. The resulting new equilibrium in the market for loanable funds would be a ___

interest rate and a ___ quantity of funds saved and invested.

6. Consider the market for loanable funds. Graphically illustrate the impact on the equilibrium interest rate and the equilibrium quantity of funds saved and invested in each of the following scenarios. **[LO 31.3, 31.4]**

   a. Due to slow growth in the economy, fewer workers are receiving pay increases and more workers are losing their jobs.

   b. The government decides to reduce the number of weeks a person is eligible for unemployment compensation.

   c. Numerous firms remain concerned about growth prospects in the economy.

   d. The government decides to reduce income tax rates, and this reduction leads to an increase in the size of the budget deficit.

7. You go to the bank and purchase a $1,000 certificate of deposit (CD). **[LO 31.5]**

   a. Who is doing the borrowing? Who is doing the lending?

   b. Which is higher, the interest rate paid on the 6-month CD or the 2-year CD? Why?

8. What does the risk premium measure? During a recession, what is likely to happen to the risk premium? **[LO 31.5]**

9. You have a sum of funds sitting in a savings account earning a modest interest rate of 3 percent. A good friend wants to borrow half of this sum, and he has agreed to pay you an interest rate of 5 percent. Should you lend your friend the money? Why or why not? **[LO 31.6]**

10. In your spare time, you help out with a magazine for high schoolers that focuses on current events related to economics and politics. While the magazine aims to be readable and entertaining, it also wants to use terminology correctly. Knowing that you've taken an economics class, the editor turns to you to look over a paragraph in a story focusing on the roles of saving and investment after the recent crisis in the housing market. Go through the following quotation and correct any errors in economic vocabulary, including an explanation for the editor about why the original was incorrect. **[LO 31.3, 31.6]**

   When Americans invest by buying securities such as stocks and bonds or putting money in a bank, they provide funds for firms wishing to engage in diversification by buying assets used to produce goods and services. Households with extra money left over after buying things they want or need consume by purchasing securities or putting their funds in savings accounts, and banks help transfer those funds to firms. By matching and working with these borrowers and lenders, banks act as a source of liquidity.

11. In each of following examples, name the financial product being described. **[LO 31.7]**

    a. A family borrows money to pay for a house.

    b. A new tech start-up offers investors the ability to purchase a small part of the company to raise needed capital.

    c. The U.S. government offers to pay investors a 3 percent return rate next year if they finance its debt today.

12. Evaluate each of the following statements and say whether it describes a loan, a bond, and/or a stock. **[LO 31.7]**

    a. It implies ownership in the issuing firm.

    b. Small businesses use these to raise funds for investment.

    c. This is also known as equity financing.

    d. We can think of this as a more liquid version of a loan.

    e. It pays some form of interest, and principal is paid at maturity.

13. Match each of the following players in the financial system with the financial product(s) they are most associated with. **[LO 31.8]**

    a. Commercial banks.   i.   Stocks.

    b. Savers.   ii. Bonds.

    c. Investment banks.   iii. Loans.

14. Rank the following actors in financial markets by the level of liquidity they are providing. **[LO 31.8]**

    a. Entrepreneurs offering equity in their businesses.

    b. The Federal Reserve offering banks the chance to borrow short-term money through the discount window.

    c. Investment banks offering shares in mutual funds, which penalize you if you withdraw your money within 30 days.

    d. A bank offering you a no-minimum reserve requirement checking account.

15. Rank the following assets based on their expected return. Then repeat the exercise, this time ranking the assets based on their expected risk. **[LO 31.9]**

    a. Real estate.

    b. Commodities.

    c. U.S. equities (stocks).

    d. Cash.

    e. U.S. fixed-income bonds.

16. Evaluate whether the following statements are true or false. **[LO 31.9]**

    a. Risk is measured by looking at the expected value (average) of an asset's returns over time.

    b. Market risk can be minimized with a well-diversified portfolio.

    c. Idiosyncratic risk is unique to a particular asset, rather than to the market as a whole.

    d. A portfolio of well-diversified assets will often be less risky for the same level of return when compared to an individual asset.

17. "Listen," your buddy says. "Have you ever noticed that you can get the same type and size of tire for $30 cheaper in the next county over? I've got a way to make profits for years—we'll buy the tires where they're cheaper and bring them back here to sell." What is the term for the transaction your friend wants to make? Would the efficient-market hypothesis predict it will be as profitable as he says? Explain. **[LO 31.10]**

18. In each of the following examples say whether the market is behaving within the principles of the efficient-market hypothesis. **[LO 31.10]**

    a. The day after unrest in the Middle East, the source of supply for much of the world's oil, the price of oil falls.

    b. Investors find very few opportunities for arbitrage in the foreign exchange market.

    c. The Dow Jones Industrial Average, a major stock market index, changes in value by 5 percent for an entire week, even though very little economic news is released.

19. In 2015, U.S. government spending was $3.8 trillion, tax revenue was $4.5 trillion, GDP was $14.12 trillion, and total consumer spending was $10.5 trillion. If the economy has no exports or imports, what was the national savings in 2015? How much was public savings? How much was private savings? **[LO 31.11]**

20. A country's government has been running a deficit for the past few years. Suppose this country decides to increase its government spending. **[LO 31.4, 31.11]**

    a. Compare the impact of the increase in government spending in a closed economy and an open economy.

    b. Are you more likely to observe crowding out in a closed economy or an open economy? Explain.

21. Consider the U.S. market for loanable funds in a closed-economy model. Answer the following questions about each scenario. **[LO 31.4, 31.11]**

    a. The government starts offering a national savings bond to increase private savings, which pays a higher return than many other options available on the market. Which way will the supply of loanable funds curve shift? Will the interest rate increase or decrease? Will there be more or less borrowing?

b. Suppose the economy is now open. Due to rapid economic expansion in China, the Chinese government decides to invest in U.S. Treasury notes with some of its surplus. Which way will the supply curve shift?

c. A new computer software program is introduced into the market that offers businesses that purchase it promising returns on their investment. Which curve will shift? Which way will it shift?

d. The government reduces the capital gains tax, which taxes earnings on assets in the stock market. Which curve will shift? Which way will it shift?

Endnotes

1. For the moment, we are talking about the real interest rate. In Chapter 33, "Inflation," we'll talk about how the nominal interest rate can differ from the real interest rate when there is inflation; don't worry about that for now.

2. In Chapter 33, "Inflation," we will also see that there are other reasons to be concerned about *deflation,* or falling prices in an economy.

3. The savings rate is measured as the difference between disposable income and spending. The measure thus reflects how much money people put in the bank minus how much they borrow. Economists estimate that changes in how much people borrow explains much of the recent variation in the measured savings rate shown in Figure 31-3. See http://www.frbsf.org/economic-research/files/el2011-01.pdf.

4. Note that the word *public* in *public companies* indicates that ownership is open to the general public; it does not imply anything about government, as in the term *public*—government—*spending.*

5. In the past, bonds had actual coupons that bondholders would clip and return to the bond issuer in exchange for interest payments. Those coupons were quite different in purpose from the ones that people use to get price reductions on goods and services.

6. The average inflation-adjusted stock return in the 50 years between 1965 and 2015 was about 7 percent. A better measure of returns is the compound annual growth rate, which shows a gain of about 5.5 percent in the same period. If you're interested in looking further into data trends, you can try the stock market return calculator at http://www.moneychimp.com/features/market_cagr.htm.

7. https://www.federalreserve.gov/releases/z1/Current/accessible/default.htm.

8. Robert Shiller, *Irrational Exuberance,* 2nd ed. (Princeton, NJ: Princeton University Press, 2005).

Money and the Monetary System

Learning Objectives

LO 32.1 Describe the three main functions of money.

LO 32.2 Describe the characteristics that make something a good choice as money and distinguish between commodity-backed and fiat money.

LO 32.3 Explain the concept of fractional-reserve banking and the money multiplier.

LO 32.4 Describe M1 and M2.

LO 32.5 Understand the role of a central bank and discuss the idea of the Federal Reserve's dual mandate.

LO 32.6 Explain the tools the Federal Reserve uses to conduct monetary policy.

LO 32.7 Understand how monetary policy affects the prevailing interest rate and supply of money.

LO 32.8 Explain how expansionary or contractionary monetary policy influences the broader economy.

CIGARETTE MONEY

During World War II, millions of soldiers were captured and sent to prisoner-of-war (POW) camps. With no formal currency and little connection with the outside economy, the camps initially functioned with little more than an internal trading system: If a soldier had an extra bar of soap and really wanted a can of salmon, he would have to find someone who had a spare can of salmon and really wanted a bar of soap. Finding these kinds of trading possibilities sometimes worked, but it was time-consuming and inefficient.

Over time, a solution evolved: Prisoners began to use cigarettes as a common currency. A simple system of exchange with standardized prices developed: Cans of food could be bought for a set quantity of cigarettes, soap for another quantity.

Why did the prisoners start using cigarettes as money? To start with, they were a lot easier to carry around than bars of soap or cans of salmon. Unlike food, cigarettes didn't spoil. And

© Hulton Archive/Getty Images

there was a fairly stable supply. Cigarettes came into the camps in shipments of food and other supplies from the Red Cross humanitarian agency and were distributed among the prisoners.

Sometimes, though, there would be a sudden influx of cigarettes—say, if the Red Cross managed to send an extra shipment one week. Soldiers, having an abundance of cigarettes, would go on spending sprees. They would outbid each other to get the things they wanted. As you might predict, that bidding would send prices skyrocketing. Soldiers would then need a lot more cigarettes to buy a bar of soap.

But what would happen if war troubles caused the Red Cross to miss a few shipments? There would be a steady decrease in the number of cigarettes in circulation, as prisoners smoked them. Prices would plummet, and overall economic activity would fall, as trading slowed to a halt. Why would this happen? The reason is obvious if you think about it: With fewer and fewer cigarettes in circulation, and uncertainty about when the next shipment might arrive, cigarettes would become increasingly rare and valuable. This would give prisoners greater incentive to hoard rather than spend their cigarettes.

This unique system of money and trade was described by a British officer named R. A. Radford, who was captured by the Nazis and sent to a series of prisoner-of-war camps, where he remained until his rescue by Allied forces. After his return to Great Britain in 1945, Radford wrote a now-classic paper, "The Economic Organisation of a P.O.W. Camp." His paper showed that money—in whatever form it might take, even cigarettes—is an intrinsic part of any economic system.

The challenges that made World War II prisoners adopt cigarettes as their currency are the same as those faced in any economy. What is money? What functions does it serve and what problems does it solve? What makes a particular item (such as cigarettes) a good or bad choice for use as money? How does the supply of money influence the broader economy, and who controls the supply?

In this chapter, we'll see how and why money works in the economy. And we'll show how the tools of economics are being used to make sure the dollar in your pocket keeps its value.

What Is Money?

We all have an intuitive grasp of what money is—we use it every day. But what is it that separates the cash we hold in our hands from any of the other items we own that have value? Economies used to work on a system in which one person could trade a few eggs from her chicken for some milk from a neighbor's cow. Why did civilization long ago abandon that system for one based on the exchange of small pieces of precious metal? And how did sheets of printed paper come to substitute for that shiny metal and then give way to records kept in a bank's computer? To answer these questions, we'll need a more formal understanding of the functions money plays in society and what makes something good as money.

Functions of money

LO 32.1   Describe the three main functions of money.

How much money do you have? When asked that question, you might answer by counting just the cash in your wallet and maybe the amount in your bank account. You also might count the total value of your car (if you own one) or any stocks, bonds, real estate, or any other assets you may be fortunate enough to own. By most definitions, money consists only of what you typically use to buy something—which includes the cash in your wallet and the balance in your bank account, but not the stocks, bonds, real estate, car, or any other asset. More precisely, **money** is the set of all assets that are regularly used to directly purchase goods and services.

> **money**
> the set of all assets that are regularly used to directly purchase goods and services

Money typically serves three major functions: it is a *store of value*, a *medium of exchange*, and a *unit of account*.

A store of value

We say that money is a **store of value** because it represents a certain amount of purchasing power that money retains over time. To have $100 or $1,000 or $1 million is to have the ability to acquire a certain quantity of goods. Money stores value in the sense that if you put a $100 bill in a safe, you can expect to be able to purchase roughly $100 worth of goods when you take the bill out, whenever that is. The value won't be absolutely the same, of course—we'll learn more shortly about how changes in prices create changes in the value of money—but holding money is nearly always the most convenient way to hold onto wealth over time. If, by contrast, you stored all your wealth in bananas, you would lose most of that wealth quickly, as the fruit spoiled.

> **store of value**
> a certain amount of purchasing power that money retains over time

A medium of exchange

Of course, items other than money also generally store value pretty well, such as stocks and land. So we need to add to our list of money's functions its role as a **medium of exchange**—that is to say, the fact that you can use it to purchase goods and services. That is, you can make a transaction by exchanging your money for the goods or services you want to buy.

> **medium of exchange**
> the ability to use money to purchase goods and services

First, imagine a world without money, where the only way to acquire something you wanted would be to engage in **barter**—to directly offer a good or service (maybe your jacket or bike, or maybe the value of your labor) in exchange for some good or service you want. The reason barter is extremely inefficient is that you have to find someone who both has what you want and wants what you have.

> **barter**
> directly offering a good or service in exchange for some good or service you want

Now add money to the world. Money makes life much easier because you need only find someone who wants what you have (say, your labor). You accept money in exchange for the labor because you are confident that, once you have money, the person who has what you want (say, groceries) will also, in turn, accept that money in exchange. There's no longer any need to find one person who fits both requirements.

Not surprisingly, an economy that uses money is dramatically more efficient than a society based on directly trading one good for another. Without money people and firms would have to search constantly for mutually agreeable trades. Using money reduces transaction costs immeasurably.

A unit of account

unit of account
a standard unit of comparison

The final role of money is also important, though it is easily overlooked: Money provides a common **unit of account**—a standard unit of comparison. Imagine that you live in an economy without money and have to choose between two competing job offers:

- A farmer offers to pay you 12 big crates of eggs a week.
- A shoemaker offers weekly wages of a pair of fine leather shoes.

Which is the better option? It's hard to tell. But if one offered you $300 a week and the other offered you $400 for the same amount of work, you could easily compare the offers. By giving us a standard unit of comparison, money allows us to make more informed decisions.

What makes for good money?

LO 32.2 Describe the characteristics that make something a good choice as money and distinguish between commodity-backed and fiat money.

Now that we understand the functions played by money, we can ask a related question: What makes for good money? Economists differ on the exact answer, but two basic considerations offer a good starting point. Something makes for good money if it has *stability of value* and *convenience.*

Stability of value

We saw the importance of stability in our chapter-opening example, in which prisoners used cigarettes as a form of money. As long as shipments arrived predictably from the Red Cross, the value of a cigarette remained fairly stable. If there was either a sudden influx or a prolonged shortage of cigarettes, the functioning of the camp economy was disrupted.

Like cigarettes in the POW camp, the earliest forms of money were chosen primarily because they offered stability of value. These early versions of money generally took the form of a physical material that is durable and has *intrinsic value,* or value unrelated to its use as money. Goods that have intrinsic value will keep a more steady value; even if their value as money falls, the good is still useful to people for other reasons. Gold is the traditional example: In early societies, gold had intrinsic value because it was durable and people liked wearing it as shiny jewelry. That's still true today. The cigarettes in the chapter opener also had intrinsic value. After all, the reason the cigarettes were being shipped to the POW camp in the first place was that many soldiers smoked.

There is no reason, though, why money needs to have intrinsic value. A dollar bill has practically no intrinsic value: People don't typically eat it, smoke it, or wear it as a necklace. We accept dollar bills because we know that everyone else values them too. Wide acceptance comes largely from the fact that dollars have stable value.[1]

Convenience

How and why did we go from gold coins to dollar bills? Paper money is more *convenient.* Compared to paper money, gold coins are heavy and hard to use for small purchases. A solid gold coin weighing just one ounce would be worth over $1,300 at the time of this writing, making it hard to use to pay for a package of gum or a soda.[2]

Ultimately, as time goes on, technology allows for the development of more convenient forms of money. For an ingenious example of making money even more convenient in the developing world, read the Real Life box "Banking with a cell phone."

Real Life

Banking with a cell phone

Imagine you grew up in a small village in rural Kenya and moved to the capital city to find work. You want to send money back to your village to support your family, but how do you do it? Your village does not have a bank branch—the nearest is hours away. You could take a wad of banknotes back to the village yourself, but that would involve a long day's travel in a crowded bus. Or you could entrust the money to someone else who is traveling back to your village, but what if no one's going soon?

A Kenyan mobile phone company called Safaricom came up with a solution to this problem. It's called M-Pesa—the M stands for mobile, while *Pesa* is the local word for money. The system allows people to transfer money simply by sending a text message.

The process is amazingly simple. You go to an M-Pesa outlet (a small store usually located in the village marketplace) and deposit money into an account. This becomes your *e-float,* essentially an electronic representation of money. In this way, it's not all that different from a deposit at a traditional bank. You can then use a text message to transfer, say, $15 worth of e-float to the account of another M-Pesa user. (The transfer costs a small fee, but that's a much smaller transaction cost than the time and money of traveling back to the village.) The recipient then goes to the local M-Pesa outlet and withdraws the e-float as cash, paying another small fee.

With this ease of use, and the fact that M-Pesa outlets outnumber bank branches five to one, M-Pesa quickly became wildly popular. In 2015, M-Pesa had over 13 million active users—over 40 percent of Kenya's adult population. Annual transfers were equal to over 42 percent of Kenyan GDP. Three-quarters of M-Pesa members say they use their e-float accounts not just to transfer money but also to save money: Using an e-float account is safer than carrying cash and much more accessible than a traditional bank account. Safaricom has now introduced a product called M-Schwari that includes interest-paying savings accounts and greatly expands access to banking services in rural areas.

The system hasn't eliminated the need for cash since not everyone uses M-Pesa. Also, since there are small fees involved in sending money, sometimes it's better to use cash (depending on the amounts involved).

M-Pesa shows how new technologies can connect underserved areas and change the concept of money. Inspired by the success in Kenya, companies in over 80 countries—including the United States—are developing similar mobile banking systems.

Sources: http://siteresources.worldbank.org/AFRICAEXT/Resources/258643-1271798012256/M-PESA_Kenya. pdf; http://www.bbc.co.uk/news/business-11793290; http://www.safaricom.co.ke/personal/m-pesa/do-more-with-m-pesa/m-shwari; http://www.techweez.com/2015/05/07/ten-takeaways-safaricom-2015-results.

Commodity-backed money versus fiat money

The earliest forms of paper money could be converted at a bank into a specified amount of a named commodity. **Commodity-backed money** is any form of money—usually paper money—that can be legally exchanged into a fixed amount of an underlying commodity, generally gold.

In the United States, the dollar was commodity-backed for over 100 years, from shortly after the Civil War until 1971. Anyone who held dollar bills before 1971 could simply go to a designated "reserve bank" and exchange those dollar bills for a fixed amount of gold, whenever they wanted to. By law, the bank was required to make that exchange.

But what of the post-1971 world? If our money is no longer backed by the value of a commodity like gold, where does its value come from? What is it backed by? Well, it's backed by nothing—nothing tangible, at least. Instead, the U.S. dollar today is backed by "the full faith and credit of the United States government." In other words, the U.S. dollar has value only to the extent that people trust the U.S. government to keep using dollars and to keep their value

commodity-backed money
any form of money that can be legally exchanged into a fixed amount of an underlying commodity

fiat money

money created by rule, without any commodity to back it

roughly constant. The formal term for this type of money is **fiat money**. Fiat money is money created by rule, without any commodity to back it. (*Fiat* is a Latin term that roughly translates to "it shall be.")

When we say "to the extent that people trust the U.S. government," what exactly are we trusting it to do, or not do? Essentially, we're trusting the government to maintain a reliable system of money—in short, to not create lots of new money. Creating lots of new money would reduce the value of existing money—just as, in our chapter-opening example, an unexpectedly large shipment of cigarettes into the POW camp reduced the value of existing cigarettes.

✓ CONCEPT CHECK

☐ What kind of exchange happens when people trade goods without using money? **[LO 32.1]**

☐ How are cigarettes a good example of commodity-backed money? **[LO 32.2]**

☐ What kind of money is the U.S. dollar? What kind was it 60 years ago? **[LO 32.2]**

Banks and the Money-Creation Process

We discussed how using actual gold coins in payment was eventually replaced by paper money that was backed by gold. We considered one obvious advantage of this: It's easier to carry around a piece of paper saying "10 gold coins" than it is to carry around 10 gold coins.

Here's another, less obvious, implication: Paper money made it possible for banks to *create money,* through a process called *fractional-reserve banking.* This is one of the most important, yet intuitively challenging, facts about our modern financial system. It's worth taking some time to make sure you understand it.

"Creating" money

LO 32.3 Explain the concept of fractional-reserve banking and the money multiplier.

The easiest way to understand how banks create money is to picture an economy making the transition from gold coins to paper money. To start with, imagine that you live in ancient times and all transactions are carried out using actual gold coins. How much money exists in the economy? That's an easy question to answer: It's simply the amount of gold.

Next, imagine that banking is invented, and now you're offered the chance to store your gold coins so you don't have to carry them around. When you deposit a gold coin in the bank, the bank gives you a piece of paper (a banknote) saying "one gold coin." At any time, you could go to the bank, give the bank back this piece of paper, and get a gold coin.

But you don't need to do this because merchants are happy to accept the banknote instead of the gold coin. They know that the note is as good as the coin itself. At any point they could take the note to the bank to get a coin. And people find it so much more convenient to use notes than lug around heavy gold coins.

Now put yourself in the bank's shoes (sandals): As a banker, you observe that on any given day, out of the 1,000 coins that are in your bank vault, people come in and ask for only 100 of them. The other 900 are just sitting there. Why not lend them out, charge an interest rate on these loans, and make a profit?

So, you decide to lend out the other 900 coins to people who want to use them to buy things—say, to pay workers to build a house. When the workers receive their coins as wages, the workers all decide to deposit them in the bank for safe keeping. For every coin they deposit, the bank gives them a piece of paper saying "one gold coin."

How much money is in the economy now? To answer that question, let's consider both the gold coins in the bank and the banknotes now available in the economy. As Table 32-1 shows, the bank again has 1,000 gold coins. But it has now issued 1,900 banknotes saying "one gold coin."

TABLE 32-1

Simple money-creation process

Gold coins in bank	Money (banknotes) in the economy
1,000 coins deposited in bank	1,000 banknotes issued in exchange for initial deposit
−900 coins loaned out (with 100 held in reserve)	
+900 coins that were loaned out and then deposited by workers	+900 banknotes issued in exchange for workers' deposits
1,000 coins in bank	**1,900 banknotes**

Because people are just as happy to trade banknotes as actual gold coins—and, thus, we can meaningfully consider the banknotes to be *money*—we can say that by making loans, the bank has *created money*. It has created 900 gold coins worth of money, to be exact. It did so simply by lending a portion of the money it had on deposit.

Money creation in today's economy

How does the money-creation process work in today's economy? Let's work through another simple example with the aid of some basic accounting tools.

Let's say that you walk into a bank with $1,000 in cash and you make a deposit. The bank takes your cash, puts it in a vault, and records $1,000 as your account balance. You can get your $1,000 back any time you ask the bank for it. Because of that fact, such deposits are called **demand deposits**—funds held in bank accounts that can be withdrawn ("demanded") by depositors at any time without advance notice.

From an accounting point of view, the $1,000 cash deposit represents two things for the bank:

- It is an *asset*—a resource the bank possesses.
- It also is a *liability*—an amount the bank owes. The bank owes you that amount and has promised that you can get your cash back at any time.

The primary way that banks earn money is by lending funds and collecting interest on those loans. So the bank wants to lend out as much of your $1,000 deposit as it (safely) can. As we saw in the example of the gold-coin bank, it's not necessary to keep on hand the total amount of the demand deposits. Instead, the bank decides to keep a certain amount on hand and to lend the rest.

We call the cash that a bank keeps in its vault its **reserves**. In practice, modern banks keep reserves either as cash or as deposits at the Federal Reserve ("the Fed"), the U.S. government's central bank. As before, lending funds enables banks to "create" money.

The Federal Reserve requires banks to keep a certain proportion of their deposits as reserves. When expressed as an amount, it is called the **required reserves**. Of course, a bank can choose to hold more in reserves than the required minimum. Any additional amount, beyond the required reserves, that the bank chooses to keep in reserve is called **excess reserves**. As with the earlier gold-coin example, banks "create" money by lending funds not kept as reserves. When the reserve requirement is expressed as a fraction, is is called the **reserve ratio**. The reserve ratio is calculated as the amount of cash kept as reserves divided by the total amount of demand deposits. We'll assume throughout our discussion that the bank keeps a reserve ratio of 10 percent.

In the example above, we saw that the $1,000 cash deposit created both an asset and a liability for the bank. Financial accounting is based on the *basic accounting equation,* which says that assets must equal the total of liabilities plus owners' equity (the claim the owners of a firm have on assets):

$$\text{Assets} = \text{Liabilities} + \text{Owners' equity}$$

demand deposits
funds held in bank accounts that can be withdrawn ("demanded") by depositors at any time without advance notice

reserves
the money that a bank keeps on hand, either in cash or in deposits at the Federal Reserve

required reserves
the minimum fraction of deposits that banks are legally required (by the Federal Reserve) to keep on hand

excess reserves
any additional amount, beyond the required reserves, that a bank chooses to keep in reserve

reserve ratio
the fraction of deposits a bank must hold as reserves; calculated as the amount of cash kept as reserves divided by the total amount of demand deposits

Companies periodically report the balances of their assets, liabilities, and owners' equity in a financial statement called a *balance sheet*. One common form of a balance sheet is called the *account form* of the balance sheet; it mimics the accounting equation by showing assets on the left and liabilities and owners' equity on the right. We'll use that form to visualize the bank's transactions. In the example we work through here, we will assume owners' equity of zero. Thus, we will assume that for the bank, assets must equal liabilities.

Panel A of Figure 32-1 shows, in a simple account-form balance sheet format, what happens to the bank's assets and liabilities when you make a $1,000 deposit. The left-hand side shows the bank's assets—in this case, the $1,000 cash deposit. The right-hand side shows the bank's liabilities (the amount owed to you, the depositor)—in this case, the demand deposits of $1,000.

Now, let's see what happens when a new customer comes into the bank wanting to *borrow* $900—say, to purchase a new refrigerator. After completing the loan-approval process, the banker takes $900 in cash out of the vault and hands over the money to the customer as a $900 loan. Panel B of Figure 32-1 shows the bank's new situation: Because the loan is an asset for the bank, the bank still has $1,000 in assets: $100 in required cash reserves plus the loan of $900. The assets and liabilities both still total $1,000, though the composition of the assets has changed.

The bank has less actual cash on hand ($100 required reserves) than the total of its deposits ($1,000). Is this reckless on the bank's part? It's not, if you remember the thinking of our ancient bank that stored gold coins: Observing that only a small number of customers wanted to convert banknotes into coins on any given day, it was happy to keep only 10 percent of its coins in its vault and lend out the rest. In the same way, modern banks count on the fact that not all of their customers will try to withdraw cash at the same time.

Here's where things get even more interesting: The appliance store sells the refrigerator and gets paid $900 in cash. The store owner goes to the bank and deposits that amount in the store's bank account. Panel C of Figure 32-1 shows the bank's position now. It now has the following assets: the $100 required cash reserves, a loan of $900, and the new cash deposit of $900, for a total of $1,900. Demand deposits total the same amount. (The bank's assets equal its liabilities.)

FIGURE 32-1

How banks create money   As the money comes in to the bank and then is lent out again, new money is created. In this example, by the time the money is lent out twice, the bank has created $1,900 from $1,000.

(A) Modern Bank

Assets		Liabilities	
Cash	$1,000	Demand deposits	$1,000
Total	$1,000	Total	$1,000

(B) Modern Bank

Assets		Liabilities	
Required reserves	$ 100	Demand deposits	$1,000
Loan	900		
Total	$1,000	Total	$1,000

(C) Modern Bank

Assets		Liabilities	
Required reserves	$ 100	Demand deposits	$1,900
Loan	900		
New cash deposit	900		
Total	$1,900	Total	$1,900

(D) Modern Bank

Assets		Liabilities	
Required reserves*	$ 190	Demand deposits	$1,900
Loans**	1,710		
Total	$1,900	Total	$1,900

*10% × $1,900
**90% × $1,900

After the new cash deposit, what happens to the required reserves? Let's say our modern bank keeps in its vault as required cash reserves 10 percent of what its customers have deposited. Experience indicates that that amount will be enough to cover day-to-day requests from its depositors for cash withdrawals.[3] With $1,900 in liabilities ($1,000 in the original deposit and the store owner's deposit of $900), the bank will now want to keep 10 percent of $1,900, or $190, required cash reserves in the vault. That means it will be happy to lend money up to the amount of $1,710 (90 percent of $1,900). The bank has already made loans of $900 and now lends another $810 to another customer in order to have lent a total of $1,710. This new situation is shown in panel D of Figure 32-1.

How far can this process continue? The bank will continue lending and taking deposits. Over time, the bank can end up creating as much as $9,000 in new loans. Why $9,000? Because you originally deposited $1,000, and the bank has to hold 10 percent of that (= $100) as required cash reserves. It then lends the rest, and eventually gets the loans back as deposits (assuming Modern Bank is the only bank in the economy).

Those deposits, in turn, create reserve requirements. By the time the bank has lent a total of $9,000, it can expect $9,000 in deposits—which creates a need for 10 percent of those deposits to be held as cash reserves too (= $900). The total sum of required cash reserves is thus $100 + $900. Thanks to your original $1,000 cash deposit, the bank has enough cash to cover that. But that's all the bank has in cash, so it can't lend more. With $9,000 in loans and $1,000 in reserves, there is no money left for new loans. Still, your original $1,000 has had quite a run: The bank has used it to create $9,000 in new money, effectively turning $1,000 into $10,000.

From one bank to an entire economy

So far, we have assumed that there's only one bank in the economy—everyone has to use that bank to borrow and save. In practice, of course, modern economies have many banks. The logic of the example still holds, though, if we think of the bank in our example as representing the *entire banking system:* The first deposit might be made into Bank of America, for example, and the next into Chase. The next might go to Citi. The key is that all money loaned out eventually gets put back into some bank within the banking system.

Let's round off our discussion with some formal terminology. In our example, the bank kept 10 percent of its deposits as reserves. If the reserve ratio were 100 percent (a situation known as *full-reserve banking*), no lending would have happened in the example. Your entire original $1,000 deposit would just sit in the bank's vault. If banks aren't lending, it would be very hard to get the money needed to buy a house or car. The entire financial system would grind to a halt.

Rarely if ever do we observe full-reserve banking. Instead, we have **fractional-reserve banking**, a banking system in which banks keep on reserve less than 100 percent of their deposits. (That is, the reserve ratio is less than 100 percent.) Fractional-reserve banking allows the bank to lend out a portion of the money deposited in the bank.

We call the ratio of money created by the lending activities of the banking system to the money created by the government's central bank the **money multiplier**. The size of the reserve determines the size of the money multiplier: As a simple approximation, we can calculate the money multiplier as $\frac{1}{R}$, where R is the reserve ratio.

EQUATION 32-1

$$\text{Money multiplier} = \frac{1}{\text{Reserve ratio}}$$
$$= \frac{1}{R}$$

Thus, a reserve ratio of 10 percent (or, equivalently, 0.10) means the money multiplier is 10:

$$\text{Money multiplier} = \frac{1}{0.10}$$
$$= 10$$

fractional-reserve banking
a banking system in which banks keep on reserve less than 100 percent of their deposits

money multiplier
the ratio of money created by the lending activities of the banking system to the money created by the government's central bank

With $1,900 in liabilities ($1,000 in the original deposit and the store owner's deposit of $900), the bank will want to keep $190 required cash reserves in the vault (10 percent of $1,900). That means it will be happy to lend money up to the amount of $1,710 (90 percent of $1,900)—the situation shown in panel D of Figure 32-1.

The bank has already made loans of $900 and now lends another $810 to another customer in order to have lent a total of $1,710. The approximation in Equation 32-1 works exactly as long as two things occur:

- People don't hold any money as cash outside the bank and
- Banks lend out as much as they can beyond what's legally required for them to hold as reserves.[4]

If either assumption fails to hold, the multiplier will be smaller than the approximation.

Ultimately, the system of fractional reserve banking is what makes possible the existence of banks as we know them. However, you may be wondering if there are big risks involved. What if too many customers turn up at the bank asking for their dollar bills at the same time? When that happens, a *bank run* occurs—the situation that arises from fear that the bank is in danger of running out of money. Read the Real Life box "Bank runs and the banking holiday" for some real-life examples.

Real Life
Bank runs and the banking holiday

In 2007, hundreds of panicked customers lined up outside branches of the British bank Northern Rock in a desperate attempt to get money out of their accounts. The media had just reported that Northern Rock had made big investments in financial products created during the U.S. housing bubble. Those investments were now nearly worthless, and the losses pushed the bank toward bankruptcy. Not surprisingly, customers suddenly wanted their money out of the bank.

British banking regulations at the time offered some protection to savers: The government pledged that customers wouldn't lose the value of their savings at Northern Rock, with a guarantee up to a limit of £35,000 (about $55,000). But many customers decided they'd prefer to withdraw their money immediately rather than risk it. About £2 billion of cash was withdrawn in just two days.

Bank runs are a problem because under a fractional-reserve system, banks don't hold enough cash to pay out more than a fraction of their depositors' money. Ironically, a bank run can *create* the very thing customers are afraid of—the bank going bust—even if their fears are unfounded. If enough customers demand their deposits back all at once, a bank will inevitably go bankrupt, no matter its initial condition.

The most important response to a bank run, therefore, is to try to reassure savers and create time for their panic to subside. During the Great Depression, in March 1933, the governor of Michigan feared that one of the largest banks in the state, the Guardian Trust Company of Detroit, was on the edge of shutting down for good. In order to keep the bank from failing, the governor took the drastic measure of stopping transactions at all of the 800 banks in the state, leaving people to get by on only the cash they had in their pockets. The move backfired. Far from quelling the panic, it only sparked greater concern. Many reasoned that if the banks could be saved only by preventing all transactions, the entire system must be in danger of collapse.

Word of bank trouble spread throughout the country, and bank runs threatened to spiral out of control, destroying people's savings and crippling the economy. In response, Congress quickly passed what became known as the "Bank Holiday," closing all banks in the country for four days (later stretched out to a week). Right before the banks were due to reopen, President Roosevelt talked to Americans through radio broadcasts known as "fireside chats" to explain what was going on. Furthermore, the Federal Reserve pledged to supply unlimited currency to banks that reopened, and so depositors essentially had 100 percent insurance on their deposits.

Amazingly, it worked. When the banks reopened, the panic had abated, and Americans replaced two-thirds of the money they had drawn out in the bank runs. The outgrowth of this holiday was the creation of the Federal Deposit Insurance Commission (FDIC) through the Glass-Steagall Act. It reassured savers that if their bank fails, the government will protect any deposit less than $100,000 (later increased to $250,000).

What happened to Northern Rock? After a second day of lines outside the bank's branches, the British government stepped in and announced that it would refund the entire value of customers' savings accounts if the bank went bust. The panic abated, and Northern Rock lived to see another day. (However, it lost so much money in the U.S. housing crash that the British government eventually had to take it over to keep it going.)

These experiences remind us that bank runs—widely thought to have been consigned to the history books—can still happen in today's economy.

Sources: http://www.nber.org/papers/w12717; https://www.bostonfed.org/-/media/Documents/education/pubs/closed.pdf.

Measuring money

LO 32.4 Describe M1 and M2.

Now that we know how money is created by the banking system, let's revisit our earlier question: How much money *is* there? If you are thinking to yourself, "That depends on what type of money you are asking about," you are exactly right. It is the job of the Federal Reserve to manage the **money supply**—the amount of money available in the economy—and the Fed provides the most common definitions of the money supply.

The Fed classifies different types of money by their *liquidity*—that is, by how easy an asset is to convert immediately to cash without losing value. The most common classifications of money are the monetary base, M1, and M2:

- The **monetary base** is the sum of currency in circulation and reserves held by banks at the Federal Reserve.
- **M1** includes currency held by the public ("cash") plus checking account balances (demand deposits, which are not exactly cash but are readily accessible for most people).
- **M2** is broader still. M2 includes everything in M1 plus savings accounts and other financial instruments where money is locked away for a specified period of time. Since these forms of savings can't be accessed quickly without penalty fees, they are slightly less liquid than other forms of money. (Certificates of deposit are an example of a less-liquid form of money.)

All three are legitimate measures of the money supply. Which one we use depends on our goals. If we want to look at spending (liquidity), we use M1. If we want to look at savings, we would use M2. You can think of M2 as a measure of the "multiplied" money. Comparing it to the monetary base (the sum of currency and reserves) can give you some sense of what the money multiplier actually is at a given point in time.

Figure 32-2 shows that the money multiplier was relatively stable over time, until the huge change sparked by the 2008 financial crisis. At that point, the monetary base rose dramatically due to actions by the Federal Reserve to combat the financial crisis by adding to banks' reserves. But banks were nervous in the face of the crisis and reluctant to lend to others. As a result, there were relatively small increases in M1 and M2, despite the big expansion in reserves.

money supply
the amount of money available in the economy

monetary base
the sum of currency in circulation and reserves held by banks at the Federal Reserve

M1
definition of money that includes cash plus checking account balances

M2
definition of money that includes everything in M1 plus savings accounts and other financial instruments where money is locked away for a specified amount of time; less liquid than M1

FIGURE 32-2

Monetary base, M1, and M2 over time

In nominal terms, all three measures of money steadily increased over this period of time, although the rate of increase of M2 sped up dramatically starting around 1995. The monetary base ("hard money") increased dramatically in 2008 as part of the effort to combat the financial crisis.

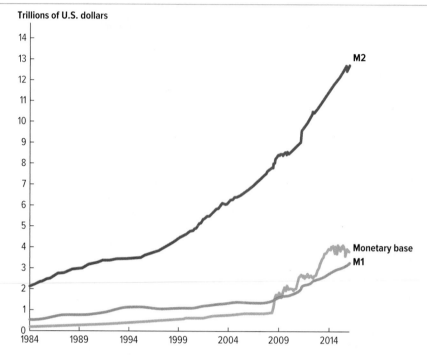

Source: Federal Reserve Economic Data, http://research.stlouisfed.org/fred2/ (accessed October 31, 2012, 2013).

At this point, you might wonder who decides how much money is going to exist. Obviously, based on our earlier discussion of money creation, the banks play a large role in M1 and M2. But who decides how much hard money there is to multiply in the first place? And who sets the required reserves ratio? We address these questions in the next section.

✓ CONCEPT CHECK

☐ What is a reserve requirement of 100 percent called? **[LO 32.3]**
☐ How does the money multiplier create money in the economy? **[LO 32.3]**
☐ What type(s) of money includes demand deposits (amounts in checking accounts)? **[LO 32.4]**

Managing the Money Supply: The Federal Reserve

On October 24, 1907, the United States was in the middle of one of the most severe financial crises in its history. Tens of thousands of depositors were descending upon banks across the country, creating a bank run of such proportions that no one was safe. Even some of the largest banks were in jeopardy and struggling to survive day to day. In this flurry of activity, a single man took responsibility for the survival of the U.S. financial system: John Pierpont Morgan, president of J.P. Morgan & Co. and the most powerful banker of the time. With many banks already near collapse, at 1:30 P.M. on October 24th, news reached Morgan that the New York Stock Exchange was simply out of money. Even someone willing to pay 100 percent interest for a loan couldn't find a lender. Stock prices were plummeting. Absent any action, all stock on the exchange would become worthless.

With only a few hours to act, Morgan convened nearly every major figure in the U.S. financial world of the time—all of the leading bankers and industrial capitalists. Even the Secretary of the Treasury, George Cortelyou, came running to see if the most powerful banker in the country could save the U.S. economy from collapse. The system needed cash—lots of it. In the face of catastrophe, the U.S. government pitched in $25 million. John D. Rockefeller offered $10 million immediately and up to $40 million if extra funds were needed. By 2:30 P.M., Morgan had collected enough money to save the system.

The reliance on a single titan of industry to save the nation from collapse was a stark reminder that the nation was ill-prepared for crisis. Six years later, in 1913, President Woodrow Wilson signed the Federal Reserve Act into law, creating the Federal Reserve. Since then, the Fed has been the centralized institution responsible for coordinating the operations of the U.S. financial system.[5]

The role of the central bank

LO 32.5 Understand the role of a central bank and discuss the idea of the Federal Reserve's dual mandate.

Almost every major nation has a central bank. A **central bank** is the institution ultimately responsible for managing the nation's money supply and coordinating the banking system to ensure a sound economy. In the United States, the central bank is the Federal Reserve. Like any central bank, the Federal Reserve has two essential functions:

- managing the money supply and
- acting as a lender of last resort.

Before we explain the two functions of a central bank, it may help to explain what a central bank *is not*. It is not the government's finance arm. In the United States, the financial operations of the government—collecting taxes, paying bills, issuing debt, and generally managing the nation's finances—are conducted by the Treasury Department. The Fed is responsible for deciding how much physical currency should be printed, but the printing itself is done by the Treasury Department's Bureau of Engraving and Printing. In short, the Treasury Department executes *fiscal policy,* while the Federal Reserve conducts *monetary policy.* Formally, **monetary policy** consists of actions by the central bank to manage the money supply, in pursuit of certain macroeconomic goals.

So, a central bank's most important function is to manage the money supply. A bit later, we'll learn more about the ways that the Fed does that. First, though, it's worth asking whether we in fact *need* a central bank to manage the money supply. Why not leave it to the private market to issue currency and control it? In principle at least, there is no reason why a privately issued currency should not gain wide acceptance. For more about one attempt to create a new currency, see the From Another Angle box "Is Bitcoin the currency of the future?"

central bank
the institution ultimately responsible for managing the nation's money supply and coordinating the banking system to ensure a sound economy

monetary policy
actions by the central bank to manage the money supply, in pursuit of certain macroeconomic goals

From Another Angle

Is Bitcoin the currency of the future?

Some online communities have their own money: The simulation game Farmville 2 has "farm cash" and Second Life has "Linden dollars." Could virtual currencies ever take over from conventional currencies such as the U.S. dollar? In principle, it's a possibility. In practice, it's hard to imagine.

Think back to our discussion of what makes for good money. One of the most important features is stability of value. Why were people through the ages happy to store their wealth in

(continued)

gold? Because they thought it was unlikely that a huge new amount of gold would be discovered; such a discovery would slash the value of the gold they had. Why are people today happy to store their wealth in U.S. dollars? Because they are reasonably confident that the Fed will not suddenly decide to print trillions upon trillions of new dollar bills, thus rendering everyone's existing dollars near-worthless.

Who has the power to "print" money in virtual worlds? Ultimately, it's the people who run those worlds. Would you really be happy to hold your life savings in a virtual currency, trusting that those in charge would never decide to create huge amounts of new money? Most of us wouldn't be so brave (or, say some, so foolish).

In 2009, a mysterious programmer using the fake name Satoshi Nakamoto created a new virtual currency—Bitcoin—that proposed a solution to this problem: Nobody is in charge of the Bitcoin money supply. Instead, the supply of money increases at a rate predetermined by a mathematical algorithm.

In its early days, the value of a Bitcoin was a tiny fraction of a cent. Users of Bitcoins were a small community of computer enthusiasts. The first real-world purchase was made, for fun, by a Florida programmer named Laszlo Hanyecz, who paid 10,000 Bitcoins to get two Papa John's pizzas delivered. (He transferred the Bitcoins to another enthusiast, who paid in dollars.) Soon, Bitcoins attracted the attention of the media, and speculators started to buy them. Their value took off, and by June 2011 the value of a Bitcoin had soared to $27. The 10,000 Bitcoins that Laszlo Hanyecz had paid for his pizza just a few months previously would have been worth over $270,000 at those prices. "I don't feel bad about it," he claims. "The pizza was really good."

With Bitcoins worth so much, hackers started to look for ways to steal them out of users' accounts. In July 2011, an Internet site called Mt. Gox, which then handled 90 percent of all Bitcoin transactions, was hacked. Other security scares followed, and one user reported that his $500,000 worth of Bitcoins was stolen. The damage to the project's credibility saw the value of Bitcoins fall to around $3 at one point. The currency has experienced big price fluctuations over time. (By 2016 a Bitcoin was valued at about $575.)

Although the creator of Bitcoin, Satoshi Nakamoto, has disappeared without a trace, there are still plenty of enthusiasts for the Bitcoin project, working to bring the technology into the mainstream. Will the story of Bitcoin eventually come to be seen as just the first chapter in how new currencies rendered central banks obsolete? Or will it be just another online idea that didn't live up to all the hype? The Bitcoin saga shows that even in the digital age, we still need to take seriously the very old problem of how to maintain stable, trustworthy currencies.

Sources: http://www.wired.com/magazine/2011/11/mf_bitcoin/all/1; http://www.dailytech.com/Digital+Black+Friday+First+Bitcoin+Depression+Hits/article21877.htm; http://www.economist.com/blogs/babbage/2011/06/virtual-currency.

Another role played by a central bank is the *lender of last resort*. What does this mean? Think back to the story of J.P. Morgan, who almost single-handedly saved the banking system in 1907. When nobody else was willing to lend to banks facing a bank run, J.P. Morgan, along with others he rallied to the table, stepped in as lenders of last resort. They became the last line of defense before an imminent financial collapse. These days, that's the Fed's job. As we'll see in Chapter 34, "Financial Crisis," the Fed played exactly this role during the U.S. financial crisis in 2008.

How does the Federal Reserve work?

Now that you know what the role of a central bank is, let's look more closely at how the Federal Reserve—the United States's central bank—actually works. We will focus on two topics: the organizational structure of the Federal Reserve and the key principles that guide the Fed in its policy-making.

How the Fed is organized

The entity we popularly call the **Federal Reserve**, or Fed for short, is actually not one organization but an entire system. The Federal Reserve System consists of 12 regional banks and a seven-member Board of Governors that act as the central bank in the United States. The seven-member Board of Governors and its staff, based in Washington, DC, are responsible for the overall governance of the system.

Supporting the efforts of the Board of Governors are 12 regional Federal Reserve banks scattered in major cities across the country, as shown in Figure 32-3. These 12 banks conduct the day-to-day affairs of the central bank. Under them are the so-called *member banks,* which include most of the banks in the United States. These banks are considered to be members of the Federal Reserve System and are subject to its regulations.

The Board of Governors is made up of experts in finance, banking, and monetary policy who are appointed by the U.S. president and confirmed by the Senate for 14-year terms. In addition, the president appoints one member of the Board of Governors to be chair for a four-year term. The chair of the Federal Reserve is one of the most important economic positions in the United States, if not the world. The chair has significant direct control over the conduct of monetary policy by the central bank.

Each of the regional Federal Reserve banks, for their part, is led by a president. The regional presidents are generally selected from the banking and business community in the region. They are responsible for overseeing the day-to-day actions of the regional banks, including regulatory oversight and implementation of monetary policy.

In addition, five of the 12 regional bank presidents serve on the *Federal Open Market Committee,* or FOMC. Four of these regional presidents serve on a rotating basis; the president of the New York regional bank is always a member, emphasizing how important the financial

Federal Reserve ("the Fed")

the system consisting of a seven-member Board of Governors and 12 regional banks that act as the central bank of the United States

---

FIGURE 32-3

The Federal Reserve System   The Federal Reserve System is made up of 12 regional banks spread across the country, headed by the Board of Governors in Washington, DC.

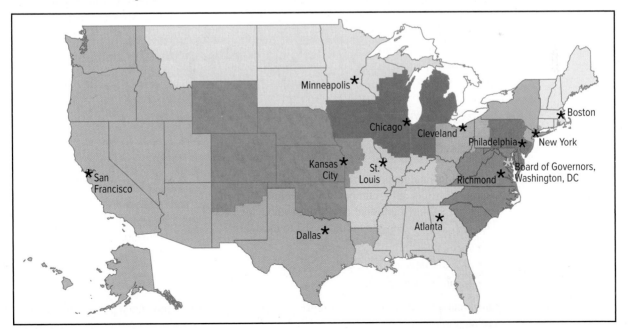

Source: http://www.federalreserve.gov/otherfrb.htm (accessed January 27, 2013).

Janet Yellen, a former business school professor at the University of California, was sworn in as chair of the Federal Reserve in February 2014.
© Mark Wilson/Getty Images

industry in the New York metropolitan area is to the nation's monetary and financial policy. The five regional bank presidents are joined on the FOMC by the seven-member Board of Governors (for a total of 12 members). The FOMC is the most important policy-making body of the Federal Reserve System. It carries full responsibility for setting the overall direction of monetary policy and guiding the money supply.

You may notice that for a governmental agency, the Federal Reserve has little connection with the rest of government. Though appointed by the government, the members of the Board of Governors enjoy the security of serving long terms, which helps them to be independent of politics. This is no accident. Politicians of all parties know the power of monetary policy. Giving the Fed a high degree of independence means that the Fed governors will not be as tempted by political pressure as someone with less independence. The Fed's independence, for example, makes it less likely to expand the money supply simply to make it cheaper for the government to repay its debt. In addition, knowing that technocrats rather than politicians are in charge tends to increase people's trust in the stability of the dollar.

How the Fed makes policy

But what exactly does it mean to manage monetary policy for the benefit of the country? The Federal Reserve has twin responsibilities—what is commonly known as a **dual mandate**: The first part of this mandate is to *ensure price stability* and the second is to *maintain full employment.*

dual mandate

the twin responsibilities of the Federal Reserve, to use monetary policy to ensure price stability and to maintain full employment

The first responsibility is what many think of when talking about monetary policy. It involves maintaining a stable money supply that meets the needs of the economy, while keeping prices relatively constant over time. For many central banks, this is as far as the mandate goes. (Maintaining price stability is, for instance, the only mandate of the European Central Bank, which manages monetary policy for much of Europe.)

In the United States, however, the Federal Reserve also has been given the second part of the mandate—to use monetary policy to maintain full employment. Monetary policy can have powerful effects on the economy. This second responsibility means using that power to keep the economy strong and stable. In the next few sections, we'll show how the Fed works to fulfill this second part of its mandate. In Chapter 33, "Inflation," we'll see how the two parts of the dual mandate can be fundamentally in conflict and how the Fed manages the tension between them.

Tools of monetary policy

LO 32.6 Explain the tools the Federal Reserve uses to conduct monetary policy.

To fulfill its dual mandate, the Fed manages the supply of money. In order to change the money supply, the Fed has a number of different options at its disposal. In this section, we'll walk through the three traditional ones to show how the Federal Reserve generally conducts business. These tools, from least commonly used to most, are

- reserve requirements,
- the discount window, and
- open-market operations.

Open-market operations are the most frequently used tool of monetary policy; the others are backup tools, rarely used.

Reserve requirements

Although it is seldom used, the most powerful tool available to the Federal Reserve is its ability to adjust the **reserve requirement**—the regulation that sets the minimum fraction of deposits banks must hold in reserve. The tool can have far-reaching effects, so policy-makers try to use it sparingly.

You'll recall that the reserve ratio a bank maintains is one of several determinants of how much money is available in the economy, and by extension how much lending occurs. If it wanted to, the Fed could even eliminate fractional-reserve banking altogether by mandating that banks hold 100 percent of their deposits in reserve, though that wouldn't be a very good idea.

Although changing the reserve requirement is a powerful tool, it is *too* powerful in most situations. Meaningfully controlling the money supply through reserve requirements would mean dramatically changing the amount of money banks are required to hold, an action almost certain to have significant and unpredictable consequences. Bank managers make their plans depending in part on a certain reserve requirement. Rapid change in the requirement would make it harder for them to manage their money. Rapid change also would have ripple effects throughout the entire economy, affecting the availability of credit and confidence in the banking system.

Despite the dangers of changing reserve requirements, some countries, most notably China, have used adjustments to the required reserve ratio as a primary tool of monetary policy (and have had mixed success). In the United States, changes to the reserve requirements are rarely used for policy unless there's a crisis. Think of changing the reserve requirement as a big shove; most of the time, monetary policy changes aim for more of a gentle push.

reserve requirement
the regulation that sets the minimum fraction of deposits banks must hold in reserve

The discount window

The second tool used by the Fed is the discount window. The **discount window** is a lending facility that allows any bank to borrow reserves from the Fed. The interest rate charged for these loans is called the **discount rate**. The discount window is one of the Fed's primary tools for providing liquidity to the markets and acting as a lender of last resort. When a bank is in trouble (because of a bank run, perhaps), the discount window can be a guaranteed source of emergency funds.

Historically, although the discount window is key to the Fed's responsibility as lender of last resort, loans from the discount window are rarely used for monetary policy. The reason is that the discount rate has generally been somewhat higher than interest rates available in the market. As a result, banks tend to look elsewhere for loans. Because of that, any bank that makes use of the window opens itself up to significant speculation about its financial health. If the bank needs to borrow on unfavorable terms to stay alive, the thinking goes, it's likely that the bank is in trouble. Such stigma makes banks reluctant to use the discount window.

Sometimes, though, banks lack better options. The stigma of discount-window loans fell away during the 2008 financial crisis: Banks in desperate need of cash were forced to put aside their reputational concerns and turn to the only place willing to lend to them. In just one week in October 2008, banks borrowed $117 billion in emergency funds from the discount window.[6]

discount window
the lending facility run by the Fed that allows any bank to borrow reserves

discount rate
the interest rate charged by the Fed for loans of reserves through the discount window

Open-market operations

The final, most used, and most important tool in the Fed's traditional toolbox is open-market operations. **Open-market operations** are sales or purchases of government securities, by the Fed to or from banks on the open (public) market. The actual process is a bit more indirect than we'll present it here, but the ultimate end is the same: The Fed sells bonds to a bank or buys bonds from it. These transactions directly result in an increase or decrease in the money supply:

open-market operations
sales or purchases of government bonds by the Fed, to or from banks, on the open market

- Increasing the money supply: When the Fed wants to increase the money supply, it can purchase a bond from one of the large banks it trades with. The Fed pays for this purchase with money it has on hand, which then translates into larger deposits and reserves in the commercial bank.

- Decreasing the money supply: On the other hand, if the Fed wants to decrease the money supply, it sells bonds, accepting as payment reserves from the buying bank. The Fed then effectively destroys the money it receives, which decreases the amount of the monetary base in existence.

How exactly do open-market operations affect the larger economy? This tool works two ways. The Fed can *buy* government bonds to pursue **expansionary monetary policy**—actions that increase the money supply in order to increase aggregate demand. When the Fed buys bonds from a bank, it pays for those bonds by increasing the bank's deposit in the Fed, which increases the bank's reserves. The bank can then lend more and set off a ripple effect that increases other banks' lending. This maneuver enables the Fed to increase the growth rate of the money supply and pursue expansionary monetary policy.[7]

When the Fed *sells* bonds to a bank, the bank pays for the transaction with money that it keeps on deposit at the Fed. The sale thus reduces the bank's reserves. This in turn reduces the bank's ability to lend. Through the multiplier effect, the reduction in lending sets off a ripple effect with other banks' lending and slows down the growth rate of the money supply. This is an important way to conduct **contractionary monetary policy**—actions that reduce the money supply in order to decrease aggregate demand.

Open-market operations have a couple of advantages over other tools of monetary policy. First, the transactions—the buying and selling of bonds—take place on a *daily* basis. Since the Fed commonly wants to make small adjustments rather than sweeping changes in the economy, the frequency of these transactions adds to this tool's flexibility. The ability to act on a day-to-day basis helps maintain the Fed's reputation for steady, credible policy.

The second advantage of open-market operations is that they affect the *federal funds rate,* the interest rate that banks charge when one bank makes a very-short-term (usually overnight) loan of reserves to another bank. The Fed uses this rate as a target in open-market operations, pushing it upward by selling bonds and pushing it downward by buying bonds.

The federal funds rate and money supply

The Federal Reserve rarely describes its policies in terms of changes in the money supply. Instead, it focuses on interest rates. Technically, the Fed announces a "target" for the **federal funds rate**—the interest rate at which banks choose to lend reserves held at the Fed to one another, usually just overnight.

Banks are required to maintain a certain level of reserves. Thus, when a bank finds itself short at the end of the day, it may choose to make up the shortfall by borrowing from another bank that has excess reserves. Since both banks have an account with the Federal Reserve, it is easy and safe to borrow money this way.

How does the Fed affect the federal funds rate? In contractionary policy, as we saw, the Fed sells bonds, taking reserves from banks as payment. This decrease in the supply of reserves pushes the federal funds rate upward. Why? By reducing the supply of reserves, the price of borrowing reserves rises, just as in the standard analysis of supply and demand in a market for goods. Other interest rates move in the same direction as the federal funds rate, so interest rates rise in general, discouraging spending on houses, cars, new machinery, and other things. Raising the federal funds rate thus helps meet the goal of contractionary policy—which is to slow the economy down.

A similar chain of logic applies to expansionary policy, in which the goal is to reduce interest rates to stimulate the economy. In expansionary policy, the logic works in the opposite direction: The Fed buys bonds, injecting reserves into the banking system, and lowers the federal funds rates.

The one caveat with expansionary monetary policy is that there is a natural limit to how low the federal funds rate (or any other nominal interest rate) can go. Since anyone in the economy

---

expansionary monetary policy
actions that increase the money supply in order to increase aggregate demand

contractionary monetary policy
actions that reduce the money supply in order to decrease aggregate demand

federal funds rate
the interest rate at which banks choose to lend reserves held at the Fed to one another

can always hold cold, hard cash, which offers a zero-percent interest rate, it is nearly impossible to push nominal interest rates on any other asset below zero. The natural lower limit on interest rates is known as the *zero lower bound,* and it has played a central role in the recent economic crises in the United States, Japan, and Europe.

These three tools—reserve requirements, the discount window, and open-market operations—comprise the traditional strategies of the Federal Reserve. We'll discuss examples of more unorthodox techniques in Chapter 34, "Financial Crisis." These innovations were used in the recent financial crisis to help shore up the entire financial system. Through use of such new policies, the Federal Reserve has rapidly adapted its toolkit to meet the changing demands of the global economy.

✓ CONCEPT CHECK

☐ What is the name of the part of the Federal Reserve in Washington, DC, that oversees the Fed's operations? **[LO 32.5]**

☐ What is the dual mandate of the Federal Reserve? **[LO 32.5]**

☐ What is the most common tool that the Federal Reserve uses to conduct monetary policy? What makes this tool more appealing than the other two? **[LO 32.6]**

The Economic Effects of Monetary Policy

To understand why the Federal Reserve's control over the money supply is so powerful, we need a better understanding of the mechanism by which monetary policy affects the economy. Some economists, known as *monetarists,* argue that over the *long run,* monetary policy is irrelevant because prices will adjust to a high or low supply of money, without any change in overall economic output. (Consequently, monetarists say that "money is neutral.") However, most economists agree that in the *short run,* at least, the Federal Reserve's control over monetary policy allows it to combat recessions and cool an overheating economy. But how does this mechanism work?

Monetary policy primarily influences the economy through changes in the interest rate. Changes in the interest rate, in turn, affect the appeal of borrowing and lending, which can have significant impacts on the economy. In this section, we'll walk through the connections in this process as well as some of the challenges of implementing monetary policy.

Interest rates and monetary policy: The liquidity-preference model

> **LO 32.7** Understand how monetary policy affects the prevailing interest rate and supply of money

When the central bank increases or decreases the money supply, it changes the balance of money supplied versus money demanded. If the words "supply" and "demand" make you think about money in a market as depicted in the supply-demand graphs we've used so far, you're on the right track.

To understand how the relationships work, we first describe the nature of the supply and demand of money using an idea, first proposed by economist John Maynard Keynes in 1936, called the *liquidity-preference model.*

The demand for money

Economists use the term "liquid" to describe the ease of turning assets into cash. Cash is highly liquid by definition, and checking accounts (demand-deposit accounts) are nearly as liquid as cash. We need cash and easy-to-access bank accounts to be able to meet our daily spending needs. In other words, we have a preference for liquidity.

Government bonds, in contrast, are not very liquid. They have to be sold in order to generate cash for spending. Of course, government bonds have an important advantage over cash: they earn interest. The advantage of interest is weighed against the disadvantage of not being very liquid.

So, when the interest rate earned on government bonds is high, most people will try to hold more bonds and less cash. And when the interest rate on bonds falls, the advantage of bonds is reduced, making cash relatively more attractive. When you don't earn much interest on bonds, you may as well hold your money in cash and other liquid forms.

liquidity-preference model

idea that the quantity of money people want to hold is a function of the interest rate

This relationship is the central idea of the **liquidity-preference model**, which explains that the quantity of money people want to hold is a function of the interest rate. In this model, the money-demand curve slopes downward, showing a negative relationship between the interest rate and how much money is demanded. Why? Think of "money" here as cash—specifically, cash as opposed to other assets such as bonds that pay interest. (No matter how high interest rates are, though, you'll still have to hold onto some money to complete day-to-day transactions.)

On the whole, the liquidity-preference model means that people aren't going to demand much money when interest rates are high; they will demand more and more money as interest rates decrease. A change in the quantity of money demanded in response to a change in the interest rate is represented by movement along the money demand curve:

- When the interest rate rises, we demand a lower quantity of money, moving leftward along the curve.
- When the interest rate falls, we demand a higher quantity of money, moving rightward along the curve.

Not all changes in the quantity of money demanded result from movement along the demand curve. Some factors instead cause the demand curve itself to shift. One such factor is the price level in the economy. The demand for money in the United States is much higher today than it was 50 years ago, for the simple reason that almost everything is far more expensive today than it was then. Higher prices mean a greater need for money to meet the everyday needs of life, and that means more money demanded at every level of the interest rate. This increase in demand is represented by shifting the money demand curve to the right.

Increases or decreases in real GDP have a similar effect on money demand:

- Increases in real GDP—more production and income—mean more money is needed to purchase goods and services.
- Decreases in real GDP would have the opposite effect: With less activity going on in the economy, less money will be needed to purchase goods and services.

In addition to these economic factors, technological advancements can also play a role. Easier use of credit cards and greater availability of ATMs, for instance, reduce the demand for money. With these tools, people need to carry around far less cash in their wallets at any given time in order to make day-to-day purchases.

Money supply

In the simple version of the liquidity-preference model, the supply of money is considered to be set only by the Federal Reserve. Regardless of the interest rate, the Fed will ensure that there is a constant quantity of money supplied in the economy. As Figure 32-4 shows, this means that the money supply curve can be represented as a vertical line in the liquidity-preference model. It also means that the only way the supply of money can change is when the Fed does so for policy reasons.

Figure 32-4 shows the basic relationship between money supply and money demand in the liquidity-preference model. The point where the supply of money meets the demand for money (r^*) will determine the *nominal interest rate,* or stated price of money in the economy.

FIGURE 32-4

The liquidity-preference model

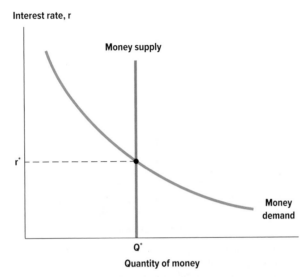

The liquidity-preference model shows the basic relationship between money supply and money demand. In this model we assume that the money supply is completely fixed by the Fed. The money demand curve slopes downward as a function of the interest rate. With high interest rates, people demand a small quantity of money, but as interest rates decrease, people demand more.

This simple model assumes that the Fed has complete control over the supply curve, but in reality an economy's money supply comes from a variety of sources. As the model currently stands, the Fed dictates the supply of the monetary base. Banks decide how much money is eventually created from the base money through the impact their lending decisions have on the money multiplier. As we'll see later, the Fed's ability to target the money supply and interest rates is not nearly as precise as this model suggests. Still, the assumption of a fixed money supply controlled by the Fed is useful for introducing the model.

Earlier, we discussed the tools the Fed has to adjust the money supply. These adjustments can be represented by shifts in the money supply curve, depending on whether the Fed wants to increase or decrease the money supply. Any actions that increase the money supply will shift the money supply curve to the right. These actions include decreasing the reserve requirement, decreasing the discount rate, or buying government bonds on the open market. In contrast, any actions that decrease the money supply will shift the money supply curve left. As you can see in Figure 32-5, changes in the money supply increase or decrease interest rates.

Knowing the slope of the money demand curve is important: The slope of the money demand curve determines how a change in the money supply will change the interest rate. If the quantity of money demanded is really responsive to changes to the interest rate (a flat, elastic demand curve), changes to the money supply will have a smaller effect on interest rates than if demand is less responsive (steeper, more inelastic). You can see this visually in Figure 32-6.

FIGURE 32-5

Shifts in the money supply curve and their effects on the interest rate

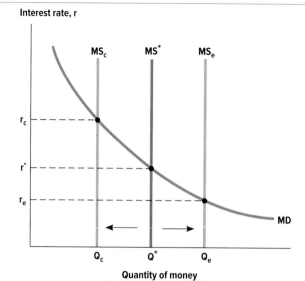

Shifting the money supply curve to the right (expanding the money supply) is called expansionary monetary policy (denoted with an e). The result is a greater amount of money in the economy, at lower interest rates. Shifting the curve to the left represents a decrease in the money supply. The result is less money in the economy, at higher interest rates.

FIGURE 32-6

The slope of the money supply curve affects the amount of change in the interest rate

(A) Elastic money demand curve

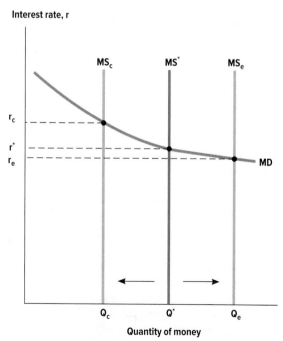

When the slope of the money demand curve is more elastic, changes in the money supply will have a smaller effect on interest rates.

(B) Inelastic money demand curve

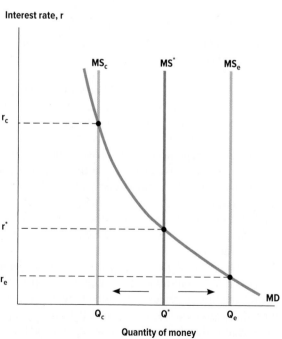

When the slope of the money demand curve is more inelastic, changes in the money supply will have a greater effect on interest rates.

Interest rates and the economy

LO 32.8 Explain how expansionary or contractionary monetary policy influences the broader economy.

The liquidity-preference model explains how the Federal Reserve's actions can change interest rates. The Fed can cause interest rates to fall by increasing the money supply, or it can cause interest rates to rise by decreasing the money supply. But why does the Fed care about the interest rate? The answer is that the interest rate has important effects in the economy. Many of the large purchases we make—buying a house, a car, or an expensive appliance—are made using money we've borrowed. Likewise, corporations borrowing to make investments must also pay the price dictated by the interest rate.

Expansionary monetary policy

Changes in interest rates affect aggregate demand and supply in an economy: Lower interest rates make it cheaper to borrow money, and less rewarding to save money. At lower interest rates, people will spend on big-ticket items instead of save, further increasing the consumption part of aggregate demand. Monetary policy is thus an important way for policy-makers to respond to changes in the health of the economy.

For an example, let's say that the economy is in a recession. Aggregate demand is low. The economy is in a short-run equilibrium marked by sluggish output and lower prices. The Fed knows that lower interest rates would spur increased borrowing and spending—shifting the aggregate demand curve to the right. The Federal Reserve chairman announces that the Fed will lower the federal funds rate. So the Fed conducts open-market operations to increase the supply of money in the economy. This action is called *expansionary monetary policy*. As you can see in panel A of Figure 32-7, lower interest rates are the result of this action. It is important to keep in mind that the lower interest rates affect the rates of return on assets throughout the economy:

- When the Fed purchases bonds on the open market, it increases the demand for those bonds, drives up their prices, and therefore lowers their expected rates of return (since investors now have to pay more for the same stream of payments).
- Since investors no longer find Treasuries as attractive as before, they shift their portfolios toward other assets, like private stocks and bonds and real estate.
- This portfolio shift then increases the prices of the other assets in the economy and reduces *their* rates of return.

Thus, the Fed's decision to lower *an* interest rate—the federal funds rate—results in an economywide increase in asset prices and rates of return.

This increase in asset prices leads to what is known as the *balance sheet channel* of monetary policy. The idea is that a rise in asset prices causes firms and households to perceive an increase in their net worth. Then, when they feel an increase in net worth, they tend to increase spending. The causes of the additional spending differ for households and firms:

- In the case of households, the most important asset tends to be the house itself. For them, the balance sheet channel refers to spending out of an increase in housing wealth.
- In the case of firms, corporations tend to hold much of their business savings in the form of financial assets. When firms see an increase in their net worth due to increased asset prices, they are usually more willing to spend on new projects. They can use those larger internal savings to self-finance their investments. (Also, of course, the opportunity cost of using those funds is lower because the interest rate is lower.)

So, lower interest rates spur borrowing and spending. They also discourage saving. With increases in consumption spending and investment, aggregate demand increases. The aggregate

FIGURE 32-7

Expansionary monetary policy

(A) Expansionary monetary policy

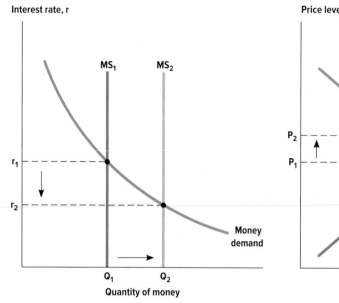

Expansionary money supply pushes interest rates lower and puts more money into the economy.

(B) Expansionary monetary policy and the AD/AS model

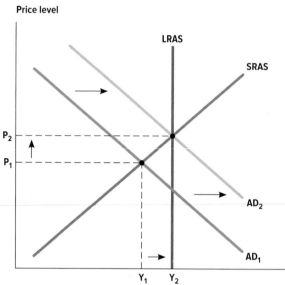

As a result people spend and borrow more, increasing aggregate demand. In this case, monetary policy was able to pull the economy out of recession.

demand curve shifts to the right as shown in panel B of Figure 32-7. Ultimately the effect is the same as that of the expansionary *fiscal* policy we discussed in Chapter 31, "The Basics of Finance." Both prices and output increase, taking the bite out of the recession.

Contractionary monetary policy

Conversely, what should the Fed do when the economy is booming, as it was in the housing bubble of 2006? Since the system was flush with cash, the aggregate demand curve was way to the right, and price levels were high. Output was also high, which made the decision of what needed to be done in this situation slightly tougher.

On the one hand, strong economic activity is obviously a good thing. On the other hand, it is possible for the economy to be operating beyond its means. When short-run output moves above long-run equilibrium, the price level will inevitably increase. Such increases in the price level are contrary to the central bank's mandate to maintain stable price levels. We'll go into this responsibility in more depth in Chapter 33, "Inflation," but for now, let's say that the Fed would be worried that these rising price levels would begin to adversely affect the economy.

When the Fed decides that the economy is a little too active—economists often call this "overheating"—it often moves to increase interest rates, as it did throughout the housing bubble. This increase in interest rates shifts the aggregate demand curve leftward, leading to lower prices and equilibrium output in the short run. That result, shown in panel B of Figure 32-8, is the effect of a contractionary monetary policy, shown in panel A of the same figure.

You'll note that we left both of these examples in the short run. In the long run, the economy will adjust to changes in the money supply, leaving only changes in the overall price level. This fact leads to one of the challenges facing the Federal Reserve: how to maintain stable price levels

FIGURE 32-8
Contractionary monetary policy

(A) Contractionary monetary policy

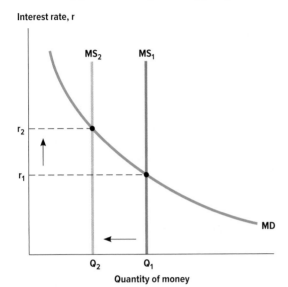

Contractionary monetary policy decreases the money supply, increasing interest rates.

(B) Contractionary monetary policy and the AD/AS model

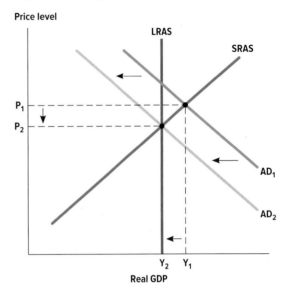

Decreasing the money supply can cool down the economy when it overheats.

while also ensuring full employment. As you'll see in Chapter 33, "Inflation," these two goals are often in fundamental conflict.

Challenges and advantages of monetary policy

The examples of the use of monetary policy, above, show how policy can work in ideal cases. It is rare for the world to work so cleanly. When we discussed fiscal policy, we noted that policy-makers face practical challenges, such as time lags and imperfect information, when they try to make policy. The Fed faces the same problems as it seeks to steer the economy using monetary policy.

Although monetary policy usually does not take as long to implement as fiscal policy, a few months can pass before the Fed's actions start to have their desired impact. By that time, the state of the economy might have changed. A boost in the money supply could push the economy past the level of long-run equilibrium output, for example, and cause the economy to overheat. Even worse, the Fed could inadvertently contract the money supply just as the economy starts sliding into a recession. This mistiming of policy would make the ensuing recession even worse.

Even so, monetary policy does have advantages compared to traditional fiscal policy. The Fed does not have to wait for politicians to come to a consensus about the best policy to help the economy. Instead, the Fed Board of Governors and Open Market Committee typically meet every six weeks or so. They can, if necessary, change monetary policy then and there. Also, the Fed is made up of prominent economic policy-makers whose job is to make sure they fully understand the nuances of the overall economy in order to apply the right policy at the right time. It does not need to make specific decisions about spending and tax policy; it merely lowers or raises interest rates and lets the market determine spending decisions.

Benefits like these make monetary policy a vitally important weapon against low employment and excessive inflation.

☐ What is the federal funds rate? **[LO 32.7]**

☐ What should the central bank do to fight low aggregate demand during a recession?
[LO 32.8]

Conclusion

In this chapter, we've explored one of the most fundamental concepts in modern economics: money. We've looked at the roles money plays in the economy. We've also looked at how central banks and the private banking system interact to determine the size of the money supply. Finally, we've seen some of the tools the central bank has to manage the money supply and how those tools allow it to exert considerable influence over the broader economy.

This unique power gives the Fed (and central banks in other countries) incredible responsibility for the economy. As you'll see in the next few chapters, this responsibility usually comes down to two main tasks: keeping price levels stable and acting as a lender of last resort. The Fed is the last line of defense when a financial crisis threatens an economy.

Key Terms

money, p. 831

store of value, p. 831

medium of exchange, p. 831

barter, p. 831

unit of account, p. 832

commodity-backed money, p. 833

fiat money, p. 834

demand deposits, p. 835

reserves, p. 835

required reserves, p. 835

excess reserves, p. 835

reserve ratio, p. 835

fractional-reserve banking, p. 837

money multiplier, p. 837

money supply, p. 839

monetary base, p. 839

M1, p. 839

M2, p. 839

central bank, p. 841

monetary policy, p. 841

Federal Reserve ("the Fed"), p. 843

dual mandate, p. 844

reserve requirement, p. 845

discount window, p. 845

discount rate, p. 845

open-market operations, p. 845

expansionary monetary policy, p. 846

contractionary monetary policy, p. 846

federal funds rate, p. 846

liquidity-preference model, p. 848

Summary

LO 32.1 Describe the three main functions of money.

The three main functions of money are as a store of value, a medium of exchange, and a unit of account. Money derives much of its true importance from its role as a medium of exchange—from the fact that you can use it to purchase the goods and services you desire. Money is also important as a way to register the value of transactions.

LO 32.2 Describe the characteristics that make something a good choice as money and distinguish between commodity-backed and fiat money.

Money needs to have *stability of value* and *be convenient.* Items whose value varies from one day to the next will not be a good store of value, and so are not suitable as money. Money also needs to be widely accepted in order to fulfill its function as a medium of exchange. The earliest forms of paper money could be legally exchanged into a specific amount of a named commodity (generally gold), making it *commodity-backed money.* Since 1971, U.S. money has been *fiat money,* which is money created by rule rather than backed by a commodity.

LO 32.3 Explain the concept of fractional-reserve banking and the money multiplier.

Banks keep on hand a portion of the money deposited, in case depositors want to withdraw money. This money is known as the bank's *reserves,* and the ratio of the original deposit to the amount kept as reserves is the *reserve ratio.* If the reserve ratio were 100 percent (a situation known as *full-reserve banking*), no lending would take place; all deposits would sit in the banks' vaults, and the financial system would grind to a halt. *Fractional-reserve banking* allows a reserve ratio of less than 100 percent, enabling banks to lend a portion of the money that has been deposited. By means of that lending, banks "create" money. The ratio of money created by the lending activities of the banking system to the money created by the government's central bank is the *money multiplier.*

The Fed classifies different types of money by their *liquidity*—by how easy an asset is to convert immediately to cash without losing value. Cash and reserves physically held at the Fed are *hard money,* which can be used in transactions without delay. *M1* includes hard money plus checkable deposits (which are not exactly cash but are fairly readily accessible for most people). *M2* includes everything in M1 as well as things like savings accounts and CDs (certificates of deposit) that are generally harder to access immediately and so slightly less liquid than other forms of money.

LO 32.5 Understand the role of a central bank and discuss the idea of the Federal Reserve's dual mandate.

In any nation, the central bank's duties generally include maintaining the money supply and coordinating the banking system. In the United States, the central bank is known as the Federal Reserve—a system consisting of a Board of Governors and 12 regional banks. It has a dual mandate: to use monetary policy to ensure price stability and maintain full employment. Price stability means maintaining a stable money supply that meets the needs of the economy, while keeping the purchasing power of a dollar relatively constant over time by preventing destabilizing levels of price changes. Full employment can be affected through monetary policy to stimulate or cool aggregate demand.

LO 32.6 Explain the tools the Federal Reserve uses to conduct monetary policy.

The Federal Reserve has three tools to conduct monetary policy. The first is changing the *reserve requirement,* or the regulation that sets the minimum fraction of deposits that banks must hold. It is usually seen as a rather blunt tool—powerful but inappropriate for most day-to-day economic maintenance. The second is the *discount window,* a lending facility run by the Fed that allows any bank to receive cash in exchange for certain noncash assets like government bonds; the interest rate charged for these loans is the *discount rate.* The discount window is one of the Fed's primary tools for providing liquidity to

the markets and acting as a lender of last resort. The final and most-used tool is *open-market operations,* in which the Federal Reserve sells or buys government bonds in the open market. Use of this tool alters bank reserves and influences overall interest rates.

LO 32.7 Understand how monetary policy affects the prevailing interest rate and supply of money.

The *liquidity-preference model* explains that the quantity of money people want to hold (the demand for money) is a function of the interest rate, which the Federal Reserve controls. As the quantity of money supplied changes, the price of that money, reflected in interest rates, will change as well. Increasing the money supply (such as by buying government bonds on the open market) decreases interest rates. Decreasing the money supply (such as by selling government bonds) will increase interest rates.

LO 32.8 Explain how expansionary or contractionary monetary policy influences the broader economy.

Depending on the circumstances, the Fed may want to engage in either expansionary or contractionary monetary policy. *Expansionary monetary policy* involves lowering interest rates; the lower rates increase aggregate demand, helping to expand the economy. This action is generally taken in response to recessionary forces. *Contractionary monetary policy* involves raising interest rates, which shrinks aggregate demand and slows the economy; it generally is taken in response to inflationary forces.

Review Questions

1. Describe how money contributes to economic activity and allows for a more complex society than barter does. **[LO 32.1]**

2. Explain how cigarettes fulfilled the three functions of money in the POW camps during World War II. **[LO 32.1]**

3. Throughout time, metals such as gold have been popular choices for money across various societies. Explain why this might be, using our criteria for what makes good money. **[LO 32.2]**

4. On the Yap Islands in the middle of the Pacific Ocean, giant stone wheels, weighing as much as a small car, were used as currency. What were some of the likely problems with this currency? **[LO 32.2]**

5. Explain why keeping a reserve ratio of zero could be a very bad idea. **[LO 32.3]**

6. If banks keep 100 percent of deposits on hand as reserves, what would this imply about the reserve requirement and the multiplier? What would it imply about banks' ability to create new money? **[LO 32.3]**

7. Explain the role of base money and the money multiplier in the Federal Reserve System's enactment of monetary policy. **[LO 32.4]**

8. Give an example where depositors changing the way they hold assets could increase the M1 measure of the money supply while leaving M2 unchanged. **[LO 32.4]**

9. What is one key way in which the mission of the Federal Reserve differs from the mission of the European Central Bank? **[LO 32.5]**

10. What do we mean when we say that the Federal Reserve System is politically independent, and how might this independence be a good thing for the U.S. economy? **[LO 32.5]**

11. Explain why using changes in reserve requirements to conduct monetary policy is generally not a good idea for the United States. **[LO 32.6]**

12. Which tool of monetary policy is used most frequently by the Federal Reserve System? What makes this tool the best choice in most circumstances? **[LO 32.6]**

13. Are there any differences in the effects of fiscal policy versus monetary policy on aggregate demand in the short-run aggregate demand and supply model? **[LO 32.7]**

14. Describe the slope of the money supply curve in the liquidity-preference model. Are the assumptions behind the supply curve realistic? **[LO 32.7]**

15. Under the liquidity-preference model, how would the slope of the money demand curve affect the power of a central bank to conduct monetary policy? **[LO 32.8]**

16. Use the liquidity-preference model to explain how the Federal Reserve can react to the threat of exceedingly high inflation via monetary policy. Be sure to include the intended effect on the interest rate and quantity of money. **[LO 32.8]**

Problems and Applications

1. Determine whether each of the following would fulfill the three functions of money. If the item does not fulfill all three, name at least one function of money that it violates. **[LO 32.1]**

    a. Salt.

    b. The barter system.

    c. Baseball cards.

2. Imagine you own a lawn-mowing business. Identify the main function of money exhibited in each situation below. **[LO 32.1]**

    a. You swipe your debit card to purchase gasoline for your lawn mower.

    b. You stuff your earnings from mowing lawns into a piggy bank.

    c. You pay your friend Cornelius $5 to help you mow lawns.

    d. You calculate your net earnings for the year on your tax return.

    e. You determine how much value your new lawn mower has added to your business.

3. From 2004 to 2009 the country of Zimbabwe underwent hyperinflation, in which prices rise rapidly. The government began printing bills as large as 100 billion Zimbabwe dollars. Explain how this situation would have affected the characteristics of good money discussed in this chapter. **[LO 32.2]**

4. Suppose you live in a country perfect for growing tulips and governed by King Balthazar, who proposes that you use the tulips for your currency. After all, says Balthazar, they are widely accepted in the community, they've been valuable for years, and they are highly portable. If you were Balthazar's economic advisor, would you recommend using the tulips? If yes, list the traits of good money they satisfy. If no, list the trait(s) of good money they do not satisfy. **[LO 32.2]**

5. You decide to take $300 out of your piggy bank at home and place it in the bank. If the reserve requirement is 5 percent, how much can your $300 increase the amount of money in the economy? **[LO 32.3]**

6. Assume that $1 million is deposited in a bank with a reserve requirement of 15 percent. What is the money supply as a result? What would change if the government decides to raise the reserve requirement to 40 percent? **[LO 32.3]**

7. Say whether each of the following are types of M1 or M2, or both. **[LO 32.4]**

    a. Checkable deposits.

    b. Dollar bills.

    c. Money in your checking account.

    d. Money in your savings account.

    e. Certificates of deposit under $100,000.

    f. Traveler's checks.

8. Which of the following statements are true regarding the differences between M1 and M2? Check all that apply. **[LO 32.4]**

    a. M1 includes cash and reserves, whereas M2 does not.

    b. M2 represents a broader measure of the money supply compared to M1.

    c. Numerically, M1 is larger than M2.

    d. All items in M1 are more liquid than all items in M2.

    e. M2 includes savings deposits, whereas M1 does not.

f. Checking account balances are part of M2 but not M1.

9. The following quotation comes from remarks given by Ben Bernanke, former chairman of the Federal Reserve. The Federal Reserve has a dual mandate. Which mandate does the quote below refer to? **[LO 32.5]**

   > The substantial ongoing slack in the labor market and the relatively slow pace of improvement remain important reasons that the Committee continues to maintain a highly accommodative monetary policy.[8]

10. Look back to the POW camps described at the beginning of this chapter. Who played the role of the central bank? **[LO 32.5]**

11. Which tool of monetary policy is most likely being described by each of the following statements? **[LO 32.6]**

    a. It's the major way the Federal Reserve System enacts monetary policy.

    b. This tool is good for emergency situations that require major, large-scale action.

    c. This tool goes through the Federal Reserve's role as lender of last resort.

    d. This tool is best for everyday monetary policy.

    e. A major disadvantage of this tool is that it requires that banks want to borrow from the Fed.

    f. Even if they aren't interested in buying, selling, or borrowing from the Fed, changes in this tool may inconvenience bank managers.

12. Name the monetary policy tool being used in each of the following examples. **[LO 32.6]**

    a. The central bank buys government securities from banks.

    b. The central bank raises the cost of borrowing money.

    c. The central bank changes the amount of money banks must hold from their depositors.

13. The economy is in recession and the Federal Reserve wants to increase the money supply. Should it increase or decrease the following? **[LO 32.6]**

    a. Reserve requirements.

    b. The discount rate.

    c. Purchases of bonds in the open market.

14. Using Figure 32P-1, answer the following questions. **[LO 32.7]**

    a. Is this economy in recession, just right, or overheating?

    b. What is the correct monetary policy in this situation—expansionary or contractionary?

    c. What is the effect on prices of that policy—will they increase or decrease?

FIGURE 32P-1

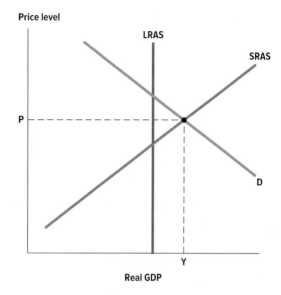

15. What would happen to each of these components of the liquidity-preference model if the Federal Reserve decides to raise the reserve requirement? **[LO 32.8]**

    a. Money supply.

    b. Interest rates.

    c. Quantity of money in the economy.

    d. Money demand curve.

16. For each of the following situations, identify whether the Federal Reserve is likely to pursue an expansionary or a contractionary monetary policy. **[LO 32.8]**

    a. The unemployment rate is at 0.5 percent.

    b. The economy is experiencing record growth in GDP.

    c. The unemployment rate is at 15 percent.

    d. Inflation has reached 10 percent, a recent high.

    e. A hurricane recently demolished a major city, causing a major recession.

Endnotes

1. This wasn't always the case: In the early days of the United States, there was no universal U.S. dollar; banks in each state produced their own currencies. In 1792 the United States started slowly phasing out the competing state currencies in favor of a standard form of money for the entire country. This was a critical decision in U.S. economic history.

2. http://www.jmbullion.com/charts/gold-price.

3. The bank has two reasons to hold reserves. First, the Federal Reserve *requires* the bank to hold a certain percentage

of deposits as reserves. It's simply the law. In the example, the Fed's reserve requirement is 10 percent. The second reason is that banks have to meet customers' needs for *liquidity,* independent of the banks' legal requirements to hold reserves. Sometimes banks find it strategic to hold extra reserves over and above the legal requirement. In the example here, the bank's legal requirement and its own judgment of customers' needs happen to coincide. So, for both reasons, the bank chooses to hold 10 percent of deposits as reserves.

4. In reality, some dollars might get held as cash rather than being deposited, but usually we're safe to ignore those very small amounts relative to the total, especially in the United States and other economies with well-developed banking systems. In some parts of the world today, however, much more money is held outside of banks and that fact would need to be taken into account.

5. Robert F. Bruner and Sean D. Carr, *The Panic of 1907: Lessons Learned from the Market's Perfect Storm* (Hoboken, NJ: John Wiley & Sons, 2007).

6. Binyamin Appelbaum and Jo Craven McGinty, "The Fed's Crisis Lending: A Billion Here, a Thousand There," *The New York Times,* April 1, 2011, p. B1, http://www.nytimes .com/2011/04/01/business/economy/01fed.html.

7. The Fed also buys bonds directly from the public–not just banks. Some of the money from the sales of those bonds gets put into banks as deposits. Those deposits increase the banks' reserves, and we see the same result as we do when the Fed buys the bonds directly from banks.

8. Speech by Chairman Ben S. Bernanke of the Federal Reserve at the New York Economic Club, New York, New York, November 20, 2012 ("The Economic Recovery and Economic Policy"), http://www.federalreserve.gov/newsevents/speech/bernanke20121120a.htm.

Inflation

LO 33.1 Define inflation, deflation, headline inflation, and core inflation.

LO 33.2 Explain the neutrality of money.

LO 33.3 Describe and illustrate the classical theory of inflation.

LO 33.4 Explain the quantity theory of money and relate it to inflation and deflation.

LO 33.5 Analyze the economic consequences of inflation.

LO 33.6 Analyze the economic consequences of deflation.

LO 33.7 Describe disinflation and hyperinflation and explain the role of monetary policy in creating both situations.

LO 33.8 Understand why policy-makers favor a small amount of inflation over zero inflation.

LO 33.9 Explain the relationship between inflation, the output gap, and monetary policy.

LO 33.10 Explain how the relationship between inflation and unemployment is modeled by the Phillips curve and integrated into the non-accelerating inflation rate of unemployment.

A LAND OF OPPORTUNITY . . . AND INFLATION

The story is a familiar one: In the closing years of the 1800s, millions of immigrants sought out the promised land—a country rich in natural resources and with the highest standards of living in the world. These immigrants sought a new life in one of the world's great cities—a modern, cosmopolitan city where the blending of cultures led to vibrancy nearly unrivaled in the world. At its peak, nearly 50 percent of the city's residents were immigrants.

These immigrants were not greeted by the Statue of Liberty. They did not pass through New York's Ellis Island. They didn't set foot in Manhattan or anywhere else in the United States. Instead, they went to Buenos Aires—their promised land was Argentina. From the late 1800s

© Simon Chavez/dpa/Corbis

to the early 1900s, more than 5 million immigrants from across Europe arrived in Argentina, a country with seemingly limitless opportunity. In 1910, Argentina's per capita GDP was relatively high, four-fifths that of the United States.

In the century that followed, though, Argentina lagged behind economically. Its per capita GDP is now less than a third of that in the United States. What caused this divergence in fortunes? You could point to the political instability that led to a series of military coups and populist dictatorships. But dig a little deeper and you will find a common thread that came to define daily life in Argentina: steadily rising prices throughout the economy—in other words, out-of-control *inflation.*

More than almost any other country in the world, Argentina has struggled with rising prices. Over the past 75 years, Argentina experienced three separate *hyperinflations* (extremely long and painful inflationary periods). The worst of these, in the late 1980s and early 1990s, saw inflation peak at over 20,000 percent per year. (In other words, prices were doubling every month or two.) If this were to happen in the United States today, an iPod costing $100 at Christmas would cost $200 in February, $400 in March, and more than $20,000 by the following Christmas.

In between the periods of hyperinflation, Argentina has seen sustained high inflation unlike almost any other country in the world. In fact, the average annual inflation rate over the last 75 years is over 200 percent—a tripling of prices every year! Argentina has brought inflation down to about 25 percent per year recently—which seems modest compared to historical levels, despite being one of the highest inflation rates in the world.[1]

A century ago, Argentina seemed on the cusp of challenging the United States for supremacy in the Americas. Of course, the difference in inflation rates was not the only policy or geographic difference between the United States and Argentina. But it does help explain why that dream is gone. What is so damaging about inflation for a nation's economy? And why do most economists believe that its opposite—deflation—is even worse?

In the chapter on money and the monetary system, we saw how money creation and the supply of money can have an enormous impact on the overall economy, and in particular on interest rates. In this chapter, we will look at the topic of inflation from various angles—theories about changing price levels, inflation in its various forms, and the effects of inflation on monetary policy.

Changing Price Levels

The price level, and especially changes in it, is one of the most important concepts in macroeconomics. The economy is driven by billions of frequently changing prices. Some of these price changes matter for the economy more than others. There are a few key questions economists address: How should we summarize the most important price changes? What causes the price level to change? And how do changes in the price level affect the economy?

Measuring inflation

LO 33.1 Define inflation, deflation, headline inflation, and core inflation.

An overall rise in prices in the economy is called **inflation**. An overall fall in prices in the economy is called **deflation**.

As we saw in Chapter 25, "The Cost of Living," the U.S. government's Bureau of Labor Statistics (BLS) measures overall prices in the economy by creating a consumption basket designed to resemble the purchases of the average urban consumer. This measure of overall prices is called the Consumer Price Index (CPI). Measuring inflation or deflation is done by calculating the percentage change in the CPI ratio of the cost of the market basket to the cost of that basket in a base year. The BLS measures two inflation numbers:

- The measure of inflation that includes *all* of the goods that the average consumer buys is called **headline inflation**. It measures the changes in prices for the entire market basket of the average urban consumer.

- **Core inflation** is a measure of inflation that excludes goods with historically volatile price changes—energy and food. It is the BLS's official measure of changes in prices through the CPI. The reason to calculate core inflation is that changes in price levels due to goods with volatile prices might simply reflect shocks to individual product markets rather than any sort of economywide inflation. In 2015, for example, the price of gasoline dropped 27.3 percent, while core inflation rose by 1.7 percent.[2]

When economists are interested in the underlying rate of inflation in the economy, they often differentiate between headline inflation and core inflation. Figure 33-1 clearly shows how much more stable core inflation (as represented by the core CPI) is than overall or headline inflation (as represented by the CPI). Although headline inflation gives a more complete picture of how changing prices are affecting the average consumer, it's useful to subtract out food and gasoline if we want to get a better feel for underlying economic trends.

inflation
an overall rise in prices in the economy

deflation
an overall fall in prices in the economy

headline inflation
measure of inflation that includes all of the goods that the average consumer buys

core inflation
measure of inflation that excludes goods with historically volatile price changes—energy and food

The neutrality of money

LO 33.2 Explain the neutrality of money.

When we say that the price level changes, what do we mean? To answer the question, it helps to think about what "output" really is. A country's GDP is simply an accounting of all of the purchases and sales that take place over a given period. In each transaction, somebody gives money to somebody else. All output, then, can be tied to the movement of money. But how do we measure that output?

It seems intuitive to measure output in terms of money, but this can become problematic. Imagine that the government were to simply add two zeros to every piece of money (automatically turning $1 into $100 and $100 into $10,000). Prices would jump, and the measured "value of output" in the economy would increase tremendously. But we would know that the real output, the goods and services traded, didn't actually change—only the numbers did. What we want to

FIGURE 33-1

Running annual change in CPI and core CPI, January 2001–January 2016   The figure shows actual annual inflation rates, as represented by CPI (representing headline or overall inflation) and core CPI (representing core inflation). Core inflation is much more stable than headline inflation.

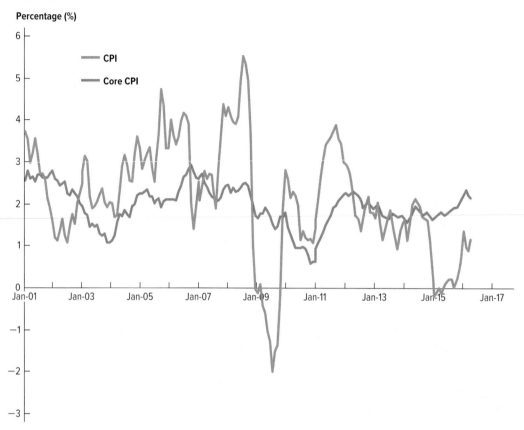

Sources: Federal Reserve Bank of St. Louis, FRED Economic Data: https://research.stlouisfed.org/fred2/series/CPIAUCSL# (CPI data) and https://research.stlouisfed.org/fred2/series/CPILFESL# (core CPI data).

measure is the output in terms of real, tangible goods and services: How many cans of soda or tons of steel were created by the country?

As you may recall from earlier chapters, we use the terms *real* and *nominal* to differentiate the quantity of tangible goods and services from the numbers associated with them:

- We call quantities measured in terms of real, tangible goods and service *real values.* They represent an accounting for the actual amount of something that is produced. That accounting is independent of how many pieces of paper with a certain number of zeros on it you would need to purchase that output.

- In contrast, values measured in terms of how much money it would take to purchase something are called *nominal values.*

We use changes in the *price level* to get from one to the other. In Chapter 25, "The Cost of Living," we described the concept of a *deflator*—the idea of using a price index like the CPI or the GDP deflator to adjust between nominal and real prices. These indexes allow us to convert nominal measures of output into real measures of output. In other words, they let us measure how much real stuff we get for our money. The **aggregate price level** is a measure of the average price level for GDP. In practice, it is measured by either the CPI or the GDP price deflator.

Now, back to the hypothetical: What if the government one day decided to add two zeros to the figure on every new and existing dollar bill (and added two zeroes to every financial

aggregate price level
a measure of the average price level for GDP; in practice, the CPI or GDP price deflator

account)? Doing this would essentially increase the money supply by 100 times. If nothing else changed in the economy, you can predict that a store-owner who previously sold a bottle of water for $1 would raise the price to $100; your $20 haircut would soon cost $2,000. And you would push for a raise from $10 an hour to $1,000 an hour in your job at the library. With that new wage, the change in the price of goods and services really wouldn't make much of a difference.

In this example, the change in the price level (prices and wages being 100 times higher than before) didn't dent your purchasing power because the *real* value of your money hasn't changed. When all prices (including wages) increase proportionately, what you could buy when you made $10 an hour is the same as what you can buy when you make $1,000 an hour. The change in the price level—that is, the change in the unit of measurement used to account for something—changed only *nominal* values, not real values.

This is the basic intuition behind what is called the **neutrality of money**—the idea that, in the long run, changes in the money supply affect nominal variables, such as prices and wages, but do not affect real outcomes in the economy. The underlying mechanism is described in the next section.

neutrality of money
the idea that, in the long run, changes in the money supply affect nominal variables, such as prices and wages, but do not affect real outcomes in the economy

The classical theory of inflation

LO 33.3 Describe and illustrate the classical theory of inflation.

In Chapter 32, "Money and the Monetary System," we touched on the idea that the level of prices in an economy is affected by the quantity of money in an economy. It's time to explain formally how this process happens, using the *classical theory of inflation*. The classical theory of inflation illustrates the relationship between money supply, output (or GDP), and the overall level of prices. It also shows the neutrality of money in the long run.

Figure 33-2 illustrates the basic framework of the classical theory using the now-familiar aggregate supply and aggregate demand perspective. Suppose the economy is in long-run

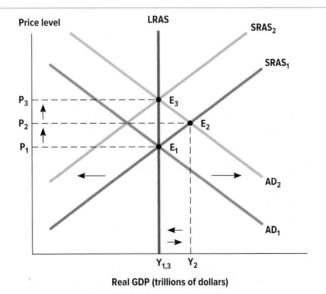

FIGURE 33-2

Increase in the money supply under the classical theory of inflation

According to the classical theory of inflation, in the long run, increases in the money supply will lead to an increase in prices only; output will stay the same. In the short run, output and prices increase as aggregate demand shifts to the right. However, workers then begin to negotiate for a higher wage, which shifts the aggregate supply curve to the left. Output returns to the original level, while prices increase even more.

equilibrium at point E_1 in the figure. Short-run aggregate demand matches short-run aggregate supply, which matches the long-run potential aggregate supply of the economy.

What happens if the Federal Reserve increases the money supply, as in expansionary monetary policy? The increased money supply will result in lower interest rates and higher levels of borrowing; in turn, aggregate demand will increase. As Figure 33-2 shows, aggregate demand shifts right, creating a new temporary equilibrium where the new short-run aggregate demand curve intersects the short-run aggregate supply curve and increasing output (real GDP). The economy is at point E_2.

We know from the idea of the neutrality of money, however, that this situation can't survive for long. Eventually, prices will rise in proportion with the increase in the money supply. In practice, this can take a little bit of time, since prices are relatively *sticky* (slow-moving). (For example, you don't get to renegotiate your wages immediately when prices go up; you have to wait until your contract is up for renewal or the time is right to renegotiate your wage.)

While it might take time for prices to rise, as long as money is neutral we know they will eventually tick upwards. The increase in prices, especially in nominal wages, in turn leads to a leftward shift in the short-run aggregate supply curve. Why? Because the higher input prices of labor and other goods used in production make it more expensive to produce a given level of output.

The economy eventually reaches a new equilibrium, indicated by point E_3 on the figure: Aggregate supply and short-run aggregate demand once again meet at exactly the level of the long-run aggregate supply curve, and real GDP has fallen back to exactly the point at which it started. (This point is often called *potential output,* a concept we'll explore later in the chapter.) In fact, the only difference is that now *the price level is higher*—reflecting the lower value of money due to the increased money supply. In other words, it will now take a higher number of dollars to buy a given good or service. (Again, think back to the effect of more cigarettes in the POW camp in Chapter 32, "Money and the Monetary System.")

The neutrality of money holds in many cases. But in extreme situations, such as the story of Argentina that we discussed in the chapter opener, the neutrality of money does break down. Extreme and sustained inflation can wreak havoc in the economy, leading to slower growth. At a minimum, stores would need to constantly reprice items. When prices change more rapidly, consumers and firms face uncertainty, and the cost of discovering (and updating) information about alternative prices rises.

It's important to emphasize that the classical theory of inflation describes a long-run equilibrium. Some economists have used the eventual neutrality of money to argue that the Federal Reserve can't meaningfully guide the economy through monetary policy. Others cite empirical evidence that suggests that there is considerable scope for the Federal Reserve to affect the economy in the short run through expansionary or contractionary policy. This is one reason our analysis may yield different answers in the short run versus the long run.

The quantity theory of money

quantity theory of money
theory that the value of money (and thus the aggregate price level) is determined by the overall quantity of money in existence (the money supply); it states that changes in the price level (inflation or deflation) are primarily the result of changes in the quantity of money

LO 33.4 Explain the quantity theory of money and relate it to inflation and deflation.

The classical theory of inflation is strongly connected to a related theory: the **quantity theory of money**. The quantity theory of money states explicitly that the value of money (and thus the aggregate price level) is determined by the overall quantity of money in existence (the money supply). Further, it states that changes in the price level (inflation or deflation) are primarily the result of changes in the quantity of money:

- An increase in the money supply leads to an increase in prices (inflation), as there are more dollar bills spent on the same number of goods and services.

- Likewise, a decrease in the money supply leads to a decrease in prices (deflation), as there are just as many goods and services but fewer dollars with which to purchase them.

The quantity theory of money depends on the velocity of money being relatively constant. The **velocity of money**, simply put, is the number of transactions a typical dollar is used in during a given period. If you buy a hamburger, some of the money you spent to purchase it goes to the waitress, another part goes to the cook, and yet another part goes to the rancher who raised the cow; some goes to the dozens of other suppliers who provided everything from the bun to the booth you are sitting in. In other words, your consumption spending is someone else's income, and that person can (and usually does) go on to spend at least part of that income on something else. Intuitively, the velocity of money is a simple concept. If the average dollar is spent five times a year, then the velocity of money for that year would be five.

velocity of money
the number of times the entire money supply turns over in a given period

We can mathematically calculate the velocity of money (V) as equal to the price level (P) multiplied by real output (Y), divided by the money supply (M):

EQUATION 33-1

$$V = \frac{P \times Y}{M}$$

For example, if an economy produces 1,000 units of output (so that Y = 1,000) with a price level of $1 (P = $1) and the money supply (M) is $500, velocity is

$$\frac{\$1 \times 1,000}{\$500} = 2$$

That means that over the course of the year, each dollar in the money supply was spent twice on average in order to generate $1,000 worth of output.

Rearranging Equation 33-1, we can see that the total amount of money in the economy (the money supply, M) multiplied by the number of times that money turns over during the year (the velocity of money, V) must equal the nominal value of output (Y). If we now adjust this formula to incorporate the concept of real output and aggregate price levels, we can see that total money supply multiplied by the velocity of money is equal to the price level times real output. This is the **quantity equation** that underlies the quantity theory of money:

quantity equation
the equation M × V = P × Y, which relates the money supply and velocity of money to the price value of real output

EQUATION 33-2

$$M \times V = P \times Y$$

We've assumed that velocity is relatively constant. But is that true in practice? Figure 33-3 shows information on the velocity of money in the United States through history. As you can see, velocity has been relatively stable historically, though the recent financial crisis temporarily caused some significant changes. This means that real output (Y) will also not change in equilibrium (as long as the production process remains the same as well). Equation 33-2 implies that any increase in M (the money supply) has to eventually lead directly to an increase in P (the aggregate price level). Of course, a decrease in M would result in a decrease in P. In other words, increasing the money supply leads to inflation, and decreasing the money supply leads to deflation.

If the velocity of money were not relatively constant, then the quantity theory of money could not hold. With rapid increases or decreases in the amount of money changing hands in the economy, it would be possible for the money supply to double while people spend their money half as fast. Rather than increasing prices, as we would otherwise expect when the money supply doubles, the amount of money moving around in the economy would stay the same, and prices would stay roughly the same as well. As an example of this, the Fed increased the size of the monetary base quite substantially in an attempt to stimulate the economy following the 2007–2009 recession. If the velocity of money had not declined during this period (as shown in Figure 33-3), the result would have been far more inflation than was actually observed.

An implication of this theory is that deflation occurs if the money supply remains constant but real output increases. Logically, the effect is the same as if real output stayed constant and the money supply declined. As we saw in Chapter 32, "Money and the Monetary System," this relationship between output and the money supply is one of the main arguments against the gold standard. Barring a sudden discovery of gold, the supply of gold-backed money is

FIGURE 33-3

Velocity of M1 in the United States   For much of the early part of this graph, the velocity of money, reflected by the amount of money spent compared to nominal GDP, slowly heats up. After oscillating between six and eight times GDP in the 80s and early 90s, money velocity increases to over 10 times GDP at the height of the housing boom. The speed of money through the economy then slowed in the recession.

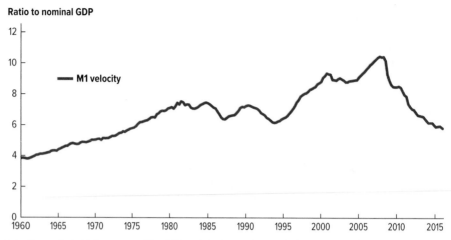

Source: Federal Reserve Bank of St. Louis, accessed from FRED economic data, August 2012, http://research.stlouisfed.org/fred2/.

relatively fixed. If M is constant, when the economy expands (that is, when Y increases), then either the velocity of money must go up or the price level must go down (or a combination of these two events will occur). And if velocity is relatively constant, then there is only one option: The price level must fall, a situation known as *deflation*. We will see in more detail later in this chapter why deflation can be extremely damaging to an economy.

The Where's George? website brings to life the idea of velocity. The site allows users to enter the serial number of a dollar bill and see where it has been (assuming other holders of that dollar have entered the bill). See the Real Life box "Where's George?" for more.

Real Life

Where's George?

Have you ever looked at a crumpled dollar bill and wondered where that piece of paper had been before it got to you? You might even have noticed a stamp on a dollar bill leading you to the Where's George? website (www.wheresgeorge.com). Now that you know more about how money works, you might find it interesting to see what happens there: Users track the adventures of millions of bills as they travel through the economy. Tracking those travels captures what economists mean when they talk about velocity.

The website works like this: Users input the serial number found at the corner of any U.S. bill. If the bill has already been entered on the site, you can see where the bill has been and how long it took for it to get around. If you are the first person to enter the serial number, the bill becomes part of the database that will record the story of that bill.

Statistics from the site can give a pretty interesting picture of who holds money in the United States. Overall, more than 263 million unique Georges have been added. The most bills are entered in California, New York, and Florida. This is not too surprising as these states are within the top five in total population.

The individual stories can also tell a lot about how money moves through the economy. The site records such statistics as the distance the bills traveled between being recorded in the site, which is also converted into a miles per day figure. Most bills travel about five miles per day on average.

One of the more intrepid Georges visited 14 cities in a 7,686-mile, four-year jaunt around the country that took it from the fast-food chain Whataburger in Tallahassee, Florida, to Aiken, South Carolina, via flashy Times Square and the hip streets of Portland, Oregon.

Most trips are far more mundane: 57 percent of the bills on the site travel only between 30 and 500 miles in the course of nine months. The website depends on users to add bills, and it has captured only a sliver of the 11.4 billion dollar bills in circulation. Still, the site reminds us that those crumpled dollars in your pocket might have already had some interesting adventures.

Sources: http://www.wheresgeorge.com/; https://www.federalreserve.gov/paymentsystems/coin_currcircvolume.htm.

Other causes of changing price levels

We've looked at how the quantity theory of money explains changes in price levels: Over the long term, any increase or decrease in the money supply—assuming that velocity and real output are held constant—will result in an increase or decrease in the price level. In addition, changes in the price level can also be created in a more temporary fashion by (1) the actions of the business cycle or (2) sudden supply shocks to a key resource in production.

We've actually discussed the changes in the price level resulting from the action of the business cycle many times before, in other chapters. Recall what happens in the aggregate supply and demand framework:

- When an economy goes through a boom, companies look to expand rapidly to meet rising demand and competition for scarce resources heats up. It becomes harder to find workers, leading employers to bid against each other for the best talent, increasing wages. This demand pulls prices higher, as too much money is spent chasing too few goods. This is *demand-pull inflation.*

- Of course, the opposite is also true. When economic activity is slow, fewer dollars are spent on the same amount of goods, pushing prices downward. This kind of demand-related deflation is relatively rare.

These two effects combine to create a rise in price levels during the boom periods and, potentially, a fall in price levels during busts. We'll explore the relationship between inflation and the business cycle, and in particular unemployment, in more detail a bit later.

The other type of change in price levels occurs when the price of any key input increases suddenly. Known as *cost-push inflation,* the rising cost causes firms to increase prices in order to maintain profits. A serious bout of cost-push inflation occurred in the mid-1970s in the United States when OPEC, the organization that controls most of the world's supply of oil, decided to cut the amount of oil they produced. Oil in its many forms is absolutely essential not only to the production of gasoline but also to many other goods, from corn to plastics. The shortage caused an increase in the price of oil, and the increase in the price of oil increased the prices of goods throughout the economy.

✓CONCEPT CHECK

- ☐ What is included in headline inflation that is left out of core inflation? **[LO 33.1]**
- ☐ Do changes in the aggregate price level change overall real output? **[LO 33.2]**
- ☐ According to the classical theory of inflation, will inflation increase or decrease if the Federal Reserve pursues expansionary monetary policy? **[LO 33.3]**
- ☐ What is the velocity of money? **[LO 33.4]**

Why Do We Care about Changing Price Levels?

At this point you may find yourself wondering why changes in the price level matter. After all, we've seen from the theory of money neutrality that the economy should adjust itself to different levels of nominal prices, leaving no change in overall output. So why be concerned about price levels?

As we'll see in this section, while the price level itself is immaterial, *changes* in the price level can have a big effect on economic behavior. We'll also see why many economists believe a modest and predictable level of inflation is a good thing, but high or unpredictable levels of inflation—and any level of deflation—are economically damaging.

Inflation

LO 33.5 Analyze the economic consequences of inflation.

We've defined inflation as an overall rise in prices (an increase in the aggregate price level). If the average price level rises 10 percent every year (that is, the prices of all the things in the economy go up by an average of 10 percent), we say that the economy is experiencing an inflation rate of 10 percent per year. The four panels of Figure 33-4 show inflation rates around the world in 1980, 1990, 2000, and 2010. Note that over the last four decades, the inflation rate has generally decreased.

Despite the generally decreasing inflation rate in the past four decades, inflation is always a threat. That makes it important to understand the costs of predictable inflation and the problems of unpredictable inflation.

FIGURE 33-4a

Inflation around the world (1980)*

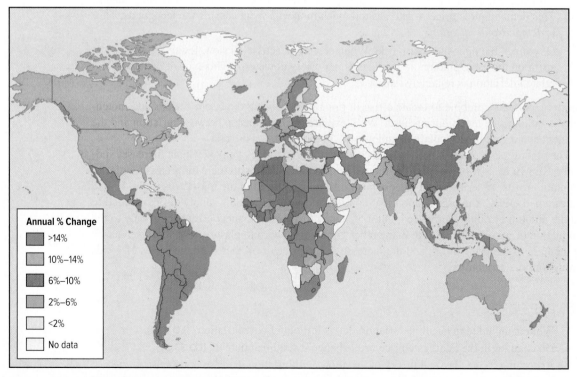

Annual % Change
>14%
10%–14%
6%–10%
2%–6%
<2%
No data

*National boundaries were slightly different in 1980, 1990, and 2000.

Source: World Bank World Development Indicators, 2012, http://data.worldbank.org/data-catalog/world-development-indicators.

FIGURE 33-4b

Inflation around the world (1990)*

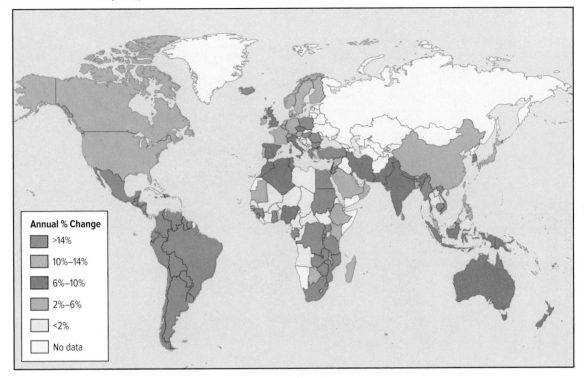

Annual % Change

- >14%
- 10%–14%
- 6%–10%
- 2%–6%
- <2%
- No data

FIGURE 33-4c

Inflation around the world (2000)*

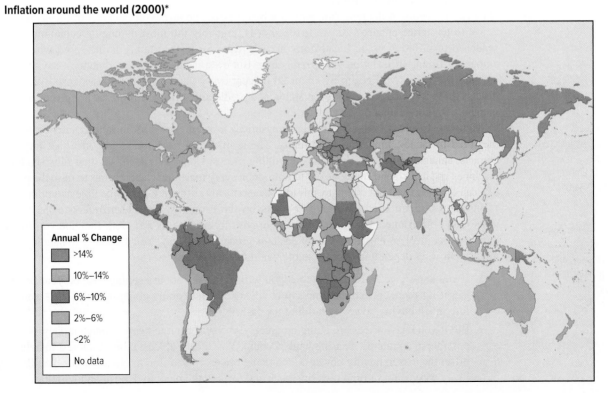

Annual % Change

- >14%
- 10%–14%
- 6%–10%
- 2%–6%
- <2%
- No data

FIGURE 33-4d

Inflation around the world (2010)

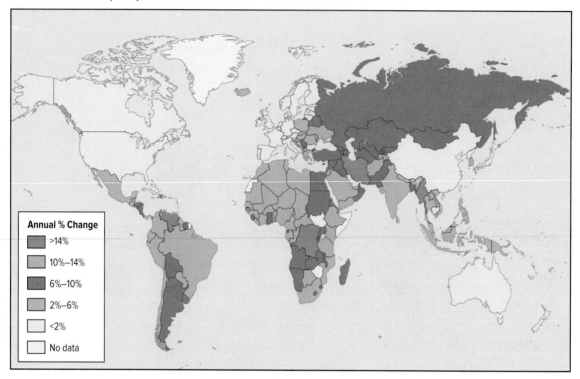

Annual % Change
- >14%
- 10%–14%
- 6%–10%
- 2%–6%
- <2%
- No data

Costs of predictable inflation

If money is neutral in the long run, why is it bad if prices go up? Won't the rest of the economy adjust to any price change? As we'll see shortly, arguably the most damaging economic consequence of inflation is the *uncertainty* it can create. Such uncertainty is increased when the amount or timing of inflation is *unpredictable*. But even if inflation is predictable—say, if you are sure that prices will go up by about 20 percent every year—it still imposes costs. We will discuss three types of costs that even stable and predictable inflation imposes on the economy: menu costs, shoe-leather costs, and tax distortions.

menu costs
the costs (measured in money, time, and opportunity) of changing prices to keep pace with inflation

Menu costs refer to the costs of changing prices to keep pace with inflation. Such costs are measured in money, time, and opportunity. The term comes from the simple idea that for restaurants, changing prices likely means reprinting menus. Consider a company that runs vending machines and has to send someone out to reprogram every machine when it wants to raise the price of a can of soda. Even if a company has to update only a website, it takes some time and effort.

shoe-leather costs
the costs (measured in time, money, and effort) of managing cash in the face of inflation

Inflation also imposes **shoe-leather costs** on the economy. That term refers to the time, money, and effort one has to spend *managing cash* in the face of inflation. Imagine you run a business that involves handling a lot of cash—a grocery store, say. You are likely to handle cash in different ways depending on how stable you think prices are:

- If you know prices are fairly stable, you will be relaxed about keeping cash on your premises if it's more convenient (and safe) to do so. If prices aren't going up much, you won't lose much buying power by holding the cash.

- But if you know prices are going up quickly, you will want to keep as much money as possible in an interest-bearing bank account. You'll earn at least a bit of interest to help offset the loss in buying power due to rising prices. In addition to other hassles, you'll likely waste a lot of time traveling back and forth to the bank to deposit and withdraw cash—wearing out your shoe leather, hence the name. (And even though with online banking your actual shoes may not wear so thin, the time you spend transferring assets from one form to another could be spent in more profitable—and enjoyable—ways.)

The third type of cost that inflation imposes on the economy is *tax distortion* (also sometimes called *bracket creep*). This one is a bit more subtle than menu costs and shoe-leather costs but can be costly all the same. Tax distortions happen because tax laws take into consideration only nominal income—not what you can buy with it. It's easiest to show the consequences with an example. Let's assume that those who earn less than $60,000 a year pay a 10 percent tax on their entire income, and those who earn $60,000 or more pay a 15 percent tax on their entire income. If a family earns $50,000 a year, they pay $5,000 in tax to the government. But imagine that inflation is 20 percent per year and the family's income adjusts to exactly keep up with inflation. They now earn $60,000, but their purchasing power is unchanged. All the same, they now have to pay a 15 percent tax rate since they just entered the higher tax bracket. Their bill to the government has now increased to $9,000, and thus the tax system is essentially penalizing the family for inflation.

In theory, the government can adjust tax brackets for inflation. In practice this doesn't always happen. In the United States, the *alternative minimum tax* (AMT) is an example of a tax that often is subject to bracket creep. The AMT was designed to impose taxes on only very wealthy individuals. But because the cutoffs were not adjusted for inflation, millions of Americans who were not super-rich were eventually hit by the tax. In 2013, Congress created new rules that automatically adjust the AMT cutoffs for inflation.

Problems of unpredictable inflation

We've just considered three costs that occur even when inflation is stable and predictable. It turns out that even worse problems arise when inflation is *not* predictable.

In many businesses, the profit margin (the difference between the cost of producing a product and the amount it can be sold for) is less than 10 percent. If the company can't be sure whether the prices of the inputs used to make its product will go up by 5 percent, 10 percent, or 20 percent over the next year, planning becomes tough. Businesses become hesitant to invest in new ideas and to hire workers.

Uncertainty also lies behind a more complex "cost" of inflation, which occurs because changing prices affect interest rates. Here, there can be a redistributive effect, effectively transferring money either from savers to borrowers, or vice versa. To see how this happens, it might help to review the difference between *nominal* and *real* interest rates:

- The **nominal interest rate** is the everyday notion of the interest rate. It is the reported interest rate, not adjusted for the effects of inflation. For example, the percentage that the bank pays you for saving (or, if you're borrowing, the percentage that you pay the lender) is the nominal interest rate. Examples of the nominal interest rate can be found in the financial pages of a newspaper such as *The Wall Street Journal* or the *New York Times* or in a loan contract.

- The **real interest rate** is the interest rate adjusted for the anticipated effects of inflation. As we know, inflation means that each dollar becomes less valuable over time.

nominal interest rate
the reported interest rate, not adjusted for the effects of inflation

real interest rate
the interest rate adjusted for the effects of inflation

Since investors do not know, however, the exact inflation rate that will prevail over the duration of the transaction, they need to adjust nominal interest rates for the *expected* rate of inflation. When you're deciding how much to save, then, you need to look at two things that work in opposite directions:

- How interest will add to the value of your savings.
- How inflation will erode the purchasing power of each dollar in your savings account.

To know which effect is dominant—that is, whether the real value of your money will increase or decrease over time—you can calculate the real interest rate by subtracting the expected inflation rate from the nominal interest rate. Since both rates are typically stated as an annual percentage of the base level, the formula for calculating the real interest rate is simple:

EQUATION 33-3   Real.interest rate = Nominal interest rate − Expected inflation rate

To see how important the difference between the nominal and real interest rates can be, look at Table 33-1. It shows an example of the same savings account with two different inflation rates. Suppose that in 2010 you had deposited $1,000 into an account with a nominal annual interest rate of 4 percent, keeping it there for five years. Here's what would happen with varying rates of inflation:

- If there is no inflation, then your real return is equal to the nominal interest rate. In that case you would end up with $1,217 in both 2015 dollars and 2010 dollars.
- If inflation runs at 3 percent per year over the five years, your real interest rate is only 1 percent (4% nominal interest rate − 3% inflation rate). Then, in 2015, you will still have $1,217 in 2015 dollars, but they are worth only $1,051 in 2010 dollars.
- If inflation is 5 percent per year, then your money actually loses value. The real interest rate is −1 percent (4% nominal interest rate − 5% inflation rate). You again end up with $1,217 at the end of the five-year period in 2015 dollars, but in this case it's worth only $951 in 2010 dollars.

Of course, the reverse situation applies to *borrowers.* Suppose you borrowed $1,000 in 2010 and agreed to pay it back at a rate of 4 percent interest. High inflation is now your friend: If inflation turns out to be 5 percent, then the real value of what you end up paying back is less than the amount you borrowed. That is good news for you!

In other words, when the inflation rate is higher than nominal interest rates (when *real* interest rates are negative), the value of both savings and debts decreases:

- Savers become worse off, as the value of what they have put in the bank becomes less valuable over time.
- Conversely, borrowers gain from inflation since inflation reduces the value of dollars; a loan made today will have a smaller value in real terms later. This debt will be easier to repay as its real value decreases.

Effectively, we can say that *high inflation redistributes wealth from those who save to those who borrow.* (We should note, however, that borrowers may eventually suffer if savers/lenders stop making loans entirely because of these losses.)

If inflation is predictable, then this redistributive effect need not happen. Even if inflation is high—say, 20 percent—savers will not lose out as long as banks offer nominal interest rates above 20 percent. However, changes in the inflation rate often come as a surprise, and it can take time for nominal interest rates to adjust. (Storekeepers cannot immediately change all prices, nor can employers immediately change wages.). And as we discussed earlier, there are other costs of inflation that apply even when its timing and amount are predictable.

TABLE 33-1

Real and nominal interest rates

Without inflation, the real and nominal interest rates are the same, so the interest rate you see is what you actually get. With inflation, the real interest you are earning is less than the nominal rate; if inflation is greater than the nominal interest rate, the investment actually becomes worth less in real value than the original investment.

Value in 2010 ($)	Nominal interest rate (%)	Inflation rate (%)	Real interest rate (%)	Nominal 2015 value ($)	Value in 2015 (2010 dollars)
1,000	4	0	4	1,217	1,217
1,000	4	3	1	1,217	1,051
1,000	4	5	−1	1,217	951

These same ideas about the economic consequences of inflation apply to governments that have taken on debt and need to repay it. The only difference is that a government can control inflation, at least to some degree, through monetary policy. A government may thus be tempted to slowly "inflate away" the amount of debt it owes. The pros and cons of such a strategy are discussed in the Real Life box "Inflating away the debt."

Real Life

Inflating away the debt

Picture this: You're the president of a country in an economic bind. Tax revenues are down. The prospect of economic growth is bleak. You face a growing government debt.

What do you do? You could cut government spending or raise taxes, but both of these options are destined to make you unpopular. Fortunately, your chief economic advisor has an idea: "Just print money! That can solve your debt problems," he says. "Printing more money would increase prices, and this increase in inflation would reduce the real value of the debt that is carried by the government."

Zimbabwe used this scheme when it found itself owing more money to foreigners and government employees than it could easily afford. To get out of the bind, the regime headed by Robert Mugabe decided to start printing Zimbabwean dollars. In 2006, the government printed 21 trillion Zimbabwean dollars (roughly $210 million U.S.) to pay off loans, and another 60 trillion (or $600 million U.S.) to pay civil servants.

Did the strategy work? In a sense, yes. The government's debts, denominated in Zimbabwean dollars, soon became almost worthless as inflation predictably spiraled out of control. Inflation in Zimbabwe reached an incredible *11 million percent* in 2008! However, such high levels of inflation caused utter chaos that crippled the Zimbabwean economy, leading to an unemployment rate of more than 80 percent.

Inflating away the debt is not always such a recipe for disaster. On a more modest scale, this strategy can have some success. In the 1940s, for example, the United States emerged from World War II with a debt-to-GDP ratio of 108.6 percent. In other words, all of the country's production for slightly more than a year would be needed to get rid of that amount of debt. According to economists Joshua Aizenman and Nancy Marion, thanks to inflation—which reached 14.4 percent in 1947—that ratio was cut by more than a third within a decade. In the meantime, the economy, buoyed by postwar economic activity, posted strong gains.

Even when the economy stays strong, inflation is not an ideal solution. Debt represents a promise made to lenders, and they stand to lose money if the government decides to print its way out of debt. In the end, nobody is going to want to lend money to a government that has a track record of inflating away its debts. Economist Alan Auerbach calculates that with the way debt is designed, inflation could wipe away only $5.4 trillion of the roughly $53 trillion budget shortfall projected for the United States over the next 75 years.

Still, it's easy to see the attraction of the idea: If you could simply print money to reduce the real value of your personal debts, wouldn't you be just a little bit tempted?

Sources: http://allafrica.com/stories/200602170023.html; http://economix.blogs.nytimes.com/2010/02/18/inflation-wont-solve-our-debt-problems/; http://www.nber.org/papers/w15562.

Deflation

LO 33.6 Analyze the economic consequences of deflation.

Inflation has a natural opposite: deflation. *Deflation* is an overall fall in prices (a decrease in the aggregate price level)—negative inflation, essentially. Periods of deflation occur far less often than inflation, and they generally occur in only the very worst economic circumstances. Deflation characterized the Great Depression of the 1930s, when aggregate prices in the United States fell by nearly half in a few years. More recently, Japan experienced a so-called lost decade of deflation in the 1990s, which continues to pose challenges for its economy.

Why is deflation such a problem? For one thing, it increases the burden of debt. As we saw in the discussion of the problems of unpredictable inflation, most loans are made in nominal terms: If you borrow $100 at an annual interest rate of 5 percent for one year, you will owe $105 at the end of the year. If the price level has gone down due to deflation, the *real* value of that $105 will be even higher. Since paying back loans eats up a greater part of what you can buy in real terms, consumption will decrease.

Of course, the flip-side is that if you are a saver in deflationary times, your savings will be worth more in real terms. In that case, won't savers spend more, given that deflation causes their savings to increase in value? Probably not. If people *expect* deflation, they will likely want to spend less. It's easy to see why: Suppose you expect prices to be 10 percent lower in a few months than they are now. Will you buy that new car now or wait a few months? The expectation that prices will fall explains at least in part why deflation can cripple an economy. In addition, companies that expect deflation to continue will be less willing to borrow money to invest. They expect the money they borrow will be worth more in real terms when they have to pay it back.

With consumption and investment both down, the net result of expected deflation is to *reduce the level of aggregate demand* in the economy. This, in turn, reduces prices, causing deflation to continue. This self-reinforcing cycle is referred to as a *deflationary spiral,* or deflationary trap.

As we saw in Chapter 32, "Money and the Monetary System," the risk of deflation is an argument against tying a currency to gold. Indeed, the pain caused by deflation was a major populist issue at end of the nineteenth century in America. Under the gold standard, prices were decreasing at the rate of 1 to 2 percent per year. This decrease consistently expanded the debts of borrowers, who were mostly poor farmers. At the 1896 Democratic Party convention, William Jennings Bryan railed against the power of the gold standard to the advantage of savers at the expense of borrowers, in what is now known as the "Cross of Gold" speech. He ended by saying, "You shall not press down upon the brow of labor this crown of thorns, you shall not crucify mankind upon a cross of gold."

Bryan instead advocated for returning to a bimetallic standard, in which silver and gold were both used as money. That change would have resulted in a substantial increase in the money supply and overall prices. This increase would have enabled farmers and workers to be able to pay off their debt more easily. In the end, Bryan's opponent, William McKinley, won the election and formally entrenched the gold standard as official policy of the United States in 1900.

Controlling inflation, or not: Disinflation and hyperinflation

> **LO 33.7** Describe disinflation and hyperinflation and explain the role of monetary policy in creating both situations.

Controlling inflation is a critical role of the Federal Reserve in managing the money supply, part of its dual mandate. When central banks succeed at controlling inflation, *disinflation* occurs. When central banks fail to control runaway inflation, *hyperinflation* occurs. Here, we look at both situations.

Disinflation

disinflation
a period in which inflation rates are falling, but still positive

Let's say the Federal Reserve wants to reduce inflation from 7 percent to 2 percent. If it succeeds, the result is **disinflation**, the term for a period during which overall inflation rates, while still positive, are falling. (Be sure not to get this concept confused with *deflation,* in which inflation rates are negative.) In general, disinflation is usually discussed in the context of the central bank (the Fed in the United States) aggressively trying to contain inflation via contractionary monetary policy.

In the United States, the Federal Reserve famously applied disinflationary tactics to slow the increase in prices experienced as a result of the OPEC oil embargo in the 1970s, when inflation hit about 10 percent per year. There were campaigns to avoid shopping at high-priced shops. A troop of Girl Scouts in Kansas hit the news when they pledged to fight inflation by keeping the price of their cookies the same as it had been two years before. Such efforts made little progress in reducing the ballooning inflation rate—until President Jimmy Carter appointed Paul Volcker as chairman of the Federal Reserve in 1979.

In a direct reversal of his predecessor's policies, Volcker advocated for "shock therapy" to gain control over the double-digit inflation. He bumped the official federal funds rate from 10 percent to 20 percent. Unsurprisingly, because the economywide rise in interest rates made it very expensive to borrow money, this increase in interest rates plunged the economy deep into recession. In protest, a group of farmers drove tractors onto C Street, in the heart of Washington, DC, and blockaded the main entrances of the Federal Reserve building. However, the shock therapy eventually worked. Inflation fell from 10.4 percent in 1981 to below 5 percent in 1983 and has stayed low ever since. Volcker's bold vision caused short-run pain, but it fixed the inflation problem in the long run.

Economists differ over how high inflation has to be before it becomes enough of a problem to merit such painful measures. Some countries have successfully coped with very high inflation (as much as 30 or 40 percent a year) for long periods of time without too much adverse effect on their economy. This is a high-risk situation, though: At such a high rate, inflation is extremely unstable, and it doesn't take much for an economy to slip further toward higher and higher inflation rates.

Hyperinflation

When inflation begins to spiral out of control, we say that a country is experiencing **hyperinflation**—extremely long-lasting and painful increases in the price level. Such increases are usually enough to render the currency completely valueless or close to it. This happened pretty quickly in Zimbabwe after the Mugabe regime started printing money to inflate away their debts in 2006.

In one of his first major involvements in public policy, John Maynard Keynes attended the meetings at Versailles that formally ended World War I. During these negotiations, Germany demanded, over the objection of Keynes, extensive reparation payments. Keynes left the Versailles meetings and returned to England to write *The Economic Consequences of the Peace* (1919). This popular work argued that the Versailles treaty demanded more in reparation payments from Germany than the German economy was capable of producing. Keynes predicted that it could lead to political and economic instability and the possibility of hyperinflation in Germany. Keynes's predictions materialized. While this was not the first or most severe hyperinflation experienced in Europe, it had far-reaching consequences: The resultant political and economic instability helped lead to the collapse of the Weimar Republic and the rise of Nazi Germany.

The worst hyperinflation ever recorded happened in Hungary in 1946. With the economy in ruins after World War II, and tax revenues covering only 15 percent of expenditures, the government began to print money to finance the gap. In January 1946, there were 16,500,000 *pengos* in circulation. By July 1946, there were 1,730,000,000,000,000,000. Prices were doubling approximately every 15 hours. Clearly, this situation was not sustainable. In August 1946

hyperinflation
extremely long-lasting and painful increases in the price level

Imagine the complications of hyperinflation in daily life. This Zimbabwean man, at the height of the country's hyperinflation, is carrying enough money to buy some milk.
© Tsvangirayi Mukwazhi/ AP Images

To try to keep up with inflation, the Zimbabwean government kept printing bills in bigger denominations. Here is a 100-trillion dollar note—not enough to buy a gallon of milk.
© Finnbarr Webster/Alamy

the government abandoned the *pengo* and introduced a new currency, the *forint,* which is still in circulation today. By backing the new currency with gold, the government instilled confidence that it would not print huge amounts of forints.

Expectations can also perpetuate hyperinflation. In Brazil during the 1990s, prices rose in part because everyone simply expected them to keep rising. The increase was slowed only by an unorthodox plan that included an entirely fake currency. The story can be found in the Real Life box "A *real* plan—with fake currency."

Real Life

A *real* plan—with fake currency

In 1993, President Itamar Franco of Brazil appointed Fernando Henrique Cardoso to be the country's fourth finance minister within seven months. As the rate of turnover suggests, it was not an enviable job. Price levels in Brazil had been steadily rising for seven years, and the inflation rate was approaching 2,000 percent per year. If he wanted to keep his job, Cardoso had to tackle the hyperinflation quickly. No one had high hopes for his success, though. Cardoso was a professor of sociology, with little training in economics. Furthermore, years of failed efforts had convinced Brazilians that the hyperinflation was invincible to government efforts.

Cardoso sought help from an academic economist named Edmar Bacha, who had been debating with colleagues about how to tame Brazil's stubbornly high inflation. Observing that the traditional tactics used to fight inflation—freezes on prices and wages—had been unsuccessful, they proposed an elegant, if slightly unorthodox solution: Brazil would create a system of fake money, called "units of real value," or URVs for short.

The plan, dubbed *Plano Real* in Portuguese or "Real Plan," worked as follows: Cardoso required everyone in the economy—grocery stores, the government, retail outlets, and all other businesses—to quote prices in both *cruzeiros* (the Brazilian currency at the time) and URVs. Even contracts with promises for future payment had to quote the payment in URVs as well as *cruzeiros.* People would pay in *cruzeiros* but would always see the price in URVs as well.

Changing conversion rates would ensure that the URV price remained stable: If prices doubled, the conversion rate between *cruzeiros* and URVs would halve, so that prices in URVs would remain the same. The price shown on a pint of milk might increase from 1,000 *cruzeiros* to 2,000 *cruzeiros,* but the price in URVs shown alongside would remain the same.

How could this simple accounting trick possibly help to get inflation under control? The genius of the idea is that it tackled what economists call the *psychological inertia* of hyperinflation. As inflation rises and rises, and all government efforts visibly fail to reduce it, people simply get used to the idea that things can only get worse. Businesses raise prices merely because they expect that prices will keep rising. When enough businesses do this, it becomes a self-fulfilling prophecy. A vicious cycle ensues.

The *Plano Real* broke this cycle. Since prices in URVs were stable, people began to trust that they would *stay* stable. Once trust in the stability of URVs developed, the government simply traded out the untrustworthy *cruzeiros* for a new currency called the *real,* which is still in use today. The government explained that one *real* was worth one URV. Convinced through experience that URV prices were stable, people expected *real* prices to be stable as well. And because they *expected* prices to be stable, they were—relatively speaking, at least. In the first few years after the *real* was introduced, inflation fell to under 20 percent.

And what of Fernando Henrique Cardoso, whose job prospects as finance minister originally seemed so uncertain? A grateful nation promptly elected him president.

Sources: http://www.econ.puc-rio.br/gfranco/rptpd.pdf; http://uk.reuters.com/article/2011/07/02/uk-brazil-president-idUKTRE76119A20110702.

Why a little inflation is good

LO 33.8 Understand why policy-makers favor a small amount of inflation over zero inflation.

If deflation is bad and inflation is bad, then central banks must try to achieve perfect price stability with an inflation rate of zero, right? Wrong. In fact, for most central banks around the world, the preferred monetary policy is to promote modest positive inflation—something around 2 or 3 percent per year. Why do most economists believe it's better to aim for modest inflation than completely stable prices? There are three main reasons for this belief, which we discuss here.

The first reason to favor modest inflation over completely stable prices is that allowing for a little inflation reduces the risk of deflation. If the inflation rate tends to hover around zero percent, and the central bank miscalculates by making monetary policy too contractionary, the result would be deflation—which can have serious impacts on the economy. Keeping inflation at a modest positive level gives a central bank some leeway to make mistakes, without running the risk of tipping the country into a deflationary spiral.

Second, keeping inflation at a modest positive level leaves more room for the central bank to engage in expansionary monetary policy. To understand why, we can work through a simple example. Suppose that inflation is at a healthy 3 percent per year. Investors are going to want an interest rate that is at or above the inflation rate to ensure that the real rate of return they earn on their money is positive. For monetary policy, this means that the overall interest rate will likely end up somewhere at or above 3 percent. This gives the Federal Reserve some room to reduce interest rates before hitting the zero lower bound.

By contrast, if inflation was zero percent, nominal interest rates would be close to zero as well. In the case of a recession, a central bank would have very little leeway to further reduce interest rates in an effort to stimulate the economy. (This situation is sometimes referred to as a *liquidity trap*. It has been a major problem in Japan for more than a decade.)

In fact, during the latest financial crisis, Olivier Blanchard, the former chief economist of the International Monetary Fund (IMF), advised central banks to increase their inflation target from the traditional 2 percent to 4 percent. That extra room, he argued, could mean the difference between effectively fighting a deep recession and hitting the zero lower bound while the economy could still use some help from monetary policy.[3]

A third reason for having a positive inflation target is that the target makes it easier for firms to adjust real wages in the labor market in response to changing labor demand and supply conditions. Reductions in labor demand or labor supply result in reductions in the equilibrium real wage. If prices are stable, reducing the real wage requires employers to reduce the nominal wage; workers may respond to a 1 percent reduction in their nominal pay by reducing their work effort. But workers generally seem less bothered if they receive a 2 percent wage increase when there is 3 percent inflation. The effect is the same—a 1 percent reduction in income—but the cause of the reduced income seems different.

Furthermore, in cases in which there is a formal labor contract, nominal wages cannot be reduced during the life of the contract. With a low inflation rate, though, all that is required for firms to lower real wages is to increase nominal wages more slowly than the inflation rate. Thus, a low and stable inflation rate may help to "grease the wheels" of the labor market, allowing for more flexible real wages and more efficient labor markets.

✓CONCEPT CHECK

☐ Why would people at the highest income level not worry about bracket creep? **[LO 33.5]**

☐ Why do people spend less in the present when deflation is expected in the future? **[LO 33.6]**

☐ What is a reduction in the overall rate of inflation known as? **[LO 33.7]**

☐ Why would lenders favor unexpected deflation, while borrowers favor unexpected inflation? **[LO 33.7]**

☐ Why does the "zero lower bound" cause problems for macroeconomic policy? **[LO 33.8]**

Inflation and Monetary Policy

We've discussed the Federal Reserve's dual mandate in conducting monetary policy: maintaining price stability and ensuring full employment. Maintaining price stability is, of course, another way of saying that inflation rates should be consistently low. Ensuring full employment simply means that the economy experiences only frictional and structural unemployment and no cyclical unemployment.

The competing goals of the dual mandate

LO 33.9 Explain the relationship between inflation, the output gap, and monetary policy.

In practice, the goals of the dual mandate are often incompatible. To understand why, it helps to think about how inflation rates change through a typical business cycle. During a recession, inflation is typically very low. Why is that? During a bust, the economy is operating well below its potential. Economists refer to an economy's **potential output** as the total amount of output the country could reasonably produce if all of its people and capital resources (i.e., machines and factories and the like) were fully engaged. In practice, this means that only frictional and structural unemployment—no cyclical unemployment—occur.

potential output
the total amount of output a country could produce if all of its resources were fully engaged

output gap
the difference between actual and potential output in an economy

The output gap and inflation

When an economy's actual output differs from its potential output at some point in time, we say that it is experiencing an **output gap**. An output gap can be negative or positive:

- If output is below potential, then the output gap is *negative.* Resources—either factories or workers—are not being fully used. Workers are unemployed and factories are sitting idle, waiting for work.

- It is also possible for an economy to operate above capacity—with factories and workers not only fully employed but also working overtime. When an economy is working above capacity, we say that it has a *positive* output gap.

Figure 33-5 shows the historical output gap for the United States. For the most part, actual output has been below potential output (a negative output gap).

FIGURE 33-5

The output gap in the United States   The output gap registers the difference between the actual GDP and the potential GDP at full employment. For the most part, actual output has stayed below potential output.

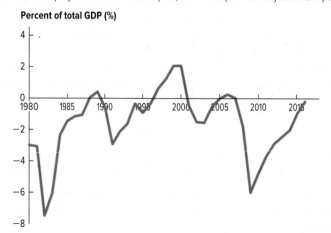

Percent of total GDP (%)

Source: IMF World Economic Outlook database, http://data.okfn.org/data/core/imf-weo#data.

What is going on when an economy has a negative output gap? As we've said, a lot of resources are not being fully used. Workers are unemployed and factories are sitting idle. In other words, the economy is experiencing recessionary conditions. During recessionary periods, there is typically little threat of a rise in inflation (unless the economy is hit by an oil crisis or similar external shock). Low rates of inflation occur in part because there is so little demand for money in an economy experiencing recession: Borrowers, for example, are much less interested in taking out loans for big-ticket items during a recession since they are less confident in their ability to pay back the loans. Firms have little incentive to borrow in an effort to expand their businesses when overall demand for goods and services is low. Why produce if you don't assume there will be buyers for the output you make? As long as the supply of money stays the same, decreased demand causes the overall price level to fall.

But what happens when the economy is experiencing a positive output gap? With nearly everyone employed (and working overtime), hiring new workers can become very expensive. Employers have to compete for workers, who can eventually command higher salaries to switch jobs. Likewise, companies are competing to buy machines, factories, or other inputs to meet soaring demand for their products. That competition leads to a rise in the prices of those inputs as well. Rising prices across the economy, of course, mean inflation.

The output gap and monetary policy

As you can see, there is typically a strong relationship between the output gap and inflation. But what does this have to do with monetary policy? To answer that question, we'll have to go back to what happens when the Fed conducts monetary policy.

We'll start with *expansionary monetary policy.* In a recession, an output gap implies that employment is low. A central bank knows that it can fix this problem by engaging in expansionary monetary policy: It increases the money supply and lowers interest rates. As a result, borrowing may increase, which may then help the economy rebound. An increase in economic activity puts more people back to work, which fulfills the mandate: Prices have increased only a little bit, and employment is high.

But as you know, this is only a short-run equilibrium. The increased demand for goods and services will put upward pressure on prices. With an increase in the money supply, more money will be spent chasing the same amount of goods. The economy will eventually fall back to the long-run equilibrium. Employment will decrease, but prices will remain elevated. So what does a central bank do? It could continue to pump money into the economy in an effort to increase employment, but these gains will be short lived and inflation will worsen.

The opposite scenario occurs when inflation is above normal. When inflation is pulled high by demand, money in the economy is spent chasing a limited amount of goods. Firms want to buy machines and inputs in an effort to expand operations, while workers receive higher wages. In this case, employment is at full, or even beyond full, capacity. If a central bank decides that it needs to curb inflation, it will pursue *contractionary monetary policy:* It will reduce the growth rate of the money supply, to work toward a higher interest rate. As we described earlier, this action slows the economy. The higher interest rate makes borrowing more expensive, and firms slow investment. Although inflation decreases, the slowing of the economy increases unemployment. Eventually, though, as the economy adjusts to lower prices and we move into the long run, employment will return to full-output levels, leaving just the decrease in overall prices.

So, you can see that central banks, no matter how they conduct monetary policy, inevitably *affect only price levels,* with no lasting impact on employment in the long run:

- Attempts to stimulate the economy through expansionary monetary policy will increase the inflation rate.
- Attempts to slow the economy through contractionary policy will lower the inflation rate, and risk causing deflation.

The Federal Reserve has to navigate this trade-off carefully.

Inflation and unemployment

> **LO 33.10** Explain how the relationship between inflation and unemployment is modeled by the Phillips curve and integrated into the non-accelerating inflation rate of unemployment.

We've seen that there is a trade-off between inflation and unemployment in the short run, which poses a challenge for the Federal Reserve's dual mandate. Ensuring full employment is really another way of saying "keeping actual output near potential output." Fulfilling this mandate through expansionary monetary policy, however, risks violating the Fed's other mandate, that of price stability. How can the Fed calculate the best way to make this trade-off?

The Phillips curve

In 1958, an economist named A. W. Phillips plotted the change in prices against unemployment over a 95-year period in Great Britain. A distinct pattern emerged:

- As inflation ran higher, unemployment was low.
- When inflation was low, unemployment was high.

Phillips curve
a model that shows the connection between inflation and unemployment in the short run

The line showing that relationship is now called the **Phillips curve**, and it forms the basis of a model that shows the connection between inflation and unemployment in the short run.

Figure 33-6 shows the most basic form of the Phillips curve. The curve, based on hypothetical data, shows that if the central bank of this economy wants zero inflation, then it will have to accept 7 percent unemployment. If it wants to target a modest positive rate of inflation of, for example, 3 percent, then it will have to accept 4 percent unemployment. If it wants to get unemployment down as low as 1 percent, it will have to accept a rate of inflation of 6 percent. And so on.

This simple formulation fits our intuition about how the output gap—and, by extension, unemployment—relates to inflation. In general:

- High amounts of unemployment in an economy will coincide with low inflation.
- Higher amounts of inflation come with lower unemployment.

We can now further investigate this relationship using the aggregate demand and aggregate supply model in the short run, as shown in panels A and B of Figure 33-7. If the economy is

---

FIGURE 33-6

Hypothetical short-run Phillips curve for an economy

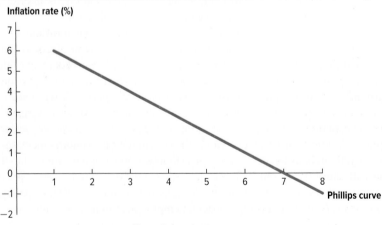

The short-run Phillips curve shows a direct relationship between the inflation rate and the unemployment rate. In an economy that is humming along, prices will increase at a faster rate, although unemployment will be low. As the unemployment rate increases, prices increase far more slowly.

FIGURE 33-7

Aggregate demand and the Phillips curve in the short run

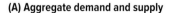

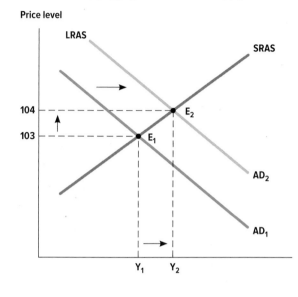

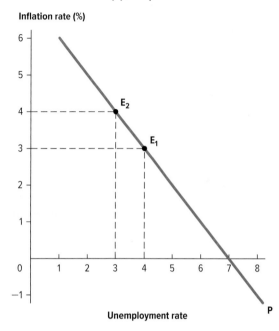

Panel A shows the result of two different aggregate demand curves. E_1 shows a short-run equilibrium with lower prices and output than point E_2 on a higher aggregate demand curve.

With more economic activity, point E_2 on the Phillips curve shows higher inflation and lower unemployment than point E_1, which represents the short-run equilibrium with lower economic activity.

at short-run equilibrium with 4 percent unemployment and 3 percent inflation, an increase in aggregate demand above expectations is going to cause the economy to be at a point higher and to the left on the Phillips curve.

However, this basic curve fails to consider an important factor: the role of *inflation expectations*. In any economy, people often come to expect whatever level of inflation has prevailed over the past few years. If inflation has been about 3 percent over the past few years, then the expectation of 3 percent inflation typically becomes "baked into" prices. If prices are rising by 3 percent per year, employees will expect raises of at least 3 percent as a matter of course, and 3 percent inflation becomes sort of a "default" for the economy.

Why does this matter? Let's assume that the economy represented in Figure 33-5 is humming along at a *long-run equilibrium* of 4 percent unemployment and 3 percent inflation. Now imagine that the central bank decides to try to reduce unemployment, accepting a slightly higher inflation rate as a result: By expanding the money supply, unemployment falls to 1 percent and inflation increases to 6 percent.

So far, the central bank has achieved the results it hoped for. However, we know that the economy was in long-run equilibrium at 4 percent unemployment. And we know from Figure 33-1, earlier in the chapter, what happens if a central bank pursues expansionary monetary policy when the economy is already at long-run equilibrium: It can increase output (and, hence, reduce unemployment), but *only in the short run*. In the long run, output returns to its earlier equilibrium, and so do levels of employment.

Our hypothetical central bank finds that unemployment is now back at 4 percent, but inflation is now running at 6 percent. Effectively, by pursuing expansionary monetary policy when the

FIGURE 33-8

The Phillips curve responds to inflation expectations

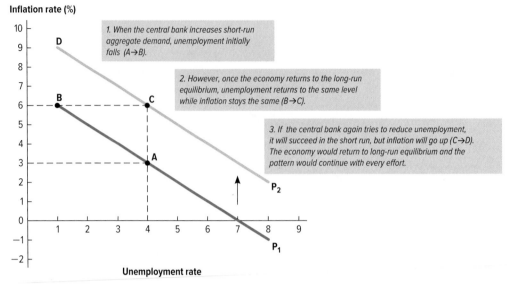

With preset expectations in the economy, the Phillips curve shifts upward by the amount of expected inflation. This means that the amount of inflation at any given amount of unemployment rises in the long run by the amount of expected inflation.

economy was already at long-run equilibrium, it has shifted the Phillips curve upward, as shown in Figure 33-8.

People in our hypothetical economy now *expect* inflation of 6 percent. What happens if the central bank, stubbornly, has another go at reducing unemployment to 1 percent? It will succeed in the short run, but as we can see from the new Phillips curve, inflation will go up to 9 percent (see point D). And in the long run, unemployment will rise again to 4 percent, but inflation will remain stubbornly at 9 percent because people will have adjusted their inflation expectations upward once again. Eventually, the central bank's efforts would simply spiral out of control, leading to more and more inflation and the unemployment rate never staying at the bank's goal in the long run.

Realizing this effect, economists proposed an improved version of the Phillips curve—one that also shows the long-run effect of changing inflation expectations. We'll now call the traditional Phillips curve the *short-run* Phillips curve. The new, improved version we call the *long-run* Phillips curve. Figure 33-9 shows both the short-run Phillips curve and the long-run Phillips curve for two different levels of inflation expectations. The two short-run Phillips curves in the figure tell us the trade-off facing monetary policy-makers between inflation and unemployment at any given time. The vertical line in the figure is the long-run Phillips curve, which is at 4 percent. This line represents the idea that in the long run in our hypothetical economy, it is impossible to get the level of unemployment below 4 percent.

To see why, we'll run through a story that we've told many times before: Let's say the economy is at 4 percent unemployment and the economy expands. In order to expand, firms need more workers, but with such a low unemployment rate, few workers are just sitting around looking for work. As a result, trying to hire more workers is going to be expensive. Wages—the price of labor—are prices, after all. With higher wages resulting from the increase in demand for labor, prices throughout the economy will increase. In Figure 33-9, the vertical line marks the lowest possible unemployment rate that will not cause the inflation rate to increase. Economists call this minimum level of unemployment the **non-accelerating inflation rate of unemployment (NAIRU)**. The NAIRU is sometimes also called the *natural rate of unemployment* or simply *full employment* (even though it's not technically 0 percent unemployment).

non-accelerating inflation rate of unemployment (NAIRU)
the lowest possible unemployment rate that will not cause the inflation rate to increase

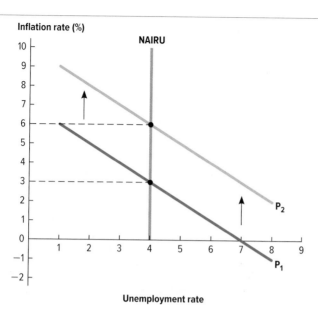

FIGURE 33-9

The long-run Phillips curve

The long-run Phillips curve represents the fact that there is no trade-off between inflation and unemployment in the long run.

The NAIRU can change over time. Take, for example, the introduction of the Internet to job searches. This innovation reduced structural unemployment (and the NAIRU) on two fronts:

- It increased opportunities available to searchers. Before the availability of sites like monster.com and indeed.com (which allow you to search millions of job listings), job hunters had to scour local classifieds and attend job fairs. They essentially confined their searches to opportunities within a very narrow geographical range. With the Internet, that range has been greatly expanded.

- The Internet has also been a boon to employers. Today, a job posting on the Internet will be seen by more job seekers and bring forward a wider pool of high-quality applicants.

Both job seekers and employers have a wider range of opportunities, with an attendant reduction in the NAIRU.

In practice, calculating the exact NAIRU is difficult. It differs among economies and over time due to variations in the structural components of unemployment, the regulatory and competitive environment, and a multitude of other factors. As a result, it can be difficult to know whether an economy is truly at full employment at any given time—which is a challenge for Federal Reserve policy-makers looking to fulfill their dual mandate. Though we may not know the *exact* location of the NAIRU, we can fairly quickly determine if we are above or below it, though:

- If unemployment is below the NAIRU, inflation generally accelerates.

- If we observe involuntary unemployment rising, unemployment is above the NAIRU.

The Phillips curve and NAIRU in practice

To understand how the NAIRU and Phillips curve work in practice, we'll return to the story from earlier in the chapter of monetary policy after the OPEC oil embargo. When the oil embargo hit, the aggregate supply curve shifted sharply to the left. At that short-run equilibrium, prices were higher and output lower. Obviously, this combination was not desirable for policy-makers; it meant either permitting high rates of inflation, in order to keep unemployment in check, or slowing the economy even further in order to rein in inflation.

FIGURE 33-10

The Phillips curve winds upward

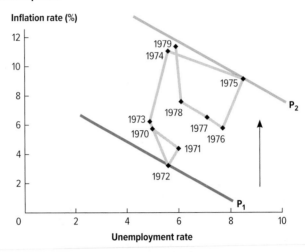

When the Fed tried to battle unemployment by allowing higher inflation, it eventually found that it had simply put the economy on a higher Phillips curve (P_2), as shown above.

During the 1970s, the Federal Reserve chose the first path. The Fed thought that unemployment was a greater danger to the economy than was inflation. The Fed even expanded the money supply to try to pick up the economy after the supply shock. As time wore on, inflation pushed higher and higher, but unemployment stayed relatively the same. You now know why: The economy had shifted to a higher Phillips curve. Since inflation was *expected* in the economy, further attempts to boost the economy simply pushed the trade-off between inflation and unemployment even higher.

By the end of the 1970s, inflation was running at double digits, with high unemployment. Figure 33-10 shows this adjustment upward toward higher Phillips curves, from an inflation rate of about 4 percent in the early 1970s to the double-digit rate by 1979.

When Paul Volcker became Fed chairman in 1979, he realized that shock therapy was needed to wean the economy off the expectation that inflation would continue to increase at relatively high rates. He employed the traditional tool used to fight inflation—Volcker decreased the money supply through increases in interest rates.

This blunt policy worked. Since people knew that the Fed was going to take a tough stand on inflation, expectations for price increases in the future evaporated. In just five years, the overall economy was in a position with a far more favorable trade-off between inflation and unemployment. In Figure 33-11 you can see the change in Phillips curves over this time period, resulting from a decrease in the inflation rate of about 14 percent in 1980 to a much tamer rate of about 4 percent in 1985.

The Phillips curve remains an essential tool for understanding how the Fed's dual mandate works in practice. Effectively, fulfillment of the mandate for full employment means ensuring that employment remains as close to the NAIRU as possible at all times. Pushing unemployment below that level all but guarantees that inflation will get out of control, violating the dual mandate by failing to maintain price stability. On the other hand, allowing unemployment to remain at a higher level than NAIRU would mean failing to maintain full employment, also violating the dual mandate.

The Fed's aim, then, is to keep unemployment levels near the NAIRU and inflation reasonably under control. As the story of the oil embargo shows, managing this trade-off is no easy task.[4]

Inflation rate (%)

FIGURE 33-11
The Phillips curve adjusts downward

When Paul Volcker became Fed chairman, inflation was running above 12 percent. In the early 1980s, he led an effort to raise interest rates, thereby decreasing the money supply and bringing down inflation. By 1985, the economy was on a lower Phillips curve (P_3).

✓CONCEPT CHECK

☐ What does it mean for the output gap to be positive? What will eventually happen if that occurs? **[LO 33.9]**

☐ What happens if unemployment is lower than the NAIRU? **[LO 33.10]**

Conclusion

In this chapter we've explored one of the most complex issues in economics: inflation. We've seen how mismanagement of the money supply can lead to runaway inflation, how even relatively modest inflation can have far-reaching consequences for healthy economies, and why deflation is a problem. We've also seen that expectations of inflation help determine whether savings will hold their value and whether it's a good time to borrow.

We've seen too that when people expect inflation to continue, those beliefs can, in themselves, perpetuate inflation. Thus, inflation can be a self-fulfilling prophecy. Getting runaway inflation under control thus requires the right monetary policy plus convincing people that inflation will indeed fall.

Key Terms

inflation, p. 861

deflation, p. 861

headline inflation, p. 861

core inflation, p. 861

aggregate price level, p. 862

neutrality of money, p. 863

quantity theory of money, p. 864

velocity of money, p. 865

quantity equation, p. 865

menu costs, p. 870

shoe-leather costs, p. 870

nominal interest rate, p. 871

real interest rate, p. 871

disinflation, p. 874

hyperinflation, p. 875

potential output, p. 878

output gap, p. 878

Phillips curve, p. 880

non-accelerating inflation rate of unemployment (NAIRU), p. 882

Summary

LO 33.1 Define inflation, deflation, headline inflation, and core inflation.

Inflation is an overall rise in prices in the economy. *Deflation* is an overall fall in prices in the economy. Economists measure inflation or deflation by calculating the percentage change in the CPI. This is the ratio of the cost of the market basket in a given year to the cost of that same basket in a base year. Two different measures of inflation are used: *Headline inflation* is the measure of inflation that includes all of the goods that the average consumer buys, while *core inflation* is the measure of inflation that excludes goods with historically volatile price changes (energy and food). The BLS's official measure uses core inflation because it is less likely to reflect shocks to individual product markets and more likely to show economywide inflation.

LO 33.2 Explain the neutrality of money.

Prices denote the nominal value of goods; the price level reflects prices when aggregated across the economy. The neutrality of money suggests that the money supply affects price levels throughout the economy, but in the long run has no effect on real variables in the economy, such as output. The neutrality of money implies that if the money supply suddenly doubled, nominal GDP would double as well, but real GDP would remain the same.

LO 33.3 Describe and illustrate the classical theory of inflation.

The classical theory of inflation describes the relationship between the money supply, output, and the price level. The theory argues that the money supply has no effect on output in the long run. However, it shows how adjusting the money supply can change output in the short run. If the Federal Reserve adopts expansionary policy, it could increase the money supply, shifting the aggregate demand curve to the right and causing output and prices to increase. The effect on the cost of production and anticipation that these high prices will continue causes the aggregate supply curve to shift leftward until it intersects the demand curve at the original level of output.

LO 33.4 Explain the quantity theory of money and relate it to inflation and deflation.

The quantity theory of money shows the relationship between the value of money in terms of the output we can buy and the quantity of it. Mathematically, the quantity theory of money indicates that the product of the velocity of money and the money supply (total spending) is identical to the product of the price level and real output (nominal GDP).

Changes in the quantity of money affect the price level. An increase in the money supply leads to inflation; a decrease in the money supply leads to deflation.

LO 33.5 Analyze the economic consequences of inflation.

Inflation is an increase in the price level in an economy. Over the long run, inflation is often caused by increases in the money supply. In the short run, it is more often a result of the business cycle. If inflation rates are unstable, they introduce uncertainty into the market, often causing a decline in output. Even a stable rate of inflation can impose costs on the economy, including menu costs and bracket creep.

LO 33.6 Analyze the economic consequences of deflation.

In contrast to inflation, deflation is a fall in the price level of an economy. Deflation is considered more dangerous than inflation. When prices are falling, borrowers have a more difficult time paying back their debts; deflation makes the debt more expensive over time, often causing borrowers to default. High default rates, in turn, lower prices, causing further defaults. A deflationary spiral often ensues, halting the economy.

LO 33.7 Describe disinflation and hyperinflation and explain the role of monetary policy in creating both situations.

When central banks succeed at controlling inflation, disinflation often occurs. Disinflation happens when inflation rates are positive but falling. A famous example of disinflation was Paul Volcker's efforts to stem inflation in the 1980s. When central banks fail to control inflation, hyperinflation can occur. Hyperinflation is an extreme rise in price levels. It can cause economic crisis and drastically reduce the value of a country's currency.

LO 33.8 Understand why policy-makers favor a small amount of inflation over zero inflation.

Although you might think that central banks want to achieve perfect price stability with an inflation rate of zero, most central banks around the world actually prefer modest positive inflation of around 2 or 3 percent per year. There are a few reasons for this. For starters, a little inflation reduces the risk of deflation, giving the central bank some leeway in case their monetary policy is too contractionary. Second, keeping inflation at a modest positive level leaves more room for the central bank to engage in expansionary monetary policy. Finally, positive inflation makes it easier for firms to adjust real wages in response to changing labor demand and supply conditions.

> **LO 33.9** Explain the relationship between inflation, the output gap, and monetary policy.

The central bank uses monetary policy to control inflation. Central banks prefer to keep inflation low but positive. When full employment occurs, the economy is said to be producing at its potential output, the total amount of output a country can produce if its resources are used efficiently. The output gap is the difference between potential and actual output. When the output gap is negative, inflation will decrease. Central banks will then pursue expansionary monetary policy by lowering interest rates, allowing inflation to rise and bringing back full employment. When the output gap is positive, inflation will increase.

> **LO 33.10** Explain how the relationship between inflation and unemployment is modeled by the Phillips curve and integrated into the non-accelerating inflation rate of unemployment.

This relationship between employment and inflation in the short run is modeled by the Phillips curve. The curve shows that a decrease in unemployment will be accompanied by an increase in inflation in the short run. The relationship does not hold over the long run, in part because of inflation expectations. If central banks pursue aggressive expansionary policy to reduce unemployment, inflation may spiral out of control. The level of unemployment at which inflation will remain stable is called the non-accelerating inflation rate of unemployment (NAIRU), or full employment.

Review Questions

1. What is the difference between the Consumer Price Index and the inflation rate? **[LO 33.1]**

2. What is the difference between core inflation and headline inflation? Why do economists calculate both types of inflation? **[LO 33.1]**

3. Your uncle comes to you with an investment idea. He tells you that the nominal GDP of Paradisia quadrupled over the past year and suggests that you invest there. Unemployment is at 20 percent, and inflation over the last year was 500 percent. Do you think it's a good idea

to invest? Draw on the neutrality theory of money to explain why or why not. **[LO 33.2]**

4. Why might we want to measure GDP in dollar terms? In output terms? How does the neutrality of money relate to your answer? **[LO 33.2]**

5. Suppose a country's currency is a gold coin. One day, speculators find a large gold mine, which doubles the supply of gold coins in the economy. What will happen to output in the short run? What about price levels? What will happen to output in the long run? What about price levels? **[LO 33.3]**

6. Explain how some analysts might use the short-run and long-run effects on the aggregate demand–aggregate supply model to argue that monetary policy can't affect employment in the long run. **[LO 33.3]**

7. Why might the velocity of money increase around the holidays? If the Federal Reserve wants to avoid inflation in those times, what should it do? **[LO 33.4]**

8. Use the quantity theory of money to explain how expansionary monetary policy can be inflationary. **[LO 33.4]**

9. Imagine you own an ice cream store in New York City. Write a brief note to your senators explaining two ways in which unpredictable inflation hurts your business. **[LO 33.5]**

10. Is inflation harmful only when it's unexpected? If yes, why? If no, name two costs that occur with even predictable inflation. **[LO 33.5]**

11. Your senators now claim that lowering prices would be good for everyone—"Who doesn't like lower prices, after all?" They tell you they plan to lobby for deflation. Explain why falling prices could lead to a bad situation. **[LO 33.6]**

12. When does inflation become hyperinflation? What causes hyperinflation? **[LO 33.6]**

13. What could have happened to prices and inflation in the years during and after the 2007–2009 recession if the government and the Federal Reserve had not intervened in the economy? How would this have affected the economy? **[LO 33.7]**

14. Are deflation and disinflation the same thing? Why or why not? **[LO 33.7]**

15. Would you expect nominal interest rates to be higher in countries that have higher target inflation rates? Why or why not? **[LO 33.8]**

16. Your friend claims that a target inflation rate of zero is a good policy because this will keep prices stable. You claim a positive target inflation rate is preferred because the country will be able to better avoid a liquidity trap. Who is right? **[LO 33.8]**

17. In the 1960s, policy based on the simple short-run Phillips curve worked better than similar attempts in the 1970s. How might better information availability have contributed to this result? **[LO 33.9]**

18. When we have a negative output gap, what is the proper monetary policy response in the short run? What are its intended effects on interest rates and employment? **[LO 33.9]**

19. Explain the effect contractionary monetary policy will have on the output gap, inflation, and unemployment if unemployment is currently at the non-accelerating inflation rate of unemployment. **[LO 33.10]**

20. Compare and contrast the effect of increased unemployment on inflation in the short and long run. **[LO 33.10]**

Problems and Applications

1. The price index values used to calculate headline and core inflation for 2012 through 2016 are found in Table 33P-1. **[LO 33.1]**

    a. Calculate the annual inflation rate for each series.

    b. Which series represents core inflation and which represents headline inflation? How do you know?

    c. Is there inflation or deflation in each year?

2. Determine whether each of the following events is likely to cause deflation, disinflation, no change in the price level, or inflation. **[LO 33.1]**

    a. A bubble in the biomedical industry just burst.

    b. A new technology is introduced into the economy, sparking an economic boom.

    c. The Federal Reserve conducts contractionary monetary policy.

    d. The Federal Reserve is successful at meeting its dual mandate of full employment and price stability.

TABLE 33P-1

Year	Series 1	Series 2
2012	132.00	122.00
2013	136.22	124.56
2014	138.26	126.68
2015	143.24	129.72
2016	144.81	131.79

3. Which of the following can be affected by the money supply in the long run? **[LO 33.2]**

    a. Nominal GDP.

    b. Real GDP.

    c. Inflation.

    d. Unemployment.

4. The average individual in a country earns an annual salary of $60,000, of which $24,000 is spent on housing, $10,800 on food, $10,800 on transportation, and $14,400 on other goods and services. Suppose the government in this country mandates that all salaries and the prices of all goods and services be reduced by 40 percent. **[LO 33.2]**

    a. How much does the average individual now earn?

    b. How much does the average individual now spend on housing, food, transportation, and other goods and services?

    c. What happened to the average individual's real salary?

5. To increase the self-esteem of dieters everywhere, powerful fashion designers lobby Congress to redefine "five pounds" as "one pound." Under this system, what would have previously been five pounds of bananas will now be one pound of bananas and a 500-pound gorilla would now weigh only 100 pounds. **[LO 33.3]**

    a. How much would someone who originally weighed 180 pounds now weigh as a result of this redefinition?

    b. Has there been a nominal change in the person's weight? A real change?

    c. How is this story similar to contractionary monetary policy via a decrease in the money supply in the long run? (*Hint:* Congress essentially shrunk the "pounds supply" by redefining the word.)

6. "Monetary policy is incredible," your friend says. "Just a little manipulation of the money supply and interest rates, and we end up at just the right price level and amount of output." Is your friend overstating the Fed's control over price levels and output? Why or why not? **[LO 33.3]**

7. Your dormitory Griffingate has appointed you central banker of its economy, which deals in the currency of wizcoins. Assume that the velocity of wizcoins in Griffingate is constant at 10,000 transactions per year. Right now, real GDP is 1,000 wizcoins and there are 2,000 wizcoins in existence. **[LO 33.4]**

    a. What will be the value of each of the variables that make up the quantity equation—M, V, and P?

    b. Now indicate how the other variables will respond to each of the following scenarios, taking each case separately and assuming that velocity remains constant.

    i. *Real GDP:* You increase the money supply to 4,000, and prices increase twofold.

    ii. *Price level:* Start with the initial values. Real GDP drops to 500 wizcoins, and the money supply remains constant.

    iii. *Real GDP:* Start with the initial values. Prices increase threefold because of a sudden scarcity of soda, and you decide to keep the supply of wizcoins constant.

    iv. *Real GDP:* Start with the initial values. You increase the money supply to 5,000 wizcoins, and prices rise by 350 percent.

8. Express the following relationships using the equation for the quantity theory of money. **[LO 33.4]**

    a. The money supply is given by nominal GDP divided by the velocity of money.

    b. The relationship of the money supply to the price level is the same as the relationship between real GDP and velocity. (*Hint:* Start by dividing the money supply by the price level.)

    c. Real GDP is given by the flow of money divided by the price level.

    d. The price level of an economy can be found by dividing the product of the money supply and its velocity by real GDP.

9. Identify whether the following individuals will be affected by bracket creep next year given the rates of taxation and levels of inflation found in Table 33P-2. **[LO 33.5]**

    a. Gabriela makes $9,500, and inflation is at 5 percent.

    b. Cooper makes $160,000, and inflation is at a record high of 20 percent.

    c. Shawna makes $140,000, and inflation is at 8 percent.

TABLE 33P-2

Marginal tax rate (%)	Income level ($)
10	0–10,000
15	10,001–30,000
18	30,001–50,000
20	50,001–100,000
23	100,001–150,000
25	150,001 and up

    d. Samuel makes $45,000, and inflation is at 6 percent.

    e. Marguerite makes $96,000, and inflation is at 6 percent.

10. Cookie Monster has decided to channel his love of cookies into a new business, "Me Want Cookies Inc.," a new partnership he has formed with Miss Piggy. They are considering different countries in which to start their venture and would like to rank the countries based on the inflationary environment. They decide to give a country 10 "menu-cost" points for each percent of actual inflation in the last year since inflation will cause their menu costs to increase. They also dislike unstable inflation, so they will give a country 20 "uncertainty" points for each percent difference in the actual inflation rate when compared to the projected inflation rate. Countries with the least total points will receive the highest rankings. Complete Table 33P-3 for Cookie Monster. **[LO 33.5]**

11. Jack recently took out a loan from Diane at an interest rate of 5 percent. Diane expected this year's inflation rate to be 2 percent and the real interest rate to be 3 percent. The loan is due at the end of this year. Complete

TABLE 33P-3

Country	Projected inflation (%)	Actual inflation (%)	Uncertainty points	Menu-cost points	Total points	Rank
Kermikopia	2	4				
Gonzoland	4	5				
Elmostan	7	8				
Oscaria	10	13				
Bertico	14	14				

TABLE 33P-4

This year's actual inflation rate (%)	Actual real interest rate (%)	Who benefits?
1		
4		
0		
−2		

TABLE 33P-6

	Year	Inflation rate (%)	Description
a.	1900	90	
b.	1901	80	
c.	1902	120	
d.	1903	40	
e.	1904	−2	

Table 33P-4, showing the real interest rate for each possible inflation rate. For each situation, determine whether the unexpected inflation level benefits Jack or Diane. **[LO 33.5]**

12. Assume the prices shown in Table 33P-5 are the prices of Big Macs in 2030, 2031, and 2032 and that changes in the price of Big Macs tend to closely keep up with inflation. For each of the four instances, determine the following. **[LO 33.6, 33.7]**

   a. The percentage changes in price levels between each consecutive year.

   b. Whether the economy was experiencing inflation, deflation, disinflation, or hyperinflation over each period. (Assume that inflation above 100 percent constitutes hyperinflation.)

13. Assuming that inflation above 100 percent is hyperinflation, categorize each of the inflation rates in Table 33P-6 as deflation, disinflation, inflation, or hyperinflation as we move from one year to the next. **[LO 33.6, 33.7]**

14. Suppose you live in Frigidia, a country near the North Pole that is experiencing hyperinflation. You work for a U.S. company that pays you a monthly income of $100 U.S. Today, you can exchange those dollars for frigids, the currency of Frigidia, at a rate of 1,000 frigids/dollar. You pay a monthly heating bill that costs

$10 U.S. Instead of paying the heating bill, you could simply burn Frigidia notes (which you can obtain in one-frigid denominations) at a rate of 1 million per month to supply heating. What would the exchange rate between frigids and U.S. dollars have to be for you to decide to burn bills instead of paying for heating? What level of inflation does this represent, assuming the real exchange rate remains the same? **[LO 33.7]**

15. "The problem wasn't having the wrong idea about interest rates," a sheepish central bank official says at a conference, "but rather not having the right idea about inflation rates." What does the official mean? How does the inflation rate affect the central bank's interest rate target, and how can a wrong prediction about inflation make monetary policy go awry? **[LO 33.7]**

16. In which scenario is monetary policy likely to be more effective? Explain. **[LO 33.8]**

   Scenario A—The inflation rate in the country has hovered close to zero for the last three years.

   Scenario B—The inflation rate in the country has averaged 3 percent for the last three years.

17. Consider a country that has experienced a decline in labor demand that results in a 2 percent reduction in the equilibrium real wage. **[LO 33.8]**

   a. If the inflation rate in the country has been at zero percent, what has to happen to the nominal wage to restore labor market equilibrium?

   b. If the inflation rate in the country has been at 4 percent, what has to happen to the nominal wage to restore labor market equilibrium?

   c. Do you think workers and employers would prefer to have a zero percent inflation rate or a 4 percent inflation rate in this case? Explain.

18. Determine whether the Federal Reserve would pursue contractionary monetary policy, expansionary monetary policy, or no change in policy in each of the following situations. **[LO 33.9]**

TABLE 33P-5

	Price in 2030 ($)	Price in 2031 ($)	Price in 2032 ($)
a.	1.00	1.02	1.03
b.	1.00	0.99	0.97
c.	0.01	0.05	1.00
d.	1.00	1.10	1.15

a. Inflation is 10 percent, above its average of 3 percent in the last several years.

b. The output gap is positive.

c. Unemployment is at a record high.

d. The economy is experiencing full employment.

e. The economy is on the brink of deflation.

f. A new technology causes output to surge.

19. Answer each of the following questions assuming the economy is experiencing a positive output gap. **[LO 33.9]**

a. Is inflation decreasing, increasing, or stable?

b. Is actual output greater than or less than potential output?

c. Is unemployment rising or falling?

d. Is the Federal Reserve more likely to pursue expansionary or contractionary monetary policy?

e. Is the economy likely experiencing an expansion or contraction?

20. Answer each of the following questions assuming the economy is experiencing a negative output gap. **[LO 33.9]**

a. Is inflation decreasing, increasing, or stable?

b. Is actual output greater than or less than potential output?

c. Is unemployment rising or falling?

d. Is the Federal Reserve more likely to pursue expansionary or contractionary monetary policy?

e. Is the economy likely experiencing an expansion or contraction?

21. Assume the Phillips curve is given by the simple equation $U = -I + 20$. The non-accelerating inflation rate of unemployment is 10 percent. If inflation changes to 15 percent, what will be the unemployment rate in the short run? What will it be in the long run? **[LO 33.10]**

22. Using what you know about the Phillips curve, determine whether the following quantities will increase, decrease, or remain the same. **[LO 33.10]**

a. Unemployment in the short run after an increase in inflation.

b. Unemployment in the long run after an increase in inflation.

c. Inflation in the short run after a decrease in unemployment.

d. Inflation in the long run after a decrease in unemployment.

Endnotes

1. "Argentina's Inflation Problem: The Price of Cooking the Books," *The Economist,* February 25, 2012, http://www.economist.com/node/21548229.

2. http://energy.gov/eere/vehicles/fact-915-march-7-2016-average-historical-annual-gasoline-pump-price-1929-2015; http://www.tradingeconomics.com/united-states/core-inflation-rate.

3. Bob Davis, "IMF Tells Bankers to Rethink Inflation," *The Wall Street Journal,* February 12, 2010, http://online.wsj.com/article/SB10001424052748704337004575059542325748142.html.

4. Marco A. Espinosa-Vega and Steven Russell, "History and Theory of the NAIRU: A Critical Review," *Economic Review* (Federal Reserve Bank of Atlanta), 1997, https://www.frbatlanta.org/-/media/Documents/research/publications/economic-review/1997/vol82no2_espinosa-russell.pdf.

Financial Crisis

LO 34.1 Describe the role of irrational expectations and leverage in the creation of financial crises.

LO 34.2 Discuss the causes of two famous historical financial crises.

LO 34.3 Trace the role of mortgage-backed securities and tranching in the rise of subprime lending.

LO 34.4 Analyze the factors that led to the housing bubble and rising levels of household debt.

LO 34.5 Explain how the collapse of the housing bubble created a credit crisis and subsequent contraction in output.

LO 34.6 Describe the monetary and fiscal policy responses to the financial crisis of 2008.

LO 34.7 Describe the different tools that can be used to stimulate the economy when interest rates are at the zero lower bound.

A FINANCIAL STORM

Guiding the economy is a bit like steering a massive cruise ship. Mostly the aim is to keep an eye on the latest data and navigate in the right direction. Every now and then the ship might need to speed up or slow down, but most of the time the job is just to keep things steady and steer forward.

Sometimes, though, ships run into huge storms, and all of a sudden the crew is fighting to keep the vessel afloat. The biggest recent *financial* storm for the U.S. economy started brewing in 2007 and reached full hurricane force in late 2008.

At 8:00 a.m. on a Friday in September 2008, Ben Bernanke, the chair of the Federal Reserve, joined Hank Paulson, the Secretary of the U.S. Treasury Department, for breakfast. They usually ate breakfast together once a week, but this morning was very different. Some of the country's biggest banks and financial companies were in desperate trouble. The firms had made risky bets about the future of the housing market, and now it was becoming clear how risky those bets were—and how badly they were turning out. What started as a simple breakfast turned out to be

© Jack Guez/AFP/Getty Images

the beginning of a week of tense meetings about how to save the economy from disaster.

Two days earlier, the investment firm Lehman Brothers announced that it had lost a staggering $4 billion on its bets. All weekend, officials at the Treasury and Federal Reserve scrambled to find a way to rescue Lehman, but the pieces didn't come together. Three days later, Lehman declared bankruptcy. Soon it became clear that Merrill Lynch, a major Wall Street Bank, also needed rescuing. So too did AIG, the insurance giant, and Washington Mutual, America's largest savings-and-loan bank. One crisis was leading to another, and related problems were intensifying in Europe. Within the month, the U.S. stock market was in free fall.

What started as a banking crisis was felt by people, rich and poor, across the country. Between 2007 and 2009, retirees saw the value of the stocks in their pensions collapse; investments built up over decades evaporated. Families lost their most valuable assets, their homes. All in all, household wealth was cut in half, and workers lost jobs, nearly nine million in all.

Over the next five years, the economy started coming back, the stock market began rising again, and companies created new jobs. But the effects of the 2007–2009 crisis are still being felt. This chapter tells the story of how the economy got into trouble and what economics teaches about tackling future crises.

Markets are a powerful tool for the efficient allocation of scarce resources. Financial markets are in many ways the purest expression of the market mechanism. Relatively free from government intervention, financial markets are a global marketplace in which sophisticated investors make billion-dollar decisions nearly every second of the day.

So, how can financial markets go so very wrong as they did in the 2007–2009 crisis? And why do the failings of financial markets reverberate through the broader economy? Developing an understanding of the common causes of financial crises has become an urgently important task.

In this chapter, we'll introduce a few of the basic concepts of financial crises. We'll talk about why things sometimes go wrong in financial markets and how those problems might be corrected. In particular, we will take a close look at the crisis that began in December of 2007 after the collapse of the housing market.

bubble
trade in an asset whose price has risen unsustainably far above historically justified levels

The Origins of Financial Crises

Financial crises often occur as the result of a financial bubble. As discussed in Chapter 31, "The Basics of Finance," a **bubble** involves trade in an asset whose price has risen unsustainably far above historically justified levels. The first recorded example of a financial bubble is a "tulip mania" that afflicted investors in Holland in 1636–1637. At the time, a single tulip bulb was worth more than a handful of diamonds. Investors paid incredible sums for bulbs, hoping to profit by selling later at even higher prices. After a few years, however, the mania surrounding tulips died out, and prices plummeted. Those who had invested in tulips lost fortunes.

This pattern has since been repeated many times. Prices go up and up and up, way higher than seems to make any rational sense, and then suddenly crash. Why does this happen? Two interconnected concepts lie at the heart of many financial crises: irrational expectations and leverage.

Irrational expectations

LO 34.1 Describe the role of irrational expectations and leverage in the creation of financial crises.

In Chapter 31, "The Basics of Finance," we talked about how financial markets are supposed to allocate funds efficiently. Ideally, they allow money to flow to the places where it is most highly valued at any given time. What's more, the efficient-market hypothesis says that financial markets should incorporate all available information, and so prices should represent the true value of an asset as correctly as possible. Where, in all of that, is there room for bubbles and crashes?

In reality, markets sometimes appear to be very irrational. The price of an asset can become inflated beyond the point where anyone can explain precisely why it should be so valuable. How does that happen? One hypothesis is that investors sometimes follow a "herd instinct," investing in something simply because everyone else is doing it. Investors are just people—albeit often well-informed people with a financial interest in making good investments. They can get caught up in the moment and act emotionally, just like anyone else. A bubble starts to inflate when investors become irrationally optimistic that an asset's price will continue to rise.

Where do irrational expectations come from? One possible explanation is a well-established cognitive bias called the *recency effect*. There is a basic human tendency to overvalue recent experience when trying to predict the future. When investors and speculators do this, it can lead to enormous miscalculations. For example, consider a company that enjoyed a spectacular few years of success: Apple Computer. In 2005, Apple's total profits were just over $1.3 billion. Then, it launched the MacBook, followed by the iPhone, and then the iPad. In 2010, Apple reported profits of more than $14 billion. That's a tenfold growth in profits over just five years.

With Apple's products still flying off the shelves, would an investor be justified in believing that Apple might continue its incredible run for another five or 10 or 15 years? After another five years of tenfold growth, Apple would be earning more than $140 billion a year. In 10 years, the company would be earning more than $1.4 trillion. By 2025, Apple would be earning $14 trillion annually—the current GDP of the entire United States! When you look at it that way, it becomes clear that there will come a time for Apple when future growth simply can't resemble past growth.

Although it's unlikely that anyone would project something quite that extreme, trends do influence our thinking. For example, in the housing markets, decades of rising house prices persuaded many Americans that it was inconceivable that they could ever fall. However, not all investors in a bubble are necessarily caught up in irrational expectations. Some may be aware that assets are overpriced but gamble on riding the rise in prices as close to the top as possible in the hope of selling at maximum profit, just before the inevitable crash. This high-stakes game is described in the From Another Angle box "Do investors rationally inflate bubbles?"

From Another Angle
Do investors rationally inflate bubbles?

On June 16, 2005, *The Economist* ran a story entitled "After the Fall." The magazine spelled out clearly why the fast-rising real estate prices around the world were a bubble that would burst, sooner or later:

> Throughout history, financial bubbles—whether in houses, equities, or tulip bulbs—have continued to inflate for longer than rational folk believed possible. It is impossible to predict when [housing] prices will turn. Yet turn they will. Prices are already sliding in Australia and Britain. America's housing market may be a year or so behind.

The question was not *if* the bubble would burst, but *when*? As it happened, housing prices in the United States stayed astronomically high for another two years after these words were written. Was this because house buyers had stubbornly plugged their ears to such warnings? Maybe. Or maybe speculators were continuing to buy real estate knowing that a crash would come but expecting that the bubble had a bit more inflating to do and hoping to maximize profits by selling at the peak price, *just before* the market came crashing down.

How do you make sure you get out just before the market goes into free fall? If the timing is off, investors can get their fingers badly burned. Fund manager Stanley Druckenmiller lost a lot of money by not selling soon enough during the bubble in tech stocks in the 1990s. He explained his mistake, using a baseball analogy, "We thought it was the eighth inning, and it was the ninth."

The problem is that no one knows exactly when the bubble will end. A bubble pops when a critical mass of investors decides that the time is right to sell. This causes prices to dip, and everyone who was sitting tight will rush to sell off as well, turning the dip into a plummet. If you haven't managed to sell before this moment comes, then you'll struggle to find anyone who wants to buy.

The existence of speculators practicing this sort of brinkmanship also complicates policy steps that could be taken to avert a crisis. If the bubble is being inflated by speculators who are poised to sell at the first sign of prices going into reverse, it might be impossible to prevent a gentle slowdown from turning into a crash landing.

Sources: http://www.princeton.edu/~markus/research/papers/bubbles_crashes.pdf; "After the Fall: Soaring House Prices Have Given a Huge Boost to the World Economy. What Happens When They Drop?" © The Economist Newspaper Limited, London (June 16, 2005).

Leverage

Irrational expectations help explain how prices get so inflated during a bubble, but we have to go further to understand why the crash is so damaging after a bubble bursts. One culprit is the extensive use of leverage, which multiplies the effect of gains and losses in financial markets. In finance, **leverage** is the practice of using borrowed money to pay for investments.

The use of leverage means that a person or company can make an investment that is much larger in value than the amount they actually own:

> **leverage**
> the practice of using borrowed money to pay for investments

- If the investment does well, you pay back the loan and get to keep the profits, which will be larger than what you would have earned if you could invest only the cash you had on hand.

- If the investment does badly, you still have to pay back the loan, and that can require digging deep into your own resources.

When financial markets are booming, leverage multiplies the gains; when they crash, leverage magnifies the losses.

On a personal level, people can leverage their funds through a "margin account." A margin account allows you to use your existing investments as collateral to either buy more financial assets or withdraw cash. For example, if you have $100 in an account that offers "2x" margin, you can effectively buy $200 worth of stocks even though you put in only $100. When stocks rise, you will earn twice as much profit, minus interest payments.

But what happens if the stock you bought goes down? Let's say it goes down 10 percent. If you did not buy on margin, your account value would go down to only $90. If you did buy on margin, however, you are going to lose $20, which would bring your account value down to $80. That doesn't sound so bad, but what if the stock goes down 50 percent? You would lose all your money since 50 percent of $200 is your entire original $100. If the stock goes down more than 50 percent, you could actually end up owing money to your broker!

In practice, brokers exercise a "margin call" to ensure that they don't lose money. If it looks like you are in danger of running through your money, the broker will force you to sell your stock and use the money to pay back the loan. Since this probably means selling at the worst possible time—just as the market is collapsing—this situation is both bad for you and potentially destabilizing for the market as a whole. A rapidly falling stock price can trigger a flood of margin calls, leading to massive sales of the stock, which pushes the price down even more.

Companies and banks can also leverage their funds. Such transactions can lead to losses on a much larger scale than personal margin accounts. For instance, an investment bank or hedge fund might use $5 million as collateral in order to buy a claim on $50 million worth of oil futures.[1] Gains or losses on that investment will be multiplied by the use of leverage in exactly the same way that they are on a personal level. If the value of the investment goes down by a lot, the company can end up owing more than it is able to pay. Just before it went bankrupt during the crash in 2008, Lehman Brothers investment bank was highly leveraged. Its total assets were valued at levels about 30 times the actual funds it owned, depending on exactly how one calculates it.

The amount of leverage a company takes on can be expressed in terms of the **leverage ratio**. That measure is the ratio of a company's assets to its equity, where equity is defined as the firm's assets minus its liabilities. In the case of Lehman Brothers, a leverage ratio of 30 implies that a 10 percent increase in the value of its assets would generate a 300 percent increase in the value of its equity.[2] This magnification of returns may sound attractive when we're considering positive changes in asset prices, but the logic also works in reverse: Small decreases in asset values can lead to catastrophic losses for highly leveraged institutions.

leverage ratio
the ratio of a company's assets to its equity, where equity is defined as the firm's assets minus its liabilities

Leverage alone is not necessarily a dangerous thing—so long as it is limited and investors understand the risks well. Unfortunately, leverage combined with irrational expectations about a market can be a brutal combination. Imagine you believed that Apple would keep growing at 60 percent a year for the next decade, and borrowed heavily to leverage your investment. When the price of Apple stock inevitably fell back to earth, you would take a huge loss.

The two-headed monster of leverage and irrational expectations is at the heart of most financial crises.

Two Famous Historical Financial Crises

LO 34.2 Discuss the causes of two famous historical financial crises.

Before we dive into a case study of the Great Recession, let's take a quick look back at how the twin dangers of irrational expectations and leverage have played out in two famous historical financial crises.

The South Seas Bubble
In the late seventeenth century, stock markets in England were in their infancy. In 1688, the East India Company made one of the first issuances of stock: Investors would be given a cut of the profits on a forthcoming voyage to India. By 1695, 140 companies were offering similar arrangements in London's Exchange Alley.

The South Seas Company took form in this new environment. The company was granted a government monopoly on trade between England and South America. Interest in the company's stock was intense. In just a single day, the price of South Seas Company stock rose from £130 to over £300. The company issued more stock, and the price jumped from £300 to £325 as investors used their existing stock as collateral to buy more. By June 1720, the bubble was in full swing, with stock of the South Seas Company trading at a price over £1,000 a share.

It was never entirely clear how the South Seas Company was going to earn enough profit to justify this fantastic share price. After all, there wasn't much trade between England and South America, which at the time was made up of colonies that were mostly controlled by Spain. The company depended on an agreement with Spain to be able to run trading ships, and Spain allowed it to run only one ship a year. Still, wild rumors circulated of the fabulous profits that would one day flow from the South Seas. Investors were caught up in the frenzy.

Con artists saw the high prices that investors were willing to pay for shares in the South Seas Company and decided to cash in on the frenzy. They concocted their own companies, which promised investors riches through fanciful schemes. One company claimed to be building a wheel of perpetual motion. Another famously invited investors to buy stock in "a company for carrying out an undertaking of great advantage, but nobody to know what it is." Eventually, the English Parliament realized the dangers and moved to regulate companies that traded stock publicly, through a law known as the Bubble Act.

Inevitably, sanity returned, and the price of stock in the South Seas Company plunged back to earth. Many investors were ruined. Sir Isaac Newton, the great mathematician and one of the investors, lost £20,000—the equivalent of about $5 million today. Kicking himself, Newton grumbled that he could "calculate the motion of heavenly bodies, but not the madness of people."

The Great Crash of 1929

While the South Seas bubble could be considered the first financial crisis of the modern stock market era, the worst was arguably the infamous stock market crash of October 1929. This event led to the Great Depression, which wreaked havoc throughout the 1930s. Production slowed and unemployment in the United States exceeded 25 percent.

The Great Crash of 1929 wreaked havoc on Wall Street—a loss the U.S. economy took 25 years to recover from.
© MPI/Getty Images

The Great Crash and resulting Great Depression had their roots in another bubble, a period of flashy exuberance known as the "Roaring Twenties." From 1922 to 1929, the total value of the stock market more than tripled, averaging an annual growth rate of over 18 percent. There was some foundation for this increase in share prices: U.S. soldiers, home from World War I, had boosted production with additional manpower. New technologies such as movies, radio, and mass-produced automobiles were causing widespread excitement. Many people began buying stocks on the margin.

If stock prices continued to rise, as many figured they would, buying on the margin could increase profits substantially. For most of the 1920s, that seemed a pretty good bet. Economist Irving Fisher infamously assured everyone that the stock market had reached a "permanently high plateau." Secretary of the Treasury Andrew Mellon stated on October 14, 1929, that there was "no cause to worry. The high tide of prosperity will continue."

Ten days later, the stock market fell apart. On October 24, 1929—"Black Thursday"—the leading index of stock prices dropped by 9 percent. Bankers tried to shore up confidence by buying up the stocks of large companies. But this buying couldn't stem the avalanche of selling as investors unloaded shares in an unprecedented, panicked sell-off. Once prices started to drop, everyone wanted to sell before the price dropped further. Of course, this rush of sales *caused* the price to drop further, making the panic a self-perpetuating problem.

On the following Monday, the stock market posted a loss of 13 percent. The next day, the market fell again by 12 percent. As more panic set in, the volume of shares traded reached a record-setting 16.4 million—more than four times the typical number.

By the time prices bottomed out in July 1932, 90 percent of the entire value of the stock market had been wiped away in just three years. It took until 1954—a full 25 years later—for the stock market to return to the peak reached in September 1929.

✓CONCEPT CHECK

☐ Why does leverage exacerbate the effect of a financial crash? **[LO 34.1]**

☐ What is the name of the period of sluggish economic activity that followed the Great Crash of 1929? **[LO 34.1]**

☐ Why did the initial stock sell-off create further panic during the Great Crash of 1929? **[LO 34.2]**

The Great Recession: A Financial-Crisis Case Study

In the 1930s, Congress passed several laws intended to prevent similar crises in the future:

- The Glass-Steagall Banking Act of 1933 required the separation of investment and commercial banks.[3]
- The Federal Deposit Insurance Corporation (FDIC) insured bank deposits against possible bank failures, among other things.
- The Securities and Exchange Act of 1932 formed the Securities and Exchange Commission (SEC), which regulates the securities industry today.

These reforms contributed to a long period of relative stability in financial markets. For decades, the U.S. economy chugged along without a major financial crisis or contraction in output. It seemed that the stock market crash of 1929 might go down in history as the beginning of a new and more predictable era. Perhaps the global economy had moved on from the days of bubbles and panics. By the mid-2000s, this idea, sometimes dubbed "the Great Moderation," had support in the academic and policy-making community. Unfortunately, less than five years later, the global economy would again find itself in a major recession.

By 2008, we were in the midst of the greatest global economic downturn since the Great Depression. Industrial and financial giants from General Motors to Merrill Lynch were under threat of collapse. Millions of people saw their life savings evaporate as housing prices collapsed and markets around the world plummeted.

In this section, we'll explore the origins of the financial crisis and the extraordinary monetary and fiscal response from the world's governments, using the macroeconomics concepts we've explored over the last few chapters. We will focus on the United States—in many ways the epicenter of the crisis—but the global crash was not just the result of problems in the United States spreading to the rest of the world. Countries from Spain to Ireland and the United Kingdom also faced enormous challenges of their own that helped feed the global crisis.

In order to really understand how the U.S. economy collapsed so suddenly, we'll start by looking at some interrelated components of the U.S. economy: subprime lending, the housing and mortgage market, and the broader world of consumer debt.

Subprime lending

LO 34.3 Trace the role of mortgage-backed securities and tranching in the rise of subprime lending.

To understand the financial crisis that rocked the country in 2008, we have to start with the housing market. From World War II to the onset of the financial crisis—a period of more than 60 years—housing prices had never fallen across the entire United States. Housing prices on the whole had stayed steady, even when the rest of the economy went into recession. Buying a house was considered the safest investment anyone could make—a path to stability, wealth, and the American Dream. Even the federal government joined the bandwagon in promoting home ownership: It implemented policies ranging from tax deductions on home mortgage interest to government-created companies like Fannie Mae and Freddie Mac, which are intended to spread access to mortgage financing.

Yet some people still couldn't obtain a traditional mortgage loan—because of poor credit, low income, or job instability. Financial innovators opened a new path to home ownership through the growing availability of *subprime mortgages.* A subprime mortgage is a mortgage loan made to a borrower with a low credit score—that is, to someone who has a history of missing payments or otherwise struggling with debts. (The word *subprime* is in contrast to *prime* borrowers, who have better credit scores.) At first, subprime mortgages were seen as a triumph: They enabled even more Americans to pursue the dream of home ownership for the first time.

Why were lenders willing to lend to subprime borrowers? The loans, after all, are especially risky. Banks had long been wary of lending to subprime-rated borrowers. That all changed with the advent of securitization. **Securitization** is the practice of packaging individual debts, like mortgage loans or credit card debts, into a single uniform asset that can be easily bought and sold. In the late 1990s, investment banks began purchasing mortgages from the local banks that had created them. They, in turn, then packaged them as *mortgage-backed securities,* which were tradable assets made up of collections of individual mortgages, whose value was tied to the revenues of those mortgages.

Securitization of mortgages allowed *local banks* to reduce their exposure to risk by effectively selling their mortgage debt to investors. The investors got the revenues from mortgage payments, but if borrowers defaulted, the investors would experience a loss. For investors, the mortgage-backed security seemed to promise diversification: By combining many mortgages into one security, the risks specific to individual mortgages (called *idiosyncratic risk*) would be diluted. As a result, the combination of mortgages would have lower total risk than any individual mortgage. The reasoning was similar to that of a bank or insurance company pooling risks, as discussed in Chapter 31, "The Basics of Finance":

- If you make a single loan and the borrower defaults, you lose everything at once.
- If, however, you make 100 loans, it's very unlikely that everyone will default at once. A bank can take a thousand loans, estimate that *on average* 250 of them will default, and set prices so that it can still earn a profit on the total package.

An investor could go out and buy a thousand different individual mortgages to diversify risk. Doing that, though, takes time: It would involve scrutinizing each mortgage to guess how likely a particular homeowner is to default and ensuring that the thousand mortgages are not highly correlated. Instead, the mortgage-backed security was supposed to be a single, uniform asset that pooled risk while still being easy to buy and sell quickly. It allowed local banks to pass the risk involved in holding mortgage debts on to investors with higher risk tolerance.

Diversification is valuable, but the logic of pooling risks depends crucially on the degree to which the loans in the pool are correlated with one another. If for any reason the risks associated with a set of loans are highly correlated, then it is much harder to diversify away the default risk. (An example of high correlation of mortgage risk, for example, would be if many loans are

securitization

the practice of packaging individual debts into a single uniform asset

issued to households who could make payments only if interest rates stayed low.) Worse yet, if investors are unaware that the underlying risks are in fact highly correlated, then they might unintentionally take on more risk than they want.

Some banks went one step further: They divided packages of debts into slices (called *tranches*), each with different risk and return characteristics. Packages of reliable, low-risk mortgages could be sold to more risk-averse investors; higher-risk subprime mortgages could be sold to risk-loving investors.

What was the point of this financial wizardry? It allowed local banks and mortgage companies to chase higher profits by making loans that they would have rejected as too risky in the past. Now they could sell those mortgages to investment banks, which in turn could chase profits by packaging them as mortgage-backed securities and selling them on.

Investors had such an appetite for mortgage-backed securities that local banks couldn't make loans fast enough. Real estate agents started pushing larger mortgages to customers, even to borrowers who wouldn't traditionally have been able to afford them. Some mortgage brokers cut corners in paperwork to be able to pump out more loans. By 2006, a full 20 percent of the mortgage market consisted of subprime loans, a category that barely even existed a decade before. The sudden explosion of subprime mortgages is shown in Figure 34-1.

The creation of the housing bubble

LO 34.4 Analyze the factors that led to the housing bubble and rising levels of household debt.

The sudden explosion of cheap and readily available mortgages encouraged people to buy bigger and better homes. A mortgage is a form of leverage—you make a down payment that is only a

FIGURE 34-1

Growth of the subprime loan market   This figure shows subprime mortgages as a percentage of all new mortgages from 2001 through 2007. Traditionally, new subprime mortgages comprised less than 10 percent of the total new mortgages in any given year. This changed in 2004, when the number of new subprime mortgages more than doubled as a share of new mortgages. Then, in 2007, the housing market collapsed, and lenders reacted by sharply reducing subprime loans.

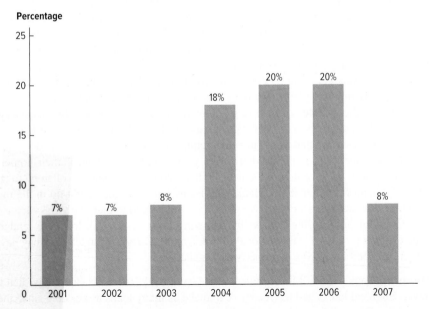

Source: *The State of the Nation's Housing*, Harvard University Joint Center for Housing Studies, 2008.

FIGURE 34-2

The housing bubble pops   The chart shows the rapid increase of housing prices from 1999 to 2006. As you can see, prices peaked in early 2007 and then quickly plummeted. The bubble was large nationally (as seen by the national composite index, represented by the blue line), as prices doubled on average in the span of seven years. The bursting of the bubble is shown by the sudden decrease in housing starts, followed by a sharp reduction in price of houses.

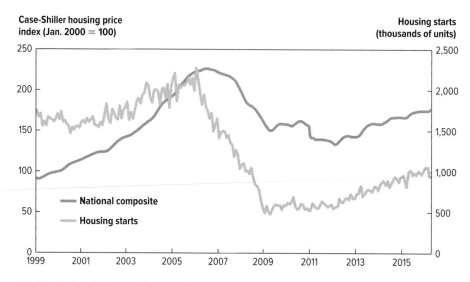

Sources: Price index data from FRED Economic Data, https://fred.stlouisfed.org/series/SPCS20RSA; housing starts data from U.S. Census Bureau, https://www.census.gov/construction/nrc/pdf/compsa.pdf.

fraction of the value of the asset (i.e., the house) that you are buying, and you borrow the rest. As down-payment requirements got smaller and loans got cheaper, many homeowners became more and more leveraged.

The frenzy of highly leveraged demand for houses was accompanied by a sharp run-up in housing prices. Figure 34-2 shows the rapid rise in U.S. home prices during this period and the number of *housing starts* (a term that means new home construction—an indicator of increasing supply in the housing market) in the same period. At the height of the real estate bubble, American homeowners were much like Lehman Brothers, with a very high ratio of home "value" to money actually paid. When housing prices stopped rising, however, millions of homeowners found themselves with payments they couldn't possibly make on highly leveraged housing properties.

Why did these loans get made? Economists continue to debate this question, but in many ways, the enormous run-up in housing prices was a classic bubble. People bought houses with the expectation that they would continue to go up in value. Banks began to offer special types of mortgages that allowed borrowers to defer payments for the first few years of the loan. Or they offered "teaser" interest rates that would increase to much higher levels a few years down the road. As long as home prices kept going up, borrowers would simply "refinance" their homes when the bills came. That is, they would use the new, higher value of the home as collateral to take out a new mortgage with friendlier terms. Banks and borrowers both got caught up in the moment. Convinced that housing prices would never go down, both agreed to incredibly risky loans.

Securitization encouraged the process by removing most of the risk from the lenders who created the original mortgage. This removal of risk from the original lender also may have contributed to misaligned incentives to properly assess risk:

- Investment banks on Wall Street relied on the local banks to assess each individual borrower. But local banks had the incentive to make as many loans as possible since they earned fees for each loan.

- Wall Street bankers made money not by ensuring local banks were making good loans, but by buying as many loans as possible, packaging them into mortgage-backed securities, and selling them to investors.

At some point up the chain, the people creating and buying complicated assets that were several steps removed from the original mortgage may not have fully understood what they were paying for.

Investors relied on the reassuringly high AAA ratings given to many of these assets by credit-rating agencies. However, the ratings agencies attracted business in part by keeping Wall Street happy. The ratings turned out to be much too optimistic. Politicians were driven by a vision of broader home ownership but failed to pay enough attention to the economics. The same tools that were intended to allocate funds and spread risk more efficiently made it difficult for everyone to stay fully informed; they diluted the incentive to do the research and to say no to bad risks.

Effects of the housing bubble collapse

LO 34.5 Explain how the collapse of the housing bubble created a credit crisis and subsequent contraction in output.

As housing prices continued to rise, consumers were simultaneously saving less and borrowing (and spending) more. Flush with the feeling of wealth from their inflated home values, many consumers used the value of their homes to secure loans and higher limits on their credit cards, taking on more and more debt to support their spending habits. In addition, consumers had become accustomed to *refinancing* their mortgages—paying off the existing mortgage and taking out a new mortgage based on the increased value of the home. Often the new mortgage was structured to result in lower payments (at least for a while), and often the appreciated value of the home enabled the homeowner to borrow some cash in the refinancing deal. These consumer responses to the housing bubble ultimately led to a credit crisis and a new equilibrium in the economy in which both prices and output had fallen.

Buying on credit

Personal debt levels in the United States had steadily been rising for decades, since the mid-1980s. As the housing market took off in the early 2000s and consumers began borrowing more, the growth in household debt accelerated rapidly, hitting a peak by the end of 2008. Figure 34-3 shows the historical trajectory of personal debt in the United States.

To understand consumer debt, economists look at a concept known as debt service. **Debt service** is the amount that consumers have to spend to pay their debts, often expressed as a percentage of disposable income. Over the two decades leading up the 2008 crisis, falling interest rates made borrowing—and therefore going into debt—much cheaper. Consumers could take on more debt without significantly increasing the amount of debt service they had to pay. Figure 34-4 shows the divergence between rising debt levels and relatively stable debt-service burdens. Unfortunately, that level of debt was sustainable only as long as interest rates remained low and home values remained high. Consumers would be facing serious trouble if anything unexpectedly went wrong—which is exactly what happened when the housing bubble popped.

debt service
the amount that consumers have to spend to pay their debts, often expressed as a percentage of disposable income

A domino effect toward reduced output

When housing prices stopped rising and began to fall in places like Nevada, Arizona, California, and Florida, consumers found themselves unable to refinance their loans. The housing collapse began in the subprime housing market. It was like a domino trail, in which the first domino that tips starts a cascading effect:

- Faced with impossibly high payments relative to their incomes, a massive wave of mortgage defaults occurred. Millions of people found themselves in *foreclosure:* Their homes

FIGURE 34-3

Historical personal debt trends in the United States   Since the 1960s, personal debt in the United States has almost doubled its share of GDP, from around 45 percent to about 80 percent of GDP today. During the financial crisis, personal debt was almost 100 percent of GDP.

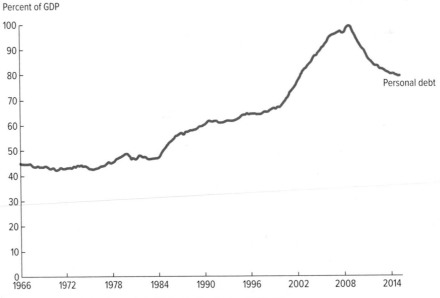

Source: FRED Economic Data, https://research.stlouisfed.org/fred2/series/HDTGPDUSQ163N.

FIGURE 34-4

Debt payments and total debt   This graph compares household financial obligations (which include payments during the year for mortgages, credit cards, property tax, and leases) and household debt (which is the total amount owed) as a percent of income. Despite the fact that household debt has risen considerably, nearly doubling from about 70 percent of total disposable income to just below 120 percent of disposable income, household payments on this debt have not increased very much, as low interest rates have kept the price of debt low.

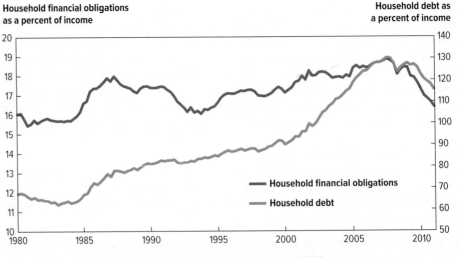

Source: Board of Governors of the Federal Reserve System, accessed on the FRED, updated June 8, 2012.

became the property of the bank when they defaulted on a mortgage loan. Often, the bank would then evict the homeowner and try to sell the house.

- The wave of foreclosed properties hit the market, creating a big increase in the supply of housing. The increase in supply depressed housing prices even further, leading to another wave of defaults.
- Consumers who had used second and third mortgages or borrowed in other ways to extract wealth from their homes suddenly found themselves "underwater," owing more in mortgage debt than their houses were worth. A vicious cycle of defaults and falling prices began; it would ultimately cause home values to fall by more than 50 percent in the hardest-hit areas.

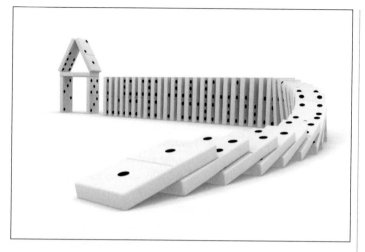

As home prices fell, consumers were unable to refinance mortgages, and a cycle of defaults and falling prices followed, eventually engulfing the entire economy.
© Anton Sokolov/123RF

- Riskier real estate investments became worthless. Even the supposedly "safe," AAA-rated investments were badly affected. Banks lost trillions of dollars.
- Because of the opaque and complicated nature of mortgage-backed securities, it was difficult to tell which banks had been hit the hardest by the crash. As a result, the *entire* borrowing and lending engine of the economy ground to a halt. Nobody wanted to lend to anybody, in case they turned out to be a bad risk.
- Even the most venerable banks teetered on the edge of collapse. Large institutions and companies that had deposited money with Wall Street's banks began withdrawing their funds, leading to a run on bank assets. Two of the largest and most respected banks—Bear Stearns and Lehman Brothers—collapsed, and the rest were perceived to be at risk as well. Figure 34-5 shows the dramatic collapse in stock prices of the largest banks.

FIGURE 34-5

Stock prices of major banks   As a result of the housing boom, the financial sector performed well in the years leading up to the crisis. This ended when many of the banks announced that they held large amounts of toxic assets. Beginning in February 2007, prices began to fall. Come September 2008, prices of stocks throughout the financial sectors plummeted as the crisis hit.

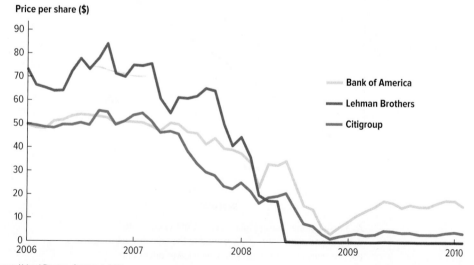

Source: Yahoo! Finance, October 4, 2011.

- Because banks were unwilling to lend, many businesses were suddenly unable to get access to credit for their day-to-day needs. Even simple tasks like buying inventory or taking delivery of a container ship full of imported goods became nearly impossible for many companies. Effectively, the aggregate productive capacity of the entire world was reduced almost overnight.
- The combination of increasing interest rates and pessimism about future economic prospects decreased investment spending: Businesses could no longer obtain credit to invest, and most would not have wanted to invest as the economy weakened anyway.
- Households found themselves struggling to pay back debts, and some faced reduced income and poor job prospects. The fall in home prices meant they were no longer as wealthy as they thought they were, and people reduced their consumption accordingly.
- With demand flagging, businesses had to cut back further. Some employees were laid off, and others saw their wages or hours cut.
- Lower incomes led naturally to lower spending and still more layoffs.

Figure 34-6 shows the combined impact of these forces: As a result of the housing-market crash, both aggregate demand and aggregate supply shifted to the left. The combined shifts put the economy at a new equilibrium, with dramatically reduced output. Prices fell because the effect of the leftward shift in the aggregate demand curve was stronger than the effect of the leftward shift in aggregate supply. The combined effect left the economy reeling.

It took barely two years for the bursting of a real estate bubble to tip the global economy into its worst downturn in over 75 years. Once housing prices collapsed and the bad loans in the financial system were revealed for what they were, it was only a matter of time before the convulsions on Wall Street led to job losses and economic pain on Main Street.

FIGURE 34-6

The financial crisis in terms of AD and AS

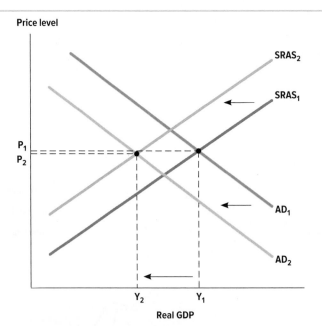

As a result of the housing-market crash, both aggregate demand and aggregate supply shifted to the left. This put the economy at a new equilibrium, with lower prices and dramatically reduced output.

The immediate response to the crisis

LO 34.6 Describe the monetary and fiscal policy responses to the financial crisis of 2008.

With the private sector reeling from the impact of the shifts in both aggregate demand and aggregate supply, many looked to the government to provide stability and ensure that the situation did not become even worse. We've talked about how the government can use monetary and fiscal policy to impact the economy. During the financial crisis, policy-makers used these tools to try to avert a catastrophic economic collapse.

With more banks failing each day, the goal of fiscal and monetary policy in 2008 was to "unstick" the frozen credit markets. Economists feared that any attempt to stimulate aggregate demand without first addressing the lack of supply would have been ineffective at best and dangerous at worst. It could potentially have led to **stagflation**—that is, high inflation despite low economic growth and high unemployment.

The challenges facing the financial system stemmed from the two fundamental issues of liquidity and solvency. The more pressing of the two was liquidity. There was great uncertainty about which banks were facing losses and which would most likely go bankrupt next. As a result, banks were not willing to lend to each other. The lack of liquidity meant that there wasn't enough money moving through the system to keep transactions going. Concerns about the amount of the liquidity in the market were reflected in interest rates: In the depths of the financial crisis, interest rates on even the most secure loans soared.

Addressing the liquidity problem fell to the world's central banks, and primarily to the U.S. Federal Reserve in its role as "lender of last resort." When a similar financial crisis shook the United States in the early 1900s, one man—J.P. Morgan—stepped in to act as the lender of last resort, averting a national financial collapse. Six years after that event, the Federal Reserve was created. In 2008, the existence of the Fed meant that the situation played out very differently. Shortly after Lehman Brothers' collapse, the Fed leapt into action: It offered nearly unlimited short-term financing to any bank that suddenly found itself short on cash. The European Central Bank and the Bank of England quickly followed suit, trying to help the financial system from seizing up completely.

Figure 34-7 shows the effect of this monetary policy response: a dramatic spike in the size of the Federal Reserve's balance sheet in September 2008. The Fed greatly expanded its

stagflation
high inflation despite low economic growth and high unemployment

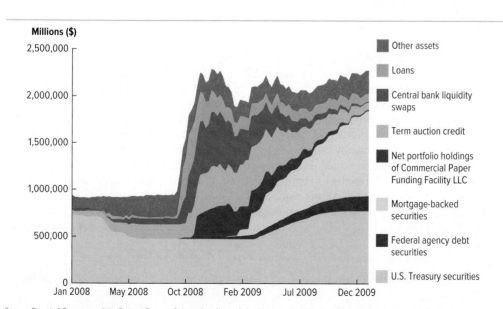

FIGURE 34-7

The Federal Reserve's balance sheet

Responding to the crisis, the Fed in fall 2008 doubled the assets on its balance sheet, over the span of just a month. Notice the rise in mortgage-backed securities beginning in early 2009, which the Fed began purchasing as a way to support the housing market.

Source: Board of Governors of the Federal Reserve System, http://www.federalreserve.gov/releases/h41/current/, updated July 5, 2012.

holdings of financial products, doubling the assets over the span of a month. The intent of the policy was to compensate for the loss of capital in the financial markets. By buying various assets, the Fed added nearly $1.5 trillion in new money to the U.S. economy. Even though you may not recognize every asset on the Fed's balance sheet, notice the rise in mortgage-backed securities beginning in early 2009, which the Fed began purchasing as a way to support the housing market.

At the same time, the U.S. Treasury began the difficult task of dealing with banks that had a solvency problem. "Solvency problem" is a gentle way of referring to banks that had lost so much money that they would inevitably go bankrupt. Hundreds of banks were allowed to fail during this period. However, certain banks were deemed **"too big to fail"**—that is, so large in terms of assets or customers or so historically important that banking regulators allow the bank to keep operating despite insolvency. The failure of one of these big banks carried the risk of causing a domino effect in the highly integrated financial system, causing widespread loss and credit seize-up.

Banks considered "too big to fail" were eventually bailed out through fiscal policy—that is, through increased government spending. The bulk of this effort came through the Troubled Asset Relief Program, commonly known as *TARP*. This program represented the first wave of the federal government's fiscal policy response to the crisis. The first wave invested more than $700 billion in failing institutions. The recipients ranged from major banks like Citigroup to insurance companies like AIG. General Motors and Chrysler, two automakers that were floundering in the weak economy, also received bailouts from the Treasury.

This one-two punch of monetary and fiscal policy averted a systemic collapse and brought stability to the global financial system. By shoring up the capital of the most heavily damaged banks and flooding the system with liquidity, the Treasury and the Federal Reserve worked together to restore the lines of credit within the economy.

Many officials argued that the bailouts were absolutely necessary to save the economy. Debate swirled around TARP as it made its way through government. Chief among the concerns was the fear that blanket bailouts would create a class of banks that *knew* they were considered to be "too big to fail" and so would continue to take unnecessary risks. This debate is covered in the Real Life box "Too big to fail?"

"too big to fail"
so large in terms of assets or customers or so historically important that banking regulators allow the bank to keep operating despite insolvency

Real Life
Too big to fail?

In 1984, the Continental Illinois Bank based in Chicago was headed for bankruptcy. The government and financial regulators had a choice: Either let the seventh-largest bank in the country fail and risk damages to the financial sector, or step in and provide it with the cash it needed to stay in business. In the end, the government decided to step in and save Continental Illinois because it feared the consequences of letting such a big bank fail.

What's the problem with a bank being "too big to fail"? Like any other firm, banks want to make profits but are usually constrained by the fact that if they make decisions that are too risky, there is a chance they could go bankrupt. However, if a bank knows the government will bail it out, the downside to risky behavior is reduced. If the risk pays off, the bank keeps the profits; if the risk goes bad, it doesn't bear all of the losses. This encourages greater risk-taking. Imagine going to the casino and knowing that if you lose everything, your parents will bail you out. Wouldn't you be more willing to gamble than if you had to bear all of the consequences yourself?

This "heads I win, tails you lose" problem creates a dilemma for government:

- On the one hand, the government doesn't want bank collapses to have negative effects on the economy.

- On the other hand, the government doesn't want to encourage risky behavior by bailing out banks whenever they get into trouble.

This dilemma came into sharp focus in 2008 when Lehman Brothers, the fourth-largest investment bank in the United States, faced bankruptcy. After many emergency meetings, the government ultimately decided *not* to bail out Lehman Brothers. That decision sent shockwaves through the financial sector. Many analysts had assumed that Lehman would be deemed "too big to fail." Though concerned about the consequences of a Lehman bankruptcy, the government decided it was more important to send a signal that it wasn't automatically going to help every bank that got itself into trouble.

The very next day, the insurance giant AIG was about to fail. This time, the government *did* step in to bail it out, to the tune of $85 billion. AIG was the country's largest insurer of commercial and industrial outfits. Policy-makers calculated that AIG could not go bust without inflicting extensive damage throughout the financial system.

Just a few weeks later, the Federal Reserve, together with the U.S. Treasury, put together TARP, essentially acknowledging that more banks were "too big to fail." As an illustration of how serious the situation had become, Ben Bernanke, chairman of the Federal Reserve, told politicians that the TARP was necessary because without it, "we might not have an economy on Monday."

Where does that leave banks today? Some have suggested that the solution to the "too big to fail" dilemma is to break up "too big" banks into smaller chunks. Those smaller banks could be allowed to fail without widespread damage to the financial system. Others argue that the "too big to fail" banks should be explicitly named and their activities more closely regulated, to reflect the risks that taxpayers are bearing.

As things stands, the dilemma remains: Any bank that faces going bust will have to wait nervously to discover if the government considers it to be more of a Lehman Brothers or an AIG.

Sources: http://www.nytimes.com/2008/10/02/business/02crisis.html; http://widerimage.reuters.com/timesofcrisis/.

The effect of the monetary and fiscal actions in the aggregate demand and aggregate supply model is shown in Figure 34-8, which builds from Figure 34-6:

- The Federal Reserve lowered interest rates to respond to the sharp reduction in the amount of credit available in the market:
- The Treasury through the TARP provided money in the market.

These two actions restored aggregate supply to its original level.

Once order was restored in the credit market, businesses were again able to finance their inventories and continue to grow their operations. This restoration pushed the SRAS curve back toward its original pre-crisis position. However, due to sluggish aggregate demand, output was still well below pre-crash levels (Y_1).

You might be wondering why all of that capital failed to stimulate aggregate demand. The short answer is that these programs did not have the same goal as traditional monetary policy conducted through the federal funds rate. Most of the offerings, instead, were used only by banks that faced problems getting the capital they needed to function normally—emergency programs for an extraordinary situation. So even as the financial sector stabilized, the United States found itself with the classic problem of most economic downturns: depressed aggregate demand.

FIGURE 34-8

Fed and Treasury intervention restores aggregate supply

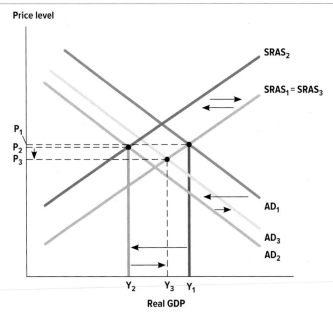

The Fed and the Treasury both responded to the sharp reduction of credit available in the market. Their responses provided enough money in the market to spur aggregate supply and demand, although due to sluggish aggregate demand, output was still well below pre-crash levels (Y_1).

Stimulus at the zero lower bound

> **LO 34.7** Describe the different tools that can be used to stimulate the economy when interest rates are at the zero lower bound.

The policy prescriptions for fixing low aggregate demand are relatively straightforward:

- The Federal Reserve can pursue expansionary monetary policy, lowering interest rates to encourage borrowing and investment spending, which pushes the aggregate demand curve to the right.
- Alternatively, the government can engage in stimulus through fiscal policy, increasing aggregate demand through tax cuts or increases in government spending.

In fact, both routes were pursued in the 2007–2009 crisis. Congress and President Obama passed fiscal stimulus legislation intended to support demand. The Federal Reserve slashed the federal funds rate from a little more than 5 percent before the crisis to 2 percent. As demand stayed weak—even after stimulus spending—the Fed continued to cut the federal funds rate.

By 2009, the economy was in an unusual situation. Interest rates were near zero and the economy had still not recovered. Households were trying to pay down their debts; there was little desire to borrow for consumption—even when borrowing was essentially free. With consumption weak, businesses were in no mood to invest in expanding their productive capacity. With interest rates already at zero, it seemed as though monetary policy was out of ammunition. After all, the Fed couldn't lower interest rates below zero. What *could* it do?

What came out of this impasse was a prescription for unorthodox monetary policy: quantitative easing. **Quantitative easing** involves policies that are designed to directly increase the money supply by a certain amount. As a policy, it contrasts with the more common practice of indirectly adjusting the money supply through interest rates. The Fed accomplished quantitative

quantitative easing
policies that are designed to directly increase the money supply by a certain amount

easing by purchasing long-term government bonds. The aim was to get more money into the economy. In all, the Fed purchased more than $1 trillion worth of long-term bonds with newly created money, thus adding $1 trillion to the money supply.

In choosing quantitative easing, the Fed wanted to avoid what happened in Japan after a housing bubble inflated in the 1980s and then popped. For years, the Japanese economy was weak, and deflation was a recurring problem. The Real Life box "Japan's lost decade" tells the story.

Real Life
Japan's lost decade

In the 1980s, Japan was one of the world's leading economies. In 1989, a real estate bubble threatened to destabilize the economy, and the Central Bank of Japan tried to gently rein in the price of housing by raising interest rates. The effect was dramatic: Housing prices fell 87 percent from their peak. This shock reverberated throughout the economy and ravaged the stock market. With the combined crashes in housing and the stock market, Japan lost the equivalent of three years of GDP, one of the largest peacetime losses of wealth in human history.

In response, the Japanese government and central bank engaged many of the traditional tools used to fight financial crises and recessions. They bailed out banks that were in danger of collapse. Banks got enough capital to keep them afloat, but it wasn't enough for normal day-to-day lending. These banks became known as "zombie banks"—banks that are nominally alive thanks to continued government bailouts but not able to play a useful role in the economy.

The government also embarked on an ambitious fiscal stimulus plan. Most of that spending went to building bridges and roads in rural areas. This stimulus also failed to improve the economy. Some argue the projects were ill-conceived. Others say the spigot of funding was turned off far too early to have a real impact.

In an especially drastic measure, the central bank dropped interest rates from 8 percent all the way down to zero. When that didn't work, the central bank said there was little else it could do—it had reached the *zero lower bound* on interest rates.

Japan's economy slipped into a downward spiral. Homeowners who had borrowed to purchase their houses when prices were high cut back on their spending so they could pay back debt. As a result, the economy became so weak that prices started to fall. The resulting deflation was incredibly damaging. Consumers held onto their money, knowing that they would be able to buy more in the future when its value increased. That reluctance to spend drove prices even further downward.

With these headwinds, the Japanese economy stayed stuck in neutral for two decades. What was originally known as the "Lost Decade" eventually became the "Lost Years." However, one economist who closely studied Japan's experience suggested that much of this stagnation was avoidable. The government could have let some of the zombie banks fail, continued stimulus spending, and tried alternative monetary policy measures, such as quantitative easing, to stimulate the economy.

Who was the economist who proposed these measures? It was Ben Bernanke, chairman of the Federal Reserve during the U.S. crisis.

Sources: http://www.nytimes.com/2010/05/21/opinion/21krugman.html; http://www.time.com/time/magazine/article/0,9171,1884815,00.html.

After the Fed's first round of quantitative easing, the overall money supply remained nearly unchanged. When the economy continued to stagnate, however, the Fed engaged in a second round of quantitative easing. The second round dramatically increased the overall level of the money supply. By mid-2011, the money supply stood at nearly $3 trillion, more than triple its level going into the crisis.

This enormous increase in the money supply was unprecedented. Critics feared that it would cause very high inflation. With the economy stagnating, however, the increase in the money supply led to only a slight increase in borrowing. Why did this happen? The money multiplier collapsed as banks were unwilling to lend and consumers and businesses were not very interested in, or capable of being approved for, borrowing. There is still debate about whether quantitative easing was successful in boosting demand. It appears, though, that the Fed's efforts at least prevented an outright fall in borrowing and lending, which would have further damaged an already weak economy.

✓ CONCEPT CHECK

- ☐ What is a subprime mortgage? **[LO 34.3]**
- ☐ Why did mortgage-backed securities lead to an increase in subprime lending? **[LO 34.4]**
- ☐ How did the 2007 financial crisis impact aggregate demand? **[LO 34.5]**
- ☐ What is the dilemma involved in deciding whether to bail out a bank that is considered "too big to fail"? **[LO 34.6]**
- ☐ Why would a central bank implement quantitative easing? **[LO 34.7]**

Conclusion

This chapter began with a simple question: Why do financial crises occur? Usually, financial crises arise from a combination of irrational expectations and leverage, which create bubbles that burst with dire consequences for the real economy. Crises have been around since the very first financial markets, as the example of the South Seas Company in the 1700s shows.

These forces surfaced once again when innovations in the subprime lending market led to a dramatic increase in home ownership and housing prices. When the real estate bubble burst in 2007, a financial crisis struck again, challenging economists' belief that economic crises had become a thing of the past.

Recent events show that we still have much to learn about the macroeconomy. Can we permanently moderate the business cycle? How will increasing global interdependency affect future crises? What can governments do to make financial markets work better? There are no quick and easy answers to these questions, but we are starting to better understand the complexity of the challenges. The unfortunate reality is that economies can collapse almost overnight, but they often take a lot longer to recover.

Key Terms

bubble, p. 894	securitization, p. 900	"too big to fail," p. 908
leverage, p. 896	debt service, p. 903	quantitative easing, p. 910
leverage ratio, p. 897	stagflation, p. 907	

Summary

LO 34.1 Describe the role of irrational expectations and leverage in the creation of financial crises.

The existence of financial crises challenges the efficient-market hypothesis, showing that markets may not always accurately reflect all available information. Irrational expectations, often based on overly optimistic projections for the future, frequently lead to overvaluations of companies' stocks. Combined with leverage, irrational expectations can create or fuel financial crises.

LO 34.2 Discuss the causes of two famous historical financial crises.

The twin dangers of irrational expectations and leverage played out in two famous historical financial crises. The South Seas Bubble of the eighteenth century is one example: Unrealistic expectations about access to trade with South America led to dramatic overvaluation of companies and spawned fanciful investment schemes. Centuries later, the optimism and rush to invest in the stock market following the Roaring Twenties gave way to the Crash of 1929 and a decade of economic decline during the Great Depression.

LO 34.3 Trace the role of mortgage-backed securities and tranching in the rise of subprime lending.

Securitization in the market for mortgage loans created a wave of subprime lending. Investment banks packaged these loans into larger mortgage-backed securities, which pooled the risk of subprime loans and enabled more loans to be made. Eventually, banks began tranching these securities, dividing them into segments with different risk and return characteristics. This process allowed the banks to tailor mortgage-backed securities to their clients' investment needs. It also contributed to asymmetric information problems, which later contributed to the crisis.

LO 34.4 Analyze the factors that led to the housing bubble and rising levels of household debt.

Securitization of mortgage loans encouraged banks to offer more subprime mortgages, increasing demand for housing and pushing up prices. At the same time, homeowners found themselves with more wealth because the price of their homes had risen. Feeling wealthier, people increased their household debt, taking out more loans at attractive low interest rates, to pay for higher levels of consumption.

LO 34.5 Explain how the collapse of the housing bubble created a credit crisis and subsequent contraction in output.

Eventually, the housing bubble popped. Many subprime borrowers defaulted on their loans after teaser rates expired; home prices dropped, and banks found themselves with mortgage-backed securities worth a fraction of their original estimate. Many banks stopped lending and many failed; credit markets dried up. Businesses were no longer able to finance economic investments. Households, facing a negative shock to wealth due to depressed housing prices, began saving more and consuming less. Both aggregate demand and aggregate

supply shifted to the left. At the new equilibrium, output was dramatically lower. Prices fell because the effect of the leftward shift in the aggregate demand curve was stronger than the effect of the leftward shift in aggregate supply. The economy entered a recession.

LO 34.6 Describe the monetary and fiscal policy responses to the financial crisis of 2008.

In response to the crisis, the federal government acted quickly to stabilize the financial system. The Federal Reserve, in its role as the lender of last resort, offered short-term financing to banks that couldn't access credit otherwise. This provided liquidity to the market, a crucial step in raising aggregate supply. The government also tackled solvency issues by bailing out several large banks through the Troubled Assets Relief Program (TARP). Once the crisis gave way to a contraction in output, the government used fiscal policy to increase aggregate demand by passing stimulus measures.

LO 34.7 Describe the different tools that can be used to stimulate the economy when interest rates are at the zero lower bound.

When the monetary policy hit the zero lower bound, the Fed undertook quantitative easing, designed to increase the money supply by a certain amount. In two rounds of quantitative easing, it directly purchased a total of $3 trillion in long-term government bonds, thus adding that amount to the money supply.

Review Questions

1. Your best friend comes to you for financial investment advice. She is wondering whether she should invest in (a) a sector of the economy that has been performing extremely well in the last five years relative to historical levels or (b) one that has been performing extremely poorly in the last five years relative to historical levels. What would you advise? How might irrational expectations affect your recommendations? **[LO 34.1]**

2. What is leverage, and how can it make an asset pricing bubble worse? **[LO 34.1]**

3. What causes a stock market bubble to form? **[LO 34.2]**

4. History suggests that all stock market bubbles will eventually pop and cause severe financial loss for many of those who purchased stock. Given this history, do you think that stock market bubbles will continue to occur? Why or why not? **[LO 34.2]**

5. Explain why it's possible for tranching to make investing in a mortgage-backed security more risky than investing in a single subprime loan. **[LO 34.3]**

6. Explain how a mortgage-backed security can increase loan availability to those with little credit or bad credit. **[LO 34.3]**

7. Explain the role that leverage played in the recent housing bubble. **[LO 34.4]**

8. How did government policies and asymmetric information problems make the recent housing bubble worse? **[LO 34.4]**

9. Many subprime borrowers entered into "adjustable-rate mortgages" with low teaser rates. These mortgages allowed borrowers to pay a low interest rate for the first two years on their mortgage, before the rate jumped to market levels. But the loan documents sometimes made it difficult for borrowers to understand that the rate would increase. Explain why this practice could lead to a bubble in housing prices. **[LO 34.5]**

10. How did the recent housing crisis affect the aggregate demand curve? **[LO 34.5]**

11. Imagine what would have happened if the Federal Reserve was not in place to act as a lender of last resort during the financial crisis. Absent government involvement, what would be the likely effect on aggregate supply? Why? What would be the likely effect on aggregate demand? Why? **[LO 34.6]**

12. As the Federal Reserve responded to the recent housing crisis, how did this affect its balance sheet? Can you think of what caused the balance sheet's size to change so much? **[LO 34.6]**

13. What is the "zero lower bound" that must be considered in monetary policy, and how can it cause problems in enacting such policy? **[LO 34.7]**

14. What is quantitative easing, and when might it be used? **[LO 34.7]**

Problems and Applications

1. Determine whether or not each of the following is an example of irrational expectations. **[LO 34.1]**

   a. The price of Amazon's stock rises after tech blogs reveal that the company plans to release a new tablet, rumored to be competitive with Apple's iPad.

   b. The CEO of a new start-up producing applications for tablets is quoted as proclaiming a new era of media, in which thirst for content will rise indefinitely as information becomes more and more convenient for people to digest. An economics blog continues the discussion a year later, discussing returns to investment that have never before been contemplated. Stock prices for media companies are consistently outperforming

   historical levels by 50 percent and seem to be on a permanent rise.

   c. After an unusually cool summer, investors in Papa's Cool-Pops decide to sell, believing demand for frozen treats will never reach historic levels again because of the weather.

   d. The Justice Department reveals allegations against the CEO of a food and beverage company, alleging misconduct within the company. A trial could cost the company millions of dollars. The stock price falls by 5 percent by the day's end.

2. Ike, an investor, is considering opening a margin account and investing $1,000 in Mike's mutual fund. The terms of the account require that he pay back the amount he borrowed on the margin by the end of the year with 10 percent interest. Ike is trying to decide what level of margin he wants. For example, if he chooses an account at the level of 50 percent, the bank will let him borrow and invest an additional $500, or 50 percent of his original $1,000. Complete Table 34P-1 by filling in Ike's account value at the end of the year, given varying levels of the margin account and mutual fund performance. Assume that Mike's mutual fund will return 40 percent per year in a stellar market and 5 percent per year in a fair market, and that in a terrible market, it will lose 30 percent. **[LO 34.1]**

3. Consider a stock whose value increases across an 8-year period as shown in Table 34P-2. **[LO 34.2]**

   a. Calculate the percentage change in the value of the stock from year to year.

   b. Calculate the percentage change in the value of the stock across the entire 8-year period.

   c. Do you think this qualifies as a bubble? Why or why not?

4. Assume that a subprime mortgage involves a loan of $1,000 and is to be paid back in full with 30 percent interest after one year. **[LO 34.3]**

   a. Sometimes borrowers will not be able to pay off the entire mortgage or may default entirely. Calculate the final amount of money an investor earns under the payback rates shown in Table 34P-3. (Note that a rate of 130 percent means that the whole loan is paid off, plus the additional 30 percent of interest.)

   b. Assume investors are unwilling to invest in these loans unless the expected rate of return is 10 percent. Calculate the expected rate of return for this loan by adding up all of the products of the final value and the probability that that value will occur. Will investors want to invest in this loan?

TABLE 34P-1

Margin account level	Account value in a stellar market	Account value in a fair market	Account value in a terrible market
No margin			
60%			
100%			
150%			
200%			

TABLE 34P-2

Year	Stock Value ($)	Percentage Change
1	50.00	n/a
2	60.00	
3	75.00	
4	86.25	
5	103.50	
6	155.25	
7	248.40	
8	372.60	

TABLE 34P-3

Amount paid (%)	Final value	Probability
130		0.6
110		0.1
100		0.1
50		0.1
0		0.1

TABLE 34P-4

Number of loans	Probability of default (%)	Weighted risk
40	3.0	40% × 3% = 1.2%
25	11.0	
15	1.5	
20	5.0	

category by multiplying the percentage of loans represented (for example, the first tier includes 40 loans, which is $\frac{40}{100} = 40\%$ of the total) times the probability of default on loans of that category. Do so for each type of loan, then add together the weighted risks to come up with an overall expected default risk for this financial investment. If the bank is willing to take on only projects for which the default risk is 6 percent or less, which option(s) should it choose? **[LO 34.3]**

6. Table 34P-5 shows hypothetical levels of average household debt and debt service payments in two years, 2010 and 2013. At what annual interest rate would consumers have had to borrow for the debt-service payments in 2013 to equal the debt-service payments in 2010, despite the increase in household debt? Assume households are paying only interest on their debt and not part of the principal. **[LO 34.4]**

TABLE 34P-5

	2010	2013
Household debt	$20,000	$80,000
Annual debt-service payments	800	?

5. A single bank is considering two options: First, it can make a $200,000 mortgage loan for a customer with a 10 percent probability of default or, second, it can buy a $200,000 security representing a bundle of 100 mortgage loans, which break down as shown in Table 34P-4. You can calculate the weighted risk for each firm

TABLE 34P-6

Year	Household income ($)	Financial obligations ($)	Financial obligations as % of income	Household debt ($)	Debt as % of income
2011	35,000	4,000			
2012	38,500	4,200			
2013	42,000	5,000			
2014	45,250	6,200			

7. Table 34P-6 gives information on income and debt for a small nation for the years 2011 through 2014. The nation had average household debt of $34,000 at the end of 2010. Use this information to fill in the blanks. **[LO 34.4]**

8. Imagine that your personal finances are summarized by the account balances shown in Table 34P-7. Assume also that your decision to save is a function of your income and net worth. More specifically, assume that your savings each year will be equal to: $0.2I - NW$, where I is your income and NW is your net worth. **[LO 34.4]**

    a. If your income is $60,000, how much will you save this year?

    b. Assume the value of your house decreases by 20 percent. What is your net worth now? How much will you save?

9. If the rate currently payable on 10-year Treasury bonds is 4.8 percent and the risk spread is 2 percent, what is the average rate on other forms of commercial lending? **[LO 34.5]**

10. Which of the following policies were used in response to the latest financial crisis? Of those used, which are examples of monetary policy? Of fiscal policy? **[LO 34.6]**

    a. Aggressive controlling of inflation by raising interest rates.

    b. Providing short-term financing directly to small businesses to jump-start investment.

    c. Bailing out banks that have large amounts of risky mortgage-backed securities.

    d. Purchasing long-term bonds to increase the money supply.

    e. Raising the Social Security eligibility age by five years to encourage people to work.

11. Table 34P-8 shows the balance sheet of a bank in millions of dollars. **[LO 34.6]**

    a. What is the bank's net worth?

    b. Assume housing prices increase and defaults on subprime mortgages rise, causing the bank's assets in subprime mortgages to decrease from $500 million to $350 million. What are total assets now? What is the bank's new net worth?

    c. How far would the value of subprime mortgages have to fall to cause the bank to be insolvent (that is, for liabilities to be greater than assets)?

TABLE 34P-7

Assets		Liabilities	
Home	$100,000	Mortgage	$ 90,000
Checking account	15,000	Student loans	20,000
Car	10,000	Credit card	10,000
Total assets	$125,000	Total liabilities	$120,000

TABLE 34P-8

Assets (in millions)		Liabilities (in millions)	
Cash	$ 800	CDs	$2,000
Commercial loans	2,000	Savings accounts	1,500
Consumer loans	600	Long-term debt	1,000
Prime mortgages	800		
Subprime mortgages	500		
Total assets	$4,700	Total liabilities	$4,500

12. Japan's economic situation throughout its Lost Decade and beyond can be explained in terms of problems with monetary policy via interest rates. Explain what happened. Identify what Japan's central bank should have done. **[LO 34.7]**

13. Consider an economy with $10 billion in base money and a multiplier of 4. The money supply is currently $10 billion × 4 = $40 billion. Now let's say that the amount of base money rises by 50 percent, to $15 billion. How must the multiplier change for the money supply to remain unaffected by this change in base money? **[LO 34.7]**

Endnotes

1. *Futures* are standardized financial contracts that obligate the buyer to either buy or sell a specified amount of some asset at a particular price at a specific future date. There are two main motivations for buying futures. One is "hedging": Companies and individuals use futures contracts to reduce uncertainty about prices in the future. The other is "speculating": Other investors use futures contracts as a way to make bets on the direction of price changes—and, they hope, to make profits by betting correctly.

2. Holding liabilities constant, equity increases by exactly as much as assets. Since assets are 30 times the size of equity, a 10 percent increase in assets amounts to a 300 percent increase in equity.

3. This provision was effectively reversed by the Gramm-Leach-Bliley Act in 1999.

Part Ten

International Policy Issues

The two chapters in Part 10 will introduce you to . . .

the international financial system and development policy. Chapter 35, "Open-Market Macroeconomics," covers the *international financial system.* If you've ever traveled abroad and traded your dollars for another currency, you've participated in one part of the international financial system. Yet it goes much further than that. Anything that was originally produced internationally and imported into the United States was made possible by the international trade of money. In this chapter, we'll introduce the markets that make this trade possible. Like the domestic financial system, the international financial system is vitally important to the smooth operation of the U.S. economy. We'll describe how it works and where it can get into trouble.

Chapter 36, "Development Economics," turns to a large and pressing question: Why is the world filled with poverty amid so much wealth? This is one of the basic questions in *development economics.* We'll describe how understandings of economic development have changed over time. We'll review the current state of research and introduce promising new methods to rigorously evaluate policies and innovations that aim to reduce poverty. Finally, we'll give some examples of solutions that draw on ideas developed in this book—solutions that are making a practical difference in people's lives.

Throughout the text we've seen how economics sheds light on many questions, decisions, and policy issues. Some (such as tax policy) are more obviously about "economics" and some less so. We hope that in reading, you've learned how to apply the economic toolkit to help you solve everyday problems at home and investigate questions about the world around us.

Open-Market Macroeconomics

FROM FACTORY TO FIGURES

The Apple iPhone has been a runaway success. Since its release in June 2007 to the end of 2015, Apple has sold over 896 million phones around the world.[1] You might think of the iPhone as an all-American success story, given that Apple is a U.S. company. Technically, though, the iPhone counts as an import. That's because, like so many consumer goods, the iPhone's component parts are put together in a factory in China before the finished product is shipped to the United States.

© Qilai Shen/Bloomberg via Getty Images

The fact that the iPhone is considered an import means that every iPhone bought in the United States contributes to the trade deficit the United States has with China. In 2015, American consumers bought $483 billion worth of goods from China, while American firms sold only $116 billion worth of goods to consumers in China. The result is an astronomical $367 billion *trade gap* between what America is buying from China and what it is selling there. Mobile phone imports account for 2.3 percent of total imports from China, according to U.S. Census data for 2015. Two economists found that in 2010 iPhones *alone* contributed $1.9 billion to the U.S.–China trade deficit.

To see what this trade gap really means, imagine for a moment that China bought exactly as much from the United States as it sold to the United States. What would happen? Americans would convert $483 billion U.S. into the Chinese currency, the yuan, and use it to buy Chinese goods. In turn, Chinese people would use those $483 billion to buy American goods. Everything would balance out.

In reality, though, the Chinese use only $116 billion to buy American goods. So there must be $367 billion still sloshing around the Chinese economy. Presumably the Chinese don't just keep this money under their mattresses. Where does it end up?

Some dollars are spent or invested at home or abroad, searching for the best return. A lot of them end up being invested in U.S. government debt, which means the Chinese use the money to make *loans to* the U.S. government. Overall, the U.S. government has borrowed more than $1.6 trillion directly from Chinese investors by selling U.S. Treasury securities.[2] The web of international financial connections is something to think about the next time you see an iPhone.

What explains trade flows? How and why does the United States accrue debt to China? Why would China lend to the United States? What determines the rate at which dollars can be converted into yuan? This chapter will answer those questions by exploring international economics. We examine the flow of goods and money around the world and then discuss related shifts in the value of a country's currency.

By showing how to understand the macroeconomy in an international context, this chapter sheds light on important policy debates about exchange rates, trade balances, and capital flows across countries.

International Flows of Goods and Capital

International trade is not a new thing. More than 3,000 years ago, China was exporting textiles along the famed Silk Road to the Mediterranean and Persian empires. Spices were traveling from India to the Roman Empire along the Spice Route. The voyage of Christopher Columbus was inspired by the desire to find a quicker route to the riches of India. Today, modern communications and ease of transportation have allowed international flows of goods and capital to reach unprecedented levels: Consumers in Europe buy freshly cut flowers from Kenya, Americans dine on shrimp from Thailand, and Chinese utility companies ship in coal from Colombia.

In this section, we look at the different ways in which goods and capital flow around the global economy today.

Imports and exports

LO 35.1 Define the balance of trade and describe the general trends of U.S. trade.

First, let's look at some patterns of trade in the United States. Figure 35-1 shows trade flows over the last 50 years. You can see that both exports and imports have increased dramatically over this period as the economy has grown. In 2015, exports of goods and services were $2.3 trillion, or approximately 13 percent of GDP. Imports the same year were $2.8 trillion, or approximately 15.5 percent of GDP.

It is interesting to look at the flows in and out, but the number that economists care the most about is the net value of these flows. Called the **balance of trade**, it is the value of exports minus the value of imports. The balance of trade can be either negative or positive:

- If a country imports more than it exports, the balance of trade is negative. Economists call this situation a **trade deficit**. For nearly every year since 1970, the United States has had a trade deficit. In 2015, the trade balance was –$500 billion, or about 2.8 percent of GDP.

- If a country exports more than it imports, the balance of trade is positive. In that case, the country is said to have a **trade surplus**. Countries like Japan, China, and Germany run large trade surpluses. For example, the 2015 trade surplus in Germany was worth around 8.8 percent of its GDP.[3]

Figure 35-1 shows the total trade balance of the United States with all the other countries in the world. If you had to guess, which countries would you expect to be the main trading partners of the United States? Because trade requires transporting goods, which costs money, countries tend to trade with their neighbors. This holds true for the United States. Two of its biggest trading

balance of trade
the value of exports minus the value of imports

trade deficit
a negative balance of trade; a greater amount of imports than exports

trade surplus
a positive balance of trade; a greater amount of exports than imports

---

FIGURE 35-1

Imports, exports, and the balance of U.S. trade since 1960 Until 1980, trade by the United States was relatively balanced; imports were roughly equal to exports. Shortly thereafter, the amount of imports grew faster than the amount of exports, which led to a negative trade balance. Now, the trade deficit stands at $500 billion.

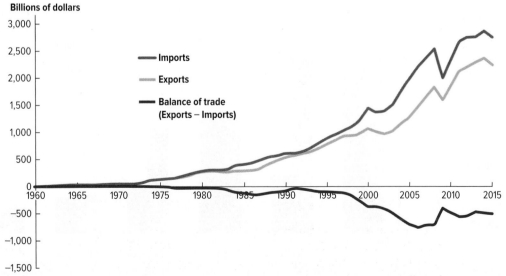

Source: U.S. Census Bureau, Historical Series: Annual Goods, Services, and Total Balance, Exports and Imports; https://www.census.gov/foreign-trade/statistics/historical/index.html.

partners are its neighbors: Canada to the north and Mexico to the south. In addition to being neighbors, trade has expanded because of the North American Free Trade Agreement (NAFTA), a pact that eliminates barriers to trade and investment among these neighbors.

Of course, as Figure 35-2 shows, not all trade partners are neighbors. In fact, the United States imports more goods from China than from any other country, including its neighbors Mexico and Canada. And the United States imports much more from China than it exports to it. This difference generates a negative trade balance with China that makes up about half of the total U.S. trade deficit for goods. As we go through this chapter, we'll examine explanations for the trade deficit with China. One factor is that Chinese products tend to be low in price. We'll also look at less-obvious factors such as the amount of savings in China and its exchange-rate policies.

We've seen how much the United States is trading and with whom—but *what* is it trading? As we described in Chapter 2, "Specialization and Exchange," there are *gains from trade* when countries specialize in producing particular goods and then trade with others to meet their other needs. Looking at trade statistics shows exactly where the gains from trade in the United States come from. Figure 35-3 shows the main categories of goods that the United States exports and imports, and the contribution to the trade balance for each category.

FIGURE 35-2

Major U.S. trading partners

Much of U.S. trade occurs with its closest neighbors, Canada and Mexico. However, the United States's biggest trading partner is China, even though it is far away. Trade between the United States and China consists mostly of imports into the United States.

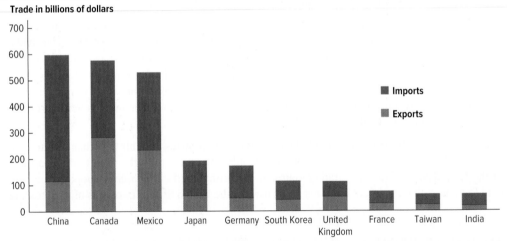

Trade in billions of dollars

Source: U.S. Census Bureau, Top Trading Partners for 2015, https://www.census.gov/foreign-trade/statistics/highlights/top/top1512yr.html.

FIGURE 35-3

What does the United States trade?

The United States imports a large amount of capital goods—things that are used to produce other goods—which also constitute the largest U.S. export. The largest difference between imports and exports is in the category of consumer goods, as the United States imports far more consumer goods than it exports.

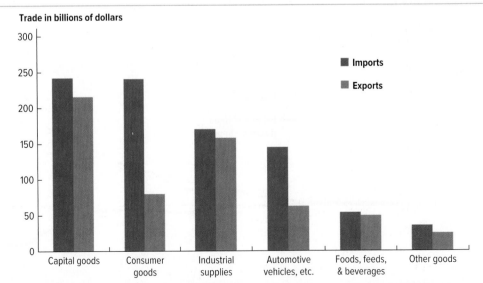

Trade in billions of dollars

Source: U.S. Census Bureau, U.S. Bureau of Economic Analysis News, July 6, 2016. Data for January through May 2016. http://www.bea.gov/newsreleases/international/trade/2016/pdf/trad0516.pdf.

The largest category of U.S. exports is capital goods—goods such as semiconductors and industrial machines. The United States exported $216 billion in capital goods in the first half of 2016. At the same time, it imported $243 billion worth of capital goods, mostly computers and telecommunications equipment. The balance of trade in capital goods was −$27 billion.

While the amount the United States imports and exports is pretty close for capital goods, consumer goods are dominated by imports—goods such as clothing, smartphones, pharmaceuticals, and toys. The balance of trade in consumer goods was nearly −$161 billion, with imports of about $241 billion and exports of about $80 billion for the first half of 2016. In fact, as of May 2016, the United States was running a negative trade balance in all categories. The "Foods, feeds, and beverages" category has the smallest trade deficit; the high value of U.S. exports of soybeans and corn, subsidized in part by the U.S. government, explains this.

Foreign investment

LO 35.2 Define portfolio investment and foreign direct investment.

Imports and exports are the most visible and straightforward aspects of international economics. Countries interact in other ways as well, including through investment. The investment when a firm runs part of its operation abroad or owns all or part of another company abroad is called **foreign direct investment (FDI)**. Foreign direct investment often makes economic sense for businesses—it helps broaden markets and can cut wage costs, for example. Some people object that such investment can encourage "sweatshops" abroad, where workers work for long hours under worse conditions than would be allowed in the United States. For a discussion of some of the issues surrounding foreign investment, see the What Do You Think? box "Are sweatshops good or bad?"

foreign direct investment (FDI) investment when a firm runs part of its operation abroad or owns all or part of another company abroad

What Do You Think?

Are sweatshops good or bad?

In 2001, an MIT graduate student named Jonah Peretti ordered a pair of sneakers from the NIKE iD service, which allows customers to personalize their shoes with a word of their choice. Peretti asked that his be emblazoned with the word "sweatshop." Nike refused, claiming that the word violated the NIKE iD terms and conditions because it was "inappropriate slang."

Peretti e-mailed back, with false innocence:

After consulting Webster's Dictionary, I discovered that "sweatshop" is in fact part of standard English, and not slang. The word means: "a shop or factory in which workers are employed for long hours at low wages and under unhealthy conditions" and its origin dates from 1892. . . . Your web site advertises that the NIKE iD program is "about freedom to choose and freedom to express who you are." I share Nike's love of freedom and personal expression. . . . I hope that you will value my freedom of statement and reconsider your decision to reject my order.

Nike again refused, doubtless not wanting the bad publicity of someone walking around in a pair of "Nike Sweatshops." But Nike got bad publicity anyway when the e-mail exchange with Peretti went viral, sparking media coverage around the globe. Peretti had a pointed goal—to shame Nike for the use of "sweatshop" labor to make its shoes. (Nike, for its part, has since taken steps to improve labor standards and monitor conditions.)

Yet here is the irony: Although they are bad for publicity, it's not entirely clear that sweatshops are always such a bad thing. Economists, including Jeffrey Sachs of Columbia University,

(continued)

argue that some kinds of sweatshops are good for an economy. After all, the fact that people choose to work in sweatshops indicates that these jobs are better for them than their other options. Outside of working in the factories, the only alternative may be backbreaking agricultural work that pays even less than the low wages offered by sweatshops. By bringing people out of agriculture, sweatshops provide a source of relative financial security and contribute toward the growth of the economy.

Those who forwarded Peretti's e-mail exchange with Nike presumably felt uneasy with Sachs's argument. Critics of sweatshops think it's wrong that workers can toil for as long as 80 hours per week for what most Americans would consider a tiny wage. Often, it is not just that wages are low by U.S. standards. In addition, workers may be unknowingly exposed to hazardous chemicals and dangerous machinery. Such a problem could be a market failure due to information asymmetry if employees are not fully aware of the risks they are taking. Even where safety regulations exist, workers may be unable to report violations to local authorities without fear of retribution.

WHAT DO YOU THINK?

1. Why do rich countries tend to have stricter labor standards than poor counties? How do you think these labor standards developed?
2. If consumers feel uneasy about buying goods made in overseas sweatshops, should they support efforts to enact minimum wage and worker safety legislation all over the world? Why or why not?

Source: "Making Nike Sweat," Village Voice, February 13, 2001.

---

foreign portfolio investment
investment funded by foreign sources but operated domestically

Of course, investment abroad doesn't have to be just in tangible assets such as factories. Often, investors also want to buy foreign financial assets, such as stocks or government-issued securities. We call this type of investment *foreign portfolio investment*. **Foreign portfolio investment** is investment funded by foreign sources but operated domestically. Portfolio investment allows investors to hold financial assets that deliver greater profit and reduce overall risk relative to financial investments available at home.

Portfolio investment can generally flow across borders quickly because it mainly involves transfers between bank accounts. When a country is small, the rapid movement of money across borders can easily overwhelm the country's financial markets. Foreign direct investment doesn't move as fast. You cannot just pick up a factory and move it across the border.

One of the largest portfolio investments comes from Chinese purchases of U.S. government debt. Part of the reason for this investment is that Chinese investors have a large reserve of U.S. dollars, so they want to buy assets that are U.S. dollar–denominated. Why do they have a large reserve of U.S. dollars? Because, as noted earlier, every time we buy Chinese goods, someone had to sell dollars in exchange for *yuan* to pay for these products. One option for what to do with all these dollars is to use them to buy U.S. Treasury bills.

net capital flow
the net flow of funds invested outside of a country; specifically, the difference between capital inflows (investment financed by savings from another country) and capital outflows (domestic savings invested abroad)

When the total amount of foreign direct investment and foreign portfolio investment is tallied, we can find the net investment position of a country. The **net capital flow** is the net flow of funds invested outside of a country. Specifically, net capital flow is the difference between capital inflows and capital outflows:

- *Capital inflows* are investments financed by savings from another country. Countries that have a trade deficit have a *net capital inflow.*
- *Capital outflows* are domestic savings invested abroad. Countries that have a trade surplus have a positive *net capital outflow.*

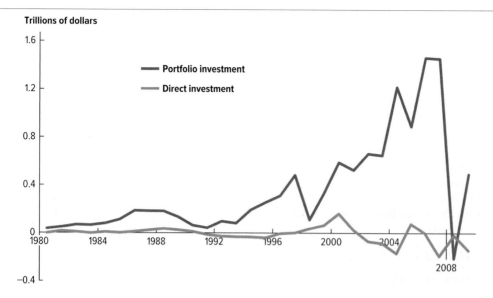

Trillions of dollars

— Portfolio investment
— Direct investment

Source: U.S. Bureau of Economic Analysis (accessed June 29, 2011).

FIGURE 35-4

Net capital flows for the United States

For a long time, portfolio and direct investment flows in the United States were small. Then, starting with the tech bubble, portfolio investment began to ramp up, blipped downward before the bubble popped, and then completely exploded in the housing bubble. The falloff from this crash was severe: In the span of one year, portfolio investment fell from $1.4 trillion to an outflow of $200 billion.

Figure 35-4 shows net capital outflow for the United States over 30 years. You can see that the capital outflow is broken down into the two types of foreign investment: direct investment and portfolio investment.

The trade in goods, services, and capital comprises trillions of dollars around the world. Keeping track of the trade balance and net capital flows helps organize these transactions. In general, the accounting for trade in goods and capital is known as the *balance of payments.*

Balance of payments

LO 35.3 Explain the connection between the balance of trade and net capital outflow.

How are countries like the United States able to sustain large deficits in trade? It turns out that trade in tangible goods and different types of capital must balance each other out, balancing trade deficits with capital surpluses. This is shown through the **balance-of-payments identity**, an equation that shows that the value of net exports equals the net capital outflow.

Recall the income-expenditure identity from Chapter 24, "Measuring GDP." The identity for a closed economy—that is, one with no imports or exports—looks like this:

$$Y = C + I + G$$

Remember also that in a closed economy, savings (S) equal investment (I). We have two kinds of savings in the economy: *private savings,* which is the money left over that households and businesses don't spend, and *public savings,* which is the money left over that the government doesn't spend. Thus, rearranging the variables in the income-expenditure identify, we find:

(1) $I = Y - C - G$

(2) $S = S_{private} + S_{public} = Y - C - G$

(3) $S = I$

What do things look like if we open up the economy and add in the variable of net exports? We get the typical equation for GDP, also known as the income-expenditure identity:

$$Y = C + I + G + NX$$

balance-of-payments identity
an equation that shows that the value of net exports equals net capital outflow

If we then rearrange the income-expenditure identity for an open economy, we get something that looks very similar to the equation above, except that savings equals investment plus net exports.

(4) $I + NX = Y - C - G$

(5) $S = S_{private} + S_{public} = Y - C - G$

(6) $S = I + NX$

Finally, assume that people can choose where they want to invest: They can invest in the home country; those investments we'll call I, as before. Or they can invest in the rest of the world; those investments we'll call NCO, which stands for "net capital outflow." The total amount of money that a country has to invest, its savings (S), must add up to $I + NCO$. Using this equation and (6) above, we find that net capital outflows to all other countries equal net exports to all other countries:

(7) $S = I + NCO$

(8) $S = I + NX$

(9) $I + NCO = I + NX$

(10) $NCO = NX$

The result—that net capital outflows equal net exports ($NCO = NX$)—is important and answers the question posed in the beginning of this section: *How are countries able to sustain large deficits in trade?* A country that exports more goods than it imports, like China, will necessarily also send out more capital than it receives. That's because China's high net exports must be balanced by high net capital outflows. The capital outflows allow countries to sustain trade imbalances for long periods of time. This idea may seem tricky, so let's work through a simplified example.

Let's assume that China and the United States are both initially closed economies; their savings equal domestic investment. Then, one day, a firm in the United States decides to buy a specialized battery made in China. The Chinese firm sends the battery to the United States, and the U.S. firm gives the Chinese firm a $100 bill.

What will the Chinese firm do with the $100 bill? It can do two things:

- Option 1: It can keep the money in America (for instance, by depositing it in a bank account in the United States, or buying bonds or stocks or financial securities in the United States).

- Option 2: It can buy something in America—say, a collection of economics books—and ship them back to China.

If the Chinese firm decides that it wants to keep the $100 in America, then it has made an investment in the U.S. economy. In other words, the *net capital outflow* from China to the United States is $100. The value of exports—the battery—from China to the United States is $100. Net exports are equal to net capital outflow.

What if, instead of investing the $100, the Chinese firm decides to use to it buy the books and import them back to China? Net exports for China are zero: The Chinese firm exported a $100 battery and imported $100 worth of books. Net capital outflow for China is also zero because the money earned from the batteries was used to buy books, rather than being invested in the United States. Thus, none of its money remains in the United States. So, for China, $NX = NCO$.

Now let's look at the same transaction from the U.S. perspective: In option 1, in which the United States has $100 of its currency owned by China, the U.S. net capital outflow is −$100. Because the U.S. firm bought the battery from China, the United States has net exports of −$100. Net capital outflow equals net exports for the United States as well.

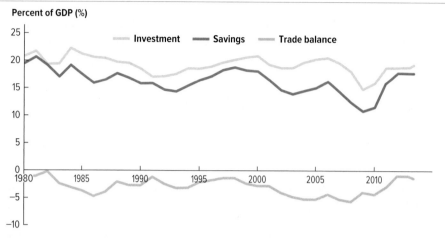

Percent of GDP (%)

Investment — Savings — Trade balance

Sources: The World Bank, http://data.worldbank.org/indicator/NE.GDI.TOTL.ZS and http://data.worldbank.org/indicator/NY.GNS.ICTR.ZS.

FIGURE 35-5

The equivalence of NCO and NX in the United States

The gap between savings and investment in the overall economy is shown by the trade balance. When investment is larger than savings, as it is in the United States, an economy will have a negative trade balance.

What happens from the U.S. perspective in option 2? When the United States initially imported the battery, it had NX of −$100. But then it exported $100 worth of books, so NX became zero. No capital has been invested in or from China, so NCO is zero. For the United States, too, NX = NCO.

The balance-of-payments identity tells us that the net capital outflow of a country equals the value of its net exports. Figure 35-5 shows savings, investment, and net exports in the United States in recent years. Notice that the gap between savings and investment is almost exactly the trade balance. (There may be small differences, which stem from the complexities of measurement.) In general, savings equals investment plus net exports, as we saw in the equations above.

✓ CONCEPT CHECK

☐ Which country is the United States's largest trading partner? **[LO 35.1]**

☐ What is portfolio investment? **[LO 35.2]**

☐ What is the relationship between net capital outflow and net exports in the balance-of-payments identity? **[LO 35.3]**

International Capital Flows

For the last three decades, seas of money have surged into the U.S. economy from abroad, in search of profitable investment opportunities. Why does capital flow into some economies and out of others? In this section, we'll develop a model to explain international capital flows.

Determinants of international capital flows

LO 35.4 Describe the determinants of international capital flows using the demand and supply for international loanable funds.

In Chapter 31, "The Basics of Finance," we developed a model of the market for loanable funds in a closed economy. In that model, the equilibrium interest rate was determined by the intersection of the domestic investment curve and the domestic savings curve—the demand and supply of domestic loanable funds.

How does this model change in an open economy? The basic idea is the same: There still is a demand for and supply of loanable funds. Exactly as before, the supply of loanable funds is the sum of national savings. Savings has a positive relationship with the interest rate. (That is, as the interest rate increases, savers will supply a greater quantity of loanable funds to the market.)

The demand for loanable funds (investment) comes from two sources:

- *Domestic investment* is the same as it was in the domestic market for loanable funds, when we considered the economy to be closed.
- *International investment* comes in two forms: capital inflow (when money from abroad is invested domestically) and capital outflow (when domestic money is invested internationally).

For the sake of this model, we will assume that all investment transactions occur through loanable funds. When we subtract capital inflows from capital outflows, we get *net capital outflows (NCO).* This NCO plus domestic investment form the demand for loanable funds in the open economy. What does this demand curve look like?

We can start with the fact that domestic investment has a negative relationship with the interest rate. (That is, lower interest rates make it cheaper for firms to invest in equipment and factories.) Let's use that knowledge to think about the intuition behind how capital inflows and outflows will be affected by U.S. interest rates. Suppose the domestic interest rate declines:

- People in the United States will start to look overseas for opportunities to earn more interest on their money. The result will be higher capital outflows.
- Meanwhile, people overseas will be less keen to invest in the United States because of the lower returns, so there will be lower capital inflows.

Higher outflows and lower inflows both push *net* outflows in the same direction: *higher.*

Now suppose the interest rate goes up. In that case, the opposite happens:

- People in the United States will be more willing to keep their savings in the country; outflows will go down.
- At the same time, people overseas will send their financial investments to the United States in pursuit of better returns; inflows will go up.

Lower outflows and higher inflows both push net outflows in the same direction: *lower.*

When we put this result together with domestic investment, as shown in Figure 35-6, we get the combined I + NCO curve—which is the *demand for loanable funds in the open economy.* In the open economy, the equilibrium interest rate is found at the intersection of national savings and the combined I + NCO curve.

For a real-life example of the power of domestic investment and capital inflows, see the Real Life box "Iceland and the banking crisis." In 2007, banks in Iceland held $90 billion in their accounts, far more than the entire country's GDP. When these banks ran into trouble, the whole country was thrown into crisis.

Real Life

Iceland and the banking crisis

Iceland is a volcanic island in the North Atlantic Ocean, located between Greenland and the United Kingdom. The country is home to some 300,000 people, and until recently was best known as the home of the eccentric singer Björk. That changed in 2010 when a collapse of the banking sector in this quiet island nation nearly brought down the entire world economy.

Until the early 2000s, Icelandic banks were small and largely focused on catering to the basic financing needs of local citizens. Then Iceland deregulated its banking industry, and the country's banks expanded throughout Europe. This process was fueled by the Icelandic central bank's determination to control inflation by keeping interest rates high. We have seen that high interest rates lead to negative NCO (that is, a net *inflow* of capital).

Sure enough, money flowed into Iceland as savers from all over Europe rushed to deposit money in Icelandic banks. The banks grew bigger and bigger, creating leverage as they borrowed against the savings, and eventually amassing foreign debt of more than $90 billion, six times larger than Iceland's entire GDP. (All the money people deposited with them constituted foreign debt.)

As the financial crisis and Great Recession of 2008 washed up on Iceland's shores, all three of its major banks collapsed. Savers saw their savings evaporate. Could the government of Iceland have decided to bail out the banks to keep the wider economy from derailing? In theory, yes. But unfortunately Iceland's banks had grown so big that even the state couldn't afford to bail them out. Iceland had to ask the International Monetary Fund, the global agency responsible for helping to maintain international financial stability, to step in with emergency funds of $6 billion to keep the country's financial system functioning.

As the Icelandic economy shrank by more than 6 percent in 2009 alone, the British and Dutch governments undertook legal action to try to recover their citizens' billions in lost banking deposits. Not surprisingly, the people of Iceland reacted badly to the idea that their taxes should have to compensate British and Dutch savers. After all, ordinary Icelanders had little to do with the risky behavior of their nation's banks.

Icelanders vented their frustration at the politicians who had allowed this mess to happen by voting an absurdist comedian in as the new mayor of the capital city. His policy platform? "We should have this huge statue of Björk at the harbor like the Statue of Liberty." Sadly, the new mayor did not find the money to enact this plan.

Sources: http://www.nytimes.com/2010/06/26/world/europe/26iceland.html; debt statistics from the Central Bank of Iceland.

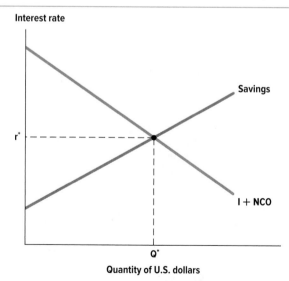

Interest rate

Savings

r*

I + NCO

Q*

Quantity of U.S. dollars

FIGURE 35-6

Expanded market for loanable funds

The market for loanable funds in the open economy is determined by both domestic and international investment as well as the amount of domestic savings. Domestic and international investment is reflected in the I + NCO curve. The interest rate is determined by the intersection of the savings curve and the combined investment + net capital outflow curve.

Effects of foreign investment

LO 35.5 Show how the international market for loanable funds can be used to explain events in the international financial system.

Using our model of international capital flows, we can begin to examine the impact of foreign investment—and understand why it's often economically beneficial. In short, foreign investment can

- Increase the GDP of the host country by giving it access to additional resources.
- Increase the GDP of the investing country by providing it with ways to earn higher returns on its capital.
- Make the world a more efficient place by moving capital from places with low returns to places with high returns.

To see how this works, imagine that financial troubles abroad trigger a "flight to quality," where investors suddenly find lower-risk U.S. government bonds more attractive as a safe haven for savings. Figure 35-7 shows what happens in this case. The shift in preferences toward investing in the United States means that the demand curve for loanable funds in the open economy will shift to the left, for two reasons. First, foreign investors are now more eager to purchase U.S. assets than they were before, so net capital outflows contract ($NCO_1 > NCO_2$). In addition, the existence of better investment opportunities in the United States means that domestic investors are also going to keep more of their money at home, which again contributes to the leftward shift of the loanable funds curve.

How does this contraction in net capital outflows affect interest rates, saving, and investment in the United States? The increase in demand for U.S. assets means that people are now willing to pay more for the same stream of payments (and investors are now paying more for the same asset), so the rate of return on these assets (that is, the interest rate) falls. The lower rate of return on financial assets makes saving less attractive for people in the United States, which can be seen

FIGURE 35-7

Effect of a flight to quality in the U.S. economy

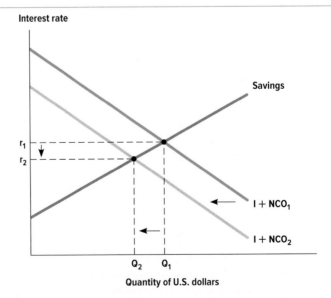

If investors at home and abroad suddenly find lower-risk U.S. government bonds more attractive, the combined investment plus net capital outflow (I + NCO) curve shifts to the left. The result is a lower interst rate, more dollers invested in physical capital, and lower national saving.

FIGURE 35-8

Effect of an increase in the government deficit

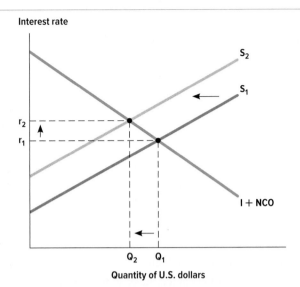

When the government spends more than it collects in revenue, it has to borrow money. This pushes the savings curve left, which results in an increase in the interest rate and lower quantity of investment.

as the leftward movement along the blue savings curve in Figure 35-7. However, the lower interest rate also makes it cheaper for firms to finance capital projects; as a result, investment demand increases. The increase in investment due to the lower interest rates helps explain why the quantity of loanable funds demanded does not fall by the full leftward shift of the I + NCO curve.

Investment is a key component of GDP, so the U.S. economy benefits when foreign investment increases. Foreign investors also benefit from better investment opportunities in the United States, adding to the GDP of their countries.

We can also examine the relationship between foreign investment and public savings. Doing so will bring us closer to understanding the trade imbalance between the United States and China. Recall that the savings curve for the economy reflects the sum of private and public savings. In order to see the connection, let's look at the case of a government budget deficit, which causes a decrease in public savings. When the government runs a deficit, the savings curve shifts to the left, as in Figure 35-8. When this happens, the new equilibrium interest rate is higher than before. With a higher interest rate, there is more incentive to invest in the United States. Less capital flows out and more capital flows in. Net capital outflow decreases and the quantity of loanable funds saved and invested in equilibrium drops.

Although net capital outflow is lower, the higher interest rate in the economy due to a decrease in savings instead means that there is a lower level of domestic investment. Foreign and domestic savings are used to finance the government budget, instead of being used to finance domestic investment. We say that the government deficit "crowds out" domestic investment; the higher interest rate reduces firms' investment in the economy.

As mentioned before, China funds much of the U.S. government deficit by buying Treasury securities. But where does all of that money come from? Ben Bernanke, a Princeton economist and former chair of the Federal Reserve, argues that China is simply saving too much.

Can a country save too much?

Saying that it is possible to save too much is like claiming that it's possible to eat too much broccoli. It's true only at the most ridiculous extremes. But perhaps China's saving rate is at that extreme. After all, it currently saves nearly 50 percent of its GDP! In comparison, the United

States saves only 18 percent of its total income.[4] High domestic savings can keep demand for local products low as people consume less. There are empty malls and vacant housing projects in China, simply waiting for customers to open their wallets. Saving too much can also lead to trade imbalances.

We mentioned this idea in Chapter 31, "The Basics of Finance," but now we have the tools to evaluate the effects of a "global savings glut." A growing propensity to save shifts out the savings curve, decreasing the equilibrium interest rate. Low interest rates in China relative to other markets encourage capital to flow abroad, raising net capital outflow—which explains why China has so much invested in the United States. The massive net capital outflow from China requires that large quantities of Chinese currency are exchanged into U.S. currency. The flip-side is the massive trade imbalance between China and the United States, which requires that large quantities of U.S. currency are exchanged into Chinese currency in order to buy the goods.

If this explanation of the trade imbalance is right, how could it be corrected? Consider a couple of possible solutions:

- One solution could be for China to reduce its savings levels and increase consumption. Imports should rise and exports should fall.

- Another solution could be for the United States to increase its own savings levels and spend a little less. The U.S. economy saves 18 percent overall, but the rate of household savings is low (usually less than 5 percent). The rate of government saving is actually negative (the government is running a budget deficit). If the United States were to increase its total savings, either because households or the government saves more, then capital outflow would increase from the United States, reducing the imbalance.

There's another story, however. Others, particularly politicians, suggest that the trade deficit between the United States and China stems from China's fixed exchange rate, an idea we explore next.

✓ CONCEPT CHECK

☐ Which two curves make up the international market for loanable funds? **[LO 35.4]**

☐ What is the difference between the closed- and open-economy versions of the market for loanable funds? **[LO 35.5]**

☐ Which way does the savings curve shift when the government reduces its deficit? **[LO 35.5]**

Exchange Rates

If you arrive in a foreign country with a pocketful of U.S. dollars, chances are you won't be able to use them locally. Most local shops and restaurants will require local currency, which you can get by exchanging your dollars at a bank or a specialized foreign currency dealer. The price at which the exchange happens is the *exchange rate*. Sometimes the exchange rate gives you lots of local currency for your dollars. Other times, the exchange rate requires you to give more of your dollars for the same amount of local currency. How does the market for currency work?

The foreign-exchange market

LO 35.6 Describe exchange rate appreciation and depreciation and understand their effects on trade.

The market for buying and selling foreign currencies is often referred to as the "forex" market, short for *foreign exchange*. Every weekday people engage in trillions of dollars of transactions around the clock. They trade dollars for euros or euros for Mexican pesos, for example.

Like any other market, in the forex market there are supply, demand, price, and quantity traded. And like any other market, the market for different currencies has a price, which is called the exchange rate. The **exchange rate** is the value of one currency expressed in terms of another currency. For example, in June 2016, one U.S. dollar—abbreviated USD—could be exchanged for 0.80 euro, 6.59 Chinese yuan, or 18.82 Mexican pesos.

exchange rate
the value of one currency expressed in terms of another currency

Exchange rates can be expressed in two ways: either in terms of the domestic currency or in terms of the foreign currency. When we examine the exchange rates between two nations' currencies, the exchange rates will be reciprocals of each other.

> ### HINT
> Recall that the *reciprocal* of a fraction or ratio is just that fraction or ratio "turned upside down" or "flipped over": The numerator (portion above the fraction line) becomes the denominator (portion below the fraction line), and the denominator becomes the numerator. The reciprocal of $\frac{3}{4}$ is $\frac{4}{3}$, and the reciprocal of 2 (equivalent to $\frac{2}{1}$) is therefore $\frac{1}{2}$.

If 1 unit of domestic currency is worth 6 units of a foreign currency, then we can express this equivalently as the foreign currency being worth $\frac{1}{6}$ of a unit of the domestic currency.

In the real world, foreign exchange rates are often expressed in decimal form rather than fraction form, but the same idea applies:

- If \$1 is worth 0.80 euro, then 1 euro is worth \$1.25 (\$1 ÷ 0.80 = 1.25 \$/euro).
- If \$1 is worth 90 yen, then 1 yen is worth \$0.01 (\$1 ÷ 90 = 0.01 \$/yen).

From this point forward, we will express exchange rates *from the point of view of the United States, using the dollar as the domestic currency.* That means that exchange rates will be expressed in terms of *units of foreign currency required to "buy" one dollar.*

Of course, we could also look at things from the perspective of another nation—for example, from Japan's point of view. In that case, the yen would be considered the home currency, and exchange rates would be expressed in terms of the units of foreign currency—dollars, yuan, euro, and so forth—required to "buy" one yen. All concepts discussed in the chapter apply no matter which nation's point of view we assume.

You might wonder if discrepancies between the forex markets, located in so many places, might arise. Is it possible for a trader to make money by taking advantage of discrepancies in currency exchange rates? For example, could a trader convert dollars to pesos in a Mexican forex market, pesos to yuan in a Chinese forex market, yuan to euros in a European forex market, and euros back to dollars in an American forex market and end up with more dollars than she started with? This possibility is known as *arbitrage,* gaining financially by taking advantage of discrepancies in currency exchange rates. Yes, it is possible that money *can* be made on such trades. Because of that possibility, forex traders have sophisticated software constantly scouring information from the world's different forex markets to see if any discrepancies

U.S. dollars can be used all over the world but need to be changed into local currency by currency exchangers. Sometimes this means a bank, and sometimes it is just a small shop, like this one in Manila.
© Joel Nito/AFP/Getty Images

exist. If they find them, they instantly trade the currencies until the discrepancy no longer exists. As a result, any opportunities for arbitrage are fleeting.

Another way in which speculators try to make money from forex is by betting on the direction that an exchange rate will move over time. The value of one currency relative to another can either increase or decrease. When the value of a currency *increases* relative to the value of another currency, we say that a currency experiences **exchange-rate appreciation**. When the currency appreciates, it can "buy" more of another currency. For example, if the U.S. dollar appreciates against the euro—say from 0.7 to 0.8 euro—the result is that one dollar can buy 0.1 more euro than before.

Who benefits when the dollar appreciates against the euro? The U.S. dollar can buy more goods that are denominated in euros, so people who have U.S. dollars and want to buy goods from Europe will benefit. For instance, American tourists in Paris will find that things are cheaper as the dollar appreciates against the euro:

- A French hotel room with a nightly rate of 70 euros would cost $100 at an exchange rate of 0.7 euro per dollar: $\left[70 \text{ euros} \times \left(\frac{\$1}{0.7\,\text{euro}}\right) = \$100\right]$.
- After the dollar appreciates against the euro, and the new exchange rate is 0.8 euro per dollar, the hotel room would cost only $87.50: $\left[70 \text{ euros} \times \left(\frac{\$1}{0.8\,\text{euro}}\right) = \$87.50\right]$.

On the other hand, a U.S. company that sells DVDs in France will find that it has fewer customers:

- A $15 DVD would sell for 10.50 euros in Paris at an exchange rate of 0.7 euro per dollar: $\left[\$15 \times \left(\frac{0.7\,\text{euro}}{\$1}\right) = 10.50 \text{ euros}\right]$.
- After the dollar appreciates against the euro, and the new exchange rate is 0.8 euro per dollar, the $15 DVD would sell for 12 euros: $\left[\$15 \times \left(\frac{0.8\,\text{euro}}{\$1}\right) = 12 \text{ euros}\right]$.

In contrast, when the value of a currency *decreases* relative to other currencies, we say that a currency experiences **exchange-rate depreciation**. When the currency depreciates, it can "buy" less of another currency. In our example, when the dollar appreciates against the euro, logic tells us that the euro has *depreciated* against the dollar. Or imagine the U.S. dollar goes from being worth 6.5 yuan to 6 yuan. We say the U.S. dollar has depreciated—it now buys fewer yuan than it did before. Who's going to be happy if the dollar depreciates against the yuan? U.S. consumers will have to pay more for Chinese goods, which they won't like. On the other hand, U.S. exporters will have an easier time selling to Chinese consumers.

The exchange rate and net exports

Exchange rates affect nearly every dimension of international economics. The flow of goods is one example:

- When the U.S. dollar appreciates against a foreign currency, U.S. goods become more expensive to people abroad, and foreign goods become cheaper for Americans. As a result, we would expect *net exports to decrease*.
- When the U.S. dollar depreciates against a foreign currency, foreign goods become more expensive for Americans, and American goods become cheaper for foreign consumers. We would expect *net exports to increase*.

Does this expectation hold empirically? Figure 35-9 shows U.S. net exports plotted against an exchange-rate index. That index represents the average value of the U.S. dollar against its main trading partners. Just as we would expect:

- When the U.S. dollar goes up in value against other currencies, net exports tend to go down soon afterward. When net exports fall, the trade deficit rises. That's why we see that when the exchange rate rises (as represented by the "Real effective exchange rate index" line in Figure 35-9), the trade deficit will usually rise too.
- Similarly, when the U.S. dollar drops in value, exports tend to go up, which reduces the trade deficit. When the exchange rate falls, so will the trade deficit.

exchange-rate appreciation
an increase in the value of a currency relative to the value of another currency

exchange-rate depreciation
a decrease in the value of a currency relative to other currencies

FIGURE 35-9

Trade deficit and the exchange rate in the United States   In the United States, there is a distinct relationship between the exchange rate (shown here relative to its 2010 level) and the trade deficit. When the exchange rate falls, the trade deficit decreases, although this effect operates on a lag, meaning that it takes time for trade to respond to changes in the exchange rate.

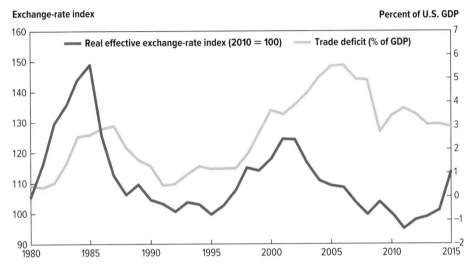

Sources: The World Bank, http://data.worldbank.org/indicator/NE.RSB.GNFS.ZS?end=2015&locations=US&start=1990 and http://data.worldbank.org/indicator/PX.REX.REER.

A model of the exchange-rate market

LO 35.7 Describe the determinants of demand and supply in the forex market.

The foreign-exchange market is a market like any other: There is demand for a currency and a supply of that currency. An equilibrium price and quantity are determined by the intersection of supply and demand. What determines demand and supply in the forex market?

Demand for foreign currency

Let's start with *demand.* Why would foreigners demand foreign currency?

The first determinant of demand for currency comes from *consumer preferences*—from foreign consumers, businesses, and governments that want to use the currency to buy goods or services in the domestic currency. For example, a British family might demand dollars to be able to vacation in Florida. A Japanese shop might demand dollars to import U.S.-made DVDs for sale to Japanese consumers. The Chinese government might demand dollars to be able to purchase financial assets such as U.S. Treasury debt.

The demand for dollars also depends on *interest rates,* both in the United States and abroad:

- High interest rates in the United States relative to overseas will attract foreign capital. These assets need to be paid for in U.S. dollars, so demand for U.S. dollars will increase.

- On the other hand, if foreign interest rates are high relative to those in the United States, demand for dollars will decrease as investors sell their dollars to buy foreign currency for investment.

The last key variable in determining the demand for a country's currency is the *perceived risk* of investing in that country against the perceived risk of investing in other countries. If investors feel confident about putting money into emerging economies such as Russia, Brazil, or

South Africa, they will invest more there, all else equal. If investors decide it is risky to invest in such countries compared to the United States, then more people will want to invest more in the United States, increasing the demand for U.S. dollars.

To make an investment, one has to have the right currency. Anything that motivates investors to invest in a particular country will therefore increase demand for the currency of that country.

Supply of foreign currency

What about factors affecting the *supply* of foreign exchange? The same three factors affect the supply: If the U.S. *interest rate* is low relative to foreign interest rates, financial investors holding U.S. assets will want to sell them and purchase foreign assets. Similarly, if investors' *confidence* in foreign economies increases, the supply of U.S. dollars will increase as investors sell off U.S. assets. Finally, *consumer preferences* also play a role. If U.S. consumers prefer foreign goods, they will sell their dollars to obtain foreign currency, increasing the supply of U.S. dollars in the forex market.

The equilibrium exchange rate

Panel A of Figure 35-10 shows how the supply of and demand for dollars determines the equilibrium exchange rate against any other given currency. The "price" of the currency is the exchange rate. As the exchange rate increases, the quantity supplied of dollars increases and the quantity demanded of dollars decreases

Panel B of Figure 35-10 shows how the equilibrium exchange rate in turn determines the level of net exports:

FIGURE 35-10

The foreign-exchange market in equilibrium

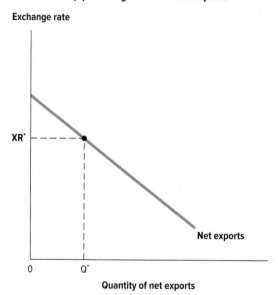

Like any other market, there is supply and demand for foreign currency. The quantity supplied of dollars increases as the exchange rate increases, and the quantity demanded decreases as the price of currency increases. The price of the currency is known as the exchange rate.

As the exchange rate from local to foreign currency decreases, the quantity of net exports decreases. With the lower price of goods, local goods will become attractive to foreigners, and foreign goods will be more expensive locally.

- When the price of dollars is high, foreigners will buy fewer goods from the United States and Americans will buy more goods from overseas. As a result, net exports are low and may even be negative.
- When the price of dollars is low, the reverse happens: It's cheap for foreigners to buy U.S. goods and expensive for Americans to buy foreign goods, so net exports will be high.

An example: Prius imports

Let's look at an example of how this model works in practice. When the Toyota Prius was released to the U.S. market in 2003, many people wanted to get their hands on the first mass-produced hybrid gas/electric vehicle. Because the Prius was manufactured by Toyota in Japan, U.S. dealers had to exchange dollars for Japanese yen to be able to buy and import Priuses. This led the supply curve of U.S. dollars to shift to the right. The exchange rate from the U.S. dollar to the Japanese yen fell as a result. The new equilibrium is shown in panel A of Figure 35-11.

What effect does the fall in the exchange rate have on net exports for the United States? As we have seen, the net export curve is a demand curve; it shows the demand for net exports at different prices (in this case, those prices are exchange rates). Just like a standard demand curve, shifts in preferences shift the net export curve. Actually, two shifts occur:

- When U.S. consumers decide they want to buy Priuses rather than cars made in America, this shift in preferences moves the net export curve to the left (because more imports mean fewer exports).

FIGURE 35-11

Increase in demand for Prius cars

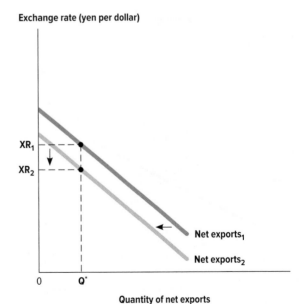

(A) Foreign-exchange market

Exchange rate (yen per dollar)

When the demand for Priuses shifts to the right, the supply of dollars at equilibrium increases as more people are trying to sell dollars in order to purchase yen. This shift increases the quantity of dollars traded, but lowers the exchange rate.

(B) Exchange rate and net exports

Exchange rate (yen per dollar)

Since Americans are now importing far more cars, the net exports curve shifts to the left. At the same time the exchange rate falls. Depending on the size of these two changes, the quantity of net exports could be higher or lower than it was before; in this instance the two cancel each other out.

- However, something else is also going on at the same time: Because the value of U.S. dollars depreciated, U.S. exports became cheaper, which increased the quantity of net exports.

Panel B of Figure 35-11 shows the combined effects of these two shifts: The effects of a greater preference for Japanese cars are counterbalanced by the effects of the depreciation in the exchange rate. Depending on which effect is bigger, the quantity of net exports could end up being higher *or* lower than before the Prius was introduced. In this case, the graph depicts the effects as canceling each other out exactly.

Another example: A rising interest rate

Now imagine another scenario: The Federal Reserve decides to tighten monetary policy by increasing the interest rate. This increase is going to affect both the demand for and the supply of U.S. dollars:

- Because the return to investment is higher in the United States as a result of the higher interest rate, foreign investors want to buy U.S. foreign assets; the demand for U.S. dollars increases.
- At the same time, U.S. investors would rather invest in their own economy instead of buying financial assets abroad, reducing the supply of U.S. dollars.

As shown in panel A of Figure 35-12, these shifts will cause the exchange rate to appreciate. Nothing in this story will shift the net exports curve, however. Therefore, panel B shows that the higher exchange rate translates directly into a reduction in net exports.

FIGURE 35-12

Tighter monetary policy in the United States

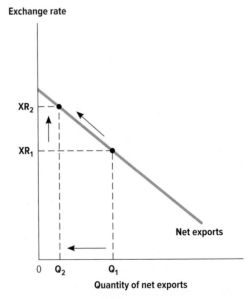

(A) Foreign-exchange market

(B) Decrease in quantity demanded for net exports

When the Federal Reserve tightens the money supply, the price of the dollar initially rises and supply decreases. Demand shifts out as well, and the price of the dollar rises and the quantity of dollars traded returns to the initial amount.

With an increase in the exchange rate of the dollar, the quantity of net exports falls, as U.S. goods are now more expensive for foreigners.

We can also look at the change in monetary policy in another way. We know that net exports equal net capital outflows (NX = NCO), so the higher exchange rate has also caused a reduction in NCO. In other words, it has caused more capital *inflows*. We know that there will be more capital flowing into the United States when interest rates go up, as foreign savers take advantage of the opportunity to get a better return.

Our model of the foreign-exchange market has shown us that monetary policy works on aggregate demand in two ways: reducing investment and reducing net exports. Remember, by raising the interest rate, the Fed is trying to cool off the economy. A higher interest rate makes borrowing more expensive, reducing investment. Increasing the interest rate also causes the exchange rate to appreciate, which reduces net exports. Because net exports are also part of aggregate demand, reducing net exports further reduces aggregate demand.

However, this result holds only in an open economy where the exchange rate is determined by the market. As we shall now see, some governments do not allow the market to determine the exchange rate for their currency.

Exchange-rate regimes

LO 35.8 Explain fixed and floating exchange rates.

The euro is used by 19 European countries, each of which previously had its own currency. Since many European countries are small, different currencies made life difficult. A 150-mile trip from Dusseldorf, Germany, to Brussels, Belgium, with a stop in Maastricht in The Netherlands, would require the use of three separate currencies—the German mark, Dutch guilder, and Belgian franc. Now, with the euro, tourists no longer have the hassle of exchanging money (and paying a commission to do so) every time they cross a border. Businesses that do a lot of trade with neighboring countries no longer have to worry about exchange-rate fluctuations changing the prices they have to pay for their inputs or will receive for their products.

There are also disadvantages, however. In being so tightly joined to other economies, the members of the euro zone give up some of their ability to conduct independent macroeconomic policy. Let's say that Germany has low unemployment: Wages are rising, and so are concerns about inflation. We know that to tackle inflation, a central bank would usually tighten monetary policy—that is, increase interest rates. Let's say at the same time Italy is experiencing *high* unemployment. There, a central bank would usually loosen monetary policy—that is, lower interest rates.

When Germany used the mark and Italy used the lira, these differing monetary policies would cause their currencies' exchange rates to change. In our example, the lira would depreciate and the mark would appreciate. The result? Italian products would become cheaper for other countries to buy, helping to boost aggregate demand in Italy and tackle unemployment. Meanwhile, just as we saw in the U.S. example presented in Figure 35-12, the appreciating German mark would help to reduce net exports in Germany, and also aggregate demand, easing the upward pressure on prices. However, when countries gave up their own currencies and joined the euro, they could no longer pursue their own monetary policies to tackle their specific macroeconomic situations.

You may be wondering why this isn't a problem among U.S. states. What if Wisconsin is experiencing high demand for labor and rising prices and wages, whereas Nebraska is experiencing high unemployment? The problem solves itself without any need for separate currencies and exchange rate changes: We would expect unemployed Nebraskans to move to Wisconsin in search of higher wages, and Wisconsin-based businesses to relocate to Nebraska in search of cheaper labor.

The difference with the euro zone is that, unlike people in Nebraska and Wisconsin, Germans and Italians speak different languages and have distinct cultures. In theory, Italian laborers can seek work in Germany and German businesses can relocate to Italy. But in practice it's not so easy—certainly not as easy as moving from one state to another in the United States.

Not all countries that share a currency are neighbors. In fact, Ecuador, a small country in South America, now uses U.S. dollars exclusively. The barriers seem even greater than between Italy and Germany: Ecuador and the United States are much farther apart geographically, and unemployed Ecuadorans don't have the legal right to seek work in the United States, as Italians do in Germany. Still, that hasn't stopped Ecuador from adopting the U.S. dollar as its currency, as the Real Life box "Dollarization: When not in the U.S. . . ." discusses.

Real Life

Dollarization: When not in the U.S. . . .

In 1998 and 1999, Ecuador experienced a wrenching financial crisis that caused the value of the Ecuadoran currency, the sucre, to fall by 50 percent in just two months. Within two years, 70 percent of Ecuador's financial institutions went out of business, sending shockwaves throughout the rest of the economy. When the crisis was over, the country's GDP, at $10 billion, was half of what it had been two years earlier.

Rather than try to reboot the sucre, the government decided to "dollarize"—to replace all sucres with U.S. dollars. This move immediately stabilized the Ecuadoran economy. In just three years, the annual inflation rate in Ecuador dropped from 20 percent to 2.7 percent.

However, dollarization has a drawback: It tied Ecuador's economy to that of the United States, for better or worse. In exchange for a stable currency and lower inflation, the government had to give up control of monetary policy. Ecuador's government cannot print U.S. dollars if the country's economy is in recession. Nor can it reduce the amount of U.S. dollars in circulation if it wants to cool an overheating economy. Only the U.S. Federal Reserve can do those things, and the Fed is not likely to take much account of Ecuador's macroeconomic needs when making decisions. If the U.S. economy is doing well while Ecuador is struggling, a contraction in the money supply would further damage the Ecuadoran economy.

Ecuador is one of 10 countries that have decided to dollarize. They have given up their own national currency and thrown in their lot with the United States in terms of monetary policy and exchange rates. Most of these countries are scattered throughout the Pacific (such as Palau and Micronesia) or Latin America (Panama and El Salvador, along with Ecuador). Although it is a rather dramatic step, for countries where inflation or financial instability is a persistent problem, the price of giving up control over monetary policy is one that's considered to be well worth paying.

Source: http://www.imf.org/external/pubs/ft/issues/issues24.

Fixed and floating rates

floating exchange rate
an exchange rate whose value is determined by the market

The dollar, euro, Mexican peso, and Japanese yen are all examples of currencies with a **floating exchange rate**. Their value is determined by the market, and the currency can be freely traded. The exchange rate of floating-rate currencies is set by the intersection of the supply and demand curves for foreign exchange, shown in panel A of Figure 35-13.

fixed exchange rate
an exchange rate that is set by the government, instead of determined by the market

Some currencies, however, have a **fixed exchange rate**—one that is set by the government, usually with reference to the U.S. dollar or some composite index of major global currencies. A fixed exchange rate can be fixed at a price that is above the market equilibrium rate or below the market equilibrium rate, as shown in panel B of Figure 35-13.

Why might a government decide to fix its currency's exchange rate? The thinking is similar to Ecuador's decision to dollarize. The theory is that a fixed rate allows for more predictability and stability. More stability helps attract foreign investment and gives businesses that depend on overseas trade more confidence to invest.

FIGURE 35-13

Floating versus fixed exchange rates

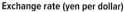

| **(A) Floating exchange rate** | **(B) Fixed exchange rate** |

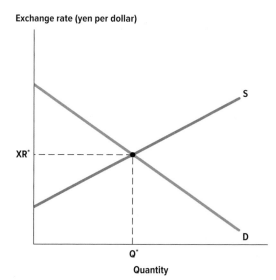

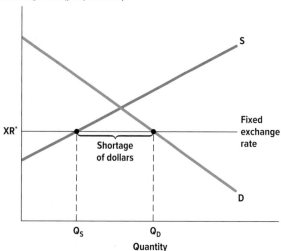

When the exchange rate is allowed to float, the market for foreign exchange will operate at the equilibrium price and quantity.

On the other hand, when there is a fixed exchange rate that is set too low, there is excess demand for the currency, which the government must cover by buying foreign currencies and selling the local currency.

How is a fixed exchange rate kept above or below market rates? To maintain a fixed exchange rate, the government needs to be prepared to intervene in the foreign-exchange market, either buying or selling foreign currency. For example, let's say that all of a sudden consumers develop a greater appetite for imported goods. If the exchange rate were allowed to float, the increased supply of local currency would push the exchange rate downward. When the exchange rate is fixed, though, the exchange rate is not allowed to depreciate. The government then has to step into the foreign-exchange market and buy up local currency to balance out the increased supply. Governments generally try to increase demand for their currency by using their own reserves of foreign currencies to buy the domestic currency.

HINT

Economists use a slightly different vocabulary to describe changes in the exchange rate when the exchange rate is fixed. Instead of saying that a currency depreciates, we say that it is *devalued* if the government lowers the level at which the fixed exchange rate is set. Likewise, instead of saying that a currency appreciates, we say that the fixed exchange rate is *revalued* if the fixed exchange rate is set higher.

Maintaining a fixed exchange rate can be tough. This is especially true when investors begin to doubt the overall health of an economy. Then investors will start to sell their investments, increasing the supply of local currency. To counter that, the government will be forced to spend large amounts of foreign reserves to prop up demand for its currency.

FIGURE 35-14

Speculative attack on the Thai baht

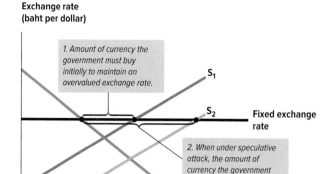

Exchange rate
(baht per dollar)

1. Amount of currency the government must buy initially to maintain an overvalued exchange rate.

S_1

S_2

Fixed exchange rate

2. When under speculative attack, the amount of currency the government must buy increases.

D

Quantity

When a country suffers from a speculative attack, the supply of currency available shifts right. This lowers the equilibrium exchange rate even further, forcing the government to spend even more to defend the fixed exchange rate.

Some investors, called *speculators,* look for these kinds of situations. The moment that they begin to doubt the ability or the resolve of a country to maintain its fixed exchange rate, they will sell that currency, converting it into a different currency, like dollars. If they dump a lot of the currency quickly, they may cause the government to run out of its stock of dollars and other foreign reserves. If that happens, the government has to give up its efforts to maintain the fixed exchange rate. The value of the currency usually drops fast. At that point, the speculators come back in and buy the cheapened currency. They pocket a profit from having sold the currency at a high price and then buying it back at a low price. When this activity is happening, we say that a currency is experiencing a *speculative attack.*

In 1997, for example, the Thai baht came under intense speculative attack from investors. The Thai government had a fixed-exchange-rate policy; when the attack began, it needed to use foreign reserves to buy baht. The government spent more than $33 billion (about 90 percent of the country's foreign reserves) trying to protect the currency. It also increased domestic interest rates to encourage investors to keep money in the country. However, the attack continued, and the government eventually could not continue to defend the baht. The only choice was to untether the currency from the fixed exchange-rate system and let the baht float. Or, rather, sink: When the rate was allowed to float, the baht lost half its value.[5] We show in Figure 35-14 how a speculative attack on the currency puts pressure on the exchange rate.

Macroeconomic policy and exchange rates

LO 35.9 Describe why monetary policy is ineffective when maintaining a fixed exchange rate.

Now that we have outlined the difference between floating and fixed exchange rates, we'll look at monetary policy under the two exchange-rate regimes. Monetary policy is more effective *under a flexible exchange rate* than a fixed exchange rate because the flexible rate can affect two key variables: investment and net exports.

Imagine there's a recession and the Federal Reserve wants to increase the money supply to stimulate aggregate demand. The lower interest rates that follow this action will make investing in the United States less attractive. Since the return on investment is lower, demand for U.S. dollars will fall. At the same time, the supply of U.S. dollars will increase as investors sell their U.S. financial assets and look to buy assets abroad instead. Under a floating exchange-rate system, the exchange rate depreciates and net exports increase.

Figure 35-15 depicts what would happen if the exchange rate were fixed. Increasing the money supply would naturally cause the value of the dollar to fall. Since the government must maintain the exchange rate, however, it must buy its own currency in the foreign-exchange market. This purchase of dollars must be exactly the same as the increase of the money supply in order to maintain a fixed exchange rate. The end result is no change in the overall money supply, leading to a key point about fixed exchange rates: It is impossible to conduct monetary policy *and* maintain a fixed exchange rate.

Is the Chinese currency undervalued?

Our discussion of monetary policy and exchange rates leads us to the second explanation for the large trade deficit between China and the United States, which we mentioned at the beginning of this chapter. During China's great economic expansion, China maintained a fixed exchange rate, keeping its currency pegged at 6.5 yuan per dollar. This rate was *below* what the market would likely set. Why did China want to do that? Its goods would be cheap when measured in other currencies, so there would be lots of demand for Chinese exports.

The Chinese government keeps the yuan's value low by selling piles of yuan in the foreign-exchange market, and it uses a portion of those dollars to buy U.S. Treasury debt. The United States argues that China's currency is intentionally undervalued. The effect is to make China's exports more attractive to U.S. consumers and make it harder for U.S. companies to export to China. Chinese government officials, in turn, blame the trade deficit on U.S. government budget deficits and lack of savings.

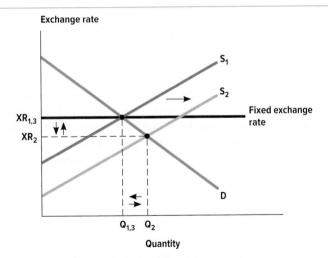

FIGURE 35-15

Loosening monetary policy with fixed exchange rates

With a fixed exchange rate, monetary policy cannot be successful. When a country expands the money supply, the supply of currency increases and the exchange rate falls. Since this is unacceptable in a fixed exchange-rate regime, the government is forced to buy back the local currency on foreign markets, restoring the exchange rate.

Would a floating exchange-rate regime eliminate the trade deficit between China and the United States? If the Chinese yuan appreciated, Chinese exports would become more expensive and imports would become cheaper, and so the Chinese trade balance would fall. The effect on the United States's overall trade balance is not so straightforward, however. The United States would import less from China, but it is possible that consumers in the United States would instead choose to import from other countries.

Suppose the United States is right and China is undervaluing its currency to promote its exports. If having a low exchange rate is good for exports, we should ask, *"Why isn't everyone already doing it?"* Well, sometimes everyone does. This situation is known as *competitive devaluation,* or a currency war. It occurs when multiple countries are trying to boost their economies by lowering their interest rates. Of course, because the value of a currency is measured relative to other currencies, it's logically impossible for *all* the world's currencies to devalue simultaneously.

There are reasons why a government might not want to have an undervalued currency, though. For one thing, it means that savers tend to send their money to be invested overseas rather than domestically, just as much of China's savings end up in the United States. This may not be the best way to develop the domestic economy. A second cost is that an undervalued currency makes imported foreign goods more expensive. For example, an undervalued Chinese currency makes goods imported from the United States relatively more expensive for Chinese consumers.

The real exchange rate

LO 35.10 Describe the difference between the real and nominal exchange rates.

As we saw in Chapter 25, "The Cost of Living," it's not only currency exchange rates that determine the relative price of goods in different countries. Even after converting exchange rates, the exact same Big Mac might be more expensive in Switzerland than in the United States, and more expensive in the United States than in China.

Up until now, we have been talking about the **nominal exchange rate**—the stated rate at which one country's currency can be traded for another country's currency. To really understand international trade, we also need to take into account the prices in two different countries by looking at the *real* exchange rate. The **real exchange rate** expresses the value of goods in one country in terms of the same goods in another country.

nominal exchange rate
the stated rate at which one country's currency can be traded for another country's currency

real exchange rate
the value of goods in one country expressed in terms of the same goods in another country

To take a simplified example, let's consider only one good—an apple. Say that you can buy an apple in the United States for $1, and in China an apple costs 3 yuan. If the nominal exchange rate is 6 yuan per dollar, then the *real* exchange rate is 2. We'll provide a standard formula for calculating the real exchange rate in a few paragraphs, but for now, let's concentrate on the intuition behind this answer. Since $1 can be exchanged for 6 yuan, and 6 yuan can buy two apples (6 yuan/3 yuan per apple = 2 apples), the dollar that can buy only one apple in the United States can buy two apples in China. Note that our dollar "goes further" (buys more) in real terms in China than in the United States—you can buy twice as many apples with that dollar in China than in the United States.

Of course, people want to buy and sell more than apples. To calculate the real exchange rate properly, we need to look at *all the prices* in the United States and compare this total to *all the prices* in China. To do so, we need to look at the *price index* in both countries—the index that measures a typical basket of goods bought by a household. The real exchange rate uses the price level in each country to convert the exchange rate into a value that is in "real" terms. Similar to what we did with the apple example, to calculate the real exchange rate, we divide the price level at home by the price level in the foreign country, and then multiply by the nominal exchange rate. Mathematically:

EQUATION 35-1 $\text{Real exchange rate} = \left(\dfrac{\text{Domestic price level}}{\text{Foreign price level}} \right) \times \text{Nominal exchange rate}$

Note that the nominal exchange rate in this formula is expressed in terms of the foreign currency per dollar, as we've done throughout the chapter. So, for example, let's say that the price of a typical basket of goods in the United States (the domestic price level) is $100; in China it (the foreign price level) is 300 yuan. Further, let's assume that the nominal exchange rate expressed in terms of yuan per dollar is 6; in other words, 1 dollar can be traded for 6 yuan. With this information, we can calculate the real exchange rate to be 2:

EQUATION 35-1A

$$\text{Real exchange rate} = \left(\frac{\text{Domestic price level}}{\text{Foreign price level}}\right) \times \text{Nominal exchange rate}$$

$$= \left(\frac{\$100}{300 \text{ yuan}}\right) \times 6 \text{ yuan/1 dollar} = 2$$

The *real* exchange rate is another way of saying "the exchange rate adjusted for *purchasing power parity*," an idea we discussed in Chapter 25, "The Cost of Living." If there were parity in purchasing power—that is, if an apple cost the same in China as in the United States, after adjusting for nominal exchange rates—then the real exchange rate would be 1.

The same factors that complicate calculations of PPP also complicate calculations of the real exchange rate. Consumers in China purchase different kinds of goods than do U.S. consumers—more rice, for example, and fewer burgers—so it's not easy to compare price levels using typical baskets of goods. Still, the real exchange rate is a useful way of comparing how far your money will go in another country.

✓ CONCEPT CHECK

- ☐ Does exchange-rate appreciation mean that the home currency gets stronger or weaker relative to other foreign currencies? **[LO 35.6]**
- ☐ When demand for a foreign good increases, what happens in the market for foreign exchange? **[LO 35.7]**
- ☐ How does the relative level of the U.S. interest rate affect the supply of foreign currency? **[LO 35.7]**
- ☐ What measurement gives the prices of the same goods in two different countries? **[LO 35.8]**
- ☐ Which variable can monetary policy affect under a flexible exchange rate that cannot be affected under a fixed exchange rate? **[LO 35.9]**
- ☐ What is another name for the real exchange rate? **[LO 35.10]**

Global Financial Crises

LO 35.11 Describe the role of the IMF and how financial crises are created by excessive debt and unsustainable exchange rates.

Although the international financial system works well most of the time, occasionally it falls out of order. In general, these crises can be labeled as one of two types: debt crises and exchange-rate crises. Throughout this section, you'll see how foreign direct investment and international flows can be fickle, which can destabilize economies when things go wrong.

The role of the IMF

Before working through some examples of disruptions in the financial system, we'll introduce the institution that is responsible for keeping the system together—the *IMF,* or *International Monetary Fund.* The IMF was created at the end of World War II. Although it's an international agency like the United Nations and World Bank, the IMF headquarters is in Washington, DC, a few blocks from the U.S. Federal Reserve headquarters and the U.S. Treasury Department.

Initially, when many countries had fixed exchange rates tied to gold, the IMF had the task of helping countries maintain their fixed rates. When countries ran into trouble maintaining their currencies, the IMF would step in and provide a loan to patch up a balance-of-payments deficit.

Now that most exchange rates are flexible, the IMF's role has changed. Today, the IMF often steps in as a lender of last resort, making loans to countries when private investors flee. The loans can help to stabilize the economy and keep fears from building on themselves. As the recent financial crises in Greece and Iceland show, international financial crises still occur, and the IMF is needed to help when things go wrong.

However, the IMF is not a magic solution for countries in need. Many IMF loans are made on the condition that the governments make certain policy changes. For example, a recipient country may be required to make efforts to reduce its budget deficit as a signal that it is committed to reform. In many cases, the IMF has been criticized for requiring economies to undertake contractionary fiscal policy and tighter monetary policy during the crisis itself. These policies usually depress the economy further and can exacerbate the crisis.

The role of the IMF and other global institutions is an area of ongoing debate. As globalization poses more risks of contagious collapse, how can the international system design institutions that will be able to prevent crises?

Debt crises

When countries need to finance their expenses, they often turn to international capital markets. The result is that a large share of government debt is often held by foreign investors. If those investors begin to worry whether the government will be able to repay the debt, the investors begin to move their money out of the country in a hurry. Why? If the government defaults, everyone who had invested in that debt stands to lose their money.

One such instance of investors losing confidence in the government's ability to repay debt occurred in Argentina in 2001. The setting for the debt crisis in Argentina started with heavy financing of a variety of industrial development projects during the 1960s and 1970s. The government then accumulated more debt in a war against the United Kingdom for control of the Falkland Islands.

As Argentina accumulated more debt, paying the interest on its debt formed a larger proportion of its budget. That wasn't the only problem, though. In an effort to curb inflation, Argentina had created a fixed exchange rate tied to the U.S. dollar, but the currency became overvalued. Domestic industry and large amounts of trade went to Argentina's neighbors, where products were cheaper. In addition, the financial crisis in Russia in 1998 made investors far more skeptical of investing money in "emerging markets" like Argentina. The combination of overvalued currency and loss in confidence raised interest rates, making it harder and more expensive to borrow more.

To try to stop the flight of capital, the government announced several attempts to reduce government spending. As you might have guessed, these promises were not kept. What followed was a painful economic spiral: Increased capital outflows from the country led to higher and higher interest rates. The increasing rates made debt payments more expensive, which created further government deficits. By 2001, the problem had spun into a full-on crisis, with bank runs and public protests. Unemployment came close to 20 percent. The government finally defaulted on its debt, unable to meet the increasingly high debt payments.[6]

We can analyze this scenario using the open-economy loanable-funds market set up earlier in the chapter. Figure 35-16 illustrates the stages of this debt crisis:

- When foreign investors started pulling their money out of the country, the net capital outflow curve shifted to the right.
- Interest rates then increased to r_2, which reduced investment. The higher interest rates also made the government's debt more expensive, and the government deficit increased.

FIGURE 35-16
The Argentine debt crisis

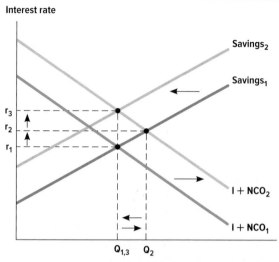

Once investors got word that the Argentine government was in danger, they pulled their investments out of the country, shifting the combined investments and net capital outflow curve to the right, increasing the interest rate. This higher interest rate made the government debt more expensive, which decreased savings. This led to a further increase in the interest rate, and a repetition of the cycle.

- As the government deficit increased, this shifted the national savings curve to the left, increasing the interest rate again (to r_3) and reducing investment yet again.

Exchange-rate crises

Loss of confidence in a government's ability to defend an exchange rate can also spook investors. If a government devalues an exchange rate, it essentially represents a loss for those holding investments in the country.

With this in mind, we turn to the story of the Asian financial crisis. In the early 1990s, emerging economies in Asia—Thailand, Indonesia, Malaysia, the Philippines—received a lot of capital from global investors. The influx of investment contributed to a remarkable spurt of growth. With all that fresh capital, banks wanted to move money, and they started making loans to riskier entrepreneurs. Soon the signs of good fortune were fading. In Thailand, especially, most economic indicators started to create worries, and investors began pulling their money out of the country.

But the crisis didn't end there. Because the world is so interconnected, crises can easily spread in a chain reaction called a *contagion.* The virus imagery is fitting. When Thailand got into trouble, investors immediately became nervous about other countries in the area, regardless of their condition. Soon, fearful investors were pulling their money out of the surrounding countries as well, creating financial crises in those countries. In other words, the crisis was contagious.

After the financial fall of Thailand in 1997, speculative attacks spread to Indonesia, the Philippines, South Korea, and Malaysia. Like Thailand, each of these countries was unable to defend its fixed currency. Not surprisingly, their currencies rapidly depreciated once the fixed exchange-rate policies were abandoned and exchange rates were made flexible. GDP in these five countries fell about 10 percent between 1997 and 1998. The crisis lasted for about a year, and millions of people suffered. The overriding lesson of the Asian financial crisis was that the combination of fast-moving capital and fixed exchange rates can lead to devastating speculative attacks with the power to shake to whole continents.[7]

✓CONCEPT CHECK

☐ What is a lender of last resort? **[LO 35.11]**
☐ Why are fixed exchange rates vulnerable to speculative attack? **[LO 35.11]**

Conclusion

In this chapter, we opened up the national economy to understand how countries trade and invest with each other. When we add net exports to our GDP equation, we get an interesting result: The difference between what a country buys and sells is also equal to the level of foreign investment. In effect, if a country is buying more than it is selling, it needs to borrow money from abroad to pay for its imports. This important equality is called the *balance-of-payments identity.* The tight link between the trade balance and capital flows is the key to understanding issues such as the U.S. trade deficit and the U.S. debt with China.

We looked at two explanations for the trade deficit with China, which turn out to be different sides of the same coin. The first explanation is that the United States is not saving nearly as much as China and is relying on investment from other countries. From the balance-of-payments identity, we know that if foreign investment is high, then there must also be a trade imbalance.

The second explanation is that exports from China are artificially cheap because the Chinese currency is set at a price below what it should be—that is, below its market price. Cheap Chinese exports mean that the balance of trade is negative, and the United States needs to borrow money to pay for its spending.

In extreme cases, we saw how international debt and fixed exchange rates can tip countries into economic crises. As the world continues to become more and more interlinked, economic policy in one part of the world will have global effects.

Macroeconomics may seem more abstract than microeconomics, with lots of moving parts. Yet trade policy, government fiscal policy, monetary policy, and the decision of how to set the exchange rate affect the daily lives of every citizen, usually in ways that are hard to see.

In the concluding chapter, we will apply the lessons you've learned throughout the book to one of the most stubborn problems in economics—international poverty.

Key Terms

balance of trade, p. 923

trade deficit, p. 923

trade surplus, p. 923

foreign direct investment (FDI), p. 925

foreign portfolio investment, p. 926

net capital flow, p. 926

balance-of-payments identity, p. 927

exchange rate, p. 935

exchange-rate appreciation, p. 936

exchange-rate depreciation, p. 936

floating exchange rate, p. 942

fixed exchange rate, p. 942

nominal exchange rate, p. 946

real exchange rate, p. 946

Summary

LO 35.1 Define the balance of trade and describe the general trends of U.S. trade.

The *balance of trade* is the value of exports less the value of imports. It is also called *net exports.* Net exports respond to the value of the exchange rate: When the exchange rate is high, domestic goods are expensive and foreign goods are cheap, so net exports are low. When the exchange rate is low, net exports are high.

LO 35.2 Define portfolio investment and direct foreign investment.

There are two types of foreign investment. *Direct investment* is when a firm invests abroad with an active interest—for example, by building a factory and managing the factory. *Portfolio investment* is investment in financial securities, such as stocks or bonds, so that domestic residents still operate firms. Together, direct investment and portfolio investment give the net capital outflow of the country, a measure of the money a country invests outside its border.

LO 35.3 Explain the connection between the balance of trade and net capital outflow.

The balance of trade and net capital outflow are related through the balance-of-payments identity, which states that NX = NCO. This identity is an accounting identity: If a country has an imbalance of trade (positive net exports), it means that it has lent money to the rest of the world (positive capital outflow) to pay for these goods.

LO 35.4 Describe the determinants of international capital flows using the demand and supply of international loanable funds.

Net capital outflows are determined by the demand and supply for net capital outflow. The supply of net capital outflows is national savings less domestic investment. The demand for net capital outflow is determined by the domestic interest rate and the foreign interest rate. When the domestic interest rate is high, net capital outflow is low because foreign money flows into the country. When the foreign interest rate is high, net capital outflow is high because money flows out of the country to take advantage of high returns.

LO 35.5 Show how the international market for loanable funds can be used to explain events in the international financial system.

Various events can influence the international supply and demand for loanable funds. An increase in confidence in an economy will cut net capital outflows and lower the interest rate. A decrease in savings from an increase in the government deficit will shift the supply curve for loanable funds to the left, increasing the interest rate and decreasing net capital outflows.

LO 35.6 Describe exchange rate appreciation and depreciation and understand their effects on trade.

The *exchange rate* is the value of one currency expressed in terms of another currency. Exchange rates can be expressed in two ways: either in terms of the domestic (home) currency or in terms of the foreign currency. Exchange rates can appreciate or depreciate, as the currencies strengthen or weaken against each other.

LO 35.7 Describe the determinants of demand and supply in the forex market.

The exchange rate is determined by demand and supply for domestic currency. Demand and supply are influenced by preferences for domestic and foreign goods and services, the domestic interest rate, the foreign interest rate, and the perceived riskiness of domestic and foreign investment.

LO 35.8 Explain fixed and floating exchange rates.

A *fixed exchange rate* is an exchange rate that is set by the government, not the market. Usually fixed exchange rates are set to maintain a steady relationship with another stable currency. A government maintains a fixed exchange rate by intervening in the foreign-exchange market, by either buying or selling foreign currency. A *floating exchange rate,* on the other hand, is set by the market. Floating exchange rates are set by the intersection of supply and demand for foreign exchange.

LO 35.9 Describe why monetary policy is ineffective when maintaining a fixed exchange rate.

A fixed exchange rate necessarily means that monetary policy will not have an effect—any change to the money supply has to be counteracted by government actions on the foreign-exchange market to maintain the exchange rate. Monetary policy is more effective under a flexible exchange rate because the flexible rate can affect both investment and net exports.

LO 35.10 Describe the difference between the real and nominal exchange rates.

The real exchange rate is the nominal exchange rate corrected for the price levels in the domestic and foreign country. The real exchange rate is measured in terms of goods instead of currency. If the real exchange rate is 1, then a good can be exchanged in one country directly for a good in another country. If this is the case, we say there is purchasing power parity between the two countries.

LO 35.11 Describe the role of the IMF and how financial crises are created by excessive debt and unsustainable exchange rates.

Although the financial system works well most of the time, financial crises can occur. The IMF often steps in as a *lender of last resort* when this happens, making loans to countries when private lenders flee. However, this is not always an ideal solution. Crises exist because countries often turn to international capital markets to finance expenses, therefore meaning investors own the countries' debts. This can backfire if investors worry that the government won't be able to repay the debt or if they lose confidence in the government's ability to defend the exchange rate.

Review Questions

1. What happens to the U.S. balance of trade as oil prices rise? **[LO 35.1]**

2. Suppose a presidential candidate criticizes his opponent by saying his opponent's economic policies have made the dollar weaker and cost American factory workers their jobs. What would be your response? **[LO 35.1]**

3. Why would a company want to make a direct investment in countries where the company's home currency has higher purchasing power? **[LO 35.2]**

4. Part of the North American Free Trade Agreement (NAFTA) opened the Mexican stock market to U.S. and Canadian investors for the first time. How would this affect direct and portfolio foreign investment in Mexico? **[LO 35.2]**

5. If many factories that once made goods in the United States move to Mexico, what must also happen in order to correct the balance of payments in the United States? **[LO 35.3]**

6. Critics of NAFTA argued that opening our borders to free trade with Mexico would result in U.S. firms moving all of their factories to Mexico and the United States running large trade deficits with Mexico. Comment on the concerns of these critics using your knowledge of international trade and net capital flows. **[LO 35.3]**

7. Rating agencies rate countries on the perceived riskiness of investing in their economies. Standard and Poor's, one of the main rating agencies, downgraded the credit rating for U.S. Treasury bonds in 2011. According to this chapter, what impact should the downgrading have had on net capital outflows and interest rates? Why? **[LO 35.4]**

8. The interest rate on 10-year U.S. Treasury bonds just before Standard and Poor's downgraded the U.S. credit rating was 2.47 percent. One year later, the interest rate on these bonds had fallen to 1.60 percent. How can one explain this result that seems to contradict the findings of this chapter? **[LO 35.4]**

9. List three policies that a government could engage in that would reduce interest rates. (*Hint:* Look back to Figures 35-6 through 35-8.) **[LO 35.5]**

10. A country doubles its rate of saving. How is this likely to affect the equilibrium interest rate and net capital outflow? What is the impact on the trade balance? **[LO 35.5]**

11. Suppose the exchange rate value of the dollar depreciates. Who wins and who loses? **[LO 35.6]**

12. Suppose the exchange rate was 102 yen per dollar in 2014 and 110 yen per dollar in 2015. Did the dollar appreciate or depreciate? What about the yen? **[LO 35.6]**

13. Identify the main reasons why people convert one currency into another currency. **[LO 35.7]**

14. During a recession the central bank lowers interest rates. How does this affect the exchange rate and net exports? **[LO 35.7]**

15. A country has a fixed exchange rate. If world interest rates rise, what will the country have to do to maintain its fixed exchange rate? Has the fixed exchange rate become relatively more undervalued or overvalued? **[LO 35.8]**

16. Suppose that in response to a severe recession, a country with an overvalued currency and a fixed exchange rate moves to a floating exchange-rate system. Who are the winners and losers in this move? **[LO 35.8]**

17. A country operates under a flexible exchange rate system. When the central bank lowers the interest rate during a recession, how does this affect investment and net exports, and ultimately aggregate demand? What if the exchange rate was fixed instead? **[LO 35.9]**

18. What are the advantages to fixing the exchange rate at an undervalued level? What are the disadvantages? **[LO 35.9]**

19. Discuss what would happen to the real exchange rate between the U.S. and Australia if oil prices fell, which dramatically reduced the cost of transporting goods. **[LO 35.10]**

20. Is it ever possible for a country's nominal exchange rate to be depreciating while its real exchange rate is appreciating? Explain. **[LO 35.10]**

21. Foreign investors in a country become worried about the stability of the government due to its rising debt level. What do you expect to happen to the interest rate and the exchange rate value of the country's currency, assuming the country has a floating exchange rate? **[LO 35.11]**

22. Foreign investors in a country become worried about the stability of the government due to its rising debt level. How might the IMF help avert a financial crisis in this country? **[LO 35.11]**

Problems and Applications

1. Suppose total U.S. exports in the month of June were $122.9 billion and total imports from foreign countries were $192.4 billion. What was the balance of trade? **[LO 35.1]**

2. Suppose a country has total GDP (Y) = $10 trillion, consumption = $7 trillion, government spending = $2 trillion, investment = $2 trillion, and taxes = $1.5 trillion. What is the level of net exports or balance of trade? What is the level of public savings? What is the level of private savings? What is the level of net capital outflow? **[LO 35.1, 35.3]**

3. In 2010, U.S. investors purchased $50 billion in foreign assets, and foreigners purchased $100 billion in U.S.

assets such as stocks and Treasury bills. In addition, U.S. businesses invested $150 billion in foreign factories and operations, while foreign companies invested $100 billion in U.S. factories and operations. What was the net capital outflow for the United States? [**LO 35.2**]

4. Define each of the following as direct or portfolio foreign investment. [**LO 35.2**]

   a. Nike (a U.S. company) builds new factories in Cambodia.

   b. A U.S. hedge fund purchases 30 percent of the shares of a Brazilian paper manufacturer.

   c. Mercedes-Benz (a German company) builds a new manufacturing plant in Alabama.

   d. Intel (a U.S. company) sets up a new call center in India.

   e. A British chocolate maker buys a smaller U.S. rival.

   f. Hilton Hotels (a U.S. company) builds a new resort in Hawaii.

5. Tom is stuck with his friends on an island that uses coconuts for currency, but they recently discovered Wilson's Island nearby. Tom's Island agrees to make only one transaction with Wilson's Island: It sells a fishing boat to Wilson's for 15 coconuts. Answer the following questions, assuming that yearly consumption on Tom's Island equals 500 coconuts and domestic investments in huts and farm equipment equals 150 coconuts. [**LO 35.3**]

   a. What are net exports for Tom's Island?

   b. What is the total national savings for Tom's Island?

   c. Suppose Tom's Island imports a volleyball net from Wilson's Island for 5 coconuts. What is the total national savings now?

   d. Now Tom purchases 1 coconut tree on Wilson Island at a cost of 10 coconuts. What is the balance of payments? (*Hint:* A coconut tree produces coconuts like a factory produces goods.)

6. Over the last five years, Portlandia's average income has risen and caused the supply curve of loanable funds to increase and shift right. [**LO 35.4, 35.5**]

   a. Would the domestic interest rate have increased or decreased?

   b. Given the change in the interest rate, would General Motors (GM) be more or less likely to open a Camaro plant in the country?

   c. If Portlandia hits a recession and interest rates fall, which way must the demand curve for loanable funds have shifted?

7. Describe what happens to the supply and/or demand curves for U.S. dollars under the following scenarios. In each scenario, does the U.S. exchange rate appreciate or depreciate, and what happens to the U.S. balance of trade? [**LO 35.6, 35.7**]

   a. A drought in Russia destroys the wheat crop, resulting in increased purchases of wheat from the United States.

   b. Bollywood movies become extremely popular in the United States, increasing demand for foreign movies.

   c. The U.S. government forces all government offices to purchase American-made computer products, instead of importing them.

8. Suppose there is major unrest in the labor market in the United States, making European investors nervous about investing in the United States. [**LO 35.6, 35.7**]

   a. Draw the supply and demand curves for U.S. dollars, and show the appropriate shift(s) in supply and demand for U.S. dollars associated with the labor unrest.

   b. Did the value of the U.S. dollar depreciate or appreciate?

9. A government has been running budget deficits for many years and decides to balance its budget. Explain how each of the following are affected under a floating exchange-rate regime. [**LO 35.5, 35.6, 35.7**]

   a. The interest rate.

   b. The exchange rate.

   c. The trade balance.

10. Suppose the new CEO for Apple Inc. decides to produce all the company's products in the United States instead of China. [**LO 35.7**]

   a. Which way will the supply for U.S. dollars shift?

   b. Which way will the demand for U.S. dollars shift?

   c. Does the value of the U.S. dollars depreciate or appreciate?

11. Suppose that in the United States last season's hot holiday gift was the iPad (which is made primarily in China), while this season's big gift is media content for the iPad (which is made in the United States). Determine whether there will be an increase, decrease, or no change for each of the following variables compared to last year. [**LO 35.6, 35.7**]

   a. Supply and demand for dollars.

   b. Exchange rate between the United States and China.

   c. Net exports for the United States.

   d. Net capital outflows for the United States.

12. In March 2009 the Canadian dollar was worth $0.78 U.S. In April 2011 the Canadian dollar was worth $1.06 U.S. What effect would this increase have on the trade balance between the United States and Canada? Why? [**LO 35.6**]

TABLE 35P-1

Exchange rate	USD	EUR	JPY
USD	1.00000	0.78230	81.200
EUR	1.27830	1.00000	103.796
JPY	0.01232	0.00963	1.000

13. Martha has $10,000 to invest in the foreign-exchange market. She's interested in trading U.S. dollars (USD) for euros (EUR) and Japanese yen (JPY). Using Table 35P-1, determine the arbitrage profit/loss Martha will make in each of the following scenarios. (*Note:* Any value less than $10 should be considered zero.) **[LO 35.6]**

    a. USD → EUR → JPY → USD.

    b. USD → JPY → EUR → USD.

    c. Now look up the current exchange rates among any three currencies. Show that there are no arbitrage opportunities for the three currencies you chose.

14. Some politicians argue for imposing trade restrictions in the hope that doing so will reduce the trade deficit of the United States. Assuming the United States has a floating exchange rate, answer the following questions regarding the impact of the trade restrictions. **[LO 35.7]**

    a. What is the impact in the foreign exchange market for dollars?

    b. What is the impact in the market for foreign currency (euros, yen, etc.)?

    c. What happens to the exchange rate of the dollar?

    d. What happens to net exports?

15. Suppose the U.S. economy slips into a recession. In response, the Federal Reserve cuts the federal funds rate in order to avoid unemployment. Consider what happens to the following under a floating exchange-rate regime. **[LO 35.8]**

    a. Domestic investment.

    b. Capital inflow.

    c. Capital outflow.

    d. Exchange rate.

    e. Net exports.

    f. Aggregate demand.

16. Reevaluate the previous problem assuming the U.S. economy follows a fixed exchange-rate regime. **[LO 35.8, 35.9]**

17. A country that has been operating under a fixed exchange-rate regime falls into recession. All attempts at using fiscal policy to lift the economy out of recession have failed. **[LO 35.9]**

    a. Can monetary policy be effective in this case? Why or why not?

    b. Should the country allow the exchange rate to float? Why or why not?

18. In Windsor, Ontario, a Big Mac from McDonald's costs C$4.16 (Canadian dollars), and across the border in Detroit it costs $3.54 in U.S. dollars. **[LO 35.10]**

    a. Suppose the nominal U.S. exchange rate with Canada is US$0.80 per Canadian dollar. Does purchasing power parity hold between the two countries?

    b. What is the purchasing power parity exchange rate for the United States?

19. Suppose the current U.S.–UK exchange rate is 0.63 pound (the pound is the UK currency) per dollar, and the aggregate price level is 170 for the United States and 140 for the UK. What is the real exchange rate? What does this real exchange rate mean in terms of the relative purchasing power of the dollar and the pound? **[LO 35.10]**

20. Imagine there are only two trading nations in the world. For each of the following scenarios, determine whether goods in one country will become more attractive relative to goods in the other country given their inflation rates and a shift in the nominal exchange rates. **[LO 35.10]**

    a. Inflation is 8 percent in the UK and 4 percent in Germany, but the UK pound–euro exchange rate remains the same.

    b. Inflation is 3 percent in the United States and 7 percent in Japan, but the exchange rate for U.S. dollars to Japanese yen increases from 70 to 80 Japanese yen.

    c. Inflation is 10 percent in the United States and 6 percent in Mexico, and the price of the Mexican peso rises from US$0.08 to US$0.15.

21. Over several years, foreign investors poured billions of dollars into a country due to its favorable growth prospects. They have now become concerned about the return on their investments because growth in the country is stagnating. As a result they are pulling their money out. Will this country be better able to withstand the financial crisis if it has a fixed or a floating exchange rate? Explain. **[LO 35.11]**

Endnotes

1. http://bgr.com/2016/04/06/iphone-sales-hit-one-billion-2016.

2. http://ticdata.treasury.gov/Publish/shla2010r.pdf.

3. http://www.ft.com/fastft/2016/05/10/german-current-account-surplus-swells-to-record.

4. http://data.worldbank.org/indicator/NY.GNS.ICTR.ZS.

5. http://fas.org/man/crs/crs-asia2.htm.

6. http://fpc.state.gov/documents/organization/8040.pdf.

7. http://fas.org/man/crs/crs-asia2.htm.

Development Economics

Learning Objectives

LO 36.1 Explain how the capabilities approach relates to economic development.

LO 36.2 Explain the relationship between economic growth and economic development.

LO 36.3 Describe how improvements to education and health can develop human capital.

LO 36.4 Explain the importance of institutions and good governance in development economics.

LO 36.5 Evaluate the role of industrial policy and clusters in development.

LO 36.6 Evaluate how migration and remittances promote development.

LO 36.7 Describe the aims of foreign aid, the role of poverty traps, the main institutions delivering aid, and criticisms of foreign aid.

LO 36.8 Understand how impact investing provides a new tool for creating social impact.

LO 36.9 Explain the need for impact evaluation and analyze the role of randomized controlled trials in measuring impact.

POVERTY AMID PLENTY

In the macroeconomics chapters, we've talked a lot about economic growth. But economic growth is not an end in itself. An economy can grow but still leave many people behind. Although the average level of real GDP per capita tripled in the second half of the twentieth century across the world as a whole, many people today still don't have enough resources for much of anything.

About 702 million of the 7.2 billion people on earth live on just $1.90 per day, the World Bank's measure of extreme poverty.[1] Billions more live on only slightly higher incomes. The depth and breadth of global poverty are not just a compelling humanitarian concern but also an economic puzzle: How can such poverty persist amid such plenty?

Some who have a more pessimistic outlook believe that poverty will always be a part of life. They point to a decades-long legacy of hopelessly failed bureaucracies and wasted foreign-aid budgets. Others who are more optimistic point to evidence of progress: Thanks to sustained

Courtesy of Robin Saidman

efforts by governments, nongovernmental organizations, and communities, many more children are attending school than even a decade or two ago. Infant mortality has dropped by half since 1960. Nine million more kids lived to celebrate their first birthday in 2006 than would have if the mortality rate had stayed at the 1960 level.

Impressively, such improvements have occurred even in places where average incomes failed to grow. So although growth is good in general, the poorest can do better even if there is little growth. Nor does lots of growth necessarily mean higher incomes for the poorest. In more technical words, overall growth and income for the poorest are correlated, but not perfectly.

So what can help the poorest lead better lives? One important step is improving access to markets and institutions that can expand opportunities and give more choices. Think of how you rely on a basic bank account to pay bills and save money. About half of the adults in the world live their lives without access to a bank. By expanding access to banks, millions would be helped to save, invest, and provide for their families. The same goes for access to improved markets for transportation, health care, education, and other basic services, backed by responsive legal and political institutions to maintain fair practices.

These are the issues taken up in the field of development economics, the topic of this chapter. Development economists tackle a series of questions that span several core economic issues: What makes some people—and some countries—richer than others? What makes others poorer? How can markets be made more efficient and wide-reaching in low-income countries? How should donors and investors choose among good options, given that resources are scarce?

In the first part of this chapter, we examine the relationship between economic growth and economic development. Then we look at the basics of economic development, taking a fresh perspective on some ideas we've encountered already in this book—human capital, good governance, investment, trade, and migration. In the final part of the chapter, we consider foreign aid—its history, the arguments for and against such aid, and how development economists are striving to understand what works.

Development and Capabilities

So far, we've talked a lot about economic *growth*. In this chapter, we talk about economic *development*. The concepts are intertwined, but distinct. Economic *growth* involves increases in GDP. However, GDP doesn't necessarily tell us much about what it's like to live in a country—its levels of inequality and poverty, what opportunities there are to better yourself if you're in the middle or at the bottom of the heap, how well basic institutions like courts and hospitals work, how many people can read and write, and so on. These are the kinds of things we're concerned about when we talk about economic *development.* Development economics looks beyond GDP growth to ask about the quality of life for all sectors of society. A helpful way to think about what matters comes from an idea called the *capabilities approach.*

The capabilities approach

LO 36.1 Explain how the capabilities approach relates to economic development.

The capabilities approach was developed by Amartya Sen, a Harvard professor who won the 1998 Nobel Prize in Economics. His idea provides a framework for economists to think about poverty, inequality, and human development. A **capability** is something a person is able to be or do. Examples of capabilities include being able to live a long and healthy life, have adequate food and shelter, get an education, speak one's mind, travel freely, live free of the fear of violence, be able to find secure and meaningful work, and be able to enjoy recreational and cultural activities.

In all, capabilities represent a vast spectrum of life—from basic survival and good health to self-expression and engagement in culture. Whereas economic growth focuses on expanding the economy, the capabilities approach to economic development instead looks to constantly improve what individuals can be and can do. Institutional and market failures restrict what people can do, and the restriction of capabilities often affects poorest citizens the most.

You might be wondering why we need a fancy new term like "capabilities" here. Aren't all of the things we've mentioned also simply things that increase utility? Why do we need to depart from the traditional economic framework of maximizing utility? Read the What Do You Think? box "Utility versus capabilities" for more on that question.

capability
something a person is able to be or do, such as to engage fully in life, including having economic and political freedoms

What Do You Think?
Utility versus capabilities

We have seen throughout this text that the idea of "maximizing utility" is the foundation of individual decision making in economics. It captures the idea that people want to obtain more of what gives them satisfaction. Can't we, then, simply use the *utility approach* to think about development? Why do we need to introduce the *capability approach* to establish the value of things like education and health and free speech? After all, aren't those capabilities also going to increase people's utility?

While the utility approach serves us well when thinking about how *individuals* make decisions, it may not guide us toward the best decisions for *society.* The early founders of the utilitarian approach, the philosophers Jeremy Bentham and John Stuart Mill, suggested that the best society is one that maximizes the collective utility of everyone in that society. Since then, other philosophers have argued that there are flaws in this idea. The capabilities approach addresses at least two of those flaws.

The first problem is that a simple utility-maximizing approach ignores the idea of fundamental rights. For example, what if slave owners received more utility from slave ownership than the utility slaves would get from being freed? Should society therefore allow slavery? Most people would say there are some rights, like not being enslaved, that are worth preserving even if it means accepting lower utility across society as a whole. As Sen says, "Happiness or desire fulfillment represents only one aspect of human existence. The capabilities approach attempts to fill the gap by looking at a much broader conception of life" (as quoted by Clark, 2011).

Second, simply trying to maximize utility ignores the *distribution* of that utility. Imagine that the president of an impoverished nation feels gnawing envy when he sees the presidents of

(continued)

richer countries flying around in private jets. His utility from owning a private jet is so great that it would outweigh the combined utility that citizens of a city would get from a new health clinic in their district. Should we, then, buy the president a private jet instead of improving health care? There seems to be something wrong with accepting this conclusion at face value.

On the other hand, by moving too far away from the utility approach, do we risk paternalistically giving the poor what we think they *ought* to want instead of what they really *do* want? In their book *Poor Economics,* Abhijit Banerjee and Esther Duflo tell of a man in a remote, dusty village in Morocco who, when asked by researchers what he would do if he had more money, said he would buy more nutritious food for his family. The researchers pointed out that he owned a television and a DVD player and asked why he'd bought these things when his family didn't have enough to eat. "Oh," he replied, "television is more important than food."

WHAT DO YOU THINK?

1. Should the World Bank and local governments be building bridges, schools, and clinics in low-income countries if citizens would rather have TVs?
2. Should development economists put more focus on capabilities or utility?

Sources: Abhijit Banerjee and Esther Duflo, *Poor Economics* (New York: Public Affairs, 2011); David A. Clark, "The Capability Approach: Its Development, Critiques and Recent Advances," http://www.gprg.org/pubs/workingpapers/pdfs/gprg-wps-032.pdf (accessed November 7, 2011).

Economic growth and economic development

LO 36.2 Explain the relationship between economic growth and economic development.

We saw in an earlier chapter that growth in countries such as China has slashed poverty rates. The average person in China now earns about $7,500 a year, compared with just $250 three decades ago.[2] Average levels of education and health have increased dramatically, too. That's not surprising. After all, when people have more money, you would expect them to spend more on improving their health and educating their children.

However, there is nothing inevitable about GDP growth improving health and education for everyone. For example, survey data show that in India, the rate of children suffering from malnutrition essentially didn't change over the span of two health surveys conducted in 1998 and 2005.[3] Clearly, it is possible for a country to experience strong economic *growth* without comparably strong economic *development.* There needs to be additional attention paid to policy mechanisms that can help to translate higher average incomes into improved capabilities for the poorest citizens.

What about the other direction of the relationship? Does economic *development* lead to economic *growth*? There are plenty of reasons to think it does. As we saw in Chapter 27, "Economic Growth," economists hotly debate the fundamentals of economic growth. There is general agreement, though, that those fundamentals include such things as property rights, the rule of law, and human capital. After all, an economy without healthy, educated workers is obviously going to have a hard time growing. We will turn now to considering in more depth some of the basic aspects of economic development.

✓ CONCEPT CHECK

- ☐ What are some examples of capabilities? **[LO 36.1]**
- ☐ Does economic growth always lead to economic development? **[LO 36.2]**
- ☐ Why may improving the education and health of the poorest help those who are more well off? **[LO 36.2]**

The Basics of Development Economics

Knowing there's a difference between economic growth and economic development, let's return with a fresh perspective to some ideas covered in earlier chapters. As we look at how countries can promote health, education, and good governance—all questions central to development economics—remember that we can think of these policies in two ways: We can see them as putting in place the conditions for economic growth, and we also can see them as translating the fruits of economic growth into greater capabilities for people in society.

Human capital

LO 36.3 Describe how improvements to education and health can develop human capital.

Countries all over the world have witnessed dramatic improvements in health and education. This is especially true in Asia, and even countries in Africa that once lagged in health and education progress are now coming close to having all children in primary school. This is good news for both development and growth. Still, though, each year millions of kids die from diseases that could be prevented. These are improvements that could happen quickly and cheaply, but don't.

Health

Why do these improvements fail to happen? Part of the problem is that health care facilities don't exist in many parts of the world. In rural areas, especially, getting to a modern clinic may involve trekking on foot for miles. Another part of the problem is that even where clinics do exist, many people don't use them. Many choose instead to resort to home remedies and traditional village "doctors" who have little or no training in medicine but charge lower fees than those charged by modern hospitals and often are more attentive.

Recognizing this, countries around the world, ranging from middle-income Thailand to poorer Ghana, have started national health insurance programs. For a nominal fee, usually a couple of dollars per year, families can visit any national clinic or hospital to receive basic services. Still, often these national health care programs are not as effective as they could be. One study showed that in India, local health care workers were absent about 40 percent of the time on average. Even when the workers do show up, clinics sometimes run out of important drugs such as quinine (which fights malaria).

One study of health care clinics in Delhi, by Jishnu Das of the World Bank and Jeffrey Hammer of Princeton, found there were plenty of clinics available to poor households, but they provided much worse care than did private clinics in wealthier areas. It's not because the doctors were badly trained. Rather, Das and Hammer found that doctors serving poor patients often operated below their "knowledge frontiers"—the doctors provided care below the standard of their medical training. One study, for example, showed doctors in public clinics failing to ask even the most basic diagnostic questions when patients appeared to be having heart attacks. Why? Partly because doctors in private clinics receive a fee for their services, while in public clinics they receive a fixed salary. Doctors have a much higher incentive to get the treatment right when their income depends on customer satisfaction.[4] One of the challenges for development economists working in health care is to figure out a way to give doctors the right incentives when their own intrinsic motivation isn't enough.

Fixing these health care challenges can contribute greatly to economic growth as well as development. Well-nourished, healthy kids do better in school, making them more productive workers as adults. Epidemics that afflict young adults can have a profound impact on GDP. The AIDS epidemic alone has been found to lower growth rates by up to 1.5 percent per year throughout sub-Saharan Africa.

Is it first necessary to achieve economic growth to be able to fix health care challenges? Figure 36-1 shows the relationship between income measured in GDP per capita and life expectancy. As you would expect, people who live in countries with higher average incomes generally live longer lives. Still, the correlation is not exact. Compare Vietnam and Nigeria, for example. Nigeria has a slightly higher average income than Vietnam, but a baby born in Vietnam is expected to live about 22 years longer on average than a baby born in Nigeria. Clearly, it must be possible to improve health outcomes dramatically even without achieving strong growth in average incomes.

Education

As with health, the reasons for investing in teachers, schools, and books are related to both growth and capabilities:

- In terms of economic growth, educated workers are generally more productive: Each additional year of schooling is worth about 10 percent more in overall earnings over the course of a lifetime.

- In terms of capabilities, education can be seen as worthwhile in itself, as well as contributing to other capabilities. For example, more-educated women tend to make better decisions about family planning. Considerable data also indicate that more education tends to make a society more democratic and reduce its levels of inequality.

In 1999, 106 million children around the world were not attending school; by 2015, that number had fallen by more than half. Even countries without strong economic growth had made strong progress in school attendance. The abolishment of school fees is a major reason why

---

FIGURE 36-1

Income and life expectancy   Overall, the higher the income within a country, the higher the life expectancy of the citizens within the country. At lower levels of income, this relationship isn't perfect, however. Some countries have made strides in income without making much progress in development in life expectancy, while others have high levels of life expectancy despite low incomes.

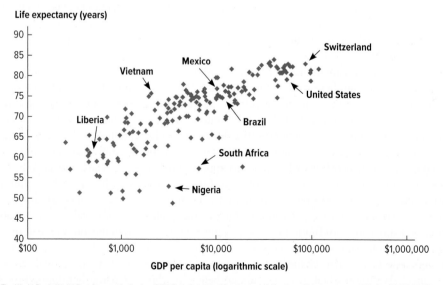

Source: The World Bank, World Development Indicators 2015 Data Set, http://databank.worldbank.org/data/reports.aspx?Code=SP.DYN.LE00. IN&id=af3ce82b&report_name=Popular_indicators&populartype=series&ispopular=y

more children are in school in a number of poorer countries. Even though the fees were usually small—about $30 a year—families living on just a few dollars per day simply could not afford them. Not surprisingly, when the fees were abolished, more kids went to school. In Kenya, for example, when school fees were eliminated in 2003, schools had to rush to find places for the 1 million more kids who enrolled around the country.

However, a sudden increase in students poses a new problem—crowded classrooms and over-burdened teachers. In some countries, there is only one teacher for 100 students. Development economists have recently started to pay more attention to the challenge of improving the *quality* of education. Even in middle-income countries such as Mexico, where all kids go to primary school, 91 percent of kids do not learn math well enough to be competitive on the international stage. The situation is worse for lower-income countries. One study in Ghana found that sixth-graders on average performed at the same level on a basic literacy test as one could achieve simply by guessing.

There are many ideas for how to improve schools. Recent research by development economists has made great strides in testing which approaches are more effective and which are not. To work with children lagging behind on basic math and reading skills, Innovations for Poverty Action tested a remedial education program in India, Kenya, and Ghana and found the program to be particularly successful. The approach included training women in the community to offer supplemental lessons to the students who were furthest behind in their learning. Other approaches, such as distributing textbooks, helped only the best students in the class. Providing parents with information about the quality of the children's schools had no effect at all.[5]

Institutions and good governance

> **LO 36.4** Explain the importance of institutions and good governance in development economics.

When we studied the determinants of economic growth, we discussed the importance of "good governance." Not surprisingly, good governance is also crucially important in economic development. Many basic capabilities rely on having a competent, well-intentioned government and good *institutions*. Economist Douglass North of Washington University in St. Louis (and co-winner of the 1993 Nobel Prize for his contributions to economic history) defines **institutions** as the humanly devised constraints that shape human interactions.[6] This definition includes *laws* enforced by the government as well as *cultural norms*, such as whether people see it as unacceptable to avoid responsibility at work, embezzle funds from your employer, cheat on your taxes, and so on. Stated informally, institutions are the "rules of the game" in a society.

institutions the humanly devised constraints that shape human interactions

The term *institutions* is also commonly used to refer to government bodies (such as senates and ministries of education), development agencies (such as the World Bank), and international groups (such as the United Nations). According to North, to avoid confusion we should think of these as examples of "organizations" instead in development economics.

What exactly constitutes "good governance"? At first it seems like a highly normative question. Some think the best government is the smallest government, staying out of people's lives as much as possible. Others think that government should have its hand in many different sectors of the economy, all in the name of promoting stability, growth, and development. Most development economists agree that the most basic and important task of any government is to create a stable political system—one that ensures the important institutions of enforceable property rights and the rule of law.

Property rights and the rule of law

Say you'd like to sell a bucketful of apples. This will probably work just fine without your having to prove you actually own the apples. You set up shop at a market, someone gives you the cash, and you give them the apples. What if you want to sell a house or a field? Would you ever buy land if you didn't have clear proof that the person selling it is the owner? No, you would want to see the *title* to the land, a document that certifies ownership of property. In many countries, the system of *titling* (providing legal documents proving ownership of assets) is weak. Now imagine you own land and you want to use it as collateral for a loan—say, to buy a tractor so you can farm the land more effectively. Do you think the bank is going to lend you the money unless you can prove you own the land?

Hernando de Soto, a Peruvian economist and president of the Institute for Liberty and Democracy, says that that the weak titling system in Latin America results in "dead capital." Millions of people may have land or other assets, but without proper titles they are effectively unable to tap the financial power of those assets. Titles would allow owners to take out billions of dollars in loans that could be used productively to invest in starting new businesses or improving their farms. If only they had titles, De Soto argues, their capital could be put to better use—it could become "alive." The evidence supporting his claim is mixed, suggesting that titling may be important only if other conditions are in place too.

One of those conditions is the *rule of law*. There's no point in being able to prove you own something if the police and courts are corrupt or incompetent and won't help you if thieves take it away. The rule of law helps to create stability and provides a set of clear guides to govern transactions. Where crime is rampant and government unhelpful—or, worse, when a country falls into outright conflict—it's hard to sustain either economic growth or economic development.[7]

Is democracy necessary?

Studies indicate a link between economic growth and political stability. The correlation between economic growth and democracy is less clear. Many of the stories of sustained growth in formerly poor countries occurred under governments that were far from democratic. Just think of China. The tiny, landlocked East African country of Rwanda is another illustration: Over the last decade and a half, growth has averaged about 7.5 percent per year, and residents are provided with basic and almost universal health insurance. Despite this growth, journalists critical of the government are routinely jailed; political opponents are routinely harassed and barred from participating in elections. The current president, Paul Kagame, won the last election with 93 percent of the vote, achieved by keeping any serious opponents from getting on the ballot.

Rwanda shows that even a relatively autocratic government can promote economic development as well as economic growth. Despite its democratic shortcomings, the government often makes good policy. Anti-corruption laws are some of the strongest in Africa. Also, women are encouraged to participate in the political process—so much so that the Rwandan parliament is one of only two in the world in which women outnumber men (Bolivia is the other).

So if good policy and fair institutions do not require democratic elections, should we care about democracy? Amartya Sen's capabilities framework suggests that we should view democracy in its own right as an essential ingredient in improving lives and sustaining basic freedoms.[8]

Investment

> **LO 36.5** Evaluate the role of industrial policy and clusters in development.

We saw in Chapter 27, "Economic Growth," that investment is a key concern in promoting growth. Foreign direct investment is an important source of funds in many countries with low savings rates. Development economists debate the best way for low-income countries to deal with these flows of capital from overseas as well as the funds that come from domestic sources. *Industrial policy* has two traditional tactics: import substitution or export-led growth. It can also involve trying to promote a cluster of industries that share linkages through the economy, so that they can develop in unison—an idea called *clustering*. Let's consider these ideas in turn.

Industrial policy

South Korea's GDP per capita in 1960 was about twice the size of Brazil's. By 2015, it was more than four times the size.[9] What accounts for these different rates of growth?

One important difference is that South Korea successfully pursued an industrial policy. **Industrial policy** is an effort by a government to favor some industries over others. The hope of such a policy is that coordinated investments in a chosen industry will help the overall economy to develop and will spur growth in the long run. The tools at governments' disposal in pursuing industrial policy include trade barriers, tax breaks, subsidies, incentives for foreign direct investment, and investment in research. Traditionally, these tools have been used as part of two opposite philosophies of industrial policy: import substitution and export-led growth.

industrial policy
effort by a government to favor some industries over others

Import substitution is the practice of using trade policy to protect domestic industries until they are efficient enough to compete on the world market. Imagine you want to nurture a successful electronics industry in your country. But new electronics firms can't get off the ground because they have to compete with cheap imports from countries with well-established electronics industries. Why not impose temporary trade barriers to stop the cheap imports, allowing time for the domestic infant industry in electronics to grow big and strong enough to compete?

Unfortunately, import substitution has failed to work well in the real world. A couple of problems related to import substitution can contribute to such failure:

- Without the spur of foreign competition to drive down costs, an infant industry might never grow up. For years, the Brazilian government protected domestic computer makers, but Brazilian-made machines still cost double the price of an American or Japanese machine.

- Decisions about which industries to protect are frequently made on the basis of *political* connections rather than real *economic* considerations. Naturally, companies would like to have their industry protected from foreign competition. That desire encourages large amounts of "rent-seeking" behavior—firms attempting to influence politicians in the name of profits. Protective policies have often persisted long after they were expected to lapse, at great cost to the taxpayer.

Realizing the problems with import substitution, some Asian countries have gone another route: *export-led growth.* This involves investing heavily in an industry through tax breaks and export subsidies (government monetary support for exporters) with the aim of selling goods around the world. Rather than walling domestic markets off from international trade, export-led growth instead selects industries to push into the world market. Success depends on picking winners. The South Korean government, for example, has managed to do just that, supporting companies

South Korea is achieving export-led growth by favoring companies, such as Hyundai, that are succeeding in the world market.
© *Jean Chung/Bloomberg via Getty Images*

such as Samsung and Hyundai. As a result, South Korea made the jump from poor to rich over the course of five decades. Japan, Singapore, and Taiwan used similar strategies to create the so-called Asian miracle.

Unfortunately, export-led growth doesn't always work. The unexpected and unprecedented success of these Asian countries led to many imitators, but not all succeeded. International markets are fickle and competition can be fierce. While the benefits of picking winners can be huge, so can the costs if you end up picking losers.

Clusters

As governments consider how to develop their industrial sectors, they often choose to focus on promoting not just one industry but *clusters*. **Clusters** are networks of interdependent firms, universities, and businesses that focus on the production of a specific type of good. Each part of the network is far less productive operating in isolation, so if governments can push each element of the cluster in unison, they should realize huge gains in productivity.

A successful example is Bangladesh's textile industry. Starting in the 1970s, the government made a concerted effort to develop a cluster around textiles. It ensured that complementary firms—such as those making fabrics and those sewing the fabric into clothes—were located in close proximity to minimize transportation costs. The government provided incentives for these firms to work together. Ready-made garments are now a multibillion-dollar industry in Bangladesh; in 2014–2015 they accounted for 81.6 percent of all the country's net export revenues.

Trade

In earlier chapters, we studied the benefits of international trade: When one country can produce a good more efficiently than another country, both can specialize in the industry in which they have comparative advantage and experience mutual gains. By opening up to foreign markets, countries gain access to a wide array of new products, save money through access to cheaper goods, and find new customers for their products. It's not surprising, then, that trade plays a major role in development economics.

In the last few decades, there has been great growth in free trade worldwide. Tariffs (taxes on imports) in low-income countries have fallen by more than 20 percent. Part of this change has been due to the efforts of the **World Trade Organization (WTO)**, designed to monitor and enforce trade agreements while also promoting free trade. But about two-thirds of the reduction in tariffs in the past 20 years comes from reforms by national governments changing their own policies or making agreements with each other.

Wealthy countries increasingly feel that trade can sometimes be a more powerful lever than aid to help poorer countries develop. In 2000, for example, the U.S. government initiated the African Growth and Opportunity Act, which gave preferential treatment to about 1,800 goods coming from Africa—especially goods like apparel and textiles, exempting them from duties and quotas. In 2005, aid donors began to offer "aid for trade" programs to fund initiatives in low-income countries that minimize barriers to trade and provide the infrastructure critical for imports and exports. While trade policy is often politically contentious, trade-related aid now accounts for over a quarter of official development assistance.

Migration

LO 36.6 Evaluate how migration and remittances promote development.

The prospect of a better life drives millions of people to move away from home to other cities, provinces, or countries thousands of miles away in search of opportunity. Research by economists Michael Clemens, Claudio Montenegro, and Lant Pritchett indicates that skilled workers in the

clusters
networks of interdependent firms, universities, and businesses that focus on the production of a specific type of good

World Trade Organization (WTO)
an international organization designed to monitor and enforce trade agreements, while also promoting free trade

United States earn about 15 times more than workers with exactly the same skills in Nigeria.[10] It's hardly surprising, then, that according to the Gallup World Values Survey, 40 percent of those living in the poorest quartile of countries would like to emigrate (move out of their home country).

However, it's difficult to legally move to a high-income country. Every year, the U.S. Diversity Visa lottery randomly gives 500,000 people from low-income countries the chance to permanently immigrate to the United States. And every year, about 14 million people apply.[11] That's a 3.5 percent chance of admission—lower than admission rates to the most competitive U.S. colleges. Some of those who are unsuccessful are so desperate to find better-paying work that they set off on perilous journeys—crossing the desert to and from Mexico or taking a rickety boat from Africa to Europe—to try to enter a high-income country illegally.

As we saw in Chapter 26, "Unemployment and the Labor Market," in host countries such as the United States, the influx of immigrants can be a highly controversial issue. But when we look at migration from the perspective of countries of origin, it presents a variety of opportunities to promote development. One important consequence of migration is remittances (money sent home by migrants). As shown in Figure 36-2, remittances are a major financial flow in some countries. The largest overall recipients of remittances are China and India, which each gets more than $60 billion per year.

Overall, remittances have become a powerful force in the world economy, growing impressively even after accounting for inflation. In 1990, less than $50 billion in inflation-adjusted dollars was transferred. In 2014, this figure was over $590 billion.

In addition to the benefits from remittances, migrants often return home after a few years working overseas, bringing with them new ideas and skills that benefit their local economy. For

FIGURE 36-2

Remittances around the world   The top 10 countries in terms of remittances received are a diverse group. India and China are large countries, with many migrants abroad. The Philippines and Mexico are countries that have traditionally been associated with remittances. As the data for France and Germany show, remittances aren't strictly a flow from rich to poor countries.

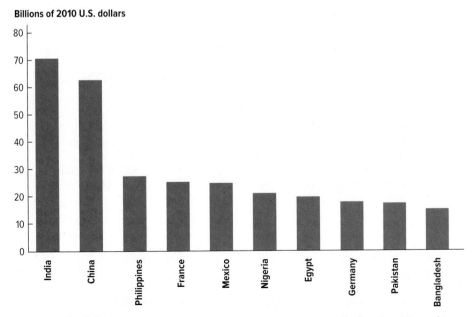

Source: The World Bank, 2014 data, http://www.worldbank.org/en/topic/migrationremittancesdiasporaissues/brief/migration-remittances-data

Michael Clemens, an economist at the Center for Global Development, and Lant Pritchett, author of the book *Let Their People Come,* the world has much to gain by loosening migration restrictions so that workers can more freely seek jobs in other places.[12] See the From Another Angle box "Trillion-dollar bills on the sidewalk?" for more.

From Another Angle
Trillion-dollar bills on the sidewalk?

In 2011, Alabama enacted HB56, a law punishing employers who hire illegal immigrants. After the law passed, tomato farmer Chad Smith found himself needing to hire Americans to pick his 85 acres of tomatoes. But picking tomatoes turned out to be hard, sweaty, poorly paid work, and most of his U.S. workers quit after just a couple of days. Without immigrant labor, Smith argued, his farm couldn't operate competitively.

This story illustrates why studies find that the available evidence often doesn't back up common concerns that immigration takes away jobs and drives down wages among the low-skilled. Often, immigrants do jobs that natives don't want.

On the flip-side, in the countries that migrants move away from, evidence suggests the shrinking labor supply pushes wages up as the supply of labor falls. One study estimated the effect of emigration from Mexico to be worth about an 8 percent raise for low-income workers who stay in Mexico. On net, then, research finds that more migration boosts incomes across the global economy.

From an economic-development perspective, there is another worry about migration: "brain drain." The workers who leave a country for better job opportunities naturally tend to be the most skilled. However, in a 2011 paper, John Gibson and David McKenzie concluded that lowering barriers to migration might actually *increase* the number of skilled workers in poorer countries. It makes sense, when you think about it: If workers in a low-income country know that it's possible to migrate, they may be more motivated to obtain crucial skills that would qualify them for jobs abroad. Not everyone in the end decides to move away—so the domestic economy ends up with more highly skilled workers as a result. This opens up the possibility of "brain gain" instead of "brain drain."

Economist Michael Clemens has done the math and found that removing just 5 percent of barriers to the movement of workers between countries has the power to lift income around the world by trillions of dollars. Overall, this 5 percent reduction would have more of an effect than removing all existing tariffs, quotas, and barriers to capital movement around the world. The impact of making migration easier could dwarf anything foreign aid can hope to achieve.

Sources: Dean Yang, "Migrant Remittances," *Journal of Economic Perspectives* 25, no. 3 (Summer 2011), pp. 129–152, http://pubs.aeaweb.org/doi/pdfplus/10.1257/jep.25.3.129; John Gibson and David McKenzie, "The Development Impact of a Best Practice Seasonal Worker Policy," Policy Research Working Paper, Impact Evaluation Series No. 48 (November 1, 2010), http://www.wds.worldbank.org/external/default/WDSContentServer/IW3P/IB/2010/11/30/000158349_20101130131212/Rendered/PDF/WPS5488.pdf; Michael Clemens; "Economics and Emigration: Trillion Dollar Bills on the Sidewalk," Center for Global Development Working Paper no. 264 (August 2011).

✓ CONCEPT CHECK

☐ What do development economists mean by "institutions"? **[LO 36.4]**

☐ What are the three types of industrial policy named in this section? **[LO 36.5]**

☐ What are remittances and how do they promote development? **[LO 36.6]**

What Can Aid Do?

Foreign aid has long been seen as part of economic development, although a controversial part. Taxes in many countries go to provide aid to the poor around the world. Many citizens in these countries also give money to private charities such as Heifer International, CARE, Save the Children, and church-based organizations. In fact, private donations are larger than the entire budget for official foreign aid provided by the United States.

Why is foreign aid often the central focus of development efforts? It has direct intuitive appeal:

Children in Sudan look on as food and supplies are delivered by Save the Children, an international relief and development nonprofit organization.
© Mike Goldwater/Alamy

- If people are poor, then surely money would help make life a little easier.
- Are children not going to school? Why not give families money so that they don't have to choose between work and school?
- Are roads full of potholes, making it costly and difficult to get to markets and jobs? Why not help governments build and repair them?

These donations can be very important, whether in easing hunger in famine-ravaged areas or providing funding to would-be entrepreneurs. The problem is how to make these funds go to the best uses. With many examples of misuse and waste, donating money often seems like a very unsure enterprise. Later in the chapter, we'll discuss how development economists are helping to discover what works—so that these donations can provide the most bang for their buck.

Perspectives on foreign aid

LO 36.7 Describe the aims of foreign aid, the role of poverty traps, the main institutions delivering aid, and criticisms of foreign aid.

Foreign aid got its start following World War II. In an unprecedented show of generosity, the United States distributed, as part of the Marshall Plan, $12 billion to help 16 European countries rebuild after the devastation of the war. In today's money (accounting for inflation between 1948 and now), the sum is the equivalent of over $100 billion. Of course, this aid wasn't entirely altruistic on the part of the United States. There was a good deal of strategic self-interest involved: It was seen as imperative to have strong European allies on the western borders of the Soviet Union.

Aid then shifted to the world's poorer regions. The 1947 Truman Doctrine pledged $650 million to help "free peoples who are resisting attempted subjugation by armed minorities or by outside pressures." In other words, the United States was willing to put forth money to spread development—and to try to halt the spread of communism. Russia, too, got involved in the aid business, trying to woo unaligned countries to join the communist bloc. During the "Cold War," a period of competition between the United States and Russia, many dams and bridges built in developing countries were the product of such altruism combined with political strategy.

The Cold War has been over since 1991. Yet foreign aid continues and is still largely dedicated toward building public goods. Remember from Chapter 18, "Externalities," that public goods tend to be underprovided, considering the positive externalities they provide to the economy. This is especially true in countries that already lack means for collecting taxes and making capital investment. The result is a **financing gap**—the difference between the savings rate within an economy and the amount of investment needed to achieve sustainable growth. To plug that

financing gap
the difference between the savings rate within an economy and the amount of investment needed to achieve sustainable growth

FIGURE 36-3

Official development assistance   In absolute terms, the amount of official development assistance (ODA) has steadily increased; over 50 years, the amount of money given by OECD countries in aid has tripled. Despite the 0.7 percent of gross national income (GNI) target set in the 1970s, the amount of ODA as a percent of the GNI has fallen and is not even half of this target.

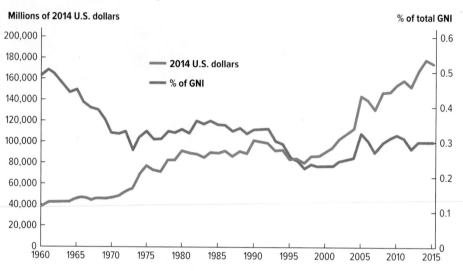

Source: Total flows by donor (ODA), http://stats.oecd.org/Index.aspx?ThemeTreeId=3#

gap, a large fraction of aid goes toward building schools, health care systems, and infrastructure networks. For much of the history of foreign aid, the financing gap has been a driving force in decisions about how much to give.

In 2002, at the Monterrey Conference on Financing for Development, the leaders of the world's most industrialized countries made a major pledge: They would devote 0.7 percent of their gross national income (GNI, a combination of GDP plus net capital flow from abroad) to foreign aid, formally called *official development assistance* (ODA). For the United States alone, this pledge would mean at least $90 billion per year. Hopes were high for what that money could accomplish.

However, actual foreign aid budgets have fallen well below that goal. Of the 22 richest countries that made the pledge, so far only six have followed through to the extent promised. As of 2015, the United States devotes only about 0.3 percent of GNI to ODA, far below the 0.7 percent target and also below the average amount given by OECD countries. As you can see in Figure 36-3, the percentage has not been rising.[13]

Over the past 55 years, the amount given in aid has increased in dollar terms, but has fallen and leveled off in terms of aid *as a share of GDP*. Should the United States meet its pledge to give 0.7 percent? See the What Do You Think? box "Should the United States give more in foreign aid?" for more on this debate.

What Do You Think?

Should the United States give more in foreign aid?

In 2015, the U.S. government spent $31.08 billion on official development assistance, about 0.17 percent of the country's gross national income and less than 1 percent of the U.S. federal government's budget. In 2010, this number was even smaller. However, when the World Public Opinion survey asked U.S. voters in 2010 what portion of government spending they believe goes toward foreign aid, the average response was a full 25 percent. When the same voters were asked how much they thought would be "appropriate" to spend on international aid, the median answer was 10 percent—10 times more than we actually spend.

Does that mean most Americans would enthusiastically support candidates who promise to spend 10 times more on foreign aid? Not necessarily. According to a Pew Research Center poll conducted in January 2013, 48 percent of Americans would like to see foreign aid *reduced,* the largest share out of any of the other options presented. In comparison, just 24 percent of those surveyed would like to see cuts to the military and to domestic anti-poverty programs. Maybe most Americans feel at a gut level that however much the United States donates to the needy abroad, it's too much.

If the United States is one of the richest countries, does it have an obligation to be generous to less-fortunate countries? Ten percent of the U.S. budget would represent an incredible (and unrealistic) sum of money. A small increase in aid, however, could potentially have large effects. Aid advocates argue that many development programs can do a lot with relatively small increases in spending. The World Food Program, which provides badly needed food aid to areas of famine around the world, costs about $4 billion per year (which is a fairly modest cost given the size of aid budgets). Researchers estimate that a yearly investment of $7 billion would be enough to reduce the global prevalence of AIDS from 38 million cases to 1 million by 2050.

The other side of the argument centers on the idea that the United States should focus on problems at home first. As the United States faces growing public debt, it has to make tough decisions about which taxes to raise or programs to cut. Money spent on foreign aid could just as easily go toward addressing domestic problems. In March 2016, the U.S. government adopted a budget that cuts spending by over $3 trillion during a 10-year period in order to control the accumulating debt. This spending cut includes removing $2.5 trillion in funding from health care programs for low- to moderate-income people. Other cuts include $125 billion from the SNAP program (formerly knows as food stamps) and about $300 billion from other entitlement programs.

WHAT DO YOU THINK?

1. At a time when U.S. government programs are facing cuts, does it make sense to help provide health insurance in Tanzania, roads in Afghanistan, hospitals in Iraq, and agricultural development in Mozambique?
2. How should the U.S. government weigh (a) providing humanitarian assistance after natural disasters abroad versus (b) investing in the long-term development of poorer countries?

Sources: http://www.worldpublicopinion.org/pipa/articles/brunitedstatescanadara/670.php?lb=btda&pnt=670&nid=&id; http://www.cbsnews.com/htdocs/pdf/poll_deficit_072909.pdf; http://www.washingtonpost.com/blogs/federal-eye/post/whats-getting-cut-in-the-fy-2011-budget/2011/04/11/AFMIynLD_blog.html; http://www.people-press.org/2013/02/22/as-sequester-deadline-looms-little-support-for-cutting-most-programs; http://www.cbpp.org/research/federal-budget/congressional-budget-plans-get-two-thirds-of-cuts-from-programs-for-people.

Poverty traps and the Millennium Development Goals

Those who argue for ramping up foreign-aid budgets often assert that aid can help countries break out of poverty traps. A **poverty trap** is a self-reinforcing mechanism that causes the poor to stay poor. For instance, a poorly nourished and undereducated population is unlikely to have the energy or know-how to develop its economy. In the long run, it will struggle to earn enough to feed itself and educate its children. Foreign aid, the theory goes, can break this negative self-reinforcing mechanism and create a *virtuous cycle,* in which improvements build on improvements.

Some theories of economic development hold that escaping from poverty traps requires there to be simultaneous investments in a wide variety of sectors as well as improvement of institutions. One variant of this idea, championed by Columbia University economist Jeffrey Sachs in his book *The End of Poverty,* is known as the "big push."[14] The idea that concerted efforts in different sectors are necessary lay behind the United Nations' decision in 2000 to create eight *Millennium Development Goals.* These goals served as targets in all of the areas covered in Sachs's

poverty trap
a self-reinforcing mechanism that causes the poor to stay poor

"big push." The goals include establishing universal primary education and halving the number of people living on one dollar per day.[15] They were supposed to be achieved by 2015. Some were, and some were not. (Looking ahead, the United Nations agreed in 2015 on a set of 17 *Sustainable Development Goals* to meet by 2030.)

Of course, if a goal is not met, it doesn't mean the effort has been wasted. Even if universal primary education was not achieved by 2015, far more kids are going to school. As a result of this push, the number of children who were not in primary school fell from 100 million in 2000 to about 57 million in 2015.[16]

To showcase the "big push" idea, the United Nations and Columbia University's Earth Institute—headed by Jeffrey Sachs—together set up 13 "Millennium Villages," scattered around sub-Saharan Africa. The villages are intended to show what can happen with sustained and targeted investment. For $110 per person per year, new schools and clinics are built, sanitation improves, farmers receive improved varieties of seeds, and so on.

However, not everyone is convinced that such "big push" ideas are the right way for foreign aid to go. Critics argue that there is no guarantee the idea could work if rolled out globally, and it would be extremely expensive to try. They suggest other, cheaper ways to kick-start economic development, such as a focus on setting up better institutions or improving the quality of credit or insurance markets.

The major distributors of aid

How do governments of wealthy countries give their foreign aid? Much of it is channeled through national development agencies or sectors of foreign-affairs ministries. The *United States Agency for International Development (USAID)* serves this purpose in the United States. About $20 billion of the $31 billion allocated by the United States toward official development assistance funds USAID, which works to improve economic growth, trade, and agriculture, among other things.[17]

World Bank
a multinational organization dedicated to providing financial and technical assistance to developing countries

Other resources are channeled through international institutions. About $2.3 billion per year comes from the **World Bank**, a multinational organization dedicated to providing financial and technical assistance to developing countries. Formed in 1948 at the same Bretton Woods conference that spawned the International Monetary Fund, the World Bank is actually two development organizations:

- Much like a bank, the International Bank for Reconstruction and Development (IBRD) makes loans that are used by middle-income and creditworthy poor countries to finance a wide variety of investment projects.

- The International Development Association (IDA), on the other hand, more closely resembles what we think of as a traditional aid agency. From 2000 to 2010, IDA funded immunizations for 310 million children and clean water for 113 million. This work has continued since, on large-scale budgets that include $19 billion worth of commitments for the year ending June 2015.

United Nations Development Program (UNDP)
a global United Nations network that provides knowledge and resources to developing countries

Much development work is also conducted through a sprawling network of organizations under the **United Nations Development Program (UNDP)**—a global United Nations network that provides knowledge and resources to developing countries. In all, the UNDP is on the ground in 166 countries, operating a diverse set of projects, including everything from halting the spread of HIV/AIDS to developing democratic institutions. Within the UNDP, specialized organizations fund more targeted types of aid. The World Food Program, for example, spent over $4.2 billion in aid in 2015, 86 percent of which went toward fighting hunger in famine-ravaged areas, as part of its Emergency Preparedness and Response program.[18] Some government aid is also funneled through private, nonprofit organizations such as Heifer, CARE, and Save the Children.

Problems with foreign aid

With such a large system of aid, it's not surprising that not everyone is on board with the idea of doling out billions of dollars to poor countries around the world. It's not hard to find these critics—including some notable economists—who believe that aid can be inefficient and even counterproductive. Jean-Claude Duvalier, president of Haiti from 1971 to 1986, lived a fantastically lavish lifestyle while ordinary Haitians lived in intense poverty. Duvalier would regularly showcase Haiti's poor to international donors and then divert much of the resulting aid (one estimate is 80 percent) into his personal bank account.

Foreign aid is now tracked more carefully than it was in Duvalier's day, and agencies and governments now require a greater degree of accountability. But problems still persist. An intriguing insight was provided in 2011 when WikiLeaks, an organization that works to make classified documents public, released 250,000 classified cables from U.S. embassies. One of these cables revealed embezzlement and misplacement of funds from the UK Department for International Development (UK DfID) in projects around the world. In one example, almost $2 million given by the UK Ministry of Defense to "support peacekeeping" in Sierra Leone was instead embezzled by top generals in the Sierra Leone Ministry of Defense to buy plasma televisions and hunting rifles. In Kenya, the Ministry of Education admitted to losing $17.3 million worth of textbooks distributed through the "Free Education" program. In Uganda, officials managed to divert almost $27 million from an education fund.

Disappearing money may be one reason why, despite the spending of half a trillion dollars in ODA from 1970 to 1994, productivity growth in developing countries was essentially zero and economic growth not much more. Another big problem is that organizations such as the World Bank are not held accountable for what happens to funds once dispersed. Abhijit Banerjee notes the example of a World Bank computer kiosk program implemented in India, which the Bank trumpeted as a rousing success in its "Empowerment" sourcebook.[19] Many of these machines, however, were sitting uselessly in buildings that didn't have electricity or Internet connections. William Easterly, an economist at NYU who spent years working at the World Bank, argues that aid agencies typically have nebulous goals—such as promoting empowerment or economic growth or governmental reform—rather than being charged with completing a task that is specific and measurable. Without measurable goals, it's not surprising that organizations have little incentive to be sure that what they are doing actually works.

There are even stronger critics of aid than Easterly. Dambisa Moyo, in her book *Dead Aid*, argues that aid actually hurts the countries that receive it.[20] In many countries, aid is a substantial part of the budget. In Kenya, for example, aid averaged 10 percent of GDP from 1970 to 2010. Such large flows can have serious effects throughout the economy, notably crowding out domestic investment. When foreign aid flows in, it also has to be traded for local currency; that currency trade bids up the price of the local currency and hurts the competitiveness of the local export sector.

Aid can be particularly counterproductive when it involves trucking in goods for free or at highly discounted prices. Such aid is known as *goods-in-kind donations*. When aid agencies or governments distribute food, clothing, or other materials, they are giving goods in kind. To see the possible side-effects of well-intentioned donations, see the From Another Angle box "In Zambia, did the Steelers win Super Bowl XLV?"

From Another Angle

In Zambia, did the Steelers win Super Bowl XLV?

Before the confetti from Super Bowl XLV was swept away, the victorious players for the Green Bay Packers donned T-shirts emblazoned with the words "Super Bowl Champions." Of course, the Packers hadn't waited until *after* the game to have those T-shirts printed; instead, they had thousands printed beforehand, in case they won. So did the losing side, the Pittsburgh Steelers.

But as soon as the Steelers lost the game, their shirts became pretty much worthless. Who's going to buy a shirt that says the wrong team won? The NFL and a charity called World Vision

(continued)

came up with a solution: Instead of letting the T-shirts sit around, getting moldy in a warehouse, they could ship the T-shirts to Africa to give to the poor and needy.

Sounds great, right? Not if you're an African T-shirt maker. As it happens, T-shirts are not desperately needed in Africa. Africa has a solid homegrown and secondhand clothing market that supplies clothes at a fair price. Very few people go without T-shirts because they cannot afford them. An influx of Steelers T-shirts, instead of helping out, distorts the market: It hurts everyone from secondhand clothes marketers to local clothing makers, who obviously can't compete with free T-shirts.

That's not the only problem with the idea of shipping all those Steelers T-shirts to Africa. Shipping costs money. One particularly glaring example of this is the *One Million Shirts* campaign, started by a young entrepreneur. In order to cover the shipping charges for the one million shirts he planned to send to Africa, the founder asked for a dollar along with each shirt. While this sounds noble, the plan comes with a considerable opportunity cost. Is shipping unneeded shirts to Africa really the best way to spend $1 million? Would it be better to spend that money on, say, buying life-saving drugs or mosquito nets? In the end, the program was shut down after a firestorm of criticism.

The lesson is that it takes more than good intentions to solve the pressing issues of development. If good intentions were all it took, aid would have lifted everyone out of poverty long ago.

Sources: http://www.freakonomics.com/2011/02/15/what-happens-to-all-those-super-bowl-t-shirts-a-guest-post-by-dean-karlan/; http://www.nber.org/papers/w17456.pdf?new_window=1; http://www.time.com/time/world/article/0,8599,1987628,00.html.

Do these problems mean all aid should be stopped? Not necessarily. The lesson may be that more effort needs to go into improving the weak governments that embezzle aid or fail to use it productively. This idea was tested by economists Craig Burnside at Duke University and David Dollar, now at the U.S. Treasury Department. They found that in the decades of the 1980s and 1990s:

- Countries with sound fiscal, monetary, and trade policies and strong rule of law, combined with large amounts of aid, grew GDP at 1 percent.
- Countries with bad policy and high amounts of aid saw GDP shrink by 1 percent over the same time period.[21]

In fact, for countries with "bad" policy, aid was actually a detriment to growth. The example of Duvalier's Haiti at the beginning of this section suggests why: With aid flowing in to embezzle, Duvalier had little incentive to work to improve Haiti's economy because such improvements would reduce or eliminate aid.

The research behind the Dollar and Burnside study has been questioned (it turns out that more recent data do not show the same patterns). Nevertheless, their logic has spurred governments and aid organizations to think harder about links between aid and policy. In 2004, the United States created the Millennium Challenge Corporation to give cash to "worthy" governments. To qualify, these governments have to meet 17 requirements, including ruling justly, tamping down corruption, and maintaining a stable economy. So far, the Millennium Challenge Corporation has given out $11 billion in arrangements called "compacts" to 26 countries.[22]

Impact investing

LO 36.8 Understand how impact investing provides a new tool for creating social impact.

Most thinking about foreign aid has little to do with business. But businesses, after all, are extremely good at generating new products, producing at the right scale, marketing, and creating efficient supply chains. Those are the exact qualities needed to solve some of the toughest social and economic problems.

Private investors and institutions are supporting this new breed of socially minded businesses through an idea called impact investing. **Impact investing** involves investing money in firms to generate both financial and social returns. In some ways, it's an alternative to foreign aid, though in fact the two ideas can work together. The firms that receive the impact-investing funds are called "social businesses." They are involved in all kinds of endeavors from building cheap but effective private schools in the slums of Nairobi, to hospitals that serve the poor for free in South India.

The guiding idea behind impact investing is simple: Markets can be powerful tools to promote human development, but not if investors are interested only in a quick financial return.[23] Impact investors, who may be foundations, wealth managers, private managers, or nonprofit organizations, are willing to be more patient and take greater risks. They sometimes accept lower financial returns as long as they're convinced that their money is being used to create social change.

One pioneering example of impact investing is the Acumen Fund, a "nonprofit global venture fund" that invests only in businesses that aim for social impact. Since its start in 2001, it has invested more than $101 million in health, housing, water, energy, education, and agriculture businesses across East Africa, West Africa, Latin America, India, and Pakistan. Among the firms supported by the Acumen Fund—to the tune of $1.5 million—is d.light design, which sells lanterns that produce light using solar energy. One out of four people in the world does not have electricity. The solar lanterns sold by d.light are a healthier solution than kerosene lanterns, which produce dangerous fumes.

Although the Acumen Fund's investments are a small fraction of the roughly $2 trillion in foreign direct investment that flows around the world each year, impact investing is growing quickly, particularly in Europe. Large banks are getting involved, as are universities: Colorado State University, for example, offers a Global Social and Sustainable Enterprise (GSSE) Master's in Business Administration. Stanford University's Entrepreneurial Design for Extreme Affordability class teaches students to design products to serve consumers at the lowest income level (and was the group that incubated the solar lantern behind d.light design).

Solar-powered lighting makes things we take for granted in the United States, like studying at night and charging a cell phone, much easier to do.
© *Mark Boulton/Alamy*

impact investing
investing money in firms to generate both financial and social returns

How do we know what works?

LO 36.9 Explain the need for impact evaluation and analyze the role of randomized controlled trials in measuring impact.

There is no shortage of ideas for how to promote economic development. The Millennium Project, for one, offers 449 ways to reduce poverty. These ideas include hydrological monitoring systems, footpaths, road maintenance, electric power grids, women's empowerment initiatives, and industrial parks. But because resources are limited, governments and aid agencies have to make some tough choices about which policies would be the best in reducing poverty. In short, *how do we know what works?*

For most of the twentieth century, development efforts proceeded on a trial-and-error basis. Certain strategies were tried. If they seemed to work, they were kept; if they looked like glaring failures, they were scrapped. The trouble is, many of the failures weren't glaring enough. Often, aid agencies simply couldn't be sure whether a particular strategy had helped or hurt.

In recent years, some development economists have started to argue against charging forward with ideas that might or might not work. Instead they promote a more informed approach by rigorously evaluating the impact of development programs and policies.

Evaluations

Impact evaluation entails answering one seemingly simple question: How did people's lives change after a program or policy, compared with how they would have changed without it? This question would be easy to answer if everything else were held constant except the program or policy—but that's not the case in the complexities of the real world.

Consider the challenge of enrolling kids in school and ensuring they learn while they are there. To achieve those goals, there are many options and promising programs:

- For example, because schools in developing countries often have to make do with old, battered learning materials, one strategy is to provide students with better textbooks.
- Another strategy might be providing kids with school uniforms. Even when schooling itself is free, many schools require students to wear uniforms; when this is an expense that families cannot afford, their kids don't go to school.

At first glance, it seems as if it would be easy to evaluate efforts like these—just measure the test scores of kids in schools who receive the textbooks or the uniforms. If they're higher than before, great; if not, then back to the drawing board. Unfortunately, that type of evaluation is far from fool-proof. Beyond the question of whether the tests measure learning in a meaningful way, how do we know that the better test scores are not the result of something else? What if there's been an especially good harvest this year, so kids are learning better because they're no longer hungry while at school? In that case, we might be mistaken in thinking the textbooks are making the difference, and we'd keep pouring money into buying more textbooks when it could be put to better use elsewhere.

randomized controlled trial (RCT)

a method that randomly assigns subjects into control and treatment groups in order to assess the causal link from an intervention to specific outcomes

One way to avoid evaluation problems is by using **randomized controlled trials**, or **RCTs** for short. Randomized controlled trials randomly assign people into groups in order to focus on the impact of a particular intervention. Some of the stories told in this book, such as the one about giving out mosquito nets to protect from malaria (see the "Paying for bednets" box in Chapter 4, "Elasticity"), have been the result of such randomized controlled trials.

How could we use the idea of RCTs to know the true impact of providing more textbooks on test scores? We could select 100 similar schools and divide them into two groups of 50 at random. The first group doesn't get the textbooks; the second group does. If it's the textbooks making the difference, then schools in the so-called *treatment group* (the one that receives the textbooks) will do better than those in the *control group*. The key to the process is dividing the schools at random: The two groups should be similar on average before the study, so any factor other than the treatment itself should affect them equally. The RCT doesn't completely control for other variables that could possibly affect schools' performance, but it's a start.

Evaluations using the RCT method can give surprising results. It turns out if you want to boost school attendance, there's something you can buy and give out that's sometimes more effective than either textbooks or uniforms—deworming pills. Worms are tiny, parasitic organisms that cause chronic sickness that keeps kids out of school. The parasites were once common in parts of the United States, and they are still common in other countries. One study in Kenya found that, overall, a deworming program led to a 7.5 percent gain in primary school participation. Deworming pills are also far cheaper than textbooks or uniforms, costing just 50 cents per child per year. In comparison, the state-run *Oportunidades* (previously called *Progresa*) safety-net program in Mexico, which links cash benefits for families to activities such as getting kids vaccinated and sending them to school, costs many times this amount.[24] (Note that programs like Oportunidades also have other goals, not just increasing school attendance.)

Figure 36-4 shows the results from an RCT study of various programs intended to increase years of education. The figure shows that there is one intervention that is even more cost-effective than deworming. When researchers crunched the numbers of the program costs versus how effective they were at increasing school enrollment, they found that a very simple program scored highest. That program involves simply informing parents of the potential benefits of giving their children an education. Many of these parents in parts of the developing world may never have attended school themselves. Explaining the benefits of education turned out to be by far the most effective intervention, resulting in 20 extra "child-years" of education for every $100 spent.

FIGURE 36-4

Impact of programs intended to increase years of education   Evaluations allow researchers to compare the cost-effectiveness of various programs. Telling parents about the benefits of education ("Information on returns") was by far the most effective intervention, and resulted in 20 extra "child-years" of education for every $100 spent. Deworming is also very cost-effective. Although other programs were also effective at increasing schooling, they were not as cost-effective as the others.

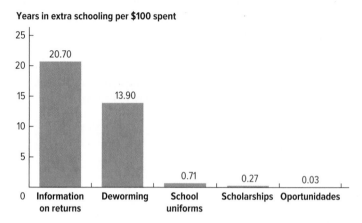

Source: https://www.povertyactionlab.org/policy-lessons/education/improving-student-participation.

Thanks to randomized controlled trials, policy-makers and program managers can more confidently channel resources to approaches that work and are cost-effective. Two organizations are dedicated to this research: One is the Abdul Latif Jameel Poverty Action Lab (J-PAL), founded by economists at MIT and Harvard. The other is Innovations for Poverty Action (IPA), a nonprofit organization started by Dean Karlan (one of the authors of this book). Many other organizations and researchers have followed their lead in using RCTs to investigate sectors as varied as microfinance, education, health, agriculture, charitable giving, corruption, and social capital. Thanks to rigorous evaluations, the remedial education program we described earlier in this chapter, for example, is now being scaled up in Ghana, with the aim of reaching thousands of schools.

This is not to say that these organizations have found the solution to global poverty. Like so many other tools, RCTs have challenges and limitations. Some questions, like the effect on economic development of changing monetary policy, simply can't be evaluated with an RCT. Even for those programs that can be evaluated, it's possible that the observed effects will change if the intervention is repeated on another continent or even in different areas of a country. And often it's hard to tell from an RCT exactly why the intervention worked or failed.

Still, using economic theory to help design experiments, and replicating experiments at different times and in different places, can be critical in moving knowledge forward. Along with other kinds of analysis, RCTs are helping to build knowledge, piece by piece, which is already pointing to some seemingly small interventions that can make large differences.

✓CONCEPT CHECK

- ☐ How do financing gaps justify foreign aid? **[LO 36.7]**
- ☐ How many countries pledged to participate in official development assistance? How many of them actually gave the amount promised? **[LO 36.7]**
- ☐ What are the Millennium Development Goals? **[LO 36.7]**
- ☐ Why might goods-in-kind donations cause problems for local producers? **[LO 36.7]**
- ☐ How does impact investing differ from foreign aid? **[LO 36.8]**
- ☐ What is a randomized controlled trial? **[LO 36.9]**

Conclusion

Although the work needed to put an end to global poverty may seem daunting, major strides have been made and continue to be made. Most obviously, decades of growth in the Chinese economy have lifted millions of people out of poverty. What worked for China was the product of a time and place that can't simply be bottled and shipped to other regions. Yet there are hopeful signs of improvements elsewhere, including Africa. Around the African continent, vigorously contested, democratic elections are taking place, and some countries are posting impressive growth figures.

Progress is being made through different mixes of good governance, aid, strengthened institutions, investment, and careful testing of what works and what does not among aid programs. While there is a long way to go, progress like this can promote the expansion of capabilities and help expand markets that truly work for the world's poor.

Key Terms

capability, p. 957

institutions, p. 961

industrial policy, p. 963

clusters, p. 964

World Trade Organization (WTO), p. 964

financing gap, p. 967

poverty trap, p. 969

World Bank, p. 970

United Nations Development Program (UNDP), p. 970

impact investing, p. 973

randomized controlled trial (RCT), p. 974

Summary

LO 36.1 Explain how the capabilities approach relates to economic development.

Development is a field of economics that studies the causes and nature of international poverty and human development. One way to think about development is known as the capabilities approach, developed by Amartya Sen. The goal of development is to increase human capabilities. There are many different types of capabilities, including very basic rights to health and education as well as other concepts like self-expression and reputation.

LO 36.2 Explain the relationship between economic growth and economic development.

The ideas of economic growth and development are similar but not identical. Economic growth can promote development. After all, when people have more money, you would expect them to spend more on improving their health and educating their children. There is general agreement, though, that the fundamentals of economic growth, including such elements as property rights, the rule of law, and human capital, will spark development.

LO 36.3 Describe how improvements to education and health can develop human capital.

By providing access to more and better schools and clinics, countries can develop human capital. Many countries are now mandating universal primary education and providing health insurance on the cheap to make great strides in basic human capital development. These efforts must be of high quality to be effective, though. Human capital is an important part of economic development, as it allows for more productive workers and greater economic growth. Improvements in human capital can also promote capacities development as people are able to lead more complete (better educated and healthier) lives.

LO 36.4 Explain the importance of institutions and good governance in development economics.

Development often takes root in places where there are strong institutions. Institutions are human-devised constraints that shape human interactions. In contrast, organizations are groups of people that act according to those constraints. Several institutions are important for development, including a strong system of property rights, the rule of law, and a government capable of implementing good policy.

LO 36.5 Evaluate the role of industrial policy and clusters in development.

Governments have turned to industrial policy in an attempt to favor some industries over others. Two popular types of industrial policy include import substitution and export-led industrialization. An alternative industrial policy is clustering, which promotes networks of interdependent firms, universities, and customers focusing on a specific type of good.

LO 36.6 Evaluate how migration and remittances promote development.

Every year, millions of people leave their home countries and villages to migrate in search of better-paying jobs. The money they send home to their families, called remittances, represents a large and growing financial flow around the world. As a result, governments and aid agencies work to make sure that these remittances best help the families back home escape poverty.

LO 36.7 Describe the aims of foreign aid, the role of poverty traps, the main institutions delivering aid, and criticisms of foreign aid.

Over the past 55 years, the amount given in foreign aid has increased in dollar terms but has fallen and leveled off as a share of GDP. Those who argue for ramping up foreign-aid budgets often assert that aid can help countries break out of *poverty traps.* Others suggest different ways to kick-start economic development, such as a focus on setting up better institutions or improving the quality of credit or insurance markets. Much of the foreign aid governments do give is channeled through national development agencies like USAID, or through global organizations like the World Bank and the United Nations. Although foreign aid can provide money needed to finance developments in infrastructure, clinic and school construction, and other important measures that simply would not happen without outside assistance, critics point to cases in which foreign aid has been a destabilizing force that was wasted at best, and destructive at worst.

LO 36.8 Understand how impact investing provides a new tool for creating social impact.

Most thinking about foreign aid has little to do with business. But private investors and institutions are supporting socially minded businesses through *impact investing,* which involves investing money in firms to generate both financial and social returns. Markets can be powerful tools to promote human development, and impact investors sometimes accept lower financial returns as long as they're convinced their money is being used to create social change.

LO 36.9 Explain the need for impact evaluation and analyze the role of randomized controlled trials in measuring impact.

Throughout history, ideas about how to spur development have mostly proceeded on a trial-and-error basis. Instead of wasting money on programs that may or may not work, economists have begun to evaluate the impact of various development programs. Impact evaluation tries to answer the question of how a particular program or policy changed people's lives. A *randomized controlled trial (RCT)* is one way to answer that question; it compares a treatment group with a control group to show the effect of a program.

Review Questions

1. Are capabilities and utility the same thing? If so, why do economists use two different terms for the same concept? If not, explain the difference, in terms of both their definitions and when each is best used in economic analysis. **[LO 36.1]**

2. Determine whether each of the following is true or false. **[LO 36.1]**

   a. The chance to see a musical is an example of a capability.

   b. The freedom to practice religion is not a capability because it is not directly related to economic development.

   c. Economists will make the same conclusions and recommendations using the utility-maximization approach as they will using the capabilities approach.

   d. The capabilities approach works better for analyzing what's best for society, while the utility-maximization approach works better for analyzing what's best for an individual.

3. Are economic growth and economic development the same? Why or why not? **[LO 36.2]**

4. Does economic growth lead to development? Or does the causation run the other way, with economic development leading to growth? Explain. **[LO 36.2]**

5. How can health and education work together to spur economic development? What does this imply about the best way to spend aid funds with the goal of increasing educational attainment in a developing nation? **[LO 36.3]**

6. Explain how better health care in a developing nation, such as increasing the number of immunized children, can have economic effects beyond fewer sick kids. **[LO 36.3]**

7. "I'm thinking about writing a paper for class on development economics," your friend tells you over lunch. "I'm going to focus on important institutions like government bodies and economic agencies." Is your friend using the term *institutions* correctly? Why or why not? **[LO 36.4]**

8. How can capital be considered "dead," and what do we mean by making this capital "alive"? **[LO 36.4]**

9. International trade is associated with economic growth and development—open economies tend to grow faster than closed economies, all else equal. Given this information, should a nation seeking to grow and develop faster use the method of import substitution or export-led growth? How would each of these two methods affect GDP through its net exports component? **[LO 36.5]**

10. Determine whether each of the following is an example of import substitution, export-led growth, or clustering. **[LO 36.5]**

    a. The government gives a $50 million grant to a leading university to work with car manufacturers and to research new ways to produce more fuel-efficient vehicles.

    b. The government gives $50 million to a domestic car company to subsidize its shipping costs to other countries.

    c. The government enacts a tariff on all cars imported from abroad.

11. How can emigration help the home economy in terms of income? Are the benefits of migration on income limited to those who actually migrate? Why or why not? **[LO 36.6]**

12. How does emigration affect wages and income in the migrant's country of origin? In the country the migrant immigrates to? **[LO 36.6]**

13. Say that the United States is considering giving direct aid to a nation run by a dictator known for his lavish lifestyle while the nation's citizens suffer through a terrible famine. What might be a problem with giving aid to this nation? Name at least one way to fix the problem. **[LO 36.7]**

14. What are goods-in-kind donations, and how can they hurt the economies they're meant to help? **[LO 36.7]**

15. How does impact investment differ from traditional foreign aid and traditional financial investment? **[LO 36.8]**

16. Explain briefly how you could set up an RCT to evaluate whether providing free breakfasts to elementary-school students helps them learn. **[LO 36.9]**

17. List three shortcomings of using an RCT to evaluate the success of a given economic program. **[LO 36.9]**

Problems and Applications

1. In a small town in the midwestern United States lives a drug dealer and manufacturer who supplies the illegal, addictive drug crystal meth. The drug dealer insists that making and selling the drug is what gives him the most satisfaction among any possible use of his time and resources. Using the utility-maximization approach, should he be allowed to continue supplying the drug? What about with the capabilities approach? Explain your answer. **[LO 36.1]**

2. Professor Bucks and Professor Liber are having a debate about the role of economic growth in contributing to economic development. Professor Bucks contends that economic growth is the only thing to consider in development, as people's utility is directly related to their income. Professor Liber agrees that income is directly related to development but says that there are other things to consider. Given what we've learned in this chapter, pick the option that is most correct according to the capabilities approach. **[LO 36.1]**

    a. Professor Bucks is correct because increases in income are the only way to measure economic development.

    b. Professor Bucks is correct because capabilities always increase when income does.

    c. Professor Liber is correct because income is unrelated to capabilities, which are the most important factor in development.

    d. Professor Liber is correct because income is related to development, but it is not the only contributor to capabilities.

3. Table 36P-1 shows the levels and annual growth rates of economic indicators for two countries, Nationavia and Countrystan. Assume these growth rates will remain constant for the foreseeable future. Use these data to determine whether each of the following statements is true, false, or indeterminable. **[LO 36.2]**

    a. The theory of income convergence (that national incomes in poor countries will "catch up" to those in wealthier countries) holds for Nationavia and Countrystan.

    b. Countrystan has higher levels of human capital than Nationavia.

    c. Inequality is greater in Nationavia.

    d. In 10 years, it's likely that Countrystan will have higher levels of human capital than Nationavia.

4. In Nation A, GDP per capita is $21,000 and is growing annually at a rate of 1.4 percent. The average citizen in Nation A lives for 51 years, and this figure is growing at 6 percent per year. Additionally, the average person in Nation A has 9 years of education, growing annually at

TABLE 36P-1

Indicator	Level	Growth rate (%)
GDP per capita—Nationavia	$50,000	3.1
GDP per capita—Countrystan	$30,000	3.0
Average years of education per capita—Nationavia	15 years	2.0
Average years of education per capita—Countrystan	5 years	8.0
Life expectancy—Nationavia	72 years	0.5
Life expectancy—Countrystan	56 years	1.8

5.1 percent, and 60 percent of Nation A's population is currently literate, growing at a rate of 2 percent.

In Nation B, GDP per capita is $40,000 and is growing annually at a rate of 0.8 percent. The average citizen in Nation B lives for 68 years, and this value is growing at 2 percent per year. The average person in Nation B has 10.5 years of education, increasing 2 percent annually, while 78 percent of its population is literate, a figure growing at 0.5 percent annually.

Which nation is experiencing more economic growth? Which is wealthier? Which currently has more capabilities for its citizens? And which is experiencing more economic development? **[LO 36.2]**

5. Imagine that you are the leader of a low-income nation. You have identified lack of access to health care as a major contributor to your nation's low income, and the United States has offered to help by providing funds to build more health clinics. Will this solve the problem? Why or why not? If it won't, what's one alternative to using these foreign aid dollars to build clinics? **[LO 36.3]**

6. While listening to the radio on the way to school, you hear a politician from a small, low-income nation say the following: "Over the last five years, there has been a 10 percent increase in the number of children attending school full time. We can expect to see these children grow up to be more productive workers because their human capital has increased." Is the politician's statement true, false, or somewhere in between? Explain your answer. **[LO 36.3]**

7. Classify each of the following as an institution or organization. **[LO 36.4]**

    a. The United States Agency for International Development, a U.S. government agency that channels aid abroad.

    b. The United Nations Development Program.

    c. The UN Declaration of Human Rights, an agreement among members of the United Nations regarding the rights of individuals.

    d. The United Nations.

    e. The Sarbanes-Oxley Act (SOX), which established rules for how publicly traded firms must report information in their financial documents.

8. A given nation has a good titling system, but theft of productive equipment is rampant, with few consequences for those who steal. What is the term development economists use for what's lacking in this economy? What effect will this lack likely have on economic growth and economic development? Give one way to improve the situation. **[LO 36.4]**

9. The small, landlocked nation of Wheatleyton is just starting to develop an agricultural sector. Firms in this sector appeal to the government to temporarily limit imports of agricultural goods from other nations with more experience and larger scale, resulting in import prices so low domestic firms can't compete. What is this desired policy called? What problems are associated with it, and how can we reduce them? **[LO 36.5]**

10. The small nation of Movieheim wants to develop a film industry. It is considering two options for doing so:

    Option A: Reimburse relocation expenses for firms and give tax breaks to acting schools, film studios, digital artists, etc., to encourage them to work together and share ideas.

    Option B: Make the purchase and exhibition of foreign films illegal for the next 10 years.

    What would development economists call each of these options? Which is more likely to encourage long-term economic development, and why? **[LO 36.5]**

11. Consider separately each of the following hypothetical scenarios about South Africa and answer the included questions. Assume in each case that medical school has an 80 percent success rate—in other words, 80 percent of people who attend medical school graduate and become doctors. **[LO 36.6]**

    a. No doctors are allowed to emigrate, and the number of people going to medical school is given by $D = 100,000 \times I$, where I is an index relating the income of doctors to those in other professions. If $I = 4$, how many students will go to medical school? How many more doctors will there be in South Africa?

b. The United States decides to offer visas for any doctors from South Africa. Additionally, I in the above equation changes to 10. Assume that 30 percent of doctors educated in South Africa immigrate to the United States. How many students will go to medical school? How many will become doctors? How many of those doctors will practice in South Africa, and how many will practice in the United States?

c. The United States decides to limit the number of doctors from South Africa who can obtain visas to no more than 10 percent of those graduating from medical school. Assume that I remains at 10. How many students will go to medical school? How many will become doctors? How many of those doctors will practice in South Africa, and how many will practice in the United States?

12. Table 36P-2 shows the size of various flows to developing countries in 2009 and 2010 in billions of dollars. **[LO 36.7]**

   a. Rank each of the flows in 2010 as a percentage of ODA (official development assistance) in 2009, from highest to lowest.

   b. Rank each of the flows in terms of their growth rates from 2009 to 2010, from highest to lowest.

13. The following equation provides an alternative calculation to determine a developing country's financing gap: **[LO 36.7]**

$$FG = (A \times g) - I_D$$

   In this equation, FG is the financing gap; A is a variable that captures the country's starting income together with its ability to turn investment into growth (expressed in dollars); g is the targeted growth rate; and I_D is the amount of domestic investment currently in the economy. Assume that A = \$50,000,000,000, g = 0.08, and I_D = \$500,000,000, and answer the questions that follow. **[LO 36.7]**

TABLE 36P-2

Financial flow	Amount in 2009 (billions of $)	Amount in 2010 (billions of $)
Official development assistance	128	119
Foreign direct investment	510	573
Remittances	307	324

a. What is the size of the financing gap?

b. Assume that the population of the United States is 300 million. How much would each U.S. citizen have to pay to fill the financing gap?

c. What percentage of GDP per capita in the United States does your answer from (b) represent if GDP per capita is currently \$45,000?

Now assume that the United States decides to donate the amount of the financing gap to the developing country as aid. Assume also that there are administrative and competitive costs associated with receiving aid. Specifically, 23 cents of every dollar spent on aid will go to administrative costs. Also, for every dollar received from abroad intended to be used for investment, 50 cents will be used for noninvestment purposes.

d. Calculate the real increase in investment dollars the aid from the United States will provide in the recipient country.

e. Calculate the new financing gap by subtracting the above from the financing gap you calculated in part (a).

14. The president of an organization specializing in foreign investment says the following at a shareholder meeting: "Our one-year program was a failure. We were hoping for a 6 percent return on our investment, but we got only 3 percent." Use the idea of impact investing to provide an alternative argument that the program was not a failure. **[LO 36.8]**

15. Table 36P-3 displays the results of a study on how to improve vaccination rates in a developing nation. The baseline numbers represent the rates of vaccination at the beginning of the study, while the endline numbers represent the rates of vaccination at the study's conclusion. Answer the following questions. **[LO 36.9]**

   a. Which campaign(s) had a positive effect on vaccination rates in comparison to the control group?

   b. Which campaign had the largest positive effect on vaccination rates in comparison to the control group?

   c. Which campaign(s) had a negative effect on vaccination rates in comparison to the control group?

   d. Which campaign(s) had no effect on vaccination rates in comparison to the control group?

16. Table 36P-4 displays the results of a study on how to improve vaccination rates in a developing nation. The baseline numbers represent the rates of vaccination at the beginning of the study, and the endline numbers represent the rates of vaccination at the study's conclusion. Rank the campaigns in order from most effective

TABLE 36P-3

Campaign	Vaccination rates (%)			
	Baseline, control	Baseline, treatment	Endline, control	Endline, treatment
Lectures	5	6	8	5
Free provision	5	4	8	8
Subsidy	5	5	8	10
Newspaper announcements	5	7	8	7

TABLE 36P-4

Campaign	Vaccination Rates (%)			
	Baseline, control	Baseline, treatment	Endline, control	Endline, treatment
Lectures	4	6	6	9
Free provision	4	7	6	8
Subsidy	4	5	6	9
Newspaper announcements	4	3	6	2

TABLE 36P-5

Campaign	Cost per person ($)
Lectures	10
Free provision	20
Subsidy	15
Newspaper announcements	5

to least effective. Then refer to Table 36P-5, which shows the cost per person of each campaign. Combining information from the two tables, rank the campaigns that resulted in an increase in vaccinations from high to low in terms of cost-effectiveness (based on treatment effect alone). **[LO 36.9]**

Endnotes

1. http://www.worldbank.org/en/news/press-release/2015/10/04/world-bank-forecasts-global-poverty-to-fall-below-10-for-first-time-major-hurdles-remain-in-goal-to-end-poverty-by-2030.

2. http://data.worldbank.org/indicator/NY.GDP.PCAP.CD.

3. http://blogs.ei.columbia.edu/2011/03/24/india-is-booming-so-why-are-nearly-half-of-its-children-malnourished-part-1/.

4. Jishnu Das and Jeffrey Hammer, "Strained Mercy: The Quality of Medical Care in Delhi," World Bank Policy Research Working Paper Series No. 3228 (2004).

5. Unpublished data from Innovations for Poverty Action.

6. Douglass C. North, "Institutions," *Journal of Economic Perspectives* 5, no. 1 (Winter 1991), pp. 97–112.

7. http://internationalpropertyrightsindex.org/introduction.

8. For evidence on the link between democracy and economic growth, see http://as.nyu.edu/docs/IO/2591/Development.pdf.

9. https://knoema.com/sijweyg/gdp-per-capita-ranking-2015-data-and-charts.

10. Michael Clemens, Claudio E. Montenegro, and Lant Pritchett, "The Place Premium: Wage Differences for Identical Workers across the U.S. Border," Center for Global Development Working Paper no. 148, July 2008.

11. https://travel.state.gov/content/dam/visas/Diversity-Visa/DVStatistics/DVApplicantEntrantsbyCountry%202013-2015.pdf.

12. Michael Clemens, "Economics and Emigration: Trillion Dollar Bills on the Sidewalk," Center for Global

Development Working Paper no. 264 (August 2011); and Lant Pritchett, *Let Their People Come* (Washington, DC: Center for Global Development, 2006).

13. The data in Figure 36-3 report *gross ODA,* which is the amount that the United States spends on ODA in a given year. Because the United States receives loan repayments from countries (due on loans made in previous years), the net outflow is smaller than gross ODA. Subtracting any loan repayments received yields *net ODA.* In 2015, net ODA provided by the United States was 0.17 percent of GNI.

14. Jeffrey Sachs, *The End of Poverty* (New York: Penguin Press, 2006).

15. http://www.unicef.org/publications/files/Children_and_the_MDGs.pdf.

16. http://www.undp.org/content/undp/en/home/librarypage/mdg/the-millennium-development-goals-report-2015.html.

17. https://www.usaid.gov/sites/default/files/documents/1869/USAIDFY2015DevelopmentBudgetFactSheet.pdf.

18. http://documents.wfp.org/stellent/groups/public/documents/reports/wfp284116.pdf.

19. Abhijit Banerjee, *Making Aid Work* (Cambridge, MA: MIT Press, 2007).

20. Dambisa Moyo, *Dead aid: Why Aid Is Not Working and How There Is a Better Way for Africa* (New York: Farrar, Straus and Giroux, 2009).

21. Craig Burnside and David Dollar, "Aid, Policies and Growth: Revisiting the Evidence," WB Policy Research Paper no. O-2834 (Washington, DC: World Bank, 2004).

22. https://www.fas.org/sgp/crs/row/RL32427.pdf.

23. Jonathan Morduch, "Not So Fast: The Realities of Impact Investing," *America's Quarterly,* Fall 2011, http://www.americasquarterly.org/not-so-fast-the-realities-of-impact-investing.

24. https://www.povertyactionlab.org/policy-lessons/education/improving-student-participation.

Guide to Data Sources

Throughout this book . . . we've used data from a wide variety of sources to present theories on phenomena ranging from international aid to financial crises. Without accurate and timely data, we couldn't reliably say nearly as much about these issues.

Before recent advances in information technology, gathering data was much more cumbersome—and data sources were far less prevalent. Today, we have the opposite problem. The amount of data already collected is astounding. With so much data available, finding the right sources can seem like a challenge.

To help you dive into the real world of economics, we provide this guide to some of the most useful and widely used data sources for the economy. Since the quality of your data will have a big impact on the quality of any investigation in economics, you'll want to be sure you have the best data out there—and, more importantly, the correct data. Going to the right source can help you ensure that your data are from a trusted organization and up to date. (In the United States, the government is often the most reliable source.)

This short guide will introduce you to the sources that many economists use to answer thousands of different questions. In the sections that follow, we provide an overview of each source, including the organization's purpose and the data it hosts, and then we look at an example of how those data have been used. To gain experience using these sources, you'll need to explore each source on your own and learn how to manipulate the data as they appear on the site. To that end, we ask you to answer a few questions using the data you find.

National (United States) Data

Bureau of Economic Analysis (BEA)

http://bea.gov

Interactive database can be found at http://www.bea.gov/itable/index.cfm

The Bureau of Economic Analysis (BEA) is an agency within the U.S. Department of Commerce. Its mission is to promote "a better understanding of the U.S. economy by providing the most timely, relevant, and accurate economic accounts data in an objective and cost effective manner."

The BEA is one of the most widely cited sources for current economic news. Partly that's because it's responsible for publishing the granddaddy of all economic indicators, GDP. GDP is part of the National Income and Product Accounts, which give a broad overview of economic activity in the United States. The BEA publishes this information quarterly and houses historical data dating back to 1929.

A sample of the indicators you can find . . .

- GDP and its components
- Personal income and outlays
- Consumer spending
- Balance of payments
- Corporate profits
- Foreign direct investment

Note: When looking for information from the BEA (and other sources), be sure to look at the databases and not just the news releases. Only the databases will provide comprehensive information about the indicator over time.

TRY IT YOURSELF

✓**APPLICATIONS**

Suppose you're an economic advisor to the president and are trying to gauge how well the economy is performing now in comparison to the last few years.

1. Find the historical database for seasonally adjusted real GDP and report the seasonally adjusted real GDP for the latest quarter available.
2. Use this same database to retrieve the quarterly data for GDP for the three most recent years in the database. Which quarter had the highest rate of GDP growth? Which quarter had the lowest? Graph these data over time.

✓**PROBLEMS**

1. Does consumer spending in the United States tend to stay at the same levels throughout the year, or are there certain months in which it's higher than others?
2. Which countries have the most foreign direct investment in the United States? Where does the United States have the most foreign direct investment?

Federal Reserve Economic Data (FRED), Federal Reserve Bank of St. Louis

http://research.stlouisfed.org/fred2

The Federal Reserve Bank of St. Louis hosts FRED, a database of more than 82,000 U.S. and international economic indicators (time series) from 55 sources. It's the most inclusive, "one-stop shop" data source available for the U.S. economy.

The FRED website allows you to download, graph, track, and compare vast amounts of data covering a wide array of categories. Those include banking, business/fiscal, employment and population, exchange rates, financial data, foreign exchange intervention, GDP, interest rates, international data, monetary aggregates, prices, reserves and monetary base, U.S. regional data, and U.S. Trade and International Transaction data.

A sample of the indicators you can find . . .

- The federal funds rate
- Yield on Treasury bills
- Money supply

TRY IT YOURSELF

✓ APPLICATIONS

Suppose you're an economist trying to examine how the Federal Reserve responds to various GDP growth rates in the economy.

1. Find the series for the monthly effective federal funds rate. (*Tip:* Use the search bar on the FRED home page.) What is the latest value for the effective federal funds rate? What was the value for the effective federal funds rate two years ago?
2. Now find the series for GDP growth. What is the average growth rate of annual GDP in the last two years?
3. Based on your answers to questions 1 and 2 (and lessons you learned from the macroeconomic chapters), do you think there's a relationship between the federal funds rate and GDP growth? If so, how would you describe that relationship?

✓ PROBLEMS

1. What was the average personal savings rate in 1950? What is it today?
2. How much money is in circulation in the United States today, using M2?

U.S. Bureau of Labor Statistics (BLS)

http://www.bls.gov

The U.S. Bureau of Labor Statistics (BLS) is a government agency that is the primary source of statistics on employment and prices. Each month, it publishes an "Employment Situation Summary," which, among other statistics, gives an account of the number of unemployed people and the unemployment rate.

Labor statistics are of interest to a diverse crowd: from labor economists trying to understand the relationship between minimum wage and employment, to college graduates attempting to predict their employment prospects. Below is an example from the news that highlights the use of labor statistics.

U.S. Teens Struggle to Find Elusive Part-Time Jobs, Often Competing with Displaced Older Workers

AP; HARTFORD, Conn.—The economic turmoil that has left many Americans without work is having a disproportionate effect on teenage job-seekers, whose quest for entry-level positions often pits them against experienced older workers willing to take any job for a paycheck.

U.S. labor figures show the 2011 unemployment rate nationwide averaged just below 9 percent, but for job-seekers ages 16 to 19, it was almost 25 percent—the third consecutive year in that range, and with some cities recording rates far higher. . . .

A sample of the indicators you can find . . .

- Unemployment rate
- Consumer Price Index (CPI)
- Consumer spending
- Wages
- Worker productivity, workplace injuries, illnesses, and fatalities

TRY IT YOURSELF

✓**APPLICATION**

Imagine you're advising a presidential candidate running against the incumbent. The candidate wants you to tell her about the employment situation, including specific information about whether certain parts of the population face higher unemployment rates than others do.

1. Find the latest Employment Situation Summary. When was it issued?
2. What was the unemployment rate for the last month? How did it compare to the unemployment rate for the month before that? Was it higher or lower?
3. Finally, look at the site's Table A-4, "Employment status of the civilian population 25 years and over by educational attainment." For the latest month available, what is the difference in the unemployment rate between those with a bachelor's degree and those without a high-school diploma?

✓**PROBLEMS**

1. What is the highest rate of unemployment the United States has experienced in the past 20 years?
2. In the past 20 years, when did the Consumer Price Index have the fastest rate of annual increase?

Congressional Budget Office (CBO)

http://www.cbo.gov

The Congressional Budget Office (CBO) is a federal agency responsible for providing objective, nonpartisan analysis to assist Congress with budgetary decisions. Whenever you hear politicians argue over whose plan to improve the economy will cost more, it's a good bet that they'll mention a projection from the CBO. The Office is responsible for projecting the costs of government programs at the request of Congress. The CBO also provides regular reports to Congress on fiscal policy through the *Budget and Economic Outlook* and cost estimates of the president's budget through its *Analysis of the President's Budget.*

A sample of the indicators you can find . . .

- The federal deficit
- Federal spending
- Federal revenue

TRY IT YOURSELF

✓**APPLICATIONS**

Imagine your professor has announced that the subject for a class debate is "Should the United States balance the budget?" You want to find the statistics that will back up your position.

1. Find the latest version of the *Budget and Economic Outlook* and navigate to the full document. Find the table titled "CBO's Baseline Budget Projections." What is the total deficit projected for this year in billions of dollars? What percentage of GDP does that represent?
2. According to the CBO's economic outlook, will the budget deficit increase, decrease, or remain the same over the next five years?

✓ PROBLEMS

1. What is the projected shortfall in Social Security in 2050?
2. What is the projected budget deficit/surplus in 2025 as a percentage of GDP?

U.S. Census Bureau

http://www.census.gov

Interactive database can be found at http://factfinder2.census.gov/faces/nav/jsf/pages/index.xhtml

The U.S. Census Bureau is an agency within the Department of Commerce. The Bureau is responsible for conducting the United States Census, which attempts to collect very detailed information about all households in the United States every 10 years. These data provide a very clear picture of the changes and trends happening throughout America. In addition to the Census, the Bureau collects data every year through the American Community Survey and other sources.

A sample of the indicators you can find . . .

- Population
- Demographic information about households (age, sex, ethnicity)
- School enrollment
- Poverty
- Health insurance
- The number of businesses in a region
- The number of houses in a region

TRY IT YOURSELF

✓ APPLICATIONS

Suppose you're a governor trying to determine whether your state's tax base will increase or decrease. As part of that effort, you want to know about population trends.

1. Find the two most recent population numbers for your state. How much did the population increase or decrease in the last decade?
2. Compare your state's population growth rate to the rate of population growth in the entire United States. Is the United States gaining population faster or slower than your state?

✓ PROBLEMS

1. What is the state with the highest percentage of people living in poverty? With the lowest?
2. How many businesses are operating in your county?

International Data

The World Bank

http://databank.worldbank.org/data/home.aspx

The World Bank is an international financial institution that seeks to reduce poverty. As part of its efforts, it collects and analyzes statistics about economies around the world. Its World Development Indicators (WDI) are a widely cited source of statistics about development; its Global Development Finance indicators provide external debt and financial flows statistics for several countries. The bank publishes these two sources in an online database called the "World Data-Bank." The World DataBank catalogs indicators about a wide array of topics including income, education, health, gender, and the environment.

The World Bank's World Development Indicators are the most prominent source of data on development. Here's one example from economists at Yale, MIT, and Oxford who test the relationship between economic growth and human development.

Paths to Success: The Relationship Between Human Development and Economic Growth

Tavneet Suri, *MIT Sloan School of Management, Cambridge, MA, U.S.A.*

Michael A. Boozer and Gustav Ranis, *Yale University, New Haven, CT, U.S.A.*

Frances Stewart, *University of Oxford, Oxford, U.K.*

Accepted 26 August 2010. Available online 17 January 2011.

Summary

This paper explores the two-way relationship between economic growth (EG) and human development (HD). We develop panel data strategies to estimate the strength of these relationships and find that HD plays an essential role in determining growth trajectories (our measure of sustained growth). Not only is HD a final product in the sense that it measures basic human well-being but it is also a critical input into EG. Our findings illustrate the empirical relevance of endogenous growth, and are consistent with threshold effect models. Our results imply that successful policy requires an early focus on HD, not only because of its direct impact but also because of its feedback effect on sustaining EG.

A sample of the indicators you can find . . .

- Government expenditure per student
- Urban population growth
- Real interest rate
- Net migration
- Gini coefficients
- Official development assistance

TRY IT YOURSELF

✓APPLICATIONS

Imagine you're an entrepreneur trying to start a global company and are looking for the best country in which to start it.

1. Navigate to the "Doing Business" database and select it. Under the "Country" drop-down, choose "Select all." Under the "Series" drop-down, scroll down to the data series called "Ease of doing business index." Select that series, and click on the small icon at the left to see metadata about the series, including a "Long definition" of the series. In your *own* words, what does the ease of doing business index represent?

2. Close the metadata window and open the "Time" drop-down, then choose "Select all." You should now have selected variables for Country, Series, and Time. Click on "Table" (at the top of the screen) to see your choices in table view. On the left-hand side of the page, switch to the "Layout" tab and set the options that will format your table with Country in rows, Series on the page, and Time in columns. Based on the latest available year in the table, what country has the highest ease of doing business? What country has the lowest?

3. What country made the most progress in the index from the earliest year available to the latest year available?

✓ PROBLEMS

1. What country has the lowest literacy rate? What is that rate?
2. Which region in the world has the highest GDP per capita? The lowest?

CIA World Factbook

https://www.cia.gov/library/publications/the-world-factbook/index.html

Despite the sound of its title, the CIA's World Factbook is not a book for spies, filled with hidden facts about the inner workings of foreign governments. Rather, The World Factbook provides information on the history, people, government, economy, geography, communications, transportation, military, and transnational issues for 267 world entities. (Of course, spies could use it if they wanted to know any of that information.) If you're looking for the population of Armenia, or the percentage of people working in the agricultural sector in Vietnam, The World Factbook is the place to go.

The main advantage of The World Factbook is its ease of navigation. Whereas finding statistics on other sites is an exercise in sleuthing and patience, The World Factbook divides statistics by country and navigates like any other website—no databases to query here.

A sample of the indicators you can find . . .

- Maps of the major world regions
- Trade statistics
- Miles of paved roads

TRY IT YOURSELF

✓ APPLICATIONS

Suppose your boss is looking at a few countries to invest in and wants you to put together a general country brief for each. Find and state the information detailed below for four countries: Bulgaria, Moldova, Romania, and Poland.

1. People and society
   a. Age structure
   b. Life expectancy at birth

2. Economy
    a. Labor force—by occupation
    b. GDP (purchasing power parity)
    c. GDP—per capita
    d. GDP—real growth rate
    e. GDP—composition, by sector of origin
    f. Exports ($ value)
    g. Exports—partners
    h. Imports ($ value)
    i. Imports—partners

✓PROBLEMS

1. What is the size, in square miles, of Eritrea? Of Ethiopia?
2. How many miles of paved roads are in Poland?

The United Nations Statistics Division

http://data.un.org

Human Development Index can be found at http://hdr.undp.org/en/data/trends

UNdata is an initiative by the United Nations Statistics Division (UNSD) that brings together several data sources hosted by the United Nations. The United Nations collects statistics from its member states on a wide variety of topics. These include crime, education, energy, environment, population, and health, among others. Among its most popular indicators is the Human Development Index, a measure of general well-being calculated across countries. The Human Development Report Office within the United Nations Development Program hosts a site devoted specifically to this indicator. In addition to providing data on HDI, the site allows users to graph the data in simple and compelling ways, distilling complex data into concise graphs.

A sample of the indicators you can find . . .

- Quantity traded of commodity goods
- Gender inequality
- CO_2 emissions
- Foreign direct investment
- Prevalence of HIV

TRY IT YOURSELF

✓APPLICATIONS

Suppose you're the head of a foundation with the mission to support governments and organizations trying to improve primary-school enrollment around the world. You want to know where to start your efforts.

1. Go to data.un.org, navigate to "The State of the World's Children" database, and view the data for "Net attendance ratio in primary education (NER)." Over what years are the observations given? What are the subgroups for the observations?
2. What country has the lowest attendance rate for males? What is it?
3. What country has the highest attendance rate for females? What is it?

✓PROBLEMS

1. What is the most populous country?
2. What country receives the most development assistance?

Other Directories of Data

Google's Public Data

http://www.google.com/publicdata/directory

Google's Public Data site publishes several publicly available datasets in an easy-to-use way. The site continues to add sources; current sources include the U.S. Bureau of Economic Analysis, World Bank, World Economic Forum, International Monetary Fund, and the U.S. Bureau of Labor Statistics, among others.

The U.S. Government

http://www.data.gov/

The U.S. government has combined several government data sources into one site. This can be a good place to start if you know what category of data you need but aren't sure where to look for it.

Williams College Economics Department

http://econ.williams.edu/students/online-resources

The Economics Department at Williams College has provided links to many different data sources on one web page, to help students like you conduct research in several areas.

glossary

A

absolute advantage the ability to produce more of a good or service than others can with a given amount of resources.

absolute poverty line a measure that defines poverty as income below a certain amount, fixed at a given point in time.

accounting profit total revenue minus explicit costs.

administrative burden the logistical costs associated with implementing a tax.

adverse selection a state that occurs when buyers and sellers have different information about the quality of a good or the riskiness of a situation, and this asymmetric information results in failure to complete transactions that would have been possible if both sides had the same information.

agent a person who carries out a task on someone else's behalf.

aggregate demand curve a curve that shows the relationship between the overall price level in the economy and total demand.

aggregate expenditure (Y) the level of aggregate expenditure that consists of consumption, government spending, net exports, and actual investment by firms.

aggregate price level a measure of the average price level for GDP; in practice, the CPI or GDP price deflator.

aggregate supply curve a curve that shows the relationship between the overall price level in the economy and total production by firms.

altruism a motive for action in which a person's utility increases simply because someone else's utility increases.

arbitrage the process of taking advantage of market inefficiencies to earn profits.

Arrow's impossibility theorem a theorem showing that no voting system can aggregate the preferences of voters over three or more options while satisfying the criteria of an ideal voting system.

autarky an economy that is self-contained and does not engage in trade with outsiders.

automatic stabilizers taxes and government spending that affect fiscal policy without specific action from policy-makers.

autonomous expenditure expenditure that is independent of the current level of aggregate income in the economy.

average fixed cost (AFC) fixed cost divided by the quantity of output.

average revenue revenue generated per product, calculated as total revenue divided by the quantity sold.

average total cost (ATC) total cost divided by the quantity of output.

average variable cost (AVC) variable cost divided by the quantity of output.

B

backward induction the process of analyzing a problem in reverse, starting with the last choice, then the second-to-last choice, and so on, to determine the optimal strategy.

balance of trade the value of exports minus the value of imports.

balance-of-payments identity an equation that shows that the value of net exports equals net capital outflow.

barter directly offering a good or service in exchange for some good or service you want.

behaving strategically acting to achieve a goal by anticipating the interplay between your own and others' decisions.

behavioral economics a field of economics that draws on insights from psychology to expand models of individual decision making.

bond a form of debt that represents a promise by the bond issuer to repay the face value of the loan, at a specified maturity date, and to pay periodic interest at a specific percentage rate.

bubble trade in an asset whose price has risen unsustainably far above historically justified levels.

budget constraint a line that is composed of all of the possible combinations of goods and services that a consumer can buy with her or his income.

budget deficit an amount of money a government spends beyond the revenue it brings in.

budget surplus an amount of revenue a government brings in beyond what it spends.

bundle a unique combination of goods and services that a person could choose to consume.

business cycle Fluctuations of output around the level of potential output in the economy.

C

capability something a person is able to be or do, such as to engage fully in life, including having economic and political freedoms.

capital manufactured goods that are used to produce new goods.

capital gains tax a tax on income earned by buying investments and selling them at a higher price.

cartel a number of firms that collude to make collective production decisions about quantities or prices.

causation a relationship between two events in which one brings about the other.

central bank the institution ultimately responsible for managing the nation's money supply and coordinating the banking system to ensure a sound economy.

choice architecture the organization of the context and process in which people make decisions.

circular flow model a simplified representation of how the economy's transactions work together.

closed economy an economy that does not interact with other countries' economies.

clusters networks of interdependent firms, universities, and businesses that focus on the production of a specific type of good.

Coase theorem the idea that even in the presence of an externality, individuals can reach an efficient equilibrium through private trades, assuming zero transaction costs.

collective-action problem a situation in which a group of people stands to gain from an action that it is not rational for any of the members to undertake individually.

collusion the act of working together to make decisions about price and quantity.

commitment device a mechanism that allows people to voluntarily restrict their choices in order to make it easier to stick to plans.

commitment strategy an agreement to submit to a penalty in the future for defecting from a given strategy.

commodity-backed money any form of money that can be legally exchanged into a fixed amount of an underlying commodity.

common resource a good that is not excludable but is rival.

comparative advantage the ability to produce a good or service at a lower opportunity cost than others.

competitive market a market in which fully informed, price-taking buyers and sellers easily trade a standardized good or service.

complements goods that are consumed together, so that purchasing one will make consumers more likely to purchase the other.

complete information state of being fully informed about the choices that relevant economic actors face.

compounding the process of accumulation that results from the additional interest paid on previously earned interest.

conditional cash transfer a program in which financial support is given only to people who engage in certain actions.

Condorcet paradox a situation in which the preferences of each individual member of a group are transitive, but the collective preferences of the group are not.

constant returns to scale returns that occur when average total cost does not depend on the quantity of output.

Consumer Price Index (CPI) a measure that tracks changes in the cost of a basket of goods and services purchased by a typical U.S. household.

consumer surplus the net benefit that a consumer receives from purchasing a good or service, measured by the difference between willingness to pay and the actual price.

consumption spending on goods and services by private individuals and households.

consumption externality an externality that occurs when a good or service is being consumed.

contractionary fiscal policy decisions about government spending and taxation intended to decrease aggregate demand.

contractionary monetary policy actions that reduce the money supply in order to decrease aggregate demand.

convergence theory the theory that countries that start out poor will initially grow faster than rich ones but will eventually converge to the same growth rate.

core inflation measure of inflation that excludes goods with historically volatile price changes—energy and food.

correlation a consistently observed relationship between two variables.

credit constraint inability to get a loan even though a person expects to be able to repay the loan plus interest.

cross-price elasticity of demand a measure of how the demand for one good changes when the price of a different good changes.

crowding out the reduction in private borrowing caused by an increase in government borrowing.

cyclical unemployment unemployment caused by short-term economic fluctuations.

D

deadweight loss a loss of total surplus that occurs because the quantity of a good that is bought and sold is below the market equilibrium quantity.

debt service the amount that consumers have to spend to pay their debts, often expressed as a percentage of disposable income.

default the failure of a borrower to pay back a loan according to the agreed-upon terms.

default rule a rule defining what will automatically occur if a chooser fails to make an active decision otherwise.

deflation an overall fall in prices in the economy.

demand curve a graph that shows the quantities of a particular good or service that consumers will demand at various prices.

demand deposits funds held in bank accounts that can be withdrawn ("demanded") by depositors at any time without advance notice.

demand schedule a table that shows the quantities of a particular good or service that consumers are willing and able to purchase (demand) at various prices.

depression a particularly severe or extended recession.

derivative an asset whose value is based on the value of another asset.

diminishing marginal product a principle stating that the marginal product of an input decreases as the quantity of the input increases.

diminishing marginal utility the principle that the additional utility gained from consuming successive units of a good or service tends to be smaller than the utility gained from the previous unit.

discount rate the interest rate charged by the Fed for loans of reserves through the discount window.

discount window the lending facility run by the Fed that allows any bank to borrow reserves.

discouraged workers people who have looked for work in the past year but have given up looking because of the condition of the labor market.

discretionary spending public expenditures that have to be approved each year.

discrimination making choices by using generalizations based on people's observable characteristics like race, gender, and age.

diseconomies of scale returns that occur when an increase in the quantity of output increases average total cost.

disinflation a period in which inflation rates are falling, but still positive.

diversification the process by which risks are shared across many different assets or people, reducing the impact of any particular risk on any one individual.

dividend a payment made periodically, typically annually or quarterly, to all shareholders of a company.

domestic savings savings for capital investment that come from within a country; equal to domestic income minus consumption spending.

dominant strategy a strategy that is the best one for a player to follow no matter what strategy other players choose.

dual mandate the twin responsibilities of the Federal Reserve, to use monetary policy to ensure price stability and to maintain full employment.

E

economic profit total revenue minus all opportunity costs, explicit and implicit.

economic rent the gains that workers and owners of capital receive from supplying their labor or machinery in factor markets.

economics the study of how people, individually and collectively, manage resources.

economies of scale returns that occur when an increase in the quantity of output decreases average total cost.

efficiency use of resources in the most productive way possible to produce the goods and services that have the greatest total economic value to society.

efficiency wage a wage that is deliberately set above the market rate to increase worker productivity.

efficient market an arrangement such that no exchange can make anyone better off without someone becoming worse off.

efficient points combinations of production possibilities that squeeze the most output possible from all available resources.

efficient scale the quantity of output at which average total cost is minimized.

efficient-market hypothesis the idea that market prices always incorporate all available information, and therefore represent true value as correctly as is possible.

elastic demand that has an absolute value of elasticity greater than 1.

elasticity a measure of how much consumers and producers will respond to a change in market conditions.

embargo a restriction or prohibition of trade in order to put political pressure on a country.

endowment effect the tendency of people to place more value on something simply because they own it.

entitlement spending public expenditure that "entitles" people to benefits by virtue of age, income, or some other factor.

equilibrium the situation in a market when the quantity supplied equals the quantity demanded; graphically, this convergence happens where the demand curve intersects the supply curve.

equilibrium aggregate expenditure the level of aggregate expenditure where unplanned investment is equal to zero, or, equivalently, where planned aggregate expenditure is equal to actual aggregate expenditure.

equilibrium price the price at which the quantity supplied equals the quantity demanded.

equilibrium quantity the quantity that is supplied and demanded at the equilibrium price.

excess reserves any additional amount, beyond the required reserves, that a bank chooses to keep in reserve.

exchange rate the value of one currency expressed in terms of another currency.

exchange-rate appreciation an increase in the value of a currency relative to the value of another currency.

exchange-rate depreciation a decrease in the value of a currency relative to other currencies.

excise tax a sales tax on a specific good or service.

excludable a characteristic of a good or service that allows owners to prevent its use by people who have not paid for it.

expansionary fiscal policy decisions about government spending and taxation intended to increase aggregate demand.

expansionary monetary policy actions that increase the money supply in order to increase aggregate demand.

expected value the average of each possible outcome of a future event, weighted by its probability of occurring.

expenditure multiplier the factor by which output increases in response to an initial change in aggregate expenditure .

explicit costs costs that require a firm to spend money.

exports goods and services that are produced domestically and consumed in other countries.

external benefits benefits that accrue without compensation to someone other than the person who caused it.

external costs costs imposed without compensation on someone other than the person who caused them.

externality a cost or benefit imposed without compensation on someone other than the person who caused it.

F

factors of production the ingredients that go into making a good or service.

federal funds rate the interest rate at which banks choose to lend reserves held at the Fed to one another.

Federal Reserve ("the Fed") the system consisting of a seven-member Board of

Governors and 12 regional banks that act as the central bank of the United States.

fiat money money created by rule, without any commodity to back it.

financial capital money saved by households that gets lent to firms for investment purposes and to governments to fund budget deficits.

financial intermediaries institutions that channel funds from people who have them to people who want them.

financial market a market in which people trade future claims on funds or goods.

financial system the group of institutions that bring together savers, borrowers, investors, and insurers in a set of interconnected markets where people trade financial products.

financing gap the difference between the savings rate within an economy and the amount of investment needed to achieve sustainable growth.

first-mover advantage benefit enjoyed by the player who chooses first and, as a result, gets a higher payoff than those who follow.

fiscal policy government decisions about the level of taxation and public spending.

fixed costs costs that do not depend on the quantity of output produced.

fixed exchange rate an exchange rate that is set by the government, instead of determined by the market.

floating exchange rate an exchange rate whose value is determined by the market.

foreign direct investment (FDI) investment when a firm runs part of its operation abroad or owns all or part of another company abroad

foreign portfolio investment investment funded by foreign sources but operated domestically.

fractional-reserve banking a banking system in which banks keep on reserve less than 100 percent of their deposits.

free-rider problem a problem that occurs when the nonexcludability of a public good leads to undersupply.

frictional unemployment unemployment caused by workers who are changing location, job, or career.

full information complete knowledge of the product being offered in the market.

fungible easily exchangeable or substitutable.

G

gains from trade the improvement in outcomes that occurs when producers specialize and exchange goods and services.

game a situation involving at least two people that requires those involved to think strategically.

game theory the study of how people behave strategically under different circumstances.

GDP deflator a measure of the overall change in prices in an economy, using the ratio between real and nominal GDP.

GDP per capita a country's GDP divided by its population.

Gini coefficient a single-number measure of income inequality; ranges from 0 to 1, with higher numbers meaning greater inequality.

government purchases spending on goods and services by all levels of government.

government-spending multiplier the amount by which GDP increases when government spending increases by $1.

green GDP an alternative measure of GDP that subtracts the environmental costs of production from the positive outputs normally counted in GDP.

gross domestic product (GDP) the sum of the market values of all final goods and services produced within a country in a given period of time.

gross national product (GNP) the sum of the market values of all final goods and services produced and capital owned by the permanent residents of a country in a given period of time.

H

headline inflation measure of inflation that includes all of the goods that the average consumer buys.

heuristic a mental shortcut for making decisions (sometimes in good ways, but sometimes not).

human capital the set of skills, knowledge, experience, and talent that determine the productivity of workers.

hyperinflation extremely long-lasting and painful increases in the price level.

I

idiosyncratic risk any risk that is unique to a particular company or asset.

impact investing investing money in firms to generate both financial and social returns.

implicit costs costs that represent forgone opportunities.

import quota a limit on the amount of a particular good that can be imported.

imports goods and services that are produced in other countries and consumed domestically.

in-kind transfer a program that provides specific goods or services, rather than cash, directly to needy recipients.

incentive something that causes people to behave in a certain way by changing the trade-offs they face.

incidence a description of who bears the burden of a tax.

income effect the change in consumption that results from a change in effective wealth due to higher or lower prices.

income elasticity of demand a measure of how much the demand for a good changes in response to a change in consumers' incomes.

income mobility the ability to improve one's economic circumstances over time.

income tax a tax charged on the earnings of individuals and corporations.

indexing the practice of automatically increasing payments in proportion to the cost of living.

indifference curve a curve showing all the different consumption bundles that provide a consumer with equal levels of utility.

industrial policy effort by a government to favor some industries over others.

inelastic demand that has an absolute value of elasticity less than 1.

inferior goods goods for which demand decreases as income increases.

inflation an overall rise in prices in the economy.

inflation rate the size of the change in the overall price level; the percent change in a price index such as the CPI from year to year.

inflationary output gap an output gap that occurs when equilibrium aggregate expenditure is above the level needed for full employment.

information asymmetry a condition in which one participant in a transaction knows more than another participant.

institutions the humanly devised constraints that shape human interactions.

interest rate the price of money, typically expressed as a percentage per dollar per unit of time; for savers, it is the price received for letting a bank use money for a specified period of time; for borrowers, it is the price of using money for a specified period of time.

inventory the stock of goods that a company produces now but does not sell immediately.

investment spending on productive inputs, such as factories, machinery, and inventories.

investment trade-off a reduction in current consumption to pay for investment in capital intended to increase future production.

K

Keynesian equilibrium a situation in which planned aggregate expenditure is equal to actual aggregate expenditure.

L

labor demand curve a graph showing the relationship between the total quantity of labor demanded by all the firms in the economy and the wage rate.

labor force people who are in the working-age population and are either employed or unemployed; people who are currently working or who are actively trying to find a job.

labor supply curve a graph showing the relationship between the total labor supplied in the economy and the wage rate.

labor unions groups of employees who join together to bargain with their employer(s) over salaries and work conditions.

labor-force participation rate the number of people in the labor force divided by the working-age population.

law of demand a fundamental characteristic of demand that states that, all else equal, quantity demanded rises as price falls.

law of supply a fundamental characteristic of supply that states that, all else equal, quantity supplied rises as price rises.

leverage the practice of using borrowed money to pay for investments.

leverage ratio the ratio of a company's assets to its equity, where equity is defined as the firm's assets minus its liabilities.

liquidity a measure of how easily a particular asset can be converted quickly to cash without much loss of value.

liquidity-preference model idea that the quantity of money people want to hold is a function of the interest rate.

loan an agreement in which a lender gives money to a borrower in exchange for a promise to repay the amount loaned plus an agreed-upon amount of interest.

Lorenz curve a graphic representation of income distribution that maps percentage of the population against cumulative percentage of income earned by those people.

loss aversion the tendency for people to put more effort into avoiding losses than achieving gains.

lump-sum tax (head tax) a tax that charges the same amount to each taxpayer, regardless of their economic behavior or circumstances.

lump-sum taxes taxes whose levels do not change when income rises or falls.

M

M1 definition of money that includes cash plus checking account balances.

M2 definition of money that includes everything in M1 plus savings accounts and other financial instruments where money is locked away for a specified amount of time; less liquid than M1.

macroeconomics the study of the economy as a whole, and how policymakers manage the growth and behavior of the overall economy.

marginal cost (MC) the additional cost incurred by a firm when it produces one additional unit of output.

marginal decision making comparison of additional benefits of a choice against the additional costs it would bring, without considering related benefits and costs of past choices.

marginal product the increase in output that is generated by an additional unit of input.

marginal propensity to consume (MPC) the amount that consumption increases when after-tax income increases by $1.

marginal rate of substitution (MRS) the rate at which a consumer is willing to trade or substitute between two goods.

marginal revenue the revenue generated by selling an additional unit of a good.

marginal tax rate the tax rate charged on the last dollar a taxpayer earns.

marginal utility the change in total utility that comes from consuming one additional unit of a good or service.

market buyers and sellers who trade a particular good or service.

market basket a list of specific goods and services in fixed quantities.

market economy an economy in which private individuals, rather than a centralized planning authority, make the decisions.

market failures situations in which the assumption of efficient, competitive markets fails to hold.

market for loanable funds a market in which savers supply funds to those who want to borrow.

market power the ability to noticeably affect market prices.

market (systemic) risk any risk that is broadly shared by the entire market or economy; also called *systemic risk*.

means-tested the characteristic of a program that defines eligibility for benefits based on recipients' income.

median-voter theorem a model stating that under certain conditions, politicians maximize their votes by taking the policy position preferred by the median voter.

medium of exchange the ability to use money to purchase goods and services.

menu costs the costs (measured in money, time, and opportunity) of changing prices to keep pace with inflation.

microeconomics the study of how individuals and firms manage resources.

mid-point method method that measures percentage change in quantity demanded (or quantity supplied) relative to a point midway between two points on a curve; used to estimate elasticity.

model a simplified representation of the important parts of a complicated situation.

monetary base the sum of currency in circulation and reserves held by banks at the Federal Reserve.

monetary policy actions by the central bank to manage the money supply, in pursuit of certain macroeconomic goals.

money the set of all assets that are regularly used to directly purchase goods and services.

money multiplier the ratio of money created by the lending activities of the banking system to the money created by the government's central bank.

money supply the amount of money available in the economy.

monopolistic competition a market with many firms that sell goods and services that are similar, but slightly different.

monopoly a firm that is the only producer of a good or service with no close substitutes.

monopsony a market in which there is only one buyer but many sellers.

moral hazard the tendency for people to behave in a riskier way or to renege on contracts when they do not face the full consequences of their actions.

multiplier effect the increase in consumer spending that occurs when spending by one person causes others to spend more too, increasing the impact on the economy of the initial spending .

mutual fund a portfolio of stocks, bonds, and other assets managed by a professional who makes decisions on behalf of clients.

N

Nash equilibrium an equilibrium reached when all players choose the best strategy they can, given the choices of all other players. It is a situation wherein, given the consequences, the player has no regrets about his or her decision.

national savings the sum of the private savings of individuals and corporations plus the public savings of the government.

natural monopoly a market in which a single firm can produce, at a lower cost than multiple firms, the entire quantity of output demanded.

natural rate of unemployment the normal level of unemployment that persists in an economy in the long run.

net capital flow the net flow of funds invested outside of a country; specifically, the difference between capital inflows (investment financed by savings from another country) and capital outflows (domestic savings invested abroad).

net exports (NX) exports minus imports; the value of goods and services produced domestically and consumed abroad minus the value of goods and services produced abroad and consumed domestically.

net present value (NPV) a measure of the current value of a stream of cash flows expected in the future.

network externality the effect that an additional user of a good or participant in an activity has on the value of that good or activity for others.

neutrality of money the idea that, in the long run, changes in the money supply affect nominal variables, such as prices and wages, but do not affect real outcomes in the economy.

nominal exchange rate the stated rate at which one country's currency can be traded for another country's currency.

nominal GDP GDP calculation in which goods and services are valued at current prices.

nominal interest rate the reported interest rate, not adjusted for the effects of inflation.

non-accelerating inflation rate of unemployment (NAIRU) the lowest possible unemployment rate that will not cause the inflation rate to increase.

nonautonomous expenditure expenditure that changes as a result of the current level of aggregate income in the economy.

normal goods goods for which demand increases as income increases.

normative statement a claim about how the world should be.

nudge an implementation of choice architecture that alters people's behavior in a deliberate and predictable way without changing economic incentives much.

O

oligopoly a market with only a few firms, which sell a similar good or service.

open economy an economy that interacts with other countries' economies.

open-market operations sales or purchases of government bonds by the Fed, to or from banks, on the open market.

opportunity cost the value to you of what you have to give up in order to get something; the value you could have gained by choosing the next-best alternative.

output gap the difference between actual and potential output in an economy.

P

payroll tax a tax on the wages paid to an employee.

pension fund a professionally managed portfolio of assets intended to provide income to retirees.

perfectly elastic demand demand for which any increase in price will cause quantity demanded to drop to zero; represented by a perfectly horizontal line.

perfectly inelastic demand demand for which quantity demanded remains the same regardless of price; represented by a perfectly vertical line.

Phillips curve a model that shows the connection between inflation and unemployment in the short run.

physical capital the stock of equipment and structures that allow for production of goods and services.

Pigovian tax a tax meant to counterbalance a negative externality.

planned aggregate expenditure (PAE) the level of aggregate expenditure that consists of consumption, planned investment, government spending, and net exports.

planned aggregate expenditure curve planned aggregate expenditure as a function of actual aggregate expenditure, holding all other factors constant.

planned investment the amount that firms actively decide to spend on new capital equipment or strategic inventory accumulation.

positive statement a factual claim about how the world actually works.

potential output the total amount of output a country could produce if all of its resources were fully engaged.

poverty line See *absolute poverty line* and *relative poverty line*.

poverty rate the percentage of the population that falls below the absolute poverty line.

poverty trap a self-reinforcing mechanism that causes the poor to stay poor.

PPP-adjustment recalculating economic statistics to account for differences in price levels across countries.

present value how much a certain amount of money that will be obtained in the future is worth today.

price ceiling a maximum legal price at which a good can be sold.

price control a regulation that sets a maximum or minimum legal price for a particular good.

price discrimination the practice of charging customers different prices for the same good.

price elasticity of demand the size of the change in the quantity demanded of a good or service when its price changes.

price elasticity of supply the size of the change in the quantity supplied of a good or service when its price changes.

price floor a minimum legal price at which a good can be sold.

price index a measure showing how much the cost of a market basket has risen or fallen relative to the cost in a base time period or location.

price taker a buyer or seller who cannot affect the market price. In a perfectly competitive market, firms are price takers as a consequence of many sellers selling standardized goods.

principal a person who entrusts someone with a task.

prisoners' dilemma a game of strategy in which two people make rational choices that lead to a less-than-ideal result for both.

private benefits benefits that accrue directly to the decision maker.

private costs costs that fall directly on an economic decision maker.

private goods goods that are both excludable and rival.

private savings the savings of individuals or corporations within a country.

producer surplus the net benefit that a producer receives from the sale of a good or service, measured by the difference between the producer's willingness to sell and the actual price.

product differentiation the creation of products that are similar to competitors' products but more attractive in some ways.

production externality an externality that occurs when a good or service is being produced.

production function the relationship between quantity of inputs and the resulting quantity of outputs.

production possibilities frontier (PPF) a line or curve that shows all the possible combinations of two outputs that can be produced using all available resources.

productivity output produced per worker.

profit the difference between total revenue and total cost.

progressive tax a tax that charges low-income people a smaller percentage of their income than high-income people.

property tax a tax on the estimated value of a home or other property.

proportional/flat tax a tax that takes the same percentage of income from all taxpayers.

protectionism a preference for policies that limit trade.

public debt the total amount of money that a government owes at a point in time; the cumulative sum of all deficits and surpluses.

public good a good that is neither excludable nor rival.

public savings the difference between government tax revenue and government spending.

purchase price the price paid to gain permanent ownership of a factor of production.

purchasing power parity (PPP) the theory that purchasing power in different countries should be the same when stated in a common currency.

purchasing power parity (PPP) index index that describes the overall difference in prices of goods between countries.

Q

quantitative easing policies that are designed to directly increase the money supply by a certain amount.

quantity demanded the amount of a particular good that buyers will purchase at a given price during a specified period.

quantity equation the equation $M \times V = P \times Y$, which relates the money supply and velocity of money to the price value of real output.

quantity supplied the amount of a particular good or service that producers will offer for sale at a given price during a specified period.

quantity theory of money theory that the value of money (and thus the aggregate price level) is determined by the overall quantity of money in existence (the money supply); it states that changes in the price level (inflation or deflation) are primarily the result of changes in the quantity of money.

quota (imports) See *import quota*.

quota rents profits earned by foreign firms or governments under a quota.

R

randomized controlled trial (RCT) a method that randomly assigns subjects into control and treatment groups in order to assess the causal link from an intervention to specific outcomes.

rational behavior making choices to achieve goals in the most effective way possible.

rational ignorance choosing to remain ignorant when the opportunity costs of gathering information outweigh the benefits.

real exchange rate the value of goods in one country expressed in terms of the same goods in another country.

real GDP GDP calculation in which goods and services are valued at constant prices.

real interest rate the interest rate adjusted for the effects of inflation.

real-wage or classical unemployment unemployment that results from wages being higher than the market-clearing level.

recession a period of significant economic decline.

recessionary output gap an output gap that occurs when equilibrium aggregate expenditure is below the level needed for full employment.

reciprocity responding to another's action with a similar action.

regressive tax a tax that charges low-income people a larger percentage of their income than it charges high-income people.

relative poverty line a measure that defines poverty in terms of the income of the rest of the population.

rent-seeking the act of pursuing privileges that increase the surplus of a person or group without increasing total surplus.

rental price the price paid to use a factor of production for a certain period or task.

repeated game a game that is played more than once.

required reserves the minimum fraction of deposits that banks are legally required (by the Federal Reserve) to keep on hand.

reserve ratio the fraction of deposits a bank must hold as reserves; calculated as the amount of cash kept as reserves divided by the total amount of demand deposits.

reserve requirement the regulation that sets the minimum fraction of deposits banks must hold in reserve.

reserves the money that a bank keeps on hand, either in cash or in deposits at the Federal Reserve.

revealed preference the idea that people's preferences can be determined by observing their choices and behavior.

rise vertical distance; calculated as the change in *y*.

risk exists when the costs or benefits of an event or choice are uncertain.

risk pooling organizing people into a group to collectively absorb the risk faced by each individual.

risk-averse having a low willingness to take on situations with risk; when faced with two options with equal expected value, the one with lower risk is preferred.

risk-free rate the interest rate at which one would lend if there were no risk of default; usually approximated by interest rates on U.S. government debt.

risk-seeking having a high willingness to take on situations with risk; when faced with two options with equal expected value, the one with higher risk is preferred.

rival in consumption (rival) the characteristic of a good for which one person's consumption prevents or decreases others' ability to consume it.

run horizontal distance; calculated as the change in *x*.

S

sales tax a tax that is charged on the value of a good or service being purchased.

savings the portion of income that is not immediately spent on consumption of goods and services.

scarcity the condition of wanting more than we can get with available resources.

screening taking action to reveal private information about someone else.

securitization the practice of packaging individual debts into a single uniform asset.

shoe-leather costs the costs (measured in time, money, and effort) of managing cash in the face of inflation.

shortage (excess demand) a situation in which the quantity of a good that is demanded is higher than the quantity supplied.

signaling taking action to reveal one's own private information.

slope the ratio of vertical distance (change in *y*) to horizontal distance (change in *x*).

social benefit the entire benefits of a decision, including both private benefits and external benefits.

social cost the entire cost of a decision, including both private costs and any external costs.

social insurance government programs under which people pay into a common pool and are eligible to draw on benefits under certain circumstances.

specialization spending all of your time producing a particular good.

stagflation high inflation despite low economic growth and high unemployment.

standard deviation a measure of how spread out a set of numbers is.

standardized good a good for which any two units have the same features and are interchangeable.

statistical discrimination distinguishing between choices by generalizing based on observable characteristics in order to fill in missing information.

status-quo bias the tendency to stick with the current situation over other options, even when it is cheap to switch.

stock a financial asset that represents partial ownership of a company.

store of value a certain amount of purchasing power that money retains over time.

structural unemployment unemployment that results from a mismatch between the skills workers can offer and the skills in demand.

subsidy a requirement that the government pay an extra amount to producers or consumers of a good.

substitutes goods that serve a similar-enough purpose that a consumer might purchase one in place of the other.

substitution effect the change in consumption that results from a change in the relative price of goods.

sunk cost a cost that has already been incurred and cannot be refunded or recovered.

supply curve a graph that shows the quantities of a particular good or service that producers will supply at various prices.

supply schedule a table that shows the quantities of a particular good or service that producers will supply at various prices.

supply shocks significant events that directly affect production and the aggregate supply curve in the short run.

surplus (efficiency) a way of measuring who benefits from transactions and by how much.

surplus (excess supply) a situation in which the quantity of a good that is supplied is higher than the quantity demanded.

T

tariff a tax on imported goods.

tax incidence the relative tax burden borne by buyers and sellers.

tax wedge the difference between the price paid by buyers and the price

received by sellers in the presence of a tax.

taxation multiplier the amount GDP decreases when taxes increase by $1.

time inconsistency a situation in which we change our minds about what we want simply because of the timing of the decision.

tit-for-tat a strategy in which a player in a repeated game takes the same action that his or her opponent did in the preceding round.

"too big to fail" so large in terms of assets or customers or so historically important that banking regulators allow the bank to keep operating despite insolvency.

total cost the amount that a firm pays for all of the inputs that go into producing goods and services.

total revenue the amount that a firm receives from the sale of goods and services; calculated as the quantity sold multiplied by the price paid for each unit.

total surplus a measure of the combined benefits that everyone receives from participating in an exchange of goods or services.

tradable allowance a production or consumption quota that can be bought and sold.

trade deficit a negative balance of trade; a greater amount of imports than exports.

trade liberalization policies and actions that reduce trade restrictions.

trade surplus a positive balance of trade; a greater amount of exports than imports.

tragedy of the commons the depletion of a common resource due to individually rational but collectively inefficient overconsumption.

transaction costs the costs incurred by buyer and seller in agreeing to and executing a sale of goods or services.

transfer payments Payments from government accounts to individuals for programs, like Social Security, that do not involve a purchase of goods or services.

Treasury securities debt-financing arrangements made by the U.S. government.

U

underemployed workers who are either working less than they would like to or are working in jobs below their skill level.

unemployment situation in which someone wants to work but cannot find a job in the current market.

unemployment insurance money paid by the government to people who are unemployed.

unemployment rate the number of unemployed people divided by the number of people in the labor force.

United Nations Development Program (UNDP) a global United Nations network that provides knowledge and resources to developing countries.

unit of account a standard unit of comparison.

unit-elastic demand that has an absolute value of elasticity exactly equal to 1.

utility a measure of the amount of satisfaction a person derives from something.

utility function a formula for calculating the total utility that a particular person derives from consuming a combination of goods and services.

V

value of the marginal product the increase in revenue generated by the last unit of an input; calculated as the output generated by an input (marginal product) times the unit price of the output.

variable costs costs that depend on the quantity of output produced.

velocity of money the number of times the entire money supply turns over in a given period.

W

willingness to pay (reservation price) the maximum price that a buyer would be willing to pay for a good or service.

willingness to sell the minimum price that a seller is willing to accept in exchange for a good or service.

World Bank a multinational organization dedicated to providing financial and technical assistance to developing countries.

World Trade Organization (WTO) an international organization designed to monitor and enforce trade agreements, while also promoting free trade.

Z

zero-sum game a situation in which whenever one person gains, another loses an equal amount, such that the net value of any transaction is zero.

index